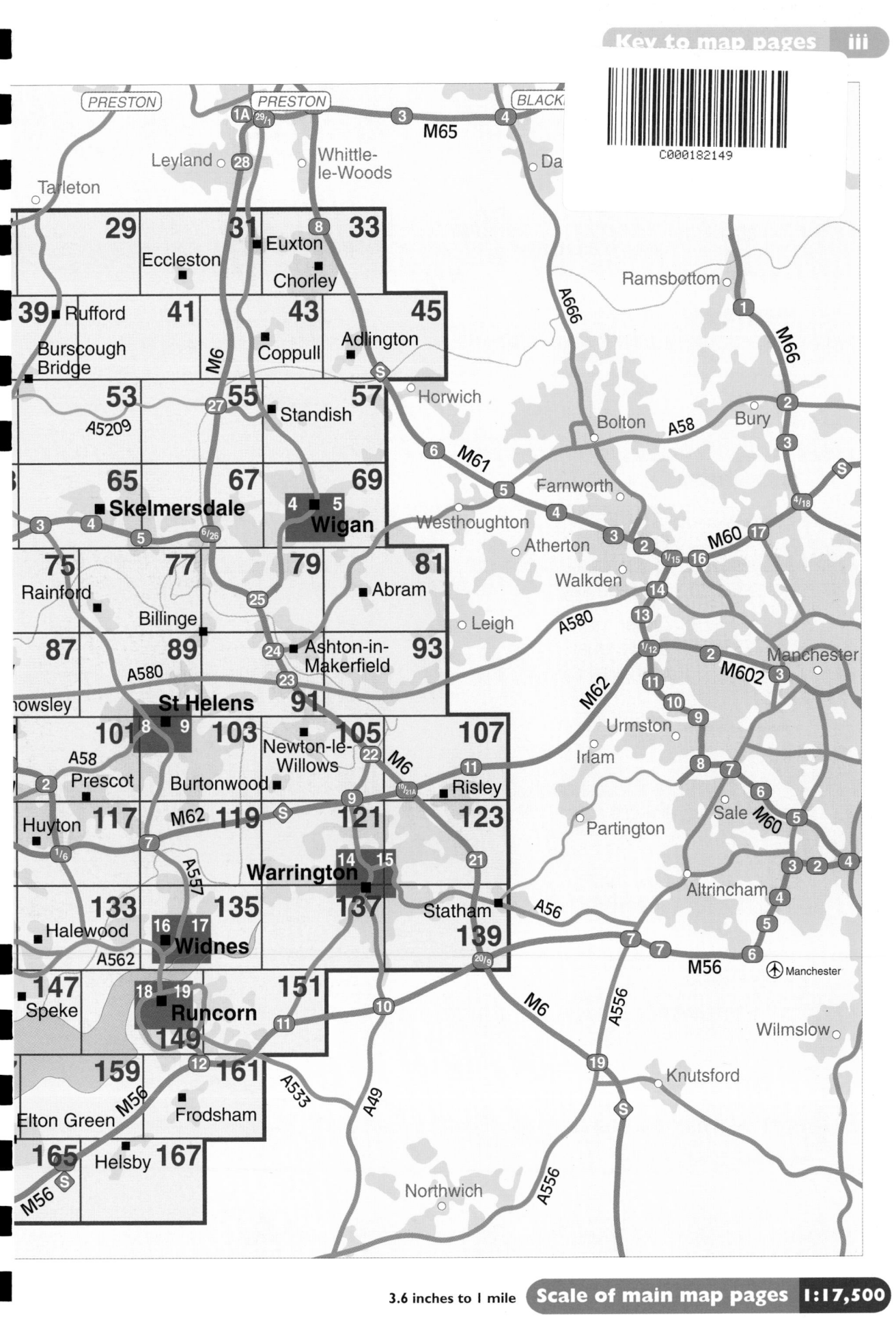

3.6 inches to 1 mile  Scale of main map pages  1:17,500

| | |
|---|---|
| Junction 9 | Motorway & junction |
| Services | Motorway service area |
| | Primary road single/dual carriageway |
| Services | Primary road service area |
| | A road single/dual carriageway |
| | B road single/dual carriageway |
| | Other road single/dual carriageway |
| | Restricted road |
| | Private road |
| ← ← | One way street |
| | Pedestrian street |
| | Track/ footpath |
| | Road under construction |
| ⊏ ─ ─ ─ ─ ⊐ | Road tunnel |
| P | Parking |

| | |
|---|---|
| P+ | Park & Ride |
| | Bus/coach station |
| | Railway & main railway station |
| | Railway & minor railway station |
| ⊖ | Underground station |
| ⊖ | Light railway & station |
| +++++++++++ | Preserved private railway |
| LC | Level crossing |
| •—•—•—•—•—• | Tramway |
| - - - - - - - | Ferry route |
| ......................... | Airport runway |
| — · — · — · — | Boundaries- borough/ district |
| ⋎⋎⋎⋎⋎⋎⋎⋎ | Mounds |
| 93 | Page continuation 1:17,500 |
| 7 | Page continuation to enlarged scale 1:10,000 |

# Street by Street

# MERSEYSIDE

## PLUS ASHTON-IN-MAKERFIELD, CHORLEY, ELLESMERE PORT, NESTON, ORMSKIRK, RUNCORN, SKELMERSDALE, WARRINGTON, WIDNES, WIGAN

Enlarged Areas Birkenhead, Bootle, Liverpool, St Helens, Southport

Ist edition May 2001

© Automobile Association Developments Limited 2001

This product includes map data licensed from Ordnance Survey® with the permission of the Controller of Her Majesty's Stationery Office. © Crown copyright 2000. All rights reserved. Licence No: 399221.

Published by AA Publishing (a trading name of Automobile Association Developments Limited, whose registered office is Norfolk House, Priestley Road, Basingstoke, Hampshire, RG24 9NY. Registered number 1878835).

Mapping produced by the Cartographic Department of The Automobile Association.

A CIP Catalogue record for this book is available from the British Library.

Printed by G. Canale & C. S.P.A., Torino, Italy

Ref: MX048

| Key to map pages | ii-iii |
| Key to map symbols | iv-1 |
| Enlarged scale pages | 2-21 |
| Street by Street | 22-167 |
| Index – towns & villages | 168 |
| Index – streets | 169-215 |
| Index – featured places | 215-222 |

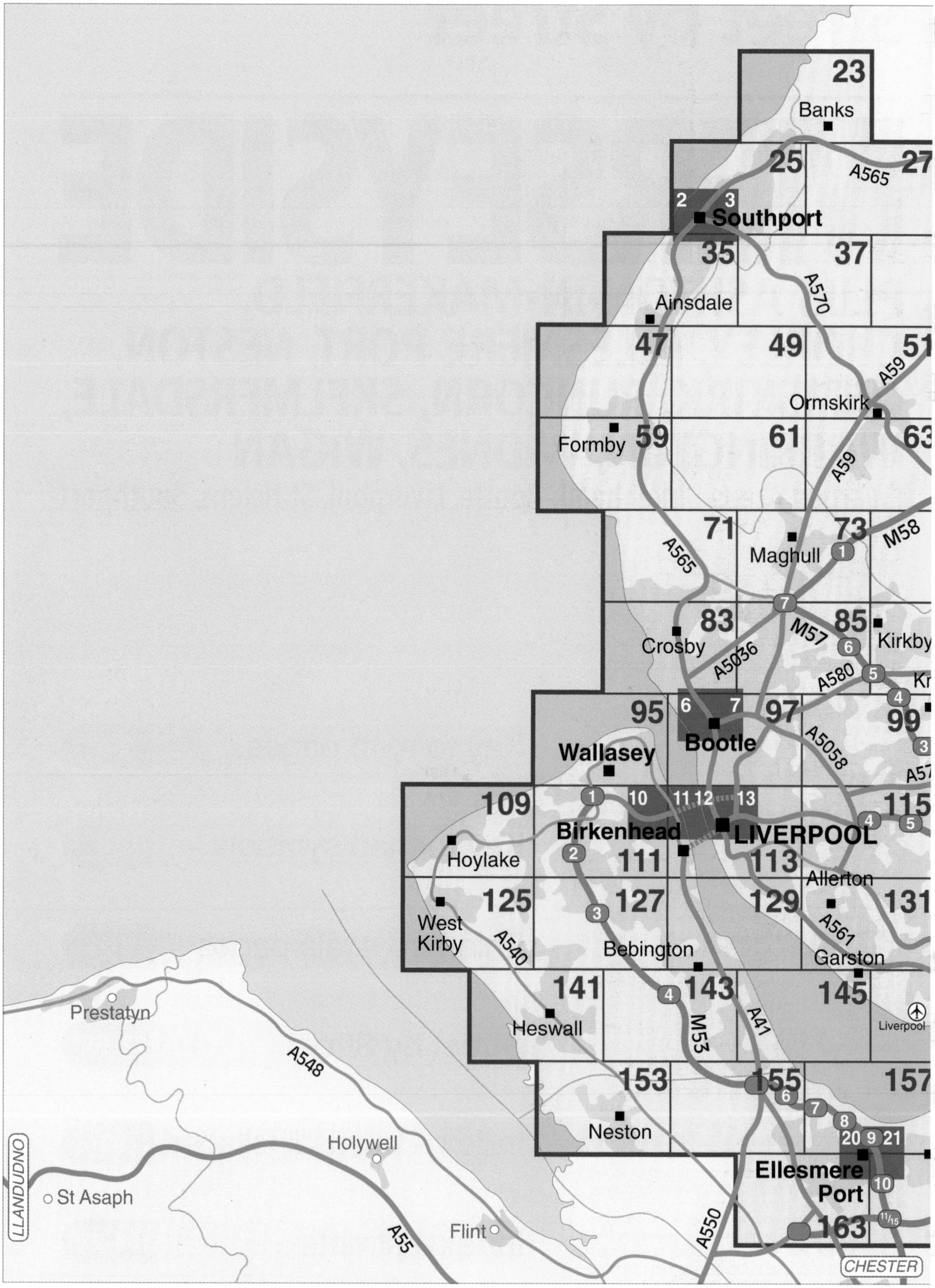

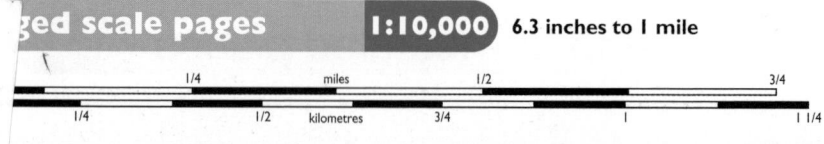

23
Banks
25
27
A565
2
3
Southport
35
37
A570
Ainsdale
47
49
51
A59
Ormskirk
Formby
59
61
63
A59
71
73
M58
Maghull
1
A565
7
83
85
Crosby
M57
6
Kirkby
A5036
A580
5
4
95
6
7
97
99
Wallasey
Bootle
A5058
3
109
1
10
11
12
13
115
Birkenhead
LIVERPOOL
4
5
Hoylake
2
111
113
Allerton
125
3
127
129
131
West
Kirby
A540
Bebington
A561
Garston
141
4
143
145
Prestatyn
Heswall
M53
A41
Liverpool
A548
153
155
157
6
7
8
Neston
20
9
21
Holywell
Ellesmere
Port
10
LLANDUDNO
St Asaph
A550
A55
Flint
163
CHESTER


ged scale pages **1:10,000** 6.3 inches to 1 mile

| | | | | | |
|---|---|---|---|---|---|
| miles | 1/4 | | 1/2 | 3/4 | |
| kilometres | 1/4 | 1/2 | 3/4 | 1 | 1 1/4 |

River/canal
lake, pier

Aqueduct
lock, weir

465
▲
Winter Hill

Peak (with
height in
metres)

Beach

Coniferous
woodland

Broadleaved
woodland

Mixed
woodland

Park

Cemetery

Built-up
area

Featured building

City wall

A&E

Accident &
Emergency
hospital

Toilet

Toilet with
disabled facilities

Petrol station

PH  Public house

PO  Post Office

Public library

i  Tourist Information
Centre

Castle

Historic house/
building

Wakehurst
Place NT

National Trust
property

M  Museum/
art gallery

†  Church/chapel

Country park

Theatre/
performing arts

Cinema

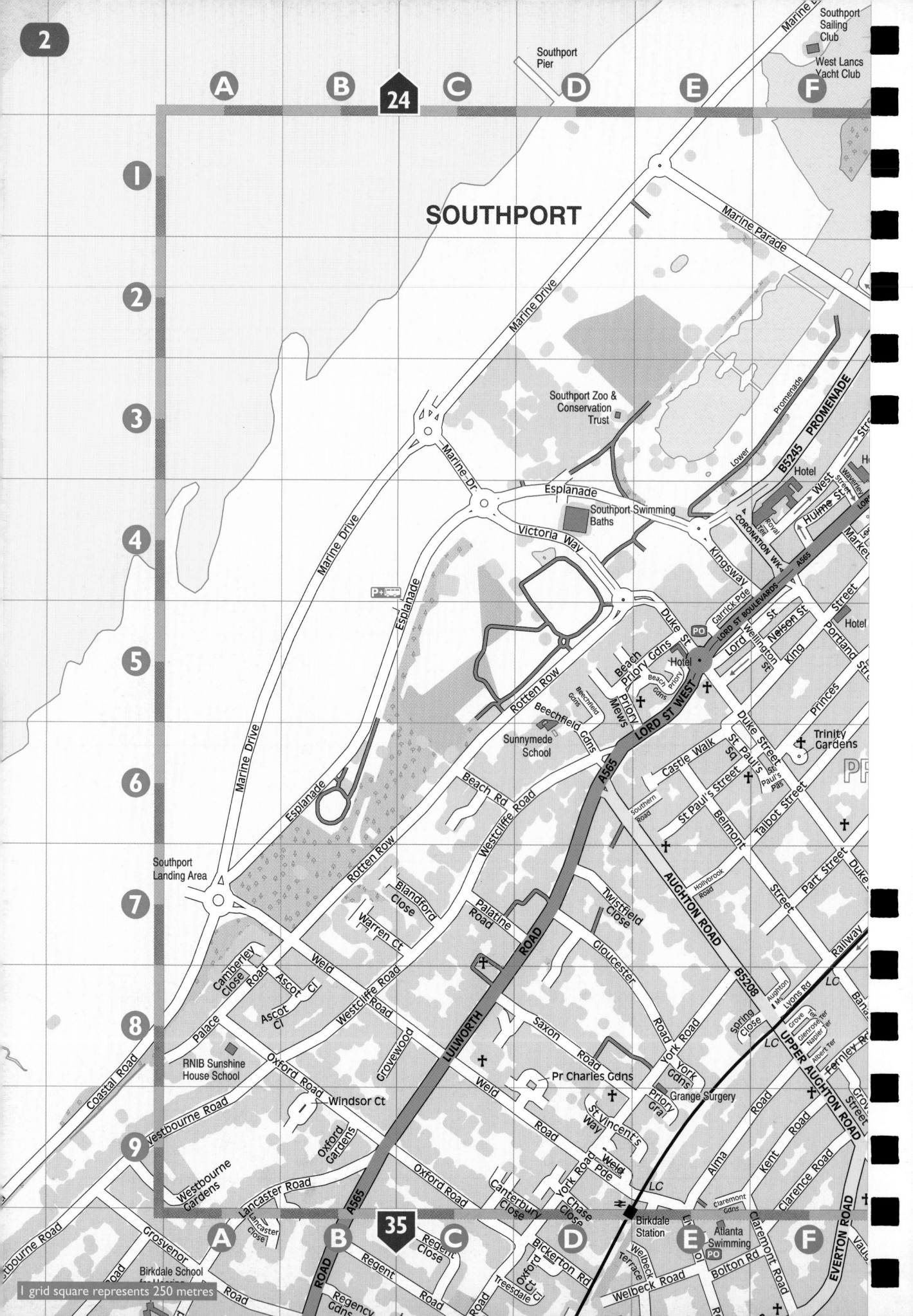

A  B  24  C  D  E  F

1

2

3

4

5

6

7

8

9

A  B  35  C  D  E  F

**SOUTHPORT**

Southport Pier

Southport
Sailing
Club

West Lancs
Yacht Club

Marine Parade

Marine Drive

Marine Dr

Esplanade

Victoria Way

Southport Zoo &
Conservation
Trust

Southport Swimming
Baths

Hotel

PROMENADE

B5245

Promenade

Lower

CORONATION WK

Hulme St

West St

Waverley

Royal Ter

Market

Street

A565

Kingsway

Garrick Pde

LORD ST BOULEVARDS

PO

Duke St

Lord St

Wellington St

Nelson St

King St

Portland St

Hotel

Beach
Priory Gdns

Hotel

Beach
Priory

Priory
Mews

Beechfield
Gdns

LORD ST WEST

Castle Walk

St Paul's
Sq

Duke Street

Princes

Trinity
Gardens

PR

Marine Drive

Esplanade

Rotten Row

Beechfield Gdns

A565

Southern
Road

St Paul's Street

St
Paul's
Pas

Belmont

Talbot Street

Part Street

Duke

Esplanade

Sunnymede
School

Beach Rd

Westcliffe Road

AUGHTON ROAD

Hollybrook

Southport
Landing Area

Rotten Row

Blandford
Close

Warren Ct

Palatine
Road

Twistfield
Close

Gloucester

Road

York Road

BS208

Railway

LC

Camberley
Close

Ascot
Ct

Westcliffe Road

LULWORTH ROAD

Saxon
Road

York
Gdns

Spring
Close

Aughton Mews

Lyons Rd

Grove

Glenrose Ter

Napier Ter

Albert Ter

LC

UPPER AUGHTON ROAD

Fernley Rd

Road

Ascot
Cl

Palace
Road

Coastal Road

RNIB Sunshine
House School

Oxford Road

Grovewood

Weld

Pr Charles Gdns

York Rd

Priory
Gra

Grange Surgery

Road

Kent Road

Crow
Street

Road

Westbourne Road

Windsor Ct

Oxford
Gardens

Weld
Road

St Vincent's
Way

Weld
Rd Pde

Atlanta
Swimming

PO

EVERTON ROAD

Westbourne
Gardens

Lancaster Road

A565

Regent
Close

Regent
Road

Canterbury
Close

York
Chase Close

Oxford
Ct Cl

Bickerton Rd

Treesdale

Birkdale
Station

Welbeck
Terrace

Alma

Bolton Rd

Welbeck Road

Claremont Road

Claremont
Gdns

Clarence Road

Grosvenor

Birkdale School
for Hearing

Regency
Gdns

Oxford Road

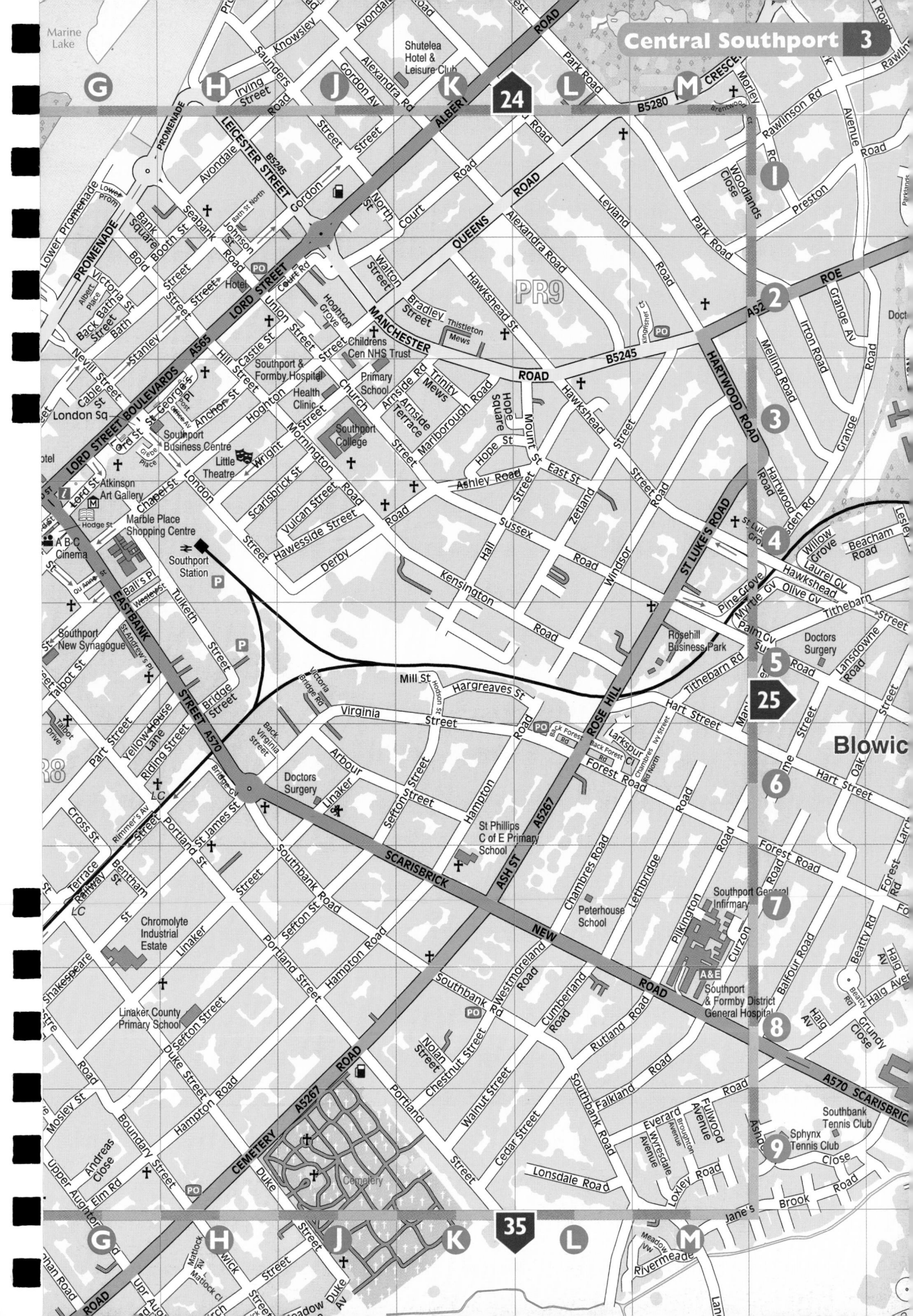

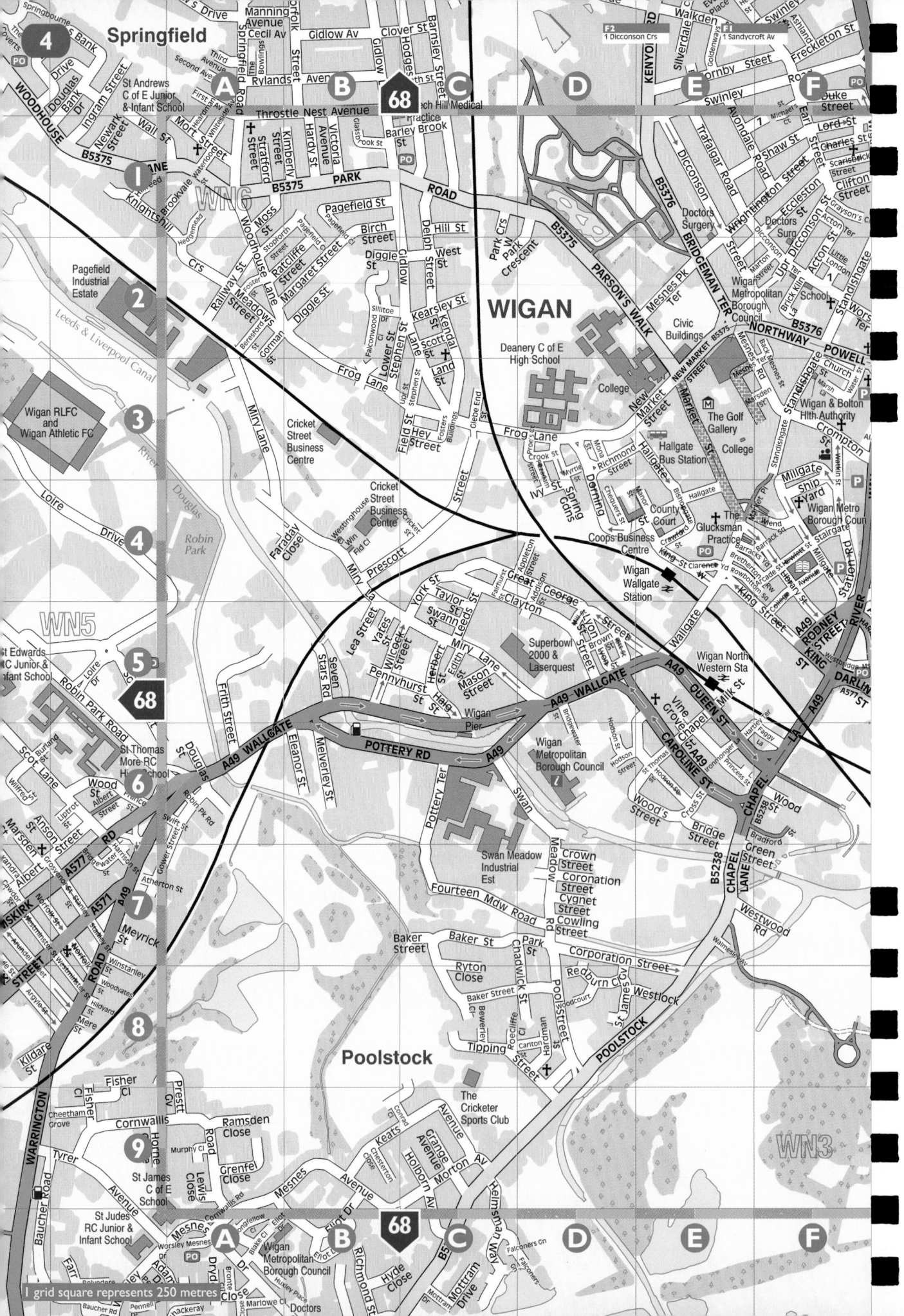

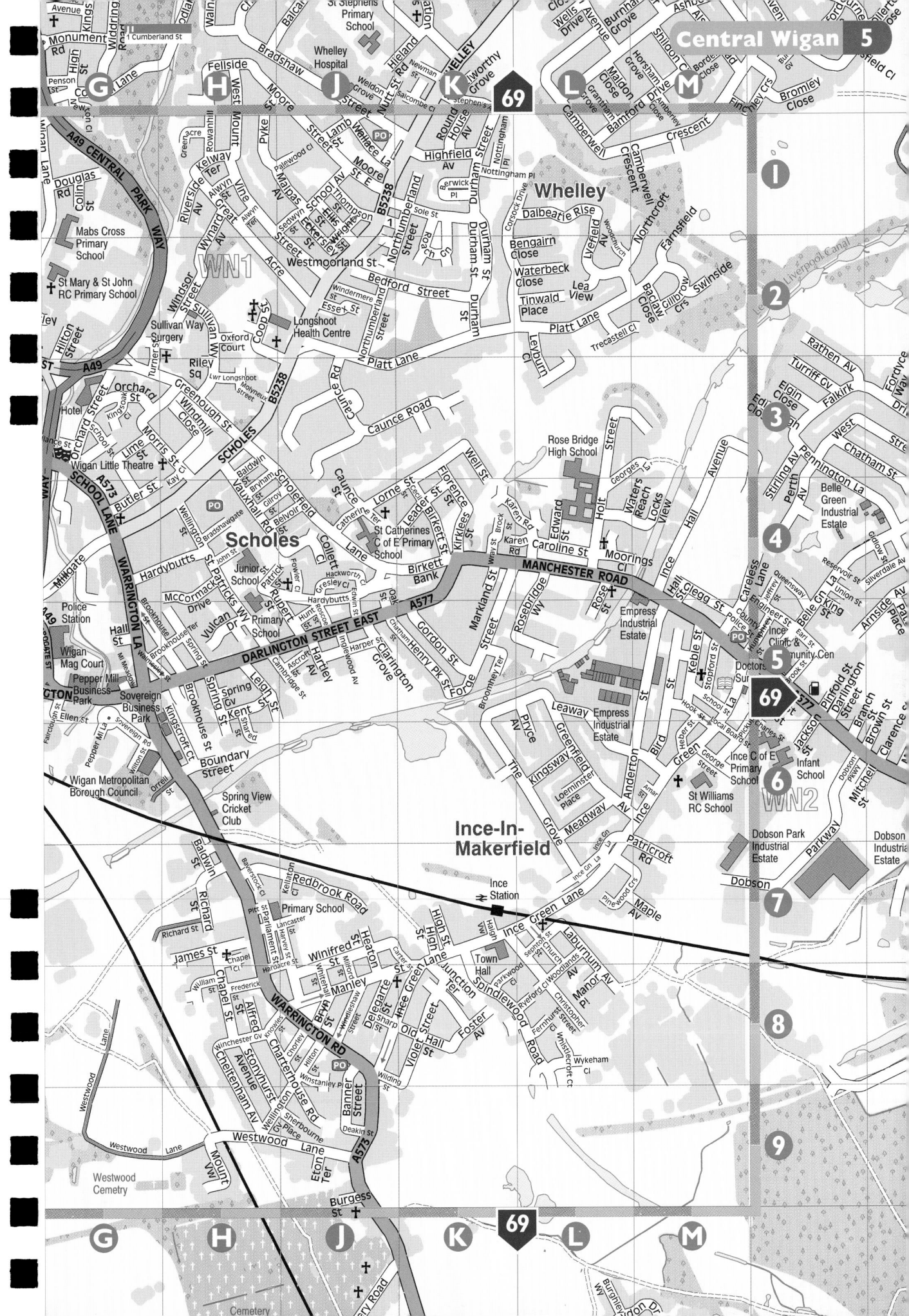

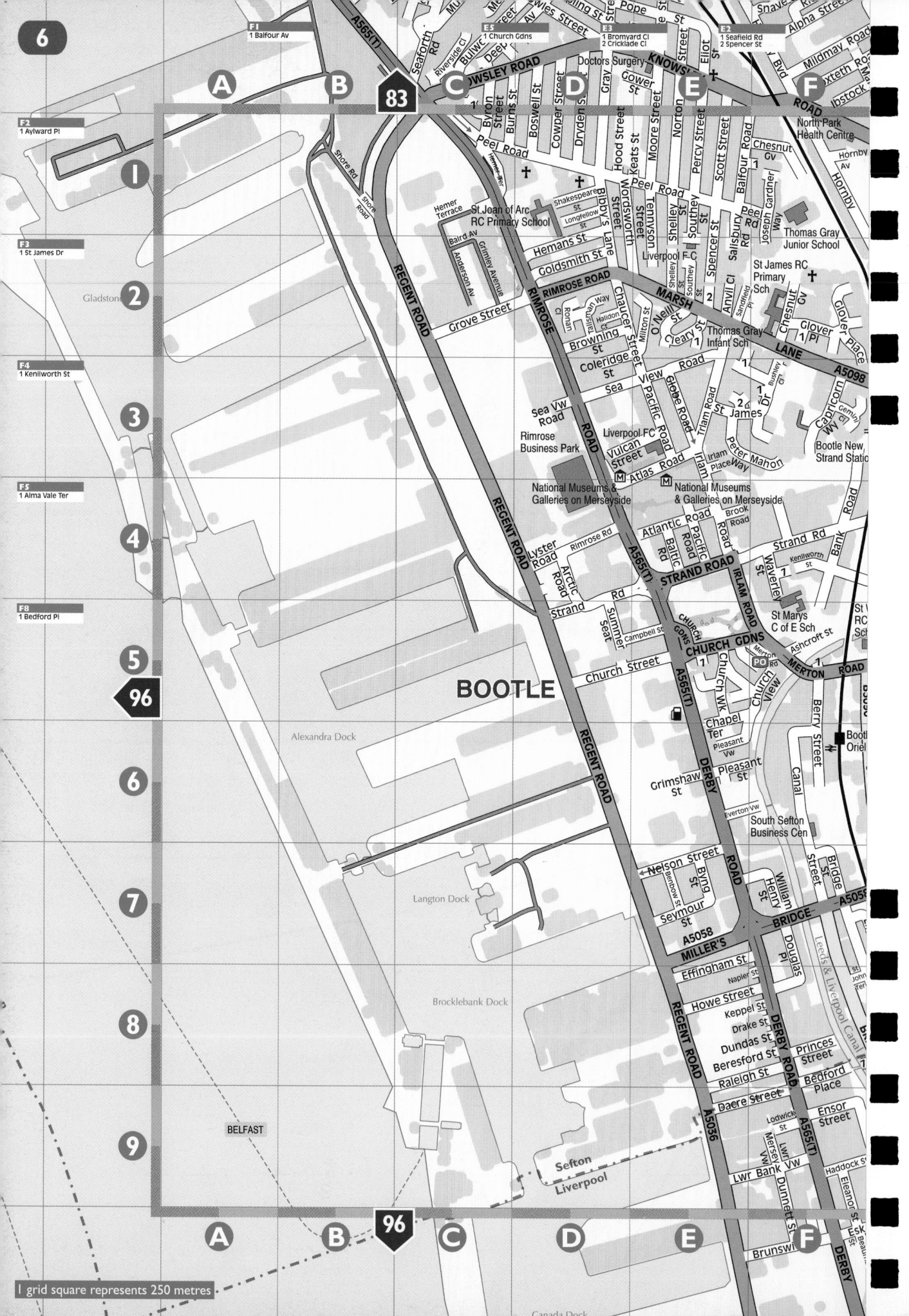

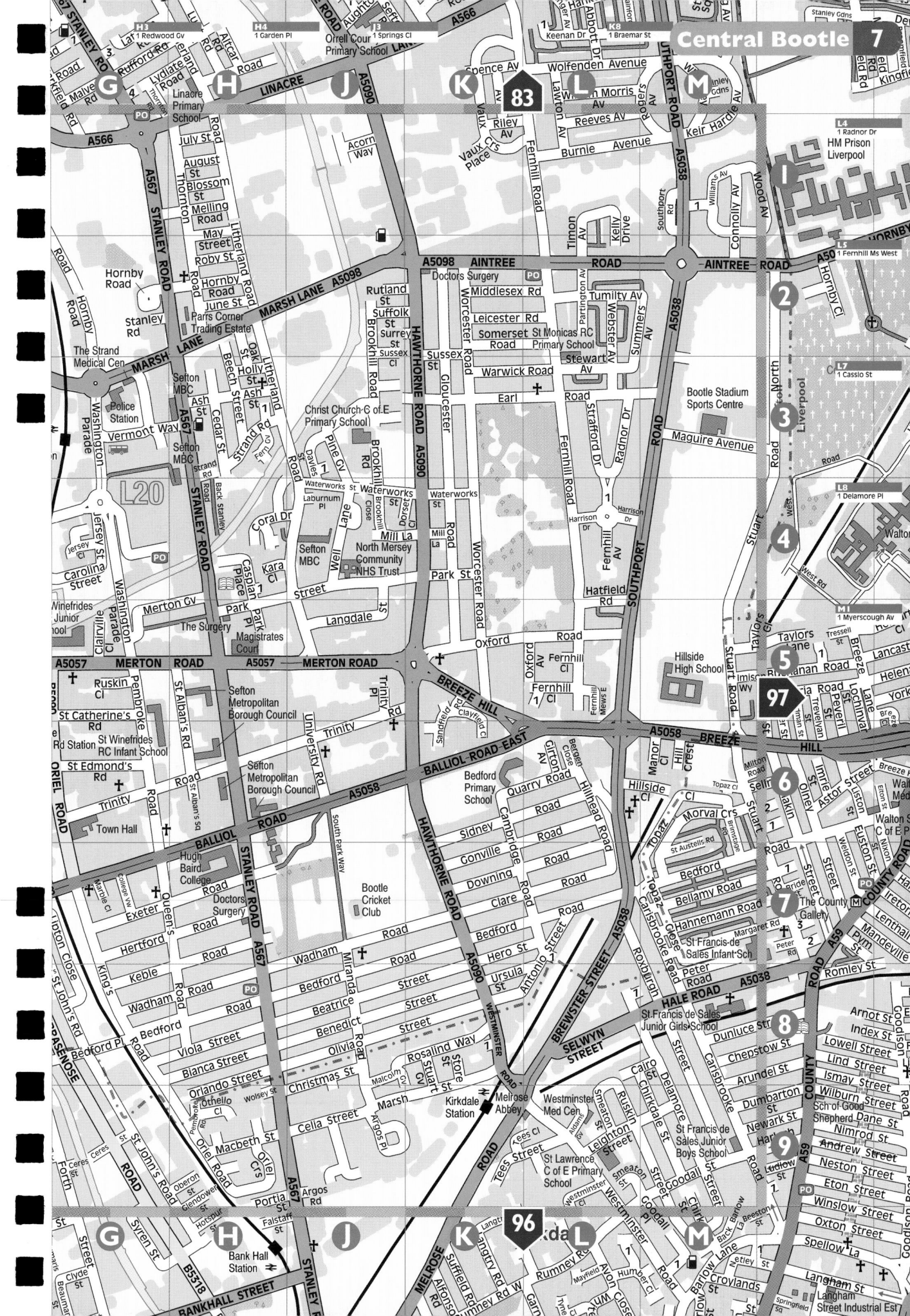

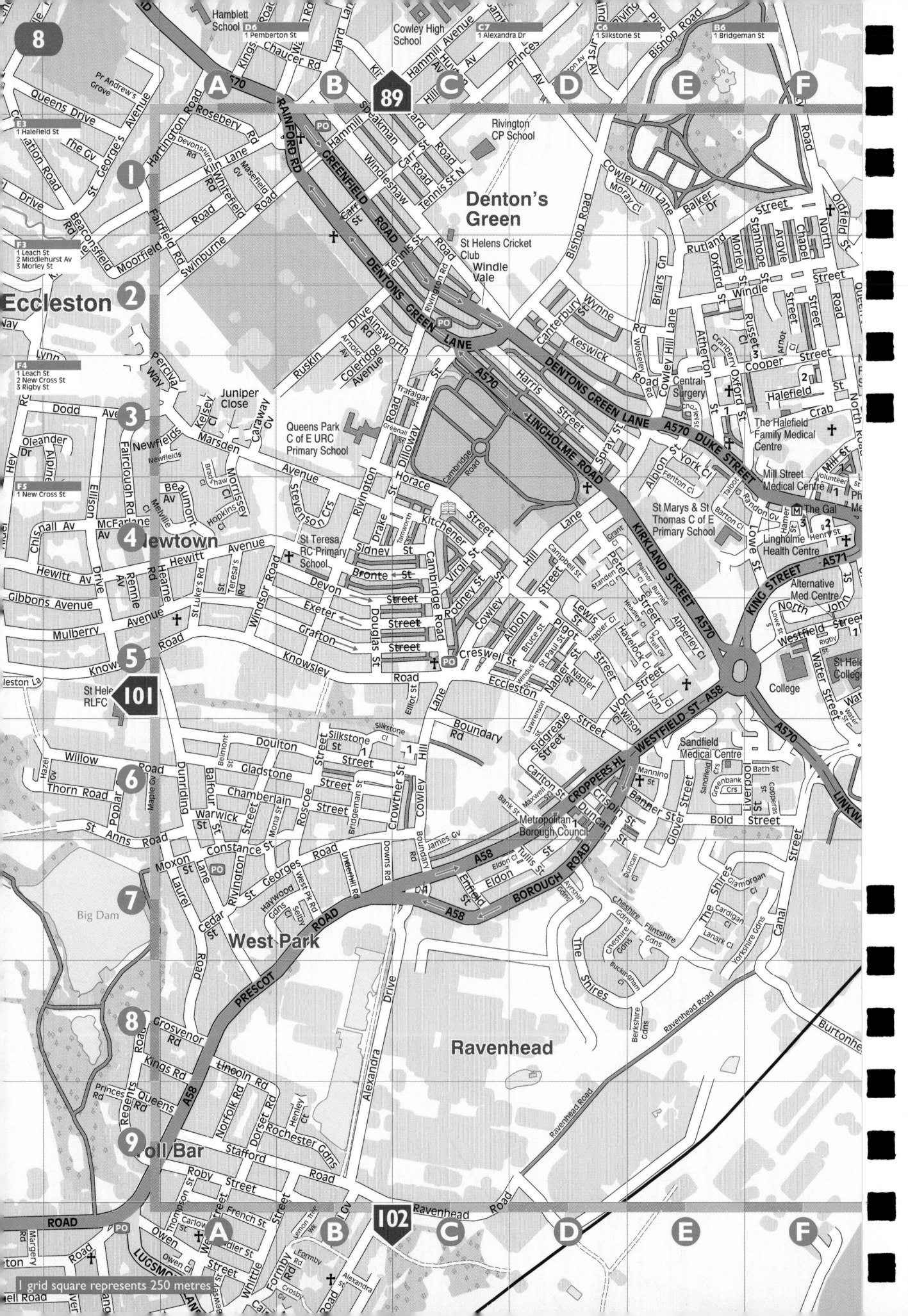

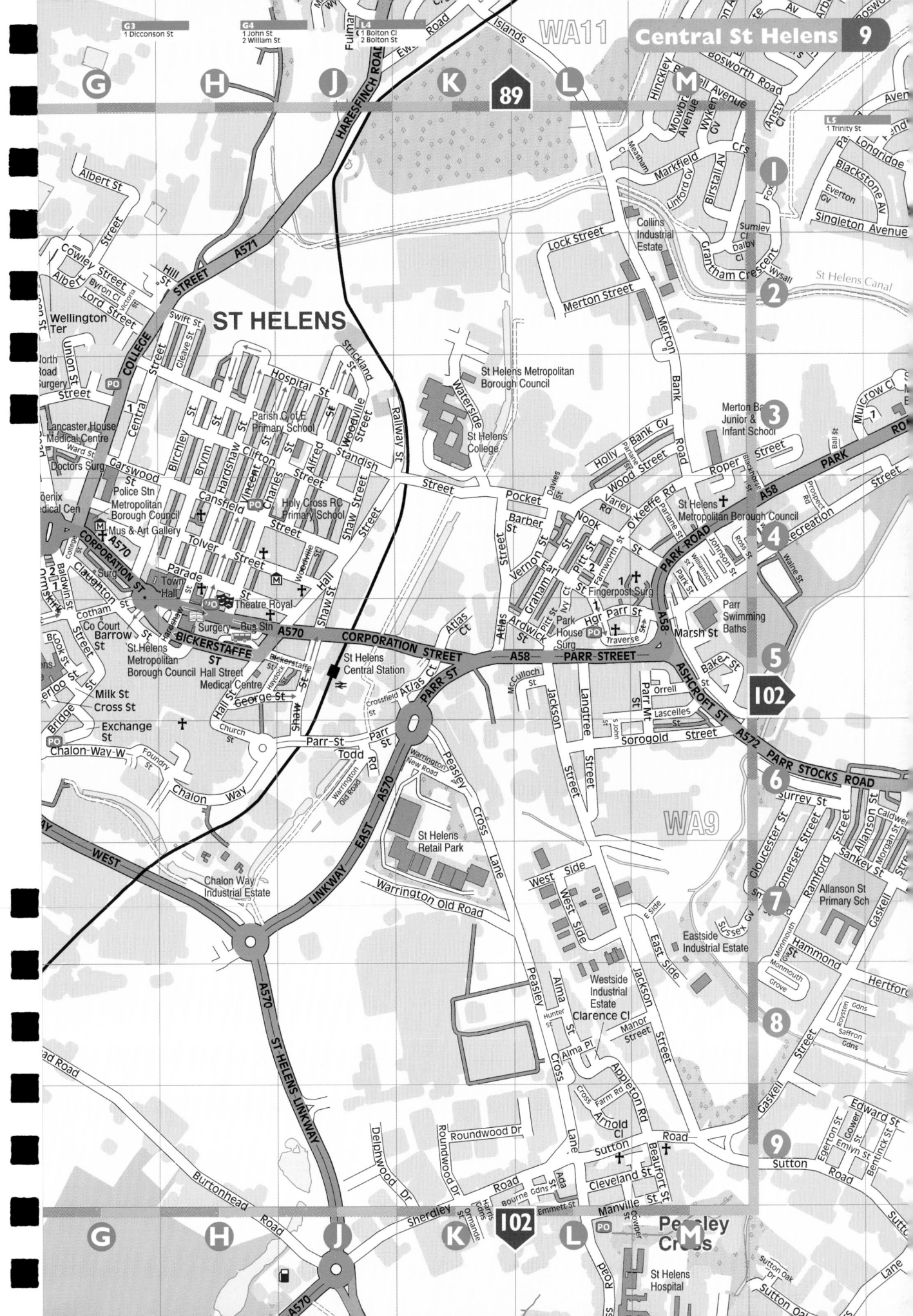

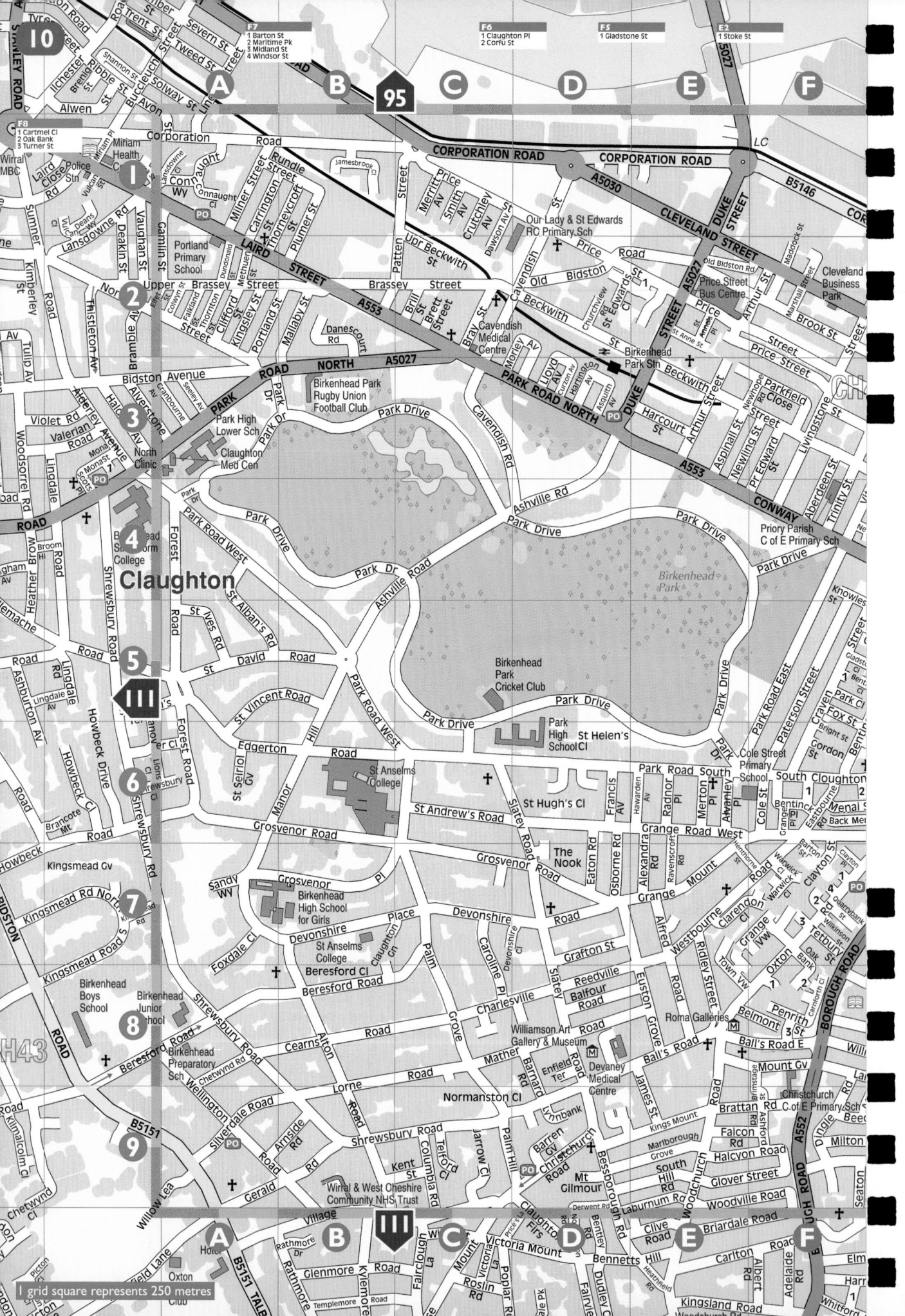

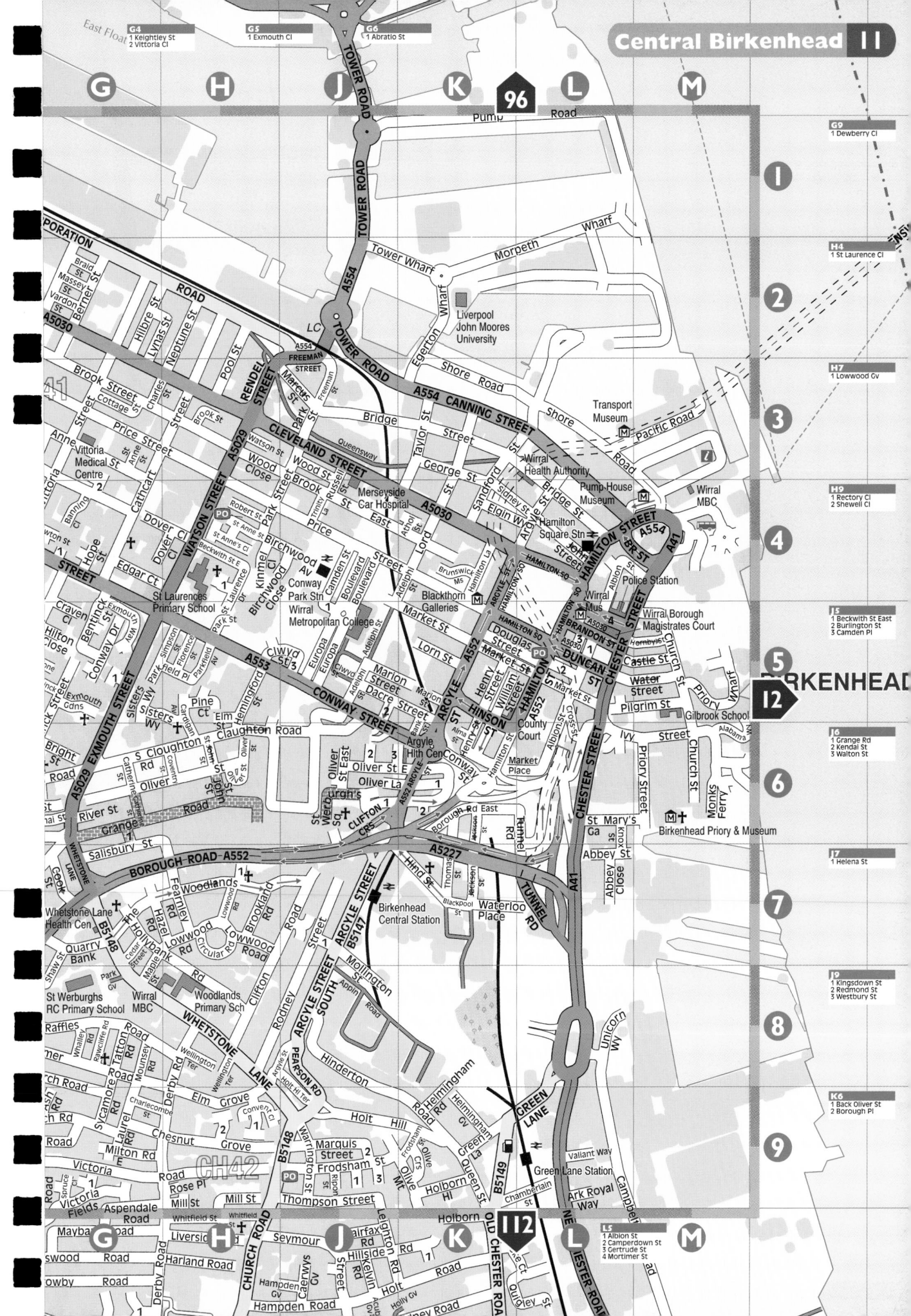

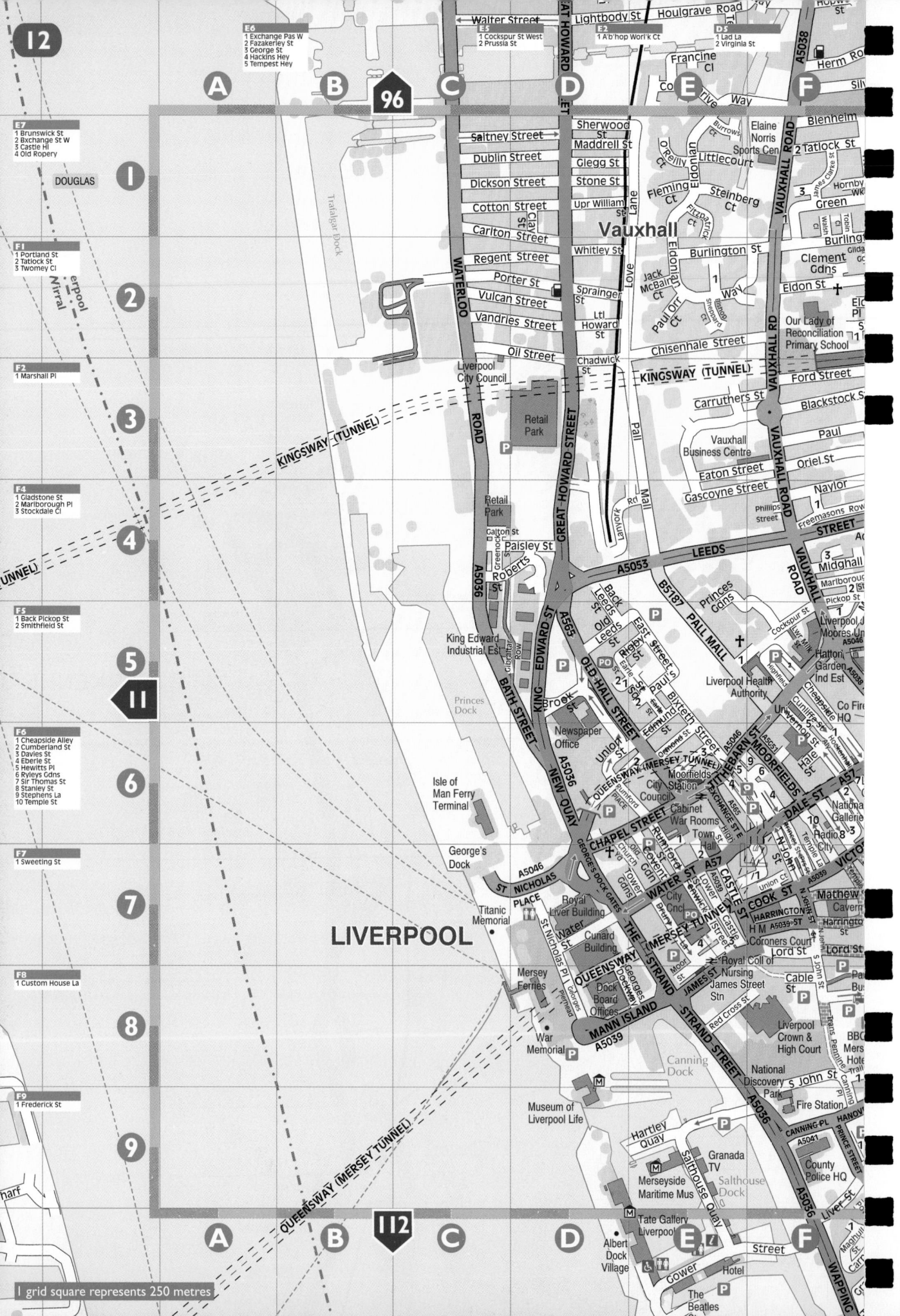

LIVERPOOL

Vauxhall

96

112

11

DOUGLAS

**E6**
1 Exchange Pas W
2 Fazakerley St
3 George St
4 Hackins Hey
5 Tempest Hey

**E5**
1 Cockspur St West
2 Prussia St

**E2**
1 A'b'hop Worl'k Ct

**D5**
1 Lad La
2 Virginia St

**E7**
1 Brunswick St
2 Exchange St W
3 Castle Hl
4 Old Ropery

**F1**
1 Portland St
2 Tatlock St
3 Twomey Cl

**F2**
1 Marshall Pl

**F4**
1 Gladstone St
2 Mariborough Pl
3 Stockdale Cl

**F5**
1 Back Pickop St
2 Smithfield St

**F6**
1 Cheapside Alley
2 Cumberland St
3 Davies St
4 Eberle St
5 Hewitts Pl
6 Ryleys Gdns
7 Sir Thomas St
8 Stanley St
9 Stephens La
10 Temple St

**F7**
1 Sweeting St

**F8**
1 Custom House La

**F9**
1 Frederick St

Trafalgar Dock

Saltney Street
Dublin Street
Dickson Street
Cotton Street
Carlton Street
Regent Street
Porter St
Vulcan Street
Vandries Street
Oil Street

Liverpool City Council

WATERLOO ROAD

KINGSWAY (TUNNEL)

Retail Park

Retail Park

King Edward Industrial Est

Princes Dock

Isle of Man Ferry Terminal

George's Dock

Titanic Memorial

Mersey Ferries

Museum of Liverpool Life

Hartley Quay

Tate Gallery Liverpool

Albert Dock Village

Gower

The Beatles

Hotel

Sherwood St
Maddrell St
Glegg St
Stone St
Upr William St
Whitley St
Sprainger St
Ltl Howard St
Chadwick St
Chisenhale Street

Love Lane

GREAT HOWARD STREET

KINGSWAY (TUNNEL)

Carruthers St

Paisley St

Galton St
Greenock St
Roberts
Gibraltar Row

KING EDWARD ST

OLD HALL STREET

A5036

A565

A5036

BATH STREET

NEW QUAY

Newspaper Office

Union St

Brook St

QUEENSWAY (MERSEY TUNNEL)

CHAPEL STREET

ST NICHOLAS PLACE

Royal Liver Building

Cunard Building

Water St

Dock Board Offices

GEORGES DOCK GATES

THE STRAND

St Nicholas Pl

Georges Pierhead

War Memorial

MANN ISLAND

A5039

Canning Dock

STRAND STREET

Salthouse Quay

Merseyside Maritime Mus

Salthouse Dock

Granada TV

CANNING PL

PRINCE STREET

A5041

County Police HQ

WAPPING

A5036

LIVERPOOL

Elaine Norris Sports Cen
Littlecourt

O'Reilly Ct
Fleming Ct
Steinberg Ct
Fitzpatrick Ct

Burlington St

Jack McBaine Ct
Paul Orr Ct

Clement Gdns

Eldon St
Eldon Pl

Our Lady of Reconciliation Primary School

Ford Street

Carruthers St

Blackstock St

Paul
Oriel St
Naylor

Vauxhall Business Centre
Eaton Street
Gascoyne Street

Phillips Street

Freemasons Row

VAUXHALL ROAD

VAUXHALL RD

STREET

Midghall

Marlborough
Pickop

LEEDS

A5053

B5187

PALL MALL

Princes Gdns

Back Leeds St
Old Leeds St
East Street
Paul's Sq

Rigby St
Earle St

PO

Bixteth Street

Edmund St
Ormond St

Liverpool John Moores Un

A5046

Hatton Garden Ind Est

Liverpool Health Authority

Cheapside

Co Fire HQ

Cunliffe St
Vernon St
Hale St

DALE ST

Exchange St E

Moorfields Station

Moorfields

City Council

Cabinet War Rooms
Town Hall

Rumford Place
Rumford
Covent Gdn
Church St
Tower Gdns
Lower Castle St

A57

City Cncl

A57

Water St

Cook St

Victoria St

National Galleries
Radio City

John St

Harrington

Cavern

Mathew St

HM Coroners Court

Lord St

Lord St

Castle St

MERSEY TUNNEL

James St

Royal Coll of Nursing

James Street Stn

Red Cross St

Liverpool Crown & High Court

National Discovery Park

John St

Fire Station

Cable St

Hanover

Liver St

1 grid square represents 250 metres

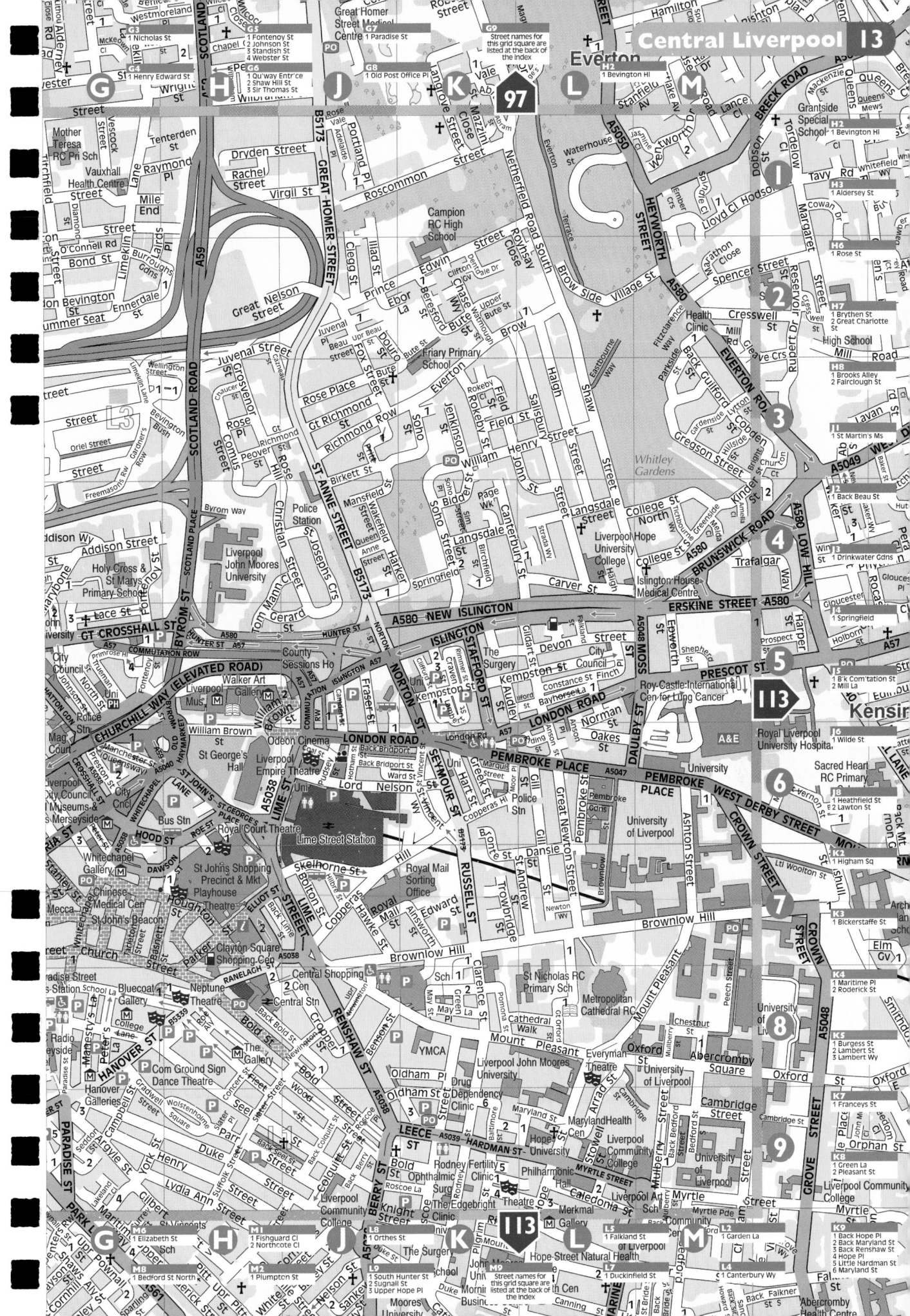

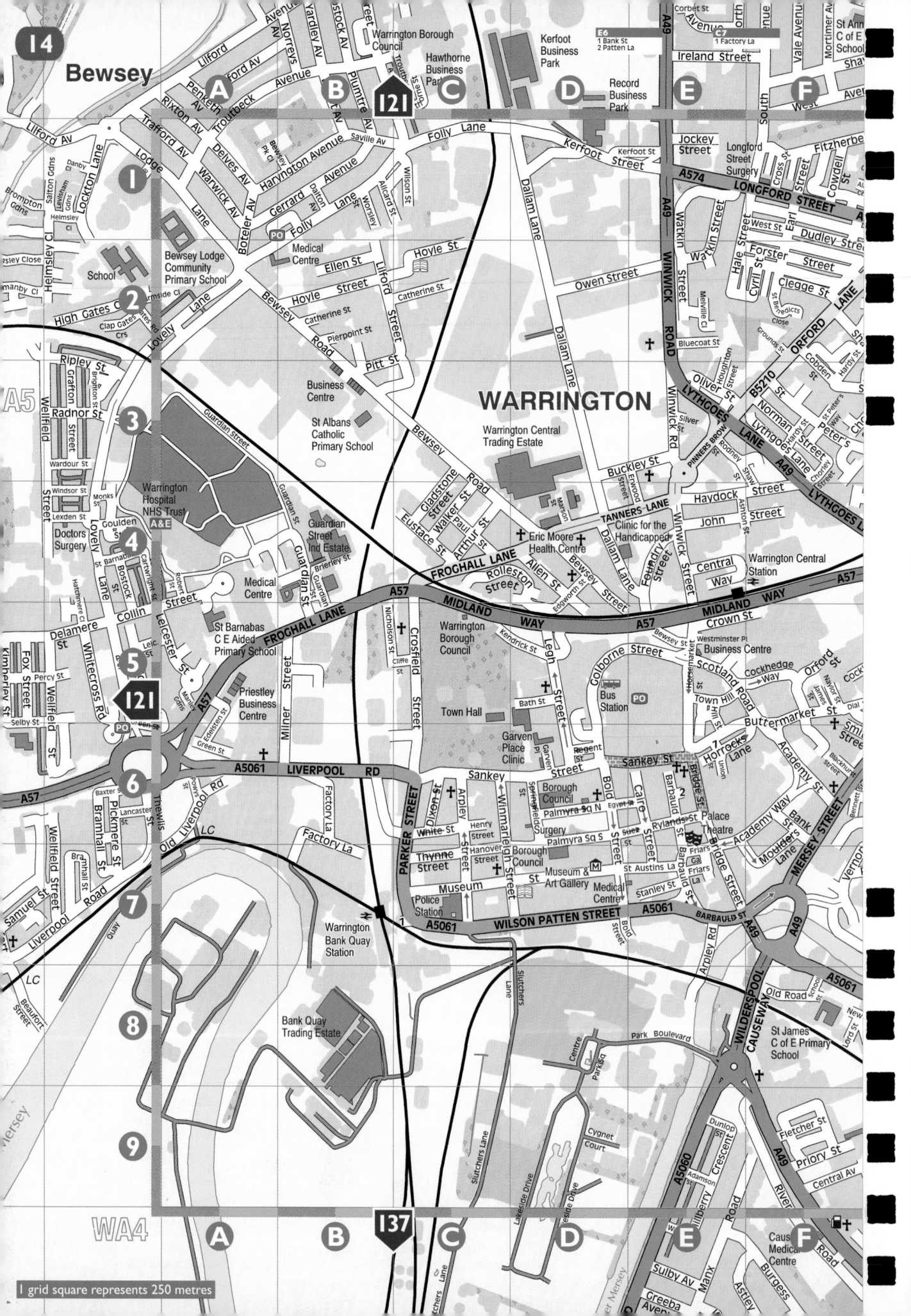

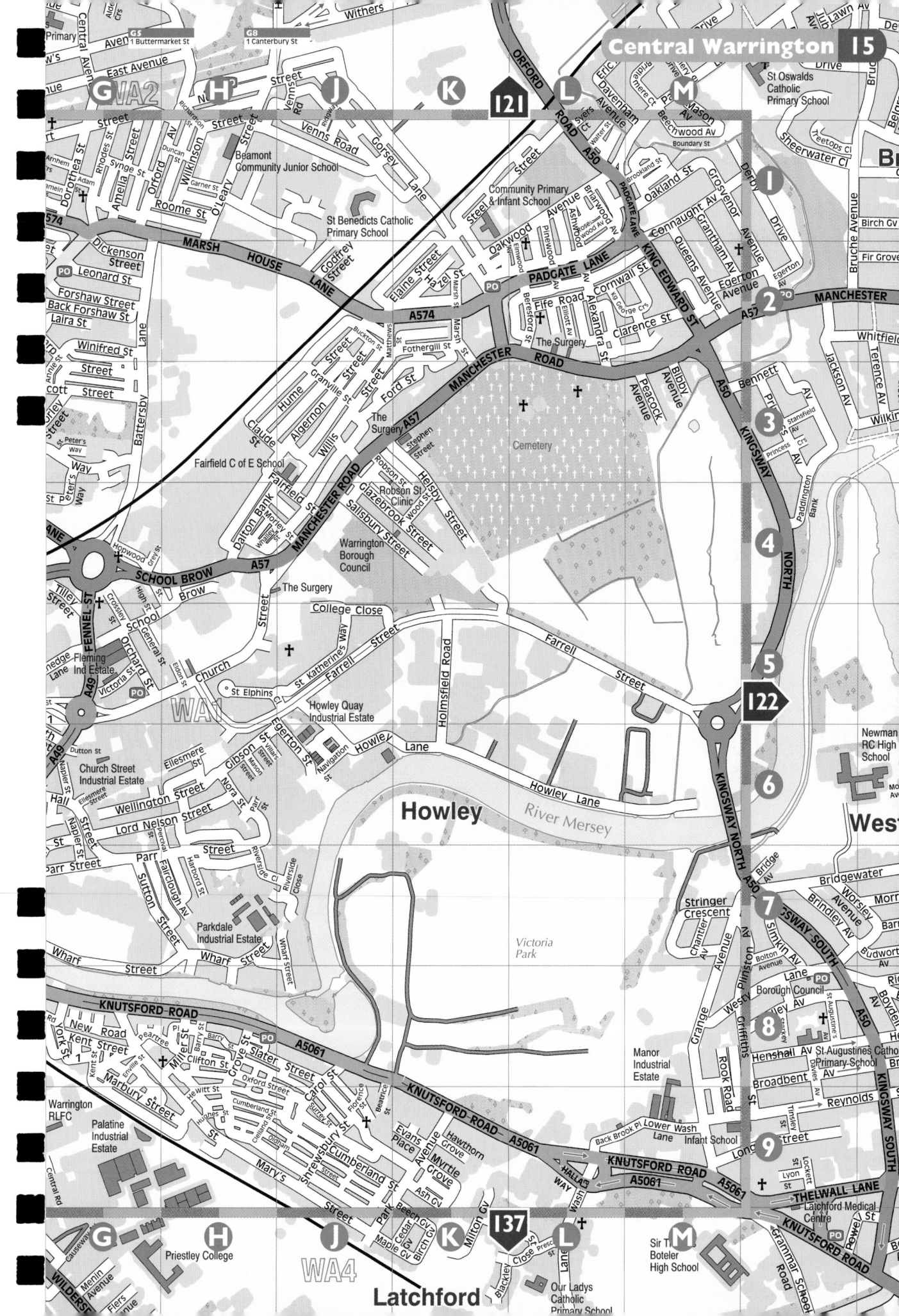

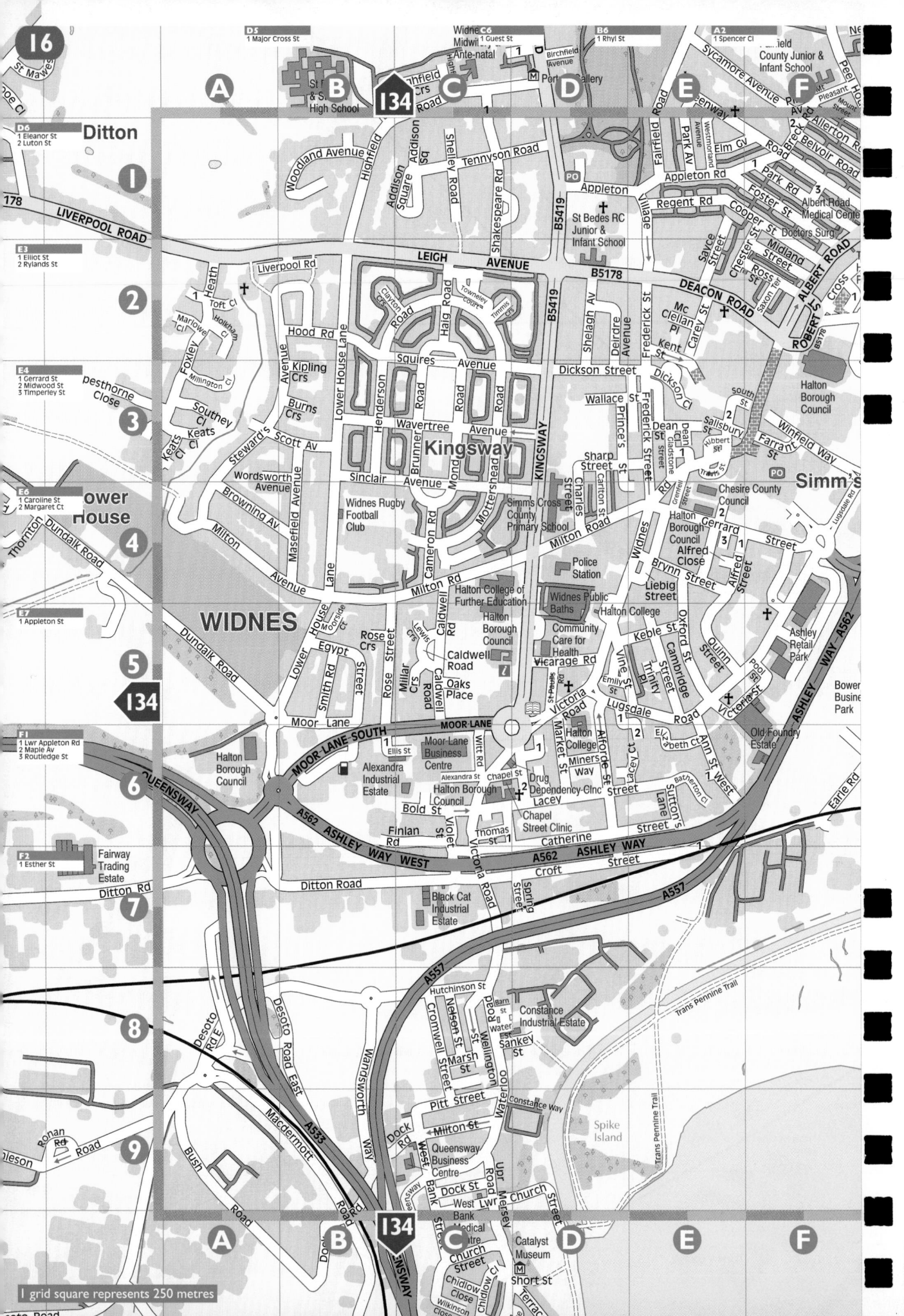

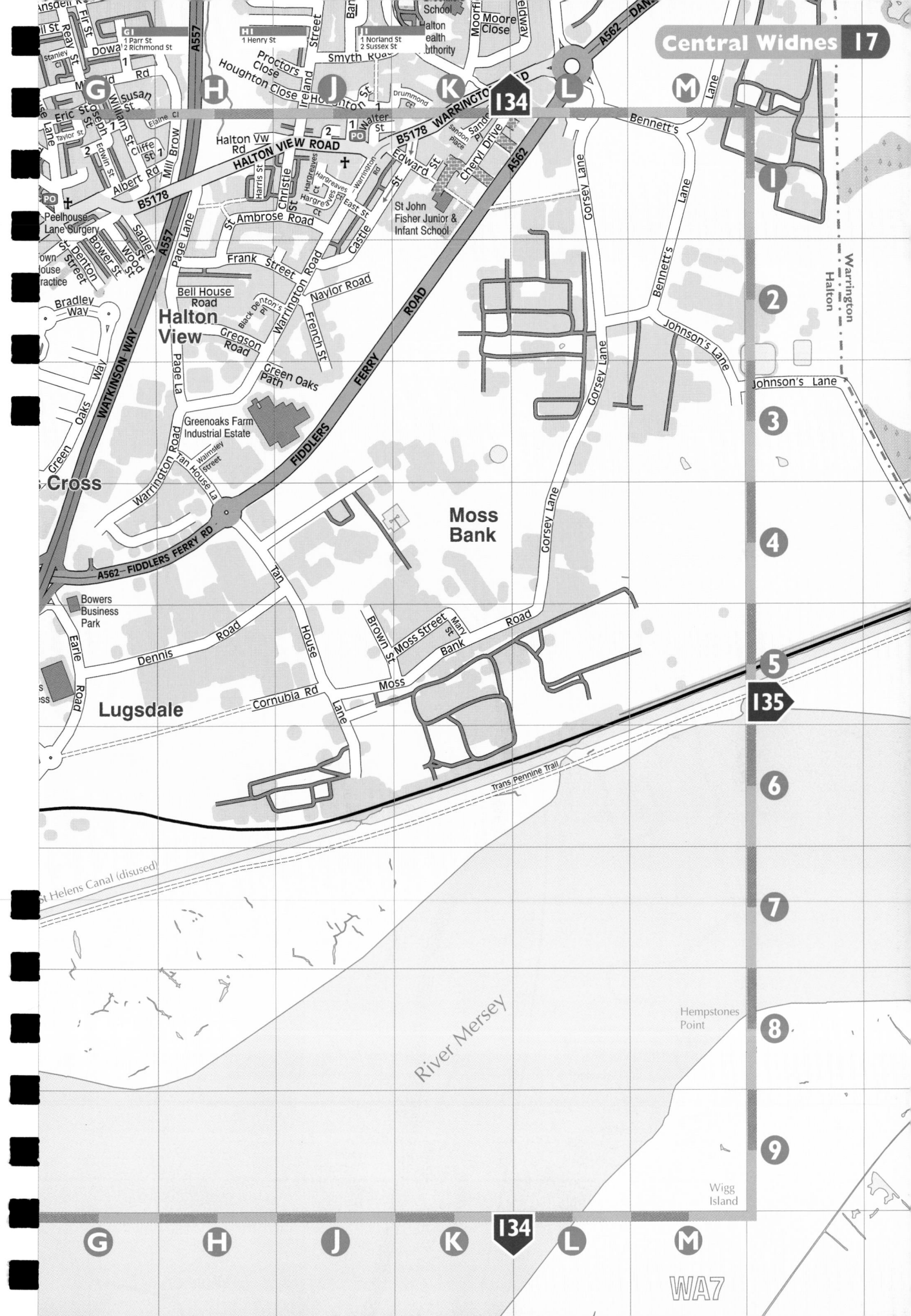

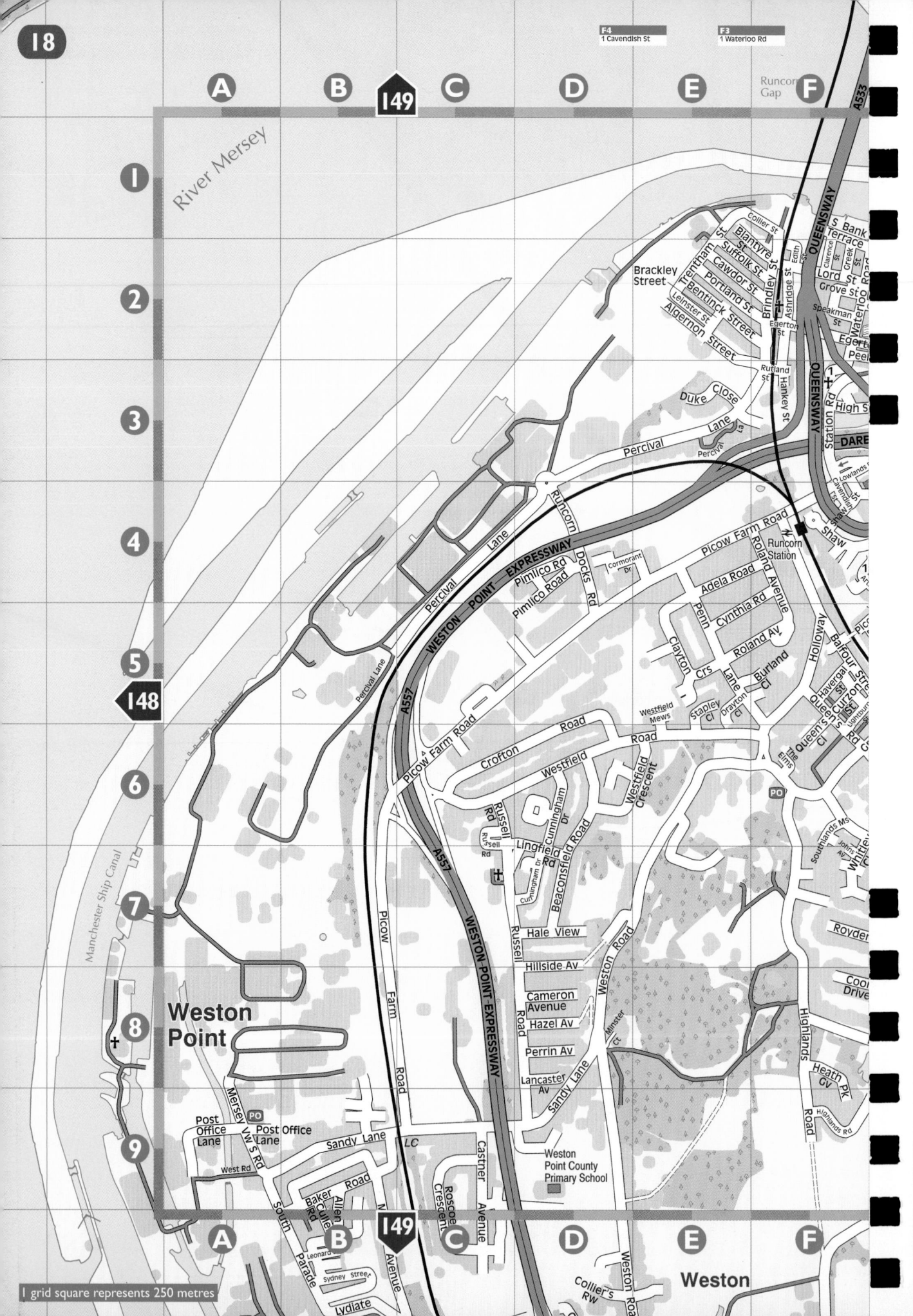

F4
1 Cavendish St

F3
1 Waterloo Rd

A    B    149    C    D    E    F

Runcorn
Gap

A533

River Mersey

1

2

Brackley
Street

Collier St
Blantyre St
Trentham St
Suffolk St
Cawdor St
Portland St
Bentinck Street
Algernon Street
Leinster St
Edith St
Brindley St
Ashridge St

S Bank
Terrace
Clarence St
Greek St
Lord
Grove St

QUEENSWAY
Speakman
Av

Egerton
St
Waterloo St
Egert
Peel

3

Duke
Lane
Close
Percival
La

Percival
Rutland
St
Hankey St

QUEENSWAY
High St
Station Rd
DARE
Lowlands

4

Percival
Lane
WESTON POINT EXPRESSWAY
Docks Rd
Pimlico Rd
Pimlico Road
Cormorant
Dr

Picow Farm Road
Roland Avenue
Adela Road
Cynthia Rd
Penn
Roland Av
Holloway
Balfour Str
Runcorn Station
Shaw

Picow

5
148

Percival Lane
A557
Clayton
Crs
Lane
Drayton
Stapley Cl
Burland
Ct
Havergal St
Queen's Cl
Curzon
Cl
Lomborn

6

Picow Farm Road
A557
Crofton
Road
Russell
Rd
Russell
Rd
Lingfield
Rd
Westfield
Road
Westfield
Mews
Westfield
Road
Cunningham
Dr
Beaconsfield Road
Westfield
Crescent
The
Elms
PO
Southlands Ms
Johns
Av
Whitlei

7

Picow
Farm
Road
WESTON POINT EXPRESSWAY
Russell
Road
Cunningham Dr
Hale View
Hillside Av
Cameron
Avenue
Hazel Av
Perrin Av
Lancaster
Av
Sandy Lane
Weston Road
Minster
Ct
Highlands
Road
Royden
Cook
Drive
Heath
Gv
Heath PK

8

Weston
Point

9

Manchester Ship Canal

Post
Office
Lane
PO
Post Office
Lane
Mersey Vw S Rd
West Rd
Sandy Lane
LC
Baker
Cullen
Rd
Allen
Rd
South
Parade
Castner
Avenue
Roscoe
Crescent
Weston
Point County
Primary School
Highlands Rd

A    B    149    C    D    E    F

Leonard
Sydney Street
Lydiate
N Avenue
Collier's
RW
Weston Roa

Weston

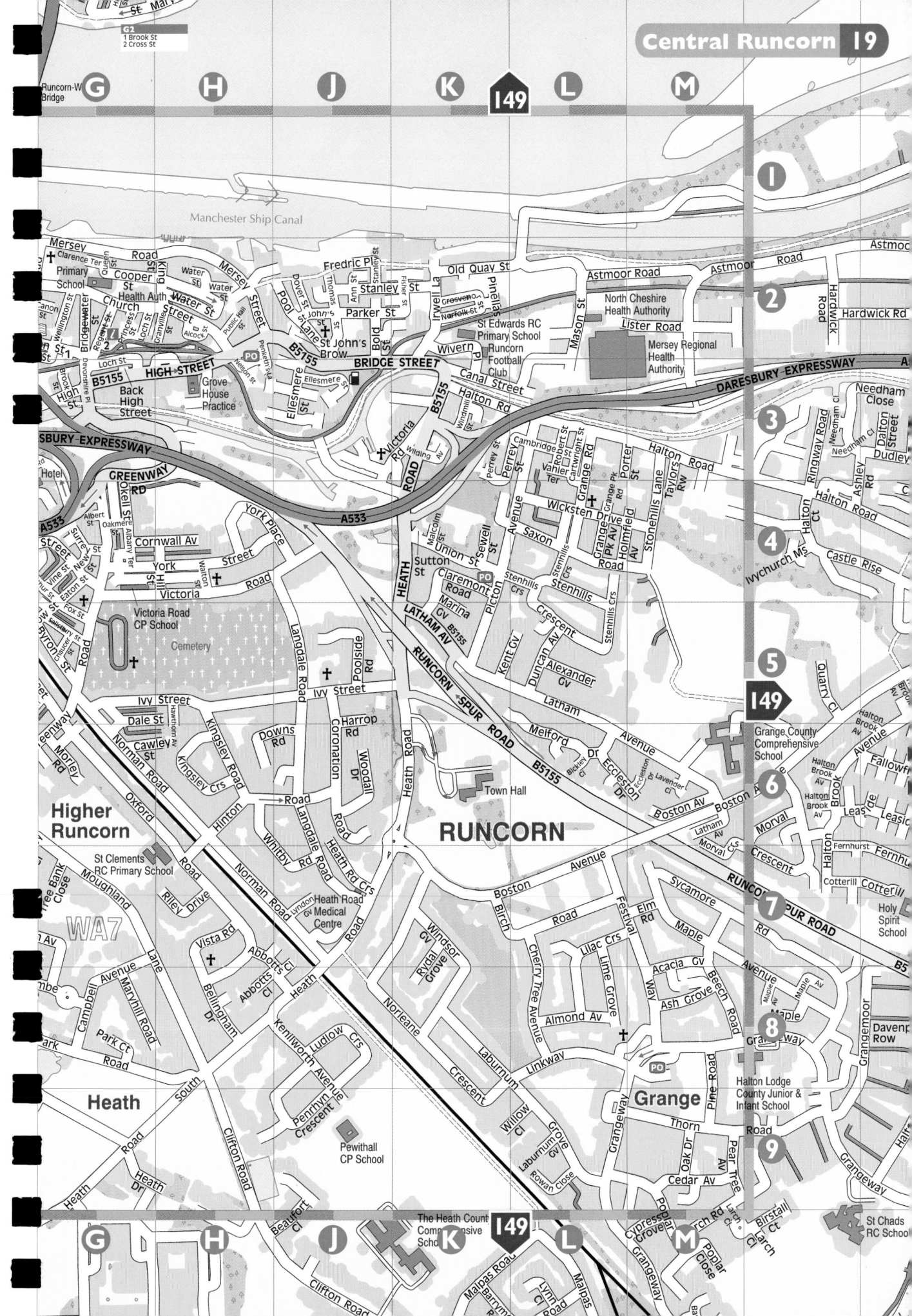

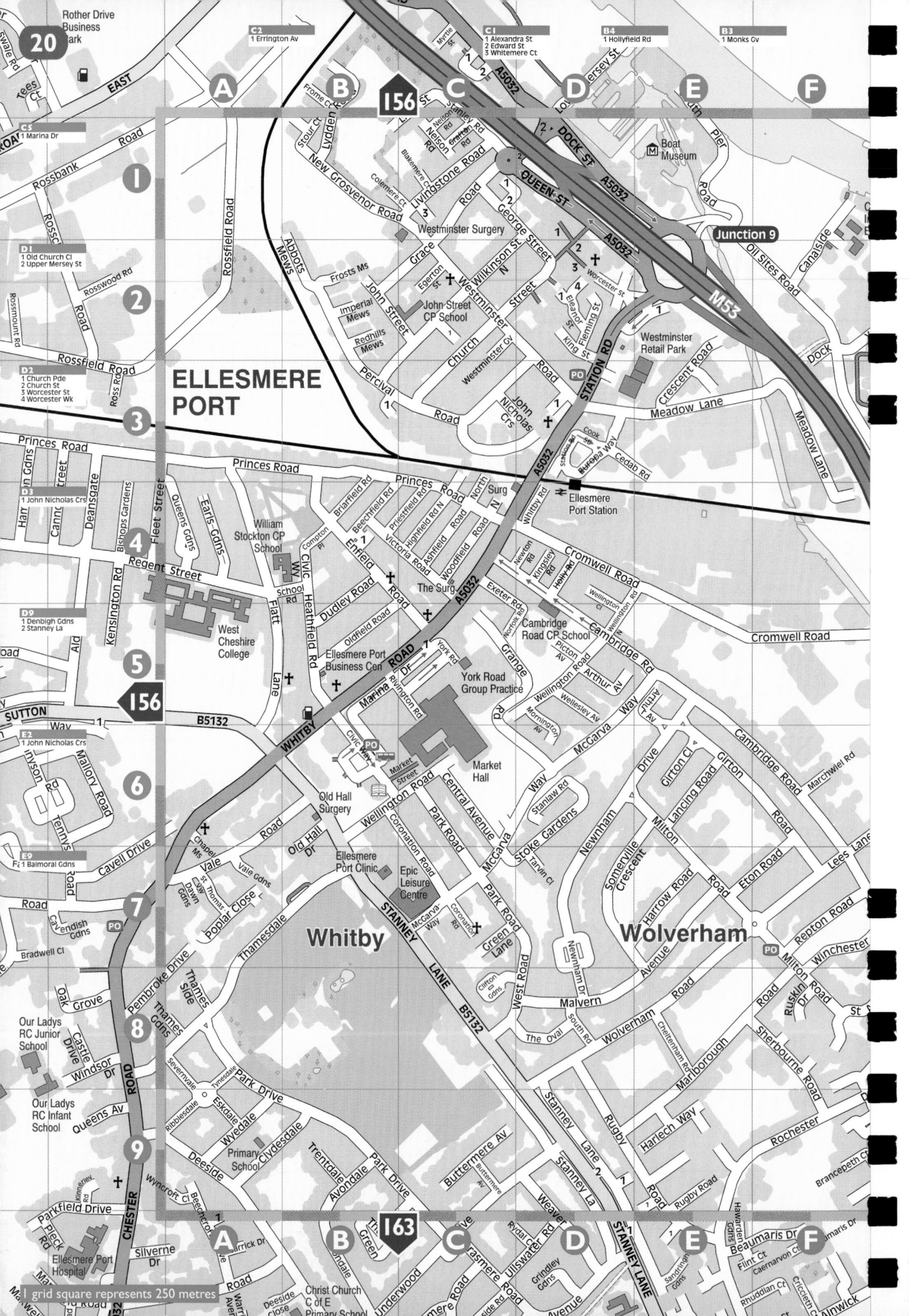

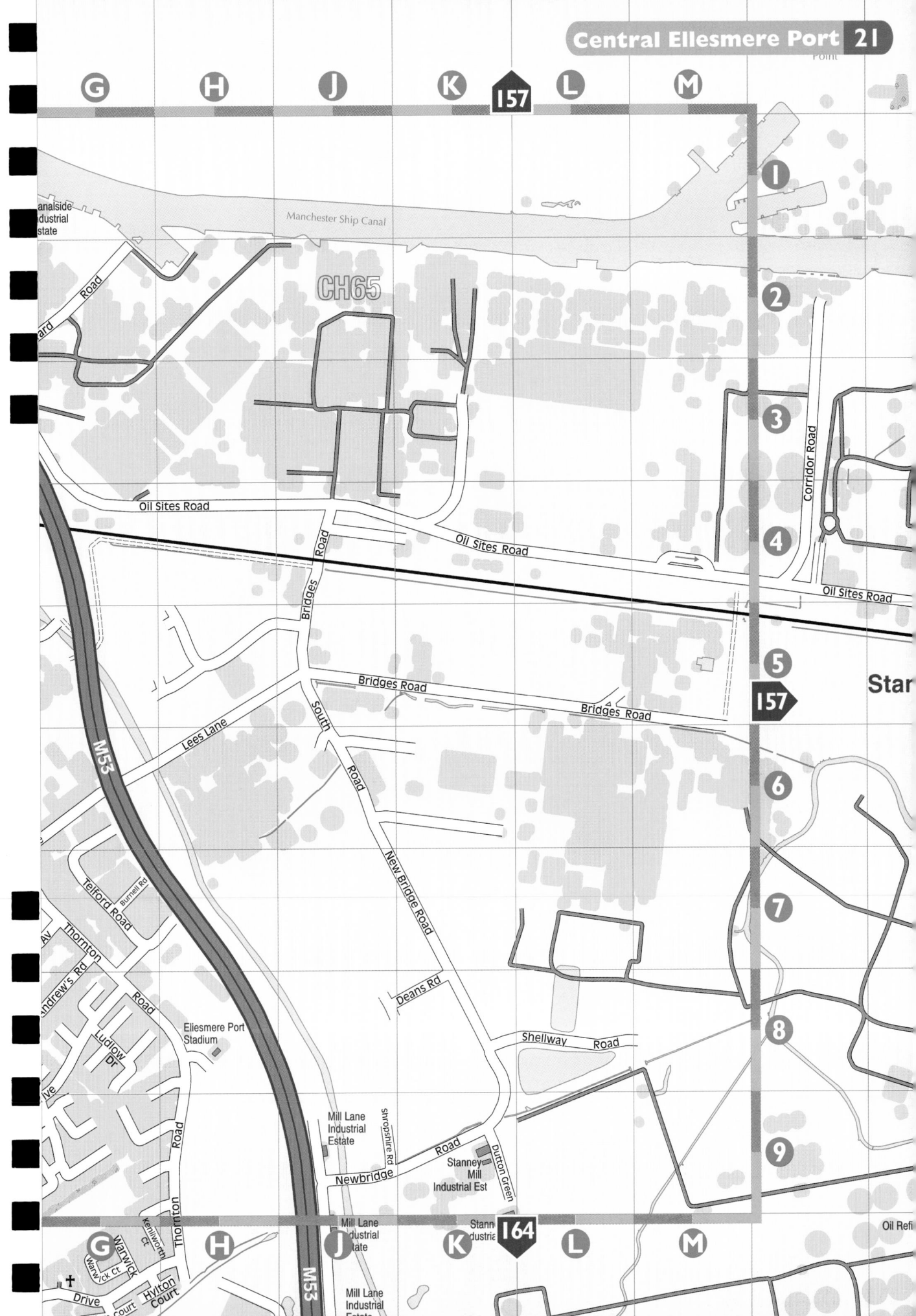

G H J K 157 L M

Point

Manchester Ship Canal

Canalside Industrial Estate

CH65

ard Road

Oil Sites Road

Oil Sites Road

Bridges Road

1

2

Corridor Road

3

4

Oil Sites Road

5

157 Star

Bridges Road

Bridges Road

Lees Lane

South Road

New Bridge Road

M53

6

7

Telford Road

Burnell Rd

AV Thornton

ndrew's Rd

Road

Ludlow Dr

ive

Eliesmere Port Stadium

Deans Rd

Shellway Road

8

9

Mill Lane Industrial Estate

Shropshire Rd

Road

Stanney Mill Industrial Est

Dutton Green

Newbridge

Thornton Road

G H J 164 K L M

Warwick Ct

Kenilworth Ct

Mill Lane Industrial Estate

Stann dustria

Oil Refi

† Warwick Drive

William Court Hylton Court

M53

Mill Lane Industrial Estate

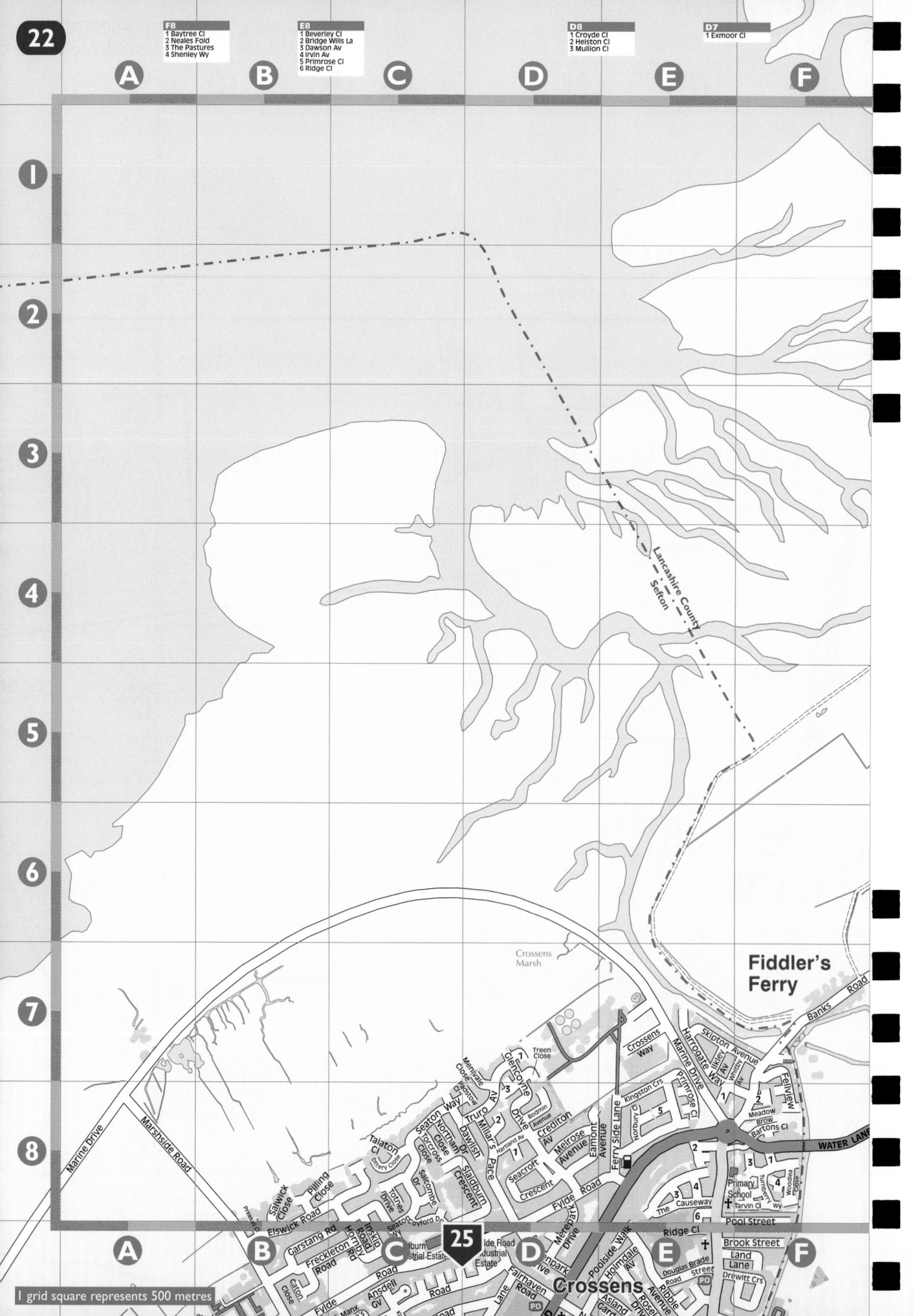

A   B   C   D   E   F

I

2

3

4

5

6

7

8

A   B   C   D   E   F

Lancashire County
Sefton

Fiddler's
Ferry

Crossens
Marsh

Banks Road

WATER LANE

Marine Drive

Marshside Road

Menivale Close

Seaton Way

Norham Dr

Truro Av

Dawlish

Talaton Cl

Ottery Close

Saltcombe Dr

Slapton Crescent

Seacroft Crescent

Millar's Pace

Hartland Av

Crediton Av

Bodmin Av

Melrose Avenue

Eamont Avenue

Ferry Side Lane

Fylde Road

Denpark Avenue

Salwick Close

Pilling Close

Elswick Road

Garstang Rd

Frecklleton Road

Prescalls Dr

Inskip Road

Hornby Rd

Seaton Wy

Oxford Dr

Kilburn Road

Industrial Estate

Industrial Estate

ide Road

Fairhaven Road

Merepark Drive

Ridge Cl

Norbury Cl

Kingston Crs

Crossens Way

Primrose Cl

Marine Drive

Harrogate Way

Skipton Avenue

Ilkley Av

White Av

Meadow Brow

Bartons Cl

Felview

Pool Street

The Causeway

Primary School

Tarvin Cl

Woodlea

Wy

Woodlea Edge

Brook Street
Land Lane

Drewitt Crs

Pooside Walk

Holmdale Av

Douglas Brade Road

Ribble Avenue

Roselea Drive

Asland Garde

Crossens

Treen Close

Glencoone Drive

Glencoone Dr

Chepstow Close

**25**

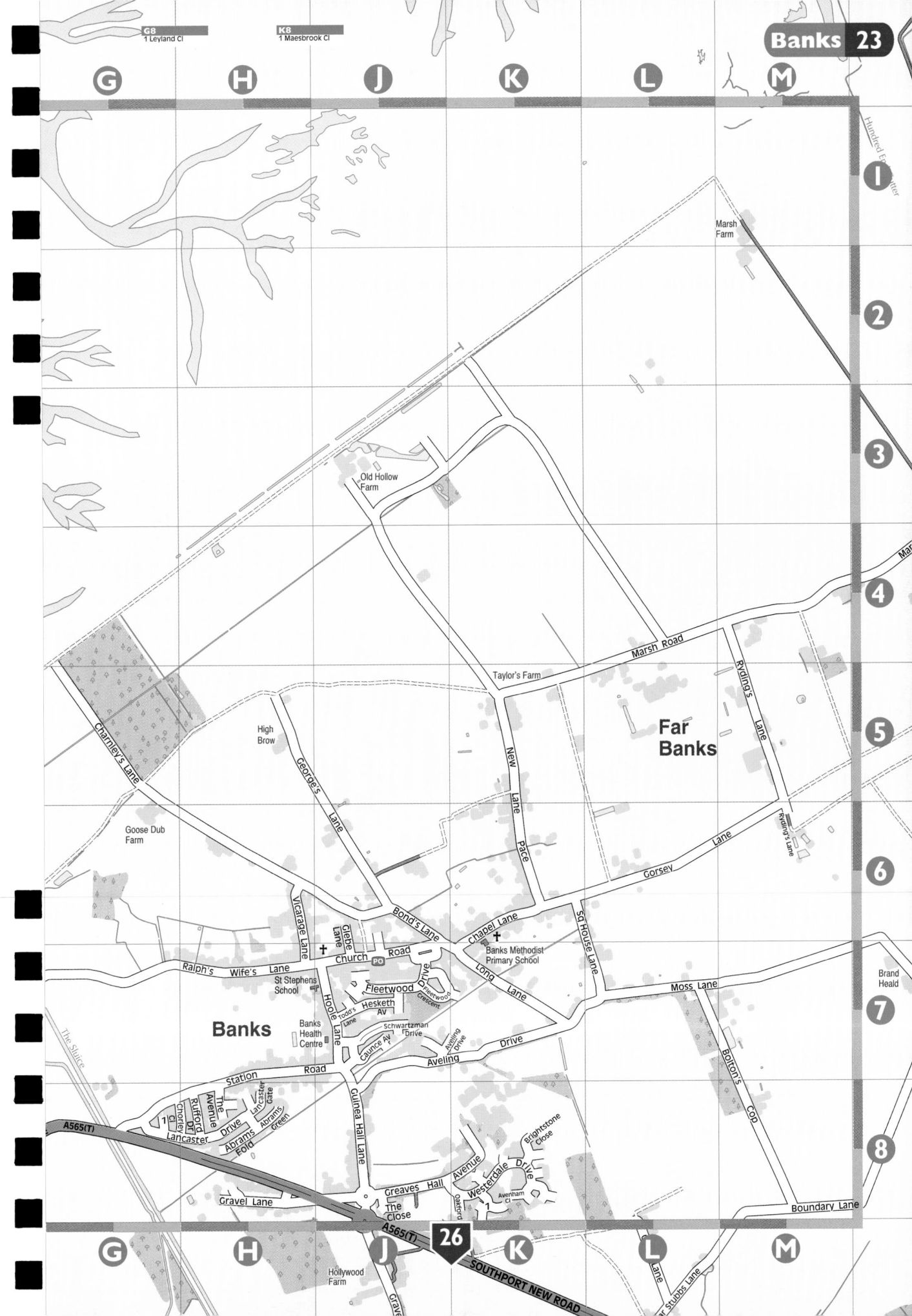

G H J K L M

1
2
3
4
5
6
7
8

Marsh Farm

Old Hollow Farm

Marsh Road

Taylor's Farm

**Far Banks**

Ryding's Lane

High Brow

George's Lane

Charnley's Lane

Goose Dub Farm

New Lane

Pace Lane

Ryding's Lane

Gorsey Lane

Vicarage Lane

Glebe Lane

Bond's Lane

Chapel Lane

Banks Methodist Primary School

Sq House Lane

Brand Heald

Ralph's Wife's Lane

Church Road

St Stephens School

PO

Fleetwood Drive

Fleetwood Crescent

Long Lane

Moss Lane

Bolton's Cop

**Banks**

Hoole Lane

Todd's Lane

Hesketh Av

Banks Health Centre

Caunce Av

Schwartzman Drive

Aveling Drive

Drive

Aveling Drive

Station Road

The Avenue

Rufford Dr

Chorley Cl

Larcaster Gate

Abrams Green

Abrams Fold

Lancaster Drive

Guinea Hall Lane

Brightstone Close

A565(T)

The Sluice

Greaves Hall Avenue

Westerdale Drive

Avenham Cl

Oakford

Boundary Lane

Gravel Lane

The Close

Hollywood Farm

Stubbs Lane

G H J K L M

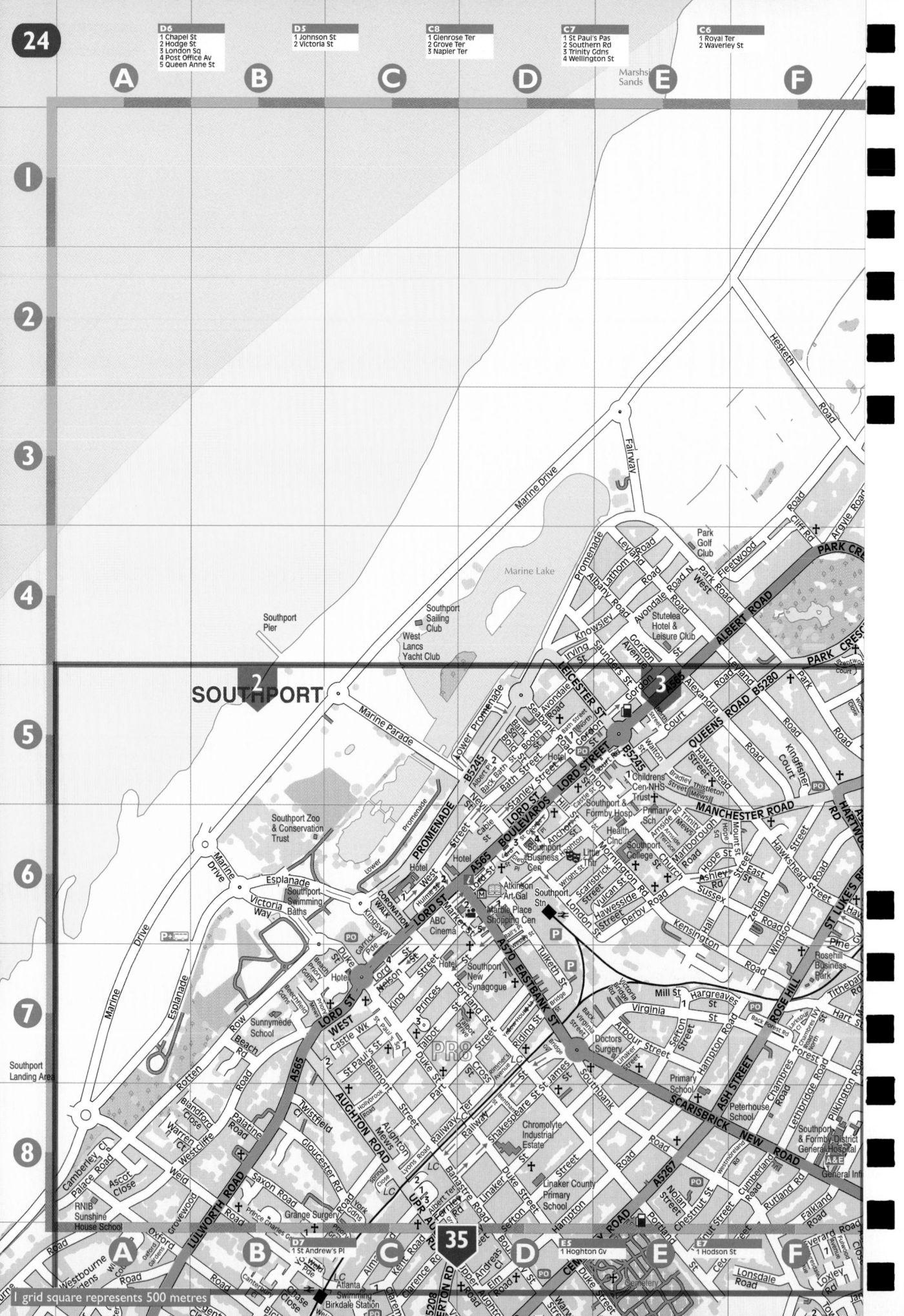

**D6**
1 Chapel St
2 Hodge St
3 London Sq
4 Post Office Av
5 Queen Anne St

**D5**
1 Johnson St
2 Victoria St

**C8**
1 Glenrose Ter
2 Grove Ter
3 Napier Ter

**C7**
1 St Paul's Pas
2 Southern Rd
3 Trinity Gdns
4 Wellington St

**C6**
1 Royal Ter
2 Waverley St

Marshside
Sands

A  B  C  D  E  F

1
2
3
4
5
6
7
8

SOUTHPORT

2

3

35

Marine Lake

Southport Pier

Southport
Sailing
Club

West
Lancs
Yacht Club

Marine Drive

Park
Golf
Club

Fleetwood

PARK CRA

ALBERT ROAD

PARK CRESC

Promenade

Albany Road

Lathom Road

Leyland Road

Knowsley Road N. West

Park Road

Stutelea
Hotel &
Leisure Club

Cliff Rd

Argyle Road

Hesketh Road

Fairway

Marine Drive

Southport Zoo
& Conservation
Trust

Marine parade

Lower Promenade

PROMENADE

Promenade

Lower Promenade

Esplanade

Southport
Swimming
Baths

Victoria
Way

Marine
Drive

Esplanade

Marine
Drive

Southport
Landing Area

Sunnymede
School

Beach
Row

Rotten Row

Blandford
Close

Warren Cr

Westcliffe

Ascot
Close

Camberley
Palace Road

RNIB
Sunshine
House School

Westbourne
Gardens

Oxford
Road

Grovewood

Prince Charles Gdns

Grange Surgery

LULWORTH ROAD

Saxon Road

Gloucester Rd

Twistfield Cl

Palatine
Road

A565

AUGHTON ROAD

Hollybrook
Road

Aughton
Mews

York
Rd

Lyons Road

Spring
Close

Railwalk Ter

Railway

LC

LC

Banastre Rd

Albert Rd

Clarence Road

Atlanta

Chase
Close

Birkdale Station

St Andrew's Pl

D7

B

A

1 grid square represents 500 metres

KINGSWAY

CORONATION WALK

Carlisle Pde

PO

Dyke St

Lord St

Hotel

Hotel

West Street

Nelson Street

King Street

Princes Street

Portland Street

Talbot Street

Duke St

St Paul's St

Belmont Street

Castle Wk

LORD ST WEST

Benchfield
Gdns

Hart St

A565

Southport
New
Synagogue

Part St

Cross Street

CENTRAL ROAD

Duke Street

Sefton Street

Linaker Street

Hampton Road

Linaker County
Primary
School

Chromolyte
Industrial
Estate

Shakespeare Street

Railway

Riding St

Ridley St

Tulketh St

A570 EASTBANK ST

A570

Bridge

Virginia St

Arbour Street

Doctors
Surgery

Primary
School

Hampton Road

Hart St

SCARISBRICK NEW ROAD

ASH STREET

ROSE HILL

Windsor Road

Rosehill
Business
Park

Pine Street

Kensington Road

Leyland Road

ST LUKE'S RD

HARTWO

Forest Road

Lethbridge Road

Pilkington Road

Peterhouse
School

Southport
& Formby District
General Hospital

A&E

A5267

General Inf

Nolan Street

Cumberland St

Rutland Rd

Falkland Road

Loxley

Lonsdale Road

Chestnut St

PO

Bradley St
Marlborough Rd

MANCHESTER ROAD

Hope St
Ashley
Rd

Church
Street

Sussex Road

Derby Road

Hawesside Street

Vulcan Street

Scarisbrick
Street

Mornington Rd

Southport
College

Health
Clnc

Southport &
Formby Hosp.

Primary
Sch

Childrens
Cen-NHS
Trust

Southport
Business
Cen

Anchor St

Little
Thtr

Wrights St

London St

Derby Road

Mount St
East

Hawkshead Street

Hawkshead
Street

Thornton Rd

Eastbourne Rd

B5280

QUEENS ROAD

Alexandra Road

Leyland Road

Kingfisher
Court

Thistleton
Street

Hawkshead
Street

Walton Street

Southport
Stn

P

P

P

Atkinson
Art Gal

Marble Place
Shopping Cen

ABC
Cinema

Southport &
Formby Hosp

B5245

Gordon Street

Saunders St

Gordon
Avenue

Avondale Road

Irving St

Knowsley Road

Seabank Road

Bath Street

Stanley Street

Booth

Bank

Back Bath St

West Street

Hotel

Hulme St

Cable St

LORD STREET

LORD ST

BOULEVARDS

B5245

LEICESTER ST

Castle St

Neville St

PO

Seabank Rd

Avondale Road

Marble St

Hoghton

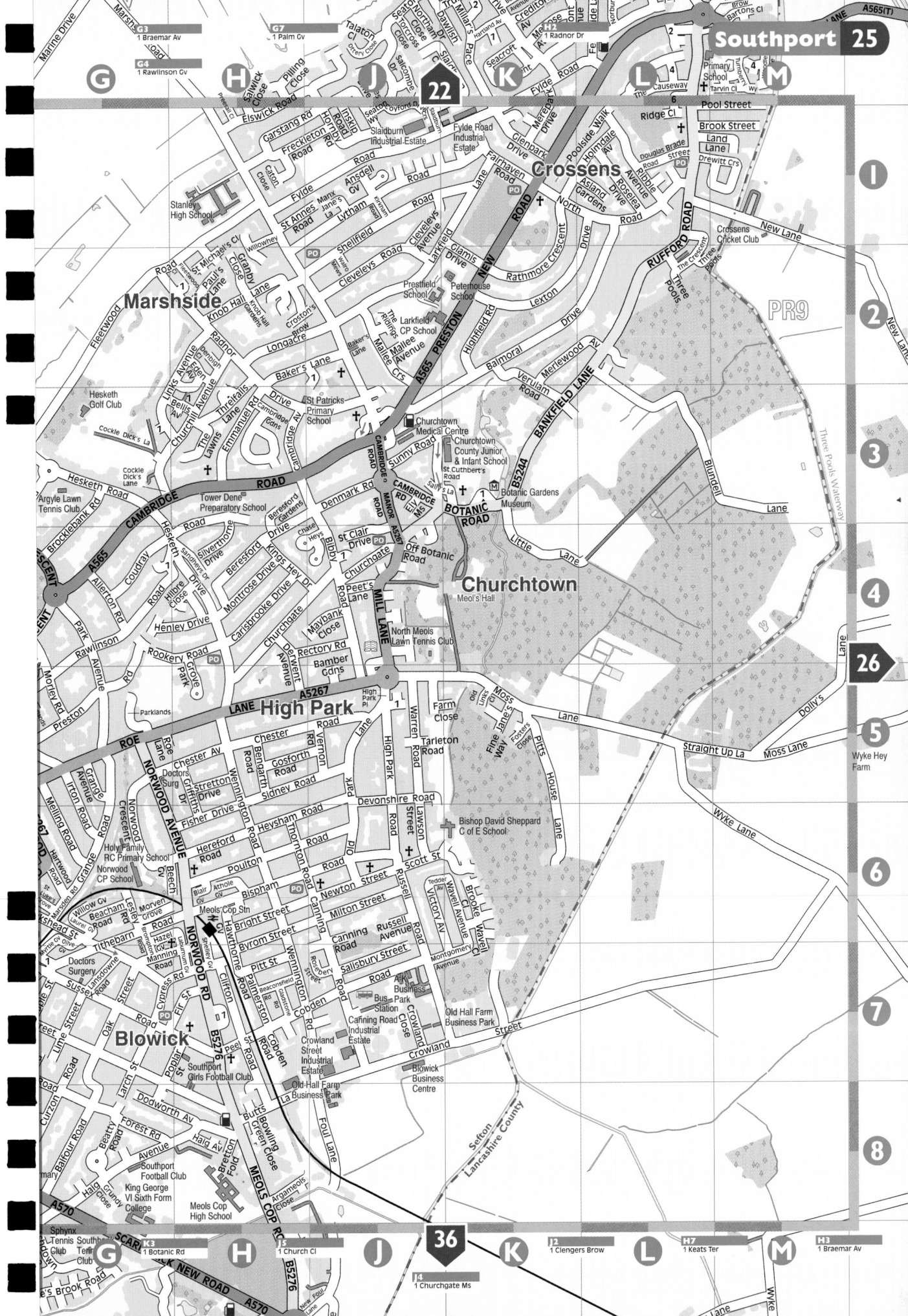

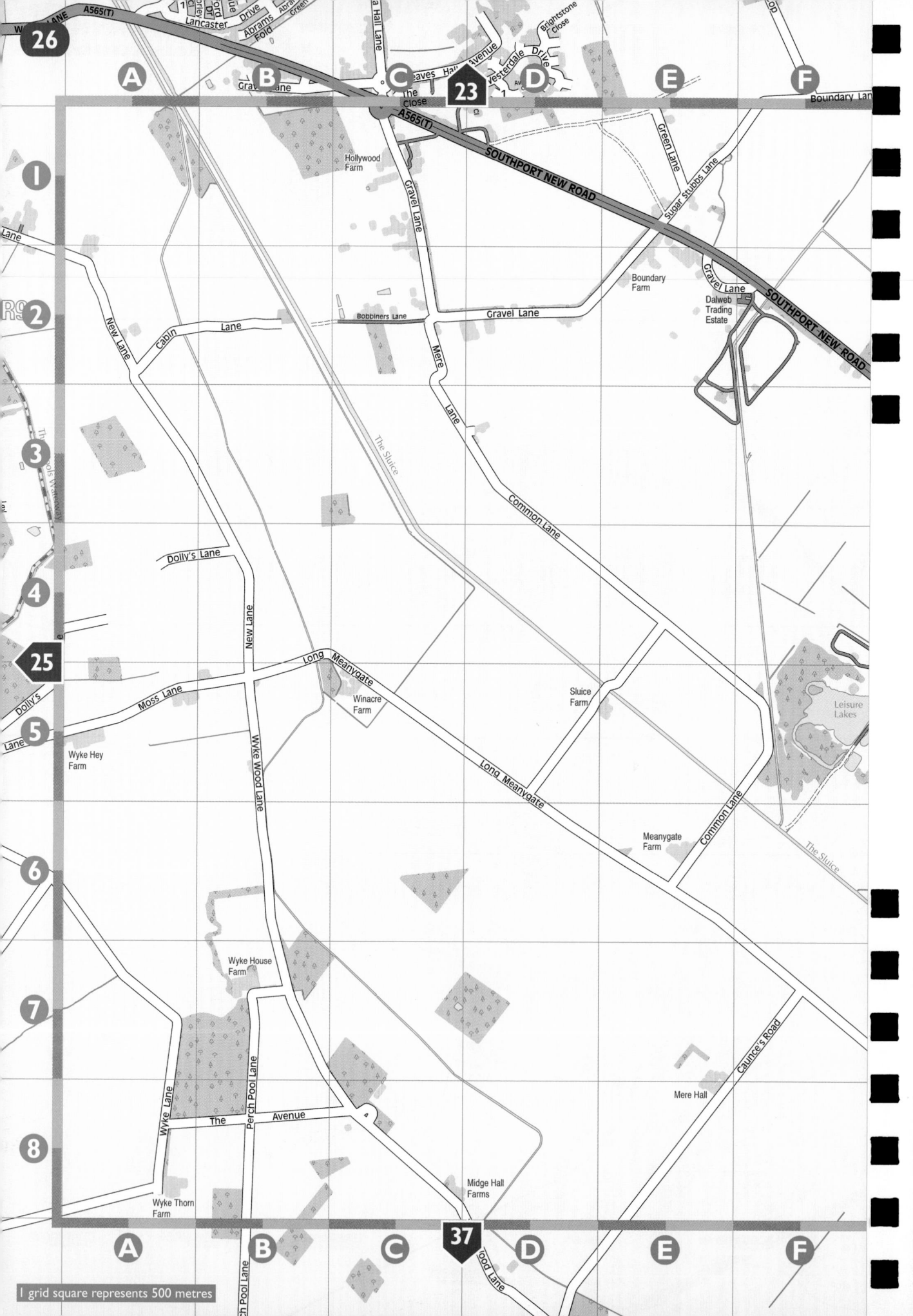

A565(T)

Lancaster

Abrams Fold

a Hall Lane

Brightstone Close

A   B   C   **23**   D   E   F

Gravel Lane

The Close

Greaves Hall Avenue

Westerdale Drive

Boundary Lan

A565(T)

SOUTHPORT NEW ROAD

Green Lane

Sugar Stubbs Lane

I

Hollywood Farm

Lane

R9 **2**

New Lane

Cabin   Lane

Bobbiners Lane

Gravel Lane

Gravel Lane

Mere Lane

The Sluice

Boundary Farm

Gravel Lane

Dalweb Trading Estate

SOUTHPORT NEW ROAD

**3**

The Pools Waterway

Common Lane

**4**

Dolly's Lane

New Lane

**25**

Dolly's

Long  Meanygate

Winacre Farm

Sluice Farm

Leisure Lakes

**5**

Lane

Moss Lane

Wyke Hey Farm

Wyke Wood Lane

Long Meanygate

Common Lane

The Sluice

**6**

Meanygate Farm

Wyke House Farm

**7**

Perch Pool Lane

Caunce's Road

Mere Hall

Wyke Lane

The   Avenue

**8**

Midge Hall Farms

Wyke Thorn Farm

ch Pool Lane

A   B   C   **37**   D   E   F

ood Lane

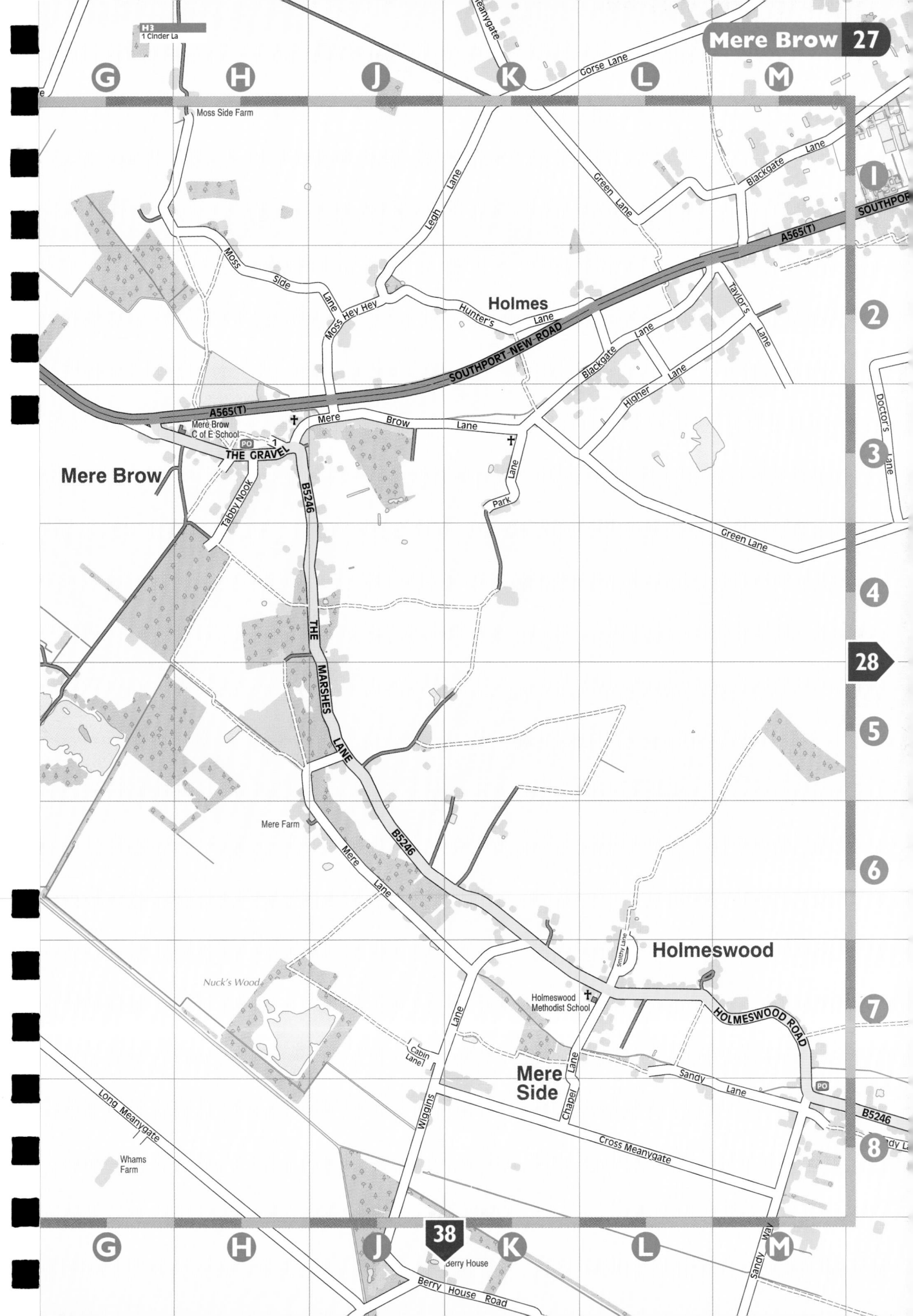

G H J K L M

H3
1 Cinder La

Moss Side Farm

Gorse Lane

Green Lane

Blackgate Lane

SOUTHPORT

A565(T)

Taylor's Lane

Doctor's Lane

Legh Lane

Moss Side Lane

Hunter's Lane

Holmes

Moss Hey Hey

SOUTHPORT NEW ROAD

Blackgate Lane

Higher Lane

A565(T)

Mere Brow
C of E School

PO

THE GRAVEL

Mere Brow Lane

Mere Brow

Tabby Nook

B5246

Park Lane

Green Lane

THE MARSHES LANE

B5246

Mere Farm

Mere Lane

Holmeswood

Smithy Lane

Nuck's Wood

Holmeswood
Methodist School

HOLMESWOOD ROAD

Cabin Lane

Wiggins Lane

Mere Side

Chapel Lane

Sandy Lane

PO

B5246

Long Meanygate

Whams Farm

Cross Meanygate

Sandy Way

G H J K L M

38

Berry House

Berry House Road

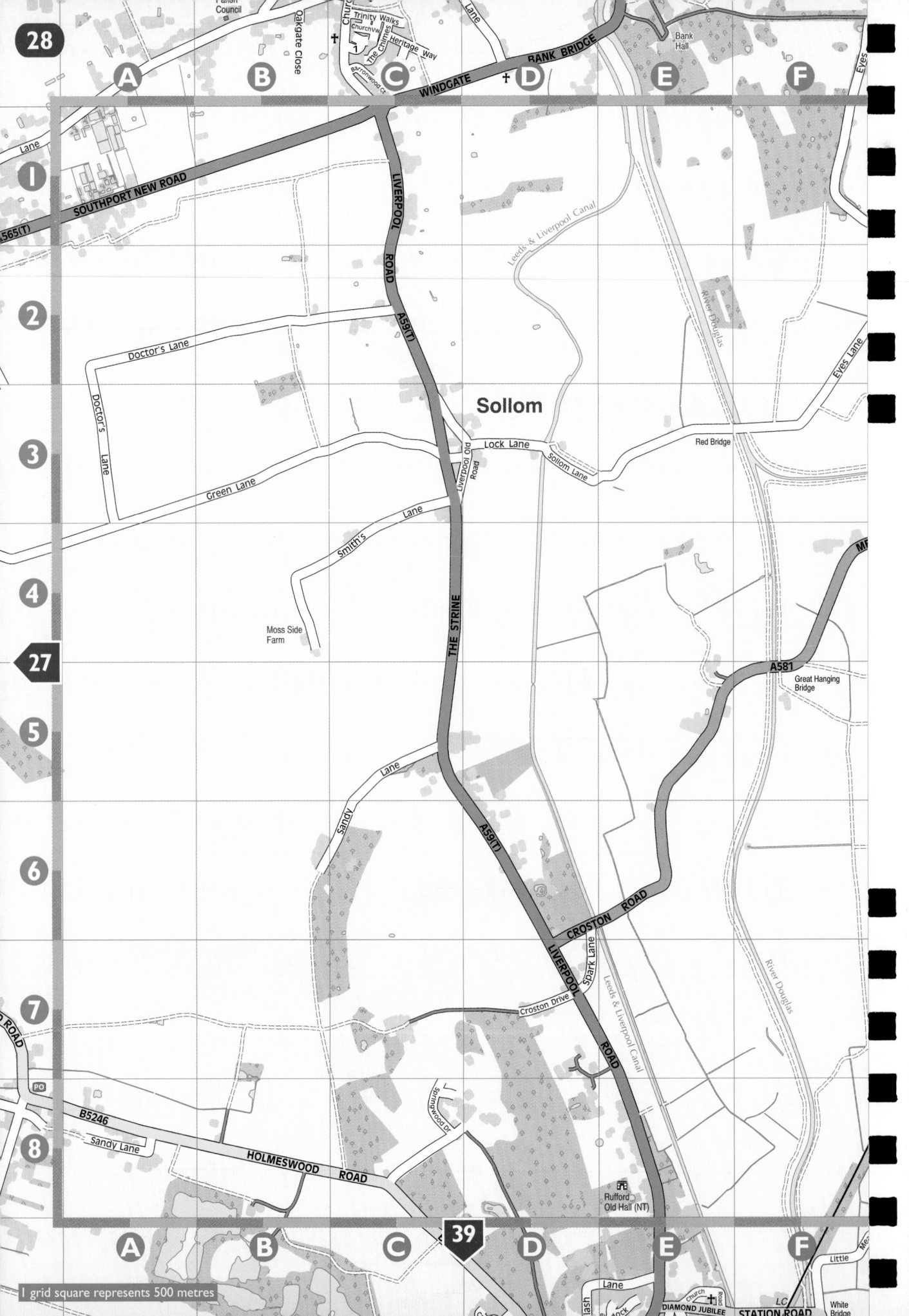

A  B  C  D  E  F

1

2

3

4

27

5

6

7

8

A  B  C  D  E  F

Lane

SOUTHPORT NEW ROAD

565(T)

Parish Council

Oakgate Close

Trinity Walks

Church

The Chimes

Heritage Way

Barronwood Ct

Churchvw

WINDGATE

BANK BRIDGE

Bank Hall

Eves

LIVERPOOL ROAD

A59(T)

Leeds & Liverpool Canal

River Douglas

Eves Lane

Doctor's Lane

Doctor's Lane

Green Lane

Sollom

Lock Lane

Liverpool Old Road

Sollom Lane

Red Bridge

Smith's Lane

Moss Side Farm

THE STRINE

A59(T)

A581

Great Hanging Bridge

Sandy Lane

CROSTON ROAD

Spark Lane

LIVERPOOL ROAD

Croston Drive

Leeds & Liverpool Canal

River Douglas

MF

ROAD

PO

B5246

Sandy Lane

HOLMESWOOD ROAD

Springwood Rd

Rufford Old Hall (NT)

Flash Lane

DIAMOND JUBILEE

church Road

STATION ROAD

LC

White Bridge

Little Eves

1 grid square represents 500 metres

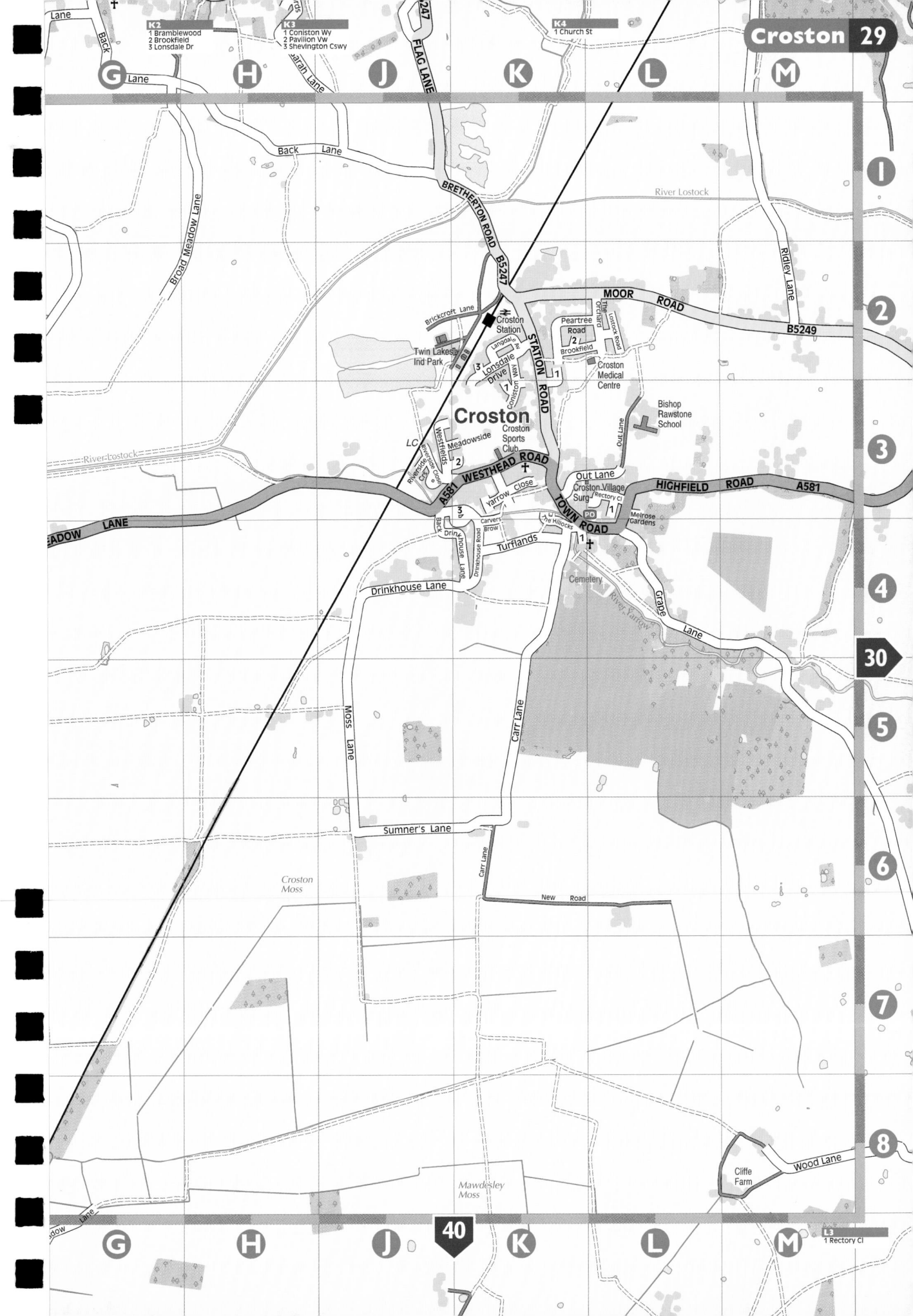

1 Bramblewood
2 Brookfield
3 Lonsdale Dr

1 Coniston Wy
2 Pavilion Vw
3 Shevington Cswy

1 Church St

**G** Lane
**H**
Sarah Lane
**J** FLAG LANE
247
**K** K4
**L**
**M**

**I**

Back Lane

BRETHERTON ROAD B5247

River Lostock

**2**
B5249

Broad Meadow Lane

Ridley Lane

Brickcroft Lane
Croston Station
Peartree Road
MOOR ROAD
Lostock Road
The Orchard
Twin Lakes Ind Park
Langdale Av
Brookfield
2
Lonsdale Drive
3
1
Croston Medical Centre
Coniston Wy
7
STATION ROAD
Bishop Rawstone School

**3**
River Lostock
**Croston**
LC
Westfields
Meadowside
Croston Sports Club
Out Lane
Riverside CI
2
WESTHEAD ROAD
A581
Out Lane
HIGHFIELD ROAD A581
Yarrow Close
Croston Village Surg
Rectory CI
Back Drin
3b
Drinkhouse Road
Carvers Brow
TOWN ROAD
1
PO
Melrose Gardens
The Hillocks
Turflands
1

**4**
Drinkhouse Lane
Cemetery
River Yarow
Grape Lane

**30**

**5**
Moss Lane
Carr Lane

**6**
Sumner's Lane
Carr Lane

New Road

**7**

**8**
Cliffe Farm
Wood Lane

Croston Moss

Mawdesley Moss

MEADOW LANE

**G**
**H**
**J** **40**
**K**
**L**
**M**
1 Rectory CI

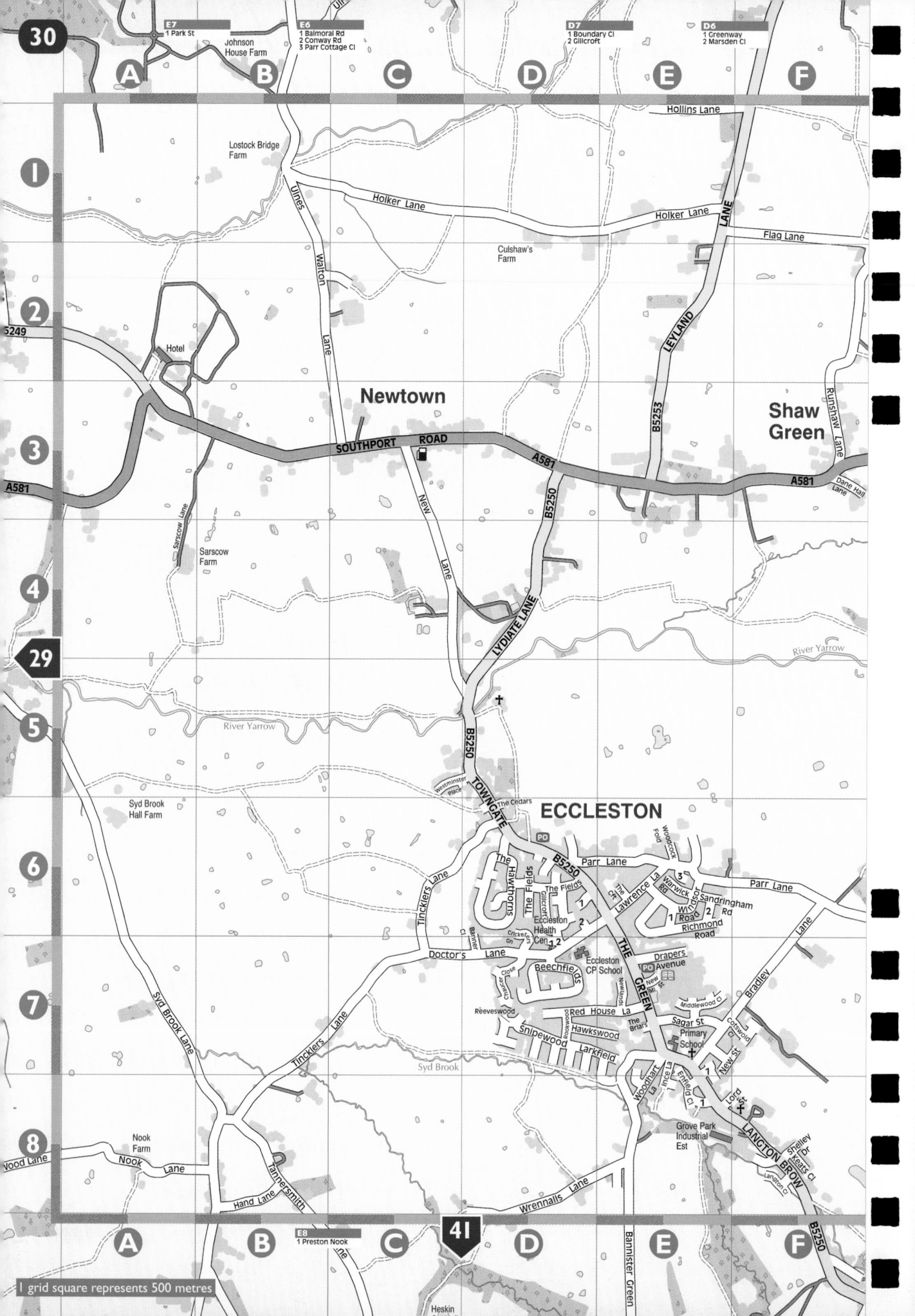

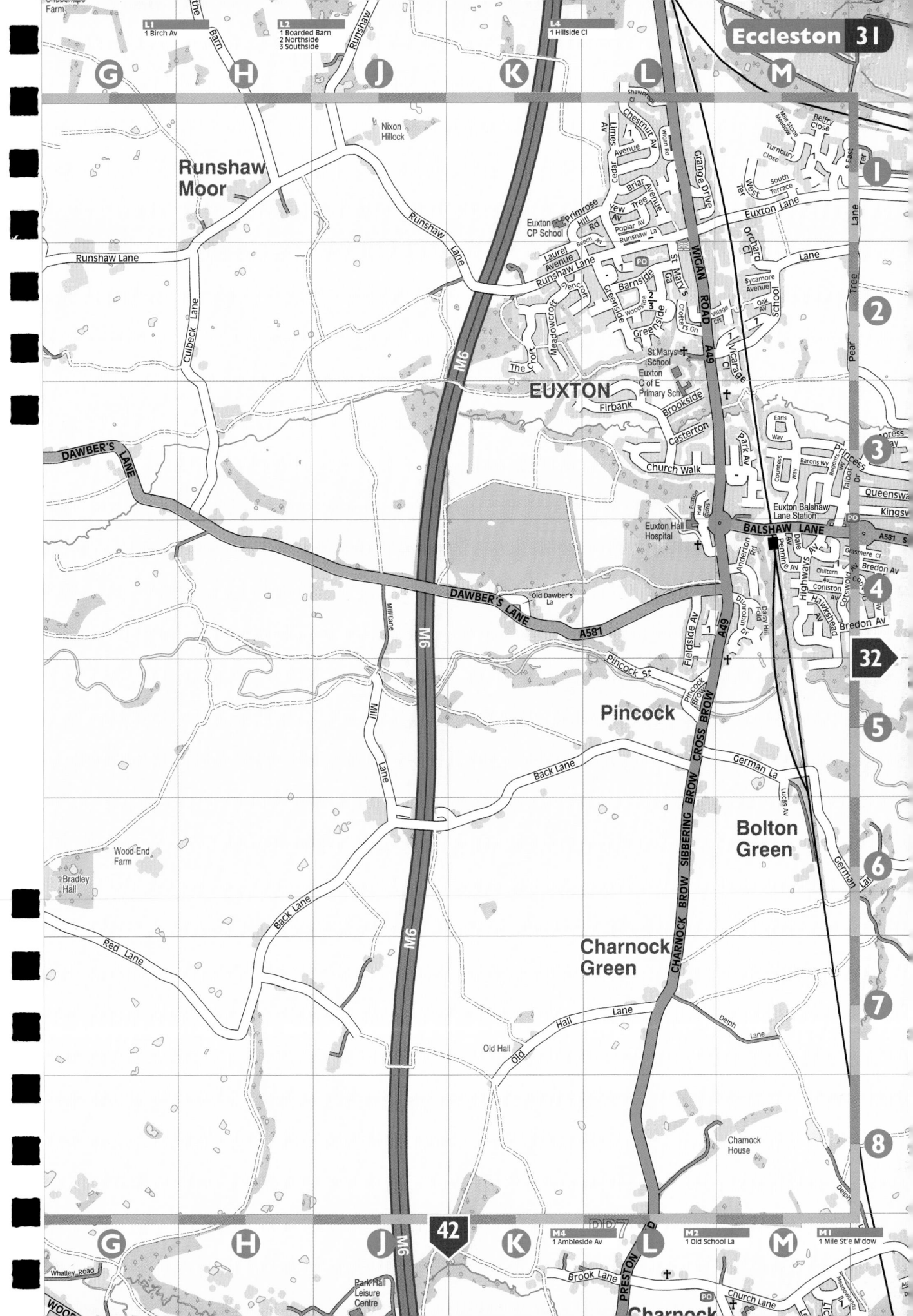

G3
1 Chestnut Av

G4
1 Fosterfield Pl
2 Morris Rd
3 Pennine Rd
4 Rossall Rd
5 Talbot St
6 Turton Dr

G2
1 Alpine Rd

Trigg Lane

PR6

G
H
J
K
L
M

I
2
3
4
5
6
7
8

A674

Junction 8

Leeds and Liverpool Canal

BLACKBURN ROAD

B6228

Guildford Av
Epsom Close
Ewell
Carleton
Dorking Road
Melford
Merton Gv
Paradise St

Barn Lane
Tithe
Chapel Lane
Scow
Coppice Lane
Croft

White Coppice

Heapey Road
Merlin Close
Tittwake
The Dingle
High Bank
The Del
The Wold
Osprey Close
Tormore Close

Higher House Lane
Morris Farm
Hollin
Morris Lane

The Colt

BOTANY BROW
M61
Northgate Dr
Larch
Daisy Fold
Mason Street
St Peters C of E Junior School
Smithills
Withnell
Dunscar
Holcombe
Bagganley La
Belmont Dr
Coppice Cl
Rivington Rd
Montcliffe Road
Froom Street
Pennine Rd
Canal Walk
The CSW
Grey Hts Vw
Eaves Lane
Dev Court
PO Wy
St James C of E School
Crosse Hall Lane
Crosse Ridge
Frederick Street
Crosse Hall Street

Knowley Brow
Bagganley Lane

B6229
Blackstone
Granville Rd
Marlborough Rd
PO
Nab
Rd
Moorfields

B6228
St Peter's St
Curate St
Foster St
Cobden St
Kershaw
Carr

Aniline St
Mossfield
Wright St
Thistle
Portsmouth
Colyton Rd
The CSW
ward
Lytham
Rosklyn Road
Worthy Street
Limbrick Rd
Cowling Brow
Croft

Primary School
Cranbourne St
Canterbury St
Fife
Richmond
Athol Gv
Quarry Rd
Fell View
Sackville St

**Cowling**

Eaves

Healey Nab

Healey Fold Lane

Crosse Hall Lane
White House

Moorland Ga
Moorland Lane
Weaver's Brow
Flag Lane
Weaver's Brow
Hogg's

Fish Barn Farm
Charnock
Back Lane

Kays Farm

Anglezarke Reservoir

Moor Road

Yarrow
Yarrow Gv
Albany High School
Primary School
Cowling Brow Industrial Estate

BOLTON

**Limbrick**

44

G
H
J
K
L
M

G
1 Blackbrook Cl
H
J2
1 Kestrel Cl
H1
1 Bromley Gn
G7
1 Hornby Rd
2 Montrose Cl

G5, G6
Street names for these grid squares are listed at the back of the index

Hallsworth Fold Farm

Lane Ends

Charnock Back

Chester
Woodside

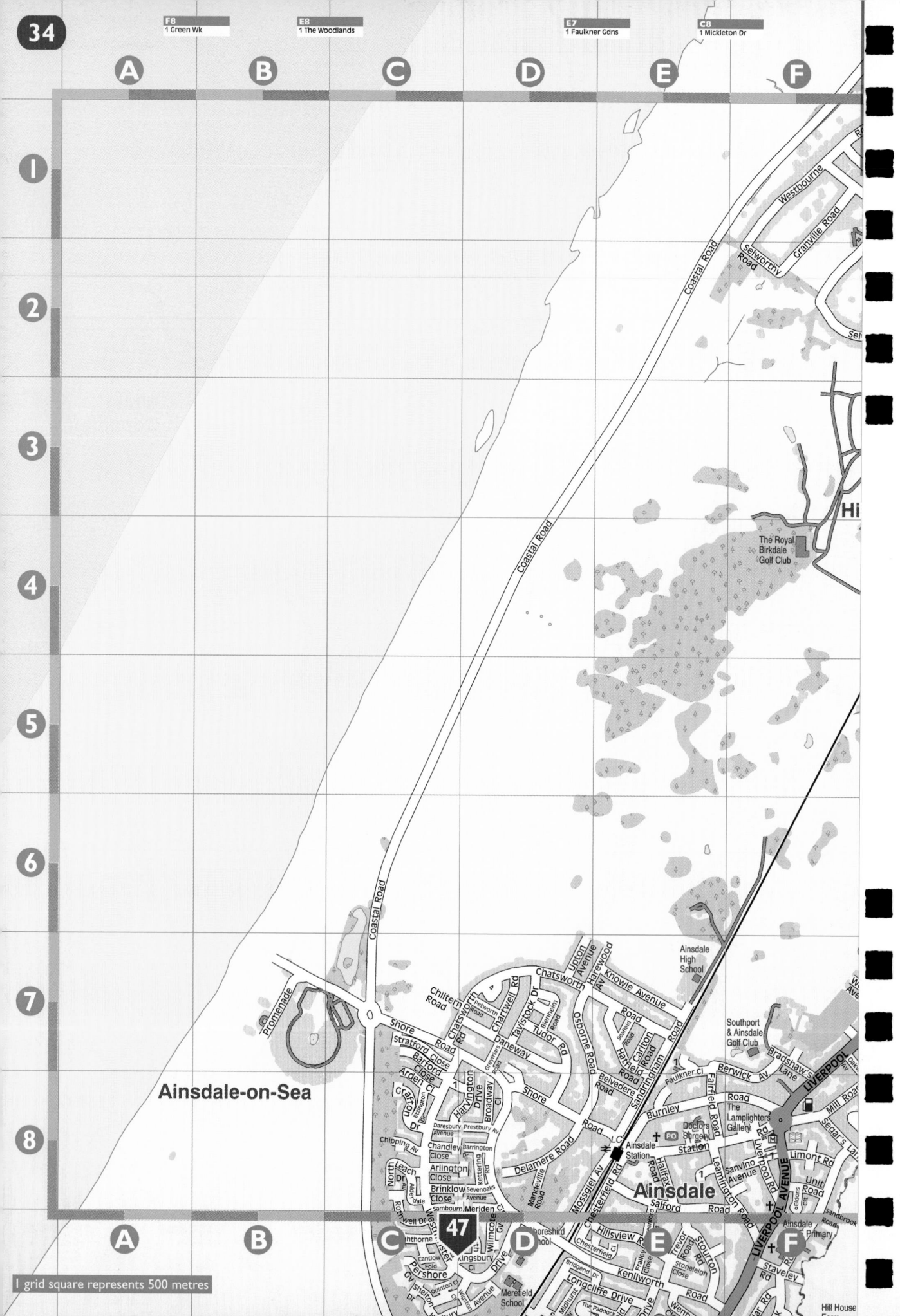

F8
1 Green Wk

E8
1 The Woodlands

E7
1 Faulkner Gdns

C8
1 Mickleton Dr

A B C D E F

1
2
3
4
5
6
7
8

Westbourne
Granville Road
Selworthy
Road
Sel

Coastal Road

Coastal Road

Hi

The Royal
Birkdale
Golf Club

Coastal Road

Ainsdale
High
School

Southport
& Ainsdale
Golf Club

Promenade

Ainsdale-on-Sea

Chiltern
Road

Chatsworth

Upton
Avenue

Harewood

Knowle Avenue

shore
Road

Chatsworth Rd

Petworth
Road
Chattwell Rd

Tavistock Dr

Tudor Rd

Osborne Road

Carlton
Road

Hatfield
Road

Saldringham
Road

Bradshaw's
Lane

LIVERPOOL

Liverpool
Road

stratford Close

Daneway

Bletherin

Sefford

Berwick Av

Fairfield Road

The
Lamplighters
Gallery

W
Ave

Barford
Close

Greymars

Faulkner Cl

Arden
Dr

Grafton

Harvington
Drive

Broadway

shore

Belvedere
Road

Burnley

Doctor's
Surgery

PO

Ri
Liverpool Ro

Segar's Lau

Daresbury
Avenue

Prestbury Av

Delamere Road

Ainsdale
Station

Mill Road

Ettington

chipping Av

Chandley
Close

Barrington
Dr

Kettering Rd

Mandeville
Road

Mossjael Av

Chesterfield Rd

Halifax
Road

Leamington Road

sanvino
Avenue

Limont Rd

Unit
Road

Leach
Dr

Arlington
Close

Ainsdale

Salford

Liverpool Ro

Sandbrook

Norm

Alder

Brinklow
Close

Sevenoaks
Avenue

sambourn

Meriden

Ainsdale
Primary

Rothwell Dr

47

Wilmcote
Drive

shoreshird
hool

Hillsview Rd

Trevor
Road

Stourton
Road

LIVERPOOL AVENUE

Alesto

anthorne

Kingsbury
Cl

Chesterfield
Cl

Talley
Close

Stoneleigh
Close

Ainsdale

Pershore

Cantlow
Fold

Quinton Cl

Bridgend Dr

Keniworth
Road

Wentw

Staveley
Rd

Hill House

shelton

Wigton

Merefield
School

Longcliffe Drive

The Paddock

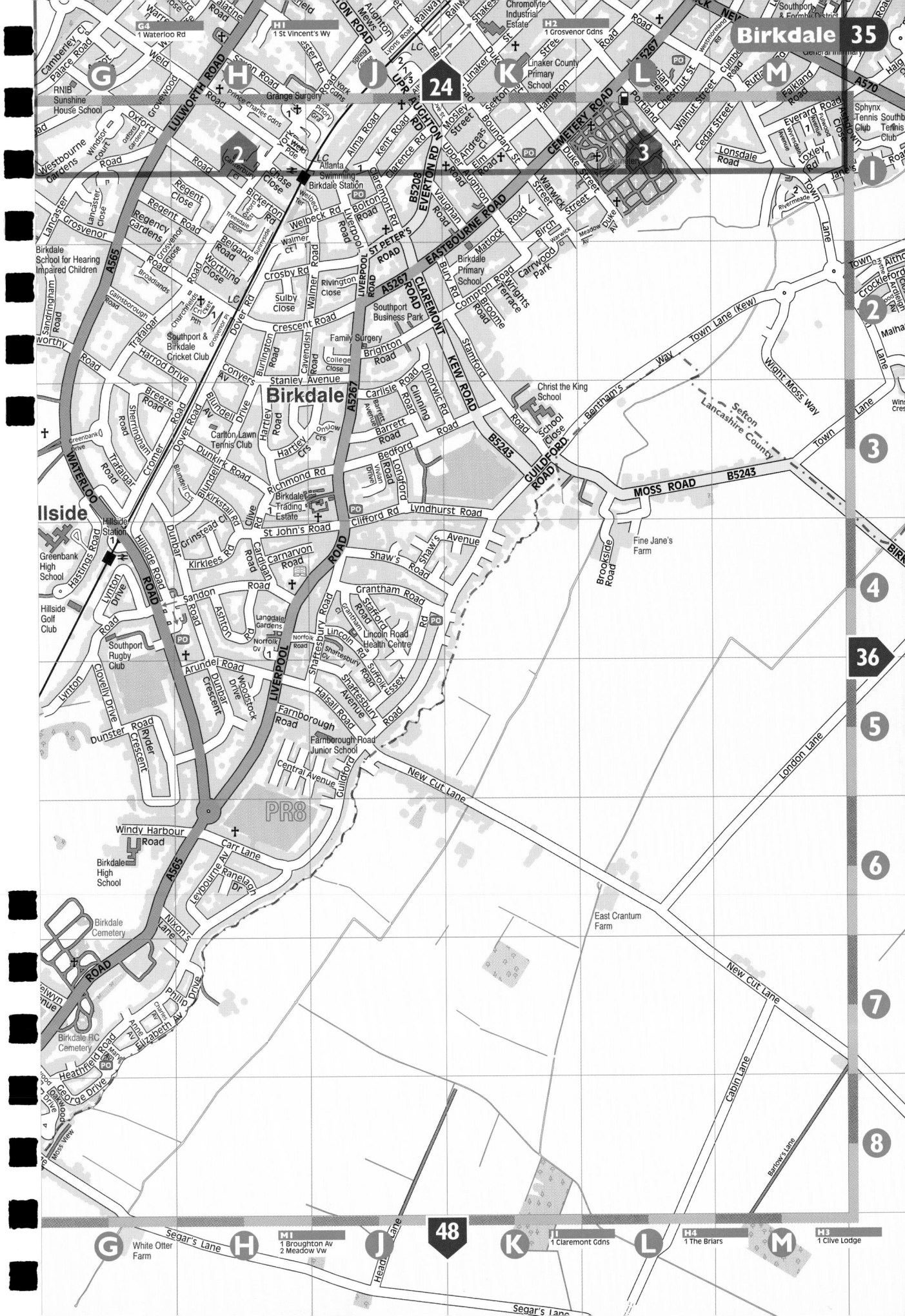

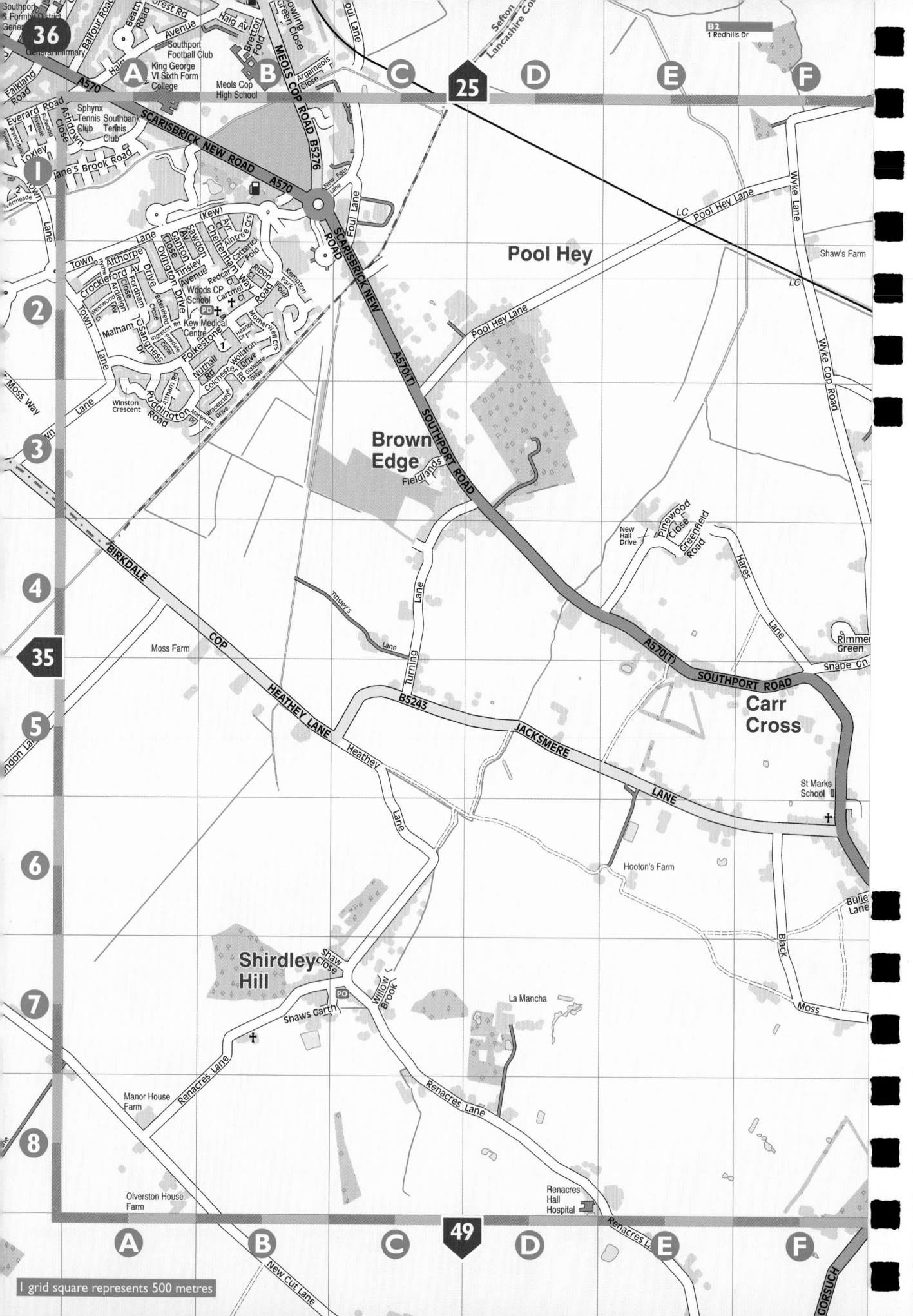

I grid square represents 500 metres

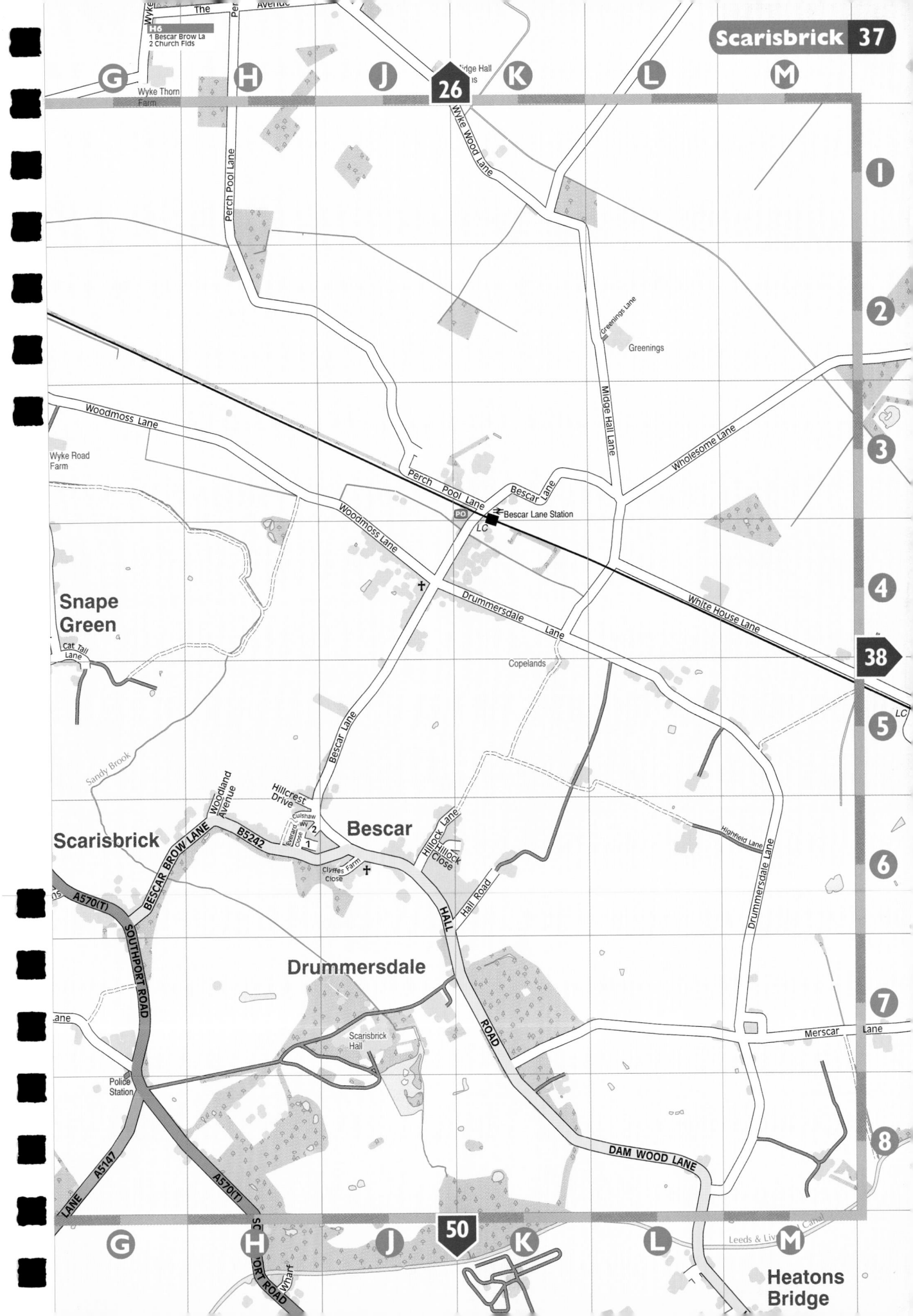

G H J 26 K L M

I
2
3
4
38
5
6
7
8

H6
1 Bescar Brow La
2 Church Flds

The
Avenue

Wyke Thorn
Farm

Perch Pool Lane

Midge Hall
Hs

Wyke Wood Lane

Greenings Lane

Greenings

Wholesome Lane

Midge Hall Lane

Woodmoss Lane

Wyke Road
Farm

Perch Pool Lane

Bescar Lane

PO
LC

Bescar Lane Station

White House Lane

Woodmoss Lane

Drummersdale Lane

**Snape
Green**

Cat Tail
Lane

Copelands

Sandy Brook

Bescar Lane

Hillcrest
Drive

Woodland Avenue

**Scarisbrick**

BESCAR BROW LANE

B5242

Culshaw
WN
1 2

Eveleard
Close

Clyffes Farm
Close

**Bescar**

Hillock Lane

Hillock
Close

Hall Road

Highfield Lane

Drummersdale Lane

Merscar
Lane

A570(T)

SOUTHPORT ROAD

**Drummersdale**

HALL

ROAD

Scarisbrick
Hall

Police
Station

LANE A5147

A570(T)

SC

Wharf

DAM WOOD LANE

Leeds & Liv Canal

G H J 50 K L M

**Heatons
Bridge**

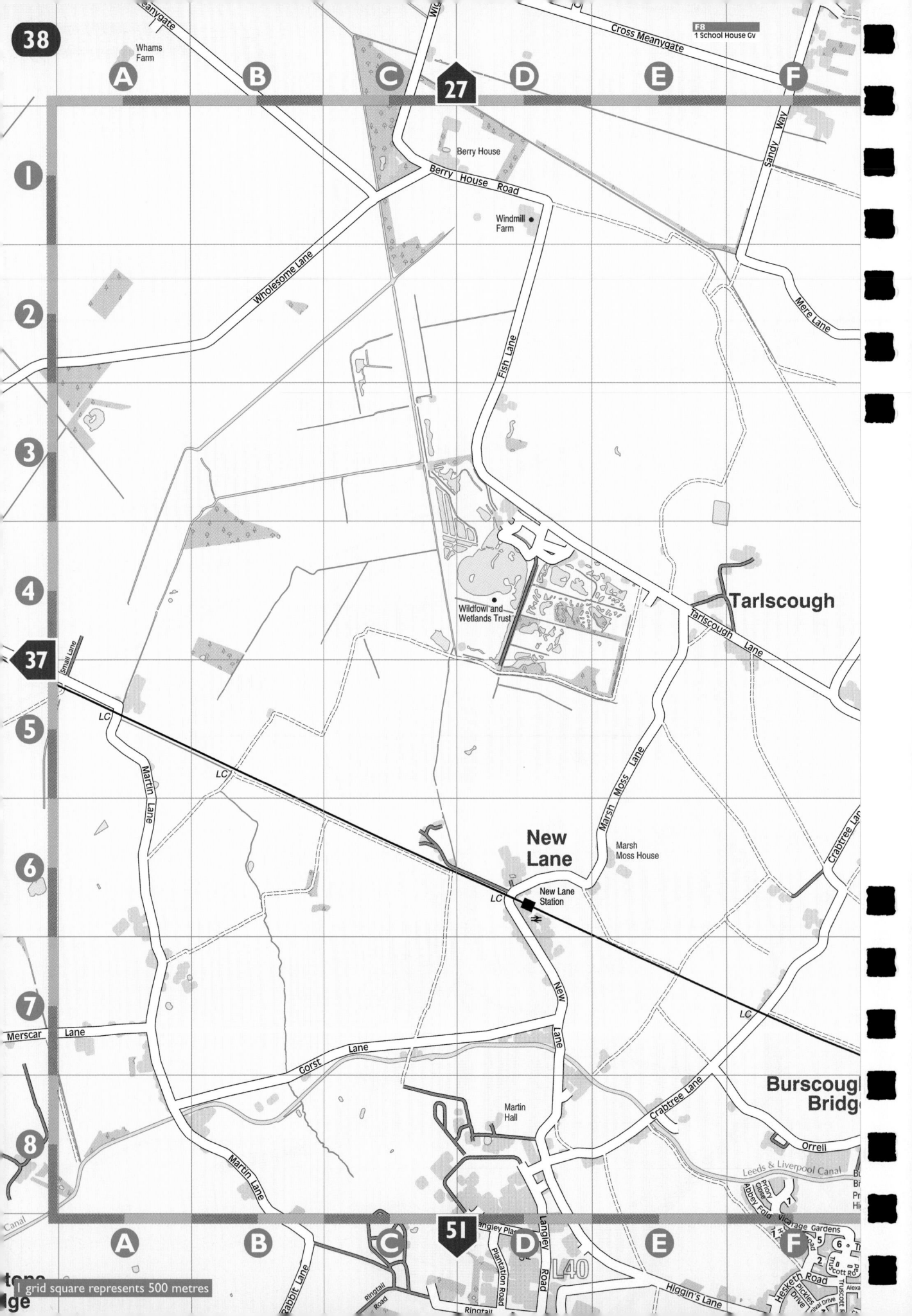

A   B   C   **27**   D   E   F

**F8**
1 School House Gv

Cross Meanygate

Whams Farm

Berry House

Berry House Road

Windmill Farm

Wholesome Lane

Fish Lane

Mere Lane

Sandy Way

Small Lane

**37**

LC

LC

Martin Lane

Wildfowl and Wetlands Trust

Tarlscough Lane

**Tarlscough**

Marsh Moss Lane

Marsh Moss House

Crabtree Lane

**New Lane**

New Lane Station

LC

Merscar Lane

Gorst Lane

New Lane

Martin Hall

Crabtree Lane

**Burscough Bridge**

Orrell

Leeds & Liverpool Canal

Martin Lane

Rabbit Lane

Canal

A   B   C   **51**   D   E   F

Langley Plac

Plantation Road

Langley Road

L40

Higgin's Lane

Hesketh Road

Vicarage Gardens

Abbey Fold

1 grid square represents 500 metres

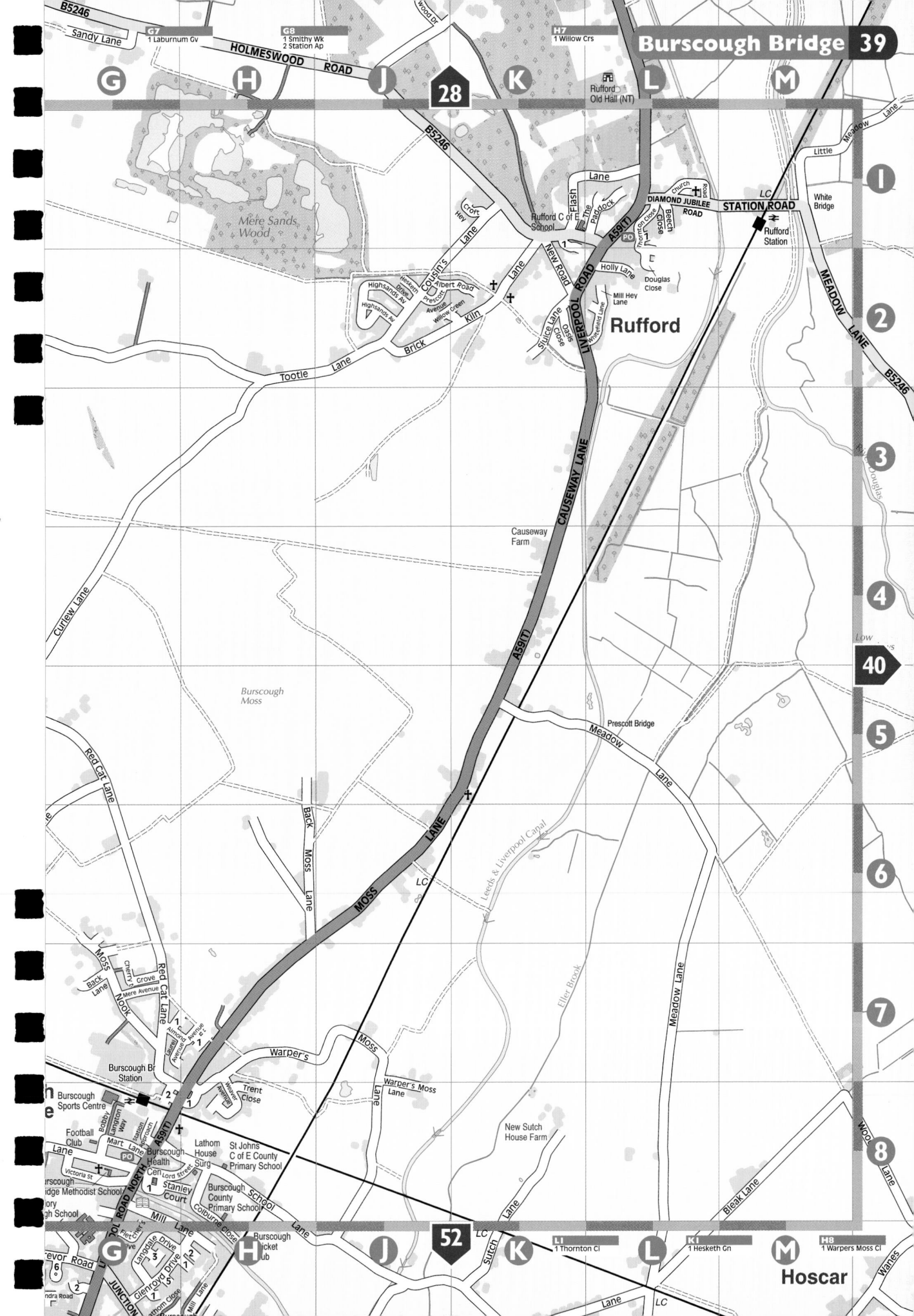

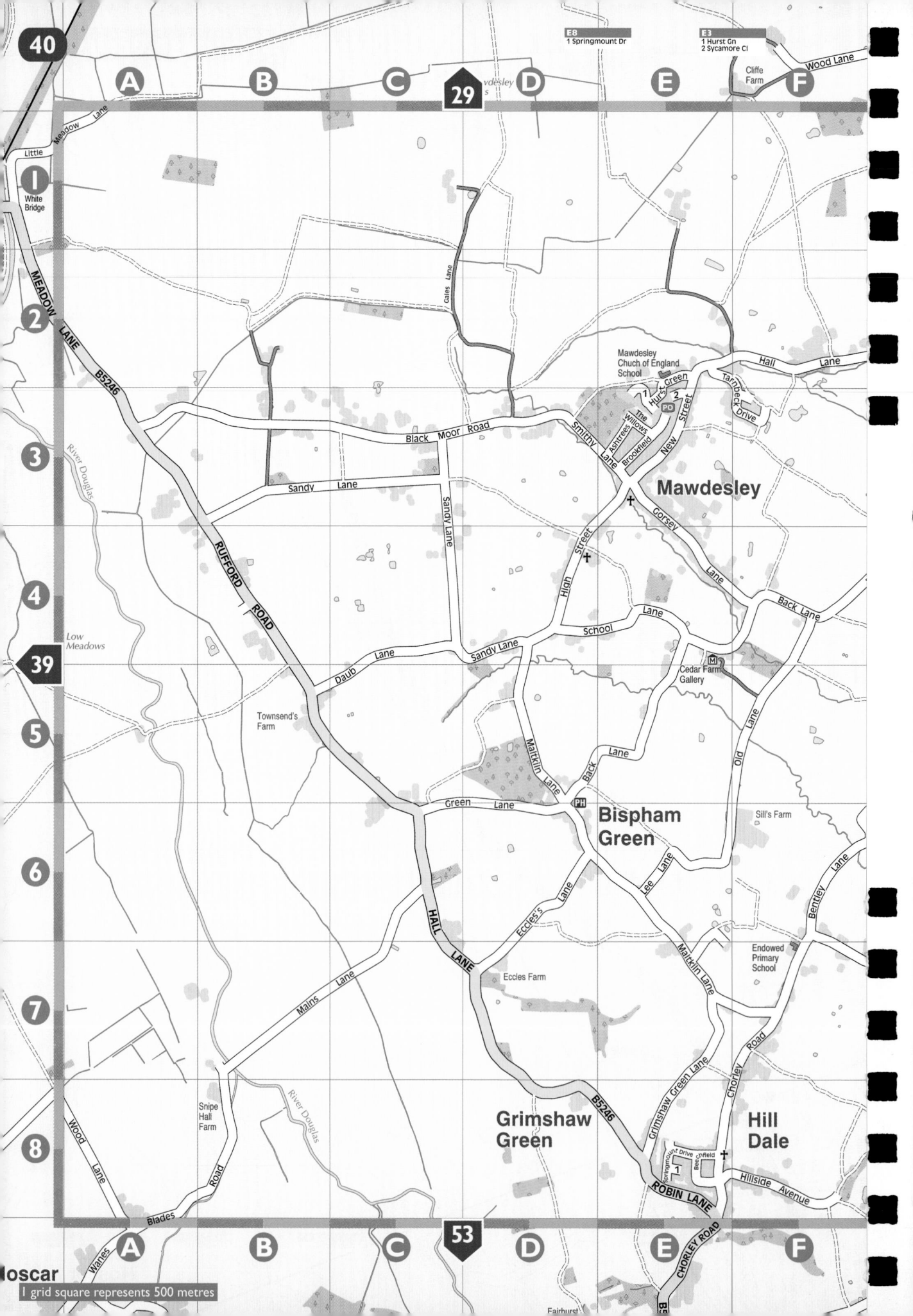

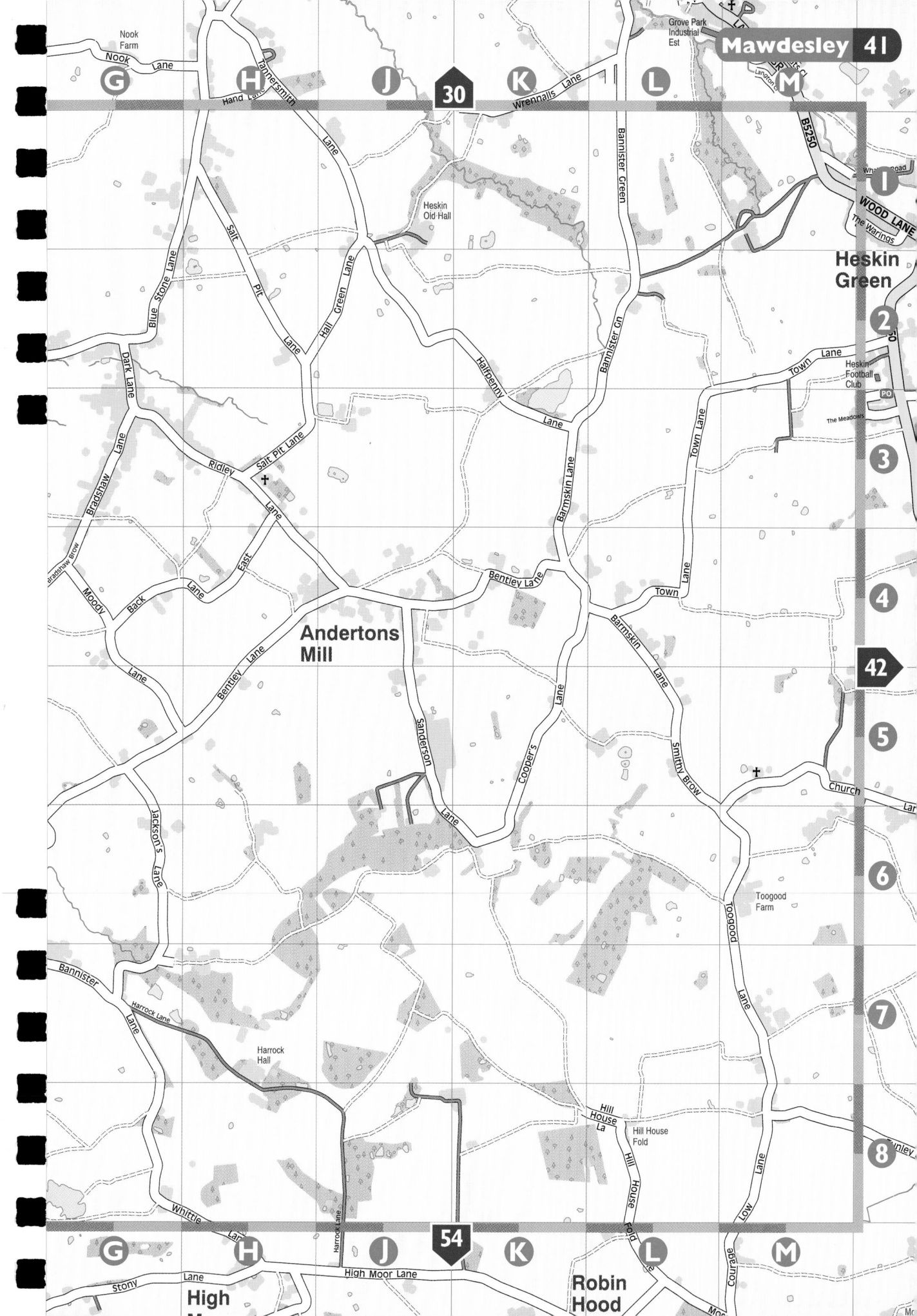

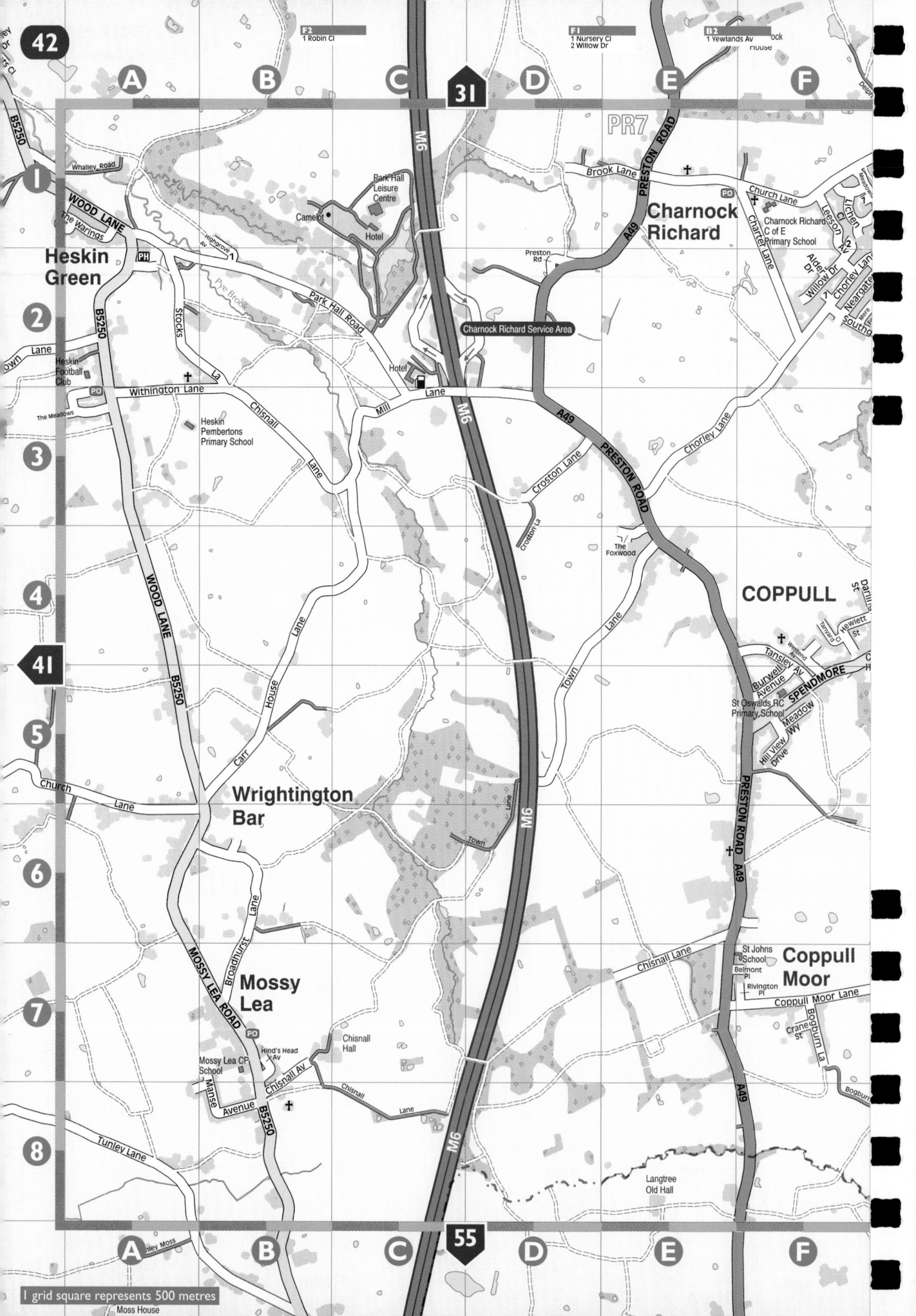

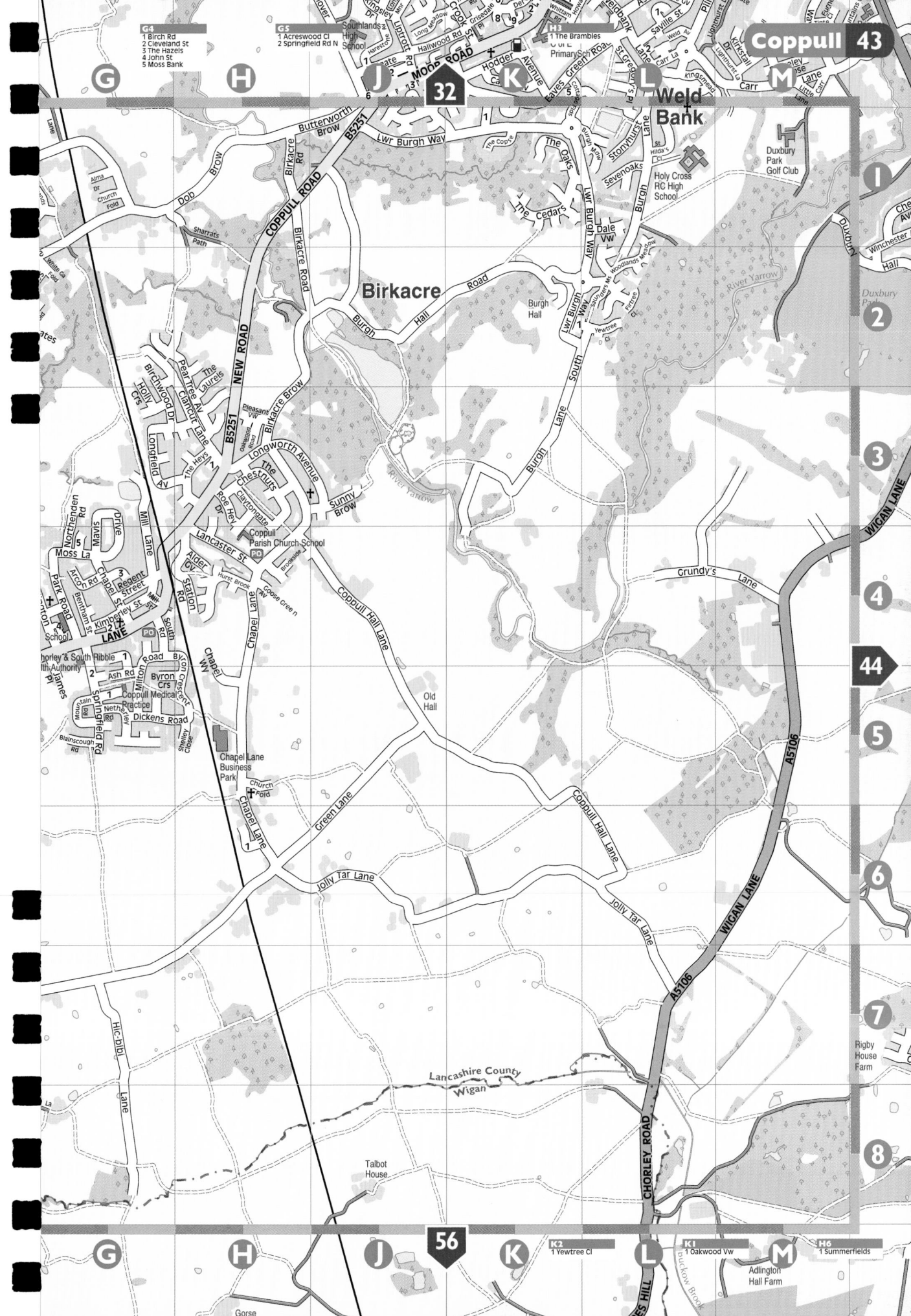

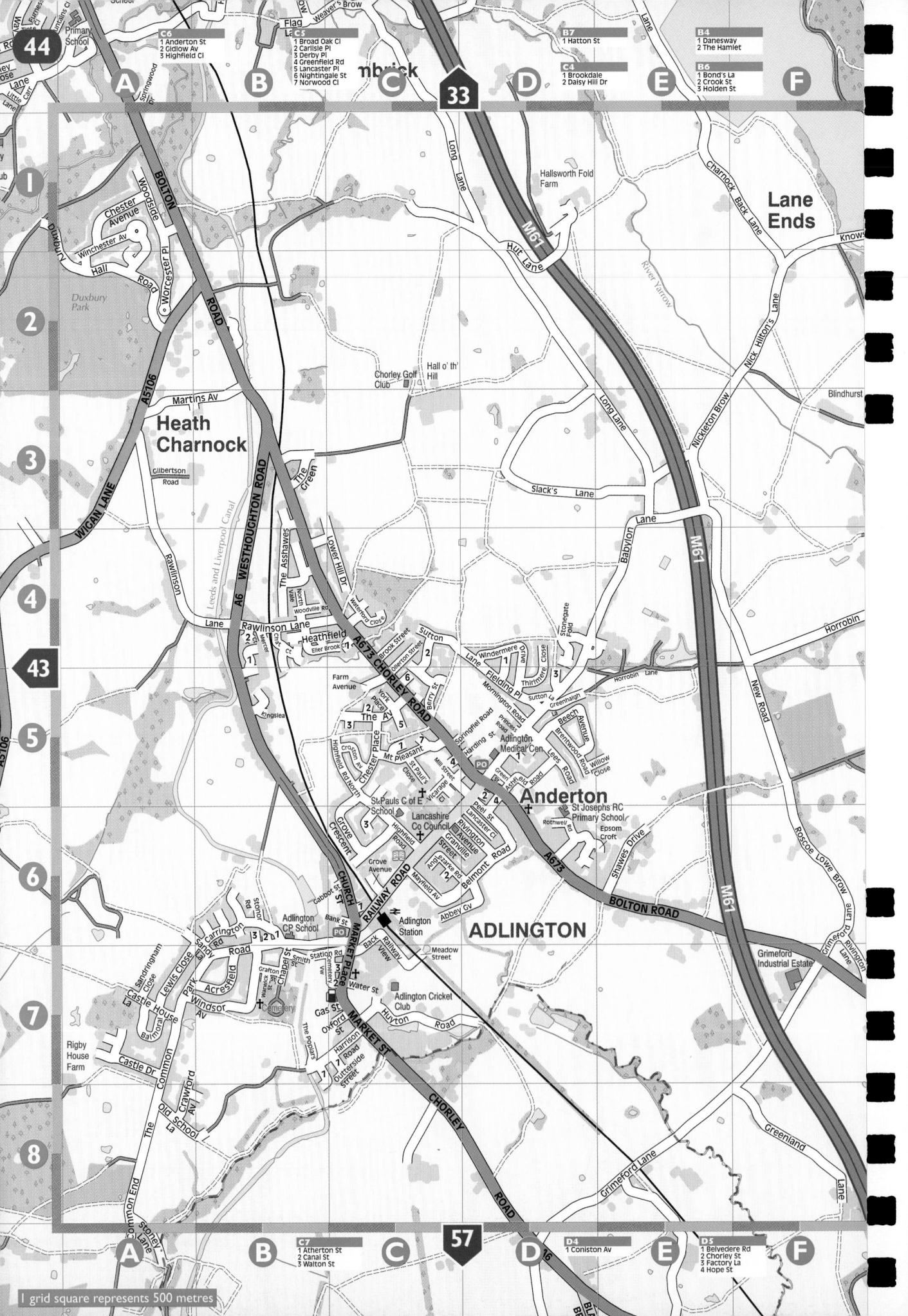

33

**C6**
1 Anderton St
2 Gidlow Av
3 Highfield Cl

**C5**
1 Broad Oak Cl
2 Carlisle Pl
3 Derby Pl
4 Greenfield Rd
5 Lancaster Pl
6 Nightingale St
7 Norwood Cl

Flag

**B7**
1 Hatton St

**C4**
1 Brookdale
2 Daisy Hill Dr

**B4**
1 Danesway
2 The Hamlet

**B6**
1 Bond's La
2 Crook St
3 Holden St

nbrick

Lane
Ends

Hallsworth Fold
Farm

River Yarrow

Chester
Avenue

Winchester Av

Woodside

Worcester Pl

BOLTON

Hall

ROAD

A5106

Duxbury
Park

Martins Av

Gilbertson
Road

Heath
Charnock

WIGAN LANE

Rawlinson

A6 WESTHOUGHTON ROAD

The Asshawes

The Green

Lower Hill Dr

Leeds and Liverpool Canal

Chorley Golf
Club

Hall o' th'
Hill

Blindhurst

Slack's Lane

Babylon Lane

M61

Hut Lane

Long Lane

Long Lane

Nickleton Brow

Nick Hilton's Lane

Charnock Back Lane

Knowl

Horrobin

New Road

Horrobin Lane

Stonegate
Fold

Sutton

Windermere Dr

Fielding Pl

Thirlmere Close

Greenhalgh
La

Beech
Avenue

Brentwood Road

Willow
Close

Leos Rd

Epsom
Croft

Shawes Drive

St Josephs RC
Primary School

Rothwell
Rd

Anderton

Adlington
Medical Cen

PO

Green
Acre Rd

Actifield
Road

Rivington
Avenue

Granville
Street

Belmont

Road

A673

BOLTON ROAD

M61

Roscoe Lowe Brow

Grimeford Lane

Rivington Lane

Grimeford
Industrial Estate

Greenland

Rawlinson Lane

Heathfield
Eller Brook

North
Vale

Woodville Rd

Waterford
Close

Farm
Avenue

Mercer

Kingsley

The

York

Highfield Rd North

Croston

Chester Place

Crove
Crescent

Grove
Avenue

Brook Street

Ollerton Street

Berry St

Sutton
Lane

Mornington Road

Springfiel Road

Harding
St

Princess
Road

Mt Pleasant

St Paul's

Vicarage

St Pauls C of E
School

Highfield
Road

Mill St

St
Peel

Lancashire
Co Council

Lancaster Cl

Sutton La

Mayfield Av

Abbey Gv

Abbey Gv

ADLINGTON

A673 CHORLEY ROAD

CHURCH ST

RAILWAY ROAD

Cabbot St

Bank St

Adlington CP School

PO

Stonor

Carrington
Rd

Sandy

Chapel St

Smith St

Station Rd

Grafton

Warwick St

Windsor
Av

Acresfield

Road

Park

Lewis Close

Castle House
La

Sandringham
Close

Balmoral

Rigby House
Farm

Castle Dr

Common

Crawford
Av

The Old School La

The Poplars

Cemetery

Gas St

Oxford

Harrison
Road

Outterside
Street

MARKET ST

MARKET PLACE

Water St

Station Rd

Railway
View

Meadow
Street

Back

Adlington Station

Adlington Cricket
Club

Huyton

Road

CHORLEY

ROAD

Common End

Stoney

Lane

**C7**
1 Atherton St
2 Canal St
3 Walton St

**D4**
1 Coniston Av

16

**D5**
1 Belvedere Rd
2 Chorley St
3 Factory La
4 Hope St

**43**

1 grid square represents 500 metres

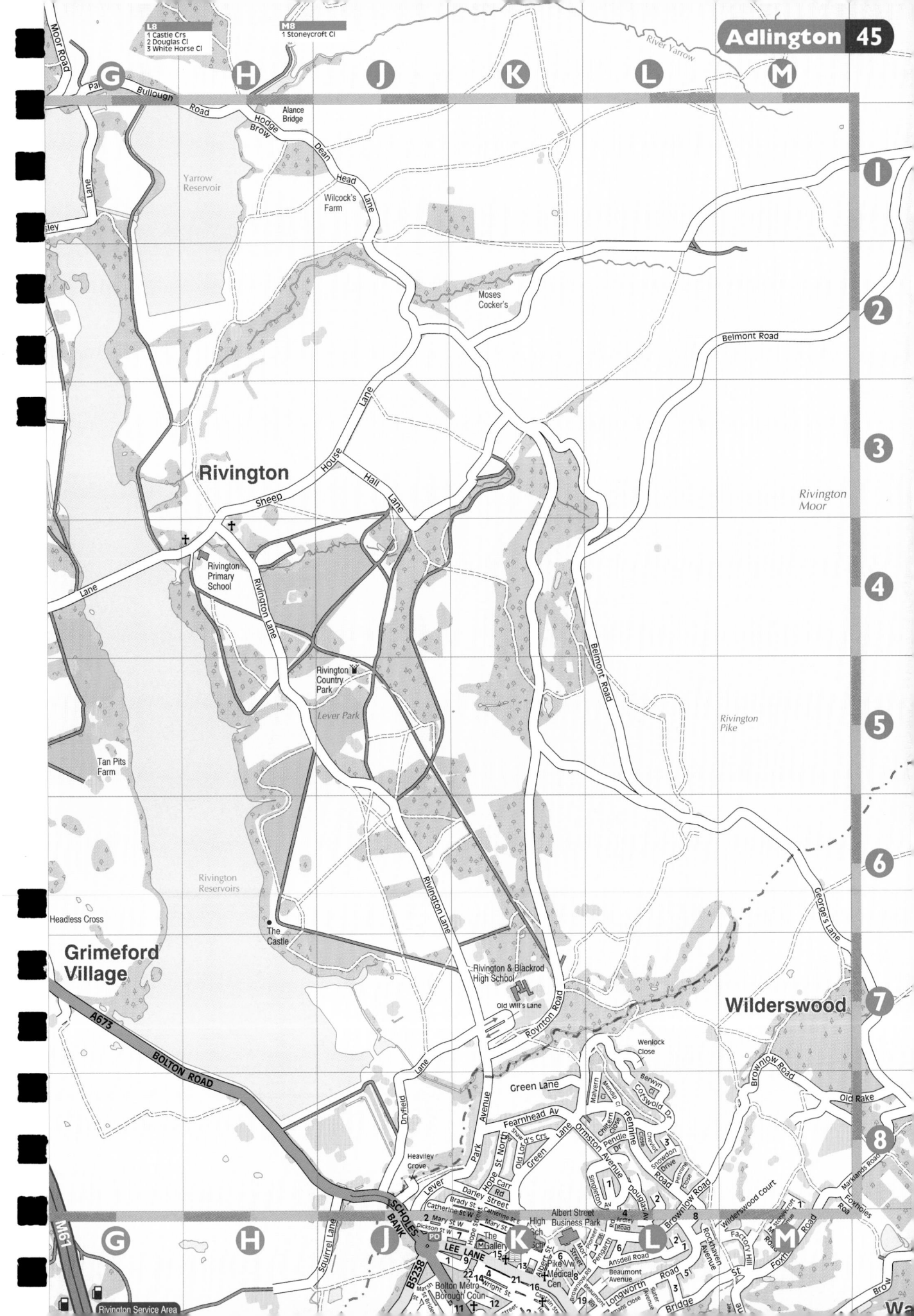

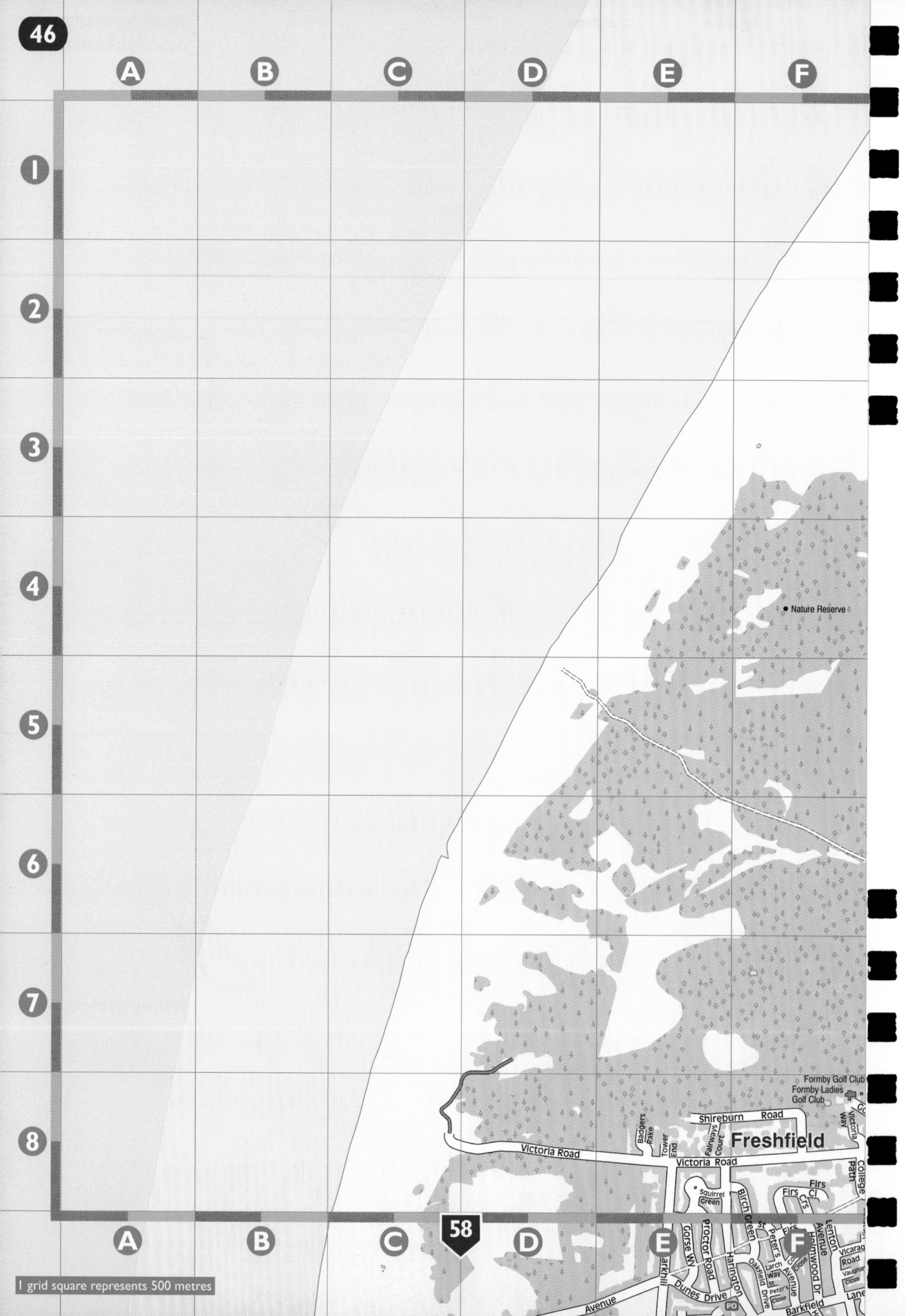

A B C D E F

1
2
3
4
5
6
7
8

A B C D E F

Nature Reserve

Formby Golf Club
Formby Ladies
Golf Club

Shireburn Road

**Freshfield**

Victoria Road
Victoria Road

Badgers Rake
Tower End
Fairways Court

Squirrel Green

Birch Green
Firs
Firs Cl
Firs Crs

Gorse Wy
Proctor Road
Harington
Larch Avenue
St. Peter's Close
Oakfield Drive
Lenton Avenue
Harnwood Dr
Vicarage Close
Vaughan Close
Victoria Way
College Path

Dunes Drive
Avenue
Barkfield
Lane
PO

1 grid square represents 500 metres

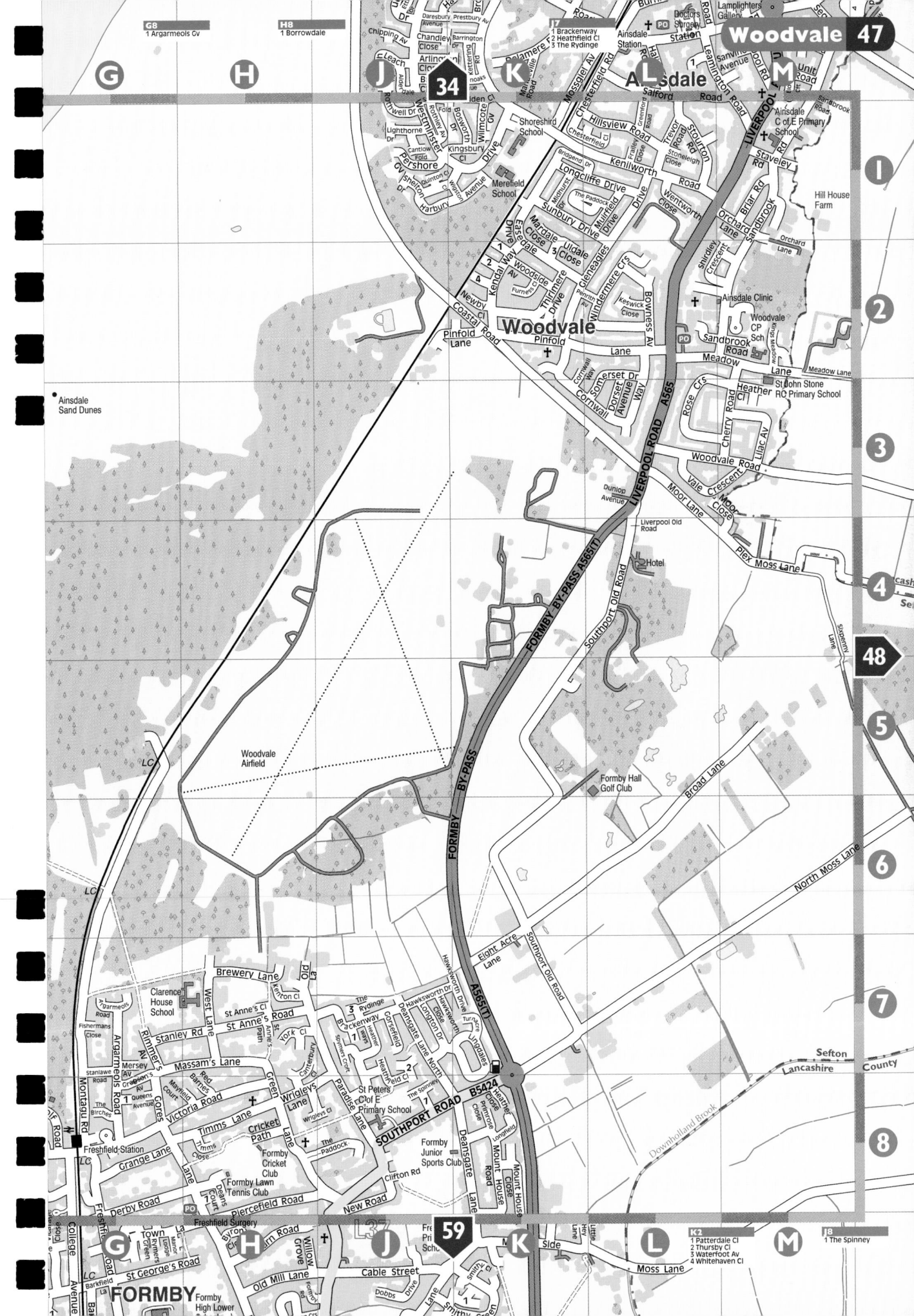

35

A B C D E F

I

Unit Road

Moss View

White Otter Farm

Segar's Lane

Segar's Lane

Headbolt Lane

Hill House Farm

spencer's Lane

Carr Moss Lane

Michael's Lane

Heather Farm

Carr Moss Lane

Meadow Lane

2

John Stone Primary School

Plex Moss

3

Woodvale Road

4

Lancashire County

Sefton

Plex Moss Lane

Gettern Farm

5

Alder Lane

Plex Moss Lane

Heathy Lane

Gorsey Lane

North Lane

6

Gorsey Lane

Shaw

7

Sefton

Lancashire County

Cheshire Lines Path

Moss Lane

8

Old Moss Lane

A B C D E F

60

Downholland Moss

I grid square represents 500 metres

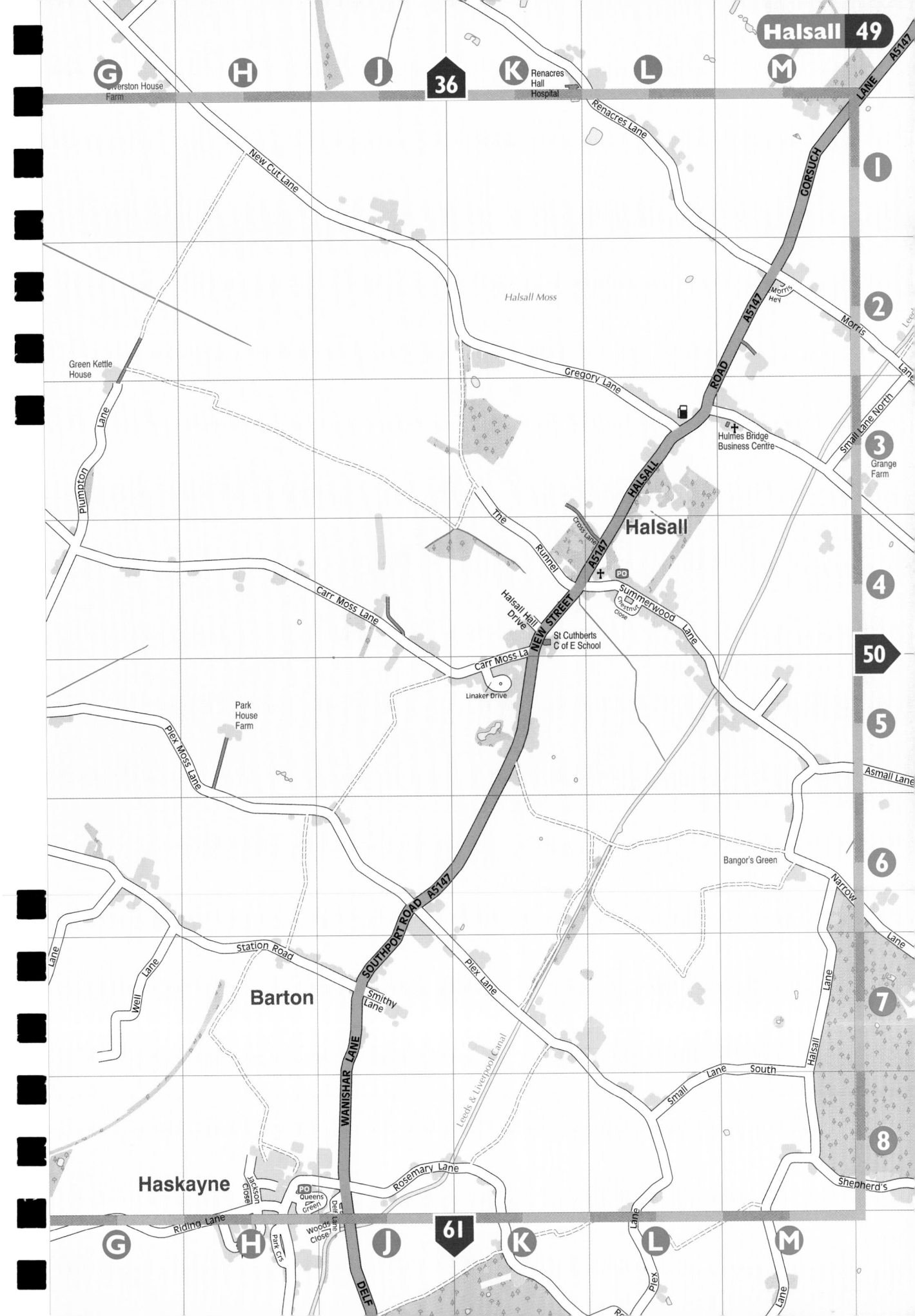

G
H
J
36
K
L
M

I
2
3
4
50
5
6
7
8

G
H
J
61
K
L
M

Green Kettle House

Iverston House Farm

Renacres Hall Hospital

Renacres Lane

GORSUCH LANE

A5147

Morris Hey

Morris Lane

Small Lane North

Grange Farm

New Cut Lane

Halsall Moss

Gregory Lane

HALSALL ROAD A5147

Hulmes Bridge Business Centre

Halsall

Plumpton Lane

The Runnel

Cross Lane

PO

Summerwood Lane

Chestnut Close

Carr Moss Lane

Halsall Hall Drive

NEW STREET A5147

St Cuthberts C of E School

Carr Moss La

Linaker Drive

Asmall Lane

Park House Farm

Plex Moss Lane

Bangor's Green

Narrow Lane

SOUTHPORT ROAD A5147

Station Road

Plex Lane

Halsall Lane

Barton

Smithy Lane

WANISHAR LANE

Leeds & Liverpool Canal

Small Lane South

Well Lane

Lane

Haskayne

Jackson Close

PO Queens Green

Rosemary Lane

Park Crs

Delf Lane

Woods Lane Close

Riding Lane

Plex Rd

Shepherd's

DELF

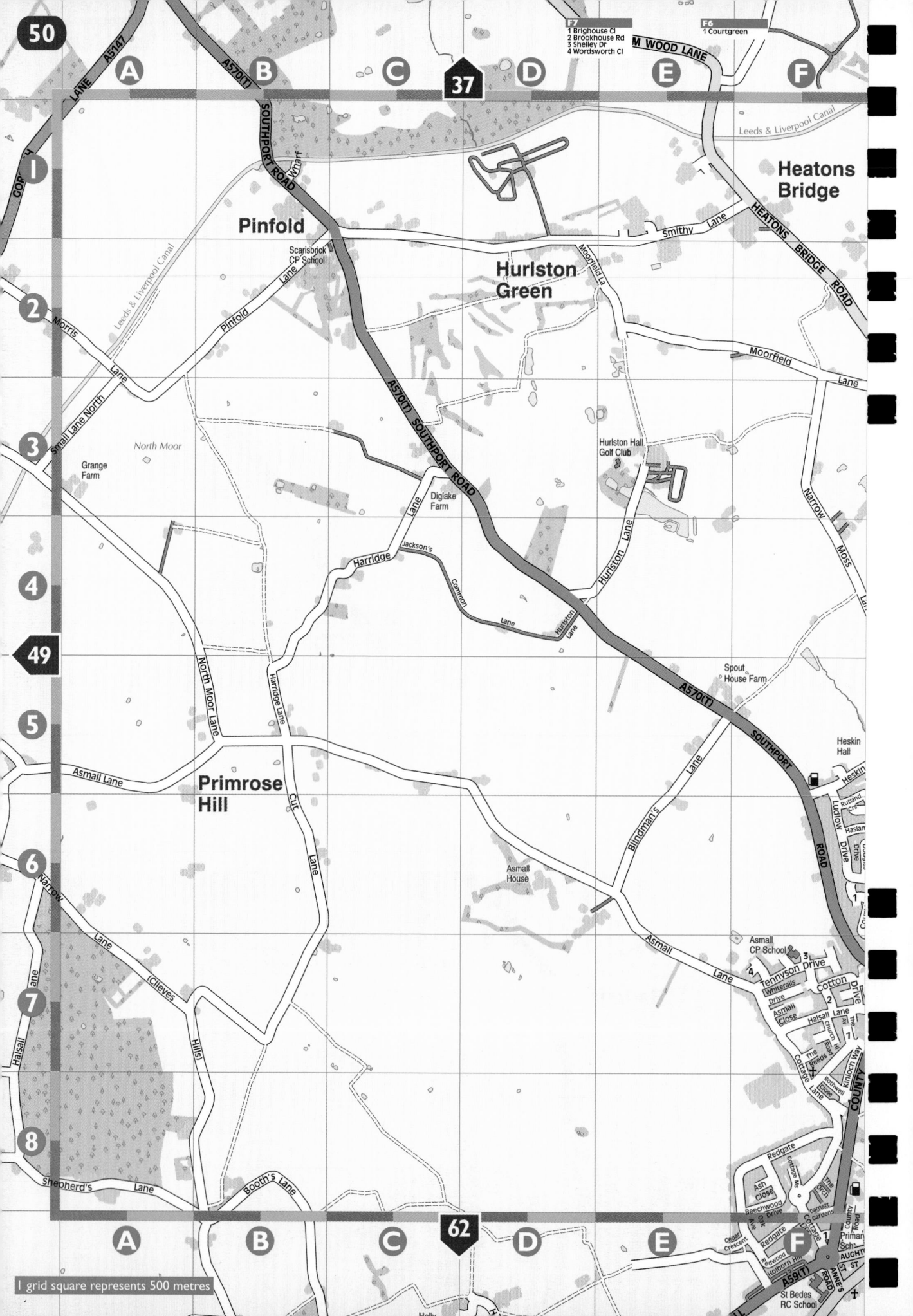

**Bridge**

Football

Leeds & Liverpool Canal

G6
1 Fairfield Dr
2 Hurlston Dr

G7
1 Alexandra Ms
2 Ellerbrook Wy
3 Green Lane Av
4 Sanfield Cl

H6
1 Croftson Av
2 Grove Pk
3 Lonsdale Av

Priory High School

G H J 38 K L M

Martin Hall

Langley Place

Langley Road

Plantation Road

Rabbit Lane

Ringtail Road

L40

Higgin's Lane

Hesketh Road

Vicarage Gardens

Harding Road

Trevor Road

Edge Farm

Ringtail Road

Ringtail Court

Ringtall Place

Tollgate Road

Christines Crs

Lordsgate Drive

Rivington Drive

A59(T)

B5242 BARRISON GREEN

PIPPIN STREET B5242

Stub Lane

Blackacre Lane

Merridale Farm

Tollgate Road

The Surgery

Lordsgate Lane

Liverpool Road

Mill Dam Lane

Springfield Close

Meadowbrook

SOUTH

ROAD

Platts Lane

Manor Crs

Manor Drive

Manor Avenue

Manor Gardens

Chapel La

**Burscough**

Hotel

Abbey Lane

Abbey Lane Industrial Est

Mill Dam Lane

Blythe Hall

**52**

Renfrey Close

Marians Drive

West End County Primary School

Whittle Drive

Mawdsley Terrace

Dawson Road

Tyler Road

Carroll Crescent

Parker Crescent

Scott Drive

Sephton Drive

Lea Crescent

Sturgess Close

HIGH LANE

Dark Lane

Sandy Lane

Lathom Lane

Lady's Walk

Ormskirk Golf Club

Fairfield Close

Highfield Road

Hayfield Rd

A59(T)

BURSCOUGH ROAD

Pine Cl

Pine Avenue

Old Boundary

Brookacre

Bath Farm

Dark Lane

Castle Lane

Ormskirk Rugby Union Football Club

Clucas Gdns

Ashcroft Avenue

Scarisbrick Street

Farrington Drive

Hillcrest Rd

B5319 BURSCOUGH STREET

Yew Tree Road

Waterworks Road

Nursery Avenue

Pendle Hill

Southport Rd

Green Lane

Pennington Avenue

Hants Lane

Ormskirk College

Station Rd

New Court Way

Haitsacre

Greetby Hill C of E Junior School

Greetby Hill

Chestive Road

Thompson

Field Walk

Rosscroft Close

Church Fields

Ormskirk Station

Railway Road

Derby Street

Derby Hill Road

Edgley Drive

Taylor Avenue

Lapp Walk

Vicarage Walk

Church Walk

Derby St West

Doctors Surg

Leyland House Surg

Aughton Street

Sunnyfields

Tower Hill

Latham Avenue

Ormskirk Swimming Pool

Aughton St

MOOR ST

PO

WIGAN ROAD

A577 CROSSHALL

Cross Hall High School

Kingsbury Sch

AUGHTON ST

PARK ROAD

ST HELEN'S ROAD

Knowsley Road

Windmill Street

Mill Street

Ormskirk & District General Hospital

G H J 63 K L BRO M

ORMSKIRK

**Westhead**

M3
1 Mill Dam La
2 Thoroughgood Cl

M1
1 Chislett Cl
2 Crabtree Cl
3 Furnival Dr
4 Heaton Cl
5 Killingbeck Cl
6 Trevor Rd

L1
1 Admiralty Cl

J8
1 Derby Hill Crs

L8
1 Quarry Mt
2 Top Delph

H8
1 Meadow Bank
2 Millers Ct
3 Oak Gn
4 Station Ap
5 Willow Gn

H7
1 Chestnut Ct
2 Jubilee Av
3 Owen Av

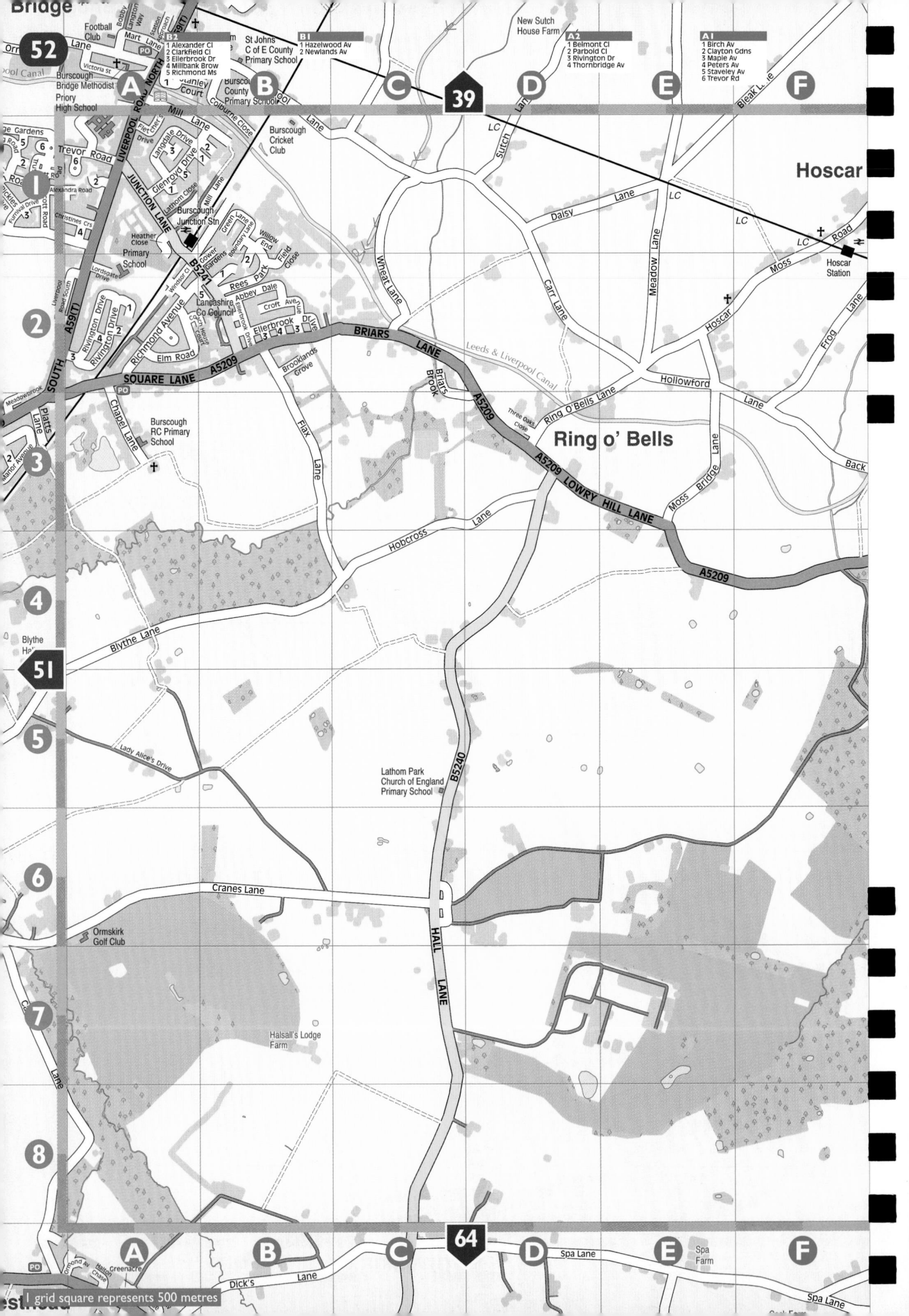

# Bridge

**B1**
1 Alexander Cl
2 Clarkfield Cl
3 Ellerbrook Dr
4 Millbank Brow
5 Richmond Ms

**B1**
1 Hazelwood Av
2 Newlands Av

New Sutch
House Farm

**A2**
1 Belmont Cl
2 Parbold Cl
3 Rivington Dr
4 Thornbridge Av

**A1**
1 Birch Av
2 Clayton Gdns
3 Maple Av
4 Peters Av
5 Staveley Av
6 Trevor Rd

Hoscar

A · B · C · **39** · D · E · F

Burscough
Bridge Methodist
Priory
High School

St Johns
C of E County
Primary School

Burscough Cricket
Club

Hoscar Station

**1**

Burscough County Primary School

Burscough Junction Stn

Daisy Lane

Meadow Lane

Hoscar Lane

Moss Lane

Frog Lane

**2**

Richmond Avenue

Square Lane A5209

Leeds & Liverpool Canal

Carr Lane

Hollowford Lane

**Ring o' Bells**

**3**

Burscough RC Primary School

Flax Lane

Briars Brook

Ring O'Bells Lane

Three Oaks Close

Moss Bridge Lane

Back Lane

**4**

Hobcross Lane

Lowry Hill Lane

A5209

Blythe Hall

**51**

**5**

Lady Alice's Drive

Lathom Park Church of England Primary School

B5240

**6**

Cranes Lane

Ormskirk Golf Club

Hall Lane

**7**

Halsall's Lodge Farm

**8**

A · B · C · **64** · D · Spa Lane · E · Spa Farm · F

Spa Lane

1 grid square represents 500 metres

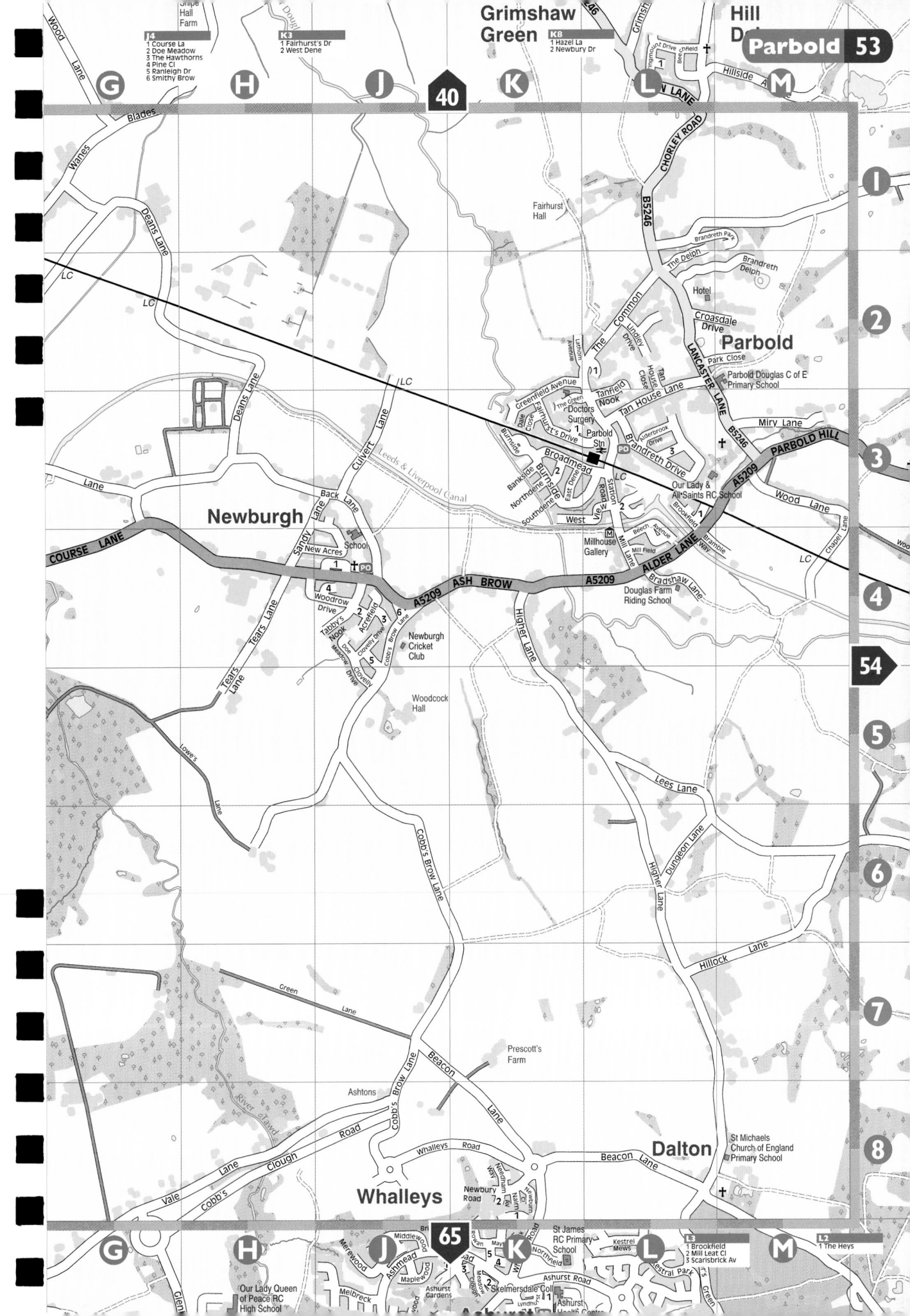

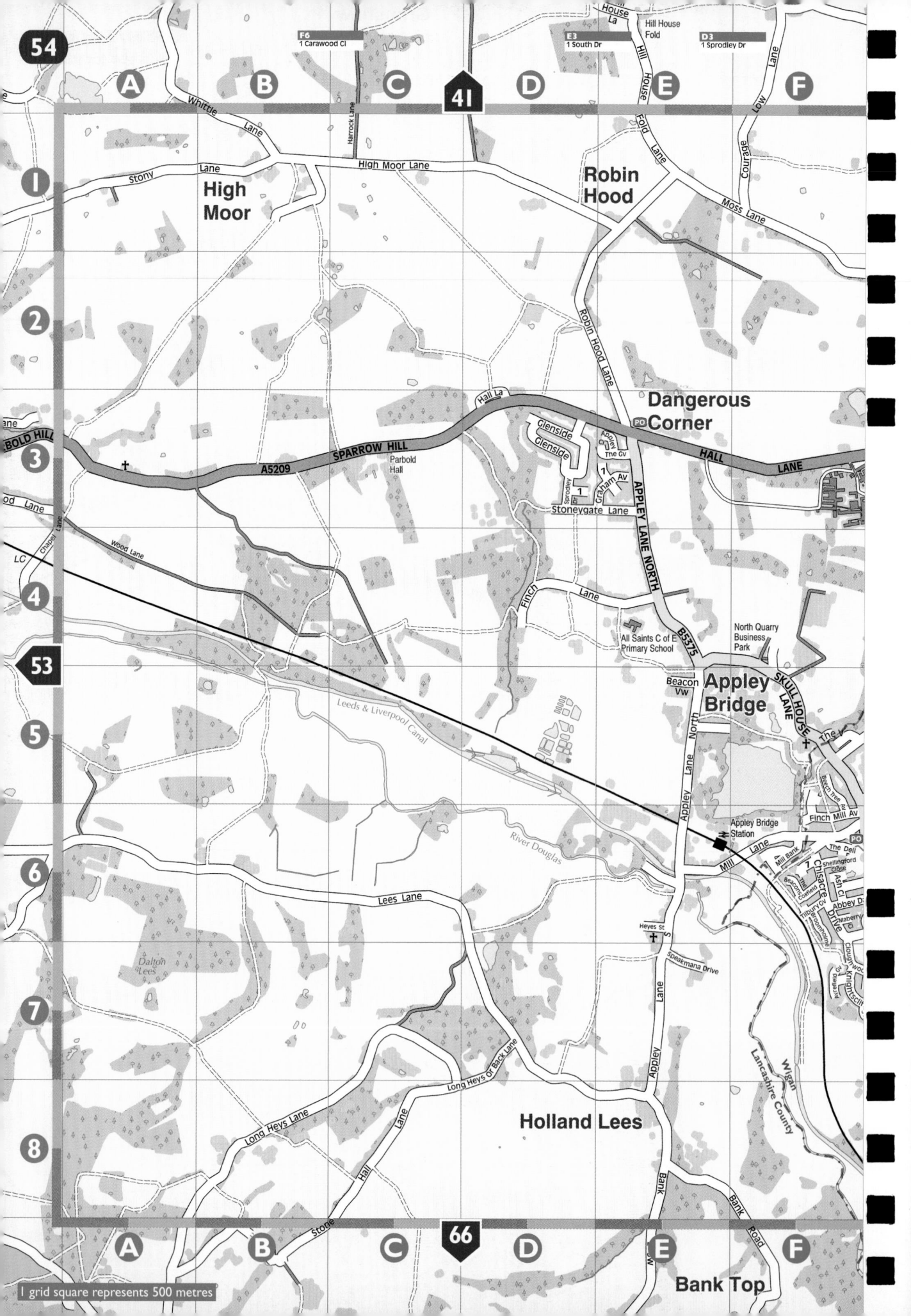

G6
1 Braidhaven

G7
1 Bankwood
2 Woodcroft

H8
1 St Anne's Ct

I3
1 Fircroft
2 Forest Dr
3 Hesketh Dr

K2
1 Richards Rd

K3
1 Barbrook Cl
2 Colnbrook

**42**

G  H  J  K  L  M

Tunley Lane

A5250

Tunley Moss

Moss House Farm

Hunger Hill

MOSSY LEA ROAD

St Josephs RC School

Mossy Lea Fold

MOSS LANE

Hotel

Boundary La

Pepper Lane

Pepper Lane

Hyatt Crs

Pepper Lane

Fairhurst Av

Langtree Lane

PRESTON ROAD

Malvern St

Ludlow St

Langtree Hall

A49

CROW ORCHARD ROAD

A5209

M6

Shevington Moor

Robin Hill Drive

Robin Hi Lane

Chisholm

Harris Rd

Douglas

Ribble Rd

Old Pepper Lane

Whiteacre

Parkway

Broadacre

Marble

Standish High School

Kenyon Rd

Primrose La

Ingleby Cl

Marwick Cl

Moores La

Greenwood Rd

James Sq

James Pl

St Maries Primary S

Foxglove Cl

Bradshaw Cl

Langham Road

Cranborne

Hempstead

Wheatsheaf Wk

Langton Rd

Wrightington Hospital N H S Trust

Cripple Ga

Junction 27

CROW ORCHARD ROAD

SHEVINGTON LANE

Cresswell

Ashurst

PK

Palace

Almond Brook

Hotel

PO

ALMOND BROOK ROAD A5209

Woodhurst Dr

Witham

Spey

School Lane

**56**

Wood Fold Primary Sch

Longendale

Wilkesley Av

Beech Walk

Back Lane

Shevington Vale

WN6

Aspinall Rd

Arbour Lane

Glen Dr

Hullet Cl

Vale Cl

Moor Av

Runshaw Av

Greaves

Whitehall Av

Rookery Av

Woodnook

Shevington Vale CP School

Hermitage Close

Hill Cl

Newgate Avenue

Grovewood Dr

Park Av

Highcr

The Nook

MILES LANE

Spearding Road

B5375

Shevington CP School

Clnc

Houghton

New Miles Lane

Manor Rd

Calico Wood Avenue

Miles Lane

Doctors Surg

PO

Naylorfarm Av

The Oval

Queensway

GATHURST LANE

BROAD O'TH LANE

Braithwaite

Highfield Av

Inward Drive

Maryland

Beechwood Avenue

Oakwood Av

Douglas Dr

Ran

Lane

St Anne's Dr

Edgewood

Vicarage Lane

Primary School

B5375

CHURCH LANE

Dixon Av

Wood Field

Fern Av

Hope Crs

Gill Av

Lower Lyndon Av

Wilton Av

Kilburn Dr

Copperas Cl

Orch

Willowbrook Dr

Paradise Farm

SHEVINGTON LANE

Park Av

Parbrook Lane

Shevington County High School

Park Play

Longbrook

Yewdale Park

Coach House Dr

Millbrook CP Sch

Elmup Avenue

Redwood

The Clade

Elmfield

Christleton

Foxfield Gv

WIGAN ROAD

Standish Hall

Shevington

Forest Fold Farm

Leeds & Liverpool Canal

**67**

G  H  J  K  L  M

M2
1 Deben Cl
2 Langham Rd
3 Leadale Cl
4 Nairn Cl
5 Simfield Cl

M3
1 Northways
2 Viola Cl
3 Whitwell Cl

L4
1 St Stephen's Rd

K4
1 Greensward Cl

I

2

3

4

5

6

7

8

Langtree Hall

Standish Hall

**A**  **B**  **C**  43  **D**  **E**  **F**

**1**

Talbot
House

Adlington
Hall Farm

Gorse
Hall

Adlington
Park

**2**

Langtree Lane

Langtree
Hall

Bradley Lane

Platt Lane

Worthington
Lakes
(Reservoirs)

BORES HILL

A5106

CHORLEY ROAD

Buckow Brook

**3**

Moore's La

James Sq

James Pl

Sheldon Avenue

Langley

Woodland

Edale Dr

Sterndale Av

Dovedale Dr

St Maries RC
Primary School

Greenwood Road

Avondale

Broomfield Rd

Bentham Pl

Bradley Lane

Churchlands

Copeland Drive

Belfry Crs

Canon Close

Ormsby

Bradley Hall
Trading
Estate

Hutton Street

Hotel

**STANDISH**

RECTORY LANE

Brookside Road

Artle Lane

**4**

Wheatsheaf Wk

Adelph

Langton Av

Collingwood

Smalley St

Market St

PO

Heaton Av

Church St

Baxter

Wilfrid's St

Perryn

Brandreth

Taberner

St Wilfrid's

Rudyard

St Wilfrid's

Standish
Medical
Practice

Fontwell Cl

St Wilfrids C of E
Primary School

B5239

Sussex

Devon Dr

Essex Rd

PO

Arley La

Arley

RED ROCK LANE B5239

**55**

Wood
Primary Sch

Withnall

Dr

Greenland Av

HIGH STREET

Southlands Av

Police
Stn

Victoria

Clinic

Grove

Grove Pl

Cranleigh

Lane

Clebe Rd

Larkhill

Rivington

**Red
Rock**

**5**

Be

Ingendale Rd

Wilkesley Av

Green Lane

Alford

Calveley Wk

Byley

Mossy

Birch Av

Ash Grove

Elm Av

Oak Av

Cedar Av

Maldon Rd

Silsbury

Judson

**Winstanleys**

Cricket
Club

Westmead

Trescott
Mews

Longridge

Rowton Rd

**6**

Beech Crs

Walk

Park Rd

Prospect Rd

Almond Crs

Kingshill Court

Highcliffe Court

Darnford Dr

A49

Hibank Dale

Serpolly

Pinevale

Briarly

Plymouth

Rowan Rd

**7**

Standish
Hall

Standish Wood Lane

Greenriggs Cl

gton Drive

Iredale Crs

Thirlmere Av

Waterfield

Coniston Park

Drive

Pilgrims Way

Cromedale

Delfhaven
Ct

Derngate

**Boar's
Head**

Raisey Ct

Boars Head

Copperbeech
Drive

Greenways

Water

Drive

Lurdin La

Ridge
Av

Richmond
Cl

Hawthorn Av

Limes Av

A5106

Pendlebury Lane

**8**

Gidlow
Cemetery

Mere Oaks
School

Elmfield Rd

Scott Av

Pendbury Rd

WIGAN

Bethersden
Road

Newbrook

Broomfield
Avenue

Brock Mill Lane

Wingates

Douglas Valley
Business Park

Sennicar Lane

Wigan Rugby Union
Football Club

**WN1**

**A**

**B**

**C**  68  **D**  **E**  **F**

Larkin

Whitley

Elkwood

Hazelwood Rd

Cranbrook
Way

Willow Tree

Galway Gv

Woodfield
Primary Sch

A49

Hall Lane

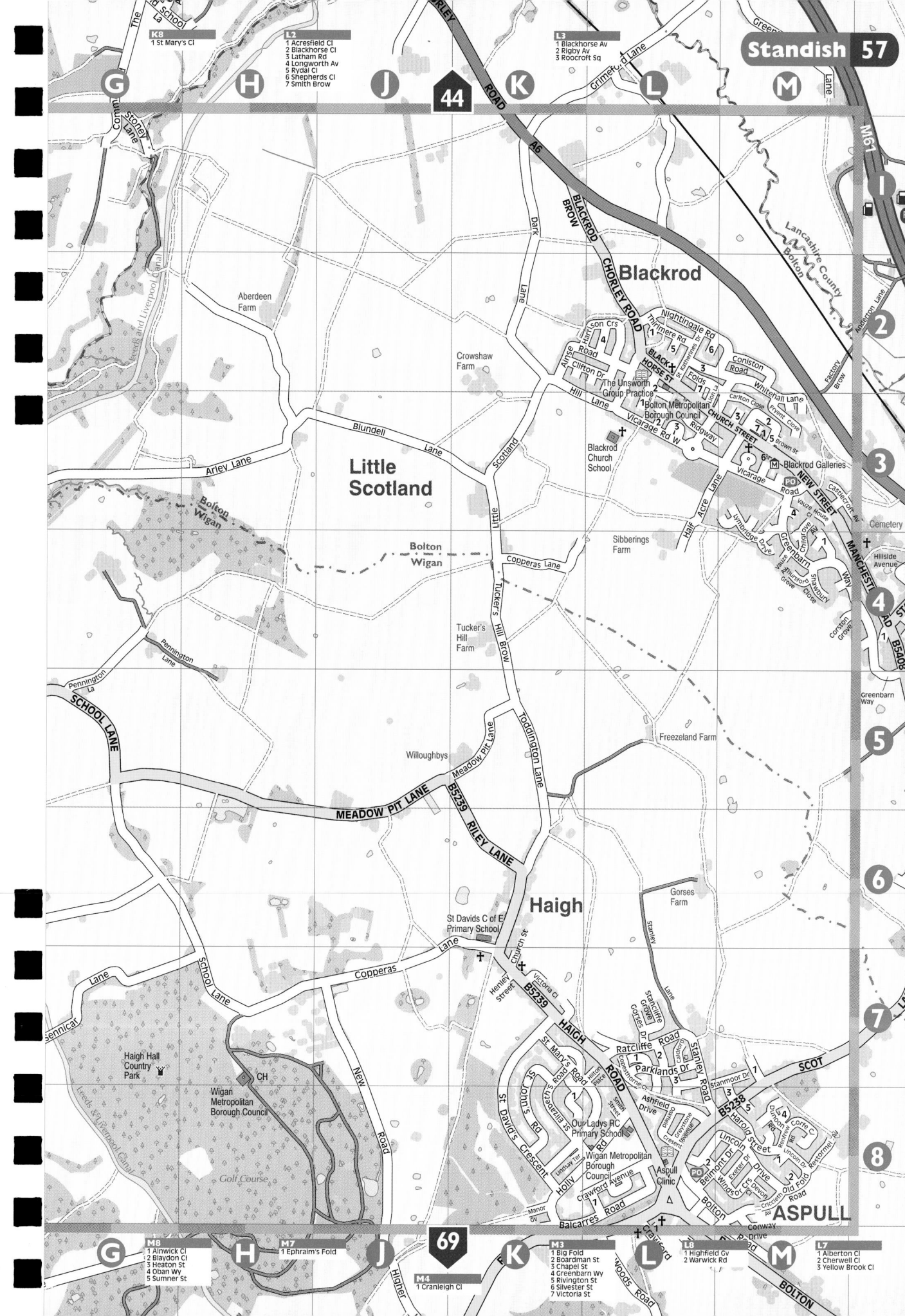

G  H  J  44  K  L  M

M61

I

2

3

4

5

6

7

8

Blackrod

Aberdeen Farm

Crowshaw Farm

Little Scotland

Bolton Wigan

Bolton Wigan

Copperas Lane

Sibberings Farm

Blackrod Church School

The Unsworth Group Practice

Bolton Metropolitan Borough Council

Blackrod Galleries

Cemetery

Hillside Avenue

Arley Lane

Blundell Lane

Bolton Wigan

Pennington Lane

Pennington La

SCHOOL LANE

Tucker's Hill Brow

Tucker's Hill Farm

Willoughbys

Meadow Pit Lane

MEADOW PIT LANE

B5239

RILEY LANE

Toddington Lane

Freezeland Farm

Greenbarn Way

Haigh

Gorses Farm

St Davids C of E Primary School

Copperas Lane

School Lane

Lane

Bennicat Lane

Haigh Hall Country Park

Wigan Metropolitan Borough Council

CH

Golf Course

Leeds & Liverpool Canal

New Road

Church St

Henley Street

B5239

HAIGH ROAD

St Mary's Road

St John's Rd

St David's Crescent

Our Ladys RC Primary School

Wigan Metropolitan Borough Council

Aspull Clinic

Ratcliffe

Parklands Dr

Stanley Road

B5238

SCOT

Crawford Avenue

Balcarres Road

Bolton Road

ASPULL

Conway Drive

BOLTON

G  H  J  69  K  L  M

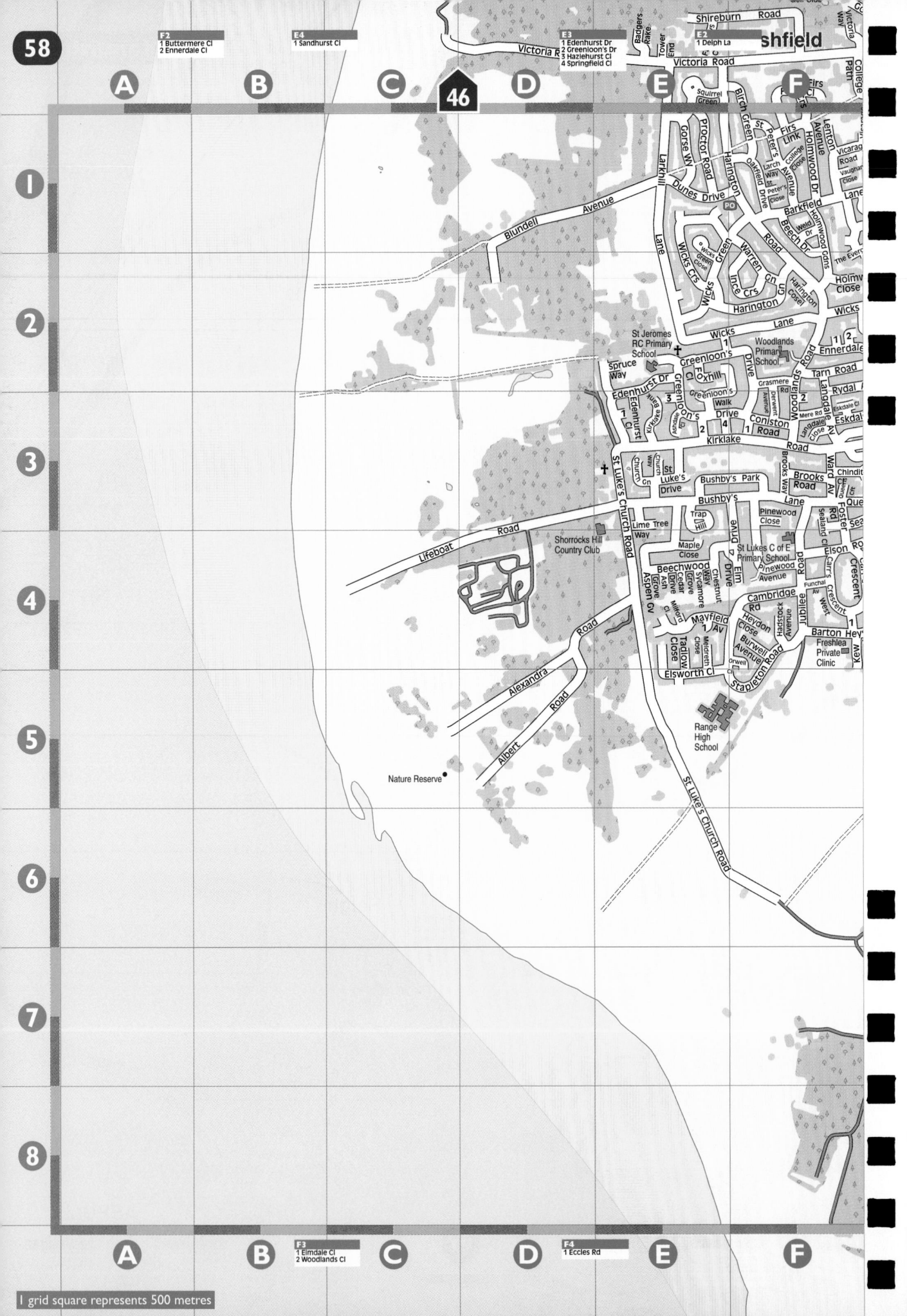

46

**F2**
1 Buttermere Cl
2 Ennerdale Cl

**E4**
1 Sandhurst Cl

**E3**
1 Edenhurst Dr
2 Greenloon's Dr
3 Hazlehurst Cl
4 Springfield Cl

**E2**
1 Delph La

shfield

Victoria R

Victoria Road

Shireburn Road

Badgers Rake

Tower End

Squirrel Green

Birch Green

Firs Link

Firs Cl

College Path

Victoria Way

Col

Co Wy

A B C D E F

1

Blundell Avenue

Gorse Wy

Proctor Road

Harington

Larkhill

Dunes Drive

PO

St Peter's Way

Oakfield Drive

Larch Close

St Peter's Close

College Close

Lenton Avenue

Holmwood Dr

Vicarage Road

Vaughan Lane

Barkfield Avenue

Weld Dr

Holmwood Gdns

Beech Dr

2

Wicks Crs

Wicks Green Close

Wicks Green

Warren Ct

Ince Crs

Harington Road

The Ever

Holmw Close

Harington Lane

Wicks

Wicks Lane

St Jeromes RC Primary School

Spruce Way

Edenhurst Dr

Edenhurst Cl

Kirklake

Greenloon's Dr

Foxhill

Greenloon's Walk

Woodlands Primary School

1 2

Ennerdale

Tarn Road

Grasmere Rd

Derwent Avenue

Rydal A

Mere Rd

Eskdale Cl

3

Church Cn

St Luke's Drive

St Luke's Church Road

Coniston Road

Kirklake Road

Langale Cl

Eskda

Langdale

Woodpdr

Ward Cl

Chindit

Cree

Qu

Sea

3

Bushby's Park

Brooks Way

Brooks Road

Bushby's Lane

Trap Hill

Pinewood Close

Lime Tree Way

4

Lifeboat Road

Shorrocks Hill Country Club

Maple Close

St Lukes C of E Primary School

Pinewood Avenue

Beechwood Grove

Cedar Grove

Ash Grove

Sycamore

Chestnut Drive

Elm Drive

Pinewood Drive

Carr's Crescent

Funchal Av

Cambridge Rd

West

Crescent

4

Road

Mayfield Av

Milford

Heydon Close

Hadstock Avenue

Barton Hey

1

Road

Tadlow Close

Meldrem Close

Burwell Close

Stapleton Road

Freshlea Private Clinic

Key

Elsworth Cl

Orwell Cl

5

Alexandra Road

Albert Road

St Luke's Church Road

Range High School

5

Nature Reserve

6

6

7

7

8

8

A B C D E F

**F3**
1 Elmdale Cl
2 Woodlands Cl

**F4**
1 Eccles Rd

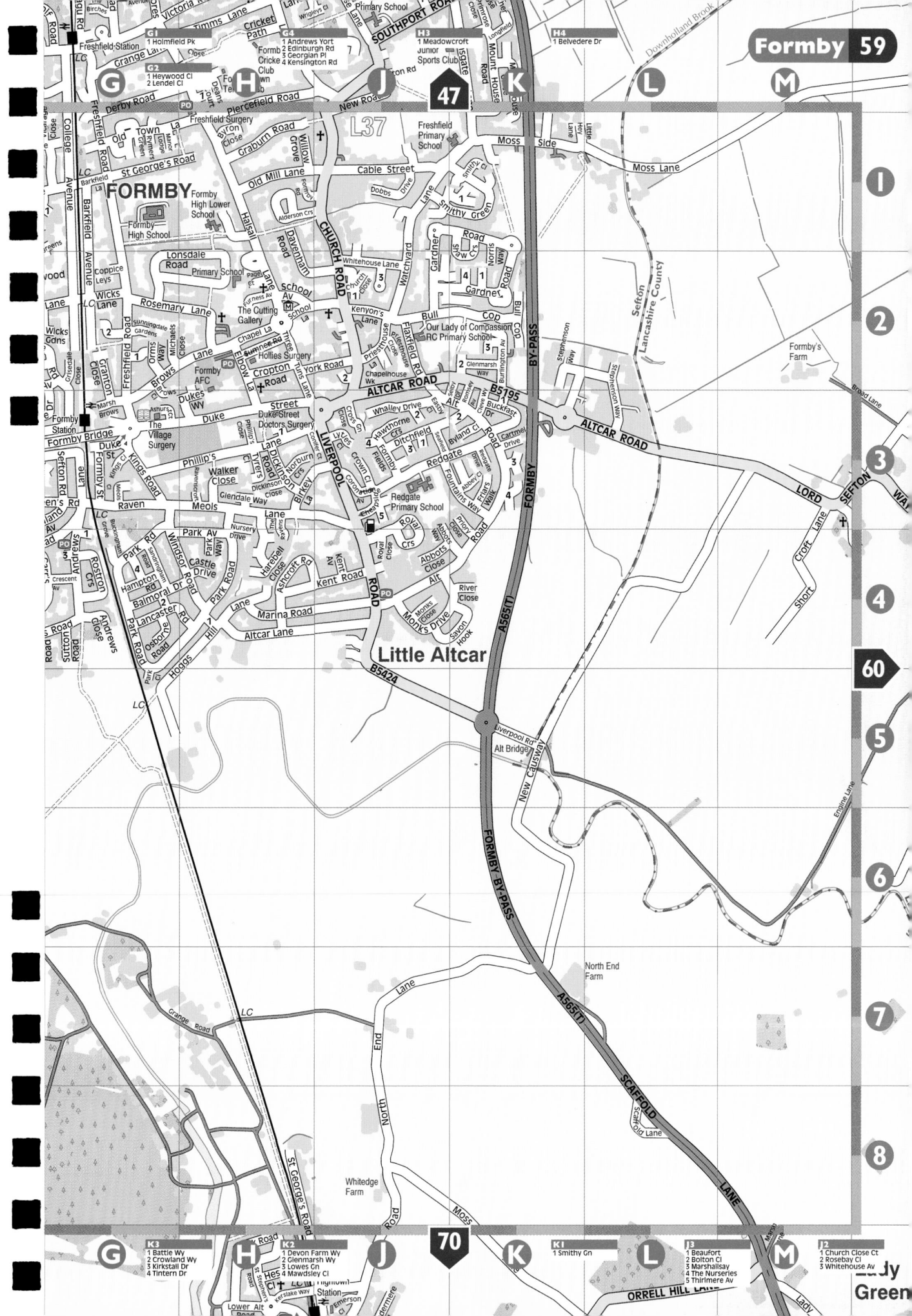

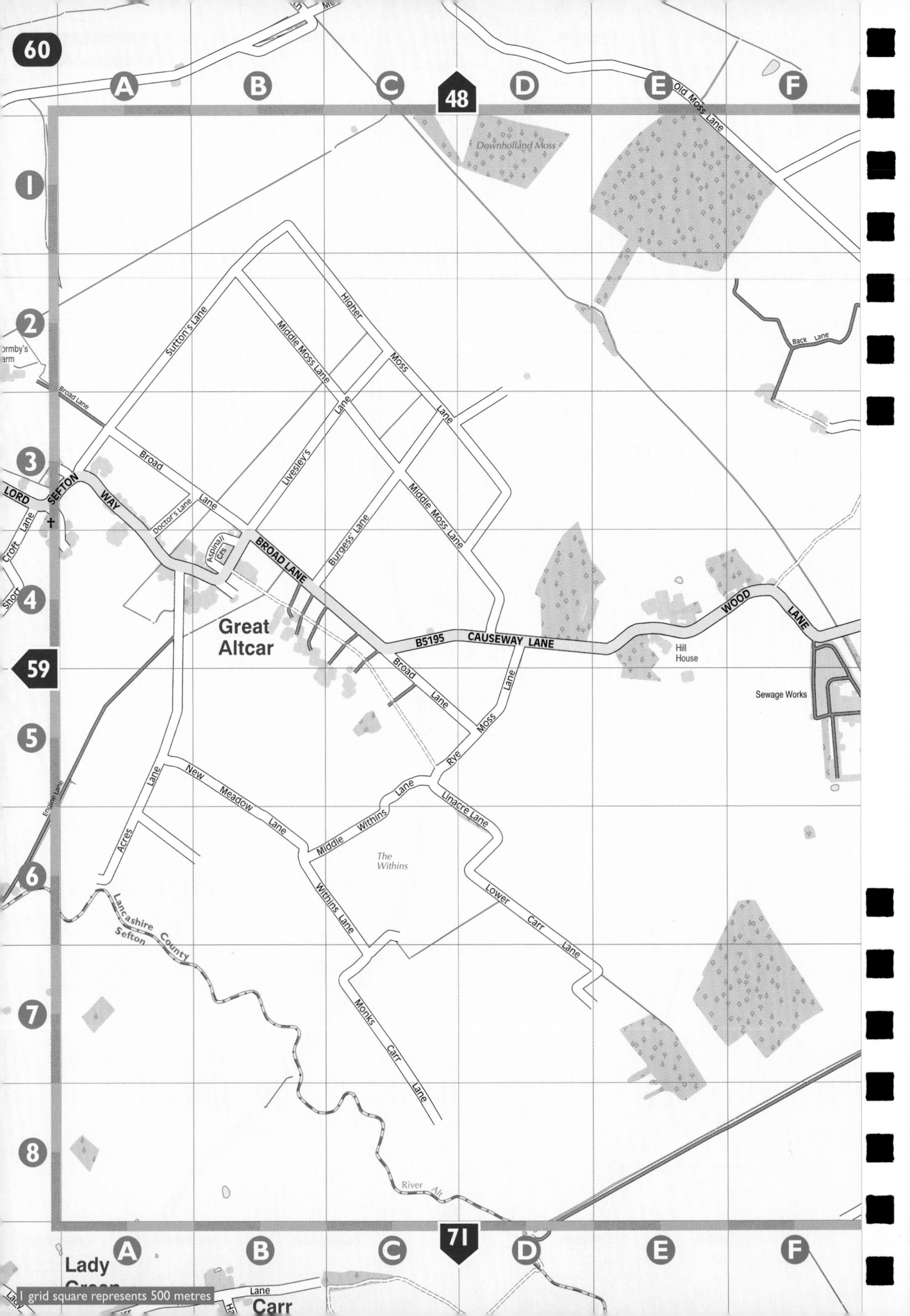

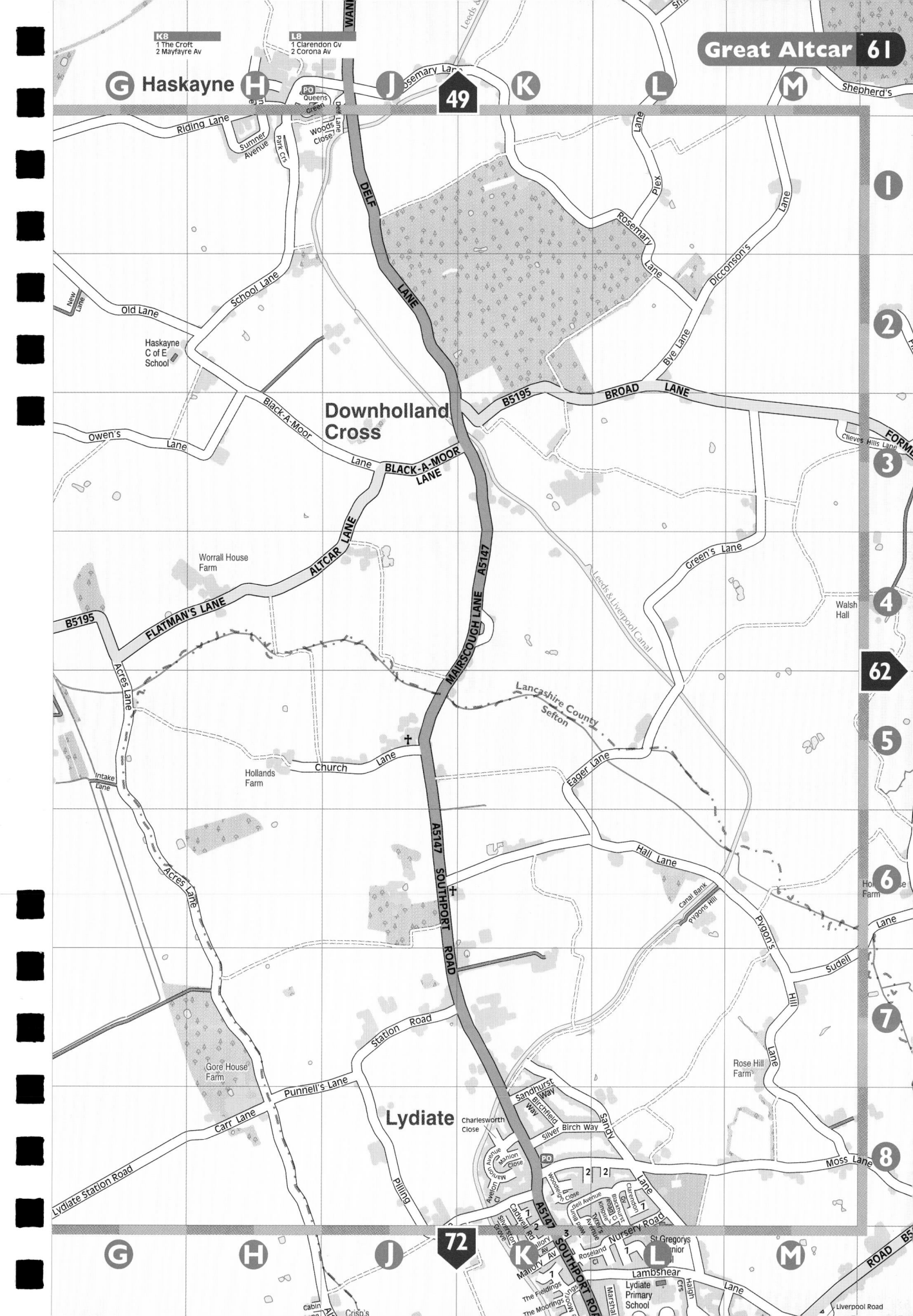

G **Haskayne** H J 49 K L M

I
2
3
4
62
5
6
7
8

K8
1 The Croft
2 Mayfayre Av

L8
1 Clarendon Gv
2 Corona Av

PO
Queens
Green

Riding Lane

Sumner Avenue

Park Crs

Woods Close

Delf Lane Close

Rosemary Lane

New Lane

Old Lane

School Lane

DELF LANE

Rosemary Lane

Plex Lane

Dicconson's Lane

Bye Lane

Clieves Hills Lane

FORME

Haskayne C of E School

**Downholland Cross**

Black-A-Moor Lane

BLACK-A-MOOR LANE

B5195

BROAD LANE

Owen's Lane

ALTCAR LANE

Worrall House Farm

Green's Lane

B5195

FLATMAN'S LANE

MAIRSCOUGH LANE

A5147

Leeds & Liverpool Canal

Walsh Hall

62

Acres Lane

Lancashire County Sefton

Hollands Farm

Church Lane

Eager Lane

Acres Lane

Intake Lane

Hall Lane

Canal Bank

Pygon's Hill

Pygon's Hill Lane

Sudell Lane

Ho... Farm

A5147 SOUTHPORT ROAD

Station Road

Gore House Farm

Rose Hill Farm

Punnell's Lane

Carr Lane

**Lydiate**

Charlesworth Close

Sandhurst Way

Birchfield Way

Silver Birch Way

Sandy Lane

Moss Lane

Lydiate Station Road

Pilling

PO

Avelon Avenue

Marion Close

Woodland Close

Dell Avenue

Clarendon

Nursery Road

St Gregorys Junior

Lydiate Primary School

ROAD B5...

Mallory Av

Roseland Cl

Lambshear Lane

Highfield Crs

Liverpool Road

Crisp's

Cabin

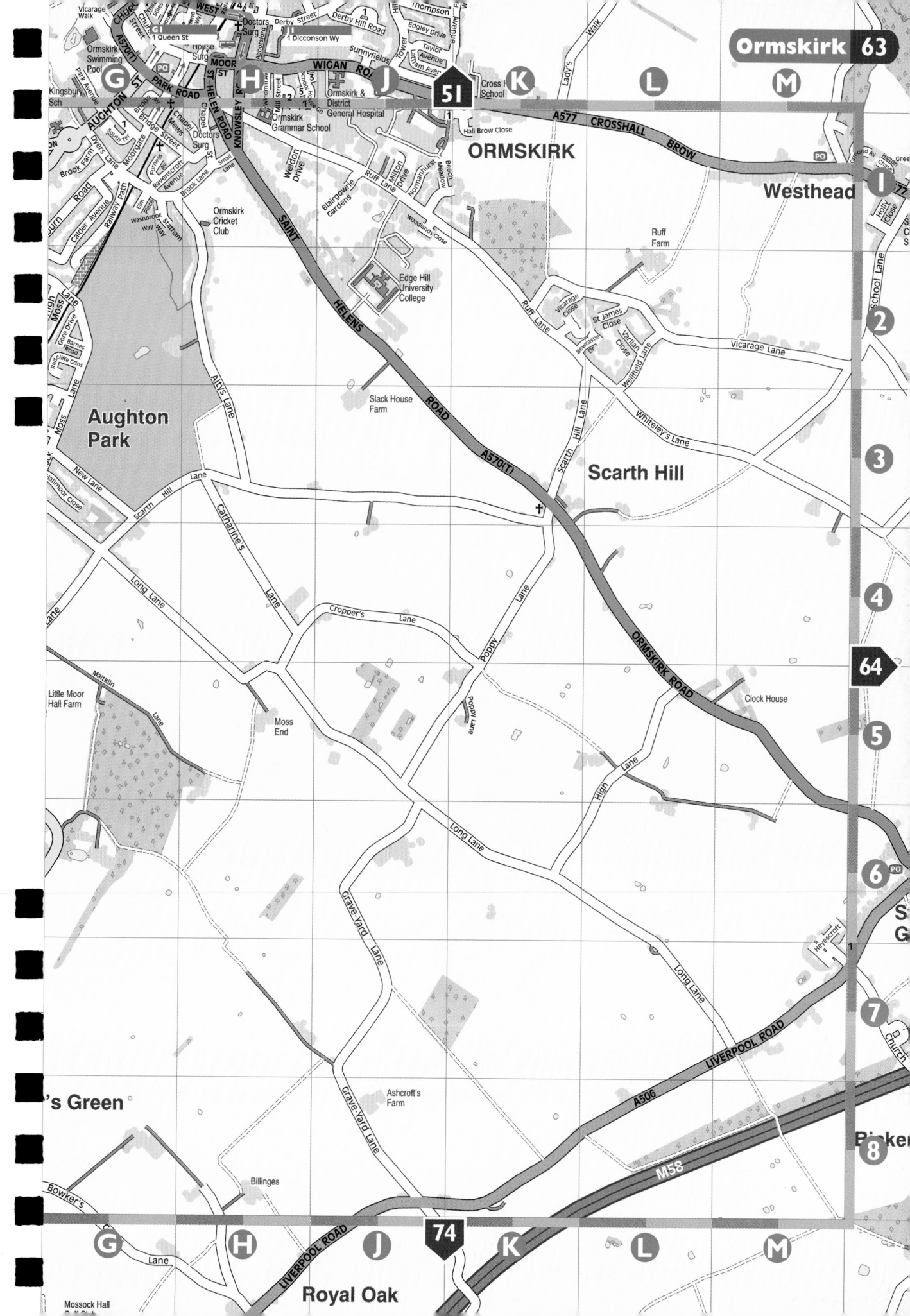

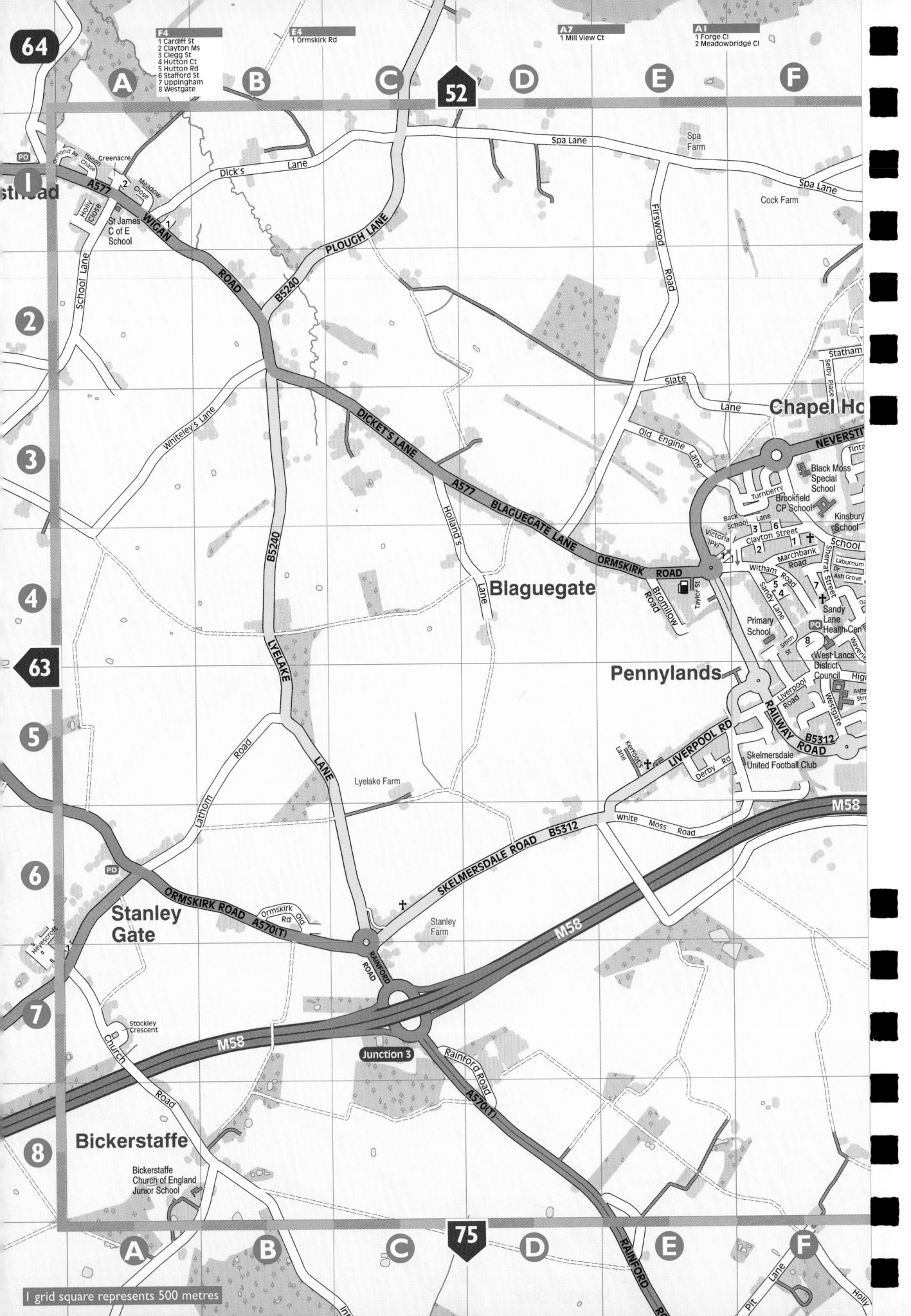

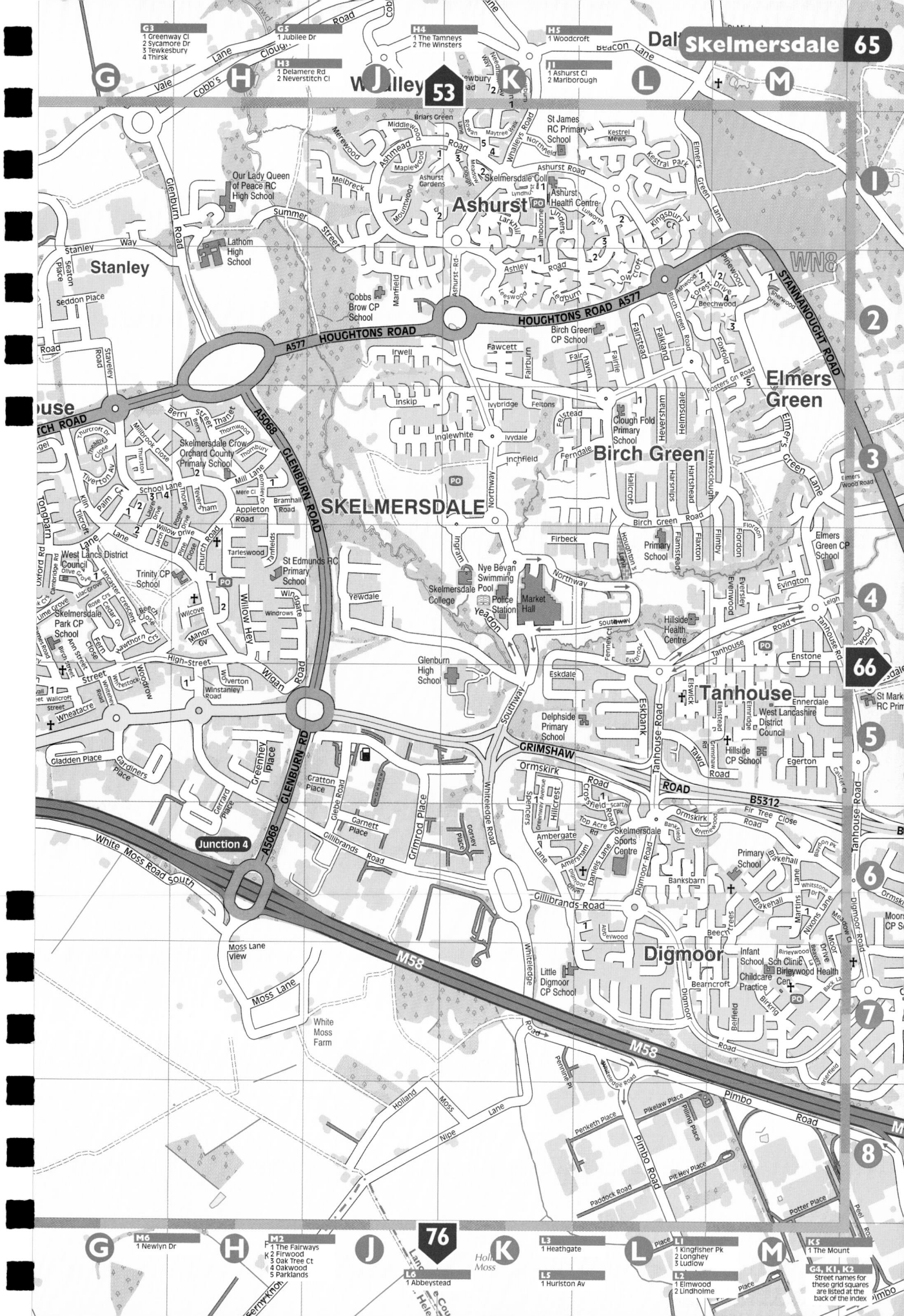

G · H · W**J**lley 53 · K · L · † · M

WN8

I

2

3

4

66

5

6

7

8

Skelmersdale

Stanley

Ashurst

Elmers Green

Birch Green

SKELMERSDALE

Tanhouse

Digmoor

Our Lady Queen of Peace RC High School

Lathom High School

St James RC Primary School

Skelmersdale Coll

Ashurst Health Centre

Cobbs Brow CP School

HOUGHTONS ROAD A577

A577 HOUGHTONS ROAD

Birch Green CP School

Clough Fold Primary School

STANNANOUGHT ROAD

A5068 GLENBURN ROAD

Skelmersdale Crow Orchard County Primary School

West Lancs District Council

Trinity CP School

St Edmunds RC Primary School

Skelmersdale Park CP School

Primary School

Elmers Green CP School

Nye Bevan Swimming Pool

Police Station

Market Hall

Skelmersdale College

Glenburn High School

Northway

Southway

Hillside Health Centre

Tanhouse Road

West Lancashire District Council

Hillside CP School

St Mark RC Prim

Delphside Primary School

GRIMSHAW

Ormskirk ROAD

B5312

Fir Tree Close Road

Skelmersdale Sports Centre

Whiteledge Road

Junction 4

A5068 GLENBURN RD

White Moss Road South

M58

Moss Lane View

Moss Lane

White Moss Farm

Little Digmoor CP School

Infant School Sch Clinic

Childcare Practice

Birleywood Health Cen

Pimbo Road

M58

M58

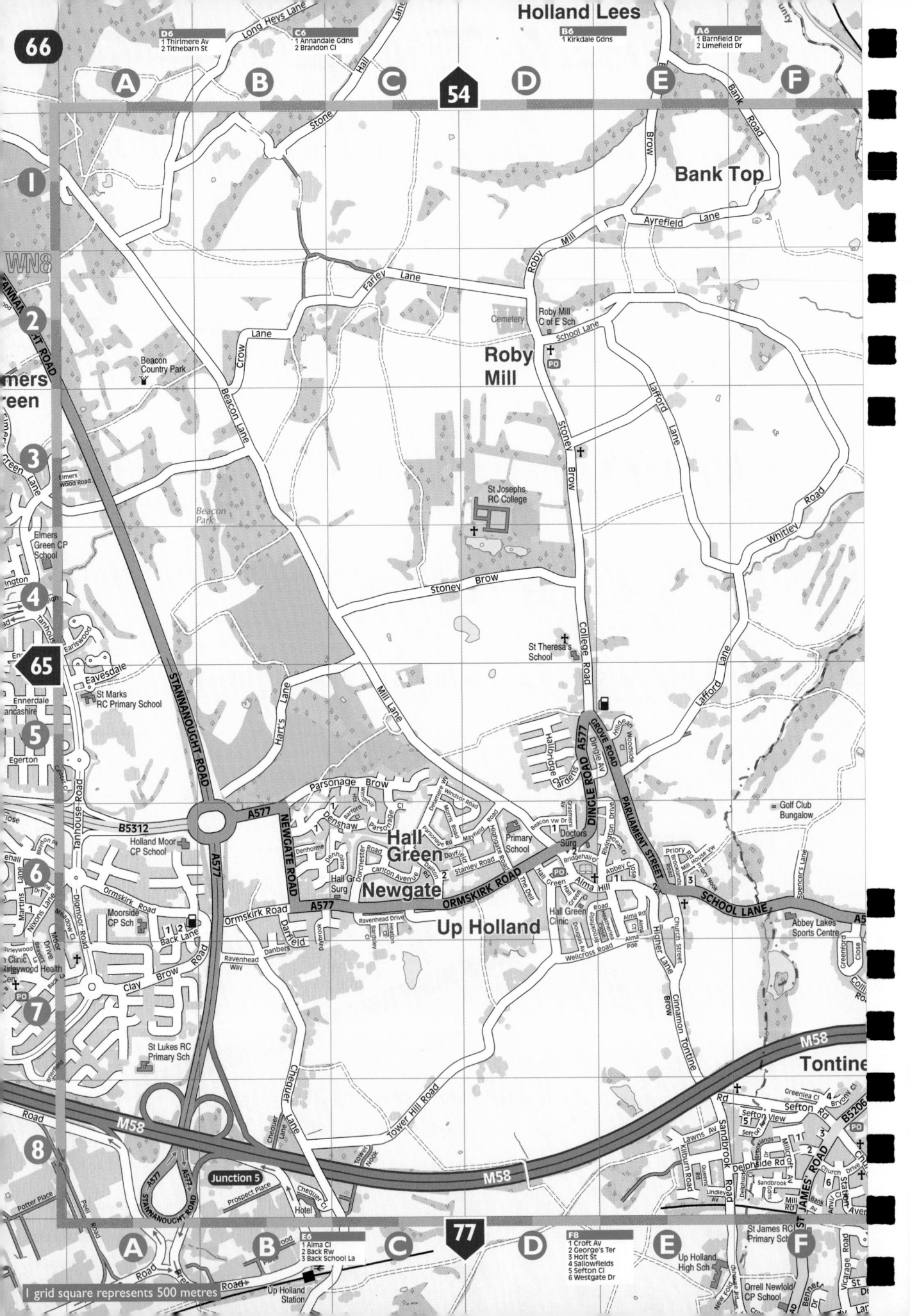

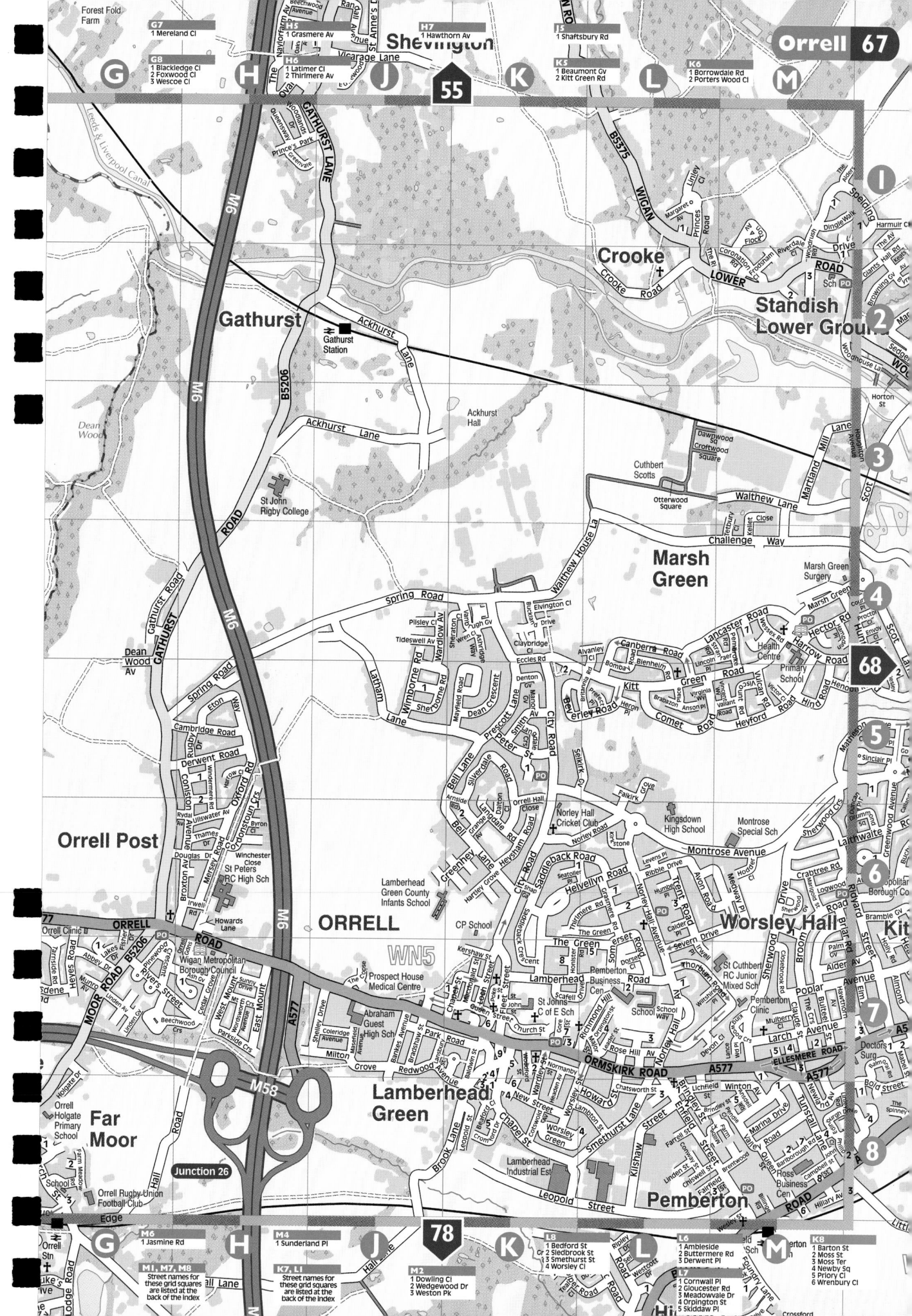

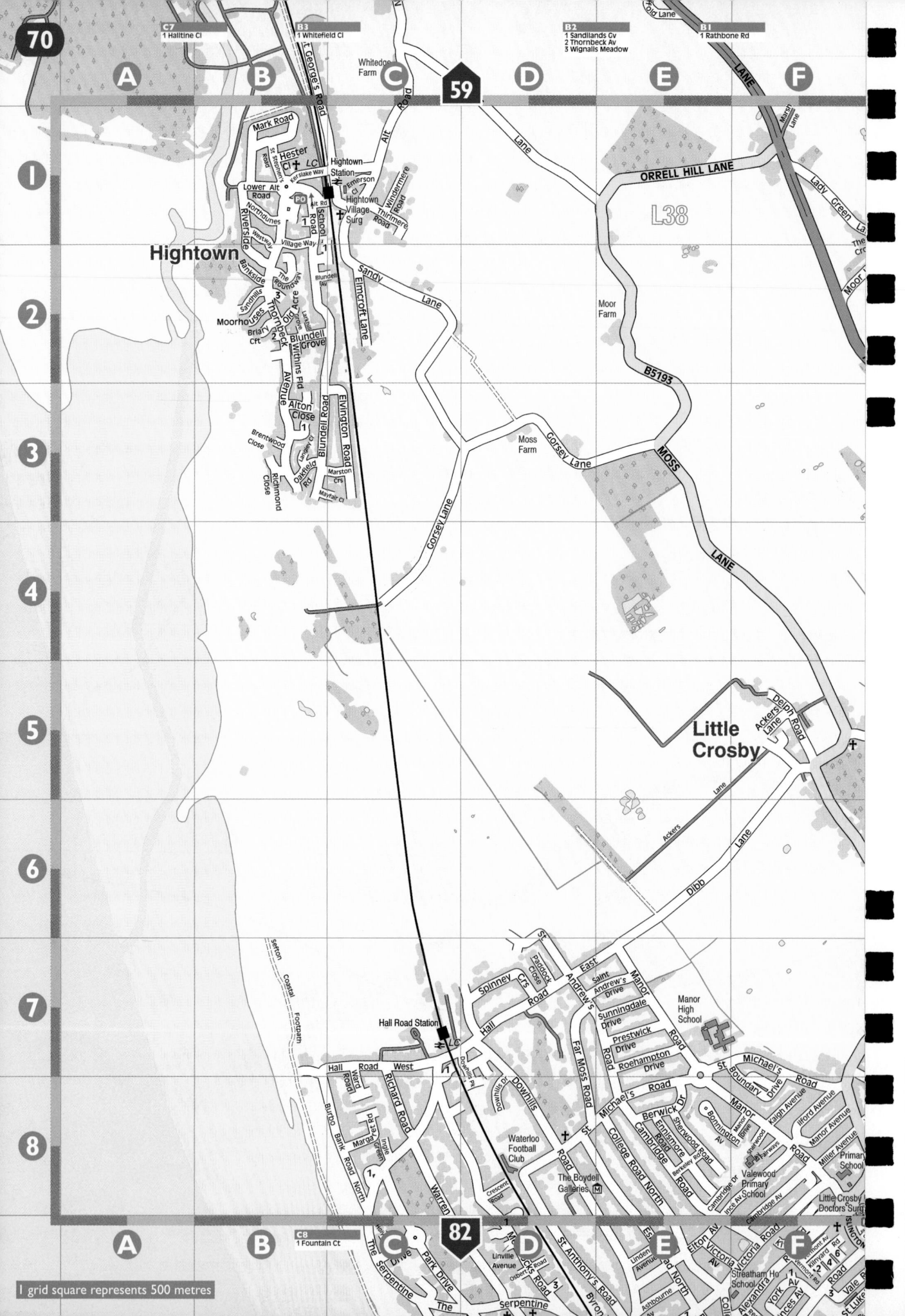

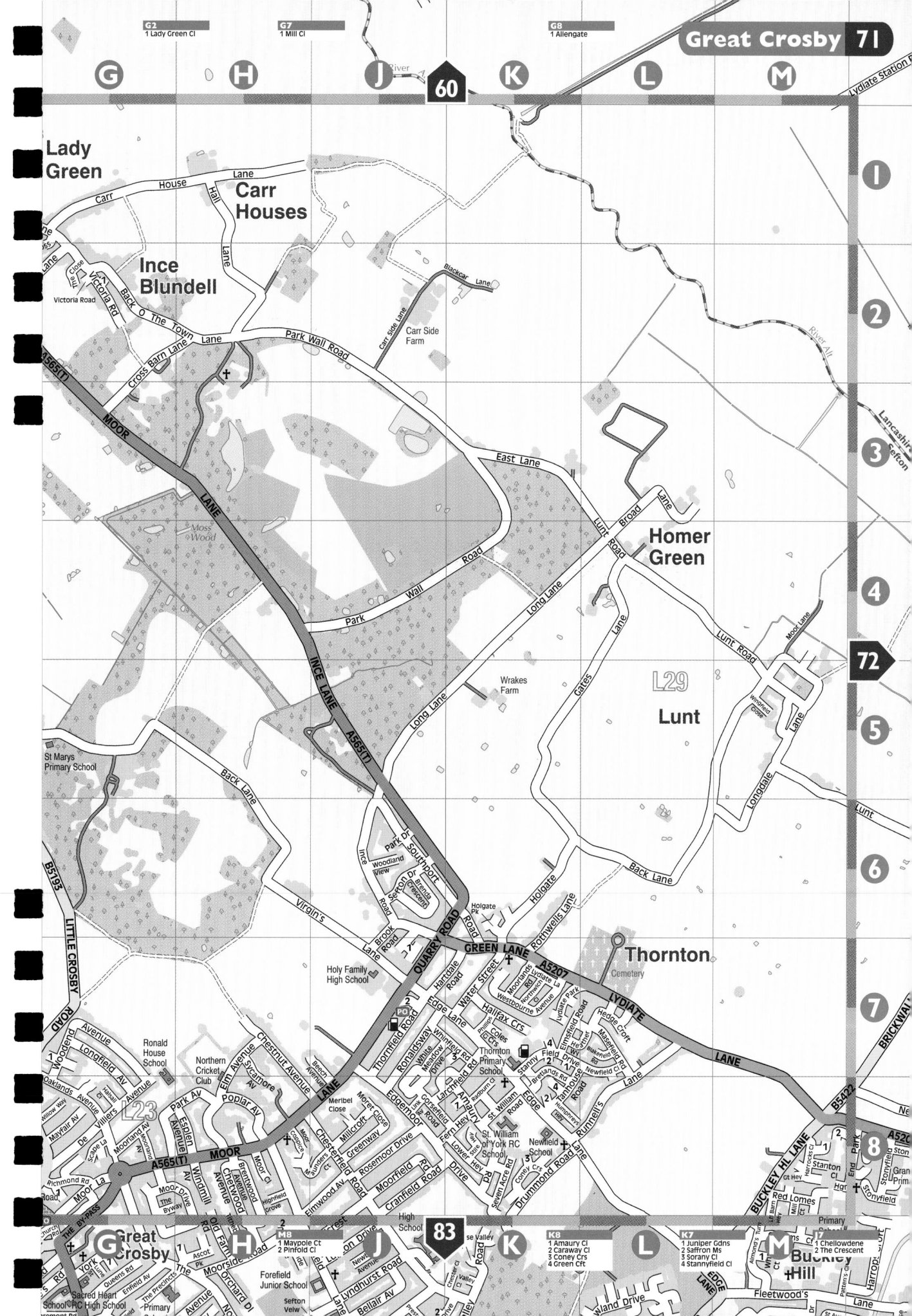

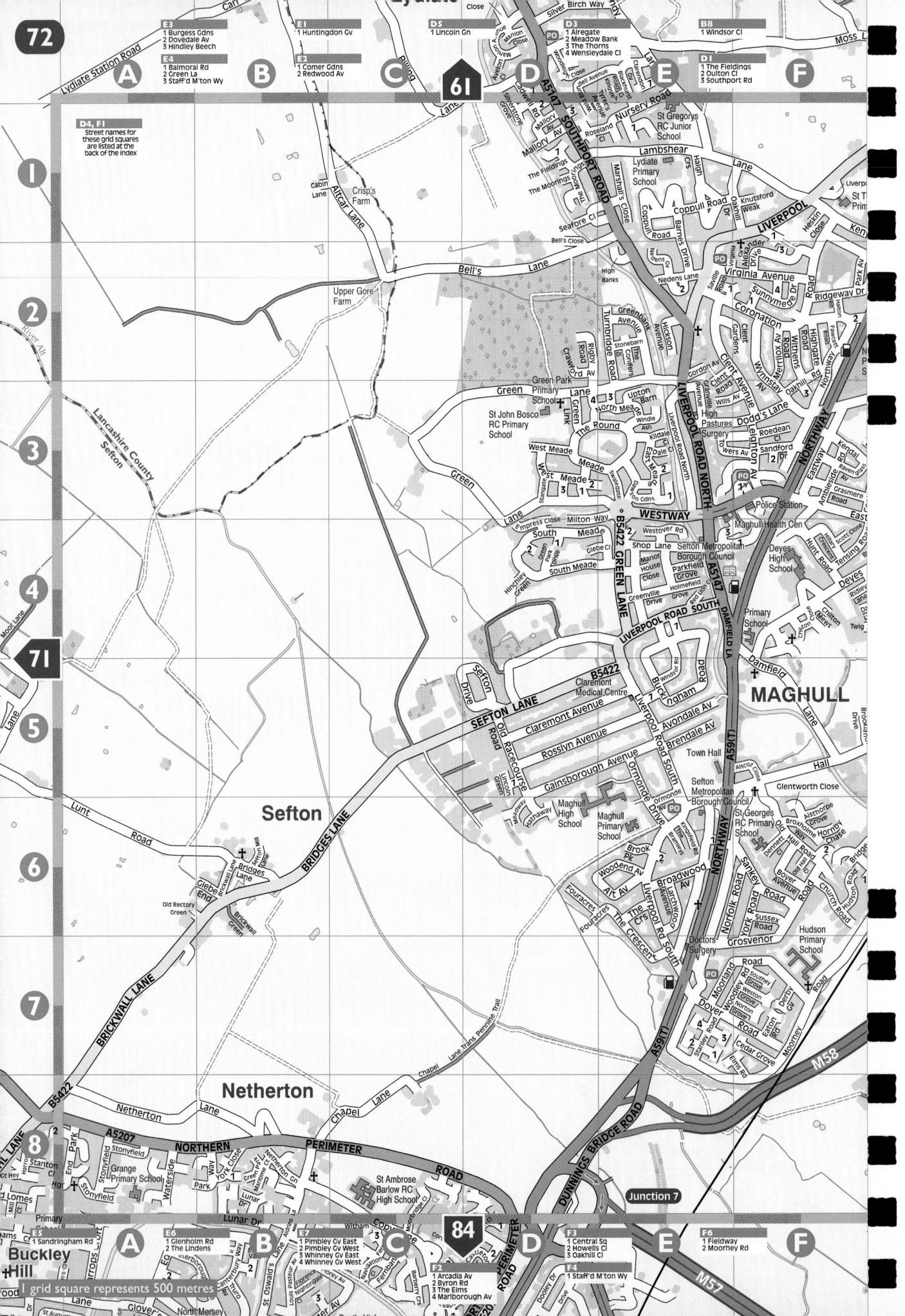

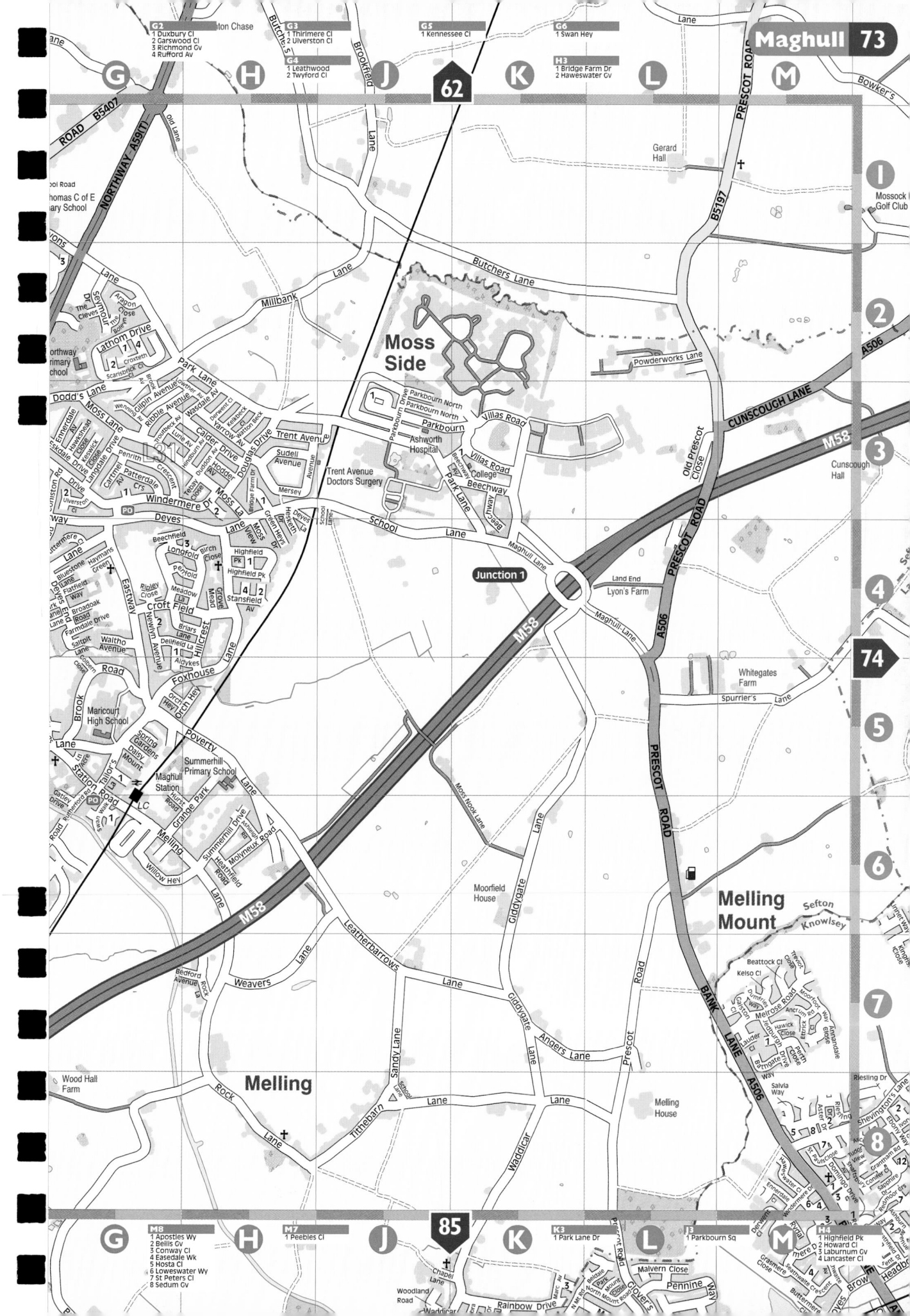

## Map labels

**G2**
1 Duxbury Cl
2 Garswood Cl
3 Richmond Gv
4 Rufford Av

**G3**
1 Thirlmere Cl
2 Ulverston Cl

**G4**
1 Leathwood
2 Twyford Cl

**G5**
1 Kennessee Cl

**G6**
1 Swan Hey

**H3**
1 Bridge Farm Dr
2 Haweswater Gv

**62**

G  H  J  K  L  M

**I**

Mossock Golf Club

Gerard Hall

**2**

A506

Butchers Lane

Powderworks Lane

CUNSCOUGH LANE

**3**

Cunscough Hall

M58

Moss Side

Parkbourn North
Parkbourn North
Parkbourn

Villas Road

Villas Road

Beechway College

Beechway

Ashworth Hospital

Trent Avenue Doctors Surgery

Park Lane

School Lane

Maghull Lane

Old Prescot Close

PRESCOT ROAD

**4**

Junction 1

M58

Land End
Lyon's Farm

Maghull Lane

A506

Whitegates Farm

**74**

Spurrier's Lane

**5**

Millbank

Lane

ROAD B5407

NORTHWAY A59(n)

Old Lane

Thomas C of E Primary School

Northway Primary School

The Cleves

Lathom Drive

Aragon Close

Croxteth

Scarisbrick Cl

Dodd's Lane

Moss Lane

Gilpin Avenue

Park Lane

Cowther Av

Wasdale Av

Calder Drive

Yarrow Av

Watton Beck

Derwent Cl

Kenwick

Wenning Av

Ribble Avenue

Lune Av

Hindburn Av

Douglas Drive

Ouseburn Av

Duddon Av

Hodder

Ribby Av

Moss La

Trent Avenue

Sudell Avenue

Mersey

Avenue

Green Heys

Hesketh

Deyes Lane

Deyes Lane View

Emmerdale

Meadhead

Hawkshead

Keswick

Eskdale Drive

Langdale Drive

Penrith Crescent

Cartmel

Patterdale Crs

Windermere Dr

Ennerdale Lane

Ulverston Cl

PO

Deyes

Beechfield

Longfold

Birch Close

Peizfold

Ripley Close

Meadow La

Grove Mead

Croft Field

Newlyn Avenue

Briars La

Delifield La

Aldykes

Highfield Pk

Highfield Pk

Stansfield Av

Bluestone Lane

Flatfield Way

Broadoak Road

Farmdale Drive

Saltpit Lane

Waltho Avenue

Foxhouse Lane

Hillcrest Road

Orchard Hey

Crown Hey

Brook Lane

Maricourt High School

Station Road

Spring Gardens

Daisy Mount

Poverty Lane

Summerhill Primary School

Maghull Station

PO

LC

Melling Lane

Willow Hey

Grange Park

Summerhill Drive

Heathfield Road

Molyneux Road

Acheson Road

M58

Bedford Avenue

Rock Lane

Weavers Lane

Leatherbarrows Lane

Melling

Rock Lane

Tithebarn Lane

School Lane

Sandy Lane

Waddicar Lane

Giddygate Lane

Angers Lane

Moss Nook Lane

Moorfield House

Prescot Road

Melling House

Melling Mount

Sefton
Knowsley

Beattock Cl
Kelso Cl

Trevor Cl

Moorfoot Way

Caiston

Dumfries Way

Galston

Lauder

Melrose Road

Ancrum Rd

Hawick Close

Penrith Drive

Reburn Dr

Kings Close

Tanracle Close

**6**

PRESCOT ROAD

BANK LANE A506

**7**

Riesling Dr

Shevington's Lane

**8**

**G**  **H**  **J**  **K**  **L**  **M**

**85**

Chapel Lane

Woodland Road

Waddicar

**M8**
1 Apostles Wy
2 Bells Gv
3 Conway Cl
4 Easedale Wk
5 Hosta Cl
6 Loweswater Wy
7 St Peters Cl
8 Sedum Gv

**M7**
1 Peebles Cl

**K3**
1 Park Lane Dr

**L**
1 Parkbourn Sq

**H4**
1 Highfield Pk
2 Howard Cl
3 Laburnum Gv
4 Lancaster Cl

Malvern Close

Pennine Way

Rainbow Drive

Grasmere Close

Buttermere

North Mount

A  B  63  C  D  E  F

I

Bowker's
Green
Lane

Mossock Hall
Golf Club

Royal Oak

Roby's
Farm

2

A506

M58

Simonswood Lane

Mercer's Lane

New Way

3  58
Cunscough
Hall

Back Lane

Bullens
Farm

New Way

Hurst's Lane

Bickerstaffe
Moss

Outlet Lane

Simonswood Lane

Back Lane

Sefton
Lancashire County

Outlet Lane

Outlet
Farm

4

73

Hall Lane

5

Grayson's
Farm

6

Sefton
Knowsley

Hall Lane

Moss Lane

Stopgate Lane

7

Weaver Avenue

Stopgate Lane

Shevington's Lane

St Peter &
St Pauls
Primary School

Greetham Avenue

Tower Hill
Health
Centre

8

Tower
Hill

Primary
School

Eastcroft Park
Primary School

Headbolt Lane

Spencer's
House

Urban
Farm

A  B  86  C  D  E  F

Overdale
Primary
School

Roughwood Drive

Tercastle Road

Perimeter Road

Depot

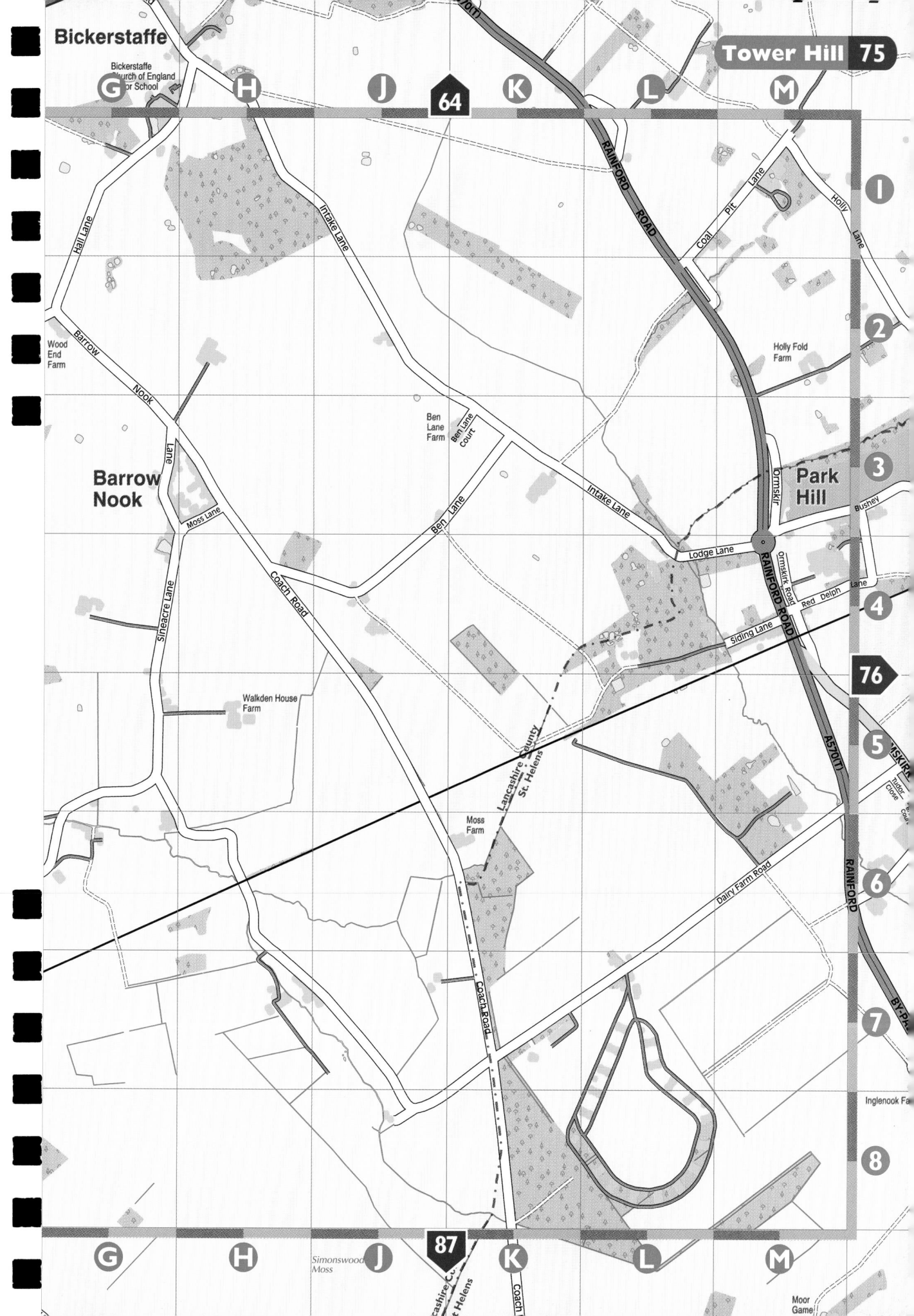

Bickerstaffe
Church of England
or School

Intake Lane

Hall Lane

Barrow Nook Lane

Wood End Farm

**Barrow Nook**

Moss Lane

Sineacre Lane

Coach Road

Walkden House Farm

Ben Lane Farm

Ben Lane Court

Ben Lane

Intake Lane

RAINFORD ROAD

Coal Pit Lane

Holly Lane

Holly Fold Farm

Ormskirk Road

**Park Hill**

Bushey

Lodge Lane

RAINFORD ROAD

Ormskirk Road

Red Delph Lane

Siding Lane

Tudor Cross Court

Lancashire County
St. Helens

Moss Farm

Dairy Farm Road

RAINFORD

Coach Road

Inglenook Fa

BY-Pa

A570(T)

**G** **H** **J** 64 **K** **L** **M**

**I**

**2**

**3**

**4**

76

**5**

**6**

**7**

**8**

**G** **H** **J** 87 **K** **L** **M**

Simonswood
Moss

Lancashire Co
St. Helens

Coach

Moor
Game

65

75

88

A B C D E F

I
2
3
4
5
6
7
8

Park
Hill
Fold

Ferny
Knoll

Holland
Moss

Lancashire County
St. Helens

Crawford

Crawford Road
Oakleigh
Holland
Court

Pit Hey Plac
Pinfold Place

Penalb
Place

LC

Duke's
Wood
Lane

Holly Fold Lane
Ferny Knoll Road
News
Lane

Rainford
Junction

News Lane
Windermere Drive
Buttermere Crs
Kendal
Close
Kendal
Spring Field
PO
Rail close
Rainford
Station
Busney
Lane
Lane

Maggots

Henderson
Drive

Brow
Reeds
Langwood
Lane

Holiday
Moss

ORMSKIRK
Knowsley
view
Junction Road
Randle
Avenue
Harrison
Drive
Eden Avenue
Tudor
Close
Randle
Court

Graysons
Road
Helen Bank Dr
Brook Lodge
Primary School
Rainford
High
School

Hyde's Brow
Rainford

Stanley Avenue
Old
Parklands
Lathom
Drive
Rainford
Road
Witton
Way
2
Scamprick
Duxbury
Close
Standish Drive
Carswood
Higher
Lane

RAINFORD

ROAD
Beech
Gardens
Pine Dale
Fern
Bank
Moss Brow
Victoria St
Central Drive
B5203
Corpus Christi
RC Primary
School
Arman Rd
Arman Wy
Corteth
Drive
Muncaster
Drive
Heyes Avenue
Heyes
Grove
Sinton
Kenway

RAINFORD
BY-PASS
Parson's
Brow
Moss Nook Lane
Inglenook Farm
Beech
Gardens
Ash Grove
The Avenue
Lime Av
CROSS PIT LANE
Leyland
Road
Pilkington Street
Southern's
Lane
Rainford
C of E
Primary
School
Lakeside
Gardens
Rainford
Health
Centre
B5205
Lakeside
Court
Eagle Crescent
Rookery Drive
Finch
Av
Heron
Gv
HIGHER
Fire Clay
Farm

CHURCH ROAD
Council Offices
The Kenneth Macrae
Medical Centre
PO
Holly Crs
MOSSBOROUGH ROAD B5203
Church
Road
Thickwood Moss
Lane
Derby
Festival Road
Walmesley
Drive
Carter
Avenue
Green
Lane
LANE
Diamond
Business Park
Hazel
Business
Park
HIGHER
LANE B5205

Rose
Drive
Rose Rookery
Hopwood
Crescent
Wellfield
Mill Lane
Sandwash

C7
1 Norwood Gv

B7
1 Elm Gdns
2 Whalley Av

B6
1 Alfred St
2 Astley Cl

B3
1 Coniston Wy
2 Keswick Wy

C8
1 Queensway

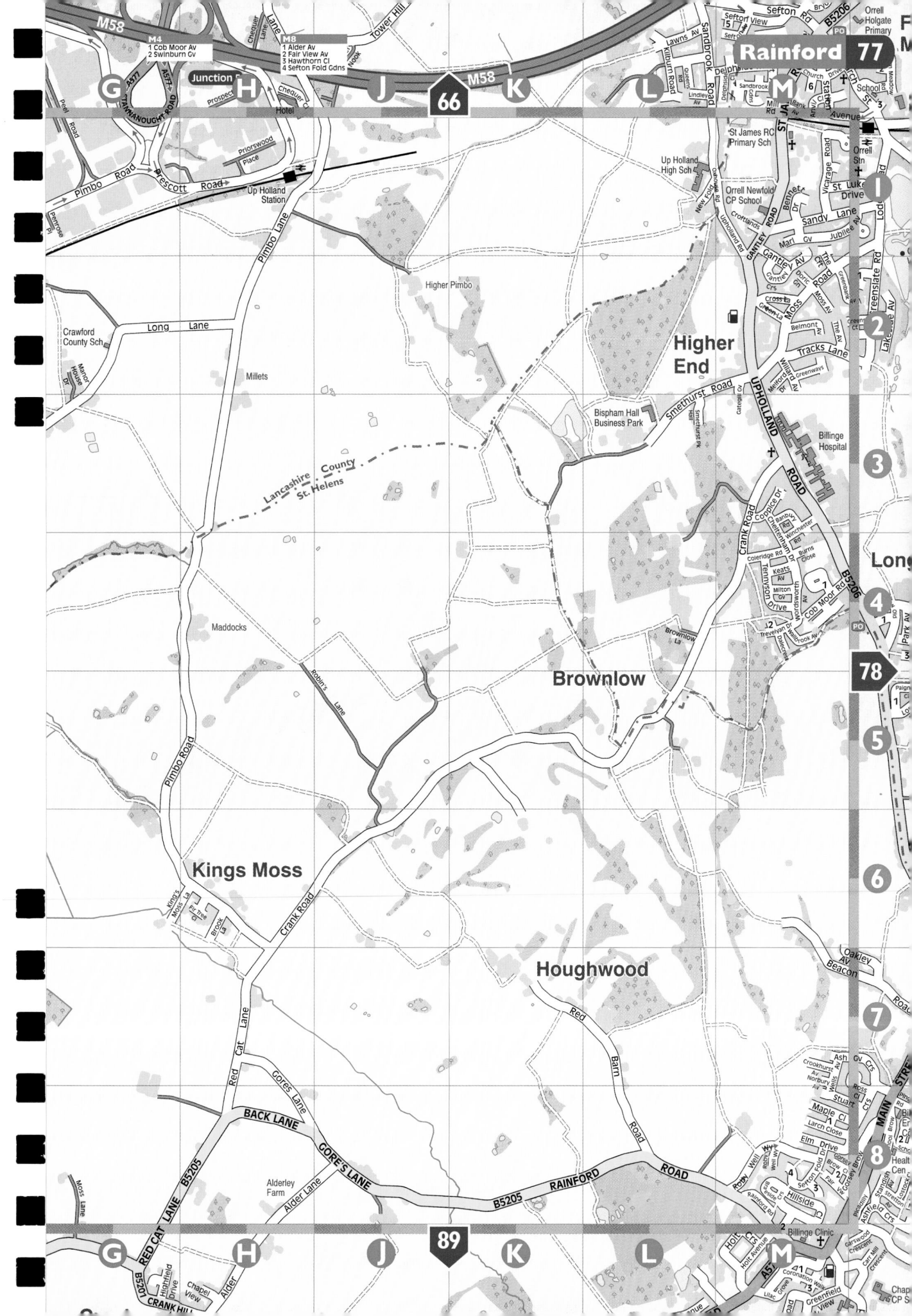

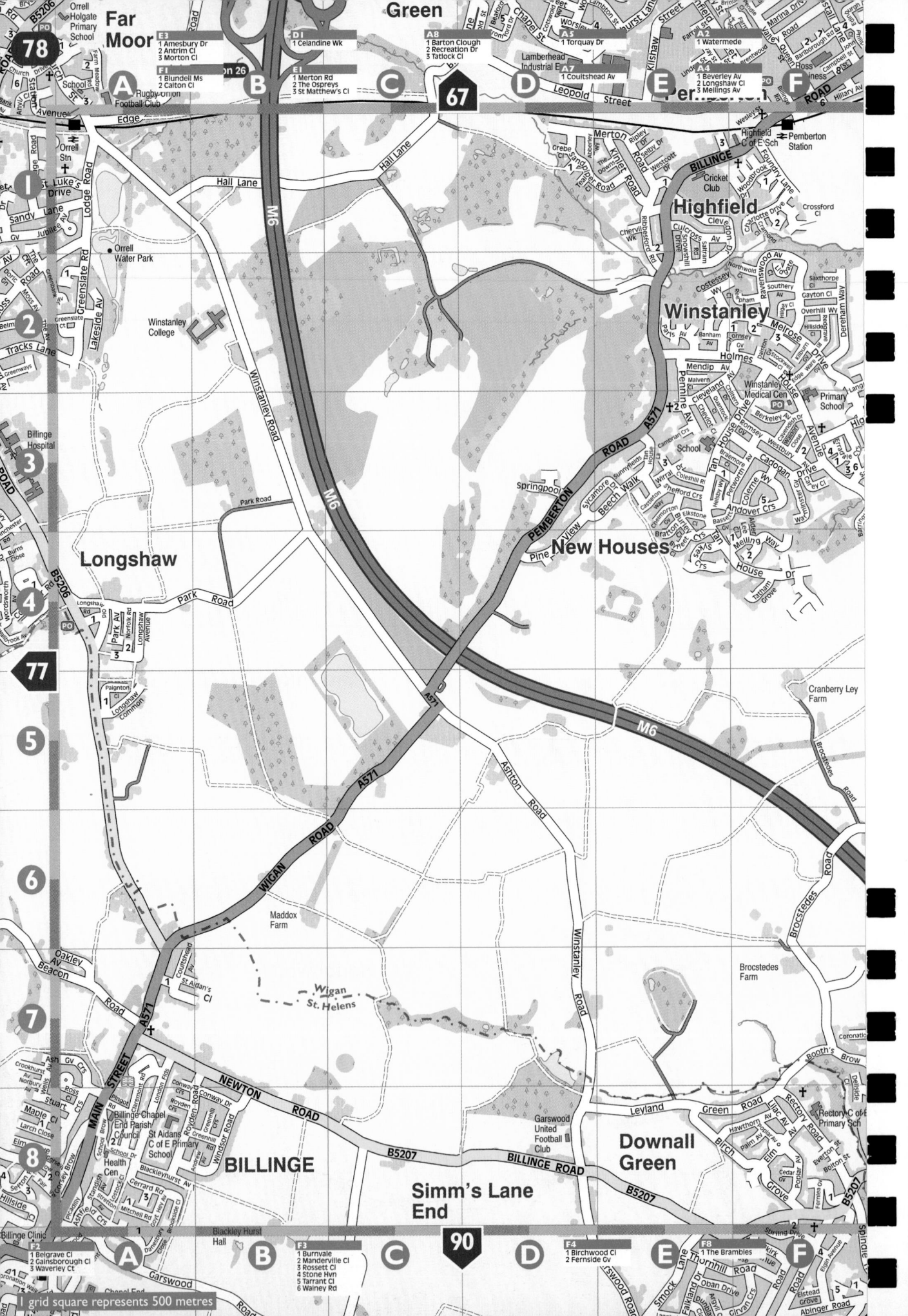

G1
1 Newburn Cl

G2
1 Kellbank Rd
2 Lea Gate Cl
3 Madeley Cl

G3
1 Clanwood Cl
2 Falstone Cl
3 Wallgarth St

H2
1 Crummock Dr
2 Ulverston Rd

H7
1 Haseldine St
2 Medway Cl
3 Myrtle Av
4 Norwood Av
5 Wilton St

H8
1 Cornelian Gv

G H J K L M

WN3
Goose
Green

Worsley
Mesnes

A571
Little Lane

WARRINGTON ROAD
A49

Snowden Avenue
Paul's
St Pauls C of E
Junior & Infant School
Ruskin Av
Kingsley Avenue
Walpole Avenue
Cranfell
Hawkley Brook
Surgery
Marus Avenue
Marus Bridge
Health Centre
Coppice Dr
Grange
Special
Sch
Forton
Caxton Cl
Wheatlea
Industrial Est
Hawkley Brook
Trading Estate
Bembridge
Court

Hawkley
Fulbeck Avenue
Navenby Road
Whitecroft
Road
Edgeway Rd
Birkside Cl
Havkrell Rd

Rosley
Road
Firbank
Ashby Rd
Colby Close
Loxton Crs
Darley Av
Thurston Av
Hawkley Hall
High School

Pearson's Flash

Scotman's Flash

Cemetery

M6

Junction 25

Haslemere
Industrial Est
Landgate
Industrial Est
Bankside
Av
Patterdale Road
Yewdale Road
Land Gate Lane
Perry Brook
Community
Primary Sch

Land Gate

Park House
Farm

Bryn Gates Lane

Three
Sisters

Downall Green
RC Primary School
DOWNALL
ROAD
Bryn
GREEN
ROAD
WIGAN ROAD
Sougher's Lane
Drummer's Lane
Dryden Avenue
Chimes Rd
Meadowcroft
Leacroft
Clough Grove
Bryn Stn
Richmond Road
Priory Road
Wentworth Road

Bryn-Cross
Surgery
Nicol Mere
Primary Sch
Doctors
Surg
Ashton
Medical
Cen

BRYN ROAD
B5207
Kingsher
Lockett Rd
Antler
Ct
Redgate Rd
Lockett Road
Beaver Ct
Kestrel Dr
Three sisters Rd

Ashton Grange
Industrial Estate

Stubshaw
Cross

BOLTON ROAD
Bolton Rd
Severn Rd

91

K8
1 Greenall St
2 Nicol Mere Dr

K2
1 Penshaw Av
2 Stanton Cl

K3
1 Woodhead Gv

L8
1 Troutbeck Rd

J4
1 Lingmoor Cl

M
1 Daleside Av
2 Dovedale Crs
3 Meadowside Av
4 Woodside Av

street names for
these grid squares
are listed at the
back of the index

Wigan Metropolitan
Borough Council

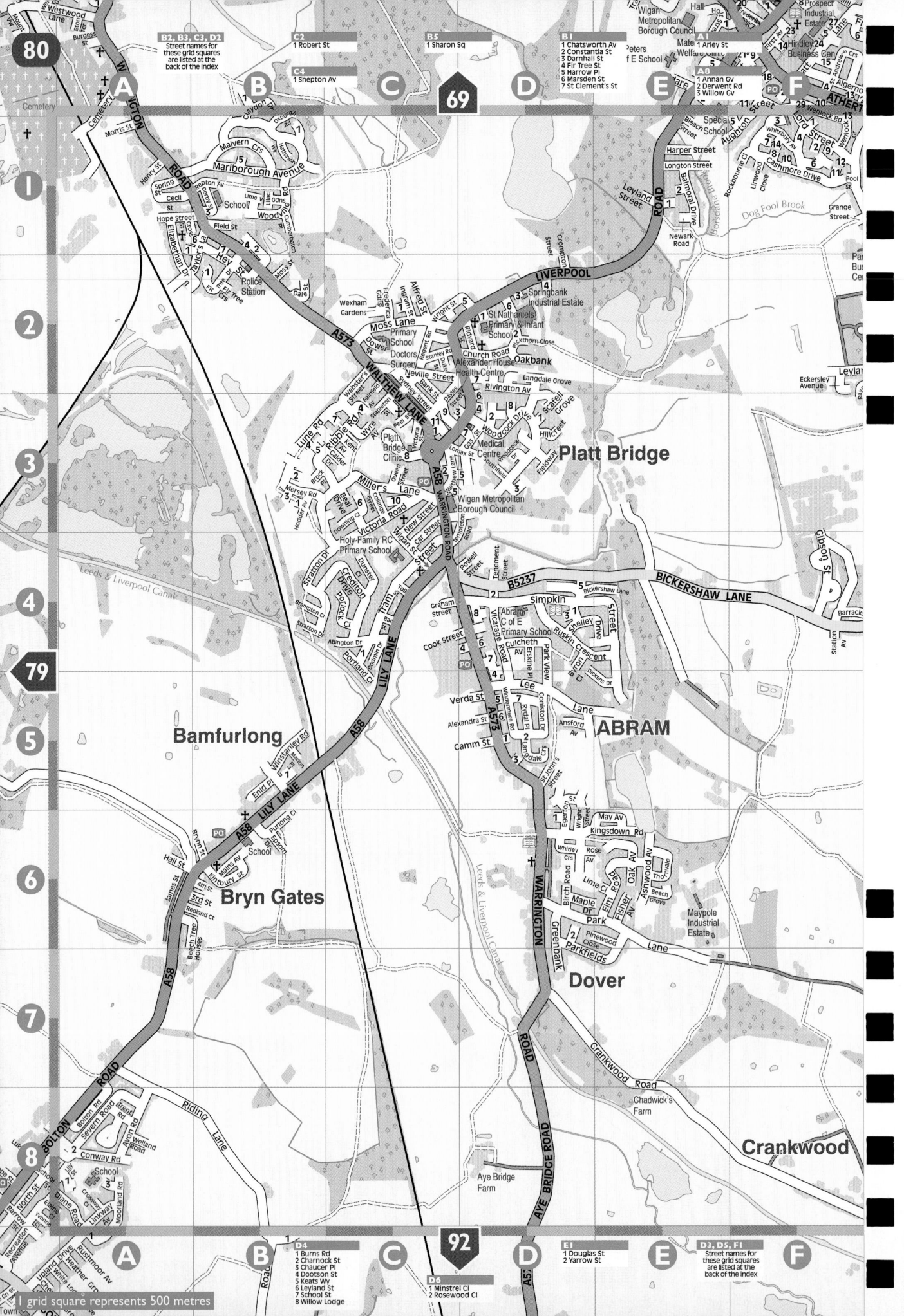

69

79

Cemetery

Marlborough Avenue

Police Station

WALTHEW LANE

Wexham Gardens

Moss Lane

LIVERPOOL ROAD

Springbank Industrial Estate

St Nathaniels) Primary & Infant School

Church Road

Alexander House Health Centre

Oakbank

Langdale Grove

Rivington Av

Scafell Grove

HillCrest

**Platt Bridge**

Lune Rd

Ribble Rd

Miller's Lane

Platt Bridge Clinic

Medical Centre

Southfield

Victoria Road

Holy Family RC Primary School

Tram Lane

LILY LANE

WARRINGTON ROAD

Wigan Metropolitan Borough Council

Bickershaw Lane

**BICKERSHAW LANE**

B5237

Simpkin Street

Graham Street

Cook Street

Abram C of E Primary School

Ruskin Crescent

Culcheth Av

Park View

**ABRAM**

Verda St

Alexandra Av

Camm St

**Bamfurlong**

A58

Leeds & Liverpool Canal

Winstanley Rd

Enid Pl

LILY LANE

A58

School

PO

**Bryn Gates**

Hall St

James St

3rd St

Beech Tree Houses

WARRINGTON ROAD

Greenbank

Kingsdown Rd

Maple Dr

Park

Pinewood Close

Parkfields

Maypole Industrial Estate

**Dover**

BOLTON ROAD

A58

Riding Lane

Conway Rd

Welland Road

School

AYE BRIDGE ROAD

Crankwood Road

Aye Bridge Farm

Chadwick's Farm

**Crankwood**

92

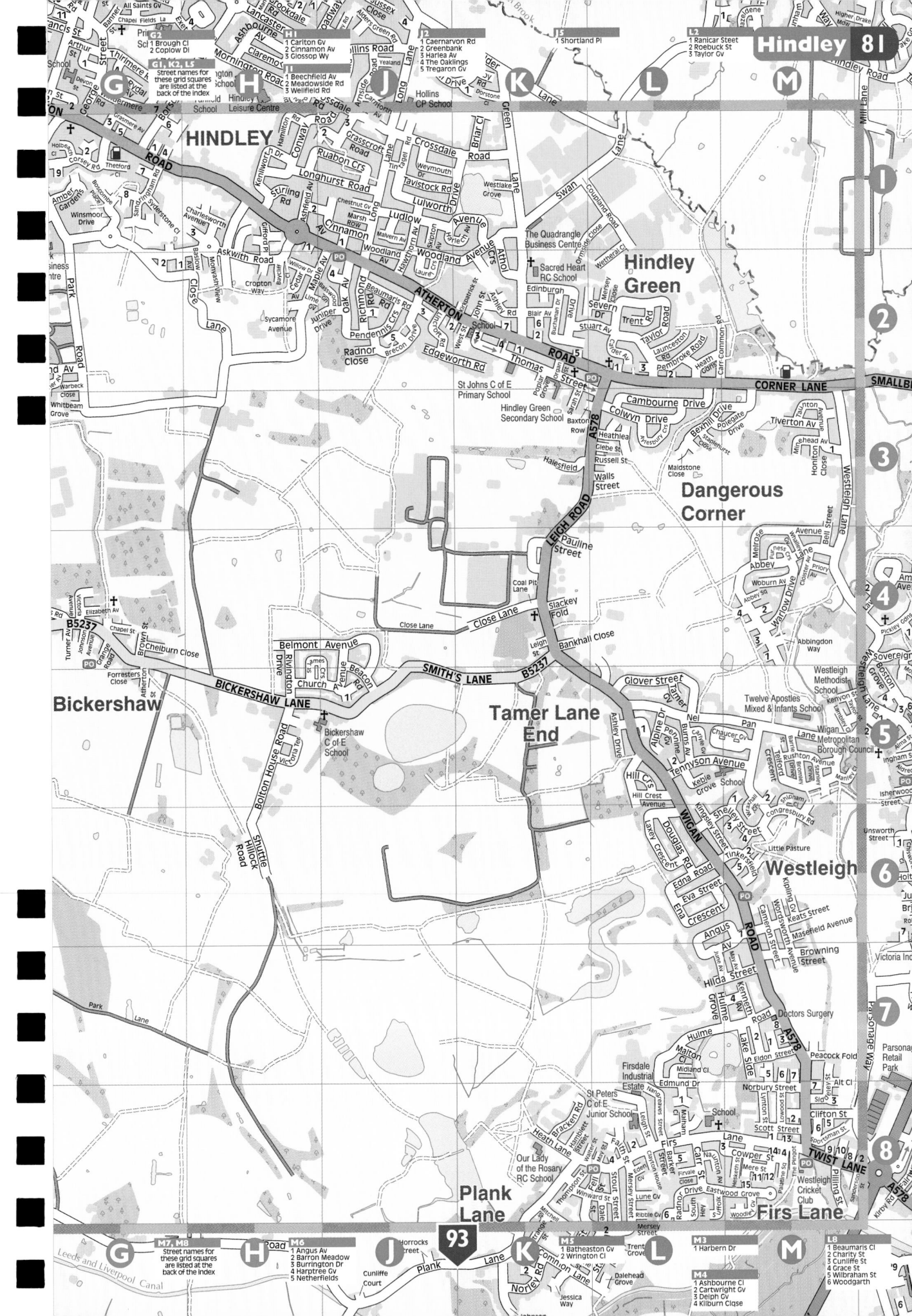

HINDLEY

Hindley Green

Dangerous Corner

Bickershaw

Tamer Lane End

Westleigh

Plank Lane

Firs Lane

G1, K2, L5
Street names for these grid squares are listed at the back of the index

G2
1 Brough Cl
2 Coplow Dl

H1
1 Carlton Gv
2 Cinnamon Av
3 Glossop Wy

J2
1 Caernarvon Rd
2 Greenbank
3 Harlea Av
4 The Oaklings
5 Tregaron Gv

L3
1 Ranicar Steet
2 Roebuck St
3 Taylor Gv

J5
1 Shortland Pl

I1
1 Beechfield Gv
2 Meadowside Rd
3 Wellfield Rd

Street names for these grid squares are listed at the back of the index

M6
1 Angus Av
2 Barron Meadow
3 Burrington Dr
4 Harptree Gv
5 Netherfields

M3
1 Batheaston Gv
2 Wrington Cl

M3
1 Harbern Dr

L8
1 Beaumaris Cl
2 Charity St
3 Cunliffe St
4 Grace St
5 Wilbraham St
6 Woodgarth

M4
1 Ashbourne Cl
2 Cartwright Gv
3 Delph Gv
4 Kilburn Clqse

**D3, F1** Street names for these grid squares are listed at the back of the index

**E2**
1 Crossdale Rd
2 Midlothian Dr

**E4**
1 Lulworth Av
2 Sandheys Ter

**E1** Blundellsands Rd East

**D2**
1 Burbo Bank Rd S
2 Burbo Crs
3 Channel Reach
4 Seathwaite Cl

**D1**
1 Birkenshaw Av
2 Clementina Rd
3 Partridge Rd

**F2**
1 The Cloisters
2 Kimberley Av
3 The Spur

**F3**
1 Browning Rd

**F4**
1 Argo Rd
2 Back Mount St
3 Canning St
4 Corona Rd
5 Denmark St
6 Midland Ter
7 Sweden Gv

**F5**
1 Deacon Cl
2 Duke St

70

95

Blundellsands

Brighton le Sands

CROSBY

Waterloo

L22

Marine Lake

BELFAST

DOUGLAS

DUBLIN

Waterloo Football Club

The Boydell Galleries

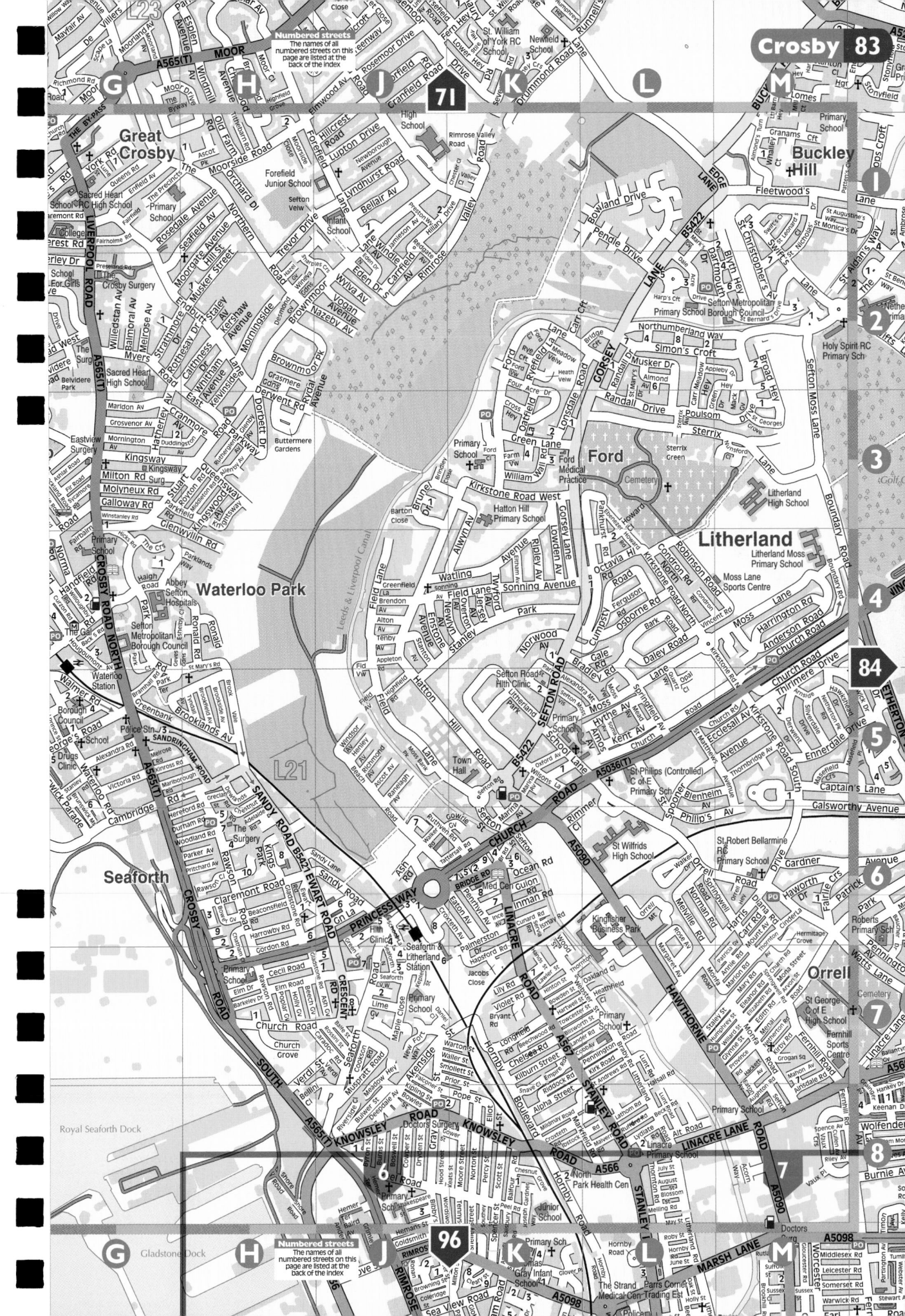

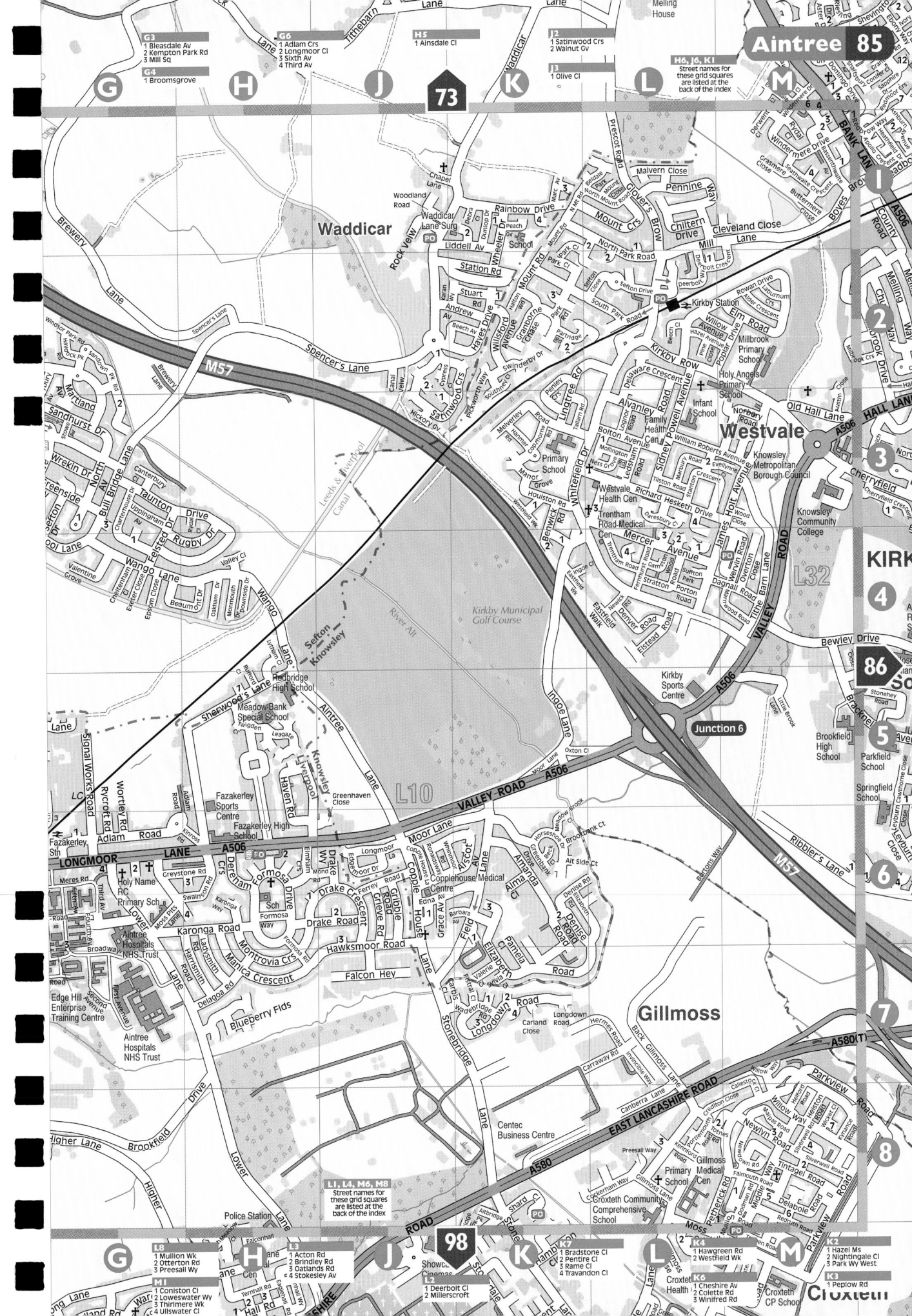

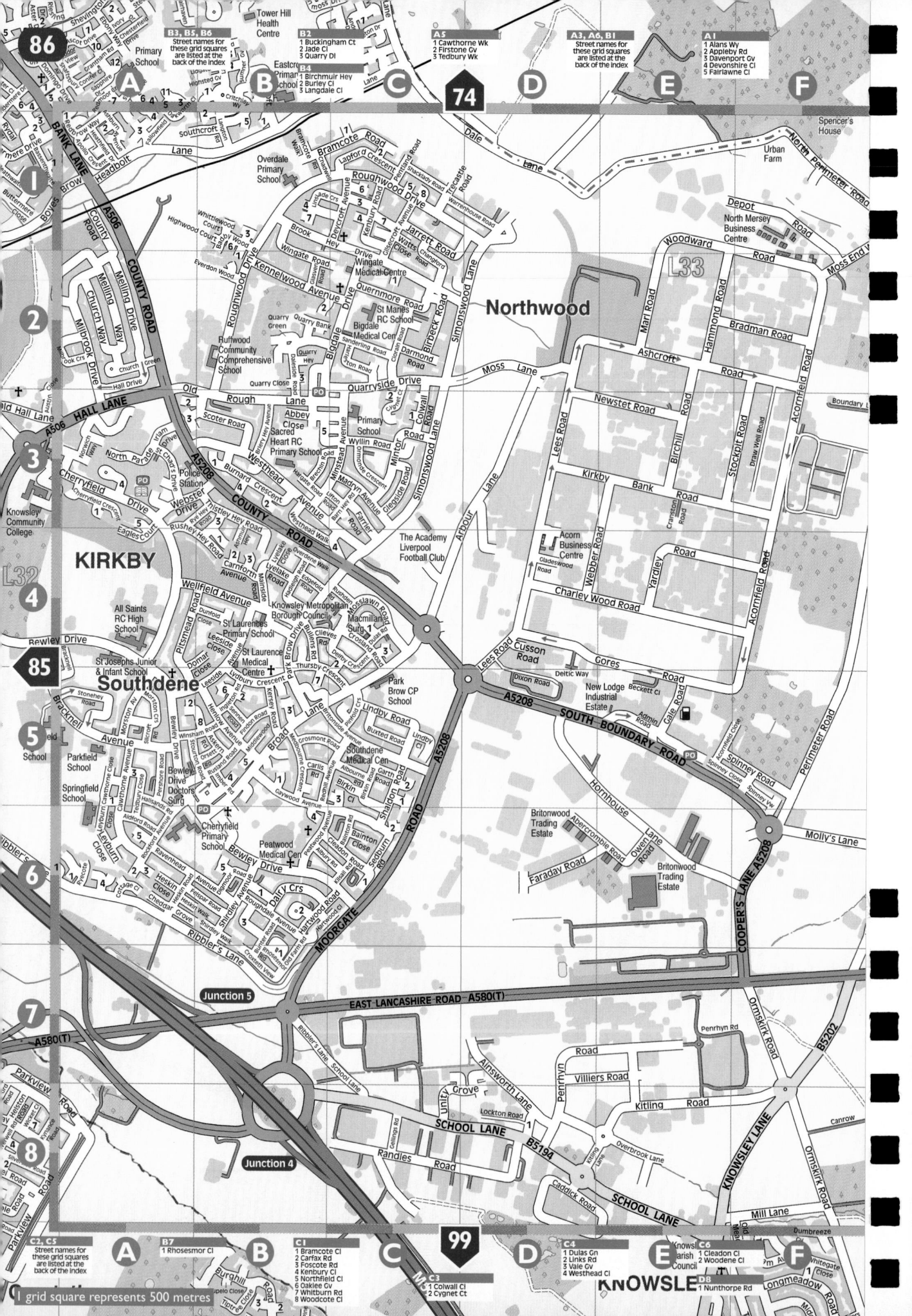

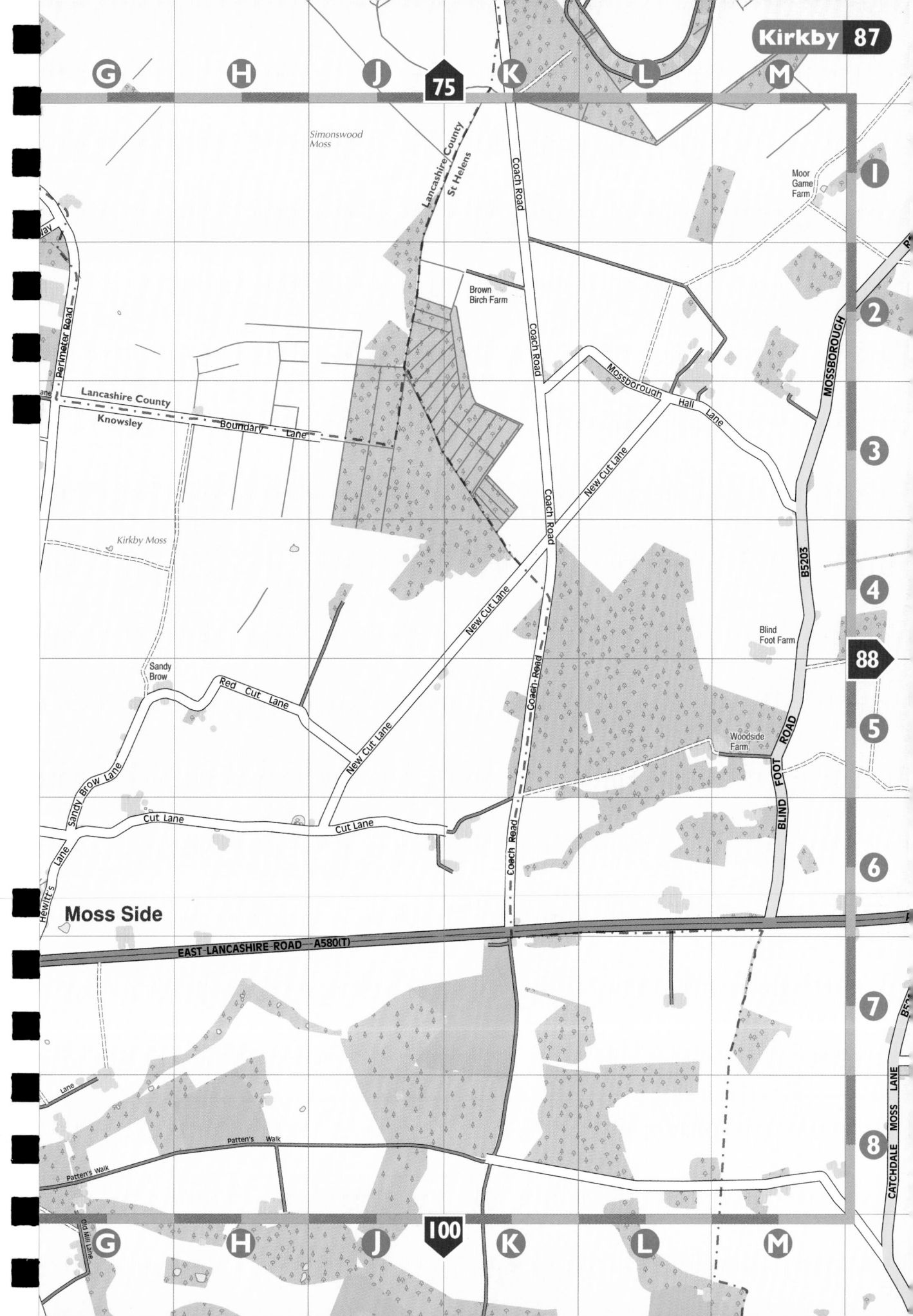

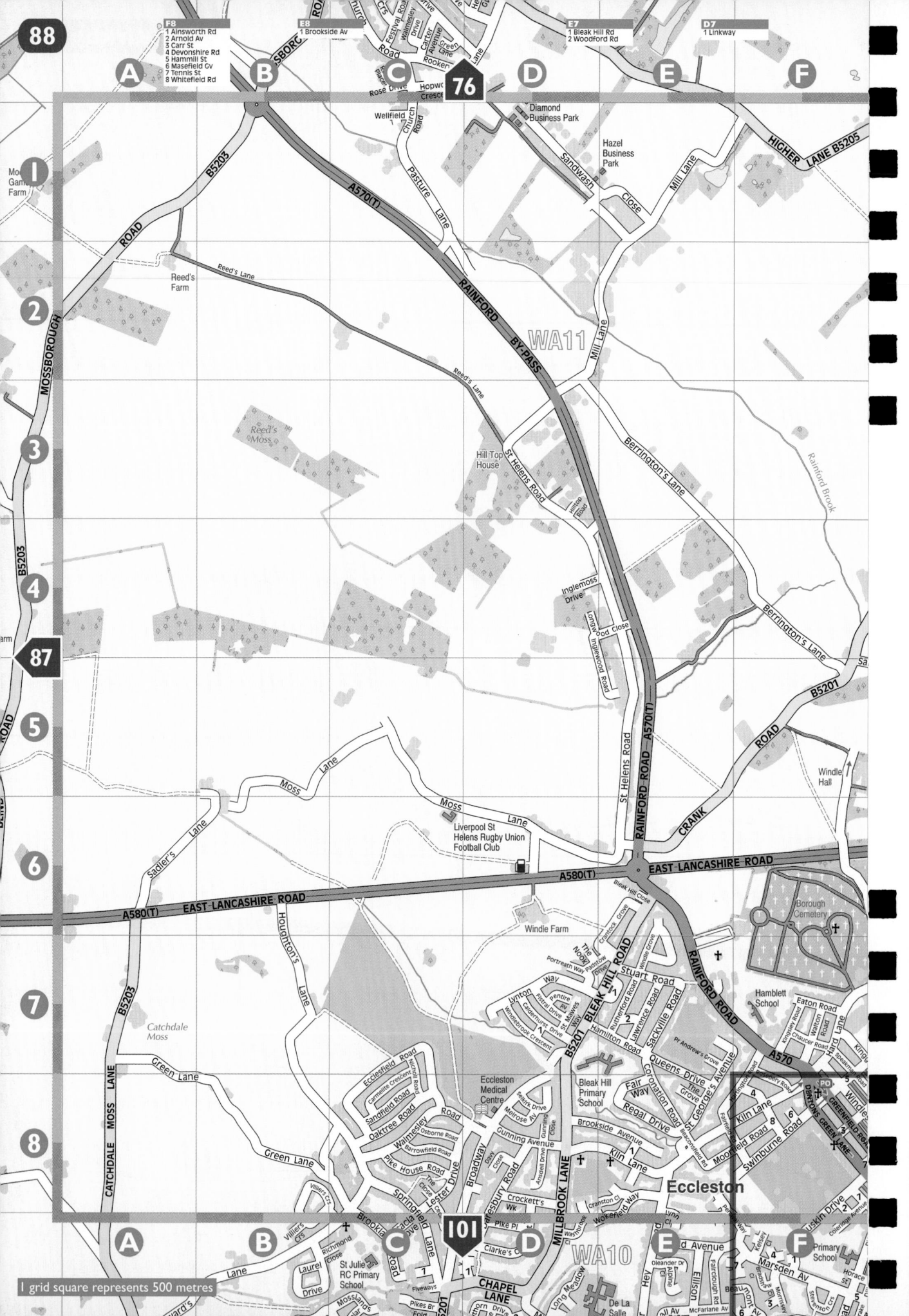

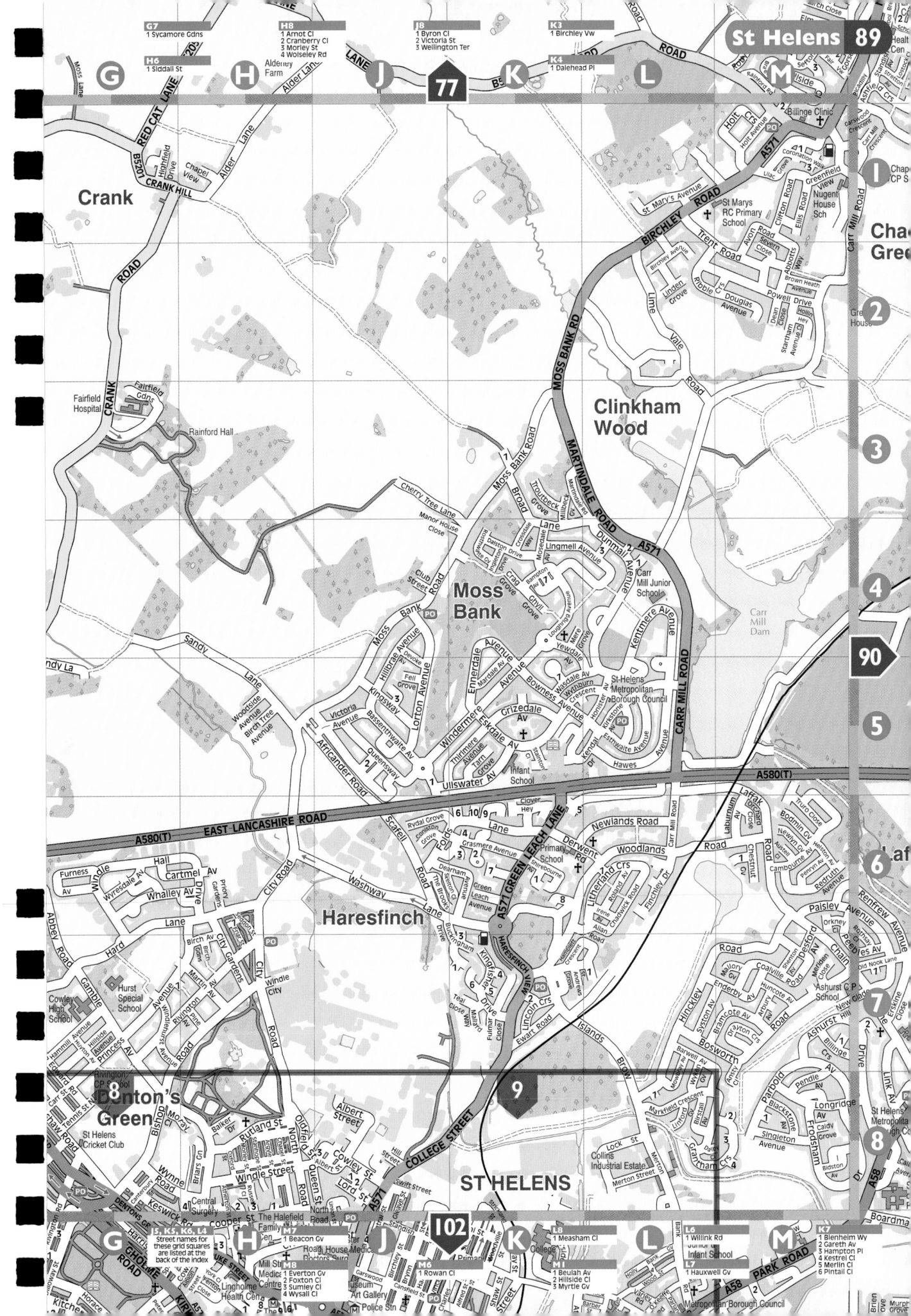

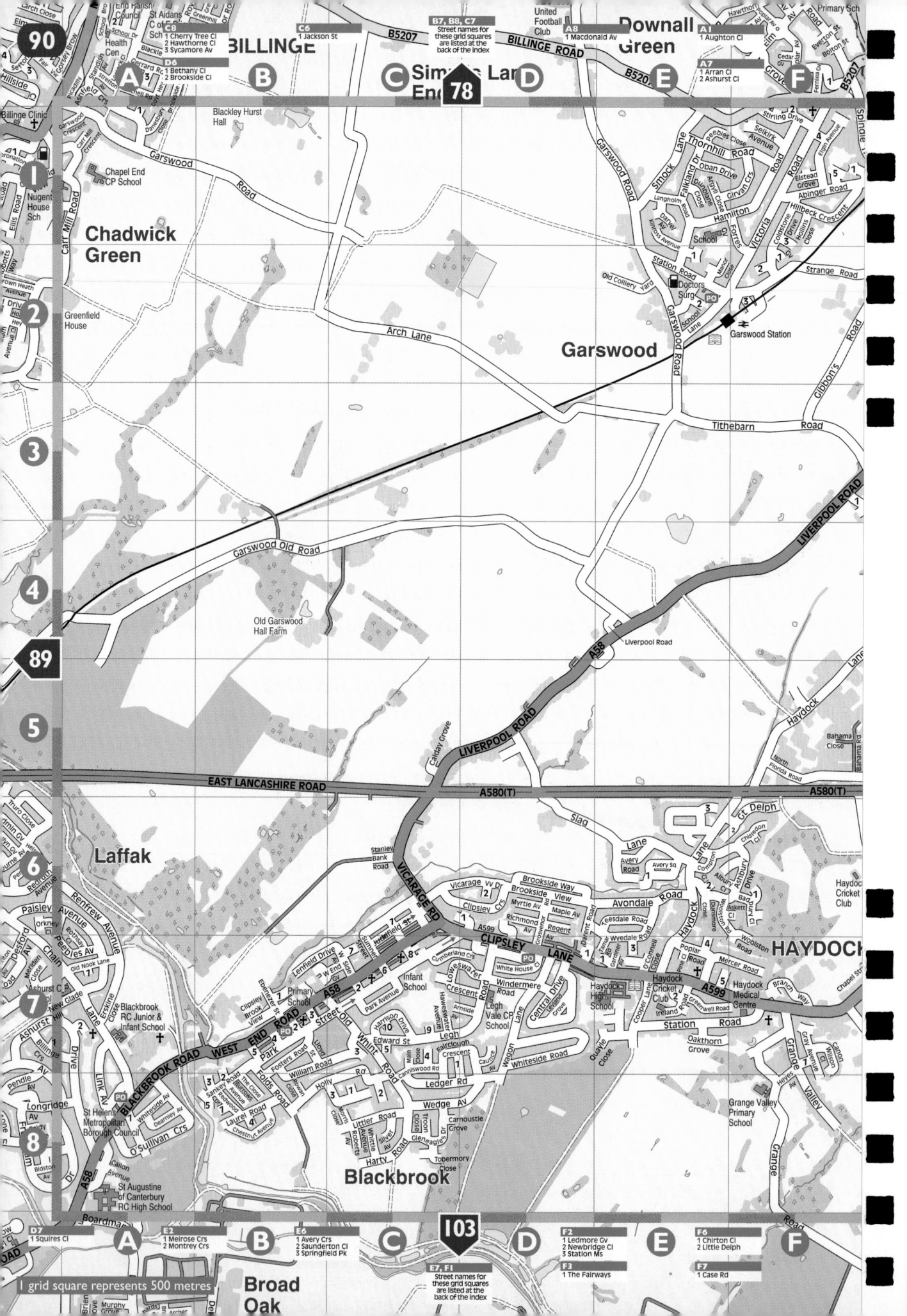

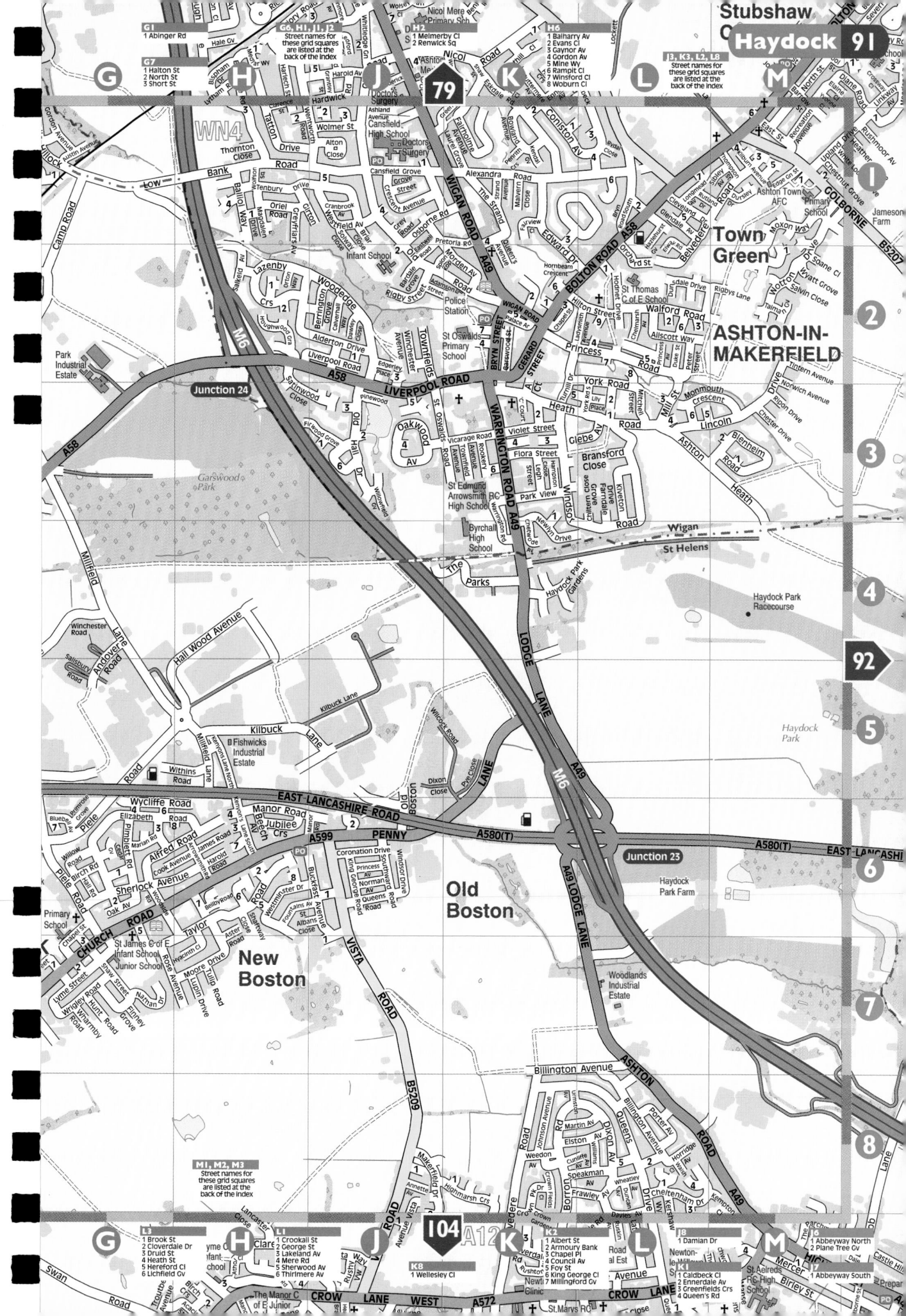

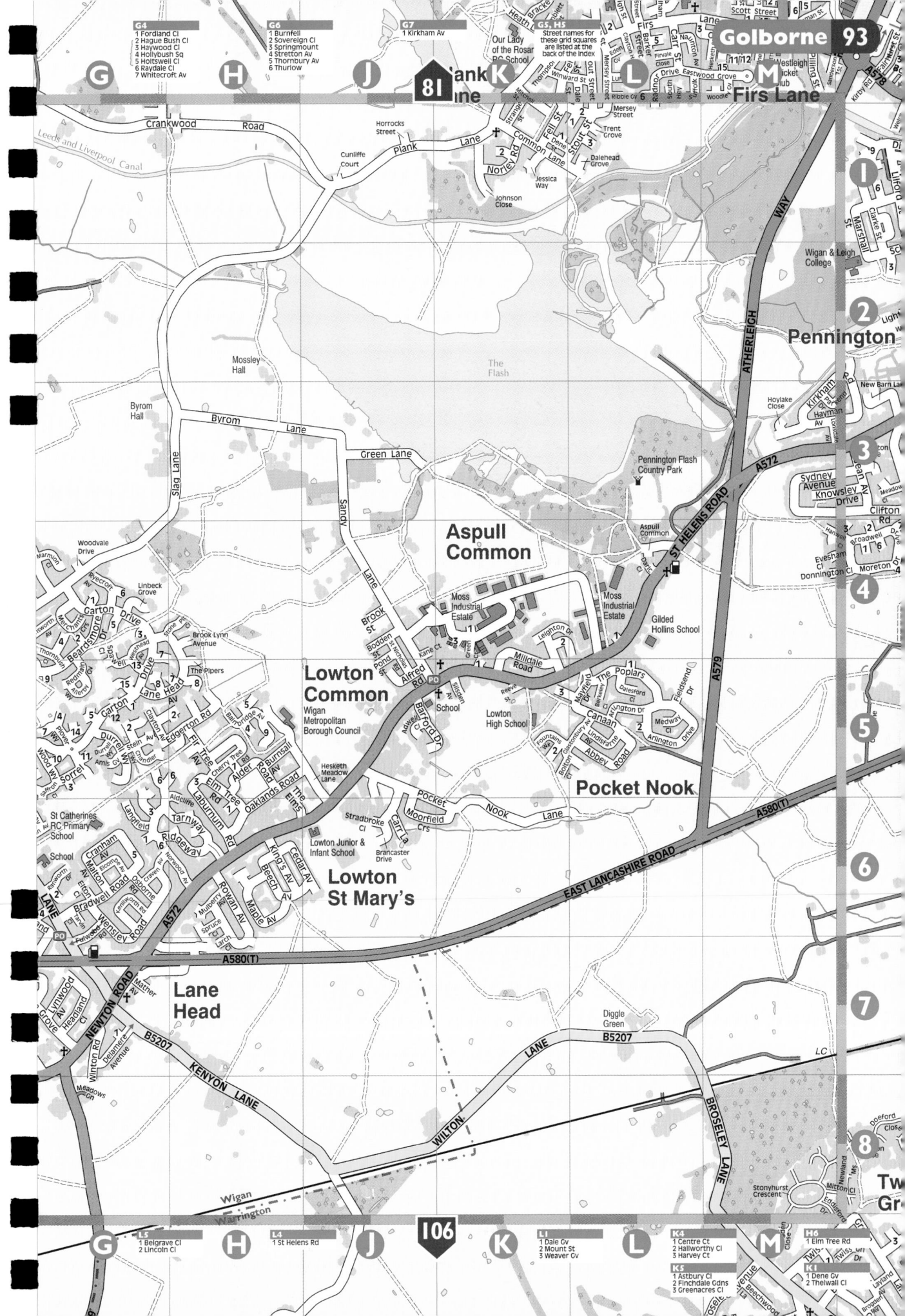

G4
1 Fordland Cl
2 Hague Bush Cl
3 Haywood Cl
4 Hollybush Sq
5 Holtswell Cl
6 Raydale Cl
7 Whitecroft Av

G6
1 Burnfell
2 Sovereign Cl
3 Springmount
4 Stretton Av
5 Thornbury Av
6 Thurlow

G7
1 Kirkham Av

Our Lady
of the Rosar
RC School

G5, H5
Street names for
these grid squares
are listed at the
back of the index

G H J K L M

Firs Lane

Wigan & Leigh
College

Pennington

New Barn Lane
Hoylake
Close

Sydney
Avenue
Knowsley
Drive

Clifton
Rd

Pennington Flash
Country Park

Leeds and Liverpool Canal

Crankwood Road

Horrocks
Street

Cunliffe
Court

Plank
Lane

Johnson
Close

Jessica
Way

The
Flash

Mossley
Hall

Byrom
Hall

Byrom Lane

Green Lane

Aspull
Common

Aspull
Common

Woodvale
Drive

Linbeck
Grove

Slag Lane

Sandy Lane

Brook St

Bodden St

Moss Industrial
Estate

Moss
Industrial
Estate

Gilded
Hollins School

Leighton Dr

Lowton
Common

Wigan
Metropolitan
Borough Council

Alfred Rd

Barford Dr

School

Lowton
High School

Milldale
Road

The
Poplars

Canaan

Abbey Road

Medway
Cl

Arlington
Drive

Fieldsend
Dr

Pocket Nook

Hesketh
Meadow
Lane

Stradbroke
Cl

Carr La

Moorfield
Crs

Brancaster
Drive

Pocket
Nook
Lane

Lowton Junior &
Infant School

St Catherines
RC Primary
School

Tarnway

Ridgeway

Cranham
Av

Malton
Cl

Osborne

Oaklands Road

Labarnum Rd

Kings Av

Cedar Av

Rowan Av

Beech Av

Maple Av

Mulberry Av

Spruce Av

Larch

Lowton
St Mary's

East Lancashire Road

A580(T)

Bradwell Road

Wensley
Road

A572

Lane
Head

Lynwood
Av

Grove

Headland

Newton Road

Wilton Rd

Delamere
Avenue

B5207 Kenyon Lane

Mather

Meadows
Gn

Wigan
Warrington

Wilton Lane

Diggle
Green

B5207

Broseley Lane

LC

Stonyhurst
Crescent

L5
1 Belgrave Cl
2 Lincoln Cl

L4
1 St Helens Rd

K4
1 Dale Gv
2 Mount St
3 Weaver Gv

K4
1 Centre Ct
2 Hallworthy Cl
3 Harvey Ct

K5
1 Astbury Cl
2 Finchdale Gdns
3 Greenacres Cl

H6
1 Elm Tree Rd

K1
1 Dene Gv
2 Thelwall Cl

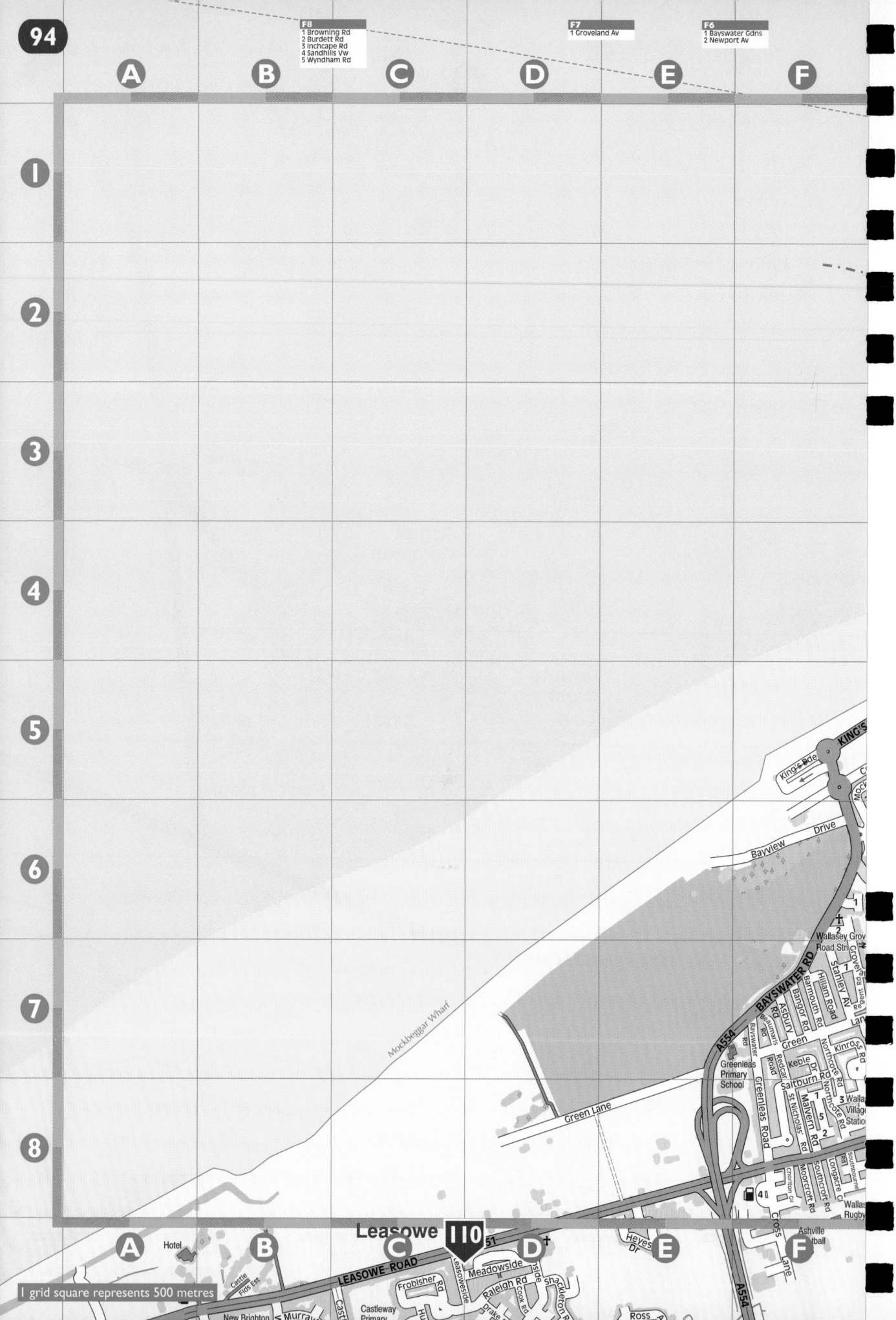

F8
1 Browning Rd
2 Burdett Rd
3 Inchcape Rd
4 Sandhills Vw
5 Wyndham Rd

F7
1 Groveland Av

F6
1 Bayswater Gdns
2 Newport Av

A B C D E F

I
2
3
4
5
6
7
8

KING'S
King's Pde
Mock

Bayview Drive

Wallasey Grove
Road Stn

BAYSWATER RD
A554
Ashburn Rd
Bangor Rd
Barmouth Rd
Hillam Rd
Stanley Av
Beaumaris Rd
Grove Rd
Green
Bayswater Rd
Keble Dr
Northcote Rd
Kinros
St Nicholas Rd
Greenleas Road
Greenleas
Primary
School
Saltburn Rd
Malvern Rd
Wallasey
Village
Station
Moorcroft Rd
Longacre Rd
Southcroft Rd
Chorlton Rd
Wallas...
Rugby

Mockbeggar Wharf

Green Lane

A554

Heyes
Dr

Ashville
...ball

Leasowe 110 51

LEASOWE ROAD

Hotel
Castle
Flds Est
New Brighton Murray...
Castleway
Primary
Frobisher
Rd
Meadowside
Leasoweside
Raleigh Rd
Cook Rd
Shackleton R...
Drake
Ross A...

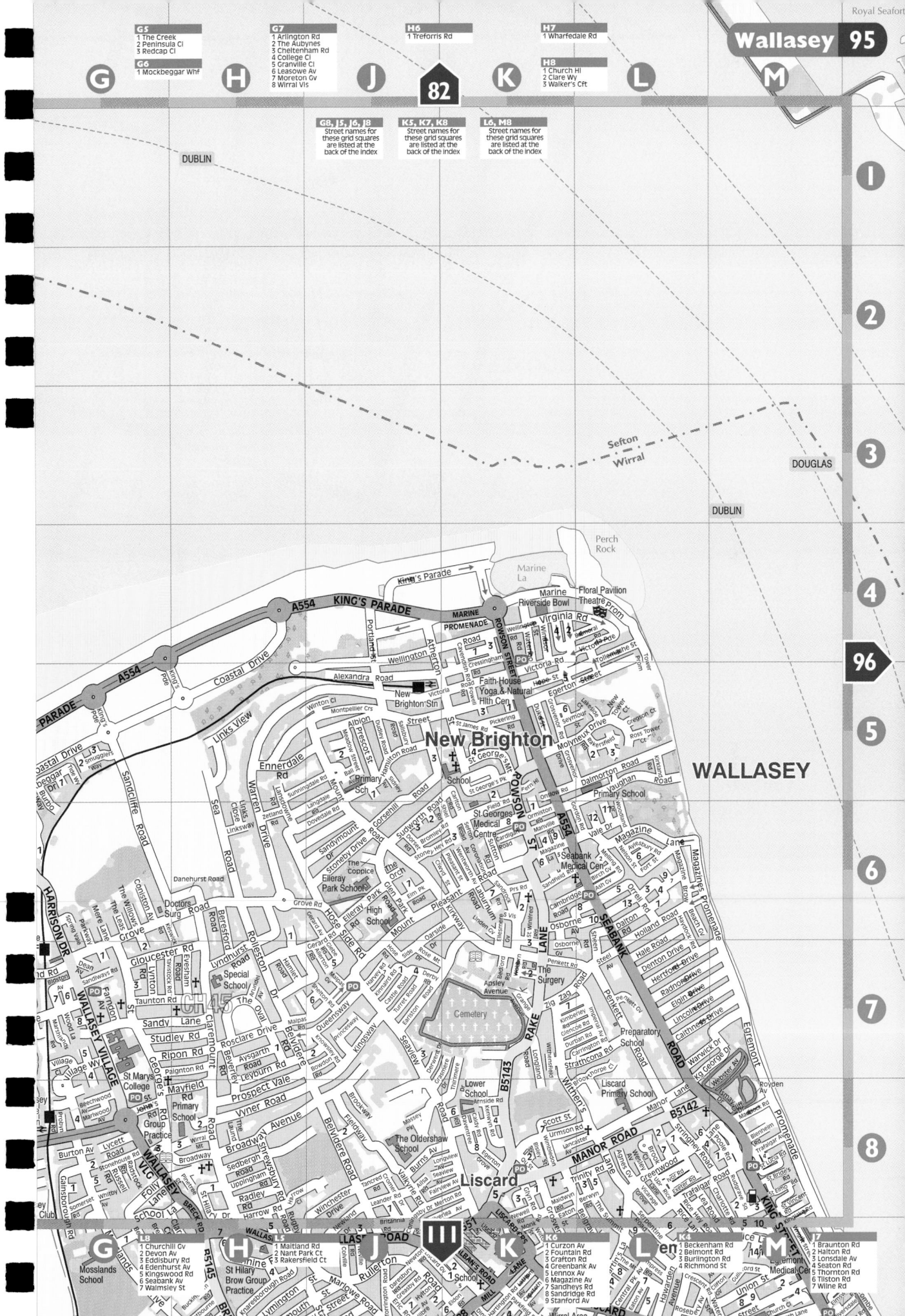

G  H  J  82  K  L  M  96

DUBLIN

Sefton

Wirral

DOUGLAS

DUBLIN

Royal Seafort

Perch Rock

Marine La

Marine Riverside Bowl

Floral Pavilion Theatre

King's Parade

A554  KING'S PARADE

MARINE PROMENADE

Virginia Rd

New Brighton Stn

New Brighton

WALLASEY

Liscard

Mosslands School

St Hilary Brow Group Practice

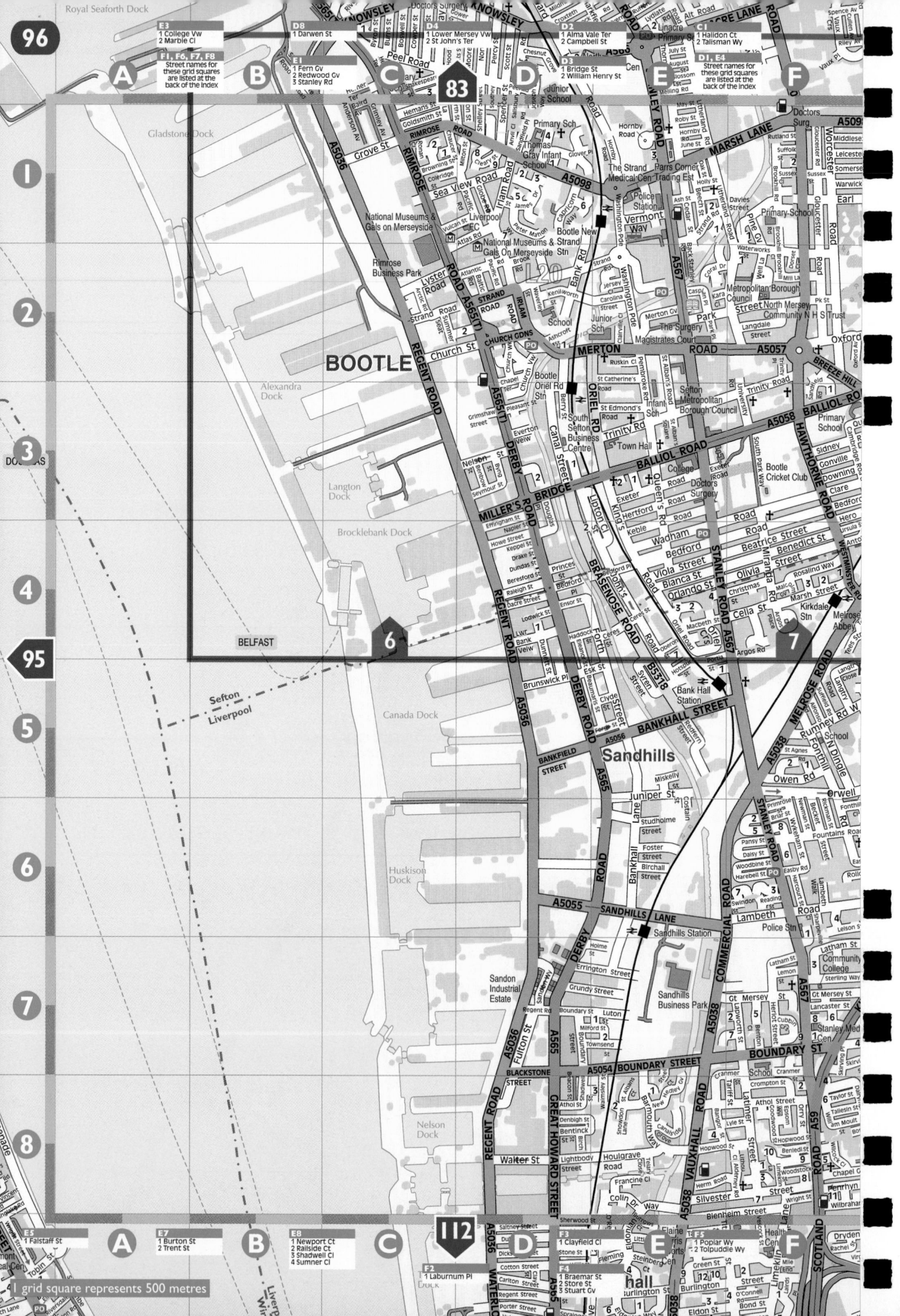

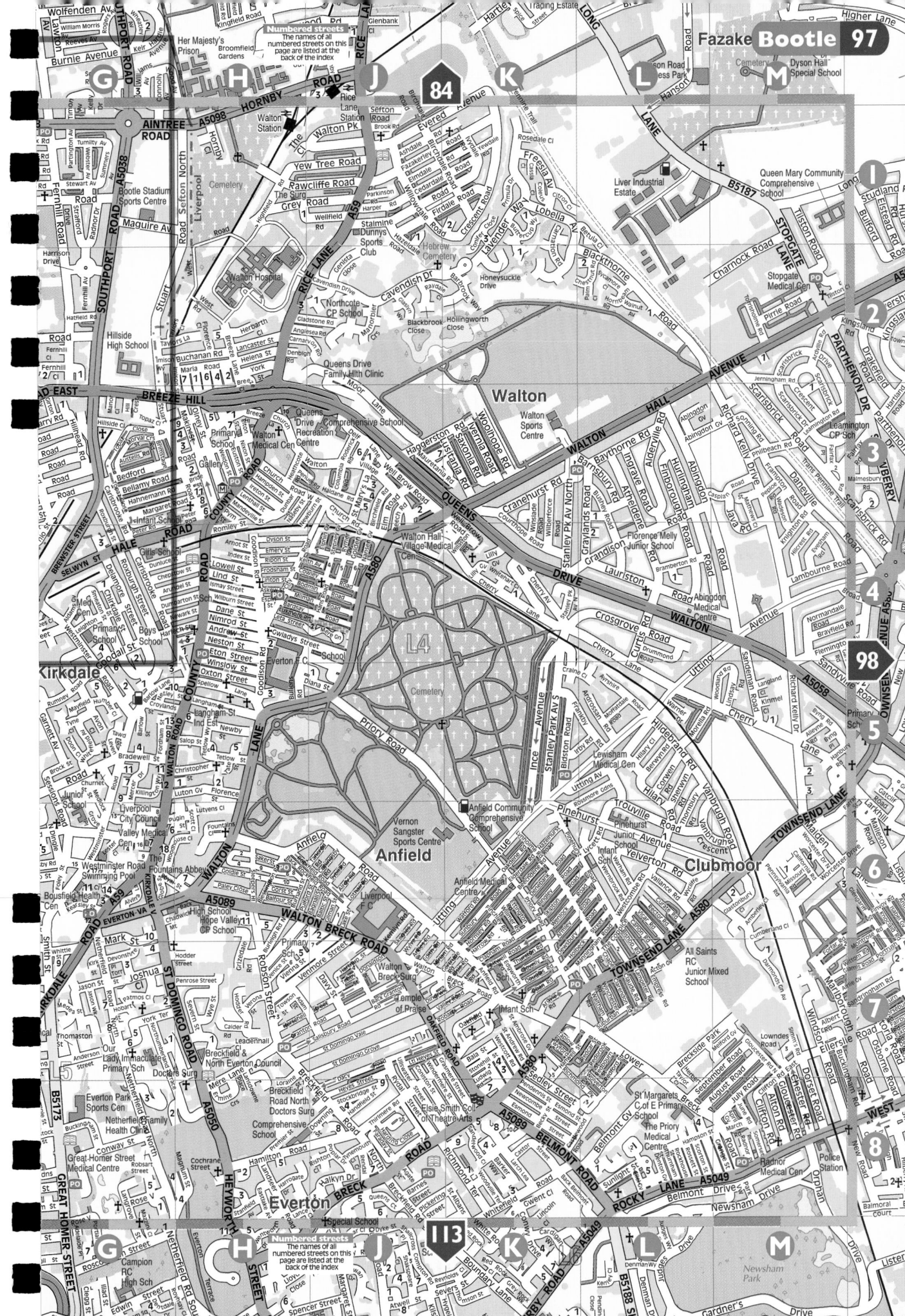

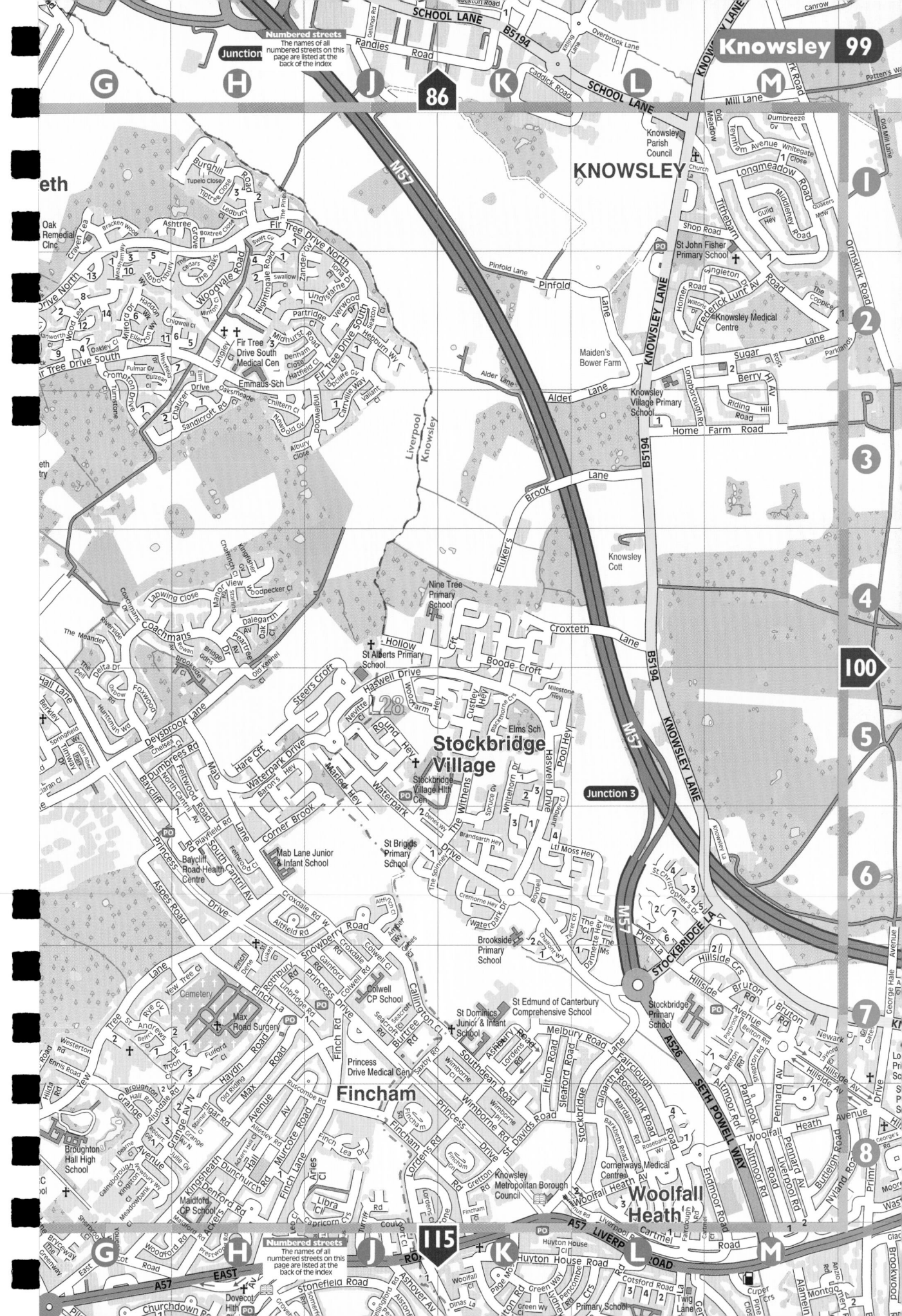

100

E7
1 Green Rd
2 Highfields
3 Vicarage Pl

Patten's

C8
1 Westminster Gv

B8
1 Jasmine Ct

A2
1 Woodview

A    B    C    87    D    E    F

Canrow

Patten's Walk

Ormskirk Road

Old Mill Lane

mbreeze

Whitegate
1 Close
dow

Middleley Road

Quakers Mow

The
Coppice

Ormskirk Road

Parklands

LANE

Knowsley
Community
College

Jack's

Knowsley
Park

Knowsley
Park

White
Man's
Dam

Entry

Brow

L34

Knowsley
Safari Park

Dark

No. 4 Reservoir

St Helens

Knowsley

99

Knowsley
Hall

6

A58

Prescot
School

The Spinney

Our Ladys
Primary
School

St Helens Road

Park Road

Prescot Association
Football Club

The Curtain
Gallery

Evans

Rowson St

Doctors

WARRINGTON

Hallatt Rd

Moss Rd

Grosvenor Rd

Natural Hlth
Clinic

Prescot Medical

Egerton rd

Police Station

Prescot Mus

Park House
Medical Cen

Houghton St

Cyprus St

Chester street

Station Road

George Hale
Avenue

Alden Long
Gv

Junction 2

PRESCOT

LIVERPOOL ROAD A57

WEST STREET

Knowsley
Metropolitan Borough
Council
Cemetery

KEMBLE ST

Williams

M57

KNOWSLEY LANE

B5194

Lyme

Cross Rd

Radway

Lyme

Lyme Cl

Chorley
Rd

Westbrook

Wood

Mitchell
Rd

Manchester

Norris
St

Central

Road

Preston

Sewell
St

bruto

Newark Cl

Gates

Longview
Primary
School

Astley Road

Marton Rd

Barford
Road

Hathersage
rd

Hazel Road

Kings
Business Park

Liverpool Rd

Beesley
Rd

South

Avenue

Avenue

Hillside

Hillside Av

St Columbas
Primary
School

Radway
Road

Hollyrood

Carr Lane

B5199

Manchester Rd

Prescot
Station

Hillside Road

Drive

St George's

Primrose

Moorcroft Rd

Hillside Road
Doctors Surg

PO

Blenheim
Dr

LIVERPOOL ROAD

Butleigh Road

Nyland Road

Heath

Pennard Av

Liverpool Av

Pennard Av

8

Hillside
House Surgery

Wastle Bridge Rd

Longview

A57

Glade Rd

Bakers Rd

Mossway Road

Moorcroft Rd

Northwood

Longview

LANE

Fairway

Whiston Lane

Mossy

116

Gol
Cour

D

F
Street names for
this grid square are
listed at the back of
the index

E

F8
1 Yates' Ct

A    B    F6
1 New Cross St    C    D    E    F

Prescot
Primary
School

1 grid square represents 500 metres

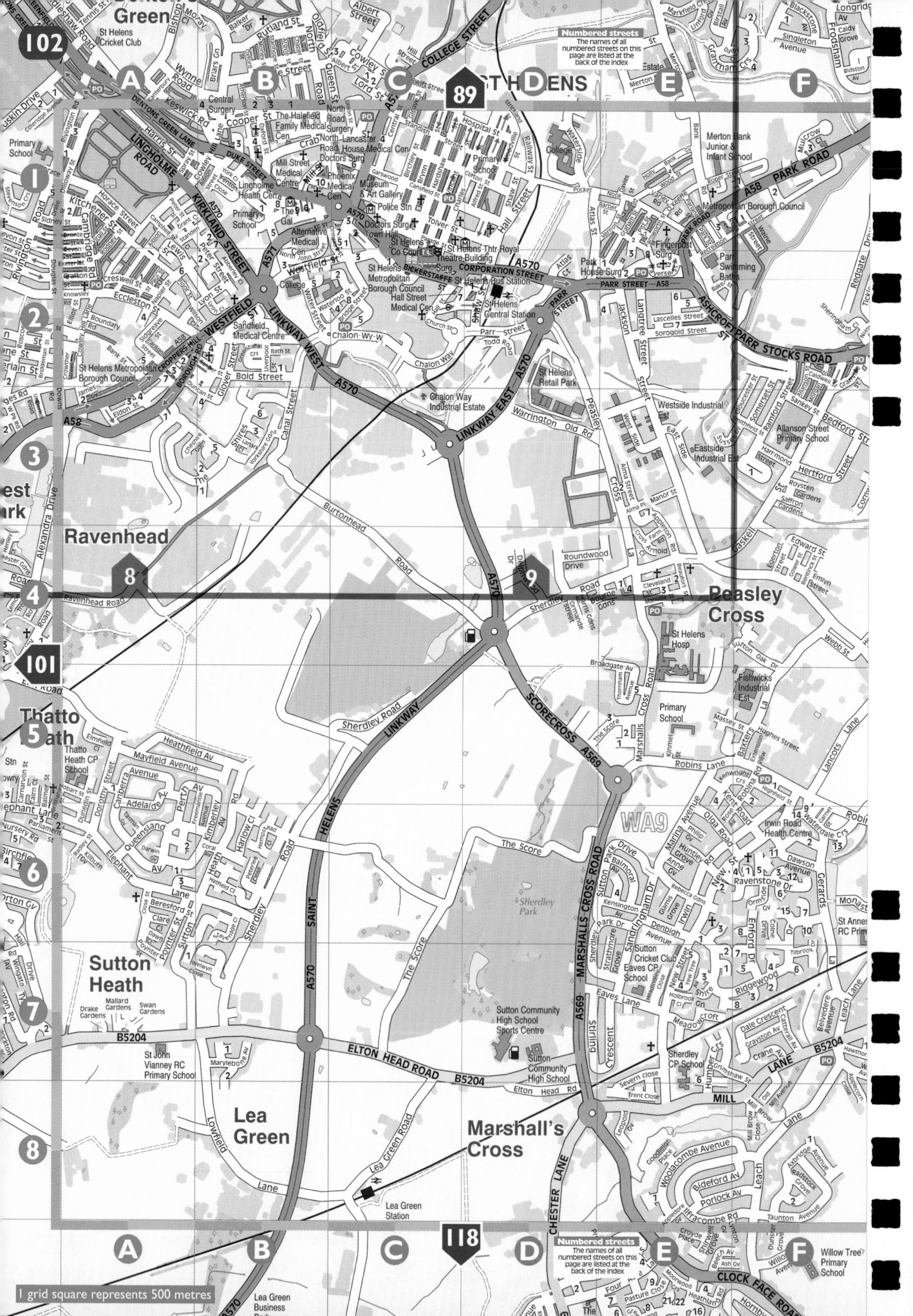

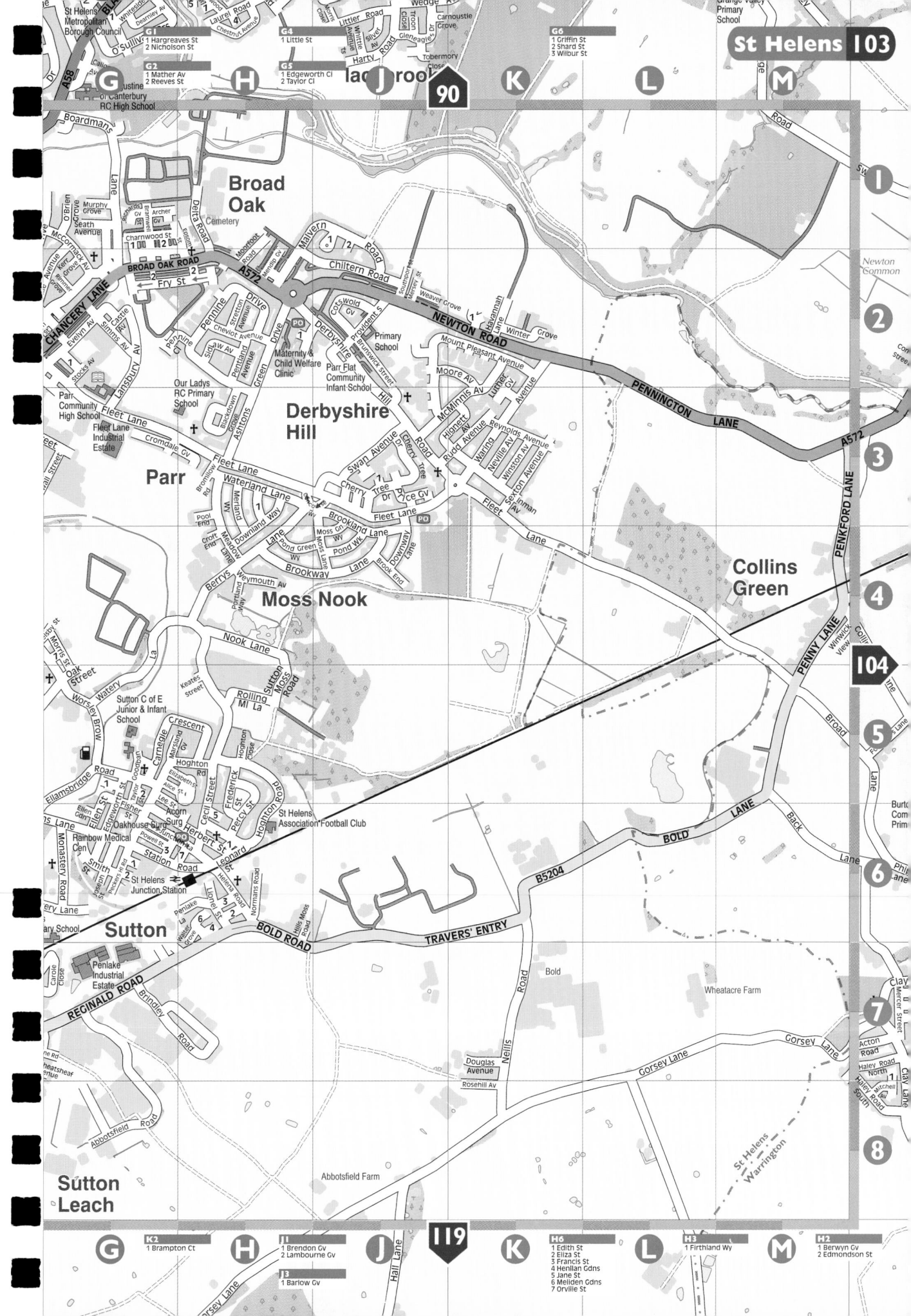

**90**

**Broad Oak**

**Derbyshire Hill**

**Parr**

**Moss Nook**

**Collins Green**

**Sutton**

**Sutton Leach**

**104**

**119**

G
H
J
K
L
M

I
2
3
4
5
6
7
8

**G3**
1 Hargreaves St
2 Nicholson St

**G2**
1 Mather Av
2 Reeves St

**G4**
1 Little St

**G5**
1 Edgeworth Cl
2 Taylor Cl

**G6**
1 Griffin St
2 Shard St
3 Wilbur St

**K2**
1 Brampton Ct

**J1**
1 Brendon Gv
2 Lambourne Gv

**J3**
1 Barlow Gv

**H6**
1 Edith St
2 Eliza St
3 Francis St
4 Henllan Gdns
5 Jane St
6 Meliden Gdns
7 Orville St

**H3**
1 Firthland Wy

**H2**
1 Berwyn Gv
2 Edmondson St

91

A — B — C — D — E — F

1

2

3

103

4

5

6

7

8

**Earlestown**

**NEWTON-LE-WILLOWS**

**Wargrave**

**Vulcan Village**

**Burtonwood**

WA12

A572

A49

A — B — C — D — E — F

1 grid square represents 500 metres

Town of Lowton

**92**

G2
1 Burkhardt Dr
2 Mill Meadow
3 Roscoe Av

G4
1 Coronation Dr

H1
1 Waterworks Dr

G   H   J   K   L   M

Lowton
Gartetts

Moss Lane

Farm

Golborne
Dale Road

Preparatory School

Castle Hill

Rob

Dale Vw

M6

PO
A49 CHURCH ST

Primary School

Hotel

Park Road North

Willow AV

SOUTHWORTH ROAD

Willowdale

Willow
Cabank Est

Holford Way

Warten

Rosemary Dr

Newton-le-Willows Station

Alfred Street

Special School

Banastre Drive

Conway Drive

Cheshire Close

Norman

A572

M6

A573

Parkside Farm

I

2

Kenyon Hall

WINWICK

A579

Newton Park Drive

Newton Park

Wayfarers Dr

WINWICK ROAD

Central Way

MILL LANE

A49

Red Bank School

Bungalow Road

Elm WY

Red Bank Avenue

St Helens Warrington

Cop Holt Farm

Red Bank

Hermitage Green Lane

Warrington St. Helens

Wood Head

PARKSIDE ROAD

M6

Wigan St. Helens

Barrow Lane

Oven Back Farm

Junction 22

3

Sandy

4

**106**

5

South Farm

NEWTON ROAD

A573

GOLBORNE ROAD

Colborne Rd

Genese Av

Hermitage Green

Old School House Lane

Green La

Green Lane

The Priory

Cem

Church Walk

PO

Waterworks

Hornby

Winwick C of E Primary School

Winwick Parish Leisure Centre

Ilex AV

Winwick

Myddleton

Ash Rd

Maple Rd

LINK ROAD

WINWICK

Highfield Lane

Southworth

Lane

6

Delph Lane

Arbury

7

Hollins Lane

Watery Lane

Warrington Community Health Care NHS Trust

Hollins La

Hollins Dr

Rectory La

Rectory Rd

Farington Road

Falcondale Rd

Linvside Av

Arbury Lane

WINWICK

Mid
Farm

8

Cemetery

Mill Lane

Junction 9

**121**

Delph

M62

G   H   J   K   L   M

Clarendon Court

Calver Rd

Calver Road

Rd

Woburn

ROAD

Elm

Birch Av

Poplar

Winwick Quay

K7
1 St Oswalds Cl

J7
1 Pilgrim Cl

M62

WA2

H2
1 Eastwood Av
2 Northwood Av
3 Woodland Av

Peel Hall

Newhaven

Mill Lane

G1
1 Burnham Cl
2 Marton Cl
3 Petersfield Gdns

G2
Street names for this grid square are listed at the back of the index

G8
1 Newton Av

H1
1 Sandown Cl

H2
1 Hampson Av
2 Newsholme Cl
3 Paythorne Cl
4 Warrington Rd

H3
1 Chatburn Ct
2 Downham Av

H7
1 Adlington Cl

T G s Green

H

J

K

L

M

wley Common

Fowley Common

Hey Shoot Lane

WARRINGTON

Moss House Farm

Moss Lane

Twiss Green Community Primary School

Sutton Av

Chiltern

Chatsworth Av

Culcheth Hall Drive

Wellfield

Culcheth Community Primary School

Hebden Av

Bevin Av

Eden Av

Churchill Avenue

Beaverbrook Av

B5212

HOLCROFT LANE

Heswall Av

Wirral

Ellesmere Rd

Burton

Kirkby Rd

Cranwell Av

Thirlby Rd

Withins Rd Drive

Withington Av

A574

Beech Av

Culcheth High School

Daisy Mill Bank Close

chmill Dr

Sefton Cl

LANE

COMMON

chill Av

Brogden Av

wley Av

Avenue

Broadhurst Av

Pendle Gdns

Jackson Av

Thompson Av

The Surgery

PO

Warrington Borough Council

Culcheth Clinic

Holcroft Clinic

Church

Kaye Av

Poplar Av

Newchurch Lane

York Av

Hampson Av

Walton Av

Carnock Rd

Culcheth Sports Club

Ribchester Gdns

**Culcheth**

Shaw St

Bent La

Shawley

Thames Road

Avon Cl

Bollin Cl

Ratcliffe House Farm

Newchurch Community Primary School

Crossfield Av

Whitegate

Dunham Rd

Do

Ribble Av

New Hall Lane

Medway Rd

Bentham Rd

Severn Road

Greenwood Cl

Cedar Ct

Howard Rd

Franks Farm

raziers Lane

New Hall La

WA3

Bates Farm

H.M. Remand Centre

Abbey Farm

Moss Side Farm

M62

M62

Silver Lane

M62

Junction 11

Silver Lane

**Gorse Covert**

Hoyles Moss Farm

M62

Clayton Cl

Melbury Ct

Leacroft Road

Raglan Cl

Roscoe Rd

Trident Industrial Est

**Risley**

Daten Avenue

Heaton Court

Risley Rd

Daten Av

Adlington Ct

Keswick

Bramshill

Fisherfield Drive

Hamsterley

Gorse

Darnaway

Falstone

Covert

Woolmer Cl

Covert Rd

Rockingham Cl

Harborough Close

Rendlesham

Primary School

PO

School Lane

Daten Av

Maxwell Cl

Kelvin Street

Reynolds Av

Arden

Sparmore

Rangemoor Cl

Ringwood

Cavendish Avenue

Ravenhurst

A574

Trinity Ct

Bramshill

Gorse Covert Rd

Gorse Covert

Gilderdale

Warrington St

Dalton St

Griffith Av

Faraday Av

Chadwick Pl

Walton Rd

Joule Street

Moss Gate

Ashdown La

Dalby Close

Langwell

Killingworth Lane

Wilson

Thompson Street

Street

Ordnance Avenue

**Birchwood**

BIRCHWOOD WAY

BIRCHWOOD

Risley Moss Nature

Omrod Far

G

Avenue

H

Adam

J

I23

K

L

M

Redshank La

Powers La

Pheasant Cl

K7
1 Inglewood Cl

K8
1 Bowland Cl
2 Charnwood Cl

J8
1 Flaxley Cl
2 Rossendale Dr
3 Westhay Crs
4 Whittlewood Cl
5 Wigmore Cl

J7
1 Applecross Cl
2 Culbin Cl
3 Dunley Cl
4 Rangemoor Cl

H8
1 Aston Av

J3
1 Derwent Cl
2 Weaver Rd

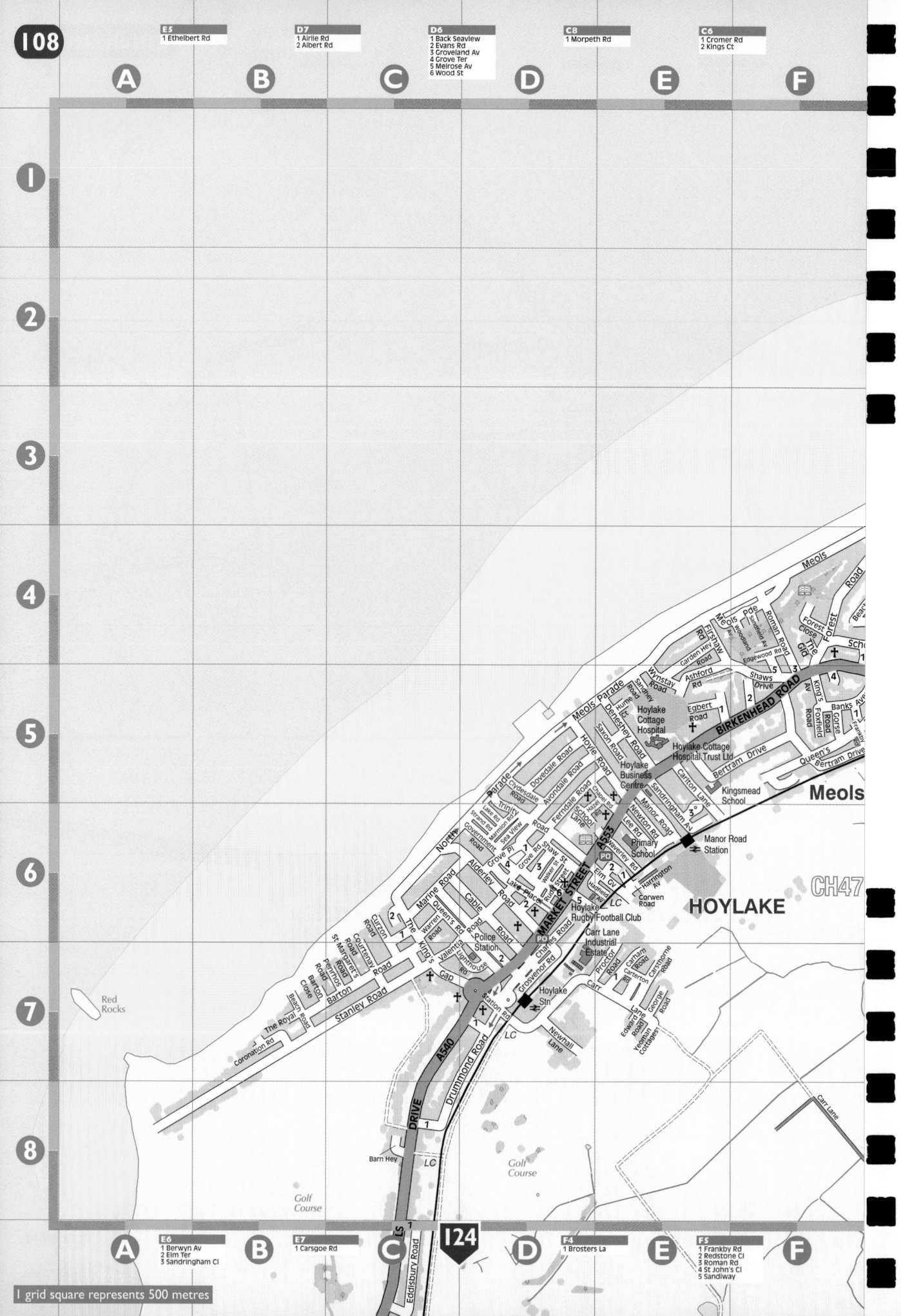

**E5**
1 Ethelbert Rd

**D7**
1 Airlie Rd
2 Albert Rd

**D6**
1 Back Seaview
2 Evans Rd
3 Groveland Av
4 Grove Ter
5 Melrose Av
6 Wood St

**C8**
1 Morpeth Rd

**C6**
1 Cromer Rd
2 Kings Ct

**E6**
1 Berwyn Av
2 Elm Ter
3 Sandringham Cl

**E7**
1 Carsgoe Rd

**124**

**F4**
1 Brosters La

**F5**
1 Frankby Rd
2 Redstone Cl
3 Roman Rd
4 St John's Cl
5 Sandiway

1 grid square represents 500 metres

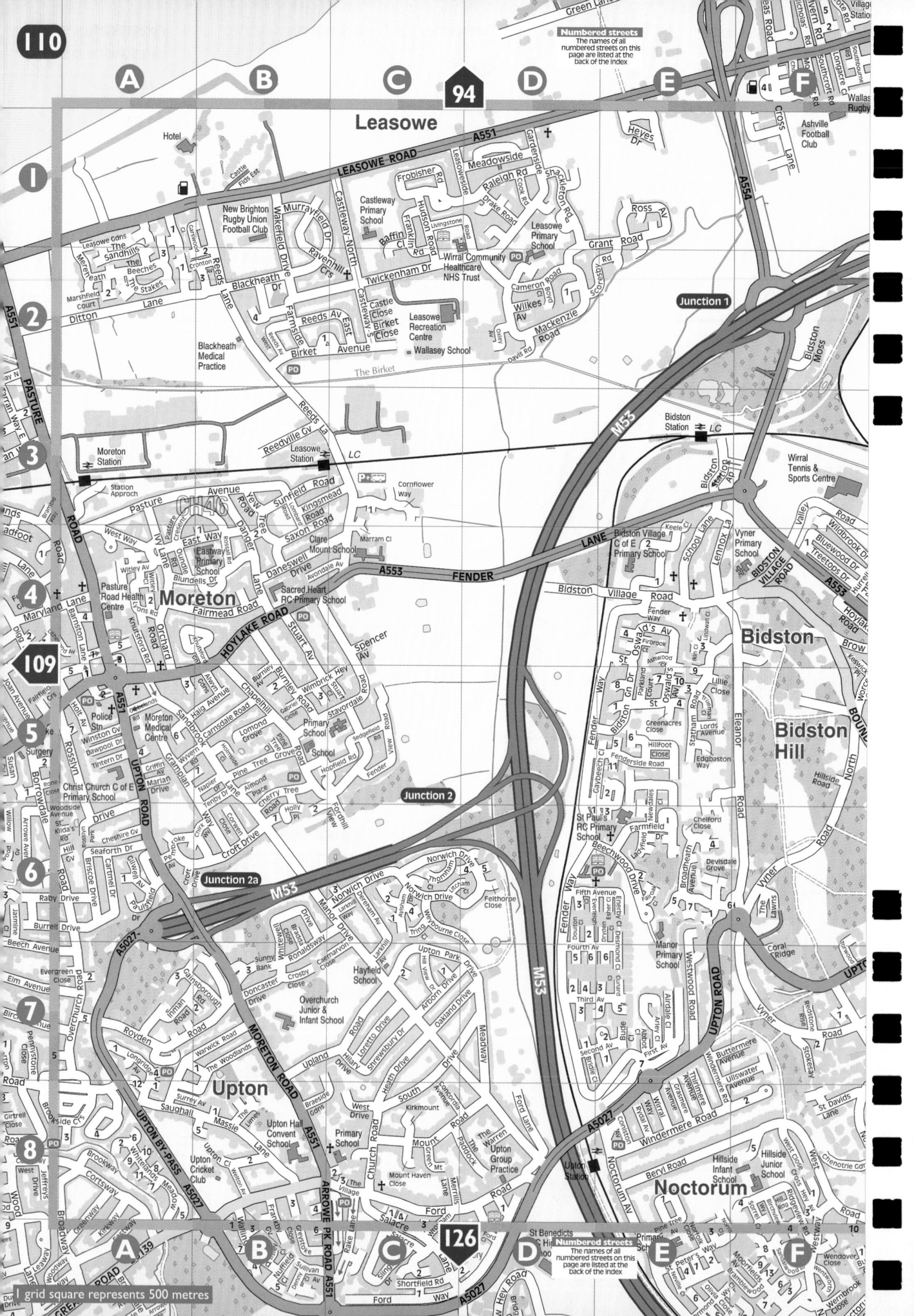

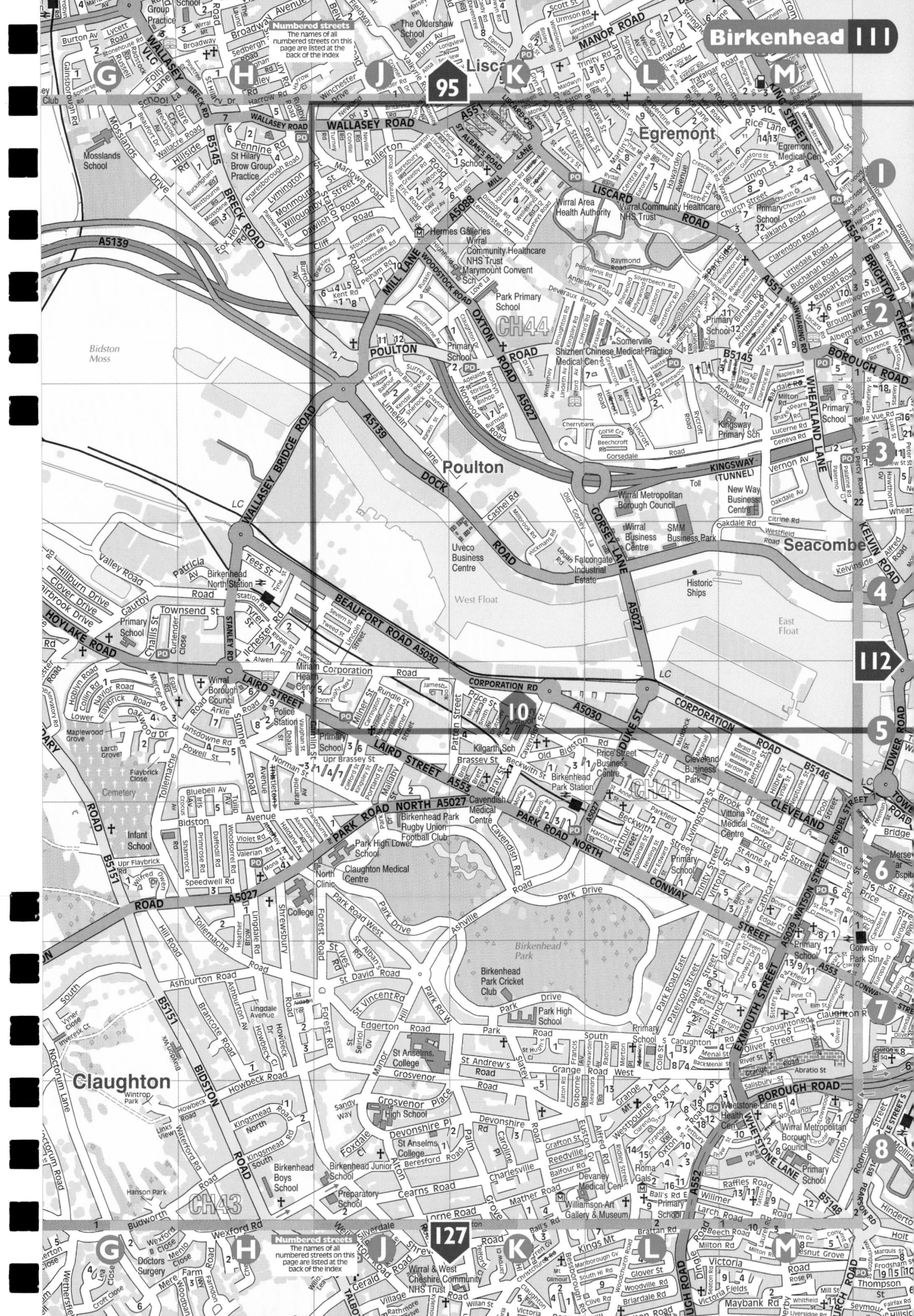

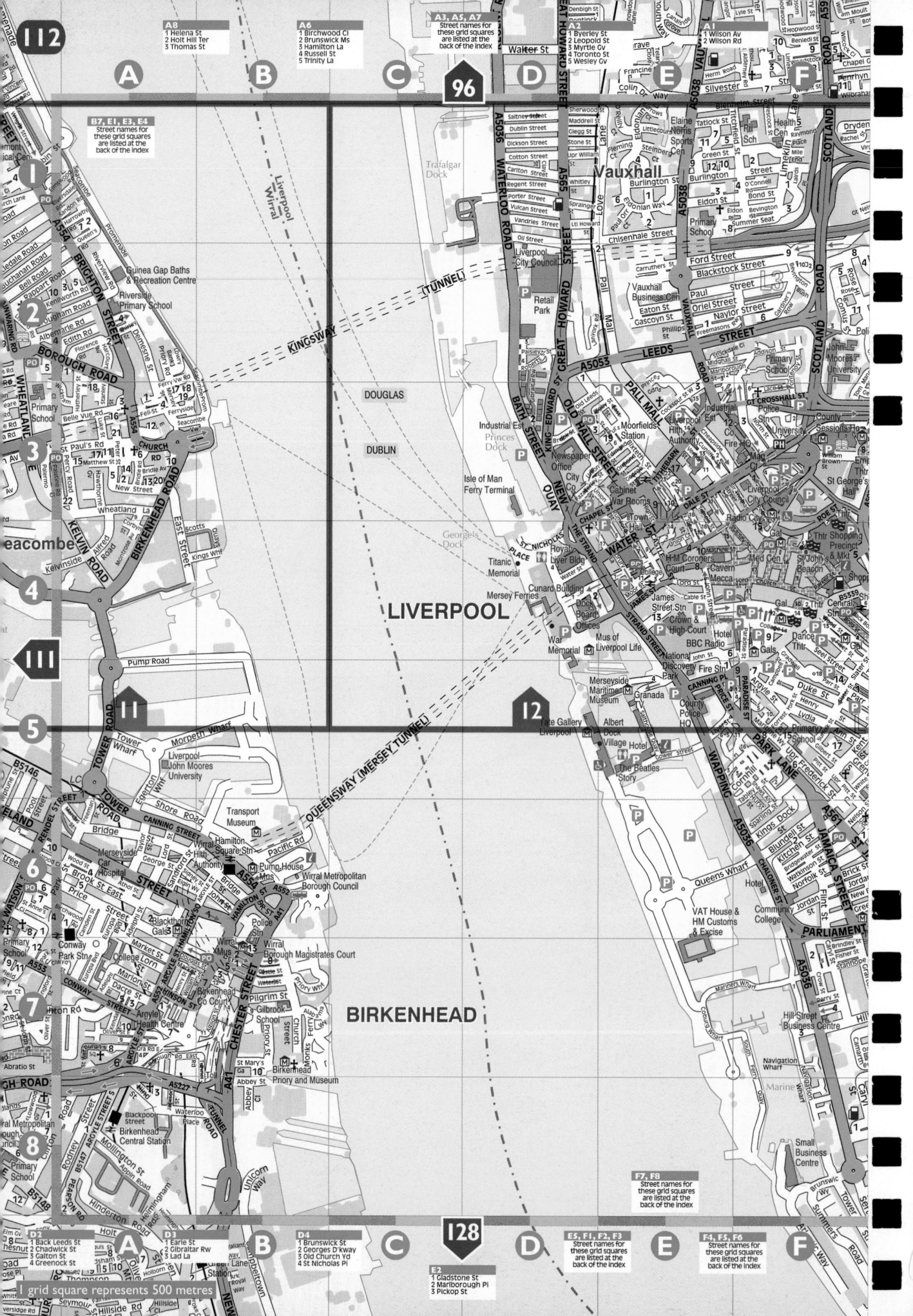

96

Vauxhall

LIVERPOOL

111

I1 I2

BIRKENHEAD

1 grid square represents 500 metres

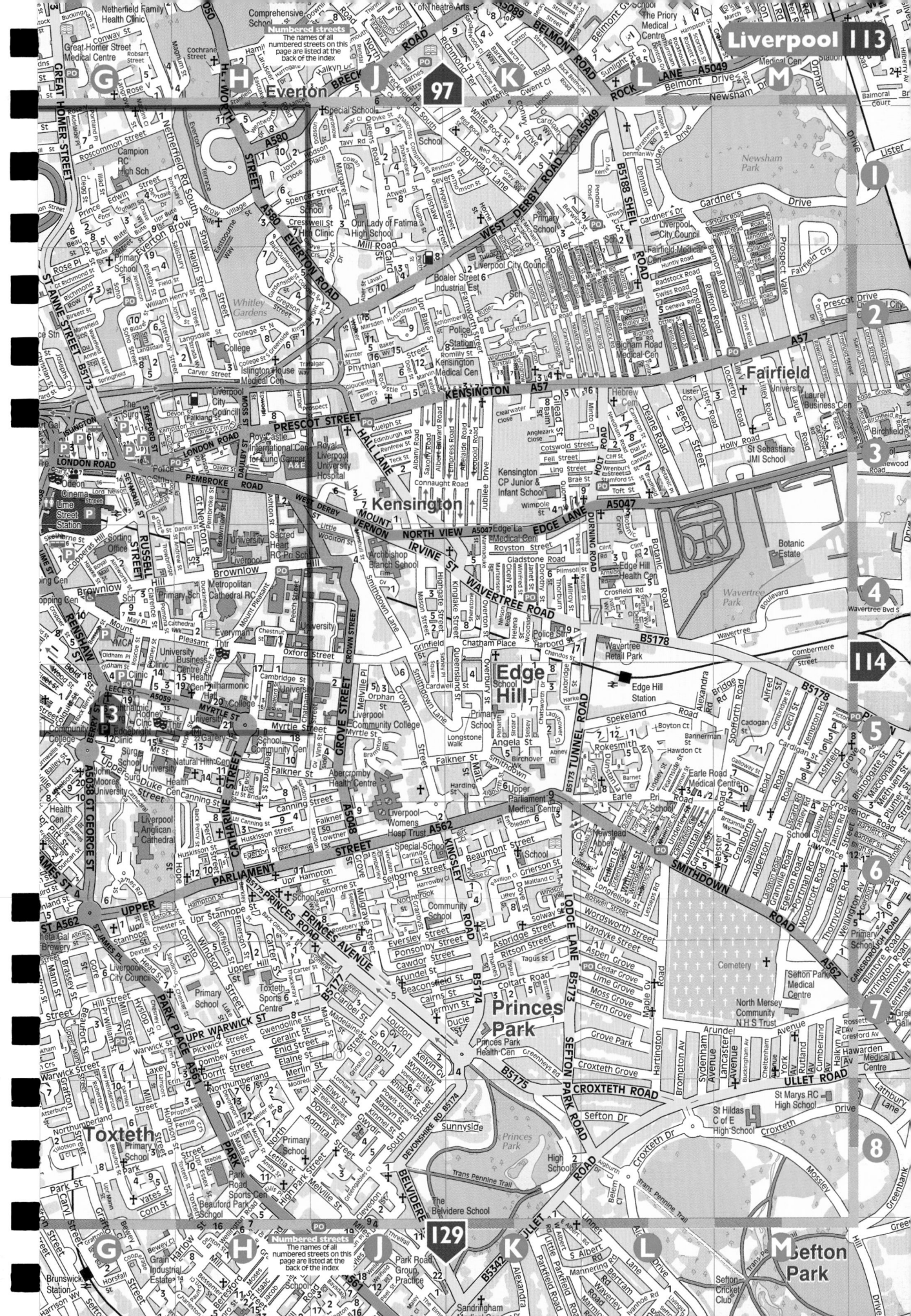

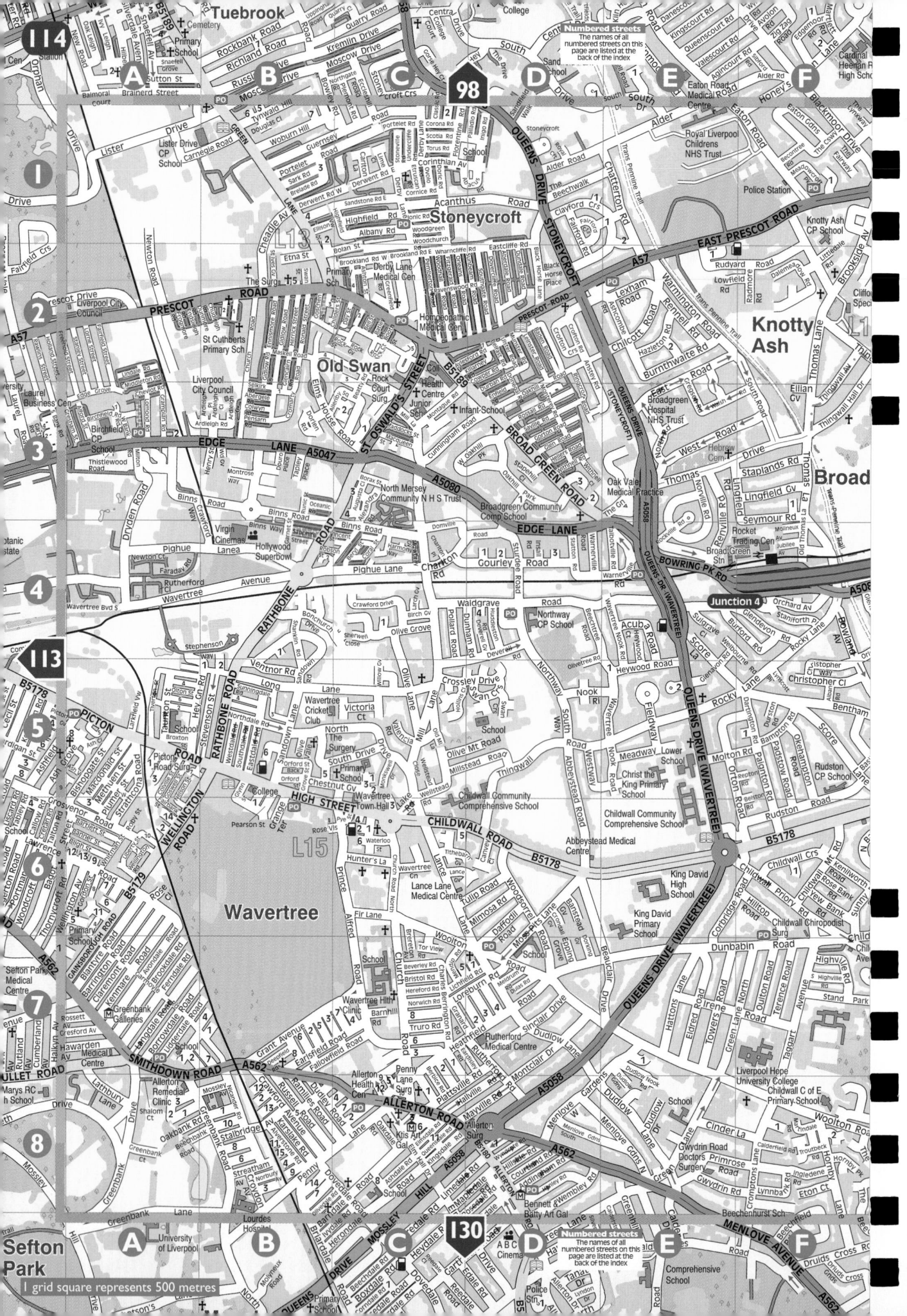

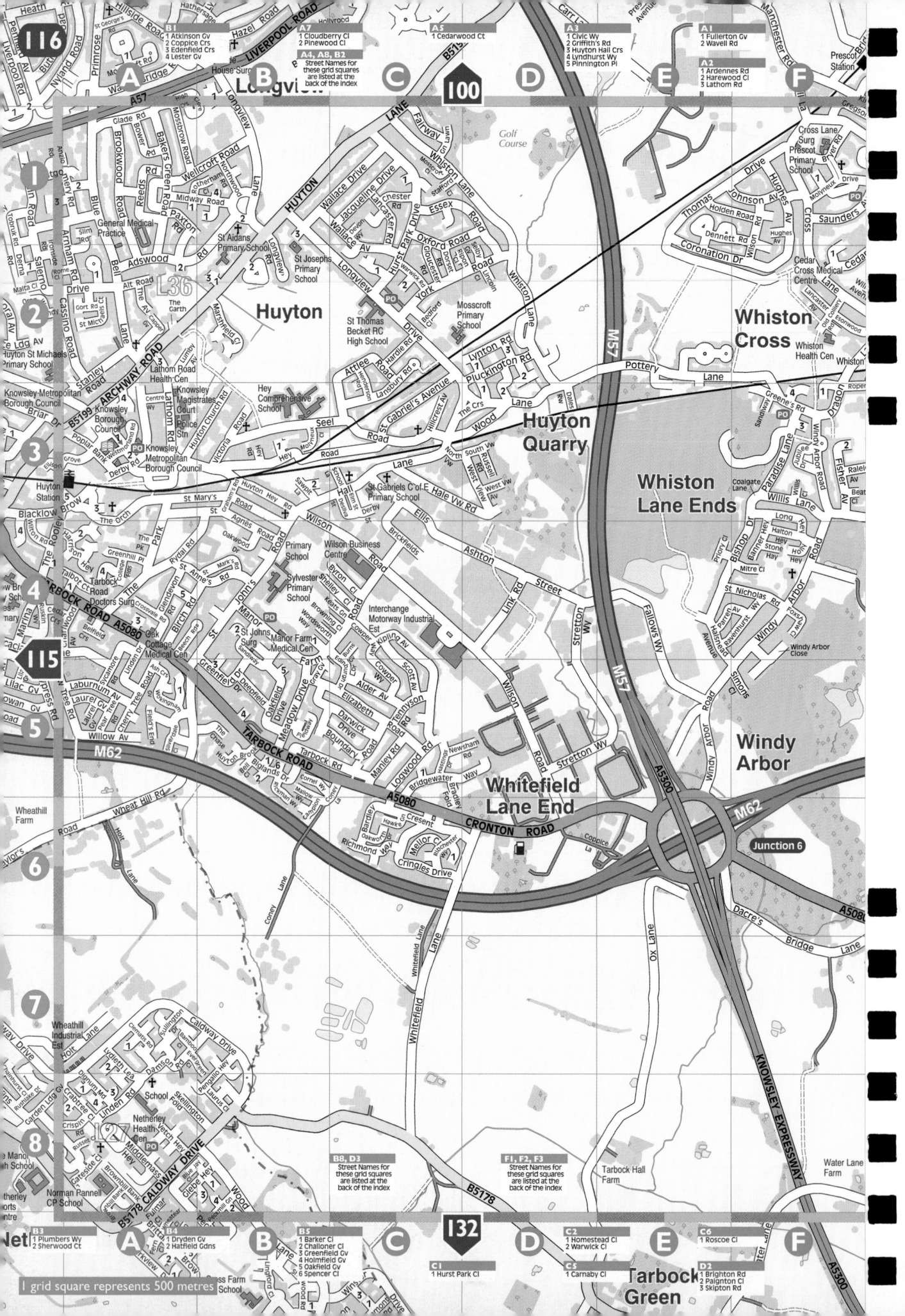

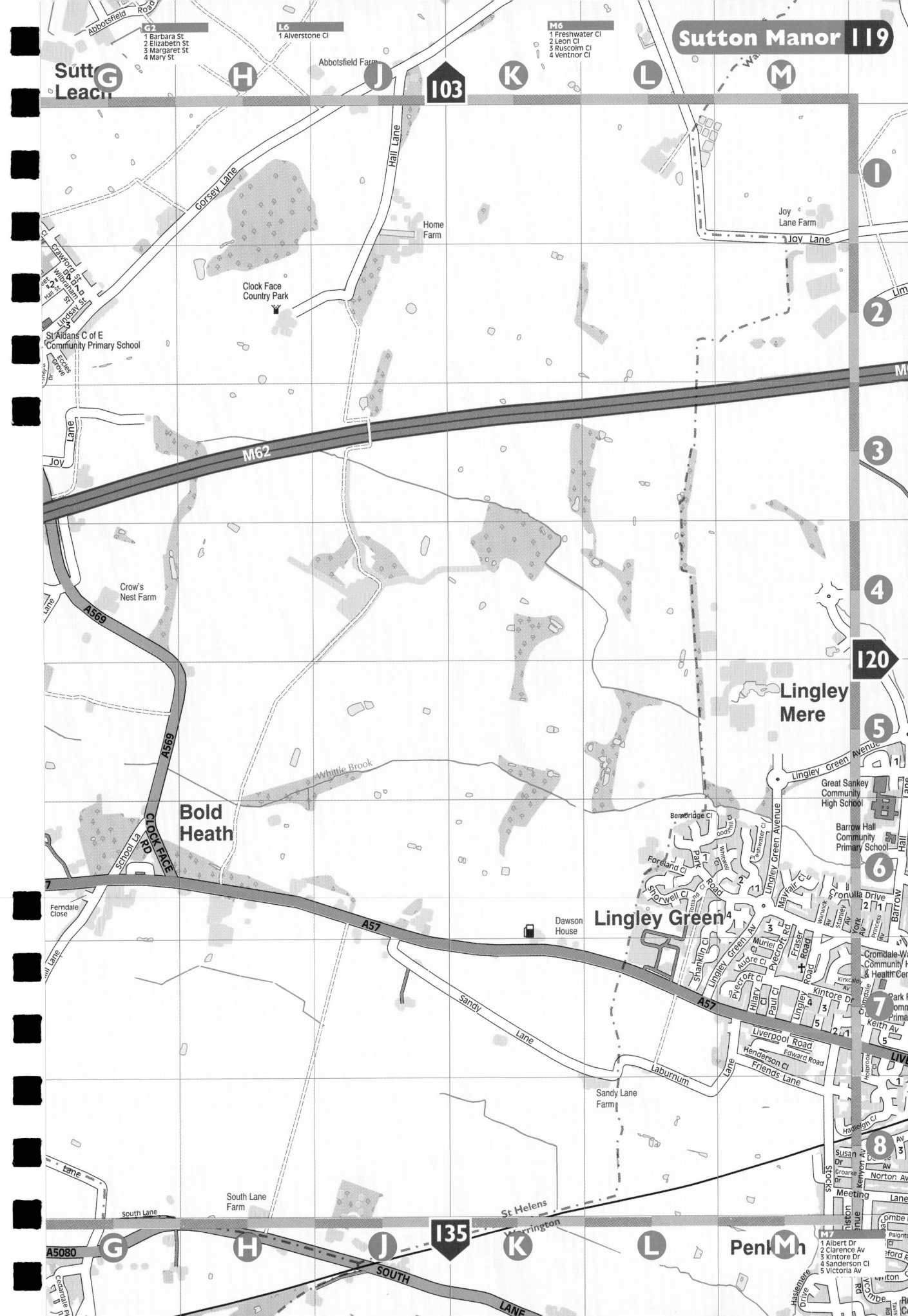

**G2**
1 Barbara St
2 Elizabeth St
3 Margaret St
4 Mary St

**L6**
1 Alverstone Cl

**M6**
1 Freshwater Cl
2 Leon Cl
3 Ruscolm Cl
4 Ventnor Cl

Abbotsfield Road

Sutt
Leach

G   H   J   **103**   K   L   M

Abbotsfield Farm

I

Crawford St
Lindsay St
Eccles Grove
St Aidans C of E
Community Primary School

Corsey Lane

Hall Lane

Home
Farm

Joy
Lane Farm

Joy Lane

2

Clock Face
Country Park

Joy
Lane

M62

3

M6

Joy

Crow's
Nest Farm

A569

4

**120**

Lingley
Mere

A569

Lingley Green Avenue

5

Lingley Green Avenue

Great Sankey
Community
High School

1

Whittle Brook

**Bold
Heath**

Bembridge Cl
Goodw
Peshwater Cl
Whitehall

Barrow Hall
Community
Primary School

6

CLOCK FACE RD
School La

Foreland Cl
Park Road

Shorwell Cl

Cronulla Drive

Warwick

Stanley
York

Princess

Barrow

Ferndale
Close

A57

Dawson
House

**Lingley Green** 4

Sharklin Cl
Lingley Green Avenue
Muriel
Aldre Cl
Pyecroft Cl

Fraser
Road

1
2
3

Cromdale Wa
Community H
& Health Cen

Hilary
Paul Cl

Pyecroft Rd

Lingley
Road

Kintore Dr

Kirkcaldy
Av

Cromdale

Park F
Comm
Ro

7

Sandy
Lane

A57

Liverpool Road

Edward Road

Henderson Close
Friends Lane

Keith Av

LIVE

Hobcroft

Laburnum
Lane

Sandy Lane
Farm

Hadleigh Cl

8

Susan
Dr

Groarke
Dr

Kenyon Rd

Norton Av

South Lane
Farm

St Helens

Warrington

Stocks
Meeting
Lane

A5080   G   H   J   **135**   K   L   **Penk M** h

South Lane

SOUTH

LANE

Cedardale Pa

**M7**
1 Albert Dr
2 Clarence Av
3 Kintore Dr
4 Sanderson Cl
5 Victoria Av

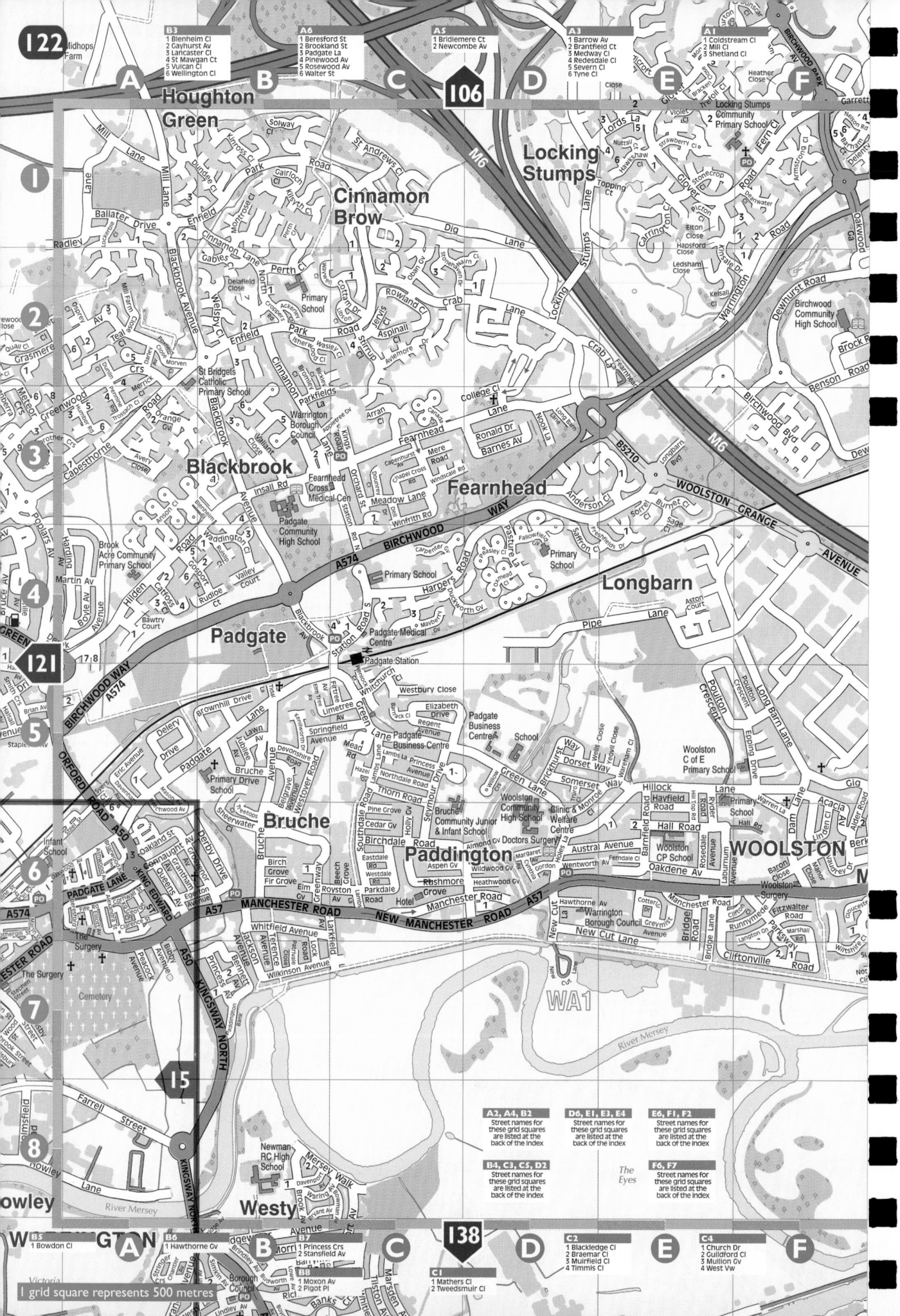

**G** · **H** · **J** · **K** · **L** · **M**

**107**

Omrod Rd

**1**

Birchwood

Oakwood

Risley Moss
Nature Park

Prospect
Farm

Prospect Lane

**2**

Rixton
Moss

Woodend Lane

**3**

Primary
School

Birchwood
Medical Cen

Birchwood
Station

Woodhouse
Close

Woolston
Moss

Holly Bush Lane

**4**

Marshall's Farm

Green Alley
Farm

**5**

M6

WOOLSTON GRANGE AVENUE

Nicol Av

Juniper Lane

BROOK LANE

A57

Brookside
Farm

**6**

Bollin
Point

Warrington
Borough
Council

B5210

M6

Manchester
Road

MANCHESTER ROAD

A57

River Mersey

Martinscroft

Junction 21

**7**

Thelwall
Viaduct

Golf Course

**8**

Statham

Laskey House

Manchester Ship Canal

Whitbarrow Road

Oldfield
Road

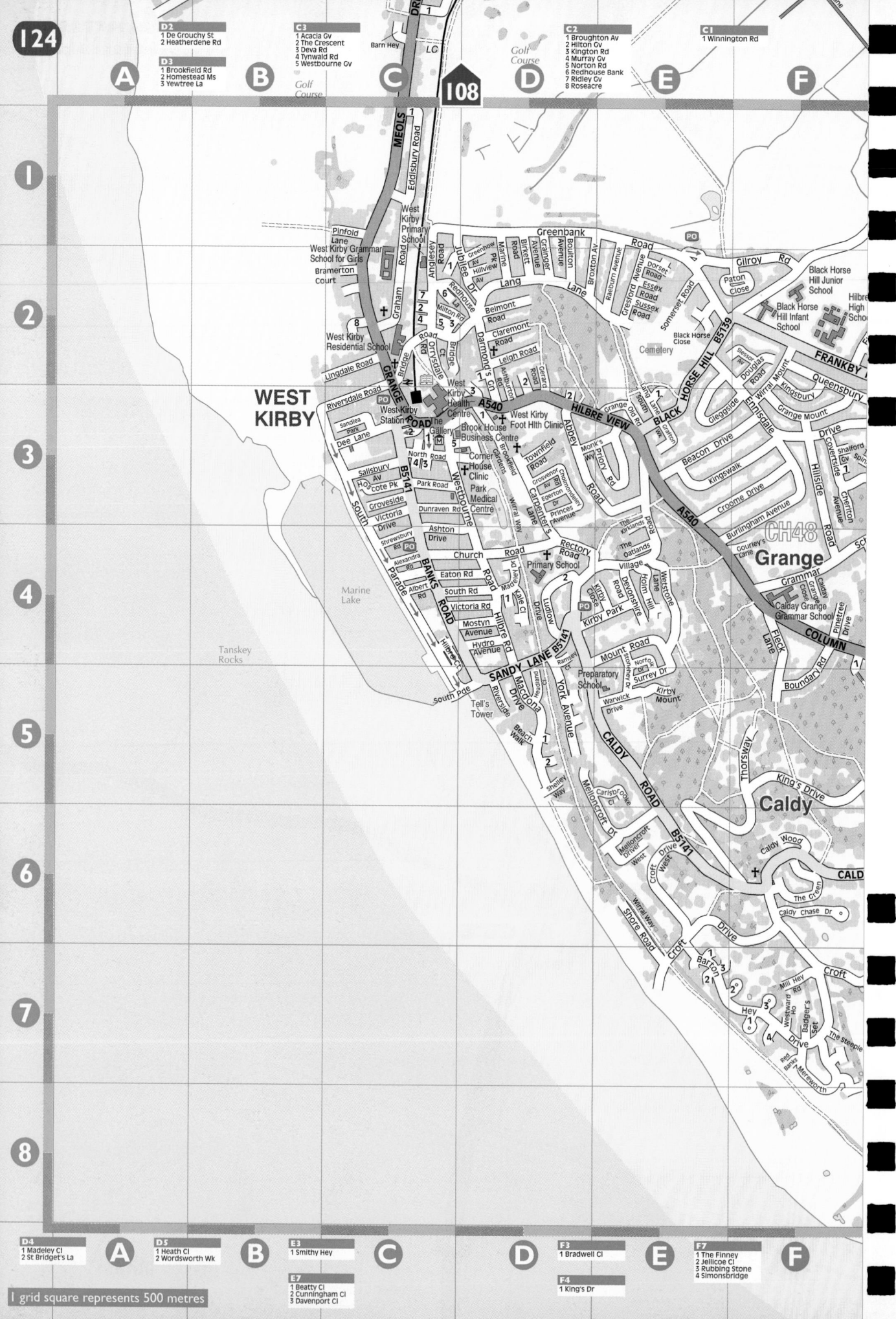

A  B  C  D  E  F

108

**WEST KIRBY**

Barn Hey

Golf Course

Golf Course

Greenbank Road

Pinfold Lane
West Kirby Grammar School for Girls
West Kirby Primary School
Bramerton Court

West Kirby Residential School

Lingdale Road

Riversdale Road
Sandiea Park
Dee Lane

Salisbury Av
cote Pk

Groveside

Victoria Drive

Shrewsbury Rd
Alexandra Rd

Church Road
Eaton Rd

South Rd

Victoria Rd

Mostyn Avenue

Hydro Avenue

Marine Lake

Tanskey Rocks

Tell's Tower

South Pde

West Kirby Station
The Gallery
Brook House Business Centre

Corner House Clinic
Park Medical Centre

North Road

Park Road

Dunraven Cl

Ashton Drive

Albert Rd

Brookfield

Townfield Road
Carpenter's Lane

Rectory Road
Primary School

West Kirby Health Centre

West Kirby Foot Hlth Clinic

Abbey Road

Monk's Way
Priory Rd

Grosvenor Av
Chomondeley Rd
Egerton Dr
Princes Avenue

The Kirklands
The Oatlands
Village

Kirby Park

Devonshire Road

Holm Hill

Kirby Mount

Mount Road

Preparatory School

Warwick Drive

Beach Walk

Shelley Way

Melloncroft Drive

Melloncroft Drive West

Shore Road

Croft Drive West

Croft Drive

Croft Drive

CALDY ROAD B5141

Thorsway

King's Drive

**Caldy**

Caldy Wood

Caldy Chase Dr

CALD

The Green

Barton Hey

Mill Hey Rd

Westward Ho
Drive

Badger's Set

Hey

The Steeple

Red Banks

Mereworth

**Grange**

CH48

Burlingham Avenue

Gourley's Lane

Calday Grange Grammar School

COLUMN

FLECK LANE

Boundary Rd

Pinetree Drive

Beacon Drive

Kingswalk

Croome Drive

A540

Black Horse Hill

BLACK HORSE HILL B5139

Cemetery

Black Horse Close

Paton Close

Gilroy Rd

Black Horse Hill Junior School

Black Horse Hill Infant School

Hilbre High School

FRANKBY

Queensbury

Wirral Mount

Kingsbury

Grange Mount

Innisdale

Grange Drive

Coverside

Shalford

Hillside

Cherton Avenue

Douglas

Strasser
Gleggside

MEOLS DR

Eddisbury Road

Graham Road

Anglesey Road

GRANGE ROAD

BANKS ROAD

B5141

South Parade

Hilbre Rd

Macdona Drive

Riverside Drive

York Avenue

SANDY LANE B5141

CALDY ROAD

Wirral Way

HILBRE VIEW

A540

A  B  C  D  E  F

1 grid square represents 500 metres

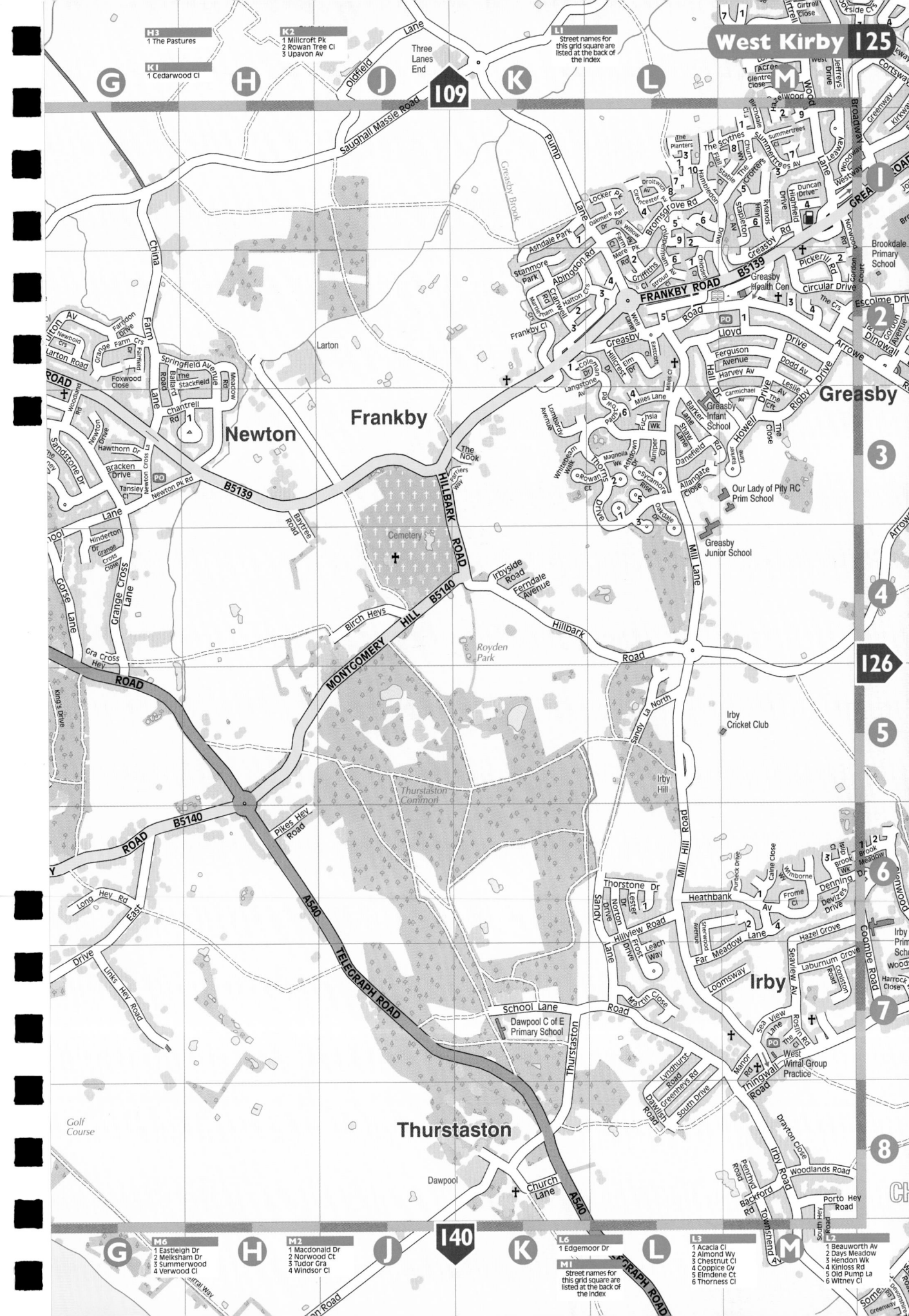

109

140

126

Newton

Frankby

Greasby

Irby

Thurstaston

Royden Park

Thurstaston Common

Golf Course

Cemetery

Irby Cricket Club

Irby Hill

Dawpool

Brookdale Primary School

Greasby Health Cen

Greasby Infant School

Our Lady of Pity RC Prim School

Greasby Junior School

Dawpool C of E Primary School

Irby Prim Schol

West Wirral Group Practice

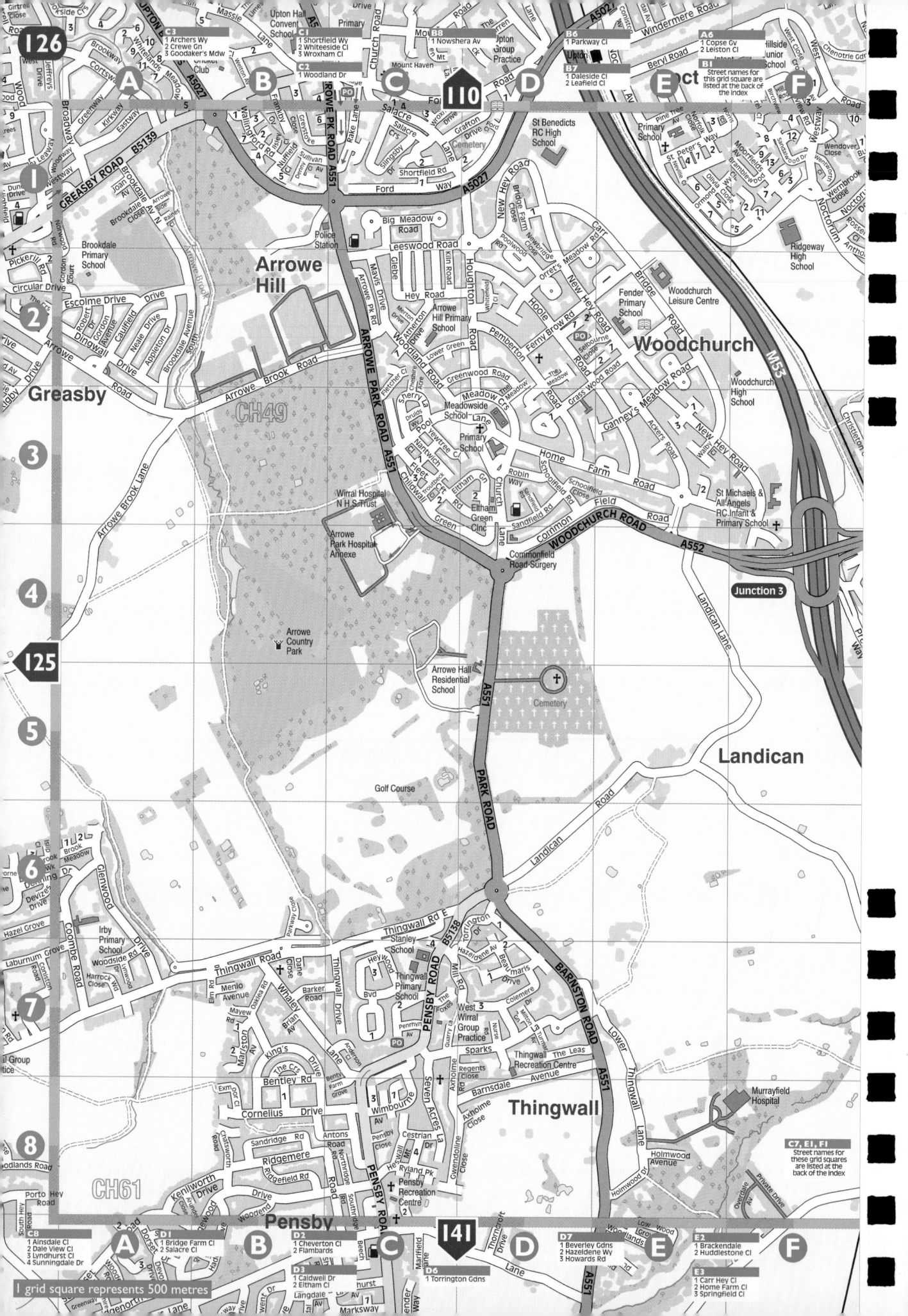

Toxteth

Sefton Park

Dingle

St Michael's Hamlet

Otterspool

Devil's Bank

River Mersey

Garston Channel

Festival Gardens

Liverpool & Wirral

H1, H2, J2
Street names for
these grid squares
are listed at the
back of the index

K2
1 Alpass Rd
2 Neilson Rd

K3
1 Rosewarne Rd
2 Springbourne Rd
3 Sunnburne Rd
4 Windbourne Rd

113

130

144

M4
1 Jericho La

L4
1 Calvados Cl

L3
Street names for
this grid square
are listed at the back
of the index

L2
1 Broadhurst St
2 Linhope Wy
3 Newland Ct

L1
1 Aigburth Dr
2 Forge Cottages
3 Hesketh St
4 Lucknow St

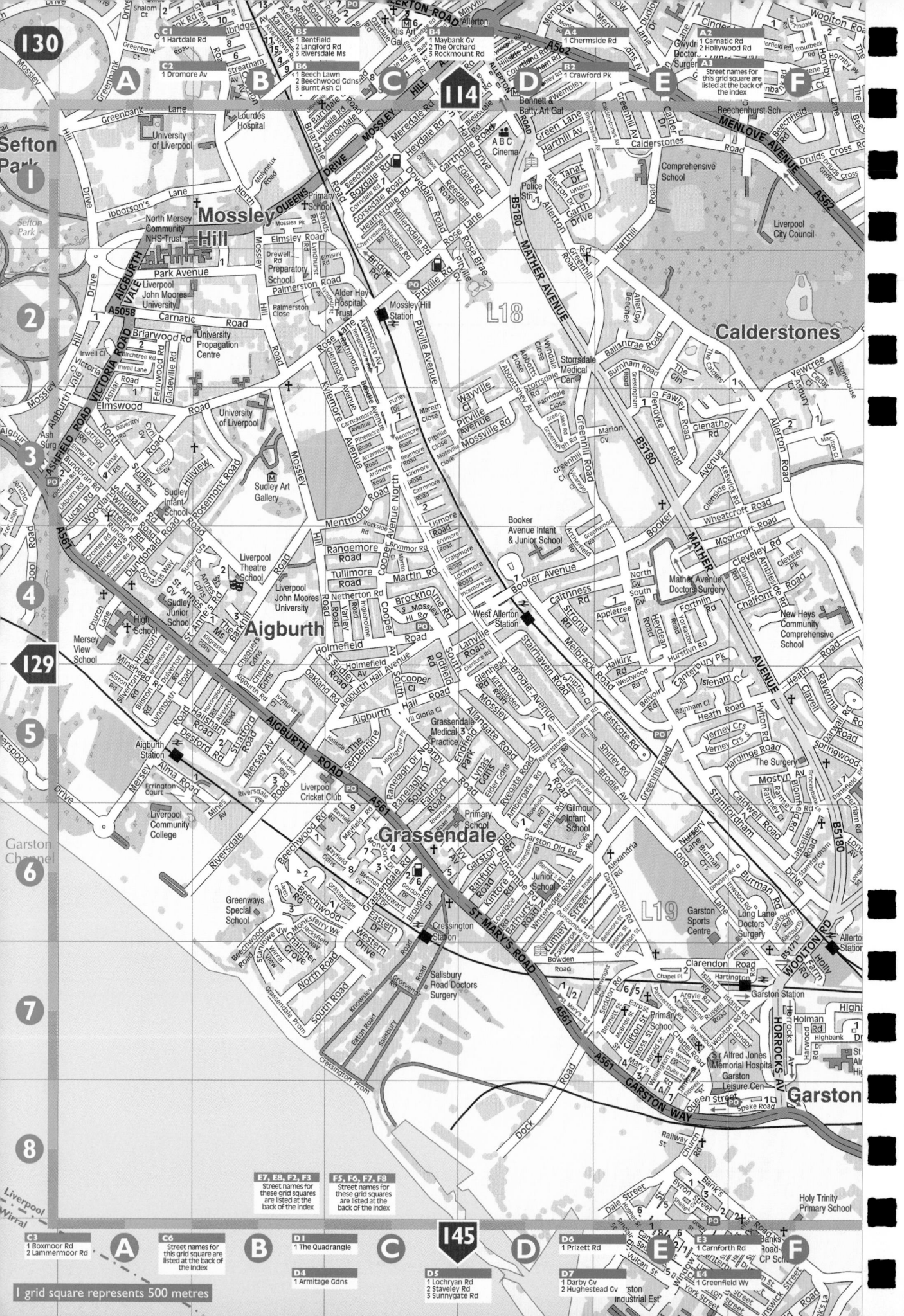

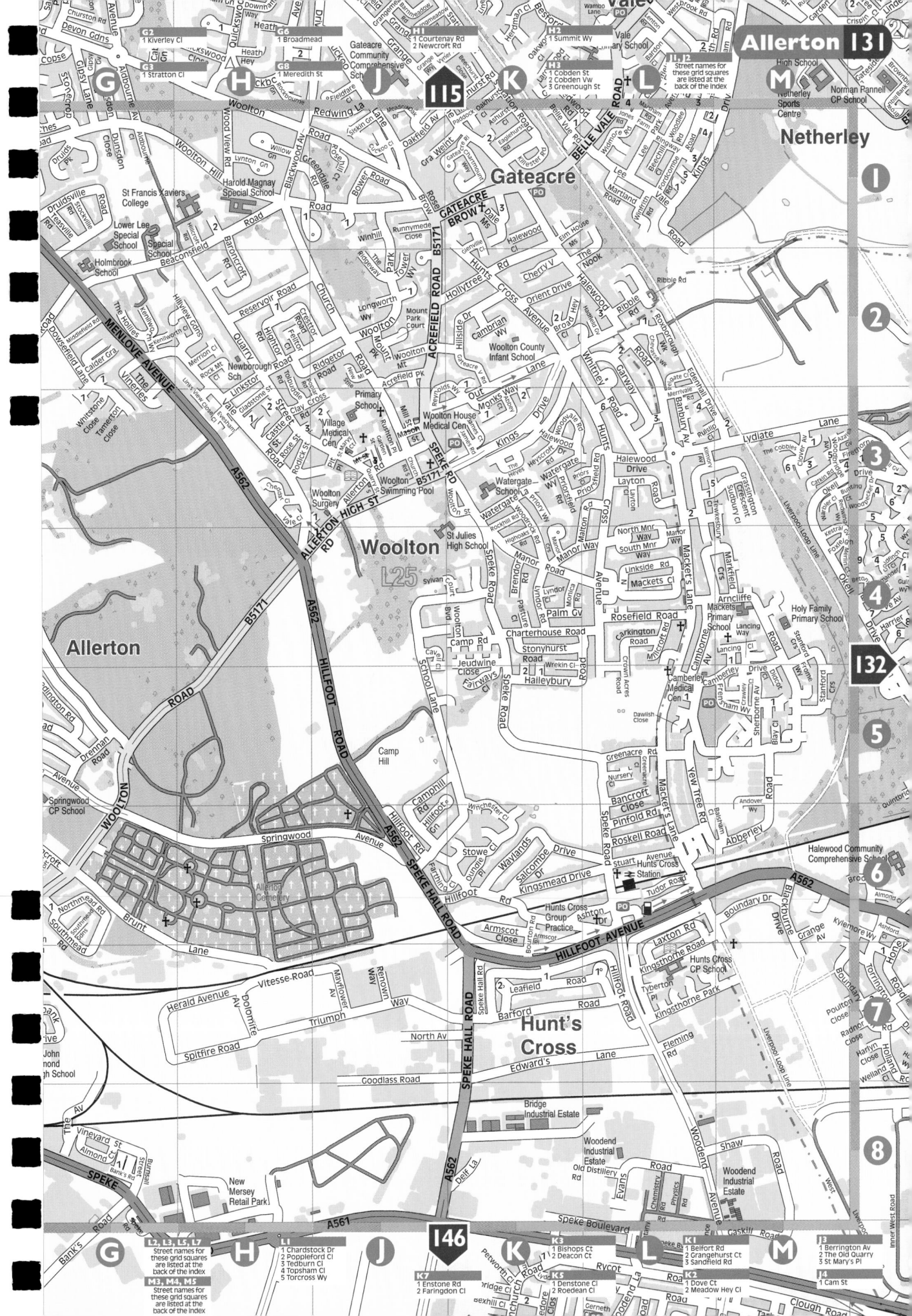

Cronton

G H J K L M

J2
1 Orchard Wy

J5
1 Beaufort Cl
2 Woodview Crs

K1
1 Billington Rd
2 Newsham Cl

K4
1 Acrefield Rd
2 Gainsborough Ct
3 Wilsden Rd

K5
1 Westminster Cl

K8
1 Church Mdw Wk
2 Cock Lane Ends

**117**

A5080

CRONTON RD

Upton

Hough Green

Ditton

SPEKE ROAD

A562

**134**

**148**

G H J K L M

M5
1 Alverton Cl
2 Poulton Dr

M3
1 Brentfield
2 Lingwell Av
3 Moyles Cl
4 Revesby Cl
5 Tate Cl

M2
1 Bloomsbury Wy
2 Shipton Cl
3 Turner Cl
4 Warnley Cl

L5
1 Kenneth Rd
2 Winchester Pl

L2, L3, L4
Street names for
these grid squares
are listed at the
back of the index

M5
1 Alverton Cl
2 Poulton Dr

M1
1 Bowen Cl
2 Chapman Cl

I 2 3 4 5 6 7 8

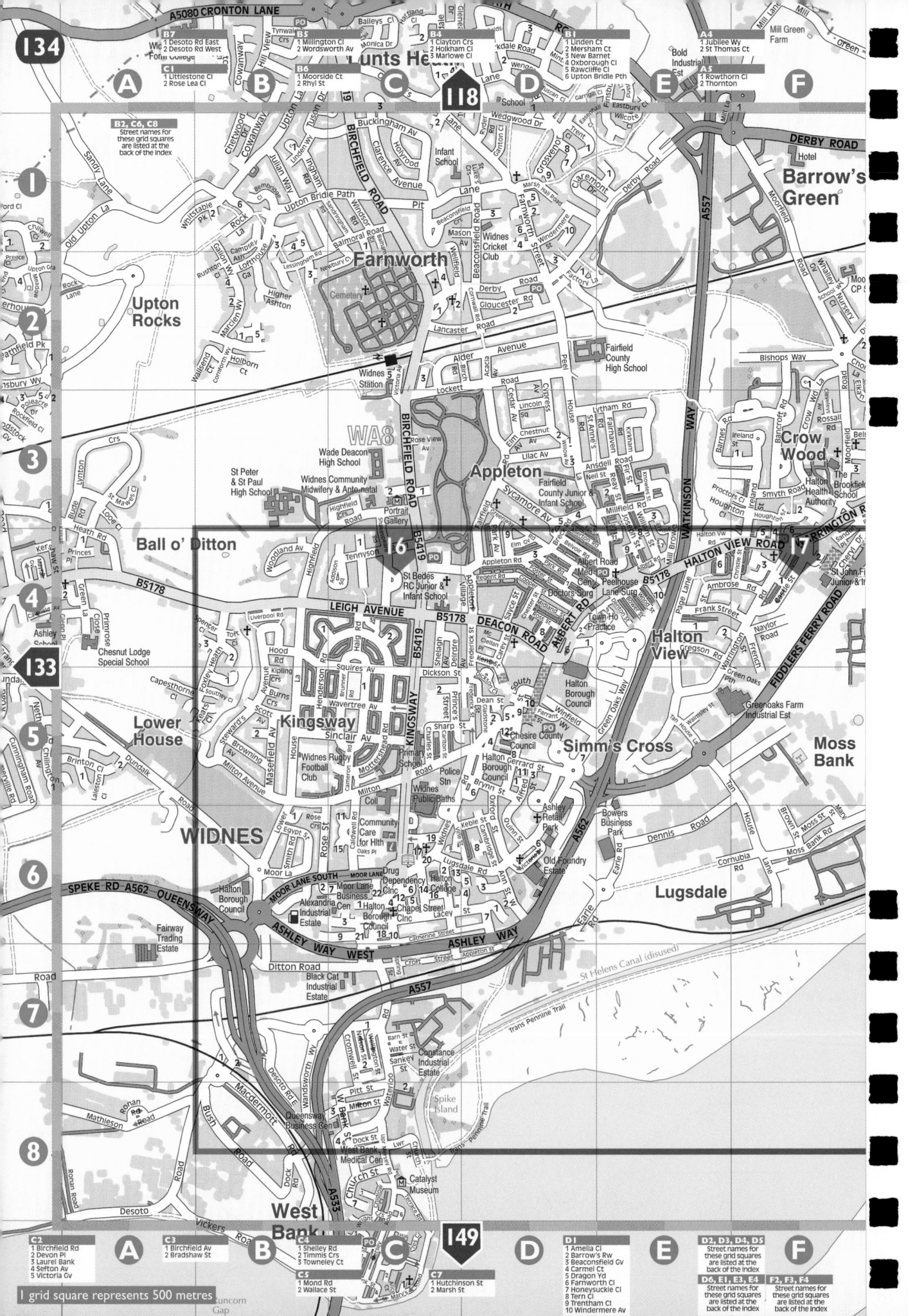

A B C D E F

117

133

1 grid square represents 500 metres

**B7**
1 Desoto Rd East
2 Desoto Rd West

**C1**
1 Littlestone Cl
2 Rose Lea Cl

**B5**
1 Millington Cl
2 Wordsworth Av

**B6**
1 Moorside Ct
2 Rhyl St

**B4**
1 Clayton Crs
2 Holkham Cl
3 Marlowe Cl

**B1**
1 Linden Ct
2 Mersham Ct
3 New Barnet
4 Oxborough Cl
5 Rawcliffe Cl
6 Upton Bridle Pth

**A4**
1 Jubilee Wy
2 St Thomas Ct

**A5**
1 Rowthorn Cl
2 Thornton

**B2, C6, C8**
Street names for
these grid squares
are listed at the
back of the index

**C2**
1 Birchfield Rd
2 Devon Pl
3 Laurel Bank
4 Sefton Av
5 Victoria Gv

**C3**
1 Birchfield Av
2 Bradshaw St

**C4**
1 Shelley Rd
2 Timmis Crs
3 Towneley Ct

**C5**
1 Mond Rd
2 Wallace St

**C7**
1 Hutchinson St
2 Marsh St

**D1**
1 Amelia Cl
2 Barrow's Rw
3 Beaconsfield Av
4 Carmel Ct
5 Dragon Yd
6 Farnworth Cl
7 Honeysuckle Cl
8 Tern Cl
9 Trentham Cl
10 Windermere Av

**D2, D3, D4, D5**
Street names for
these grid squares
are listed at the
back of the index

**D6, E1, E3, E4**
Street names for
these grid squares
are listed at the
back of the index

**F2, F3, F4**
Street names for
these grid squares
are listed at the
back of the index

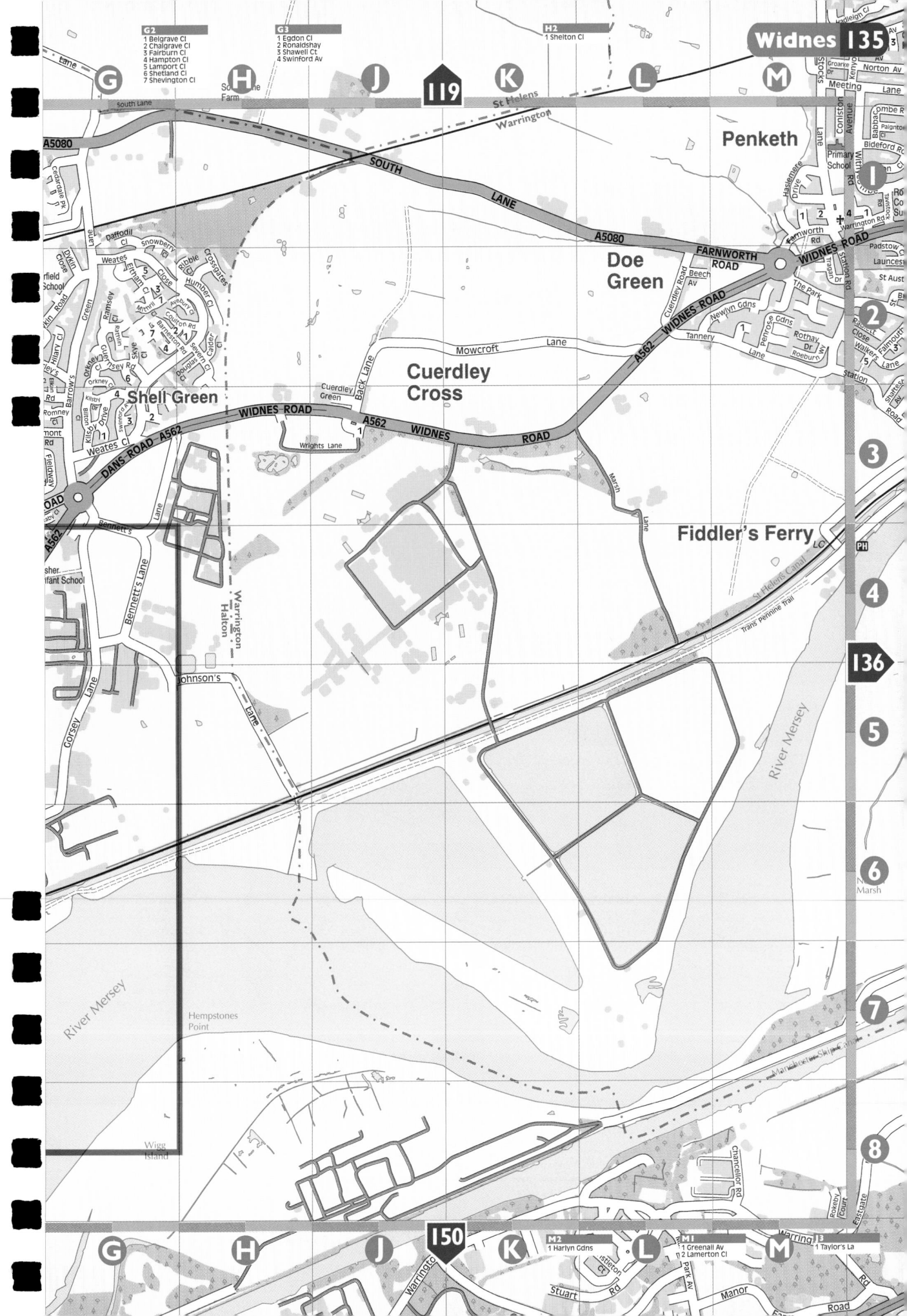

G

**Penketh**

Primary School

H

J

**119**

St Helens

Warrington

South Lane

SOUTH

LANE

A5080

A5080

FARNWORTH ROAD

**Doe Green**

WIDNES ROAD

A562

WIDNES ROAD

Tannery

Newlyn Gdns

Penrose Gdns

Beech Av

Cuerdley Road

Rothay Dr

Roeburn Wy

The Park

Widnes Road

Farnworth Rd

Stocks

Groarke Rd

Kenyon

Norton Av

Coniston Av

Withins Rd

Babbacombe R

Paignton

Bideford Rd

Meeting Lane

Padstow

Launceston

St Aust

Station Rd

Tragan Dr

Shelton Rd

Walker's Lane

Falmouth

Radnott Close

K

L

M

I

2

3

4

**136**

5

6

N Marsh

7

8

Mowcroft

Lane

**Cuerdley Cross**

Cuerdley Green

Back Lane

WIDNES ROAD

A562

WIDNES

ROAD

Wrights Lane

1

Marsh

Lane

**Fiddler's Ferry**

LC

PH

St Helens Canal

Trans Pennine Trail

**Shell Green**

WIDNES ROAD

DANS ROAD A562

Weates

Fieldway

Daffodil Cl

Snowberry

Weates

Eltham Cl

Ribble

Humber Cl

Crossgates

Cedardale Pk

Lane

Green

Ramsey

Avebury Rd

Courton Rd

Severn Cl

Barnoldswick Rd

Ribley

Rartun

Douglas Cl

Orkney

Clwyd

Kilsby

Barrow's

Elton

Romney

Orksey

Kilsby Drive

Swinford Av

Daffodil Cl

Dykin Close

erfield School

Green Road

Fanshawe

fermont Rd

A5080

A562

ROAD

Bennett's

Lane

Bennett's Lane

sher.

fant School

Corsey Lane

Johnson's

Warrington Halton

**River Mersey**

Hempstones Point

Wigg Island

G

H

J

**150**

Warrington

K

Ct

steton

Rd

Stuart Rd

L

Park Av

Manor Road

Warring

3

1 Taylor's La

M

Chancellor Rd

Eastgate

Manchester Ship Canal

**River Mersey**

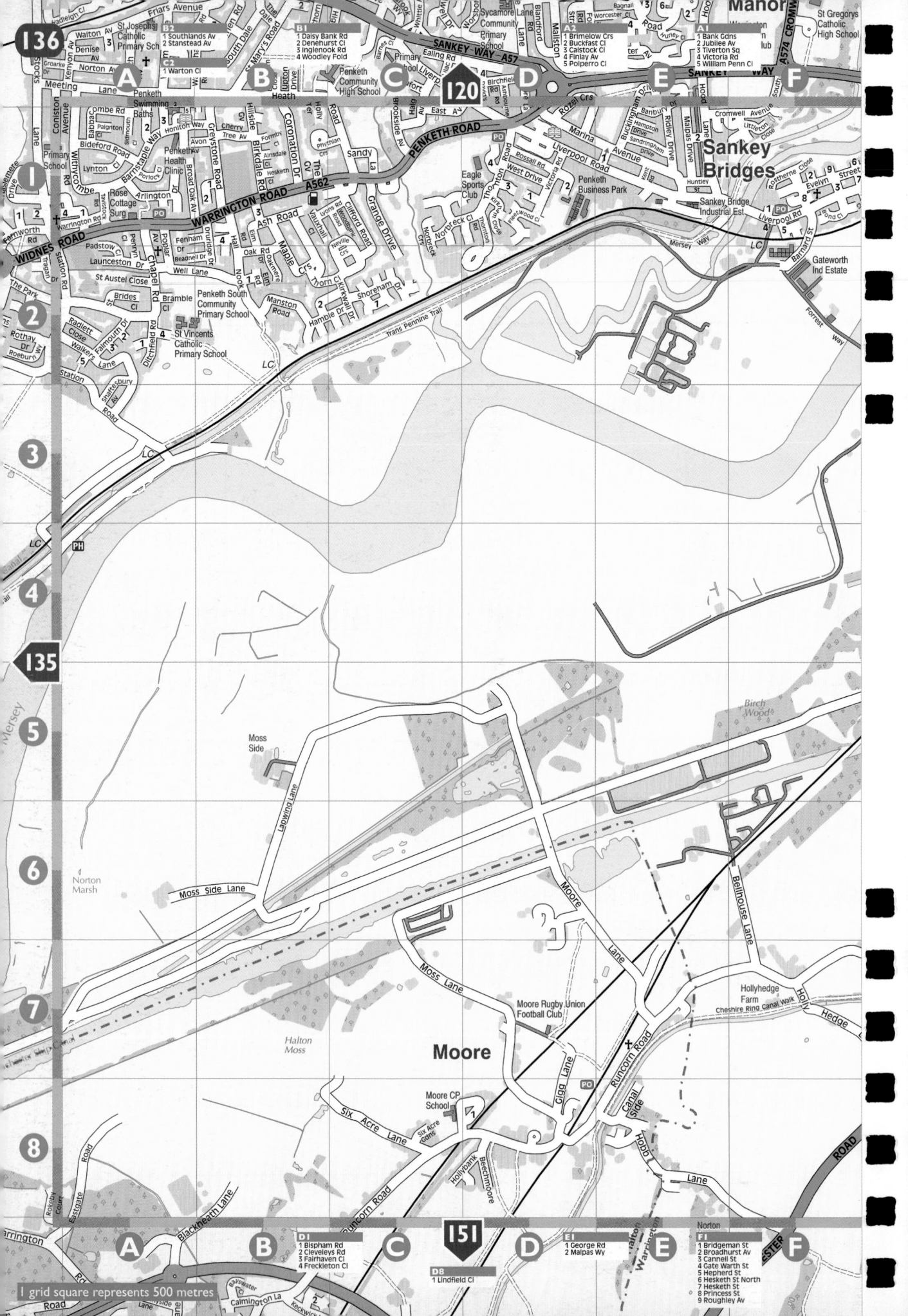

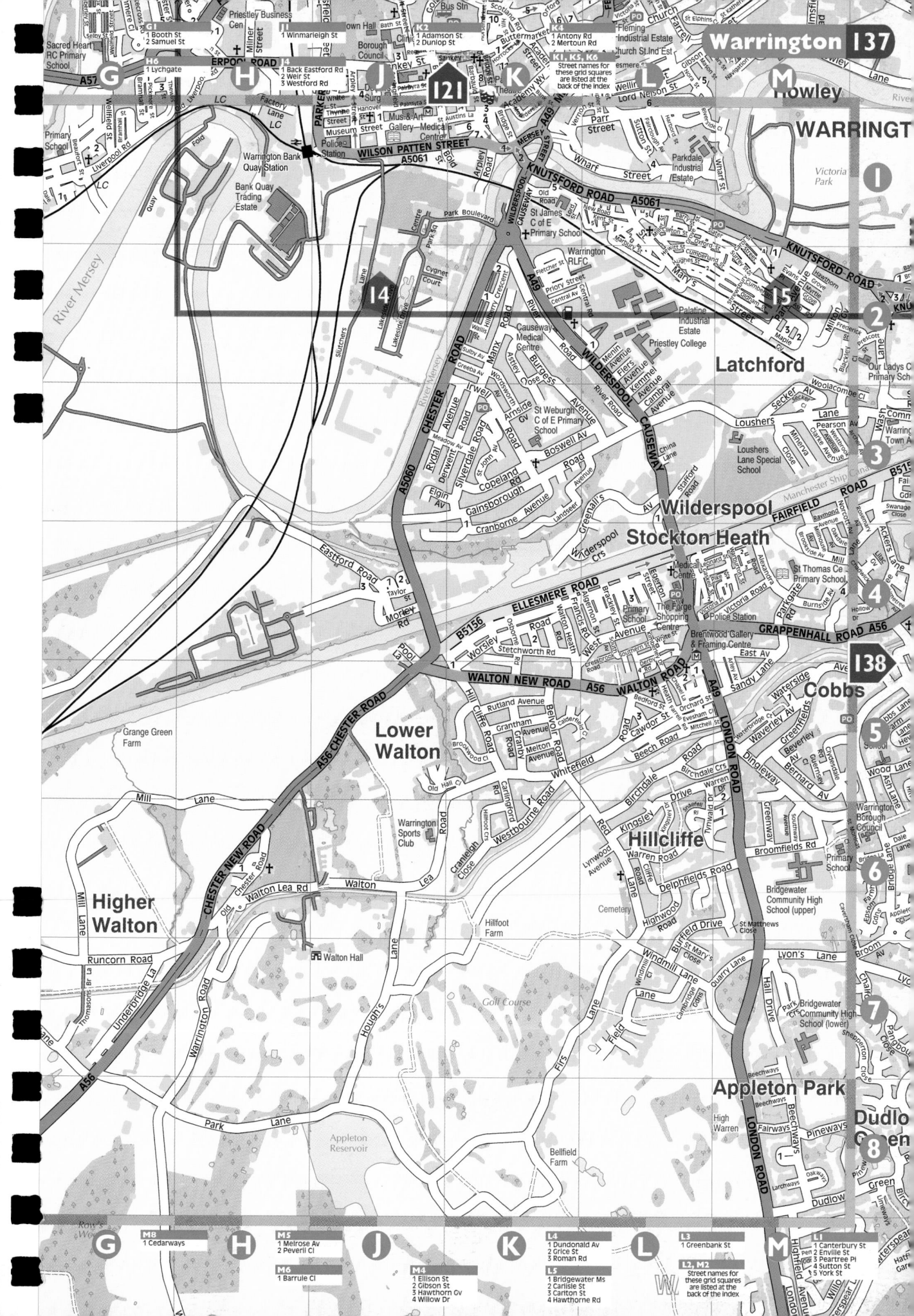

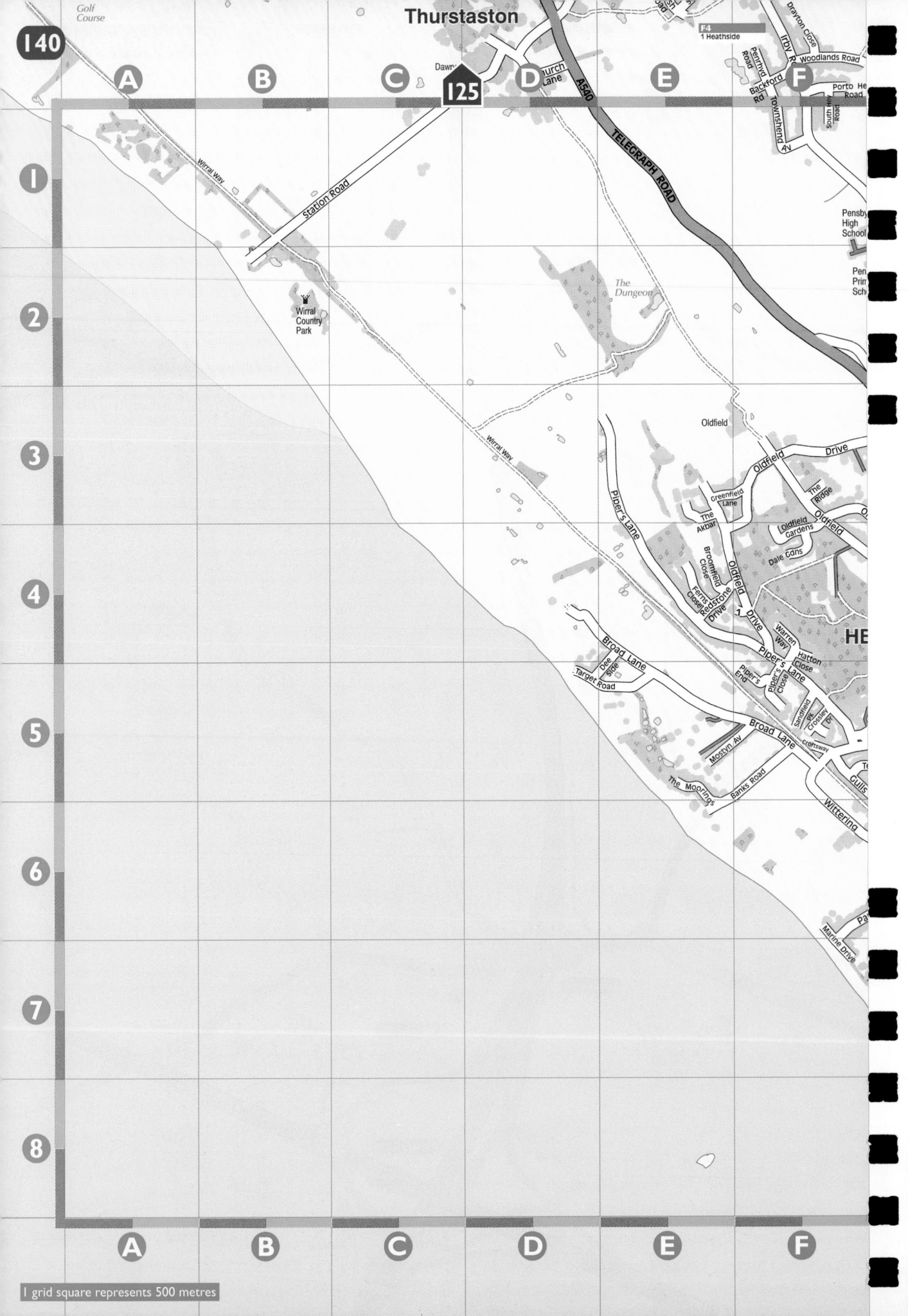

Golf
Course

Thurstaston

F4
1 Heathside

Irby Rd

Woodlands Road

A      B      C      125      D      Church Lane      E      F      Porto He
Road

Drayton close

Penthyd Road

Backford Rd

Townshend Av

South Hey Road

Pensby High School

Pen Prim Sch

Wirral Way

Station Road

1

Wirral Country Park

2

The Dungeon

Oldfield

Wirral Way

3

Piper's Lane

Oldfield Drive

The Ridge

Greenfield Lane

The Akbar

Oldfield Gardens

Oldfield

Dale Gdns

Broomfield Close

Oldfield Drive

4

Farms Close

Redstone Drive

Warren Way

Hatton Close

HE

Broad Lane

Dee Side

Piper's Lane

Piper's End

Piper's Close

Target Road

Sandfield

Crossley Dr

5

Mostyn Av

Broad Lane

Croftsway

Culls

The Moorings

Banks Road

Wittering

6

7

Marine Drive

Pa

8

A      B      C      D      E      F

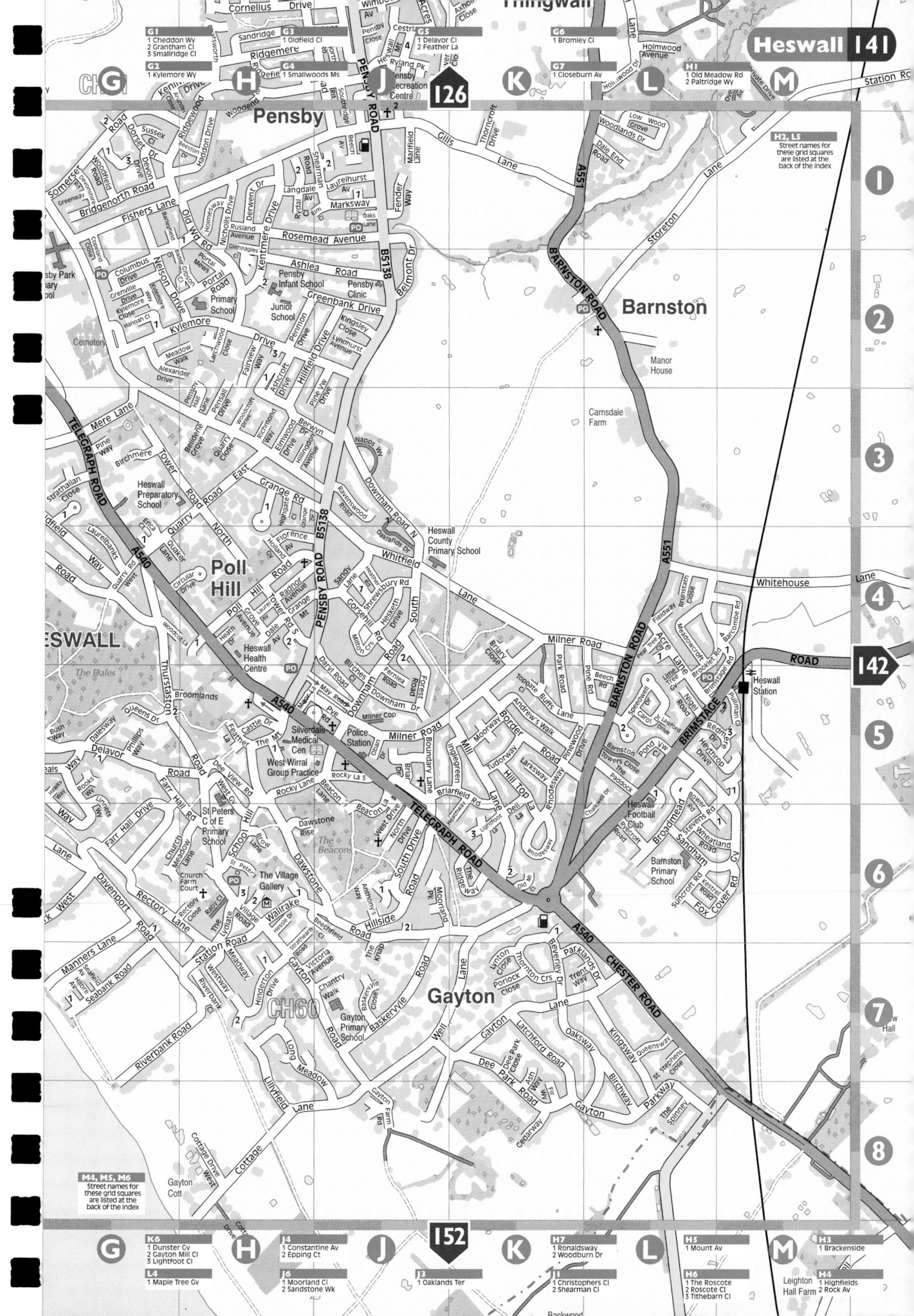

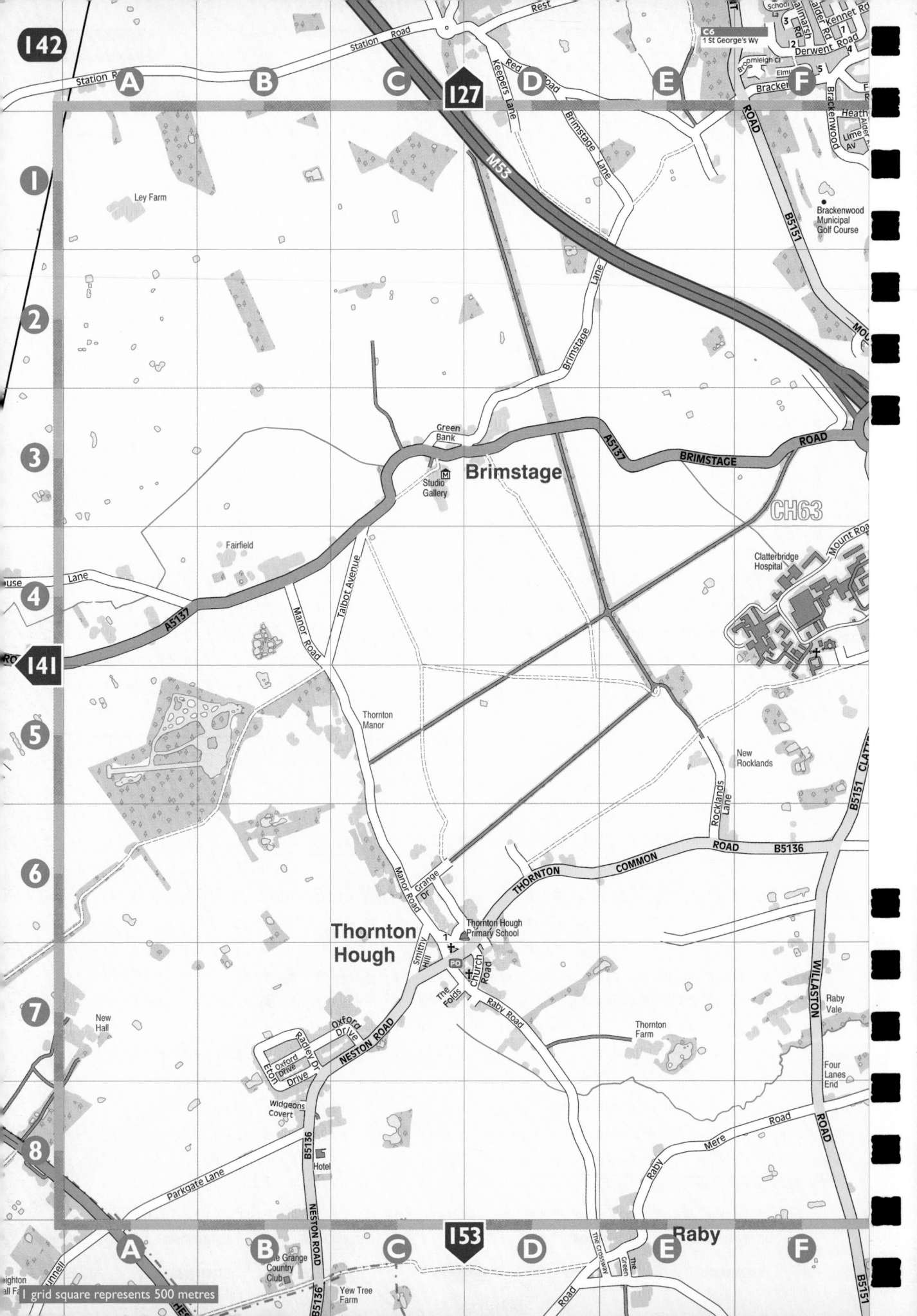

127

141

153

**Brimstage**

**Thornton Hough**

**Raby**

Ley Farm

Green Bank

Studio Gallery

Fairfield

Thornton Manor

Clatterbridge Hospital

New Rocklands

Thornton Hough Primary School

Thornton Farm

New Hall

Raby Vale

Four Lanes End

The Folds

Widgeons Covert

Hotel

Yew Tree Farm

The Grange Country Club

The Green

Brackenwood Municipal Golf Course

CH63

C6
1 St George's Wy

Station Rd

Station Road

Rest

Red Keepers Lane

Red Road

Brimstage Lane

Brimstage Lane

M53

A5137

BRIMSTAGE ROAD

A5137

Lane

Manor Road

Talbot Avenue

Manor Road

Grange Dr

THORNTON COMMON ROAD B5136

Rocklands Lane

B5151 CLATT

Mount Road

MOU

B5151

Brackenwood Av

Heath

Lime Av

Smithy Hill

Church Road

PO

Raby Road

Oxford Drive

Radley Dr

NESTON ROAD

Eton Drive

B5136

NESTON ROAD B5136

Parkgate Lane

Mere Road

Raby Road

Raby Road

WILLASTON

School Jammarsh Rd
Calder Rd Kennet Rd
Derwent Road
Broomleigh Cl Elmr
Bracke

A

B

C

D

E

F

1

2

3

4

5

6

7

8

A

B

C

D

E

F

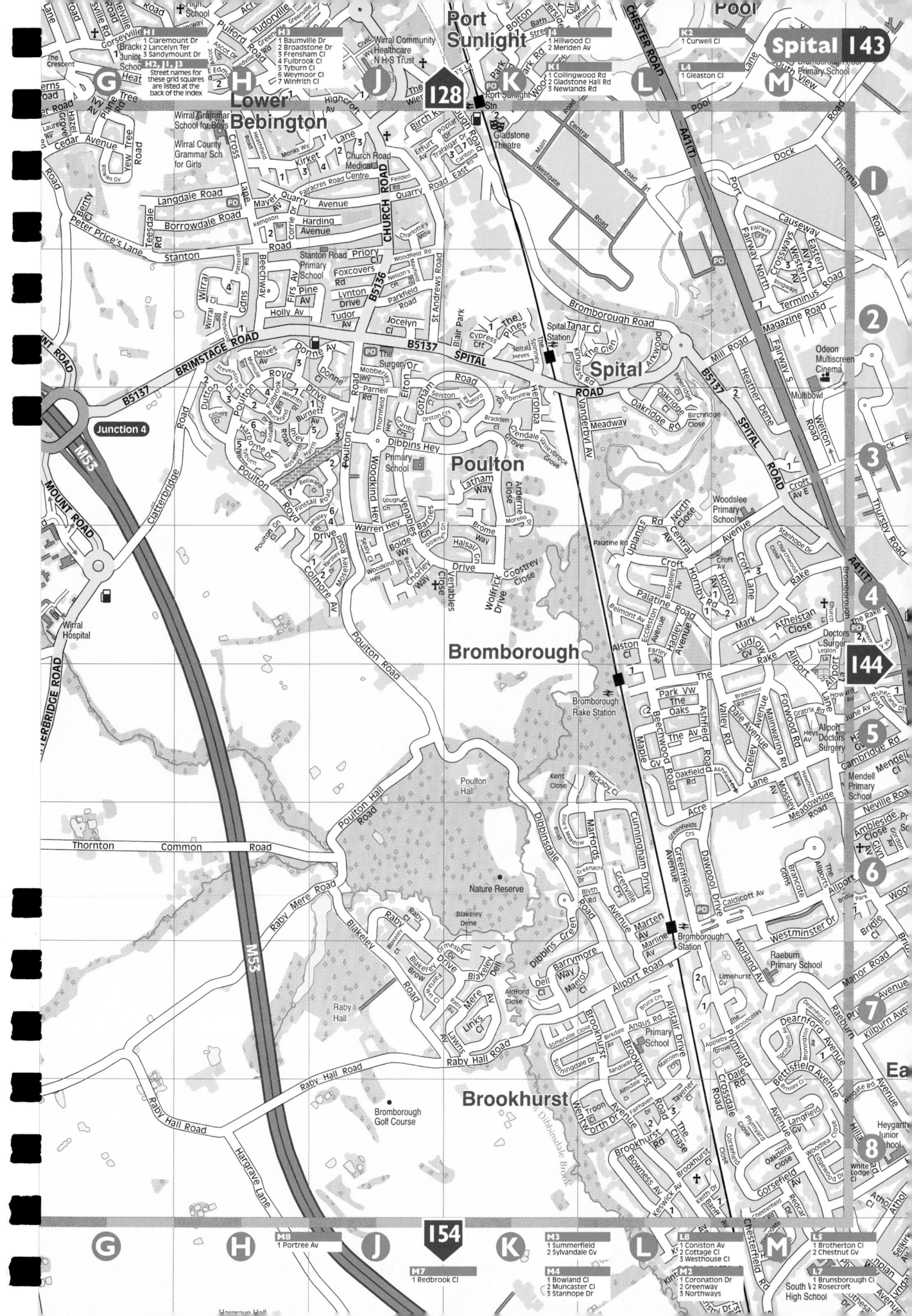

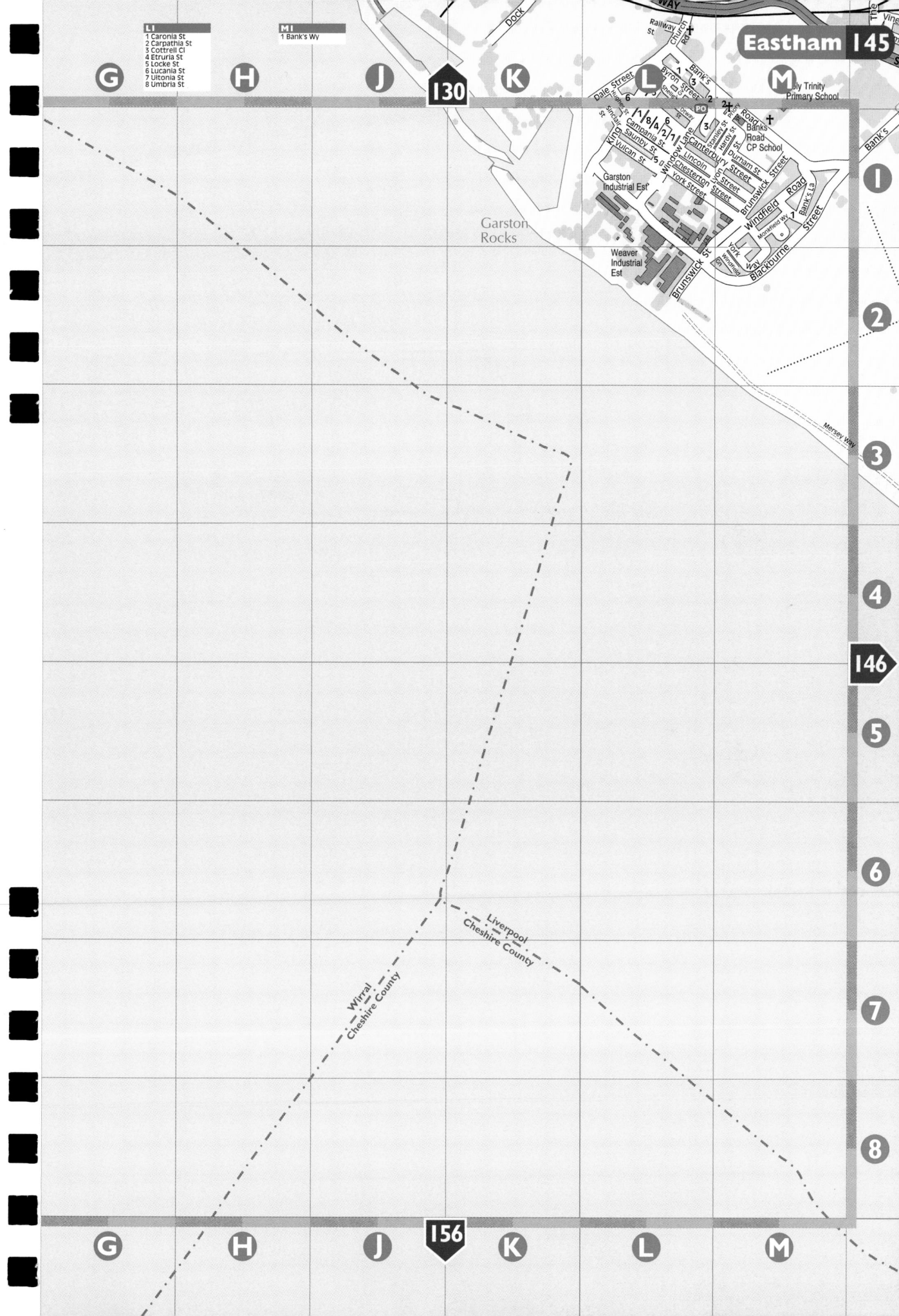

L1
1 Caronia St
2 Carpathia St
3 Cottrell Cl
4 Etruria St
5 Locke St
6 Lucania St
7 Ultonia St
8 Umbria St

M1
1 Bank's Wy

G    H    J    **130**    K    L    M

I

2

3

4

**146**

5

6

7

8

Garston
Rocks

Garston
Industrial Est

Weaver
Industrial
Est

Brunswick St.

York
Street

Railway
St.

Church
Rd

Bank's
Road

Dale Street

Byron Street

Holy Trinity
Primary School

Banks
Road
CP School

Windfield    Road

Windfield Way

Bank's La

Blackburne Street

Brunswick Street

Durham Street

Canterbury Street

Lincoln
Street

Chesterton
Street

York Street

Campania St

Gt. Saunby St

Kr. Vulcan St

Mersey Way

PO

Liverpool
Cheshire County

Wirral
Cheshire County

G    H    J    **156**    K    L    M

**A** **B** **C** **D** **E** **F**

I
2
3
4
5
6
7
8

131

145

157

**F2**
1 Fenton Cl
2 Harefield Gn
3 Wellbrook Gn
4 Welton Cl
5 Welton Gn

**F1**
1 Wellbrook Cl

**E1**
1 Ramsbrook Cl

**D1**
1 Bognor Cl
2 Lenham Wy
3 Sudbury Wy

**F3**
1 Fenton Gn
2 Marton Cl
3 Marton Gn

Holy Trinity Primary School

SPEKE Road

Bank's Road

ROAD

A561

Speke Boulevard

Liverpool Airport

Mersey Way

Bank's Lane

Spindus Road

Speke Hall (NT)

Speke Hall Avenue

The Walk

Blenheim Wy

Owen Dr

Dunlop Road

Liverpool Airport

Mersey Way

River Mersey

Vineyard St

Almond

Street

Petworth Rd

Tonbridge Cl

Bexhill Cl

Sandgate Cl

Speke Hall Av

Barnham Dr

Dymchurch Rd

Lydd Cl

Appledore

Speke Town La

Rycot

Bray

Woodend La

Road

School Wy

Gerneth Cl

Speke Church Rd

Greyhound Cl

Ramsbrook

Blackrock

Stockton Wd Rd

Stockton Wood JMI School

All Saints

Hale Road

Oglet Lane

Dam Wood Road

Clough Road

Tarbock Road

St Christophers Infant School

St Christophers Junior Sch

Blackcat Hall Road

Goldfinch Farm Road

Western Avenue

Linner Road

Stapleton Avenue

Speke Comprehensive School

Harefield Road

Lovel Wy

Central Avenue

Lovel Road

Speke Community Comprehensive School

Sutton Wood Rd

Tewit Hall Rd

Tewit Hall

Delf La

Evans Road

Botany Rd

Science Rd

Physics Rd

Speke Blvd

Gaskill Road

Woodend Industrial Estate

Estate Old Distillery Rd

West

L24

O

G1
1 Eastham Gn
2 Northern Rd
3 Penketh Gn

G2
1 Prenton Gn
2 Upton Cl
3 Upton Gn

G3
1 Bramhall Cl
2 Ganworth Cl
3 Southern Rd

G

H

J

132

K

L

M

1

2

3

148

4

5

6

7

8

Burn
Mill

Carr Lane

Higher Road

Lane

Inner West Road

Liverpool Loop Line

A561

SPEKE BOULEVARD

South Road

East Road

Middle Rd

Central Road

Inner S Road

Middle Road

Clough Road

Millwood Road Doctors Surgery

Millwood Road

East

Millwood Road

Ramsfield

Maintree Crs

West Mains

Cassley Rd

Oak Vw

Sandiath Rd

Leveret Rd

Miners W

The Margaret Thompson Medical Cen

Speke

Conleach Road

3 2 1

Millwood Road

Heaton Close

Harland Gn

Elloway Rd

Croxde Rd

Mains Rd

Dr

Austin Rawlinson Sports Cen

Alder

Wood

Avenue

Greenway Rd

Ganworth Road

Alderwood CP School

Oldbridge Rd

Ardwick Rd

Withington Rd

Catford Gn

Police Station

North Parade

Speke Family Health Clinic

Hlth Authority

South Parade

PO

Central

Way

School

St Ambrose Primary School

Alderfield

Critchley Rd

Wood Rd

Alderfield

Little Heath

Burnage Cl

McIlwain

Eastern

Dam

Heathgate Av

Churchway Rd

Dam Wood Road

Hale Road

Hale Drive

Eastern

East

Dam

Liverpool

Halton

Ramsbrook Lane

Brook Farm

Hale

Morcott Lane

Carlow Cl

Arklow

Wexford

Langford

Langford

Pheasant

Aran Cl

High

Street

Drive

Malin Cl

Ennis

Holly Cl

Pepper St

Trevor La

Hale Primary School

PO

Curlender W

Ivy Farm Court Doctors Surg

School

Ireland Road

Erinwood Cl

Hale Police Station

Dungeon Lane

Lane

Bailey's

Mersey Way

Mersey Way

Church End

Church Road

Lighthouse

glet

Oglet Lane

Mersey Way

Mersey Way

Liverpool
Cheshire County

Halton
Cheshire County

G

H

J

158

K

L

M

M3
1 Bandon Cl
2 Greenore Dr

J3
1 Almeda Rd
2 Daneswell Rd

J2
1 Harland Gn
2 Ringsfield Rd

J1
1 Huttfield Rd
2 Millway Rd

A B C 133 D E F

1

Burn Mill

Carr Lane

I

Hale Bank

Mersey View Road

2

Carr Lane

Hale Gate Road

Potters La

Halebank C of E Controlled Primary School

Baguley Ave

Heathview Rd

Kenview Cl

Blackburne Avenue

Gate Crescent

Fou

Pickering Road

F6 1 Cullen Rd

A3 1 Assheton Wk 2 Wellington Ga

dry La

Garnetts Lane

Pickerings Pasture

Trans Pennine Trail

River Mersey

3

ale

Lane Police Station

Errwood Cl

Curlender Wy

Western Road

Town Lane

Hoghton Rd

Ernie

Holly Cl

Pepper St La

Ivy Farm Court Doctors Surg

School

Ireland Road

Halegate Farm

Trans Pennine Trail

4

PO

Church End

Vicarage Close

Within Way

147

Church Road

Weston Point

Mersey Vw S Rd

PO

Post Office La

5

Lighthouse Road

Mersey Way

Sandy Lane

West Road

Baker Road

South Parade

6

Hale Head

Leonard St

Sydney St

Picow Farm Rd

7

Halton Cheshire County

8

A B C 159 D E F

1 grid square represents 500 metres

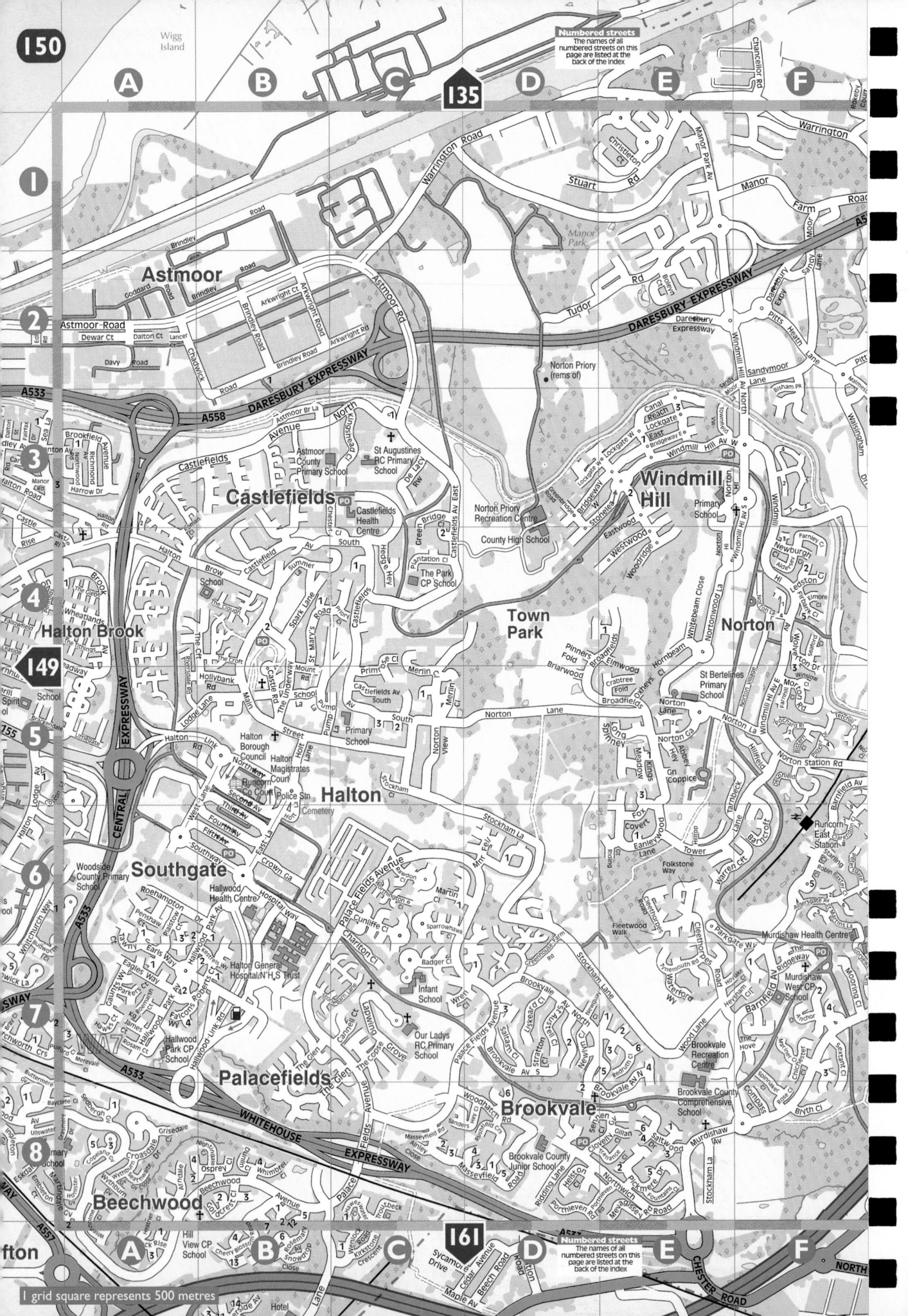

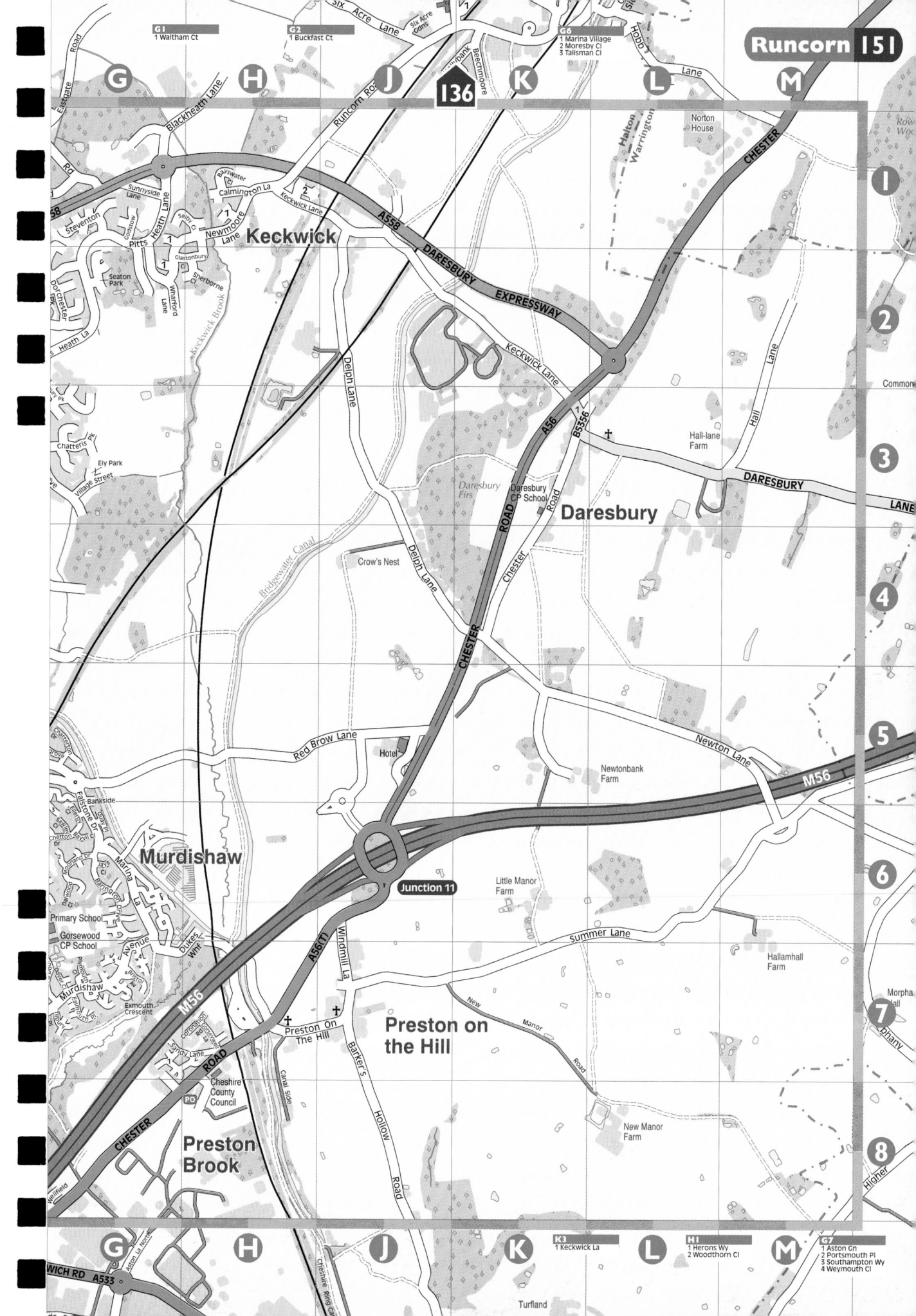

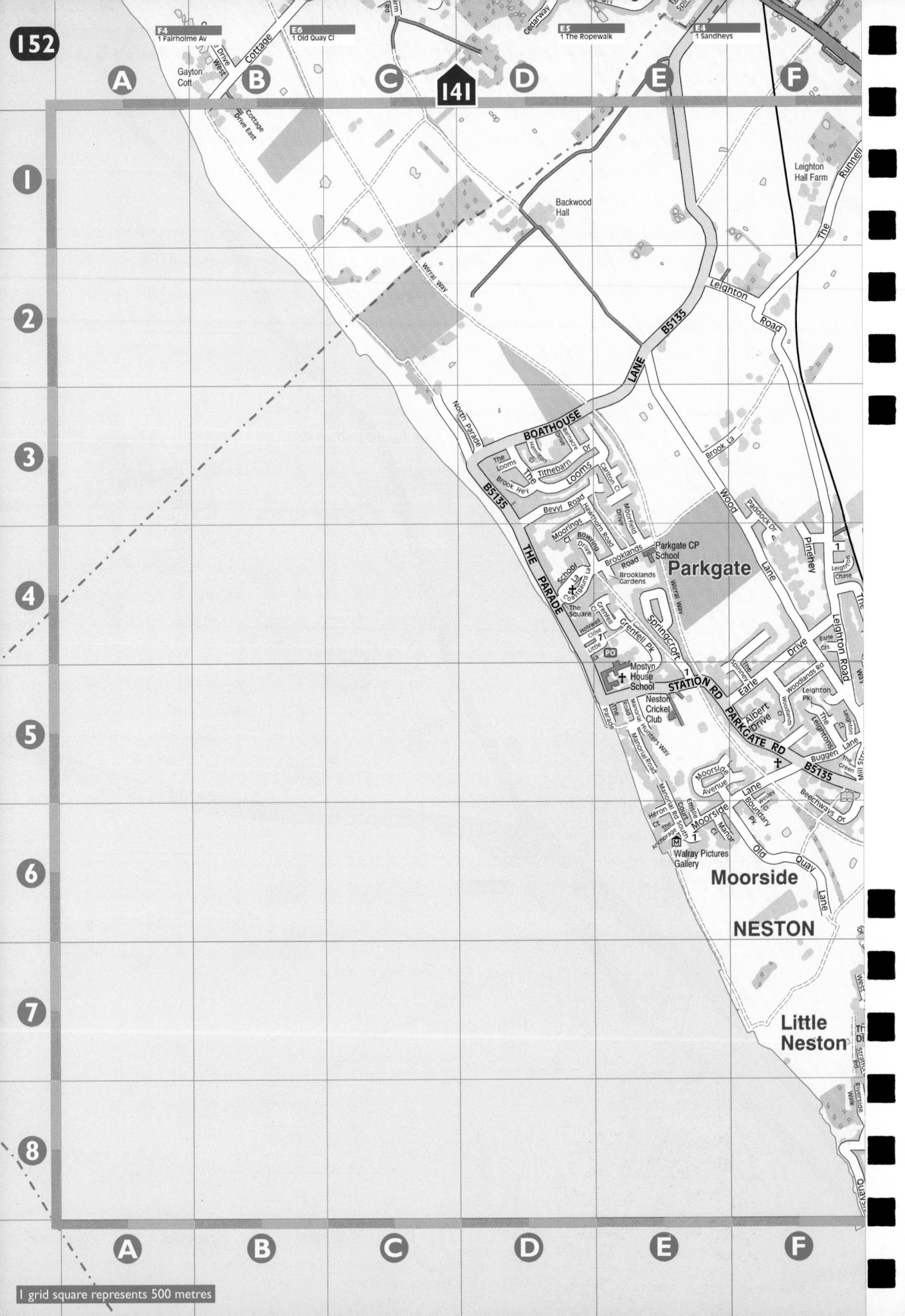

141

A B C D E F

1

2

3

4

5

6

7

8

F4
1 Fairholme Av

E6
1 Old Quay Cl

E5
1 The Ropewalk

E4
1 Sandheys

Leighton Hall Farm

The Runnell

Gayton Cott

Cottage Drive West

Cottage Drive East

Wirral Way

Backwood Hall

Leighton Road

B5135

LANE

BOATHOUSE

North Parade

The Looms

Brook Hey

Hamilton Drive

Birchacre Dr

Tithebarn

The Looms

Carlton Cl

Moorfield Drive

Brook La

Wood

Paddock Dr

Pinehey

B5135

THE PARADE

Bevyl Road

Hawthorn Road

Moorings Cl

Bowling

School

Brooklands Road

Crenfell PK

Castleyard La

Parkgate CP School

Brooklands Gardens

Wirral Way

Parkgate

Leighton Chase

1 Leighton Chase

Leighton Road

The Square

Holywell

Little Close

PO

Crenfell Cl

Springcroft

Earle Cirs

The Way

Mostyn House School

STATION RD

Earle

Albert Drive

PARKGATE RD

Woodlands Rd

Woodlands

Leighton Pk

The Leighton

The Green

Buggen Lane

B5135

Mill Street

Neston Cricket Club

The Parade

Memorial Road

Bunkers Way

Moorside Avenue

Emilie Court

Moorside

Manor Lane

Wesley Cl

Boundary Pk

Beechways Dr

Heron Ct

The Anchorage

1

M

Old Quay Lane

Walray Pictures Gallery

Moorside

NESTON

Little Neston

West

The Dr

Stratton Rd

Riverside Walk

Quay

1 grid square represents 500 metres

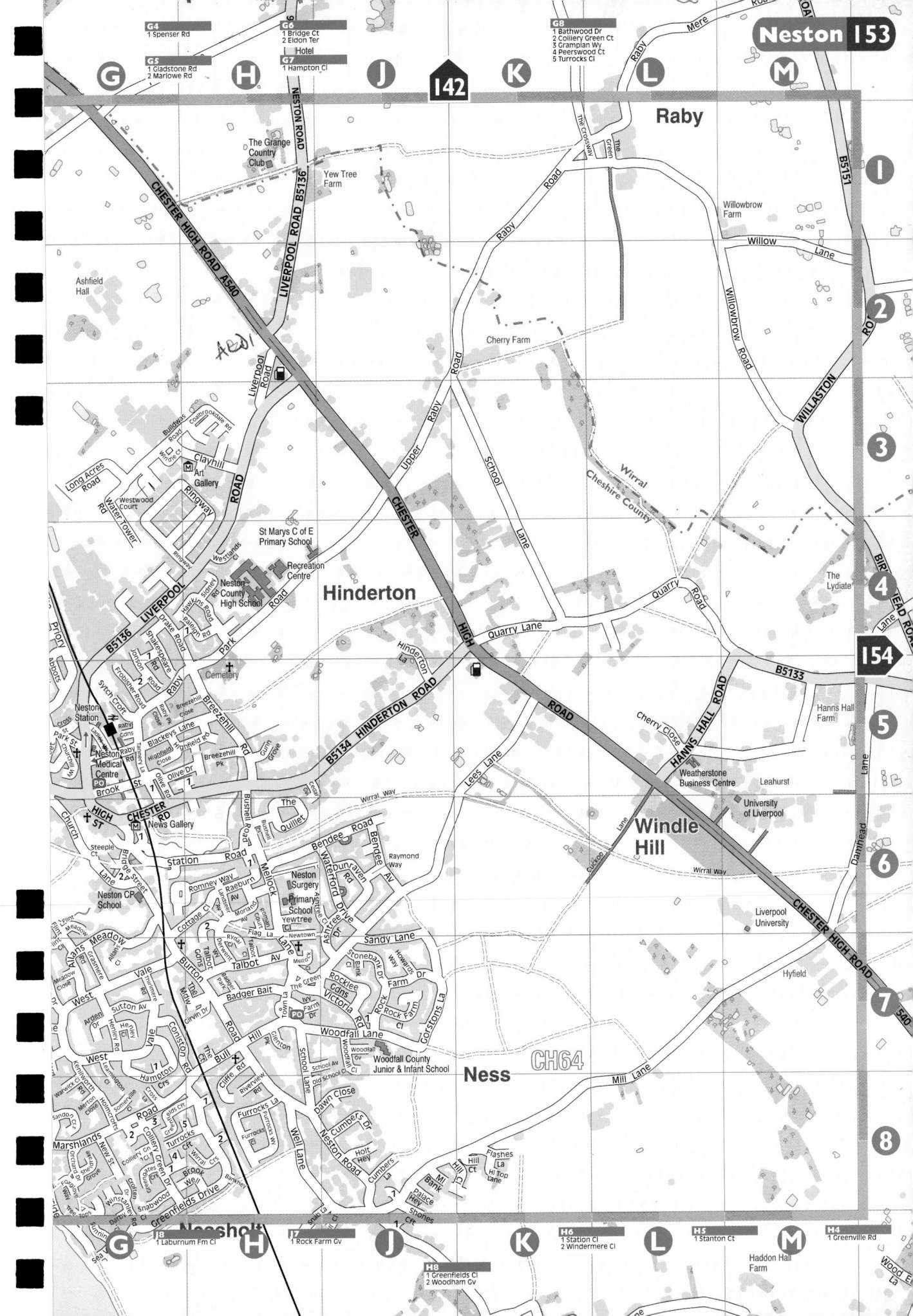

G4
1 Spenser Rd

G6
1 Bridge Ct
2 Eldon Ter

G7
1 Hampton Cl

G5
1 Gladstone Rd
2 Marlowe Rd

G8
1 Bathwood Dr
2 Colliery Green Ct
3 Grampian Wy
4 Peerswood Cl
5 Turrocks Cl

**G** **H** **J** **142** **K** **L** **M**

**I**

Raby

The Grange
Country
Club

Yew Tree
Farm

The Crossway

The Green

Willowbrow
Farm

Willow Lane

**2**

Ashfield
Hall

Cherry Farm

Willowbrow Road

WILLASTON ROAD

CHESTER HIGH ROAD A540

LIVERPOOL ROAD B5136

**3**

Raby Road

Long Acres
Road

Bullwargs
Road

Coalbrookdale Rd

Clayhill
Art
Gallery

Wirral

Cheshire County

Westwood
Court

Water Tower
Rd

Ringway

Ringway

St Marys C of E
Primary School

Recreation
Centre

School Lane

Upper Raby Road

The
Lydiate

**4**

BIRKENHEAD ROAD

Liverpool Road

Neston
County
High School

**Hinderton**

Quarry Road

B5133

**154**

LIVERPOOL B5136

ROAD

Westlands

Hawkins Road

Sydney Rd

Park Road

Shakespeare Rd

Cemetery

Hinderton La

HIGH

Quarry Lane

Quarry Lane

Hanns Hall
Farm

**5**

Neston
Station

Neston
Medical
Centre

PO

Priory

Cross St

Park St

Churchill

Syrch Croft

Frobisher Road

Jonson Rd

Raby Rd

Raby
Gdns

Drake Road

Blackeys Lane

Breezehill
Close

Highfield
Close

Olive Dr

Olive Dr

Breezehill Rd

Enfield Rd

Breezehill
Pk

Gum Grove

Cherry Close

CHESTER ROAD

Lees Lane

HANNS HALL ROAD

Weatherstone
Business Centre

Leahurst

**6**

Brook St

HIGH
ST

CHESTER
RD

M

News Gallery

Steeple
Ct

Bridge Street

Station Road

Bushel Road

Bushell Rd

The
Quillet

Wirral Way

Cuckoo Lane

University
of Liverpool

**Windle
Hill**

Wirral Way

Church

Neston CP
School

Romney Way

Raeburn
Av

Melock

Bendee Road

Bendee Av

Raymond
Way

Liverpool
University

Hyfield

CHESTER HIGH ROAD

**7**

Adlans
Meadow

Meadow
Close

WEST

Arden
Dr

WEST

Cottage Cl

Talbot
Gdns

Ashtree
Dr

Ashtree
Dr

Howards Dr

Neston
Surgery

Primary
School

Yewtree

Newtown

Morland
Rd

Talbot
Av

Flag La

Stonebank Dr

Sandy Lane

Rockfee
Farm

Way

Sutton Av

VALE

Burton
Road

Badger Bait

The
Green

Ivy
Farm
Dr

Rockiee
Gdns

Victoria
Rd

Rock
Farm

Corstons La

**Ness**

CH64

**8**

Conston Rd

HAMPTON

Warwick Rd

Merton Cl

Somerville

Riverview
Rd

Cliffe Rd

School Road

Hill

Woodfall Lane

Dawn Close

Cumbers Dr

Woodfall
Lane

School Av

Old School Cl

Woodfall County
Junior & Infant School

Mill Lane

Marshlands

New St

Colliery Green Dr

Colliery Gn

Turrocks
Cft

Furrocks La

Furrocks Cl

Furrocks Wy

Well
Lane

Wirral Crs

Holt
Hey

Cumbers
La

Flashes
La

Hl Top
Lane

Palace Hey

Shones
Ct

**Nesholt**

**G** J8
1 Laburnum Fm Cl

**H** J7
1 Rock Farm Gv

**J** H8
1 Greenfields Cl
2 Woodham Gv

**K** H6
1 Station Cl
2 Windermere Cl

**L** H5
1 Stanton Ct

**M** H4
1 Greenville Rd

Haddon Hall
Farm

Greenfields Drive

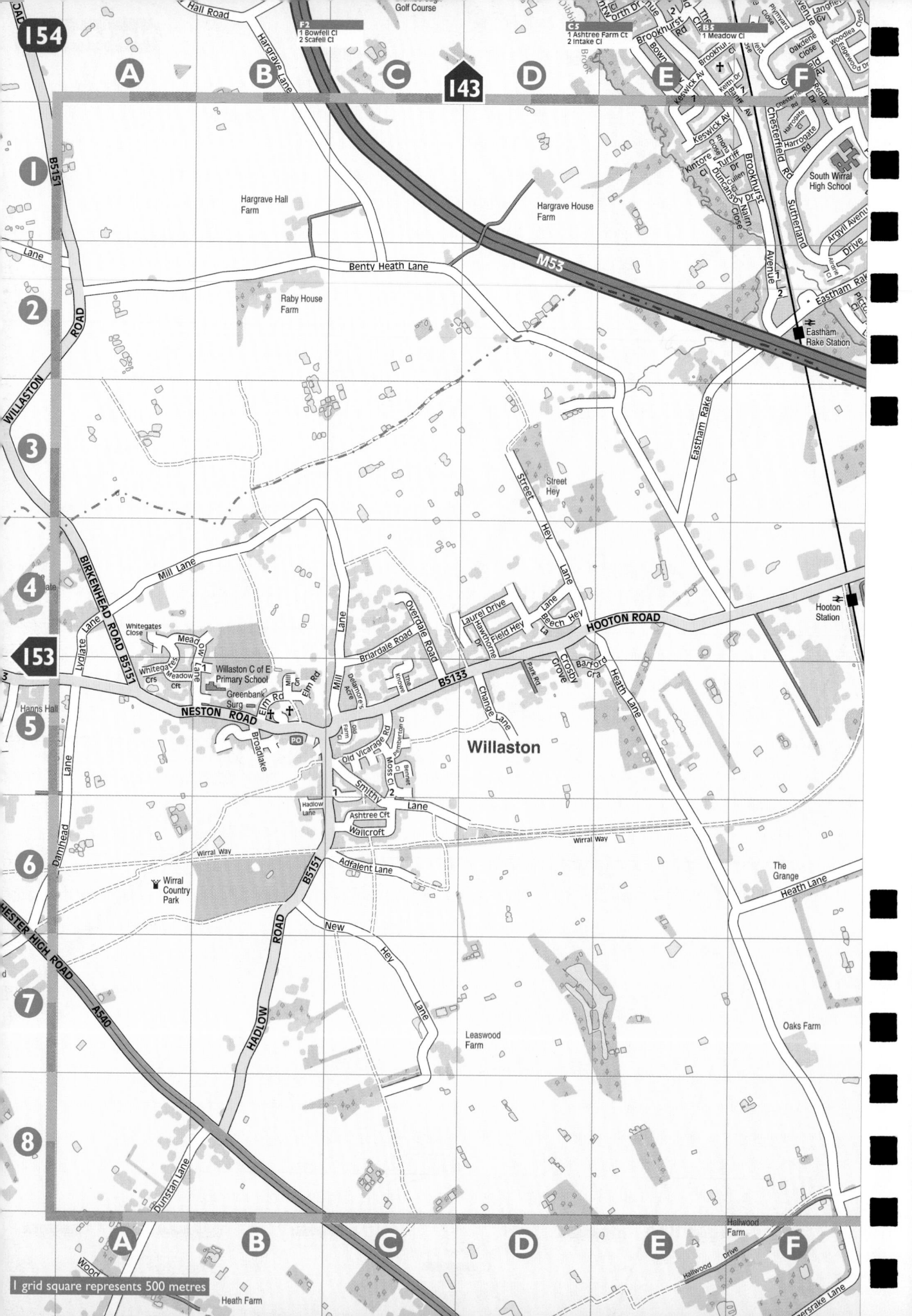

A    B    C    143    D    E    F

Hall Road

Hargrave Lane

Golf Course

F2
1 Bowfell Cl
2 Scafell Cl

C5
1 Ashtree Farm Ct
2 Intake Cl

B5
1 Meadow Cl

Brookhurst

Keswick Av

Kintore Cl

Duncansby Dr

South Wirral
High School

Argyll Avenue

Chesterfield Rd

Sutherland

Hargrave Hall
Farm

Hargrave House
Farm

Benty Heath Lane

M53

Eastham
Rake Station

Raby House
Farm

Willaston
Road

B5151

Birkenhead Road B5151

Lydiate Lane

Mill Lane

Whitegates
Close

Meadow Lane

Whitegates
Crs

Meadow
Cft

Willaston C of E
Primary School

Greenbank
Surg

Neston Road

Elm Rd

Broadlake

PO

Hadlow
Lane

Hanns Hall
Lane

Dunnhead

Lane

Wirral
Country
Park

Wirral Way

B5151

Neston Road

Adfalent Lane

New

Hey

Lane

Hadlow

Road

Chester High Road

A540

Dunstan Lane

Wood

Heath Farm

Overdale Road

Briardale Road

Mill Lane

Delamere's
Acre

Mill
Grn

Old Vicarage Rd

Moss Cl

Pemberton Cl

Bennett

Smithy

Lane

Ashtree Cft

Wallcroft

Street Hey

Street
Hey

Lane

Laurel Drive

Hawthorne

Field Hey

Lane

Beech Hey

Crosby
Grove

Hooton Road

B5133

Change Lane

Willaston

Park Rd

Barford
Gra

Heath Lane

Eastham Rake

Hooton
Station

Wirral Way

The
Grange

Heath Lane

Oaks Farm

Leaswood
Farm

Hallwood
Farm

I grid square represents 500 metres

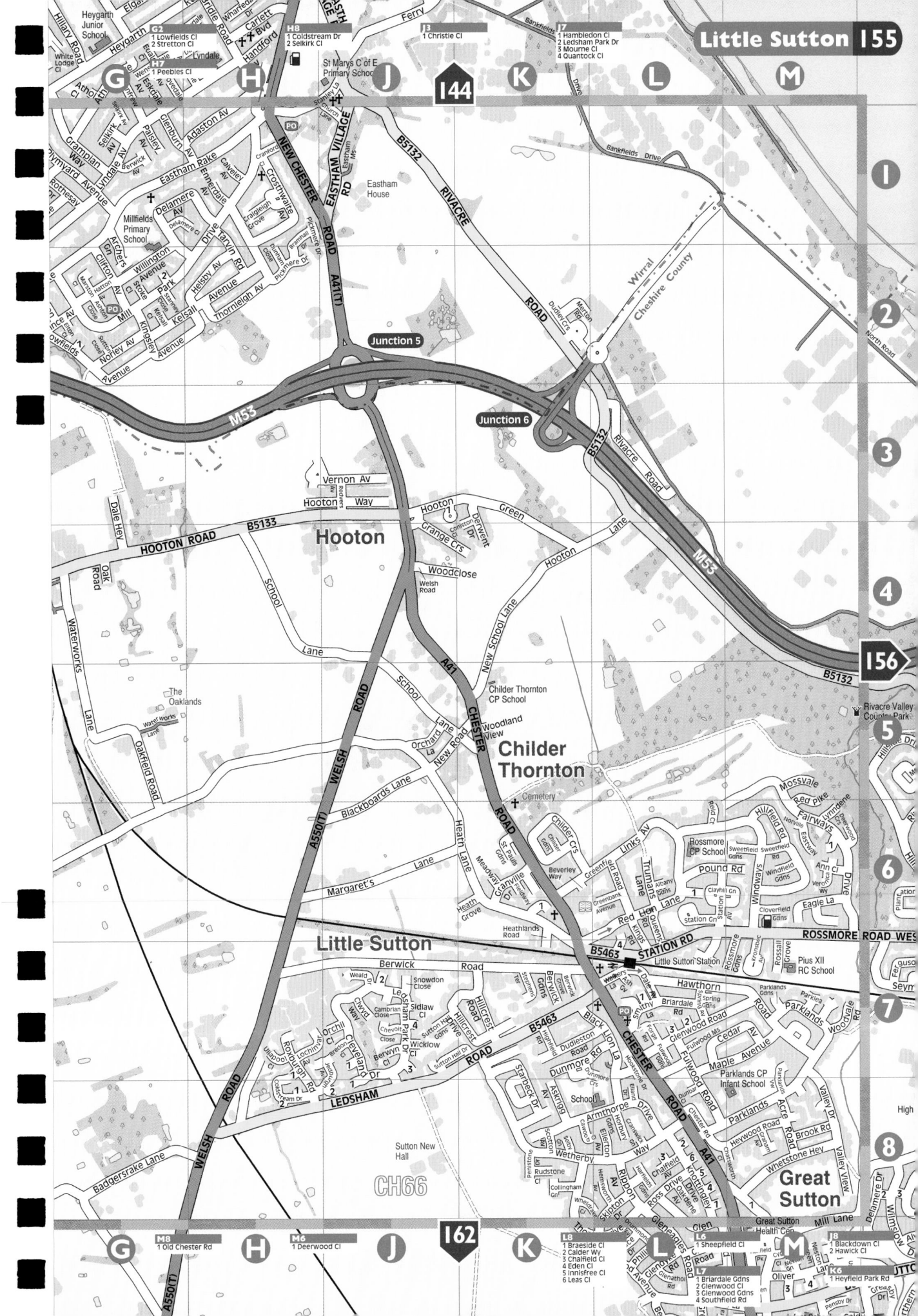

G H J 146 K L M

1

2

3

4

158

5

6

21

Manchester Ship Canal

Canalside
Industrial
Estate

CH65

rd Road

Oil Sites Road

Stanlow
Point

Manch

7

Corridor Road

Oil Sites Road

8

South Road

Bridges Road

**Stanlow**

Stanlow & Thornton
Station

Lees

New

G H J 164 K L M

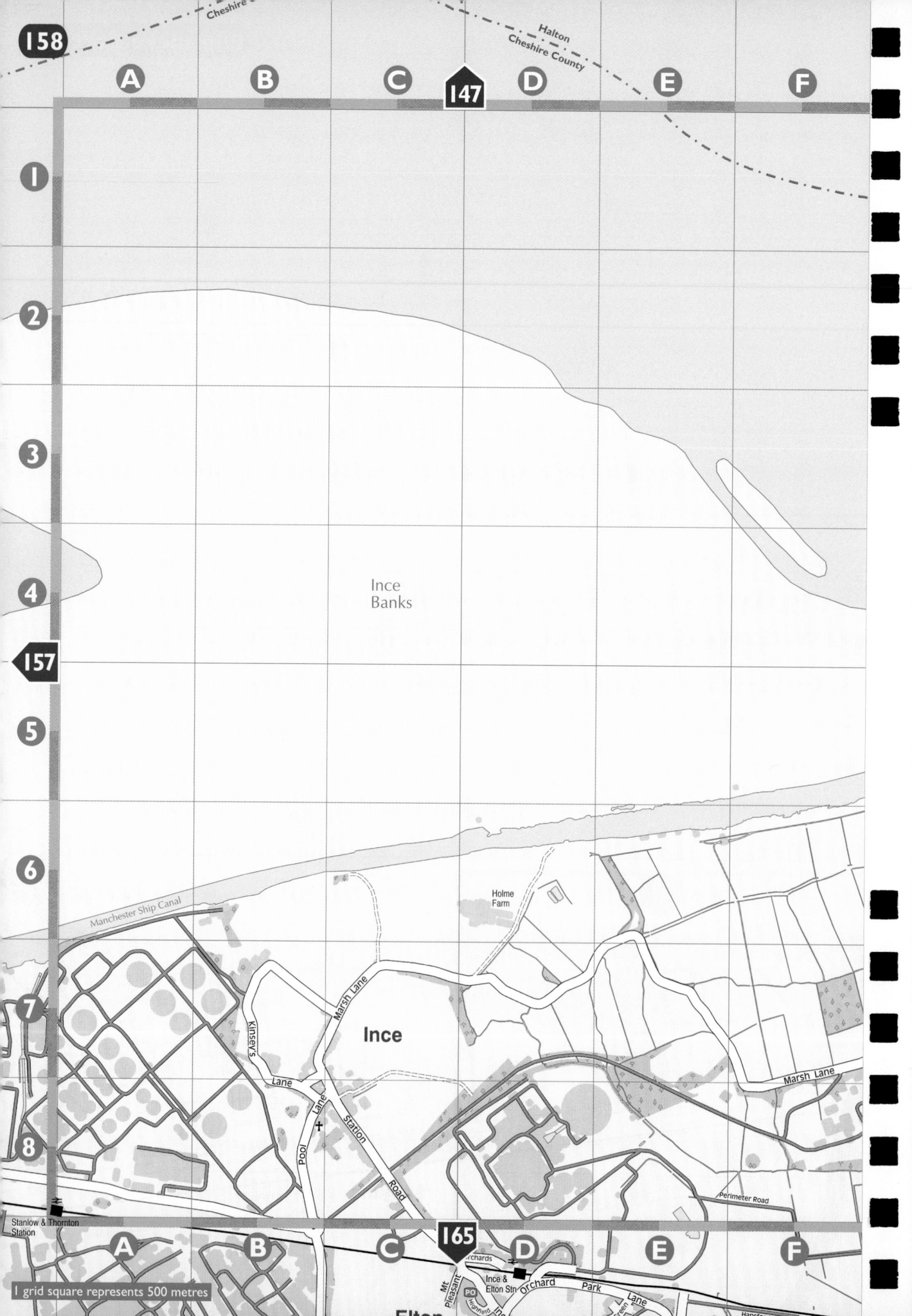

A B C 147 D E F

158

Cheshire

Halton
Cheshire County

1

2

3

Ince
Banks

4

157

5

6

Manchester Ship Canal

Holme
Farm

7

Ince

Kinsey's
Lane

Marsh Lane

Marsh Lane

Pool Lane

Station Road

8

Stanlow & Thornton
Station

Perimeter Road

A B C 165 D E F

Orchards

Mt Pleasant

Highfield

Ince &
Elton Stn

PO

Orchard Park

Lane

Green

Elton

L8
1 Dove Cl

G  H  J  **148**  K  L  M

1

2

Frodsham
Marsh
Farm

Alder Lane

Alder Lane

Bro

3

Moorditch Lane

Moorditch Lane

Tadgers Lane

4

**160**

Cross Lane

5

Manchester Ship Canal

Lordship Lane

Straight

6

Elton Lordship Lane

Lordship Lane

Ince
Marshes

Rake Lane

7

Hill View
Farm

M56

Hornsmill Brook

Helsby
Marsh

8

by Co
Scho

Hoolpool Lane

Smithy Lane

Holly Ct

Plovers
Lane

Cem

Elton Lane

G  H  J  **166**  K  L  M

Lower Rake Lane

Vale Gdns

The
Beeches

Hallastone Rd

House

Bank
Lane

Vicarage Lane

High View

School

Hall View Road

Conery

Cambridge
Gdns

Old Chester Road

Foxhill Cy

Profits Cy

Helsby
Station

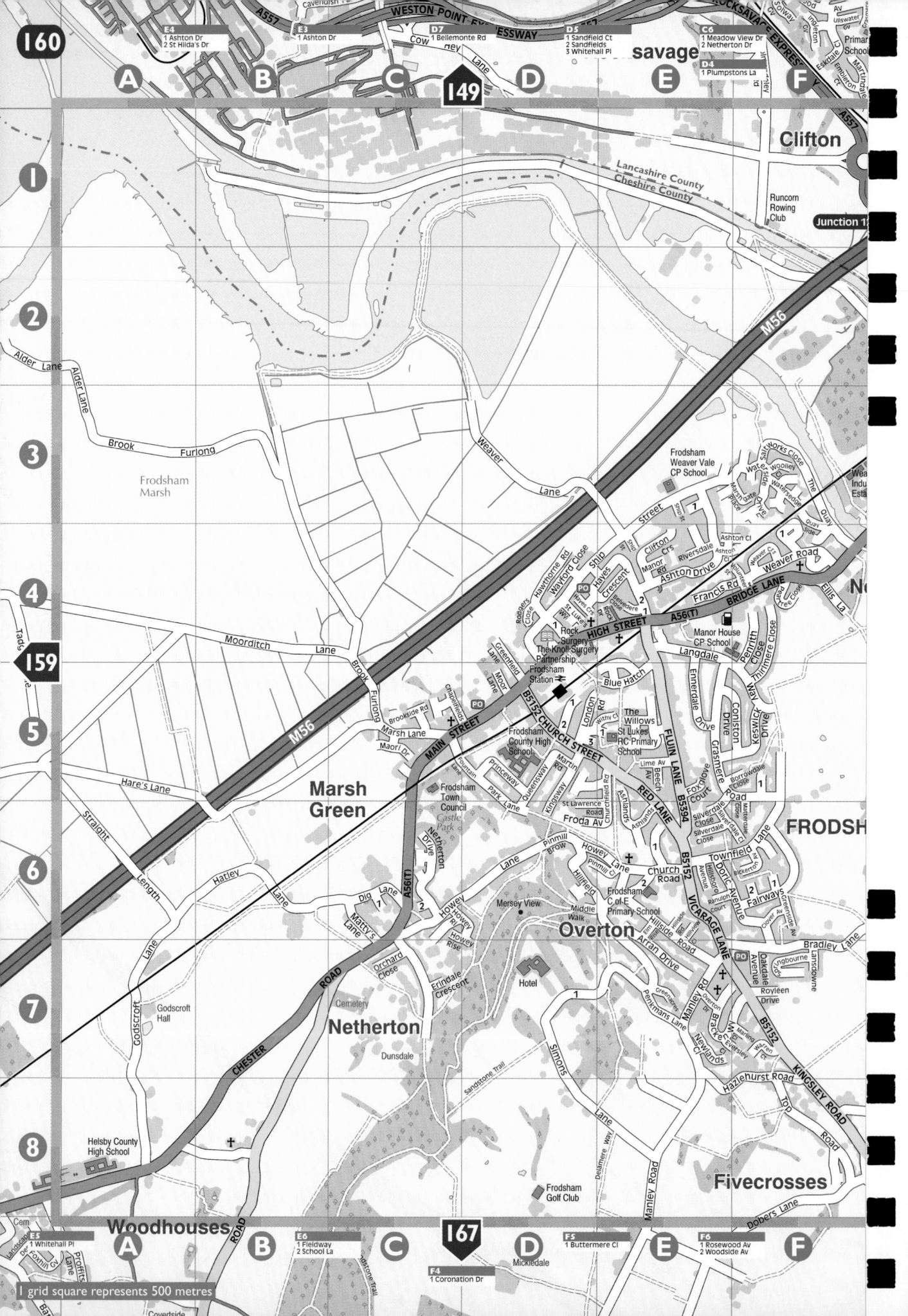

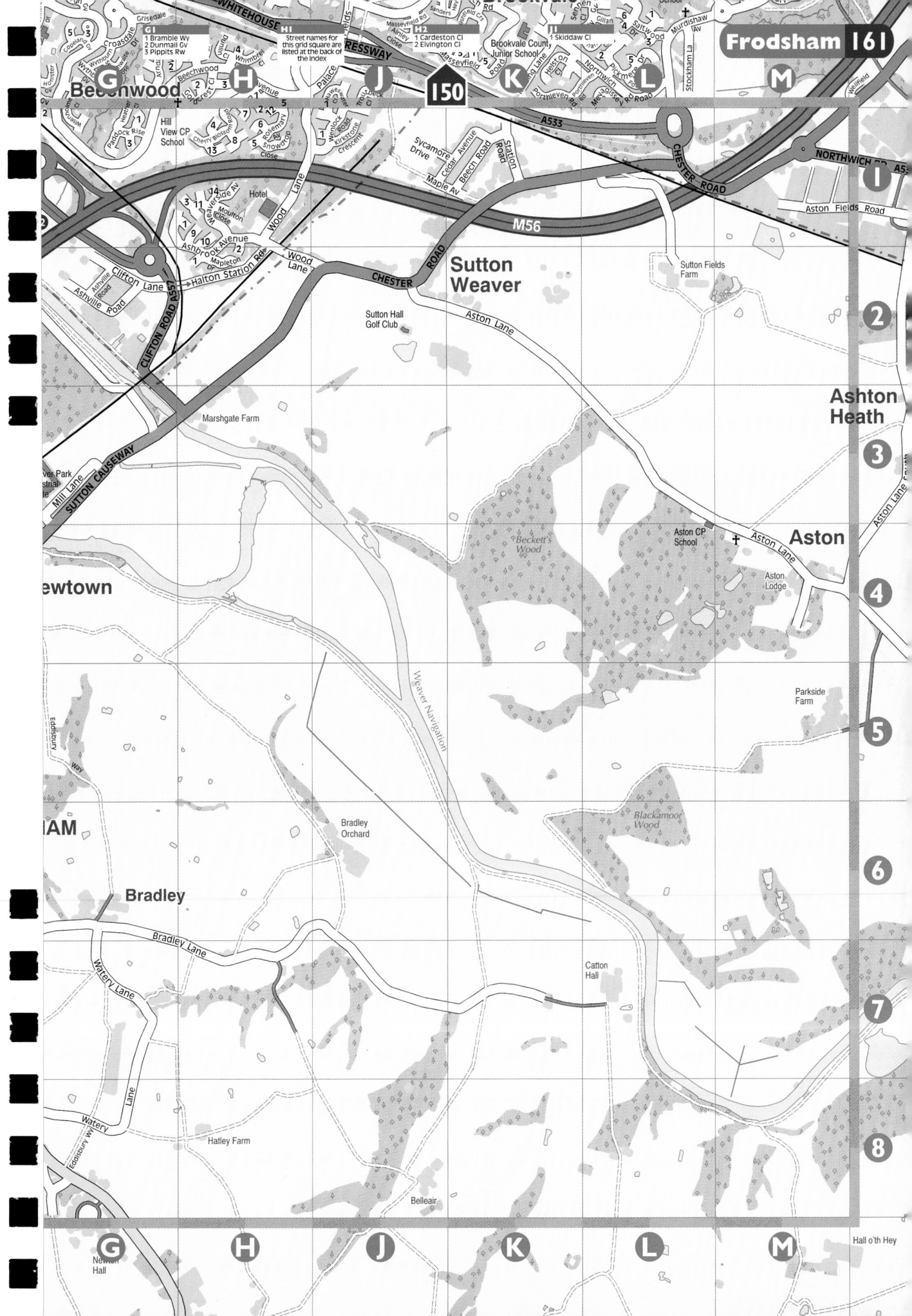

WHITEHOUSE

Grisedale

G1
1 Bramble Wy
2 Dunmail Gv
3 Pippits Rw

H1

Street names for
this grid square are
listed at the back of
the index

H2
1 Cardeston Cl
2 Elvington Cl

J1
1 Skiddaw Cl

Brookvale County
Junior School

**G** Beechwood

**H**

**J**

**150**

**K**

**L**

**M**

Paddock Rise

Hill
View CP
School

Ashbrook Avenue

Wood Lane

Palace

CHESTER ROAD

A533

M56

CHESTER ROAD

Sycamore
Drive

Cedar Avenue

Maple Av

Beech Road

Station
Road

**Sutton
Weaver**

NORTHWICH RD A533

Aston Fields Road

Sutton Fields
Farm

Clifton Lane

Ashville
Road

Ashville Road

CLIFTON ROAD A557

Halton Station Rd

Wood
Lane

Sutton Hall
Golf Club

Aston Lane

**1**

**2**

**Ashton
Heath**

**3**

ewtown

Marshgate Farm

Mill Lane

SUTTON CAUSEWAY

ver Park
Industrial
tate

Beckett's
Wood

Aston CP
School

Aston Lane

**Aston**

Aston
Lodge

Aston Lane South

**4**

Eddisbury
Way

Weaver Navigation

Parkside
Farm

**5**

IAM

Bradley
Orchard

Blackamoor
Wood

**6**

**Bradley**

Bradley Lane

Watery Lane

Catton
Hall

**7**

Watery
Lane

Eddisbury Lane

Hatley Farm

**8**

Belleair

**G**

**H**

Newton
Hall

**J**

**K**

**L**

**M**

Hall o'th Hey

A   B   C   66   155   D   E   F Great Sutton

Sutton New Hall

E3
1 Barnfield Cl

E2
1 The Harn

Rudstone

Collingham Gn

1
2
3
4
5
6
7
8

WELSH ROAD
A550(T)
Ledsham Lane

Ledsham

Works

Sutton Green

Gorsthills CP School

Pennington Green

Rectory Lane

Manorfield Close

Capenhurst Lane

Capenhurst Primary School

Capenhurst Station

Capenhurst Lane

Penfold Close

Dunkirk Lane

Capenhurst

Two Mills Farm

A550(T)

Malden Dr

Two Mills

Shotwick Lane

PARKGATE

Woodbank

ROAD

A540

Gibbet Mill

New Covert

F3
1 Hemingford Cl

Ashcroft Farm

Powey Lane

A5117(T)

Old Hall Farm

Dunkirk Trading Estate

Strawberry Lane

F4
1 Ashwood Cl
2 Birchwood Cl

Hill Farm

A   B   C   D   E   F

1 grid square represents 500 metres

7(T)

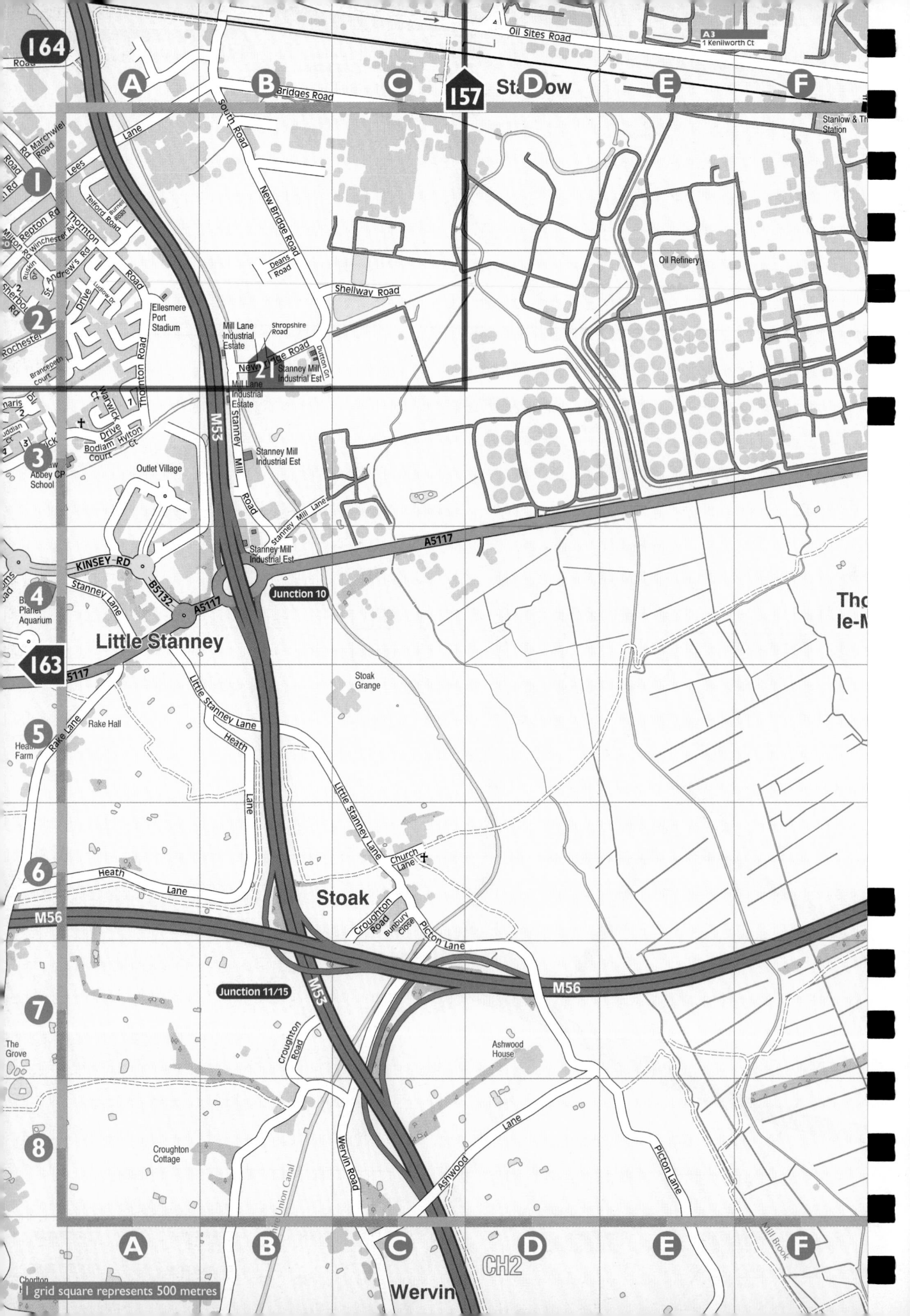

157 Stanlow

163

1 grid square represents 500 metres

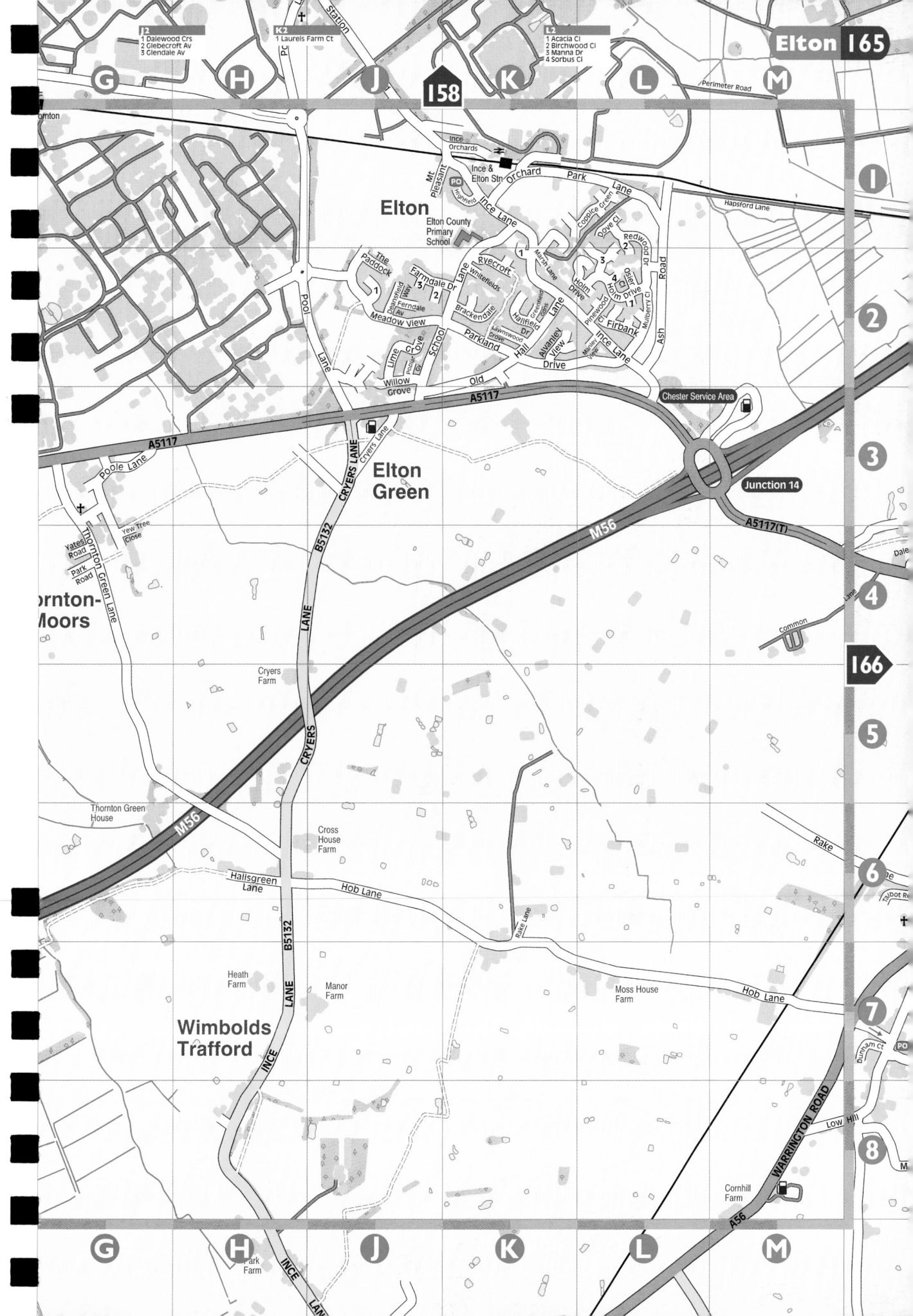

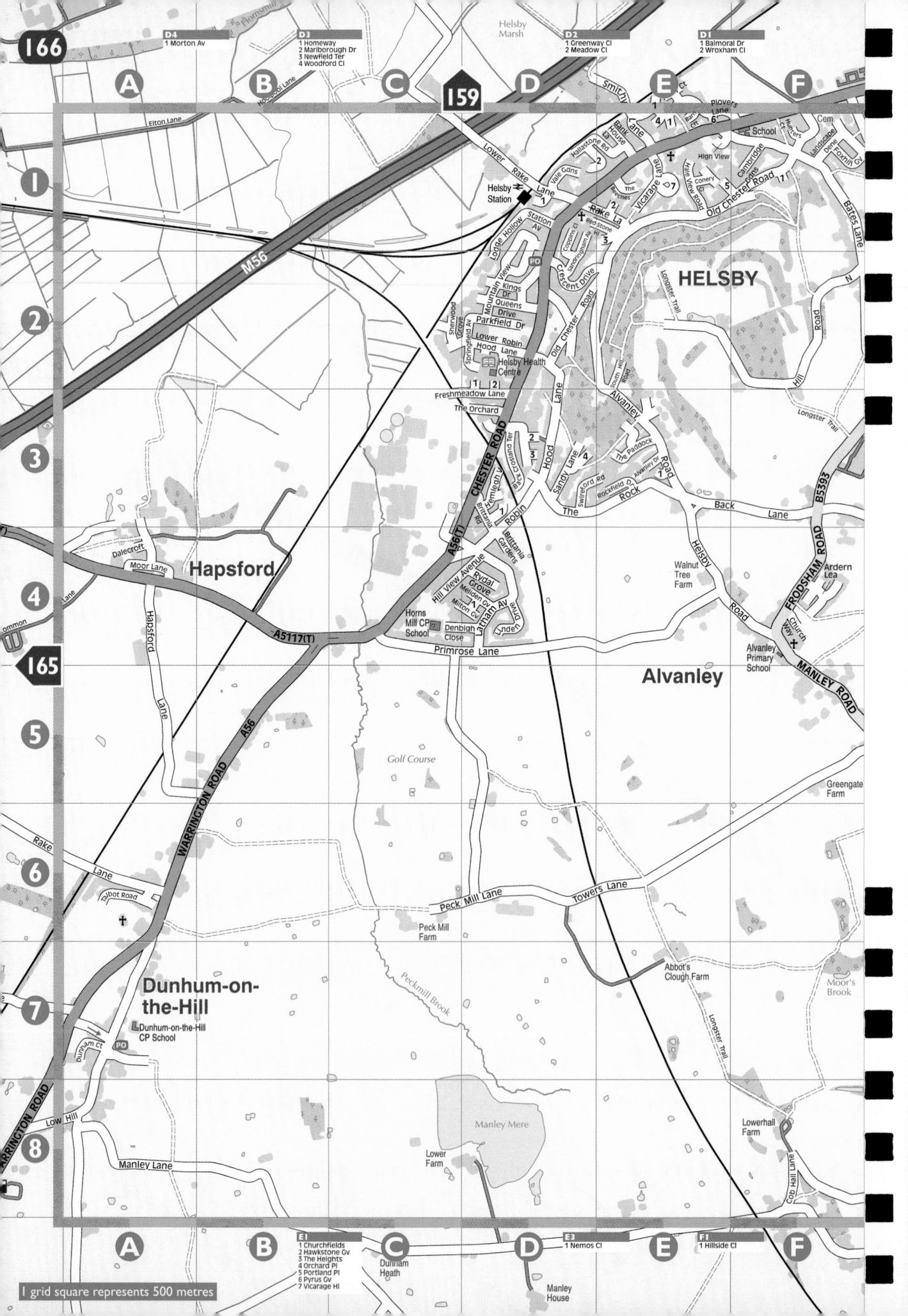

D4
1 Morton Av

D3
1 Homeway
2 Marlborough Dr
3 Newfield Ter
4 Woodford Cl

D2
1 Greenway Cl
2 Meadow Cl

D1
1 Balmoral Dr
2 Wroxham Cl

A  B  C  D  E  F

159

Helsby Marsh

Hornsmill

Hapswood Lane

Elton Lane

M56

Lower Rake Lane

Helsby Station

Lodge Hollow

Station Av

Mountain View

Sherwood Grove

Springfield Av

Lower Robin Hood Lane

Helsby Health Centre

Freshmeadow Lane

The Orchard

CHESTER ROAD

A56(T)

Crossfield Ter

Hemleigh V

Brittania

Britannia Gardens

Robin

Hood Lane

The

Hill View Avenue

Rydal Grove

Meiden Gv

Milton Gv

Latham Av

Under

Horns Mill CP School

Denbigh Close

Primrose Lane

Kings Dr

Queens Drive

Parkfield Dr

Crescent Drive

Old Chester Road

Smith

Bank House

Hallstone Rd

Vale Gdns

Rake La

The Beeches

Red stone

Coppice Cl

Sandymeadow

Vicarage Lane

High View

Conery

Cambridge

Mile View Road

Old Chester Road

Plovers Lane

Landscape

Dene

Foxhill Gv

School

Cem

Bates Lane

HELSBY

Longster Trail

Alvanley

Sandy Lane

Swirford Rd

The Paddock

Rockfield Dr

Alvanley Dr

The ROCK

Back Lane

B5393

FRODSHAM ROAD

MANLEY ROAD

Walnut Tree Farm

Helsby Road

Ardern Lea

Church Way

Alvanley Primary School

Alvanley

Greengate Farm

Hapsford

Dalecroft

Moor Lane

Common Lane

Hapsford Lane

A5117(T)

A56

WARRINGTON ROAD

165

Golf Course

Rake Lane

Talbot Road

Dunhum-on-the-Hill

Dunhum-on-the-Hill CP School

Dunhum Ct

PO

WARRINGTON ROAD

Low Hill

Manley Lane

Peck Mill Lane

Towers Lane

Peck Mill Farm

Peckmill Brook

Abbot's Clough Farm

Longster Trail

Moor's Brook

Manley Mere

Lower Farm

Lowerhall Farm

Cob Hall Lane

Dunham Heath

Manley House

E4
1 Churchfields
2 Hawkstone Gv
3 The Heights
4 Orchard Pl
5 Portland Pl
6 Pyrus Gv
7 Vicarage Hl

E3
1 Nemos Cl

F1
1 Hillside Cl

1 grid square represents 500 metres

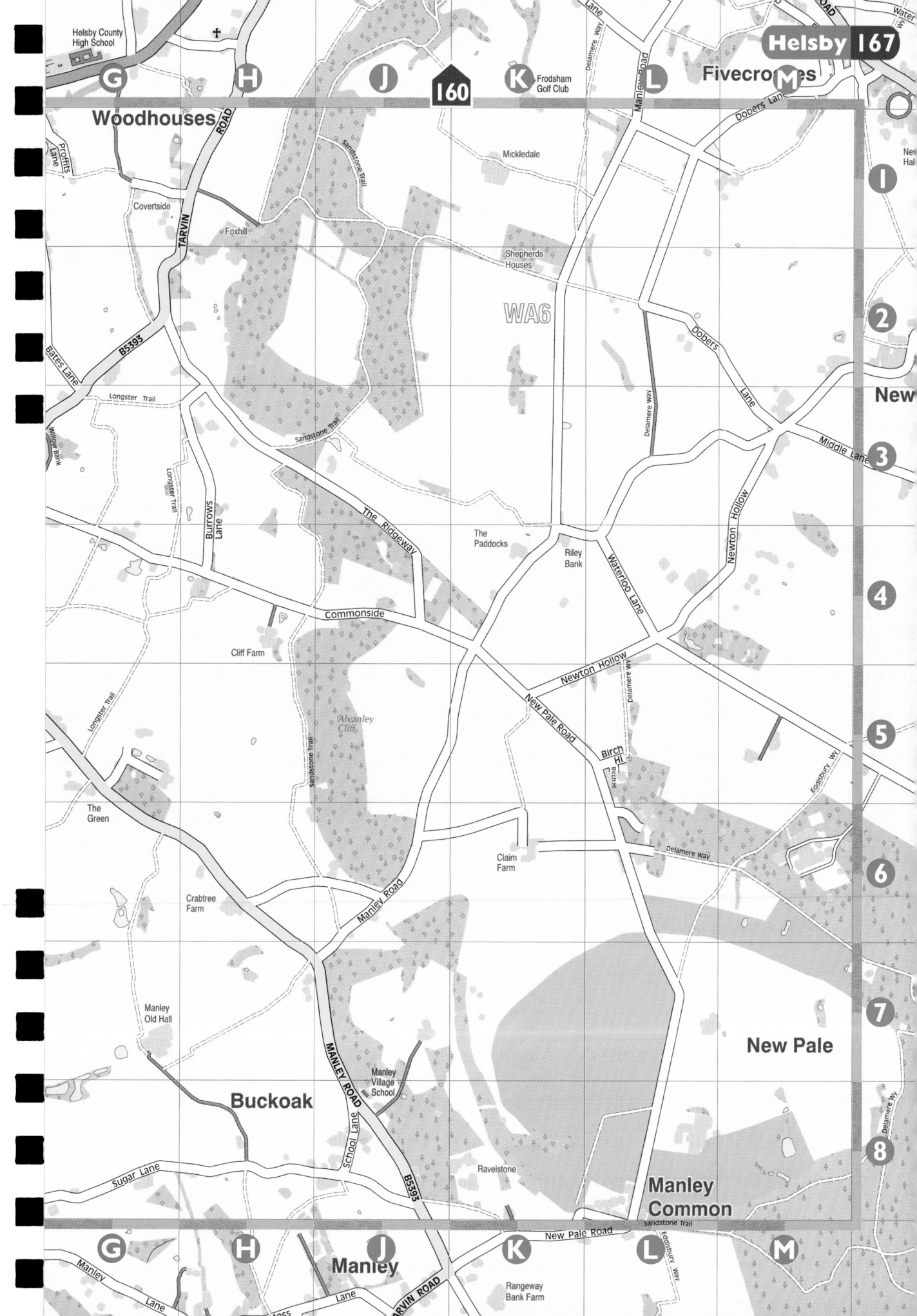

G H J **160** K L M

**Fivecromes**

**Woodhouses**

Helsby County
High School

†

Covertside

Foxhill

Profits Lane

TARVIN ROAD

B5393

Bates Lane

Longster Trail

Willow Bank

Longster Trail

Burrows Lane

Sandstone Trail

Sandstone Trail

The Ridgeway

Commonside

Cliff Farm

Alvanley Cliff

Longster Trail

The Green

Crabtree Farm

Manley Old Hall

Manley Road

MANLEY ROAD

SCHOOL LANE

B5393

Sugar Lane

**Buckoak**

Manley Village School

Mickledale

Shepherds Houses

WA6

The Paddocks

Riley Bank

Delamere Way

Manley Road

Waterloo Lane

New Pale Road

Newton Hollow

Dobers Lane

Dobers Lane

Middle Lane

Newton Hollow

Newton Hollow

Delamere Wy

Birch Hl

Birch Hl

Claim Farm

Delamere Way

Frodsham Golf Club

Egdsbury Wy

**New Pale**

Delamere Wy

Ravelstone

New Pale Road

Sandstone Trail

**Manley Common**

Egdsbury Wy

I
2
3
4
5
6
7
8

New

New Hal

Water

**Manley**

Manley Lane

TARVIN ROAD

Lane

M55

Rangeway Bank Farm

| | | | | |
|---|---|---|---|---|
| Abram 80 E5 | Croft 106 D5 | High Park 25 H5 | Netherton 72 B8 | Southgate 150 A6 |
| Adlington 44 D6 | Cronton 117 K8 | Hightown 70 A2 | Netherton 160 B7 | Southport 2 C1 |
| Aigburth 130 B4 | Crooke 67 L2 | Hillcliffe 137 L6 | New Boston 91 H7 | Speke 147 G2 |
| Ainsdale 34 E8 | Crosby 82 D4 | Hill Dale 40 F8 | New Brighton 95 J5 | Spital 143 L2 |
| Ainsdale-on-Sea 34 A8 | Crossens 25 K1 | Hillside 34 F3 | New Ferry 128 E6 | Springfield 68 B3 |
| Aintree 84 F3 | Croston 29 K3 | Hinderton 153 J4 | Newgate 66 C6 | Standish 56 B4 |
| Allerton 131 G4 | Crow Wood 134 F3 | Hindley 81 H1 | New Houses 78 D4 | Standish Lower Ground 67 M2 |
| Alvanley 166 E5 | Croxteth 98 F1 | Hindley Green 81 L2 | New Lane 38 D6 | Stanley 65 G2 |
| Anderton 44 D5 | Cuerdley Cross 135 J2 | Holland Lees 54 D8 | New Lane End 106 C3 | Stanley Gate 64 A6 |
| Andertons Mill 41 H4 | Culcheth 107 J2 | Holmes 27 K2 | New Pale 167 M7 | Stanlow 157 K8 |
| Anfield 97 J6 | Dallam 121 H4 | Holmeswood 27 L7 | New Springs 69 G3 | Statham 139 M1 |
| Appleton 134 D3 | Dalton 53 L8 | Holt 101 J8 | Newton 125 H3 | Stoak 164 B6 |
| Appleton Park 137 M8 | Dangerous Corner 54 E3 | Holt Green 62 D6 | Newton-Le-Willows 104 F2 | Stockbridge Village 99 J5 |
| Appley Bridge 54 E5 | Dangerous Corner 81 L3 | Homer Green 71 L4 | Newton Park 105 H3 | Stockton Heath 137 L4 |
| Arrowe Hill 126 B2 | Daresbury 151 K3 | Hood Manor 120 E8 | Newtown 30 C3 | Stoneycroft 114 C1 |
| Ashton Heath 161 M3 | Denton's Green 8 C1 | Hooton 155 H4 | Newtown 68 A7 | Storeton 127 K8 |
| Ashton-in-Makerfield 91 M2 | Derbyshire Hill 103 H3 | Hoscar 52 F1 | Newtown 101 L1 | Stubshaw Cross 79 M8 |
| Ashurst 65 K1 | Digmoor 65 L7 | Hough Green 133 J4 | Newtown 160 F4 | Sutton 103 G6 |
| Aspull 57 M8 | Dingle 129 J2 | Houghton Green 106 A8 | Noctorum 110 E8 | Sutton Green 162 D2 |
| Aspull Common 93 K4 | Ditton 133 K6 | Houghwood 77 J7 | Norris Green 98 B4 | Sutton Heath 102 A7 |
| Astmoor 150 A2 | Doe Green 135 L2 | Howley 15 K6 | Northwood 86 D2 | Sutton Leach 103 G8 |
| Aston 161 M4 | Dog & Gun 98 C2 | Hoylake 108 E6 | Norton 150 E4 | Sutton Manor 118 C3 |
| Aughton 62 B6 | Dovecot 115 H2 | Hulme 121 K2 | Nut Grove 101 L7 | Sutton Weaver 161 K2 |
| Aughton Park 63 G3 | Dover 80 D7 | Hunger Hill 55 H2 | Oakwood 123 H1 | Swanside 115 H2 |
| Backford Cross 163 H6 | Downall Green 78 E8 | Hunt's Cross 131 K7 | Oglet 146 F5 | Tamer Lane End 81 K5 |
| Ball o' Ditton 134 A4 | Downholland Cross 61 J3 | Hurlston Green 50 D2 | Old Boston 91 K6 | Tanhouse 65 L5 |
| Bamfurlong 80 A5 | Drummersdale 37 H7 | Huyton 116 B2 | Old Swan 114 B2 | Tarbock Green 132 E1 |
| Banks 23 H7 | Dudlows Green 138 A8 | Huyton Park 115 L4 | Orford 121 M4 | Tarlscough 38 F4 |
| Bank Top 66 E1 | Dunham-On-The-Hill 166 A7 | Huyton Quarry 116 D3 | Ormskirk 63 K1 | Thatto Heath 101 M5 |
| Barnston 141 L2 | Dunkirk 163 G6 | Huyton-With-Roby 115 L2 | Orrell 67 J6 | Thelwall 139 G2 |
| Barrow Nook 75 G3 | Earlestown 104 B2 | Ince 158 C7 | Orrell 83 M7 | Thingwall 126 D8 |
| Barrow's Green 134 F1 | Eastham 144 A7 | Ince Blundell 71 G2 | Orrell Post 67 G6 | Thornton 71 L7 |
| Barton 49 H7 | Eastham Ferry 144 C5 | Ince-in-Makerfield 5 K6 | Otterspool 129 M4 | Thornton Hough 142 B6 |
| Bebington 128 A4 | Eccleston 30 D6 | Irby 125 M7 | Overpool 156 B6 | Thornton-le-Moors 164 F4 |
| Beech Hill 68 B3 | Eccleston 88 E8 | Keckwick 151 H1 | Overton 160 D6 | Thurstaston 125 J8 |
| Beechwood 150 A8 | Eccleston Park 101 J6 | Kensington 113 J3 | Oxton 127 H1 | Toll Bar 101 L4 |
| Belle Vale 115 L8 | Edge Green 92 B2 | Kenyon 106 C1 | Paddington 122 C6 | Tontine 66 F7 |
| Bescar 37 J6 | Edge Hill 113 K5 | Kings Moss 77 H6 | Padgate 122 B4 | Top Lock 69 K3 |
| Bewsey 121 G5 | Egremont 111 L1 | Kingsway 16 C3 | Page Moss 115 K2 | Tower Hill 74 A8 |
| Bickershaw 81 G5 | Ellesmere Port 20 A3 | Kingswood 120 C2 | Palacefields 150 B8 | Town End 117 L7 |
| Bickerstaffe 64 A8 | Elmers Green 65 M2 | Kirkby 86 A4 | Parbold 53 M2 | Town Green 62 F6 |
| Bidston 110 F4 | Elton 165 J1 | Kirkdale 96 F5 | Parkgate 152 E4 | Town Green 91 M1 |
| Bidston Hill 110 F5 | Elton Green 165 J3 | Kitt Green 68 A6 | Park Hill 75 M3 | Town of Lowton 92 C8 |
| Billinge 78 B8 | Euxton 31 K3 | Knotty Ash 114 F2 | Parr 103 G3 | Town Park 150 D4 |
| Birch Green 65 L3 | Everton 97 H8 | Knowsley 99 L1 | Peasley Cross 102 E4 | Toxteth 113 G8 |
| Birchwood 123 G1 | Fairfield 113 M2 | Lady Green 71 G1 | Pemberton 67 L8 | Tranmere 128 A2 |
| Birkacre 43 J2 | Far Banks 23 L5 | Laffak 90 A6 | Penketh 135 M1 | Tuebrook 98 B8 |
| Birkdale 35 H3 | Far Moor 67 G8 | Lamberhead Green 67 J8 | Pennington 93 M2 | Two Mills 162 A6 |
| Birkenhead 112 C7 | Farnworth 134 C2 | Land Gate 79 J6 | Pennylands 64 E5 | Up Holland 66 C6 |
| Bispham Green 40 E6 | Fazakerley 84 E8 | Landican 126 E5 | Pensby 141 H1 | Upton 110 B8 |
| Blackbrook 90 C8 | Fearnhead 122 C3 | Lane Ends 44 F1 | Pincock 31 L5 | Upton 133 K3 |
| Blackbrook 122 A3 | Fiddler's Ferry 22 F7 | Lane Head 93 H7 | Pinfold 50 B1 | Upton Rocks 134 A2 |
| Blackrod 57 L2 | Fiddler's Ferry 135 L4 | Latchford 137 L2 | Plank Lane 81 K8 | Vauxhall 12 D1 |
| Blaguegate 64 D4 | Fincham 99 J8 | Lea Green 102 B8 | Platt Bridge 80 D3 | Vulcan Village 104 E5 |
| Blowick 25 G7 | Firs Lane 81 M8 | Leasowe 110 C1 | Pocket Nook 93 L5 | Waddicar 85 J1 |
| Blundellsands 82 B1 | Fivecrosses 160 E8 | Ledsham 162 B3 | Poll Hill 141 H4 | Wallasey 95 L5 |
| Boar's Head 56 C7 | Ford 83 L3 | Limbrick 33 J8 | Pool Hey 36 D2 | Walton 97 K3 |
| Bold Heath 119 G6 | Formby 59 G1 | Lingley Green 119 L6 | Poolstock 4 B8 | Wargrave 104 E4 |
| Bolton Green 31 M6 | Frankby 125 J3 | Lingley Mere 119 M5 | Portico 101 J5 | Warrington 14 C3 |
| Bootle 6 C5 | Freshfield 46 E8 | Liscard 95 K8 | Port Sunlight 128 D8 | Waterloo 82 F3 |
| Bowing Park 115 K5 | Frodsham 160 F6 | Litherland 83 L4 | Poulton 111 J3 | Waterloo Park 83 H4 |
| Bowker's Green 62 F8 | Garston 130 F8 | Little Altcar 59 J4 | Poulton 143 K3 | Wavertree 114 B6 |
| Bradley 161 G6 | Garswood 90 D2 | Little Crosby 70 E5 | Prenton 127 J4 | Weld Bank 32 E8 |
| Brighton le Sands 82 C2 | Gateacre 131 K1 | Little Neston 152 F7 | Prescot 100 D7 | West Bank 134 B8 |
| Brimstage 142 D3 | Gathurst 67 H2 | Little Scotland 57 J3 | Preston Brook 151 H8 | Westbrook 120 C4 |
| Broad Green 114 F3 | Gayton 141 J7 | Little Stanney 164 A4 | Preston on the Hill 151 J7 | Westhead 63 H1 |
| Broad Oak 103 H1 | Gemini 120 F2 | Little Sutton 155 H7 | Primrose Hill 50 B5 | West Kirby 124 B3 |
| Bromborough 143 K4 | Gillar's Green 101 G2 | Little Town 106 D3 | Princes Park 113 K7 | Westleigh 81 M6 |
| Bromborough Pool 128 F8 | Gillmoss 85 L7 | Liverpool 12 B7 | Raby 153 L1 | Weston 149 H7 |
| Brookhurst 143 K8 | Golborne 92 D6 | Locking Stumps 122 D1 | Rainford 76 C6 | Weston Point 18 A8 |
| Brookvale 150 D8 | Goose Green 79 G1 | Longbarn 122 E4 | Rainford Junction 76 B3 | West Park 8 A7 |
| Brown Edge 36 C3 | Gorse Covert 107 K7 | Longford 121 K4 | Rainhill 117 M2 | Westvale 85 M3 |
| Brown Edge 101 L6 | Grange 19 M9 | Longshaw 78 A4 | Rainhill Stoops 118 A3 | Westy 122 B8 |
| Brownlow 77 K5 | Grange 124 F4 | Longview 100 B8 | Ravenhead 8 C8 | Whalleys 53 J8 |
| Bruche 122 B6 | Grange Park 101 K5 | Lower Bebington 128 B8 | Red Rock 56 F5 | Whelley 5 L1 |
| Bryn 79 H7 | Grappenhall 138 D3 | Lower House 134 A5 | Ring o' Bells 52 D3 | Whiston 117 G2 |
| Bryn Gates 80 B6 | Grassendale 130 C6 | Lower Walton 137 J5 | Risley 107 G7 | Whiston Cross 116 F2 |
| Buckley Hill 83 M1 | Greasby 125 M3 | Lowton 92 F5 | Rivington 45 H3 | Whiston Lane Ends 116 E3 |
| Buckoak 167 H8 | Great Altcar 60 B4 | Lowton Common 93 J5 | Robin Hood 54 D1 | Whitby 20 B7 |
| Burscough 51 L3 | Great Crosby 83 G1 | Lowton Heath 92 E7 | Roby 115 K3 | Whitbyheath 163 H4 |
| Burscough Bridge 38 F7 | Great Sankey 120 D7 | Lowton St Mary's 93 J6 | Roby Mill 66 D2 | White Coppice 33 M3 |
| Burtonwood 104 C7 | Great Sutton 155 M8 | Lugsdale 17 G5 | Rock Ferry 128 B3 | Whitefield Lane End 116 D5 |
| Calderstones 130 E2 | Grimeford Village 45 G7 | Lunt 71 L5 | Rocksavage 149 K8 | Whitley 68 C2 |
| Caldy 124 F6 | Grimshaw Green 40 D8 | Lunts Heath 118 C8 | Royal Oak 74 B1 | Widnes 16 A5 |
| Callands 120 F3 | Haigh 57 K6 | Lydiate 61 J8 | Rufford 39 L2 | Wigan 4 C2 |
| Capenhurst 162 D5 | Hale 147 M3 | Maghull 72 F5 | Runcorn 19 M5 | Wilderspool 137 L3 |
| Carr Cross 36 F5 | Hale Bank 148 D1 | Manley Common 167 L8 | Runshaw Moor 31 H1 | Wilderswood 45 M7 |
| Carr Houses 71 H1 | Halewood 132 B5 | Marshall's Cross 102 D8 | St Helens 9 H2 | Willaston 154 D5 |
| Castlefields 150 B3 | Hall Green 66 C6 | Marsh Green 67 L4 | St Michael's Hamlet 129 K3 | Wimbolds Trafford 165 H7 |
| Chadwick Green 90 A1 | Halsall 49 L4 | Marsh Green 160 B5 | Sandhills 96 E5 | Windle Hill 153 L6 |
| Chapel House 64 F3 | Halton 150 B5 | Marshside 25 G2 | Sankey Bridges 136 E1 | Windmill Hill 150 E3 |
| Charnock Green 31 K7 | Halton Brook 149 M4 | Martinscroft 122 F6 | Saughall Massie 109 K7 | Windy Arbor 116 F5 |
| Charnock Richard 42 E1 | Halton View 17 H2 | Marylebone 68 F2 | Scarisbrick 37 G6 | Winstanley 78 E2 |
| Childer Thornton 155 K5 | Hapsford 166 A4 | Mawdesley 40 E3 | Scarth Hill 63 L3 | Winstanleys 55 E6 |
| Childwall 115 H7 | Haresfinch 89 J6 | Melling 73 H8 | Scholes 5 H4 | Winwick 105 K6 |
| Chorley 32 D4 | Hartwood 32 E3 | Melling Mount 73 M6 | Seacombe 111 M4 | Winwick Quay 121 K1 |
| Churchtown 25 K4 | Haskayne 49 G8 | Meols 108 F5 | Seaforth 83 G6 | Wirral 126 B5 |
| Cinnamon Brow 122 C1 | Hawkley 79 J2 | Mere Brow 27 G3 | Sefton 72 B6 | Wolverham 20 D7 |
| Claughton 111 G8 | Haydock 90 F7 | Mere Side 27 K8 | Sefton Park 129 M1 | Woodbank 162 A7 |
| Clifton 160 F1 | Heath 19 G9 | Moore 136 C2 | Shaw Green 30 F3 | Woodchurch 126 E2 |
| Clinkham Wood 89 J3 | Heath Charnock 44 A3 | Moorside 152 E6 | Shell Green 135 G3 | Woodhey 128 B6 |
| Clock Face 118 F2 | Heaton's Bridge 50 F1 | Moreton 110 A4 | Shevington 55 J8 | Woodhouses 167 G1 |
| Clubmoor 97 L6 | Helsby 166 E1 | Moss Bank 17 K4 | Shevington Moor 55 J3 | Woodvale 47 K2 |
| Cobbs 137 M5 | Hermitage Green 105 K5 | Moss Bank 89 K4 | Shevington Vale 55 H5 | Woolfall Heath 99 L8 |
| Collins Green 103 M4 | Heskin Green 41 M2 | Mossley Hill 130 B1 | Shirdley Hill 36 B7 | Woolston 122 E6 |
| Coppull 42 F4 | Heswall 140 F4 | Moss Nook 103 H4 | Simm's Cross 16 F4 | Woolton 131 J4 |
| Coppull Moor 42 F7 | Higher Bebington 127 K6 | Moss Side 73 J2 | Simm's Lane End 78 C8 | Worsley Hall 67 M6 |
| Court Hey 115 H4 | Higher End 77 L2 | Moss Side 87 G6 | Skelmersdale 65 J3 | Worsley Mesnes 79 H1 |
| Cowling 33 G7 | Higher Runcorn 19 G6 | Mossy Lea 42 B7 | Snape Green 37 G4 | Wrightington Bar 42 B5 |
| Crank 89 G1 | Higher Walton 137 G6 | Ness 153 K8 | Sollom 28 D3 | Wrights Green 138 C8 |
| Crankwood 80 F8 | Highfield 78 E1 | Neston 152 F6 | Southdene 86 A5 | |
| Crawford 76 E3 | High Moor 54 B1 | Netherley 131 M1 | | |

## USING THE STREET INDEX

Street names are listed alphabetically. Each street name is followed by its postal town or area locality, the Postcode District, the page number, and the reference to the square in which the name is found.

Example: **Abbeyfields** *WGNNW/ST* WN6 ............... **68** A2 🔢

Some entries are followed by a number in a blue box. This number indicates the location of the street within the referenced grid square. The full street name is listed at the side of the map page.

169

## GENERAL ABBREVIATIONS

ACC ACCESS
ALY ALLEY
AP APPROACH
AR ARCADE
ASS ASSOCIATION
AV AVENUE
BCH BEACH
BLDS BUILDINGS
BND BEND
BNK BANK
BR BRIDGE
BRK BROOK
BTM BOTTOM
BUS BUSINESS
BVD BOULEVARD
BY BYPASS
CATH CATHEDRAL
CEM CEMETERY
CEN CENTRE
CFT CROFT
CH CHURCH
CHA CHASE
CHYD CHURCHYARD
CIR CIRCLE
CIRC CIRCUS
CL CLOSE
CLFS CLIFFS
CMP CAMP
CNR CORNER
CO COUNTY
COLL COLLEGE
COM COMMON
COMM COMMISSION
CON CONVENT
COT COTTAGE
COTS COTTAGES
CP CAPE
CPS COPSE
CR CREEK
CREM CREMATORIUM
CRS CRESCENT
CSWY CAUSEWAY
CT COURT
CTRL CENTRAL
CTS COURTS
CTYD COURTYARD
CUTT CUTTINGS
CV COVE
CYN CANYON
DEPT DEPARTMENT
DL DALE
DM DAM
DR DRIVE
DRO DROVE
DRY DRIVEWAY
DWGS DWELLINGS
E EAST
EMB EMBANKMENT
EMBY EMBASSY
ESP ESPLANADE
EST ESTATE
EX EXCHANGE
EXPY EXPRESSWAY
EXT EXTENSION
F/O FLYOVER
FC FOOTBALL CLUB
FK FORK
FLD FIELD
FLDS FIELDS
FLS FALLS
FLS FLATS
FM FARM
FT FORT
FWY FREEWAY
FY FERRY
GA GATE
GAL GALLERY
GDN GARDEN
GDNS GARDENS
GLD GLADE
GLN GLEN
GN GREEN
GND GROUND
GRA GRANGE
GRG GARAGE
GT GREAT
GTWY GATEWAY
GV GROVE
HGR HIGHER
HL HILL
HLS HILLS
HO HOUSE
HOL HOLLOW
HOSP HOSPITAL
HRB HARBOUR
HTH HEATH
HTS HEIGHTS
HVN HAVEN
HWY HIGHWAY
IMP IMPERIAL
IN INLET
IND EST INDUSTRIAL ESTATE
INF INFIRMARY
INFO INFORMATION
INT INTERCHANGE
IS ISLAND
JCT JUNCTION
JTY JETTY
KG KING
KNL KNOLL
L LAKE
LA LANE
LDG LODGE
LGT LIGHT
LK LOCK
LKS LAKES
LNDG LANDING
LTL LITTLE
LWR LOWER
MAG MAGISTRATE
MAN MANSIONS
MD MEAD
MDW MEADOWS
MEM MEMORIAL
MKT MARKET
MKTS MARKETS
ML MALL
ML MILL
MNR MANOR
MS MEWS
MSN MISSION
MT MOUNT
MTN MOUNTAIN
MTS MOUNTAINS
MUS MUSEUM
MWY MOTORWAY
N NORTH
NE NORTH EAST
NW NORTH WEST
O/P OVERPASS
OFF OFFICE
ORCH ORCHARD
OV OVAL
PAL PALACE
PAS PASSAGE
PAV PAVILION
PDE PARADE
PH PUBLIC HOUSE
PK PARK
PKWY PARKWAY
PL PLACE
PLN PLAIN
PLNS PLAINS
PLZ PLAZA
POL POLICE STATION
PR PRINCE
PREC PRECINCT
PREP PREPARATORY
PRIM PRIMARY
PROM PROMENADE
PRS PRINCESS
PRT PORT
PT POINT
PTH PATH
PZ PIAZZA
QD QUADRANT
QU QUEEN
QY QUAY
R RIVER
RBT ROUNDABOUT
RD ROAD
RDG RIDGE
REP REPUBLIC
RES RESERVOIR
RFC RUGBY FOOTBALL CLUB
RI RISE
RP RAMP
RW ROW
S SOUTH
SCH SCHOOL
SE SOUTH EAST
SER SERVICE AREA
SH SHORE
SHOP SHOPPING
SKWY SKYWAY
SMT SUMMIT
SOC SOCIETY
SP SPUR
SPR SPRING
SQ SQUARE
ST STREET
STN STATION
STR STREAM
STRD STRAND
SW SOUTH WEST
TDG TRADING
TER TERRACE
THWY THROUGHWAY
TNL TUNNEL
TOLL TOLLWAY
TPK TURNPIKE
TR TRACK
TRL TRAIL
TWR TOWER
U/P UNDERPASS
UNI UNIVERSITY
UPR UPPER
V VALE
VA VALLEY
VIAD VIADUCT
VIL VILLA
VIS VISTA
VLG VILLAGE
VLS VILLAS
VW VIEW
W WEST
WD WOOD
WHF WHARF
WK WALK
WKS WALKS
WLS WELLS
WY WAY
YD YARD
YHA YOUTH HOSTEL

## POSTCODE TOWNS AND AREA ABBREVIATIONS

AIG/SPK Aigburth/Sefton Park
AIMK Ashton-in-Makerfield
AIN/FAZ Aintree/Fazakerley
ALL/GAR Allerton/Garston
ANF/KKDL Anfield/Kirkdale
BEB Bebington
BIRK Birkenhead
BRSC Burscough
BTL Bootle
CALD/MH Calderstones/Mossley Hill
CH/BCN Chester/Blacon
CHLDW Childwall
CHLY/EC Chorley/Eccleston
CHLYE Chorley east/Adlington/Whittle-le-Woods
CHNE Chester northeast
CHTN/BK Churchtown/Banks
CL/PREN Claughton/Prenton
CLB/OSW/ST Clubmoor/Old Swan/Stoneycroft
CLVP Central Liverpool
CLVPS Central Liverpool south
CSBY/BLUN Crosby/Blundellsands
CSBY/WL Crosby/Waterloo
DV/KA/FCH Dovecot/Knotty Ash/Fincham
ECCL Eccleston
EHL/KEN Edge Hill/Kensington
EP Ellesmere Port
EV Everton
FMBY Formby
FROD/HEL Frodsham/Helsby
GOL/RIS/CUL Golborne/Risley/Culcheth
GR/UP/WCH Greasby/Upton/Woodchurch
GTS/LS Great Sutton/Little Sutton
HES Heswall
HLWD Halewood
HOR/BR Horwich/Blackrod
HOY Hoylake
HTWN Hightown
HUY Huyton
KIRK/FR/WAR Kirkham Freckleton/Warton
KKBY Kirkby
LEIGH Leigh
LEY/BBR Leyland/Bamber Bridge
LITH Litherland
LYMM Lymm
MGHL Maghull
MOR/LEA Moreton/Leasowe
NEWLW Newton-le-Willows
NG/CROX Norris Green/Croxteth
NPK/KEN Newsham Park/Kensington
NSTN Neston
NTHLY Netherley
NTHTN Netherton
NWD/KWIPK Northwood/Knowsley Industrial Park
ORM Ormskirk
PEN/TH Pensby/Thingwall
PR/KW Prescot/Knowsley
PS/BROM Port Sunlight/Bromborough
RAIN/WH Rainhill/Whiston
RF/TRAN Rock Ferry/Tranmere
RNFD/HAY Rainford/Haydock
RUNC Runcorn
SFTN Sefton
SKEL Skelmersdale
SPK/HALE Speke/Hale
STBRV Stockbridge Village
STHEL St Helens
STHP Southport
TOX Toxteth
VAUX/LVPD Vauxhall/Liverpool Docks
WAL/EG Wallasey/Egremont
WAL/NB Wallasey/New Brighton
WARR Warrington
WARRN/WOL Warrington north/Woolston
WARRS Warrington south
WARRW/BUR Warrington west/Burtonwood
WAV Wavertree
WD/CROXPK West Derby/Croxteth Park
WDN Widnes
WGN Wigan
WGNE/HIN Wigan east/Hindley
WGNNW/ST Wigan northwest/Standish
WGNS/IIMK Wigan south/Ince-in-Makerfield
WGNW/BIL/OR Wigan west/Billinge/Orrell
WHTN Westhoughton
WKBY West Kirby
WLT/FAZ Walton/Fazakerley
WLTN Woolton

## Index - streets

3rd - Ain


**3rd St** *WGNE/HIN* WN2 **80** A6
**4th St** *WGNE/HIN* WN2 **80** B6

## A

**Abacus Rd** *CLB/OSW/ST* L13 **114** C1
**Abberley Cl** *ECCL* WA10 **8** E5
**Abberley Rd** *WLTN* L25 **131** M6
**Abberley Wy** *WGNS/IIMK* WN3 **78** D1
**Abbey Cl** *BIRK* CH41 **11** L7
*FMBY* L37 **59** K3
*GOL/RIS/CU* WA3 **106** C5
*NWD/KWIPK* L33 **86** B3
*SKEL* WN8 **66** E6
*WDN* WA8 **133** L5
**Abbey Ct** *WGNNW/ST* WN6 **68** A3
*WLTN* L25 **131** K3
**Abbey Dl** *BRSC* L40 **52** B2
*WGNNW/ST* WN6 **54** F6
**Abbey Dr** *WGNW/BIL/O* WN5 **67** G7
**Abbeyfield Dr** *WD/CROXPK* L12 **98** F3
**Abbeyfields** *WGNNW/ST* WN6 **68** A2
**Abbey Fold** *BRSC* L40 **38** F8
**Abbey Gv** *CHLYE* PR6 **44** C6
**Abbey Hey** *RUNC* WA7 **150** E5
**Abbey La** *BRSC* L40 **51** L5
*LEIGH* WN7 **81** M4
**Abbey Rd** *ECCL* WA10 **89** G6
*GOL/RIS/CU* WA3 **93** L5
*RNFD/HAY* WA11 **91** G6
*WDN* WA8 **133** K5
*WKBY* CH48 **124** D3
**Abbey Sq** *LEIGH* WN7 **81** M4
**Abbeystead** *SKEL* WN8 **65** L6
**Abbeystead Av** *NTHTN* L30 **84** C4
**Abbeystead Rd** *WAV* L15 **114** D5
**Abbey St** *BIRK* CH41 **11** L7
**Abbeyvale Dr** *NTHLY* L27 **115** L7
**Abbey Vw** *CHLDW* L16 **115** G6
**Abbeyway North**
*RNFD/HAY* WA11 **91** J6
**Abbeyway South**
*RNFD/HAY* WA11 **91** J7
**Abbeywood** *SKEL* WN8 **65** L6
**Abbeywood Gv**
*RAIN/WH* L35 **117** H3
**Abbingdon Wy** *LEIGH* WN7 **81** M4
**Abbot Cl** *CL/PREN* CH43 **110** E7
**Abbotsbury Wy**
*WD/CROXPK* L12 **99** G2
**Abbots Cl** *FMBY* L37 **59** J4
**Abbots Dr** *BEB* CH63 **143** J1
**Abbotsfield Cl** *WARRS* WA4 **138** A7
**Abbotsfield Rd** *STHEL* WA9 **103** G8
**Abbotsford** *ORM* L39 **51** H8
**Abbotsford Cl**
*GOL/RIS/CU* WA3 **92** F4
**Abbotsford Gdns**
*CSBY/BLUN* L23 **82** E2
**Abbotsford Rd** *CSBY/BLUN* L23 **82** E2
*NG/CROX* L11 **98** A3
**Abbotsford St** *WAL/EG* CH44 **112** A3
**Abbots Hall Av** *STHEL* WA9 **118** F2
**Abbots Ms** *EP* CH65 **20** B2
**Abbots Wy** *FMBY* L37 **59** J3
*NSTN* CH64 **152** F4
**Abbott Dr** *BTL* L20 **84** A8
**Abbotts Cl** *CALD/MH* L18 **130** D2
*RUNC* WA7 **19** H8
**Abbottshey Av** *CALD/MH* L18 **130** D2
**Abbott St** *WGNE/HIN* WN2 **69** L7
**Abbotts Wy** *WGNW/BIL/O* WN5 **89** M2
**Abdale Rd** *NG/CROX* L11 **98** B2
**Abercrombie Rd**
*NWD/KWIPK* L33 **86** D6
**Abercromby Sq** *EHL/KEN* L7 **13** M8
**Aberdale Rd** *CLB/OSW/ST* L13 **114** D2
**Aberdare Cl** *WARRW/BUR* WA5 **121** G4
**Aberdeen St** *BIRK* CH41 **10** F4
**Aberford Av** *WAL/NB* CH45 **95** G8
**Abergele Rd** *CLB/OSW/ST* L13 **114** B3
**Aber St** *NPK/KEN* L6 **113** J2
**Abingdon Av** *WARR* WA1 **123** G6
**Abingdon Gv** *ANF/KKDL* L4 **97** L3
*HLWD* L26 **132** C4
**Abingdon Rd** *ANF/KKDL* L4 **97** L3
*GR/UP/WCH* CH49 **125** K2
**Abinger Rd** *AIMK* WN4 **91** G1
**Abington Dr** *WGNE/HIN* WN2 **80** C4
**Abney Cl** *EHL/KEN* L7 **113** K5
**Aboyne Cl** *WLT/FAZ* L9 **97** J1
**Abrams Fold** *CHTN/BK* PR9 **23** H8
**Abrams Gn** *CHTN/BK* PR9 **23** H8
**Abram St** *EV* L5 **13** K1
*EV* L5 **97** G8
**Abratio St** *BIRK* CH41 **11** G6
**Abstone Cl** *WARR* WA1 **122** E6
**Abyssinia Cl** *WAV* L15 **114** A6
**Acacia Av** *HUY* L36 **115** M4
*WARR* WA1 **122** F5
*WDN* WA8 **134** D2
**Acacia Cl** *CHNE* CH2 **165** L2
*GR/UP/WCH* CH49 **125** L3
**Acacia Crs** *WGNNW/ST* WN6 **68** B2
**Acacia Dr** *GTS/LS* CH66 **163** H4
**Acacia Gv** *ECCL* WA10 **101** J1
*RUNC* WA7 **19** M8
*WAL/EG* CH44 **112** A3
*WKBY* CH48 **124** C3
*WLT/FAZ* L9 **84** D7
**Acacia St** *NEWLW* WA12 **104** B1
**Academy St** *WARR* WA1 **14** F6
**Academy Wy** *WARR* WA1 **14** E7
**Acanthus Rd** *CLB/OSW/ST* L13 **114** C1
**Access Rd** *WD/CROXPK* L12 **98** F6
**Acer Leigh** *AIG/SPK* L17 **129** M4
**Acheson Rd** *CLB/OSW/ST* L13 **98** A7
**Achilles Av** *WARRN/WOL* WA2 **121** K3
**Ackerley Cl** *WARRN/WOL* WA2 **122** B2
**Ackers Hall Av** *DV/KA/FCH* L14 **115** H1
**Ackers Hall Cl** *DV/KA/FCH* L14 **99** H8
**Ackers La** *ECCL* WA10 **101** L1
*HTWN* L38 **70** F5
*WARRS* WA4 **138** A4
**Ackers Rd** *GR/UP/WCH* CH49 **126** E3
*WARRS* WA4 **138** A3
**Ackhurst La** *WGNW/BIL/O* WN5 **67** J2
**Ackhurst Rd** *CHLY/EC* PR7 **32** B5
**Acland Rd** *WAL/EG* CH44 **111** K1
**Aconbury Cl** *NG/CROX* L11 **98** B2
**Aconbury Pl** *NG/CROX* L11 **98** B2
**Acorn Cl** *BEB* CH63 **127** M7
*STHEL* WA9 **118** E1
**Acorn Dr** *EP* CH65 **163** K4
**Acornfield Cl** *NWD/KWIPK* L33 **86** E5
**Acornfield Rd** *NWD/KWIPK* L33 **86** F4
**Acorn St** *NEWLW* WA12 **104** E2
**Acorn Wy** *BTL* L20 **7** J1
**A Ct** *AIMK* WN4 **91** K3
**Acrefield** *SKEL* WN8 **53** J4
**Acrefield Pk** *WLTN* L25 **131** J2
**Acrefield Rd** *RF/TRAN* CH42 **127** K4
*WDN* WA8 **133** K4
*WLTN* L25 **131** J2
**Acre Gn** *HLWD* L26 **132** C7
**Acre La** *HES* CH60 **141** L4
*PS/BROM* CH62 **143** L6
**Acre Rd** *GTS/LS* CH66 **155** M8
**Acresfield** *CHLY/EC* PR7 **44** B7
**Acresfield Cl** *HOR/BR* BL6 **57** L2
**Acresgate Ct** *WLTN* L25 **115** J8
**Acres La** *FMBY* L37 **60** A6
*ORM* L39 **61** G6
**Acres Rd** *BEB* CH63 **128** B7
*HOY* CH47 **109** G6
**Acreswood Cl** *CHLY/EC* PR7 **43** G5
**Acreville Rd** *BEB* CH63 **128** B8
**Acton Cl** *RNFD/HAY* WA11 **90** E7
**Acton Gv** *NPK/KEN* L6 **97** L7
**Acton La** *MOR/LEA* CH46 **109** L6
**Acton Rd** *KKBY* L32 **85** L3
*RF/TRAN* CH42 **128** C4
*WARRW/BUR* WA5 **104** A7
**Acton St** *WGN* WN1 **4** F2
**Acton Ter** *WGN* WN1 **4** F1
**Acton Wy** *EHL/KEN* L7 **113** L5
**Acuba Gv** *BIRK* CH41 **128** A1
**Acuba Rd** *WAV* L15 **114** E4
**Adair Pl** *CLB/OSW/ST* L13 **98** A6
**Adair Rd** *CLB/OSW/ST* L13 **98** A6
**Adam Av** *GTS/LS* CH66 **162** E2
**Adam Cl** *GTS/LS* CH66 **162** F1
**Adams Cl** *NEWLW* WA12 **104** F3
**Adams Dr** *WGNS/IIMK* WN3 **68** B8
**Adamson Ct** *WARRS* WA4 **138** D3
**Adamson St** *AIMK* WN4 **91** J2
*EHL/KEN* L7 **113** M3
*WARRS* WA4 **14** E9
**Adam St** *EV* L5 **97** H7
*WARRN/WOL* WA2 **15** G1
**Adaston Av** *PS/BROM* CH62 **155** H1
**Ada St** *STHEL* WA9 **9** L9
**Adcote Cl** *DV/KA/FCH* L14 **115** H2
**Adcote Rd** *DV/KA/FCH* L14 **115** H2
**Adderley St** *EHL/KEN* L7 **113** K3
**Addingham Av** *WDN* WA8 **133** L6
**Addingham Rd** *CALD/MH* L18 **114** D8
**Addington St** *WAL/EG* CH44 **111** M2
**Addison Sq** *WDN* WA8 **16** C1
**Addison St** *BTL* L20 **83** J8
*VAUX/LVPD* L3 **13** G4
*WGNS/IIMK* WN3 **4** D5
**Addison Wy** *VAUX/LVPD* L3 **12** F4
**Adelaide Av** *STHEL* WA9 **102** A6
**Adelaide Pl** *EV* L5 **13** J1
**Adelaide Rd** *EHL/KEN* L7 **113** K3
*LITH* L21 **83** H6
*RF/TRAN* CH42 **127** L1
**Adelaide St** *WAL/EG* CH44 **111** K3
**Adelaide Ter** *CSBY/WL* L22 **82** E4
**Adela Rd** *RUNC* WA7 **18** E4
**Adele Thompson Dr** *TOX* L8 **113** J6
**Adelphi St** *BIRK* CH41 **11** J5
*WGNNW/ST* WN6 **56** A4
**Adfalent La** *NSTN* CH64 **154** C6
**Adkins St** *EV* L5 **97** J7
**Adlam Crs** *WLT/FAZ* L9 **85** G6
**Adlam Rd** *AIN/FAZ* L10 **85** G6
**Adlington Ct**
*GOL/RIS/CU* WA3 **107** H7
*GOL/RIS/CU* WA3 **107** H7
**Adlington Rd** *RUNC* WA7 **150** F3
**Admin Rd** *NWD/KWIPK* L33 **86** E5
**Admirals Rd** *GOL/RIS/CU* WA3 **123** G2
**Admiral St** *TOX* L8 **113** H8
**Admiralty Cl** *BRSC* L40 **51** L3
**Adrian's Wy** *KKBY* L32 **86** A3
**Adshead Rd** *CLB/OSW/ST* L13 **98** A6
**Adstone Rd** *WLTN* L25 **115** L8
**Adswood Rd** *HUY* L36 **116** A2
**Adwell Cl** *GOL/RIS/CU* WA3 **93** J5
**Africander Rd** *RNFD/HAY* WA11 **89** J5
**Afton** *WDN* WA8 **133** J3
**Agar Rd** *NG/CROX* L11 **98** B6
**Agate St** *NPK/KEN* L6 **97** J8
**Agincourt Rd** *WD/CROXPK* L12 **98** E8
**Agnes Gv** *WAL/EG* CH44 **95** L8
**Agnes Rd** *CSBY/BLUN* L23 **82** E2
*RF/TRAN* CH42 **127** M2
**Agnes St** *STHEL* WA9 **118** E2
**Agnes Wy** *EHL/KEN* L7 **113** K4
**Aiden Long Gv** *PR/KW* L34 **100** A7
**Aigburth Dr** *AIG/SPK* L17 **129** L1
**Aigburth Hall Av** *ALL/GAR* L19 **130** C5
**Aigburth Hall Rd** *ALL/GAR* L19 **130** C5
**Aigburth Rd** *AIG/SPK* L17 **129** K2
*ALL/GAR* L19 **130** B5
**Aigburth St** *TOX* L8 **113** K5
**Aigburth V** *AIG/SPK* L17 **129** M3
*CALD/MH* L18 **130** A2
**Ailsa Rd** *WAL/NB* CH45 **95** J8
**Ainley Cl** *RUNC* WA7 **150** C8
**Ainscough Rd** *GOL/RIS/CU* WA3 **123** G2
**Ainsdale Cl** *AIN/FAZ* L10 **85** H5
*BEB* CH63 **143** L8
*PEN/TH* CH61 **126** C8
*WARRW/BUR* WA5 **136** B1
**Ainsdale Rd** *BTL* L20 **83** M8
**Ainse Rd** *HOR/BR* BL6 **57** K2
**Ainsworth Av** *MOR/LEA* CH46 **109** L7
**Ainsworth La** *PR/KW* L34 **86** D7
**Ainsworth Rd** *ECCL* WA10 **8** B2
**Ainsworth St** *VAUX/LVPD* L3 **13** K7
**Aintree Crs** *STHP* PR8 **36** B2
**Aintree Gv** *GTS/LS* CH66 **162** F2
**Aintree La** *AIN/FAZ* L10 **84** E3
**Aintree Rd** *BTL* L20 **7** K2
*WLT/FAZ* L9 **84** F7

Airdale Cl *CL/PREN* CH43 .......... 110 E7
Airdale Rd *WAV* L15 .......... 114 B7
Airdrie Cl *PS/BROM* CH62 .......... 154 F2
Aire *WDN* WA8 .......... 133 K3
Airedale Cl *WARRW/BUR* WA5.......... 16 B6
Airegate *MGHL* L31 .......... 72 D3
Airlie Gv *LYMM* WA13 .......... 139 M1
Airlie Rd *HOY* CH47 .......... 108 D7
Airton Rd *WLT/FAZ* L9 .......... 79 K2
Aisthorpe Gv *MGHL* L31 .......... 72 F6
Ajax Av *WARRN/WOL* WA2 .......... 121 K3
The Akbar *HES* CH60 .......... 140 E4
Akenside St *BTL* L20 .......... 83 J7
Alabama Wy *BIRK* CH41 .......... 11 M6
Alamein Crs *WARRN/WOL* WA2 .......... 14 F1
Alamein Rd *HUY* L36 .......... 115 M1
Alance Br *CHLYE* PR6 .......... 45 H1
Alans Wy *NWD/KWIPK* L33 .......... 86 A1
Alastair Crs *CL/PREN* CH43 .......... 127 H4
Alban Rd *CHLDW* L16 .......... 114 F5
Albany Av *PR/KW* L34 .......... 101 H6
Albany Crs *LYMM* WA13 .......... 139 M1
Albany Gv *LYMM* WA13 .......... 139 L1
Albany Rd *CLB/OSW/ST* L13 .......... 114 C4
  *EHL/KEN* L7 .......... 113 J3
  *LYMM* WA13 .......... 139 L2
  *PR/KW* L34 .......... 101 G7
  *RF/TRAN* CH42 .......... 128 A3
  *STHP* PR8 .......... 24 D4
  *WLT/FAZ* L9 .......... 84 D6
Albany Ter *RUNC* WA7 .......... 19 G4
Albemarle Rd *WAL/EG* CH44 .......... 111 M2
Albert Dr *BTL* L20 .......... 84 B7
  *NSTN* CH64 .......... 152 F5
  *WARRW/BUR* WA5 .......... 119 M7
Albert Edward Rd *EHL/KEN* L7 .......... 113 J3
Albert Gv *CSBY/BLUN* L23 .......... 82 F1
  *WAV* L15 .......... 114 C5
Alberton Cl *WGNE/HIN* WN2 .......... 57 L7
Albert Pk *AIG/SPK* L17 .......... 113 K6
Albert Pl *STHP* PR8 .......... 3 G2
Albert Rd *BRSC* L40 .......... 39 J2
  *CHTN/BK* PR9 .......... 3 K1
  *CLB/OSW/ST* L13 .......... 97 M7
  *CSBY/WL* L22 .......... 82 F4
  *FMBY* L37 .......... 58 D5
  *HOY* CH47 .......... 108 D7
  *RF/TRAN* CH42 .......... 127 L1
  *WARRS* WA4 .......... 138 C3
  *WDN* WA8 .......... 16 F2
  *WKBY* CH48 .......... 124 C4
**Albert Schweitzer Av**
  *NTHTN* L30 .......... 84 B2
Albert St *AIMK* WN4 .......... 91 K2
  *CHLY/EC* PR7 .......... 32 F6
  *ECCL* WA10 .......... 9 G1
  *EHL/KEN* L7 .......... 113 J4
  *RUNC* WA7 .......... 19 G4
  *WGNE/HIN* WN2 .......... 69 M8
  *WGNW/BIL/O* WN5 .......... 68 B7
Albert Ter *STHP* PR8 .......... 2 F8
Albion Dr *WDN* WA8 .......... 16 F4
Albion Pl *WAL/NB* CH45 .......... 95 K5
Albion St *BIRK* CH41 .......... 11 L5
  *CHLY/EC* PR7 .......... 32 E6
  *ECCL* WA10 .......... 9 G7
  *EV* L5 .......... 97 G7
  *WAL/NB* CH45 .......... 95 J5
  *WGNE/HIN* WN2 .......... 69 K3
  *WGNE/HIN* WN2 .......... 80 C3
Albourne Rd *KKBY* L32 .......... 86 C5
Albury Cl *RNFD/HAY* WA11 .......... 90 E6
  *WD/CROXPK* L12 .......... 99 H3
Albury Rd *KKBY* L32 .......... 86 B6
Albury Wy *WGNE/HIN* WN2 .......... 69 H3
Alcester Rd *WD/CROXPK* L12 .......... 98 E7
Alcock St *RUNC* WA7 .......... 19 H2
Aldams Gv *ANF/KKDL* L4 .......... 7 L9
Aldbourne Av *CALD/MH* L18 .......... 115 G8
Aldbourne Rd *WLTN* L25 .......... 131 G1
Aldcliffe *GOL/RIS/CU* WA3 .......... 93 H6
Alder Av *AIMK* WN4 .......... 79 L6
  *HUY* L36 .......... 116 C5
  *WDN* WA8 .......... 134 C2
  *WGNW/BIL/O* WN5 .......... 67 M7
  *WGNW/BIL/O* WN5 .......... 77 M8
**Alderbank Rd**
  *WARRW/BUR* WA5 .......... 120 C7
Alderbrook Dr *SKEL* WN8 .......... 53 L3
Alder Cl *PR/KW* L34 .......... 101 H7
Alder Crs *KKBY* L32 .......... 85 M2
  *WARRN/WOL* WA2 .......... 121 L5
Alderdale Av *STHP* PR8 .......... 34 C8
Alder Dr *CHLY/EC* PR7 .......... 42 F2
  *GTS/LS* CH66 .......... 163 H4
Alderfield Dr *SPK/HALE* L24 .......... 147 J3
Alder Gv *CHLY/EC* PR7 .......... 43 H4
  *CSBY/WL* L22 .......... 82 F3
Alder Hey Rd *ECCL* WA10 .......... 101 L1
Alder La *FROD/HEL* WA6 .......... 159 M2
  *ORM* L39 .......... 48 A5
  *PR/KW* L34 .......... 99 K3
  *RNFD/HAY* WA11 .......... 77 H8
  *SKEL* WN8 .......... 53 L4
  *WARRN/WOL* WA2 .......... 121 K5
  *WARRW/BUR* WA5 .......... 104 C6
  *WDN* WA8 .......... 133 H1
Alder Lee Cl *WGNS/IIMK* WN3 .......... 78 B3
Alderley Av *BIRK* CH41 .......... 111 H6
  *GOL/RIS/CU* WA3 .......... 92 F6
Alderley Rd *HOY* CH47 .......... 108 D6
  *WAL/EG* CH44 .......... 111 K2
  *WARRS* WA4 .......... 138 A3
Alderney Cl *EP* CH65 .......... 163 L4
Alderney Dr *WGNS/IIMK* WN3 .......... 79 J2
Alderney Rd *EV* L5 .......... 96 F8
Alder Rd *BEB* CH63 .......... 142 F1
  *GOL/RIS/CU* WA3 .......... 93 H5
  *PR/KW* L34 .......... 101 H7
  *WARR* WA1 .......... 122 F6
  *WD/CROXPK* L12 .......... 114 D1
**Alder Root La**
  *WARRN/WOL* WA2 .......... 104 C3
Aldersey Cl *RUNC* WA7 .......... 187 J8
Aldersey St *VAUX/LVPD* L3 .......... 13 H3
Aldersgate *RF/TRAN* CH42 .......... 128 B3

Aldersgate Av *RUNC* WA7 .......... 150 F6
Aldersgate Dr *HLWD* L26 .......... 132 C7
Alderson Crs *FMBY* L37 .......... 59 H1
Alderson Rd *WAV* L15 .......... 113 M6
Alder St *NEWLW* WA12 .......... 104 E2
Alderton Dr *AIMK* WN4 .......... 91 J2
Alderville Rd *ANF/KKDL* L4 .......... 97 J3
Alder Wood Av *SPK/HALE* L24 .......... 147 G2
Aldewood Cl *GOL/RIS/CU* WA3 .......... 107 J7
Aldford Cl *BEB* CH63 .......... 143 K7
  *CL/PREN* CH43 .......... 127 G3
Aldford Rd *KKBY* L32 .......... 86 A6
Aldford Wy *WGNNW/ST* WN6 .......... 56 A5
Aldgate *EP* CH65 .......... 156 C8
Aldred St *WGNE/HIN* WN2 .......... 80 F1
Aldridge Cl *WD/CROXPK* L12 .......... 99 G2
  *WGNS/IIMK* WN3 .......... 79 K2
Aldridge Dr *WARRW/BUR* WA5 .......... 104 B6
Aldrins La *NTHTN* L30 .......... 84 B1
Aldwark Rd *DV/KA/FCH* L14 .......... 115 J1
Aldwych Rd *WD/CROXPK* L12 .......... 98 E7
Aldykes *MGHL* L31 .......... 73 G5
Alexander Cl *BRSC* L40 .......... 52 B2
Alexander Dr *MGHL* L31 .......... 72 F2
  *PEN/TH* CH61 .......... 141 G2
  *WDN* WA8 .......... 133 M5
**Alexander Fleming Av**
  *NTHTN* L30 .......... 84 B1
Alexander Gv *RUNC* WA7 .......... 19 L5
Alexandra Ct *NPK/KEN* L6 .......... 113 K2
**Alexandra Crs**
  *WGNW/BIL/O* WN5 .......... 68 A7
Alexandra Dr *AIG/SPK* L17 .......... 129 K1
  *BTL* L20 .......... 84 A7
  *ECCL* WA10 .......... 8 C7
  *RF/TRAN* CH42 .......... 128 A4
Alexandra Ms *ORM* L39 .......... 51 G7
Alexandra Mt *LITH* L21 .......... 83 K5
Alexandra Pk *AIG/SPK* L17 .......... 129 K2
Alexandra Pk *AIMK* WN4 .......... 91 K1
  *BRSC* L40 .......... 51 M1
  *CHTN/BK* PR9 .......... 3 K1
  *CL/PREN* CH43 .......... 10 E7
  *CLB/OSW/ST* L13 .......... 114 C4
  *CSBY/BLUN* L23 .......... 82 F1
  *CSBY/WL* L22 .......... 83 G5
  *EHL/KEN* L7 .......... 113 L5
  *FMBY* L37 .......... 58 D5
  *WAL/NB* CH45 .......... 95 J5
  *WARRS* WA4 .......... 138 B3
  *WKBY* CH48 .......... 124 C4
Alexandra St *ECCL* WA10 .......... 101 M4
  *EP* CH65 .......... 20 C1
  *WARR* WA1 .......... 15 L2
  *WDN* WA8 .......... 16 C6
  *WGNE/HIN* WN2 .......... 80 C5
  *WGNW/BIL/O* WN5 .......... 68 B7
Alexandria Rd *WD/CROXPK* L12 .......... 130 E6
Alfonso Rd *ANF/KKDL* L4 .......... 96 F5
Alford Av *STHEL* WA9 .......... 118 D1
Alforde St *WDN* WA8 .......... 16 D6
Alford St *EHL/KEN* L7 .......... 114 A3
Alfred Cl *WDN* WA8 .......... 16 E4
Alfred Dr *WDN* WA8 .......... 16 E4
Alfred Rd *CL/PREN* CH43 .......... 10 E7
  *GOL/RIS/CU* WA3 .......... 93 J5
  *RNFD/HAY* WA11 .......... 91 G6
  *WAL/EG* CH44 .......... 112 A4
Alfred St *ECCL* WA10 .......... 9 J3
  *NEWLW* WA12 .......... 105 G2
  *RNFD/HAY* WA11 .......... 76 B6
  *WAV* L15 .......... 113 M5
  *WDN* WA8 .......... 16 E4
  *WGN* WN1 .......... 68 D3
  *WGNE/HIN* WN2 .......... 80 C2
  *WGNS/IIMK* WN3 .......... 5 H8
Alfriston Rd *WD/CROXPK* L12 .......... 98 F7
Algernon St *RUNC* WA7 .......... 18 E2
  *WARR* WA1 .......... 15 J3
  *WARRS* WA4 .......... 137 L4
  *WGNE/HIN* WN2 .......... 69 M8
  *WGNS/IIMK* WN3 .......... 79 J1
Alice Ct *WDN* WA8 .......... 149 J1
Alice St *STHEL* WA9 .......... 103 G5
Alison Av *RF/TRAN* CH42 .......... 128 B2
Alison Pl *CLB/OSW/ST* L13 .......... 98 A6
Alison Rd *CLB/OSW/ST* L13 .......... 98 A6
Alistair Dr *BEB* CH63 .......... 143 L7
Alker La *CHLYE* PR6 .......... 32 C2
Alker St *CHLY/EC* PR7 .......... 32 E6
  *WGNW/BIL/O* WN5 .......... 68 B7
Allangate Cl *GR/UP/WCH* CH49 .......... 125 L3
Allangate Rd *ALL/GAR* L19 .......... 130 D5
Allan Rd *RNFD/HAY* WA11 .......... 89 L6
Allans Cl *NSTN* CH64 .......... 153 G7
Allans Meadow *NSTN* CH64 .......... 153 G7
Allanson St *STHEL* WA9 .......... 102 F3
Allcard St *WARRW/BUR* WA5 .......... 14 B7
Allcot Av *RF/TRAN* CH42 .......... 127 M3
Allen Av *GOL/RIS/CU* WA3 .......... 107 L1
Allenby Av *CSBY/WL* L22 .......... 83 H1
Allenby Sq *CLB/OSW/ST* L13 .......... 114 B3
Allendale *RUNC* WA7 .......... 150 D7
  *RAIN/WH* L35 .......... 117 M2
  *WLT/FAZ* L9 .......... 84 D6
Allengate *CSBY/BLUN* L23 .......... 71 G8
Allen Rd *RUNC* WA7 .......... 18 B9
Allen St *WARRN/WOL* WA2 .......... 14 D4
Allerby Wy *GOL/RIS/CU* WA3 .......... 93 M5
Allerford Rd *WD/CROXPK* L12 .......... 98 F5
Allerton Beeches *CALD/MH* L18 .......... 130 D2
Allerton Dr *CALD/MH* L18 .......... 130 D1
Allerton Gv *RF/TRAN* CH42 .......... 127 M2
Allerton Rd *CALD/MH* L18 .......... 114 D8
  *CHTN/BK* PR9 .......... 25 G4
  *RF/TRAN* CH42 .......... 127 M2
  *WAL/NB* CH45 .......... 95 J5
  *WDN* WA8 .......... 16 F1
  *WGN* WN1 .......... 131 H4
Allesley Rd *DV/KA/FCH* L14 .......... 99 H8
Alleyne Rd *ANF/KKDL* L4 .......... 97 M5
Alliance Av *WGN* WN1 .......... 4 F3
Allington St *AIG/SPK* L17 .......... 129 K2
Allonby Cl *CL/PREN* CH43 .......... 127 G1
Allport La *PS/BROM* CH62 .......... 143 M4
Allport Rd *BEB* CH63 .......... 143 L7
The Allports *PS/BROM* CH62 .......... 143 M6
All Saints Cl *NTHTN* L30 .......... 84 A1

All Saints Dr *WARRS* WA4 .......... 139 G2
All Saints Rd *SPK/HALE* L24 .......... 146 E2
Allscott Wy *AIMK* WN4 .......... 91 L2
Allscott Rd *AIN/FAZ* L10 .......... 85 K6
  *SKEL* WN8 .......... 66 E6
Alma Ct *SKEL* WN8 .......... 66 E6
Almacs Cl *CSBY/BLUN* L23 .......... 82 D2
Alma Dr *CHLY/EC* PR7 .......... 43 G1
Alma Gv *WGNS/IIMK* WN3 .......... 79 G3
Alma Hl *SKEL* WN8 .......... 66 E7
Alma Pde *SKEL* WN8 .......... 66 E7
Alma Pl *STHEL* WA9 .......... 9 L8
Alma Rd *AIG/SPK* L17 .......... 130 A5
  *SKEL* WN8 .......... 66 E6
  *STHP* PR8 .......... 2 E9
Alma St *BIRK* CH41 .......... 11 K6
  *NEWLW* WA12 .......... 104 D2
  *PS/BROM* CH62 .......... 128 C6
  *STHEL* WA9 .......... 9 L8
Alma Vale Ter *BTL* L20 .......... 6 F5
Almeda Rd *SPK/HALE* L24 .......... 147 J3
Almer Dr *WARRW/BUR* WA5 .......... 120 E8
Almond Av *BRSC* L40 .......... 39 G7
  *NTHTN* L30 .......... 83 J2
  *RUNC* WA7 .......... 19 L8
**Almond Brook Rd**
  *WGNNW/ST* WN6 .......... 55 K3
Almond Cl *HLWD* L26 .......... 132 A6
  *RNFD/HAY* WA11 .......... 90 B8
Almond Ct *ALL/GAR* L19 .......... 131 G8
Almond Crs *WGNNW/ST* WN6 .......... 56 B6
Almond Dr *WARRW/BUR* WA5 .......... 104 B7
Almond Gv *WARR* WA1 .......... 122 D6
  *WGNW/BIL/O* WN5 .......... 68 A7
Almond Pl *MOR/LEA* CH46 .......... 110 B5
Almond's Gn *WD/CROXPK* L12 .......... 98 C5
Almond's Gv *WD/CROXPK* L12 .......... 98 C6
Almonds Pk *WD/CROXPK* L12 .......... 98 C5
Almond's Turn *NTHTN* L30 .......... 83 M1
**Almond Wy**
  *GR/UP/WCH* CH49 .......... 125 L3
Alness Dr *RAIN/WH* L35 .......... 117 M3
Alnwick Cl *WGNE/HIN* WN2 .......... 57 M8
Alnwick Dr *EP* CH65 .......... 163 M5
  *MOR/LEA* CH46 .......... 109 J3
Alpass Rd *AIG/SPK* L17 .......... 129 K2
Alpha Dr *RF/TRAN* CH42 .......... 128 C4
Alpha St *LITH* L21 .......... 83 K8
Alpine Cl *ECCL* WA10 .......... 101 L1
Alpine Dr *LEIGH* WN7 .......... 81 L5
Alpine Rd *CHLYE* PR6 .......... 33 G2
  *NEWLW* WA12 .......... 104 C2
Airesford Rd *ALL/GAR* L19 .......... 130 B5
Alroy Rd *ANF/KKDL* L4 .......... 97 J6
Alscot Av *AIN/FAZ* L10 .......... 85 K6
Alscot Cl *MGHL* L31 .......... 72 F5
Alston Cl *PS/BROM* CH62 .......... 144 B6
Alston Rd *AIG/SPK* L17 .......... 130 A5
  *WGNE/HIN* WN2 .......... 69 H3
Alt *WDN* WA8 .......... 133 K3
Alt Av *MGHL* L31 .......... 72 E6
Altbridge Pk *NG/CROX* L11 .......... 85 K8
Alt Bridge Rd *HUY* L36 .......... 115 M1
Altcar Av *WAV* L15 .......... 113 M6
Altcar Dr *MOR/LEA* CH46 .......... 109 M6
Altcar La *FMBY* L37 .......... 59 H4
  *MGHL* L31 .......... 72 C1
  *ORM* L39 .......... 61 H4
Altcar Rd *FMBY* L37 .......... 59 K3
Alt Cl *LEIGH* WN7 .......... 81 M8
Altcross Rd *NG/CROX* L11 .......... 98 E2
Altcross Wy *NG/CROX* L11 .......... 98 E1
Altfield Rd *DV/KA/FCH* L14 .......... 99 H6
Altfinch Cl *DV/KA/FCH* L14 .......... 99 J6
Altham Rd *NG/CROX* L11 .......... 98 B6
  *STHP* PR8 .......... 36 A3
Althorpe Dr *STHP* PR8 .......... 36 A2
Althorp St *TOX* L8 .......... 129 H2
Alt Cl *LEIGH* WN7 .......... 81 M8
Alton Av *LITH* L21 .......... 83 J4
Alton Cl *AIMK* WN4 .......... 91 J1
  *HTWN* L38 .......... 70 B3
Alton Rd *CL/PREN* CH43 .......... 10 B8
  *NPK/KEN* L6 .......... 97 M8
Alt Rd *BTL* L20 .......... 83 L8
  *FMBY* L37 .......... 59 J4
  *HTWN* L38 .......... 70 B1
  *HUY* L36 .......... 116 A2
Alt Side Ct *AIN/FAZ* L10 .......... 85 K6
Alt St *TOX* L8 .......... 113 K6
Altway *AIN/FAZ* L10 .......... 84 E2
Altys La *ORM* L39 .......... 63 H2
Alundale Rd *FROD/HEL* WA6 .......... 166 E3
Alvanley Cl *WGNW/BIL/O* WN5 .......... 67 K4
Alvanley Dr *FROD/HEL* WA6 .......... 166 E3
Alvanley Pl *CL/PREN* CH43 .......... 10 E6
Alvanley Rd *FROD/HEL* WA6 .......... 166 E3
  *GTS/LS* CH66 .......... 163 G1
  *KKBY* L32 .......... 85 L3
  *WD/CROXPK* L12 .......... 98 E8
Alvanley Vw *CHNE* CH2 .......... 165 K2
Alvega Dr *PS/BROM* CH62 .......... 128 E6
Alverstone Av *BIRK* CH41 .......... 111 H6
**Alverstone Cl**
  *WARRW/BUR* WA5 .......... 119 L6
Alverstone Rd *CALD/MH* L18 .......... 114 B8
  *WAL/EG* CH44 .......... 111 M2
Alverton Cl *WDN* WA8 .......... 133 M5
Alvina La *ANF/KKDL* L4 .......... 97 G6
  *NWD/KWIPK* L33 .......... 74 C8
Alwain Gn *SPK/HALE* L24 .......... 147 H3
Alwen St *BIRK* CH41 .......... 111 H4
Alwyn Av *LITH* L21 .......... 83 K4
Alwyn Gdns *MOR/LEA* CH46 .......... 110 B5
Alwyn St *AIG/SPK* L17 .......... 129 K2
  *WGN* WN1 .......... 5 H1
Alwyn Ter *WGN* WN1 .......... 5 H1
Amanda Rd *AIN/FAZ* L10 .......... 85 K6
  *RAIN/WH* L35 .......... 101 K3
Amanda Wy *MGHL* L31 .......... 85 K1
Amar St *WGNE/HIN* WN2 .......... 5 M6
Amaryllis Cl *WGNE/HIN* WN2 .......... 69 J3
Amaury Cl *CSBY/BLUN* L23 .......... 71 K8
Amaury Rd *CSBY/BLUN* L23 .......... 71 K8
Ambassador Dr *HLWD* L26 .......... 132 C4
Amber Gdns *WGNE/HIN* WN2 .......... 81 C1
Ambergate *SKEL* WN8 .......... 65 K6

Ambergate Cl *STHEL* WA9 .......... 102 F6
Ambergate Rd *ALL/GAR* L19 .......... 130 D6
Amberley Av *MOR/LEA* CH46 .......... 109 L6
Amberley Cl *MOR/LEA* CH46 .......... 109 L6
  *NPK/KEN* L6 .......... 97 M6
  *WGNE/HIN* WN2 .......... 69 H3
Amberswood Cl *WGNE/HIN* WN2 .......... 69 K6
Amber Wy *DV/KA/FCH* L14 .......... 99 J6
Ambleside Wy *WGNE/HIN* WN2 .......... 69 K5
  *WGNW/BIL/O* WN5 .......... 67 L6
Ambleside Av *CHLY/EC* PR7 .......... 31 M4
  *MOR/LEA* CH46 .......... 109 M5
Ambleside Cl *PEN/TH* CH61 .......... 126 C7
  *PS/BROM* CH62 .......... 144 A6
**Ambleside Crs**
  *WARRN/WOL* WA2 .......... 121 L2
Ambleside Rd *CALD/MH* L18 .......... 130 F4
  *EP* CH65 .......... 163 L3
  *MGHL* L31 .......... 72 F3
Amelia Cl *NPK/KEN* L6 .......... 13 M4
  *WDN* WA8 .......... 134 D1
Amelia St *WARRN/WOL* WA2 .......... 15 G1
Amersham St *CALD/MH* L18 .......... 65 K6
Amersham Rd *ANF/KKDL* L4 .......... 97 L3
Amery Gv *RF/TRAN* CH42 .......... 127 L3
**Amesbury Dr**
  *WGNS/IIMK* WN3 .......... 78 E3
Amherst Rd *AIG/SPK* L17 .......... 129 L3
Amis Gv *GOL/RIS/CU* WA3 .......... 93 G5
Amity St *TOX* L8 .......... 113 H8
Amos Av *LITH* L21 .......... 83 L5
Ampleforth Cl *KKBY* L32 .......... 85 L4
Ampthill Rd *AIG/SPK* L17 .......... 129 L3
Ampulla Rd *NG/CROX* L11 .......... 98 E2
Ancaster Rd *AIG/SPK* L17 .......... 129 L3
Ancholme Cl *RAIN/WH* L35 .......... 101 J7
**The Anchorage** *LYMM* WA13 .......... 139 M2
  *NSTN* CH64 .......... 152 E6
  *VAUX/LVPD* L3 .......... 112 F7
Anchor Cl *RUNC* WA7 .......... 150 F7
Anchor St *CHTN/BK* PR9 .......... 3 H3
Ancient Mdw *WLT/FAZ* L9 .......... 84 D6
Ancroft Rd *DV/KA/FCH* L14 .......... 115 J1
Ancrum Rd *NWD/KWIPK* L33 .......... 73 M7
Anders Dr *NWD/KWIPK* L33 .......... 74 C8
Anderson Av *BTL* L20 .......... 6 C2
Anderson Cl *PEN/TH* CH61 .......... 117 M4
  *RAIN/WH* L35 .......... 117 M4
  *WARRN/WOL* WA2 .......... 122 D3
Anderson Rd *LITH* L21 .......... 83 M4
Anderson St *EV* L5 .......... 97 G7
Anderton Rd *CHLY/EC* PR7 .......... 31 M4
Anderton St *CHLY/EC* PR7 .......... 32 E6
  *CHLYE* PR6 .......... 44 C5
  *WGNE/HIN* WN2 .......... 5 L6
Anderton Ter *HUY* L36 .......... 116 A3
Anderton Wy *WGNE/HIN* WN2 .......... 69 K3
**Andover Cl**
  *WARRN/WOL* WA2 .......... 122 A4
Andover Crs *WGNS/IIMK* WN3 .......... 78 E3
Andover Rd *RNFD/HAY* WA11 .......... 91 G5
Andover Wy *WLTN* L25 .......... 131 M5
Andreas Cl *STHP* PR8 .......... 3 G9
Andrew Av *MGHL* L31 .......... 85 J2
  *WGNW/BIL/O* WN5 .......... 78 A8
Andrew Cl *WDN* WA8 .......... 133 L5
Andrews Cl *FMBY* L37 .......... 59 G4
Andrews La *FMBY* L37 .......... 59 G4
Andrew St *ANF/KKDL* L4 .......... 97 H4
Andrew's Wk *HES* CH60 .......... 141 K5
Andrews Yort *FMBY* L37 .......... 59 G4
Anfield Rd *ANF/KKDL* L4 .......... 97 H6
Angela St *EHL/KEN* L7 .......... 113 K5
Angers La *MGHL* L31 .......... 73 K7
Anglesea Rd *WLT/FAZ* L9 .......... 97 H2
Anglesea Wy *TOX* L8 .......... 129 H1
Anglesey Cl *EP* CH65 .......... 163 L4
Anglesey Rd *WAL/EG* CH44 .......... 95 K8
  *WKBY* CH48 .......... 124 C2
Anglezark Cl *EHL/KEN* L7 .......... 113 K5
Anglezarke Rd *CHLYE* PR6 .......... 44 C6
Anglo Cl *WLT/FAZ* L9 .......... 84 E5
Angus Av *LEIGH* WN7 .......... 81 M6
Angus Rd *BEB* CH63 .......... 143 L7
  *NG/CROX* L11 .......... 98 B5
Aniline St *CHLYE* PR6 .......... 33 G5
Anjou Bvd *WGNW/BIL/O* WN5 .......... 68 A5
Annandale Cl *NWD/KWIPK* L33 .......... 73 M7
Annandale Gdns *SKEL* WN8 .......... 66 C6
Annan Gv *AIMK* WN4 .......... 80 A3
Ann Cl *GTS/LS* CH66 .......... 155 M6
Anne Av *STHP* PR8 .......... 35 G7
Anne Gv *STHEL* WA9 .......... 102 E6
Annerley St *EHL/KEN* L7 .......... 113 L5
Annesley Crs *WGNS/IIMK* WN3 .......... 79 H2
Annesley Rd *AIG/SPK* L17 .......... 129 L3
  *WAL/EG* CH44 .......... 111 K2
Anne St *STHEL* WA9 .......... 118 F2
Annette Av *NEWLW* WA12 .......... 91 J8
Annie Rd *BTL* L20 .......... 83 M7
Annie St *WARRN/WOL* WA2 .......... 15 G3
Ann St *RUNC* WA7 .......... 19 J2
  *SKEL* WN8 .......... 65 G4
Ann St West *WDN* WA8 .......... 16 E6
Anscot Av *BEB* CH63 .......... 128 B7
Ansdell Dr *ECCL* WA10 .......... 88 D8
Ansdell Gv *CHTN/BK* PR9 .......... 25 J1
Ansdell Rd *WDN* WA8 .......... 134 D3
  *WGNW/BIL/O* WN5 .......... 67 M8
Ansdell Villas' Rd *RAIN/WH* L35 .......... 117 L1
Ansford Rd *WGNE/HIN* WN2 .......... 80 D5
Anson Cl *WARRN/WOL* WA2 .......... 122 A3
Anson Pl *VAUX/LVPD* L3 .......... 13 L5
  *WGNW/BIL/O* WN5 .......... 67 L5
Anson St *VAUX/LVPD* L3 .......... 13 L6
  *WGNW/BIL/O* WN5 .......... 68 B7
Anstey Cl *MOR/LEA* CH46 .......... 109 K4
Anstey Rd *CLB/OSW/ST* L13 .......... 114 D2
Ansty Cl *RNFD/HAY* WA11 .......... 89 M8
Anthony's Wy *HES* CH60 .......... 141 M4
Anthorn Cl *CL/PREN* CH43 .......... 126 F1
Anthorn Rd *WGNS/IIMK* WN3 .......... 79 G2
Antler Cl *AIMK* WN4 .......... 79 K7
Antonio St *BTL* L20 .......... 7 L8
Antons Cl *HLWD* L26 .......... 132 B7
Antons Rd *HLWD* L26 .......... 132 B7
  *PEN/TH* CH61 .......... 126 B8
Antony Rd *WARRS* WA4 .......... 137 K4

Antrim Cl *RNFD/HAY* WA11 .......... 90 E7
  *WGNS/IIMK* WN3 .......... 78 E3
Antrim Dr *GTS/LS* CH66 .......... 163 H3
Antrim Rd *WARRN/WOL* WA2 .......... 121 J3
Antrim St *CLB/OSW/ST* L13 .......... 98 A6
Anvil Cl *EP* CH65 .......... 6 E2
  *WGNW/BIL/O* WN5 .......... 66 F8
The Anzacs *PS/BROM* CH62 .......... 128 E7
Anzio Rd *HUY* L36 .......... 115 M1
Apollo Crs *NWD/KWIPK* L33 .......... 86 A1
Apollo Wy *NPK/KEN* L6 .......... 97 K8
  *NTHTN* L30 .......... 84 B1
Apostles Wy *NWD/KWIPK* L33 .......... 73 M8
Appin Rd *BIRK* CH41 .......... 11 J8
Appleby Cl *WDN* WA8 .......... 133 L5
Appleby Dr *NTHTN* L30 .......... 83 L2
Appleby Gn *WD/CROXPK* L12 .......... 98 F7
Appleby Gv *PS/BROM* CH62 .......... 143 L7
Appleby Rd *NTHLY* L27 .......... 132 C1
  *NWD/KWIPK* L33 .......... 86 A1
  *WARRN/WOL* WA2 .......... 121 L2
Applecorn Cl *STHEL* WA9 .......... 102 F7
**Applecross Cl**
  *GOL/RIS/CU* WA3 .......... 107 J7
Appledale Dr *GTS/LS* CH66 .......... 163 J5
**Apple Dell Av**
  *GOL/RIS/CU* WA3 .......... 92 E4
Appledore Cl *SPK/HALE* L24 .......... 146 D1
Appledore Gv *STHEL* WA9 .......... 118 C1
Appleford Cl *WARRS* WA4 .......... 138 A6
Applegarth *MOR/LEA* CH46 .......... 109 L2
Applethwaite *WGNE/HIN* WN2 .......... 69 K5
Appleton Dr *EP* CH65 .......... 163 H2
  *GR/UP/WCH* CH49 .......... 126 A2
Appleton Rd *ANF/KKDL* L4 .......... 97 J4
  *LITH* L21 .......... 83 J4
  *SKEL* WN8 .......... 65 H3
  *STHEL* WA9 .......... 9 L8
  *WDN* WA8 .......... 16 E1
Appleton St *WDN* WA8 .......... 16 E7
  *WGNS/IIMK* WN3 .......... 4 D4
Appleton Village *WDN* WA8 .......... 16 D1
Appletree Cl *CALD/MH* L18 .......... 130 F4
Apple Tree Cl *STBRV* L28 .......... 99 K5
Apple Tree Gv *GTS/LS* CH66 .......... 163 H5
Appletree Gv *WARRN/WOL* WA2 .......... 122 B3
Appley Cl *WGNNW/ST* WN6 .......... 54 E3
**Appley La North**
  *WGNNW/ST* WN6 .......... 54 E6
Appley La South *SKEL* WN8 .......... 54 E6
April Gv *NPK/KEN* L6 .......... 97 M8
April Ri *NTHTN* L30 .......... 84 A2
Apsley Av *WAL/NB* CH45 .......... 95 H5
Apsley Brow *MGHL* L31 .......... 72 D4
Apsley Gv *BEB* CH63 .......... 128 C3
Apsley Rd *PS/BROM* CH62 .......... 128 D5
  *WD/CROXPK* L12 .......... 98 E7
**Aquarius Cl** *DV/KA/FCH* L14 .......... 115 J1
Aragon Cl *MGHL* L31 .......... 73 G2
Aran Cl *SPK/HALE* L24 .......... 147 M3
Arborn Dr *GR/UP/WCH* CH49 .......... 110 C7
Arbour La *NWD/KWIPK* L33 .......... 86 C3
  *WGNNW/ST* WN6 .......... 55 K4
Arbour St *STHP* PR8 .......... 3 J6
Arbury Av *RNFD/HAY* WA11 .......... 89 M7
Arbury La *WARRN/WOL* WA2 .......... 105 L7
Arcade St *WGN* WN1 .......... 4 F4
Arcadia Av *MGHL* L31 .......... 72 F2
**Archbishop Worlock Ct**
  *VAUX/LVPD* L3 .......... 12 E2
Archer Av *WARRS* WA4 .......... 138 A3
Archer Cl *ANF/KKDL* L4 .......... 97 G6
Archerfield Rd *CALD/MH* L18 .......... 130 D4
Archer Gv *STHEL* WA9 .......... 103 G1
Archers Gn *PS/BROM* CH62 .......... 155 G1
Archer St *ANF/KKDL* L4 .......... 97 G6
**Archers Wy**
  *GR/UP/WCH* CH49 .......... 126 C3
  *GTS/LS* CH66 .......... 163 G4
Arch La *AIMK* WN4 .......... 90 C2
Archway Rd *HUY* L36 .......... 116 A3
Arcon Rd *CHLY/EC* PR7 .......... 43 G4
Arctic Rd *BTL* L20 .......... 6 D4
Arden *WDN* WA8 .......... 133 J3
Arden Cl *GOL/RIS/CU* WA3 .......... 107 K7
  *STHP* PR8 .......... 34 C7
Arden Dr *NSTN* CH64 .......... 153 G7
Ardenne Cl *BEB* CH63 .......... 143 K3
Ardern Lea *FROD/HEL* WA6 .......... 166 F4
Ardleigh Av *STHP* PR8 .......... 36 A2
Ardleigh Cl *CLB/OSW/ST* L13 .......... 114 B3
Ardleigh Gv *CLB/OSW/ST* L13 .......... 114 B3
Ardleigh Pl *CLB/OSW/ST* L13 .......... 114 B3
Ardleigh Rd *CLB/OSW/ST* L13 .......... 114 A3
Ardmore Rd *CALD/MH* L18 .......... 130 C3
Ardrossan Rd *ANF/KKDL* L4 .......... 97 L5
Ardville Rd *NG/CROX* L11 .......... 97 M2
Ardwick Rd *SPK/HALE* L24 .......... 147 H2
Ardwick St *STHEL* WA9 .......... 103 G2
Argameols Cl *STHP* PR8 .......... 25 H8
Argarmeols Gv *FMBY* L37 .......... 47 G8
Argarmeols Rd *FMBY* L37 .......... 47 G7
Argo Rd *CSBY/WL* L22 .......... 82 F4
Argos Pl *BTL* L20 .......... 7 J9
Argos Rd *BTL* L20 .......... 7 J9
Argyle Rd *ALL/GAR* L19 .......... 130 E7
  *ANF/KKDL* L4 .......... 97 K7
  *CHTN/BK* PR9 .......... 24 F4
Argyle St *BIRK* CH41 .......... 11 J7
  *CLVPS* L1 .......... 13 G9
  *ECCL* WA10 .......... 8 F1
  *WGNE/HIN* WN2 .......... 69 M8
  *WGNW/BIL/O* WN5 .......... 68 B7
**Argyle Street Hamilton Sq**
  *BIRK* CH41 .......... 11 K5
Argyle St South *BIRK* CH41 .......... 11 H6
Argyll Av *PS/BROM* CH62 .......... 154 F1
Argyll Cl *AIMK* WN4 .......... 90 E1
Aries Cl *DV/KA/FCH* L14 .......... 99 J8
Ariss Gv *RAIN/WH* L35 .......... 101 J8
**Arkenshaw Rd**
  *GOL/RIS/CU* WA3 .......... 106 C6
Arkenstone Cl *WDN* WA8 .......... 133 L3
Arkle Cl *CL/PREN* CH43 .......... 111 H5
Arkles Rd *ANF/KKDL* L4 .......... 97 J7
Arklow Dr *SPK/HALE* L24 .......... 147 M3
Ark Royal Wy *BIRK* CH41 .......... 11 L9

**Arkwood Cl** *PS/BROM* CH62 ........ 143 L2
**Arkwright Ct** *RUNC* WA7 ............ 150 B2
**Arkwright Rd** *RUNC* WA7 ........... 150 B2
**Arlescourt Rd** *WD/CROXPK* L12 .... 98 E8
**Arley Av** *WARRS* WA4 ................ 137 M4
**Arley Cl** *CL/PREN* CH43 .............. 110 E7
*WGNE/HIN* WN2 ........................ 69 K3
**Arley Dr** *WDN* WA8 ..................... 133 K3
**Arley La** *CHLY/EC* PR7 ................. 57 H3
*WGN* WN1 ................................. 56 F4
*WGNE/HIN* WN2 ........................ 56 F5
**Arley St** *CHLY/EC* PR7 .................. 32 F5
*WGNE/HIN* WN2 ........................ 80 A1
**Arlington Av** *CALD/MH* L18 ....... 114 B8
**Arlington Cl** *STHP* PR8 ................ 34 C8
**Arlington Dr** *GOL/RIS/CU* WA3 ...... 93 L5
*LEIGH* WN7 ............................... 93 L5
*WARRW/BUR* WA5 ..................... 136 A1
**Arlington Rd** *WAL/NB* CH45 ........ 95 G7
**Armill Rd** *NG/CROX* L11 ................ 98 E2
**Armitage Gdns**
*CALD/MH* L18 ........................... 130 D4
**Armitstead St**
*WGNE/HIN* WN2 ......................... 80 F1
**Armley Rd** *ANF/KKDL* L4 ............... 97 K6
**Armour Av**
*WARRN/WOL* WA2 ..................... 121 K3
**Armoury Bank** *AIMK* WN4 ............. 91 K2
**The Armoury**
*WD/CROXPK* L12 ........................ 98 D6
**Armscot Cl** *WLTN* L25 .................. 131 K6
**Armscot Pl** *WLTN* L25 .................. 131 K6
**Armstrong Cl** *GOL/RIS/CU* WA3 .. 122 F1
**Armstrong Quay**
*VAUX/LVPD* L3 .......................... 129 H2
**Armstrong St** *WGNE/HIN* WN2 .. 69 J2
**Armthorpe Dr** *GTS/LS* CH66 ....... 155 K8
**Arncliffe Dr**
*WARRW/BUR* WA5 ..................... 104 B7
**Arncliffe Rd** *WLTN* L25 ................ 131 M4
**Arndale** *RUNC* WA7 ...................... 150 A8
**Arnham Rd** *HUY* L36 ................... 115 M1
**Arnhem Crs** *WARRN/WOL* WA2 ....... 14 F1
**Arnian Rd** *RNFD/HAY* WA11 ........... 76 B6
**Arnian Wy** *RNFD/HAY* WA11 .......... 76 B6
**Arnold Av** *ECCL* WA10 ..................... 8 B2
**Arnold Cl** *STHEL* WA9 ..................... 9 L9
*TOX* L8 ...................................... 113 J7
**Arnold Gv** *WAV* L15 ..................... 114 C5
**Arnold Pl** *CHLY/EC* PR7 ................. 32 C8
*WDN* WA8 .................................. 133 L6
**Arnold St** *TOX* L8 ........................ 113 H7
*WAL/NB* CH45 ............................ 95 K8
**Arno Rd** *CL/PREN* CH43 .............. 127 K2
**Arnot Cl** *ECCL* WA10 ....................... 8 F2
**Arnot St** *ANF/KKDL* L4 ................... 97 H4
**Arnot Wy** *BEB* CH63 .................... 127 M7
**Arnside** *LITH* L21 .......................... 83 M5
**Arnside Av** *RAIN/WH* L35 ............ 117 J1
*RNFD/HAY* WA11 ........................ 90 C7
*WGNE/HIN* WN2 ......................... 69 J6
**Arnside Gv** *WARRS* WA4 .............. 137 K3
**Arnside Rd** *CHTN/BK* PR9 ................ 3 K3
*CL/PREN* CH43 ............................ 10 B9
*EHL/KEN* L7 ............................... 113 L4
*HUY* L36 .................................... 115 K3
*WAL/NB* CH45 ............................. 95 K8
*WGNW/BIL/O* WN5 ........................ 67 J5
**Arnside Ter** *CHTN/BK* PR9 ............... 3 K3
**Arpley Rd** *WARR* WA1 ..................... 14 E8
**Arpley St** *WARR* WA1 ..................... 14 C6
**Arrad St** *EHL/KEN* L7 ..................... 13 L9
**Arran Av** *EP* CH65 ........................ 163 L4
**Arran Cl** *RNFD/HAY* WA11 ............. 90 A7
*WARRN/WOL* WA2 ....................... 122 C3
**Arran Dr** *FROD/HEL* WA6 .............. 160 E6
**Arranmore Rd** *CALD/MH* L18 ........ 130 C3
**Arrowe Av** *MOR/LEA* CH46 .......... 109 M6
**Arrowe Brook La**
*GR/UP/WCH* CH49 ...................... 126 A4
**Arrowe Brook Rd**
*GR/UP/WCH* CH49 ...................... 126 B3
**Arrowe Park Rd**
*GR/UP/WCH* CH49 ...................... 126 C2
**Arrowe Rd** *GR/UP/WCH* CH49 ...... 125 M2
**Arrowe Side** *GR/UP/WCH* CH49 .. 126 A1
**Arrowsmith Rd** *RNFD/HAY* WA11 .. 91 H6
**Arthur Av** *EP* CH65 ........................ 20 D5
**Arthur St** *ALL/GAR* L19 ............... 130 F8
*BIRK* CH41 .................................. 10 E3
*RUNC* WA7 ................................... 18 F4
*WARRN/WOL* WA2 ......................... 14 C4
**Arundel Av** *AIG/SPK* L17 .............. 113 L7
*WAL/NB* CH45 ............................. 95 H7
**Arundel Cl** *PEN/TH* CH61 .............. 126 A8
**Arundel Rd** *STHP* PR8 .................... 35 H5
**Arundel St** *ANF/KKDL* L4 ................. 7 M9
*TOX* L8 ...................................... 113 J7
*WGNW/BIL/O* WN5 ........................ 68 B7
**Arvon St** *BTL* L20 ........................... 83 M7
**Asbridge St** *TOX* L8 ...................... 113 K7
**Asbury Cl** *CALD/MH* L18 ................. 130 F1
**Asbury Rd** *WAL/NB* CH45 ................ 94 F7
**Ascot Av** *LITH* L21 .......................... 83 J5
*RUNC* WA7 ................................... 149 K7
**Ascot Cl** *STHP* PR8 ......................... 2 A8
*WARR* WA1 ................................ 123 G6
*WARRS* WA4 ................................ 138 E3
**Ascot Dr** *BEB* CH63 ...................... 128 B8
*GTS/LS* CH66 ............................... 162 F2
*NWD/KWIPK* L33 ............................ 74 A8
**Ascot Gv** *BEB* CH63 ...................... 128 B8
**Ascot Pk** *CSBY/BLUN* L23 ............. 83 H1
**Ascroft Av** *WGNNW/ST* WN6 .......... 68 B2
**Ascroft Rd** *WLT/FAZ* L9 ................. 84 D5
**Ascroft St** *WGN* WN1 ........................ 5 J5
**Ash Av** *NEWLW* WA12 ................... 104 E3
**Ashbank Rd** *NG/CROX* L11 .............. 98 C3
**Ashberry Dr** *WARRS* WA4 .............. 138 D8
**Ashbourne Av** *CSBY/BLUN* L23 ....... 82 E1
*NTHTN* L30 .................................. 84 A3
*RUNC* WA7 .................................. 149 K7
*WGNE/HIN* WN2 ........................... 69 H3
**Ashbourne Cl** *GTS/LS* CH66 .......... 163 G5
*LEIGH* WN7 ................................... 81 M4
**Ashbourne Crs** *HUY* L36 ................ 115 K3
**Ashbourne Rd** *AIG/SPK* L17 ........... 129 L4
*WARRW/BUR* WA5 ......................... 120 D8
**Ashbrook Av** *RUNC* WA7 .............. 161 H1
**Ashbrook Crs**
*WARRN/WOL* WA2 ......................... 121 M5
**Ashbrook Dr** *WLT/FAZ* L9 ............... 84 E7
**Ash Brow** *SKEL* WN8 ....................... 53 K4
**Ashburn Av** *NWD/KWIPK* L33 .......... 86 A1
**Ashburton Av** *CL/PREN* CH43 ........ 111 H7
**Ashburton Rd** *CL/PREN* CH43 ........ 111 G7
*WAL/EG* CH44 ............................... 111 K1
*WKBY* CH48 ................................. 124 D2
**Ashbury Cl** *RUNC* WA7 .................. 150 F3
**Ashbury Dr** *RNFD/HAY* WA11 ........... 90 F6
**Ashbury Rd** *DV/KA/FCH* L14 ............ 99 K7
**Ashby Cl** *HOY* CH47 ....................... 109 K4
**Ashby Gv** *LEIGH* WN7 ...................... 81 L5
**Ashby Rd** *WGNS/IIMK* WN3 .............. 79 K2
**Ashby St** *CHLY/EC* PR7 ..................... 32 E7
**Ash Cl** *GTS/LS* CH66 ....................... 163 H4
*ORM* L39 ....................................... 50 F8
*WAV* L15 ....................................... 114 A5
*WGNNW/ST* WN6 .............................. 54 F6
**Ashcombe Rd** *DV/KA/FCH* L14 ......... 114 E2
**Ash Crs** *HUY* L36 ............................ 116 A5
**Ashcroft Av** *ORM* L39 ....................... 51 H7
**Ashcroft Dr** *PEN/TH* CH61 ............... 141 H3
**Ashcroft Rd** *FMBY* L37 ....................... 59 H4
*NWD/KWIPK* L33 ................................ 86 E2
**Ashcroft St** *BTL* L20 ............................ 6 F5
*STHEL* WA9 ....................................... 9 M5
*WGNE/HIN* WN2 ................................ 81 G1
**Ashdale** *HUY* L36 ............................. 115 M3
**Ashdale Cl** *FMBY* L37 ........................ 58 E3
**Ashdale Pk** *GR/UP/WCH* CH49 ......... 125 K2
**Ashdale Rd** *CALD/MH* L18 ................. 114 C8
*CSBY/WL* L22 .................................... 82 F3
*WGNS/IIMK* WN3 ................................ 79 J3
*WLT/FAZ* L9 ....................................... 97 J1
**Ashdown Crs** *STHEL* WA9 ................... 118 E1
**Ashdown Dr** *GR/UP/WCH* CH49 .. 125 L3
**Ashdown Gv** *HLWD* L26 ..................... 132 C4
**Ashdown La** *GOL/RIS/CU* WA3 .... 107 J8
**Ashfarm Ct** *DV/KA/FCH* L14 ......... 115 H2
**Ashfield** *RAIN/WH* L35 ................... 117 M2
*WAV* L15 ......................................... 113 M5
**Ashfield Av** *WGNE/HIN* WN2 ............ 81 H1
**Ashfield Crs** *PS/BROM* CH62 .......... 143 M5
*WGNW/BIL/O* WN5 ............................ 78 A8
**Ashfield Dr** *WGNE/HIN* WN2 .............. 57 L8
**Ashfield Park Dr**
*WGNNW/ST* WN6 ................................ 56 B5
**Ashfield Rd** *AIG/SPK* L17 ................. 129 M3
*CHLY/EC* PR7 ..................................... 32 D6
*CHLYE* PR6 ........................................ 44 D5
*PS/BROM* CH62 ................................. 143 L5
**Ashfield Rd North** *EP* CH65 .............. 20 C4
**Ashford Cl** *HLWD* L26 ...................... 132 A6
**Ashford Ri** *WGN* WN1 ........................ 68 D1
**Ashford Rd** *BIRK* CH41 ....................... 10 F9
*HOY* CH47 ......................................... 108 E5
**Ash Gv** *CHLY/EC* PR7 ......................... 32 E8
*FMBY* L37 ........................................... 58 E4
*GTS/LS* CH66 ..................................... 155 L7
*LITH* L21 ............................................ 83 J7
*RAIN/WH* L35 .................................... 117 G1
*RNFD/HAY* WA11 .................................. 76 B7
*RUNC* WA7 .......................................... 19 M8
*SKEL* WN8 ........................................... 64 F4
*STHEL* WA9 ......................................... 118 E1
*WAL/NB* CH45 ..................................... 95 L6
*WARRS* WA4 ........................................ 15 K9
*WAV* L15 ........................................... 113 M5
*WGNNW/ST* WN6 .................................. 56 B5
*WGNW/BIL/O* WN5 ................................ 67 H7
**Ash Grove Crs**
*WGNW/BIL/O* WN5 ................................ 77 M7
**Ashland Av** *AIMK* WN4 ......................... 91 J1
*WGN* WN1 ............................................ 68 E3
**Ashlands** *FROD/HEL* WA6 ................... 160 E6
**Ash La** *WARRS* WA4 ........................... 138 A5
*WDN* WA8 ........................................... 133 H5
*WGNE/HIN* WN2 .................................... 69 J3
**Ashlar Gv** *AIG/SPK* L17 .................... 130 A3
**Ashlar Rd** *AIG/SPK* L17 ..................... 130 A3
*CSBY/WL* L22 ........................................ 83 G3
**Ashlea Rd** *PEN/TH* CH61 ................... 141 H2
**Ashleigh Rd** *MGHL* L31 ........................ 73 H6
**Ashley Av** *HOY* CH47 ......................... 109 H4
**Ashley Cl** *NWD/KWIPK* L33 ................. 74 A8
*RAIN/WH* L35 ...................................... 117 M3
*WARRS* WA4 ........................................ 138 E2
**Ashley Dr** *LEIGH* WN7 .......................... 81 L5
**Ashley Rd** *CHTN/BK* PR9 ........................ 3 K4
*RUNC* WA7 ........................................... 149 M3
*SKEL* WN8 ............................................. 65 K2
*WGNE/HIN* WN2 ..................................... 81 K2
**Ashley St** *RF/TRAN* CH42 ................... 128 B3
**Ashley Wy** *WDN* WA8 ............................ 16 D7
**Ashley Wy West** *WDN* WA8 ................... 16 B6
**Ashmead Rd** *SKEL* WN8 ........................ 65 J1
**Ashmore Cl** *GOL/RIS/CU* WA3 ............ 123 J2
**Ashmuir Hey** *KKBY* L32 ......................... 86 B4
**Ashover Av** *DV/KA/FCH* L14 ............... 115 J1
**Ash Priors** *WDN* WA8 .......................... 133 M2
**Ashridge St** *RUNC* WA7 ......................... 18 F2
**Ashridge Wy** *WGNW/BIL/O* WN5 .. 67 K4
**Ash Rd** *BEB* CH63 ................................ 128 B6
*CHLY/EC* PR7 ......................................... 43 G5
*CHNE* CH2 ............................................. 165 L2
*LITH* L21 ................................................ 83 J6
*LYMM* WA13 .......................................... 139 L2
*RF/TRAN* CH42 ........................................ 11 G9
*RNFD/HAY* WA11 ..................................... 91 G6
*WARRN/WOL* WA2 .................................. 105 K7
*WARRW/BUR* WA5 ................................... 136 B1
**Ash St** *BTL* L20 ....................................... 7 H3
*GOL/RIS/CU* WA3 ..................................... 92 D3
*STHP* PR8 ................................................. 3 K7
**Ashton Av** *RAIN/WH* L35 ...................... 117 L3
**Ashton Cl** *FROD/HEL* WA6 ..................... 160 E4
*PS/BROM* CH62 ........................................ 155 G2
*RUNC* WA7 ............................................. 149 H7
**Ashton Dr** *FROD/HEL* WA6 ..................... 160 E3
*FROD/HEL* WA6 ........................................ 160 E4
*WKBY* CH48 ............................................. 124 C4
*WLTN* L25 ................................................ 131 K6
**Ashton Heath** *AIMK* WN4 ......................... 91 L3
**Ashton Rd** *GOL/RIS/CU* WA3 ................... 92 B3
*NEWLW* WA12 ............................................ 91 L7
*STHP* PR8 ................................................... 35 H4
*WGNW/BIL/O* WN5 ....................................... 78 D5
**Ashtons Green Dr** *STHEL* WA9 .............. 103 H3
**Ashton St** *CLB/OSW/ST* L13 .................. 114 C2
*VAUX/LVPD* L3 ........................................... 13 M6
*WARRN/WOL* WA2 ......................................... 14 E4
**Ashtree Cl** *NSTN* CH64 ............................ 153 H6
**Ashtree Cft** *NSTN* CH64 ........................... 154 C6
**Ashtree Dr** *NSTN* CH64 ............................. 153 J7
**Ashtree Farm Ct** *NSTN* CH64 ... 154 C5
**Ashtree Gv** *WD/CROXPK* L12 ..................... 99 G1
**Ashtrees** *BRSC* L40 ..................................... 40 E3
**Ashurst Cl** *RNFD/HAY* WA11 ....................... 90 A7
*SKEL* WN8 ................................................... 65 J1
*WLTN* L25 ................................................... 131 K1
**Ashurst Ct** *FMBY* L37 .................................. 59 G3
**Ashurst Dr** *RNFD/HAY* WA11 ........................ 89 M7
**Ashurst Gdns** *SKEL* WN8 ............................. 65 J1
**Ashurst Rd** *SKEL* WN8 ................................ 65 K1
*WGNNW/ST* WN6 ............................................ 55 J3
**Ash V** *WAV* L15 ........................................ 114 A5
**Ashville Rd** *BIRK* CH41 ................................. 10 D4
*RUNC* WA7 .................................................... 161 G2
*WAL/EG* CH44 ............................................... 111 L3
**Ashwall St** *SKEL* WN8 .................................... 64 F5
**Ashwater Rd** *NG/CROX* L11 ............................ 98 E3
**Ash Wy** *HES* CH60 ....................................... 141 K8
**Ashwell Av** *GOL/RIS/CU* WA3 .......................... 92 F4
**Ashwell St** *TOX* L8 ....................................... 113 G6
**Ashwood** *SKEL* WN8 ........................................ 65 L2
**Ashwood Av** *AIMK* WN4 .................................... 91 J3
*GOL/RIS/CU* WA3 ............................................... 92 F5
*WARR* WA1 ....................................................... 15 L1
*WGNE/HIN* WN2 .................................................. 80 E6
**Ashwood Cl** *GTS/LS* CH66 ............................. 162 F4
*NWD/KWIPK* L33 .................................................. 74 A8
**Ashwood Ct** *CL/PREN* CH43 ............................ 110 E4
**Ashwood Dr** *WD/CROXPK* L12 ........................... 98 F2
**Ashwood La** *CHNE* CH2 ..................................... 164 C8
**Askern Rd** *KKBY* L32 ........................................... 86 B5
**Askett Cl** *RNFD/HAY* WA11 ................................. 90 E6
**Askew Cl** *WAL/EG* CH44 .................................. 111 M1
**Askew St** *ANF/KKDL* L4 .......................................... 97 H4
**Askham Cl** *TOX* L8 ................................................ 113 K6
**Askrigg Av** *GTS/LS* CH66 ....................................... 155 K8
**Askwith Rd** *WGNE/HIN* WN2 ...................................... 81 H2
**Asland Gdns** *CHTN/BK* PR9 ......................................... 25 L1
**Asmall Cl** *ORM* L39 ..................................................... 50 F7
**Asmall La** *ORM* L39 ....................................................... 50 A5
**Aspen Cl** *GTS/LS* CH66 ................................................. 163 G4
*HES* CH60 .......................................................................... 141 M5
*NWD/KWIPK* L33 ................................................................. 74 B7
**Aspendale Rd**
*RF/TRAN* CH42 ................................................................... 127 M1
**Aspen Gdns** *CHLY/EC* PR7 ............................................... 32 D7
**Aspen Gv** *FMBY* L37 ............................................................ 58 E4
*TOX* L8 ................................................................................. 113 L7
*WARR* WA1 .......................................................................... 122 C6
**Aspenwood** *AIMK* WN4 ............................................................ 91 J3
**Aspes Rd** *WD/CROXPK* L12 ....................................................... 99 G6
**Aspinall Cl** *WARRN/WOL* WA2 ............................................ 122 C2
**Aspinall Crs** *FMBY* L37 ........................................................... 60 B4
**Aspinall Rd** *WGNNW/ST* WN6 ................................................... 55 K4
**Aspinall St** *BIRK* CH41 ........................................................... 10 E3
*WGNE/HIN* WN2 ........................................................................ 80 C3
**Aspinal St** *PR/KW* L34 ........................................................ 100 F7
**Aspull Cl** *GOL/RIS/CU* WA3 ............................................... 122 E1
**Aspull Common** *LEIGH* WN7 ....................................................... 93 L4
**Asquith Av** *BIRK* CH41 ................................................................ 10 D3
**Asser Rd** *NG/CROX* L11 .................................................................. 98 A5
**The Asshawes** *CHLYE* PR6 .................................................................. 44 B4
**Assheton Wk** *SPK/HALE* L24 .... 148 A3
**Assissian Crs** *NTHTN* L30 ........................................................................ 84 A1
**Astbury Cl** *GOL/RIS/CU* WA3 ............................................................................ 93 K5
**Aster Crs** *RUNC* WA7 ..................................................................................... 161 H1
**Aster Dr** *NWD/KWIPK* L33 ............................................................................... 73 M8
**Asterfield Av** *BEB* CH63 .................................................................................... 128 A6
**Aster Rd** *RNFD/HAY* WA11 ..................................................................................... 91 H7
**Astley Cl** *RNFD/HAY* WA11 ...................................................................................... 76 B6
*WARRS* WA4 .......................................................................................................... 137 K2
*WDN* WA8 ................................................................................................................ 133 L2
**Astley Rd** *CHLY/EC* PR7 .................................................................................................. 32 D4
*HUY* L36 ........................................................................................................................... 100 A7
**Astley St** *CHLY/EC* PR7 ....................................................................................................... 32 E4
**Astmoor Bridge La** *RUNC* WA7 .... 150 B3
**Astmoor Rd** *RUNC* WA7 .......................................................................................................... 19 M2
**Aston Av** *GOL/RIS/CU* WA3 ........ 107 H8
**Aston Cl** *CL/PREN* CH43 .............. 127 H2
**Aston Ct** *WARR* WA1 ..................... 122 E4
**Aston Fields Rd** *RUNC* WA7 .......... 161 M1
**Aston Gn** *RUNC* WA7 ..................... 151 G7
**Aston La** *RUNC* WA7 ...................... 161 K2
**Aston St** *ALL/GAR* L19 .................. 130 F8
**Astonwood Rd**
*RF/TRAN* CH42 .............................. 127 M2
**Astor Dr** *WARRS* WA4 .................... 138 B5
**Astor St** *ANF/KKDL* L4 ..................... 97 H3
**Atheldene Rd** *ANF/KKDL* L4 ............ 97 L3
**Athelstan Cl** *PS/BROM* CH62 ......... 143 M4
**Atherleigh Wy** *LEIGH* WN7 ............... 93 M2
**Atherton Cl** *EV* L5 ............................ 97 G8
**Atherton Dr** *GR/UP/WCH* CH49 .. 126 C2
**Atherton Rd** *EP* CH65 ..................... 156 B7
*WGNE/HIN* WN2 ................................ 69 M8
*WLT/FAZ* L9 ...................................... 84 E7
**Atherton St** *CHLY/EC* PR7 ................ 44 C7
*ECCL* WA10 ......................................... 8 E2
*PR/KW* L34 ....................................... 100 F7
*WAL/NB* CH45 ..................................... 95 J4
*WGNE/HIN* WN2 .................................. 81 G5
*WGNW/BIL/O* WN5 ............................... 68 B7
**Athlone Rd** *WARRN/WOL* WA2 ........... 121 J4
**Athol Cl** *NEWLW* WA12 ..................... 104 B1
*PS/BROM* CH62 ................................... 144 A8
**Athol Crs** *WGNE/HIN* WN2 .................. 81 K1
**Athol Dr** *PS/BROM* CH62 .................... 144 A8
**Athole Gv** *CHTN/BK* PR9 ...................... 25 H6
**Athol Gv** *CHLYE* PR6 ........................... 33 G7
**Atholl Crs** *AIN/FAZ* L10 ....................... 84 F3
**Atholl Gv** *WGNS/IIMK* WN3 .................. 79 J2
**Athol St** *BIRK* CH41 .............................. 11 K4
*EV* L5 ................................................... 96 F8
**Atkinson Gv** *HUY* L36 ........................ 116 B1
**Atkinson St** *WGNE/HIN* WN2 ................ 80 D5
**Atlantic Rd** *BTL* L20 ............................. 6 E4
**Atlantic Wy** *NTHTN* L30 ........................ 84 A5
*VAUX/LVPD* L3 ..................................... 128 F1
**Atlas Ct** *STHEL* WA9 ............................... 9 K5
**Atlas Rd** *BTL* L20 ................................... 6 D4
**Atlas St** *STHEL* WA9 ............................... 9 K5
**Atterbury Cl** *WDN* WA8 ......................... 133 L3
**Atterbury St** *TOX* L8 ............................. 113 G8
**Attlee Av** *GOL/RIS/CU* WA3 ................... 107 K1
**Attlee Rd** *HUY* L36 ................................ 116 C2
**Attwood St** *ANF/KKDL* L4 ......................... 97 H6
**Atwell St** *NPK/KEN* L6 .............................. 113 J1
**Aubourn Cl** *WDN* WA8 ............................... 133 L2
**Aubrey Ct** *NPK/KEN* L6 ................................ 113 J1
**Auburn Rd** *CLB/OSW/ST* L13 ......................... 98 A8
*WAL/NB* CH45 ............................................... 95 J6
**The Aubynes** *WAL/NB* CH45 ........................... 95 G7
**Auckery Av** *GTS/LS* CH66 .............................. 162 F2
**Audie Murphy Rd**
*WARRW/BUR* WA5 ........................................... 120 D7
**Audlem Av** *CL/PREN* CH43 ............................ 127 H2
**Audlem Cl** *RUNC* WA7 .................................... 161 H1
**Audley St** *VAUX/LVPD* L3 ................................ 13 K5
**Audre Cl** *WARRW/BUR* WA5 ............................ 119 M7
**Aughton Cl**
*WGNW/BIL/O* WN5 ............................................. 90 A1
**Aughton Ms** *STHP* PR8 ...................................... 2 F8
**Aughton Park Dr** *ORM* L39 ................................ 62 F3
**Aughton Rd** *BTL* L20 ......................................... 83 M8
*STHP* PR8 .......................................................... 2 E7
**Aughton St** *ORM* L39 ........................................ 62 F1
*WGNE/HIN* WN2 ................................................... 80 E1
**Augusta Cl** *CLB/OSW/ST* L13 ............................. 114 C3
**August Rd** *NPK/KEN* L6 ....................................... 97 L8
**August St** *BTL* L20 ................................................ 7 H1
**Aukland Gv** *RAIN/WH* L35 .................................... 101 M6
**Aukland Rd** *CALD/MH* L18 ..................................... 114 C8
**Aurorean Cl** *NTHLY* L27 ........................................ 115 M7
**Austell Cl** *RNFD/HAY* WA11 ...................................... 89 M6
**Austin Av** *AIMK* WN4 ................................................ 91 G1
*ECCL* WA10 ............................................................. 101 L5
**Austin Cl** *KKBY* L32 ...................................................... 85 M3
**Austin St** *LEIGH* WN7 .................................................... 81 M8
*WAL/EG* CH44 ............................................................... 111 J3
**Austral Av** *WARR* WA1 ................................................... 122 D6
**Australia La** *WARRS* WA4 ................................................ 138 E4
**Autumn Gv** *RF/TRAN* CH42 ................................................ 128 A5
**Avebury Cl** *GOL/RIS/CU* WA3 ............................................. 93 G5
*WDN* WA8 ........................................................................ 135 G2
**Aveley Cl** *WARR* WA1 .......................................................... 122 D6
**Aveling Dr** *CHTN/BK* PR9 ......................................................... 23 K8
**Avelon Cl** *CL/PREN* CH43 .............................................................. 110 F8
*MGHL* L31 ...................................................................................... 61 K8
**Avenham Cl** *CHTN/BK* PR9 ............................................................... 23 K8
**Avenham Rd** *CHLY/EC* PR7 ................................................................. 32 E6
**The Avenue** *ALL/GAR* L19 ..................................................................... 131 G8
*CHLYE* PR6 .......................................................................................... 44 C5
*CHTN/BK* PR9 ........................................................................................ 23 H8
*CHTN/BK* PR9 ........................................................................................ 26 B8
*ECCL* WA10 ........................................................................................... 101 K2
*HLWD* L26 ............................................................................................. 132 A6
*HUY* L36 ............................................................................................... 116 A2
*LYMM* WA13 ......................................................................................... 139 L4
*NEWLW* WA12 ....................................................................................... 104 E1
*ORM* L39 .................................................................................................. 50 F7
*PS/BROM* CH62 ........................................................................................ 143 L5
*RNFD/HAY* WA11 ......................................................................................... 76 B7
*WGN* WN1 ................................................................................................... 68 F3
*WGNNW/ST* WN6 ......................................................................................... 68 A1
*WGNW/BIL/O* WN5 ......................................................................................... 77 M2
**Averham Cl** *AIMK* WN4 .................................................................................. 91 K3
**Avery Cl** *WARRN/WOL* WA2 ............................................................................. 122 A3
**Avery Crs** *RNFD/HAY* WA11 ............................................................................... 90 E6
**Avery Rd** *RNFD/HAY* WA11 ................................................................................ 90 E6
**Avery Sq** *RNFD/HAY* WA11 ................................................................................. 90 E6
**Aviemore Cl** *AIMK* WN4 ........................................................................................ 90 F1
**Aviemore Dr** *WARRN/WOL* WA2 .. 122 C2
**Aviemore Rd**
*CLB/OSW/ST* L13 ............................................................................................. 114 B2
**Avocet Cl** *NEWLW* WA12 ............................................................................................ 104 E1
*WARRN/WOL* WA2 ........................................................................................................ 121 M2
**Avolon Rd** *WD/CROXPK* L12 .......................................................................................... 98 F8
**Avon** *WDN* WA8 ............................................................................................................ 133 J3
**Avon Av** *WARRW/BUR* WA5 ........................................................................................... 136 A1
**Avon Cl** *ANF/KKDL* L4 ....................................................................................................... 97 G5
*NWD/KWIPK* L33 ................................................................................................................ 74 B7
**Avondale** *EP* CH65 ............................................................................................................... 20 B9
**Avondale Av** *MGHL* L31 .............................................................................................................. 61 G7
*MOR/LEA* CH46 .......................................................................................................................... 110 B4
*PS/BROM* CH62 ............................................................................................................................... 144 A8
**Avondale Dr** *WDN* WA8 ................................................................................................................... 133 K4
**Avondale Rd** *CHLY/EC* PR7 .................................................................................................................. 32 E6
*CHTN/BK* PR9 ....................................................................................................................................... 3 H1
*HOY* CH47 ............................................................................................................................................ 108 D6
*RNFD/HAY* WA11 .................................................................................................................................... 90 E6
*WAV* L15 .............................................................................................................................................. 114 A7
*WGN* WN1 ............................................................................................................................................... 68 E3
**Avondale Rd North**
*CHTN/BK* PR9 ............................................................................................................................................ 24 E4
**Avondale St** *WGNNW/ST* WN6 .. 56 A3
**Avonmore Av** *CALD/MH* L18 ...... 130 C2
**Avon Rd** *AIMK* WN4 ................... 80 A8
*GOL/RIS/CU* WA3 .......................... 107 J3
*WGNW/BIL/O* WN5 .......................... 67 L6
*WGNW/BIL/O* WN5 .......................... 89 M2
**Avon St** *BIRK* CH41 ...................... 111 H4
*NPK/KEN* L6 ..................................... 97 K8
**Awelon Cl** *WD/CROXPK* L12 ............ 98 E5
**Axbridge Av** *STHEL* WA9 ............... 102 F8
**Axholme Cl** *PEN/TH* CH61 .............. 126 D8
**Axholme Rd** *PEN/TH* CH61 .............. 126 C8
**Ayala Cl** *BTL* L20 ............................ 84 B6
**Aycliffe Rd** *RAIN/WH* L35 ............... 101 M7
**Aye Bridge Rd** *GOL/RIS/CU* WA3 .. 80 D8
**Aylesbury Av** *CL/PREN* CH43 ............ 127 G3
**Aylesbury Cl** *GTS/LS* CH66 ............... 162 E2
**Aylesbury Crs** *WGNE/HIN* WN2 .......... 81 L3
**Aylesbury Rd** *WAL/NB* CH45 ................ 95 L6
**Aylesford Rd** *CLB/OSW/ST* L13 .......... 114 C2
**Aylsham Cl** *WDN* WA8 .......................... 133 L2
**Aylsham Dr** *GR/UP/WCH* CH49 ............ 110 C6
**Aylton Rd** *HUY* L36 ................................ 115 K1
**Aylward Pl** *BTL* L20 ................................. 6 F2
**Ayr Cl** *STHP* PR8 ..................................... 36 B1
**Ayrefield Gv** *WGNNW/ST* WN6 .................. 54 F7
**Ayrefield La** *SKEL* WN8 ............................ 66 E1
**Ayrshire Gdns** *ECCL* WA10 ........................ 8 D7
**Ayrshire Rd** *ANF/KKDL* L4 ......................... 97 L5
**Aysgarth Av** *WD/CROXPK* L12 .................... 98 E7
**Aysgarth Rd** *WAL/NB* CH45 ........................ 95 H7
**Azalea Gv** *HLWD* L26 ................................. 131 M3
*RUNC* WA7 ................................................... 161 H1

# B

**Babbacombe Rd** *CHLDW* L16 ...... 115 G7
*WARRW/BUR* WA5 ........................ 136 A1
**Babylon La** *CHLYE* PR6 .................. 44 E4
**Back Ashby St** *CHLY/EC* PR7 ......... 32 E7
**Back Barlow La** *ANF/KKDL* L4 .... 97 G5
**Back Bath St** *STHP* PR8 ..................... 3 G2
**Back Beau St** *EV* L5 ......................... 13 J2
**Back Bedford St** *EHL/KEN* L7 .......... 13 M9
**Back Belmont Rd** *NPK/KEN* L6 ......... 97 K8
**Back Berry St** *CLVPS* L1 .................... 13 J9
**Back Blackfield Ter**
*ANF/KKDL* L4 ..................................... 96 F6
**Back Bold St** *CLVPS* L1 ...................... 13 H8
**Back Booth St** *NEWLW* WA12 .. 104 C2
**Back Boundary St** *EV* L5 ................... 96 F7
**Back Bridge St**
*NEWLW* WA12 ................................... 104 D2
**Back Bridport St** *VAUX/LVPD* L3 .... 13 J6
**Back Bk Pl** *WARRS* WA4 ..................... 15 L9
**Back Canning St** *TOX* L8 ................. 113 H5
**Back Catharine St** *TOX* L8 .............. 113 H5
**Back Chadwick Mt** *EV* L5 .................. 97 H6
**Back Chatham Pl**
*EHL/KEN* L7 ....................................... 113 K4
**Back Colquitt St** *CLVPS* L1 ................ 13 J9
**Back Commutation St**
*VAUX/LVPD* L3 ..................................... 13 J5
**Back Crosland Ter**
*FROD/HEL* WA6 .................................. 166 D3
**Back Cross La** *NEWLW* WA12 ... 104 D1
**Back Drinkhouse La**
*LEY/BBR* PR5 ........................................ 29 J3
**Back Eastford Rd**
*WARRS* WA4 ......................................... 137 J4
**Back Egerton St North**
*TOX* L8 ................................................ 113 H6
**Back Falkner St South**
*TOX* L8 ................................................ 113 J5
**Backford Cl** *CL/PREN* CH43 ............ 127 G2
*RUNC* WA7 ........................................ 150 E8
**Backford Gdns** *GTS/LS* CH66 .... 163 H6
**Backford Rd** *PEN/TH* CH61 .............. 125 M8
**Backford Wy** *CL/PREN* CH43 ........... 127 G2
**Back Forest Rd** *STHP* PR8 .................. 3 L6
**Back Forshaw St**
*WARRN/WOL* WA2 .................................. 15 G2
**Back Gibson St** *TOX* L8 .................... 113 H6
**Back Gillmoss La** *NG/CROX* L11 .... 85 L7
**Back Granton Rd** *EV* L5 ..................... 97 J7
**Back Guilford St** *NPK/KEN* L6 ........... 13 M2
**Back High St** *RUNC* WA7 .................... 19 G3
**Back Holland Pl** *EHL/KEN* L7 .... 113 K4
**Back Hope Pl** *CLVPS* L1 .................... 13 K9
**Back Huskisson St** *TOX* L8 ........... 113 H6
**Back Kelvin Gv** *TOX* L8 .................... 113 J7
**Back Knight St** *CLVPS* L1 ................. 113 G5
**Back La** *BRSC* L40 ............................. 39 G7
*BRSC* L40 ............................................. 40 D5
*BRSC* L40 ............................................. 52 F3
*CHLY/EC* PR7 ........................................ 31 H6
*CHLY/EC* PR7 ........................................ 31 K5
*CSBY/BLUN* L23 ..................................... 71 H5
*FROD/HEL* WA6 ..................................... 166 E3
*LEY/BBR* PR5 ........................................ 29 H1
*ORM* L39 ............................................... 60 F2
*ORM* L39 ............................................... 62 B7
*ORM* L39 ............................................... 74 C2
*RNFD/HAY* WA11 .................................... 77 H8
*SFTN* L29 ............................................... 71 L6
*SKEL* WN8 ............................................... 53 J3
*SKEL* WN8 ............................................... 65 M7
*SKEL* WN8 ............................................... 66 A7
*WARRW/BUR* WA5 ................................... 103 M6
*WARRW/BUR* WA5 ................................... 135 J3
*WGNNW/ST* WN6 ...................................... 55 H4
**Back La East** *BRSC* L40 ...................... 41 G4
**Back Lawrence St**
*NEWLW* WA12 ....................................... 104 C2
**Back Leeds St** *VAUX/LVPD* L3 ............ 12 D4
**Back Legh St** *NEWLW* WA12 ............. 104 C2
**Back Lime St** *CLVPS* L1 ........................ 13 H7
**Back Little Canning St**
*TOX* L8 ............................................... 113 H6
**Back Luton Gv** *ANF/KKDL* L4 ............. 97 H5
**Back Market St** *NEWLW* WA12 ......... 104 C1
*WGNE/HIN* WN2 ..................................... 69 M8
**Back Maryland St** *CLVPS* L1 ............... 13 K9
**Back Mersey Vw** *CSBY/WL* L22 ............ 82 E3
**Back Mesnes St** *WGN* WN1 .................... 4 F2
**Back Moss La** *BRSC* L40 ....................... 39 H6
**Back Mt** *CHLY/EC* PR7 ......................... 32 E5
**Back Mount St** *CSBY/WL* L22 ............. 82 F4
**Back Mount Vernon Gn**
*EHL/KEN* L7 ......................................... 113 J3
**Back Mulberry St** *TOX* L8 .................. 113 H5
**Back Oliver St** *BIRK* CH41 ................... 11 K6
**Back Orford St** *WAV* L15 ................... 114 B5
**Back O the Town La** *HTWN* L38 .... 71 G2
**Back Percy St** *TOX* L8 ........................ 113 H6
**Back Pickop St** *VAUX/LVPD* L3 .. 12 F5
**Back Railway Vw** *CHLY/EC* PR7 .... 44 C7
**Back Renshaw St** *CLVPS* L1 ............... 13 K9
**Back Rockfield Rd** *ANF/KKDL* L4 .. 97 H6
**Back Rw** *SKEL* WN8 ............................. 66 E6
**Back St Bride St** *TOX* L8 ................... 113 H5
**Back Sandon St** *TOX* L8 ..................... 113 H6
**Back Sandstone Rd**
*CLB/OSW/ST* L13 ................................... 114 B1
**Back School La** *SKEL* WN8 .................... 64 E3
*SKEL* WN8 ............................................ 66 E6
**Back Seaview** *HOY* CH47 .................... 108 D6
**Back Seel St** *CLVPS* L1 ........................ 13 H9
**Back Sir Howard St** *TOX* L8 ............. 113 H5
**Back South Rd** *CSBY/WL* L22 ............... 83 G4
**Back Stanley Rd** *BTL* L20 ..................... 7 H4
**Back Towerlands St**
*EHL/KEN* L7 ......................................... 113 K4
**Back Virginia St** *STHP* PR8 .................. 3 H6
**Back Wellesley Rd** *TOX* L8 ............... 129 J1
**Back Westminster Rd**
*ANF/KKDL* L4 ........................................ 97 G5
**Back Windsor Vw** *TOX* L8 ................. 113 K6
**Back Winstanley Rd**
*CSBY/WL* L22 ......................................... 83 G3

Back York Ter EV L5 .......... 97 G7
Baclaw Cl WGN WN1 .......... 5 M2
Badbury Cl RNFD/HAY WA11 ... 90 F6
Badby Wd NWD/KWIPK L33 ..... 86 B1
Baden Cl GOL/OSW/ST L13 ..... 114 D2
Bader Cl PEN/TH CH61 .......... 141 G2
Badger Bait NSTN CH64 ......... 153 H7
Badger Cl RUNC WA7 ........... 150 C7
Badgers Cl GTS/LS CH66 ....... 163 H5
Badgers Pk NSTN CH64 ......... 153 H7
Badgers Rake FMBY L37 ........ 46 E8
Badger's Set WKBY CH48 ....... 124 F7
Badger Wy CL/PREN CH43 ...... 127 C5
Badminton St TOX L8 ........... 129 H2
Baffin Cl MOR/LEA CH46 ........ 110 C1
Bagganley La CHLYE PR6 ....... 33 C4
Bagnall Av WARRW/BUR WA5 ... 120 E8
Bagnall St ANF/KKDL L4 ........ 97 J6
Bagot Av WARRW/BUR WA5 ..... 121 H5
Bagot St WAV L15 .............. 113 M6
Baguley Av WDN WA8 ........... 133 J8
Bahama Cl RNFD/HAY WA11 ..... 90 F5
Bahama Rd RNFD/HAY WA11 .... 90 F5
Bailey Av EP CH65 .............. 156 B7
Bailey Dr BTL L20 .............. 84 A7
Baileys Cl WDN WA8 ............ 118 C8
Baileys La HLWD L26 ........... 132 C5
SPK/HALE L24.................. 147 J4
Bailey St CLVPS L1 ............. 113 G5
Bainbridge Av GOL/RIS/CU WA3.. 93 H5
Bainton Cl KKBY L32 ........... 86 C6
Bainton Rd KKBY L32 ........... 86 C6
Baird Av BTL L20 ............... 6 C2
Baker Dr GTS/LS CH66 .......... 163 G2
Baker Rd RUNC WA7 ............ 18 B9
Bakers Green Rd HUY L36 ...... 116 A1
Baker's La CHTN/BK PR9 ........ 25 H2
Baker St NPK/KEN L6 ........... 113 J2
STHEL WA9...................... 9 M5
WGNS/IIMK WN3................. 4 C8
Bakewell Av NPK/KEN L6 ........ 113 J2
Bakewell Cl GTS/LS CH66 ....... 163 G5
Bakewell Dr WGNNW/ST WN6 ... 68 C3
Bakewell Gv WLT/FAZ L9 ....... 84 D6
Bakewell Rd WARRW/BUR WA5.. 104 C6
Bala Cl WARRW/BUR WA5 ....... 121 C3
Bala Gv WAL/EG CH44 .......... 111 J2
Bala St ANF/KKDL L4 ........... 97 K7
Balcarres Av CALD/MH L18 ...... 114 B8
WGN WN1....................... 69 G3
Balcarres Rd CHLY/EC PR7 ...... 32 D8
WGNE/HIN WN2.................. 69 K1
Baldock Cl WARRS WA4 ......... 138 E2
Baldwin Av CHLDW L16 ......... 115 H5
Baldwin St ECCL WA10 ......... 9 C4
WGN WN1....................... 5 H3
WGNE/HIN WN2.................. 81 K2
WGNS/IIMK WN3................. 5 H6
WGNW/BIL/O WN5............... 67 K8
The Bales NTHTN L30 ........... 84 C1
Balfe St LITH L21 .............. 83 J7
Balfour Av BTL L20 ............. 6 F1
Balfour Rd BTL L20 ............. 6 E1
CL/PREN CH43.................. 10 D8
STHP PR8...................... 25 G8
WAL/EG CH44................... 111 J3
Balfour St ANF/KKDL L4 ........ 97 H6
ECCL WA10..................... 8 A6
RUNC WA7...................... 18 F5
Balham Av WDN WA8 ........... 134 C1
Balharry Av RNFD/HAY WA11 ... 91 H6
Balker Dr ECCL WA10 .......... 8 E1
Ballantrae Rd CALD/MH L18 .... 130 C2
Ballantyne Dr CL/PREN CH43 .. 110 E4
Ballantyne Gv BTL L20 ......... 84 A7
CLB/OSW/ST L13................ 98 A6
Ballantyne Pl CLB/OSW/ST L13.. 98 A6
Ballantyne Rd CLB/OSW/ST L13.. 98 A7
Ballantyne Wy
GOL/RIS/CU WA3 .............. 93 G5
Ballard Rd WKBY CH48 ......... 125 G2
Ballater Dr WARRN/WOL WA2 .. 122 A1
Ball Av WAL/NB CH45 .......... 95 J5
Balliol Cl CL/PREN CH43 ....... 110 E4
Balliol Gv CSBY/WL L22 ........ 82 D3
Balliol Rd BTL L20 ............. 7 H7
Balliol Rd East BTL L20 ........ 7 K6
Balliol Wy AIMK WN4 .......... 91 H1
Ball's Pl STHP PR8 ............. 3 C4
Ball's Rd CL/PREN CH43 ........ 10 E8
Ball's Rd East BIRK CH41 ...... 10 E8
Balmer St STHEL WA9 .......... 101 M6
Balmoral CHLY/EC PR7 ......... 44 A7
Balmoral Av CSBY/BLUN L23 ... 83 G2
GOL/RIS/CU WA3................ 92 F4
STHEL WA9..................... 102 E6
Balmoral Cl NWD/KWIPK L33 ... 74 A8
Balmoral Ct CLB/OSW/ST L13 .. 98 A8
Balmoral Dr CHTN/BK PR9 ...... 25 K2
FMBY L37...................... 59 J3
FROD/HEL WA6.................. 166 D1
WGNE/HIN WN2.................. 80 E1
Balmoral Gdns EP CH65 ........ 20 E9
Balmoral Rd AIMK WN4 ......... 91 J1
CHLY/EC PR7................... 30 E6
CHLY/EC PR7................... 32 D5
MGHL L31...................... 72 E4
NPK/KEN L6.................... 113 L2
WAL/NB CH45................... 95 K4
WARRS WA4..................... 138 B3
WDN WA8....................... 134 C1
WGNW/BIL/O WN5............... 68 A7
WLT/FAZ L9.................... 84 C7
Balm St EHL/KEN L7 ........... 113 K3
Balniel Cl CHLY/EC PR7 ........ 32 D6
Balniel St STHEL WA9 .......... 118 F2
Balsham Cl WLTN L25 .......... 131 L6
Balshaw La CHLY/EC PR7 ....... 31 M4
Baltic Rd BTL L20 ............. 6 E4
Baltic St ANF/KKDL L4 ......... 97 J5
Baltimore St CLVPS L1 ......... 13 K9
Bamber St CHLY/EC PR7 ........ 32 D8
Bamboo Cl NTHLY L27 .......... 116 A7
Bamburgh Pl AIMK WN4 ........ 79 J8
Bamford Cl WGNE/HIN WN2 .... 5 L1
Bamford Dr WGNE/HIN WN2 ... 5 L1
Bampton Av RNFD/HAY WA11 ... 89 K4

Bampton Rd CHLDW L16 ........ 114 F5
Banastre CHLY/EC PR7 ......... 32 C3
Banastre Dr NEWLW WA12 ..... 105 H2
Banastre Rd STHP PR8 ......... 2 E8
Banbury Av WLTN L25 .......... 131 L3
Banbury Dr WARRW/BUR WA5 .. 120 E1
Banbury Rd WGNW/BIL/O WN5.. 77 M3
Banbury Wy CL/PREN CH43 .... 127 C3
Bancroft Cl WLTN L25 ......... 131 L6
Bancroft Rd WDN WA8 ......... 134 F3
Bandon Cl SPK/HALE L24 ...... 147 M3
Banff Av BEB CH63 ............ 143 L8
Bangor Cl GTS/LS CH66 ....... 163 H5
Bangor Rd WAL/NB CH45 ...... 94 F7
Bangor St EV L5 .............. 96 E8
Banham Av WGNS/IIMK WN3 .. 78 E2
Bank Av WGNW/BIL/O WN5 .... 67 J7
Bankbrook Cl WARRW/BUR WA5 67 M1
Bank Brow SKEL WN8 .......... 54 E8
Bank Cl NSTN CH64 ........... 153 J7
Bank Dene RF/TRAN CH42 ..... 128 C5
Bankes' La RUNC WA7 ......... 149 G7
Bankfield SKEL WN8 ........... 65 L6
Bankfield Ct CLB/OSW/ST L13 . 98 A8
Bankfield La CHTN/BK PR9 .... 25 K3
Bankfield St CLB/OSW/ST L13 . 98 B8
WDN WA8...................... 133 K4
Bankfields Dr PS/BROM CH62 . 144 D8
Bankfield St BTL L20 ......... 96 D5
Bank Gdns
WARRW/BUR WA5 ............. 136 A1
Bankhall Cl WGNE/HIN WN2 ... 81 K4
Bankhall La BTL L20 .......... 96 E6
Bankhall St BTL L20 .......... 96 E5
Bankhey NSTN CH64 ........... 153 H8
Bank House La FROD/HEL WA6 . 166 F1
Bankland Rd CLB/OSW/ST L13 . 98 B8
Bank La MGHL L31 ............ 73 L7
NWD/KWIPK L33............... 85 M1
Bank Pas GOL/RIS/CU WA3 .... 92 C4
Bank Rd BTL L20 ............. 6 F4
SKEL WN8..................... 54 E8
Banks Av HOY CH47 .......... 108 F5
Banksbarn SKEL WN8 ......... 65 L6
Banks Ct LEIGH WN7 ......... 81 M8
Banks Crs WARRS WA4 ....... 138 B1
Bankside HTWN L38 .......... 70 B2
RUNC WA7..................... 151 C6
SKEL WN8..................... 53 K3
Bankside Av AIMK WN4 ....... 79 J5
Bankside Rd RF/TRAN CH42 ... 128 B5
Bank's La ALL/GAR L19 ....... 145 M1
SPK/HALE L24................. 146 B3
Bank Sq CHTN/BK PR9 ........ 3 C1
Bank's Rd ALL/GAR L19 ....... 130 E8
CHTN/BK PR9.................. 22 F7
HES CH60..................... 140 E5
SPK/HALE L24................. 146 A1
WKBY CH48.................... 124 C4
Bank's Wy ALL/GAR L19 ...... 145 M1
Bankville Rd RF/TRAN CH42 ... 128 A2
Bankwood WGNNW/ST WN6 ... 55 C7
Banner Cl CHLY/EC PR7 ....... 30 D6
Banner Hey RAIN/WH L35 ..... 116 F4
Bannerman St EHL/KEN L7 .... 113 L5
Bannerman Ter CHLYE PR6 ... 32 F3
Banner St ECCL WA10 ........ 8 E6
WAV L15...................... 114 A6
WGNS/IIMK WN3............... 5 J9
Banning Cl BIRK CH41 ........ 11 C4
Bannister Gn CHLY/EC PR7 ... 41 L2
Bannister La BRSC L40 ....... 41 C7
Bannister St CHLY/EC PR7 .... 32 E6
Banstead Gv WAV L15 ........ 114 D6
Barbara Av AIN/FAZ L10 ...... 85 J6
Barbara St STHEL WA9 ....... 119 C2
Barbauld St WARR WA1 ...... 14 E6
Barberry Cl MOR/LEA CH46 .. 109 K5
Barberry Crs NTHTN L30 ..... 84 C1
Barber St STHEL WA9 ........ 9 K4
Barbondale Cl
WARRW/BUR WA5 ............. 120 B6
Barbour Dr BTL L20 .......... 84 A7
Barbrook Cl WARRW/BUR WA5 . 55 K3
Barbrook Wy WLT/FAZ L9 .... 97 K2
Barchester Dr AIG/SPK L17 ... 129 L4
Barclay St TOX L8 ........... 129 H1
Barcombe Rd HES CH60 ...... 141 M4
Bardale Gv AIMK WN4 ........ 91 J2
Bardley Crs HUY L36 ......... 116 C6
Bardney Av GOL/RIS/CU WA3 . 92 B3
Bardon Cl WLTN L25 ......... 115 L8
Bardsay Rd ANF/KKDL L4 ..... 97 H4
Bardsey Cl EP CH65 .......... 163 L4
Bardsley Av WARRW/BUR WA5 . 121 H3
Bardsley Cl SKEL WN8 ........ 66 C6
Barford Cl CL/PREN CH43 .... 110 D7
SKEL WN8..................... 66 C6
STHP PR8..................... 34 C7
WARRW/BUR WA5.............. 120 D4
Barford Dr GOL/RIS/CU WA3 .. 93 J5
Barford Gra NSTN CH64 ...... 154 D5
Barford Rd HUY L36 ......... 100 B7
SPK/HALE L24................. 131 K7
Barford Rd GOL/RIS/CU WA3 . 92 B3
Barkbeth Rd HUY L36 ........ 99 L8
Barkeley Dr LITH L21 ......... 83 H7
Barker La GR/UP/WCH CH49 .. 125 M3
Barker Rd PEN/TH CH61 ...... 126 B7
Barker's Hollow Rd
WARRS WA4 .................. 151 J7
Barker St LEIGH WN7 ........ 81 L8
Barkerville Cl
CLB/OSW/ST L13 ............. 97 M6

Barker Wy NPK/KEN L6 ....... 97 K8
Barkfield Av FMBY L37 ....... 59 G1
Barkfield La FMBY L37 ....... 58 F1
Barkhill Rd AIG/SPK L17 ..... 130 B4
Barkiss Cl TOX L8 ........... 113 H8
Bark Rd LITH L21 ............ 83 L4
Barlborough Rd
WGNW/BIL/O WN5 ............ 67 M8
Barley Brook St WGNNW/ST WN6 4 B1
Barleycastle La WARRS WA4 .. 138 F8
Barleyfield PEN/TH CH61 ..... 141 G1
Barley Mow Cl CH/BCN CH1 .. 162 E3
Barley Rd WARRS WA4 ....... 138 E3
Barlow Av BEB CH63 ......... 128 C6
Barlow Gv STHEL WA9 ....... 103 J3
Barlow La ANF/KKDL L4 ...... 97 G5
Barlows Cl WLT/FAZ L9 ...... 84 F5
Barlows La WLT/FAZ L9 ...... 84 F5
Barlow St ANF/KKDL L4 ...... 97 G5
Barmouth Cl WARRW/BUR WA5. 121 C3
Barmouth Rd WAL/NB CH45 .. 94 F7
Barmouth Wy EV L5 .......... 96 E8
Barmskin La CHLY/EC PR7 .... 41 L4
Barnack Cl WARR WA1 ....... 122 C5
Barnacre Dr NSTN CH64 ..... 152 D3
Barnacre La WKBY CH48 ..... 109 K7
Barnard Rd CL/PREN CH43 ... 10 D8
Barnard St WARRW/BUR WA5 . 136 F2
Barn Cl NTHTN L30 .......... 84 C1
Barn Cft FROD/HEL WA6 ..... 166 F1
Barncroft RUNC WA7 ........ 150 F6
Barn Croft Rd HLWD L26 .... 132 C6
The Barncroft
GR/UP/WCH CH49 ............ 125 M1
Barndale Rd CALD/MH L18 ... 130 B1
Barnes Av WARRN/WOL WA2 . 122 D3
Barnes Cl WARRW/BUR WA5 .. 120 C8
WDN WA8..................... 134 F3
Barnes Dr FROD/HEL WA6 .... 166 F1
Barnes Gn BEB CH63 ......... 143 J4
Barnes Rd ORM L39 .......... 63 G2
SKEL WN8..................... 64 F4
WDN WA8..................... 134 E3
Barnes St NPK/KEN L6 ....... 97 J8
Barneston Rd WDN WA8 ..... 135 G2
Barnet Cl EHL/KEN L7 ....... 113 L5
Barnett Av NEWLW WA12 .... 104 A2
Barnfield Cl GTS/LS CH66 .... 162 E3
HOY CH47..................... 109 C4
NTHTN L30.................... 84 A3
WD/CROXPK L12............... 98 D7
Barnfield Dr SKEL WN8 ...... 66 A6
WD/CROXPK L12............... 98 D7
Barnfield Rd WARR WA1 ..... 122 E6
Barngill Gv WGNS/IIMK WN3 . 79 G2
Barnham Cl GOL/RIS/CU WA3 . 92 C5
SPK/HALE L24................. 146 D1
Barnham Dr CHLDW L16 ..... 115 C6
Barn Hey Crs HOY CH47 ..... 108 C8
Barn Hey Gn WD/CROXPK L12 . 98 D7
Barn Hey Rd NWD/KWIPK L33 . 86 C3
Barnhill Rd WAV L15 ........ 114 C7
Barnhurst Cl CHLDW L16 .... 115 G6
Barnhurst Rd CHLDW L16 ... 115 G6
Barn La GOL/RIS/CU WA3 .... 92 B6
Barnmeadow Rd WLTN L25 .. 115 J8
Barnsbury Rd ANF/KKDL L4 .. 97 K3
Barnsdale Av PEN/TH CH61 .. 126 D8
Barnside CHLY/EC PR7 ....... 31 L2
Barnside Ct CHLDW L16 ..... 115 G6
Barnsley Cl STNNW/ST WN6 . 68 C2
Barnstaple Wy
WARRW/BUR WA5 ............ 136 A1
Barnston La MOR/LEA CH46 . 110 A5
Barnston Rd HES CH60 ...... 141 L5
PEN/TH CH61.................. 126 D7
WLT/FAZ L9................... 84 C7
Barnston Towers Cl HES CH60 . 141 L1
Barn St WDN WA8 ........... 16 C8
Barnswood Cl WARRS WA4 .. 138 F8
Barnton Cl GOL/RIS/CU WA3 . 92 F6
Barn Wy NEWLW WA12 ...... 104 D2
Barnwell Av GOL/RIS/CU WA3 . 106 F1
WAL/EG CH44.................. 95 K8
Barnwood Rd HUY L36 ...... 115 K1
Baron Cl WARR WA1 ........ 122 F6
Baroncroft Rd WLTN L25 .... 131 H1
Baron's Cl WDN WA8 ....... 133 L5
Baron's Hey STBRV L28 ..... 99 H5
Barons Wy CHLY/EC PR7 .... 31 M3
Barrack Sq WGN WN1 ....... 4 F4
Barracks Rd WGNE/HIN WN2 . 80 F4
Barracks Yd WGNE/HIN WN2 . 80 F4
Barren Gv CL/PREN CH43 .... 10 D9
Barrett Av STHP PR8 ........ 35 J3
Barrett Rd STHP PR8 ........ 35 J3
Barrie St LEIGH WN7 ........ 81 M5
Barrington Cl WGNS/IIMK WN3 . 78 F4
Barrington Dr STHP PR8 ..... 34 D8
Barrington Rd WAL/EG CH44 . 111 L2
WAV L15...................... 114 A7
Barrison Gn BRSC L40 ....... 51 G3
Barron Meadow LEIGH WN7 . 81 M6
Barrow Av WARRN/WOL WA2 . 122 A3
Barrow Cl WD/CROXPK L12 .. 98 E4
Barrowdale Rd GOL/RIS/CU WA3. 92 D5
Barrowfield Rd ECCL WA10 .. 88 C8
Barrow Hall La
WARRW/BUR WA5 ............ 120 A7
Barrow La GOL/RIS/CU WA3 .. 75 G2
Barrow Nook La ORM L39 ... 75 C2
Barrow's Green La WDN WA8 . 135 G2
Barrow's Rw WDN WA8 ...... 134 D1
Barrow St AIMK WN4 ........ 79 M4
ECCL WA10.................... 9 C5
Barrule Cl WARRS WA4 ...... 137 M6
Barrymore Av
CLB/OSW/ST L13 ............. 114 B2
RUNC WA7.................... 149 K6
Barrymore Wy BEB CH63 .... 143 K7
Barry St WARRS WA4 ........ 15 H8
Barsbank Cl LYMM WA13 .... 139 L2
Barsbank La LYMM WA13 .... 139 L2
Barston Av EP CH65 ......... 156 B8

Bar St WGNE/HIN WN2 ....... 80 C4
Bartholomew Cl RAIN/WH L35 . 118 A4
Bartlegate Cl RUNC WA7 .... 150 D8
Bartlett St LITH L21 ........ 114 A6
Barton Av WARRS WA4 ...... 138 C3
WGN WN1..................... 68 D3
Barton Cl ECCL WA10 ....... 8 E4
HOY CH47..................... 108 B7
LITH L21..................... 83 J7
RUNC WA7.................... 150 F6
Barton Clough
WGNW/BIL/O WN5 ............ 78 A8
Barton Hey Dr WKBY CH48 .. 124 E7
Barton Heys Rd WKBY CH48 . 58 F4
Barton Rd HOY CH47 ........ 108 C7
WLT/FAZ L9................... 97 H1
Bartons Cl CHTN/BK PR9 .... 22 F7
CL/PREN CH43................ 10 F6
GOL/RIS/CU WA3.............. 92 C5
WGNE/HIN WN2................ 80 D2
WGNW/BIL/O WN5............. 67 J8
Barton St BIRK CH41 ........ 10 F7
CL/PREN CH43................ 10 F6
Barwell Av RNFD/HAY WA11 .. 89 L7
Basil Cl CHLDW L16 ......... 115 C5
Basildon Cl STHEL WA9 ..... 102 A7
Basil Rd CHLDW L16 ........ 114 F5
Basing St ALL/GAR L19 ..... 130 E7
Baskervyle Cl HES CH60 .... 141 J7
Baskervyle Rd HES CH60 .... 141 J7
Baslow Av WGNE/HIN WN2 .. 81 H1
Basnett St CLVPS L1 ........ 13 G7
Bassendale Rd PS/BROM CH62. 144 A3
Bassenthwaite Av
CL/PREN CH43 .............. 110 F8
NWD/KWIPK L33............... 85 M1
RNFD/HAY WA11............... 89 J5
Bassett Av WGNS/IIMK WN3 . 78 E3
Basswood Gv WGNE/HIN WN2. 81 J2
Bates Crs ECCL WA10 ....... 101 M5
Bates La FROD/HEL WA6 ..... 166 F1
Batey Av RAIN/WH L35 ...... 117 K1
Batheaston Gv LEIGH WN7 .. 81 M5
Bathgate Wy NWD/KWIPK L33. 73 M7
Batherton Cl WDN WA8 ..... 16 E6
Bath St CSBY/WL L22 ....... 82 F5
ECCL WA10.................... 8 F6
PS/BROM CH62................ 128 D8
STHP PR8..................... 3 G2
VAUX/LVPD L3................. 12 C5
WARR WA1.................... 14 D5
WGNE/HIN WN2................ 69 H3
Bath St North CHTN/BK PR9 . 3 H1
Bathurst Rd ALL/GAR L19 ... 130 D6
Bathwood Dr NSTN CH64 ... 153 G8
Batley St WGNE/HIN WN2 ... 69 K5
Battenberg St EHL/KEN L7 .. 113 J3
Battersby La WARRN/WOL WA2. 15 C3
Battersby St WGNE/HIN WN2 . 69 K5
Battersea Ct WDN WA8 ..... 134 B2
Battery Cl AIG/SPK L17 ..... 129 L3
Battery La WARR WA1 ....... 123 H7
Battle Wy FMBY L37 ........ 59 K3
Baucher Dr BTL L20 ........ 84 A6
Baucher Rd WGNS/IIMK WN3. 68 B8
Baumville Dr BEB CH63 ..... 143 H8
Baverstock Cl WGNS/IIMK WN3. 5 H7
Bawtry Ct WARRN/WOL WA2 . 122 A4
Baxter Cl RUNC WA7 ........ 150 F6
Baxters La STHEL WA9 ...... 102 F5
Baxter's Rw WGNE/HIN WN2 . 69 J5
Baxter St WARRW/BUR WA5 .. 121 G8
Bayciff Cl WGNE/HIN WN2 .. 81 H2
Baycliffe LYMM WA13 ....... 139 M3
Baycliffe Cl RUNC WA7 ..... 149 M6
Baycliff Rd WD/CROXPK L12 . 99 G5
Bayfield Rd ALL/GAR L19 ... 130 C6
Bayhorse La VAUX/LVPD L3 .. 13 L5
Baysdale Cl TOX L8 ......... 129 J1
Bayswater Cl RUNC WA7 .... 151 H1
Bayswater Gdns
WAL/NB CH45 ............... 94 F6
Bayswater Rd WAL/NB CH45 . 94 F7
Baythorne Rd ANF/KKDL L4 . 97 L3
Baytree Cl CHTN/BK PR9 .... 22 F8
GTS/LS CH66.................. 163 H4
Baytree Rd RF/TRAN CH42 .. 128 A2
WGNNW/ST WN6............... 68 B3
WKBY CH48.................... 125 H3
Bayview Dr WAL/NB CH45 ... 94 F6
Bayvil Cl RUNC WA7 ........ 151 G6
Beacham Rd STHP PR8 ...... 25 G6
Beachcroft Rd HOY CH47 ... 108 F4
Beach Gv WAL/NB CH45 .... 95 H4
Beach Lawn CSBY/WL L22 .. 82 E4
Beach Priory Gdns STHP PR8. 2 E5
Beach Rd HOY CH47 ........ 108 F4
LITH L21..................... 83 K6
STHP PR8..................... 2 C6
Beach Wk WKBY CH48 ...... 124 C5
Beacon Dr WKBY CH48 ...... 124 E8
Beacon Gv RNFD/HAY WA11 . 89 M7
Beacon La BRSC L40 ........ 53 L8
EV L5........................ 97 H7
HES CH60..................... 141 J5
SKEL WN8..................... 53 L8
SKEL WN8..................... 66 B3
Beacon Rd WGNE/HIN WN2 .. 81 J5
WGNNW/ST WN6............... 55 H9
WGNW/BIL/O WN5............. 55 H9
Beaconsfield Cl BIRK CH41 .. 128 B2
Beaconsfield Crs WDN WA8 . 134 C1
Beaconsfield Gv WDN WA8 .. 134 D1
Beaconsfield Rd CHTN/BK PR9. 25 H7
ECCL WA10.................... 88 C8
LITH L21..................... 83 L7
PS/BROM CH62................ 128 D6
RUNC WA7.................... 18 D2
WDN WA8..................... 134 D2
WLTN L25..................... 131 G2
Beaconsfield St TOX L8 ..... 113 G6
Beaconsfield Ter CHLYE PR6.. 32 F3
The Beacons WGNNW/ST WN6. 54 F6
Beacon St CHLY/EC PR7 ..... 32 F5
EV L5........................ 96 D7
Beacon Vw WGNNW/ST WN6 . 54 E5
Beacon View Dr SKEL WN8 .. 66 D6

Beadnell Dr WARRW/BUR WA5. 136 A2
Beaford Cl WGNW/BIL/O WN5 . 67 K8
Beal Dr WGNE/HIN WN2 ..... 80 C3
Beames Cl EHL/KEN L7 ..... 113 L4
Beamont St WDN WA8 ...... 149 J1
Beardsmore Dr
GOL/RIS/CU WA3 ............ 93 C5
Bearncroft SKEL WN8 ....... 65 L7
Beasley Cl GTS/LS CH66 .... 162 F2
Beatrice Av BEB CH63 ...... 128 A6
Beatrice St BTL L20 ........ 7 J8
WARRS WA4................... 15 J9
Beattock Cl NWD/KWIPK L33. 73 M7
Beatty Av CHLY/EC PR7 ..... 32 D7
WARRN/WOL WA2.............. 121 L4
Beatty Cl RAIN/WH L35 ..... 116 F3
WKBY CH48.................... 124 E7
Beatty Rd CLB/OSW/ST L13 .. 114 C3
STHEL WA9.................... 25 G8
Beauclair Dr WAV L15 ...... 114 D7
Beaufort FMBY L37 ......... 59 J3
Beaufort Cl ORM L39 ....... 62 C4
RUNC WA7.................... 149 K6
WARRW/BUR WA5.............. 120 C8
WDN WA8..................... 133 J5
Beaufort Dr WAL/EG CH44 .. 111 G1
Beaufort Rd BIRK CH41 ..... 111 J4
Beaufort St STHEL WA9 ..... 9 M9
TOX L8....................... 113 G7
WARRW/BUR WA5.............. 137 G1
WGNE/HIN WN2................ 69 M8
WGNW/BIL/O WN5............. 68 A7
Beaumaris Cl LEIGH WN7 ... 81 L8
Beaumaris Dr EP CH65 ...... 163 H3
PEN/TH CH61.................. 126 D7
Beaumaris Rd WAL/NB CH45. 94 F7
WGNE/HIN WN2................ 81 J2
Beaumaris St BTL L20 ...... 96 D5
Beaumont Av ECCL WA10 ... 8 A4
Beaumont Crs ORM L39 ..... 62 F3
Beaumont Dr AIN/FAZ L10 .. 85 G4
Beaumont Gv
WGNW/BIL/O WN5 ........... 67 K5
Beaumont St TOX L8 ........ 113 K6
Beau St VAUX/LVPD L3 ..... 13 J2
Beauworth Av
GR/UP/WCH CH49 ............ 125 L2
Beaverbrook Av
GOL/RIS/CU WA3 ............ 107 K1
Beaver Ct AIMK WN4 ....... 79 L7
Beaver Gv WLT/FAZ L9 ..... 84 C7
Beavers La SKEL WN8 ....... 65 M7
Bebington Rd GTS/LS CH66 . 162 F1
PS/BROM CH62................ 128 C2
RF/TRAN CH42................. 127 M3
Bebles Rd ORM L39 ......... 62 C2
Bebington St WDN WA8 ..... 133 K2
Bechers Rw WLT/FAZ L9 .... 84 B6
Beck Cl AIN/FAZ L10 ....... 85 K6
Beckenham Av
CALD/MH L18 ............... 114 B8
Beckenham Rd WAL/NB CH45. 95 K4
Becket St ANF/KKDL L4 ..... 96 F6
Beckett Cl NWD/KWIPK L33 . 86 E5
Beckett Gv BEB CH63 ....... 127 M6
Beck Gv RNFD/HAY WA11 ... 89 K5
Beck Rd BTL L20 ........... 83 L8
Beckwith WGNE/HIN WN2 ... 80 D2
Beckwith St BIRK CH41 ..... 10 E3
CLVPS L1..................... 13 G7
Beckwith St East BIRK CH41. 11 J5
Becky St NPK/KEN L6 ....... 97 K8
Becontree Rd WD/CROXPK L12. 114 F1
Bective St EHL/KEN L7 ..... 113 L5
Bedburn Dr HUY L36 ....... 115 J2
Bedford Av EP CH65 ........ 163 J3
MGHL L31..................... 73 C7
RF/TRAN CH42................. 128 A4
TOX L8....................... 113 H5
Bedford Av East EP CH65 ... 163 K3
Bedford Cl HUY L36 ........ 116 C2
TOX L8....................... 113 H5
Bedford Pl AIMK WN4 ....... 79 J8
BTL L20...................... 6 F8
LITH L21..................... 83 H6
RF/TRAN CH42................. 128 C3
Bedford Rd ANF/KKDL L4 ... 7 M7
BTL L20...................... 7 G8
RF/TRAN CH42................. 128 B3
STHP PR8..................... 35 J3
WAL/NB CH45................. 95 K7
Bedford Rd East
RF/TRAN CH42 .............. 128 C3
Bedford St STHEL WA9 ..... 102 F3
WARRS WA4................... 137 L5
WGN WN1..................... 5 J7
WGNW/BIL/O WN5............. 67 L8
Bedford St North
EHL/KEN L7 ................ 13 M8
Bedford St South EHL/KEN L7. 13 M9
Beecham Cl HUY L36 ....... 115 M4
Beech Av AIG/SPK L17 ...... 129 K3
CHLY/EC PR7.................. 31 K2
CHLYE PR6.................... 44 D5
CSBY/BLUN L25................ 71 J7
FROD/HEL WA6................. 160 E5
GOL/RIS/CU WA3.............. 93 H6
GOL/RIS/CU WA3.............. 107 J2
GR/UP/WCH CH49.............. 109 M7
MGHL L31..................... 85 K2
PEN/TH CH61.................. 141 J1
PR/KW L34.................... 101 H7
RNFD/HAY WA11............... 91 H6
SKEL WN8..................... 53 L4
STHEL WA9.................... 118 L1
WARRS WA4................... 138 F2
WARRW/BUR WA5.............. 120 C8
Beechbank Rd AIG/SPK L17 . 114 A8
Beechburn Crs HUY L36 .... 115 K2
Beechburn Rd HUY L36 ..... 115 J2
Beech Cl BRSC L40 ......... 39 L1
KKBY L32..................... 85 L1
NEWLW WA12.................. 104 E3
SKEL WN8..................... 65 G4
WD/CROXPK L12............... 98 F2
Beech Ct CALD/MH L18 ..... 130 F2
Beech Crs WGNNW/ST WN6 . 56 A5
Beechcroft Dr EP CH65 ..... 20 A9
Beechcroft Rd WAL/EG CH44. 111 C3
Beechdale Rd CALD/MH L18. 130 C1

Beechdene Rd ANF/KKDL L4 .... 97 K6
Beech Dr FMBY L37 .... 58 F1
The Beeches CALD/MH L18 .... 114 F8
  FROD/HEL WA6 .... 166 E1
  MOR/LEA CH46 .... 110 A2
Beechfield MGHL L31 .... 73 C4
  SKEL WN8 .... 40 E8
Beechfield Av WGNE/HIN WN2 .. 81 J1
Beechfield Cl HES CH60 .... 141 H6
Beechfield Gdns STHP PR8 .... 2 D5
Beechfield Rd CALD/MH L18 .... 130 F1
  EP CH65 .... 20 B4
  WARRS WA4 .... 138 C4
Beechfields CHLY/EC PR7 .... 30 D7
Beech Gdns RNFD/HAY WA11 .... 76 A6
Beech Gn WD/CROXPK L12 .... 98 C5
Beech Gv CHTN/BK PR9 .... 25 G6
  GTS/LS CH66 .... 163 J5
  LITH L21 .... 83 H7
  LYMM WA13 .... 139 K3
  NTHTN L30 .... 84 C3
  WARR WA1 .... 122 C6
  WARRS WA4 .... 15 K9
  WGNE/HIN WN2 .... 80 E6
  WGNNW/ST WN6 .... 68 A2
  WLT/FAZ L9 .... 84 D7
Beech Hall St WGNNW/ST WN6 ... 68 C3
Beech Hey La NSTN CH64 .... 154 D4
Beech Hill Av WGNNW/ST WN6 .. 68 A2
Beech Hill La WGNE/HIN WN2 .... 68 A3
Beechill Cl WLTN L25 .... 131 L1
Beech Lawn ALL/GAR L19 .... 130 B6
Beech Meadow ORM L39 .... 63 J1
Beechmill Dr GOL/RIS/CU WA3 ... 106 F2
Beechmoore WARRS WA4 .... 136 D8
Beech Pk WD/CROXPK L12 .... 98 C7
Beech Rd ANF/KKDL L4 .... 97 J4
  BEB CH63 .... 128 B6
  GOL/RIS/CU WA3 .... 92 C4
  HES CH60 .... 141 L5
  HUY L36 .... 116 A4
  ORM L39 .... 62 C7
  RF/TRAN CH42 .... 10 F9
  RUNC WA7 .... 19 M8
  RUNC WA7 .... 161 K1
  WARRS WA4 .... 137 L5
Beech St BTL L20 .... 7 H2
  ECCL WA10 .... 101 M5
  EHL/KEN L7 .... 113 L3
Beech Tree Av WGNNW/ST WN6 .. 54 F5
Beech Tree Houses
  WGNE/HIN WN2 .... 80 A7
Beechtree Rd WAV L15 .... 114 E5
Beechtrees SKEL WN8 .... 65 L6
Beechurst Cl WLTN L25 .... 115 K8
Beechurst Rd WLTN L25 .... 115 K8
Beech Wk WGNNW/ST WN6 .... 55 M5
  WGNS/IIMK WN3 .... 78 E3
The Beechwalk BEB CH63 .... 143 H2
  MGHL L31 .... 73 K3
Beechway Av MGHL L31 .... 73 J3
Beechways WARRS WA4 .... 137 M8
Beechways Dr NSTN CH64 .... 152 F5
Beechwood SKEL WN8 .... 65 L2
Beechwood Av AIMK WN4 .... 91 J5
  HLWD L26 .... 132 A6
  NEWLW WA12 .... 104 F1
  RUNC WA7 .... 149 M8
  RUNC WA7 .... 150 B8
  WAL/NB CH45 .... 95 G8
  WARR WA1 .... 122 A5
  WARRW/BUR WA5 .... 120 B8
  WGNNW/ST WN6 .... 55 H8
Beechwood Cl ALL/GAR L19 .... 130 C6
  RAIN/WH L35 .... 117 G1
Beechwood Crs
  WGNW/BIL/O WN5 .... 67 G7
Beechwood Dr CL/PREN CH43 .... 110 D6
  FMBY L37 .... 58 E4
  GTS/LS CH66 .... 162 F4
  ORM L39 .... 62 F1
Beechwood Gdns
  ALL/GAR L19 .... 130 B6
Beechwood La
  GOL/RIS/CU WA3 .... 106 F1
Beechwood Rd ALL/GAR L19 .... 130 B6
  CHLY/EC PR7 .... 32 F7
  LITH L21 .... 83 K7
  PS/BROM CH62 .... 143 L5
Beecroft Cl WARRW/BUR WA5 ... 120 F4
Beesands Cl NTHLY L27 .... 132 B1
Beesley Rd PR/KW L34 .... 100 E7
Beeston Cl CL/PREN CH43 .... 110 E7
  GOL/RIS/CU WA3 .... 122 F1
Beeston Dr PEN/TH CH61 .... 141 G1
Beeston Gn GTS/LS CH66 .... 156 A8
Beeston Gv ALL/GAR L19 .... 130 C6
Beeston Gv ANF/KKDL L4 .... 97 G5
Beilby Rd RNFD/HAY WA11 .... 91 H6
Beldale Pk KKBY L32 .... 85 L1
Beldon Crs HUY L36 .... 115 K2
Belem Cl AIG/SPK L17 .... 113 L8
Belfast Rd CLB/OSW/ST L13 .... 114 D2
Belfield SKEL WN8 .... 65 M7
Belfield Crs HUY L36 .... 116 A4
Belfield Dr CL/PREN CH43 .... 127 K2
Belford Dr MOR/LEA CH46 .... 109 L5
Belfort Rd WLTN L25 .... 131 K1
Belfry Cl CHLYE PR6 .... 31 M1
  MOR/LEA CH46 .... 109 K4
  WD/CROXPK L12 .... 99 G7
Belfry Crs WGNNW/ST WN6 .... 56 B8
Belgarve Av WAL/EG CH44 .... 111 L1
  WARR WA1 .... 122 B6
Belgrave AIG/SPK L17 .... 129 K2
  LITH L21 .... 83 H6
Belgrave St WAL/NB CH45 .... 95 L8
Belhaven Rd CALD/MH L18 .... 114 B8
Bellair Av CSBY/BLUN L23 .... 83 J1
Bellairs Rd NG/CROX L11 .... 98 A5
Bellamy Rd ANF/KKDL L4 .... 7 M7
Bell Cl HUY L36 .... 116 B5

Belldean WGNE/HIN WN2 .... 69 J5
Belldene Gv HES CH60 .... 141 H3
Bellefield Av WD/CROXPK L12 .... 98 D7
Belle Green La WGNE/HIN WN2 .. 69 J5
Belle Vale Rd WLTN L25 .... 131 K1
Belle Vue Rd WAL/EG CH44 .... 112 A3
  WLTN L25 .... 115 K8
Belle Vue St
  WGNW/BIL/O WN5 .... 67 M8
Bellew Rd NG/CROX L11 .... 98 B6
Bellfield Crs WAL/NB CH45 .... 95 J5
Bellgreen Rd NG/CROX L11 .... 98 C3
Bellhouse La WARRS WA4 .... 136 F6
Bell House Rd WDN WA8 .... 17 H2
Bellingham Av WGN WN1 .... 68 E3
Bellingham Dr RUNC WA7 .... 19 H8
  WGN WN1 .... 68 E3
Bellingham Mt WGN WN1 .... 68 E3
Bellini Cl LITH L21 .... 83 H8
Bellis Av CHTN/BK PR9 .... 25 G3
Bellis Gv NWD/KWIPK L33 .... 73 M8
Bell La RAIN/WH L35 .... 118 C3
  WARRS WA4 .... 139 G1
  WGNW/BIL/O WN5 .... 67 M8
Bellmore St ALL/GAR L19 .... 130 E6
Bell Rd WAL/EG CH44 .... 111 M2
Bell's Cl MGHL L31 .... 72 D2
Bell St CLB/OSW/ST L13 .... 114 C2
  LEIGH WN7 .... 81 J8
Bellward Cl BEB CH63 .... 143 H3
Belmont BIRK CH41 .... 10 E8
Belmont Av GOL/RIS/CU WA3 .... 92 E4
  PS/BROM CH62 .... 143 L4
  WARRS WA4 .... 138 B2
  WGNE/HIN WN2 .... 81 H4
  WGNW/BIL/O WN5 .... 77 M2
Belmont Cl BRSC L40 .... 52 A2
Belmont Crs WARRW/BUR WA5 .. 120 B7
Belmont Dr CHLYE PR6 .... 33 C4
  NPK/KEN L6 .... 97 L8
  PEN/TH CH61 .... 141 J2
  WGNE/HIN WN2 .... 57 L8
Belmont Gv NPK/KEN L6 .... 97 L8
Belmont Pl CHLY/EC PR7 .... 42 E7
Belmont Rd CHLYE PR6 .... 44 D6
  HOR/BR BL6 .... 45 L4
  NPK/KEN L6 .... 97 K8
  WAL/NB CH45 .... 95 K4
  WDN WA8 .... 138 A3
  WKBY CH48 .... 124 D2
Belmont St ECCL WA10 .... 8 A6
  STHP PR8 .... 2 E6
Beloe St TOX L8 .... 129 H1
Belper St ALL/GAR L19 .... 130 D7
Belston Rd CHLDW L16 .... 114 F6
Belton Rd HUY L36 .... 99 M7
Belvedere Av STHEL WA9 .... 102 F7
Belvedere Cl FROD/HEL WA6 .... 160 E4
  PR/KW L34 .... 101 G6
Belvedere Dr CHLY/EC PR7 .... 32 D5
  FMBY L37 .... 59 H4
Belvedere Pk ORM L39 .... 62 E6
Belvedere Pl WGNS/IIMK WN3 .... 68 B8
Belvedere Rd AIMK WN4 .... 91 K7
  CHLYE PR6 .... 44 D5
  NEWLW WA12 .... 104 D1
  STHP PR8 .... 34 E8
Belvoir Rd CALD/MH L18 .... 130 E5
  WARRS WA4 .... 137 K5
  WDN WA8 .... 16 F1
Belvoir St WGN WN1 .... 5 H4
Bembridge Cl
  WARRW/BUR WA5 .... 119 L6
  WDN WA8 .... 134 B1
Bembridge Ct WGNS/IIMK WN3 .. 79 G3
Bempton Rd AIG/SPK L17 .... 129 K3
Benbow St EV L5 .... 6 E7
Bendee Av NSTN CH64 .... 153 J6
Bendee Rd NSTN CH64 .... 153 H6
Benedict St BTL L20 .... 7 J8
Bengairn Cl WLTN L25 .... 5 K2
Bengarth Rd CHTN/BK PR9 .... 25 H5
Bengel St EHL/KEN L7 .... 113 J3
Benjamin Fold AIMK WN4 .... 79 K8
Ben La RNFD/HAY WA11 .... 75 K3
Ben Lane Ct ORM L39 .... 75 K3
Benledi St EV L5 .... 96 F3
Benmore Rd CALD/MH L18 .... 130 C3
Bennet Cl NSTN CH64 .... 153 G8
Bennet's La HOY CH47 .... 109 G3
Bennett Av WARR WA1 .... 15 M3
Bennett Dr WGNW/BIL/O WN5 ... 77 M1
Bennetts Hl CL/PREN CH43 .... 127 K1
Bennett's La WDN WA8 .... 17 M1
Bennett St ALL/GAR L19 .... 130 E7
  WARR WA1 .... 14 F6
Ben Nevis Rd RF/TRAN CH42 .... 127 K8
Bennison Dr ALL/GAR L19 .... 130 C6
Benson Cl GR/UP/WCH CH49 .... 126 B3
Benson Rd GOL/RIS/CU WA3 .... 122 F3
Benson St CLVPS L1 .... 13 J8
Bentfield AIG/SPK L17 .... 130 B5
Bentfield Cl BEB CH63 .... 127 M6
Bentfield Gdns BEB CH63 .... 127 M6
Bentham Av WARRN/WOL WA2 .. 121 L2
Bentham Cl CL/PREN CH43 .... 127 G2
Bentham Dr CHLDW L16 .... 114 F5
Bentham Pl WGNNW/ST WN6 .... 56 B3
Bentham Rd GOL/RIS/CU WA3 ... 107 J3
  WGNNW/ST WN6 .... 56 A4
Bentham St CHLY/EC PR7 .... 43 G4
  STHP PR8 .... 3 G7
Bentham's Wy STHP PR8 .... 35 L3
Bentinck Cl BIRK CH41 .... 10 F6
Bentinck Pl BIRK CH41 .... 11 G5
Bentinck St BIRK CH41 .... 10 F6
  EV L5 .... 96 D8
  RUNC WA7 .... 18 E2
  STHEL WA9 .... 102 F4

WGNS/IIMK WN3 .... 79 G1
Bent La GOL/RIS/CU WA3 .... 107 J3
Bentley La BRSC L40 .... 40 F6
Bentley Rd CL/PREN CH43 .... 127 K1
  PEN/TH CH61 .... 126 B8
  TOX L8 .... 113 K7
Bentley St STHEL WA9 .... 118 E1
Benton Cl EV L5 .... 96 F7
Benty Cl BEB CH63 .... 143 G5
Benty Farm Gv PEN/TH CH61 ... 126 C8
Benty Heath La NSTN CH64 .... 154 C2
Benwick Rd KKBY L32 .... 85 K4
Berbice Rd WAV L15 .... 114 C7
Beresford Av BEB CH63 .... 128 C7
Beresford Cl CL/PREN CH43 .... 10 B3
Beresford Dr CHTN/BK PR9 .... 25 H4
Beresford Gdns CHTN/BK PR9 .... 25 H3
Beresford Rd CL/PREN CH43 .... 10 B3
  TOX L8 .... 129 H1
  WAL/NB CH45 .... 95 H6
Beresford St BTL L20 .... 6 E8
  EV L5 .... 13 K2
  STHEL WA9 .... 102 A6
  WARR WA1 .... 15 L2
  WGNNW/ST WN6 .... 4 A2
Bergen Cl BTL L20 .... 7 L6
Berkeley Av CL/PREN CH43 .... 127 G4
  WGNS/IIMK WN3 .... 78 F3
Berkeley Cl CHLY/EC PR7 .... 32 F8
  LEIGH WN7 .... 93 L5
Berkeley Dr WAL/NB CH45 .... 95 L6
Berkeley Rd CSBY/BLUN L23 .... 70 E8
Berkeswell Rd NG/CROX L11 .... 98 C4
Berkley Av WD/CROXPK L12 .... 98 D5
Berkley St TOX L8 .... 113 H7
Berkshire Dr WARR WA1 .... 122 F6
Berkshire Gdns ECCL WA10 .... 8 E8
Bermuda Rd MOR/LEA CH46 .... 109 L5
Bernard Av WAL/NB CH45 .... 95 L6
  WARRS WA4 .... 137 M5
Berner's Rd ALL/GAR L19 .... 130 D6
Berner St BIRK CH41 .... 11 G2
Berrington Av WLTN L25 .... 131 J3
Berrington Gv WARRN/WOL WA2 .. 91 J2
Berrington's La
  RNFD/HAY WA11 .... 88 E3
Berry Cl GTS/LS CH66 .... 162 E2
  SKEL WN8 .... 65 H3
Berry Dr GTS/LS CH66 .... 162 E1
Berry Hill Av PR/KW L34 .... 99 M2
Berry Hill Rd BRSC L40 .... 38 C1
Berrylands Cl
  MOR/LEA CH46 .... 109 M4
Berrylands Rd MOR/LEA CH46 ... 109 M3
Berry Rd WDN WA8 .... 133 M4
Berrys La STHEL WA9 .... 103 H4
Berry St BTL L20 .... 6 F5
  CHLYE PR6 .... 44 C5
  CLVPS L1 .... 113 G5
  SKEL WN8 .... 65 G3
Berrywood Dr RAIN/WH L35 .... 117 J1
Bertha St BIRK CH41 .... 111 H5
Bertram Dr HOY CH47 .... 108 E5
Bertram Dr North HOY CH47 .... 108 F5
Bertram Rd AIG/SPK L17 .... 129 L1
Bertram St NEWLW WA12 .... 104 B2
  STHP PR8 .... 34 E8
Berwick Av PS/BROM CH62 .... 155 G1
  STHP PR8 .... 34 F8
Berwick Cl CL/PREN CH43 .... 110 E7
  MOR/LEA CH46 .... 109 M4
  NPK/KEN L6 .... 113 K1
  WARR WA1 .... 123 G7
Berwick Dr CSBY/BLUN L23 .... 70 E8
Berwick Gdns GTS/LS CH66 .... 155 K7
Berwick Gv GTS/LS CH66 .... 155 K7
Berwick Pl WGN WN1 .... 5 K1
Berwick Rd GTS/LS CH66 .... 155 J7
Berwick St NPK/KEN L6 .... 113 K1
Berwyn Av HOY CH47 .... 108 E6
  PEN/TH CH61 .... 126 C7
Berwyn Bvd BEB CH63 .... 128 C5
Berwyn Cl GTS/LS CH66 .... 155 J7
  HOR/BR BL6 .... 45 L8
Berwyn Dr PEN/TH CH61 .... 141 G1
Berwyn Gv STHEL WA9 .... 103 H2
Berwyn Rd ANF/KKDL L4 .... 97 L5
  WAL/EG CH44 .... 95 L8
Beryl Rd CL/PREN CH43 .... 110 B8
Beryl St CLB/OSW/ST L13 .... 114 F1
Bescar Brow La BRSC L40 .... 37 H6
Bescar La BRSC L40 .... 37 J5
Besford Rd WLTN L25 .... 115 K8
Bessborough Rd CL/PREN CH43 .. 10 D9
Bessbrook Rd AIG/SPK L17 .... 130 A3
Bessemer St TOX L8 .... 129 H1
Bessie's Well Pl
  WGNNW/ST WN6 .... 56 B5
Beta Cl PS/BROM CH62 .... 128 C6
Betchworth Crs RUNC WA7 .... 149 M7
Bethany Cl RNFD/HAY WA11 .... 90 D6
Bethersden Rd WGN WN1 .... 56 D8
Betjeman Cl WARR WA1 .... 138 B1
Betjeman Gv CHLDW L16 .... 115 G5
Betony Cl HLWD L26 .... 132 A4
Betsyfield Dr GOL/RIS/CU WA3 .. 106 C3
Bettisfield Av PS/BROM CH62 ... 143 M8
Betula Cl WLT/FAZ L9 .... 97 L1
Beulah Av WGNW/BIL/O WN5 ... 89 H1
Bevan Cl STHEL WA9 .... 101 M7
Bevan's La WD/CROXPK L12 .... 98 E5
Beverley Av WARRS WA4 .... 137 M5
  WGNW/BIL/O WN5 .... 78 A4
Beverley Cl CHTN/BK PR9 .... 22 E8
Beverley Dr HES CH60 .... 141 K6
Beverley Gdns PEN/TH CH61 .... 126 D7
Beverley Rd PS/BROM CH62 .... 128 D5
  WAL/NB CH45 .... 95 H4
  WARRW/BUR WA5 .... 120 C7
  WAV L15 .... 114 C4
  WGNW/BIL/O WN5 .... 67 K5
Beverley Wy GTS/LS CH66 .... 155 K7
Beversbrook Rd NG/CROX L11 ... 98 B7
Bevin Cl GOL/RIS/CU WA3 .... 107 K1
Bevington Bush VAUX/LVPD L3 .. 13 H3
Bevington Hl VAUX/LVPD L3 .... 13 H2
Bevington St AIMK WN4 .... 79 H3
  VAUX/LVPD L3 .... 13 G2

Bevyl Rd NSTN CH64 .... 152 D3
Bewcastle Dr BRSC L40 .... 63 K2
Bewerley Cl WGNS/IIMK WN3 .... 4 C8
Bewey Cl TOX L8 .... 129 G1
Bewley Dr KKBY L32 .... 85 M4
Bewsey Farm Cl
  WARRW/BUR WA5 .... 120 F6
Bewsey Park Cl
  WARRW/BUR WA5 .... 14 A1
Bewsey Rd WARRW/BUR WA5 ... 14 A2
Bewsey St ECCL WA10 .... 101 M4
  WARR WA1 .... 14 E5
  WARRW/WOL WA2 .... 14 D4
Bexhill Av WARRN/WOL WA2 .... 121 K1
Bexhill Cl SPK/HALE L24 .... 146 D1
Bexhill Dr WGNE/HIN WN2 .... 81 L3
Bexley St WGNE/HIN WN2 .... 81 K2
Bianca St BTL L20 .... 7 H8
Bibby Av WARR WA1 .... 15 M3
Bibby Rd CHTN/BK PR9 .... 25 J4
Bibby's La BTL L20 .... 6 D1
Bibby St CLB/OSW/ST L13 .... 114 B2
Bickershaw La WGNE/HIN WN2 .. 80 D4
Bickerstaffe St ECCL WA10 .... 9 H5
  VAUX/LVPD L3 .... 13 K3
Bickerton Av BEB CH63 .... 127 M5
  FROD/HEL WA6 .... 160 F6
Bickerton Cl
  GOL/RIS/CU WA3 .... 122 F1
Bickerton Rd STHP PR8 .... 35 H1
Bickerton St AIG/SPK L17 .... 129 L2
Bickley Cl RUNC WA7 .... 19 L6
  WARRN/WOL WA2 .... 122 B2
Bicknell Cl WARRW/BUR WA5 .... 120 D5
Bidder St VAUX/LVPD L3 .... 13 K4
Bideford Av STHEL WA9 .... 102 E8
Bideford Rd WARRW/BUR WA5 .. 136 A1
Bidston Av BIRK CH41 .... 111 H6
  RNFD/HAY WA11 .... 89 M8
  WARRS WA4 .... 137 M5
Bidston Gn GTS/LS CH66 .... 162 F1
Bidston Green Ct
  CL/PREN CH43 .... 110 E5
Bidston Green Dr
  CL/PREN CH43 .... 110 E5
Bidston Moss WAL/EG CH44 .... 110 F4
Bidston Rd ANF/KKDL L4 .... 97 K5
  CL/PREN CH43 .... 111 H7
Bidston Station Ap
  CL/PREN CH43 .... 110 E3
Bidston Village Rd
  CL/PREN CH43 .... 110 D4
Big Fold HOR/BR BL6 .... 57 M3
Biggin Ct WARRN/WOL WA2 .... 122 A4
Bigham Rd NPK/KEN L6 .... 113 L2
Biglands Dr HUY L36 .... 116 B5
Big Meadow Rd
  GR/UP/WCH CH49 .... 126 C1
Billinge Crs RNFD/HAY WA11 .... 89 M7
Billinge Rd AIMK WN4 .... 78 D8
  WGNS/IIMK WN3 .... 78 E1
  WGNW/BIL/O WN5 .... 67 M8
Billingham Rd RAIN/WH L35 .... 101 M6
Billings Cl EV L5 .... 96 F7
Billington Av NEWLW WA12 .... 91 K7
Billington Cl
  WARRW/BUR WA5 .... 120 A5
Billington Rd WDN WA8 .... 133 K1
Bilston Rd AIG/SPK L17 .... 130 A5
Bilton Cl WDN WA8 .... 135 G3
Binbrook Pl CHLY/EC PR7 .... 32 C5
Bingley Rd ANF/KKDL L4 .... 97 K6
Binns Rd CLB/OSW/ST L13 .... 114 C4
Binns Wy CLB/OSW/ST L13 .... 114 B4
Binsey Cl GR/UP/WCH CH49 .... 109 M8
Birbeck Rd NWD/KWIPK L33 .... 86 C2
Birchall Av GOL/RIS/CU WA3 .... 106 F1
Birchall St BTL L20 .... 96 E6
Birch Av BRSC L40 .... 52 A1
  CHLY/EC PR7 .... 31 L1
  ECCL WA10 .... 89 H7
  GR/UP/WCH CH49 .... 109 M7
  WARRN/WOL WA2 .... 121 J1
  WGNNW/ST WN6 .... 56 B5
  WLT/FAZ L9 .... 84 D7
Birchcliffe Rd RF/TRAN CH42 .... 128 B3
Birch Cl CL/PREN CH43 .... 127 K2
  MGHL L31 .... 73 J4
  RAIN/WH L35 .... 117 G1
Birch Crs NEWLW WA12 .... 104 B1
Birchdale
  GR/UP/WCH CH49 .... 125 M1
Birchdale Crs WARRS WA4 .... 137 L5
Birchdale Rd CSBY/WL L22 .... 82 F5
  WARR WA1 .... 122 C6
  WARRS WA4 .... 137 L6
  WLT/FAZ L9 .... 84 C8
Birchden Rd HLWD L26 .... 132 C6
Birch Dr RAIN/WH L35 .... 116 F2
Birches Cl HES CH60 .... 141 J4
The Birches FMBY L37 .... 47 G8
  STBRV L28 .... 99 J8
  WAL/EG CH44 .... 112 A3
Birchfield MOR/LEA CH46 .... 109 M4
Birchfield Av WDN WA8 .... 134 C3
Birchfield Cl EHL/KEN L7 .... 114 A3
  MOR/LEA CH46 .... 109 L7
Birchfield Rd ANF/KKDL L4 .... 97 J4
  EHL/KEN L7 .... 114 A3
  WARRW/BUR WA5 .... 120 D8
  WDN WA8 .... 16 D1
  WDN WA8 .... 134 C2
Birchfield St RAIN/WH L35 .... 101 M6
  VAUX/LVPD L3 .... 13 K4
Birchfield Wy MGHL L31 .... 61 L8
Birch Gn FMBY L37 .... 46 F8
Birch Green Rd SKEL WN8 .... 78 A3
Birch Gv AIMK WN4 .... 78 B8
  GTS/LS CH66 .... 115 M3
  HUY L36 .... 115 M3
  RAIN/WH L35 .... 117 G1
  WAL/NB CH45 .... 95 L6
  WARR WA1 .... 122 B6
  WARRS WA4 .... 137 M2
  WAV L15 .... 114 C4
Birch Heys WKBY CH48 .... 125 J4

Birch Hl FROD/HEL WA6 .... 167 L5
Birchill Rd NWD/KWIPK L33 .... 86 E3
Birchley Av WGNW/BIL/O WN5 ... 89 L2
Birchley Rd WGNW/BIL/O WN5 .. 89 L2
Birchley St ECCL WA10 .... 9 H3
Birchley Vw RNFD/HAY WA11 ... 89 K3
Birchmere HES CH60 .... 141 G3
Birchley Hey KKBY L32 .... 86 B4
Birchover Wk EHL/KEN L7 .... 113 K5
Birchridge Cl PS/BROM CH62 .... 143 J5
Birch Rd BEB CH63 .... 143 J1
  CHLY/EC PR7 .... 43 G4
  CLYE PR6 .... 32 F3
  CL/PREN CH43 .... 127 K2
  HOY CH47 .... 109 G5
  HUY L36 .... 116 A4
  RNFD/HAY WA11 .... 91 G6
  RUNC WA7 .... 19 K7
  WDN WA8 .... 134 C2
  WGNE/HIN WN2 .... 80 D6
Birch St EV L5 .... 96 G4
  SKEL WN8 .... 65 G4
  STHP PR8 .... 35 K1
  WGNE/HIN WN2 .... 69 M8
  WGNNW/ST WN6 .... 4 B1
Birch Tree Av RNFD/HAY WA11.... 89 K3
Birch Tree Ct WD/CROXPK L12 .. 98 C7
Birchtree Rd AIG/SPK L17 .... 130 A3
Birch Tree Rd
  GOL/RIS/CU WA3 .... 93 H5
Birchview Wy CL/PREN CH43 .... 110 F8
Birchway HES CH60 .... 141 L7
Birchways WARRS WA4 .... 138 A8
Birchwood Av BIRK CH41 .... 11 H4
Birchwood Bvd
  GOL/RIS/CU WA3 .... 122 F3
Birchwood Cl BIRK CH41 .... 11 H5
  CHTN CH42 .... 165 L2
  GTS/LS CH66 .... 162 F4
  WGNS/IIMK WN3 .... 78 F4
Birchwood Dr CHLY/EC PR7 .... 43 G2
Birchwood Park Av
  GOL/RIS/CU WA3 .... 106 F8
Birchwood Wy
  GOL/RIS/CU WA3 .... 123 H1
  WARRN/WOL WA2 .... 122 A5
  WGNE/HIN WN2 .... 5 M6
Bird St EHL/KEN L7 .... 113 L6
Birdwell Dr WARRW/BUR WA5 ... 120 C8
Birdwood Rd NG/CROX L11 .... 98 B5
Birkacre Brow CHLY/EC PR7 .... 43 H5
Birkacre Rd CHLY/EC PR7 .... 43 H1
Birkdale Av BEB CH63 .... 143 L7
  NPK/KEN L6 .... 97 M7
Birkdale Cl HUY L36 .... 115 L4
  NPK/KEN L6 .... 97 M7
Birkdale Cop STHP PR8 .... 36 A4
Birkdale Rd WARRW/BUR WA5 .. 136 B1
  WDN WA8 .... 118 D8
Birkenhead Rd HOY CH47 .... 108 E5
  NSTN CH64 .... 154 A4
  WAL/EG CH44 .... 112 A4
Birkenshaw Av
  CSBY/BLUN L23 .... 82 D1
Birket Av MOR/LEA CH46 .... 110 B2
Birket Cl MOR/LEA CH46 .... 110 C2
Birket Sq MOR/LEA CH46 .... 110 B2
Birkett Av EP CH65 .... 163 L3
Birkett Bank WGN WN1 .... 5 K4
Birkett Rd RF/TRAN CH42 .... 128 A4
  WKBY CH48 .... 124 D1
Birkett St VAUX/LVPD L3 .... 13 J4
  WGN WN1 .... 5 K4
Birkey La FMBY L37 .... 59 H3
Birkin Cl KKBY L32 .... 86 C5
Birkin Rd KKBY L32 .... 86 C5
Birkrig SKEL WN8 .... 65 M7
Birley Cl WGNNW/ST WN6 .... 55 H5
Birley Ct TOX L8 .... 113 H6
Birley St NEWLW WA12 .... 104 F1
Birleywood SKEL WN8 .... 65 M7
Birnam Dr RAIN/WH L35 .... 117 M3
Birnam Rd WAL/EG CH44 .... 111 M2
Birstall Av RNFD/HAY WA11 .... 9 M1
Birstall Ct RUNC WA7 .... 149 M6
Birstall Rd NPK/KEN L6 .... 113 K2
Birt Cl TOX L8 .... 113 K6
Birtles Rd WARRN/WOL WA2 .... 121 L4
Bisham Pk RUNC WA7 .... 150 F3
Bishopdale Cl
  WARRW/BUR WA5 .... 120 B6
Bishopdale Dr RAIN/WH L35 .... 117 M3
Bishop Dr RAIN/WH L35 .... 116 F2
Bishopgate WGN WN1 .... 4 E4
Bishopgate St WAV L15 .... 114 A6
Bishop Reeves Rd
  RNFD/HAY WA11 .... 91 G3
Bishop Rd ECCL WA10 .... 8 D2
  NPK/KEN L6 .... 97 L6
  WAL/EG CH44 .... 111 K3
Bishops Ct WARRN/WOL WA2 ... 121 H1
  WLTN L25 .... 131 K1
Bishops Gdns EP CH65 .... 156 C8
Bishop Sheppard Ct
  VAUX/LVPD L3 .... 12 E2
Bishops Wy WDN WA8 .... 134 F2
Bisley St WAL/NB CH45 .... 95 K8
  WAV L15 .... 114 A6
Bispham Dr AIMK WN4 .... 79 H8
  HOY CH47 .... 109 G6
Bispham Rd CHTN/BK PR9 .... 25 H6
  WARRW/BUR WA5 .... 136 D1
Bittern Cl RUNC WA7 .... 150 F5
  WARRN/WOL WA2 .... 121 M2
Bixteth St VAUX/LVPD L3 .... 12 E5
Blackacre La BRSC L40 .... 51 H4
Black-a-moor La ORM L39 .... 61 J3
Blackberry Gv HLWD L26 .... 131 M3
Blackboards La GTS/LS CH66 .... 155 J6
Blackbrook Av
  WARRN/WOL WA2 .... 122 D3
Blackbrook Cl CHLYE PR6 .... 33 J5
  WDN WA8 .... 133 L2
  WLT/FAZ L9 .... 97 J2
Blackbrook Rd RNFD/HAY WA11.. 90 A8
Blackburn Brow CHLYE PR6 .... 33 G3
Blackburn Cl GOL/RIS/CU WA3 .. 93 H5
Blackburne Av WDN WA8 .... 133 K8

Blackburne Cl
  *WARRN/WOL* WA2 ......... **122** E3 🔲
Blackburne Dr *WLTN* L25.... **131** M6
Blackburne Pl *TOX* L8 ......... **113** H5 🔲
Blackburn St *SPK/HALE* L24 **145** M2
Blackburn St *CHLYE* PR6 ...... **32** F6
Blackcar La *SFTN* L29 ......... **71** J2
Black Denton's Pl *WDN* WA8 .. **17** H2
Blackdown Cl *GTS/LS* CH66 ... **155** J8 🔲
Blackdown Gv *STHEL* WA9 ..... **103** H3
Blackeys La *NSTN* CH64 ....... **153** C5
Blackfield St *EV* L5 .............. **96** F7 🔲
Blackgate La *KIRK/FR/WA* PR4.. **27** L2
Blackheath Dr *MOR/LEA* CH46.. **110** B2
Blackheath La *RUNC* WA7 ...... **151** C1
Blackhorse Av *HOR/BR* BL6 .... **57** L3 🔲
Blackhorse Cl *HOR/BR* BL6 .... **57** L2 🔲
Black Horse Hl *WKBY* CH48 .... **124** E2
Black Horse Hl *WKBY* CH48 .... **124** E3
Black Horse La
  *CLB/OSW/ST* L13 ............ **114** D2
Black Horse Pl
  *CLB/OSW/ST* L13 ............ **114** D2
Black Horse St *CHLY/EC* PR7 .. **32** D7 🔲
  *HOR/BR* BL6 ..................... **57** L2
Blackhorse St *STHEL* WA9 ...... **9** M3
  *STHEL* WA9 ..................... **102** F1 🔲
Blackhurst Rd *MGHL* L31 ....... **61** L8
Blackhurst St *WARR* WA1 ...... **14** F6
Blackledge Cl
  *WARRN/WOL* WA2 ............ **122** C2 🔲
  *WGNW/BIL/O* WN5 ........... **67** C8 🔲
Blackley Cl *WARRS* WA4 ........ **137** M2
Blackley Gv *NWD/KWIPK* L33 .. **74** C7 🔲
Blackleyhurst Av
  *WGNW/BIL/O* WN5 ........... **78** A3
Black Lion La *GTS/LS* CH66 .... **155** K7
Blacklock Hall Rd
  *SPK/HALE* L24................. **146** E2
Blacklow Brow *HUY* L36 ........ **115** M3
Blackmoor Dr *WD/CROXPK* L12.. **98** E2
Black Moor Rd *SKEL* WN8 ...... **40** C3
Black Moss La *BRSC* L40 ........ **36** F6
  *ORM* L39 ........................ **62** F3
Blackpool St *BIRK* CH41 ........ **11** K7
Blackrod Av *SPK/HALE* L24 .... **146** E2
Blackrod Brow *HOR/BR* BL6 ... **57** K1
Blackshaw Dr
  *WARRW/BUR* WA5 ........... **120** D4
Blackstock St *RNFD/HAY* WA11..**89** M8
Blackstone Rd *CHLYE* PR6 ...... **33** G4
Blackstone St *EV* L5 ............. **96** D8
Blackthorn Cl *WGNNW/ST* WN6 .. **68** B2
Blackthorn Cl
  *MOR/LEA* CH46 .............. **110** B6 🔲
Blackthorne Av *GTS/LS* CH66 .. **163** J5
Blackthorne Crs *STBRV* L28 .... **99** K5
Blackthorne Rd *WLT/FAZ* L9 ... **97** L2
Blackwater Rd *NG/CROX* L11 ... **98** F1
Blackwood Av *WLTN* L25 ....... **131** H1
Blaguegate La *SKEL* WN8 ....... **64** D3
Blainscough Rd *CHLY/EC* PR7 .. **43** G5
Blair Av *WGNE/HIN* WN2 ....... **81** H4
Blair Dr *WDN* WA8 .............. **133** K2
Blairgowrie Gdns *ORM* L39..... **63** J1
Blair Gv *CHTN/BK* PR9 .......... **25** H6
Blair Pk *BEB* CH63 ............... **143** K2
Blair St *TOX* L8 ................... **113** G6
Blaisdon Cl *NG/CROX* L11 ...... **98** C4
Blakeacre Cl *HLWD* L26 ........ **132** B7 🔲
Blakeacre Rd *HLWD* L26 ........ **132** B7
Blake Cl *WGNS/IIMK* WN3 ...... **68** C8
Blakefield Rd *CSBY/BLUN* L23 .. **71** L7
Blakehall *SKEL* WN8 ............. **65** M6
Blakeley Brow *BEB* CH63 ...... **143** J7
Blakeley Ct *BEB* CH63 .......... **143** J7
Blakeley Dell *BEB* CH63 ........ **143** K7
Blakeley Dene *BEB* CH63 ...... **143** K6
Blakeley Rd *BEB* CH63 .......... **143** K6
Blakemere Ct *EP* CH65 ........... **20** C1
Blakeney Cl
  *GR/UP/WCH* CH49 .......... **110** C6 🔲
Blakenhall Wy
  *GR/UP/WCH* CH49 .......... **109** M7 🔲
Blaking Dr *PR/KW* L34 .......... **99** M1 🔲
Blandford Cl *STHP* PR8 ........... **2** B7
Blandford Rd
  *WARRW/BUR* WA5 ........... **120** D8
Blantyre Rd *WAV* L15 .......... **114** A7
Blantyre St *RUNC* WA7 .......... **18** E1
Blay Cl *WLTN* L25 ............... **131** M5
Blaydon Cl *NTHTN* L30 .......... **84** C4 🔲
  *WGNE/HIN* WN2 ............... **57** M8 🔲
Blaydon Gv *RAIN/WH* L35 ..... **101** M6 🔲
Blaydon Pk *SKEL* WN8 .......... **65** M6
Blaydon Wk *CL/PREN* CH43 .... **111** H7
Bleach St *WGNE/HIN* WN2...... **80** E1
Bleak Hill Cl *ECCL* WA10 ....... **88** E6
Bleak Hill Rd *ECCL* WA10 ...... **88** E7 🔲
Bleak La *BRSC* L40 ............... **39** M8
Bleaklow Cl *WGNS/IIMK* WN3 .. **79** K3
Bleasdale Av *AIN/FAZ* L10 ...... **85** C3 🔲
Bleasdale Cl
  *GR/UP/WCH* CH49 .......... **110** A7 🔲
  *ORM* L39 ......................... **62** F6
Bleasdale Rd *CALD/MH* L18 .... **130** D1
  *NEWLW* WA12 ................. **104** C1 🔲
Blenheim Av *LITH* L21 .......... **83** L5
Blenheim Cl
  *WARRN/WOL* WA2 ........... **122** B3 🔲
Blenheim Dr *HUY* L36 .......... **100** B8
Blenheim Rd *AIMK* WN4 ........ **91** M3
  *CALD/MH* L18 ................. **114** B8 🔲
  *STHP* PR8 ........................ **34** D7
  *WAL/EG* CH44 .................. **95** M8
  *WGNW/BIL/O* WN5 ........... **67** L5
Blenheim St *EV* L5 .............. **12** F1
Blenheim Wy
  *RNFD/HAY* WA11 ............. **89** K7 🔲
  *SPK/HALE* L24 ................ **146** D2 🔲
Blessington Rd *ANF/KKDL* L4 .. **97** H6
Bletchley Av *WAL/EG* CH44 ... **111** H1 🔲
Bligh St *WAV* L15 ................ **114** A6
Blind Foot Rd *RNFD/HAY* WA11.. **87** M6
Blindman's La *ORM* L39 ........ **50** E6
Blissford Cl *WGNE/HIN* WN2 ... **80** F1
Blisworth St *LITH* L21 ........... **83** K7

Blomfield Rd *ALL/GAR* L19 ..... **130** F5
Bloomsbury Wy *WDN* WA8 .... **133** M2 🔲
Blossom St *BTL* L20 .............. **7** H1
Blucher St *CSBY/WL* L22 ....... **82** E4
Bluebell Av *BIRK* CH41 ......... **111** H5
  *RNFD/HAY* WA11 ............. **91** G6
Bluebell Ct *CSBY/WL* L22 ...... **83** G4 🔲
Bluebell Ct *RUNC* WA7 ........ **161** H1 🔲
Blue Bell La *HUY* L36 ........... **116** A1
Blueberry Flds *AIN/FAZ* L10 ... **85** H7
Bluecoat St *WARRN/WOL* WA2 .. **14** E2
Bluefields St *TOX* L8 ............. **113** H6
Blue Hatch *FROD/HEL* WA6.... **160** E5
Blue Jay Cl *NTHLY* L27 .......... **116** A8 🔲
Blue Stone La *BRSC* L40 ........ **41** C2
Bluestone La *MGHL* L31 ........ **73** G4
Bluewood Dr *BIRK* CH41 ....... **110** F4
Blundell Av *FMBY* L37 ........... **58** D1
  *HTWN* L38 ....................... **70** B2
  *STHP* PR8 ........................ **35** H3
Blundell Crs *STHP* PR8 .......... **35** H3
Blundell Dr *STHP* PR8 ........... **35** H3
Blundell Gv *HTWN* L38 .......... **70** B2
Blundell La *CHTN/BK* PR9 ...... **25** L3
  *HOR/BR* BL6 ..................... **57** J1
Blundell Ms *WGNS/IIMK* WN3 .. **78** F1 🔲
Blundell Rd *HTWN* L38 .......... **70** B3
  *WDN* WA8 ...................... **133** M5
Blundellsands Rd East
  *CSBY/BLUN* L23 ............... **82** E1 🔲
Blundellsands Rd West
  *CSBY/BLUN* L23 ............... **82** D2
Blundells Dr *MOR/LEA* CH46 .. **110** A4
Blundell's La *RAIN/WH* L35 .... **117** J4
Blundell St *CLVPS* L1 ........... **112** F6
Blyth Cl *RUNC* WA7 ............. **150** F8
Blythe Av *WDN* WA8 ........... **118** D8 🔲
Blythe La *BRSC* L40 ............. **52** A4
Blythewood *SKEL* WN8 ......... **65** L6
Blyth Hey *NTHTN* L30 .......... **83** M2
Blyth Rd *BEB* CH63 ............. **143** L6
Blythswood St *AIG/SPK* L17 ... **129** K2
Boaler St *NPK/KEN* L6 .......... **113** K2
Boarded Barn *CHLY/EC* PR7 ... **31** L2 🔲
Boardman's La *STHEL* WA9 .... **103** G1
Boardman St *HOR/BR* BL6 .... **57** M3 🔲
Boars Head Av *WGNNW/ST* WN6.. **56** C5
Boathouse La *NSTN* CH64 ...... **152** D3
Bobbies La *ECCL* WA10 ......... **101** J1
Bobbiners La *CHTN/BK* PR9 .... **26** C2
Bobby Langton Wy *BRSC* L40 .. **39** G8
Bodden St *GOL/RIS/CU* WA3 ... **93** J4
  *STHEL* WA9 ..................... **118** F1
Bodiam Ct *EP* CH65 ............. **164** A3
Bodley St *ANF/KKDL* L4 ........ **97** H6 🔲
Bodmin Av *CHTN/BK* PR9 ...... **25** J6
Bodmin Cl *RUNC* WA7 ......... **150** D7 🔲
Bodmin Dr *WGNE/HIN* WN2 ... **80** C4
Bodmin Gv *RNFD/HAY* WA11 .. **89** M6
Bodmin Rd *ANF/KKDL* L4 ....... **97** H4
Bodmin Wy *HLWD* L26 ......... **132** A5
Bogburn La *CHLY/EC* PR7 ...... **42** F8
Bognor Cl *SPK/HALE* L24 ...... **146** D1 🔲
Bolan St *CLB/OSW/ST* L13 .... **114** C2
Bolderwood Dr
  *WGNE/HIN* WN2 ............... **80** F1 🔲
Bolde Wy *BEB* CH63 ............ **143** J4
Bold Av *ORM* L39 ............... **62** D6
  *WARRW/BUR* WA5 ........... **103** L6
Bold Rd *STHEL* WA9 ............ **103** H6
Bold St *CHTN/BK* PR9 ............ **3** G2
  *CLVPS* L1 ......................... **13** H8
  *ECCL* WA10 ....................... **8** E6
  *RUNC* WA7 ....................... **19** J2
  *WARR* WA1 ....................... **14** D6
  *WDN* WA8 ........................ **16** C6
  *WGNW/BIL/O* WN5 ........... **68** A8
Boleyn Ct *RUNC* WA7 .......... **150** E2
The Boleyn *MGHL* L31 .......... **73** G2
Bollin Cl *GOL/RIS/CU* WA3 .... **107** J3
Bollington Cl *CL/PREN* CH43 .. **127** H2 🔲
Bolney St *WGNE/HIN* WN2 ..... **69** J2
Bolton Av *KKBY* L32 ............. **85** L3
  *WARRS* WA4 ................... **138** B1 🔲
Bolton Cl *FMBY* L37 ............. **59** J3 🔲
  *GOL/RIS/CU* WA3 ............. **93** K5
  *STHEL* WA9 ........................ **9** L4 🔲
Bolton House Rd
  *WGNE/HIN* WN2 ............... **81** H6
Bolton Rd *AIMK* WN4 ........... **79** M8
  *CHLY/EC* PR7 .................... **32** F7
  *CHLYE* PR6 ........................ **44** E6
  *PS/BROM* CH62 ............... **128** E7
  *STHP* PR8 ......................... **35** J1
  *WGNE/HIN* WN2 ............... **57** L8
Bolton Rd East *PS/BROM* CH62.. **128** E7
Bolton's Cop *CHTN/BK* PR9.... **23** M7
Bolton St *AIMK* WN4 ............ **78** F8
  *CHLY/EC* PR7 .................... **32** F7
  *STHEL* WA9 ........................ **9** L4 🔲
  *VAUX/LVPD* L3 .................. **13** J7
Bombay Rd *WGNW/BIL/O* WN5.. **67** L5
Bonchurch Dr *WAV* L15 ....... **114** B4
Bond Cl *WARRW/BUR* WA5 ... **136** F1
Bond's La *CHLY/EC* PR7 ........ **44** B6 🔲
  *CHTN/BK* PR9 ................... **23** J6
Bond St *PR/KW* L34 ............ **100** F3 🔲
  *VAUX/LVPD* L3 .................. **13** G2
Bonnington Av *CSBY/BLUN* L23.. **70** E3
Bonsall Rd *WD/CROXPK* L12 .. **98** D7
Boode Cft *STBRV* L28 ........... **99** K4
Booker Av *ALL/GAR* L19 ....... **130** D4
Booth's Brow Rd *AIMK* WN4... **78** F7
Booths Hill Cl *LYMM* WA13 ... **139** M3 🔲
Booth's Hill La *LYMM* WA13 .. **139** L2
Booth's Hill Rd *LYMM* WA13 .. **139** L2
Booth's La *LYMM* WA13 ....... **139** K3
  *ORM* L39 ........................ **50** B8
Booth St *CHTN/BK* PR9 .......... **3** G2
  *CLB/OSW/ST* L13 ............ **129** H2 🔲
  *NEWLW* WA12 ................. **104** C2 🔲
  *RAIN/WH* L35 ................. **101** M6
  *WARRW/BUR* WA5 ........... **137** G1 🔲
Boothwood Cl *EHL/KEN* L7 ... **113** K5 🔲
Bor Av *WGNS/IIMK* WN3 ....... **79** K1
Borax St *CLB/OSW/ST* L13 .... **114** C3
Borden Cl *WGNE/HIN* WN2 .... **69** H3

Border Rd *HES* CH60 ........... **141** K5
Borella Rd *CLB/OSW/ST* L13 .. **98** B7
Bores Hl *WGN* WN1 ............. **56** E1
Borough Pl *BIRK* CH41 .......... **11** K6
Borough Rd *BIRK* CH41 .......... **11** C7
  *ECCL* WA10 ........................ **8** D7
  *RF/TRAN* CH42 .................. **10** F8
  *WAL/EG* CH44 ................. **111** M2
Borough Rd East *BIRK* CH41... **11** K6
Borron Rd *NEWLW* WA12 ...... **91** K8
Borrowdale Av
  *WARRN/WOL* WA2 ........... **121** K2
Borrowdale Cl *FROD/HEL* WA6.. **160** F5
Borrowdale Rd *BEB* CH63 ..... **143** C1
  *ECCL* WA10 ..................... **101** L5 🔲
  *MOR/LEA* CH46 .............. **109** M5
  *WAV* L15 ........................ **114** A7
  *WDN* WA8 ...................... **133** L5
  *WGNW/BIL/O* WN5 .......... **67** K6 🔲
Borsdane Av *WGNE/HIN* WN2 .. **81** C1
Boscombe Pl *WGNE/HIN* WN2 .. **81** L1
Boscow Crs *STHEL* WA9 ....... **102** F6 🔲
Bosnia St *TOX* L8 ................ **129** J2
Bostock Gn *EP* CH65 ........... **156** B8
Bostock St *EV* L5 ................. **96** F8
  *WARRN/BUR* WA5 ........... **121** G7 🔲
Boston Av *RUNC* WA7 ........... **19** K7
Boston Cl *GOL/RIS/CU* WA3 .. **107** H1
Boswell Av *WARRS* WA4 ...... **137** K3
Boswell St *TOX* L8 ................ **113** M8
Boswell Rd *CL/PREN* CH43 .... **127** H4
Bosworth Cl *BEB* CH63 ........ **127** M8
Bosworth Dr *STHP* PR8 .......... **47** L1
Bosworth Rd *RNFD/HAY* WA11.. **89** L7
Botanic Gv *EHL/KEN* L7 ..... **113** L3
Botanic Pl *EHL/KEN* L7 ........ **113** L3
Botanic Rd *CHTN/BK* PR9 ..... **25** K3 🔲
  *EHL/KEN* L7 .................... **113** L4
Botany Brow *CHLYE* PR6........ **33** G3
Botany Cl *WGNE/HIN* WN2 .... **69** J5
Botany Rd *SPK/HALE* L24 ..... **146** E1
Boteler Av *WARRW/BUR* WA5 .. **14** A2
Botley Cl *GR/UP/WCH* CH49 .. **109** M8 🔲
The Boulevard *EP* CH65 ....... **163** H1
  *WD/CROXPK* L12 .............. **98** D5
Boulting Av *WARRW/BUR* WA5.. **121** H3
Boulton Av *PS/BROM* CH62 ... **128** D5
  *WKBY* CH48 .................... **124** D1
Boundary Dr *CSBY/BLUN* L23.. **70** E7
  *WLTN* L25 ...................... **131** M6
Boundary Farm Rd *HLWD* L26.. **131** M7
Boundary La *BRSC* L40 .......... **52** B2
  *CHTN/BK* PR9 ................... **23** M8
  *HES* CH60 ....................... **141** J5
  *NPK/KEN* L6 .................... **113** K1
  *NWD/KWIPK* L33 .............. **86** F3
  *WGNNW/ST* WN6 .............. **55** J2
Boundary Pk *NSTN* CH64 ..... **152** F5
Boundary Rd *CL/PREN* CH43.. **110** F5
  *ECCL* WA10 ........................ **8** C6
  *HUY* L36 ......................... **116** B5
  *LITH* L21 ......................... **83** M4
  *PS/BROM* CH62 ............... **128** D6
  *WKBY* CH48 .................... **124** F5
Boundary St *EV* L5 ............... **96** D7
  *STHP* PR8 ......................... **3** C9
  *WARR* WA1 ...................... **15** M1
  *WGN* WN1 ........................ **5** H6
Boundary Street East *EV* L5 ... **96** F7 🔲
Bourne Av *GOL/RIS/CU* WA3 .. **92** F5
Bourne Gdns *STHEL* WA9 ..... **102** D4
Bournemouth Cl *RUNC* WA7.. **150** F7 🔲
Bourne St *NPK/KEN* L6 ........ **113** K2 🔲
Bourton Rd *WLTN* L25 ......... **131** K7
Bousfield St *ANF/KKDL* L4 .... **97** C6 🔲
  *GOL/RIS/CU* WA3 ............ **107** H1
  *WD/CROXPK* L12 .............. **99** G3
Bowden Cl *ECCL* WA10 ........ **101** K3 🔲
  *GOL/RIS/CU* WA3 ............ **107** H1
Bowden St *LITH* L21 ............ **83** L1
Bowdon Cl *WARR* WA1 ....... **122** B5 🔲
Bowdon Rd *WAL/NB* CH45 ..... **95** J7
Bowen Cl *WDN* WA8 ........... **133** M1 🔲
Bower Gv *LITH* L21 .............. **83** H6
Bower Rd *HES* CH60 ........... **141** L5
  *HUY* L36 ......................... **116** A1
  *WLTN* L25 ...................... **131** J1
Bower St *WDN* WA8 ............. **17** G1
Bowfell Cl *BEB* CH63 ........... **154** F2 🔲
Bowfield Rd *ALL/GAR* L19 .... **130** D4
Bowgreen Cl *CL/PREN* CH43 .. **110** E6 🔲
Bowker's Green La *ORM* L39 .. **63** G8
Bowland Av *AIMK* WN4 ........ **91** K1
  *CHLDW* L16 .................... **114** F4
  *CHLYE* PR6 ....................... **32** F5 🔲
  *GOL/RIS/CU* WA3 ............ **92** E4 🔲
  *STHEL* WA9 ..................... **118** C2
Bowland Cl *GOL/RIS/CU* WA3 .. **107** K8 🔲
  *PS/BROM* CH62 ............... **143** M4 🔲
  *RUNC* WA7 ..................... **150** A8 🔲
Bowland Dr *LITH* L21 ........... **83** L1
Bowles St *BTL* L20 ............... **83** J8
Bowley Rd *CLB/OSW/ST* L13 .. **98** B8
Bowling Green Cl *STHP* PR8 ... **25** H8
The Bowlings
  *WGNNW/ST* WN6 .............. **68** C3 🔲
Bowman Av *WARRS* WA4 ..... **122** C6
Bowness Av *BEB* CH63 ........ **143** L8
  *CL/PREN* CH43 ................ **127** J3
  *RNFD/HAY* WA11 ............. **89** K5
  *STHP* PR8 ........................ **47** L2
  *WGNE/HIN* WN2 ............... **81** L3
Bowness Pl *WGNE/HIN* WN2 .. **69** K5 🔲
Bowood Ct
  *WARRN/WOL* WA2 ........... **121** J1 🔲
Bowood St *TOX* L8 .............. **129** H2 🔲
Bowring Dr *NSTN* CH64 ....... **152** D4
Bowring Park Av *CHLDW* L16.. **115** J3 🔲
Bowring Park Rd
  *DV/KA/FCH* L14 ............... **115** H3 🔲
Bowring St *TOX* L8 .............. **129** J1 🔲

Bowscale Cl
  *GR/UP/WCH* CH49 .......... **110** A8 🔲
Bowscale Rd *NG/CROX* L11 ... **98** C4
Boxdale Rd *CALD/MH* L18 ..... **130** C1
Boxgrove Cl *WDN* WA8 ........ **134** D2 🔲
Boxmoor Rd *CALD/MH* L18 ... **130** C3
Boxtree Cl *WD/CROXPK* L12 ... **99** H1
Boxwood Cl *HUY* L36 .......... **115** L3
Boycott St *EV* L5 ................. **97** J7 🔲
Boyd Cl *MOR/LEA* CH46 ...... **110** D2
  *WGNNW/ST* WN6 .............. **56** B5
Boydell Av *WARRS* WA4 ...... **138** D3 🔲
Boydell St *STBRV* L28 ........... **99** K6
Boyer Av *MGHL* L31 ............. **72** F6
Boyes Brow *NWD/KWIPK* L33.. **85** M1
Boyle Av *WARRN/WOL* WA2 .. **122** A4
Boyton Ct *EHL/KEN* L7 ........ **113** L5
Brabant Rd *AIG/SPK* L17 ...... **130** A4
Brabazon Pl *WGNW/BIL/O* WN5.. **67** L5
Braby Rd *LITH* L21 ............... **83** L7
Bracebridge Dr *STHP* PR8 ..... **36** B3
Bracewell St *STHEL* WA9 ...... **102** E7 🔲
Bracken Cl *CHLYE* PR6 .......... **33** G5
  *GOL/RIS/CU* WA3 ............ **106** E8
Bracken Ct *STHEL* WA9 ........ **118** E1 🔲
Brackendale *CHNE* CH2 ....... **165** K2
  *GR/UP/WCH* CH49 .......... **126** E2 🔲
  *RUNC* WA7 ..................... **149** M5
Brackendale Av *WLT/FAZ* L9 .. **84** D6 🔲
Bracken Dr *WKBY* CH48 ...... **125** G3
Brackenhurst Dr
  *WAL/NB* CH45 .................. **95** L6 🔲
Brackenhurst Gn
  *NWD/KWIPK* L33 .............. **86** A3 🔲
Bracken La *BEB* CH63 .......... **127** M8
Bracken Rd *GTS/LS* CH66 ..... **163** G1
  *LEIGH* WN7 ...................... **81** K8
Brackenside *HES* CH60 ........ **141** H3 🔲
Brackenway *FMBY* L37 .......... **47** J7 🔲
Bracken Wy *FROD/HEL* WA6.. **160** E7
Bracken Wd *WD/CROXPK* L12.. **99** G1
Brackenwood Gv
  *RAIN/WH* L35 .................. **117** H2 🔲
Brackenwood Rd *BEB* CH63 .. **127** M8
Brackley Cl *WAL/EG* CH44 .... **111** J2
Brackley St *RUNC* WA7 ......... **18** E2
Bracknell Av *KKBY* L32 ........ **85** M5
Bracknell Cl *KKBY* L32 ......... **86** A4
Bracknel Wy *ORM* L39 ......... **62** C4 🔲
Bradbourne Cl
  *WD/CROXPK* L12 .............. **99** G2 🔲
Bradda Cl *GR/UP/WCH* CH49 .. **110** B6
Braddan Cl *CLB/OSW/ST* L13 .. **98** A8 🔲
Braddock Cl *BIRK* CH41 ........ **143** K3
Brade St *CHTN/BK* PR9 .......... **25** L1
Bradewell Cl *ANF/KKDL* L4 ... **97** G5 🔲
Bradewell St *ANF/KKDL* L4 ... **97** G5
Bradfield Av *AIN/FAZ* L10 ..... **84** E2 🔲
Bradfield St *EHL/KEN* L7 ...... **113** L3
Bradford St *WGNS/IIMK* WN3 ... **4** E6
Bradgate Cl *HOY* CH47 ........ **109** K4
Bradlegh Rd *NEWLW* WA12 .. **104** E3
Bradley Bvd *WARRW/BUR* WA5.. **120** D7
Bradley Fold *RAIN/WH* L35 ... **116** C5
Bradley La *CHLY/EC* PR7 ....... **30** F7
  *FROD/HEL* WA6 ............... **160** F7
  *WARRW/BUR* WA5 ........... **104** B3
  *WGNNW/ST* WN6 .............. **56** B3
Bradley Rd *BTL* L20 ............. **83** K4
Bradley St *CHTN/BK* PR9 ........ **3** K2
Bradley Wy *WDN* WA8 ........... **17** C7
Bradman Rd *MOR/LEA* CH46 .. **109** L4
  *NWD/KWIPK* L33 .............. **86** E2
Bradmoor Rd *PS/BROM* CH62.. **143** M5
Bradshaw Brow *BRSC* L40 ..... **41** C4
Bradshaw Cl *ECCL* WA10 ....... **8** A3
  *WGNNW/ST* WN6 .............. **55** M4
Bradshawgate *WGN* WN1 ....... **5** H4
Bradshaw La *BRSC* L40 ......... **41** C3
  *SKEL* WN8 ....................... **53** L4
  *WARRS* WA4 ................... **138** D2
Bradshaw's La *STHP* PR8 ...... **34** F7
Bradshaw St *WDN* WA8 ....... **134** C3 🔲
  *WGN* WN1 ......................... **5** J7
  *WGNW/BIL/O* WN5 ........... **67** J7
Bradstone Cl *NG/CROX* L11 ... **85** K7 🔲
Bradville Rd *WLT/FAZ* L9 ...... **84** E6
Bradwell Cl *EP* CH65 ........... **163** J1
  *WKBY* CH48 .................... **124** F3 🔲
Bradwell Rd *GOL/RIS/CU* WA3.. **93** G6
Brady St *HOR/BR* BL6 ........... **45** J8
Braeburn Ct *LEIGH* WN7 ....... **81** M8 🔲
Braehaven Rd *WAL/NB* CH45 .. **95** L6 🔲
Braemar Av *CHTN/BK* PR9 .... **25** G3 🔲
  *CHTN/BK* PR9 ................... **25** H3 🔲
Braemar Cl *RAIN/WH* L35 .... **117** H2 🔲
  *WARRN/WOL* WA2 ........... **122** C2 🔲
Braemar St *BTL* L20 .............. **7** K8 🔲
Braemore Cl *WGNS/IIMK* WN3 .. **78** D8
Braemore Rd *WAL/EG* CH44 .. **111** H1 🔲
Braeside Cl *GTS/LS* CH66 ..... **155** L8 🔲
Braeside Crs *WGNW/BIL/O* WN5.. **77** M8 🔲
Braeside Gdns
  *GR/UP/WCH* CH49 .......... **110** B8
Brae St *EHL/KEN* L7 ............ **113** K3
Brahms Cl *TOX* L8 ............... **113** L6
Braid St *BIRK* CH41 ............. **111** H4
Braidhaven *WGNNW/ST* WN6 .. **55** C6 🔲
Braid St *BIRK* CH41 ............. **111** H4
Brainerd St *CLB/OSW/ST* L13 .. **98** A8
Braithwaite Cl *RAIN/WH* L35 .. **117** L2 🔲
  *RUNC* WA7 ..................... **148** C2
Braithwaite Rd *GOL/RIS/CU* WA3.. **92** F4
Brakenwood Ms *WARRS* WA4.. **138** E4 🔲
Bramberton Pl *ANF/KKDL* L4 .. **97** L4 🔲
Bramberton Rd *ANF/KKDL* L4.. **97** L4
Bramble Av *BIRK* CH41 ........ **111** H6
Bramble Cl *WARRW/BUR* WA5.. **136** A2
Bramble Gv *WGNW/BIL/O* WN5.. **68** A6
The Brambles *AIMK* WN4 ...... **78** E8 🔲
  *CHLYE* PR7 ....................... **43** H5 🔲
Bramble Wy *MOR/LEA* CH46.. **109** M3
  *RUNC* WA7 ..................... **161** G1 🔲
  *SKEL* WN8 ....................... **53** L4
Bramblewood *LEY/BBR* PR5 .. **29** K2 🔲
Bramblewood Cl
  *CL/PREN* CH43 ................ **126** E1

*NTHLY* L27 ....................... **116** A8 🔲
Brambling Cl *RUNC* WA7 ..... **150** A8 🔲
Brambling Pk *HLWD* L26 ...... **132** A4
Brambling Wy
  *GOL/RIS/CU* WA3 ............ **93** C5 🔲
Bramcote Av *RNFD/HAY* WA11.. **89** M7
Bramcote Cl *NWD/KWIPK* L33.. **86** C1 🔲
Bramcote Rd *NWD/KWIPK* L33.. **86** B1
Bramcote Wk *NWD/KWIPK* L33.. **86** B1
Bramerton Ct *WKBY* CH48 .... **124** B2
Bramford Cl
  *GR/UP/WCH* CH49 .......... **110** A8 🔲
Bramhall Cl *SPK/HALE* L24 ... **147** C3 🔲
Bramhall Dr *PS/BROM* CH62 .. **155** H2
Bramhall Rd *CSBY/WL* L22 .... **83** G5
  *SKEL* WN8 ....................... **65** H3
Bramhall St *WARRW/BUR* WA5.. **121** G8
Bramley Av *BEB* CH63 ......... **128** A6
Bramley Cl *GTS/LS* CH66 ..... **163** H5 🔲
  *NTHLY* L27 ..................... **116** A8 🔲
The Bramleys *MGHL* L31 ...... **72** E6
Brampton Ct *WGNE/HIN* WN2.. **80** B4
Brampton Ct *STHEL* WA9 ..... **103** K2 🔲
Brampton Dr *TOX* L8 ........... **113** J5
Bramshill Cl *GOL/RIS/CU* WA3.. **107** J7
Bramwell Av *CL/PREN* CH43 .. **127** J4
Bramwell St *STHEL* WA9 ...... **103** G1
Brancaster Dr *GOL/RIS/CU* WA3.. **93** J6
Brancepeth Ct *EP* CH65 ........ **20** F9
Branch St *WGNE/HIN* WN2 .... **69** J6
Branch Wy *RNFD/HAY* WA11.. **90** F7
Brancker Av *RAIN/WH* L35 ... **117** K1
Brancker St *CHLY/EC* PR7 ..... **32** C3 🔲
Brancote Gdns *PS/BROM* CH62.. **143** M6
Brancote Mt *CL/PREN* CH43 .. **111** H7
Brancote Rd *CL/PREN* CH43 .. **111** H7
Brandearth Hey *STBRV* L28 ... **99** K6
Brandon *WDN* WA8 ............. **133** J3
Brandon St *SKEL* WN8 .......... **66** C6 🔲
Brandon St *BIRK* CH41 .......... **11** L5
Brandreth Cl *RAIN/WH* L35 ... **117** L2 🔲
Brandreth Delph *SKEL* WN8 ... **53** M2
Brandreth Dr *SKEL* WN8 ....... **53** L3
Brandreth Pk *SKEL* WN8 ....... **53** L1
Brandreth Pl *WGNNW/ST* WN6.. **56** B4
Brandwood Av
  *WARRN/WOL* WA2 ........... **121** K3 🔲
Branfield Cl *WD/CROXPK* L12.. **99** G2 🔲
Bransdale Cl *WARRW/BUR* WA5.. **120** A6
Bransfield Cl *WGNS/IIMK* WN3.. **79** J2
Bransford Cl *AIMK* WN4 ........ **91** L3
Branstree Av *NG/CROX* L11 ... **98** B3
Brantfield Ct
  *WARRN/WOL* WA2 ........... **122** A3 🔲
Branthwaite *WGNE/HIN* WN2.. **69** K4
Branthwaite Cl *NG/CROX* L11.. **98** C4 🔲
Branthwaite Crs *NG/CROX* L11.. **98** C4
Branthwaite Gv *NG/CROX* L11.. **98** C4 🔲
Brasenose Rd *BTL* L20 ........... **6** F8
Brassey St *BIRK* CH41 .......... **10** B2
  *TOX* L8 ........................... **113** G7
Brathay Cl *WARRN/WOL* WA2.. **121** L2
Brattan Rd *RF/TRAN* CH42 ... **10** E9
Bratton Cl *WGNS/IIMK* WN3 .. **78** E4
Braunton Rd *AIG/SPK* L17 .... **130** A5
  *WAL/NB* CH45 ................... **95** J7
Braybrooke Rd *NG/CROX* L11.. **98** C2
Bray Cl *RUNC* WA7 ............. **149** M7
Braydon Cl *WLTN* L25 ......... **131** L7 🔲
Brayfield Rd *ANF/KKDL* L4 .... **97** M4
Bray Rd *SPK/HALE* L24 ....... **146** E1
Bray St *BIRK* CH41 .............. **10** C2
Brayton Ct *WGNE/HIN* WN2 .. **69** M7
Brechin Rd *NWD/KWIPK* L33 .. **86** B3
Breckfield Pl *EV* L5 .............. **97** H8 🔲
Breckfield Rd North *EV* L5 .... **97** H7
Breckfield Rd South
  *NPK/KEN* L6 ..................... **97** J8
Breck Pl *WAL/EG* CH44 ....... **111** J2 🔲
Breckside Pk *NPK/KEN* L6 .... **97** L7
The Breck *GTS/LS* CH66 ...... **156** A6
Brecon Av *NTHTN* L30 ......... **84** B4
Brecon Cl *WARRS* WA4 ........ **80** D5 🔲
Brecon Dr *GTS/LS* CH66 ...... **163** G4
  *WGNE/HIN* WN2 ............... **81** J2
Brecon Rd *RF/TRAN* CH42 ... **127** L4
Bredon Av *CHLY/EC* PR7 ....... **31** M4
Bredon Ct *GTS/LS* CH66 ...... **155** J7
Breeze Cl *WLT/FAZ* L9 ......... **97** H3
Breeze Hl *ANF/KKDL* L4 ......... **7** M6
  *BTL* L20 ........................... **7** K5
  *WGNNW/ST* WN6 .............. **56** D6
Breezehill Cl *NSTN* CH64 ..... **153** G5
Breezehill Pk *NSTN* CH64 .... **153** H5
Breezehill Rd *NSTN* CH64 .... **153** H5
Breeze La *WLT/FAZ* L9 ......... **97** H2
Breeze Rd *STHP* PR8 ............ **35** G3
Brelade Rd *CLB/OSW/ST* L13.. **114** B1
Bremhill Rd *NG/CROX* L11 .... **98** B2
Bremner Cl *EHL/KEN* L7 ...... **113** L4 🔲
Brenda Crs *CSBY/BLUN* L23 .. **71** J6
Brendale Av *MGHL* L31 ........ **72** E5
Brendon Av *LITH* L21 ........... **83** J4
  *WARRN/WOL* WA2 ........... **121** J2 🔲
Brendon Gv *STHEL* WA9 ...... **103** J1 🔲
Brendor Rd *WLTN* L25 ......... **131** K4
Brenig St *BIRK* CH41 ........... **111** H4 🔲
Brenka Av *WLT/FAZ* L9 ........ **84** D4
Brentfield *WDN* WA8 ........... **133** M3 🔲
Brentnall Cl
  *WARRW/BUR* WA5 ........... **120** A8 🔲
Brent Wy *HLWD* L26 ........... **132** B7
Brentwood Av *WGNW/BIL/O* WN5.. **67** K6 🔲
Brentwood Av *AIG/SPK* L17 .. **129** L2
  *CSBY/BLUN* L23 ............... **71** H8
Brentwood Cl *ECCL* WA10 .... **101** K2 🔲
  *HTWN* L38 ...................... **70** B3
Brentwood Ct *CHTN/BK* PR9 .. **24** F4
Brentwood Rd *CHLYE* PR6 .... **44** D5
Brentwood St *WAL/EG* CH44 .. **111** L3
Brereton Av *BEB* CH63 ........ **128** C7
  *WAV* L15 ........................ **114** C6
Brereton Cl *RUNC* WA7 ....... **150** C5 🔲
Bretherton Pl *RAIN/WH* L35 .. **117** L1 🔲

Bretherton Rd LEY/BBR PR5 29 J1
PR/KW L34 101 G7
Bretherton Rw WGN WN1 4 E4
Bretherton St WGNE/HIN WN2 69 L7
Bretlands Rd CSBY/BLUN L23 71 K8
Bretton Fold STHP PR8 25 H8
Brett St BIRK CH41 10 C2
Brewery La FMBY L37 47 H7
MGHL L31 85 G1
Brewster St ANF/KKDL L4 7 L8
Brian Av PEN/TH CH61 126 B7
WARRN/WOL WA2 121 M5
WARRS WA4 138 A4
Briar Av CHLY/EC PR7 31 L1
Briar Cl AIMK WN4 91 J1
WGNE/HIN WN2 81 K1
Briardale Gdns GTS/LS CH66 155 L7
Briardale Rd BEB CH63 128 B6
CALD/MH L18 130 B1
GTS/LS CH66 155 L7
NSTN CH64 154 C5
RF/TRAN CH42 127 L1
WAL/EG CH44 112 A3
Briar Dr HES CH60 141 J5
HUY L36 115 M3
Briarfield Av WDN WA8 133 J4
Briarfield Rd EP CH65 20 B4
HES CH60 141 J5
Briarly WGNNW/ST WN6 56 C6
Briar Rd GOL/RIS/CU WA3 92 D5
STHP PR8 47 M1
WGNW/BIL/O WN5 67 M6
Briars Brook BRSC L40 52 C2
Briars Cl RAIN/WH L35 117 M4
Briars Gn ECCL WA10 8 E2
SKEL WN8 65 J1
Briars La BRSC L40 52 C2
MGHL L31 73 G4
The Briars CHLY/EC PR7 30 E7
STHP PR8 35 H4
Briar St ANF/KKDL L4 96 F6
Briarswood Cl RAIN/WH L35 117 H3
RF/TRAN CH42 128 B5
Briarwood RUNC WA7 150 D4
Briarwood Av WARR WA1 15 L1
Briarwood Rd AIG/SPK L17 130 A2
Briary Cl HES CH60 141 K4
Briary Cft HTWN L38 70 B2
Brickcroft La LEY/BBR PR5 29 J2
Brickfields HUY L36 116 C4
Brickhurst Wy WARR WA1 122 D5
Brick Kiln La BRSC L40 39 J2
WGN WN1 4 F2
Brick St CLVPS L1 112 F6
NEWLW WA12 104 B2
Brickwall Gn SFTN L29 72 B6
Brickwall La SFTN L29 72 B6
Bride St ANF/KKDL L4 97 H3
Bridge Av ORM L39 63 G1
WARRS WA4 138 B1
Bridge Ct NSTN CH64 153 G6
WKBY CH48 124 C2
Bridge Cft LITH L21 83 L2
Bridgecroft Rd WAL/NB CH45 95 K7
Bridge Farm Cl
GR/UP/WCH CH49 126 D1
Bridge Farm Dr MGHL L31 73 H3
Bridgefield Cl WLTN L25 115 K6
Bridgeford Av
WD/CROXPK L12 98 C6
Bridge Gdns WD/CROXPK L12 99 H4
Bridge Gv STHP PR8 3 H6
Bridgehall Dr SKEL WN8 66 D6
Bridge La FROD/HEL WA6 160 E4
NTHTN L30 84 A2
WARR WA1 122 E7
WARRS WA4 138 A6
Bridgeman St ECCL WA10 8 B6
WARRW/BUR WA5 136 F1
Bridgeman Ter WGN WN1 4 E1
Bridge Meadow GTS/LS CH66 163 H3
Bridgend Cl WDN WA8 133 M2
Bridgend Dr STHP PR8 47 K1
Bridgenorth Rd PEN/TH CH61 141 G1
Bridge Rd CALD/MH L18 130 C2
CSBY/BLUN L23 82 E2
EHL/KEN L7 113 M5
HUY L36 115 L3
LITH L21 83 J6
MGHL L31 72 F6
PR/KW L34 100 F8
STHEL WA9 118 F3
WARR WA1 122 E6
WKBY CH48 124 C2
Bridges La SFTN L29 72 B6
Bridges Rd EP CH65 21 J5
Bridge St BIRK CH41 11 L4
BTL L20 6 F7
ECCL WA10 9 G6
GOL/RIS/CU WA3 92 C6
NEWLW WA12 92 C6
NEWLW WA12 104 D2
NSTN CH64 153 G6
ORM L39 63 G1
RUNC WA7 19 J3
STHP PR8 3 H5
WARR WA1 14 E6
WGNE/HIN WN2 69 J2
WGNE/HIN WN2 69 M7
WGNS/IIMK WN3 4 E6
Bridge View Cl WDN WA8 149 J1
Bridgeview Dr
NWD/KWIPK L33 86 B1
Bridgewater Av WARRS WA4 138 B1
Bridgewater Cl LITH L21 83 J3
Bridgewater Ms WARRS WA4 137 L5
Bridgewater St CLVPS L1 112 F6
RUNC WA7 19 G2
WGNS/IIMK WN3 4 D5
WGNW/BIL/O WN5 68 B7
Bridgewater Wy HUY L36 116 C5
Bridgeway NG/CROX L11 98 A4
Bridgeway East RUNC WA7 150 E3
Bridgeway West RUNC WA7 150 D3
Bridge Wills La CHTN/BK PR9 22 E8
Bridgewood Dr GTS/LS CH66 162 E3
Bridle Av WAL/EG CH44 112 A3
Bridle Cl CL/PREN CH43 110 D7
PS/BROM CH62 144 A6
Bridle Ct STHEL WA9 102 E5
Bridlemere Ct WARR WA1 122 A5
Bridle Pk PS/BROM CH62 143 M6
Bridle Rd NTHTN L30 84 C5
PS/BROM CH62 144 A6
WAL/EG CH44 112 A3
Bridle Wy GTS/LS CH66 162 F2
NTHTN L30 84 B5
Briercliffe Rd CHLYE PR6 32 F4
Brierfield SKEL WN8 65 M8
Brierfield Rd WAV L15 114 B7
Brierley Cl NTHTN L30 84 D1
Brierley St WARRW/BUR WA5 14 B4
Briers Cl WARRN/WOL WA2 122 B2
Briery Hey Av NWD/KWIPK L33 86 B3
Brighouse Cl ORM L39 50 F7
Brightgate Cl EHL/KEN L7 113 K5
Brighton Rd CSBY/WL L22 82 F4
HUY L36 116 D2
STHP PR8 35 J2
Brighton St CHLYE PR6 33 C5
WAL/EG CH44 112 A2
WARRW/BUR WA5 121 G7
Brighton V CSBY/WL L22 82 E3
Brightstone Cl CHTN/BK PR9 23 K8
Bright St BIRK CH41 10 F6
CHTN/BK PR9 25 H6
NPK/KEN L6 113 J2
Brightwell Cl
GR/UP/WCH CH49 126 B1
WARRW/BUR WA5 120 A8
Brignall Gv GOL/RIS/CU WA3 92 F4
Brill St BIRK CH41 10 C2
Brimelow Crs
WARRW/BUR WA5 136 A2
Brimstage Av BEB CH63 127 M5
Brimstage Cl HES CH60 141 L5
Brimstage Gn HES CH60 141 M5
Brimstage La BEB CH63 142 D1
Brimstage Rd ANF/KKDL L4 7 M6
BEB CH63 142 E3
HES CH60 141 L5
Brimstage St BIRK CH41 10 F9
Brindle St CHLY/EC PR7 32 E7
Brindley Av WARRS WA4 138 B1
Brindley Cl LITH L21 83 J3
Brindley Rd KKBY L32 85 L3
RUNC WA7 150 B2
STHEL WA9 103 G7
Brindley St RUNC WA7 18 F2
TOX L8 112 F7
WGNW/BIL/O WN5 67 L8
Brinklow Cl STHP PR8 34 C8
Brinley Cl PS/BROM CH62 143 M8
Brinton Cl NTHLY L27 115 L7
WDN WA8 134 A5
Brisbane Av WAL/NB CH45 95 J5
Brisbane St STHEL WA9 101 M6
Briscoe Dr MOR/LEA CH46 110 A6
Bristol Av RUNC WA7 151 G7
WAL/EG CH44 111 L1
Bristol Dr GTS/LS CH66 163 G4
Bristol Rd WAV L15 114 C7
Bristow Cl WARRW/BUR WA5 120 C5
Britannia Av EHL/KEN L7 113 M6
Britannia Crs TOX L8 129 H2
Britannia Rd WAL/NB CH45 111 J1
WGNW/BIL/O WN5 67 L5
Britonside Av KKBY L32 86 B5
Brittania Gdns FROD/HEL WA6 166 D4
Brittania Rd FROD/HEL WA6 166 D3
Brittarge Brow NTHLY L27 132 A1
Britten Cl TOX L8 113 K7
Broadacre WGNNW/ST WN6 55 J3
Broadbelt St ANF/KKDL L4 97 H3
Broadbent Av WARRS WA4 138 B1
Broadfield Av CL/PREN CH43 110 E5
Broadfield Cl CL/PREN CH43 110 D6
Broadfields CHLY/EC PR7 32 D3
RUNC WA7 150 E5
Broadgate Av STHEL WA9 102 D4
Broad Green Rd
CLB/OSW/ST L13 114 D3
Broadheath Av CL/PREN CH43 110 E6
Broad Hey NTHTN L30 83 M2
Broad Hey Cl WLTN L25 131 K2
Broadheys La KNUT WA16 139 M7
Broadhurst Av
GOL/RIS/CU WA3 107 H3
WARRW/BUR WA5 136 F1
Broadhurst La WGNNW/ST WN6 42 B7
Broadhurst St AIG/SPK L17 129 L2
Broadlake NSTN CH64 154 B5
Broadland Gdns GTS/LS CH66 163 H3
Broadland Rd GTS/LS CH66 163 H3
Broadlands STHP PR8 35 G2
WGNNW/ST WN6 55 K7
Broad La ANF/KKDL L4 97 M4
FMBY L37 47 L6
FMBY L37 60 A3
HES CH60 140 E4
KKBY L32 86 B5
NG/CROX L11 98 C4
ORM L39 61 L3
RNFD/HAY WA11 89 K3
SFTN L29 71 L4
WARRS WA4 138 D5
WARRW/BUR WA5 103 M5
Broadley Av GOL/RIS/CU WA3 92 E6
Broadmead ALL/GAR L19 131 G6
HES CH60 141 L6
SKEL WN8 53 K3
Broad Meadow La LEY/BBR PR5 29 G2
Broad Oak Av
RNFD/HAY WA11 90 C7
WARRW/BUR WA5 136 A1
Broad Oak Cl CHLYE PR6 44 C5
Broadoak Rd DV/KA/FCH L14 115 H2
MGHL L31 73 G4
Broad Oak Rd STHEL WA9 103 G2
Broadoaks
GR/UP/WCH CH49 110 A7
Broad O' Th' La WGNNW/ST WN6 55 J7
Broad Pl NG/CROX L11 98 B5
Broadriding Rd
WGNNW/ST WN6 55 G7
Broad Sq NG/CROX L11 98 B5
Broadstone Dr BEB CH63 143 H3
Broad Vw NG/CROX L11 98 B5
Broadway BEB CH63 127 M6
ECCL WA10 88 D8
ECCL WA10 101 L5
GR/UP/WCH CH49 109 M8
NG/CROX L11 98 A4
WAL/NB CH45 95 H8
WDN WA8 133 J4
Broadway Av WAL/NB CH45 95 H8
Broadway Cl STHP PR8 34 D8
Broadwood Av MGHL L31 72 E6
Broadwood St WAV L15 114 A6
Brockenhurst Rd WLT/FAZ L9 84 C8
Brockhall Cl RAIN/WH L35 101 J7
Brock Hall Cl STHEL WA9 118 E1
Brockholme Rd CALD/MH L18 130 C4
Brocklebank La ALL/GAR L19 130 F5
Brocklebank Rd CHTN/BK PR9 25 G4
Brock Mill La WGN WN1 56 E8
Brock Pl WGNE/HIN WN2 80 B3
Brock Rd CHLYE PR6 32 F4
GOL/RIS/CU WA3 122 F2
Brockstedes Av AIMK WN4 79 G7
Brock St ANF/KKDL L4 97 G5
WGN WN1 5 K4
Brocstedes Rd AIMK WN4 78 F6
Brodie Av ALL/GAR L19 130 D5
CALD/MH L18 130 C2
Brogden Av GOL/RIS/CU WA3 107 G1
Bromborough Rd BEB CH63 128 C8
Bromborough Village Rd
PS/BROM CH62 143 M4
Brome Wy BEB CH63 143 K3
Bromilow Rd SKEL WN8 64 E4
STHEL WA9 103 H3
Bromley Av CALD/MH L18 114 B8
GOL/RIS/CU WA3 92 F6
Bromley Cl HES CH60 141 G6
WARRN/WOL WA2 122 B2
WGNE/HIN WN2 69 J3
Bromley Dr LEIGH WN7 81 M5
Bromley Gn CHLYE PR6 33 H1
Bromley Rd WAL/NB CH45 95 J6
Brompton Av AIG/SPK L17 113 L8
CSBY/BLUN L23 82 E2
WAL/EG CH44 111 L1
Brompton Gdns
WARRW/BUR WA5 121 G6
Brompton Rd STHP PR8 25 G6
Brompton Wy GTS/LS CH66 163 G4
Bromsgrove Rd
GR/UP/WCH CH49 125 L1
Bromyard Cl BTL L20 6 E3
Bronington Av PS/BROM CH62 143 M7
Bronte Cl CSBY/BLUN L23 82 D1
WGNS/IIMK WN3 68 C8
Bronte St ECCL WA10 8 B4
VAUX/LVPD L3 13 K6
Brook Av MGHL L31 73 G2
WARRS WA4 122 B8
WARRS WA4 138 A4
Brookbank Ct AIN/FAZ L10 85 K6
Brookbridge Rd
CLB/OSW/ST L13 98 A7
Brook Cl WAL/EG CH44 95 L8
WDN WA8 117 L7
Brookdale CHLYE PR6 44 C4
RAIN/WH L35 133 J2
Brookdale Av North
GR/UP/WCH CH49 126 A1
Brookdale Av South
GR/UP/WCH CH49 126 A2
Brookdale Cl GR/UP/WCH CH49 126 A1
Brookdale Rd WAV L15 114 A7
Brook Dr WARRW/BUR WA5 120 C8
Brooke Cl CHTN/BK PR9 25 K6
Brook End STHEL WA9 103 J4
Brooke Rd East CSBY/WL L22 82 F3
Brooke Rd West CSBY/WL L22 82 E3
Brooke St CHLYE PR6 32 F6
Brook Farm ORM L39 63 G1
Brookfield BRSC L40 40 E3
LEY/BBR PR5 29 K2
SKEL WN8 53 L3
Brookfield Av CSBY/BLUN L23 82 F2
CSBY/WL L22 83 H5
RAIN/WH L35 101 L8
RUNC WA7 150 A3
Brookfield Cl LYMM WA13 139 M2
Brookfield Dr WLT/FAZ L9 84 E8
Brookfield Gdns WKBY CH48 124 D3
Brookfield La ORM L39 62 C8
Brookfield Pk WARRS WA4 138 C3
Brookfield Rd GOL/RIS/CU WA3 106 E1
LYMM WA13 139 M2
SKEL WN8 66 E7
WKBY CH48 124 D3
Brookfield St NEWLW WA12 104 D2
Brook Furlong FROD/HEL WA6 160 A3
Brook Hey NSTN CH64 152 D3
Brook Hey Dr NWD/KWIPK L33 86 B1
Brookhill Cl BTL L20 7 J4
Brookhill Rd BTL L20 7 J3
Brook House Gv ECCL WA10 101 J2
Brookhouse Rd ORM L39 50 F7
Brookhouse St WGN WN1 5 G4
Brookhouse Ter WGN WN1 5 G5
Brookhurst Av BEB CH63 143 L7
Brookhurst Cl BEB CH63 143 L8
Brookhurst Rd BEB CH63 143 L7
Brookland Av
WGNE/HIN WN2 69 M8
Brookland La STHEL WA9 103 J3
Brookland Rd BIRK CH41 11 H7
WGN WN1 68 D2
Brookland Rd East
CLB/OSW/ST L13 114 C2
Brookland Rd West
CLB/OSW/ST L13 114 C2
Brooklands ORM L39 51 H7
Brooklands Av AIMK WN4 91 M3
CSBY/WL L22 83 G5
Brooklands Dr MGHL L31 72 F5
WGNW/BIL/O WN5 66 F8
Brooklands Gdns NSTN CH64 152 E4
Brooklands Gv BRSC L40 52 B2
Brooklands Rd ECCL WA10 101 J1
NSTN CH64 152 E4
SKEL WN8 66 E6
The Brooklands HUY L36 116 A4
Brookland St WARR WA1 15 M1
Brook La CHLY/EC PR7 42 D1
GOL/RIS/CU WA3 123 J5
NSTN CH64 152 E3
ORM L39 63 G1
RNFD/HAY WA11 77 H6
WGNW/BIL/O WN5 67 J8
Brooklet Rd HES CH60 141 L5
Brooklyn Dr EP CH65 156 B8
Brook Lynn Av GOL/RIS/CU WA3 93 H4
Brook Meadow PEN/TH CH61 126 A6
Brook Pk MGHL L31 72 E6
Brook Rd BTL L20 6 E4
CSBY/BLUN L23 71 J7
GTS/LS CH66 155 M8
LYMM WA13 139 M1
MGHL L31 73 G5
WLT/FAZ L9 97 J1
Brooks Aly CLVPS L1 13 H8
Brookside CHLY/EC PR7 31 L3
CHLY/EC PR7 43 H4
Brookside Av AIMK WN4 79 H5
CSBY/WL L22 83 H5
DV/KA/FCH L14 114 F2
ECCL WA10 88 E8
LYMM WA13 139 L1
RNFD/HAY WA11 76 A6
WARRS WA4 137 M4
WARRW/BUR WA5 120 C8
Brookside Cl RAIN/WH L35 117 G1
RNFD/HAY WA11 90 D6
WD/CROXPK L12 99 H4
WGNW/BIL/O WN5 90 A1
Brookside Crs
GR/UP/WCH CH49 109 M8
Brookside Dr
GR/UP/WCH CH49 110 A8
Brookside Rd FROD/HEL WA6 160 C5
RAIN/WH L35 117 G1
STHP PR8 35 L4
WGN WN1 56 D4
Brookside Vw RNFD/HAY WA11 90 D6
Brookside Wy RNFD/HAY WA11 90 D6
Brooks Rd FMBY L37 58 F3
The Brooks RNFD/HAY WA11 89 J6
Brook St AIMK WN4 91 L3
BIRK CH41 10 F2
CHLYE PR6 44 C4
CHTN/BK PR9 25 L1
ECCL WA10 9 G5
GOL/RIS/CU WA3 92 C6
GOL/RIS/CU WA3 93 J4
NSTN CH64 153 G5
PS/BROM CH62 128 C7
RAIN/WH L35 101 H8
RUNC WA7 19 G2
VAUX/LVPD L3 12 D5
WGNE/HIN WN2 69 J6
WGNS/IIMK WN3 79 H1
Brook St East BIRK CH41 11 J4
Brooks Wy FMBY L37 58 F3
Brookthorpe Cl WAL/NB CH45 95 K8
Brook V CSBY/WL L22 83 H5
Brookvale Av North RUNC WA7 150 D8
Brookvale Av South RUNC WA7 150 D7
Brookvale Cl WARRW/BUR WA5 104 B7
Brookview WGNE/HIN WN2 80 F1
Brook Wk PEN/TH CH61 125 M6
Brookway CL/PREN CH43 127 G4
GR/UP/WCH CH49 110 A8
WAL/NB CH45 95 J8
Brook Wy WARRW/BUR WA5 120 C8
Brookway La STHEL WA9 103 H4
Brook Well NSTN CH64 153 G8
Brookwood Cl WARRS WA4 137 K5
Brookwood Rd HUY L36 116 A1
Broom Av WARRS WA4 138 A7
Broom Cl PR/KW L34 101 H7
Broome Ct RUNC WA7 150 D8
Broome Rd STHP PR8 35 K2
Broomfield Cl HES CH60 140 E4
Broomfield Gdns WLT/FAZ L9 84 B8
Broomfield Pl
WGNNW/ST WN6 56 A4
Broomfield Rd WGNNW/ST WN6 56 A4
WLT/FAZ L9 84 B8
WLT/FAZ L9 84 B8
Broomfields Rd WARRS WA4 137 M6
Broomflat Cl
WGNNW/ST WN6 56 A4
Broomhey Av WGN WN1 56 E8
Broomhey Ter WGNE/HIN WN2 5 K5
Broom Hl CL/PREN CH43 111 H6
Broomhill Cl NTHLY L27 115 L7
Broomholme WGNNW/ST WN6 54 F6
Broomlands HES CH60 141 G5
Broomleigh Cl BEB CH63 127 M8
Broom Rd ECCL WA10 101 K5
WGNW/BIL/O WN5 67 M7
Broomsgrove AIN/FAZ L10 85 G4
Broom Wy HLWD L26 131 M6
Broseley Av GOL/RIS/CU WA3 106 F1
PS/BROM CH62 143 L4
Broseley La GOL/RIS/CU WA3 93 M8
Broster Av MOR/LEA CH46 109 L5
Broster Cl MOR/LEA CH46 109 L5
Brosters La HOY CH47 108 F4
Brotherton Cl
PS/BROM CH62 143 L5
Brougham Av BIRK CH41 128 B2
Brougham Rd WAL/EG CH44 111 M2
Brough Cl WGNE/HIN WN2 81 G2
Broughton Av GOL/RIS/CU WA3 92 F6
STHP PR8 3 M9
WKBY CH48 124 C2
Broughton Dr ALL/GAR L19 130 C6
Broughton Hall Rd
WD/CROXPK L12 99 G8
Broughton Rd WAL/EG CH44 111 K2
Brow La HES CH60 141 H6
Browmere Dr GOL/RIS/CU WA3 106 C6
Brownbill Bank NTHLY L27 116 A8
Brown Heath Av
WGNW/BIL/O WN5 89 M2
Brownhill Dr WARR WA1 122 B5
Browning Av RF/TRAN CH42 128 B4
WDN WA8 16 A4
WGNS/IIMK WN3 79 H1
Browning Cl HUY L36 116 B4
Browning Dr EP CH65 163 H1
Browning Gv WGNNW/ST WN6 68 A2
Browning Rd CSBY/WL L22 82 F3
WAL/NB CH45 94 F8
Browning St BTL L20 6 D2
LEIGH WN7 81 M7
Brownley St CHLYE PR6 33 G6
Brownlow Av WGNE/HIN WN2 69 K6
Brownlow Hl VAUX/LVPD L3 13 J7
Brownlow La WGNW/BIL/O WN5 77 L4
Brownlow Rd PS/BROM CH62 128 D6
Brownlow St VAUX/LVPD L3 13 L7
Brownmere WGNNW/ST WN6 68 B3
Brownmoor La
CSBY/BLUN L23 83 J1
Brownmoor Pk CSBY/BLUN L23 83 H2
Browns Hey CHLY/EC PR7 32 C3
Brown's La NTHTN L30 84 C2
Brown St CHLYE PR6 32 F5
HOR/BR BL6 57 M3
WDN WA8 17 J5
WGNE/HIN WN2 69 J6
WGNE/HIN WN2 81 G4
WGNS/IIMK WN3 4 D5
Brownville Rd
CLB/OSW/ST L13 97 M7
Brow Rd CL/PREN CH43 110 F4
Brows Cl FMBY L37 59 G2
Brow Side EV L5 13 L2
Brows La FMBY L37 59 G2
Broxholme Wy MGHL L31 72 F6
Broxton Av CL/PREN CH43 127 H3
WGNW/BIL/O WN5 67 H6
WKBY CH48 124 D2
Broxton Cl WDN WA8 133 L2
Broxton Rd GTS/LS CH66 156 A8
Broxton St WAV L15 114 A5
Bruce Av WARRN/WOL WA2 121 M4
Bruce Crs BEB CH63 143 L7
Bruce Dr GTS/LS CH66 162 E1
Bruce St ECCL WA10 8 D5
TOX L8 129 J1
Bruche Av WARR WA1 122 B6
Bruche Dr WARR WA1 122 B5
Bruera Rd EP CH65 163 H1
Brunel Dr LITH L21 83 J3
Brunner Rd WDN WA8 16 C3
Brunsborough Cl
PS/BROM CH62 143 L7
Brunsfield Cl MOR/LEA CH46 109 L6
Brunstath Cl HES CH60 141 L4
Brunswick Cl ANF/KKDL L4 97 G5
Brunswick Crs GTS/LS CH66 163 G2
Brunswick Ms BIRK CH41 11 K4
CSBY/WL L22 83 G5
Brunswick Pde CSBY/WL L22 82 F5
Brunswick Pl BTL L20 96 D5
Brunswick Rd NEWLW WA12 104 B1
NPK/KEN L6 13 M4
Brunswick St ALL/GAR L19 145 M1
CHLY/EC PR7 32 F5
CLVP L2 12 E7
STHEL WA9 103 J2
Brunswick Wy VAUX/LVPD L3 112 F8
Brunt La ALL/GAR L19 131 G6
Bruntleigh Av WARRS WA4 138 C2
Bruton Rd HUY L36 99 M7
Bryanston Rd AIG/SPK L17 129 K2
RF/TRAN CH42 127 J3
Bryant Av WARRS WA4 138 B1
Bryant Rd LITH L21 83 K7
The Bryceway WD/CROXPK L12 114 F1
Brydges St EHL/KEN L7 113 J4
Bryer Rd RAIN/WH L35 116 F1
Bryham St WGN WN1 5 H4
Bryn Bank WAL/EG CH44 111 L1
Bryn Gates La AIMK WN4 79 L5
Brynmor Rd CALD/MH L18 130 C4
Brynmoss Av WAL/EG CH44 111 H1
Brynn St ECCL WA10 9 H3
WDN WA8 16 E4
WGNE/HIN WN2 80 A6
Bryn Rd AIMK WN4 79 J7
Bryn Rd South AIMK WN4 91 L1
Bryn St AIMK WN4 91 K2
WGNS/IIMK WN3 5 J8
Bryony Cl WGNW/BIL/O WN5 66 F8
Bryony Wy RF/TRAN CH42 128 B5
Brythen St CLVPS L1 13 H7
Buchanan Dr WGNE/HIN WN2 81 K2
Buchanan Rd WAL/EG CH44 111 M2
WGNW/BIL/O WN5 68 A6
WLT/FAZ L9 97 H2
Buchanan St CHLYE PR6 32 F6
Buchan Cl WARRW/BUR WA5 120 D5
Buckfast Av RNFD/HAY WA11 91 H6
Buckfast Cl NTHTN L30 84 B1
WARRW/BUR WA5 136 A2
Buckfast Ct RUNC WA7 151 G2
Buckfast Dr FMBY L37 59 K3
Buckingham Av AIG/SPK L17 113 M8
BEB CH63 128 A6
CL/PREN CH43 111 H6
WDN WA8 134 C1
Buckingham Cl ECCL WA10 8 D8
WGNW/BIL/O WN5 68 A8
Buckingham Ct
NWD/KWIPK L33 86 B2
Buckingham Dr
RNFD/HAY WA11 89 J6
WARRW/BUR WA5 136 E1
Buckingham Gdns EP CH65 163 M3
Buckingham Gv FMBY L37 59 G3
Buckingham Rd
CLB/OSW/ST L13 97 M7
MGHL L31 72 E5
WAL/EG CH44 111 H1
WLT/FAZ L9 84 C7
Buckingham St CHLYE PR6 32 F6
EV L5 97 G8
Buckland Cl WDN WA8 133 M6
Buckland Dr BEB CH63 143 H3
WGNW/BIL/O WN5 67 K4
Buckland St AIG/SPK L17 129 K2

Buckley Hill La *NTHTN* L30 ......... **71** M8
Buckley St *WARRN/WOL* WA2 ...... **14** D3
*WGNNW/ST* WN6 ......................... **68** C3
Buckley St West
*WGNNW/ST* WN6 ......................... **68** C3
Buckshaw Hall CI *CHLY/EC* PR7 ... **32** D3
Buckthorn CI *STBRV* L28 ............. **99** K6 🔢
Buckthorn Gdns
*RAIN/WH* L35 ............................. **101** L7 🔢
Buckton St *WARR* WA1 ................... **15** J2
Bude CI *CL/PREN* CH43 ............... **110** E7
Bude Rd *WDN* WA8 ...................... **134** A3
Budworth Av *STHEL* WA9 ............ **118** D2
*WARRS* WA4 .............................. **138** B1
*WDN* WA8 .................................. **133** M3
Budworth CI *CL/PREN* CH43 ....... **127** G1 🔢
*RUNC* WA7 ................................ **149** M6
Budworth Dr *WLTN* L25 ............... **131** L3 🔢
Budworth Rd *CL/PREN* CH43 ....... **127** C1
*GTS/LS* CH66 ............................. **163** G3
Buer Av *WGNS/IIMK* WN3 ............ **79** H1
Buerton CI *CL/PREN* CH43 .......... **126** F1
Buffs La *HES* CH60 ..................... **141** K5
Buggen La *NSTN* CH64 ................ **152** F5
Buildwas Rd *NSTN* CH64 ............. **153** C3
Bulford Rd *WLT/FAZ* L9 ............... **98** A1
Bulkeley Rd *WAL/EG* CH44 .......... **111** M2 🔢
Bull Bridge La *AIN/FAZ* L10 ......... **85** C3
Bull Cop *FMBY* L37 ...................... **59** K2
Bullens La *BRSC* L40 .................... **36** F6
Bullens Rd *ANF/KKDL* L4 ............. **97** H5
*KKBY* L32 ................................... **86** B4
Bullfinch Ct *HLWD* L26 ................ **132** A4 🔢
Bull HI *NSTN* CH64 ...................... **153** H7
Bull La *WLT/FAZ* L9 ..................... **84** D6
The Bulrushes *AIG/SPK* L17 ......... **129** H2 🔢
Bulteel St *WGNW/BIL/O* WN5 ...... **67** M7
Bulwer St *BTL* L20 ....................... **83** J8
*EV* L5 ......................................... **97** J8 🔢
Bunbury CI *CHNE* CH2 ................ **164** C6
Bunbury Dr *RUNC* WA7 ............... **149** L7
Bundoran Rd *AIG/SPK* L17 .......... **130** K3
Bunter Rd *KKBY* L32 .................... **86** B7
Bunting CI *GOL/RIS/CU* WA3 ...... **93** C5 🔢
Bunting Ct *HLWD* L26 .................. **131** M3
Buntingford Rd *WARRS* WA4 ....... **138** E2 🔢
Burbo Bank Rd *CSBY/BLUN* L23 .. **82** C1
Burbo Bank Rd North
*CSBY/BLUN* L23 ........................ **70** B8
Burbo Bank Rd South
*CSBY/BLUN* L23 ........................ **82** D2 🔢
Burbo Crs *CSBY/BLUN* L23 ......... **82** D2 🔢
Burbo Wy *WAL/NB* CH45 ............. **95** C5
Burden Rd *MOR/LEA* CH46 ......... **109** L3
Burdett Av *BEB* CH63 .................. **143** H3
Burdett CI *BEB* CH63 .................. **143** J5 🔢
Burdett Rd *CSBY/WL* L22 ............ **82** F4
*GTS/LS* CH66 ............................. **163** G3
*WAL/NB* CH45 ............................ **94** F8 🔢
Burdett St *AIG/SPK* L17 .............. **129** L2
Burfield Dr *WARRS* WA4 ............. **137** L7
Burford Av *WAL/EG* CH44 ........... **111** H2
Burford Rd *CHLDW* L16 ............... **114** E4
Burgess Av *WARRS* WA4 ............. **137** K5
Burgess Gdns *MGHL* L31 ............. **72** E3 🔢
Burgess' La *FMBY* L37 ................. **59** C3
Burgess St *VAUX/LVPD* L3 ......... **13** K5 🔢
*WGNS/IIMK* WN3 ......................... **5** J9
Burgh Hall Rd *CHLY/EC* PR7 ....... **43** J1
Burghill Rd *WD/CROXPK* L12 ...... **99** H1
Burgh La *CHLY/EC* PR7 ............... **43** L3
Burgh La South *CHLY/EC* PR7 ..... **43** K3
Burghley Wy *WGNE/HIN* WN2 ..... **69** H8 🔢
Burgh Mdw *CHLY/EC* PR7 ........... **43** K1
Burgundy CI *NEWLW* WA12 ........ **105** G2 🔢
Burkhardt Dr *NEWLW* WA12 ....... **105** G2
Burland CI *RUNC* WA7 ................. **18** F5
Burland St *WGNW/BIL/O* WN5 .... **68** B6 🔢
Burleigh Rd North *EV* L5 ............. **97** H7
Burleigh Rd South *EV* L5 ............ **97** H6 🔢
Burley Av *GOL/RIS/CU* WA3........ **93** H5
Burley CI *KKBY* L32 ..................... **86** B4 🔢
Burley Crs *WGNS/IIMK* WN3 ....... **78** E3
Burlingham Av *WKBY* CH48 ........ **124** E4
Burlington Av *FMBY* L37 ............. **59** K2
Burlington Rd *STHP* PR8 ............. **35** H2
*WAL/NB* CH45 ............................ **95** K4
Burlington St *BIRK* CH41 ............. **11** J5 🔢
*CHLY/EC* PR7 .............................. **32** F6 🔢
*VAUX/LVPD* L3 .......................... **12** E2
Burlton Gv *WGNE/HIN* WN2 ........ **69** J3 🔢
Burman Crs *ALL/GAR* L19 ........... **130** E6
Burman Rd *ALL/GAR* L19 ............ **130** F6
Burnage Av *STHEL* WA9 .............. **118** F4
Burnage CI *SPK/HALE* L24 .......... **147** H3
Burnand St *ANF/KKDL* L4 ........... **97** H6
Burnard CI *NWD/KWIPK* L33 ....... **86** B3 🔢
Burnard Crs *NWD/KWIPK* L33 ..... **86** B3
Burnaston Gv
*WGNW/BIL/O* WN5 ................... **67** M8 🔢
Burnell CI *ECCL* WA10 ................ **8** E4
Burnell Rd *EP* CH65 ................... **21** C7
Burnet Rd *WARRN/WOL* WA2 ...... **122** C3
Burnfell *GOL/RIS/CU* WA3 ......... **93** G6 🔢
Burnham CI
*GOL/RIS/CU* WA3 ..................... **107** G1 🔢
*WARRW/BUR* WA5 ..................... **120** B3
*WDN* WA8 .................................. **133** L2 🔢
Burnham Gv *WGNE/HIN* WN2 ..... **69** H3 🔢
Burnham Rd *CALD/MH* L18 ........ **130** C2
Burnhill Ct *WGNNW/ST* WN6 ...... **56** A5 🔢
Burnie Av *BTL* L20 ....................... **7** L1
Burnley Av *MOR/LEA* CH46 ........ **110** B5
Burnley Rd *NPK/KEN* L6 ............. **113** J1 🔢
Burnley Rd *MOR/LEA* CH46 ........ **110** B5
*STHP* PR8 .................................. **34** E8
Burnsall Av *GOL/RIS/CU* WA3 .... **93** H5
Burnsall Dr *WDN* WA8 ................ **133** L2
Burnsall St *ALL/GAR* L19 ............ **131** C8
Burns Av *LEIGH* WN7 ................... **81** L5
*WAL/NB* CH45 ............................. **95** J8
Burns CI *AIMK* WN4 ..................... **79** H7
*CHLDW* L16 ................................ **115** H5
*GTS/LS* CH66 ............................. **163** G1
*RAIN/WH* L35 ............................. **117** C2
*WGNS/IIMK* WN3 ........................ **79** J1
*WGNW/BIL/O* WN5 .................... **77** M4
Burns Crs *WDN* WA8 ................... **16** B5

Burns Gv *HUY* L36 ...................... **116** C4
*WARRN/WOL* WA2 ..................... **121** L3
Burnside *SKEL* WN8 ..................... **53** K3
Burnside Av *WAL/EG* CH44 ......... **111** K3 🔢
*WARRS* WA4 .............................. **137** M4
Burnside Rd *WAL/EG* CH44 ......... **111** K3
*WGNE/HIN* WN2 ........................ **80** D4 🔢
Burns St *BTL* L20 ......................... **6** C1
Burnt Ash CI *ALL/GAR* L19 ......... **130** B6 🔢
Burnthwaite Rd
*DV/KA/FCH* L14 ......................... **114** E2
Burnvale *WGNS/IIMK* WN3 .......... **78** F3 🔢
Burrell Dr *RF/TRAN* CH42 .......... **127** L4
Burrell Rd *RF/TRAN* CH42 .......... **127** L4
Burrell St *ANF/KKDL* L4 .............. **97** H5 🔢
Burrington Dr *LEIGH* WN7 .......... **81** M6 🔢
Burrough St *GOL/RIS/CU* WA3 .... **123** H2
Burrows Av *RNFD/HAY* WA11 ...... **90** B8
Burrows Ct *VAUX/LVPD* L3 ......... **12** E1
Burrow's La *ECCL* WA10 ............. **101** G3
*FROD/HEL* WA6 ......................... **167** H4
Burrows St *RNFD/HAY* WA11 ...... **90** C7 🔢
Bursar CI *NEWLW* WA12 .............. **104** F1
Burscough Rd *ORM* L39 .............. **51** H7
Burscough St *ORM* L39 ............... **51** C8
Burton Av *RAIN/WH* L35 .............. **117** J1
*WAL/NB* CH45 ............................ **95** C8
Burton CI *CLVPS* L1 .................... **112** F5 🔢
*GOL/RIS/CU* WA3 ...................... **107** H2
*RAIN/WH* L35 ............................. **117** J1
*WDN* WA8 .................................. **134** B2 🔢
Burton Gn *GTS/LS* CH66 ............. **162** F1 🔢
Burtonhead Rd *STHEL* WA9 ........ **8** F8
Burton Rd *NSTN* CH64 ................ **153** G7
*WARRN/WOL* WA2 ..................... **121** M4
Burton St *EV* L5 .......................... **96** E7 🔢
Burtonwood Rd
*WARRW/BUR* WA5 ..................... **120** C5
Burtree Rd *DV/KA/FCH* L14 ........ **99** J7
Burwell Av *CHLY/EC* PR7 ............ **43** L7
Burwell CI *WLT/FAZ* L9 .............. **84** B7
Bury Rd *STHP* PR8 ....................... **35** J2
Busby's Cottages
*WAL/NB* CH45 ............................ **95** K5 🔢
Bushby's La *FMBY* L37 ................ **58** E3
Bushby's Pk *FMBY* L37 ............... **58** E3
Bushell CI *NSTN* CH64 ................ **153** H6
Bushell Rd *NSTN* CH64 ............... **153** H5
Bushel's Dr *STHEL* WA9 .............. **118** F3
Bushey La *RNFD/HAY* WA11 ........ **76** A3
Bushey Rd *ANF/KKDL* L4 ............ **97** L3
Bushley CI *BTL* L20 ..................... **6** F5
Bush Rd *WDN* WA8 ...................... **16** A9
Bush Wy *HES* CH60 ..................... **141** G5
Butchers La *ORM* L39 .................. **62** B8
Bute St *EV* L5 .............................. **13** K2
*VAUX/LVPD* L3 .......................... **13** J3
Butleigh Rd *HUY* L36 .................. **99** M8
Butler Crs *NPK/KEN* L6 ............... **113** K2
Butler St *NPK/KEN* L6 ................. **113** K1
*WGN* WN1 .................................. **5** C4
Buttercup CI *MOR/LEA* CH46 ...... **110** C3 🔢
Buttercup Wy *WLT/FAZ* L9 .......... **97** K1
Butterfield Gdns *ORM* L39 .......... **62** F2 🔢
Butterfield St *ANF/KKDL* L4 ........ **97** H6 🔢
Buttermarket St *WARR* WA1 ....... **15** G5 🔢
Buttermere Av *AIMK* WN4 ........... **79** K8
*CHLY/EC* PR7 ............................ **32** C7
*CL/PREN* CH43 .......................... **110** E7
*EP* CH65 .................................... **20** D5
*RNFD/HAY* WA11 ...................... **89** J5 🔢
*WARRN/WOL* WA2 ..................... **121** J2
Buttermere CI *FMBY* L37 ............ **58** F2 🔢
*FROD/HEL* WA6 ......................... **160** F5 🔢
*MGHL* L31 .................................. **72** F4
*NWD/KWIPK* L33 ....................... **85** M1
Buttermere Crs
*CSBY/BLUN* L23 ........................ **83** H3 🔢
Buttermere Gdns
*CSBY/BLUN* L23 ........................ **83** H3
Buttermere Gv *RUNC* WA7 .......... **149** M7
Buttermere Rd *CHLDW* L16 ......... **115** J5
*WGNW/BIL/O* WN5 .................... **67** L6 🔢
Buttermere St *TOX* L8 ................. **113** K6 🔢
Butterton Av
*GR/UP/WCH* CH49 ..................... **109** M7
Butterwick Dr
*WD/CROXPK* L12 ...................... **99** G2 🔢
Butterworth Brow *CHLY/EC* PR7.. **43** H1
Butts La *STHP* PR8 ...................... **25** H8
Buxted Rd *KKBY* L32 .................. **86** C5
Buxton CI *WARRW/BUR* WA5 ...... **120** C5
Exchange St West *CLVP* L2 ......... **12** E7 🔢
Bye La *ORM* L39 .......................... **61** L2
Byerley St *WAL/EG* CH44 ............ **112** A2 🔢
Byfleet CI *WGNS/IIMK* WN3 ........ **78** E4
Byland CI *FMBY* L37 ................... **59** K3
*WDN* WA8 .................................. **118** A8
Byles St *TOX* L8 .......................... **129** J1
Byley Ri *WGNNW/ST* WN6 .......... **56** A5
Byng PI *ANF/KKDL* L4 ................. **97** M5
Byng Rd *ANF/KKDL* L4 ............... **97** M5
Byng St *BTL* L20 ......................... **6** C1
The By-pass *CSBY/BLUN* L23 ...... **83** G1
Byrne Av *RF/TRAN* CH42 ............ **128** B3 🔢
Byrom La *GOL/RIS/CU* WA3........ **93** H3
Byrom St *CHTN/BK* PR9 .............. **25** H7
*VAUX/LVPD* L3 .......................... **13** H5
Byrom Wy *VAUX/LVPD* L3 .......... **13** H4
Byron Av *RAIN/WH* L35 ............... **117** H2
*WGNE/HIN* WN2 ........................ **69** M8 🔢
Byron CI *CL/PREN* CH43 ............. **127** H5 🔢
*ECCL* WA10 ................................ **9** G2
*FMBY* L37 .................................. **59** H1
*HUY* L36 .................................... **116** B4
*WGNE/HIN* WN2 ........................ **80** D5
*WGNNW/ST* WN6 ....................... **68** A2
Byron Ct *WARRN/WOL* WA2 ....... **121** J3
Byron Crs *CHLY/EC* PR7 ............. **43** G5
Byron Rd *CSBY/BLUN* L23 .......... **82** D1
*MGHL* L31 .................................. **72** F2 🔢
Byron St *ALL/GAR* L19 ................ **130** E8

## C

*BTL* L20 ...................................... **6** C1
*CHLY/EC* PR7 .............................. **32** F5 🔢
*RUNC* WA7 ................................. **18** F5
The Byway *CSBY/BLUN* L23 ........ **71** G8

Cabes CI *DV/KA/FCH* L14 ............ **99** J7
Cabin La *CHTN/BK* PR9 ............... **26** A2
*KIRK/FR/WA* PR4 ....................... **27** J7
*MGHL* L31 .................................. **72** B1
*ORM* L39 .................................... **35** M8
Cable Rd *HOY* CH47 .................... **108** D6
*RAIN/WH* L35 ............................. **101** H8
Cable St *CLVPS* L1 ...................... **12** F8
*FMBY* L37 .................................. **59** J1
*STHP* PR8 .................................. **3** G3
Cabot CI *WARRW/BUR* WA5 ........ **120** E4 🔢
Cadbot Gn *WLTN* L25 .................. **115** C8
Caddick Rd *PR/KW* L34 ............... **86** D8
Cadman Gv *WGNE/HIN* WN2 ...... **80** F1 🔢
Cadnam Rd *WLTN* L25 ................. **115** M8
Cadogan Dr *WGNS/IIMK* WN3 .... **78** F3
Cadogan St *WAV* L15 ................... **113** M5
Cadshaw CI *GOL/RIS/CU* WA3 .... **106** H3
Cadwell Rd *MGHL* L31 ................ **61** K8
Caernarvon CI
*GR/UP/WCH* CH49 ..................... **110** B7
Caernarvon Ct *EP* CH65 .............. **163** M3 🔢
Caernarvon Rd
*WGNE/HIN* WN2 ........................ **81** J2 🔢
Caerwys Gv *RF/TRAN* CH42 ....... **128** A1
Caird St *NPK/KEN* L6 .................. **113** J2
Cairn Ct *STHEL* WA9 ................... **101** M6
Cairnmore Rd *CALD/MH* L18 ...... **130** C3
Cairns St *TOX* L8 ........................ **113** J7
Cairo St *ANF/KKDL* L4 ................ **7** L8
*ECCL* WA10 ................................ **101** M4
*WARR* WA1 ................................ **14** E6
Caister CI *SKEL* WN8 .................. **65** M5
Caithness Dr *CSBY/BLUN* L23 ..... **83** H2 🔢
*WAL/NB* CH45 ............................ **95** L7
Caithness Rd *CALD/MH* L18 ....... **130** D4
Calday Grange CI *WKBY* CH48 .... **124** F4
Calday Gv *RNFD/HAY* WA11 ....... **90** C5
Caldbeck Av
*WARRN/WOL* WA2 ..................... **121** M3 🔢
Caldbeck CI *AIMK* WN4 .............. **91** K1 🔢
Caldbeck Gv *RNFD/HAY* WA11 ... **89** L4 🔢
Caldbeck Rd *PS/BROM* CH62 ..... **144** A3
Calder Av *CHLY/EC* PR7 ............. **32** D8
*CL/PREN* CH43 .......................... **127** J3 🔢
*ORM* L39 .................................... **63** G1
*WGNE/HIN* WN2 ........................ **81** L2
Calderbank St
*WGNW/BIL/O* WN5 ................... **68** A8 🔢
Calder CI *NWD/KWIPK* L33 ......... **74** B7
*WDN* WA8 .................................. **135** H2
Calder Dr *CALD/MH* L18 ............. **114** E8
*MGHL* L31 .................................. **73** H3
*RAIN/WH* L35 ............................. **117** K2
*WGNE/HIN* WN2 ........................ **80** C3
Calderfield CI *WARRS* WA4 ........ **137** K5
Calderfield Rd *CALD/MH* L18 ..... **114** F8
Calder Gra *WLTN* L25 .................. **131** G2
Calderhurst Dr *ECCL* WA10 ........ **88** D7
Calderstones Av *CALD/MH* L18 ... **114** E3
Calderstones Rd *CALD/MH* L18 ... **130** E1
Calder Wy *GTS/LS* CH66 ............. **155** L8 🔢
Caldicott Av *PS/BROM* CH62 ...... **143** M6
Caldway Dr *NTHLY* L27 ............... **115** M7
Caldwell Av *WARRW/BUR* WA5 .. **121** H3
Caldwell CI *NWD/KWIPK* L33 ...... **74** B8 🔢
*NWD/KWIPK* L33 ....................... **86** B1 🔢
Caldwell Dr
*GR/UP/WCH* CH49 ..................... **126** D3 🔢
Caldwell Rd *ALL/GAR* L19 .......... **130** F5
*WDN* WA8 .................................. **16** C5
Caldwell St *STHEL* WA9 .............. **102** F2
Caldy Chase Dr *WKBY* CH48 ...... **124** F6
Caldy Dr *GTS/LS* CH66 ............... **162** F1
Caldy Gv *RNFD/HAY* WA11 ........ **90** B8
Caldy Rd *WAL/NB* CH45 ............. **95** K8
*WKBY* CH48 .............................. **124** F6
*WLT/FAZ* L9 ............................... **84** C6
Caldy Wd *WKBY* CH48 ............... **124** F6
Caldywood Dr *RAIN/WH* L35 ...... **117** G2
Caledonia St *EHL/KEN* L7 ........... **13** L9
*TOX* L8 ...................................... **113** H5 🔢
Cale La *WGNE/HIN* WN2 ............. **69** K3
Calgarth Rd *HUY* L36 .................. **99** L8
Calico Wood Av
*WGNNW/ST* WN6 ....................... **55** H7
California CI *WARRW/BUR* WA5 .. **120** E5
California Rd *CLB/OSW/ST* L13 .... **97** M6
Callaghan CI *EV* L5 ..................... **96** F8 🔢
Callander Ct *WARRW/BUR* WA5 .. **68** A8
Callander Rd *NPK/KEN* L6 .......... **113** M2
Callands Rd *WARRW/BUR* WA5 .. **120** F3
Callestock CI *NG/CROX* L11 ........ **85** M8
Callington CI *DV/KA/FCH* L14 ..... **99** J7
Callon Av *RNFD/HAY* WA11 ........ **90** A8
Callow Rd *WAV* L15 .................... **113** M6
Calmet CI *EV* L5 .......................... **97** G7 🔢
Calmington La *RUNC* WA7 .......... **151** H1
Calne CI *PEN/TH* CH61 ............... **125** M6
Calstock CI
*WARRW/BUR* WA5 ..................... **136** A2 🔢
Calthorpe St *ALL/GAR* L19 ......... **130** D7
Calthorpe Wy *CL/PREN* CH43 .... **110** F7 🔢
Calton Av *CALD/MH* L18 ............. **114** C8 🔢
Calton CI *WGNS/IIMK* WN3 ........ **78** F3 🔢
Calvados CI *AIG/SPK* L17 ........... **129** L4 🔢
Calveley Av *PS/BROM* CH62 ....... **155** H1
Calveley Wk *WGNNW/ST* WN6 ... **56** A5
Calverhall Av *AIMK* WN4 ............ **91** J2
Calverly CI *RUNC* WA7 ................ **150** E8 🔢
Calver Rd *WARRN/WOL* WA2 ...... **121** H1
Camarthen Crs *TOX* L8 ............... **112** F7
Camberley CI *STHP* PR8 .............. **2** A8

Camberley Dr *WLTN* L25 ............. **131** L5
Camborne Av *WLTN* L25 ............. **131** L5
Camborne CI *RUNC* WA7 ............. **150** E7 🔢
Cambourne Av *RNFD/HAY* WA11.. **89**M6
Cambourne CI *WGNE/HIN* WN2 .. **81** L3
Cambourne Rd
*WARRW/BUR* WA5 ..................... **104** B7
Cambrai Av *WARRS* WA4 ............ **137** L3
Cambrian CI *GTS/LS* CH66 ......... **155** F7 🔢
*MOR/LEA* CH46 .......................... **109** K3
Cambrian Crs *WGNS/IIMK* WN3 .. **78** E3
Cambrian Rd *MOR/LEA* CH46 ..... **109** L3
Cambrian Wy *WLTN* L25 ............. **131** K2
Cambria St *NPK/KEN* L6 ............. **113** K2
Cambridge Av *RAIN/WH* PR9 ...... **25** H3
*CSBY/BLUN* L23 ........................ **82** F1
*LITH* L21 ................................... **83** K5 🔢
Cambridge CI *WARRS* WA4 ........ **137** K6 🔢
Cambridge Dr *CSBY/BLUN* L23 ... **70** E8
*HLWD* L26 .................................. **132** B5 🔢
Cambridge Gdns *CHTN/BK* PR9 .. **25** H3
*FROD/HEL* WA6 ......................... **166** F1
*WARRS* WA4 .............................. **137** L7
Cambridge Rd *BTL* L20 ............... **7** K6
*CHTN/BK* PR9 ............................ **25** H3
*CSBY/BLUN* L23 ........................ **70** E8
*ECCL* WA10 ................................ **8** C4
*EP* CH65 .................................... **20** D5
*FMBY* L37 .................................. **58** F4
*LITH* L21 ................................... **83** G6
Cambridge St *CHLY/EC* PR7 ....... **32** E6 🔢
*CHTN/BK* PR9 ............................ **25** H3
*CSBY/BLUN* L23 ........................ **70** E8
*EHL/KEN* L7 ............................... **13** L9
*EHL/KEN* L7 ............................... **113** J5 🔢
*PR/KW* L34 ................................ **100** F7 🔢
*RUNC* WA7 ................................ **19** L3
*WAV* L15 .................................... **113** M5
*WDN* WA8 .................................. **16** E5
*WGN* WN1 ................................... **5** H5
Camdale CI *STBRV* L28 .............. **99** K6 🔢
Camden Ct *RUNC* WA7 ............... **150** F4 🔢
Camden PI *BIRK* CH41 ................ **11** J5 🔢
Camden Rd *EP* CH65 ................... **156** C8
Camden St *BIRK* CH41 ................ **11** J4
*VAUX/LVPD* L3 .......................... **13** J5
Camelford Rd *NG/CROX* L11 ...... **85** M8 🔢
Camelia CI *AIG/SPK* L17 ............. **129** J3
Camelot CI *NEWLW* WA12 .......... **104** B1 🔢
Cameron Av *RUNC* WA7 ............. **18** D8
Cameron Ct *WARRN/WOL* WA2 .. **121** J1
Cameron Cft *CHLYE* PR6 ............ **32** F5 🔢
Cameron PI *WGNW/BIL/O* WN5 .. **68** A5
Cameron Rd *MOR/LEA* CH46 ...... **110** D2
*WDN* WA8 .................................. **16** C4
Cameron St *EHL/KEN* L7 ............ **113** L3
*LEIGH* WN7 ................................ **81**M6
Camm St *WGNE/HIN* WN2 ......... **80** C5
Camomile CI *CHLY/EC* PR7 ........ **32** C5 🔢
Campania St *ALL/GAR* L19 ......... **145** L1
Campbell Crs
*WARRW/BUR* WA5 ..................... **120** B7
Campbell Dr *DV/KA/FCH* L14 ..... **115** G2
Campbell St *BTL* L20 ................... **6** D5
*CLVPS* L1 ................................... **13** G9
*ECCL* WA10 ................................ **8** D4
*WGNW/BIL/O* WN5 .................... **67**M8
Camperdown St *BIRK* CH41 ........ **11** L5
Camphill Rd *WLTN* L25 ............... **131** J6
Campion CI *GOL/RIS/CU* WA3 .... **92** K6 🔢
*RNFD/HAY* WA11 ...................... **89** G6 🔢
Campion Gv *AIMK* WN4 .............. **91** H1
Campion Wy *HUY* L36 ................ **116** B6
Camp Rd *AIMK* WN4 ................... **91** G2
*WLTN* L25 .................................. **131** K4
Campsey Ash *WDN* WA8 ............. **134** B2
Camrose CI *RUNC* WA7 ............... **149** L7
Camsley La *LYMM* WA13 ........... **139** K2
Cam St *WLTN* L25 ....................... **131** J4 🔢
Canaan St *GOL/RIS/CU* WA3 ...... **93** L5
Canada CI *WARRN/WOL* WA2 .... **122** C3
Canal Bank Pygons HI
*MGHL* L31 .................................. **61** L6
Canal Reach *RUNC* WA7 ............ **150** E3
Canalside *EP* CH65 ..................... **20** F7
Canal Side *WARRS* WA4 ............. **136** E8
*WARRS* WA4 .............................. **138** E4
*WARRS* WA4 .............................. **151** H7
Canalside Gv *EV* L5 .................... **96** E8
Canal St *BTL* L20 ........................ **6** C1
*CHLY/EC* PR7 ............................ **44** C7 🔢
*ECCL* WA10 ................................ **8** F7
*NEWLW* WA12 ........................... **104** B3
*RUNC* WA7 ................................ **19** K3
*WGNNW/ST* WN6 ....................... **68** A4
Canal Vw *MGHL* L31 ................... **85** J3
Canberra Av *STHEL* WA9 ............ **102** A6
Canberra La *NG/CROX* L11 ......... **85** L8
Canberra Rd *WGNW/BIL/O* WN5 . **54** C7
Canberra Sq *WARRN/WOL* WA2 .. **121**M3
Candleston CI
*WARRW/BUR* WA5 ..................... **121** G3
Canford Ct *WARRW/BUR* WA5 ... **120** E7
Cannell Ct *RUNC* WA7 ................. **150** C7
Cannell St *WARRW/BUR* WA5 .... **136** F1 🔢
Canning PI *CLVPS* L1 ................... **12** F8
Canning Rd *CHTN/BK* PR9 .......... **25** J6
Canning St *BIRK* CH41 ............... **11** K3
*CLVPS* L1 ................................... **113** H3
*CSBY/WL* L22 ............................ **82** F4 🔢
Canniswood Rd
*RNFD/HAY* WA11 ...................... **90** C8
Cann La *WARRS* WA4 ................. **138** C3
Cannock CI *GTS/LS* CH66 ........... **163** G5
Cannock Gn *MGHL* L31 ............... **72** D4 🔢
Cannon St *EP* CH65 ..................... **156** C8
*STHEL* WA9 ................................ **118** C2
Canon CI *RUNC* WA7 ................... **56** B3
Canon Rd *NPK/KEN* L6 ............... **97** L6
Canons Rd *WARRW/BUR* WA5 .... **120** F7
Canon St *RUNC* WA7 ................... **18** F2

Canon Wilson CI
*RNFD/HAY* WA11 ...................... **90** F7
Canrow La *PR/KW* L34 ................ **86** F8
Cansfield Gv *AIMK* WN4 .............. **91** J1
Cansfield St *ECCL* WA10 ............. **9** H4
*GOL/RIS/CU* WA3 ...................... **92** F4 🔢
Canterbury Av *AIN/FAZ* L10 ....... **85** G3
*FMBY* L37 .................................. **47** H8
*GTS/LS* CH66 ............................. **155** L2
*PR/KW* L34 ................................ **101** G6 🔢
*STHP* PR8 .................................. **35** L2
Canterbury Pk *CALD/MH* L18 ..... **130** E5
Canterbury Rd *RF/TRAN* CH42 ... **128** C4
*WAL/EG* CH44 ........................... **111** L2
*WDN* WA8 .................................. **133** L6
Canterbury St *ALL/GAR* L19 ....... **145** L1
*CHLYE* PR6 ................................ **33** G7
*ECCL* WA10 ................................ **8** D2
*VAUX/LVPD* L3 .......................... **13** K4
*WARRS* WA4 .............................. **15** G8 🔢
Canterbury Wy *NTHTN* L30 ........ **84** B1
*VAUX/LVPD* L3 .......................... **13** L4 🔢
Canter CI *WLT/FAZ* L9 ................ **84** F5 🔢
Cantley CI *RUNC* WA7 ................. **149** M7 🔢
Cantlow Fold *STHP* PR8 .............. **47** J1
Cantsfield St *EHL/KEN* L7 ........... **113** L6
Canvey CI *WAV* L15 ..................... **114** D6
Capenhurst Av
*WARRN/WOL* WA2 ..................... **122** C3
Capenhurst La *CH/BCN* CH1 ....... **162** C6
*EP* CH65 .................................... **163** J2
Cape Rd *WLT/FAZ* L9 .................. **84** E7 🔢
Capesthorne CI *WDN* WA8 .......... **134** A5
Capesthorne Rd
*WARRN/WOL* WA2 ..................... **121**M4
Capilano Pk *ORM* L39 ................. **62** E5
Capper Gv *HUY* L36 .................... **116** A2
Capps St *WGNE/HIN* WN2 .......... **80** D2 🔢
Capricorn Crs *DV/KA/FCH* L14 .... **99** H8
Capricorn Wy *BTL* L20 ................ **6** F3
Captain's La *AIMK* WN4 .............. **91** L2 🔢
*NTHTN* L30 ................................ **83**M5
Caradoc Rd *LITH* L21 ................. **83** H7
Caraway CI *CSBY/BLUN* L23 ...... **71** K8 🔢
Caraway Gv *ECCL* WA10 ............. **8** A3
Carawood CI *WGNNW/ST* WN6 .. **54** F6 🔢
Carbis CI *AIN/FAZ* L10 ................ **85** J7
Carden CI *ANF/KKDL* L4 ............. **97** G6 🔢
*GOL/RIS/CU* WA3 ...................... **122** F1 🔢
Cardeston CI *RUNC* WA7 ............ **161** H2 🔢
Cardiff CI *GTS/LS* CH66 ............. **163** G5
Cardiff St *SKEL* WN8 .................. **64** F4 🔢
Cardigan Av *BIRK* CH41 ............. **11** H5
Cardigan CI *ECCL* WA10 ............. **8** E7
*WARRW/BUR* WA5 ..................... **120** F3
Cardigan Rd *STHP* PR8 .............. **35** H4
*WAL/NB* CH45 ............................ **95** K6
Cardigan St *WAV* L15 ................. **113**M5
Cardigan Wy *NPK/KEN* L6 .......... **113** K1
*NTHTN* L30 ................................ **84** D7 🔢
Cardus Rd *MOR/LEA* CH46 ......... **109** K5 🔢
Cardwell Rd *ALL/GAR* L19 .......... **130** F7
Cardwell St *EHL/KEN* L7 ............. **113** J5
Careless La *WGNE/HIN* WN2 ...... **5**M5
Carey Av *BEB* CH63 .................... **127**M7
Carey CI *WGNS/IIMK* WN3 ......... **78** F3
Carey St *WDN* WA8 ..................... **16** K2
Carfax Rd *NWD/KWIPK* L33 ....... **86** C1 🔢
Cargill Gv *RF/TRAN* CH42 .......... **128** D5
Carham Rd *HOY* CH47 ................ **108** E7
Carisbrooke CI *WKBY* CH48 ....... **124** E4
Carisbrooke Dr *CHTN/BK* PR9 .... **25** H4
Carisbrooke PI *ANF/KKDL* L4 ..... **97** H4 🔢
Carkington Rd *WLTN* L25 ........... **131** L4
Carland CI *NG/CROX* L11 ........... **85** K7
Carlaw Rd *RF/TRAN* CH42 ......... **127** J3
Carleen CI *AIG/SPK* L17 ............. **129** K3
Carleton St *AIMK* WN4 ............... **91** J1 🔢
*HOR/BR* BL6 .............................. **57**M3
*NSTN* CH64 ............................... **152** E3
Carleton Crs *GTS/LS* CH66 ......... **156** A5
Carleton Gv *WGNE/HIN* WN2 ..... **81** H1 🔢
Carleton La *CLB/OSW/ST* L13 .... **114** C1
*HOY* CH47 .................................. **108** E5
Carleton Rd *BEB* CH63 ............... **143** K1
*GOL/RIS/CU* WA3 ...................... **92** F4
*RF/TRAN* CH42 .......................... **127** L1
*STHP* PR8 .................................. **34** E7
*WAL/NB* CH45 ............................ **95** K5
Carlton St *ECCL* WA10 ............... **8** D6
*PR/KW* L34 ................................ **100** F7 🔢
*VAUX/LVPD* L3 .......................... **12** C1
*WARRS* WA4 .............................. **137** L5 🔢
*WDN* WA8 .................................. **16** B3
*WGNS/IIMK* WN3 ....................... **4** D8
Carlyle Crs *GTS/LS* CH66 ........... **163** G1
Carlyle Gv *LEIGH* WN7 ............... **132** A5 🔢
Carlyon Wy *HLWD* L26 ............... **132** A5 🔢
Carmarthen CI
*WARRW/BUR* WA5 ..................... **120** F3
Carmel CI *ORM* L39 ..................... **50** C8
Carmel Ct *WDN* WA8 ................... **134** D1 🔢
Carmelite Crs *ECCL* WA10 .......... **88** C6 🔢
Carmichael Av
*GR/UP/WCH* CH49 ..................... **125**M3
Carnaby CI *HUY* L36 ................... **116** C5 🔢
Carnarvon Rd *STHP* PR8 ............. **35** H4
*WLT/FAZ* L9 ............................... **97** H2
Carnarvon St *STHEL* WA9 .......... **101** M6
Carnatic Rd *AIG/SPK* L17 ........... **130** A2 🔢

CALD/MH L18 .......... 130 A2
Carnation Rd WLT/FAZ L9 ..... 97 K1
Carnegie Av CSBY/BLUN L23.... 82 F2
Carnegie Crs STHEL WA9 ..... 103 G5
Carnegie Dr AIMK WN4 ..... 79 J8
Carnegie Rd CLB/OSW/ST L13 .. 114 A1
Carnforth Av KKBY L32 ..... 86 B4
Carnforth Cl BIRK CH41 ..... 10 F8
   WD/CROXPK L12 ..... 98 E4
Carnforth Rd CALD/MH L18 .. 130 E3
Carno St WAV L15 ..... 114 A5
Carnoustie Cl MOR/LEA CH46 .. 109 K4
   WD/CROXPK L12 ..... 99 H7
Carnoustie Gv RAIN/WH WA11.... 90 C8
Carnsdale Rd MOR/LEA CH46.... 110 B5
Carol Dr HES CH60 ..... 141 L5
Carole Cl STHEL WA9 ..... 103 G7
Carolina St ALL/GAR L19 ..... 145 L1
Caroline Pl CL/PREN CH43 ..... 10 C7
Caroline St WDN WA8 ..... 16 E6
   WGN WN1 ..... 5 L4
   WGNS/IIMK WN3 ..... 4 E6
Carol St WARRS WA4 ..... 15 J9
Caronia St ALL/GAR L19 ..... 145 L1
Carpathia St ALL/GAR L19 ..... 145 L1
Carpenter Gv WARRN/WOL WA2 ..... 122 C4
Carpenter's La WKBY CH48.... 124 D3
Carpenters Rw CLVPS L1 ..... 112 F5
Carradon Dr WCNNW/ST WN6 .. 56 A4
Carraway Rd NG/CROX L11..... 85 K7
Carr Bridge Rd
   GR/UP/WCH CH49 ..... 126 D1
Carr Cl NG/CROX L11 ..... 98 D3
Carr Common Rd
   WGNE/HIN WN2 ..... 81 M2
Carr Cft LITH L21 ..... 83 K2
Carrfield Av CSBY/BLUN L23.... 83 J2
Carr Ga MOR/LEA CH46 ..... 109 K6
Carr Hey MOR/LEA CH46 ..... 109 K6
Carr Hey Cl
   GR/UP/WCH CH49 ..... 126 E3
Carr House La HTWN L38 ..... 71 G1
   MOR/LEA CH46 ..... 109 K5
   WGNNW/ST WN6 ..... 42 B5
Carrick Dr EP CH65 ..... 163 K3
Carrickmore Av CALD/MH L18 .. 130 C3
Carrington Cl GOL/RIS/CU WA3 .. 122 E1
Carrington Rd CHLY/EC PR7 .. 32 D6
   CHLY/EC PR7 ..... 44 B6
   WAL/NB CH45 ..... 95 K7
Carrington St BIRK CH41 ..... 10 A1
Carr La BRSC L40 ..... 29 K6
   BRSC L40 ..... 52 D2
   CHLY/EC PR7 ..... 32 F8
   GOL/RIS/CU WA3 ..... 93 J6
   HOY CH47 ..... 108 D7
   HUY L36 ..... 115 L4
   LEY/BBR PR5 ..... 29 K5
   MGHL L31 ..... 61 H8
   NG/CROX L11 ..... 98 B3
   PR/KW L34 ..... 100 D8
   SPK/HALE L24 ..... 147 M3
   STHP PR8 ..... 35 H6
   WGNS/IIMK WN3 ..... 79 J2
   WKBY CH48 ..... 108 F8
Carr La East NG/CROX L11..... 98 D3
Carr Meadow Hey NTHTN L30.... 83 L3
Carr Mill Crs WGNW/BIL/O WN5 .... 90 A1
Carr Mill Rd RNFD/HAY WA11 .... 89 L5
   WGNW/BIL/O WN5 ..... 90 A2
Carr Moss La ORM L39 ..... 48 E2
   ORM L39 ..... 49 K5
Carrock Rd PS/BROM CH62 .. 144 A3
Carroll Crs ORM L39 ..... 51 H6
Carrow Cl MOR/LEA CH46 .. 109 K6
Carr Rd BTL L20 ..... 83 M6
   HOR/BR BL6 ..... 45 K8
Carr's Crs FMBY L37 ..... 58 F4
Carr's Crs West FMBY L37 ..... 58 F4
Carr Side La HTWN L38 ..... 71 J2
Carr St CHLYE PR6 ..... 33 G4
   ECCL WA10 ..... 8 C1
   LEIGH WN7 ..... 81 L8
   WGNE/HIN WN2 ..... 69 M7
Carruthers St VAUX/LVPD L3 .. 12 E3
Carrville Wy WD/CROXPK L12.... 99 J3
Carrwood Pk STHP PR8 ..... 35 K2
Carsdale Rd CALD/MH L18 .. 114 C8
Carsgoe Rd HOY CH47 ..... 108 E7
Carsington Rd NG/CROX L11.... 98 C3
Carstairs Rd NPK/KEN L6 .. 113 L1
Carsthorne Rd HOY CH47 ..... 108 E7
Car St WGNE/HIN WN2 ..... 80 C4
Cartbridge La HLWD L26 .. 132 B4
Carter Av RNFD/HAY WA11 .... 76 C8
The Carters
   GR/UP/WCH CH49 ..... 125 L1
   NTHTN L30 ..... 84 C1
Carter St TOX L8 ..... 113 H7
   WGNS/IIMK WN3 ..... 5 J7
Carterton Rd HOY CH47 ..... 108 E7
Cartier Cl WARRW/BUR WA5 .. 120 E4
Cartmel Av ECCL WA10 ..... 89 G6
   MGHL L31 ..... 73 G3
   WARRN/WOL WA2 ..... 121 L2
   WGN WN1 ..... 68 D2
Cartmel Cl BIRK CH41 ..... 10 F8
   HUY L36 ..... 115 M1
   STHP PR8 ..... 36 B2
   WARRW/BUR WA5 ..... 121 G3
Cartmel Dr FMBY L37 ..... 59 K3
   GTS/LS CH66 ..... 163 H6
   MOR/LEA CH46 ..... 110 A6
   RAIN/WH L35 ..... 117 J1
   WD/CROXPK L12 ..... 98 E4
Cartmell Cl RUNC WA7 ..... 149 K7
Cartmel Rd HUY L36 ..... 115 M1
Cartmel Wy HUY L36 ..... 115 L1
Cartridge La WARRS WA4 .. 138 F7
Cartwright Gv LEIGH WN7 .. 81 M4
Cartwright St WAV L14 ..... 19 L4
   WARRW/BUR WA5 ..... 121 G7
Carvers Brow LEY/BBR PR5 .. 29 K4
Carver St VAUX/LVPD L3 .. 13 L4
Caryl Gv TOX L8 ..... 129 G1
Caryl St TOX L8 ..... 112 F8

Case Gv RAIN/WH L35 ..... 101 G8
Case Rd RNFD/HAY WA11 .... 90 F7
Cashel Rd BIRK CH41 ..... 111 K3
Cashmore Dr WGNE/HIN WN2 .. 80 F1
Caspian Pl BTL L20 ..... 7 H4
Caspian Rd ANF/KKDL L4 ..... 97 K1
Cassia St WLT/FAZ L9 ..... 97 K1
Cassino Rd HUY L36 ..... 115 M2
Cassio St BTL L20 ..... 7 L7
Cassley Rd SPK/HALE L24 ..... 147 J2
Cassville Rd CALD/MH L18 .. 114 C7
Castell Gv ECCL WA10 ..... 8 E5
Casterton Av CHLY/EC PR7 .. 31 L3
Casterton St EHL/KEN L7 .. 113 L5
Castle Av STHEL WA9 ..... 103 G2
Castle Cl MOR/LEA CH46 ..... 110 C2
Castle Crs HOR/BR BL6 ..... 45 L8
Castlecroft Av HOR/BR BL6 ..... 57 M3
Castle Dr CHLY/EC PR7 ..... 44 A7
   EP CH65 ..... 163 J2
   FMBY L37 ..... 59 H4
   HES CH60 ..... 141 H5
Castlefield Av South RUNC WA7 .. 150 B4
Castlefield Cl WD/CROXPK L12 .. 98 C5
Castlefield Rd WD/CROXPK L12.. 98 C6
Castlefields Av East RUNC WA7.. 150 C4
Castlefields Av North
   RUNC WA7 ..... 150 C3
Castlefields Av South
   RUNC WA7 ..... 150 C5
Castle Fields Est
   MOR/LEA CH46 ..... 110 B1
Castleford Ri MOR/LEA CH46 .. 110 B2
Castleford St WAV L15 ..... 114 C6
Castlegate Gv WD/CROXPK L12 .. 98 C6
Castlegrange Cl
   MOR/LEA CH46 ..... 110 A1
Castleheath Cl
   MOR/LEA CH46 ..... 110 A2
Castle HI CLVP L2 ..... 12 E7
   NEWLW WA12 ..... 105 G1
Castle House La CHLY/EC PR7 .... 44 A7
Castle La BRSC L40 ..... 51 M7
Castle Ri RUNC WA7 ..... 149 M3
Castle Rd RUNC WA7 ..... 150 B5
   WAL/NB CH45 ..... 95 J7
Castlesite Rd WD/CROXPK L12.. 98 D6
Castle St BIRK CH41 ..... 11 L5
   CHLY/EC PR7 ..... 32 F6
   CHTN/BK PR9 ..... 3 H3
   CLVP L2 ..... 12 E7
   WDN WA8 ..... 17 J2
   WLTN L25 ..... 131 H3
Castleton Dr NTHTN L30 ..... 84 D1
Castleton Wy WGNS/IIMK WN3 .. 78 E3
Castletown Cl CHLDW L16........ 115 G5
Castleview Rd WD/CROXPK L12.. 98 D6
Castle Wk CHLYE PR8 ..... 2 E6
Castleway North
   MOR/LEA CH46 ..... 110 C1
Castleway South
   MOR/LEA CH46 ..... 110 C2
Castlewood Rd NPK/KEN L6 .. 97 K8
Castner Av RUNC WA7 ..... 18 C9
Castor St NPK/KEN L6 ..... 97 K8
Catchdale Moss La ECCL WA10.... 88 A4
Catford Cl WDN WA8 ..... 133 L4
Catford Gn SPK/HALE L24 .. 147 H2
Catfoss Cl WARRN/WOL WA2 .. 122 A4
Catharine's La ORM L39 ..... 63 H3
Catharine St TOX L8 ..... 113 H6
Cathcart St BIRK CH41 ..... 11 G4
Cathedral Ga CLVPS L1 ..... 113 G5
Cathedral Rd NPK/KEN L6 .. 97 L7
Cathedral Wk VAUX/LVPD L3 .. 13 K8
Catherine St BIRK CH41 ..... 11 G6
   CHLY/EC PR7 ..... 32 E7
   LITH L21 ..... 83 K7
   WARRW/BUR WA5 ..... 14 B2
   WDN WA8 ..... 16 D7
Catherine St East HOR/BR BL6.... 45 K8
Catherine St West HOR/BR BL6.. 45 J8
Catherine Ter WGN WN1 ..... 5 J4
Catherine Wy NEWLW WA12 .. 104 D3
   RNFD/HAY WA11 ..... 90 B7
Catkin Rd HLWD L26 ..... 131 M3
Caton Cl CHTN/BK PR9 ..... 25 H1
Catonfield Rd CALD/MH L18.. 114 F8
Cat Tail La STHP PR8 ..... 37 G4
Catterall Av STHEL WA9 ..... 102 F7
   WARRN/WOL WA2 ..... 121 M3
Catterick Cl HLWD L26 ..... 132 B5
Catterick Fold STHP PR8 ..... 36 B2
Caulfield Cl GR/UP/WCH CH49 .. 126 A2
Caunce Av CHTN/BK PR9 ..... 23 J7
   GOL/RIS/CU WA3 ..... 92 C6
   RNFD/HAY WA11 ..... 90 D7
Caunce Rd WGN WN1 ..... 5 J3
Caunce's Rd CHTN/BK PR9 .. 26 F7
Caunce St WGN WN1 ..... 5 H3
Causeway Av WARRS WA4 .. 137 L2
Causeway Cl PS/BROM CH62 .. 128 D7
Causeway La BRSC L40 ..... 39 K4
   FMBY L37 ..... 60 D4
The Causeway CHLYE PR6 .. 33 G5
   CHTN/BK PR9 ..... 22 E8
   PS/BROM CH62 ..... 128 D8
   WD/CROXPK L12 ..... 114 F1
Cavan Rd NG/CROX L11 ..... 98 A5
Cavell Cl WLTN L25 ..... 131 L4
Cavell Dr EP CH65 ..... 163 J1
Cavendish Av GOL/RIS/CU WA3 .. 107 G8
Cavendish Cl WAV L15 ..... 114 C6
Cavendish Dr RF/TRAN CH42 .. 127 M4
   WGNS/IIMK WN3 ..... 78 F3
   WLT/FAZ L9 ..... 97 J2
Cavendish Farm Rd RUNC WA7.. 149 H8
Cavendish Gdns EP CH65 ..... 163 J1
Cavendish Rd BIRK CH41 ..... 10 C3
   CSBY/BLUN L23 ..... 82 E2
   STHP PR8 ..... 35 H2
   WAL/NB CH45 ..... 95 M4
Cavendish St CHLYE PR6 ..... 33 G6
   RUNC WA7 ..... 18 F4
Caversham Cl WARRS WA4 .. 137 M6
Cawdor St RUNC WA7 ..... 18 E2
   TOX L8 ..... 113 J7

WARRS WA4 ..... 137 L5
WGNW/BIL/O WN5 ..... 68 B7
Cawfield Av WDN WA8 ..... 133 M4
Cawley Av GOL/RIS/CU WA3 .. 107 G1
Cawley St RUNC WA7 ..... 19 G6
Cawood Cl GTS/LS CH66 ..... 155 L8
Cawthorne Av KKBY L32 ..... 86 A6
   WARRS WA4 ..... 138 C3
Cawthorne Cl KKBY L32 ..... 86 A5
Cawthorne Wk KKBY L32 ..... 86 A5
Caxton Cl CL/PREN CH43 ..... 110 E7
   WDN WA8 ..... 133 L2
   WGNS/IIMK WN3 ..... 79 H3
Caxton Rd RAIN/WH L35 ..... 118 A4
Cazneau St VAUX/LVPD L3 .. 13 H2
C Ct AIMK WN4 ..... 91 K3
Cearns Rd CL/PREN CH43 ..... 10 B8
Cecil Av WGNW/BIL/O WN5 .. 68 C3
Cecil Dr ECCL WA10 ..... 88 C8
Cecil Rd LITH L21 ..... 83 H7
   PS/BROM CH62 ..... 128 D5
   RF/TRAN CH42 ..... 127 K3
   WAL/EG CH44 ..... 111 J1
Cecil St STHEL WA9 ..... 103 H6
   WAV L15 ..... 113 M5
   WGN WN1 ..... 5 K4
   WGNE/HIN WN2 ..... 80 A1
Cedab Rd EP CH65 ..... 20 D3
Cedar Av BEB CH63 ..... 143 G1
   CHLY/EC PR7 ..... 31 L3
   GOL/RIS/CU WA3 ..... 93 H6
   GTS/LS CH66 ..... 155 L7
   RUNC WA7 ..... 19 M9
   RUNC WA7 ..... 161 J1
   WDN WA8 ..... 134 D2
   WGNE/HIN WN2 ..... 81 H2
   WGNNW/ST WN6 ..... 56 B5
Cedar Cl CALD/MH L18 ..... 130 F2
   RAIN/WH L35 ..... 117 G1
Cedar Ct GOL/RIS/CU WA3 .. 107 H3
Cedar Crs HUY L36 ..... 115 M4
   NEWLW WA12 ..... 104 F3
   ORM L39 ..... 62 E1
Cedardale Dr GTS/LS CH66 .. 163 H4
Cedardale Pk WDN WA8 ..... 135 G1
Cedardale Rd WLT/FAZ L9 .. 97 J1
Cedar Dr FMBY L37 ..... 58 E4
Cedar Gv AIMK WN4 ..... 78 F8
   CSBY/WL L22 ..... 82 F3
   MGHL L31 ..... 72 F7
   NSTN CH64 ..... 153 H5
   RNFD/HAY WA11 ..... 91 G6
   SKEL WN8 ..... 65 G4
   TOX L8 ..... 113 L7
   WARR WA1 ..... 122 C6
   WARRS WA4 ..... 137 M2
   WGNW/BIL/O WN5 ..... 67 H7
Cedar Rd CHLYE PR6 ..... 32 F3
   RAIN/WH L35 ..... 116 F2
   WARRW/BUR WA5 ..... 120 B7
   WLT/FAZ L9 ..... 84 D7
The Cedars CHLY/EC PR7...... 30 D6
   CHLY/EC PR7 ..... 43 K1
   MOR/LEA CH46 ..... 109 L6
   WD/CROXPK L12 ..... 99 H2
Cedar St BIRK CH41 ..... 11 G7
   BTL L20 ..... 7 H3
   ECCL WA10 ..... 8 A6
   NEWLW WA12 ..... 104 E3
   STHP PR8 ..... 3 K9
Cedarway HES CH60 ..... 141 M8
Cedarways WARRS WA4 .. 137 M8
Cedarwood Cl
   GR/UP/WCH CH49 ..... 125 K1
Cedarwood Ct HUY L36 ..... 116 A5
Celandine Wk
   WGNS/IIMK WN3 ..... 78 D1
Celebration Dr NPK/KEN L6 .. 97 L8
Celedine Cl WAV L15 ..... 114 B5
Celia St BTL L20 ..... 7 J9
Celtic Rd HOY CH47 ..... 109 G4
Celtic St TOX L8 ..... 113 J7
Celt St NPK/KEN L6 ..... 113 L1
Cemetery Rd STHP PR8 ..... 3 H9
   WGNS/IIMK WN3 ..... 80 A1
Cemetery Vw CHLY/EC PR7.... 44 B7
Central Av EP CH65 ..... 20 C6
Central Dr RNFD/HAY WA11 .. 76 B6
   RNFD/HAY WA11 ..... 90 D7
   WD/CROXPK L12 ..... 98 D8
   WGNNW/ST WN6 ..... 55 K7
Central Avnue STHP PR8 ..... 35 H5
Central Dr RNFD/HAY WA11 .. 89 J1
   RNFD/HAY WA11 ..... 90 D7
   WD/CROXPK L12 ..... 98 D8
   WGNNW/ST WN6 ..... 55 K7
Central Expy RUNC WA7 ..... 149 M7
Central Park Av WAL/EG CH44 .. 111 L1
Central Park Wy WGN WN1 .... 5 G1
Central Rd PS/BROM CH62 .. 128 D6
   WARRS WA4 ..... 15 C9
Central Sq MGHL L31 ..... 72 F3
Central St ECCL WA10 ..... 9 G3
Central Wy NEWLW WA12 .. 105 G3
   SPK/HALE L24 ..... 147 G3
   WARRN/WOL WA2 ..... 14 E4
Centre Ct LEIGH WN7 ..... 93 K4
Centre Park Sq WARR WA1 .... 14 D8
Centreville Rd CALD/MH L18 .. 114 C7
Centre Wy HUY L36 ..... 116 A3
Centurion Cl
   GOL/RIS/CU WA3 ..... 122 F1
   HOY CH47 ..... 109 G4
Centurion Dr HOY CH47 ..... 109 G4
Ceres St BTL L20 ..... 7 G3
Cestrian Dr PEN/TH CH61 .. 126 C8
Chadlow Rd KKBY L32 ..... 86 B6
Chadwell Rd NWD/KWIPK L33.... 86 B1
Chadwick Av GOL/RIS/CU WA3.. 106 D6
Chadwick Pl GOL/RIS/CU WA3 .. 107 G8
Chadwick Rd RNFD/HAY WA11.... 89 L6
   RUNC WA7 ..... 150 A2
Chadwick St MOR/LEA CH46 .. 110 A5
   VAUX/LVPD L3 ..... 12 D3

WGNS/IIMK WN3 ..... 4 C7
WD/CROXPK L12 ..... 99 H4
Chaffinch Cl GOL/RIS/CU WA3 .. 123 H2
Chaffinch Gld HLWD L26 .. 132 A4
Chainhurst Cl NTHLY L27..... 115 M7
Chalbury Cl WGNE/HIN WN2 .. 80 F1
Chalcombe Av GTS/LS CH66 .. 155 L8
Chalfield Cl GTS/LS CH66 .. 155 L8
Chalfont Gv WARRS WA4 .. 138 C3
Chalfont Rd CALD/MH L18 .. 130 F4
Chalfont Wy STBRV L28 ..... 99 K6
Chalgrave Cl WDN WA8 .. 135 G2
Chalkwell Dr HES CH60 ..... 141 L6
Challenge Wy
   WGNW/BIL/O WN5 ..... 67 L4
Challis St BIRK CH41 ..... 111 G4
Challoner Cl HUY L36 ..... 116 B5
Chaloner Gv ALL/GAR L19 .. 130 B6
Chaloner St VAUX/LVPD L3 .. 112 F6
Chalon Wy ECCL WA10 ..... 9 H6
Chalon Wy West ECCL WA10.... 9 G6
Chamberlain St BIRK CH41 .. 11 K9
   ECCL WA10 ..... 8 A6
   WAL/EG CH44 ..... 111 J3
Chambres Rd STHP PR8 ..... 3 J7
Chambres Rd North STHP PR8.... 3 M6
Chancellor Rd RUNC WA7 .. 135 M8
Chancel St ANF/KKDL L4 .. 97 G6
Chancery La STHEL WA9 ..... 103 G2
Chancery Rd CHLY/EC PR7.... 32 C4
Chandler Wy GOL/RIS/CU WA3.. 93 G5
Chandley Cl STHP PR8 ..... 34 C8
Chandos St EHL/KEN L7 ..... 113 K4
Changford Rd NWD/KWIPK L33.. 86 C2
Channell Rd NPK/KEN L6 .. 113 L2
Channel Reach
   CSBY/BLUN L23 ..... 82 D2
Channel Rd CSBY/BLUN L23 .. 82 D2
Chantler Av WARRS WA4 .. 15 M7
Chantrell Rd WKBY CH48 .. 125 G3
Chantry Cl CL/PREN CH43 .. 110 E7
Chantry Wk AIMK WN4 ..... 79 H8
   HES CH60 ..... 141 J7
Chapel Av WLT/FAZ L9 ..... 84 C8
Chapel Cl WGNS/IIMK WN3 .... 5 H7
Chapel Cross Rd
   WARRN/WOL WA2 ..... 122 C3
Chapelfields FROD/HEL WA6 .. 160 C5
Chapel Gdns EV L5 ..... 96 F5
Chapelhill Rd MOR/LEA CH46 .. 110 B5
Chapelhouse Wk FMBY L37 .. 59 J2
Chapel La BRSC L40 ..... 52 A3
   CHLY/EC PR7 ..... 43 H5
   CHTN/BK PR9 ..... 23 K7
   ECCL WA10 ..... 101 K1
   FMBY L37 ..... 59 H2
   KIRK/FR/WA PR4 ..... 27 K8
   MGHL L31 ..... 85 J1
   NTHTN L30 ..... 72 C8
   RAIN/WH L35 ..... 118 B3
   SKEL WN8 ..... 53 M4
   WARRS WA4 ..... 137 L5
   WARRW/BUR WA5 ..... 104 B7
   WDN WA8 ..... 117 L8
   WGNS/IIMK WN3 ..... 4 F7
Chapel Ms EP CH65 ..... 20 A6
   ORM L39 ..... 63 G1
Chapel Pl AIMK WN4 ..... 91 K2
   ALL/GAR L19 ..... 130 E7
Chapel Rd ALL/GAR L19 ..... 130 E7
   HOY CH47 ..... 108 D5
   NPK/KEN L6 ..... 97 L7
   WARRW/BUR WA5 ..... 136 A2
Chapel St AIMK WN4 ..... 91 K2
   CHLY/EC PR7 ..... 32 F6
   CHLY/EC PR7 ..... 43 G4
   CHLY/EC PR7 ..... 44 B7
   ECCL WA10 ..... 8 F1
   HOR/BR BL6 ..... 57 M3
   NEWLW WA12 ..... 104 D2
   ORM L39 ..... 51 H8
   PR/KW L34 ..... 100 F7
   RNFD/HAY WA11 ..... 90 F7
   STHP PR8 ..... 3 G4
   VAUX/LVPD L3 ..... 12 D7
   WDN WA8 ..... 16 C6
   WGNE/HIN WN2 ..... 69 J2
   WGNE/HIN WN2 ..... 69 M8
   WGNE/HIN WN2 ..... 80 C3
   WGNE/HIN WN2 ..... 81 G4
   WGNS/IIMK WN3 ..... 4 E6
   WGNS/IIMK WN3 ..... 5 H8
   WGNS/IIMK WN3 ..... 67 K7
Chapel Ter BTL L20 ..... 6 E6
Chapel Vw RNFD/HAY WA11 .. 89 H1
Chapel Wy CHLY/EC PR7 ..... 43 H4
Chapel Yd WAV L15 ..... 114 C6
Chapman Cl TOX L8 ..... 113 G8
   WDN WA8 ..... 133 M1
Chapman Gv PR/KW L34 ..... 101 G4
Chardstock Dr WLTN L25 ..... 131 L1
Charity St LEIGH WN7 ..... 81 L8
Charlecombe St RF/TRAN CH42.. 11 G9
Charlecote St TOX L8 ..... 129 H2
Charles Av STHP PR8 ..... 35 G7
   WARRW/BUR WA5 ..... 120 B7
Charles Berrington Rd
   WAV L15 ..... 114 C7
Charlesbye Av ORM L39 ..... 51 J7
Charles Rd HOY CH47 ..... 108 D7
Charles St BIRK CH41 ..... 11 G5
   ECCL WA10 ..... 9 H4
   GOL/RIS/CU WA3 ..... 92 C4
   WDN WA8 ..... 16 D3
   WGN WN1 ..... 4 F1
Charleston Cl GTS/LS CH66 .. 162 F2
Charleston Rd TOX L8 ..... 129 H1
Charlesville CL/PREN CH43 .. 10 C8
Charles Wk DV/KA/FCH L14.... 115 H2
Charlesworth Av
   WGNE/HIN WN2 ..... 81 H1
Charlesworth Cl MGHL L31 .. 61 K8
Charley Wood Rd
   NWD/KWIPK L33 ..... 86 D4
Charlotte Dr WGNS/IIMK WN3 .. 78 F1
Charlotte Rd WAL/EG CH44.... 95 M8

Charlotte's Meadow BEB CH63 .. 143 J1
Charlton Cl RUNC WA7 ..... 150 C6
Charlton Pl CLB/OSW/ST L13.. 114 C4
Charlton Rd CLB/OSW/ST L13.. 114 C4
Charlton St WARRS WA4 .. 138 B2
Charlwood Av HUY L36 ..... 116 A4
Charlwood Cl CL/PREN CH43 .. 110 E7
Charminster Cl
   WARRW/BUR WA5 ..... 120 D8
Charmouth Cl
   WD/CROXPK L12 ..... 99 G2
Charnley's La CHTN/BK PR9.... 23 G5
Charnock Av NEWLW WA12 .. 104 D2
Charnock Back La CHLYE PR6.... 33 K7
Charnock Brow Preston Rd
   CHLY/EC PR7 ..... 31 L7
Charnock Rd GOL/RIS/CU WA3.. 107 H2
   WLT/FAZ L9 ..... 97 M2
Charnock St CHLYE PR6...... 32 F6
   WGNE/HIN WN2 ..... 80 D4
Charnwood Cl
   GOL/RIS/CU WA3 ..... 107 K8
Charnwood Rd HUY L36 ..... 115 K2
Charnwood St STHEL WA9 .. 103 G2
Charter Av WARRW/BUR WA5 .. 121 J5
Charter Crs GTS/LS CH66 .. 163 G2
Charterhouse Dr AIN/FAZ L10 .. 85 G3
Charterhouse Rd
   WGNS/IIMK WN3 ..... 5 H8
   WLTN L25 ..... 131 K4
Charter La CHLY/EC PR7 .. 42 F1
Chartmount Wy WLTN L25 .. 131 K1
Chartwell Gv HLWD L26 .. 132 C4
Chartwell Rd STHP PR8 ..... 34 D7
Chase Cl STHP PR8 ..... 2 D9
Chase Dr GTS/LS CH66 ..... 163 G3
Chase Heys CHTN/BK PR9 .. 25 H4
Chaser Cl WLT/FAZ L9 ..... 84 E5
The Chase BEB CH63 ..... 143 L8
   HUY L36 ..... 116 B5
Chase Wy EV L5 ..... 13 K2
   GTS/LS CH66 ..... 162 F3
Chatburn Av GOL/RIS/CU WA3 .. 92 E4
Chatburn Ct
   GOL/RIS/CU WA3 ..... 107 H3
Chatburn Wk TOX L8 ..... 129 H1
Chater Cl RAIN/WH L35 ..... 101 J7
Chatfield Dr GOL/RIS/CU WA3 .. 123 G3
Chatham Cl LITH L21 ..... 83 H6
Chatham Pl CHLYE PR6 ..... 33 G5
   EHL/KEN L7 ..... 113 K4
Chatham Rd RF/TRAN CH42 .. 128 C3
Chatham St WGN WN1 ..... 5 J5
   WGNE/HIN WN2 ..... 69 J3
Chatsworth Av
   GOL/RIS/CU WA3 ..... 107 H1
   WAL/EG CH44 ..... 111 L1
   WGNE/HIN WN2 ..... 80 B1
   WLT/FAZ L9 ..... 84 B8
Chatsworth Cl AIMK WN4 ..... 91 H1
   CHLY/EC PR7 ..... 32 D5
   GTS/LS CH66 ..... 155 L8
Chatsworth Ct CHLYE PR6 .. 44 B4
Chatsworth Dr EHL/KEN L7 .. 113 K5
   WDN WA8 ..... 133 L2
Chatsworth Rd PEN/TH CH61 .. 126 B8
   RAIN/WH L35 ..... 117 K1
   RF/TRAN CH42 ..... 128 C3
   STHP PR8 ..... 34 C7
Chatsworth St
   WGNW/BIL/O WN5 ..... 67 L8
Chatteris Cl WGNE/HIN WN2 .. 81 G1
Chatteris Pk RUNC WA7 ..... 151 G3
Chatterton Dr RUNC WA7 .. 151 G5
Chatterton Rd DV/KA/FCH L14.... 114 E1
Chatwell Gdns WARRS WA4 .. 138 B3
Chaucer Cl CHLY/EC PR7 .. 30 D7
Chaucer Dr WD/CROXPK L12 .. 99 H3
Chaucer Gv LEIGH WN7 ..... 81 L5
Chaucer Pl WARRS WA4 .. 138 B1
   WGN WN1 ..... 68 E2
   WGNE/HIN WN2 ..... 80 D4
Chaucer Rd ECCL WA10 ..... 88 F7
Chaucer St BTL L20 ..... 6 D2
   RUNC WA7 ..... 19 G5
   VAUX/LVPD L3 ..... 13 H3
Cheadle Av CLB/OSW/ST L13.. 114 B2
Cheam Av CHLY/EC PR7 ..... 32 F7
Cheapside CHLY/EC PR7 .. 32 E6
   CLVP L2 ..... 12 F5
   FMBY L37 ..... 59 J3
Cheapside Aly CLVP L2 ..... 12 F6
Cheddar Cl WLTN L25 ..... 131 H3
Cheddar Gv KKBY L32 ..... 86 A6
   WARRW/BUR WA5 ..... 104 B6
Cheddon Wy PEN/TH CH61 .. 141 G1
Chedworth Dr WDN WA8 .. 133 L1
Chedworth Dr DV/KA/FCH L14 .. 115 G1
Cheetham Gv
   WGNS/IIMK WN3 ..... 68 B8
Chelburn Cl WGNE/HIN WN2.... 81 G4
Cheldon Rd NG/CROX L11 .. 98 C3
Chelford Av GOL/RIS/CU WA3.. 92 F6
Chelford Cl CL/PREN CH43 .. 110 E6
   WGNS/IIMK WN3 ..... 79 H3
Chellowdene CSBY/BLUN L23 .. 71 J7
Chelmarsh Av AIMK WN4 ..... 91 L2
Chelmorton Gv WGNS/IIMK WN3.. 78 E3
Chelmsford Dr WGNS/IIMK WN3 .. 79 J1
Chelmsford Gv CHLY/EC PR7 .. 32 D6
Chelmsford Ms WGN WN1 .. 68 E3
Chelmsford Pl CHLY/EC PR7 .. 32 D7
Chelsea Ct WD/CROXPK L12 .. 99 G3
Chelsea Rd LITH L21 ..... 83 K7
   WLT/FAZ L9 ..... 84 C7
Cheltenham Av AIG/SPK L17.. 113 M8
   WGNS/IIMK WN3 ..... 5 H8
Cheltenham Crs HUY L36 .. 115 M4
   RUNC WA7 ..... 149 K7
Cheltenham Rd EP CH65 ..... 20 E8
   WAL/NB CH45 ..... 95 G7
Cheltenham St
   WGNE/HIN WN2 ..... 69 H3

178 Che - Cli

Cheltenham Wy STHP PR8 36 B1
Chelwood Av CHLDW L16 115 H5
Chemical St NEWLW WA12 104 D2 3
Chemistry Rd SPK/HALE L24 131 L8
Chenotrie Gdns CL/PREN CH43 110 F8
Chepstow Av WAL/EG CH44 111 L1 6
Chepstow Cl WARRW/BUR WA5 121 G2
Chepstow St ANF/KKDL L4 7 M8
Chequer Cl SKEL WN8 66 B8
Chequer La SKEL WN8 66 B7
Chequers Gdns ALL/GAR L19 130 B5
Chequers St WGN WN1 4 D4
Cheriton Av WKBY CH48 124 F3
Cheriton Cl HLWD L26 132 A5 2
Chermside Rd AIG/SPK L17 130 A4 1
Cherry Av ANF/KKDL L4 97 K4
Cherrybank WAL/EG CH44 111 K3
Cherry Blossom Rd
RUNC WA7 150 B8 1
Cherry Cl ANF/KKDL L4 97 K4 1
NEWLW WA12 104 B1 2
NSTN CH64 153 L5
Cherry Cnr LYMM WA13 139 J7
Cherrydale Rd CALD/MH L18 130 C1
Cherryfield Crs KKBY L32 86 A3
Cherryfield Dr KKBY L32 85 M3
Cherry Gn ORM L39 62 D4 1
Cherry Gv BRSC L40 39 G7
GTS/LS CH66 163 J4
WGNNW/ST WN6 68 B2
Cherry La ANF/KKDL L4 97 M5
LYMM WA13 139 K5
Cherry Rd STHP PR8 47 M3
Cherrysutton WDN WA8 133 K2
Cherry Tree Av LYMM WA13 139 M3 2
RUNC WA7 19 L7
WARRW/BUR WA5 136 B1
Cherry Tree Cl RAIN/WH L35 116 F2 1
RNFD/HAY WA11 90 C8 1
Cherry Tree Dr STHEL WA9 103 J3
Cherry Tree Gv CHLYE PR6 32 E2
LEIGH WN7 81 M7 1
Cherry Tree La ORM L39 62 D4
RNFD/HAY WA11 89 J3
Cherry Tree Rd GOL/RIS/CU WA3 93 H5
HUY L36 116 A5
MOR/LEA CH46 110 B6
Cherry V WLTN L25 131 K2
Cherry Vw NWD/KWIPK L33 74 B8
Chervil Wk WGNS/IIMK WN3 78 E1
Cherwell Cl
WARRN/WOL WA2 121 M3 3
WGNE/HIN WN2 57 L7 2
Cheryl Dr WDN WA8 17 K1
Cheshire Acre
GR/UP/WCH CH49 126 C3
Cheshire Av AIN/FAZ L10 85 K6 1
Cheshire Cl NEWLW WA12 105 G2
Cheshire Gdns ECCL WA10 8 D7
Cheshire Gv MOR/LEA CH46 110 A6
Cheshire Lines Pth FMBY L37 48 B7
Cheshire Ring Canal Wk
WARRS WA4 136 E7
Cheshyre Dr RUNC WA7 150 B4 1
Cheshyre's La RUNC WA7 149 G7
Chesnell Gv NWD/KWIPK L33 74 B8 2
Chesney Cl TOX L8 113 G7
Chesnut Gv BTL L20 6 F2
RF/TRAN CH42 11 G9
Chessington Cl WARRS WA4 138 B6
Chester Av CHLY/EC PR7 44 A1
CHTN/BK PR9 25 H5
GOL/RIS/CU WA3 92 F5
NTHTN L30 84 B4
Chester Cl CSBY/BLUN L23 83 K1
RUNC WA7 150 B3
Chester Dr AIMK WN4 91 M3
Chesterfield Cl STHP PR8 47 K1
Chesterfield Dr NWD/KWIPK L33 74 A8
Chesterfield Rd CSBY/BLUN L23 71 J8
PS/BROM CH62 154 F1
STHP PR8 47 K1
Chesterfield St TOX L8 113 G6 1
Chester High Rd NSTN CH64 153 G1
Chester La STHEL WA9 118 D1
Chester New Rd WARRS WA4 137 H6
Chester Pl CHLYE PR6 44 C5
Chester Rd CHTN/BK PR9 25 H5
EP CH65 163 J2
FROD/HEL WA6 160 B7
GTS/LS CH66 155 L8
HES CH60 141 L7
HUY L36 116 C1
NPK/KEN L6 97 M7
NSTN CH64 153 G6
RUNC WA7 151 G8
WARRS WA4 137 J3
Chester St BIRK CH41 11 L5
PR/KW L34 100 F7
TOX L8 113 G6
WAL/EG CH44 111 J2 3
WDN WA8 16 E2
Chesterton Cl WGNS/IIMK WN3 4 B9
Chesterton St ALL/GAR L19 145 L1
Chestnut Av CHLY/EC PR7 31 L1
CHLYE PR6 33 G3 1
CSBY/BLUN L23 71 H7
GTS/LS CH66 163 H4
HUY L36 115 M5
RNFD/HAY WA11 90 B8
WARRW/BUR WA5 120 B7
WDN WA8 134 D3
Chestnut Cl
GR/UP/WCH CH49 125 L3 3
ORM L39 49 L4
RAIN/WH L35 117 G1
Chestnut Ct ORM L39 51 H7 1
Chestnut Gv AIMK WN4 91 M1
GOL/RIS/CU WA3 93 H5 3
PS/BROM CH62 143 L5 2
RNFD/HAY WA11 89 M6
WAV L15 114 B5
WGNE/HIN WN2 81 J1
Chestnut Rd LITH L21 83 H6
WGN WN1 68 F3
WLT/FAZ L9 97 K2
The Chestnuts CHLY/EC PR7 43 H3
Chestnut St EHL/KEN L7 13 M8

STHP PR8 3 K9
Chestnut Wy FMBY L37 58 E4
Cheswood Cl RAIN/WH L35 117 G3 1
Chetham Ct WARRN/WOL WA2 121 J2
Chetton Dr RUNC WA7 151 G6
Chetwode Av AIMK WN4 91 K3
Chetwood Av CSBY/BLUN L23 71 H8
Chetwood Dr WDN WA8 134 B1
Chetwynd Cl CL/PREN CH43 127 H1
Chetwynd Rd CL/PREN CH43 10 A8
Chetwynd St AIG/SPK L17 129 K2
Chevasse Wk WLTN L25 131 L2
Cheverton Cl
GR/UP/WCH CH49 126 D2 1
Cheviot Av STHEL WA9 103 H2
WARRN/WOL WA2 121 J2
Cheviot Cl HOR/BR BL6 45 L8
RF/TRAN CH42 127 M4 1
WGNS/IIMK WN3 78 E3
Cheviot Rd EHL/KEN L7 114 A3
RF/TRAN CH42 127 L4
Cheviot Wy NWD/KWIPK L33 74 B7
Chevoit Cl GTS/LS CH66 155 J7
Cheyne Gdns ALL/GAR L19 130 B5
Cheyne Wk STHEL WA9 102 B7 1
Chichester Cl RUNC WA7 150 F7
WAV L15 113 M5 1
Chidden Cl GR/UP/WCH CH49 125 L2
Chidlow Cl WDN WA8 134 C8 1
Chigwell Cl WD/CROXPK L12 99 G2
Chilcott Rd CLB/OSW/ST L13 114 E2
Childer Crs GTS/LS CH66 155 K6
Childer Gdns GTS/LS CH66 155 K6
Childers St CLB/OSW/ST L13 114 C2
Childwall Abbey Rd CHLDW L16 114 F7
Childwall Av MOR/LEA CH46 109 M6
WAV L15 113 M6 2
Childwall Bank Rd
CHLDW L16 114 F6 1
Childwall Cl MOR/LEA CH46 109 M6 1
Childwall Crs CHLDW L16 114 F6
Childwall Gn GR/UP/WCH CH49 126 C3
Childwall Hts WLTN L25 115 H6
Childwall La DV/KA/FCH L14 115 J3
WLTN L25 115 H7
Childwall Mount Rd
CHLDW L16 114 F6
Childwall Park Av CHLDW L16 115 G7
Childwall Priory Rd CHLDW L16 114 F6
Childwall Rd GTS/LS CH66 156 A5
WAV L15 114 C6
Childwall Valley Rd CHLDW L16 114 F6
WLTN L25 115 H5
Chilgrove Av HOR/BR BL6 57 M4
Chilham St WGNW/BIL/O WN5 67 K7 1
Chilhem Cl TOX L8 129 H1 4
Chilington Av WDN WA8 133 M5
Chillerton Rd WD/CROXPK L12 98 F5
Chillingham St TOX L8 129 J1
Chiltern Av CHLY/EC PR7 31 M4
WARRN/WOL WA2 121 J2 2
Chiltern Cl AIMK WN4 91 L3
HOR/BR BL6 45 L8
WD/CROXPK L12 99 H3
Chiltern Crs
WARRN/WOL WA2 121 J2 3
Chiltern Dr KKBY L32 85 L1
WGNS/IIMK WN3 78 E2
Chiltern Rd GOL/RIS/CU WA3 107 G1
RF/TRAN CH42 127 L4
STHEL WA9 103 J2
STHP PR8 34 C7
WARRN/WOL WA2 121 J2
Chilton Cl MGHL L31 72 F4
Chilton Dr GTS/LS CH66 163 H3 2
Chilton Ms MGHL L31 72 F4
Chilwell Cl WDN WA8 133 M1
Chimes Rd AIMK WN4 79 H7
China Farm La WKBY CH48 125 G1
China La WARRS WA4 137 L3
Chindit Cl FMBY L37 58 F3
Chippenham Av
GR/UP/WCH CH49 125 L1
Chipping Av STHP PR8 34 C8
Chippingdall Cl
WARRW/BUR WA5 120 E8 2
Chirkdale St ANF/KKDL L4 7 L8
Chirk Wy MOR/LEA CH46 110 B6
Chirton Cl RNFD/HAY WA11 90 F6 1
Chisacre Dr WGNNW/ST WN6 54 F6
Chisenhale St VAUX/LVPD L3 12 E2
Chisholm Cl WGNNW/ST WN6 55 K2
Chisledon Cl RNFD/HAY WA11 90 F6
Chislehurst Av WLTN L25 115 K7
Chislett Cl BRSC L40 51 M1 1
Chisnall Av ECCL WA10 101 L1
WGNNW/ST WN6 42 B8
Chisnall La CHLY/EC PR7 42 C8
Chiswell St EHL/KEN L7 113 L3 1
WGNW/BIL/O WN5 67 L8
Chiswick Cl RUNC WA7 150 F6 3
Chiswick Gdns WARRS WA4 138 B7
Cholmondeley Rd EP CH65 163 H1
RUNC WA7 149 M8
WKBY CH48 124 D3
Cholmondeley St WDN WA8 149 J1 3
Cholsey Cl GR/UP/WCH CH49 126 B1 3
Chorley Cl CHTN/BK PR9 23 G8
Chorley Hall Rd CHLY/EC PR7 32 E3
Chorley La CHLY/EC PR7 42 E3
Chorley Rd CHLY/EC PR7 43 M5
CHLYE PR6 44 C4
HOR/BR BL6 57 L2
PR/KW L34 100 D7
SKEL WN8 40 F8
WGN WN1 43 L8
WGN WN1 56 D4 1
Chorley's La WDN WA8 134 F2
Chorley St CHLYE PR6 44 D5 2
ECCL WA10 8 E3
WARRN/WOL WA2 14 F3
WGNS/IIMK WN3 5 J8
Chorley Wy BEB CH63 143 J4
Chorlton Cl CHLDW L16 115 H5
RUNC WA7 150 F4 2
Chorlton Gv WAL/NB CH45 94 F8
Christchurch Rd CL/PREN CH43 10 D9
Christian St VAUX/LVPD L3 13 H4

Christie Cl GTS/LS CH66 155 J3 1
Christie St WDN WA8 17 J1
Christines Crs BRSC L40 51 M1
Christleton WGNNW/ST WN6 55 K7
Christleton Cl CL/PREN CH43 126 F3
Christleton Ct RUNC WA7 150 E1
Christleton Dr GTS/LS CH66 156 A7
Christmas St BTL L20 7 J9
Christopher Cl CHLDW L16 114 F5
Christopher Dr PS/BROM CH62 144 C8
Christophers Cl
PEN/TH CH61 141 J1 1
Christopher St ANF/KKDL L4 97 H5
WGNS/IIMK WN3 5 L8
Christopher Wy CHLDW L16 114 F5
Chris Ward Cl EHL/KEN L7 113 L4 3
Chudleigh Cl HLWD L26 132 A4 3
Chudleigh Rd CLB/OSW/ST L13 114 B2
Church Av WGNE/HIN WN2 81 H5
WLT/FAZ L9 84 D6
Church Cl CHTN/BK PR9 25 J5 1
FMBY L37 59 J2
WAL/EG CH44 111 M1
Church Close Ct FMBY L37 59 J2 1
Church Crs WAL/EG CH44 112 A3 6
Churchdown Gv
DV/KA/FCH L14 115 G1 1
Churchdown Rd
DV/KA/FCH L14 115 G1
Church Dr NEWLW WA12 104 E4
PS/BROM CH62 128 D7
WARRN/WOL WA2 122 C4 1
WGNW/BIL/O WN5 66 F8
Church End SPK/HALE L24 147 M4
Church Farm Ct HES CH60 141 H6
Churchfield WGNNW/ST WN6 55 J7
Churchfield Rd FROD/HEL WA6 160 E6
WLTN L25 115 L8
Churchfields FROD/HEL WA6 166 E1 1
GOL/RIS/CU WA3 106 D6
STHEL WA9 118 E1 4
STHP PR8 35 H2
WDN WA8 118 D8
Church Flds BRSC L40 37 H6 2
ORM L39 51 G8
Church Fold CHLY/EC PR7 43 G1
CHLY/EC PR7 43 H5
Church Gdns BTL L20 6 E5 1
WAL/EG CH44 111 M1 2
Churchgate CHTN/BK PR9 25 H4
Churchgate Ms CHTN/BK PR9 25 J4 1
Church Gn CHLDW L16 115 H6
FMBY L37 58 E3
KKBY L32 86 A2
Church Gv LITH L21 83 H7
Church Hl WAL/EG CH44 95 H8 1
Church Hill Rd ORM L39 50 F7
Churchill Av CHTN/BK PR9 25 H3
GOL/RIS/CU WA3 107 K1
Churchill Gv WAL/EG CH44 95 L8 1
Churchill Wy NSTN CH64 153 G5
Churchill Wy (Elevated Rd)
CLVPS L1 13 G6
Churchlands La
WGNNW/ST WN6 56 B4
Church La AIG/SPK L17 130 A4
ANF/KKDL L4 97 H3
CHLY/EC PR7 42 F1
CHNE CH2 164 C6
ECCL WA10 101 J1
GOL/RIS/CU WA3 92 F6
GOL/RIS/CU WA3 107 H2
GR/UP/WCH CH49 126 D3
GTS/LS CH66 162 F1
NSTN CH64 153 G6
ORM L39 61 H5
ORM L39 62 C6
PEN/TH CH61 125 K8
PR/KW L34 99 L1
PS/BROM CH62 143 M4
PS/BROM CH62 144 C8
PS/BROM CH62 155 H1
WAL/EG CH44 111 M1 5
WARRS WA4 138 D4
WGNNW/ST WN6 41 M5
WGNNW/ST WN6 55 J7
Churchmeadow Cl
WAL/EG CH44 111 M1 4
Church Meadow La HES CH60 141 G6
Church Meadow Wk
WDN WA8 133 K8 1
Church Mt EHL/KEN L7 113 K4 5
Church Pde EP CH65 20 D2 1
Church Rd ALL/GAR L19 130 E8
ANF/KKDL L4 97 J3
BEB CH63 142 D7
BEB CH63 143 J1
BRSC L40 39 L1
BTL L20 83 M7
CHTN/BK PR9 23 J7
CLB/OSW/ST L13 114 B2
CSBY/BLUN L23 83 G1
CSBY/WL L22 83 G5 1
FMBY L37 59 J1
FROD/HEL WA6 160 E6
GR/UP/WCH CH49 110 C8
HLWD L26 132 B4
HUY L36 115 L2
LITH L21 83 M4
LYMM WA13 139 M3
MGHL L31 72 F6
ORM L39 64 A7
RF/TRAN CH42 127 M1
RNFD/HAY WA11 76 B7
RNFD/HAY WA11 88 C1
RNFD/HAY WA11 91 G7
SKEL WN8 65 H4
SPK/HALE L24 148 A5
WAL/EG CH44 112 A3
WAV L15 114 C7
WGNE/HIN WN2 80 D2
WKBY CH48 124 C4
WLTN L25 131 J2
Church Rd North WAV L15 114 C6
Church Rd South WLTN L25 131 J3
Church Rd West ANF/KKDL L4 97 H3
Church St BIRK CH41 11 M6
BTL L20 6 D5

CHLY/EC PR7 32 E6 5
CHLYE PR6 44 C6
CHTN/BK PR9 3 J3
CLVPS L1 13 G7
ECCL WA10 9 H6
EP CH65 20 D2 2
FROD/HEL WA6 160 D5
GOL/RIS/CU WA3 92 D4 1
HOR/BR BL6 57 L3
LEY/BBR PR5 29 K4 1
NEWLW WA12 105 G1
ORM L39 51 G8
PR/KW L34 100 F7 6
RUNC WA7 19 G2
SKEL WN8 66 E6
WAL/EG CH44 111 M1
WARR WA1 15 H5
WDN WA8 134 C8
WGN WN1 4 F3
WGNE/HIN WN2 57 K7
WGNE/HIN WN2 69 M8 9
WGNNW/ST WN6 56 A4
WGNS/IIMK WN3 5 L7
WGNW/BIL/O WN5 66 F8
WGNW/BIL/O WN5 67 K7
Church Ter RF/TRAN CH42 127 M2
Church Vw BTL L20 6 F5
ORM L39 62 C6
Churchview Rd BIRK CH41 10 D2
Church Wk BTL L20 6 E5
CHLY/EC PR7 31 L3
WARRN/WOL WA2 105 J7
Church Wy FMBY L37 58 E3
FROD/HEL WA6 166 F4
KKBY L32 86 A2
Churchway Rd SPK/HALE L24 147 J3
Churchwood Cl
PS/BROM CH62 143 M4
Churnet St ANF/KKDL L4 97 G5
Churn Wy GR/UP/WCH CH49 125 M1
Churston Rd CHLDW L16 115 G8
Churton Av CL/PREN CH43 127 H2
Churton Ct NPK/KEN L6 113 J2 2
Churton Gv WGNNW/ST WN6 55 K3
Ciaran Cl WD/CROXPK L12 98 F5
Cicely St EHL/KEN L7 113 K4
Cinder La BTL L20 83 M6
CALD/MH L18 114 E8
KIRK/FR/WA PR4 27 H3 1
WARRS WA4 139 H5
Cinnamon Av WGNE/HIN WN2 81 H1 2
Cinnamon Brow SKEL WN8 66 E7
Cinnamon La WARRN/WOL WA2 122 B2
Cinnamon La North
WARRN/WOL WA2 122 B1
Circular Dr GR/UP/WCH CH49 125 M2
HES CH60 141 G4
PS/BROM CH62 128 D6
Circular Rd BIRK CH41 11 H7
Circular Rd East NG/CROX L11 98 B5
Circular Rd West NG/CROX L11 98 B4
Cirencester Av
GR/UP/WCH CH49 125 L1
Cirrus Dr ORM L39 62 C4
Citrine Rd WAL/EG CH44 111 M3
Citron Cl WLT/FAZ L9 97 K1
City Gdns ECCL WA10 89 H7
City Rd ANF/KKDL L4 97 H4
ECCL WA10 89 H7
WGNW/BIL/O WN5 67 K6
Civic Wy EP CH65 20 B4
HUY L36 116 A3 1
Clairville Cl BTL L20 7 G5
Clairville Wy CLB/OSW/ST L13 98 A8 2
Clancut La CHLY/EC PR7 43 H3
Clandon Rd CALD/MH L18 130 F4
Clanfield Av WDN WA8 133 L2
Clanfield Rd NG/CROX L11 98 D4
Clanwood Cl WGNS/IIMK WN3 79 G3 1
Clap Gate Crs WDN WA8 133 K8
Clap Gate La WGNS/IIMK WN3 79 G2
Clap Gates Rd
WARRW/BUR WA5 121 G6
Clapham Rd ANF/KKDL L4 97 K7
Clare Cl STHEL WA9 102 A6
Clare Crs WAL/EG CH44 111 G1
Clare Dr EP CH65 163 K4
Claremont Av CHLY/EC PR7 32 D6
MGHL L31 72 D5
WDN WA8 134 E1 1
Claremont Cl LITH L21 83 H6 3
Claremont Dr ORM L39 62 F2
WDN WA8 134 D1
Claremont Gdns STHP PR8 2 E9
Claremont Rd CHLY/EC PR7 32 D8 3
CSBY/BLUN L23 82 F1
GOL/RIS/CU WA3 106 F1
LITH L21 83 H6
RUNC WA7 19 K4
WAV L15 114 A7
WGNW/BIL/O WN5 78 A8
WKBY CH48 124 D2
Claremont Wy BEB CH63 127 M5
Claremount Dr BEB CH63 143 H1 1
Claremount Rd WAL/NB CH45 95 H7
Clarence Av
WARRW/BUR WA5 119 M7 2
WDN WA8 134 C1
Clarence Cl STHEL WA9 9 L8
Clarence Rd RF/TRAN CH42 127 L2 1
STHP PR8 35 J1
WAL/EG CH44 111 M3
WARRS WA4 138 D3
Clarence St AIMK WN4 91 H1
CHLY/EC PR7 32 F6 4
GOL/RIS/CU WA3 92 C4
NEWLW WA12 104 B1
RUNC WA7 18 F2
VAUX/LVPD L3 13 K7
WARR WA1 15 L2
WGNE/HIN WN2 69 J6
Clarence Ter RUNC WA7 19 G2
Clarence Yd WGN WN1 4 E4
Clarendon Cl CL/PREN CH43 10 E7
RUNC WA7 150 F6
Clarendon Ct WARRN/WOL WA2 121 H1
Clarendon Gv MGHL L31 61 L8 1
Clarendon Rd ALL/GAR L19 130 E7

LITH L21 83 H7 1
NPK/KEN L6 97 L7
WAL/EG CH44 111 M2
Clarendon St CHLYE PR6 33 G6 3
Clare Rd BTL L20 7 K7
Clares Farm Cl WARR WA1 123 H6 1
Claret Cl AIG/SPK L17 129 L4
Clare Wy WAL/NB CH45 95 H8 2
Claribel St TOX L8 113 J7
Clarington Gv WGN WN1 5 J5
Clarke Av GOL/RIS/CU WA3 107 H1
RF/TRAN CH42 128 A3
WARRS WA4 137 M3
Clarke's Crs ECCL WA10 101 K1
Clarkfield Cl BRSC L40 52 B2 2
Classic Rd CLB/OSW/ST L13 114 C1
Clatterbridge Rd BEB CH63 142 F5
Claude Rd NPK/KEN L6 97 L7
Claude St WARR WA1 15 H3
WGNW/BIL/O WN5 67 M7
Claughton Cl EHL/KEN L7 113 L4 4
Claughton Dr WAL/EG CH44 111 K2
Claughton Firs CL/PREN CH43 10 D9
Claughton Gn CL/PREN CH43 10 B8
Claughton Pl BIRK CH41 10 F6 1
Claughton Rd BIRK CH41 11 H6
Claughton St ECCL WA10 9 G4
Clavell Rd ALL/GAR L19 130 F5
Claverton Cl RUNC WA7 149 K7 2
Claybridge Cl WGNW/BIL/O WN5 67 K4
Clay Brow Rd SKEL WN8 66 A7
Clayburn Cl CHLYE PR6 32 F3 2
Clay Cross Rd WLTN L25 131 H3
Claydon Ct HLWD L26 132 C4
Claydon Dr WGNE/HIN WN2 80 B1
Clayfield Cl BTL L20 7 K5
Clayford Crs DV/KA/FCH L14 114 D1
Clayford Pl DV/KA/FCH L14 114 D1 1
Clayford Rd DV/KA/FCH L14 114 E1 1
Clayford Wy DV/KA/FCH L14 114 E1 2
Clayhill NSTN CH64 153 H3
Clayhill Gn GTS/LS CH66 155 L6
Clay La ECCL WA10 101 G2
WARRW/BUR WA5 104 A7
Claypole Cl EHL/KEN L7 113 L5 5
Clay St VAUX/LVPD L3 12 D1
Clayton Av GOL/RIS/CU WA3 93 G5
Clayton Crs RUNC WA7 18 E5
WDN WA8 16 B2
Clayton Gdns BRSC L40 52 A1 2
Claytongate CHLY/EC PR7 43 H3
Clayton House LEIGH WN7 81 L8
Clayton La WAL/EG CH44 111 J3
Clayton Ms SKEL WN8 64 F4 2
Clayton Pl CL/PREN CH43 10 F7
Clayton Rd GOL/RIS/CU WA3 107 H7
Clayton St SKEL WN8 64 F4
WGNS/IIMK WN3 4 C4
Cleadon Cl KKBY L32 86 C6 1
Cleadon Rd KKBY L32 86 B6
Clearwater Cl EHL/KEN L7 113 K3
Cleary St BTL L20 6 E2
Clee Hill Rd RF/TRAN CH42 127 L4
Cleethorpes Rd RUNC WA7 150 E6
Clegge St WARRN/WOL WA2 14 F2
Clegg St EV L5 13 J2
SKEL WN8 64 F4 3
Clelland St WARRS WA4 15 H9
Clematis Cl CHLY/EC PR7 32 C2
Clematis Rd NTHLY L27 116 A7
Clement Gdns VAUX/LVPD L3 12 F2
Clementina Rd
CSBY/BLUN L23 82 D1 2
Clemmey Dr BTL L20 84 A7
Clengers Brow CHTN/BK PR9 25 J2 1
Clent Av MGHL L31 72 E2
Clent Gdns MGHL L31 72 F2
Clent Rd MGHL L31 72 E3
Cleopas St TOX L8 129 H1 5
Clevedon Dr WGNS/IIMK WN3 78 E1
Clevedon St TOX L8 129 J1
Cleveland Av WGNS/IIMK WN3 78 E3
Cleveland Buildings CLVPS L1 13 G9 1
Cleveland Cl KKBY L32 85 L1
Cleveland Dr AIMK WN4 91 L1
GOL/RIS/CU WA3 92 F5
GTS/LS CH66 155 J7
Cleveland Rd WARRN/WOL WA2 121 K2
Cleveland Sq CLVPS L1 13 G9 2
Cleveland St BIRK CH41 10 E1
CHLY/EC PR7 32 E5
CHLY/EC PR7 43 G4 2
STHEL WA9 9 L9
Cleveley Pk CALD/MH L18 130 F4
Cleveley Rd CALD/MH L18 130 F4
HOY CH47 109 G5
Cleveleys Av CHTN/BK PR9 25 J1
WDN WA8 134 F2
Cleveleys Rd CHTN/BK PR9 25 J2
WARRW/BUR WA5 136 D1 2
The Cleves MGHL L31 73 G2
Cleve Wy FMBY L37 59 K3
Clieves Hills La ORM L39 61 M3
Clieves Rd KKBY L32 86 B4
Cliff Dr WAL/EG CH44 95 M8
Cliffe Rd NSTN CH64 153 H8
WARRS WA4 137 L6
Cliffe St WARR WA1 14 B5
WDN WA8 17 G1
Cliff La LYMM WA13 139 K7
WARRS WA4 138 F3
WARRS WA4 139 H6
Clifford Rd STHP PR8 35 J4
WAL/EG CH44 111 K2
WARRW/BUR WA5 136 C1
Clifford St CHLY/EC PR7 32 F5
VAUX/LVPD L3 13 K5
Cliff Rd CHTN/BK PR9 24 F3
WAL/EG CH44 111 J2
Cliff St EHL/KEN L7 113 L3
Clifton Av GOL/RIS/CU WA3 106 F2
HLWD L26 132 A4
PS/BROM CH62 155 G2
Clifton Cl WARR WA1 122 E6
Clifton Crs BIRK CH41 11 J6
FROD/HEL WA6 160 E4
Clifton Cresent WGN WN1 68 E3
Clifton Dr AIN/FAZ L10 84 F3

HOR/BR BL6 ............... 57 K2
Clifton Gdns EP CH65 ........ 20 C8
Clifton Gv CHLY/EC PR7 ..... 32 D6 🔲
EV L5 ....................... 13 K2
WAL/EG CH44 ............. 111 M1
Clifton La RUNC WA7 ....... 161 G2
Cliftonmill Mdw
GOL/RIS/CU WA3 ......... 92 B5 🔲
Clifton Rd AIMK WN4 ...... 79 H7
BIRK CH41 ................ 11 H8
FMBY L37 ................. 47 J8
NPK/KEN L6 .............. 97 M8
RUNC WA7 ................ 19 H1
STHP PR8 ................. 25 H7
WGNW/BIL/O WN5 ........ 89 M1
Clifton Rd East NPK/KEN L6 .. 97 M8
Clifton St ALL/GAR L19 ..... 130 E7
ECCL WA10 ................ 9 H3
LEIGH WN7 ............... 81 M8
WARRS WA4 .............. 15 H4
WGN WN1 ................. 4 F1
WGNS/IIMK WN3 ......... 79 J1
Cliftonville Rd PR/KW L34 .. 101 G7 🔲
WARR WA1 ............... 122 E7
Clincton Cl WDN WA8 ....... 133 J5
Clincton Vw WDN WA8 ...... 133 H3
Clinning Rd STHP PR8 ....... 35 J3
Clinton Pl WD/CROXPK L12 ... 98 B6
Clinton Rd WD/CROXPK L12 .. 98 B6
Clint Rd EHL/KEN L7 ........ 113 L4
Clipper Vw PS/BROM CH62 .. 128 D5
Clipsley Brook Vw
RNFD/HAY WA11 ......... 90 B7
Clipsley Crs RNFD/HAY WA11 . 90 D6
Clipsley La RNFD/HAY WA11 .. 90 B7
Clive Av WARRN/WOL WA2 .. 121 L4
Clive Ldg STHP PR8 ........ 35 H3 🔲
Clive Rd CL/PREN CH43 ..... 127 L1
STHP PR8 ................. 35 H3
Clock Face Rd STHEL WA9 ... 118 E1
WDN WA8 ................. 119 C6
Cloister Av LEIGH WN7 ..... 81 M4
The Cloisters CSBY/BLUN L23 . 82 F2 🔲
ECCL WA10 .............. 101 K1
Clorain Rd NWD/KWIPK L33 .. 86 C2
Closebrook Rd
WGNW/BIL/O WN5 ........ 67 M7
Closeburn Av HES CH60 .... 141 G7 🔲
Close La WGNE/HIN WN2 ..... 81 H2
WGNE/HIN WN2 .......... 81 K4
Close St STHEL WA9 ....... 102 A6
The Close CHTN/BK PR9 ..... 23 J8
CSBY/BLUN L23 ........... 82 F2
ECCL WA10 ............... 88 C4
GR/UP/WCH CH49 ........ 125 M3
HTWN L38 ................ 71 G2
PEN/TH CH61 ............ 125 M7
RF/TRAN CH42 .......... 127 M4
RNFD/HAY WA11 ......... 90 B8
STBRV L28 ................ 99 L6
WLT/FAZ L9 .............. 97 K4
Cloudberry Cl NTHLY L27 ... 116 A7 🔲
Clough Acre CHLY/EC PR7 ... 32 C3
Clough Av WARRN/WOL WA2 . 121 K3 🔲
Clough Gv AIMK WN4 ....... 79 H8
Clough Rd SPK/HALE L24 ... 146 F1
The Clough RUNC WA7 ..... 150 B4
Cloughwood Crs
WGNNW/ST WN6 .......... 54 F6
Clovelly Av STHEL WA9 .... 102 F7 🔲
WARRW/BUR WA5 ........ 120 A6 🔲
STHP PR8 ................. 35 G5
Clovelly Gv RUNC WA7 ..... 150 D8
Clovelly Rd ANF/KKDL L4 .... 97 K7
Clover Av FROD/HEL WA6 ... 160 F6
HLWD L26 ................ 131 M3
Clover Ct RUNC WA7 ....... 150 D8 🔲
Cloverdale Dr AIMK WN4 ... 91 L3 🔲
Cloverdale Rd WLTN L25 ... 115 K6 🔲
Clover Dr BIRK CH41 ....... 111 C4
Cloverfield RUNC WA7 ..... 150 E6 🔲
Cloverfield Gdns GTS/LS CH66 155 M6 🔲
Clover Hey RNFD/HAY WA11 . 89 K6
Clover Rd CHLY/EC PR7 .... 32 C8
Clover St WGNNW/ST WN6 .. 68 C3
Club St RNFD/HAY WA11 .... 89 J4
Clucas Gdns ORM L39 ...... 51 G7
Clwyd Gv WD/CROXPK L12 .. 98 D5 🔲
Clwyd St BIRK CH41 ....... 11 H5
WAL/NB CH45 ............ 95 J6
Clwyd Wy GTS/LS CH66 .... 155 J7
Clyde Rd CLB/OSW/ST L13 .. 114 A3 🔲
Clydesdale EP CH65 ....... 20 A9
Clydesdale Rd HOY CH47 ... 108 D5
WAL/EG CH44 ........... 111 M1 🔲
WARRS WA4 ............. 137 M5
Clyde St BTL L20 .......... 96 E5
RF/TRAN CH42 .......... 128 B3
Clyffes Farm Cl BRSC L40 ... 37 J6
Coach House Ct BRSC L40 ... 52 A2
Coach House Dr
WGNNW/ST WN6 .......... 55 F7
Coachmans Dr WD/CROXPK L12 99 G4
Coach Rd ORM L39 ......... 75 H4
PR/KW L34 .............. 87 K6
Coalbrookdale Rd NSTN CH64 153 H3
Coalgate La RAIN/WH L35 ... 116 F3 🔲
Coalpit La CH/BCN CH1 ..... 163 D3
Coal Pit La ORM L39 ....... 75 L1
WGNE/HIN WN2 .......... 81 K4
Coal St CLVPS L1 .......... 13 J6
Coalville Rd RNFD/HAY WA11 . 89 M7
Coastal Dr WAL/NB CH45 ... 94 F5
Coastal Rd STHP PR8 ...... 34 C7
Coastgaurd La NSTN CH64 .. 152 D4
Cobb Av LITH L21 .......... 83 K7
The Cobbles HLWD L26 .... 131 M4
Cobb's Brow La SKEL WN8 .. 53 J6
Cobb's Clough Rd BRSC L40 . 53 H8
Cobbs La WARRS WA4 ..... 138 A5
Cobden Av BIRK CH41 ..... 128 B2
Cobden Ct BIRK CH41 ...... 128 B2 🔲
Cobden Pl RF/TRAN CH42 .. 128 B2 🔲
Cobden St CHTN/BK PR9 ... 25 H7
CHLYE PR6 ............... 33 G4
NEWLW WA12 ............ 104 F1 🔲
NPK/KEN L6 ............. 113 M3

WARRN/WOL WA2 ....... 14 F2
WLTN L25 ................ 131 H3 🔲
Cobden Vw WLTN L25 ..... 131 H3 🔲
Cob Hall La FROD/HEL WA6 .. 166 F8
Cobham Av WLT/FAZ L9 .... 84 B7
Cobham Rd MOR/LEA CH46 . 109 M5
Cob Moor Av
WGNW/BIL/O WN5 ........ 77 M4 🔲
Cob Moor Rd WGNW/BIL/O WN5 77 M4
Coburg Whf VAUX/LVPD L3 .. 112 E7
Cochrane St EV L5 ......... 97 H8
Cockburn St TOX L8 ....... 129 H1
Cockerell Cl ANF/KKDL L4 .. 97 G6 🔲
Cockerham Wy NG/CROX L11 . 85 K8
Cockhedge La WARR WA1 ... 14 E5
Cockhedge Wy WARR WA1 .. 14 E5
Cocklade La SPK/HALE L24 . 147 M4
Cock Lane Ends WDN WA8 . 133 K8 🔲
Cockle Dick's La CHTN/BK PR9 25 C3
Cockshead Rd WLTN L25 .. 115 K8
Cockshead Wy WLTN L25 .. 115 K7 🔲
Cockspur St VAUX/LVPD L3 . 12 F5
Cockspur St West
VAUX/LVPD L3 ........... 12 E5 🔲
Coerton Rd WLT/FAZ L9 .... 84 D6
The Cokers BEB CH63 ..... 128 A5
Colbern Cl MGHL L31 ...... 73 G5
Colbrooke Rd AIG/SPK L17 . 129 K2
Colburn Rd WGNS/IIMK WN3 . 79 J3 🔲
Colburne Cl BRSC L40 ...... 39 H8
Colby Cl CHLDW L16 ....... 115 G5
Colby Rd WGNS/IIMK WN3 .. 79 K2
Colchester Rd STHP PR8 ... 36 B3
Coldstone Dr AIMK WN4 ... 90 F1
Coldstream Cl
WARRN/WOL WA2 ....... 122 A1 🔲
Coldstream Dr GTS/LS CH66 . 155 H8 🔲
Cole Av NEWLW WA12 ..... 104 E1
Colebrook Cl
GOL/RIS/CU WA3 ........ 123 J1 🔲
Coleclough Pl GOL/RIS/CU WA3 107 H1
Cole Crs ORM L39 ......... 62 E5
Coleman Dr GR/UP/WCH CH49 125 K2
Colemere Ct EP CH65 ...... 20 B1
Colemere Dr PEN/TH CH61 . 126 D7
Coleridge Av ECCL WA10 ... 8 B3
WGNW/BIL/O WN5 ........ 67 J7
Coleridge Rd WGNW/BIL/O WN5 77 M4
Coleridge St BTL L20 ...... 6 D3
NPK/KEN L6 ............. 113 K2
Coleshill Ri WGNS/IIMK WN3 . 78 E3
Coleshill Rd NG/CROX L11 .. 98 A2
Cole St CL/PREN CH43 ..... 10 F6
Colette Rd AIN/FAZ L10 .... 85 K6 🔲
Coleus Cl WLT/FAZ L9 ..... 97 K1
Colin Cl HUY L36 .......... 115 L4 🔲
Colindale Rd CHLDW L16 .. 115 G6 🔲
Colin Dr VAUX/LVPD L3 .... 96 A3
Colinmander Gdns ORM L39 . 62 E2 🔲
Colin St WGN WN1 ......... 5 G1
Colinton St WAV L15 ...... 114 A5 🔲
College Av CSBY/BLUN L23 .. 82 F2
FMBY L37 ................ 59 G1
WGN WN1 ................ 4 F5
College Cl CL/PREN CH43 .. 110 D7 🔲
FMBY L37 ................ 58 F1
STHP PR8 ................ 35 J2
WAL/NB CH45 ........... 95 G7 🔲
WARR WA1 ............... 15 J5
WARRN/WOL WA2 ....... 122 C3
College Ct WD/CROXPK L12 . 98 E8 🔲
College Dr BEB CH63 ...... 128 C6 🔲
College Flds HUY L36 ...... 116 A4
College La CLVPS L1 ....... 13 G8
College Pth FMBY L37 ..... 46 F8
College Rd CSBY/BLUN L23 . 82 F2
SKEL WN8 ................ 66 D4
College Rd North
CSBY/BLUN L23 .......... 70 E8
College St ECCL WA10 ..... 9 G8
College St North NPK/KEN L6 . 13 L4
College St South NPK/KEN L6 . 13 M4
College Vw BTL L20 ....... 7 G7
Collett Cl WGN WN1 ....... 5 J4
Collier's Rw RUNC WA7 .... 149 G6
Collier St RUNC WA7 ...... 18 E1
WGNE/HIN WN2 .......... 69 M7 🔲
Colliery Green Cl NSTN CH64 153 G8
Colliery Green La NSTN CH64 153 G8 🔲
Colliery Green Dr NSTN CH64 153 G8
Collinge St WGNE/HIN WN2 . 80 C3
Collingham Gn GTS/LS CH66 155 K8
Collingwood Rd BEB CH63 . 143 K1 🔲
CHLY/EC PR7 ............. 32 C6
NEWLW WA12 ............ 104 D2
Collingwood St
WGNNW/ST WN6 .......... 56 A4
Collin Rd CL/PREN CH43 ... 111 C5
Collins Cl BTL L20 ......... 83 J8 🔲
Collins Green La
WARR WARRW/BUR WA5 .. 104 A4
Collin St WARRW/BUR WA5 . 121 G8
Collisdene Rd
WGNW/BIL/O WN5 ........ 66 F7
Collison Av CHLY/EC PR7 ... 32 D5
Colmore Av BEB CH63 ..... 143 H4
Colmore Rd NG/CROX L11 .. 98 A3
Colnbrook WGNNW/ST WN6 . 55 K3 🔲
Colne Dr STHEL WA9 ...... 102 F6
Colne Rd WARRW/BUR WA5 104 B7 🔲
Colorado Cl NEWLW WA12 . 104 E3
Colquitt St CLVPS L1 ...... 13 J9
Coltart Rd TOX L8 ......... 113 K7
Colton Rd WLTN L25 ...... 115 H6
Coltsfoot Dr CHLYE PR6 ... 32 F5
Columba St NTHLY L30 .... 83 J2
Columbia Rd ANF/KKDL L4 . 97 J3
CL/PREN CH43 ........... 10 C9
PR/KW L34 ............... 101 C2
Columbine Cl CHLY/EC PR7 . 32 C2 🔲
WDN WA8 ................ 133 K1
Columbus Dr PEN/TH CH61 141 G2
Columbus Quay VAUX/LVPD L3 129 C2
Columbus Wy LITH L21 .... 83 K6 🔲
Column Rd WKBY CH48 .... 124 F4

Colville Ct WARRN/WOL WA2 121 J2
Colville Rd WAL/EG CH44 .. 111 J1
Colville St WAV L15 ....... 114 A5
Colwall Cl NWD/KWIPK L33 . 86 C3
Colwall Rd NWD/KWIPK L33 . 86 C3
Colwell Cl DV/KA/FCH L14 . 99 J6
Colwell Rd DV/KA/FCH L14 . 99 J7
Colwyn Cl WARRW/BUR WA5 121 G3
Colwyn Dr WGNE/HIN WN2 . 81 L3
Colwyn Rd CLB/OSW/ST L13 114 B3
Colwyn St BIRK CH41 ...... 10 A2
Colyton Av STHEL WA9 .... 102 F8 🔲
Colyton Cl CHLYE PR6 ..... 33 G5 🔲
Colyton Rd East CHLYE PR6 . 33 G5 🔲
Combermere St TOX L8 .... 113 H7 🔲
WAV L15 ................. 113 M4
Comely Av WAL/EG CH44 .. 111 L1
Comely Bank Rd
WAL/EG CH44 ........... 111 M1 🔲
Comer Gdns MGHL L31 .... 72 E2 🔲
Comet Cl WGNW/BIL/O WN5 . 67 L5
Comfrey Gv HLWD L26 .... 132 A3 🔲
Commercial Rd CHLY/EC PR7 32 E4 🔲
EV L5 .................... 96 F7
PS/BROM CH62 .......... 144 A2
Commodore Pl
WGNW/BIL/O WN5 ........ 68 A4 🔲
Common Bank La CHLY/EC PR7 32 A6
Common End CHLY/EC PR7 . 57 G1
Common Field Rd
GR/UP/WCH CH49 ....... 126 D4
Common La CHTN/BK PR9 .. 26 D3
FROD/HEL WA6 .......... 165 M4
GOL/RIS/CU WA3 ........ 106 F1
LEIGH WN7 .............. 93 K1
WARRS WA4 ............. 138 A3
Common Rd NEWLW WA12 104 A2
Commonside FROD/HEL WA6 167 J4
Common St NEWLW WA12 . 104 A2
STHEL WA9 .............. 101 M6 🔲
The Common CHLY/EC PR7 . 44 A8
SKEL WN8 ................ 53 L2
Commutation Rw
VAUX/LVPD L3 ........... 13 G5
Company's Cl RUNC WA7 .. 149 H7 🔲
Compass Cl RUNC WA7 ... 150 F8
Compton Cl RNFD/HAY WA11 90 E6
Compton Pl EP CH65 ...... 20 B4
Compton Rd BIRK CH41 ... 110 F4 🔲
NPK/KEN L6 ............. 113 J1
STHP PR8 ................ 35 K2
Compton Wy HLWD L26 .. 132 A7
Comus St VAUX/LVPD L3 ... 13 H3
Concert St CLVPS L1 ...... 13 H9
Concord Av WGNS/IIMK WN3 79 K2
Concorde Pl
WARRN/WOL WA2 ....... 121 M3 🔲
Concordia Av
GR/UP/WCH CH49 ....... 110 C8
Concourse Wy STHEL WA9 . 103 H3
Condor Cl ALL/GAR L19 .... 130 F7
Condron Rd LITH L21 ...... 83 L4
Condron Rd North LITH L21 . 83 L4
Conery Cl FROD/HEL WA6 .. 166 E1
Coney Crs CSBY/BLUN L23 . 71 K8 🔲
Coney Gv RUNC WA7 ..... 150 D8 🔲
Coney La HUY L36 ........ 116 B6
RAIN/WH L35 ............ 116 B6
Coney Wk
GR/UP/WCH CH49 ....... 109 M7 🔲
Congresbury Rd LEIGH WN7 . 81 M6
Congress St CHLY/EC PR7 . 32 E4 🔲
Conifer Cl GTS/LS CH66 ... 163 J5
NWD/KWIPK L33 ......... 74 A3
WLT/FAZ L9 .............. 97 K2
Conifer Ct FMBY L37 ...... 59 H3
Conifer Gv WARRW/BUR WA5 120 B6
The Conifers MGHL L31 ... 72 E2
Coningsby Dr WAL/NB CH45 111 J1
Coningsby Rd ANF/KKDL L4 . 97 J5
Coniston Av AIMK WN4 .... 91 K1
BEB CH63 ................ 143 L8 🔲
CHLY/EC PR7 ............. 31 M4
CHLYE PR6 ............... 44 D4 🔲
CL/PREN CH43 ........... 110 E8
PR/KW L34 .............. 101 H7
WAL/NB CH45 ........... 95 G6
WARRW/BUR WA5 ....... 135 M1
WGN WN1 ................ 6 D2
WGNE/HIN WN2 .......... 69 K6
WGNW/BIL/O WN5 ....... 67 H5
Coniston Cl GTS/LS CH66 .. 155 J4
NWD/KWIPK L33 ......... 85 M1 🔲
RUNC WA7 ............... 149 M7
WLT/FAZ L9 .............. 84 D6 🔲
Coniston Dr FROD/HEL WA6 160 F5
WGNE/HIN WN2 .......... 80 D5
Coniston Gv RNFD/HAY WA11 89 J6
Coniston Park Dr
WGNNW/ST WN6 .......... 56 C6
Coniston Rd CHLY/EC PR7 .. 32 D7
FMBY L37 ................ 58 F3
HOY/BR BL6 ............. 57 M2
MGHL L31 ............... 73 G3
NSTN CH64 .............. 153 G7
PEN/TH CH61 ............ 125 M7
Coniston St EV L5 ......... 97 J7
Coniston Wy LEY/BBR PR5 . 76 B3 🔲
RNFD/HAY WA11 ......... 76 B3 🔲
Conleach Rd SPK/HALE L24 147 G2
Connaught Av WARR WA1 . 15 M1
Connaught Cl BIRK CH41 ... 10 A1
Connaught Dr NEWLW WA12 104 E3
Connaught Rd EHL/KEN L7 . 113 J3
Connaught Wy BIRK CH41 . 10 A1
Connolly Av BTL L20 ...... 7 M2
Conrad Cl WGNS/IIMK WN3 . 4 B9
Conroy Wy NEWLW WA12 . 104 E4
Consett Rd RAIN/WH L35 . 101 M7
Constables Cl RUNC WA7 . 150 C4
Constance St ECCL WA10 .. 8 A7
VAUX/LVPD L3 ........... 13 L3
Constance Wy WDN WA8 .. 18 F7
Constantia Rd WGNE/HIN WN2 80 B1 🔲
Constantine Av HES CH60 . 141 J4 🔲
Convent Cl ALL/GAR L19 .. 130 C6 🔲

ORM L39 ................. 62 F3
RF/TRAN CH42 .......... 11 H9
Conville Bvd BEB CH63 .... 128 A5
Conway Av WARRW/BUR WA5 121 H5
CHLY/EC PR7 ............. 30 E6 🔲
NWD/KWIPK L33 ......... 73 M8 🔲
WARRW/BUR WA5 ....... 120 B7 🔲
Conway Cl BEB CH63 ..... 127 M8
CHLY/EC PR7 ............. 30 E6 🔲
NEWLW WA12 ............ 105 G2
WGNE/HIN WN2 .......... 69 M1
WGNW/BIL/O WN5 ....... 78 B8
Conway Crs WGNW/BIL/O WN5 78 A7
Conway Dr BIRK CH41 ..... 11 C5
NEWLW WA12 ............ 105 G2
WGNE/HIN WN2 .......... 69 M1
WGNW/BIL/O WN5 ....... 78 B8
Conway Rd AIMK WN4 ..... 80 A8
CHLY/EC PR7 ............. 30 E6 🔲
WGNE/HIN WN2 .......... 81 H1
Conway St BIRK CH41 ..... 10 F4
EV L5 .................... 96 F7
WAL/EG CH44 ........... 111 K1 🔲
WGNW/BIL/O WN5 ....... 67 L8
Conwy Dr NPK/KEN L6 .... 97 K8
Conyers Av STHP PR8 ..... 35 H2
Coogee Av
WARRW/BUR WA5 ....... 120 A6 🔲
Cook Av RNFD/HAY WA11 .. 91 G6
Cooke St AIMK WN4 ....... 79 H7
Cook Rd MOR/LEA CH46 .. 110 D1
Cookson Rd LITH L21 ...... 83 J7
Cookson St CLVPS L1 ...... 13 G6
Cook St CLVP L2 ........... 12 F7
EP CH65 ................. 20 D3
RAIN/WH L35 ............ 101 H3
WGNE/HIN WN2 .......... 80 C4
Coombe Dr RUNC WA7 .... 18 F3
Coombe Rd PEN/TH CH61 . 126 A6
Cooperage Cl TOX L8 ..... 129 G1
Cooper Av North CALD/MH L18 130 C4
Cooper Av South CALD/MH L18 130 C4
Cooper Cl ALL/GAR L19 ... 130 C5
Cooper La RNFD/HAY WA11 . 90 E7
Coopers Gln WGNE/HIN WN2 69 J5 🔲
Cooper's La CHLY/EC PR7 .. 41 K5
NWD/KWIPK L33 ......... 86 F7
Cooper St ECCL WA10 ..... 8 E1
RUNC WA7 ............... 19 C2
WDN WA8 ................ 16 E1
Coop St WGN WN1 ........ 5 H2
Copeland Cl PEN/TH CH61 . 141 G1
Copeland Gv WGNNW/ST WN6 56 B3
Copeland Gv RUNC WA7 .. 150 A8
Copeland Rd WARRS WA4 . 137 K3
Copesthorne Cl WGNE/HIN WN2 57 L7
Coplow Dl WGNE/HIN WN2 . 81 G2 🔲
Copperas Cl WGNNW/ST WN6 55 J6
Copperas Hl VAUX/LVPD L3 . 13 G5
Copperas La HOR/BR BL6 .. 57 K4
WGNE/HIN WN2 .......... 57 J7
Copperas St ECCL WA10 ... 8 F6
Copperbeech Dr
WGNNW/ST WN6 .......... 56 D6
Copperfield Cl
GOL/RIS/CU WA3 ........ 106 E8 🔲
TOX L8 .................. 113 H8 🔲
Copperfield Cl
GOL/RIS/CU WA3 ........ 106 E8 🔲
Copperwood Dr RAIN/WH L35 117 G3
Copperwood Wy CHLY/EC PR7 32 B6
Coppice Cl CHLYE PR6 ..... 33 L1 🔲
CL/PREN CH43 ........... 110 D7 🔲
Coppice Dr WGNS/IIMK WN3 79 H7
WGNW/BIL/O WN5 ....... 77 M3
Coppice Gra MOR/LEA CH46 109 L6
Coppice Gn CHNE CH2 .... 165 L1
WARRW/BUR WA5 ....... 120 D3
Coppice Gv
GR/UP/WCH CH49 ....... 125 L3 🔲
Coppice La CHLYE PR6 .... 33 L1
RAIN/WH L35 ............ 116 D6
Coppice Leys FMBY L37 ... 59 G2
The Coppice NPK/KEN L6 .. 97 L7
PR/KW L34 .............. 99 M2
WAL/NB CH45 ........... 95 J6
Coppins Cl FROD/HEL WA6 . 166 D2
The Coppins
WARRN/WOL WA2 ....... 121 L3 🔲
Copple House La AIN/FAZ L10 85 J6 🔲
Coppull Hall La CHLY/EC PR7 43 J4
Coppull La WGN WN1 ..... 68 F3
Coppull Moor La CHLY/EC PR7 42 F7
Coppull Rd CHLY/EC PR7 .. 43 H1
MGHL L31 ............... 72 E7
Copse Gv PEN/TH CH61 ... 126 A6 🔲
The Copse CALD/MH L18 .. 114 F8
CHLY/EC PR7 ............. 43 K1
NEWLW WA12 ............ 104 C1
RUNC WA7 ............... 150 C7
WGNW/BIL/O WN5 ....... 67 J7
Copthorne Rd KKBY L32 ... 85 K3
Copy La NTHLY L30 ....... 84 C1
Coral Av HUY L36 ......... 115 M2
STHEL WA9 .............. 102 B6
Coral Dr BTL L20 ......... 7 L4
Coralin Wy AIMK WN4 .... 79 H6
Coral Rdg CL/PREN CH43 . 110 F7
Coral St CLB/OSW/ST L13 . 114 C4
WGNNW/ST WN6 .......... 68 C2
Corbet Av WARRN/WOL WA2 121 K5
Corbet Cl WARRN/WOL WA2 121 K5 🔲
Corbridge Rd CHLDW L16 . 114 F7
Corbyn St WAL/EG CH44 .. 112 A4
Corfe Cl WGNE/HIN WN2 .. 57 M8
Corfu St BIRK CH41 ....... 10 F6 🔲
Corinthian Av CLB/OSW/ST L13 114 C1
Corinthian St LITH L21 .... 83 H6 🔲
RF/TRAN CH42 .......... 128 B3 🔲
Corinto St TOX L8 ........ 113 H6
Cormorant Dr RUNC WA7 .. 18 D4
Corncroft Rd HUY L36 .... 99 M2 🔲
Corndale Rd CALD/MH L18 130 C1
Cornelian Gv AIMK WN4 ... 79 H8
Cornelius Dr PEN/TH CH61 126 A6
Cornel Wy HUY L36 ...... 116 B5
Corner Brook STBRV L28 .. 99 J4
Cornerhouse La WDN WA8 133 M2
Corner La WGNE/HIN WN2 . 81 M3

Cornett Rd WLT/FAZ L9 .... 84 D6
Corney St EHL/KEN L7 ..... 113 L6
Cornfield Cl GTS/LS CH66 . 163 H4
Cornflower Cl CHLYE PR6 .. 32 F3 🔲
Cornflower Wy MOR/LEA CH46 110 C3
Cornforth Wy WDN WA8 .. 134 B2 🔲
Cornhill CLVPS L1 ......... 112 F5
Cornice Rd CLB/OSW/ST L13 114 C1
Corniche Rd PS/BROM CH62 128 D7
Corn St LEIGH WN7 ....... 81 M8 🔲
TOX L8 .................. 113 G8
Cornubia Rd WDN WA8 ... 17 H5
Cornwall Av RUNC WA7 ... 19 C4
Cornwall Cl PS/BROM CH62 128 D5
Cornwall Crs WGN WN1 ... 56 D4 🔲
Cornwall Dr CL/PREN CH43 127 J4
Cornwallis Rd WGNS/IIMK WN3 68 C8 🔲
Cornwallis St CLVPS L1 .... 112 F5
Cornwall Pl
WGNW/BIL/O WN5 ....... 67 L7 🔲
Cornwall Rd WDN WA8 ... 134 D2
Cornwall St STHEL WA9 .. 102 F3 🔲
WARR WA1 ............... 15 L2
Cornwall Wy STHP PR8 ... 47 K3
Cornwood Cl HUY L36 .... 115 K6
Corona Av MGHL L31 ..... 61 L8 🔲
Corona Rd CLB/OSW/ST L13 114 C1
CSBY/WL L22 ............ 82 F4 🔲
PS/BROM CH62 .......... 144 D2
Coronation Av DV/KA/FCH L14 115 G2
FMBY L37 ................ 59 J3
WAL/NB CH45 ........... 95 K6
WARRS WA4 ............. 138 E3 🔲
Coronation Dr CSBY/BLUN L23 82 F2
DV/KA/FCH L14 ......... 115 G2
FROD/HEL WA6 .......... 160 F4 🔲
NEWLW WA12 ............ 105 G4 🔲
PS/BROM CH62 .......... 143 M2 🔲
RAIN/WH L35 ............ 116 E2
RNFD/HAY WA11 ......... 91 J6
WARRW/BUR WA5 ....... 136 B1
WDN WA8 ................ 133 K5
Coronation Rd CSBY/BLUN L23 82 F2
ECCL WA10 .............. 88 E7
EP CH65 ................. 20 C7
HOY CH47 ............... 108 B7
MGHL L31 ............... 72 F2
RUNC WA7 ............... 19 J5
RUNC WA7 ............... 151 H7
WGNNW/ST WN6 .......... 67 M2
Coronation St AIMK WN4 .. 78 F7
WGNS/IIMK WN3 ......... 4 D7
Coronation Wk STHP PR8 . 2 E4
WGNW/BIL/O WN5 ....... 89 M1
Coroner's La WDN WA8 ... 118 C8
Coronet Rd NG/CROX L11 . 98 E2
Coronet Wy WDN WA8 ... 133 K5
Corporation Rd BIRK CH41 . 10 C1
Corporation St CHLYE PR6 . 32 F4
ECCL WA10 .............. 9 G4
WGNS/IIMK WN3 ......... 4 D7
Corridor Rd EP CH65 ..... 157 K8
Corrie Dr BEB CH63 ...... 143 H1
Corsewall St EHL/KEN L7 . 113 M5 🔲
Corsey Av NTHTN L30 .... 83 L2
Corsey Rd WGNE/HIN WN2 . 81 G1
Corsham Rd HLWD L26 ... 132 A7
Corsican Gdns RAIN/WH L35 101 L6 🔲
Corsock St WGN WN1 .... 5 K1
Corston Gv HOR/BR BL6 .. 57 M4
Cortsway GR/UP/WCH CH49 110 A8
Cortsway West
GR/UP/WCH CH49 ....... 109 M8
Corwen Cl CL/PREN CH43 . 110 D7 🔲
MOR/LEA CH46 .......... 110 B6
WARRW/BUR WA5 ....... 121 G4
Corwen Crs DV/KA/FCH L14 115 H3
Corwen Dr NTHTN L30 .... 84 C1
Corwen Rd ANF/KKDL L4 .. 97 L5
HOY CH47 ............... 108 E6
Cosgrove Av NPK/KEN L6 . 97 M6 🔲
Cossack Av
WARRN/WOL WA2 ....... 121 L4 🔲
Costain St BTL L20 ....... 96 E5
Costessey Wy WGNS/IIMK WN3 78 E2
Cote Lea Ct RUNC WA7 ... 150 B7 🔲
Cotham St ECCL WA10 .... 9 G5
Cotsford Cl HUY L36 ...... 115 L1
Cotsford Pl HUY L36 ...... 115 L1 🔲
Cotsford Rd HUY L36 ..... 115 L1
Cotsford Wy HUY L36 ..... 115 L1 🔲
Cotswold Av CHLY/EC PR7 . 31 M4
GOL/RIS/CU WA3 ........ 92 F7
WGNW/BIL/O WN5 ....... 67 K8
Cotswold Dr HOR/BR BL6 .. 45 L8
Cotswold Gv STHEL WA9 .. 103 J2
Cotswold Rd CHLY/EC PR7 . 32 E7
RF/TRAN CH42 .......... 127 L4
WARRN/WOL WA2 ....... 122 B2
Cotswolds Crs HLWD L26 . 132 A6 🔲
Cotswold St EHL/KEN L7 .. 113 K3
Cottage Cl BEB CH63 ..... 143 L8 🔲
KKBY L32 ................ 86 A6
NSTN CH64 .............. 153 C6
ORM L39 ................. 62 F1 🔲
Cottage Dr East HES CH60 . 152 B1
Cottage Dr West HES CH60 . 141 H8
Cottage Flds CHLY/EC PR7 . 32 D8
Cottage La HES CH60 ..... 141 H8
ORM L39 ................. 50 F7
Cottage Ms ORM L39 ..... 50 F8
Cottage Pl STHEL WA9 .... 118 F4 🔲
Cottage St BIRK CH41 .... 11 G3
Cottam Dr WARRN/WOL WA2 122 C2
Cottam St CHLY/EC PR7 ... 32 E7 🔲
Cottenham St EHL/KEN L7 . 113 K2 🔲
Cotterdale Cl STHEL WA9 . 102 F7 🔲
WDN WA8 ................ 120 B6
Cotterill RUNC WA7 ...... 149 M5
Cotterill Dr WARR WA1 ... 122 E6
Cottesbrook Cl NG/CROX L11 98 C2
Cottesbrook Pl NG/CROX L11 98 C2 🔲
Cottesbrook Rd NG/CROX L11 98 C2
Cottesmore Dr HES CH60 . 141 M5 🔲
Cottesmore Wy
GOL/RIS/CU WA3 ........ 92 D4
Cotton Dr ORM L39 ....... 50 F7

Cotton La RUNC WA7 149 M5
Cotton St LEIGH WN7 81 M8 6
VAUX/LVPD L3 12 C1
Cottonwood AIG/SPK L17 129 H2
Cottrell Cl ALL/GAR L19 145 L1 3
Coudray Rd CHTN/BK PR9 25 G4
Coulport Cl DV/KA/FCH L14 115 J1
Coulsdon Pl TOX L8 129 J1
Coulthard Rd RF/TRAN CH42 128 C5 1
Coulton Rd WDN WA8 135 G2
Coultshead Av
WGNW/BIL/O WN5 78 A7 1
Council Av AIMK WN4 91 K2 4
Council St RAIN/WH L35 101 J8
Countess Pk NG/CROX L11 98 E3
Countess Wy CHLY/EC PR7 31 M3
Countisbury Dr CHLDW L16 115 G7
County Police St WGNE/HIN WN2 5 M5
County Rd ANF/KKDL L4 97 H5
KKBY L32 86 A1
ORM L39 50 F8
Coupland Rd WGNE/HIN WN2 81 K1
Courage Low La
WGNNW/ST WN6 54 F1
Courier Pl WGNW/BIL/O WN5 68 A4
Course La BRSC L40 53 G4
SKEL WN8 53 J4 1
Court Av HLWD L26 132 C4
Courtenay Av CSBY/WL L22 82 E3
Courtenay Rd CSBY/WL L22 82 E3
HOY CH47 108 C6
WLTN L25 131 H1 1
Courtfield ORM L39 50 F6
Courtfields Cl WD/CROXPK L12 98 D8
Courtgreen ORM L39 50 F6 1
Court Hey Av DV/KA/FCH L14 115 J3
Court Hey Dr CHLDW L16 115 H4
Court Hey Rd CHLDW L16 115 H4
Courthope Rd ANF/KKDL L4 97 K3
Courtland Rd CALD/MH L18 114 D8
Courtney Av WAL/EG CH44 111 J2 4
Courtney Rd RF/TRAN CH42 128 C5 2
Court Rd CHTN/BK PR9 3 K1
The Court NSTN CH64 153 H7
Cousin's La BRSC L40 39 J2
Covent Gdn CLVP L2 12 E7
Coventry Av GTS/LS CH66 163 G5
Coventry Rd WAV L15 114 C7 3
Coventry St BIRK CH41 11 H6
CHLY/EC PR7 32 E7 3
Coverdale Av RAIN/WH L35 117 M3
Coverdale Cl WARRW/BUR WA5 120 B6
Covertside WKBY CH48 124 F3
The Coverts WGNNW/ST WN6 68 B3 2
Cowan Dr NPK/KEN L6 113 J1
Cowanway WDN WA8 118 B8
Cowburn St LEIGH WN7 81 M8 7
Cowdell St WARRN/WOL WA2 14 F1
Cowdrey Av CL/PREN CH43 110 E4 3
Cow Hey La RUNC WA7 149 J8
Cowley Cl GR/UP/WCH CH49 109 M8 3
Cowley Hill La ECCL WA10 8 D1
Cowley Rd ANF/KKDL L4 97 H4
Cowley St ECCL WA10 9 G2
Cowling Brow CHLYE PR6 33 G6
Cowling St WGNS/IIMK WN3 4 D7
Cowper Rd CLB/OSW/ST L13 114 D3
Cowper St BTL L20 6 D1
LEIGH WN7 81 M8
Cowper Wy HUY L36 116 C5
Cowslip Wy CHLYE PR6 32 F3 4
Coxfield WGNNW/ST WN6 54 F6
Coyford Dr CHTN/BK PR9 22 C8
Coylton Av RAIN/WH L35 117 M3
Crab La WARRN/WOL WA2 122 C2
Crab St ECCL WA10 8 F3
Crabtree Cl BRSC L40 51 M1 2
NTHLY L27 115 M8
Crabtree Fold RUNC WA7 150 E5
Crabtree La BRSC L40 38 E8
Crabtree Rd WGNW/BIL/O WN5 67 M6
Cradley WDN WA8 133 L3
Crag Gv RNFD/HAY WA11 89 K4
Craigburn Rd CLB/OSW/ST L13 98 A7
Craig Gdns GTS/LS CH66 156 A6
Craighurst Rd WLTN L25 115 J6
Craigleigh Gv PS/BROM CH62 155 H1
Craigmore Rd CALD/MH L18 130 C4
Craigside Av WD/CROXPK L12 98 C6 2
Craigs Rd CLB/OSW/ST L13 98 A7
Craigwood Wy HUY L36 115 K2 1
Craine Cl ANF/KKDL L4 97 K5
Cramond Av CALD/MH L18 114 C8 4
Cramond Cl WGNS/IIMK WN3 78 F1
Cranage Cl RUNC WA7 149 M6 1
Cranberry Av WGNNW/ST WN6 68 B2
Cranberry Cl ECCL WA10 8 E2
Cranborne Av HOY CH47 109 G4
WARRS WA4 137 K4
Cranborne Cl WGNNW/ST WN6 55 M4
Cranborne Rd WAV L15 113 M6
Cranbourne Av BIRK CH41 111 H6
MOR/LEA CH46 109 M6
Cranbourne Dr CHLYE PR6 33 G6
Cranbourne St CHLYE PR6 32 F6
Cranbrook Av AIMK WN4 91 J1
Cranbrook St WGN WN1 68 D1
Cranby St WGNE/HIN WN2 69 M8 10
Crane Av STHEL WA9 102 F7
Cranehurst Rd ANF/KKDL L4 97 K3
Cranes La BRSC L40 52 B6
Crane St CHLY/EC PR7 42 F7
Cranfield Rd CSBY/BLUN L23 71 J8
WGNS/IIMK WN3 79 J2
Cranford Cl PS/BROM CH62 155 H1
Cranford Rd ALL/GAR L19 130 D5
Cranford St WAL/EG CH44 111 L3 4
Cranham Av GOL/RIS/CU WA3 93 G6
Crank Hl RNFD/HAY WA11 89 G1
Crank Rd RNFD/HAY WA11 77 H6
RNFD/HAY WA11 88 E6
Crankwood Rd WGNE/HIN WN2 80 D7
Cranleigh WGNNW/ST WN6 56 B5
Cranleigh Cl HOR/BR BL6 57 M4 1
WARRS WA4 137 K6
Cranleigh Pl WLTN L25 115 J7 1
Cranleigh Rd WLTN L25 115 J8
Cranmer St EV L5 96 F7
Cranmore Av CSBY/BLUN L23 83 G3
Cranshaw Av STHEL WA9 118 F2
Cranshaw La WDN WA8 118 D8
Cranston Cl ECCL WA10 88 D8
Cranston Rd NWD/KWIPK L33 86 E3
Cranswick Gn GTS/LS CH66 155 L8
Crantock Cl HLWD L26 132 B5
NG/CROX L11 98 E1 2
Crantock Gv ECCL WA10 88 E7
Cranwell Av GOL/RIS/CU WA3 107 H1
Cranwell Cl AIN/FAZ L10 84 E3
Cranwell Rd GR/UP/WCH CH49 125 K2
WLTN L25 115 J6
Craven Av GOL/RIS/CU WA3 93 G6
Craven Cl BIRK CH41 11 G5
Craven Ct WARRN/WOL WA2 121 H1
Craven Lea WD/CROXPK L12 99 G2
Craven Rd RAIN/WH L35 117 L2
WD/CROXPK L12 98 E7 1
Craven St BIRK CH41 10 F6
VAUX/LVPD L3 13 K5
Cravenwood Rd HLWD L26 132 B6
Crawford Av CALD/MH L18 114 B8
CHLY/EC PR7 32 D6
CHLY/EC PR7 44 A8
MGHL L31 72 D2
WDN WA8 133 K4
WGNE/HIN WN2 57 K8
Crawford Cl STHEL WA9 118 F1
WD/CROXPK L12 98 F6
Crawford Dr WAV L15 114 C4
Crawford Pk CALD/MH L18 130 B2 1
Crawford Pl RUNC WA7 149 K7
Crawford Rd SKEL WN8 76 F3
Crawford St STHEL WA9 119 G1
WGN WN1 4 E4
WGNE/HIN WN2 69 L1
Crawford Wy CLB/OSW/ST L13 114 A3
Crawley Av
WARRN/WOL WA2 121 J2 4
Crawley Cl WLTN L25 131 M5
Crediton Av CHTN/BK PR9 22 D8
Crediton Cl NG/CROX L11 85 L8
Crediton Dr WGNE/HIN WN2 80 C4
The Creek WAL/NB CH45 95 G5 1
Cremorne Hey STBRV L28 99 K6
Crescent Av AIMK WN4 91 J1
FMBY L37 59 G4
Crescent Dr FROD/HEL WA6 166 D2
Crescent Gn ORM L39 62 D4
Crescent Rd CSBY/BLUN L23 70 D8
EP CH65 20 E3
LITH L21 83 J7
STHP PR8 35 H2
WAL/EG CH44 111 L1
WLT/FAZ L9 97 K1
The Crescent BEB CH63 128 A8
CHLY/EC PR7 32 E3
CHTN/BK PR9 25 L2
CSBY/BLUN L23 71 J7 2
CSBY/WL L22 83 G4
EP CH65 156 B8
GR/UP/WCH CH49 125 M2
HUY L36 116 C3
MGHL L31 72 E6
PEN/TH CH61 126 B7
RAIN/WH L35 117 H1
WGNW/BIL/O WN5 67 M7
WKBY CH48 124 C3 2
Cressbrook Rd WARRS WA4 137 L5
Cressell Pk WGNNW/ST WN6 55 J3
Cressingham Rd WAL/NB CH45 95 K5
Cressington Av RF/TRAN CH42 127 M4
Cressington Prom ALL/GAR L19 130 B7
Cresswell Cl NTHTN L30 84 B4
WARRW/BUR WA5 120 F3 1
Cresswell St NPK/KEN L6 13 M2
NPK/KEN L6 113 J1 3
Cresta Dr RUNC WA7 149 H7 3
Cresttor Rd WLTN L25 131 H2
Crestwood Av WGNS/IIMK WN3 79 G2
Creswell St ECCL WA10 8 C5
Cretan Rd WAV L15 113 M6
Crewe Gn GR/UP/WCH CH49 126 C3 2
Criccieth Av WGNE/HIN WN2 57 M8
Criccieth Ct EP CH65 163 M3 3
Cricketers Gn CHLY/EC PR7 30 D6
Cricket Pth FMBY L37 47 H8
STHP PR8 35 H2
Cricket St WGNNW/ST WN6 4 C4
Cricklade Cl BTL L20 6 E3 2
Criftin Cl GTS/LS CH66 162 E3
Cringles Dr RAIN/WH L35 116 F6
Cripple Ga WGNNW/ST WN6 55 H3
Crispin Rd NTHLY L27 115 M8
Crispin St ECCL WA10 8 D6
Critchley Rd SPK/HALE L24 147 J3
Critchley Wy NWD/KWIPK L33 74 B8
Croal Av WGNE/HIN WN2 80 C3 4
Croasdale Dr RUNC WA7 150 A8
SKEL WN8 53 L2
Crockett's Wk ECCL WA10 88 D8
Crockleford Av STHP PR8 36 A2
Crocus Av BIRK CH41 111 H5
Crocus St EV L5 96 F6 2
Croesmere Dr GTS/LS CH66 162 F3
Croft Av BRSC L40 52 D1
GOL/RIS/CU WA3 92 B3 1
PS/BROM CH62 143 L4
WGNW/BIL/O WN5 66 F8 1
Croft Av East PS/BROM CH62 143 M3
Croft Cl CL/PREN CH43 127 G1
Croft Dr GR/UP/WCH CH49 110 A6
MOR/LEA CH46 110 B6
WKBY CH48 124 E7
Croft Dr East WKBY CH48 124 F7
Croft Dr West WKBY CH48 124 E6
Croft Edge CL/PREN CH43 127 K2
Croft End STHEL WA9 103 H4
Croften Dr NSTN CH64 153 G8
Crofters Cl GTS/LS CH66 163 G4 1
Crofters Gn CHLY/EC PR7 31 L2
Crofters Heath GTS/LS CH66 163 G4
The Crofters GR/UP/WCH CH49 125 M1
Croft Fld MGHL L31 73 G4
Croft Gdns WARRS WA4 138 C6
Croft Heath Gdns
GOL/RIS/CU WA3 106 C5 1
Croft Hey BRSC L40 39 K1
Croft Heys ORM L39 62 D4
Croftlands WGNW/BIL/O WN5 77 M1
Croft La PS/BROM CH62 143 M4
WLT/FAZ L9 84 F6
Crofton Cl WARRS WA4 138 E8
Crofton Crs CLB/OSW/ST L13 114 D2
Crofton Gdns
GOL/RIS/CU WA3 107 G2 1
Crofton Rd CLB/OSW/ST L13 114 D2
RF/TRAN CH42 128 A2
RUNC WA7 18 C6
Croft Rd CHLYE PR6 33 G6
Croftside WARR WA1 123 H6
Croftson Av ORM L39 51 H6 1
Croft St GOL/RIS/CU WA3 92 C5 2
WDN WA8 16 D7
Croftsway HES CH60 140 F5
The Croft CHLY/EC PR7 30 E6
CHLY/EC PR7 31 K2
GR/UP/WCH CH49 125 M3
MGHL L31 61 K8 1
RUNC WA7 150 A4
WD/CROXPK L12 98 D6
WGNW/BIL/O WN5 77 M1
Croftwood Sq
WGNW/BIL/O WN5 67 L3
Cromarty Rd CLB/OSW/ST L13 114 B3
WAL/EG CH44 111 H1 4
Cromdale Gv STHEL WA9 103 G3
Cromdale Wy
WARRW/BUR WA5 120 A7
Cromedale Crs WGNNW/ST WN6 56 C5
Cromer Dr WAL/NB CH45 95 J8
Cromer Rd AIG/SPK L17 130 A4
HOY CH47 108 C6 1
STHP PR8 35 G3
WGNS/IIMK WN3 79 G2
Cromer Wy HLWD L26 132 B7
Cromfield ORM L39 62 E3
Cromford Dr WGNW/BIL/O WN5 67 K8
Cromford Rd HUY L36 100 A8 1
Crompton Dr WD/CROXPK L12 99 G2
Cromptons La CALD/MH L18 114 F8
Crompton St EV L5 96 F8
WGN WN1 4 F3
WGNE/HIN WN2 80 B2 1
Cromwell Av WARRW/BUR WA5 120 E5
Cromwell Av South
WARRW/BUR WA5 136 E1
Cromwell Cl ORM L39 62 E3
Cromwell Rd ANF/KKDL L4 97 H3 3
EP CH65 20 D4
Cromwell St WDN WA8 16 C8
Crondall Gv WAV L15 114 D6
Cronton Av MOR/LEA CH46 110 A2
Cronton La RAIN/WH L35 117 K4
WDN WA8 117 K5
Cronton Park Cl WDN WA8 117 L7 1
Cronton Rd RAIN/WH L35 116 D6
WAV L15 114 C8 3
Cronulla Dr WARRW/BUR WA5 119 M6
Crookall St AIMK WN4 91 L1 1
Crooke Rd WGNNW/ST WN6 67 L2
Crookhurst Av
WGNW/BIL/O WN5 77 M7
Crook St CHLY/EC PR7 32 D8
CHLY/EC PR7 44 B6 2
WGN WN1 4 D3
WGNE/HIN WN2 80 F1 2
Croome Dr WKBY CH48 124 E3
Croppers Hl ECCL WA10 8 D6
Cropper's La ORM L39 63 J4
Croppers Rd WARRN/WOL WA2 122 B2
Cropper St CLVPS L1 13 J8
Cropton Rd FMBY L37 59 H2
Cropton Wy WGNE/HIN WN2 81 H2
Crosby Av WARRW/BUR WA5 121 J5
Crosby Cl GR/UP/WCH CH49 110 B7
Crosby Gn WD/CROXPK L12 98 C6
Crosby Gv ECCL WA10 101 M4 3
NSTN CH64 154 D4
Crosby Rd STHP PR8 35 H2
Crosby Rd North CSBY/WL L22 83 G4
Crosby Rd South CSBY/WL L22 83 G5
LITH L21 83 H6
Crosender Rd CSBY/BLUN L23 82 E2
Crosfield Cl EHL/KEN L7 113 L4 3
Crosfield Rd EHL/KEN L7 113 L4
RAIN/WH L35 117 H1
WAL/EG CH44 111 L2 1
Crosfield St WARR WA1 14 C5
Crosgrove Rd ANF/KKDL L4 97 L4
Crosland Rd KKBY L32 86 C4
Crossacre Rd WLTN L25 115 K6
Cross Barn La HTWN L38 71 G3
Cross Brow Preston Rd
CHLY/EC PR7 31 L5
Crossdale Rd CSBY/BLUN L23 82 E2 1
PS/BROM CH62 143 M7
WGNE/HIN WN2 81 J1
Crossdale Wy RNFD/HAY WA11 89 K4
Crosse Hall La CHLYE PR6 33 G6
Crosse Hall St CHLYE PR6 33 H6
Crossens Wy CHTN/BK PR9 22 E7
Cross Farm Rd STHEL WA9 9 L9
Crossfield Av GOL/RIS/CU WA3 107 H3
Crossfield Rd SKEL WN8 65 L5
Crossfield St STHEL WA9 9 J5
Crossford Cl WGNS/IIMK WN3 78 F1
Crossgates WDN WA8 135 H2
Cross Green Cl FMBY L37 59 J3
Crosshall Brow BRSC L40 63 L1
Crosshall St CLVPS L1 13 G6
Cross Hey LITH L21 83 K3
Cross Hey Av CL/PREN CH43 110 F8
Cross Hillocks La RAIN/WH L35 133 G2
The Crossings NEWLW WA12 104 E2 1
Cross La BEB CH63 143 H1
FROD/HEL WA6 159 K5
GOL/RIS/CU WA3 106 F6
NEWLW WA12 104 D2
NSTN CH64 153 G8
ORM L39 49 K4
RAIN/WH L35 116 F1
WAL/NB CH45 94 F8
WARRS WA4 138 C3
WGNW/BIL/O WN5 77 M2
Cross La South
GOL/RIS/CU WA3 106 F7
Crossley Av GTS/LS CH66 156 A7
Crossley Dr HES CH60 140 F5
WAV L15 114 C5
Crossley Rd ECCL WA10 101 M5
Crossley St WARR WA1 15 G4
Cross Meanygate
KIRK/FR/WA PR4 27 L8
Cross Pit La RNFD/HAY WA11 76 B7
Cross St BIRK CH41 11 L5
CHLY/EC PR7 32 E4 4
CSBY/WL L22 82 F5
ECCL WA10 9 G5
GOL/RIS/CU WA3 92 C6
NSTN CH64 153 G5
PR/KW L34 100 F6
PS/BROM CH62 128 D8 1
RUNC WA7 19 G2 2
STHP PR8 3 G6
WARRN/WOL WA2 14 F1
WDN WA8 16 F2
WGNE/HIN WN2 69 M8
WGNNW/ST WN6 56 A4
WGNS/IIMK WN3 4 E6
WGNW/BIL/O WN5 67 K7 2
The Cross HTWN L38 70 F2
Crossvale Rd HUY L36 116 A4
Crossway CL/PREN CH43 111 G5 1
WDN WA8 133 M5
Crossway Cl AIMK WN4 80 A8
Crossways PS/BROM CH62 143 M2
The Crossway BEB CH63 153 K1
Crosswood Crs HUY L36 115 L2
Crosthwaite Av
PS/BROM CH62 155 H1
Croston Av CHLYE PR6 44 C5
RAIN/WH L35 101 K8
Croston Cl WDN WA8 133 L1
Croston Dr BRSC L40 28 D7
Croston La CHLY/EC PR7 42 D4
Croston Rd BRSC L40 28 D7
Croston's Brow CHTN/BK PR9 25 H2
Croston St WGNE/HIN WN2 69 L7 2
Crouch St EV L5 97 J7 3
STHEL WA9 102 F5 1
Croughton Rd CHNE CH2 164 C6
GTS/LS CH66 156 B5
Crowe Av WARRN/WOL WA2 121 K2
Crowhurst Dr WGN WN1 68 D2
Crowland Cl CHTN/BK PR9 25 J7
Crowland St CHTN/BK PR9 25 J7
Crowland Wy FMBY L37 59 K3 2
Crow La SKEL WN8 66 B2
Crow La East NEWLW WA12 104 E1
Crow La West NEWLW WA12 104 C1
Crowmarsh Cl
GR/UP/WCH CH49 126 B1 4
Cronton Acres Rd WLTN L25 131 L4
Crown Av WDN WA8 133 K5
Crown Cl FMBY L37 59 J3
Crown Fields Cl NEWLW WA12 91 K8
Crown Gdns NEWLW WA12 104 D1
Crown Ga RUNC WA7 150 B6
Crown Park Dr NEWLW WA12 104 D1
Crown Rd WD/CROXPK L12 98 E6
Crown St CHLY/EC PR7 32 E5
EHL/KEN L7 13 M6
NEWLW WA12 104 C2
STHEL WA9 101 M6 3
TOX L8 113 J6 2
WARR WA1 14 E5
WGNE/HIN WN2 69 L7
WGNS/IIMK WN3 4 D7
Crownway HUY L36 115 M1
Crow Orchard Rd
WGNNW/ST WN6 55 H3
Crow St TOX L8 112 F7
Crowther St ECCL WA10 8 C6
Crow Wood La WDN WA8 134 F3
Crow Wood Pl WDN WA8 134 F2 1
Crow Wood Rd GOL/RIS/CU WA3 92 F4
Croxdale Rd DV/KA/FCH L14 99 J6
Croxdale Rd West
DV/KA/FCH L14 99 H6
Croxteth Av LITH L21 83 J6
WAL/EG CH44 111 K1
Croxteth Cl MGHL L31 73 G2
Croxteth Dr AIG/SPK L17 113 L8
RNFD/HAY WA11 76 B6
Croxteth Gv TOX L8 113 K7
Croxteth Hall La NG/CROX L11 98 E2
WD/CROXPK L12 98 E3
Croxteth La STBRV L28 99 K4
Croxteth Rd BTL L20 83 L8 1
TOX L8 113 K8
Croxteth Vw KKBY L32 86 B7
Croyde Cl CHTN/BK PR9 22 D8 1
Croyde Pl STHEL WA9 118 E1
Croyde Rd SPK/HALE L24 147 J2
Croydon Av CALD/MH L18 114 B8
Croylands St ANF/KKDL L4 97 G5
Crucian Wy WD/CROXPK L12 98 F2
Crummock Dr
WGNS/IIMK WN3 79 H2 1
Crump St CLVPS L1 113 G6 2
Crutchley Av BIRK CH41 10 C2
Cryers La CHNE CH2 165 J3
Cubbin Crs EV L5 96 F7
Cubert Rd NG/CROX L11 98 E1
Cuckoo Cl WLTN L25 131 J1
Cuckoo La NSTN CH64 153 K6
WLTN L25 115 J8
Cuerden St CHLYE PR6 33 G6 4
Cuerdley Gn WDN WA8 135 J3
Cuerdley Rd WARRW/BUR WA5 135 L2
Cuerdon Dr WARRS WA4 138 F4
Culbeck La CHLY/EC PR7 31 H2
Culbin Cl GOL/RIS/CU WA3 107 J7 2
Culcheth Av WGNE/HIN WN2 80 D4
Culcheth Hall Dr
GOL/RIS/CU WA3 107 H1
Culcross Av WGNS/IIMK WN3 78 E1
Culford Cl RUNC WA7 150 F4 3
Cullen Av BTL L20 83 M8
Cullen Cl BEB CH63 154 E1
WGNE/HIN WN2 69 J5
Cullen Rd RUNC WA7 18 B9
RUNC WA7 148 F6 1
Cullen St TOX L8 113 L6
Culme Rd WD/CROXPK L12 98 B6
Culshaw Wy BRSC L40 37 H6
Culvert La SKEL WN8 53 J3
Culvert St WGNNW/ST WN6 68 C3
Culzean Cl WD/CROXPK L12 99 G2
Cumberbatch Pl
WGNE/HIN WN2 80 B1
Cumberland Av AIG/SPK L17 113 M7
CL/PREN CH43 127 J3
ECCL WA10 101 K5
NTHTN L30 83 L2 2
Cumberland Cl NPK/KEN L6 97 M7
Cumberland Crs
RNFD/HAY WA11 90 C7
Cumberland Ga NTHTN L30 84 C2
Cumberland Gv GTS/LS CH66 162 E2
Cumberland Rd STHP PR8 3 L8
WAL/NB CH45 95 L6 3
Cumberland St CLVPS L1 12 F6 2
WARRS WA4 15 H9
WGN WN1 5 J1 1
Cumber La RAIN/WH L35 117 H2
Cumbers Dr NSTN CH64 153 J8
Cumbers La NSTN CH64 153 J8
Cumbrae Dr EP CH65 163 L4
Cumbrian Cl WGNE/HIN WN2 80 D3 2
Cumbria Wy WD/CROXPK L12 98 E4
Cummings St CLVPS L1 113 G5 2
Cumpsty Rd LITH L21 83 L4
Cunard Cl CL/PREN CH43 110 E7
Cunard Rd LITH L21 83 K6
Cunliffe Av NEWLW WA12 91 K8
Cunliffe Cl RUNC WA7 150 C6
Cunliffe Ct LEIGH WN7 93 J1
Cunliffe St CHLY/EC PR7 32 E6
CLVP L2 12 F5
LEIGH WN7 81 L8 3
Cunningham Av CHLY/EC PR7 32 C7
Cunningham Cl
WARRW/BUR WA5 120 B8 2
WKBY CH48 124 E7 2
Cunningham Dr BEB CH63 143 L6
RUNC WA7 18 D7
Cunningham Rd
CLB/OSW/ST L13 114 C3
WDN WA8 133 M5
Cunscough La MGHL L31 73 M3
Cuper Crs HUY L36 115 M1
Curate Rd NPK/KEN L6 97 L6
Curate St CHLYE PR6 32 F4
Curlender Cl BIRK CH41 111 G4
Curlender Wy SPK/HALE L24 148 A3
Curlew Av GR/UP/WCH CH49 109 M7
Curlew Cl GOL/RIS/CU WA3 92 F5 1
GR/UP/WCH CH49 109 M7 3
Curlew Ct MOR/LEA CH46 109 L4
Curlew Gv GOL/RIS/CU WA3 123 G2
Curlew La BRSC L40 39 G4
Curlew Wy MOR/LEA CH46 109 L4
Currans Rd
WARRN/WOL WA2 121 J3 1
Curtana Crs NG/CROX L11 98 E2
Curtis Rd ANF/KKDL L4 97 L4
Curtis St WGNW/BIL/O WN5 67 M7 2
Curwell Cl BEB CH63 143 K2 1
Curzon Av BIRK CH41 10 D3
WAL/NB CH45 95 K6 1
Curzon Dr WARRS WA4 138 C6
Curzon Rd CSBY/WL L22 83 G4
HOY CH47 108 C6
RF/TRAN CH42 127 K3
STHP PR8 3 M7
Curzon St RUNC WA7 18 F5
Cusson Rd NWD/KWIPK L33 86 D4
Custley Hey STBRV L28 99 K5
Custom House La CLVPS L1 12 F8 1
Cuthbert St
WGNW/BIL/O WN5 67 M7 3
Cut La BRSC L40 50 B6
NWD/KWIPK L33 87 G6
Cygnet Cl GTS/LS CH66 162 F1
ORM L39 62 E3
Cygnet Ct NWD/KWIPK L33 86 C3 2
WARR WA1 14 D9
Cygnet St WGNS/IIMK WN3 4 D7
Cynthia Av WARR WA1 122 D6
Cynthia Rd RUNC WA7 18 E5
Cypress Av GTS/LS CH66 163 H4
WDN WA8 134 D2
Cypress Cl MGHL L31 85 J2
WARR WA1 123 G6 1
Cypress Cft BEB CH63 143 K2
Cypress Gdns RAIN/WH L35 101 L6 2
Cypress Gv RUNC WA7 149 L6
Cypress Rd HUY L36 115 M5
STHP PR8 25 G7
WGNW/BIL/O WN5 68 A7
Cyprus St PR/KW L34 100 F7
Cyril Gv AIG/SPK L17 130 A3
Cyril St WARRN/WOL WA2 14 F2


# D


Dacre's Bridge La RAIN/WH L35 116 F6
Dacre St BIRK CH41 11 J5
BTL L20 6 E9
Dacy Rd EV L5 97 J8
Daffodil Cl WDN WA8 135 G1
Daffodil Rd BIRK CH41 111 H6
WAV L15 114 D6
Dagnall Av WARRW/BUR WA5 121 H3
Dagnall Rd KKBY L32 85 L4
Dahlia Cl WLT/FAZ L9 97 K1 1
Dailton Rd SKEL WN8 66 C6
Dairy Farm Rd RNFD/HAY WA11 75 M6
Daisy Av NEWLW WA12 104 E3
Daisybank Cl
WGNE/HIN WN2 69 M8 11
Daisy Bank Rd LYMM WA13 139 L2
WARRW/BUR WA5 136 B1 1
Daisy Fold CHLYE PR6 33 G3
Daisy Hill Dr CHLYE PR6 44 C4 2
Daisy Hill Fold CHLY/EC PR7 31 M4
Daisy La BRSC L40 52 D1

Daisy Mill Bank Cl
GOL/RIS/CU WA3 107 G2
Daisy Mt MGHL L31 73 G5
Daisy Rd WGNW/BIL/O WN5 68 A7
Daisy St EV L5 96 F6
Dalbeatie Ri WGN WN1 5 L1
Dalby Cl GOL/RIS/CU WA3 107 K8
RNFD/HAY WA11 9 M2
Dale Acre Dr NTHTN L30 83 L2
Dale Av CHLY/EC PR7 31 M4
GTS/LS CH66 155 L7
HES CH60 141 H4
PS/BROM CH62 143 M5
Dalebrook Cl WLTN L25 115 K6
Dale Cl MGHL L31 72 E3
SKEL WN8 53 K3
WARRW/BUR WA5 136 F1
WDN WA8 133 J5
Dale Crs STHEL WA9 102 F7
Dalecrest WGNW/BIL/O WN5 77 M4
Dalecroft FROD/HEL WA6 166 A4
Dale Dr EP CH65 156 B8
Dale End Rd PEN/TH CH61 141 L1
Dale Gdns HES CH60 140 F4
Dalegarth Av WD/CROXPK L12 99 H4
Dale Gv LEIGH WN7 93 L1 1
Dalehead Gv LEIGH WN7 93 L1
Dalehead Pl RNFD/HAY WA11 89 K4 1
Dale Hey GTS/LS CH66 155 G3
WAL/EG CH44 111 K2
Dalehurst Cl WAL/EG CH44 111 M1 7
Dale La NWD/KWIPK L33 86 C1
WARRS WA4 138 A6
Dalemeadow Rd
DV/KA/FCH L14 114 F2
Dale Ms WLTN L25 131 K1
Dale Rd GOL/RIS/CU WA3 92 C6
PS/BROM CH62 143 M8
Dalesford Cl LEIGH WN7 93 L5
Daleside Av AIMK WN4 79 J5 1
Daleside Cl PEN/TH CH61 126 B7 1
Daleside Rd NWD/KWIPK L33 86 B2
Dales Rw HUY L36 116 D3
Dale St ALL/GAR L19 130 E8
CLVP L2 12 F6
CLVPS L1 12 F6
LEIGH WN7 81 L8
RUNC WA7 19 G6
WGNE/HIN WN2 80 B2
Dalesway HES CH60 141 G5
The Dale NSTN CH64 152 F7
WARRW/BUR WA5 120 B8
Dale Vw CHLY/EC PR7 43 L1
NEWLW WA12 105 G1
Dale View Cl PEN/TH CH61 126 C8 2
Dalewood WD/CROXPK L12 99 G2 6
Dalewood Crs CHNE CH2 165 J2 1
Dalewood Gdns
RAIN/WH L35 117 H3 3
Daley Pl BTL L20 84 A6
Daley Rd LITH L21 83 L4
Dallam La WARRN/WOL WA2 14 D4
Dallas Gv WLT/FAZ L9 84 C7
Dalmeny St AIG/SPK L17 129 K2
Dalmorton Rd WAL/NB CH45 95 L5
Dalry Crs KKBY L32 86 B6
Dalrymple St EV L5 96 F8
Dalston Dr RNFD/HAY WA11 89 K4
Dalston Gv WGNS/IIMK WN3 78 F2
Dalton Av WARRW/BUR WA5 14 B1
Dalton Bank WARR WA1 15 H4
Dalton Cl WD/CROXPK L12 98 E3
WGNW/BIL/O WN5 67 K6
Dalton Ct RUNC WA7 150 A2
Dalton Dr WGNS/IIMK WN3 79 G2
Dalton Gv AIMK WN4 91 J1 3
Dalton Rd WAL/NB CH45 95 L6
Dalton St GOL/RIS/CU WA3 107 G7
RUNC WA7 149 M3
Daltry Cl WD/CROXPK L12 98 C6
Dalwood Cl RUNC WA7 151 G6
Damerham Ms WLTN L25 115 J6
Damfield La MGHL L31 72 E4
Damhead La NSTN CH64 154 A6
Damian Dr NEWLW WA12 91 J8 1
Dam La GOL/RIS/CU WA3 92 B2
GOL/RIS/CU WA3 106 B6
WARR WA1 122 F6
Damson Rd NTHLY L27 116 A8
Dam Wood La BRSC L40 37 L8
Dam Wood Rd SPK/HALE L24 146 F3
Danbers SKEL WN8 66 B7
Danby Cl EV L5 97 H8 2
RUNC WA7 149 M7 2
WARRW/BUR WA5 121 G6 2
Danby Fold RAIN/WH L35 117 K2 1
Danebury Cl WGNE/HIN WN2 80 F1 10
Dane Cl GR/UP/WCH CH49 126 B7
Danefield Pl ALL/GAR L19 130 F5 1
Danefield Rd ALL/GAR L19 130 F5
GR/UP/WCH CH49 125 L3
Dane Hall La CHLY/EC PR7 30 F3
Danehurst Rd WAL/NB CH45 95 H6
WLT/FAZ L9 84 D6 6
Danesbury Cl WGNW/BIL/O WN5 90 A1
Danescourt Rd BIRK CH41 10 B2
WD/CROXPK L12 98 E8
Danescroft WDN WA8 133 K2
Dane St ANF/KKDL L4 97 H4
Danesway CHLY/EC PR7 44 B4 1
WGN WN1 68 D2
Daneswell Dr MOR/LEA CH46 110 B4
Daneswell Rd SPK/HALE L24 147 J3 2
Daneville Rd ANF/KKDL L4 97 M3
Daneway STHP PR8 34 D7
Danger La MOR/LEA CH46 110 B3
Daniel Cl GOL/RIS/CU WA3 123 J1
LITH L21 83 J7
Daniel Davies Dr TOX L8 113 J6 3
Daniels La SKEL WN8 65 L6
Dannette Hey STBRV L28 99 L7
Dansie St VAUX/LVPD L3 13 L7
Dans Rd WDN WA8 135 G3
Dante Cl WLT/FAZ L9 84 E5
Danube St TOX L8 113 L6 2
Darby Gv ALL/GAR L19 130 D7 1
Darby La WGNE/HIN WN2 69 M7
Darby Rd ALL/GAR L19 130 C5
Darent Rd RNFD/HAY WA11 90 D7
Daresbury Av STHP PR8 34 C8
Daresbury Cl KKBY L32 85 L3
Daresbury Expy RUNC WA7 18 F3
WARRS WA4 151 J2
Daresbury La WARRS WA4 151 M3
Daresbury Rd ECCL WA10 101 K1
WAL/EG CH44 111 J1
Darfield SKEL WN8 66 B6
Daric Cl LEIGH WN7 93 L4
Dark Entry PR/KW L34 100 A4
Dark La BRSC L40 41 G2
BRSC L40 51 K7
HOR/BR BL6 57 K1
MGHL L31 72 F4
Darley Av WARRN/WOL WA2 122 A2
Darley Cl WDN WA8 133 K2
Darleydale Dr PS/BROM CH62 144 B8
Darley Dr WD/CROXPK L12 98 E7
Darley Rd WGNS/IIMK WN3 79 K2
Darley St HOR/BR BL6 45 K8
Darlington Cl WAL/EG CH44 111 M1 8
Darlington St CHLY/EC PR7 42 F4
WAL/EG CH44 111 M1 9
WGN WN1 4 F5
WGNE/HIN WN2 69 J6 2
Darlington St East WGN WN1 5 H5
Darmond Rd NWD/KWIPK L33 86 C2
Darmond's Gn WKBY CH48 124 D2
Darmonds Green Av
NPK/KEN L6 97 M7
Darnaway Cl GOL/RIS/CU WA3 107 K7
Darnhall St WGNE/HIN WN2 80 B1 3
Darnley St TOX L8 113 G8
Darran Av WGNS/IIMK WN3 79 H2
Darrel Dr EHL/KEN L7 113 L6 3
Darsefield Rd CHLDW L16 115 G6
Dartington Rd CHLDW L16 114 F5
Dartmouth Av AIN/FAZ L10 84 E3
Dartmouth Dr NTHTN L30 83 L1
Darvel Av AIMK WN4 90 E1
Darwall Rd ALL/GAR L19 130 F5
Darwen St EV L5 96 D8 1
Darwick Dr HUY L36 116 C5
Darwin Gv STHEL WA9 102 A6
Daryl Rd HES CH60 141 J4
Daten Av GOL/RIS/CU WA3 107 H7
Daub La BRSC L40 40 C5
Daulby St VAUX/LVPD L3 13 M6
Dauntsey Brow WLTN L25 115 K6 3
Dauntsey Ms WLTN L25 115 K6
Davenham Av CL/PREN CH43 127 H2
WARR WA1 122 A5
Davenham Cl CL/PREN CH43 127 H3 1
Davenham Rd FMBY L37 59 H1
Davenhill Pk WLT/FAZ L9 84 E3
Davenport Av WARRS WA4 122 B8
Davenport Cl WKBY CH48 124 E7 3
Davenport Gv
NWD/KWIPK L33 86 A1 3
Davenport Rd HES CH60 141 G6
Davenport Rw RUNC WA7 149 M5 1
Daventree Rd WAL/NB CH45 95 K8
Daventry Rd AIG/SPK L17 130 A3
David Rd LYMM WA13 139 L2
David's Av WARRW/BUR WA5 120 D8
Davidson Rd
CLB/OSW/ST L13 114 B2 4
David St TOX L8 129 H1
Davids Wk WLTN L25 131 L2 1
Davies Av NEWLW WA12 104 E1
WARRS WA4 138 B1
Davies Cl WDN WA8 149 J1
Davies St BTL L20 7 J3
CLVPS L1 12 F6 3
STHEL WA9 9 L4
WGNE/HIN WN2 80 C3
Davies Wy LYMM WA13 139 M2
Davis Rd MOR/LEA CH46 110 D2
Davy Av GOL/RIS/CU WA3 107 G8
Davy Cl ECCL WA10 88 D8
Davy Rd RUNC WA7 150 A2
Davy St EV L5 97 J7
Dawber Cl NPK/KEN L6 113 J1 4
Dawber's La CHLY/EC PR7 31 G3
Dawber St AIMK WN4 91 M1 1
Dawley Cl AIMK WN4 91 J2
Dawlish Cl WLTN L25 131 L5
Dawlish Dr CHTN/BK PR9 22 C8
Dawlish Rd PEN/TH CH61 125 L8
WAL/EG CH44 111 H1
Dawn Cl NSTN CH64 153 H8
STHEL WA9 102 A6
Dawn Gdns EP CH65 20 A7
Dawnwood Sq
WGNW/BIL/O WN5 67 L3
Dawpool Dr MOR/LEA CH46 110 A5
PS/BROM CH62 143 L6
Dawson Av BIRK CH41 10 C2
CHTN/BK PR9 22 E8 3
STHEL WA9 102 F6
WGNNW/ST WN6 68 C2
Dawson Gdns MGHL L31 72 E3
Dawson Rd ORM L39 51 H6
Dawson St CLVPS L1 13 G7
Dawstone Ri HES CH60 141 H6
Dawstone Rd HES CH60 141 H6
Daybrook SKEL WN8 66 B7
Dayfield SKEL WN8 66 C6
Days Meadow
GR/UP/WCH CH49 125 L2 2
Day St CLB/OSW/ST L13 114 C2
Deacon Cl CSBY/WL L22 82 F5 1
GOL/RIS/CU WA3 106 C5
Deacon Ct CSBY/WL L22 82 F5
WLTN L25 131 K3 2
Deacon Rd WDN WA8 16 E2
Deakin St BIRK CH41 111 H5
WGNS/IIMK WN3 5 J9
Dean Av WAL/NB CH45 95 G7
Dean Cl SKEL WN8 66 E6
WDN WA8 16 E3
WGNW/BIL/O WN5 89 M2
Dean Ct GOL/RIS/CU WA3 92 C6 2
Dean Crs WARRN/WOL WA2 121 K3 5
WGNW/BIL/O WN5 67 K5
Deane Rd EHL/KEN L7 113 L3
Dean Head La CHLYE PR6 45 J1
Dean Meadow NEWLW WA12 104 E1 1
Dean Rd GOL/RIS/CU WA3 92 C6
Deansburn Rd CLB/OSW/ST L13 98 A7
Deanscales Rd NG/CROX L11 98 B3
Deans Ct FMBY L37 47 H8
Deansfield Wy CHNE CH2 165 J2
Deansgate EP CH65 156 C8
Deansgate La FMBY L37 47 K8
Deansgate La North FMBY L37 47 J7
Deans La BRSC L40 53 G1
SKEL WN8 53 H3
WARRS WA4 139 H2
Deans Rd EP CH65 21 K8
Dean St CSBY/WL L22 82 F5
WDN WA8 16 E3
Deans Wy CL/PREN CH43 111 H5 2
Deansway WDN WA8 133 L5
Deanwater Cl GOL/RIS/CU WA3 122 F1
Dean Wy STHEL WA9 118 D2
Dean Wood Av
WGNW/BIL/O WN5 67 G4
Dean Wood Cl RAIN/WH L35 117 H3 4
Dearham Av RNFD/HAY WA11 89 J6
Dearne Cl WD/CROXPK L12 99 G8
Dearnford Av PS/BROM CH62 143 M7
Dearnford Cl PS/BROM CH62 143 M7
Dearnley Av RNFD/HAY WA11 90 A8
Deauville Rd WLT/FAZ L9 84 E6
Deben Cl WGNNW/ST WN6 55 M4 1
Debra Cl GTS/LS CH66 162 E1
MGHL L31 85 K1
Debra Rd GTS/LS CH66 162 E2
Dee Cl NWD/KWIPK L33 74 B7
Dee La WKBY CH48 124 C3
Deeley Cl EHL/KEN L7 113 L4
Dee Park Cl HES CH60 141 K7
Dee Park Rd HES CH60 141 K7
Deep Dl WARRW/BUR WA5 120 B7
Deepdale WDN WA8 133 L2
Deepdale Av BTL L20 83 J8
RNFD/HAY WA11 89 L4 2
Deepdale Cl CL/PREN CH43 110 E7 6
Deepdale Dr RAIN/WH L35 117 M2
Deepdale Rd WLTN L25 115 J6
Deepfield Dr HUY L36 116 B5
Deepfield Rd WAV L15 114 B7
Deepwood Gv RAIN/WH L35 117 G3 2
Deerbarn Dr NTHTN L30 84 D2
Deerbolt Cl KKBY L32 85 L2 1
Deerbolt Crs KKBY L32 85 L2
Deerbolt Wy KKBY L32 85 L2
Deerfold CHLY/EC PR7 32 D3
Dee Rd RAIN/WH L35 117 K2
Deer Park Ct RUNC WA7 150 B7 2
Deerwood Cl GTS/LS CH66 155 M6 1
Deerwood Crs GTS/LS CH66 155 M6
Deeside EP CH65 20 A9
Dee Side HES CH60 140 E5
Deeside Cl CL/PREN CH43 110 D7 5
EP CH65 163 K3
Dee View Rd HES CH60 141 H5
De Grouchy St WKBY CH48 124 D2 1
Deighton Rd CHLY/EC PR7 32 D7 3
Deirdre Av WDN WA8 16 D2
Delabole Rd NG/CROX L11 85 M8
De Lacy Rw RUNC WA7 150 C3
Delafield Cl WARRN/WOL WA2 122 B2
Delagoa Rd AIN/FAZ L10 85 H7
Delamain Rd CLB/OSW/ST L13 98 A7
Delamere Av GOL/RIS/CU WA3 93 G7
GTS/LS CH66 156 A8 2
PS/BROM CH62 155 G1
STHEL WA9 118 C2
WDN WA8 133 L4
Delamere Cl CL/PREN CH43 110 D7 6
PS/BROM CH62 155 G1
WD/CROXPK L12 98 F2 2
Delamere Dr GTS/LS CH66 163 G1
Delamere Gv WAL/EG CH44 112 A3 7
Delamere Pl CHLYE PR6 32 F5
Delamere Rd SKEL WN8 65 H3 1
STHP PR8 34 D8
Delamere St WARRW/BUR WA5 121 G8
Delamere Wy FROD/HEL WA6 160 E8
SKEL WN8 66 C6
Delamore Pl ANF/KKDL L4 7 L8 1
Delamore's Acre NSTN CH64 154 C5
Delamore St ANF/KKDL L4 7 M8
Delavor Cl HES CH60 141 G5 1
Delavor Rd HES CH60 141 G5
Delaware Crs KKBY L32 85 L2
Delegarte St WGNS/IIMK WN3 5 J8
Delenty Dr GOL/RIS/CU WA3 122 F1
Delery Dr WARR WA1 122 A5
Delfby Crs KKBY L32 86 C4
Delfhaven Ct WGNNW/ST WN6 56 C6
Delf La ANF/KKDL L4 97 J3
ORM L39 49 J8
SPK/HALE L24 131 K8
Dell Av WGNNW/ST WN6 68 A2
Dell Cl BEB CH63 143 K7
Dell Dr WARRN/WOL WA2 122 C3
Dellfield La MGHL L31 73 G4
Dell Gv RF/TRAN CH42 128 C5
Dell La HES CH60 141 K6
Dellside Cl AIMK WN4 78 F7
Dellside Gv STHEL WA9 102 E5 2
Dell St EHL/KEN L7 113 L3 2
The Dell CHLYE PR6 33 J2
RF/TRAN CH42 128 D4
SKEL WN8 66 D6
WD/CROXPK L12 99 G4
WGNNW/ST WN6 54 F6
Delph Common Rd ORM L39 62 D4
Delphfields Rd WARRS WA4 137 L6
Delph Gv LEIGH WN7 81 M4 3
Delphield RUNC WA7 150 F5
Delph La CHLY/EC PR7 31 M7
FMBY L37 58 E2 1
ORM L39 62 E4
RAIN/WH L35 117 H1
WARRN/WOL WA2 106 A7
WARRS WA4 151 J2
Delph Park Av ORM L39 62 D4
Delph Rd HTWN L38 70 F5
Delphside Cl WGNW/BIL/O WN5 66 F8
Delphside Rd WGNW/BIL/O WN5 66 E8
Delph St WGNNW/ST WN6 4 C1
The Delph SKEL WN8 53 L2
Delphwood Dr STHEL WA9 9 J9
Delta Dr WD/CROXPK L12 99 G5
Delta Rd LITH L21 83 K6 3
STHEL WA9 103 H1
Delta Rd East RF/TRAN CH42 128 D4 1
Delta Rd West
RF/TRAN CH42 128 D4 2
Deltic Wy NTHTN L30 84 C5
NWD/KWIPK L33 86 D5
Delves Av BEB CH63 143 H2
WARRW/BUR WA5 14 A1
Delyn Cl RF/TRAN CH42 128 A4
Demage Dr GTS/LS CH66 162 F2
Demesne St WAL/EG CH44 112 A2
Denbigh Av CHTN/BK PR9 25 H2
STHEL WA9 102 E6
Denbigh Cl FROD/HEL WA6 166 C4
Denbigh Gdns EP CH65 20 D9 1
Denbigh Rd WLT/FAZ L9 97 H2
Denbigh St EV L5 96 D8
Denbury Av WARRS WA4 138 B3
Dencourt Rd NG/CROX L11 98 D4
Dene Av NEWLW WA12 104 B1
Denebank Rd ANF/KKDL L4 97 K6
Dene Gv LEIGH WN7 93 K1 1
Denehurst Cl
WARRW/BUR WA5 136 B1 2
Deneshey Rd HOY CH47 108 E5
Dene St LEIGH WN7 93 K1
Denes Wy STBRV L28 99 J6
Denford Cl WGNS/IIMK WN3 79 H2
Denford Rd DV/KA/FCH L14 99 H8
Denham Av WARRW/BUR WA5 120 D8
Denham Cl WD/CROXPK L12 99 H2
Denham Dr WGNS/IIMK WN3 79 J2
Denholme SKEL WN8 66 B6
Denise Av WARRW/BUR WA5 120 A8
Denise Rd AIN/FAZ L10 85 K6
Denison Gv STHEL WA9 102 A6 1
Denman Dr NPK/KEN L6 113 L1
Denman Gv WAL/EG CH44 112 A3 3
Denman St EHL/KEN L7 113 K2 4
Denman Wy NPK/KEN L6 113 L1
Denmark Rd CHTN/BK PR9 25 J3
Denmark St CSBY/WL L22 82 F4 5
Dennett Cl MGHL L31 72 F6
WARR WA1 123 G7
Dennett Rd RAIN/WH L35 116 E1
Denning Dr PEN/TH CH61 125 M6
Dennis Av ECCL WA10 101 L6
Dennis Rd WDN WA8 17 G5
Denny Cl GR/UP/WCH CH49 126 B1
Densham Av WARRN/WOL WA2 121 K3
Denshaw SKEL WN8 66 B6
Denston Cl CL/PREN CH43 110 D6 2
Denstone Av AIN/FAZ L10 84 F3
Denstone Cl WLTN L25 131 K5 1
Denstone Crs DV/KA/FCH L14 115 J1
Dentdale Dr EV L5 13 K2
Denton Dr WAL/NB CH45 95 L7
Denton Gv NPK/KEN L6 97 L8
WGNW/BIL/O WN5 67 K5
Dentons Green La ECCL WA10 8 B2
Denton St TOX L8 129 H1
WDN WA8 17 G2
Dentwood St TOX L8 129 J1 5
Denver Rd KKBY L32 85 L4
WARRS WA4 138 C2 2
Depot Rd NWD/KWIPK L33 86 E1
Derby Cl NEWLW WA12 104 D2 4
Derby Dr RNFD/HAY WA11 76 C8
WARR WA1 15 M1
Derby Gv MGHL L31 72 F7
Derby Hill Crs ORM L39 51 J8 1
Derby Hill Rd ORM L39 51 J8
Derby La CLB/OSW/ST L13 114 C2 1
Derby Pl CHLYE PR6 44 C5 3
Derby Rd BTL L20 6 E6
CHTN/BK PR9 3 J4
EV L5 96 D7
FMBY L37 59 G1
GOL/RIS/CU WA3 92 E4
HUY L36 116 A3
RF/TRAN CH42 127 M1
SKEL WN8 64 E5
WAL/NB CH45 95 J7
WARRS WA4 137 L5
WDN WA8 134 F1
Derby Rw NEWLW WA12 104 F5
Derbyshire Hill Rd STHEL WA9 103 J2
Derby Sq PR/KW L34 101 G7 2
Derby St CLB/OSW/ST L13 114 B2 5
HUY L36 116 C3
NEWLW WA12 104 D2
ORM L39 51 H8
WGNE/HIN WN2 80 B1
Derby St West ORM L39 51 G8
Dereham Av GR/UP/WCH CH49 110 C6
Dereham Crs AIN/FAZ L10 85 H6
Dereham Wy WGNS/IIMK WN3 78 F2
Derek Av WARRN/WOL WA2 121 M4
Derna Rd HUY L36 115 M2
Derngate Dr WGNNW/ST WN6 56 C6
Derringstone Cl ECCL WA10 101 M4 4
Derwent Av CHTN/BK PR9 25 H4
FMBY L37 58 F3
GOL/RIS/CU WA3 92 E4 4
PR/KW L34 101 H7
WGNE/HIN WN2 69 K6
Derwent Cl BEB CH63 127 M8 1
GOL/RIS/CU WA3 107 J3 1
MGHL L31 73 H3
NWD/KWIPK L33 85 M1
RAIN/WH L35 117 K2
Derwent Dr GTS/LS CH66 155 K3
LITH L21 83 M5
PEN/TH CH61 141 H1
WAL/NB CH45 95 J7
Derwent Pl WGNW/BIL/O WN5 67 L6 3
Derwent Rd AIMK WN4 80 A8 2
BEB CH63 127 M8
CHLY/EC PR7 32 D8
CL/PREN CH43 127 K1 2
CSBY/BLUN L23 83 H3
HOY CH47 109 C5
RNFD/HAY WA11 89 K6
WARRS WA4 137 J3
WDN WA8 133 L4
WGNW/BIL/O WN5 67 H5
Derwent Rd East
CLB/OSW/ST L13 114 C1
Derwent Rd West
CLB/OSW/ST L13 114 B1
Derwent Sq
CLB/OSW/ST L13 114 C1 1
Derwent Wy NSTN CH64 153 H7
Desborough Crs
WD/CROXPK L12 98 C6 3
Desford Av RNFD/HAY WA11 89 M7
Desford Cl MOR/LEA CH46 109 K4
Desford Rd ALL/GAR L19 130 A5
Desilva St HUY L36 116 C3
Desmond Cl CL/PREN CH43 110 E6
Desmond Gv CSBY/BLUN L23 83 H2
Desoto Rd WDN WA8 134 A8
Desoto Rd East WDN WA8 16 A8
De Trafford Dr WGNE/HIN WN2 69 K5
Deva Cl NWD/KWIPK L33 74 A6
Deva Rd WKBY CH48 124 C3 3
Deveraux Dr WAL/EG CH44 111 L2
Deveraux Rd WAL/EG CH44 111 K2
Deverell Gv WAV L15 114 D4
Deverell Rd WAV L15 114 D4
Deverill Rd RF/TRAN CH42 128 A4
De Villiers Av CSBY/BLUN L23 71 G8
Devisdale Gv CL/PREN CH43 110 E6
Devizes Dr PEN/TH CH61 125 M6
Devizes Ms WLTN L25 115 K6
Devoke Av RNFD/HAY WA11 89 J4
Devon Av WAL/EG CH44 95 L8 2
Devon Cl CSBY/BLUN L23 82 C1
WGNE/HIN WN2 57 M8
WGNW/BIL/O WN5 67 L7
Devondale Rd CALD/MH L18 114 C8 6
Devon Dr PEN/TH CH61 141 G1
WGN WN1 56 D4
Devon Farm Wy FMBY L37 59 K2 1
Devonfield Rd WLT/FAZ L9 84 B8
Devon Gdns CHLDW L16 115 G8
RF/TRAN CH42 128 B4 1
Devon Pl WDN WA8 134 C2 2
Devonport St TOX L8 113 H8
Devonport Wy CHLYE PR6 33 G5
Devonshire Cl
NWD/KWIPK L33 86 A1 4
Devonshire Gdns NEWLW WA12 104 E3
Devonshire Pl CL/PREN CH43 10 B7
EV L5 97 G7 4
RUNC WA7 19 G2
Devonshire Rd CHLY/EC PR7 32 E6
CHTN/BK PR9 25 J6
CL/PREN CH43 10 C7
CSBY/WL L22 82 E3
ECCL WA10 8 A1
GR/UP/WCH CH49 110 A8 4
PEN/TH CH61 141 G1
TOX L8 113 J8
WAL/EG CH44 111 K1 4
WARR WA1 122 B5
WKBY CH48 124 E4
Devonshire Rd West TOX L8 113 J8 1
Devon St ECCL WA10 8 B4
VAUX/LVPD L3 13 L5
Devon Wy CHLDW L16 115 G7
HUY L36 116 C1
Dewar Ct RUNC WA7 150 A2
Dewar St GOL/RIS/CU WA3 107 G8
Dewberry Cl RF/TRAN CH42 11 G9 1
Dewey Av WLT/FAZ L9 84 D5
Dewhurst Rd GOL/RIS/CU WA3 122 F3
Dewlands Rd LITH L21 83 H5
Dewsbury Rd ANF/KKDL L4 97 K7
Dexter St TOX L8 113 G7
Deycroft Av NWD/KWIPK L33 86 C1
Deyes End MGHL L31 73 G4
Deyes La MGHL L31 72 F4
Deysbrook La WD/CROXPK L12 98 E7
Deysbrook Side
WD/CROXPK L12 98 E7 2
Deysbrook Wy WD/CROXPK L12 98 F5
Dial Rd RF/TRAN CH42 127 M2
Dial St EHL/KEN L7 113 L3
WARR WA1 14 F5
Diamond Jubilee Rd BRSC L40 39 L1
Diamond St EV L5 13 G1
WGNNW/ST WN6 68 C2
Diana Rd BTL L20 83 M6
Diana St ANF/KKDL L4 97 H5
Diane Rd AIMK WN4 79 M8
AIMK WN4 92 A1 1
Dibbinsdale Rd BEB CH63 143 K6
Dibbins Gn BEB CH63 143 K7
Dibbins Hey BEB CH63 143 J3
Dibbinview Gv BEB CH63 143 K3
Dibb La CSBY/BLUN L23 70 E6
Dicconson Crs WGN WN1 4 F2 1
Dicconson's La ORM L39 61 L2
Dicconson St ECCL WA10 9 G3 1
WGN WN1 4 E1
Dicconson Ter WGN WN1 4 E1
Dicconson Wy ORM L39 63 J1 1
Dickens Av CL/PREN CH43 127 H4 1
Dickens Cl CL/PREN CH43 127 H4 2
Dickens Dr WGNE/HIN WN2 80 D5
Dickenson St CLVPS L1 112 F5 6
WARRN/WOL WA2 15 G2
WGNE/HIN WN2 81 G1 4
Dickens Pl WGNS/IIMK WN3 79 H1
Dickens Rd CHLY/EC PR7 43 G5
ECCL WA10 101 L5
Dickens St TOX L8 113 H7 4
Dicket's La SKEL WN8 64 C3
Dickinson Cl FMBY L37 59 H3
RNFD/HAY WA11 90 C7 4
Dickinson Rd FMBY L37 59 H3
Dick's La BRSC L40 64 B1
Dickson Cl WDN WA8 16 E3
Dickson St VAUX/LVPD L3 12 C1
WDN WA8 16 D3
Didcot Cl WLTN L25 131 M5
Didsbury Cl NWD/KWIPK L33 86 B3 2
Didsbury Gv
WGNE/HIN WN2 69 M8 12
Digg La MOR/LEA CH46 109 M4
Diggle St WGNNW/ST WN6 4 B2

Dig La FROD/HEL WA6 160 C6
WARRN/WOL WA2 122 C1
Digmoor Dr SKEL WN8 65 K6
Digmoor Rd KKBY L32 86 B6
SKEL WN8 65 L6
Dignum Md NTHLY L27 116 A7
Dilloway St ECCL WA10 8 C3
Dinas La HUY L36 115 J1
Dinesen Rd ALL/GAR L19 130 E6
Dingle Av NEWLW WA12 104 B3
SKEL WN8 66 D5
Dingle Brow TOX L8 129 J2
Dingle Cl ORM L39 62 E4
Dingle Gv TOX L8 129 J1
Dingle La TOX L8 129 J2
WARRS WA4 138 B7
Dingle Mt TOX L8 129 J2
Dingle Rd RF/TRAN CH42 10 F9
SKEL WN8 66 D6
TOX L8 129 H2
The Dingle CHLYE PR6 33 J2
Dingle V TOX L8 129 J2
Dingle Wk WGNNW/ST WN6 67 M1
Dingleway WARRS WA4 137 M5
Dingley Av WLT/FAZ L9 84 B7
Dingwall Dr GR/UP/WCH CH49 126 A2
Dinmore Rd WAL/EG CH44 111 K1
Dinorwic Rd ANF/KKDL L4 97 J7
STHP PR8 35 J2
Ditchfield FMBY L37 59 J3
Ditchfield Pl WDN WA8 133 K5
Ditchfield Rd
WARRW/BUR WA5 136 A2
WDN WA8 133 J5
Ditton La MOR/LEA CH46 110 A2
Ditton Rd WDN WA8 16 B7
Dixon Av NEWLW WA12 91 L8
WGNNW/ST WN6 55 J8
Dixon Cl RNFD/HAY WA11 91 J5
Dixon Dr WGNNW/ST WN6 55 J8
Dixon St WARR WA1 14 C6
Dob Brow CHLY/EC PR7 43 H1
Dobbs Dr FMBY L37 59 J1
Dobers La FROD/HEL WA6 167 L2
Dobson Pkwy WGNE/HIN WN2 5 M7
Dobson St NPK/KEN L6 113 J1
Dock Rd ALL/GAR L19 130 D8
BIRK CH41 111 J3
WDN WA8 16 B9
Dock Rd North PS/BROM CH62 128 E7
Dock Rd South PS/BROM CH62 143 M1
Dock St EP CH65 20 D1
WDN WA8 16 C9
Dock Yard Rd EP CH65 20 F3
Doctor's La CHLY/EC PR7 30 C7
FMBY L37 60 A4
KIRK/FR/WA PR4 28 A3
Dodd Av ECCL WA10 101 L1
GR/UP/WCH CH49 125 M2
Doddridge Rd TOX L8 113 G8
Dodd's La MGHL L31 72 F3
Dodleston Cl CL/PREN CH43 126 F1
Dodman Rd NG/CROX L11 85 M8
Dodworth Av STHP PR8 25 G8
Doel St NPK/KEN L6 113 J2
Doe Meadow SKEL WN8 53 J4
Doe's Meadow Rd BEB CH63 143 K6
Dole La CHLY/EC PR7 32 E5
Dolly's La CHTN/BK PR9 25 M5
Dolomite Av ALL/GAR L19 131 H7
Dolphin Crs GTS/LS CH66 163 G3
Domar Cl KKBY L32 86 A5
Dombey St TOX L8 113 H7
Domingo Dr NWD/KWIPK L33 73 M8
Dominic Cl CHLDW L16 115 G5
Dominic Rd CHLDW L16 115 G5
Dominion St NPK/KEN L6 97 L8
Domville RAIN/WH L35 117 G3
Domville Rd CLB/OSW/ST L13 114 C4
Donaldson St EV L5 97 J7
Donalds Wy AIG/SPK L17 130 A4
Doncaster Dr
GR/UP/WCH CH49 110 B7
Donegal Rd CLB/OSW/ST L13 114 D2
Donne Av BEB CH63 143 H2
Donne Cl BEB CH63 143 J2
Donnington Cl HUY L36 115 M5
LEIGH WN7 93 M4
Donsby Rd WLT/FAZ L9 84 D7
Dood's La WARRS WA4 138 C8
Dooley Dr NTHTN L30 84 D1
Doon Cl ANF/KKDL L4 97 G5
Dootson St WGNE/HIN WN2 80 D4
Dorbett Dr CSBY/BLUN L23 83 H3
Dorchester Cl
GR/UP/WCH CH49 126 B1
Dorchester Pk RUNC WA7 150 F2
WLTN L25 115 K7
Dorchester Rd SKEL WN8 66 C6
WARRW/BUR WA5 120 D8
Dorchester Wy
WARRW/BUR WA5 104 B7
Doreen Av MOR/LEA CH46 109 M5
Dorgan Cl RAIN/WH L35 117 K1
Doric Av FROD/HEL WA6 160 E6
Doric Gn WGNW/BIL/O WN5 77 M2
Doric Rd CLB/OSW/ST L13 114 C1
Doric St LITH L21 83 H6
RF/TRAN CH42 128 B3
Dorien Rd CLB/OSW/ST L13 114 B3
Doris St CHLYE PR6 32 F4
Dorking Gv WAV L15 114 D6
Dorking Rd CHLYE PR6 33 H1
Dorney Cl WARRS WA4 138 A7
Dorning St WGN WN1 4 D3
Dorothea St WARRN/WOL WA2 15 G1
Dorothy St EHL/KEN L7 113 K4
STHEL WA9 102 A6
Dorrington Cl RUNC WA7 150 F5
Dorrit St TOX L8 113 H7
Dorset Av STHP PR8 47 L3
WAV L15 113 M6
Dorset Cl BTL L20 7 K4
WGNW/BIL/O WN5 67 L7
Dorset Dr PEN/TH CH61 141 G1
Dorset Rd ECCL WA10 8 A9
HUY L36 116 C2
NPK/KEN L6 97 M7
WAL/NB CH45 95 J6
WGN WN1 56 D4
WKBY CH48 124 E2
Dorset Wy WARR WA1 122 D5
Douglas Av HOR/BR BL6 45 L8
SKEL WN8 66 D6
STHEL WA9 103 K7
WGNW/BIL/O WN5 89 M2
Douglas Bank Dr
WGNNW/ST WN6 68 B4
Douglas Cl BRSC L40 39 L2
CLB/OSW/ST L13 114 B1
HOR/BR BL6 45 L8
WDN WA8 135 H2
Douglas Dr MGHL L31 73 H3
MOR/LEA CH46 109 L5
ORM L39 50 F6
WGNNW/ST WN6 55 H8
WGNW/BIL/O WN5 67 G6
Douglas Pl BTL L20 6 F7
Douglas Rd ANF/KKDL L4 97 K7
CHTN/BK PR9 25 L1
LEIGH WN7 81 L6
WGN WN1 5 G1
WGNNW/ST WN6 55 K3
WKBY CH48 124 F2
Douglas St BIRK CH41 11 K5
ECCL WA10 8 B5
WGNE/HIN WN2 80 E1
WGNW/BIL/O WN5 4 A6
Douglas Wy NWD/KWIPK L33 74 B7
Doulton Cl CL/PREN CH43 110 D6
Doulton St ECCL WA10 8 A6
Dounrey Cl WARRN/WOL WA2 122 C3
Douro Pl CLB/OSW/ST L13 114 B3
Douro St EV L5 13 J2
Dove Cl CHNE CH2 165 L1
EP CH65 156 B6
FROD/HEL WA6 159 L8
GOL/RIS/CU WA3 123 H1
Dovecot Av DV/KA/FCH L14 115 H1
Dovecote Gn
WARRW/BUR WA5 120 C4
Dove Ct WLTN L25 131 K2
Dovedale Av MGHL L31 72 E3
PS/BROM CH62 144 A8
Dovedale Cl CL/PREN CH43 127 H3
WARRN/WOL WA2 122 A2
Dovedale Crs AIMK WN4 79 J5
Dovedale Dr WGNNW/ST WN6 56 A3
Dovedale Rd AIMK WN4 79 J5
CALD/MH L18 114 B8
HOY CH47 108 D5
WAL/NB CH45 95 J6
Dovenby Fold WGNE/HIN WN2 69 J6
Dovepoint Rd HOY CH47 109 G5
Dovercliffe Rd
CLB/OSW/ST L13 114 D2
Dover Cl BIRK CH41 11 G4
RUNC WA7 151 G7
Dover Dr EP CH65 163 M3
Dover Gv CHLDW L16 115 H5
Dover Rd MGHL L31 72 E7
STHP PR8 35 H3
WARRS WA4 138 C2
WLT/FAZ L9 84 B7
Dover St RUNC WA7 19 J2
Dovesmead Rd HES CH60 141 M6
Dovestone Cl EHL/KEN L7 113 K5
Dove St GOL/RIS/CU WA3 92 C3
TOX L8 113 K6
Dovey St TOX L8 113 H8
Doward St WDN WA8 134 E3
Dower St WGNE/HIN WN2 80 C2
Dowhills Dr CSBY/BLUN L23 70 D8
Dowhills Pk CSBY/BLUN L23 70 D7
Dowhills Rd CSBY/BLUN L23 70 D8
Dowling Cl WGNNW/ST WN6 67 M2
Downall Green Rd AIMK WN4 79 G7
Downes Gn BEB CH63 143 J4
Downham Av
GOL/RIS/CU WA3 107 H3
Downham Cl WLTN L25 115 H8
Downham Dr HES CH60 141 J5
Downham Gn WLTN L25 115 H8
Downham Rd RF/TRAN CH42 128 A2
Downham Rd North
PEN/TH CH61 141 J3
Downham Rd South HES CH60 141 J5
Downham Wy WLTN L25 115 H8
Downing Cl CL/PREN CH43 127 K2
WGNE/HIN WN2 80 C4
Downing Rd BTL L20 7 K7
Downing St EV L5 97 J8
Downland Wy STHEL WA9 103 H4
Downside WDN WA8 133 K2
Downside Cl NTHTN L30 84 A1
Downside Dr AIN/FAZ L10 85 H4
Downs Rd ECCL WA10 8 B7
RUNC WA7 19 H6
The Downs WGNS/IIMK WN3 78 E1
Downton Av
WGNE/HIN WN2 80 F1
Downway La STHEL WA9 103 J4
Dowsefield La CALD/MH L18 131 G2
Dragon Cl NG/CROX L11 98 E1
Dragon Crs RAIN/WH L35 117 H1
Dragon La RAIN/WH L35 116 F3
Dragon Yd WDN WA8 134 D1
Drake Cl AIN/FAZ L10 85 J6
ORM L39 62 E3
RAIN/WH L35 117 G3
WARRW/BUR WA5 120 F4
Drake Crs AIN/FAZ L10 85 J6
Drakefield Rd NG/CROX L11 98 A2
Drake Gdns STHEL WA9 102 A7
Drake Pl AIN/FAZ L10 85 H6
Drake Rd AIN/FAZ L10 85 H6
MOR/LEA CH46 110 D1
NSTN CH64 153 G4
Drake St BTL L20 6 E8
ECCL WA10 8 B4
Drake Wy AIN/FAZ L10 85 J6
Drapers Av CHLY/EC PR7 30 E7
Draycott St TOX L8 129 H2
Drayton Cl PEN/TH CH61 125 M8
RUNC WA7 18 E5
Drayton Crs RNFD/HAY WA11 89 M7
Drayton Rd ANF/KKDL L4 97 J3
WAL/EG CH44 111 M2
Drennan Rd ALL/GAR L19 131 G5
Drewell Rd CALD/MH L18 130 B2
Drewitt Crs CHTN/BK PR9 25 L1
Driffield Rd PR/KW L34 100 E7
Drinkhouse La LEY/BBR PR5 29 J4
Drinkhouse Rd LEY/BBR PR5 29 K4
Drinkwater Gdns
VAUX/LVPD L3 13 J3
The Drive WD/CROXPK L12 98 D8
Drive Wy RAIN/WH L35 117 G3
Driveway RAIN/WH L35 117 H2
RAIN/WH L35 117 H3
Droitwich Av
GR/UP/WCH CH49 125 L1
Dromore Av CALD/MH L18 130 C2
Dronfield Wy WLTN L25 115 H6
Druids Cross Gdns
CALD/MH L18 130 F1
Druids Cross Rd CALD/MH L18 131 G1
Druids Pk CALD/MH L18 131 G1
Druid St AIMK WN4 91 L3
Druidsville Rd CALD/MH L18 131 G1
Druids Wy GR/UP/WCH CH49 126 C3
Drummersdale La BRSC L40 37 K4
Drummer's La AIMK WN4 79 G6
Drummond Av GTS/LS CH66 162 E1
Drummond Ct WDN WA8 134 F3
Drummond Rd ANF/KKDL L4 97 L4
CSBY/BLUN L23 71 K8
HOY CH47 108 C8
Drummond Sq
WGNW/BIL/O WN5 68 A6
Druridge Dr WARRW/BUR WA5 136 B1
Drury La CLVP L2 12 E7
Dryden Av AIMK WN4 79 H6
Dryden Cl CL/PREN CH43 110 E6
RAIN/WH L35 117 G2
WGNS/IIMK WN3 68 C8
Dryden Gv HUY L36 116 B4
Dryden Pl WARRN/WOL WA2 121 L3
Dryden Rd EHL/KEN L7 114 A4
Dryden St BTL L20 6 D1
EV L5 13 H1
Dryebeck Gv STHEL WA9 102 F7
Dryfield Cl
GR/UP/WCH CH49 125 M1
Dryfield La HOR/BR BL6 45 J8
Drysdale St TOX L8 129 J1
Drysdale Wk TOX L8 129 J1
Dublin Cft GTS/LS CH66 163 G4
Dublin St VAUX/LVPD L3 12 C1
Ducie St TOX L8 113 K7
Duckinfield St VAUX/LVPD L3 13 L7
Duck Pond La RF/TRAN CH42 127 J3
Duckworth Gv
WARRN/WOL WA2 122 C4
Duddingston Av
CALD/MH L18 114 C8
CSBY/BLUN L23 83 G3
Duddon Av MGHL L31 73 H3
Duddon Cl CL/PREN CH43 127 H2
Dudleston Rd GTS/LS CH66 155 K7
Dudley Av RUNC WA7 149 M3
Dudley Cl CL/PREN CH43 127 K1
Dudley Crs PS/BROM CH62 155 K2
Dudley Gv CSBY/BLUN L23 83 G3
Dudley Rd CALD/MH L18 114 B8
EP CH65 20 B5
WAL/NB CH45 95 J5
Dudley St AIMK WN4 79 J8
WARRN/WOL WA2 14 F1
Dudlow Dr CALD/MH L18 114 E8
Dudlow Gdns CALD/MH L18 114 E7
Dudlow Green Rd WARRS WA4 137 M8
Dudlow La CALD/MH L18 114 D7
Dudlow Nook Rd CALD/MH L18 114 E7
Dugdale Cl ALL/GAR L19 130 C6
Duke Av STHP PR8 35 L1
Duke Cl RUNC WA7 18 E3
Dukes Rd EV L5 97 G7
Duke St AIMK WN4 91 L2
ALL/GAR L19 130 E7
BIRK CH41 10 D3
CHLY/EC PR7 32 E7
CLVPS L1 13 H9
CSBY/WL L22 82 F5
ECCL WA10 8 E3
FMBY L37 59 G3
GOL/RIS/CU WA3 92 C4
NEWLW WA12 104 D2
PR/KW L34 100 F7
STHP PR8 2 E5
WAL/NB CH45 95 K5
WGN WN1 68 E3
WGNE/HIN WN2 80 C2
WGNS/IIMK WN3 79 H1
Duke Street La CLVPS L1 13 G9
Dukes Wy FMBY L37 59 H3
Dukes Whf RUNC WA7 151 H7
Duke's Wood La SKEL WN8 76 F2
Dulas Gn KKBY L32 86 C4
Dulas Rd KKBY L32 86 C4
WAV L15 114 D7
Dulverton Rd AIG/SPK L17 130 A5
Dumbarton Gn WGNNW/ST WN6 68 A3
Dumbarton St ANF/KKDL L4 7 M9
Dumbrees Rd WD/CROXPK L12 99 G5
Dumbreeze Gv PR/KW L34 99 M1
Dumfries Wy NWD/KWIPK L33 73 M7
Dunacre Wy HLWD L26 132 B6
Dunbabin Rd CHLDW L16 114 E7
Dunbar Cl GTS/LS CH66 155 L8
Dunbar Crs STHP PR8 35 H5
Dunbar Rd STHP PR8 35 G4
Dunbar St ANF/KKDL L4 97 H3
Dunbeath Av RAIN/WH L35 117 M4
Dunbeath Cl RAIN/WH L35 117 M4
Dunblane Cl AIMK WN4 90 E1
Duncan Av NEWLW WA12 91 L8
RUNC WA7 19 L5
Duncan Cl ECCL WA10 8 E7
Duncan Dr GR/UP/WCH CH49 125 M1
Duncan Pl WGNW/BIL/O WN5 68 A6
Duncansby Crs
WARRW/BUR WA5 120 A7
Duncansby Dr BEB CH63 154 E1
Duncan St BIRK CH41 11 L5
CLVPS L1 113 G6
ECCL WA10 8 D6
WARRN/WOL WA2 15 H1
Dunchurch Rd DV/KA/FCH L14 99 H8
Duncombe Rd North
ALL/GAR L19 130 D6
Duncombe Rd South
ALL/GAR L19 130 D6
Duncote Cl RAIN/WH L35 101 J8
Dundale Rd CLB/OSW/ST L13 114 D2
Dundalk La WDN WA8 133 M5
Dundalk Rd WDN WA8 134 A5
Dundas St BTL L20 6 E8
Dundee Cl WARRN/WOL WA2 122 A1
Dundee Gv WAL/EG CH44 111 J2
Dundonald Av WARRS WA4 137 L4
Dundonald Rd AIG/SPK L17 130 A4
Dundonald St BIRK CH41 10 A2
Dunedin St STHEL WA9 102 A6
Dunes Dr FMBY L37 58 E1
Dunfold Cl KKBY L32 86 B4
Dungeon La SKEL WN8 53 L6
SPK/HALE L24 147 H4
Dunham Av GOL/RIS/CU WA3 92 B4
Dunham Cl PS/BROM CH62 155 H1
Dunham Ct FROD/HEL WA6 166 A7
Dunham Rd WAV L15 114 C4
Dunkeld Cl NPK/KEN L6 113 J2
Dunkeld St NPK/KEN L6 113 J2
Dunkirk Dr EP CH65 163 J4
Dunkirk La CH/BCN CH1 162 E5
GTS/LS CH66 163 J4
Dunkirk Rd STHP PR8 35 H3
Dunley Cl GOL/RIS/CU WA3 107 J7
Dunlin Av NEWLW WA12 104 E1
Dunlin Cl NTHLY L27 132 A1
RUNC WA7 150 B8
WARRN/WOL WA2 122 A2
Dunlop Av STHP PR8 47 L3
Dunlop Dr MGHL L31 85 K1
Dunlop Rd SPK/HALE L24 146 D3
Dunlop St WARRS WA4 14 E9
Dunluce St ANF/KKDL L4 7 M8
Dunmail Av RNFD/HAY WA11 89 L4
Dunmail Gv RUNC WA7 161 G1
Dunmore Crs GTS/LS CH66 155 K7
Dunmore Rd CLB/OSW/ST L13 114 A2
GTS/LS CH66 155 K7
Dunmow Rd WARRS WA4 138 E2
Dunmow Wy WLTN L25 131 L5
Dunnerdale Rd NG/CROX L11 98 C3
Dunnett St BTL L20 6 F9
Dunning Cl
GR/UP/WCH CH49 110 A8
Dunnings Bridge Rd NTHTN L30 84 A4
Dunnock Cl
WARRN/WOL WA2 122 A2
WLTN L25 115 J8
Dunnock Gv GOL/RIS/CU WA3 123 G1
Dunoon Rd WGNE/HIN WN2 57 M8
Dunraven Rd NSTN CH64 153 J6
WKBY CH48 124 C3
Dunriding La ECCL WA10 8 A6
Dunrobin Dr CHLY/EC PR7 31 M4
Dunscar Cl GOL/RIS/CU WA3 106 F8
Dunscar Dr CHLYE PR6 33 G4
Dunscore Rd WGNS/IIMK WN3 79 G2
Dunscroft STHEL WA9 102 F6
Dunsdale Dr AIMK WN4 91 L2
Dunsdon Cl CALD/MH L18 131 G1
Dunsdon Rd CALD/MH L18 115 G8
Dunsford WDN WA8 133 L2
Dunsmore Cl RNFD/HAY WA11 90 E6
Dunsop Av STHEL WA9 118 F1
Dunstan La EHL/KEN L7 113 L5
Dunstan St WAV L15 114 A5
Dunster Cl WGNE/HIN WN2 80 C4
Dunster Gv HES CH60 141 K6
STHEL WA9 118 F1
Dunster Rd STHP PR8 35 G5
Durban Rd CLB/OSW/ST L13 114 D3
WAL/NB CH45 95 K7
Durden St EHL/KEN L7 113 L6
Durham Av NTHTN L30 84 C4
Durham Cl WARR WA1 123 G6
Durham Ms East NTHTN L30 84 C4
Durham Ms West NTHTN L30 84 C4
Durham Rd LITH L21 83 G6
WDN WA8 134 D2
Durham St ALL/GAR L19 145 M1
WGN WN1 5 K2
Durham Wy NTHTN L30 84 C4
Durley Dr CL/PREN CH43 127 G4
Durley Rd WLT/FAZ L9 84 D7
Durliston Cl WDN WA8 133 L3
Durning Rd EHL/KEN L7 113 L3
Durrant Rd NG/CROX L11 98 A5
Durrell Wy GOL/RIS/CU WA3 93 G5
Dursley RAIN/WH L35 117 H3
Dursley Dr AIMK WN4 91 M1
Durston Rd CHLDW L16 114 F5
Durweston Wk NTHLY L27 115 L7
Dutch Barn Cl CHLY/EC PR7 32 D3
Dutton Dr BEB CH63 143 H3
Dutton Gn EP CH65 21 K9
Dutton St WARR WA1 15 G6
Duxbury Cl MGHL L31 73 G2
RNFD/HAY WA11 76 B6
Duxbury Hall Rd CHLY/EC PR7 43 M1
Duxford Ct
WARRN/WOL WA2 122 A4
Dwerryhouse La NG/CROX L11 98 D3
Dwerryhouse St TOX L8 112 F7
Dyers La ORM L39 63 G1
Dyer St GOL/RIS/CU WA3 92 B5
Dyke St NPK/KEN L6 113 J1
Dykin Cl WDN WA8 135 G2
Dykin Rd WDN WA8 134 F2
Dymchurch Rd SPK/HALE L24 146 D1
Dymoke Rd NG/CROX L11 98 E2
Dyson Hall Dr WLT/FAZ L9 84 F8
Dyson St ANF/KKDL L4 97 H4


## E


Eager La MGHL L31 61 K5
Eagle Brow LYMM WA13 139 M2
Eagle Crs RNFD/HAY WA11 76 C7
Eaglehall Rd WLT/FAZ L9 98 B1
Eaglehurst Rd WLTN L25 131 K1
Eagle La GTS/LS CH66 155 M6
Eagles Ct KKBY L32 86 A4
Eaglesfield Cl STHEL WA9 102 F6
Eagles Wy RUNC WA7 150 A7
Ealing Gv CHLYE PR6 33 H1
Ealing Rd WARRW/BUR WA5 120 C8
WLT/FAZ L9 84 D6
Eamont Av CHTN/BK PR9 22 D8
Eanleywood La RUNC WA7 150 E6
Eardisley Rd WAV L15 114 C7
Earle Cl NEWLW WA12 104 B2
Earle Crs NSTN CH64 152 F4
Earle Dr NSTN CH64 152 F5
Earle Rd EHL/KEN L7 113 L5
WDN WA8 16 F6
Earle St NEWLW WA12 104 B3
VAUX/LVPD L3 12 D5
Earl Rd BTL L20 7 K3
Earl's Cl CSBY/BLUN L23 82 F2
Earlsfield Rd WAV L15 114 B7
Earls Gdns EP CH65 20 A4
Earlston Rd WAL/NB CH45 95 J7
Earl St PS/BROM CH62 128 D6
STHEL WA9 9 L4
WARRN/WOL WA2 14 F1
WGN WN1 68 E3
WGNE/HIN WN2 69 J6
Earls Wy CHLY/EC PR7 31 M3
RUNC WA7 150 A6
Earlswood SKEL WN8 66 A4
Earlswood Cl HOY CH47 109 K5
Earlwood Gdns
RAIN/WH L35 117 G3
Earp St ALL/GAR L19 130 E7
Easby Cl FMBY L37 59 J3
Easby Rd ANF/KKDL L4 96 F6
Easedale Dr STHP PR8 47 K1
Easedale Wk
NWD/KWIPK L33 73 M8
Easenhall Cl WDN WA8 134 D1
Easington Rd RAIN/WH L35 101 M7
East Albert Rd AIG/SPK L17 129 K1
East Av GOL/RIS/CU WA3 92 E4
WARRN/WOL WA2 121 L5
WARRS WA4 137 M4
WARRW/BUR WA5 136 C1
Eastbank St STHP PR8 3 G4
Eastbourne Rd CL/PREN CH43 10 F6
CSBY/WL L22 82 D3
STHP PR8 35 J2
WLT/FAZ L9 84 D6
Eastbourne Wy NPK/KEN L6 13 L3
Eastbury Cl WDN WA8 118 E8
Eastcliffe Rd CLB/OSW/ST L13 114 D2
East Cl PR/KW L34 101 J6
Eastcote Rd ALL/GAR L19 130 E5
Eastcott Cl GR/UP/WCH CH49 125 L2
Eastcroft NWD/KWIPK L33 74 B8
Eastcroft Rd WAL/EG CH44 111 L2
Eastdale Rd WARR WA1 122 C6
WAV L15 114 B5
East Dam Wood Rd
SPK/HALE L24 147 H3
East Dene SKEL WN8 53 K3
Easter Ct WARRW/BUR WA5 120 D3
Eastern Av PS/BROM CH62 143 M1
SPK/HALE L24 147 H3
Eastern Dr ALL/GAR L19 130 C6
Eastfield Dr AIG/SPK L17 129 L2
Eastfield Wk KKBY L32 85 K4
Eastford Rd WARRS WA4 137 J4
East Front RAIN/WH L35 117 G4
Eastgarth WGNE/HIN WN2 80 D3
Eastgate Rd RUNC WA7 151 G1
Eastham Cl CHLDW L16 115 H4
Eastham Crs STHEL WA9 118 E1
Eastham Gn SPK/HALE L24 147 G1
Eastham Ms PS/BROM CH62 155 J1
Eastham Rake GTS/LS CH66 154 E3
Eastham Village Rd
PS/BROM CH62 144 C8
Eastlake Av EV L5 97 H8
East Lancashire Rd ECCL WA10 89 H6
GOL/RIS/CU WA3 92 D7
NG/CROX L11 85 K8
NWD/KWIPK L33 86 C7
RNFD/HAY WA11 89 M5
East La RUNC WA7 150 B6
SFTN L29 71 K3
East Leigh SKEL WN8 65 M4
Eastleigh Dr PEN/TH CH61 125 M6
East Mains SPK/HALE L24 147 J2
Eastman Rd CLB/OSW/ST L13 98 A6
East Md ORM L39 62 D4
East Meade MGHL L31 72 E3
East Millwood Rd
SPK/HALE L24 147 J1
East Mt WGNW/BIL/O WN5 67 H7
Easton Cl WGNS/IIMK WN3 79 J3
Easton Rd HUY L36 115 J2
PS/BROM CH62 128 D5
East Orchard La WLT/FAZ L9 84 F6
East Prescot Rd
DV/KA/FCH L14 115 G1
East Rd DV/KA/FCH L14 114 E3
SPK/HALE L24 132 D8
East Side STHEL WA9 9 M7
East St AIMK WN4 91 M1
CHTN/BK PR9 3 L3
CSBY/WL L22 82 F4
PR/KW L34 101 G7
VAUX/LVPD L3 12 E5
WAL/EG CH44 112 A3
WDN WA8 17 J1
WGNE/HIN WN2 81 K2
East Ter CHLYE PR6 32 A1
East Vw WARRS WA4 138 D3
Eastview Cl CL/PREN CH43 126 F1
East Wy CHLYE PR6 32 F5

Eastway GR/UP/WCH CH49 ...... 126 A1
GTS/LS CH66 ...... 155 M6
MGHL L31 ...... 72 F3
East Wy MOR/LEA CH46 ...... 110 A4
Eastway WDN WA8 ...... 133 M4
Eastwell Rd AIMK WN4 ...... 91 J2
WGNNW/ST WN6 ...... 68 B2
Eastwood AIG/SPK L17 ...... 129 J2
RUNC WA7 ...... 150 E4
Eastwood Av NEWLW WA12 ...... 105 H2
Eastwood Gv LEIGH WN7 ...... 81 L8
Eastwood Rd
WARRW/BUR WA5 ...... 104 B6
Eatock Brow Rd
GOL/RIS/CU WA3 ...... 106 D6
Eaton Av BTL L20 ...... 83 M7
LITH L21 ...... 83 K6
WAL/EG CH44 ...... 111 L1
Eaton CI HUY L36 ...... 115 L3
WD/CROXPK L12 ...... 98 C6
Eaton Gdns WD/CROXPK L12 ...... 98 F8
Eaton Rd ALL/GAR L19 ...... 130 C7
CL/PREN CH43 ...... 10 D7
ECCL WA10 ...... 88 F7
MGHL L31 ...... 72 F7
WD/CROXPK L12 ...... 98 D6
WKBY CH48 ...... 124 C4
Eaton Rd North
WD/CROXPK L12 ...... 98 C6
Eaton St PR/KW L34 ...... 100 F7
RUNC WA7 ...... 19 G4
VAUX/LVPD L3 ...... 12 E4
WAL/EG CH44 ...... 111 K1
Eaves Brow Rd
GOL/RIS/CU WA3 ...... 106 D6
Eavesdale SKEL WN8 ...... 66 A5
Eaves Green Rd CHLY/EC PR7 ...... 32 D8
Eaves La CHLYE PR6 ...... 33 G6
STHEL WA9 ...... 102 D7
Ebenezer Howard Rd LITH L21 ...... 83 L3
Ebenezer Rd EHL/KEN L7 ...... 113 L2
Ebenezer St RF/TRAN CH42 ...... 128 C3
RNFD/HAY WA11 ...... 90 F7
Eberle St CLVP L2 ...... 12 F6
Ebony CI MOR/LEA CH46 ...... 109 K5
Ebony Wy NWD/KWIPK L33 ...... 74 A8
Ebor La EV L5 ...... 13 J2
Ebrington St ALL/GAR L19 ...... 130 E7
Ecclesall Av LITH L21 ...... 83 L8
Ecclesfield Rd ECCL WA10 ...... 88 C8
Eccles Dr WLTN L25 ...... 115 K6
Eccles Gv STHEL WA9 ...... 119 G2
Eccleshall Rd PS/BROM CH62 ...... 128 E7
Eccleshill Rd CLB/OSW/ST L13 ...... 98 C8
Eccles Rd FMBY L37 ...... 58 F4
WGNNW/BIL/O WN5 ...... 67 K5
Eccles's La BRSC L40 ...... 40 D6
Eccleston Av GTS/LS CH66 ...... 156 A8
PS/BROM CH62 ...... 143 L4
Eccleston CI CL/PREN CH43 ...... 127 H2
GOL/RIS/CU WA3 ...... 106 E8
Eccleston Dr RUNC WA7 ...... 19 M6
Eccleston Gdns ECCL WA10 ...... 101 J4
Eccleston Rd WLT/FAZ L9 ...... 84 B7
Eccleston St ECCL WA10 ...... 8 C5
PR/KW L34 ...... 100 F7
WGN WN1 ...... 4 F1
Eckersley Av WGNE/HIN WN2 ...... 80 F2
Eckersley St WGN WN1 ...... 5 J1
Edale CI PS/BROM CH62 ...... 144 A8
Edale Dr WGNNW/ST WN6 ...... 56 A3
Edale Rd CALD/MH L18 ...... 130 C1
Eddisbury Rd GTS/LS CH66 ...... 163 H3
WAL/EG CH44 ...... 95 L8
WKBY CH48 ...... 124 C4
Eddisbury Wy WD/CROXPK L12 ...... 98 C6
Eddleston St AIMK WN4 ...... 79 H7
Edelsten St WARRW/BUR WA5 ...... 14 A6
Eden Av CHTN/BK PR9 ...... 25 H2
GOL/RIS/CU WA3 ...... 107 L1
RNFD/HAY WA11 ...... 76 A4
Eden CI GTS/LS CH66 ...... 155 L8
NWD/KWIPK L33 ...... 74 B7
RAIN/WH L35 ...... 117 K3
Edendale WDN WA8 ...... 16 A4
Eden Dr North CSBY/BLUN L23 ...... 83 J1
Eden Dr South CSBY/BLUN L23 ...... 83 J2
Edenfield CI STHP PR8 ...... 36 A2
Edenfield Crs HUY L36 ...... 116 B1
Edenfield Rd WAV L15 ...... 114 B7
Eden Gv LEIGH WN7 ...... 81 L8
Edenhall Dr WLTN L25 ...... 131 M3
Edenhurst Av CHLDW L16 ...... 115 J3
WAL/EG CH44 ...... 95 L8
Edenhurst CI FMBY L37 ...... 58 E3
Edenhurst Dr FMBY L37 ...... 58 E3
Edenpark Rd RF/TRAN CH42 ...... 127 L2
Edensor CI WGNNW/ST WN6 ...... 68 C1
Eden V NTHTN L30 ...... 84 B1
Edgar Ct BIRK CH41 ...... 11 G4
LITH L21 ...... 83 K4
Edgars Dr WARRN/WOL WA2 ...... 122 C3
Edgbaston CI HUY L36 ...... 115 L4
Edgbaston Wy CL/PREN CH43 ...... 110 E5
Edgefield CHLY/EC PR7 ...... 32 D3
Edgefield CI CL/PREN CH43 ...... 126 F1
Edgefold Rd KKBY L32 ...... 86 B4
Edge Green La GOL/RIS/CU WA3 ...... 92 B3
Edge Green Rd GOL/RIS/CU WA3 ...... 92 B2
Edge Green St AIMK WN4 ...... 91 M1
Edge Gv EHL/KEN L7 ...... 114 A3
Edge Hall Rd WGNW/BIL/O WN5 ...... 78 A1
Edgehill Rd MOR/LEA CH46 ...... 109 L5
Edge La CLB/OSW/ST L13 ...... 114 A3
CSBY/BLUN L23 ...... 71 J7
EHL/KEN L7 ...... 113 K4
Edge Lane Dr CLB/OSW/ST L13 ...... 114 D4
Edgeley Gdns WGNS/IIMK WN3 ...... 78 F2
Edgemoor CI CL/PREN CH43 ...... 110 D6
WD/CROXPK L12 ...... 98 F8
Edgemoor Dr AIN/FAZ L10 ...... 85 J6
CSBY/BLUN L23 ...... 71 J8
PEN/TH CH61 ...... 125 L6
Edgemoor Rd WD/CROXPK L12 ...... 98 F8
Edgerton Rd GOL/RIS/CU WA3 ...... 93 G5
Edge St RAIN/WH L35 ...... 101 L4
Edge Ware Gv WGNS/IIMK WN3 ...... 78 F2
Edgeway Rd WGNS/IIMK WN3 ...... 79 J4

Edgewood WGNNW/ST WN6 ...... 55 J8
Edgewood Dr PS/BROM CH62 ...... 143 M8
Edgewood Rd
GR/UP/WCH CH49 ...... 110 B7
HOY CH47 ...... 108 F4
Edgeworth CI STHEL WA9 ...... 103 G5
Edgeworth Rd
GOL/RIS/CU WA3 ...... 92 B4
WGNE/HIN WN2 ...... 81 J2
Edgeworth St WARR WA1 ...... 103 G6
Edgley Dr ORM L39 ...... 51 J8
Edgworth Rd ANF/KKDL L4 ...... 97 K7
Edinburgh CI NTHTN L30 ...... 84 B5
WGNE/HIN WN2 ...... 69 J5
Edinburgh Dr CL/PREN CH43 ...... 127 J3
HUY L36 ...... 116 C5
WGNE/HIN WN2 ...... 81 K2
WGNW/BIL/O WN5 ...... 67 M8
Edinburgh Rd EHL/KEN L7 ...... 113 K3
FMBY L37 ...... 59 G4
WAL/NB CH45 ...... 95 K8
WDN WA8 ...... 133 J5
Edington St WAV L15 ...... 114 A5
Edison Rd RUNC WA7 ...... 149 M2
Edith Rd ANF/KKDL L4 ...... 97 J7
BTL L20 ...... 83 M7
WAL/EG CH44 ...... 112 A2
Edith St STHEL WA9 ...... 103 H6
WGNS/IIMK WN3 ...... 4 C5
Edmondson St STHEL WA9 ...... 103 H2
Edmonton CI EV L5 ...... 96 F7
Edmund Dr LEIGH WN7 ...... 81 L8
Edmund St VAUX/LVPD L3 ...... 12 E6
Edna Av AIN/FAZ L10 ...... 85 J6
Edna Rd LEIGH WN7 ...... 81 L6
Edrich Av CL/PREN CH43 ...... 110 E5
Edward Dr AIMK WN4 ...... 91 K1
Edward Gdns WARR WA1 ...... 123 H7
Edward Jenner Av NTHTN L30 ...... 84 B2
Edward Rd HOY CH47 ...... 108 E7
RAIN/WH L35 ...... 101 H8
WARRW/BUR WA5 ...... 119 M7
Edward's La SPK/HALE L24 ...... 131 K7
Edward Steet WGN WN1 ...... 68 E3
Edward St CHLYE PR6 ...... 32 F6
EP CH65 ...... 20 C1
RNFD/HAY WA11 ...... 90 C7
STHEL WA9 ...... 102 F4
VAUX/LVPD L3 ...... 13 K7
WDN WA8 ...... 18 D1
WGN WN1 ...... 5 L4
Edwards Wy WDN WA8 ...... 133 L5
Edwin St WDN WA8 ...... 17 G1
WGN WN1 ...... 5 J4
Effingham St BTL L20 ...... 6 E8
Egan Rd CL/PREN CH43 ...... 111 G5
Egbert Rd HOY CH47 ...... 108 E5
Egdon CI WDN WA8 ...... 135 G3
Egerton SKEL WN8 ...... 65 M5
Egerton Dr WARR WA1 ...... 15 M2
Egerton Dr WKBY CH48 ...... 124 F3
Egerton Gdns RF/TRAN CH42 ...... 128 A4
Egerton Gv CHLY/EC PR7 ...... 32 D7
WAL/NB CH45 ...... 95 K8
Egerton Park CI RF/TRAN CH42 ...... 128 A4
Egerton Rd LYMM WA13 ...... 139 L3
PR/KW L34 ...... 100 E7
PS/BROM CH62 ...... 128 D6
WAV L15 ...... 113 M6
Egerton St EP CH65 ...... 20 C2
RUNC WA7 ...... 18 F2
STHEL WA9 ...... 102 F4
TOX L8 ...... 113 H6
WAL/NB CH45 ...... 95 K5
WARR WA1 ...... 15 H5
WARRS WA4 ...... 137 L4
WGNE/HIN WN2 ...... 80 D6
Egerton Whf BIRK CH41 ...... 11 K3
Eglington Av RAIN/WH L35 ...... 116 F3
Egremont CI WLT/FAZ L9 ...... 84 F6
Egremont Prom WAL/EG CH44 ...... 95 M7
Egremont Rd NTHLY L27 ...... 132 C1
Egypt St WARR WA1 ...... 14 D6
WDN WA8 ...... 16 B5
Eight Acre La FMBY L37 ...... 47 K7
Eighth Av WLT/FAZ L9 ...... 84 F6
Eilian Gv DV/KA/FCH L14 ...... 114 F3
Eisenhower CI
WARRW/BUR WA5 ...... 120 D8
Elaine CI AIMK WN4 ...... 79 M8
GTS/LS CH66 ...... 162 L1
WDN WA8 ...... 17 G1
Elaine St TOX L8 ...... 113 H7
WARR WA1 ...... 15 K2
Elbow La FMBY L37 ...... 59 H2
Elbow St CHLY/EC PR7 ...... 32 E6
Elcombe Av GOL/RIS/CU WA3 ...... 93 G6
Elderberry CI WGN WN1 ...... 68 D1
Elderdale Rd ANF/KKDL L4 ...... 97 K6
Elder Gdns ALL/GAR L19 ...... 130 D5
Eldersfield Rd NG/CROX L11 ...... 98 D3
Elderswood Rd RAIN/WH L35 ...... 117 L1
Elderwood Rd
RF/TRAN CH42 ...... 128 A2
Eldon CI ECCL WA10 ...... 8 C7
Eldon Gdns AIMK WN4 ...... 79 J7
Eldonian Wy VAUX/LVPD L3 ...... 12 C1
Eldon PI VAUX/LVPD L3 ...... 12 C1
Eldon Rd RF/TRAN CH42 ...... 128 B3
WAL/EG CH44 ...... 111 K1
Eldons Cft STHP PR8 ...... 34 F8
Eldon St CHLYE PR6 ...... 32 F6
ECCL WA10 ...... 8 C7
LEIGH WN7 ...... 81 M7
VAUX/LVPD L3 ...... 12 F2
WARR WA1 ...... 15 H5
Eldon Ter NSTN CH64 ...... 153 G6
Eldred Rd CHLDW L16 ...... 114 E2
Eleanor Rd BTL L20 ...... 83 M7
CL/PREN CH43 ...... 110 F5
MOR/LEA CH46 ...... 109 L4
Eleanor St BTL L20 ...... 6 F9
EP CH65 ...... 20 D2
WDN WA8 ...... 16 D6
WGNS/IIMK WN3 ...... 4 B6
Elephant La RAIN/WH L35 ...... 101 M6

STHEL WA9 ...... 102 A6
Elfet St BIRK CH41 ...... 111 H5
Elgar Av PS/BROM CH62 ...... 144 A8
Elgar CI EP CH65 ...... 163 H2
Elgar Rd DV/KA/FCH L14 ...... 99 H8
Elgin Av AIMK WN4 ...... 90 F1
WARRS WA4 ...... 137 J3
Elgin CI WGNE/HIN WN2 ...... 69 J5
Elgin Dr WAL/NB CH45 ...... 95 L7
Elgin Wy BIRK CH41 ...... 11 K4
Eliot CI PS/BROM CH62 ...... 128 C6
Eliot St BTL L20 ...... 83 K8
Elizabethan Dr WGNE/HIN WN2 ...... 80 A1
WGNE/HIN WN2 ...... 81 G4
Elizabeth Av STHP PR8 ...... 35 G7
WGNE/HIN WN2 ...... 81 G4
Elizabeth Ct WDN WA8 ...... 16 E6
Elizabeth Dr WARR WA1 ...... 122 C5
Elizabeth Rd AIN/FAZ L10 ...... 85 K6
BTL L20 ...... 83 M7
HUY L36 ...... 116 C5
RNFD/HAY WA11 ...... 91 G6
Elizabeth St STHEL WA9 ...... 119 G2
VAUX/LVPD L3 ...... 13 M6
WGNE/HIN WN2 ...... 69 K5
Eliza St STHEL WA9 ...... 103 H6
Elkan CI WDN WA8 ...... 134 F2
Elkan Rd WDN WA8 ...... 135 G2
Elkstone CI WGNS/IIMK WN3 ...... 78 E3
Elkstone Rd NG/CROX L11 ...... 98 D4
Elkwood CI WGN WN1 ...... 68 D1
Ellaby Rd RAIN/WH L35 ...... 117 L1
Ellamsbridge Rd STHEL WA9 ...... 103 G6
Elland Dr GTS/LS CH66 ...... 155 L8
Ellel Gv NPK/KEN L6 ...... 97 L8
Ellen Gdn STHEL WA9 ...... 103 G6
Ellen's CI NPK/KEN L6 ...... 113 J3
Ellen's La BEB CH63 ...... 128 C8
Ellen St STHEL WA9 ...... 103 G6
WARRW/BUR WA5 ...... 14 B2
WGN WN1 ...... 5 C5
Elleray Park Rd WAL/NB CH45 ...... 95 J6
Eller Brook CI CHLYE PR6 ...... 44 B4
Ellerbrook Dr BRSC L40 ...... 52 B2
BRSC L40 ...... 52 B2
Ellerby RUNC WA7 ...... 151 G6
Ellergreen Rd NG/CROX L11 ...... 98 B3
Ellerman Rd VAUX/LVPD L3 ...... 129 H2
Ellerslie Av RAIN/WH L35 ...... 101 L8
Ellerslie Rd CLB/OSW/ST L13 ...... 97 M7
Ellerton Av GTS/LS CH66 ...... 155 L8
Ellerton CI WDN WA8 ...... 133 M2
Ellerton Wy WD/CROXPK L12 ...... 99 G2
Ellesmere Dr AIN/FAZ L10 ...... 84 E3
Ellesmere Gv WAL/NB CH45 ...... 95 K7
Ellesmere Rd AIMK WN4 ...... 79 H8
GOL/RIS/CU WA3 ...... 107 G1
WARRS WA4 ...... 137 K4
WGNW/BIL/O WN5 ...... 67 M7
Ellesmere St RUNC WA7 ...... 19 J3
WARR WA1 ...... 15 G6
Ellesworth CI
WARRW/BUR WA5 ...... 120 E5
Elliot St CLVPS L1 ...... 13 H7
ECCL WA10 ...... 8 C5
Elliott Av GOL/RIS/CU WA3 ...... 92 D4
WARR WA1 ...... 15 L2
Elliott Dr WGNE/HIN WN2 ...... 69 M6
Ellis Ashton St HUY L36 ...... 116 C3
Ellis La FROD/HEL WA6 ...... 160 F4
Ellison Dr ECCL WA10 ...... 101 L1
Ellison Gv HUY L36 ...... 115 M3
Ellison St CLB/OSW/ST L13 ...... 114 B1
WARRS WA4 ...... 137 M4
Ellis PI TOX L8 ...... 113 H8
Ellis Rd WGNW/BIL/O WN5 ...... 89 M1
Ellis St WDN WA8 ...... 16 B6
WGN WN1 ...... 5 J1
Ellon Av RAIN/WH L35 ...... 117 M3
Elloway Rd SPK/HALE L24 ...... 147 J2
Elmar Rd AIG/SPK L17 ...... 130 A3
Elm Av AIMK WN4 ...... 78 F8
CSBY/BLUN L23 ...... 71 H8
GOL/RIS/CU WA3 ...... 92 C4
GR/UP/WCH CH49 ...... 109 M7
WDN WA8 ...... 134 D3
WGNNW/ST WN6 ...... 56 B5
WGNW/BIL/O WN5 ...... 68 A7
Elmbank Rd CALD/MH L18 ...... 114 A8
PS/BROM CH62 ...... 128 D7
Elmbank St WAL/EG CH44 ...... 111 L2
Elm CI PEN/TH CH61 ...... 141 H1
WD/CROXPK L12 ...... 99 H2
Elm Cft WGN WN1 ...... 68 D1
Elmcroft La HTWN L38 ...... 70 C2
Elmdale CI FMBY L37 ...... 58 F3
Elmdale Rd WLT/FAZ L9 ...... 97 J1
Elmdene Ct
GR/UP/WCH CH49 ...... 125 L3
Elm Dr FMBY L37 ...... 58 F4
GR/UP/WCH CH49 ...... 125 L2
LITH L21 ...... 83 H7
WGNW/BIL/O WN5 ...... 77 M8
Elmer's Green La SKEL WN8 ...... 65 M3
Elmers Wood Rd SKEL WN8 ...... 65 M4
Elmfield WGNNW/ST WN6 ...... 55 K7
Elmfield CI STHEL WA9 ...... 102 A5
Elmfield Rd WGN WN1 ...... 56 D8
WLT/FAZ L9 ...... 84 C8
Elm Gdns LITH L21 ...... 83 J7
RNFD/HAY WA11 ...... 76 B7
Elm Gv CHLYE PR6 ...... 33 G3
EHL/KEN L7 ...... 113 J4
GTS/LS CH66 ...... 163 J4
HOY CH47 ...... 108 D6
PR/KW L34 ...... 101 H6
RF/TRAN CH42 ...... 11 H9
SKEL WN8 ...... 65 G4
WARR WA1 ...... 122 B6
WDN WA8 ...... 16 E1

RUNC WA7 ...... 150 F4
Elm Park Rd WAL/NB CH45 ...... 95 J6
Elm PI ORM L39 ...... 63 G1
Elmridge SKEL WN8 ...... 65 M5
Elm Ri FROD/HEL WA6 ...... 160 E6
Elm Rd ANF/KKDL L4 ...... 97 J4
BEB CH63 ...... 128 B6
BRSC L40 ...... 52 A2
ECCL WA10 ...... 101 M5
KKBY L32 ...... 85 M2
LITH L21 ...... 83 H7
NSTN CH64 ...... 154 B5
PEN/TH CH61 ...... 126 B7
RF/TRAN CH42 ...... 127 M2
RNFD/HAY WA11 ...... 91 G6
RUNC WA7 ...... 19 M7
STHP PR8 ...... 3 G9
WARRN/WOL WA2 ...... 121 K1
WARRW/BUR WA5 ...... 136 B2
WGNE/HIN WN2 ...... 80 E6
Elm Rd North RF/TRAN CH42 ...... 127 K3
Elmsbury St AIMK WN4 ...... 79 J8
Elmsdale Rd CALD/MH L18 ...... 114 C8
Elmsett CI WARRW/BUR WA5 ...... 120 A8
Elmsfield CI WLTN L25 ...... 115 J8
Elmsfield Pk ORM L39 ...... 62 C7
Elmsfield Rd CSBY/BLUN L23 ...... 71 K7
Elms House Rd
CLB/OSW/ST L13 ...... 114 B2
Elmsley Rd CALD/MH L18 ...... 130 B1
Elms Rd MGHL L31 ...... 72 E7
Elmstead SKEL WN8 ...... 65 M5
The Elms GOL/RIS/CU WA3 ...... 93 H5
MGHL L31 ...... 72 F3
RUNC WA7 ...... 18 F6
TOX L8 ...... 129 J1
Elm St BIRK CH41 ...... 11 H5
HUY L36 ...... 116 C3
WGNE/HIN WN2 ...... 80 C3
Elmswood Av RAIN/WH L35 ...... 117 M3
Elmswood Gv HUY L36 ...... 115 L2
Elmswood Rd AIG/SPK L17 ...... 130 A3
RF/TRAN CH42 ...... 127 L1
WAL/EG CH44 ...... 111 M1
Elm Ter HOY CH47 ...... 108 E6
Elm Tree Av LYMM WA13 ...... 139 M3
WARR WA1 ...... 122 B5
Elmtree CI WD/CROXPK L12 ...... 98 E6
Elmtree Gv CL/PREN CH43 ...... 111 G5
Elm Tree Rd GOL/RIS/CU WA3 ...... 93 H6
LYMM WA13 ...... 139 M3
Elmure Av BEB CH63 ...... 127 M8
Elm V NPK/KEN L6 ...... 113 M2
Elmwood CHLY/EC PR7 ...... 32 D4
RUNC WA7 ...... 150 E4
SKEL WN8 ...... 65 L2
Elmwood Av AIMK WN4 ...... 91 J3
CSBY/BLUN L23 ...... 83 H1
WARR WA1 ...... 15 L2
Elmwood Dr PEN/TH CH61 ...... 141 H3
Elnup Av WGNNW/ST WN6 ...... 55 K7
Elphin Gv ANF/KKDL L4 ...... 97 J4
Eisbeck Gv STHEL WA9 ...... 102 F7
Elsie Rd ANF/KKDL L4 ...... 97 K7
Elsmere Av AIG/SPK L17 ...... 129 L2
Elson Rd FMBY L37 ...... 58 F4
Elstead Gv AIMK WN4 ...... 90 F1
Elstead Rd KKBY L32 ...... 85 L4
WLT/FAZ L9 ...... 98 A1
Elston Av NEWLW WA12 ...... 91 K8
Elstow St WGNW/BIL/O WN5 ...... 96 F6
Elstree Rd NPK/KEN L6 ...... 113 M2
Elswick SKEL WN8 ...... 65 L5
Elswick Rd CHTN/BK PR9 ...... 25 H1
Elswick St TOX L8 ...... 129 H2
Elsworth CI FMBY L37 ...... 58 E5
Eltham Av LITH L21 ...... 83 K4
Eltham CI AIMK WN4 ...... 91 M2
GR/UP/WCH CH49 ...... 126 D3
Eltham Gn GR/UP/WCH CH49 ...... 126 C3
Eltham St EHL/KEN L7 ...... 113 M3
Elton Av CSBY/BLUN L23 ...... 82 E1
NTHTN L30 ...... 84 A2
Elton CI GOL/RIS/CU WA3 ...... 93 G6
GOL/RIS/CU WA3 ...... 122 E1
PS/BROM CH62 ...... 155 G2
Elton Dr BEB CH63 ...... 143 J3
Elton Head Rd STHEL WA9 ...... 101 M8
Elton La FROD/HEL WA6 ...... 166 A1
Elton Lordship La
FROD/HEL WA6 ...... 159 J6
Elton St ANF/KKDL L4 ...... 97 H3
Elvington CI RUNC WA7 ...... 161 H2
WGNNW/BIL/O WN5 ...... 67 K4
Elvington Rd HTWN L38 ...... 70 C3
Elway Rd AIMK WN4 ...... 91 L2
Elworth Av WDN WA8 ...... 118 C8
Elworthy Av HLWD L26 ...... 132 B4
Elworthy Gv WGN WN1 ...... 69 G3
Elwyn Dr HLWD L26 ...... 132 B5
Elwyn Rd HOY CH47 ...... 109 G4
Elwy St TOX L8 ...... 113 J8
Ely Av MOR/LEA CH46 ...... 109 L5
Ely CI GTS/LS CH66 ...... 163 G5
NTHTN L30 ...... 84 B4
Ely Ms CHTN/BK PR9 ...... 25 J3
Ely Pk RUNC WA7 ...... 151 G3
Ember Crs NPK/KEN L6 ...... 13 M1
Embledon St TOX L8 ...... 113 K6
Embleton Ct RUNC WA7 ...... 149 M8
Emerald CI NTHTN L30 ...... 84 D2
Emerald St TOX L8 ...... 129 J2
Emerson CI HTWN L38 ...... 70 C1
Emerson St TOX L8 ...... 113 H6
Emery St ANF/KKDL L4 ...... 97 H4
Emily Av RAIN/WH L35 ...... 101 L4
Emily St WDN WA8 ...... 16 B5
Emlyn St STHEL WA9 ...... 102 F4
Emmanuel Rd CHTN/BK PR9 ...... 25 H3
Empire Rd LITH L21 ...... 83 K7
Empress CI MGHL L31 ...... 72 D4
Empress Rd EHL/KEN L7 ...... 113 K3
NPK/KEN L6 ...... 97 L7
WAL/EG CH44 ...... 111 L1
Empress Wy CHLY/EC PR7 ...... 32 A3
Emslie Ct NSTN CH64 ...... 152 E1

Ena Crs LEIGH WN7 ...... 81 L6
Endborne Rd WLT/FAZ L9 ...... 84 C7
Endbutt La CSBY/BLUN L23 ...... 83 G2
Enderby Av RNFD/HAY WA11 ...... 89 L7
Endfield Pk ALL/GAR L19 ...... 130 D5
Endmoor Rd HUY L36 ...... 99 H8
Endsleigh Rd CLB/OSW/ST L13 ...... 114 A2
CSBY/WL L22 ...... 82 D3
Enerby CI CL/PREN CH43 ...... 110 E6
Enfield Av CSBY/BLUN L23 ...... 83 G1
Enfield CI CHLY/EC PR7 ...... 30 C1
Enfield Park Rd
WARRN/WOL WA2 ...... 122 A1
Enfield Rd CLB/OSW/ST L13 ...... 114 D3
EP CH65 ...... 20 B4
Enfield St ECCL WA10 ...... 8 C7
WGNNW/BIL/O WN5 ...... 67 L8
Enfield Ter CL/PREN CH43 ...... 10 D8
Enford Dr STHEL WA9 ...... 102 F6
Engineer St WGNE/HIN WN2 ...... 69 J6
Engine La FMBY L37 ...... 59 M6
Enid PI WGNE/HIN WN2 ...... 80 B5
Enid St TOX L8 ...... 113 H7
Ennerdale Av AIMK WN4 ...... 91 K1
MGHL L31 ...... 73 G3
PS/BROM CH62 ...... 155 H1
RNFD/HAY WA11 ...... 89 K5
WARRN/WOL WA2 ...... 121 K2
Ennerdale CI FMBY L37 ...... 58 F2
NWD/KWIPK L33 ...... 73 M8
Ennerdale Dr FROD/HEL WA6 ...... 160 E5
NTHTN L30 ...... 83 M5
ORM L39 ...... 62 D3
Ennerdale PI WGNE/HIN WN2 ...... 69 K5
Ennerdale Rd CHLY/EC PR7 ...... 32 C5
CL/PREN CH43 ...... 127 G4
FMBY L37 ...... 58 F2
WAL/NB CH45 ...... 95 H5
Ennerdale St VAUX/LVPD L3 ...... 13 G2
Ennis CI SPK/HALE L24 ...... 147 M3
Ennisdale Dr WKBY CH48 ...... 124 F3
Ennismore Rd CLB/OSW/ST L13 ...... 114 B2
CSBY/BLUN L23 ...... 70 E8
Ennis Rd WD/CROXPK L12 ...... 99 G7
Ensor St BTL L20 ...... 6 F9
Enstone SKEL WN8 ...... 65 M4
Enstone Av LITH L21 ...... 83 J4
Enstone Rd WLTN L25 ...... 131 K7
Ensworth Rd CALD/MH L18 ...... 114 D8
Enville St WARRS WA4 ...... 15 G8
Envoy CI WGNW/BIL/O WN5 ...... 68 A4
Ephraim's Fold
WGNE/HIN WN2 ...... 57 M7
Epping Av STHEL WA9 ...... 118 D2
Epping CI RAIN/WH L35 ...... 117 M3
Epping Ct HES CH60 ...... 141 J4
Epping Dr WARR WA1 ...... 122 F5
Epping Gv WAV L15 ...... 114 D7
Epping PI CHLYE PR6 ...... 32 F5
Epping St CHLYE PR6 ...... 33 H1
WLT/FAZ L9 ...... 85 G4
Epsom Cft CHLYE PR6 ...... 44 E6
Epsom Av WGNE/HIN WN2 ...... 80 B6
Epsom Gdns WARRS WA4 ...... 138 A6
Epsom Gv NWD/KWIPK L33 ...... 74 C7
Epsom St STHEL WA9 ...... 103 H1
Epsom Wy EV L5 ...... 96 F8
Epworth St NPK/KEN L6 ...... 13 M5
Eremon CI WLT/FAZ L9 ...... 84 F5
Erfurt Av BEB CH63 ...... 143 J1
Erica Ct HES CH60 ...... 141 G3
Eric Av WARR WA1 ...... 122 A5
Eric Gv WAL/EG CH44 ...... 111 J1
Eric Rd WAL/EG CH44 ...... 111 J1
Eric St WDN WA8 ...... 17 G1
Eridge St TOX L8 ...... 129 J1
Erin CI TOX L8 ...... 113 G7
Erindale Crs FROD/HEL WA6 ...... 160 C7
Erl St WLT/FAZ L9 ...... 84 C7
Ermine Crs EV L5 ...... 97 H8
Erradale Crs WGNS/IIMK WN3 ...... 78 F3
Errington Av EP CH65 ...... 20 C2
Errington Ct AIG/SPK L17 ...... 130 A5
Errington St EV L5 ...... 96 D7
Errol St AIG/SPK L17 ...... 129 K2
Errwood St SPK/HALE L24 ...... 148 A3
Erskine CI RNFD/HAY WA11 ...... 90 A7
Erskine PI WGNE/HIN WN2 ...... 80 D4
Erskine Rd CHLYE PR6 ...... 33 G4
WAL/EG CH44 ...... 111 L2
Erskine St NPK/KEN L6 ...... 13 M5
Erwood St WARRN/WOL WA2 ...... 14 A7
Erylmore Rd CALD/MH L18 ...... 130 C4
Escolme Dr GR/UP/WCH CH49 ...... 126 A7
Escor Rd WLTN L25 ...... 115 H7
Eshelby CI CSBY/WL L22 ...... 83 G4
Esher CI CL/PREN CH43 ...... 110 E6
Eshe Rd CSBY/BLUN L23 ...... 82 E1
Eshe Rd North CSBY/BLUN L23 ...... 82 E1
Esher Rd NPK/KEN L6 ...... 113 L2
RF/TRAN CH42 ...... 128 D5
Eskbank SKEL WN8 ...... 65 L5
Eskbrook SKEL WN8 ...... 65 L4
Eskburn Rd CLB/OSW/ST L13 ...... 98 A3
Eskdale EP CH65 ...... 20 A9
SKEL WN8 ...... 65 K5
Eskdale Av ORM L39 ...... 62 E3
PS/BROM CH62 ...... 144 A8
RNFD/HAY WA11 ...... 89 K5
WGN WN1 ...... 68 D2
Eskdale CI FMBY L37 ...... 58 F2
RUNC WA7 ...... 149 M8
Eskdale Dr FMBY L37 ...... 58 F2
MGHL L31 ...... 72 F3
Eskdale Rd AIMK WN4 ...... 79 K8
WLT/FAZ L9 ...... 84 C7
Esk St BTL L20 ...... 96 B2
Eslington St ALL/GAR L19 ...... 130 C6
Esmond St NPK/KEN L6 ...... 97 K8
Esonwood Rd RAIN/WH L35 ...... 116 F2
Espin St ANF/KKDL L4 ...... 97 H4
Esplanade STHP PR8 ...... 2 D4
Esplen Av CSBY/BLUN L23 ...... 71 G7
Essex Rd HUY L36 ...... 116 C1
STHP PR8 ...... 35 J5
WGN WN1 ...... 56 D8
WKBY CH48 ...... 124 E2

Essex St TOX L8 .... 113 H8
WGN WN1 .... 5 J2
Esther St WDN WA8 .... 16 F2
Esthwaite Av RNFD/HAY WA11 .... 89 L5
Etal Cl NG/CROX L11 .... 98 D4
Ethelbert Rd HOY CH47 .... 108 E5
Ethel Rd WAL/EG CH44 .... 111 M2
Etna St CLB/OSW/ST L13 .... 114 B2
Eton Ct CALD/MH L18 .... 114 F8
Eton Dr ANF/FAZ L10 .... 84 B7
BEB CH63 .... 142 B7
Eton Hall Dr STHEL WA9 .... 102 E6
Eton Rd EP CH65 .... 20 E7
Eton St ANF/KKDL L4 .... 97 H4
Eton Ter WGNS/IIMK WN3 .... 5 J9
Eton Wy WGNW/BIL/O WN5 .... 67 H5
Etruria ALL/GAR L19 .... 145 L1
Etruscan Rd CLB/OSW/ST L13 .... 114 C1
Ettington Dr STHP PR8 .... 34 C8
Ettington Rd ANF/KKDL L4 .... 97 K6
Ettrick Cl NWD/KWIPK L33 .... 73 M7
Euclid Av WARRS WA4 .... 138 D3
Eurolink STHEL WA9 .... 118 B1
Europa Bvd BIRK CH41 .... 11 J4
WARRW/BUR WA5 .... 120 D2
Europa Wy EP CH65 .... 20 D3
Eustace St WARRN/WOL WA2 .... 14 C4
Euston Gv CL/PREN CH43 .... 10 E8
Euston St ANF/KKDL L4 .... 97 H3
Euxton Hall Gdns CHLY/EC PR7 .... 31 L5
Euxton La CHLY/EC PR7 .... 31 M1
CHLY/EC PR7 .... 32 D2
Evans Rd HOY CH47 .... 91 H6
Evans Pl WARRS WA4 .... 15 K9
Evans Rd HOY CH47 .... 108 D6
SPK/HALE L24 .... 131 L8
Evans St PR/KW L34 .... 100 F6
Eva St LEIGH WN7 .... 81 L6
Evellynne Cl KKBY L32 .... 85 L3
Evelyn Av PR/KW L34 .... 101 C7
STHEL WA9 .... 103 G2
Evelyn Rd WAL/EG CH44 .... 111 L2
Evelyn St WARRW/BUR WA5 .... 136 F1
Evenwood SKEL WN8 .... 65 M4
STHEL WA9 .... 102 E7
Everard Cl BRSC L40 .... 37 H6
Everard Rd STHP PR8 .... 3 M9
Everdon Rd NWD/KWIPK L33 .... 86 A2
Evered Av WLT/FAZ L9 .... 97 J1
Everest Cl GTS/LS CH66 .... 163 H2
Everest Rd WGN WN1 .... 68 E3
Everest Rd CSBY/BLUN L23 .... 82 F1
RF/TRAN CH42 .... 127 M3
Evergreen Cl
GR/UP/WCH CH49 .... 109 M7
NTHLY L27 .... 116 A7
The Evergreens FMBY L37 .... 58 F2
Everite Rd WDN WA8 .... 133 K6
Everleigh Cl CL/PREN CH43 .... 110 E6
Eversley SKEL WN8 .... 65 M4
WDN WA8 .... 133 K3
Eversley Cl FROD/HEL WA6 .... 160 E7
WARRS WA4 .... 138 B8
Eversley St TOX L8 .... 113 J7
Everton Brow VAUX/LVPD L3 .... 13 K3
Everton Rd RNFD/HAY WA11 .... 89 M8
Everton St NPK/KEN L6 .... 13 M2
STHP PR8 .... 35 J1
Everton St WAR WN4 .... 78 F8
Everton Ter EV L5 .... 13 L1
Everton Va ANF/KKDL L4 .... 97 G6
Everton Vw BTL L20 .... 6 E6
Every St NPK/KEN L6 .... 113 K1
Evesham Av LEIGH WN7 .... 93 M4
WARRS WA4 .... 137 L5
WLTN L25 .... 131 H3
Evesham Rd ANF/KKDL L4 .... 97 M4
WAL/NB CH45 .... 95 H7
Evington SKEL WN8 .... 65 M4
Ewanville HUY L36 .... 116 A4
Ewart Rd CHLDW L16 .... 115 J5
LITH L21 .... 83 H6
RNFD/HAY WA11 .... 89 K7
Ewden Cl CHLDW L16 .... 115 G6
Ewell Cl CHLYE PR6 .... 33 H1
Ewloe Ct EP CH65 .... 163 M3
Exchange Pas West CLVP L2 .... 12 E6
Exchange Pl RAIN/WH L35 .... 117 L2
Exchange St ECCL WA10 .... 9 G6
Exchange St East CLVP L2 .... 12 E6
Exeley RAIN/WH L35 .... 117 C3
Exeter Cl WLT/FAZ L9 .... 85 G4
Exeter Dr WGNE/HIN WN2 .... 57 M8
Exeter Rd BTL L20 .... 7 G7
EP CH65 .... 20 C4
WAL/EG CH44 .... 95 L8
Exeter St ECCL WA10 .... 8 B5
Exford Av WGNS/IIMK WN3 .... 79 K1
Exford Rd WD/CROXPK L12 .... 98 F5
PEN/TH CH61 .... 126 B8
Exmoor Cl CHTN/BK PR9 .... 22 D7
Exmouth Cl BIRK CH41 .... 11 G5
Exmouth Crs RUNC WA7 .... 151 G2
Exmouth Gdns BIRK CH41 .... 11 G5
Exmouth St BIRK CH41 .... 11 G6
Exmouth Wy BIRK CH41 .... 11 G5
WARRW/BUR WA5 .... 104 B7
Extension Vw STHEL WA9 .... 102 F5
Eyes La LEY/BBR PR5 .... 28 F2

## F

Factory Brow HOR/BR BL6 .... 57 M2
Factory Fold WGNE/HIN WN2 .... 69 J6
Factory La CHLYE PR6 .... 44 D5
WARR WA1 .... 14 C7
WDN WA8 .... 134 D2
Faggy La WGNS/IIMK WN3 .... 4 F6
Fairacre Rd ALL/GAR L19 .... 130 C4
Fairacres WGNNW/ST WN6 .... 55 K4
Fairacres BEB CH63 .... 143 H1
Fairbairn Rd CSBY/WL L22 .... 83 C4
Fairbank St WAV L15 .... 114 A6
Fairbeech Ct CL/PREN CH43 .... 110 E6

Fairbourne Av
WGNS/IIMK WN3 .... 79 J1
Fairbourne Cl
WARRW/BUR WA5 .... 121 G2
Fairbrook Dr BIRK CH41 .... 110 F8
Fairbrother Crs
WARRN/WOL WA2 .... 121 M3
Fairburn SKEL WN8 .... 65 K2
Fairburn Rd CLB/OSW/ST L13 .... 98 A7
Fairburn Rd WDN WA8 .... 135 G2
Fairclough Av WARR WA1 .... 15 G1
Fairclough La RNFD/HAY WA11 .... 90 C7
Fairclough La CL/PREN CH43 .... 127 K1
HUY L36 .... 99 L7
RAIN/WH L35 .... 117 K2
Fairclough St CLVPS L1 .... 13 H8
NEWLW WA12 .... 104 D2
WARRW/BUR WA5 .... 104 A7
WGN WN1 .... 5 G6
WGNE/HIN WN2 .... 69 M7
Fairfax Dr RUNC WA7 .... 149 M3
Fairfax Pl NG/CROX L11 .... 97 M3
Fairfax Rd NG/CROX L11 .... 98 A3
RF/TRAN CH42 .... 128 A1
Fairfield Av DV/KA/FCH L14 .... 115 J3
EP CH65 .... 163 J3
WDN WA8 .... 80 C3
WGNW/BIL/O WN5 .... 67 M3
Fairfield Cl HUY L36 .... 115 J3
ORM L39 .... 51 G6
Fairfield Crs HUY L36 .... 115 J3
MOR/LEA CH46 .... 109 M5
NPK/KEN L6 .... 113 M2
Fairfield Dr ORM L39 .... 51 G6
WKBY CH48 .... 125 G2
Fairfield Gdns RNFD/HAY WA11 .... 89 G3
WARRS WA4 .... 138 A3
Fairfield Rd ECCL WA10 .... 88 C8
RF/TRAN CH42 .... 128 A3
STHP PR8 .... 34 E7
WARRS WA4 .... 137 M3
WDN WA8 .... 16 E1
Fairfield St EHL/KEN L7 .... 114 A2
WARR WA1 .... 15 H3
WGNW/BIL/O WN5 .... 67 L8
Fairford Crs DV/KA/FCH L14 .... 114 D1
Fairford Rd DV/KA/FCH L14 .... 114 D1
Fairhaven NWD/KWIPK L33 .... 74 A8
SKEL WN8 .... 65 L3
Fairhaven Cl RF/TRAN CH42 .... 128 B5
WARRW/BUR WA5 .... 136 D1
Fairhaven Dr BEB CH63 .... 143 L8
Fairhaven Rd CHTN/BK PR9 .... 25 K1
WDN WA8 .... 134 E3
Fairholme Av AIMK WN4 .... 91 K1
NSTN CH64 .... 152 F4
PR/KW L34 .... 101 J7
Fairholme Cl WD/CROXPK L12 .... 98 C8
Fairholme Rd CSBY/BLUN L23 .... 83 G1
Fairhurst's Dr SKEL WN8 .... 53 K3
Fairhurst St WGNS/IIMK WN3 .... 4 C4
Fairlawn Cl BEB CH63 .... 143 J7
Fairlawne Cl NWD/KWIPK L33 .... 74 A8
NWD/KWIPK L33 .... 86 A1
Fairlie SKEL WN8 .... 65 L2
Fairlie Crs BTL L20 .... 83 M6
Fairlie Dr RAIN/WH L35 .... 117 M3
Fairmead Rd MOR/LEA CH46 .... 110 A4
NG/CROX L11 .... 98 A3
Fairoak Cl CL/PREN CH43 .... 110 E6
Fairstead SKEL WN8 .... 65 L2
Fair Vw WGNW/BIL/O WN5 .... 77 M8
Fairview Av WAL/NB CH45 .... 95 J8
Fair View Av
WGNW/BIL/O WN5 .... 77 M8
Fairview Cl AIMK WN4 .... 91 K1
CL/PREN CH43 .... 127 K2
Fair View Pl TOX L8 .... 129 J1
Fairview Rd CL/PREN CH43 .... 127 K2
GTS/LS CH66 .... 163 J3
Fairview Wy PEN/TH CH61 .... 141 H2
Fair Wy ECCL WA10 .... 88 E8
Fairway CHLY/EC PR7 .... 32 E3
CHTN/BK PR9 .... 24 E3
HUY L36 .... 116 C1
Fairway Crs PS/BROM CH62 .... 143 M1
Fairway North PS/BROM CH62 .... 143 M1
Fairways CSBY/BLUN L23 .... 70 F8
FROD/HEL WA6 .... 160 F6
WARRS WA4 .... 137 M8
Fairways Cl WLTN L25 .... 131 K5
Fairways Ct FMBY L37 .... 46 E8
Fairways Dr GTS/LS CH66 .... 155 M6
Fairway South PS/BROM CH62 .... 143 M2
The Fairways AIMK WN4 .... 90 F3
SKEL WN8 .... 65 M2
The Fairway WD/CROXPK L12 .... 114 F1
Faith St LEIGH WN7 .... 81 L8
Falcondale Rd
WARRN/WOL WA2 .... 105 K7
Falconers Gn
WARRW/BUR WA5 .... 120 D3
WGNS/IIMK WN3 .... 68 D3
Falconer St BTL L20 .... 83 J7
Falconhall Rd WLT/FAZ L9 .... 98 B1
Falcon Hey AIN/FAZ L10 .... 85 J7
Falcon Rd GTS/LS CH66 .... 163 H2
RF/TRAN CH42 .... 10 E9
Falcons Wy RUNC WA7 .... 150 A7
Falconwood Cl WGNNW/ST WN6 .... 4 B2
Falkirk Dr WGNE/HIN WN2 .... 69 J3
Falkirk Gv WGNW/BIL/O WN5 .... 67 L5
Falkland SKEL WN8 .... 65 L2
Falkland Dr AIMK WN4 .... 90 E1
Falkland Rd STHP PR8 .... 3 J9
WAL/EG CH44 .... 111 M1
Falklands Ap NG/CROX L11 .... 98 A3
Falkland St BIRK CH41 .... 10 A2
VAUX/LVPD L3 .... 13 L5
Falkner Sq TOX L8 .... 113 J6
Falkner St TOX L8 .... 113 H5
Fallbrook Dr WD/CROXPK L12 .... 98 E8
Fallow Cl STHEL WA9 .... 118 E1
Fallowfield NWD/KWIPK L33 .... 74 A8
RUNC WA7 .... 149 M4

Fallowfield Gv
WARRN/WOL WA2 .... 122 D4
Fallowfield Rd WAV L15 .... 114 B7
Fallows Wy RAIN/WH L35 .... 116 E4
Falmouth Dr WARRW/BUR WA5 .... 136 A2
Falmouth Pl RUNC WA7 .... 151 G7
Falmouth Rd NG/CROX L11 .... 85 M8
Falstaff St BTL L20 .... 96 E5
Falstone Cl GOL/RIS/CU WA3 .... 107 K7
WGNS/IIMK WN3 .... 79 G3
Falstone Dr RUNC WA7 .... 151 G5
Fanner's La KNUT WA16 .... 139 L8
Faraday Cl CLB/OSW/ST L13 .... 114 A4
Faraday Rd CLB/OSW/ST L13 .... 114 A4
EP CH65 .... 163 J1
NWD/KWIPK L33 .... 86 D6
Faraday St EV L5 .... 97 J8
GOL/RIS/CU WA3 .... 107 C8
Fardon Cl WGNS/IIMK WN3 .... 79 H2
Farefield Av GOL/RIS/CU WA3 .... 92 B3
Fareham Rd EHL/KEN L7 .... 113 M3
Faringdon Cl WLTN L25 .... 131 K7
Faringdon Rd
WARRN/WOL WA2 .... 105 K7
Farley Av PS/BROM CH62 .... 143 L4
Farley La SKEL WN8 .... 66 C3
Farlow Rd RF/TRAN CH42 .... 128 B4
Farm Av CHLYE PR6 .... 44 C5
Farmbrook Rd WLTN L25 .... 115 K7
Farm Cl CHTN/BK PR9 .... 25 J7
GR/UP/WCH CH49 .... 125 L1
Farmdale Cl CALD/MH L18 .... 130 D3
Farmdale Dr CHNE CH2 .... 165 J2
MGHL L31 .... 73 C4
Far Meadow La PEN/TH CH61 .... 125 L7
Farmer Pl BTL L20 .... 84 A6
Farmers Heath GTS/LS CH66 .... 162 F3
Farmer's La WARRW/BUR WA5 .... 104 C7
Farmfield Dr CL/PREN CH43 .... 110 E6
Farm La WARRS WA4 .... 138 A5
WGNE/HIN WN2 .... 69 J3
Farmleigh Gdns
WARRW/BUR WA5 .... 120 B6
Farm Meadow Rd
WGNW/BIL/O WN5 .... 67 G8
Far Moss Rd CSBY/BLUN L23 .... 70 D7
Farm Rd STHEL WA9 .... 118 F2
Farmside MOR/LEA CH46 .... 110 B2
Farmside Cl
WARRW/BUR WA5 .... 121 G6
Farmstead Wy GTS/LS CH66 .... 163 G4
Farm Vw LITH L21 .... 83 K3
Farmview Cl NTHLY L27 .... 115 L6
Farm Wy NEWLW WA12 .... 105 G4
Farnborough Gv HLWD L26 .... 132 B4
Farnborough Rd STHP PR8 .... 35 H5
Farndale WDN WA8 .... 118 C8
Farndale Cl WARRW/BUR WA5 .... 120 B6
Farndale Gv AIMK WN4 .... 91 L3
Farndon Av STHEL WA9 .... 118 D1
WAL/NB CH45 .... 95 G7
Farndon Dr WKBY CH48 .... 125 G2
Farndon Gv GTS/LS CH66 .... 156 A7
Farndon Wy CL/PREN CH43 .... 127 L1
Farne Cl EP CH65 .... 163 L5
Farnham Cl WARRS WA4 .... 138 A6
Farnhill Cl RUNC WA7 .... 150 F5
Farnham Cl RUNC WA7 .... 150 F4
Farnsfield WGN WN1 .... 5 M2
Farnworth Av
MOR/LEA CH46 .... 110 B2
Farnworth Cl WDN WA8 .... 134 D1
Farnworth Gv
NWD/KWIPK L33 .... 74 A8
Farnworth Rd
WARRW/BUR WA5 .... 135 M1
Farnworth St NPK/KEN L6 .... 113 K2
STHEL WA9 .... 9 L4
WDN WA8 .... 134 D1
Farrant St WDN WA8 .... 16 F3
Farrar St CLB/OSW/ST L13 .... 97 M6
Farr Cl WGNS/IIMK WN3 .... 68 B8
Farrell Cl MGHL L31 .... 85 K1
Farrell Rd WARRS WA4 .... 137 L5
Farrell St WARR WA1 .... 15 J5
WGNW/BIL/O WN5 .... 67 L8
Farr Hall Dr HES CH60 .... 141 G6
Farr Hall Rd HES CH60 .... 141 G5
Farrier's Cft WGNNW/ST WN6 .... 68 A2
Farriers Wy WKBY CH48 .... 125 J3
Farrier Wk STHEL WA9 .... 118 E1
Farringdon Cl STHEL WA9 .... 102 B7
Farrington Dr ORM L39 .... 51 G7
Farrington St CHLY/EC PR7 .... 32 E5
Farthing Cl WLTN L25 .... 131 J6
The Farthings CHLY/EC PR7 .... 32 B4
Farthingstone Cl
RAIN/WH L35 .... 101 J7
Fatherside Dr NTHTN L30 .... 83 L2
Faulkner Cl STHP PR8 .... 34 E8
Faulkner Gdns STHP PR8 .... 34 E7
Faversham Rd NG/CROX L11 .... 98 A2
Fawcett SKEL WN8 .... 65 K2
Fawcett Rd MGHL L31 .... 72 F2
Fawley Rd CALD/MH L18 .... 130 E3
RAIN/WH L35 .... 118 A4
Fazakerley Rd RAIN/WH L35 .... 117 G1
WLT/FAZ L9 .... 97 J1
Fazakerley St CHLY/EC PR7 .... 32 E5
VAUX/LVPD L3 .... 12 E6
Fearnhead Av HOR/BR BL6 .... 45 K8
Fearnhead La
WARRN/WOL WA2 .... 122 A3
WARRN/WOL WA2 .... 122 B2
Fearnley Rd BIRK CH41 .... 11 H7
Fearnside St EHL/KEN L7 .... 114 A2
Feather La HES CH60 .... 141 G5
Feeny St STHEL WA9 .... 118 D3
Feilden Rd BEB CH63 .... 143 J1
Felicity Gv MOR/LEA CH46 .... 109 M4
Fellery St CHLY/EC PR7 .... 32 E5
Fell Gv RNFD/HAY WA11 .... 89 J5
Fellside WGN WN1 .... 68 F3
Fell St EHL/KEN L7 .... 113 K3
LEIGH WN7 .... 81 L8
WAL/EG CH44 .... 112 A3
Felltor Cl WLTN L25 .... 131 H2

Fell Vw CHLYE PR6 .... 33 G7
Fellview CHTN/BK PR9 .... 22 F7
Fellwood Gv RAIN/WH L35 .... 117 G3
Felmersham Gn NG/CROX L11 .... 98 B2
Felspar Rd KKBY L32 .... 86 A6
Felstead SKEL WN8 .... 65 K3
Felsted Av WLTN L25 .... 131 L3
Felthorpe Cl GR/UP/WCH CH49 .... 110 D6
Felton Gv CLB/OSW/ST L13 .... 114 B1
Feltons SKEL WN8 .... 65 K3
Feltwell Rd ANF/KKDL L4 .... 97 K7
Feltwood Rd WD/CROXPK L12 .... 99 H6
Feltwood Wk WD/CROXPK L12 .... 99 H5
Fender La MOR/LEA CH46 .... 110 C5
Fenderside Rd CL/PREN CH43 .... 110 E5
Fender View Rd
MOR/LEA CH46 .... 110 C5
Fender Wy CL/PREN CH43 .... 110 D5
PEN/TH CH61 .... 141 J1
Fenham Dr WARRW/BUR WA5 .... 136 A1
Fennel St WARR WA1 .... 15 G5
Fenney Ct SKEL WN8 .... 65 L4
Fenton Cl ECCL WA10 .... 8 E3
NTHTN L30 .... 84 D5
SPK/HALE L24 .... 146 F2
WDN WA8 .... 133 L2
Fenton Gn SPK/HALE L24 .... 146 F3
Fenwick Av STHEL WA9 .... 118 F2
Fenwick La RUNC WA7 .... 149 M7
Fenwick Rd GTS/LS CH66 .... 163 G3
Fenwick St CLVP L2 .... 12 E7
Ferguson Av GR/UP/WCH CH49 .... 125 L2
GTS/LS CH66 .... 156 A7
Ferguson Dr
WARRN/WOL WA2 .... 121 M4
Ferguson Ri
WGNW/BIL/O WN5 .... 68 A5
Ferguson Rd LITH L21 .... 83 L4
NG/CROX L11 .... 98 A5
Fern Av NEWLW WA12 .... 104 F3
WGNE/HIN WN2 .... 69 J3
Fern Bank CHLYE PR6 .... 32 F2
RNFD/HAY WA11 .... 76 A6
Fernbank Av HUY L36 .... 115 M3
Fern Cl GOL/RIS/CU WA3 .... 123 G1
NTHLY L27 .... 132 A1
SKEL WN8 .... 65 G4
WGNNW/ST WN6 .... 55 J7
Ferndale SKEL WN8 .... 65 K3
Ferndale Av CHNE CH2 .... 165 J2
WAL/EG CH44 .... 111 L7
WKBY CH48 .... 125 K4
Ferndale Cl WARR WA1 .... 122 E6
WDN WA8 .... 119 G6
WLT/FAZ L9 .... 84 C6
Ferndale Rd CSBY/WL L22 .... 82 F3
HOY CH47 .... 108 D6
WAV L15 .... 114 A7
Fern Gdns PR/KW L34 .... 101 H6
Fern Gv BTL L20 .... 7 H3
CL/PREN CH43 .... 126 F1
TOX L8 .... 113 L7
Fern Hey CSBY/BLUN L23 .... 71 J8
Fern Hl WAL/NB CH45 .... 95 K5
Fernhill Av BTL L20 .... 7 L4
Fernhill Cl BTL L20 .... 7 L5
Fernhill Dr TOX L8 .... 113 J7
Fernhill Ms East BTL L20 .... 7 L5
Fernhill Ms West BTL L20 .... 7 L5
Fernhill Rd BTL L20 .... 83 M8
Fernhurst RUNC WA7 .... 149 M5
Fernhurst Cl WGNS/IIMK WN3 .... 5 L8
Fernhurst Ga ORM L39 .... 62 D3
Fernhurst Rd KKBY L32 .... 85 L4
Fernie Crs TOX L8 .... 113 G8
Fernlea Av RAIN/WH L35 .... 101 M6
Fernlea Gv AIMK WN4 .... 78 F8
Fernlea Ms CL/PREN CH43 .... 110 E5
Fernlea Rd HES CH60 .... 141 J5
Fernleigh Rd
CLB/OSW/ST L13 .... 114 D2
Fernley Rd STHP PR8 .... 2 F8
Fern Rd EP CH65 .... 163 J3
Ferns Cl HES CH60 .... 140 E4
Fernside Gv WGNS/IIMK WN3 .... 78 F4
Ferns Rd BEB CH63 .... 127 M8
Fernwood Dr HLWD L26 .... 132 B5
Fernwood Rd AIG/SPK L17 .... 130 A3
Ferny Brow Rd
GR/UP/WCH CH49 .... 126 D2
Ferny Knoll Rd RNFD/HAY WA11 .... 76 B1
Ferrer St AIMK WN4 .... 79 H7
Ferrey Rd AIN/FAZ L10 .... 85 J6
Ferries Cl RF/TRAN CH42 .... 128 C5
Ferry La WARRS WA4 .... 139 G1
Ferry Rd PS/BROM CH62 .... 144 C8
Ferryside WAL/EG CH44 .... 112 A3
Ferry Side La CHTN/BK PR9 .... 22 E8
Ferry View Rd WAL/EG CH44 .... 112 A3
Festival Av WARRN/WOL WA2 .... 121 M3
Festival Crs WARRN/WOL WA2 .... 121 M3
Festival Rd EP CH65 .... 156 B8
RNFD/HAY WA11 .... 76 C3
Festival Wy RUNC WA7 .... 19 L7
Ffrancon Dr BEB CH63 .... 128 B6
Fiddlers Ferry Rd WDN WA8 .... 17 J3
Fidler St ECCL WA10 .... 101 M4
Field Av LITH L21 .... 83 J5
Field Cl BRSC L40 .... 52 B2
PS/BROM CH62 .... 128 D5
Fielden St CHLYE PR6 .... 33 K7
Fieldfare Cl GOL/RIS/CU WA3 .... 92 F5
GOL/RIS/CU WA3 .... 123 H1
WLTN L25 .... 115 J8
Fieldgate WDN WA8 .... 133 K7
Field Hey La NSTN CH64 .... 154 D4
Fielding Pl CHLYE PR6 .... 44 D5
Fielding St EHL/KEN L7 .... 113 J3
Fieldlands STHP PR8 .... 36 C3
Field La AIN/FAZ L10 .... 85 K6
LITH L21 .... 83 J4
WARRS WA4 .... 137 L7
Field Rd STHEL WA9 .... 118 F2
WAL/NB CH45 .... 95 K6
Field's End HUY L36 .... 116 A5

Fieldsend Cl NTHLY L27 .... 132 A1
Fieldsend Dr LEIGH WN7 .... 93 L5
Fieldside Rd CHLY/EC PR7 .... 31 L5
Fieldside Rd RF/TRAN CH42 .... 128 A3
The Fields CHLY/EC PR7 .... 30 D6
WGNE/HIN WN2 .... 69 L1
Field St VAUX/LVPD L3 .... 13 K3
WGNE/HIN WN2 .... 81 G3
WGNNW/ST WN6 .... 4 C3
Fieldsway HOY CH47 .... 149 J7
Fieldton Rd NG/CROX L11 .... 98 D2
Field Vw LITH L21 .... 83 J4
Fieldview Dr WARRN/WOL WA2 .... 121 L4
Field Wk ORM L39 .... 51 K8
Field Wy RAIN/WH L35 .... 101 L8
Fieldway BEB CH63 .... 127 M5
FROD/HEL WA6 .... 160 E6
GTS/LS CH66 .... 155 K6
HES CH47 .... 141 L4
HOY CH47 .... 109 H6
HUY L36 .... 116 B5
MGHL L31 .... 72 F6
WAL/NB CH45 .... 95 J8
WAV L15 .... 114 E5
WDN WA8 .... 135 G3
WGNE/HIN WN2 .... 80 D3
Fife Cl CHLYE PR6 .... 33 G7
Fife Rd WARR WA1 .... 15 L2
Fifth Av CL/PREN CH43 .... 110 D6
RUNC WA7 .... 150 B6
WLT/FAZ L9 .... 84 F6
Filbert Cl NWD/KWIPK L33 .... 74 B7
Fildes Cl WARRW/BUR WA5 .... 120 E8
File St CHLY/EC PR7 .... 32 E6
Filton Rd DV/KA/FCH L14 .... 99 K8
Finborough Rd ANF/KKDL L4 .... 97 L3
Fincham Cl DV/KA/FCH L14 .... 99 K8
Fincham Gn DV/KA/FCH L14 .... 99 K8
Fincham Rd DV/KA/FCH L14 .... 99 J8
Fincham Sq DV/KA/FCH L14 .... 99 J8
Finch Av RNFD/HAY WA11 .... 76 C8
Finch Cl DV/KA/FCH L14 .... 99 J7
STHEL WA9 .... 118 F2
Finchdale Gdns
GOL/RIS/CU WA3 .... 93 K5
Finchdean Cl
GR/UP/WCH CH49 .... 125 L1
Finch Dene DV/KA/FCH L14 .... 99 H7
Finch La DV/KA/FCH L14 .... 99 H7
HLWD L26 .... 132 D7
WGNNW/ST WN6 .... 54 D4
Finch Lea Dr DV/KA/FCH L14 .... 99 J8
Finchley Crs WGNE/HIN WN2 .... 69 J3
Finchley Dr RNFD/HAY WA11 .... 89 L6
Finchley Rd ANF/KKDL L4 .... 97 K6
Finch Meadow Cl WLT/FAZ L9 .... 98 B1
Finch Mill Av WGNNW/ST WN6 .... 54 F6
Finch Pl VAUX/LVPD L3 .... 13 L5
Finch Rd DV/KA/FCH L14 .... 99 J7
Finch Wy DV/KA/FCH L14 .... 99 H8
Findlay Cl NEWLW WA12 .... 104 E3
Findley Dr MOR/LEA CH46 .... 110 B2
Findon Rd KKBY L32 .... 86 B5
Fine Jane's Wy CHTN/BK PR9 .... 25 K5
Fingall Rd WAV L15 .... 114 D7
Finger House La WDN WA8 .... 118 F4
Fingland Rd WAV L15 .... 114 A6
Finlan Rd WDN WA8 .... 16 B6
Finlay Av WARRW/BUR WA5 .... 136 A2
Finlay Ct WGNW/BIL/O WN5 .... 68 A5
Finlay St NPK/KEN L6 .... 113 L2
Finney Gv RNFD/HAY WA11 .... 91 G7
The Finney WKBY CH48 .... 124 F7
Finningley Dr
WARRN/WOL WA2 .... 122 A4
Finsbury Pk WDN WA8 .... 118 E8
Finstall Rd BEB CH63 .... 143 H3
Finvoy Rd CLB/OSW/ST L13 .... 98 A6
Fir Avennue HLWD L26 .... 132 C5
Firbank CHLY/EC PR7 .... 31 L3
CHNE CH2 .... 165 L2
Firbank Cl RUNC WA7 .... 150 F4
Firbank Rd WGNS/IIMK WN3 .... 79 K2
Firbeck SKEL WN8 .... 65 K4
Firbrook Ct CL/PREN CH43 .... 110 E4
Fir Cl HLWD L26 .... 132 C5
Fircroft WGNNW/ST WN6 .... 55 J3
Firdale Rd WLT/FAZ L9 .... 97 J1
Firdene Crs CL/PREN CH43 .... 127 L3
Fire Station Rd RAIN/WH L35 .... 101 H8
Firethorne Rd HLWD L26 .... 131 M3
Fir Gv WARR WA1 .... 122 B6
WCNNW/ST WN6 .... 68 C2
WLT/FAZ L9 .... 84 E5
Fir La WAV L15 .... 114 C6
Firman Cl WARRW/BUR WA5 .... 120 D5
Fir Rd CSBY/WL L22 .... 83 G3
Firs Av BEB CH63 .... 143 H2
Firs Cl FMBY L37 .... 46 F8
Firs Crs FMBY L37 .... 46 F8
Firshaw Rd HOY CH47 .... 108 E4
Firs La LEIGH WN7 .... 81 L8
ORM L39 .... 62 A2
WARRS WA4 .... 137 K7
Firs Link FMBY L37 .... 58 F1
Firs Park Crs WGNE/HIN WN2 .... 69 M4
First Av CL/PREN CH43 .... 110 E7
CSBY/BLUN L23 .... 82 F1
RAIN/WH L35 .... 117 K1
WGNE/HIN WN2 .... 69 M8
WGNNW/ST WN6 .... 68 C3
WLT/FAZ L9 .... 84 E6
Firstone Gv KKBY L32 .... 86 A5
Fir St ECCL WA10 .... 101 L5
STHP PR8 .... 35 H7
WDN WA8 .... 134 E3
Firswood Rd BRSC L40 .... 39 G2
Firth Av GOL/RIS/CU WA3 .... 93 H5
Firtree Av WARR WA1 .... 122 C5
Fir Tree Cl CHLY/EC PR7 .... 43 L2
Fir Tree Cl RNFD/HAY WA11 .... 77 H6
SKEL WN8 .... 65 M6
Fir Tree Crs WGNE/HIN WN2 .... 80 B2
Fir Tree Dr WGNE/HIN WN2 .... 80 B2
Fir Tree Dr North
WD/CROXPK L12 .... 98 F2

**Fir Tree Dr South**
WD/CROXPK L12 .................. 98 F2
Firtree Gv CTS/LS CH66 .......... 163 J5
**Fir Tree La** ORM L39 ................ 62 C3
WARRW/BUR WA5 ............. 104 C7
Fir Tree St WGNE/HIN WN2 ...... 80 B1
Firvale Cl LEIGH WN7 .............. 81 L8
**Fir Wy** HES CH60 .................. 141 K8
Firwood Gv AIMK WN4 ............ 91 H3
**Fisher Av** RAIN/WH L35 .......... 116 F3
WARRN/WOL WA2 ............. 121 K4
WGNE/HIN WN2 ................. 80 E6
Fisher Cl WGNS/IIMK WN3 ........ 68 B7
WGNW/BIL/O WN5 ............. 67 G7
Fisherfield Dr GOL/RIS/CU WA3 .. 107 J7
Fishermans Cl FMBY L37 .......... 47 G7
Fisher Pl RAIN/WH L35 ........... 116 F3
Fishers La PEN/TH CH61 .......... 141 G1
**Fisher St** RUNC WA7 .............. 19 K2
STHEL WA9 .................... 103 G6
TOX L8 .......................... 112 F7
Fishguard Cl NPK/KEN L6 .......... 13 M1
Fish La BRSC L40 .................. 38 D2
Fistral Cl AIN/FAZ L10 ............. 85 K7
Fistral Dr ECCL WA10 .............. 88 D7
Fitzadam Cl WGN WN1 .............. 4 D3
Fitzclarence Wy NPK/KEN L6 ...... 13 M2
Fitzgerald Rd CLB/OSW/ST L13 .. 114 C1
Fitzherbert St WARRN/WOL WA2 .. 14 F1
Fitzpatrick Ct VAUX/LVPD L3 ...... 12 E1
Fitzroy Wy NPK/KEN L6 ........... 113 J2
Fitzwalter Rd WARR WA1 ......... 122 F6
Fiveways ECCL WA10 .............. 101 J1
**Flag La** CHLYE PR6 ................ 33 H8
LEY/BBR PR5 ..................... 30 F1
NSTN CH64 .................... 153 H6
Flail Cl GR/UP/WCH CH49 ........ 125 L1
**Flambards**
GR/UP/WCH CH49 ............. 126 D2
Flamstead SKEL WN8 .............. 65 L4
Flander Cl WDN WA8 .............. 133 L3
Flashes La NSTN CH64 ........... 153 K8
Flash La BRSC L40 ................. 39 K1
Flatfield Wy MGHL L31 ............. 73 G4
Flatman's La ORM L39 ............. 61 C4
**Flatt La** CL/PREN CH43 .......... 127 H2
EP CH65 ....................... 20 A4
Flawn Rd NG/CROX L11 ........... 98 A5
Flaxfield Rd FMBY L37 ............. 59 J2
Flaxhill MOR/LEA CH46 .......... 109 M4
Flax La BRSC L40 .................. 52 B3
Flaxley Cl GOL/RIS/CU WA3 ..... 107 J8
Flaxman St EHL/KEN L7 .......... 113 L3
Flaxton SKEL WN8 ................. 65 L4
Flaybrick Cl CL/PREN CH43 ...... 111 G5
Fleck La WKBY CH48 .............. 124 F4
**Fleet Croft Rd**
GR/UP/WCH CH49 ............. 126 C3
Fleet La STHEL WA9 ............... 103 K3
**Fleet St** CHLY/EC PR7 ............ 32 C5
CLVPS L1 ........................ 13 H8
EP CH65 ....................... 156 C8
WGNW/BIL/O WN5 ............. 67 K7
Fleetwood Crs CHTN/BK PR9 ..... 25 H2
WARRW/BUR WA5 ............. 136 D1
Fleetwood Crs CHTN/BK PR9 ..... 23 J7
Fleetwood Dr CHTN/BK PR9 ...... 23 J7
Fleetwood Rd CHTN/BK PR9 ...... 24 E4
Fleetwood Wk RUNC WA7 ....... 150 E6
Fleming Ct VAUX/LVPD L3 ........ 12 E1
Fleming Rd SPK/HALE L24 ....... 131 L7
Fleming St EP CH65 ............... 20 D2
Flemington Av ANF/KKDL L4 ..... 97 M4
Flers Av WARRS WA4 ............. 137 L2
Fletcher Av PR/KW L34 .......... 101 G6
RF/TRAN CH42 .................. 128 A3
Fletcher Cl GR/UP/WCH CH49 ... 126 C3
Fletcher Dr ALL/GAR L19 ......... 130 C6
Fletcher's Dr BRSC L40 ........... 52 A1
Fletcher St WARRS WA4 .......... 14 F9
Flimby SKEL WN8 ................. 65 M4
Flint Cl NSTN CH64 ............... 153 G6
Flint Ct EP CH65 ................. 163 M3
Flint Dr NSTN CH64 .............. 153 G6
Flint Meadow NSTN CH64 ........ 153 G6
Flintshire Gdns ECCL WA10 ....... 8 E7
Flint St CLVPS L1 ................ 112 F6
Flockton Av WGNNW/ST WN6 .... 67 M1
Floral Wd AIG/SPK L17 .......... 129 H3
Flora St AIMK WN4 ............... 91 K3
Flordon SKEL WN8 ................ 65 M4
Florence Av HES CH60 ........... 141 H4
Florence Cl WLT/FAZ L9 .......... 97 H2
**Florence Nightingale Cl**
NTHTN L30 ..................... 84 B1
Florence Rd WAL/EG CH44 ...... 112 A2
**Florence St** ANF/KKDL L4 ....... 97 H5
BIRK CH41 ...................... 11 H5
RAIN/WH L35 .................. 101 L6
WARRS WA4 .................... 15 J9
WGN WN1 ....................... 5 K3
Florentine Rd CLB/OSW/ST L13 .. 114 C1
Florida Cl WARRW/BUR WA5 .... 120 E6
Florida St ALL/GAR L19 .......... 130 D5
Flowermead Cl HOY CH47 ....... 109 H4
Fluin La FROD/HEL WA6 ......... 160 D3
Fluker's Brook La PR/KW L34 .... 99 K4
Foinavon Cl BTL L20 .............. 84 B6
Folds HOR/BR BL6 ................ 57 L2
Folds La RNFD/HAY WA11 ........ 89 J6
Folds Rd RNFD/HAY WA11 ........ 90 B7
The Folds BEB CH63 ............. 142 C7
Fold St GOL/RIS/CU WA3 ......... 92 C4
Foley St ANF/KKDL L4 ............ 97 H6
WGNE/HIN WN2 ................ 69 M8
Folkestone Rd STHP PR8 ......... 36 A2
Folkstone Wy RUNC WA7 ........ 150 E6
**Folly La** WAL/EG CH44 ........... 95 G8
WARRW/BUR WA5 ............. 14 B1
Fontenoy St VAUX/LVPD L3 ....... 13 G5
VAUX/LVPD L3 .................. 13 G5
Fonthill Cl ANF/KKDL L4 .......... 96 F6
Fonthill Rd ANF/KKDL L4 ......... 96 F5
Fontwell Cl WCNNW/ST WN6 .... 56 B4
Forbes Cl GOL/RIS/CU WA3 ..... 123 G1

**Ford Cl** BTL L20 ................. 84 A6
GR/UP/WCH CH49 ............. 126 D1
LITH L21 ........................ 83 K3
Fordcombe Rd WLTN L25 ........ 131 L1
Ford Dr GR/UP/WCH CH49 ...... 110 D8
Fordham St ANF/KKDL L4 ........ 97 G5
Fordhill Vw MOR/LEA CH46 ..... 110 C5
**Fordington Rd**
WARRW/BUR WA5 ............. 120 D8
Fordland Cl GOL/RIS/CU WA3 .... 93 C4
Ford La GR/UP/WCH CH49 ...... 110 D8
LITH L21 ........................ 83 K2
Fordlea Rd WD/CROXPK L12 ..... 98 D5
Fordlea Wy WD/CROXPK L12 .... 98 D5
Ford Rd GR/UP/WCH CH49 ...... 110 C8
RAIN/WH L35 .................. 101 H7
**Ford St** VAUX/LVPD L3 .......... 12 F3
WARR WA1 ...................... 15 J3
Ford Vw LITH L21 ................. 83 K2
Ford Wy GR/UP/WCH CH49 ...... 126 C1
Fordyce Wy WGNE/HIN WN2 ..... 69 J3
Forefield La CSBY/BLUN L23 ...... 83 H1
Foreland Cl WARRW/BUR WA5 ... 119 L6
Forest Av WGNNW/ST WN6 ...... 68 A2
Forest Dr HOY CH47 ............. 108 F4
SKEL WN8 ....................... 65 L2
WGNNW/ST WN6 .............. 55 J3
Forest Gn WD/CROXPK L12 ...... 98 D5
Forest Gv PR/KW L34 ............ 101 H6
Forest Lawn WD/CROXPK L12 .... 98 D5
Forest Md ECCL WA10 ........... 101 J2
**Forest Rd** CL/PREN CH43 ....... 10 A5
CTS/LS CH66 ................... 156 A6
HES CH60 ....................... 141 J5
HOY CH47 ...................... 108 F4
STHEL WA9 .................... 118 C2
STHP PR8 ........................ 3 L6
Forfar Rd CLB/OSW/ST L13 ...... 97 M7
**Forge Cl** BRSC L40 .............. 64 A1
WDN WA8 ...................... 117 L8
Forge Cottages AIG/SPK L17 .... 129 L1
Forge Gv CTS/LS CH66 ........... 155 L7
WARRW/BUR WA5 ............. 120 B8
Forge St BTL L20 ................. 96 E5
WGNE/HIN WN2 .................. 5 K5
**Formby Br** FMBY L37 ............ 59 J3
Formby By-pass FMBY L37 ....... 47 K4
Formby Cl WARRW/BUR WA5 .... 136 B1
Formby Flds FMBY L37 ........... 59 J3
Formby La ORM L39 .............. 62 A3
Formby Rd ECCL WA10 .......... 101 M4
FMBY L37 ...................... 59 H1
Formby St FMBY L37 ............. 59 G3
Formosa Dr AIN/FAZ L10 ......... 85 H6
Formosa Rd AIN/FAZ L10 ......... 85 H6
Formosa Wy AIN/FAZ L10 ........ 85 H6
Fornalls Green La HOY CH47 .... 109 G6
Forres Gv AIMK WN4 .............. 90 E1
Forrester Av RAIN/WH L35 ...... 101 L6
Forresters Cl WGNE/HIN WN2 .... 81 G5
Forrest St CLVPS L1 .............. 13 G9
Forrest Wy WARRW/BUR WA5 ... 136 F2
Forshaw Av ECCL WA10 .......... 101 L5
**Forshaw's La**
WARRW/BUR WA5 ............. 104 A5
Forshaw St WARRN/WOL WA2 ... 15 G2
Forster St GOL/RIS/CU WA3 ...... 92 C4
WARRN/WOL WA2 ............. 14 F2
Forsythia Cl WLT/FAZ L9 .......... 97 L2
Forthlin Rd CALD/MH L18 ....... 130 E4
Forton Rd WGNS/IIMK WN3 ...... 79 H3
Fort St WAL/NB CH45 ............. 95 L6
Forwood Rd PS/BROM CH62 .... 143 M5
Foscote Rd NWD/KWIPK L33 .... 86 C1
Foster Av WGNS/IIMK WN3 ........ 5 K8
Foster Cl RAIN/WH L35 .......... 101 J8
Fosterfield Pl CHLYE PR6 ........ 33 G4
Foster Rd FMBY L37 .............. 58 F3
**Fosters Buildings**
WGNNW/ST WN6 ................ 4 C3
Fosters Cl CHTN/BK PR9 ......... 25 K5
Fosters Green Rd SKEL WN8 ..... 65 L3
Fosters Gv RNFD/HAY WA11 ..... 90 B8
Fosters Rd RNFD/HAY WA11 ..... 90 B7
**Foster St** BTL L20 ............... 96 E6
CHLYE PR6 ....................... 33 G4
WDN WA8 ...................... 16 F1
WGNNW/ST WN6 ................. 4 A2
Fotherby Pl WGNS/IIMK WN3 .... 79 J2
Fothergill St WARR WA1 ......... 15 K2
Foul La STHP PR8 ................ 36 C1
Foundry La WDN WA8 ........... 133 K8
WGNS/IIMK WN3 ............... 78 F1
Foundry St CHLY/EC PR7 ......... 32 E5
ECCL WA10 ....................... 9 G6
NEWLW WA12 .................. 104 D2
WARRN/WOL WA2 ............. 14 E4
Fountain Ct CSBY/BLUN L23 ..... 70 C8
Fountain Rd PR/KW L34 .......... 99 M2
WAL/NB CH45 .................. 95 G8
Fountains Av RNFD/HAY WA11 ... 91 H6
Fountains Cl ANF/KKDL L4 ....... 97 G6
CHLY/EC PR7 .................... 32 F8
RUNC WA7 .................... 150 E8
Fountains St RAIN/WH L35 ...... 101 L7
RF/TRAN CH42 ................. 127 L2
Fountains Wk GOL/RIS/CU WA3 .. 93 K5
Fountains Wy FMBY L37 .......... 59 J3
Four Acre Dr LITH L21 ............ 83 K2
Fouracres MGHL L31 ............. 72 D6
**Fourteen Meadows Rd**
WGNS/IIMK WN3 ................ 4 C7
Fourth Av CL/PREN CH43 ....... 110 D7
RUNC WA7 .................... 150 B6
WLT/FAZ L9 ..................... 84 F6
Fourways Cl NTHLY L27 ......... 115 M6
Fowell Rd WAL/NB CH45 ......... 95 K5
Fowler Cl EHL/KEN L7 ........... 113 L4
WGN WN1 ........................ 5 J4
Foxall Wy CTS/LS CH66 .......... 162 F3

Foxcote CHLY/EC PR7 ............ 32 D3
WDN WA8 ...................... 133 K3
Fox Cover Rd HES CH60 .......... 141 L6
Foxcovers Rd BEB CH63 ......... 143 J2
Fox Covert RUNC WA7 .......... 150 E6
Foxdale Cl CL/PREN CH43 ....... 10 A8
STHP PR8 ........................ 36 A2
Foxdale Rd WAV L15 ............ 114 B7
Foxdene Gv WGNS/IIMK WN3 .... 79 G3
Foxes Foxfield WARRN/WOL WA2 .. 122 A2
The Foxes PEN/TH CH61 ........ 126 C7
Foxfield Gv WCNNW/ST WN6 .... 55 K7
Foxfield Rd HOY CH47 ........... 108 F5
Foxfold SKEL WN8 ................ 65 M2
Fox Gdns LYMM WA13 .......... 139 L1
Foxglove Av HLWD L26 ......... 132 A4
Foxglove Cl WGNNW/ST WN6 .... 55 M3
WLT/FAZ L9 ..................... 98 B1
Foxglove Ct FROD/HEL WA6 .... 160 E5
Foxglove Rd BIRK CH41 ......... 111 H6
Foxglove Wy NSTN CH64 ........ 153 G8
Foxhill Cl FMBY L37 .............. 58 E2
Foxhill La HLWD L26 ............ 132 B3
Foxhill Gv FROD/HEL WA6 ....... 166 F1
Foxhole Rd CHLY/EC PR7 ......... 32 B5
Foxholes Rd HOR/BR BL6 ........ 45 M8
Foxhouse La MGHL L31 ........... 73 G5
Foxhunter Dr WLT/FAZ L9 ....... 84 E5
Foxleigh HLWD L26 .............. 131 M4
Foxley Heath WDN WA8 ......... 16 A3
Fox's Bank La RAIN/WH L35 .... 117 H6
WDN WA8 ...................... 117 H4
Foxshaw Cl RAIN/WH L35 ....... 116 F4
**Fox St** BIRK CH41 ............... 10 F5
RUNC WA7 ...................... 19 G5
VAUX/LVPD L3 .................. 13 J2
WARRW/BUR WA5 ............. 121 G8
Foxton Cl HOY CH47 ............ 109 K4
RNFD/HAY WA11 ............... 89 M8
Foxwood RAIN/WH L35 .......... 101 L6
WD/CROXPK L12 ............... 99 C5
**Foxwood Cl**
WGNW/BIL/O WN5 ............. 67 G8
WKBY CH48 .................... 125 G2
**The Foxwood** CHLY/EC PR7 ..... 42 E4
Foy St AIMK WN4 ................. 91 K2
Frailey Cl STHP PR8 .............. 47 L1
Frampton Rd ANF/KKDL L4 ...... 97 M3
France St WGNE/HIN WN2 ....... 69 M7
WGNW/BIL/O WN5 ............. 68 B6
Franceys St VAUX/LVPD L3 ...... 13 K7
Francine Cl EV L5 ................. 96 E8
Francis Av CL/PREN CH43 ....... 10 D6
MOR/LEA CH46 ............... 109 M5
Francis Cl RAIN/WH L35 ......... 117 L1
WDN WA8 ...................... 16 D3
Francis Rd FROD/HEL WA6 ...... 160 E4
WARRS WA4 ................... 137 K4
Francis St STHEL WA9 .......... 103 H6
WGNE/HIN WN2 ................ 69 M8
Francis Wy CHLDW L16 ......... 115 G5
Frankby Av WAL/EG CH44 ...... 111 J1
Frankby Cl GR/UP/WCH CH49 ... 125 K2
Frankby Gv GR/UP/WCH CH49 .. 110 B8
Frankby Rd ANF/KKDL L4 ........ 97 K5
GR/UP/WCH CH49 ............. 125 L2
HOY CH47 ...................... 108 F5
WKBY CH48 .................... 124 F2
Franklin Cl WARRW/BUR WA5 ... 120 E5
Franklin Pl NPK/KEN L6 .......... 97 K8
Franklin Rd MOR/LEA CH46 .... 110 C1
Frank St WDN WA8 ............... 17 H2
Fraser Rd WARRW/BUR WA5 .... 119 M7
WGNW/BIL/O WN5 ............. 68 A6
Fraser St VAUX/LVPD L3 .......... 13 J3
Frawley Av NEWLW WA12 ....... 91 K3
**Freckleton Cl**
WARRW/BUR WA5 ............. 136 D1
Freckleton Dr NWD/KWIPK L33 .. 74 C8
Freckleton Rd CHTN/BK PR9 ..... 25 H1
ECCL WA10 ..................... 101 K4
Freckleton St WGN WN1 ......... 68 E3
Freda Av STHEL WA9 ........... 102 E7
Frederica Gdns WGNE/HIN WN2 .. 80 C2
**Frederick Banting Cl**
NTHTN L30 ..................... 84 B1
Frederick Gv WAV L15 .......... 114 C5
Frederick Lunt Av PR/KW L34 .... 99 L2
**Frederick St** AIMK WN4 .......... 79 J8
CHLYE PR6 ...................... 33 G6
CLVPS L1 ........................ 12 F9
STHEL WA9 .................... 103 H6
WARRS WA4 ................... 137 M2
WDN WA8 ...................... 16 E2
WGNE/HIN WN2 ................ 69 M8
WGNS/IIMK WN3 ................ 5 H8
Fredric St RUNC WA7 ............. 19 J2
Freedom Cl EHL/KEN L7 ........ 113 L5
Freehold St EHL/KEN L7 ....... 113 M2
Freeland St ANF/KKDL L4 ........ 97 G6
Freeman St BIRK CH41 .......... 11 J3
EHL/KEN L7 ................... 113 L5
Freemantle Av STHEL WA9 ..... 102 B6
Freemasons Rw VAUX/LVPD L3 .. 12 F4
Fremont Bd WD/CROXPK L12 ... 98 C6
Freeport Gv WLT/FAZ L9 ......... 84 D2
Freesia Av WLT/FAZ L9 ........... 97 K1
Freme Cl NG/CROX L11 .......... 98 D2
French St WDN WA8 .............. 17 J2
**Frenchwood Ct**
WGNE/HIN WN2 ................ 69 L1
Frensham Cl BEB CH63 ......... 143 H3
Frensham Wy WLTN L25 ........ 131 M5
Freshfield Cl HUY L36 .......... 115 L2
Freshfield Rd FMBY L37 .......... 47 G8
WAV L15 ...................... 114 B7
WGNS/IIMK WN3 ............... 79 C2
**Freshfields**
WARRN/WOL WA2 ............. 122 D4
Freshford STHEL WA9 .......... 102 F7
**Freshmeadow La**
FROD/HEL WA6 ............... 166 C3
Freshwater WARRW/BUR WA5 .. 119 M6
**Freshwater Cl**
WARRW/BUR WA5 ............. 119 M6

Friars Av WARRW/BUR WA5 .... 120 A8
Friars Cl BEB CH63 .............. 128 B8
Friars Ga WARR WA1 ............. 14 E7
Friars La WARR WA1 .............. 14 E7
**Friar St** ECCL WA10 .............. 89 H6
EV L5 ........................... 97 J8
Friary Cl CHLY/EC PR7 ........... 32 F5
CHLYE PR6 ...................... 32 F5
Friday St CHLY/EC PR7 ........... 32 E5
Friends La WARRW/BUR WA5 ... 119 M7
Frinsted Rd NG/CROX L11 ....... 98 C4
Frith St WGNNW/ST WN6 ......... 4 A5
**Frobisher Ct**
WARRW/BUR WA5 ............. 120 F5
Frobisher Rd MOR/LEA CH46 ... 110 C1
NSTN CH64 .................... 153 G5
Froda Av FROD/HEL WA6 ....... 160 D6
Frodsham Cl WARRW/BUR WA5 .. 67 M2
Frodsham Dr RNFD/HAY WA11 .. 89 M8
Frodsham Rd FROD/HEL WA6 .. 166 F4
Frodsham St ANF/KKDL L4 ....... 97 H4
BIRK CH41 ...................... 11 J9
Froghall La WARR WA1 .......... 14 B4
WARRN/WOL WA2 ............. 14 C4
WARRS WA4 ................... 14 A5
Frog La BRSC L40 ................. 52 F2
WGNNW/ST WN6 ................ 4 B3
Frogmore Rd CLB/OSW/ST L13 .. 114 A2
Frome Cl PEN/TH CH61 ......... 125 M6
Frome Ct EP CH65 ............... 156 D6
Frome Wy WLTN L25 ........... 131 M4
Froom St CHLYE PR6 ............. 33 G5
Frost Dr PEN/TH CH61 .......... 125 L6
Frosts Ms EP CH65 ............... 20 B2
Frost St EHL/KEN L7 ............ 113 L3
WGNE/HIN WN2 ................ 69 M8
Fry St STHEL WA9 ............... 103 G2
Fryent Cl HOR/BR BL6 ........... 57 M3
Fry St STHEL WA9 ............... 103 G2
**Fuchsia Cl** CTS/LS CH66 ....... 163 H4
Fuchsia Wk GR/UP/WCH CH49 .. 125 L3
Fulbeck WDN WA8 ............... 133 L3
Fulbeck Av WGNS/IIMK WN3 .... 79 J3
Fulbeck Dr BEB CH63 ........... 143 H5
Fulbrook Cl BEB CH63 ........... 143 H5
Fulbrook Rd BEB CH63 .......... 143 H5
Fulford Cl DV/KA/FCH L14 ....... 99 H7
Fullerton Gv HUY L36 ........... 116 A1
**Fulmar Cl** NTHLY L27 .......... 132 A1
RNFD/HAY WA11 ............... 89 K7
Fulmar Gv WD/CROXPK L12 ..... 99 G2
Fulshaw Cl NTHLY L27 .......... 115 M7
Fulton Av WKBY CH48 .......... 124 F2
Fulton St EV L5 .................. 96 D7
**Fulwood Av** STHP PR8 ........... 3 M9
Fulwood Cl AIG/SPK L17 ........ 129 M3
Fulwood Dr AIG/SPK L17 ........ 129 L3
Fulwood Gdns CTS/LS CH66 .... 155 L7
Fulwood Ms CTS/LS CH66 ...... 155 L7
Fulwood Pk AIG/SPK L17 ........ 129 L4
Fulwood Rd AIG/SPK L17 ........ 129 L3
GOL/RIS/CU WA3 .............. 93 G7
CTS/LS CH66 .................. 155 L7
Funchal Av FMBY L37 ............ 58 F4
Furlong Cl WGNE/HIN WN2 ...... 80 B6
WLT/FAZ L9 ..................... 84 F5
**Furness Av** ECCL WA10 .......... 89 G6
FMBY L37 ....................... 59 H2
ORM L39 ........................ 63 G1
WD/CROXPK L12 ............... 98 E4
Furness Cl CHLY/EC PR7 ........ 32 F8
STHP PR8 ........................ 47 K2
Furness Crs LEIGH WN7 ......... 81 M4
Furness St ANF/KKDL L4 ......... 97 G6
Furnival Dr BRSC L40 ........... 51 M1
Furrocks Cl NSTN CH64 ........ 153 H8
Furrocks La NSTN CH64 ......... 153 H8
Furrocks Wy NSTN CH64 ........ 153 H8
The Furrows GTS/LS CH66 ...... 163 G5
Fylde Dr CHTN/BK PR9 .......... 22 D8

## G

Gabbot St CHLY/EC PR7 .......... 44 B6
Gable Ct NG/CROX L11 ........... 98 A2
Gables Cl WARRN/WOL WA2 .... 122 B2
Gable St NEWLW WA12 ......... 104 C2
Gabriel Cl MOR/LEA CH46 ...... 110 B5
Gainford Cl WDN WA8 .......... 133 L2
Gainford Rd DV/KA/FCH L14 ..... 99 J7
Gainsborough Av MGHL L31 ..... 72 D5
**Gainsborough Cl**
WD/CROXPK L12 ............... 99 G8
WGNS/IIMK WN3 ............... 78 F2
Gainsborough Ct WDN WA8 .... 133 K4
**Gainsborough Rd**
GR/UP/WCH CH49 ............. 110 A7
STHP PR8 ........................ 35 G2
WAL/NB CH45 .................. 95 G8
WARRS WA4 ................... 137 K3
WAV L15 ...................... 114 A7
Gairloch Cl WARRN/WOL WA2 .. 122 B1
Gaisgill Ct WDN WA8 ........... 133 L4
Gale Av WARRW/BUR WA5 ..... 121 H4
Galemeade NG/CROX L11 ....... 98 D2
Gale Rd LITH L21 ................ 83 L4
NWD/KWIPK L33 ............... 86 C5
Gales La BRSC L40 ............... 40 C2
Galion Wy WDN WA8 ........... 134 B1
Galloway Rd CSBY/WL L22 ...... 83 G3
Galloway St EHL/KEN L7 ....... 113 M5
Galston Av RAIN/WH L35 ....... 117 M3
Galsworthy Av NTHTN L30 ..... 83 M8
Galsworthy Pl NTHTN L30 ...... 84 A5
Galton St VAUX/LVPD L3 ........ 12 C4
Galtres Pk BEB CH63 ........... 128 A5
Galwey Gv WGN WN1 ............ 68 E1
Gamble Av ECCL WA10 .......... 89 G7
Gamlin St BIRK CH41 ........... 111 H5
Gamston Wd KKBY L32 .......... 85 L4
**Ganney's Meadow Rd**
GR/UP/WCH CH49 ............. 126 B3
Gannock St EHL/KEN L7 ........ 113 L3
Gantley Av WGNW/BIL/O WN5 .. 77 M1
Gantley Crs WGNW/BIL/O WN5 .. 77 M2
Gantley Rd WGNW/BIL/O WN5 .. 77 M2
Ganton Cl STHP PR8 ............. 36 A1
WDN WA8 ...................... 134 D1

Ganworth Cl SPK/HALE L24 .... 147 G3
Ganworth Rd SPK/HALE L24 .... 147 G3
Garage St EHL/KEN L7 .......... 132 B8
**Gardeners Vw**
NWD/KWIPK L33 ............... 74 B7
Gardeners Wy RAIN/WH L35 .... 101 L8
**Garden Hey Rd** HOY CH47 ..... 108 C5
MOR/LEA CH46 ............... 109 K6
Gardenia Gv AIG/SPK L17 ...... 129 J3
Garden La WARR/LEA CH46 .... 110 A4
VAUX/LVPD L3 .................. 13 L2
WLT/FAZ L9 ..................... 84 F6
**Garden Lodge Gv** NTHLY L27 .. 115 M8
Garden Pl BTL L20 ................. 7 H4
Gardenside MOR/LEA CH46 .... 110 D1
Gardenside St NPK/KEN L6 ...... 13 M3
Gardens Rd BEB CH63 .......... 128 D8
Garden St WLTN L25 ............ 131 J3
Garden Wk PR/KW L34 .......... 100 F8
Gardiner Av RNFD/HAY WA11 .. 90 E7
Gardiners Pl SKEL WN8 .......... 65 G5
Gardner Av BTL L20 ............. 83 M6
Gardner Rd CLB/OSW/ST L13 ... 98 A8
FMBY L37 ....................... 59 J2
Gardner's Dr NPK/KEN L6 ...... 113 L1
Gardner's Rw VAUX/LVPD L3 .... 13 G3
Gareth Av RNFD/HAY WA11 ..... 89 K7
Garfield Ter CHLYE PR6 ......... 32 C3
GR/UP/WCH CH49 ............. 110 C8
Garforth Cl ALL/GAR L19 ....... 130 F6
Garforth Rd ALL/GAR L19 ....... 130 F6
Garmoyle Cl WAV L15 .......... 114 A6
Garmoyle Rd WAV L15 ......... 114 A7
Garner St WARRN/WOL WA2 .... 15 H1
Garnet St CLB/OSW/ST L13 .... 114 B4
STHEL WA9 .................... 102 F6
Garnett Av ANF/KKDL L4 ......... 97 G5
WARRS WA4 ................... 138 B1
Garnett Gn ORM L39 ............ 62 F1
Garnett Pl SKEL WN8 ............ 65 J6
Garnetts La WDN WA8 .......... 148 C2
Garrett Fld GOL/RIS/CU WA3 ... 106 F8
Garrick Av MOR/LEA CH46 .... 109 L5
Garrick Pde STHP PR8 ............ 2 E5
Garrick St CL/PREN CH43 ....... 127 H5
Garrick St EHL/KEN L7 .......... 113 L6
Garrigill Cl WDN WA8 ........... 118 D8
Garrowby Dr HUY L36 .......... 115 L2
Garsdale Av RAIN/WH L35 ...... 117 M3
**Garsdale Cl**
WARRW/BUR WA5 ............. 120 B6
Garsfield Rd ANF/KKDL L4 ....... 97 M4
Garside Av GOL/RIS/CU WA3 .... 92 F5
Garside Gv WGNS/IIMK WN3 .... 79 G3
Garstang Rd CHTN/BK PR9 ...... 25 H1
Garston Old Rd ALL/GAR L19 .. 130 D6
Garston Wy ALL/GAR L19 ...... 130 E7
Garswood Av RNFD/HAY WA11 .. 76 C4
Garswood Cl MGHL L31 ......... 73 G2
MOR/LEA CH46 ............... 110 A1
**Garswood Crs**
WGNW/BIL/O WN5 ............. 89 M1
Garswood Old Rd AIMK WN4 .... 90 B4
Garswood Rd AIMK WN4 ........ 90 C2
WGNW/BIL/O WN5 ............. 90 A1
Garswood St AIMK WN4 ........ 91 K2
ECCL WA10 ...................... 9 G3
TOX L8 ......................... 129 H2
Garter Cl NG/CROX L11 .......... 98 E2
Garth Bvd BEB CH63 ........... 128 A5
Garthdale Rd CALD/MH L18 .... 130 C1
Garth Dr CALD/MH L18 ......... 130 D1
Garthowen Rd EHL/KEN L7 .... 113 M3
Garth Rd KKBY L32 .............. 86 C5
The Garth HUY L36 .............. 116 A2
Garton Dr GOL/RIS/CU WA3 ..... 93 G4
Gartons La STHEL WA9 ......... 118 E2
Garven Pl WARR WA1 ............ 14 D6
Garway WLTN L25 ............... 131 L2
Garwood Cl WARRW/BUR WA5 .. 120 D5
Gascoyne St VAUX/LVPD L3 ...... 12 E4
Gaskell Av WARRS WA4 ......... 138 C2
Gaskell's Brow AIMK WN4 ....... 79 C5
Gaskell St CHLYE PR6 ........... 33 G5
STHEL WA9 .................... 102 F4
WARRS WA4 ................... 137 L4
Gaskill Rd SPK/HALE L24 ....... 146 F1
Gas St CHLY/EC PR7 .............. 44 B7
WGNE/HIN WN2 ................ 80 D3
Gatclif Rd CLB/OSW/ST L13 ..... 98 A5
Gateacre Brow WLTN L25 ....... 131 J1
Gateacre Park Dr WLTN L25 .... 115 H7
Gateacre Ri WLTN L25 .......... 131 K1
Gateacre Vale Rd WLTN L25 .... 131 K2
Gategill Gv WGNW/BIL/O WN5 .. 77 M3
Gateside Cl NTHLY L27 ......... 116 A8
Gates La SFTN L29 ............... 71 K5
**Gate Warth St**
WARRW/BUR WA5 ............. 136 F1
Gathurst La WGNNW/ST WN6 .. 55 H8
Gathurst Rd WGNW/BIL/O WN5 .. 67 G4
Gatley Dr MGHL L31 .............. 73 G5
Gaunts Wy RUNC WA7 .......... 150 A7
Gautby Rd BIRK CH41 .......... 111 C4
Gavin Rd WDN WA8 ............ 133 K6
Gaw Hill La ORM L39 ............ 62 C2
Gaw Hill Vw ORM L39 ........... 62 C2
**Gawsworth Cl**
CL/PREN CH43 ................. 127 H2
ECCL WA10 .................... 101 K2
**Gawsworth Rd**
GOL/RIS/CU WA3 .............. 92 B4
GTS/LS CH66 .................. 163 G1
Gaybeech Cl CL/PREN CH43 .... 110 C5
**Gayhurst Av**
WARRN/WOL WA2 ............. 122 B3
Gayhurst Crs NG/CROX L11 ..... 98 C3
Gaynor Av RNFD/HAY WA11 ..... 91 H6
Gayton Av BEB CH63 ........... 127 L5
WAL/NB CH45 .................. 95 K5
Gayton Cl WGNS/IIMK WN3 ..... 78 F2
Gayton Farm Rd HES CH60 ..... 141 J8
Gayton La HES CH60 ............ 141 K7
Gayton Mill Cl HES CH60 ....... 141 K6
Gayton Pkwy HES CH60 ........ 141 K8
Gayton Rd HES CH60 ........... 141 H7
Gaywood Av KKBY L32 .......... 85 M4

Gaywood Cl CL/PREN CH43 ..... 110 E6 🖸
  KKBY L32 ..... 86 B5 🖸
Gellings Rd PR/KW L34 ..... 115 G8
Gelling St TOX L8 ..... 113 H8 🖸
Gemini Cl BTL L20 ..... 6 F3
Gemini Dr DV/KA/FCH L14 ..... 115 H1
General St WARR WA1 ..... 15 G5
Geneva Rd NPK/KEN L6 ..... 113 L2
  WAL/EG WA44 ..... 111 M3
Genista Cl WLT/FAZ L9 ..... 97 J2 🖸
Genoa Cl WLTN L25 ..... 115 L6
Gentwood Rd HUY L36 ..... 115 L1
Geoffrey St CHLYE PR6 ..... 32 F4
George Dr STHP PR8 ..... 35 G8
George Hale Av PR/KW L34 ..... 100 A7
George Harrison Cl
  NPK/KEN L6 ..... 113 K2 🖸
George Rd HOY CH47 ..... 108 E7
  WARRW/BUR WA5 ..... 136 E1 🖸
Georges Crs WARRS WA4 ..... 138 D3
George's Dock Gates
  VAUX/LVPD L3 ..... 12 D6
Georges Dockway VAUX/LVPD L3... 12 D8
George's La CHTN/BK PR9 ..... 23 H5
  HOR/BR BL6 ..... 45 M6
  WGN WN1 ..... 5 L4
Georges Pierhead
  VAUX/LVPD L3 ..... 12 D8
George's Ter
  WGNW/BIL/O WN5 ..... 66 F8 🖸
George St AIMK WN4 ..... 91 L1 🖸
  BIRK CH41 ..... 11 K3
  CHLY/EC PR7 ..... 32 E6
  ECCL WA10 ..... 9 H5
  EP CH65 ..... 20 C1
  NEWLW WA12 ..... 104 C1 🖸
  VAUX/LVPD L3 ..... 12 E6 🖸
  WGNE/HIN WN2 ..... 5 M6
Georgia Av PS/BROM CH62... 144 A2
Georgian Cl HLWD L26 ..... 132 B7 🖸
  RAIN/WH L35 ..... 101 J7 🖸
Georgian Pl LEIGH L37 ..... 59 G4 🖸
Geraint St TOX L8 ..... 113 H7
Gerald Rd CL/PREN CH43 ..... 127 J1
Gerard Av WAL/NB CH45 ..... 95 J6
Gerard Rd WAL/NB CH45 ..... 95 J7
  WKBY CH48 ..... 124 D2
Gerards La STHEL WA9 ..... 102 F6
Gerard St AIMK WN4 ..... 91 K2
  VAUX/LVPD L3 ..... 13 H5
Germander Cl HLWD L26 ..... 132 A4
German La CHLY/EC PR7 ..... 31 M5
Gerneth Cl SPK/HALE L24 ..... 146 E1
Gerneth Rd SPK/HALE L24 ..... 146 D2
Gerosa Av WARRN/WOL WA2 ... 105 K5
Gerrard Av GTS/LS CH66 ..... 162 E1
  WARRW/BUR WA5 ..... 14 A1
Gerrard Cl WGNE/HIN WN2 ... 69 M3 🖸
Gerrard Pl SKEL WN8 ..... 65 H6
Gerrard Rd GOL/RIS/CU WA3 ... 106 C6
  WGNW/BIL/O WN5 ..... 78 A8
Gerrard's La HLWD L26 ..... 132 A3
Gerrard St WDN WA8 ..... 16 E4 🖸
Gertrude Rd ANF/KKDL L4 ..... 97 J7
Gertrude St BIRK CH41 ..... 11 L5 🖸
  RAIN/WH L35 ..... 101 L7
Geves Gdns CSBY/WL L22 ..... 83 G4
Ghyll Gv RNFD/HAY WA11 ..... 88 F3
Giants Hall Rd WGNNW/ST WN6... 68 A4
Gibbons Av ECCL WA10 ..... 101 L2
Gibbon's Rd AIMK WN4 ..... 90 F3
Gibraltar Rw VAUX/LVPD L3 ..... 12 D5
Gibson Cl PEN/TH CH61 ..... 141 H2
Gibson St TOX L8 ..... 113 H6 🖸
  WARR WA1 ..... 15 H6
  WARRS WA4 ..... 137 M4 🖸
  WGNE/HIN WN2 ..... 80 F3
Giddygate La MGHL L31 ..... 71 J6
Gidlow Av CHLYE PR6 ..... 44 C6 🖸
  WGNNW/ST WN6 ..... 68 C3
Gidlow La WGNNW/ST WN6 ..... 4 B2
Gidlow Rd CLB/OSW/ST L13 ... 114 B2
Gidlow Rd South
  CLB/OSW/ST L13 ..... 114 B2
Gidlow St WGNE/HIN WN2 ..... 69 J5 🖸
Gifford Pl WGNE/HIN WN2 ..... 81 H1
Gigg La WARRS WA4 ..... 136 D8
  WARRS WA4 ..... 139 G1
Gig La WARR WA1 ..... 122 F5
Gilbert Cl BEB CH63 ..... 143 H3
Gilbert Pl RASD L40 ..... 51 K1
Gilbert Rd RAIN/WH L35 ..... 101 H8
Gilbertson Rd CHLY/EC PR7 ..... 44 A3
Gilbert St CHLY/EC PR7 ..... 32 E7 🖸
  CLVPS L1 ..... 13 G9
  CLVPS L1 ..... 112 F5
  WGNE/HIN WN2 ..... 69 L8
Gildarts Gdns VAUX/LVPD L3... 12 F2
Gildart St VAUX/LVPD L3 ..... 13 L5
Gilderdale Cl GOL/RIS/CU WA3 ... 107 K8
Gilead St EHL/KEN L7 ..... 113 K5
Gillan Cl RUNC WA7 ..... 150 E8
Gillan Rd WGNNW/ST WN6 ..... 68 D3
Gillars Green Dr ECCL WA10 ..... 101 H2
Gillar's La ECCL WA10 ..... 101 G2
Gill Av WGNNW/ST WN6 ..... 55 K7
Gillbrow Crs WGN WN1 ..... 5 M2
Gillcroft CHLY/EC PR7 ..... 30 D7 🖸
Gilleney Gv RAIN/WH L35 ..... 101 J3
Gillibrands Rd SKEL WN8 ..... 65 J6
Gillibrand St CHLY/EC PR7 ..... 32 E6
Gillibrand Wks CHLY/EC PR7... 32 E7
Gillmoss Cl NG/CROX L11 ..... 98 E1
Gillmoss La NG/CROX L11 ..... 85 L3
Gills La PEN/TH CH61 ..... 141 J1
Gill St VAUX/LVPD L3 ..... 13 L6
Gilman St ANF/KKDL L4 ..... 97 J6
Gilpin Av MGHL L31 ..... 73 G3
Gilpin Pl WGNE/HIN WN2 ..... 80 B3 🖸
Gilroy Rd NPK/KEN L6 ..... 113 K2
  WKBY CH48 ..... 124 F2
Gilroy St WGN WN1 ..... 5 H4
Gin Bow CHLY/EC PR7 ..... 32 F7 🖸

The Ginnel PS/BROM CH62 ..... 128 D8
Gipsy Gv CALD/MH L18 ..... 115 G8
Gipsy La CALD/MH L18 ..... 115 G8
Girton Av AIMK WN4 ..... 91 H1
  BTL L20 ..... 7 L6
Girton Cl EP CH65 ..... 20 E6
Girton Rd EP CH65 ..... 20 E6
Girtrell Cl GR/UP/WCH CH49 ... 109 M8
Girtrell Rd GR/UP/WCH CH49 ... 109 M8
Girvan Crs AIMK WN4 ..... 90 E1
Girvin Dr NSTN CH64 ..... 153 G7
Gisburn Av WD/CROXPK L12 ..... 92 B3
Givenchy Cl CHLDW L16 ..... 115 G5
Glade Rd HUY L36 ..... 116 A1
Gladeswood Rd
  NWD/KWIPK L33 ..... 86 D4
The Glade HOY CH47 ..... 108 F4
  WGNNW/ST WN6 ..... 55 K7
Gladeville Rd AIG/SPK L17 ..... 130 A3
Gladeville Av CHLDW L16 ..... 115 J5
  LITH L21 ..... 83 H6 🖸
Gladstone Hall Rd
  PS/BROM CH62 ..... 143 K1 🖸
Gladstone Rd ALL/GAR L19 ..... 130 E7
  CHTN/BK PR9 ..... 25 H7
  EHL/KEN L7 ..... 113 K4
  LITH L21 ..... 83 H6
  NSTN CH64 ..... 153 G5 🖸
  RF/TRAN CH42 ..... 128 B2 🖸
  WAL/EG WA44 ..... 111 M2 🖸
  WLT/FAZ L9 ..... 97 H2
Gladstone St BIRK CH41 ..... 10 F5 🖸
  ECCL WA10 ..... 8 A6
  VAUX/LVPD L3 ..... 12 F4 🖸
  WARRN/WOL WA2 ..... 14 C4
  WDN WA8 ..... 16 E3
  WGNE/HIN WN2 ..... 131 H3
Glaisdale Cl AIMK WN4 ..... 91 L2 🖸
Glaisdale Dr STHP PR8 ..... 36 B2
Glaisher St EV L5 ..... 97 J7 🖸
Glamis Dr CHLY/EC PR7 ..... 32 D5
  CHTN/BK PR9 ..... 25 K2
Glamis Gv STHEL WA9 ..... 102 E6
Glamis Rd CLB/OSW/ST L13 ..... 97 M7
Glamorgan Cl ECCL WA10 ..... 8 E7
Glan Aber Pk WD/CROXPK L12 ... 99 G5
Glasier Rd MOR/LEA CH46 ..... 109 L4
Glaslyn Wy WLT/FAZ L9 ..... 97 J2
Glassbrook St WGNNW/ST WN6... 4 B1
Glassonby Crs NG/CROX L11 ... 98 C4 🖸
Glassonby Wy NG/CROX L11 ... 98 C4 🖸
Glastonbury Av
  GOL/RIS/CU WA3 ..... 93 K5
Glastonbury Cl NPK/KEN L6 ... 97 M6
  RUNC WA7 ..... 151 G2
Glasven Rd NWD/KWIPK L33 ... 86 B2
Glazebrook St WARR WA1 ..... 15 J4
Glaziers La GOL/RIS/CU WA3 ... 106 F3
Gleadmere WDN WA8 ..... 133 L3
Gleaston Cl PS/BROM CH62 ... 143 L4 🖸
Gleave Crs NPK/KEN L6 ..... 13 M2 🖸
Gleave Rd WARRW/BUR WA5 ... 104 B7 🖸
Gleave St ECCL WA10 ..... 9 H3
Glebe Av AIMK WN4 ..... 91 K3
  WARRS WA4 ..... 138 E4
Glebe Cl MGHL L31 ..... 72 D4
  WGNNW/ST WN6 ..... 56 B4 🖸
Glebecroft Av CHNE CH2 ..... 165 J2 🖸
Glebe End SFTN L29 ..... 71 M6
Glebe End St WGNNW/ST WN6... 4 C3
Glebe Hey Rd
  GR/UP/WCH CH49 ..... 126 C2
Glebeland GOL/RIS/CU WA3 ... 107 G2
Glebelands Rd MOR/LEA CH46 ... 110 A5
Glebe La CHTN/BK PR9 ..... 23 J6
  WDN WA8 ..... 118 C8
Glebe Pl STHP PR8 ..... 3 G3
Glebe Rd SKEL WN8 ..... 65 J6
  WAL/NB CH45 ..... 95 J7
  WGNNW/ST WN6 ..... 56 B5
Glebe St WGNE/HIN WN2 ..... 81 L3
The Glebe RUNC WA7 ..... 150 A4
Gleggside WKBY CH48 ..... 124 E3
Glegg St VAUX/LVPD L3 ..... 12 D1
Glegside Rd NWD/KWIPK L33 ... 86 C3
Glemsford Cl WGNS/IIMK WN3 ... 79 K2
Glenalmond Rd
  WAL/EG WA44 ..... 111 M1 🖸
Glenathol Rd CALD/MH L18 ... 130 E3
  GTS/LS CH66 ..... 162 E1
Glenavon Rd CHLDW L16 ..... 114 E5
  CL/PREN CH43 ..... 127 J4
Glenbank CSBY/WL L22 ..... 82 E3
Glenbank Cl WLT/FAZ L9 ..... 84 C8
Glenbranter Av
  WGNE/HIN WN2 ..... 69 J5 🖸
Glenburn Av PS/BROM CH62 ... 155 G1
Glenburn Rd SKEL WN8 ..... 65 G1
  WAL/EG WA44 ..... 111 M2 🖸
Glenby Av CSBY/BLUN L23 ..... 83 H3
Glencairn Cl CLB/OSW/ST L13... 114 B3
Glencoe Rd WAL/NB CH45 ..... 95 K7
Glenconner Rd CHLDW L16 ..... 115 G4
Glencourse Rd WDN WA8 ..... 118 C8 🖸
Glencoyne Dr CHTN/BK PR9 ... 22 D7
Glencroft Cl HUY L36 ..... 99 L8 🖸
Glendale Av AIMK WN4 ..... 91 L1
  CHNE CH2 ..... 165 J2 🖸
Glendale Cl TOX L8 ..... 129 H2 🖸
Glendale Gv BEB CH63 ..... 143 K3
Glendale Wy FMBY L37 ..... 59 H3
Glendevon Rd CHLDW L16 ..... 114 F4
  HUY L36 ..... 116 A4
Glendower Rd CSBY/WL L22 ... 83 G4 🖸
Glen D WGNNW/ST WN6 ..... 55 G5
Glendyke Rd CALD/MH L18 ..... 130 E3
  GTS/LS CH66 ..... 162 E1
Gleneagles Cl PEN/TH CH61 ... 141 H2
Gleneagles Dr RNFD/HAY WA11 ... 90 C8
  STHP PR8 ..... 47 K2
  WDN WA8 ..... 118 C8
Gleneagles Rd CHLDW L16 ..... 114 F4
  GTS/LS CH66 ..... 162 E1

Glenesk Rd GTS/LS CH66 ..... 162 E1
Glenfield Cl CL/PREN CH43 ..... 110 E5 🖸
  MOR/LEA CH46 ..... 109 K4 🖸
Glenfield Rd WAV L15 ..... 114 C7 🖸
Glengariff St CLB/OSW/ST L13 ... 98 A6
Glenhead Rd ALL/GAR L19 ..... 130 D5
Glenholm Rd MGHL L31 ..... 72 E6 🖸
Glenluce Rd ALL/GAR L19 ..... 130 D5
Glenmarsh Cl BEB CH63 ..... 127 M8 🖸
  WD/CROXPK L12 ..... 98 E7 🖸
Glenmaye Cl WD/CROXPK L12 ... 99 G3 🖸
Glenmaye Rd GTS/LS CH66 ..... 162 E1
Glenmore Av CALD/MH L18 ..... 130 C2
Glenmore Rd CL/PREN CH43 ..... 127 J1
Glen Pk WDN WA8 ..... 133 M4
Glen Rd CLB/OSW/ST L13 ..... 114 D3
  GTS/LS CH66 ..... 162 E1
Glen Ronald Dr
  GR/UP/WCH CH49 ..... 109 M8 🖸
Glenrose Ter STHP PR8 ..... 2 F8
Glenroyd Dr BRSC L40 ..... 52 A1
Glenside CALD/MH L18 ..... 130 E3
  WGNNW/ST WN6 ..... 54 D3
The Glen CALD/MH L18 ..... 130 E2
  PS/BROM CH62 ..... 143 L2
  RUNC WA7 ..... 150 B7
Glenton Pk NSTN CH64 ..... 153 H7
Glentrees Cl GR/UP/WCH CH49 ... 109 M8
Glentrees Rd WD/CROXPK L12 ... 98 D5
Glentworth Cl MGHL L31 ..... 72 F5
Glenville Cl RUNC WA7 ..... 149 K7 🖸
  WLTN L25 ..... 131 K2
Glen Vine Cl CHLDW L16 ..... 115 H5 🖸
Glenway NWD/KWIPK L33 ..... 74 B7
Glenwood Cl GTS/LS CH66 ..... 155 L7 🖸
Glenwood Dr PEN/TH CH61 ..... 126 A6
Glenwood Gdns GTS/LS CH66 ... 155 L7 🖸
Glenwood Rd GTS/LS CH66 ..... 155 L7
Glenwyllin Rd CSBY/WL L22 ..... 83 G3
Globe Rd BTL L20 ..... 6 E3
Globe St ANF/KKDL L4 ..... 97 G6
Glossop Wy WGNE/HIN WN2 ... 81 H1 🖸
Gloucester Av GOL/RIS/CU WA3... 92 D4
  WARR WA1 ..... 122 F6
Gloucester Cl GTS/LS CH66 ..... 163 H5 🖸
Gloucester Pl NPK/KEN L6 ..... 113 J2 🖸
Gloucester Rd BTL L20 ..... 7 K3
  CHLY/EC PR7 ..... 32 E8
  HUY L36 ..... 116 C2
  NPK/KEN L6 ..... 97 M8
  STHP PR8 ..... 2 D7
  WAL/NB CH45 ..... 95 G7
  WDN WA8 ..... 134 D2
  WGNW/BIL/O WN5 ..... 67 L7 🖸
Gloucester Rd North
  NPK/KEN L6 ..... 97 M7
Gloucester St STHEL WA9 ..... 102 F3
Glover Pl BTL L20 ..... 6 F2
Glover Rd GOL/RIS/CU WA3 ..... 106 E8
Glover's Brow KIRK L32 ..... 85 L1
Glover's La NTHTN L30 ..... 84 A1
Glover St ECCL WA10 ..... 8 E7
  LEIGH WN7 ..... 81 L5
  NEWLW WA12 ..... 104 E2 🖸
  RF/TRAN CH42 ..... 10 E9
Glyn Av PS/BROM CH62 ..... 144 A6
Glynne Gv CHLDW L16 ..... 115 J5
Glynne St BTL L20 ..... 83 M7
Glynn St WAV L15 ..... 114 B6
Glyn Rd WAL/EG WA44 ..... 95 K8
Goddard Rd RUNC WA7 ..... 150 A2
Godetia Cl WLT/FAZ L9 ..... 98 B1 🖸
Godfrey St WARRN/WOL WA2 ... 15 J2
Godscroft La FROD/HEL WA6 ... 160 A7
Godshill Cl WARRW/BUR WA5 ... 119 H1
Godstow RUNC WA7 ..... 151 G1
Golborne Dale Rd NEWLW WA12... 92 C8
Golborne Rd AIMK WN4 ..... 91 M1
  GOL/RIS/CU WA3 ..... 92 E5
  WARRN/WOL WA2 ..... 105 J6
Golborne St NEWLW WA12 ..... 105 G1
  WARR WA1 ..... 14 D5
Goldcliffe Cl WARRW/BUR WA5 ... 120 F3
Goldcrest Cl RUNC WA7 ..... 150 B8
  WD/CROXPK L12 ..... 99 H1 🖸
Goldcrest Ms HLWD L26 ..... 132 A4 🖸
Golden Gv ANF/KKDL L4 ..... 97 J4
Goldenways WGN WN1 ..... 68 E3 🖸
Goldfinch Cl HLWD L26 ..... 132 A4
Goldfinch Farm Rd
  SPK/HALE L24 ..... 146 E2
Goldfinch La
  GOL/RIS/CU WA3 ..... 123 G1 🖸
Goldie St ANF/KKDL L4 ..... 97 H6
Goldsmith Pl WGNS/IIMK WN3 ... 79 J1
Goldsmith Rd CL/PREN CH43 ... 127 H4 🖸
Goldsmith St BTL L20 ..... 6 D2
  NPK/KEN L6 ..... 113 K2 🖸
Goldsmith Wy
  CL/PREN CH43 ..... 127 H4 🖸
Goldsworth Fold
  RAIN/WH L35 ..... 117 K2 🖸
Golf Links Rd RF/TRAN CH42 ... 127 K4
Golf Rd FMBY L37 ..... 46 F3
Gondover Av WLT/FAZ L9 ..... 84 B7
Gonville Rd BTL L20 ..... 7 K7
Gooch Dr NEWLW WA12 ..... 104 F3
Goodacre Rd WLT/FAZ L9 ..... 84 D6
Good Shepherd Cl
  NG/CROX L11 ..... 98 D3 🖸
Goodwood Cl HUY L36 ..... 115 M4 🖸
Goodwood Gv GTS/LS CH66 ..... 162 F2 🖸
Goodwood St EV L5 ..... 96 F8
Gooseberry La RUNC WA7 ..... 150 F4 🖸

Goose Green Av CHLY/EC PR7 ..... 43 H4
Goostrey Cl BEB CH63 ..... 143 K4
Gordale Cl WARRW/BUR WA5 ... 120 B6
Gordon Av WDN WA4 ..... 91 G1
  CHTN/BK PR9 ..... 24 E4
  CSBY/WL L22 ..... 82 E3 🖸
  GR/UP/WCH CH49 ..... 126 A2
  MGHL L31 ..... 72 E2
  PS/BROM CH62 ..... 144 A2
  RNFD/HAY WA11 ..... 91 H6 🖸
  WARR WA1 ..... 122 D6
Gordon Ct WGNW/BIL/O WN5 ... 68 A5
Gordon Ct GR/UP/WCH CH49 ... 126 A2
Gordon Dr ALL/GAR L19 ..... 130 C6
  DV/KA/FCH L14 ..... 115 G2
Gordon La CHNE CH2 ..... 163 K8
Gordon Rd LITH L21 ..... 83 H7
  WAL/NB CH45 ..... 95 K6
Gordonstoun Crs
  WGNW/BIL/O WN5 ..... 67 K6
Gordon St BIRK CH41 ..... 10 F6
  CHLYE PR6 ..... 32 F5
  CHTN/BK PR9 ..... 3 J1
  WAV L15 ..... 5 K5
  WGNE/HIN WN2 ..... 67 G7
Gore Dr ORM L39 ..... 63 G2
Gores La FMBY L37 ..... 47 G8
  RNFD/HAY WA11 ..... 77 H7
  RNFD/HAY WA11 ..... 77 J8
Gores Rd NWD/KWIPK L33 ..... 86 D4
Gore St TOX L8 ..... 113 G7
  WGNW/BIL/O WN5 ..... 67 K7
Goring Cl CHLY/EC PR7 ..... 32 F6
Gorman St WGNNW/ST WN6 ..... 4 A3
Gorse Av WD/CROXPK L12 ..... 98 D4
Gorsebank Rd CALD/MH L18 ... 114 A8 🖸
Gorsebank St WAL/EG WA44 ... 111 L2 🖸
Gorseburn Rd CLB/OSW/ST L13 ... 98 A7
Gorse Covert Rd
  GOL/RIS/CU WA3 ..... 107 J8
Gorse Crs WAL/EG WA44 ..... 111 L3
Gorsedale Pk WAL/EG WA44 ... 111 M3 🖸
Gorsedale Rd CALD/MH L18 ... 130 C1
  WAL/EG WA44 ..... 111 L3
Gorsefield FMBY L37 ..... 47 J7
  RAIN/WH L35 ..... 101 M6 🖸
Gorsefield Av PS/BROM CH62 ... 143 M8 🖸
Gorsefield Cl PS/BROM CH62 ... 143 M8
Gorsefield Rd CSBY/BLUN L23 ... 71 J8
  RF/TRAN CH42 ..... 127 L2
Gorse Hey Ct WD/CROXPK L12 ... 98 C8
Gorsehill Rd HES CH60 ..... 141 J4
  WAL/NB CH45 ..... 95 J6
Gorse La WKBY CH48 ..... 125 G4
Gorse Rd HOY CH47 ..... 108 F5
Gorses Dr WGNE/HIN WN2 ..... 57 L7 🖸
Gorse Wy FMBY L37 ..... 58 E1
Gorsewood Gv WLTN L25 ..... 115 K8 🖸
Gorsewood Rd RUNC WA7 ..... 150 F7
  WLTN L25 ..... 115 K8
Gorsey Brow WGNW/BIL/O WN5 ... 77 M8
Gorsey Brow Cl
  WGNW/BIL/O WN5 ..... 77 M8
Gorsey Cop Wy WLTN L25 ..... 115 J7
Gorsey Cft PR/KW L34 ..... 101 H6
Gorsey La BRSC L40 ..... 40 E3
  CHTN/BK PR9 ..... 23 L6
  HTWN L38 ..... 70 F2
  LITH L21 ..... 83 L4 🖸
  NTHTN L30 ..... 83 L2
  ORM L39 ..... 48 C6
  STHEL WA9 ..... 119 H1
  WAL/EG WA44 ..... 111 K3
  WARRN/WOL WA2 ..... 15 J1
  WDN WA8 ..... 17 L4
Gorsey Pl SKEL WN8 ..... 65 K6
Gorseyville Crs BEB CH63 ..... 128 A3 🖸
Gorseyville Rd BEB CH63 ..... 128 A8
Gorseywell La RUNC WA7 ..... 151 H7
Gorst La CHTN/BK PR9 ..... 38 B7
Gorstons La NSTN CH64 ..... 153 J7
Gorst St ANF/KKDL L4 ..... 97 H6
Gorsuch La BRSC L40 ..... 49 M1
Gorton Rd CLB/OSW/ST L13 ... 114 D3
Gort Rd HUY L36 ..... 116 A2
Goschen St BIRK CH41 ..... 111 H5 🖸
  CLB/OSW/ST L13 ..... 114 B2
  EV L5 ..... 97 H6 🖸
Gosford St TOX L8 ..... 129 H1
Gosforth Rd CHTN/BK PR9 ..... 25 H5
Gosling Rd GOL/RIS/CU WA3 ... 106 D6
Gosport Cl WARRN/WOL WA2 ... 122 A4
Goswell St WAV L15 ..... 114 A6
Gotham Rd BEB CH63 ..... 143 J3
Gothic St RF/TRAN CH42 ..... 128 B3
Gough Av WARRN/WOL WA2 ... 121 K3
Gough Rd CLB/OSW/ST L13 ..... 98 A6
Goulden St WARRW/BUR WA5 ... 121 K2
Goulders Ct RUNC WA7 ..... 150 D8 🖸
Goulding St CL/PREN CH43 ..... 127 F7
Gourley Rd CLB/OSW/ST L13 ... 114 D4
Gourley's La WKBY CH48 ..... 124 F4
Government Rd HOY CH47 ..... 108 D6
Govett Rd RAIN/WH L35 ..... 101 L6
Gower Gdns BRSC L40 ..... 52 B2
Gower St BTL L20 ..... 83 J8
  STHEL WA9 ..... 102 F4
  VAUX/LVPD L3 ..... 112 E5
  WGNW/BIL/O WN5 ..... 68 B7
Gowrie Gv LITH L21 ..... 83 J6
Goyt Hey Av WGNW/BIL/O WN5 ... 90 A1
Graburn Rd FMBY L37 ..... 59 H1
Grace Av AIN/FAZ L10 ..... 85 J6
  WARRN/WOL WA2 ..... 121 K5
Grace Rd EP CH65 ..... 20 C2
  WLT/FAZ L9 ..... 84 C7
Grace St LEIGH WN7 ..... 81 L8 🖸
  TOX L8 ..... 129 H1
Gradwell St CLVPS L1 ..... 13 G8
Grafton Ct CHLY/EC PR7 ..... 32 D8 🖸
Grafton Dr GR/UP/WCH CH49 ... 126 C1
  STHP PR8 ..... 34 C8
Grafton Gv TOX L8 ..... 129 G1
Grafton Rd EP CH65 ..... 20 C1
  WAL/NB CH45 ..... 95 K6 🖸
Grafton St CHLY/EC PR7 ..... 32 D8 🖸
  CL/PREN CH43 ..... 10 D7
  ECCL WA10 ..... 8 B5

NEWLW WA12 ..... 104 D2 🖸
  TOX L8 ..... 112 F7
  TOX L8 ..... 113 G7 🖸
  WARRW/BUR WA5 ..... 121 G7
Grafton Wk WKBY CH48 ..... 124 E3
Graham Av GTS/LS CH66 ..... 155 M8 🖸
  WGNNW/ST WN6 ..... 54 E3
Graham Cl WDN WA8 ..... 133 L4 🖸
Graham Dr HLWD L26 ..... 132 C5 🖸
Graham Rd WDN WA8 ..... 133 L5
  WKBY CH48 ..... 124 C2
Graham's Rd HUY L36 ..... 116 B3
Graham St STHEL WA9 ..... 9 L5
  WGNE/HIN WN2 ..... 80 C4
Grainger Av BTL L20 ..... 84 A7
  CL/PREN CH43 ..... 127 H3
  WKBY CH48 ..... 124 D1
Graley Cl HLWD L26 ..... 132 B7
Grammar School La
  WKBY CH48 ..... 124 F4
Grammar School Rd
  WARRS WA4 ..... 138 B2
Grampian Av MOR/LEA CH46 ... 110 B5 🖸
Grampian Rd EHL/KEN L7 ..... 114 A3
Grampian Wy GOL/RIS/CU WA3 ... 92 F4
  MOR/LEA CH46 ..... 110 A5
  NSTN CH64 ..... 153 G8 🖸
  PS/BROM CH62 ..... 155 G1
Granams Cft NTHTN L30 ..... 83 M1
Granard Rd WAV L15 ..... 114 C7
Granary Wy GTS/LS CH66 ..... 112 F7 🖸
Granborne Cha KKBY L32 ..... 85 K2
Granby Cl CHTN/BK PR9 ..... 25 H2
Granby Crs BEB CH63 ..... 143 J5
Granby Rd WARRS WA4 ..... 137 K5
Granby St TOX L8 ..... 113 J6
Grandison Rd ANF/KKDL L4 ..... 97 L4
Grange Av CHTN/BK PR9 ..... 25 G5
  WAL/NB CH45 ..... 95 K7
  WARRS WA4 ..... 15 M8
  WD/CROXPK L12 ..... 99 G8
  WGNS/IIMK WN3 ..... 4 C9
  WGNW/BIL/O WN5 ..... 67 K6
  WLTN L25 ..... 131 H6
Grange Av North
  DV/KA/FCH L14 ..... 99 H8
  WD/CROXPK L12 ..... 99 H8
Grange Cl GOL/RIS/CU WA3 ..... 92 F7
Grange Crs GTS/LS CH66 ..... 155 J4
Grange Cross Cl WKBY CH48 ... 125 G4
Grange Cross Hey WKBY CH48 ... 125 G4
Grange Cross La WKBY CH48 ... 125 G4
Grange Dr BEB CH63 ..... 142 C6
  CHLYE PR6 ..... 31 L1
  ECCL WA10 ..... 101 K4
  HES CH60 ..... 141 H4
  WARRW/BUR WA5 ..... 136 C1
  WDN WA8 ..... 133 M4
Grange Farm Crs WKBY CH48... 125 G4
Grangehurst Ct WLTN L25 ..... 131 K1 🖸
Grange La FMBY L37 ..... 47 G8
  WLTN L25 ..... 115 J8
Grangemeadow Rd WLTN L25 ... 115 J8
Grangemoor RUNC WA7 ..... 149 M6
Grange Mt CL/PREN CH43 ..... 10 E7
  HES CH60 ..... 141 H4
  WKBY CH48 ..... 124 F3
Grange Old Rd WKBY CH48 ..... 124 E3
Grange Pk MGHL L31 ..... 73 G6
Grange Park Av RUNC WA7 ..... 19 L4
Grange Park Rd ECCL WA10 ... 101 L4
  RUNC WA7 ..... 19 L4
Grange Pl CL/PREN CH43 ..... 10 E6
Grange Rd AIMK WN4 ..... 79 H7
  BIRK CH41 ..... 11 J6 🖸
  CHTN/BK PR9 ..... 25 G6
  EP CH65 ..... 20 C5
  HES CH60 ..... 141 H3
  HTWN L38 ..... 59 G7
  NTHTN L30 ..... 84 D3
  RNFD/HAY WA11 ..... 90 F8
  RUNC WA7 ..... 19 L4
  WGNE/HIN WN2 ..... 81 G4
  WKBY CH48 ..... 124 D3
Grange Rd West CL/PREN CH43... 10 E6
Grangeside WLTN L25 ..... 115 J8
Grange St NPK/KEN L6 ..... 97 M8
  WGNE/HIN WN2 ..... 80 F1
Grange Ter WAV L15 ..... 114 B6
The Grange WAL/EG WA44 ..... 111 L1 🖸
Grange V RF/TRAN CH42 ..... 128 C4
Grange Va RNFD/HAY WA11 ..... 90 F7
Grange Vw CL/PREN CH43 ..... 10 E7
Grangeway RUNC WA7 ..... 19 J4
Grange Wy WLTN L25 ..... 115 J8
Grange Weint WLTN L25 ..... 131 J1
Grangewood CHLDW L16 ..... 115 H4
Granston Cl
  WARRW/BUR WA5 ..... 121 G3 🖸
Grant Av WAV L15 ..... 114 D7 🖸
Grant Cl DV/KA/FCH L14 ..... 115 J2
  ECCL WA10 ..... 8 D4
  WARRW/BUR WA5 ..... 120 F4
Grantham Av WARR WA1 ..... 15 M1
  WARRS WA4 ..... 137 K5
Grantham Cl PEN/TH CH61 ..... 141 G1 🖸
  STHP PR8 ..... 35 J4
Grantham Crs RNFD/HAY WA11 ... 9 M2
Grantham Gv WGNE/HIN WN2 ... 69 H3 🖸
Grantham Rd NWD/KWIPK L33 ... 74 A8
  STHP PR8 ..... 35 J4
Grantham St NPK/KEN L6 ..... 113 K2
Grantham Wy NTHTN L30 ..... 84 C1
Grantley Rd WAV L15 ..... 114 D7 🖸
Grantley St AIMK WN4 ..... 79 J8
Granton Cl FMBY L37 ..... 59 G2
Granton Rd EV L5 ..... 97 H7
Grant Rd DV/KA/FCH L14 ..... 115 H2 🖸
  MOR/LEA CH46 ..... 110 D1
  WARRW/BUR WA5 ..... 120 D7 🖸
  WGNS/IIMK WN3 ..... 79 J2
Grantwood AIMK WN4 ..... 79 J8 🖸
Granville Av MGHL L31 ..... 72 C3
Granville Cl ORM L39 ..... 62 D4
  WAL/NB CH45 ..... 95 G7 🖸
Granville Dr GTS/LS CH66 ..... 155 K6
Granville Pk ORM L39 ..... 62 D5

Granville Pk West ORM L39 62 D5
Granville Rd ALL/GAR L19 130 E7 1
CHLYE PR6 33 G4
STHP PR8 34 F2
WAV L15 113 M6
Granville St CHLYE PR6 44 C6
RUNC WA7 19 H2
STHEL WA9 102 F2
WARR WA1 15 J3
Grape La LEY/BBR PR5 29 L4
Grappenhall La WARRS WA4 138 F7
Grappenhall Rd EP CH65 163 H2
WARRS WA4 137 M4
Grappenhall Wy
CL/PREN CH43 110 E6 4
Grasmere Av CL/PREN CH43 110 E8
PR/KW L34 101 H7
RNFD/HAY WA11 89 K6
SKEL WN8 66 D5
WARRN/WOL WA2 121 M2
WGNE/HIN WN2 69 J6
WGNE/HIN WN2 81 G1
WGNW/BIL/O WN5 67 H5 1
Grasmere Cl CHLY/EC PR7 31 M4
NWD/KWIPK L33 85 M1
RNFD/HAY WA11 89 K6 2
Grasmere Ct RNFD/HAY WA11 89 K6 3
Grasmere Dr AIMK WN4 79 K8
LITH L21 84 A4
RUNC WA7 149 M8
WAL/NB CH45 95 J8
Grasmere Fold
RNFD/HAY WA11 89 K6 4
Grasmere Gdns CSBY/BLUN L23 83 H2
Grasmere Rd EP CH65 163 L3
FMBY L37 58 F2
FROD/HEL WA6 160 E5
MGHL L31 72 F3
NSTN CH64 153 G7
WGNW/BIL/O WN5 67 L6
Grasmere St EV L5 97 J7
Grasmere Ter CHLY/EC PR7 32 D8
WGNE/HIN WN2 80 D5 2
Grasscroft Rd WGNE/HIN WN2 81 J1
Grassendale La ALL/GAR L19 130 C6
Grassendale Prom
ALL/GAR L19 130 B7
Grassendale Rd ALL/GAR L19 130 C6
Grassington Crs WLTN L25 131 M3
Grassmoor Cl
PS/BROM CH62 144 A5 1
Grass Wood Rd
GR/UP/WCH CH49 126 D3
Grasville Rd RF/TRAN CH42 128 A2
Gratrix Rd PS/BROM CH62 143 M5
Gratton Pl SKEL WN8 65 J5
Gravel La CHTN/BK PR9 23 H8
CHTN/BK PR9 26 C1
The Gravel KIRK/FR/WA PR4 27 H3
Grave-yard La ORM L39 63 J6
Gray Av RNFD/HAY WA11 90 F7
Gray Cl WGNE/HIN WN2 69 J3
Gray Gv HUY L36 116 B5
Graylag Cl RUNC WA7 150 B8 2
Graylands Pl ANF/KKDL L4 97 L4 2
Graylands Rd ANF/KKDL L4 97 L4
PS/BROM CH62 128 E7
Grayling Dr WD/CROXPK L12 98 F2
Grays Av RAIN/WH L35 101 H7
Grayson's Cl WGN WN1 4 F1
Graysons Rd RNFD/HAY WA11 76 B5
Grayson St CLVPS L1 112 E5 3
Grayston Av STHEL WA9 102 F7
Gray St BTL L20 83 J8
Greasby Dr GTS/LS CH66 163 G1
Greasby Rd GR/UP/WCH CH49 125 L2
WAL/EG CH44 111 J1
Great Acre WGN WN1 5 H1
Great Ashfield WDN WA8 133 M2
Great Charlotte St CLVPS L1 13 H7 2
CLVPS L1 13 H7 2
Great Crosshall St VAUX/LVPD L3 12 F5
Great Delph RNFD/HAY WA11 90 F6
Great George Pl CLVPS L1 113 G6 3
Great George's Rd CSBY/WL L22 82 F5
Great George St CLVPS L1 113 G5 8
WGNS/IIMK WN3 4 C4
Great Hanging Br LEY/BBR PR5 28 F5
Great Hey NTHTN L30 71 M8
Great Homer St EV L5 97 G8
Great Howard St EV L5 96 D8
VAUX/LVPD L3 12 D4
Great Meadow CHLY/EC PR7 32 C3
Great Mersey St EV L5 96 F7
Great Nelson St VAUX/LVPD L3 13 H2
Great Newton St VAUX/LVPD L3 13 L6
Great Orford St VAUX/LVPD L3 13 L8
Great Richmond St
VAUX/LVPD L3 13 J3
Great Riding RUNC WA7 150 E6
Greaves Cl WGNNW/ST WN6 55 H5
Greaves Hall Av CHTN/BK PR9 23 J8
Greaves St TOX L8 129 H1 6
Grebe Av ECCL WA10 101 J5
Grebe Cl WGNS/IIMK WN3 78 D1
Grecian St LITH L21 83 H5
Grecian Ter EV L5 97 H7 2
Gredington St TOX L8 129 J1 10
Greeba Av WARRS WA4 137 K2
Greek St RUNC WA7 18 F2
VAUX/LVPD L3 13 K6
Greenacre BRSC L40 64 A1
WGN WN1 5 H1
Greenacre Cl WLTN L25 131 L5
Greenacre Dr BEB CH63 143 K6
Greenacre Rd WLTN L25 131 L5
Greenacres FROD/HEL WA6 160 E7
Greenacres Cl CL/PREN CH43 110 E5
GOL/RIS/CU WA3 93 K5 3
Greenall Av
WARRW/BUR WA5 135 M1 1
Greenall's Av WARRS WA4 137 L4
Greenall St AIMK WN4 79 K8 1
ECCL WA10 8 B3
Green Bank BEB CH63 142 C3
Greenbank CSBY/WL L22 83 G5
WGNE/HIN WN2 80 D6
WGNE/HIN WN2 81 J2 2
Greenbank Av GTS/LS CH66 155 L6
MGHL L31 72 E2
WAL/NB CH45 95 K6 4
WGNW/BIL/O WN5 77 M2
Greenbank Ct AIG/SPK L17 114 A8
Greenbank Crs ECCL WA10 8 E6
Greenbank Dr AIG/SPK L17 114 A8
AIN/FAZ L10 85 K6
PEN/TH CH61 141 H2
STHP PR8 35 G3
Greenbank Gdns WARRS WA4 138 B3
Greenbank La AIG/SPK L17 130 A1
Greenbank Rd CALD/MH L18 114 B8
RF/TRAN CH42 127 L2
WARRS WA4 138 B3
WKBY CH48 124 D1
Greenbank St WARRS WA4 137 L3 1
Greenbarn Wy HOR/BR BL6 57 M3 4
Green Bridge Cl RUNC WA7 150 C4 2
Greenbridge Rd RUNC WA7 150 D3
Greenburn Av
RNFD/HAY WA11 89 L4 3
Green Coppice RUNC WA7 150 E5
Green Ct GOL/RIS/CU WA3 93 K4
Green Cft CSBY/BLUN L23 71 K8 4
Greencroft Rd WAL/EG CH44 111 L2
Greendale Rd PS/BROM CH62 128 C7
WLTN L25 131 H1
Green End La STHEL WA9 102 E5 3
Green End Pk
WD/CROXPK L12 98 C6 4
Greene's Rd RAIN/WH L35 116 F3
Greenfield Av SKEL WN8 53 K3
WGNE/HIN WN2 5 L6
Greenfield Dr HUY L36 116 B5
Greenfield Gdns CHNE CH2 165 K2
Greenfield Gv HUY L36 116 B5 3
Greenfield La FROD/HEL WA6 160 D4
HES CH60 140 E3
LITH L21 83 J4
Greenfield Rd CHLYE PR6 33 G5 5
CHLYE PR6 44 C5 4
CLB/OSW/ST L13 114 C2
ECCL WA10 8 B1
GTS/LS CH66 155 K6
STHP PR8 36 E4
Greenfields WGNNW/ST WN6 68 C1
Greenfields Av PS/BROM CH62 143 L6
WARRS WA4 137 M5
Greenfields Cl NEWLW WA12 104 E1 3
NSTN CH64 153 H8 1
WARR WA1 122 E6 2
Greenfields Crs AIMK WN4 91 K1 3
PS/BROM CH62 143 L6
Greenfields Cft NSTN CH64 153 G8
Greenfield Vw
WGNW/BIL/O WN5 89 M1
Greenfield Wy CALD/MH L18 130 E4 1
Greenfinch Cl HLWD L26 132 A4 5
WD/CROXPK L12 99 H2 1
Greenford Cl WGNW/BIL/O WN5 66 F7
Greenford Rd STHP PR8 47 L1
Greengables Cl TOX L8 113 J8
Green Gates HUY L36 100 A7
Greengates Crs NSTN CH64 153 G8
Greenhalgh La CHLYE PR6 44 D5
Greenham Av NWD/KWIPK L33 74 B7
Greenhaven Cl AIN/FAZ L10 85 J5
Green Hayes Av WGN WN1 68 E2
Greenheath Wy
MOR/LEA CH46 110 B2 4
Greenhey WGNW/BIL/O WN5 67 J6
Green Hey Dr NTHTN L30 83 L3
Greenhey Pl SKEL WN8 65 H5
Green Heys Dr MGHL L31 73 H3
Greenheys Rd PEN/TH CH61 125 L8
TOX L8 113 K7
WAL/EG CH44 111 K1
Greenhill Av CALD/MH L18 114 E8
Greenhill Cl CALD/MH L18 130 D3
Greenhill Crs WGNW/BIL/O WN5 78 B8
Greenhill Pl HUY L36 116 A4
Greenhill Rd ALL/GAR L19 130 E5
CALD/MH L18 130 D1
WGNW/BIL/O WN5 78 A8
Greenholme Cl NG/CROX L11 98 C2 2
Greenhouse Farm Rd
RUNC WA7 150 D7
Greenhow Av WKBY CH48 124 D2
Greenings La CHTN/BK PR9 37 L2
Green Jones Brow
WARRW/BUR WA5 104 B7
Greenlake Rd CALD/MH L18 130 D3
Greenland Av WGNNW/ST WN6 56 A5
Greenland La CHLYE PR6 44 F8
Greenlands HUY L36 116 A4 3
Greenland St CLVPS L1 113 G6 4
Green La BEB CH63 128 B8
BIRK CH41 11 K9
BRSC L40 40 C6
BRSC L40 52 B1
BRSC L40 53 H7
CALD/MH L18 114 E8
CALD/MH L18 130 D1
CHLY/EC PR7 43 J6
CHTN/BK PR9 26 E1
CLB/OSW/ST L13 114 B1
CSBY/BLUN L23 71 K7
CSBY/WL L22 82 E3
ECCL WA10 88 A7
EP CH65 20 C7
FMBY L37 47 H7
GOL/RIS/CU WA3 93 J3
GTS/LS CH66 162 F1
HOR/BR BL6 45 K8
KIRK/FR/WA PR4 27 L1
LITH L21 83 J6
LITH L21 83 K3
MGHL L31 72 E4 2
ORM L39 51 G7
RNFD/HAY WA11 76 C8
VAUX/LVPD L3 13 K8 1
WAL/NB CH45 94 D8
WARR WA1 122 C5
WARRN/WOL WA2 105 J6
WARRS WA4 138 C8
WARRW/BUR WA5 104 A6
WDN WA8 134 A4
WGNNW/ST WN6 56 A5
WGNW/BIL/O WN5 77 M2
Green Lane Av ORM L39 51 G7 3
Green Lane Cl
WARRN/WOL WA2 105 J6
Green La North CHLDW L16 114 E7
Green Lawn HUY L36 116 C1
RF/TRAN CH42 128 B4
Green Lawn Gv
RF/TRAN CH42 128 B4 2
Green Lawns Dr GTS/LS CH66 163 H5 3
Green Leach Av
RNFD/HAY WA11 89 K6
Green Leach Ct
RNFD/HAY WA11 89 K6 5
Green Leach La RNFD/HAY WA11 89 K6
Greenlea Cl BEB CH63 128 B7
EP CH65 163 K3
WGNW/BIL/O WN5 66 F8
Greenleaf St TOX L8 113 L6
Greenleas Rd WAL/NB CH45 94 F7
Greenleigh Rd CALD/MH L18 130 D3
Green Link MGHL L31 72 D3
Greenloon's Dr FMBY L37 58 E3 2
Greenloon's Wk FMBY L37 58 E3
Green Mt GR/UP/WCH CH49 110 C8
Green Oaks Pth WDN WA8 17 H3
Green Oaks Wy WDN WA8 17 G3
Greenock St VAUX/LVPD L3 12 C4
Greenodd Av WD/CROXPK L12 98 E4
Greenore Dr SPK/HALE L24 147 M3 2
Greenough Av RAIN/WH L35 101 L8 1
Greenough St WGN WN1 5 H3
WLTN L25 131 H3 3
Green Pk NTHTN L30 72 B8
Green Park Dr MGHL L31 72 D4
Greenrigg Cl WGNNW/ST WN6 56 B6
Green Rd PR/KW L34 100 E7 1
Greensbridge La HLWD L26 132 D4
Greenshank Cl NEWLW WA12 104 E1 4
Greenside CHLY/EC PR7 31 L2
NPK/KEN L6 13 M4
Greenside Av AIN/FAZ L10 84 F3
FROD/HEL WA6 160 F6
WAV L15 114 C6 3
Greenside Cl NWD/KWIPK L33 74 C7 3
Green's La MGHL L31 61 L4
Greenslate Ct
WGNW/BIL/O WN5 77 M2
Greenslate Rd
WGNW/BIL/O WN5 78 A2
Green Strawberry EP CH65 163 J5
Green St CHLY/EC PR7 32 C8 3
CHLYE PR6 44 D5
EV L5 12 F1
WARRW/BUR WA5 14 A6
WARRW/BUR WA5 121 G8 2
WGNE/HIN WN2 80 D3 4
WGNS/IIMK WN3 4 E7
Greensward Cl
WGNNW/ST WN6 55 K4 1
The Green BEB CH63 153 L1
CHLY/EC PR7 30 E7
CHLYE PR6 44 B3
CLB/OSW/ST L13 114 E3
EP CH65 163 K3
NSTN CH64 152 F5
NSTN CH64 153 H7
PR/KW L34 101 G6
PS/BROM CH62 129 G8
RUNC WA7 150 B4 2
SKEL WN8 53 K3
WGNW/BIL/O WN5 67 K7
WKBY CH48 124 F6
Greenvale WGNNW/ST WN6 67 H1
Greenville Cl BEB CH63 128 B8
Greenville Dr MGHL L31 72 E4
Greenville Rd BEB CH63 128 B8
NSTN CH64 153 H4 1
Green Wk STHP PR8 34 F8 1
Green Wy HUY L36 115 K1
Greenway AIMK WN4 91 J1
CHLY/EC PR7 30 D6 1
CSBY/BLUN L23 71 J8
GR/UP/WCH CH49 126 A1
PEN/TH CH61 141 G1
PS/BROM CH62 143 M2 2
WARR WA1 122 B6
WARRS WA4 137 M6
WARRW/BUR WA5 120 A6 3
Greenway Av SKEL WN8 65 K6
Greenway Cl FROD/HEL WA6 166 D2 1
Green Way Cl HUY L36 115 K1
Greenway Cl SKEL WN8 65 G3 1
Greenway Rd RF/TRAN CH42 127 M2
RUNC WA7 18 F6
SPK/HALE L24 147 J2
WDN WA8 134 D3
Greenways WGNNW/ST WN6 56 C7
WGNW/BIL/O WN5 77 M2
The Greenway
WD/CROXPK L12 115 G1
Greenwell Rd RNFD/HAY WA11 90 E7
Greenwich Ct WLT/FAZ L9 84 D5
Greenwich Rd WLT/FAZ L9 84 D5
Greenwood Av
WGNW/BIL/O WN5 68 A6
Greenwood Cl
GOL/RIS/CU WA3 107 H3
ORM L39 62 E4
PR/KW L34 101 G7
Greenwood Ct STHEL WA9 118 E1
Greenwood Crs
WARRN/WOL WA2 121 M3 3
Greenwood Dr NEWLW WA12 104 F3
Greenwood La WAL/EG CH44 95 L8
Greenwood Rd CALD/MH L18 130 D4
GR/UP/WCH CH49 126 C2
WGNNW/ST WN6 56 A3
Greetby Hl ORM L39 51 J8
Greetham St CLVPS L1 112 F5 8
Gregory Cl CHLDW L16 115 G5 2
WARRW/BUR WA5 120 E6
Gregory La ORM L39 49 K2
Gregory St WGNE/HIN WN2 69 L7 3
Gregory Wy CHLDW L16 115 G5
Gregson Ct WAL/NB CH45 95 L5
Gregson Rd DV/KA/FCH L14 114 E2
RAIN/WH L35 100 F8
WDN WA8 17 H2
Gregson's Av FMBY L37 47 G8
Gregson St NPK/KEN L6 13 M3
Grenfel Cl WGNS/IIMK WN3 4 A9
Grenfell Cl NSTN CH64 152 E4
Grenfell Pk NSTN CH64 152 E4
Grenfell Rd CLB/OSW/ST L13 98 A5
Grenfell St WDN WA8 16 E4
The Grennan WAL/NB CH45 95 K5 4
Grenville Crs BEB CH63 143 L6
Grenville Dr PEN/TH CH61 141 G2
Grenville Rd RF/TRAN CH42 128 B2
Grenville St South CLVPS L1 112 F5
Grenville Wy RF/TRAN CH42 128 B2 7
Gresford Av AIG/SPK L17 113 M7
CL/PREN CH43 127 J3
WKBY CH48 124 E2
Gresford Cl RAIN/WH L35 117 H2 3
WARRW/BUR WA5 120 F3 2
Gresham St EHL/KEN L7 113 M3
Gresley Cl EHL/KEN L7 113 L4 7
WGN WN1 5 J4
Gressingham Rd CALD/MH L18 130 E2
Gretton Rd DV/KA/FCH L14 99 K8
Greyfriars AIMK WN4 91 H1
Greyfriars Rd STHP PR8 34 D7
Grey Heights Vw CHLYE PR6 33 G5
Greyhound Farm Rd
SPK/HALE L24 146 E2
Greymist Av WARR WA1 122 E6
Grey Rd AIMK WN4 91 J1
WLT/FAZ L9 97 H1
Grey Rock Wk NPK/KEN L6 113 K1
Greystoke Cl GR/UP/WCH CH49 126 B1
Greystokes ORM L39 62 F3
Greystone Av WGNE/HIN WN2 57 L8
Greystone Crs
DV/KA/FCH L14 115 G2 1
Greystone Pl AIN/FAZ L10 85 H6 3
Greystone Rd AIN/FAZ L10 85 G6
DV/KA/FCH L14 115 G3
WARRW/BUR WA5 136 B1
Greystones GTS/LS CH66 162 F1
Grey St TOX L8 113 H6 7
TOX L8 113 H7 5
WARR WA1 15 G4
Gribble Rd AIN/FAZ L10 85 J6
Grice St WARRS WA4 137 L4 2
Grierson St TOX L8 113 K6
Grieve Rd AIN/FAZ L10 85 J6
Griffin Av MOR/LEA CH46 110 A5
Griffin Cl ECCL WA10 101 H1
NG/CROX L11 98 E1
WARRW/BUR WA5 104 A7 1
Griffin Ms WDN WA8 134 D2 3
Griffin St STHEL WA9 103 G6 1
Griffith Av GOL/RIS/CU WA3 107 G8
Griffiths Cl GR/UP/WCH CH49 125 L2
Griffiths Dr CHTN/BK PR9 25 H5
Griffith's Rd HUY L36 116 A3 2
Griffiths St CLVPS L1 113 G5 9
WARRS WA4 15 M8
WARRS WA4 138 B1
Grimeford La CHLYE PR6 44 F7
HOR/BR BL6 44 E8
Grime St CHLY/EC PR7 32 F7
Grimley Av BTL L20 6 C2
Grimrod Pl SKEL WN8 65 J6
Grimshaw Green La SKEL WN8 40 E8
Grimshaw La ORM L39 51 G7
Grimshaw Rd SKEL WN8 65 M5
Grimshaw St BTL L20 6 E6
GOL/RIS/CU WA3 92 C4
STHEL WA9 102 E7
Grindley Gdns EP CH65 163 L3 1
Grinfield St EHL/KEN L7 113 J4
Grinshill Cl TOX L8 113 J7
Grinstead Cl STHP PR8 35 H4
Grinton Crs HUY L36 115 M3
Grisedale Av
WARRN/WOL WA2 121 K2 1
Grisedale Cl FMBY L37 59 G2
RUNC WA7 150 A8
Grisedale Pl CHLY/EC PR7 32 D8
Grisedale Rd PS/BROM CH62 144 A5
Grizedale WDN WA8 133 K3
Grizedale Av RNFD/HAY WA11 89 K5
Grizedale Dr WGNE/HIN WN2 69 J6
Grizedale Rd EV L5 97 H7
Groarke Dr WARRW/BUR WA5 119 M8
Groes Rd ALL/GAR L19 130 D6
Grogan Sq BTL L20 83 M7
Gronow Pl BTL L20 84 A7 2
Grosmont Rd KKBY L32 86 B5
Grosvenor Av CSBY/BLUN L23 83 G3
GOL/RIS/CU WA3 92 F5 2
WARR WA1 15 M1
WKBY CH48 124 D3
Grosvenor Cl STHP PR8 35 G2
WARRW/BUR WA5 120 E8 4
Grosvenor Dr WAL/NB CH45 95 K5
Grosvenor Gdns NEWLW WA12 104 D3
STHP PR8 35 H2 1
Grosvenor Pl CL/PREN CH43 10 A7
STHP PR8 35 H2
Grosvenor Rd ALL/GAR L19 130 C7
ANF/KKDL L4 97 H3 4
CHLY/EC PR7 32 C7
CL/PREN CH43 10 A6
ECCL WA10 101 L3
HOY CH47 108 D7
LEIGH WN7 81 M7 2
MGHL L31 72 E7
PR/KW L34 100 F7
RNFD/HAY WA11 90 D7
STHP PR8 35 G1
WAL/NB CH45 95 K5
WAV L15 113 M6
WDN WA8 134 D1
Grosvenor St RUNC WA7 19 K2
VAUX/LVPD L3 13 H3
WAL/EG CH44 95 K8
WGNE/HIN WN2 69 M8 15
WGNW/BIL/O WN5 68 B7 5
Grounds St WARRN/WOL WA2 14 F2
Grove Av CHLYE PR6 44 C6
HES CH60 141 H4
LYMM WA13 139 L2
Grove Crs CHLYE PR6 44 C6
Grovedale Rd CALD/MH L18 114 B8 7
Grovehurst Av DV/KA/FCH L14 115 H1
Groveland Av HOY CH47 108 D6 3
WAL/NB CH45 94 F7 1
Groveland Rd WAL/NB CH45 94 F7
Grove La WGNNW/ST WN6 56 B5
Grove Md MGHL L31 73 H4
Grovenor Cl NTHTN L30 84 B2 1
Grove Pk CHTN/BK PR9 25 H4
ORM L39 51 H6 2
TOX L8 113 L7
Grove Park Av WD/CROXPK L12 98 D5
Grove Pl ANF/KKDL L4 97 G6
HOY CH47 108 D6
WGNNW/ST WN6 56 B5
Grove Rd CH/BCN CH1 163 G8
HOY CH47 108 D6
NPK/KEN L6 113 M2
RF/TRAN CH42 128 B3
SKEL WN8 66 D5
WAL/NB CH45 95 G7
Grove Side EHL/KEN L7 113 J5
Groveside WKBY CH48 124 C3
Grove Sq PS/BROM CH62 128 C6
The Groves EP CH65 163 J5
KKBY L32 86 A6 1
Grove St AIMK WN4 91 J1
BTL L20 6 C2
PS/BROM CH62 128 D6
RUNC WA7 18 F2
STHP PR8 2 F9
TOX L8 113 J5
WARRS WA4 15 H8
WAV L15 114 B5
Grove Ter HOY CH47 108 D6 4
STHP PR8 2 F8
The Grove BEB CH63 128 C8
CHLYE PR6 32 E3
CL/PREN CH43 127 K2
CLB/OSW/ST L13 98 B8 2
ECCL WA10 88 E8
GOL/RIS/CU WA3 92 F4
ORM L39 62 E6
STBRV L28 99 L7 1
WAL/EG CH44 111 L2
WARRW/BUR WA5 136 B1
WGNE/HIN WN2 5 K6
WGNNW/ST WN6 54 E3
Grove Wy EHL/KEN L7 113 J5 4
Grovewood STHP PR8 2 B8
Grovewood Dr WGNNW/ST WN6 55 G6
Grovewood Gdns RAIN/WH L35 117 G2
Grundy Cl STHP PR8 25 G8
WDN WA8 134 B2 4
Grundy's La CHLY/EC PR7 43 L4
Grundy St EV L5 96 D7
GOL/RIS/CU WA3 92 C6
Guardian St WARRW/BUR WA5 14 B4
Guelph St EHL/KEN L7 113 J3
Guernsey Cl WARRS WA4 137 M5
Guernsey Dr EP CH65 163 L4
Guernsey Rd CLB/OSW/ST L13 114 B1
WDN WA8 135 G2
Guest St WDN WA8 16 C6 1
Guffitts Cl HOY CH47 109 G4
Guffitt's Rake HOY CH47 109 G4
Guildford Av CHLYE PR6 33 H1
Guildford Cl
WARRN/WOL WA2 122 C4 2
Guildford Crs WGNNW/ST WN6 68 B2
Guildford Rd STHP PR8 35 J5
Guildford St WAL/EG CH44 111 M1
Guildhall Rd WLT/FAZ L9 84 C7
Guild Hey PR/KW L34 99 M1
Guillemot Wy HLWD L26 132 A4
Guilsted Rd NG/CROX L11 98 C3
Guinea Hall La CHTN/BK PR9 23 J8
Guion Rd LITH L21 83 K6
Guion St NPK/KEN L6 113 K1 3
Gulls Wy HES CH60 140 F5
Gunn Gv NSTN CH64 153 H5
Gunning Av ECCL WA10 88 D8
Gunning Cl ECCL WA10 88 D8
Gurnall St ANF/KKDL L4 97 H6 6
Gutticar Rd WDN WA8 133 K5
Gwendoline Cl PEN/TH CH61 126 C8
Gwendoline St TOX L8 113 H7
Gwenfron Rd NPK/KEN L6 113 K2 7
Gwent Cl NPK/KEN L6 97 K8
Gwent St TOX L8 113 J7
Gwladys St ANF/KKDL L4 97 H4
Gwydir St TOX L8 113 J8
Gwydrin Rd CALD/MH L18 114 E8


## H


Hackett Av BTL L20 83 M7
Hackins Hey CLVP L2 12 E6 4
Hackthorpe St EV L5 97 G6 10
Hackworth Cl WGN WN1 5 J4
Hadassah Gv AIG/SPK L17 129 L1
Hadden Cl RAIN/WH L35 117 J1 1
Haddock St BTL L20 6 F9
Haddon Av WLT/FAZ L9 84 B7
Haddon Dr PEN/TH CH61 141 H1
WDN WA8 133 L2
Haddon Rd GOL/RIS/CU WA3 92 F4
RF/TRAN CH42 128 C3
WGNS/IIMK WN3 79 G2
Haddon Wk WD/CROXPK L12 99 G2
Hadfield Av HOY CH47 108 D6
Hadfield Gv WLTN L25 131 L2
Hadleigh Cl WARRW/BUR WA5 119 M8
Hadleigh Rd KKBY L32 86 B4
Hadley Av PS/BROM CH62 143 L4
Hadlow La NSTN CH64 154 B6
Hadlow Rd NSTN CH64 154 B7
Hadstock Av FMBY L37 58 F4
Haggerston Rd ANF/KKDL L4 97 J3
Hague Bush Cl
GOL/RIS/CU WA3 93 G4 2
Hahnemann Rd ANF/KKDL L4 7 M7
Haig Av MOR/LEA CH46 110 A5
STHP PR8 25 G8

WARRW/BUR WA5 ..... 136 C1
Haigh Cl CHLY/EC PR7 ..... 32 C6
Haigh Crs CHLY/EC PR7 ..... 32 C6
　MGHL L31 ..... 72 E1
Haigh Rd CSBY/WL L22 ..... 83 C4
　WGNE/HIN WN2 ..... 57 K7
Haigh St VAUX/LVPD L3 ..... 13 L4
Haigh Vw WDN WN1 ..... 68 F3
　WGNS/IIMK WN3 ..... 5 K7
Haig Rd WDN WA8 ..... 16 C2
Haig St WGNS/IIMK WN3 ..... 4 C5
Haileybury Av AIN/FAZ L10 ..... 84 F3
Haileybury Rd WLTN L25 ..... 131 K5
Hailsham Rd ALL/GAR L19 ..... 130 E1
Halby Rd WLT/FAZ L9 ..... 84 D7 1
Halcombe Rd WD/CROXPK L12 ..... 98 F5
Halcyon Rd RF/TRAN CH42 ..... 10 E9
Haldane Av WARRS WA4 ..... 139 G2
Haldane Rd ANF/KKDL L4 ..... 97 J3
Hale Bank Rd WDN WA8 ..... 133 C8
Hale Dr SPK/HALE L24 ..... 147 H3
Halefield St ECCL WA10 ..... 8 E3 1
Hale Gate Rd WDN WA8 ..... 148 B2
Hale Gv AIMK WN4 ..... 79 H8
　WARRW/BUR WA5 ..... 120 C7 1
Hale Rd ANF/KKDL L4 ..... 7 M8
　SPK/HALE L24 ..... 146 E2
　WAL/NB CH45 ..... 95 L7
　WDN WA8 ..... 133 K7
Halesfield WGNE/HIN WN2 ..... 81 K3
Hale St CLVP L2 ..... 12 F6
　WARRN/WOL WA2 ..... 14 E2
Hale Vw RUNC WA7 ..... 18 D7
Hale View Rd FROD/HEL WA6 ..... 166 E1
　HUY L36 ..... 116 C3
Halewood Av GOL/RIS/CU WA3 ..... 92 B4
Halewood Cl WLTN L25 ..... 131 K1
Halewood Dr WLTN L25 ..... 131 J1
Halewood Pl WLTN L25 ..... 131 L2 1
Halewood Rd WLTN L25 ..... 131 K1
Halewood Wy WLTN L25 ..... 131 L3 1
Haley Rd North
　WARRW/BUR WA5 ..... 104 A7
Haley Rd South
　WARRW/BUR WA5 ..... 104 A7
Half Acre La HOR/BR BL6 ..... 57 L4
Halfacre La WARRS WA4 ..... 139 G2
Halfpenny La CHLY/EC PR7 ..... 41 K2
Halidon Ct BTL L20 ..... 96 C1
Halifax Cl WARRN/WOL WA2 ..... 121 M3 1
Halifax Crs CSBY/BLUN L23 ..... 71 K7
Halifax Rd STHP PR8 ..... 34 E8
Halkirk Rd CALD/MH L18 ..... 130 E5
Halkyn Dr EV L5 ..... 97 J8 1
Hallastone Rd FROD/HEL WA6 ..... 166 J1
Hall Av WDN WA8 ..... 133 J4
Halla-way WARRS WA4 ..... 15 L3
Hallbridge Gdns SKEL WN8 ..... 66 D5
Hall Brow Cl BRSC L40 ..... 63 K1
Hall Cl WGNNW/ST WN6 ..... 55 J7
Hallcroft SKEL WN8 ..... 65 L3
Hallcroft Pl WARRS WA4 ..... 138 C3
Hall Dr GR/UP/WCH CH49 ..... 125 L2
　KKBY L32 ..... 86 A3
　WARRS WA4 ..... 137 M7
Hallfield Dr CHNE CH2 ..... 165 K2
Hallfield Pk GTS/LS CH66 ..... 162 F1
Hallfields Rd WARRN/WOL WA2 ..... 121 M5
Hall Ga CHLY/EC PR7 ..... 32 C4
Hall Gn SKEL WN8 ..... 66 D6
Hall Green Cl SKEL WN8 ..... 66 D6
Hall Green La CHLY/EC PR7 ..... 41 J2
Halliday St GOL/RIS/CU WA3 ..... 123 H2
Halliwell La CHLYE PR6 ..... 32 E6 1
Halliwell Pl CHLY/EC PR7 ..... 32 E6 1
Halliwell St CHLY/EC PR7 ..... 32 E6
Hall La BRSC L40 ..... 40 C6
　BRSC L40 ..... 40 F2
　BRSC L40 ..... 52 C6
　EHL/KEN L7 ..... 113 K4
　HOR/BR BL6 ..... 45 J3
　HTWN L38 ..... 71 H1
　HUY L36 ..... 116 C3
　KKBY L32 ..... 86 A3
　MGHL L31 ..... 61 L6
　MGHL L31 ..... 72 D6
　NWD/KWIPK L33 ..... 74 B7
　ORM L39 ..... 75 G1
　PR/KW L34 ..... 100 F8
　RAIN/WH L35 ..... 117 L4
　STHEL WA9 ..... 119 J1
　WARRS WA4 ..... 138 D5
　WARRS WA4 ..... 151 M3
　WARRW/BUR WA5 ..... 104 D5
　WDN WA8 ..... 117 M7
　WGN WN1 ..... 68 F1
　WGNE/HIN WN2 ..... 69 M3
　WGNNW/ST WN6 ..... 54 D3
　WGNW/BIL/O WN5 ..... 78 B1
　WLT/FAZ L9 ..... 84 D6
Hall Lane Gv WGNE/HIN WN2 ..... 69 M5
Hallmoor Cl ORM L39 ..... 62 F3
Hall Nook WARRW/BUR WA5 ..... 136 B1
Hallows Av WARRN/WOL WA2 ..... 121 M5
Hall Rd BRSC L40 ..... 37 K6
　RNFD/HAY WA11 ..... 91 G6
　WARR WA1 ..... 122 F6
Hall Rd East CSBY/BLUN L23 ..... 70 D7 1
Hall Rd West CSBY/BLUN L23 ..... 70 C7
Hallsalls Rd KKBY L32 ..... 86 A5
Hallsgreen La CHNE CH2 ..... 165 H6
Hallside Cl ALL/GAR L19 ..... 130 C5
Hall St CHTN/BK PR9 ..... 3 K4
　ECCL WA10 ..... 9 H5
　STHEL WA9 ..... 119 G2
　WARR WA1 ..... 15 G4
　WGN WN1 ..... 5 C5
　WGNE/HIN WN2 ..... 5 M4
Hall Ter WARRW/BUR WA5 ..... 136 B4
Halitine CSBY/BLUN L23 ..... 70 C7 1
Hallville Rd CALD/MH L18 ..... 114 C8
Hall Wood Av RNFD/HAY WA11 ..... 91 H5
Hallwood Cl RUNC WA7 ..... 149 K7
Hallwood Link Rd RUNC WA7 ..... 150 A7
Hallwood Park Av RUNC WA7 ..... 150 B7
Hallwood Rd CHLY/EC PR7 ..... 32 C8

Hallworthy Cl LEIGH WN7 ..... 93 K4 1
Halsall Av WARRN/WOL WA2 ..... 121 M5
Halsall Cl CSBY/BLUN L23 ..... 71 G8
　RUNC WA7 ..... 150 E8 1
Halsall Gn BEB CH63 ..... 143 K4
Halsall Hall Dr ORM L39 ..... 49 K4
Halsall La FMBY L37 ..... 59 H1
　ORM L39 ..... 49 M7
　ORM L39 ..... 50 F7
Halsall Rd BTL L20 ..... 83 L8
　ORM L39 ..... 49 L3
　STHP PR8 ..... 35 J5
Halsall St PR/KW L34 ..... 100 F6
Halsbury Rd NPK/KEN L6 ..... 113 L2
　WAL/NB CH45 ..... 95 K7 2
Halsey Av WD/CROXPK L12 ..... 98 B6
Halsey Crs WD/CROXPK L12 ..... 98 B6
Halsnead Av RAIN/WH L35 ..... 116 A3
Halstead Rd WAL/EG CH44 ..... 111 L2
　WLT/FAZ L9 ..... 84 B7
Halton Brook Av RUNC WA7 ..... 149 M4
Halton Brow RUNC WA7 ..... 150 A4
Halton Cha BRSC L40 ..... 64 A1
Halton Ct RUNC WA7 ..... 149 M3
Halton Crs GR/UP/WCH CH49 ..... 125 K2
　GTS/LS CH66 ..... 163 H3
Halton Hey RAIN/WH L35 ..... 116 F4
Halton Link Rd RUNC WA7 ..... 150 A5
Halton Lodge Av RUNC WA7 ..... 149 M6
Halton Rd GTS/LS CH66 ..... 163 G4
　MGHL L31 ..... 72 F2
　RUNC WA7 ..... 19 K3
　WAL/NB CH45 ..... 95 J7 2
　WARRW/BUR WA5 ..... 120 B7
Halton Station Rd RUNC WA7 ..... 161 H2
Halton St RNFD/HAY WA11 ..... 91 G7 1
Halton View Rd WDN WA8 ..... 17 H1
Halton Wy GTS/LS CH66 ..... 163 G4
Halton Wd KKBY L32 ..... 85 K2
Halville Rd WAL/EG CH44 ..... 111 L2
Halton GTS/LS CH66 ..... 163 G4
Hambledon Cl GTS/LS CH66 ..... 155 J7 1
Hambledon Dr
　GR/UP/WCH CH49 ..... 125 L1
Hamble Dr WARRW/BUR WA5 ..... 136 B2
Hambleton Cl NG/CROX L11 ..... 98 D1
　WDN WA8 ..... 133 L2 2
Hamblett Crs RNFD/HAY WA11 ..... 89 K7
Hamblett St LEIGH WN7 ..... 81 K8
Hamer St ECCL WA10 ..... 8 F4
Hamil Cl HOY CH47 ..... 109 G4
Hamilton Cl NSTN CH64 ..... 152 D3
Hamilton La BIRK CH41 ..... 11 K4
Hamilton Rd AIMK WN4 ..... 90 E1
　CHLY/EC PR7 ..... 32 D6
　ECCL WA10 ..... 88 D7
　EV L5 ..... 97 H8
　WAL/NB CH45 ..... 95 J5
　WGNE/HIN WN2 ..... 81 H1
Hamilton Sq BIRK CH41 ..... 11 L4
Hamilton St BIRK CH41 ..... 11 K6
　LEIGH WN7 ..... 81 M7 1
Hamlet Rd WAL/NB CH45 ..... 95 H7
The Hamlet CHLY/EC PR7 ..... 44 B4 2
Hammersley Av STHEL WA9 ..... 118 E2
Hammersley St STHEL WA9 ..... 118 E2 1
Hammill Av ECCL WA10 ..... 89 G7
Hammill St ECCL WA10 ..... 8 B1
Hammond Rd NWD/KWIPK L33 ..... 86 E2
Hammond St STHEL WA9 ..... 102 F3
Hamnett Cl GOL/RIS/CU WA3 ..... 123 G2 1
Hamnett Rd PR/KW L34 ..... 101 G6
Hampden Gv RF/TRAN CH42 ..... 128 A1 3
Hampden Pl WGNW/BIL/O WN5 ..... 67 M4 1
Hampden Rd RF/TRAN CH42 ..... 127 M1
Hampden St ANF/KKDL L4 ..... 97 H5
　WGNW/BIL/O WN5 ..... 78 B1
Hampshire Av NTHTN L30 ..... 83 L2 1
Hampson Av
　GOL/RIS/CU WA3 ..... 107 H2 1
Hampson Cl AIMK WN4 ..... 91 K3
Hampson St NPK/KEN L6 ..... 97 L8
Hampstead Rd NPK/KEN L6 ..... 113 M1
　WAL/EG CH44 ..... 111 L2
　WGNNW/ST WN6 ..... 55 M4
Hampton Cl CHLY/EC PR7 ..... 32 C4
　NSTN CH64 ..... 153 G7 1
　WDN WA8 ..... 135 G2 1
Hampton Court Rd
　WD/CROXPK L12 ..... 98 E8
Hampton Crs NSTN CH64 ..... 153 G8
Hampton Dr WARRW/BUR WA5 ..... 136 E1
　WDN WA8 ..... 117 L8
Hampton Gdns EP CH65 ..... 156 C8
Hampton Pl RNFD/HAY WA11 ..... 89 K7 1
Hampton Rd FMBY L37 ..... 59 G4
　STHP PR8 ..... 3 K6
Hampton St TOX L8 ..... 113 H6
Hamsterley Cl GOL/RIS/CU WA3 ..... 107 K7
Hanbury Rd ANF/KKDL L4 ..... 97 M5
Handel Rd NTHLY L27 ..... 115 M7 2
Handfield Pl EV L5 ..... 97 J8 2
Handfield Rd CSBY/WL L22 ..... 83 G4
Handfield St EV L5 ..... 97 J8
Handford Av PS/BROM CH62 ..... 144 B8
Handforth Cl WARRS WA4 ..... 138 E1
Handforth La RUNC WA7 ..... 149 M7 3
Hand La CHLY/EC PR7 ..... 30 D8
Handley Ct ALL/GAR L19 ..... 130 B5
Hands St LITH L21 ..... 83 K7
Hanford Av WLT/FAZ L9 ..... 84 B7
Hankey Dr BTL L20 ..... 84 A8
Hankey St RUNC WA7 ..... 18 F3
Hankin St EV L5 ..... 96 F8 1
Hanley Cl WDN WA8 ..... 133 L4
Hanley Rd WDN WA8 ..... 133 L4
Hanlon Av BTL L20 ..... 83 M7 1
Hanmer Rd KKBY L32 ..... 85 K2
Hanmer St WGNE/HIN WN2 ..... 69 M8 16
Hannan Rd NPK/KEN L6 ..... 113 L2
Hanns Hall Rd NSTN CH64 ..... 152 A6
Hanover Cl CL/PREN CH43 ..... 111 H7 2
Hanover St CLVPS L1 ..... 12 F9
　WARR WA1 ..... 14 C7
Hanson Pk CL/PREN CH43 ..... 111 G8
Hanson Rd WLT/FAZ L9 ..... 84 E8
Hans Rd ANF/KKDL L4 ..... 97 J4 2

Hants La ORM L39 ..... 51 G7
Hanwell Cl LEIGH WN7 ..... 93 M4
Hanwell St NPK/KEN L6 ..... 97 K7
Hapsford Cl GOL/RIS/CU WA3 ..... 122 E1
Hapsford La CHNE CH2 ..... 165 M1
　FROD/HEL WA6 ..... 166 A4
Hapton St EV L5 ..... 97 G7 3
Harbern Cl RNFD/HAY WA11 ..... 83 K7
Harbern Dr LEIGH WN7 ..... 81 M3 1
Harbord Rd CSBY/WL L22 ..... 82 E4
Harbord St EHL/KEN L7 ..... 113 K4
　WARR WA1 ..... 15 H7
Harborne Dr BEB CH63 ..... 143 H3
Harbury Av STHP PR8 ..... 47 J1
Harbury Cl WGNNW/ST WN6 ..... 68 B3
Harcourt Av WAL/EG CH44 ..... 112 A2
Harcourt Cl GOL/RIS/CU WA3 ..... 123 G2
Harcourt St ANF/KKDL L4 ..... 96 F6
　BIRK CH41 ..... 10 E3
Hardacre St ORM L39 ..... 51 H7
Hardie Av MOR/LEA CH46 ..... 109 L4
Hardie Cl STHEL WA9 ..... 118 C2 1
Hardie Rd HUY L36 ..... 116 C2
Harding Av BEB CH63 ..... 143 H1
　WARRN/WOL WA2 ..... 121 M4
Harding Cl EV L5 ..... 97 J8
Harding Rd BRSC L40 ..... 51 M1
Harding St CHLYE PR6 ..... 44 D5
　TOX L8 ..... 113 K5
Hardknott Rd PS/BROM CH62 ..... 144 A4
Hard La ECCL WA10 ..... 88 F7
Hardman St CLVPS L1 ..... 13 K9
　WGNS/IIMK WN3 ..... 4 D8
Hardrow Cl WGNS/IIMK WN3 ..... 79 K3
Hardshaw St ECCL WA10 ..... 9 H4
Hardwick Rd AIMK WN4 ..... 79 J8
　RUNC WA7 ..... 149 M2
Hardybutts WGN WN1 ..... 5 G4
　WGN WN1 ..... 5 J5
Hardy Cl GTS/LS CH66 ..... 163 H2
Hardy Dr CHLY/EC PR7 ..... 32 C6
Hardy Rd LYMM WA13 ..... 139 L3
Hardy St ALL/GAR L19 ..... 145 M1
　CLVPS L1 ..... 112 F6 1
　CLVPS L1 ..... 113 G5 13
　WARRN/WOL WA2 ..... 14 F3
　WGNNW/ST WN6 ..... 4 B1
Harebell Cl FMBY L37 ..... 59 H4
Hare Cft STBRV L28 ..... 99 H5
Harefield Gn SPK/HALE L24 ..... 146 F2 2
Harefield Rd SPK/HALE L24 ..... 146 F2
Haresfinch Rd RNFD/HAY WA11 ..... 9 J1
Haresfinch Vw RNFD/HAY WA11 ..... 89 K7
Hare's La FROD/HEL WA6 ..... 160 A5
Harestone Av CHLY/EC PR7 ..... 32 C8
Harewell Rd NG/CROX L11 ..... 98 C4
Harewood Av GTS/LS CH66 ..... 162 E1
　STHP PR8 ..... 34 E7
Harewood Cl HUY L36 ..... 116 A2 1
Harewood Rd WAL/NB CH45 ..... 95 J6 1
　WGNE/HIN WN2 ..... 69 L7
Harfield Gdns GTS/LS CH66 ..... 155 L8
Hargate Rd NWD/KWIPK L33 ..... 86 B5
Hargrave Av CL/PREN CH43 ..... 127 G2
Hargrave Cl CL/PREN CH43 ..... 127 G2 1
Hargrave Dr GTS/LS CH66 ..... 156 A8
Hargrave La BEB CH63 ..... 143 H8
Hargreaves Ct WDN WA8 ..... 17 J1
Hargreaves Rd AIG/SPK L17 ..... 129 L2
Hargreaves St STHEL WA9 ..... 103 G1
　STHP PR8 ..... 3 K5
Harington Cl FMBY L37 ..... 58 F2
Harington Gn FMBY L37 ..... 58 F2
Harington Rd FMBY L37 ..... 58 E1
Harker St VAUX/LVPD L3 ..... 13 J4
Harke St EHL/KEN L7 ..... 113 K5
Harland Dr AIMK WN4 ..... 91 L2 3
Harland Gn SPK/HALE L24 ..... 147 J2
Harland Rd RF/TRAN CH42 ..... 127 M1
Harlea Av WGNE/HIN WN2 ..... 81 J2
Harlech Av WGNE/HIN WN2 ..... 81 J1
Harlech Cl WARRW/BUR WA5 ..... 121 G3
Harlech Rd CSBY/BLUN L23 ..... 82 E2
Harlech St AIMK WN4 ..... 79 H8
　WAL/EG CH44 ..... 112 A3
Harlech Wy EP CH65 ..... 20 E9
Harleston Rd NWD/KWIPK L33 ..... 86 C2
Harley Av BEB CH63 ..... 127 L5
Harley St WLT/FAZ L9 ..... 84 C7
Harlian Av MOR/LEA CH46 ..... 109 M6
Harlow St TOX L8 ..... 113 G8
Harlyn Cl HLWD L26 ..... 132 A7
Harlyn Gdns
　WARRW/BUR WA5 ..... 135 M2
Harmony Wy CLB/OSW/ST L13 ..... 114 C4
Harmuir Cl WGNNW/ST WN6 ..... 68 A1
The Harn GTS/LS CH66 ..... 162 E2
Harold Av AIMK WN4 ..... 79 J8
Harold Rd RNFD/HAY WA11 ..... 91 H6
Harold St WGNE/HIN WN2 ..... 57 M8
Harper Cl GTS/LS CH66 ..... 162 F1
Harperley CHLY/EC PR7 ..... 32 D3
Harper Rd WLT/FAZ L9 ..... 97 J1
Harper's La CHLY/EC PR7 ..... 32 C4
Harpers Rd WARRN/WOL WA2 ..... 122 C4
Harper St WGN WN1 ..... 5 J5
Harp's Cft NTHTN L30 ..... 80 L1
Harptree Cl RAIN/WH L35 ..... 117 G2
Harptree Wy STHEL WA9 ..... 81 M6
Harradon Rd WLT/FAZ L9 ..... 84 D6
Harridge La BRSC L40 ..... 50 B5
Harrier Dr HLWD L26 ..... 132 A4
Harringay Av CALD/MH L18 ..... 114 D8
Harrington Av HOY CH47 ..... 108 E6
Harrington Rd CHLY/EC PR7 ..... 32 D5
　CSBY/BLUN L23 ..... 82 F1
　LITH L21 ..... 83 M4
　VAUX/LVPD L3 ..... 129 L1

Harrington St CLVP L2 ..... 12 F7
Harris Cl BEB CH63 ..... 143 H3
Harris Dr BTL L20 ..... 83 M6
Harrismith Rd AIN/FAZ L10 ..... 85 H6
Harrison Crs HOR/BR BL6 ..... 57 L2
Harrison Dr BTL L20 ..... 7 L4
　RNFD/HAY WA11 ..... 76 B5
　RNFD/HAY WA11 ..... 90 C7
　WAL/NB CH45 ..... 95 G6
Harrison Hey HUY L36 ..... 115 M4
Harrison Rd CHLY/EC PR7 ..... 32 E7
Harrison St WDN WA8 ..... 133 K7
　WGNE/HIN WN2 ..... 81 K2
Harrison Wy NEWLW WA12 ..... 104 E1
　VAUX/LVPD L3 ..... 12 E1
Harris Rd WGNNW/ST WN6 ..... 55 K3
Harris St WDN WA8 ..... 17 H1
Harrock La BRSC L40 ..... 41 G7
　WGNNW/ST WN6 ..... 54 C1
Harrocks Cl NTHTN L30 ..... 71 M8
Harrock Wood Cl PEN/TH CH61 ..... 126 A7
Harrod Dr STHP PR8 ..... 35 G2
Harrogate Cl PS/BROM CH62 ..... 154 F1
　WARRW/BUR WA5 ..... 120 C5
Harrogate Dr EV L5 ..... 97 H8
Harrogate Rd PS/BROM CH62 ..... 154 F1
　RF/TRAN CH42 ..... 128 C3
Harrogate St WGN WN1 ..... 4 F5
Harrogate Wy CHTN/BK PR9 ..... 22 E7
Harrop Rd RUNC WA7 ..... 19 J3
Harrops Cft NTHTN L30 ..... 84 A1
Harrowby Cl TOX L8 ..... 113 J6 4
Harrowby Rd LITH L21 ..... 83 H6
　RF/TRAN CH42 ..... 127 L1
　WAL/EG CH44 ..... 112 A1
Harrowby Rd South
　RF/TRAN CH42 ..... 127 L1 3
Harrowby St TOX L8 ..... 113 J6 4
　WGNW/BIL/O WN5 ..... 67 H5
Harrow Cl NTHTN L30 ..... 84 B2
　WAL/EG CH44 ..... 95 H8
　WARRS WA4 ..... 138 A7
　WGNW/BIL/O WN5 ..... 67 H5
Harrow Dr AIN/FAZ L10 ..... 84 F3
　RUNC WA7 ..... 150 A3
Harrow Gv PS/BROM CH62 ..... 144 C4
Harrow Pl WGNE/HIN WN2 ..... 80 B1 3
Harrow Rd ANF/KKDL L4 ..... 97 K7
　EP CH65 ..... 20 E7
　WAL/EG CH44 ..... 111 H1
　WGNW/BIL/O WN5 ..... 67 M4
Harsnips SKEL WN8 ..... 65 L3
Hartdale Rd CALD/MH L18 ..... 130 C1 6
　CSBY/BLUN L23 ..... 71 J7
Hartford Cl CL/PREN CH43 ..... 127 H2
Hartford Dr EP CH65 ..... 163 H1
Harthill Av CALD/MH L18 ..... 130 D1
Harthill Rd CALD/MH L18 ..... 130 E2
Hartington Av BIRK CH41 ..... 10 D3
Hartington Dr WGNNW/ST WN6 ..... 56 B6
Hartington Rd ALL/GAR L19 ..... 130 E7
　ECCL WA10 ..... 88 E8
　TOX L8 ..... 113 L7
　WAL/EG CH44 ..... 111 K1
　WD/CROXPK L12 ..... 98 E4
Hartismere Rd WAL/EG CH44 ..... 111 M2
Hartland Av CHTN/BK PR9 ..... 22 D8
Hartland Cl WDN WA8 ..... 118 C8
Hartland Rd NG/CROX L11 ..... 98 A3
Hartley Av WGN WN1 ..... 5 J5
　WLT/FAZ L9 ..... 84 D8
Hartley Cl ANF/KKDL L4 ..... 97 H6 2
Hartley Crs STHP PR8 ..... 35 H3
Hartley Gv ECCL WA10 ..... 101 L5
　WGNW/BIL/O WN5 ..... 67 K6
Hartley Quay VAUX/LVPD L3 ..... 12 E9
Hartley Rd STHP PR8 ..... 35 H3
Hartley St WGNW/BIL/O WN5 ..... 67 K7 3
Hartley Ter WGNS/IIMK WN3 ..... 4 E6
Hartnup St EV L5 ..... 97 H7 3
Hartopp Rd WLTN L25 ..... 115 J7
Hartsbourne Av WLTN L25 ..... 115 H6
Hartsbourne Cl WLTN L25 ..... 115 H6 2
Hartsbourne Wk WLTN L25 ..... 115 J6
Hartshead SKEL WN8 ..... 65 L3
Hart's La SKEL WN8 ..... 66 B5
Hart St STHP PR8 ..... 3 M5
　VAUX/LVPD L3 ..... 13 J8
Hartswell Cl GOL/RIS/CU WA3 ..... 92 C3 1
Hartwell St LITH L21 ..... 83 K7
Hartwood Cl KKBY L32 ..... 86 B6
Hartwood Gn CHLYE PR6 ..... 32 E2
Hartwood Rd CHTN/BK PR9 ..... 3 M2
　KKBY L32 ..... 86 B6
Hartwood Sq KKBY L32 ..... 86 B6 2
Harty Rd RNFD/HAY WA11 ..... 90 C8
Harvard Cl RUNC WA7 ..... 150 F3 3
Harvard Ct WARRN/WOL WA2 ..... 121 J2 3
Harvest Av GR/UP/WCH CH49 ..... 125 M2
　NEWLW WA12 ..... 104 B2 3
Harvester Wy
　GR/UP/WCH CH49 ..... 125 L1 3
　NTHTN L30 ..... 84 C1
Harvest La MOR/LEA CH46 ..... 109 M4
Harvest Wy STHEL WA9 ..... 118 C1 3
Harvey Av GR/UP/WCH CH49 ..... 125 M2
　NEWLW WA12 ..... 104 B2 3
Harvey Ct GOL/RIS/CU WA3 ..... 93 K4 3
　WARRN/WOL WA2 ..... 121 K2 3
Harvey La GOL/RIS/CU WA3 ..... 92 B4
Harvey Rd WAL/NB CH45 ..... 95 J7
Harvey St WGNS/IIMK WN3 ..... 5 H7
Harvington Dr STHP PR8 ..... 34 C8
Harwich Gv CHLDW L16 ..... 115 H5 3
Harwood Gdns WARRS WA4 ..... 138 C3
Harwood Rd ALL/GAR L19 ..... 130 F7
Haryngton Av
　WARRW/BUR WA5 ..... 14 A1
Haselbeech Cl NG/CROX L11 ..... 98 B2
Haselbeech Crs NG/CROX L11 ..... 98 B2
Haseldine La MARDALE ..... 79 H7 11
Hasfield Rd NG/CROX L11 ..... 98 B3
Haslam Dr ORM L39 ..... 50 F6
Haslemere RAIN/WH L35 ..... 117 H2
Haslemere Dr
　WARRW/BUR WA5 ..... 135 M1

Haslemere Rd WLTN L25 ..... 115 J7
Haslemere Wy WLTN L25 ..... 115 K7 3
Haslingden Cl
　CLB/OSW/ST L13 ..... 114 D3 3
Haslington Gv HLWD L26 ..... 132 C7 3
Hassal Rd RF/TRAN CH42 ..... 128 C5
Hassnes Cl WGNS/IIMK WN3 ..... 79 K3
Hastings Av WARRN/WOL WA2 ..... 121 K1
Hastings Dr HUY L36 ..... 116 C5
Hastings Rd CSBY/WL L22 ..... 82 D3
　STHP PR8 ..... 35 G4
Haswell Dr STBRV L28 ..... 99 J5
Hatchmere Cl CL/PREN CH43 ..... 127 H2 3
　WARRW/BUR WA5 ..... 121 G8
Hatfield Cl STHEL WA9 ..... 102 B6
　WD/CROXPK L12 ..... 99 H2
Hatfield Gdns HUY L36 ..... 116 B4 3
Hatfield Rd BTL L20 ..... 7 L4
　STHP PR8 ..... 34 F7
Hathaway MGHL L31 ..... 72 D6
Hathaway Cl WLTN L25 ..... 115 J7
Hathaway Rd WLTN L25 ..... 115 J7
Hathaway Wk WGNNW/ST WN6 ..... 80 B1
Hatherley Av CSBY/WL L22 ..... 83 G3
Hatherley Cl TOX L8 ..... 113 J6 8
Hatherley St TOX L8 ..... 113 J6 8
　WAL/EG CH44 ..... 112 A3
Hathersage Rd HUY L36 ..... 100 A8
Hatley La FROD/HEL WA6 ..... 160 B6
Hatton Av PS/BROM CH62 ..... 155 G2
Hatton Cl HES CH60 ..... 140 F4
Hatton Gdn VAUX/LVPD L3 ..... 12 F5
Hatton Hill Rd LITH L21 ..... 83 J5
Hattons La CHLDW L16 ..... 114 E3
Hatton St CHLY/EC PR7 ..... 44 B7 3
Hauxwell Dr RNFD/HAY WA11 ..... 89 L7 3
Havannah La STHEL WA9 ..... 103 K2
Havelock Cl ECCL WA10 ..... 8 D5
Haven Brow ORM L39 ..... 62 E5
Haven Rd AIN/FAZ L10 ..... 85 H5
Havenwood Rd WGN WN1 ..... 68 D1
Havercroft Cl WGNS/IIMK WN3 ..... 79 G2
Havergal St RUNC WA7 ..... 18 F5
Haverstock Rd NPK/KEN L6 ..... 113 M2 3
Haverton Wk
　WD/CROXPK L12 ..... 99 G2 3
Havisham Cl GOL/RIS/CU WA3 ..... 106 F8
Hawarden Av AIG/SPK L17 ..... 113 M7
　CL/PREN CH43 ..... 10 E6
　WAL/EG CH44 ..... 111 L1
Hawarden Gdns EP CH65 ..... 20 E9
　EP CH65 ..... 163 M3 3
Hawarden Gv LITH L21 ..... 83 J7 3
Hawdon Ct EHL/KEN L7 ..... 113 L5
Hawes Av RNFD/HAY WA11 ..... 89 L5
Hawes Crs AIMK WN4 ..... 79 K8
Hawesside St CHTN/BK PR9 ..... 3 H4
Haweswater Av CHLY/EC PR7 ..... 32 D7
　RNFD/HAY WA11 ..... 90 C7
　WGNE/HIN WN2 ..... 69 K6
Haweswater Cl NWD/KWIPK L33 ..... 73 M8
　RUNC WA7 ..... 150 C8 3
Haweswater Gv MGHL L31 ..... 73 H3 3
Hawgreen Rd KKBY L32 ..... 85 K4 3
Hawick Cl GTS/LS CH66 ..... 155 J8 3
　NWD/KWIPK L33 ..... 73 M7
Hawke Gn HUY L36 ..... 116 C6
Hawkeshead Rd
　PS/BROM CH62 ..... 144 A4 3
Hawke St VAUX/LVPD L3 ..... 13 J7
Hawkesworth St ANF/KKDL L4 ..... 97 H7 3
Hawkhurst Cl TOX L8 ..... 129 H1 7
Hawkins Rd NSTN CH64 ..... 153 H4
Hawkins St NPK/KEN L6 ..... 113 K2
Hawkley Av WGNS/IIMK WN3 ..... 79 H3
Hawkrigg Cl WGNNW/ST WN6 ..... 56 B6 3
Hawksclough SKEL WN8 ..... 65 L3
Hawks Ct RUNC WA7 ..... 150 A7
Hawkshaw Cl GOL/RIS/CU WA3 ..... 122 E1
　WGNE/HIN WN2 ..... 69 J2 3
Hawkshead Av CHLY/EC PR7 ..... 31 M4
　WD/CROXPK L12 ..... 98 E4
Hawkshead Cl MGHL L31 ..... 73 G3
　RUNC WA7 ..... 150 C8 3
Hawkshead Dr LITH L21 ..... 83 M5
Hawkshead Rd
　WARRW/BUR WA5 ..... 104 A7
Hawkshead St CHTN/BK PR9 ..... 3 K4
Hawksmoor Cl NG/CROX L11 ..... 85 J6 3
Hawksmoor Rd AIN/FAZ L10 ..... 85 J7
Hawksmore Cl
　GR/UP/WCH CH49 ..... 109 M7 3
Hawkstone Gv
　FROD/HEL WA6 ..... 166 E1 3
Hawkstone St TOX L8 ..... 113 J8 3
　TOX L8 ..... 129 J1 11
Hawks Wy HES CH60 ..... 141 G5
Hawkswood Cl CHLY/EC PR7 ..... 30 D7
Hawksworth Cl FMBY L37 ..... 47 J5
Hawksworth Dr FMBY L37 ..... 47 J7
Hawley's La WARRN/WOL WA2 ..... 121 J4
Haworth Dr BTL L20 ..... 83 M6
Haworth St WGNE/HIN WN2 ..... 69 M7 3
Hawthorn Av AIMK WN4 ..... 78 E8
　NEWLW WA12 ..... 104 E2
　RUNC WA7 ..... 19 H5
　WDN WA8 ..... 134 D3 3
　WGN WN1 ..... 56 D7
　WGNE/HIN WN2 ..... 81 J2
　WGNW/BIL/O WN5 ..... 67 H7 3
Hawthorn Cl
　WGNW/BIL/O WN5 ..... 77 M8 3
Hawthorn Crs SKEL WN8 ..... 65 G4
Hawthorn Dr ECCL WA10 ..... 101 K1
　PEN/TH CH61 ..... 141 H2 3
　WKBY CH48 ..... 125 G3
Hawthorne Av HLWD L26 ..... 132 A7
　WARR WA1 ..... 122 D6
　WARRW/BUR WA5 ..... 120 B7
Hawthorne Cl
　RNFD/HAY WA11 ..... 90 C8 3
Hawthorne Crs FMBY L37 ..... 59 J3
Hawthorne Dr NSTN CH64 ..... 154 D4
Hawthorne Gv CHTN/BK PR9 ..... 25 H7
　WAL/EG CH44 ..... 112 A3
　WARR WA1 ..... 122 D6 3
Hawthorne Rd BTL L20 ..... 7 K6
　FROD/HEL WA6 ..... 160 D4

LITH L21 83 K6
RF/TRAN CH42 127 M2
STHEL WA9 102 F7
WARRS WA4 137 L5
The Hawthornes NTHLY L27 115 L7
Hawthorne St
WARRW/BUR WA5 121 J5
Hawthorn Gv EHL/KEN L7 113 K4
WARRS WA4 15 K9
WARRS WA4 137 M4
Hawthorn La PS/BROM CH62 143 M5
Hawthorn Rd GTS/LS CH66 155 L7
HUY L36 115 L3
LYMM WA13 139 L2
NSTN CH64 152 D3
PR/KW L34 101 G7
Hawthorns Gv WD/CROXPK L12 98 D7
The Hawthorns CHLY/EC PR7 30 D6
SKEL WN8 53 J4
Haxted Gdns ALL/GAR L19 130 F7
Haycastle Cl WARRW/BUR WA5 121 G4
Haycroft Cl GTS/LS CH66 162 F3
Haydn Rd DV/KA/FCH L14 99 H8
Haydock La RNFD/HAY WA11 90 E7
Haydock Park Gdns
NEWLW WA12 91 K4
Haydock Park Rd AIN/FAZ L10 85 G2
Haydock Rd WAL/NB CH45 95 L6
Haydock St AIMK WN4 91 K3
ECCL WA10 9 H5
NEWLW WA12 104 C1
WARRN/WOL WA2 14 E4
Hayes Av RAIN/WH L35 101 G8
Hayes Crs FROD/HEL WA6 160 D4
Hayes Dr MGHL L31 85 K2
Hayes St ECCL WA10 101 L5
Hayfell Rd WGNS/IIMK WN3 79 J4
Hayfield Rd ORM L39 51 G6
WARR WA1 122 E5
Hayfield St ANF/KKDL L4 97 H6
Hayles Cl WLTN L25 115 J7
Hayles Gn WLTN L25 115 J7
Hayles Gv WLTN L25 115 J7
Haylock Cl TOX L8 129 H1
Hayman Av LEIGH WN7 93 M3
Hayman's Cl WD/CROXPK L12 98 C6
Haymans Gn MGHL L31 73 G4
WD/CROXPK L12 98 C6
Hayman's Gv WD/CROXPK L12 98 C6
Haywood Cl GOL/RIS/CU WA3 93 G4
Haywood Crs RUNC WA7 150 F3
Haywood Gdns ECCL WA10 8 A7
Hazel Av KKBY L32 85 L2
RAIN/WH L35 117 G1
RUNC WA7 18 D8
WGNNW/ST WN6 68 C1
Hazelborough Cl
GOL/RIS/CU WA3 107 K7
Hazel Cl GTS/LS CH66 163 H4
Hazeldale Rd WLT/FAZ L9 97 J1
Hazeldene Av PEN/TH CH61 126 C7
WAL/NB CH45 95 J8
Hazeldene Wy PEN/TH CH61 126 D7
Hazelfield Ct STHEL WA9 118 E1
Hazel Gv BEB CH63 143 G1
CHLYE PR6 32 E2
CSBY/BLUN L23 83 H2
ECCL WA10 101 L2
GOL/RIS/CU WA3 92 D5
PEN/TH CH61 125 M6
STHP PR8 25 G6
WARR WA1 122 C5
WLT/FAZ L9 84 D7
Hazelhurst Rd ANF/KKDL L4 97 K6
Hazel La SKEL WN8 53 K8
Hazelmere Gdns
WGNE/HIN WN2 81 G1
Hazel Ms MGHL L31 85 K2
Hazel Rd BIRK CH41 11 G7
HOY CH47 108 D6
HUY L36 100 B8
Hazelslack Rd NG/CROX L11 98 C3
The Hazels CHLY/EC PR7 43 G4
Hazel St WARR WA1 15 K2
Hazelwood GR/UP/WCH CH49 125 M1
Hazelwood Av BRSC L40 52 B1
Hazelwood Cl STHEL WA9 118 D2
Hazelwood Gv HLWD L26 131 M3
Hazelwood Ms WARRS WA4 138 E4
Hazelwood Rd WGN WN1 68 D1
Hazlehurst Cl FMBY L37 58 E3
Hazlehurst Gv AIMK WN4 91 L2
Hazlehurst Rd FROD/HEL WA6 160 E8
Hazleton Rd DV/KA/FCH L14 114 E2
Headbolt La NWD/KWIPK L33 74 C8
STHP PR8 48 C1
Headbourne Cl WLTN L25 115 H6
Headen Av WGNW/BIL/O WN5 67 K8
Headingley Cl HUY L36 115 L5
STHEL WA9 102 E7
Headington Rd
GR/UP/WCH CH49 109 M8
Headland Cl GOL/RIS/CU WA3 93 G7
WKBY CH48 124 D5
Headley Cl ECCL WA10 8 D5
Head St TOX L8 113 G7
Heald St CHLYE PR6 33 G5
NEWLW WA12 104 B2
Heanor Dr STHP PR8 36 B2
Heapey Fold La CHLYE PR6 33 L5
Heapey Rd CHLYE PR6 33 J2
Heardman Av WGNNW/ST WN6 4 A1
Heath Av GTS/LS CH66 163 J4
Heathbank Av PEN/TH CH61 125 L6
WAL/EG CH44 111 J2
Heathbank Rd RF/TRAN CH42 127 M2
Heath Cl PR/KW L34 101 H6
WKBY CH48 124 D5
WLTN L25 115 H8
Heathcote Cl EHL/KEN L7 113 L5
Heathcote Gdns BEB CH63 128 B8
Heathcote Rd ANF/KKDL L4 97 H3
Heath Dl BEB CH63 143 H2
Heath Dr GR/UP/WCH CH49 110 C8
HES CH60 141 H4
RUNC WA7 19 G9
Heather Bank BEB CH63 127 M7
Heather Brae NEWLW WA12 104 C1
Heather Brow CL/PREN CH43 111 H7
Heather Cl ANF/KKDL L4 97 H5
BRSC L40 52 A1
FMBY L37 47 K8
GOL/RIS/CU WA3 106 F8
GTS/LS CH66 163 G2
RUNC WA7 150 A8
STHP PR8 47 M3
Heatherdale Cl CL/PREN CH43 127 K2
Heatherdale Rd CALD/MH L18 130 C1
Heather Dene PS/BROM CH62 143 M2
Heatherdene Rd WKBY CH48 124 D2
Heather Gv AIMK WN4 92 A1
WGNW/BIL/O WN5 68 A6
Heatherlea Cl SKEL WN8 66 E6
Heather Rd BEB CH63 142 F1
HES CH60 141 J4
Heathers Cft NTHTN L30 84 A2
Heather Wy CSBY/BLUN L23 71 K7
Heatherways FMBY L37 47 J7
Heathey La STHP PR8 36 C5
Heathfield CHLYE PR6 44 B4
Heathfield Av STHEL WA9 102 A5
Heathfield Cl FMBY L37 47 J7
LITH L21 83 L7
Heathfield Dr
NWD/KWIPK L33 74 A8
Heathfield Pk WARRS WA4 138 C3
WDN WA8 133 M2
Heathfield Rd BEB CH63 143 H1
CL/PREN CH43 127 L1
CSBY/WL L22 82 E3
EP CH65 20 B4
MGHL L31 73 H6
STHP PR8 35 G8
WAV L15 114 C7
Heathfield St CLVPS L1 13 J8
CLVPS L1 13 J8
Heath Gdns WGNE/HIN WN2 81 L2
Heathgate SKEL WN8 65 L3
Heathgate Av SPK/HALE L24 147 J3
Heath Gv GTS/LS CH66 155 K6
Heath Hey WLTN L25 115 H8
Heathland Rd STHEL WA9 118 E1
Heathlands Rd GTS/LS CH66 155 K6
The Heathlands
MOR/LEA CH46 110 A2
Heath La CHNE CH2 164 A6
GOL/RIS/CU WA3 92 F7
GOL/RIS/CU WA3 106 C3
GTS/LS CH66 155 J6
LEIGH WN7 81 K8
NSTN CH64 154 E5
Heathlea WGNE/HIN WN2 81 L3
Heathmoor Av GOL/RIS/CU WA3 92 F7
Heathmoor Rd MOR/LEA CH46 109 M4
Heath Park Gv RUNC WA7 18 F8
Heath Rd AIMK WN4 91 K3
ALL/GAR L19 130 F5
BEB CH63 128 A8
HUY L36 99 L8
RUNC WA7 19 J8
WARRW/BUR WA5 120 B8
WDN WA8 134 A4
Heath Road Crs RUNC WA7 19 J6
Heath Rd South RUNC WA7 149 H6
Heathrow Pl CHLY/EC PR7 32 C6
Heathside HES CH60 140 F4
Heath St AIMK WN4 91 L3
GOL/RIS/CU WA3 92 C5
RAIN/WH L35 101 M6
WARRS WA4 137 L5
Heath Vw LITH L21 83 K2
Heathview Rd WDN WA8 148 C1
Heathwaite Crs NG/CROX L11 98 C4
Heathway HES CH60 141 K6
Heathwood WD/CROXPK L12 98 D8
Heathwood Gv WARR WA1 122 D6
Heathy La ORM L39 48 C5
Heatley Cl CL/PREN CH43 110 E6
Heaton Cl BRSC L40 51 M1
SKEL WN8 66 C6
SPK/HALE L24 147 H2
Heaton Ct GOL/RIS/CU WA3 107 H7
Heatons Bridge Rd BRSC L40 50 F1
Heaton St WGN WN1 68 E3
WGNE/HIN WN2 57 M8
WGNNW/ST WN6 56 A4
WGNS/IIMK WN3 5 J7
Heaviley Gv HOR/BR BL6 45 J8
Hebburn Wy WD/CROXPK L12 99 J2
Hebden Av GOL/RIS/CU WA3 107 K1
Hebden Rd NG/CROX L11 98 D2
Hebdon Cl AIMK WN4 79 J8
Heber St WGNE/HIN WN2 5 M6
Hector Rd WGNW/BIL/O WN5 67 M4
Hedgebank Cl WLT/FAZ L9 84 F5
Hedgecroft CSBY/BLUN L23 71 L7
Hedgefield Rd WLTN L25 115 K8
Hedge Hey RUNC WA7 150 C4
Hedgemead WGNNW/ST WN6 4 A2
Hedges Crs CLB/OSW/ST L13 98 A6
Hedingham Cl HLWD L26 132 C4
Heeley St WGN WN1 68 D3
The Heights FROD/HEL WA6 166 E1
Helena Rd STHEL WA9 103 H6
Helena St BIRK CH41 11 J7
EHL/KEN L7 113 K4
WLT/FAZ L9 97 H2
Helen Bank Dr RNFD/HAY WA11 76 B5
Helen St AIMK WN4 91 J1
GOL/RIS/CU WA3 92 B3
Helford Cl RAIN/WH L35 101 J7
Helford Rd NG/CROX L11 85 M8
Heliers Rd CLB/OSW/ST L13 114 D3
Hell Nook GOL/RIS/CU WA3 92 A4
Helmdon Cl NG/CROX L11 98 C4
Helmingham Gv BIRK CH41 11 K9
Helmingham Rd BIRK CH41 11 K9
Helmsdale SKEL WN8 65 L3
Helmsdale La
WARRW/BUR WA5 120 E7
Helmsley Cl WARRW/BUR WA5 121 G6
Helmsley Rd HLWD L26 132 B6
Helmsman Wy WGNS/IIMK WN3 4 C9
Helsby Av PS/BROM CH62 155 H2
Helsby Rd FROD/HEL WA6 166 E4
WLT/FAZ L9 84 D6
Helsby St EHL/KEN L7 113 J4
STHEL WA9 102 F4
WARR WA1 15 K3
Helsby Wy WGNS/IIMK WN3 78 E3
Helston Av HLWD L26 132 B4
RNFD/HAY WA11 89 M6
Helston Cl CHTN/BK PR9 22 D8
RUNC WA7 150 D8
WARRW/BUR WA5 120 A8
Helston Rd NG/CROX L11 85 M8
Helton Cl CL/PREN CH43 127 G2
Helvellyn Rd WGNW/BIL/O WN5 67 K6
Hemans St BTL L20 6 D2
Hemer Ter BTL L20 6 C1
Hemfield Ct WGNE/HIN WN2 69 L5
Hemfield Rd WGNE/HIN WN2 69 L5
Hemingford Cl GTS/LS CH66 162 F3
Hemingford St BIRK CH41 11 H6
Hemlegh Vw FROD/HEL WA6 166 D3
Hemlock Cl WD/CROXPK L12 98 F2
Hempstead Cl STHEL WA9 102 B6
Hemsworth Av GTS/LS CH66 155 L8
Henbury Pl RUNC WA7 149 K7
Henderson Cl
GR/UP/WCH CH49 109 M7
WARRW/BUR WA5 119 M7
Henderson Dr RNFD/HAY WA11 76 C5
Henderson Rd HUY L36 116 C2
WDN WA8 16 B3
Hendon Rd NPK/KEN L6 113 M1
WGNW/BIL/O WN5 67 M5
Hendon Wk
GR/UP/WCH CH49 125 L2
Henglers Cl NPK/KEN L6 113 J2
Henley Av LITH L21 83 J5
Henley Cl BEB CH63 143 J3
NSTN CH64 153 G7
WARRS WA4 138 A7
Henley Ct ECCL WA10 8 B9
RUNC WA7 149 M3
Henley Dr CHTN/BK PR9 25 G4
Henley Mnr GOL/RIS/CU WA3 106 F1
Henley Rd CALD/MH L18 114 D8
NSTN CH64 153 G7
Henley St WGNE/HIN WN2 57 K7
Henllan Gdns STHEL WA9 103 H6
Henlow Av KKBY L32 86 B5
Hennawood Cl NPK/KEN L6 97 K8
Henry Edward St
VAUX/LVPD L3 13 G4
Henry Park St WGN WN1 5 K5
Henry St BIRK CH41 11 K6
CLB/OSW/ST L13 114 B3
CLVPS L1 13 G9
ECCL WA10 8 F4
WARR WA1 14 C6
WDN WA8 17 H1
WGNE/HIN WN2 80 A1
Henshall Av WARRS WA4 138 B1
Henthorne Rd PS/BROM CH62 128 D5
Henthorne St CL/PREN CH43 10 E6
Hepherd St
WARRW/BUR WA5 136 F1
Hepworth Cl GOL/RIS/CU WA3 92 B3
Herald Av ALL/GAR L19 131 G7
Herald Cl NG/CROX L11 98 E2
Heralds Cl WDN WA8 133 K5
Heralds Gn WARRW/BUR WA5 120 C3
Herald St ALL/GAR L19 130 E7
Herbarth Cl WLT/FAZ L9 97 H2
Herbert St STHEL WA9 103 H6
WARRW/BUR WA5 104 A7
WGNS/IIMK WN3 4 C5
Herbert Taylor Cl NPK/KEN L6 97 L7
Herculaneum Ct TOX L8 129 H2
Herculaneum Rd TOX L8 129 G1
Herdman Cl WLTN L25 115 K8
Hereford Av GOL/RIS/CU WA3 92 D5
GR/UP/WCH CH49 110 B7
GTS/LS CH66 163 G5
Hereford Cl AIMK WN4 91 L3
WARR WA1 122 F6
Hereford Dr NTHTN L30 84 B4
Hereford Rd CHTN/BK PR9 25 H6
LITH L21 83 G6
WAV L15 114 C7
Heriot St EV L5 96 F7
Hermes Cl NTHTN L30 84 A5
Hermes Rd NG/CROX L11 85 L7
Hermitage Cl WGNNW/ST WN6 55 G6
Hermitage Green La
WARRN/WOL WA2 105 J5
Hermitage Gv BTL L20 83 M6
Herm Rd EV L5 96 E8
Heron Cl RUNC WA7 150 F5
Heron Ct HLWD L26 132 A4
NSTN CH64 152 E6
Herondale Rd CALD/MH L18 130 B1
Heron Dr WGNS/IIMK WN3 79 G3
Heron Gv RNFD/HAY WA11 76 D8
Heronhall Rd WLT/FAZ L9 98 B1
Heronpark Wy BEB CH63 143 K2
Heron Pl WGNW/BIL/O WN5 67 L5
Heron Rd WKBY CH48 109 J7
Herons Wy RUNC WA7 151 H1
Hero St BTL L20 7 K7
Herrick St CLB/OSW/ST L13 114 B2
Herschell St EV L5 97 H7
Hertford Cl HLWD L26 132 B6
WARR WA1 123 G6
Hertford Dr WAL/NB CH45 95 L7
Hertford Rd BTL L20 7 G7
Hertford St STHEL WA9 102 F3
Hesketh Av CHTN/BK PR9 23 J7
RF/TRAN CH42 127 M4
Hesketh Cl WARRW/BUR WA5 136 B1
Hesketh Dr BRSC L40 39 J2
CHTN/BK PR9 25 G3
HES CH60 141 J4
MGHL L31 73 H3
WGNNW/ST WN6 55 J3
WLT/FAZ L9 84 F7
Hesketh Gn BRSC L40 39 K1
Hesketh Meadow La
GOL/RIS/CU WA3 93 J5
Hesketh Rd BRSC L40 51 M1
CHTN/BK PR9 25 G3
SPK/HALE L24 148 A3
Hesketh St North
WARRW/BUR WA5 136 F1
Hesketh St AIG/SPK L17 129 L1
LEIGH WN7 81 M8
WARRW/BUR WA5 136 F1
WGNW/BIL/O WN5 68 A6
Heskin Cl KKBY L32 86 A6
MGHL L31 72 F1
RAIN/WH L35 117 K2
Heskin La ORM L39 50 F5
Heskin Rd KKBY L32 86 A6
Heskin Wk KKBY L32 86 A6
Hessle Dr HES CH60 141 H6
Hester Cl HTWN L38 70 B1
Heswall Av BEB CH63 127 L5
GOL/RIS/CU WA3 107 G5
STHEL WA9 118 D1
Heswall Mt PEN/TH CH61 126 C8
Heswall Rd GTS/LS CH66 162 F1
WLT/FAZ L9 84 D6
Hever Dr HLWD L26 132 C4
Heversham SKEL WN8 65 L3
Heward Av STHEL WA9 102 E7
Hewitson Av CLB/OSW/ST L13 98 B7
Hewitson Rd CLB/OSW/ST L13 98 B7
Hewitt Av ECCL WA10 101 L1
Hewitt's La PR/KW L34 87 G6
Hewitts Pl CLVP L2 12 F6
Hewitt St WARRS WA4 15 H9
Hewlett St CHLY/EC PR7 42 F4
WGN WN1 4 F4
Hexham Av WGNS/IIMK WN3 79 H2
Hexham Cl RAIN/WH L35 101 M7
Heyburn Rd CLB/OSW/ST L13 98 A7
Heydale Rd CALD/MH L18 130 C1
Heydean Rd CALD/MH L18 130 E4
Heydon Cl FMBY L37 58 F4
Heyes Av RNFD/HAY WA11 76 C7
RNFD/HAY WA11 90 F8
Heyescroft ORM L39 63 M7
Heyes Dr LYMM WA13 139 L3
WAL/NB CH45 110 E1
Heyes Gv RNFD/HAY WA11 76 C7
Heyes La WARRS WA4 138 A5
Heyes Mt RAIN/WH L35 117 L3
Heyes Rd WDN WA8 133 L5
WGNW/BIL/O WN5 67 G7
Heyes St EV L5 97 J8
SKEL WN8 54 E6
The Heyes WLTN L25 131 K3
Heyfield Park Rd
GTS/LS CH66 155 K6
Heyford Rd WGNW/BIL/O WN5 67 M5
Heygarth Dr
GR/UP/WCH CH49 125 M1
Heygarth Rd PS/BROM CH62 144 A8
Hey Green Rd WAV L15 114 A5
Hey Lock Cl NEWLW WA12 104 E5
Hey Rd HUY L36 116 B3
Heys Av PS/BROM CH62 143 M5
Heyscroft Rd WLTN L25 131 K3
Heysham Cl RUNC WA7 150 E7
Heysham Rd CHTN/BK PR9 25 H6
NTHLY L27 132 C1
NTHTN L30 84 C3
WGNW/BIL/O WN5 67 K6
The Heys CHLY/EC PR7 43 H3
RUNC WA7 150 A4
SKEL WN8 53 L2
Hey St WGNE/HIN WN2 80 B2
WGNNW/ST WN6 4 C3
The Hey STBRV L28 99 L6
Heythrop Dr HES CH60 141 L5
Heyville Rd BEB CH63 128 A7
Heywood Av GOL/RIS/CU WA3 92 D4
Heywood Bvd PEN/TH CH61 126 C7
Heywood Cl FMBY L37 59 G2
Hey Wood Cl NEWLW WA12 104 E5
Heywood Cl PEN/TH CH61 126 C7
Heywood Ct WAV L15 114 E4
Heywood Gdns RAIN/WH L35 117 G3
Heywood Rd GTS/LS CH66 155 M8
WAV L15 114 E5
Heyworth St EV L5 97 H8
NPK/KEN L6 13 M1
Hibbert St WDN WA8 16 E3
Hic-bibi La CHLY/EC PR7 43 G7
Hickmans Rd BIRK CH41 111 K4
Hickory Cl WARR WA1 123 G6
Hickory Gv MGHL L31 85 J3
Hickson Av MGHL L31 72 E2
Hicks Rd CSBY/WL L22 83 G4
LITH L21 83 J6
Hieland Rd WGN WN1 69 G3
Higgin's La BRSC L40 51 L1
Highacre Rd WAL/NB CH45 95 J6
Higham Av ECCL WA10 101 H2
WARRW/BUR WA5 121 H4
Higham Sq EV L5 13 K2
High Bank CHLYE PR6 33 J2
High Bank Cl CL/PREN CH43 110 F8
Highbank Dr ALL/GAR L19 130 F7
High Banks MGHL L31 72 E2
High Beeches CHLDW L16 115 H4
High Beeches Crs AIMK WN4 79 J7
High Carrs HUY L36 115 K3
High Clere Crs HUY L36 100 A8
Highcliffe Ct WGNNW/ST WN6 56 B6
Highcroft Av BEB CH63 128 C8
Highcroft Gn BEB CH63 128 C8
The Highcroft BEB CH63 128 B8
Higher Ashton WDN WA8 134 B2
Higher Bebington Rd
BEB CH63 128 A7
Higher End Pk NTHTN L30 71 M8
Higher House La CHLYE PR6 33 J2
Higher La KIRK/FR/WA PR4 27 L3
RNFD/HAY WA11 76 C6
SKEL WN8 53 L6
SKEL WN8 66 E6
WGNE/HIN WN2 69 J1
WLT/FAZ L9 84 F7
Higher Moss La FMBY L37 60 C2
Higher Parr St STHEL WA9 9 L5
Higher Rd HLWD L26 132 C7
SPK/HALE L24 132 D8
Highfield CHNE CH2 165 K1
NWD/KWIPK L33 74 B7
Highfield Av GOL/RIS/CU WA3 92 B5
WARRW/BUR WA5 120 C8
WGN WN1 5 K1
WGNNW/ST WN6 55 J7
Highfield Cl CHLYE PR6 44 C6
NSTN CH64 153 G5
WAL/EG CH44 111 J2
Highfield Crs RF/TRAN CH42 128 B4
WDN WA8 134 C3
Highfield Dr GR/UP/WCH CH49 125 M1
LYMM WA13 139 L3
RNFD/HAY WA11 89 G1
WGNNW/ST WN6 56 B6
Highfield Grange Av
WGNS/IIMK WN3 78 F3
Highfield Gv CSBY/BLUN L23 71 H8
RF/TRAN CH42 128 B4
WGNE/HIN WN2 57 L8
Highfield La BRSC L40 37 L6
GOL/RIS/CU WA3 92 E8
WARRN/WOL WA2 105 L5
Highfield Pk MGHL L31 73 H4
Highfield Pl PR/KW L34 100 F7
Highfield Rd CHLYE PR6 44 C6
CHTN/BK PR9 25 K2
CLB/OSW/ST L13 114 C1
GTS/LS CH66 155 K7
LEY/BBR PR5 29 L3
LITH L21 83 J5
LYMM WA13 139 L3
NSTN CH64 153 G5
ORM L39 51 G7
RF/TRAN CH42 128 B4
WDN WA8 16 B1
WLT/FAZ L9 97 H1
Highfield Rd North CHLY/EC PR7 32 E3
CHLYE PR6 44 C5
EP CH65 20 C4
Highfield Rd South
CHLY/EC PR7 32 E4
Highfields HES CH60 141 H4
PR/KW L34 100 E7
Highfield South RF/TRAN CH42 128 B4
Highfield St STHEL WA9 102 F5
VAUX/LVPD L3 12 F5
Highfield Vw CLB/OSW/ST L13 114 B1
Highgate Cl HES CH60 141 H4
Highgate Crs WGNNW/ST WN6 55 G6
Highgate Rd MGHL L31 72 F2
SKEL WN8 66 D6
High Gates Cl
WARRW/BUR WA5 121 G6
Highgate St EHL/KEN L7 113 J4
Highgreen Rd RF/TRAN CH42 127 L2
Highgrove Av CHLY/EC PR7 42 B1
Highgrove Pk ALL/GAR L19 130 C5
Highlands Rd RUNC WA7 18 F9
High La BRSC L40 51 J5
ORM L39 63 L5
Highmarsh Crs NEWLW WA12 91 K8
High Moor La WGNNW/ST WN6 54 C1
High Moss ORM L39 63 G2
Highoaks Rd WLTN L25 131 K4
High Pk WGNNW/ST WN6 55 L7
High Park Pl CHTN/BK PR9 25 J5
High Park Rd CHTN/BK PR9 25 J5
Highpark Rd RF/TRAN CH42 127 L2
High Park St TOX L8 113 H8
Highsands Av BRSC L40 39 J2
Highsted Gv NWD/KWIPK L33 74 A8
High St BRSC L40 40 D4
CHLY/EC PR7 32 E5
CLVP L2 12 E6
FROD/HEL WA6 160 D4
GOL/RIS/CU WA3 92 C5
NEWLW WA12 104 F1
NSTN CH64 153 G6
PR/KW L34 100 F7
PS/BROM CH62 144 A4
RUNC WA7 18 F3
SKEL WN8 64 F5
SPK/HALE L24 147 M4
WARR WA1 15 G4
WAV L15 114 B6
WGN WN1 68 F3
WGNE/HIN WN2 69 K2
WGNNW/ST WN6 56 A4
WGNS/IIMK WN3 5 K7
WLTN L25 131 J3
Hightor Rd WLTN L25 131 H2
High Vw FROD/HEL WA6 166 E1
Highville Rd CHLDW L16 114 F7
Highways Av CHLY/EC PR7 31 M4
Highwood Ct NWD/KWIPK L33 86 A1
Highwood Rd WARRS WA4 137 L6
Highwoods Cl AIMK WN4 79 J8
Hignett Av STHEL WA9 103 J3
Hilary Av DV/KA/FCH L14 115 G3
GOL/RIS/CU WA3 92 F4
Hilary Cl ANF/KKDL L4 97 L5
PR/KW L34 101 G6
WARRW/BUR WA5 119 M7
WDN WA8 135 G2
Hilary Dr GR/UP/WCH CH49 110 C7
Hilary Rd ANF/KKDL L4 97 L5
Hilberry Av CLB/OSW/ST L13 98 A8
Hilbre Av HES CH60 141 G7
WAL/EG CH44 111 J1
Hilbre Cl CHTN/BK PR9 25 G4
Hilbre Ct WKBY CH48 124 C4
Hilbre Dr EP CH65 163 L4
Hilbre Rd WKBY CH48 124 D4
Hilbre St BIRK CH41 11 G2
VAUX/LVPD L3 13 J7
Hilbre Vw WKBY CH48 124 D3
Hilcrest Rd ANF/KKDL L4 97 M4
Hilda Rd WD/CROXPK L12 99 G8
Hilda St LEIGH WN7 81 L7
Hildebrand Rd ANF/KKDL L4 97 L5
Hilden Rd WARRN/WOL WA2 122 A4
Hildyard St
WGNW/BIL/O WN5 68 B7
Hilgay Cl WGNS/IIMK WN3 78 F2
Hillam Rd WAL/NB CH45 94 F7
Hillary Av WGNW/BIL/O WN5 67 M8
Hillary Crs MGHL L31 72 F4
Hillary Dr CSBY/BLUN L23 83 J1
Hillary Rd PS/BROM CH62 144 A8

**Hillary Wk** *CSBY/BLUN* L23 ........ 83 J1 2
**Hillbank** *WGNNW/ST* WN6 .............. 56 C6
**Hillbark Rd** *WKBY* CH48 ................ 125 J3
**Hillbeck Crs** *AIMK* WN4 ................. 90 F1
**Hillberry Crs** *WARRS* WA4 ........... 137 K2
**Hillbrae Av** *RNFD/HAY* WA11 ......... 89 J5
**Hillburn Dr** *BIRK* CH41 ................. 111 G4
**Hill Cliffe Rd** *WARRS* WA4 ......... 137 K5 1
**Hill Cl** *NSTN* CH64 ......................... 153 J8
*WGNNW/ST* WN6 ............................. 55 G6
**Hill Ct** *NSTN* CH64 ......................... 153 K8
**Hill Crs** *LEIGH* WN7 ....................... 81 L5
**Hill Crest** *ANF/KKDL* L4 .................... 7 M6
**Hillcrest** *MGHL* L31 ......................... 73 H5
*SKEL* WN8 ........................................... 65 K6
*WGNE/HIN* WN2 .................................. 80 D3
**Hillcrest Av** *HUY* L36 ...................... 116 C3
**Hill Crest Av** *LEIGH* WN7 ................. 81 L5
**Hillcrest Dr** *BRSC* L40 ..................... 37 H5
*GR/UP/WCH* CH49 ............................. 125 L2
*GTS/LS* CH66 ..................................... 155 J7
**Hillcrest Rd** *CSBY/BLUN* L23 ........... 83 J1
*GTS/LS* CH66 ..................................... 155 K7
*ORM* L39 ............................................... 51 G7
**Hillcroft Rd** *WAL/EG* CH44 .............. 111 L3
*WLTN* L25 ............................................ 131 H1
**Hilldean** *SKEL* WN8 ......................... 66 E5
**Hillerton Cl** *NG/CROX* L11 ........... 98 E3 1
**Hillfield** *FROD/HEL* WA6 .................. 160 D6
*RUNC* WA7 ........................................... 150 F5
**Hillfield Dr** *PEN/TH* CH61 ................ 141 H2
**Hillfield Rd** *GTS/LS* CH66 ............... 155 M6
**Hillfoot Av** *WLTN* L25 ...................... 131 K7
**Hillfoot Cl** *CL/PREN* CH43 ............... 110 E5
**Hillfoot Crs** *WARRS* WA4 ................. 137 K6
**Hillfoot Gn** *WLTN* L25 ...................... 131 J6
**Hillfoot Rd** *WLTN* L25 ...................... 131 L7
**Hill Gv** *MOR/LEA* CH46 ..................... 110 A6
**Hillhead Rd** *BTL* L20 ........................... 7 L6
**Hill House Fold La**
*WGNNW/ST* WN6 ................................. 41 L8
**Hill House La** *WGNNW/ST* WN6 ....... 41 L8
**Hillingden Av** *HLWD* L26 ................. 132 B6
**Hillingdon Av** *PEN/TH* CH61 ............ 141 H3
**Hillingdon Rd** *WAV* L15 ............. 114 D7 3
**Hill La** *HOR/BR* BL6 ............................ 57 K2
**Hillock Cl** *BRSC* L40 .......................... 37 J6
**Hillock La** *BRSC* L40 .......................... 37 J6
*SKEL* WN8 ............................................. 53 L7
*WARR* WA1 ......................................... 122 E5
**The Hillocks** *LEY/BBR* PR5 ................ 29 K3
**Hillreed** *WGNNW/ST* WN6 ............ 68 B4 1
**Hill Rdg** *CL/PREN* CH43 .................... 110 F8
**Hill Rise Vw** *ORM* L39 ........................ 62 C4
**Hill Rd** *CL/PREN* CH43 ...................... 111 G6
**Hill Rd North** *FROD/HEL* WA6 ......... 166 F2
**Hillsboro Av** *FROD/HEL* WA6 ........... 160 E6
**Hill School Rd** *ECCL* WA10 ............... 101 J5
**Hillsdown Wy** *GTS/LS* CH66 ............ 162 E3
**Hillside Av** *AIMK* WN4 ....................... 79 H5
*ECCL* WA10 ............................................ 89 G7
*HUY* L36 ................................................. 99 L7
*NEWLW* WA12 ...................................... 104 B3
*ORM* L39 ................................................. 62 F1
*RUNC* WA7 ............................................. 18 D8
*SKEL* WN8 ............................................. 40 F8
**Hillside Cl** *BIRK* CH41 ...................... 128 A1
*BTL* L20 .................................................... 7 L6
*CHLY/EC* PR7 ................................. 31 L4 1
*FROD/HEL* WA6 ............................ 166 F1 1
*WGNS/IIMK* WN3 .................................. 78 F2
*WGNW/BIL/O* WN5 .......................... 89 M1 2
**Hillside Crs** *HUY* L36 ........................ 99 L7
**Hillside Dr** *GTS/LS* CH66 ................ 156 A6
*WLTN* L25 ............................................ 131 K2
**Hillside Gv** *WARRW/BUR* WA5 ....... 120 B8
**Hillside Rd** *BIRK* CH41 ..................... 128 A1
*CALD/MH* L18 ...................................... 114 D8
*CL/PREN* CH43 .................................... 110 F5
*FROD/HEL* WA6 ................................... 160 E6
*HES* CH60 ........................................... 141 J6
*HUY* L36 ............................................... 100 A8
*STHP* PR8 .............................................. 35 G4
*WAL/EG* CH44 ..................................... 111 G1
*WKBY* CH48 ........................................ 124 F3
**Hillside St** *NPK/KEN* L6 .................... 13 M3
**Hillside Vw** *CL/PREN* CH43 ............ 127 J2
**Hills Moss Rd** *STHEL* WA9 .............. 103 H6
**Hills Pl** *WAV* L15 ......................... 114 C6 4
**Hill St** *CHTN/BK* PR9 ............................ 3 H2
*CSBY/BLUN* L23 ..................................... 83 H2
*ECCL* WA10 .............................................. 9 H2
*RUNC* WA7 ............................................. 19 H4
*TOX* L8 .................................................. 112 F7
*WARR* WA1 ............................................. 14 E5
*WGNE/HIN* WN2 .................................... 69 M7
*WGNNW/ST* WN6 ..................................... 4 C1
**Hillsview Rd** *STHP* PR8 ..................... 47 L1
**Hilltop** *RUNC* WA7 ............................. 150 E6
**Hill Top La** *HES* CH60 ....................... 141 K5
*NSTN* CH64 .......................................... 153 K8
**Hilltop Rd** *CHLDW* L16 .................... 114 F6
*LYMM* WA13 ......................................... 139 L3
*RNFD/HAY* WA11 .................................. 88 D3
**Hill Top Rd** *WARR* WA1 .................... 122 E5
*WARRS* WA4 ......................................... 138 B3
**Hilltop Wk** *ORM* L39 ............................ 62 E2
**Hillview** *AIG/SPK* L17 ......................... 130 A3
**Hill Vw** *WDN* WA8 ............................... 118 B8
**Hill View Av** *FROD/HEL* WA6 ........... 166 C4
**Hillview Av** *WKBY* CH48 ................... 124 D2
**Hillview Cl** *FROD/HEL* WA6 ............. 160 E6
**Hill View Dr** *CHLY/EC* PR7 .................. 42 F5
*GR/UP/WCH* CH49 ............................... 110 C7
**Hillview Gdns** *WLTN* L25 .................. 131 G2
**Hillview Rd** *PEN/TH* CH61 ................ 125 L7
**Hillwood Cl** *BEB* CH63 .............. 143 J4 1
**Hilton Av** *WARRW/BUR* WA5 ..... 120 D8 3
**Hilton Cl** *BIRK* CH41 ............................ 10 F5
**Hilton Gv** *WKBY* CH48 .............. 124 C2 2
**Hilton Pl** *WGNE/HIN* WN2 ................... 57 L7
**Hilton St** *AIMK* WN4 ............................. 91 K2
*WGN* WN1 ................................................. 5 G2
*WGNS/IIMK* WN3 ...................................... 5 J8
**Hinchley Gn** *MGHL* L31 ....................... 72 D4
**Hinckley Rd** *RNFD/HAY* WA11 .............. 89 L7
**Hindburn Av** *MGHL* L31 ....................... 73 H3
**Hinderton Dr** *HES* CH60 .................... 141 H7
*WKBY* CH48 ........................................... 125 G4
**Hinderton La** *NSTN* CH64 ................. 153 J4
**Hinderton Rd** *BIRK* CH41 ................... 11 J8
*NSTN* CH64 ........................................... 153 J5
**Hindle Av** *WARRW/BUR* WA5 ... 121 H4 1
**Hindley Beech** *MGHL* L31 ............. 72 E3 3
**Hindley St** *CHLY/EC* PR7 ..................... 32 D7
**Hindlip St** *TOX* L8 ...................... 129 J2 3
**Hind Rd** *WGNW/BIL/O* WN5 ................. 67 M5
**Hind's Head Av** *WGNNW/ST* WN6 ...... 42 B7
**Hind St** *BIRK* CH41 ................................ 11 K7
**Hinson St** *BIRK* CH41 ............................ 11 K5
**Hinton Crs** *WARRS* WA4 ................... 138 A5
**Hinton Rd** *RUNC* WA7 ........................ 19 H6
**Hinton St** *LITH* L21 ................................ 83 K7
*NPK/KEN* L6 .................................... 113 L2 1
**Hitchen's Cl** *RUNC* WA7 ............ 150 F6 4
**Hobart Dr** *NWD/KWIPK* L33 ................. 74 A7
**Hobart St** *EV* L5 ..................................... 97 G7
*STHEL* WA9 ........................................... 101 M5
**Hobb La** *WARRS* WA4 ......................... 136 E8
**Hobby Ct** *RUNC* WA7 ................... 150 A7 1
**Hobcross La** *BRSC* L40 ......................... 52 C4
**Hob Hey La** *GOL/RIS/CU* WA3 ........ 106 F2
**Hob La** *CHNE* CH2 ................................ 165 J6
**Hoblyn Rd** *CL/PREN* CH43 ................. 111 G5
**Hockenhall Aly** *CLVP* L2 ....................... 12 F6
**Hockenhull Cl** *BEB* CH63 ........... 143 J3 3
**Hodder Av** *CHLY/EC* PR7 ...................... 32 D8
*MGHL* L31 ................................................ 73 H3
*WGNE/HIN* WN2 ....................................... 80 B3
**Hodder Cl** *RNFD/HAY* WA11 ......... 89 K6 6
*WGNW/BIL/O* WN5 .................................. 67 M6
**Hodder Rd** *EV* L5 .................................... 97 H7
**Hodder St** *EV* L5 ..................................... 97 H7
**Hodge Brow** *CHLYE* PR6 ........................ 45 H1
**Hodges St** *WGNNW/ST* WN6 .................. 68 C3
**Hodge St** *STHP* PR8 ................................. 3 G4
**Hodgkinson Av**
*WARRW/BUR* WA5 ................................ 121 H4
**Hodnet Dr** *AIMK* WN4 ............................. 91 L2
**Hodson Pl** *NPK/KEN* L6 ......................... 13 M1
**Hodson St** *STHP* PR8 ............................... 3 K5
*WGNS/IIMK* WN3 ........................................ 4 D6
**Hogarth St** *LITH* L21 ................... 83 J7 3
**Hoggs Hill La** *FMBY* L37 ........................ 59 G5
**Hogg's La** *CHLYE* PR6 ............................. 33 H8
**Hoghton Cl** *STHEL* WA9 ......................... 103 H5
**Hoghton Gv** *CHTN/BK* PR9 ......................... 3 J2
**Hoghton Rd** *SPK/HALE* L24 ................. 148 A4
*STHEL* WA9 ............................................. 103 G5
**Hoghton St** *CHTN/BK* PR9 ......................... 3 H3
**Holbeach Cl** *WGNE/HIN* WN2 ................. 81 G1
**Holbeck St** *ANF/KKDL* L4 ...................... 97 K7
**Holborn Av** *WGNS/IIMK* WN3 ................... 4 C9
**Holborn Ct** *WDN* WA8 ............................ 134 B2
**Holborn Dr** *ORM* L39 ................................ 62 E2
**Holborn Hl** *BIRK* CH41 ............................ 11 K9
*ORM* L39 ..................................................... 62 E2
**Holborn Sq** *BIRK* CH41 ......................... 128 A1
**Holbrook Cl** *STHEL* WA9 ........................ 102 E7
*WARRW/BUR* WA5 .................................... 120 A8
**Holcombe Av** *GOL/RIS/CU* WA3 ..... 92 E5
**Holcombe Cl**
*GR/UP/WCH* CH49 ........................... 125 M1 5
**Holcombe Gv** *CHLYE* PR6 ..................... 33 G4
**Holcroft La** *GOL/RIS/CU* WA3 .............. 107 L2
**Holden Gv** *CSBY/WL* L22 ................ 82 E3 3
**Holden Rd** *CSBY/WL* L22 ....................... 82 D3
*RAIN/WH* L35 ............................................ 116 E1
**Holden Rd East** *CSBY/WL* L22 .... 82 E3 4
**Holden St** *CHLY/EC* PR7 ................... 44 B6 3
**Holden Ter** *CSBY/WL* L22 ................ 82 E3 5
**Holding St** *WGNE/HIN* WN2 ......... 69 M7 3
**Holdsworth St** *EHL/KEN* L7 ....... 113 L3 5
**Holes La** *WARR* WA1 ............................. 122 D6
**Holford Av** *WARRW/BUR* WA5 ............ 121 H5
**Holford Wy** *NEWLW* WA12 ................... 105 H2
**Holgate** *CSBY/BLUN* L23 ........................ 71 K6
**Holgate Dr** *WGNW/BIL/O* WN5 ............. 67 G8
**Holgate Pk** *CSBY/BLUN* L23 .................. 71 K6
**Holker La** *LEY/BBR* PR5 .......................... 30 C1
**Holkham Cl** *WDN* WA8 .............................. 16 A2
**Holland Ct** *SKEL* WN8 .............................. 76 F3
**Holland Gv** *HES* CH60 ............................. 141 H4
**Holland Moss** *SKEL* WN8 .......................... 65 J8
**Holland Rd** *HLWD* L26 ............................ 132 A7
*SPK/HALE* L24 ............................................ 147 G3
*WAL/NB* CH45 ............................................... 95 L6
**Holland's La** *SKEL* WN8 ........................... 64 C3
**Holland St** *EHL/KEN* L7 ........................ 113 M2
**Holland Wy** *HLWD* L26 ........................... 132 A7
**Hollies Rd** *HLWD* L26 ............................ 132 B6
**The Hollies** *WGN* WN1 ............................... 68 F2
*WLTN* L25 ................................................... 131 G2
**Hollinbrook** *WGNNW/ST* WN6 ...... 68 B3 3
**Hollingbourne Pl**
*NG/CROX* L11 .................................... 98 C2 3
**Hollingbourne Rd** *NG/CROX* L11 .. 98 C2
**Hollingwood Cl** *AIMK* WN4 .......... 91 J2 1
**Hollingworth Cl** *WLT/FAZ* L9 .............. 97 K2
**Hollin Hey Cl** *WGNW/BIL/O* WN5 .. 89 M2
**Hollin La** *CHLYE* PR6 ................................ 33 L3
**Hollins Cl** *AIMK* WN4 ................................ 90 F1
*WAV* L15 ...................................................... 114 C5
**Hollins Dr** *WARRN/WOL* WA2 ................ 105 J7
**Hollinshead St** *CHLY/EC* PR7 ............... 32 E5
**Hollins La** *LEY/BBR* PR5 .......................... 30 E1
*WARRN/WOL* WA2 ..................................... 105 H7
**Hollocombe Rd** *NG/CROX* L11 ........... 98 E3
**Holloway** *RUNC* WA7 .................................. 18 F5
**Hollow Cft** *STBRV* L28 ................................ 99 J4
**Hollow Dr** *WARRS* WA4 ........................... 138 A4
**Hollowford La** *BRSC* L40 .......................... 52 E2
**Holly Av** *BEB* CH63 ................................. 143 H2
*NEWLW* WA12 ............................................ 104 F2
**Hollybank** *WARRS* WA4 .......................... 136 C8
**Holly Bank Gv** *STHEL* WA9 ........................ 9 L3
**Hollybank Rd** *BIRK* CH41 ........................ 11 G7
*CALD/MH* L18 ..................................... 114 A8 3
*RUNC* WA7 ................................................ 150 B5
**Hollybrook Rd** *STHP* PR8 ........................... 2 E7
**Holly Bush La** *GOL/RIS/CU* WA3 .. 123 L4
**Hollybush Sq**
*GOL/RIS/CU* WA3 ............................... 93 G4 4
**Holly Cl** *BRSC* L40 ...................................... 64 A1
*ECCL* WA10 ................................................ 101 K1
*SKEL* WN8 .............................................. 65 G4 2
*SPK/HALE* L24 .......................................... 147 M4
**Holly Ct** *FROD/HEL* WA6 ...................... 159 L8
**Holly Crs** *CHLY/EC* PR7 ............................ 43 G2
*RNFD/HAY* WA11 ......................................... 76 C8
**Hollydale Rd** *CALD/MH* L18 ...... 114 C8 3
**Holly Farm Rd** *ALL/GAR* L19 ............... 130 F7
**Hollyfield Rd** *EP* CH65 ................... 20 B4 1
*WLT/FAZ* L9 .................................................. 84 B8
**Holly Fold La** *RNFD/HAY* WA11 ........... 76 A2
**Holly Gv** *BIRK* CH41 ............................ 128 A1 3
*HUY* L36 ..................................................... 115 K3
*LITH* L21 ...................................................... 83 H7
*WARR* WA1 ................................................ 122 C6
**Holly Heath Dr** *WGN* WN1 .......... 68 D1 2
**Holly Hedge La** *WARRS* WA4 ............... 136 F7
**Holly Hey** *RAIN/WH* L35 ....................... 116 F4
**Holly La** *BRSC* L40 ..................................... 39 L2
*ORM* L39 ...................................................... 62 D1
*SKEL* WN8 ..................................................... 75 M1
**Holly Mt** *WD/CROXPK* L12 ....................... 98 C7
**Holly Pl** *MOR/LEA* CH46 ........................ 110 B6
**Holly Rd** *EHL/KEN* L7 ............................ 113 M3
*EP* CH65 ....................................................... 20 D4
*GOL/RIS/CU* WA3 ......................................... 92 E5
*RNFD/HAY* WA11 .......................................... 90 B8
*WARRW/BUR* WA5 ..................................... 120 A8
*WGNE/HIN* WN2 ............................................ 57 K8
*WGNW/BIL/O* WN5 ....................................... 68 A6
**Hollyrood** *PR/KW* L34 ............................ 100 B8
**Holly St** *BTL* L20 .......................................... 7 H3
*WGNE/HIN* WN2 ............................................ 69 H3
**Holly Ter** *WARRW/BUR* WA5 ................ 120 B8
**Hollytree Rd** *WLTN* L25 ........................ 131 K2
**Hollywood Rd** *AIG/SPK* L17 ........ 130 A2 2
**Holman Rd** *ALL/GAR* L19 ....................... 130 F7
**Holm Cottages**
*CL/PREN* CH43 ..................................... 127 H3 2
**Holmcrofts** *NSTN* CH64 ......................... 153 G8
**Holmdale Av** *CHTN/BK* PR9 ...................... 25 L1
**Holm Dr** *CHNE* CH2 ................................. 165 L2
**Holme Av** *WGN* WN1 .................................. 68 E3
**Holme Cl** *PR/KW* L34 .............................. 101 J6
**Holmefield Av** *ALL/GAR* L19 ............... 130 C5
**Holmefield Gv** *MGHL* L31 ......................... 72 E4
**Holmefield Rd** *ALL/GAR* L19 ................. 130 B4
**Holme Rd** *ECCL* WA10 ............................ 101 K3
**Holmes Ct** *GOL/RIS/CU* WA3 .... 122 E1 3
**Holmes House Av**
*WGNS/IIMK* WN3 .......................................... 78 E2
**Holmes La** *LITH* L21 ................................ 83 J6 5
**Holmes St** *TOX* L8 ................................... 113 L6
**Holme St** *EV* L5 .......................................... 96 D7
**Holmesway** *PEN/TH* CH61 ..................... 141 H1
**Holmeswood Rd**
*KIRK/FR/WA* PR4 ......................................... 27 M7
**Holme Ter** *WGN* WN1 .................................. 68 D2
**Holmfield Av** *RUNC* WA7 .......................... 19 L4
**Holmfield Dr** *GTS/LS* CH66 .................... 162 F2
**Holmfield Gv** *HUY* L36 ...................... 116 B5 4
**Holmfield Pk** *FMBY* L37 ....................... 59 G1 1
**Holm Hey Rd** *CL/PREN* CH43 ............... 127 H3
**Holm Hl** *WKBY* CH48 ................................ 124 E4
**Holmlands Crs**
*CL/PREN* CH43 ..................................... 127 G3 1
**Holmlands Dr** *CL/PREN* CH43 ...... 127 G3
**Holmlands Wy**
*CL/PREN* CH43 ..................................... 127 G3 2
**Holm La** *CL/PREN* CH43 .......................... 127 H3
**Holmleigh Rd** *WLTN* L25 ................. 115 J7 5
**Holm Oak Wy** *GTS/LS* CH66 ................ 163 G5
**Holmrook Rd** *NG/CROX* L11 ..................... 98 C3
**Holmsfield Cl** *WGNE/HIN* WN2 ... 69 J3 5
**Holmsfield Rd** *WARR* WA1 ........................ 15 K6
**Holmside Cl** *MOR/LEA* CH46 ............... 110 B5
**Holmside La** *CL/PREN* CH43 .................. 127 H3
**Holm View Cl** *CL/PREN* CH43 ............... 127 J2
**Holmville Rd** *BEB* CH63 .......................... 128 A8
**Holmway** *BEB* CH63 ................................. 128 B8
**Holmwood Av** *PEN/TH* CH61 .................. 126 E8
**Holmwood Cl** *AIMK* WN4 .................... 79 J8 6
*FMBY* L37 ....................................................... 58 F2
**Holmwood Dr** *EP* CH65 .................. 163 K3 1
*FMBY* L37 ........................................................ 58 F1
*PEN/TH* CH61 .............................................. 126 E8
**Holmwood Gdns** *FMBY* L37 ....................... 58 F1
**Holt Av** *MOR/LEA* CH46 ........................... 110 A5
*WGNW/BIL/O* WN5 ........................................ 89 M1
**Holt Coppice** *ORM* L39 .......................... 62 C6 1
**Holt Crs** *WGNW/BIL/O* WN5 .................... 89 M1
**Holt Hey** *NSTN* CH64 ................................. 153 J8
**Holt Hl** *BIRK* CH41 ....................................... 11 J9
**Holt Hill Ter** *BIRK* CH41 ............................ 11 H8
**Holt La** *NTHLY* L27 .................................... 115 M7
*RAIN/WH* L35 ............................................... 117 J1
*RUNC* WA7 ..................................................... 150 B5
**Holt Rd** *BIRK* CH41 ..................................... 128 A1
*EHL/KEN* L7 ................................................... 113 L3
**Holt St** *WGN* WN1 ............................................ 5 L4
*WGNE/HIN* WN2 .............................................. 69 L8
*WGNNW/ST* WN6 ............................................. 68 B4
*WGNS/IIMK* WN3 ............................................. 79 J1
*WGNW/BIL/O* WN5 ................................... 66 F8 5
**Holtswell Cl** *GOL/RIS/CU* WA3 ...... 93 G4 5
**Holyhead Cl** *WARRW/BUR* WA5 .. 120 F2
**Holyrood** *CSBY/BLUN* L23 .......................... 82 C1
**Holyrood Av** *WDN* WA8 ............................ 134 C1
**Holywell Cl** *NSTN* CH64 .......................... 152 D4
*STHEL* WA9 ............................................ 102 F7 5
**Home Farm Cl**
*GR/UP/WCH* CH49 ............................... 126 E3 2
**Home Farm Rd**
*GR/UP/WCH* CH49 ....................................... 126 D3
*PR/KW* L34 ........................................................ 99 L3
**Homer Rd** *PR/KW* L34 .................................. 99 L2
**Homerton Rd** *NPK/KEN* L6 ............ 113 M2 2
**Homestall Rd** *NG/CROX* L11 ..................... 98 C3
**Homestead Av** *NTHTN* L30 ......................... 84 D2
*RNFD/HAY* WA11 ........................................ 91 G6 5
**Homestead Cl** *HUY* L36 ..................... 116 C2 1
**Homestead Ms** *WKBY* CH48 ....... 124 D3 2
**Homeway** *FROD/HEL* WA6 ................. 166 D3 1
**Honeybourne Dr** *RAIN/WH* L35 .. 101 J7
**Honey Hall Rd** *HLWD* L26 ......................... 132 A7
**Honeys Green Cl**
*WD/CROXPK* L12 .................................... 98 F8 2
**Honey's Green La**
*WD/CROXPK* L12 ............................................ 98 F8
**Honey St** *RAIN/WH* L35 ..................... 101 L6 3
**Honeysuckle Av**
*WGNNW/ST* WN6 ............................................. 68 B2
**Honeysuckle Cl** *GTS/LS* CH66 ...... 163 H5
*HLWD* L26 ...................................................... 131 M3 4
*WDN* WA8 .................................................... 134 D1 7
**Honeysuckle Dr** *WLT/FAZ* L9 ................. 97 K2
**Honister Av** *RNFD/HAY* WA11 ................. 89 L5
*WARRN/WOL* WA2 ........................................ 121 L3
**Honister Cl** *NTHLY* L27 ........................... 132 C2
**Honister Gv** *RUNC* WA7 ........................... 150 A8
**Honister Rd** *WGNW/BIL/O* WN5 .... 67 K7
**Honiston Av** *RAIN/WH* L35 ...................... 117 K1
**Honiton Cl** *LEIGH* WN7 ............................... 81 M3
**Honiton Rd** *AIG/SPK* L17 .......................... 130 A5
**Honiton Wy** *WARRW/BUR* WA5 .. 136 A1
**Hood La** *WARRW/BUR* WA5 ...................... 120 E8
**Hood La North**
*WARRW/BUR* WA5 ......................................... 120 E7
**Hood Rd** *WDN* WA8 ....................................... 16 B2
**Hood St** *BTL* L20 .............................................. 6 D1
*CLVPS* L1 .......................................................... 13 G6
*WAL/EG* CH44 ...................................... 111 M2 7
**Hookstone Dr** *GTS/LS* CH66 ................... 155 L7
**Hook St** *WGNE/HIN* WN2 ............................... 5 M5
**Hoole La** *CHTN/BK* PR9 .................................. 23 J7
**Hoole Rd** *GR/UP/WCH* CH49 ................... 126 D2
**Hoolpool La** *FROD/HEL* WA6 .................... 159 H8
**Hooton Gn** *GTS/LS* CH66 ............................ 155 J3
**Hooton La** *GTS/LS* CH66 ............................. 155 K4
**Hooton Rd** *NSTN* CH64 ................................ 154 D4
*WLT/FAZ* L9 ....................................................... 84 D6
**Hooton Wy** *GTS/LS* CH66 ............................ 155 H3
**Hope Crs** *WGNNW/ST* WN6 ............................ 55 K7
**Hope Cft** *GTS/LS* CH66 ................................. 163 H3
**Hope Farm Rd** *GTS/LS* CH66 .................... 163 G4
**Hope Pl** *CLVPS* L1 .................................... 13 K9 4
**Hope Sq** *CHTN/BK* PR9 ..................................... 3 K3
**Hope St** *AIMK* WN4 ........................................ 79 M8
*CHLY/EC* PR7 ..................................................... 32 E4
*CHLYE* PR6 ............................................. 44 D5 4
*CHTN/BK* PR9 ........................................................ 3 K3
*CLVPS* L1 ........................................................... 113 H6
*NEWLW* WA12 .................................................... 104 D2
*PR/KW* L34 ........................................................ 100 F7
*TOX* L8 ................................................................. 113 H5
*WAL/NB* CH45 ..................................................... 95 K5
*WGNE/HIN* WN2 .................................................. 80 A1
**Hope St North** *HOR/BR* BL6 .......................... 45 K8
**Hope Wy** *TOX* L8 ................................. 113 H5 14
**Hopfield Rd** *MOR/LEA* CH46 .................... 110 B5
**Hopkins Cl** *ECCL* WA10 ..................................... 8 A4
**Hopwood Cl** *GOL/RIS/CU* WA3 .. 93 H5 4
**Hopwood Crs** *RNFD/HAY* WA11 ...... 76 C8
**Hopwood St** *EV* L5 ........................................... 96 F8
*WARR* WA1 .............................................................. 15 G4
**Horace St** *ECCL* WA10 ........................................ 8 C4
**Horbury Gdns** *GTS/LS* CH66 ......................... 155 L8
**Hornbeam Av** *GTS/LS* CH66 .......................... 163 H4
**Hornbeam Cl** *MOR/LEA* CH46 .. 109 K5 5
*RNFD/HAY* WA11 ....................................... 90 B8 3
*RUNC* WA7 ............................................................ 150 E5
**Hornbeam Crs** *AIMK* WN4 ................................ 91 K2
**Hornbeam Rd** *HLWD* L26 ................................ 132 C6
*WLT/FAZ* L9 ............................................................ 97 L2
**Hornby Av** *BTL* L20 ................................................. 6 F1
*PS/BROM* CH62 .................................................... 143 M4
**Hornby Bvd** *LITH* L21 ............................................. 83 K7
**Hornby Cha** *MGHL* L31 ........................................ 72 F6
**Hornby Cl** *WLT/FAZ* L9 .......................................... 97 H1
**Hornby Crs** *STHEL* WA9 ...................................... 118 F1
**Hornby La** *CALD/MH* L18 .................................... 114 F8
*WARRN/WOL* WA2 ..................................................... 105 J7
**Hornby Pk** *CALD/MH* L18 ..................................... 114 F8
**Hornby Pl** *WLT/FAZ* L9 ............................................ 84 C8
**Hornby Rd** *BTL* L20 ..................................................... 6 F1
*CHLYE* PR6 ................................................................ 33 G7 1
*CHTN/BK* PR9 ................................................................ 25 J1
*PS/BROM* CH62 ........................................................ 143 L4
*WLT/FAZ* L9 .................................................................... 97 H1
**Hornby Steet** *WGN* WN1 .............................................. 68 E3
**Hornby St** *BIRK* CH41 ................................................... 11 L5
*CSBY/BLUN* L23 ...................................................... 83 G1 1
*LITH* L21 ....................................................................... 83 J7 4
**Hornby Wk** *EV* L5 ............................................................ 12 F1
**Horncastle Cl**
*GOL/RIS/CU* WA3 ........................................................... 93 H5 5
**Hornchurch Dr** *CHLY/EC* PR7 ....................................... 32 C5
**Horne Gv** *WGNS/IIMK* WN3 ............................................. 68 B8
**Horne St** *NPK/KEN* L6 .................................................. 113 K1
**Hornhouse La** *NWD/KWIPK* L33 ..................................... 86 D5
**Hornsey Gv** *WGNS/IIMK* WN3 ........................................... 78 F2
**Hornsey Rd** *ANF/KKDL* L4 ................................................. 97 K7
**Hornspit La** *WD/CROXPK* L12 ............................................ 98 C5
**Horridge Av** *NEWLW* WA12 ................................................. 91 L8
**Horringford Rd** *ALL/GAR* L19 ............................................ 130 B5
**Horrobin La** *CHLYE* PR6 ........................................................ 44 E5
**Horrocks Av** *ALL/GAR* L19 .................................................. 130 F7
**Horrocks Cl** *HUY* L36 ..................................................... 115 M1 3
**Horrocks La** *WARR* WA1 ........................................................ 14 E6
**Horrocks Rd** *HUY* L36 ..................................................... 115 M2 1
**Horrocks St** *LEIGH* WN7 ........................................................... 93 J1
**Horseman Pl** *WAL/EG* CH44 ............................................ 112 A3 10
**Horsemarket St** *WARR* WA1 .................................................... 14 E5
**Horseshoe Crs**
*WARRN/WOL* WA2 ................................................................. 122 A2 3
**Horseshoe Dr** *AIN/FAZ* L10 ........................................................ 85 K6
**Horsfall Gv** *TOX* L8 .................................................................. 129 G1 2
**Horsfall St** *TOX* L8 ......................................................................... 129 G1
**Horsham Gv** *WGNE/HIN* WN2 .......................................... 69 H3 5
**Horstone Crs** *GTS/LS* CH66 ........................................................ 163 H3
**Horstone Gdns** *GTS/LS* CH66 ................................................... 163 H3
**Horstone Rd** *GTS/LS* CH66 ........................................................... 163 H3
**Horton St** *WGNNW/ST* WN6 ................................................................ 68 A3
**Horwood Av** *RAIN/WH* L35 .............................................................. 117 K1
**Horwood Cl** *NG/CROX* L11 ........................................................ 98 E3 2
**Hoscar Moss Rd** *BRSC* L40 ................................................................. 52 E2
**Hoscote Pk** *WKBY* CH48 ...................................................................... 124 C3
**Hose Side Rd** *WAL/NB* CH45 ..................................................................... 95 J7
**Hospital St** *ECCL* WA10 ............................................................................... 9 H3
**Hospital Wy** *RUNC* WA7 ...................................................................... 150 B6
**Hosta Cl** *NWD/KWIPK* L33 ................................................................. 73 M8 5
**Hostock Cl** *RAIN/WH* L35 ....................................................................... 116 F3 3
**Hotel St** *NEWLW* WA12 ....................................................................... 104 D2 7
**Hotham St** *VAUX/LVPD* L3 ..................................................................... 13 J6
**Hothfield Rd** *WAL/EG* CH44 .......................................................... 111 M2 8
**Hotspur St** *BTL* L20 ........................................................................................ 96 E5
**Hough Green Rd** *WDN* WA8 ............................................................................ 133 J3
**Hough's La** *WARRS* WA4 .................................................................................... 137 J7
**Houghton Av** *WGNW/BIL/O* WN5 .. 68 A3
**Houghton Cl** *NEWLW* WA12 ..... 104 D2 8
*WDN* WA8 ........................................... 134 E3
**Houghton Cft** *WDN* WA8 ................... 117 L7
**Houghton La** *WGNNW/ST* WN6 ......... 55 H7
**Houghton Rd**
*GR/UP/WCH* CH49 .............................. 126 D2
**Houghton's La** *ECCL* WA10 .................. 88 B6
*SKEL* WN8 ................................................. 65 L4
**Houghtons Rd** *SKEL* WN8 ..................... 65 J2
**Houghton St** *CHLYE* PR6 .............. 32 F5 6
*CLVPS* L1 .................................................... 13 H7
*NEWLW* WA12 ................................. 104 D2 9
*PR/KW* L34 ............................................. 100 F7
*RAIN/WH* L35 ................................ 117 L2 4
*WARRN/WOL* WA2 .................................. 14 E3
*WDN* WA8 ................................................ 134 F3
**Houghwood Gra** *AIMK* WN4 ............... 91 H2
**Hougoumont Av** *CSBY/WL* L22 ...... 83 G4
**Hougoumont Gv**
*CSBY/WL* L22 ................................ 83 G4 3
**Houlding St** *ANF/KKDL* L4 ........... 97 J7 6
**Houlgrave Rd** *EV* L5 ................................ 96 E8
**Houlston Rd** *KKBY* L32 ........................... 85 K3
**Houlton St** *EHL/KEN* L7 ............ 113 L3 6
**Housley Cl** *WGNS/IIMK* WN3 .................. 79 J1
**The Hove** *RUNC* WA7 .............................. 150 F7
**Howard Av** *PS/BROM* CH62 .............. 143 M5
**Howard Cl** *LITH* L21 .................................. 83 L3
*MGHL* L31 ......................................... 73 H4 2
**Howard Dr** *ALL/GAR* L19 ..................... 130 C6
**Howard Florey Av** *NTHTN* L30 ........ 84 B1
**Howard Rd** *CHLY/EC* PR7 ......................... 32 D8
*GOL/RIS/CU* WA3 ...................................... 107 J3
**Howard's La** *ECCL* WA10 ......................... 101 G1
*WGNW/BIL/O* WN5 ....................................... 67 H6
**Howards Rd** *PEN/TH* CH61 ............ 126 D7 3
**Howard St** *ECCL* WA10 ..................... 101 L5 4
*WGNW/BIL/O* WN5 ......................................... 67 L8
**Howards Wy** *NSTN* CH64 ........................ 153 J7
**Howbeck Cl** *CL/PREN* CH43 .................. 111 H7
**Howbeck Dr** *CL/PREN* CH43 ................... 111 H7
**Howbeck Rd** *CL/PREN* CH43 ................... 111 H8
**Howden Dr** *HUY* L36 ................................... 115 J3
*WGNS/IIMK* WN3 ............................................ 79 J1
**Howe Gv** *CHLY/EC* PR7 ............................... 32 C6
**Howell Dr** *GR/UP/WCH* CH49 ................ 125 M3
**Howell Rd** *PS/BROM* CH62 ........... 128 C6 3
**Howells Av** *GTS/LS* CH66 ......................... 162 E2
**Howells Cl** *MGHL* L31 ......................... 72 F3 2
**Howe St** *BTL* L20 ............................................. 6 E8
**Howey La** *FROD/HEL* WA6 ......................... 160 C6
**Howey Ri** *FROD/HEL* WA6 ......................... 160 C6
**Howley La** *WARR* WA1 .................................. 15 J6
**Howson Rd** *WARRN/WOL* WA2 .... 121 L3
**Howson St** *RF/TRAN* CH42 ...................... 128 B3
**Hoylake Cl** *LEIGH* WN7 ................................ 93 M3
*RUNC* WA7 ....................................................... 150 E7
**Hoylake Gv** *STHEL* WA9 .................. 118 E1 10
**Hoylake Rd** *BIRK* CH41 .............................. 111 G4
*CL/PREN* CH43 ................................................. 110 F4
*MOR/LEA* CH46 ............................................... 109 K6
**Hoyle Rd** *HOY* CH47 ...................................... 108 D5
**Hoyle St** *WARRW/BUR* WA5 ......................... 14 B2
**Huddlestone Cl**
*GR/UP/WCH* CH49 ................................ 126 E2 2
**Huddleston Rd** *WAV* L15 ............................ 114 D4
**Hudson Cl** *WARRW/BUR* WA5 .................. 120 F5
**Hudson Rd** *MGHL* L31 ...................................... 72 F6
*MOR/LEA* CH46 ................................................. 110 C1
**Hudswell Cl** *NTHTN* L30 ................................. 84 D4
**Hughenden Rd** *CLB/OSW/ST* L13 .. 98 B8
**Hughes Av** *RAIN/WH* L35 ............................... 116 F1
*WARRN/WOL* WA2 ............................................... 121 M3
**Hughes Cl** *EHL/KEN* L7 .................................. 113 L4 1
**Hughes Dr** *BTL* L20 ......................................... 84 A7
**Hughes La** *CL/PREN* CH43 ............................ 127 K2
**Hughes Pl** *WARRN/WOL* WA2 .. 121 M3 7
**Hughes St** *ALL/GAR* L19 ............................... 130 E8
*NPK/KEN* L6 ..................................................... 113 J2 8
*STHEL* WA9 ............................................................. 102 F5
*WARRS* WA4 ................................................................ 15 H9
**Hughestead Gv** *ALL/GAR* L19 .. 130 D7 2
**Hughson St** *TOX* L8 ................................................ 113 G8
**Hullet Cl** *WGNNW/ST* WN6 ......................................... 55 G5
**Hulme Gv** *LEIGH* WN7 ................................................... 81 L7
**Hulme Rd** *LEIGH* WN7 .................................................... 81 L7
**Hulme St** *STHP* PR8 ............................................................ 2 F4
**Hulmewood** *BEB* CH63 ...................................... 128 C6 4
**Hulton Av** *RAIN/WH* L35 ................................................ 117 H1
**Humber Cl** *ANF/KKDL* L4 ..................................................... 97 G5
*WDN* WA8 ................................................................................ 135 H2
**Humber Crs** *STHEL* WA9 .................................................... 102 E8
**Humber Pl** *WGNW/BIL/O* WN5 ............................................. 67 L6
**Humber Rd** *GTS/LS* CH66 ..................................................... 163 H3
*WARRN/WOL* WA2 ......................................................................... 122 A3
**Hume Ct** *HOY* CH47 ....................................................................... 108 E5
**Hume St** *WARR* WA1 ............................................................................ 15 J3
**Humphrey's Cl** *RUNC* WA7 ............................................... 150 F6 5
**Humphreys Hey** *CSBY/BLUN* L23 .. 71 K6
**Humphrey St** *BTL* L20 ................................................................ 83 L7
**Huncote Av** *RNFD/HAY* WA11 ...................................................... 89 M7
**Hunslett Rd** *WLT/FAZ* L9 ..................................................................... 84 D7
**Hunstanton Cl**
*GR/UP/WCH* CH49 ....................................................................... 110 C6 2
**Hunt Cl** *WARRW/BUR* WA5 ........................................................... 120 D5 4
**Hunter Av** *WARRN/WOL* WA2 .......................................................... 121 K3
**Hunter Rd** *WGNW/BIL/O* WN5 ............................................................ 68 A4
**Hunters Ct** *FROD/HEL* WA6 ................................................................... 166 F1
*RUNC* WA7 ............................................................................................ 150 A7 3
**Hunter's La** *KIRK/FR/WA* PR4 ...................................................................... 27 K2
*WAV* L15 ......................................................................................................... 114 C6
**Hunter St** *STHEL* WA9 ................................................................................... 9 L8
*VAUX/LVPD* L3 ..................................................................................................... 13 H5
**Hunters Wy** *NSTN* CH64 ................................................................................. 152 E5
**Huntingdon Cl**
*MOR/LEA* CH46 ........................................................................................ 109 K5 6
**Huntingdon Gv** *MGHL* L31 ............................................................................ 72 E1 1
**Huntley Gv** *STHEL* WA9 ....................................................................................... 102 E6
**Huntley St** *WARRW/BUR* WA5 ............................................................................... 136 E1
**Huntly Rd** *NPK/KEN* L6 ................................................................................................. 113 L2
**Hunt Rd** *MGHL* L31 .............................................................................................................. 72 F4
*RNFD/HAY* WA11 .................................................................................................................... 91 G7
**Hunts Cross Av** *WLTN* L25 .................................................................................................... 131 K2
**Hunts La** *WARRS* WA4 ............................................................................................................ 138 B3
**Huntsman Wd** *WD/CROXPK* L12 .. 99 G5
**Hunt St** *WGN* WN1 ........................................................................................................................... 5 J5
**Hurford Av** *EP* CH65 ........................................................................................................................ 163 H1

Hurley Cl WARRW/BUR WA5 .... 120 E8
Hurlingham Rd ANF/KKDL L4 .... 97 L3
Hurlston Dr ORM L39 ......... 51 G6
Hurlston Av SKEL WN8 ........ 65 L5
Hurlston La BRSC L40 ........ 50 D4
Hurn Gv WLT/FAZ L9 .......... 32 C6
Hurrell Rd BIRK CH41 ........ 110 F4
Hursley Rd WLT/FAZ L9 ....... 98 A1
Hurst Bank RF/TRAN CH42 ..... 128 B5
Hurst Brook CHLY/EC PR7 ..... 43 H4
Hurst Gn BRSC L40 ........... 40 E3
Hurstlyn Rd CALD/MH L18 ..... 130 E4
Hurst Park Cl HUY L36 ....... 116 C1
Hurst Park Dr HUY L36 ....... 116 C2
Hurst Rd MGHL L31 ........... 73 C6
Hurst's La ORM L39 .......... 74 C3
Hurst St CLVPS L1 ........... 112 F5
  WDN WA8 ................... 149 J1
  WGNE/HIN WN2 .............. 69 L7
Huskisson St CLVPS L1 ....... 113 H6
Hutchinson St NPK/KEN L6 .... 113 J2
  WDN WA8 ................... 16 C8
Hutchinson Wk NPK/KEN L6 ... 113 J2
Hut La CHLYE PR6 ............ 44 D1
Huttfield Rd SPK/HALE L24 ... 147 J1
Hutton Ct SKEL WN8 .......... 64 F4
Hutton Rd SKEL WN8 .......... 64 F4
Hutton St WGN WN1 ........... 56 C2
Huxley Av ECCL WA10 ......... 89 C7
Huxley Pl WGNS/IIMK WN3 .... 68 C8
Huxley St CLB/OSW/ST L13 .... 98 A6
Huyton Av ECCL WA10 ......... 89 G7
Huyton Brook HUY L36 ........ 116 B5
Huyton Church Rd HUY L36 ... 116 A3
Huyton Hall Crs HUY L36 ..... 116 A3
Huyton Hey Rd HUY L36 ....... 116 B3
Huyton House Cl HUY L36 ..... 115 K1
Huyton House Rd HUY L36 .... 115 K1
Huyton La HUY L36 ........... 116 B2
Huyton Rd CHLY/EC PR7 ....... 44 C7
Hyacinth Cl RNFD/HAY WA11 .. 91 H7
Hyatt Crs WGNNW/ST WN6 .... 55 L2
Hyde Cl EP CH65 ............. 163 H1
  RUNC WA7 .................. 149 M7
  WGNS/IIMK WN3 ............. 68 C8
Hyde Rd CSBY/WL L22 ......... 82 F4
Hyde's Brow RNFD/HAY WA11 .. 76 C5
Hydro Av WKBY CH48 .......... 124 D4
Hygeia St NPK/KEN L6 ........ 113 J1
Hylton Av WAL/EG CH44 ....... 111 J1
Hylton Ct EP CH65 ........... 164 A3
Hylton Rd ALL/GAR L19 ....... 130 F5
Hyslop St TOX L8 ............ 113 G7
Hythe Av LITH L21 ........... 85 L5
Hythe Av STHP PR8 ........... 36 A2
Hythedale Cl AIG/SPK L17 .... 129 L3

**I**

Ibbotson's La AIG/SPK L17 .... 130 A1
Ibstock Rd BTL L20 .......... 83 K8
Iffley Cl GR/UP/WCH CH49 .... 109 M8
Ikin Cl CL/PREN CH43 ........ 110 E4
Ilchester Rd BIRK CH41 ...... 111 H4
  CHLDW L16 ................. 115 C4
  WAL/EG CH44 ............... 111 M2
Ilex Av WARRN/WOL WA2 ....... 105 C7
Ilford Av CSBY/BLUN L23 ..... 70 F8
  WAL/EG CH44 ............... 111 K3
Ilford St VAUX/LVPD L3 ...... 13 K5
Ilfracombe Rd STHEL WA9 ..... 102 E3
Iliad St EV L5 .............. 13 J2
Ilkley Av CHTN/BK PR9 ....... 22 E7
Ilsley Cl GR/UP/WCH CH49 ... 126 B1
Imber Rd KKBY L32 ........... 86 B5
Imison St WLT/FAZ L9 ........ 97 H2
Imison Wy WLT/FAZ L9 ........ 7 M5
Imperial Av WAL/NB CH45 ..... 95 J7
Imperial Ms EP CH65 ......... 20 B2
Imrie St ANF/KKDL L4 ........ 97 H3
Ince Av ANF/KKDL L4 ......... 97 K5
  CSBY/BLUN L23 ............. 70 E8
  LITH L21 .................. 83 K6
  PS/BROM CH62 .............. 155 G2
Ince Cl CL/PREN CH43 ........ 127 H1
Ince Crs FMBY L37 ........... 58 F2
Ince Green La WGNE/HIN WN2 .. 5 M6
  WGNS/IIMK WN3 ............. 5 K8
Ince Gv CL/PREN CH43 ........ 127 H2
Ince Hall Av WGNE/HIN WN2 ... 5 M4
Ince La CHLY/EC PR7 ......... 30 E1
  CHNE CH2 .................. 165 K1
  CSBY/BLUN L23 ............. 71 H4
Incemore Rd CALD/MH L18 .... 130 D4
Ince Orchards CHNE CH2 ..... 165 K1
Ince Rd CSBY/BLUN L23 ....... 71 J6
Inchcape Rd CHLDW L16 ...... 115 C4
  WAL/NB CH45 ............... 94 F8
Inchfield SKEL WN8 .......... 65 L3
Index St ANF/KKDL L4 ........ 97 H4
Ingestre Rd CL/PREN CH43 .... 127 J2
Ingham Rd WDN WA8 .......... 134 B1
Ingleborough Rd
  RF/TRAN CH42 .............. 127 M3
Ingleby Cl WGNNW/ST WN6 .... 55 M3
Ingleby Rd PS/BROM CH62 .... 128 D5
  WAL/EG CH44 ............... 111 J2
Ingledene Rd CALD/MH L18 ... 114 F8
Ingle Gn CSBY/BLUN L23 ...... 70 C8
Inglegreen HES CH60 ......... 141 J5
Ingleholme Gdns PR/KW L34 .. 101 J6
Ingleholme Rd CALD/MH L18 .. 130 C4
Inglemere Rd RF/TRAN CH42 .. 128 A4
Ingle Ms CHLYE PR6 .......... 32 F4
Inglemoss Dr RNFD/HAY WA11.. 88 D4
Inglenook Rd
  WARRW/BUR WA5 ............ 136 B1
Ingleton Cl
  GR/UP/WCH CH49 ........... 125 M1
  NEWLW WA12 ............... 104 D1
Ingleton Dr RNFD/HAY WA11 .. 89 K4
Ingleton Gn KKBY L32 ........ 86 B3
Ingleton Gv RUNC WA7 ....... 149 M8
Ingleton Rd CALD/MH L18 .... 114 B8
  KKBY L32 .................. 86 B5
  STHP PR8 .................. 36 A2

Inglewhite SKEL WN8 ......... 65 J3
Inglewhite Av WGN WN1 ...... 68 E3
Inglewhite Crs WGN WN1 ..... 68 E3
Inglewood WD/CROXPK L12 .... 99 J3
Inglewood Av
  MOR/LEA CH46 ............. 109 M6
  WGN WN1 .................. 5 J5
Inglewood Cl
  GOL/RIS/CU WA3 ........... 107 K7
Inglewood Rd RNFD/HAY WA11.. 88 D4
Inglis Rd WLT/FAZ L9 ........ 84 D5
Ingoe Cl KKBY L32 ........... 85 K4
Ingoe La KKBY L32 ........... 85 K5
Ingram SKEL WN8 ............. 65 K4
Ingram St WGNE/HIN WN2 ..... 80 C2
  WGNNW/ST WN6 ............. 68 B4
Ingrave Rd ANF/KKDL L4 ...... 97 L3
Ingrow Rd NPK/KEN L6 ........ 113 K2
Inigo Rd CLB/OSW/ST L13 .... 114 D1
Inley Cl BEB CH63 ........... 143 H3
Inley Rd BEB CH63 ........... 143 H3
Inman Av STHEL WA9 .......... 103 K3
Inman Rd GR/UP/WCH CH49 .... 110 A7
  LITH L21 .................. 83 K6
Inner Central Rd SPK/HALE L24 . 132 B8
Inner Forum NG/CROX L11 .... 98 A2
Inner South Rd SPK/HALE L24 . 147 H1
Inner West Rd SPK/HALE L24 . 147 G1
Innisfree Cl GTS/LS CH66 .... 155 L8
Insall Rd CLB/OSW/ST L13 .... 114 D4
  WARRN/WOL WA2 ............ 122 B3
Inskip SKEL WN8 ............. 65 J3
Inskip Rd CHTN/BK PR9 ....... 25 J1
Intake Cl NSTN CH64 ......... 154 C5
  ORM L39 ................... 75 J1
Inveresk Ct CL/PREN CH43 .... 111 G7
Invincible Cl NTHTN L30 ..... 84 A5
Invincible Wy NG/CROX L11 ... 85 L7
Inward Dr WGNNW/ST WN6 .... 55 J5
Inwood Rd ALL/GAR L19 ...... 130 E6
Iona Cl WD/CROXPK L12 ...... 99 J2
Ionic Rd CLB/OSW/ST L13 .... 114 C1
Ionic St LITH L21 ........... 83 H6
  RF/TRAN CH42 ............. 128 B3
Irby Av WAL/EG CH44 ......... 111 J1
Irby Cl GTS/LS CH66 ......... 163 G1
Irby Rd ANF/KKDL L4 ......... 97 K5
  PEN/TH CH61 .............. 125 M8
Irbyside Rd WKBY CH48 ...... 125 K4
Iredale Crs WGNNW/ST WN6 .. 56 B6
Ireland Rd RNFD/HAY WA11 ... 90 E7
  SPK/HALE L24 ............. 148 A4
Ireland St WARRN/WOL WA2 .. 121 K5
  WDN WA8 .................. 134 F3
Irene Av RNFD/HAY WA11 ..... 89 L6
Irene Rd CHLDW L16 ......... 114 E7
Ireton St ANF/KKDL L4 ....... 97 H3
Iris Av BIRK CH41 ........... 111 H5
Iris St WDN WA8 ............. 133 L3
Irlam Dr KKBY L32 ........... 86 A3
Irlam Pl BTL L20 ............ 6 E3
Irlam Rd BTL L20 ............ 6 E3
  RUNC WA7 .................. 19 K2
Irlam St BIRK CH41 .......... 11 L6
Ironbridge Vw TOX L8 ........ 12 E5
Ironmonger La WGNS/IIMK WN3.. 4 E6
Ironside Rd HUY L36 ......... 115 M1
Irton Rd CHTN/BK PR9 ........ 25 G5
Irvin Av CHTN/BK PR9 ........ 22 E8
Irvine Rd RF/TRAN CH42 ...... 127 M3
Irvine St EHL/KEN L7 ........ 113 L4
Irving St CHTN/BK PR9 ....... 24 D4
Irwell SKEL WN8 ............. 65 J2
Irwell Cl AIG/SPK L17 ....... 130 A2
Irwell La AIG/SPK L17 ....... 130 A2
  RUNC WA7 .................. 19 K2
Irwell Pl WCNW/BIL/O WN5 ... 67 L7
Irwell Rd WARRS WA4 ......... 137 K3
  WGNW/BIL/O WN5 ........... 67 H6
Irwell St WDN WA8 ........... 149 J1
Irwin Rd STHEL WA9 .......... 102 E6
Isaac St TOX L8 ............. 129 H1
Isabel Gv CLB/OSW/ST L13 ... 98 A6
Isherwood Cl
  WARRN/WOL WA2 ............ 122 B2
Island Pl ALL/GAR L19 ....... 130 E7
Island Rd ALL/GAR L19 ....... 130 E7
Island Rd South ALL/GAR L19 . 130 E7
Islands Brow RNFD/HAY WA11.. 89 K7
Islay Cl EP CH65 ............ 163 L5
Isleham Cl CALD/MH L18 ..... 130 E5
Isleworth Dr CHLY/EC PR7 ... 32 D6
Islington CSBY/BLUN L23 ..... 70 F8
  VAUX/LVPD L3 ............. 13 J5
Islip Cl PEN/TH CH61 ........ 125 M6
Ismay Dr WAL/EG CH44 ....... 95 M8
Ismay Rd LITH L21 ........... 83 J4
Ismay St ANF/KKDL L4 ........ 97 H4
Ivanhoe Av GOL/RIS/CU WA3 .. 92 F4
Ivanhoe Rd AIG/SPK L17 ..... 129 L1
  CSBY/BLUN L23 ............. 82 G2
Ivatt Wy EHL/KEN L7 ......... 113 L4
Iveagh Cl RUNC WA7 ......... 150 C6
Iver Cl WDN WA8 ............. 117 J7
Ivernia Rd ANF/KKDL L4 ...... 97 K3
Ivor Rd WAL/EG CH44 ......... 95 J4
Ivory Dr NWD/KWIPK L33 ..... 74 A8
Ivy Av ALL/GAR L19 ......... 130 C6
  BEB CH63 ................. 128 A8
  NEWLW WA12 ............... 104 E3
Ivybridge SKEL WN8 ......... 65 L5
Ivychurch Ms RUNC WA7 ..... 149 M3
Ivy Ct STHEL WA9 ........... 9 L5
Ivydale SKEL WN8 ........... 65 K3
Ivydale Rd CALD/MH L18 ..... 130 B1
  RF/TRAN CH42 ............. 128 A2
  WLT/FAZ L9 ............... 97 L1
Ivy Farm Dr NSTN CH64 ...... 153 H7
Ivy Farm Gdns
  GOL/RIS/CU WA3 ........... 106 F1
Ivy Farm Rd RAIN/WH L35 .... 117 K1
Ivy House Rd
  GOL/RIS/CU WA3 ........... 92 F4
Ivyhurst Cl ALL/GAR L19 ..... 130 B5
Ivy La MOR/LEA CH46 ........ 110 A4
Ivy Leigh CLB/OSW/ST L13 ... 98 A8
Ivy Rd GOL/RIS/CU WA3 ...... 92 D5
  WARR WA1 ................. 123 G6
Ivy St BIRK CH41 ........... 11 L6
  RUNC WA7 .................. 19 C5
  STHP PR8 .................. 3 M6
  WGNNW/ST WN6 ............. 4 D4

**J**

Jack Mcbain Ct VAUX/LVPD L3 . 12 E2
Jack's Brow PR/KW L34 ....... 100 B3
Jacksfield Wy ALL/GAR L19 ... 130 B6
Jacksmere La BRSC L40 ....... 36 D5
Jackson Av GOL/RIS/CU WA3 .. 107 G2
  WARR WA1 ................. 122 B6
Jackson Cl BEB CH63 ......... 128 B5
  ORM L39 .................. 49 H8
  RAIN/WH L35 .............. 117 M4
Jackson Rd CHLY/EC PR7 ..... 32 C8
Jackson's Common La BRSC L40 . 50 C4
Jackson's La BRSC L40 ....... 41 G6
Jackson St ALL/GAR L19 ...... 130 E7
  BIRK CH41 ................ 11 K7
  CHLY/EC PR7 .............. 32 F7
  RNFD/HAY WA11 ............ 90 C6
  STHEL WA9 ................ 9 J3
  WARRW/BUR WA5 ............ 104 A7
  WGNE/HIN WN2 ............. 69 J6
Jacobs Cl LITH L21 .......... 83 K7
  WGNE/HIN WN2 ............. 69 M7
Jacqueline Dr HUY L36 ....... 116 C1
Jade Cl NWD/KWIPK L33 ...... 86 B2
Jamaica St CLVPS L1 ......... 112 F6
James Av GTS/LS CH66 ........ 162 E2
James Clarke St EV L5 ....... 12 F1
James Ct WDN WA8 ........... 149 J1
James Gv ECCL WA10 ......... 8 C7
James Holt Av KKBY L32 ..... 85 M4
James Larkin Wy
  ANF/KKDL L4 .............. 96 F6
James Pl CHLY/EC PR7 ........ 43 G5
  WGNNW/ST WN6 ............. 55 M3
James Rd RNFD/HAY WA11 ..... 91 H6
  WLTN L25 ................. 131 K3
James Sq WGNNW/ST WN6 ..... 55 M3
James St ALL/GAR L19 ........ 130 E8
  CL/PREN CH43 ............. 10 E8
  CLVPS L1 ................. 12 E8
  STHEL WA9 ................ 118 F2
  WAL/EG CH44 .............. 112 A3
  WARR WA1 ................. 14 F5
  WGNE/HIN WN2 ............. 80 A6
  WGNS/IIMK WN3 ............ 5 H7
Jamieson Av CSBY/BLUN L23 .. 83 J1
Jane's Brook Rd STHP PR8 ... 35 M1
Jane St STHEL WA9 .......... 103 H6
Janet St EHL/KEN L7 ........ 113 K4
Jarrett Rd NWD/KWIPK L33 ... 86 C1
Jarrow Cl CL/PREN CH43 ..... 10 C9
Jasmine Cl EV L5 ........... 13 L1
  MOR/LEA CH46 ............. 109 M6
Jasmine Ct HUY L36 ......... 100 B8
Jasmine Ms AIG/SPK L17 ..... 129 J2
Jasmine Rd
  WGNW/BIL/O WN5 .......... 67 M6
Jason St EV L5 ............. 97 G7
Jason Wk EV L5 ............. 97 G7
Java Rd ANF/KKDL L4 ........ 97 M3
Jay Cl GOL/RIS/CU WA3 ...... 123 J1
Jays Cl RUNC WA7 ........... 151 K6
Jedburgh Av GTS/LS CH66 .... 155 J7
Jedburgh Dr NWD/KWIPK L33 .. 73 M7
Jeffereys Crs HUY L36 ....... 115 K3
Jeffereys Dr HUY L36 ........ 115 J2
Jeffreys Dr GR/UP/WCH CH49 . 109 M8
Jeffrey St WGNE/HIN WN2 ..... 69 K6
Jellicoe Cl WKBY CH48 ...... 124 F7
Jenkinson St VAUX/LVPD L3 .. 13 H3
  WGNE/HIN WN2 ............. 69 M7
Jennet Hey AIMK WN4 ........ 79 H7
Jericho Cl AIG/SPK L17 ...... 129 M5
Jericho Farm Cl AIG/SPK L17 . 129 M4
Jericho La AIG/SPK L17 ...... 129 M4
Jermyn St TOX L8 ........... 113 J7
Jerningham Rd NG/CROX L11 .. 97 M2
Jersey Av EP CH65 ........... 163 L4
  LITH L21 ................. 83 K4
Jersey Cl BTL L20 ........... 7 G4
Jersey St BTL L20 ........... 7 G4
  STHEL WA9 ................ 118 E2
Jervis Cl WARRN/WOL WA2 .... 122 C2
Jesmond St WAV L15 ......... 113 M5
Jessamine Rd RF/TRAN CH42 .. 128 A2
Jessica Wy LEIGH WN7 ....... 93 K1
Joan Av GR/UP/WCH CH49 .... 126 A1
  MOR/LEA CH46 ............. 109 M5
Jocelyn Cl BEB CH63 ........ 143 J2
Jockey St WARRN/WOL WA2 ... 14 F1
John Bagot Cl EV L5 ........ 97 G8
John Hunter Wy NTHTN L30 .. 84 B2
John Lennon Dr NPK/KEN L6 . 113 K2
John Moores Cl EHL/KEN L7 . 113 J5
John Nicholas Crs EP CH65 .. 20 E2
  EP CH65 .................. 20 E2
Johns Av RUNC WA7 ......... 18 F6
Johnson Av NEWLW WA12 ..... 91 K8
  RAIN/WH L35 ............. 116 E1
  WGNE/HIN WN2 ............ 81 G4
Johnson Cl LEIGH WN7 ...... 93 K1
Johnson Gv WD/CROXPK L12 .. 99 G8
Johnson Rd CL/PREN CH43 ... 127 H4
Johnson's La CHTN/BK PR9 .. 3 H1
Johnston Av BTL L20 ....... 84 A7
John St AIMK WN4 .......... 79 M8
  BIRK CH41 ............... 11 L4
  CHLY/EC PR7 ............. 43 G4
  ECCL WA10 ............... 8 C7
  EP CH65 ................. 20 B2
  GOL/RIS/CU WA3 .......... 92 C5

  VAUX/LVPD L3 ............. 13 K3
  WARRN/WOL WA2 ........... 14 E4
  WGN WN1 ................. 5 H1
  WGNE/HIN WN2 ............ 81 K2
  WGNW/BIL/O WN5 .......... 67 M8
Jolly Tar La CHLY/EC PR7 .... 43 J6
Jones Farm Rd WLTN L25 ..... 131 L1
Jonson Rd NSTN CH64 ........ 153 G4
Jonville Rd WLT/FAZ L9 ...... 84 E6
Jordan St CLVPS L1 .......... 112 F6
Joseph Gardner Wy BTL L20 .. 6 F2
Joseph Lister Cl NTHTN L30 .. 84 B2
Joseph St STHEL WA9 ......... 103 G6
  WDN WA8 .................. 134 E3
Joshua Cl EV L5 ............ 97 G7
Joule Cl GOL/RIS/CU WA3 .... 107 H8
Joy La WARRW/BUR WA5 ...... 119 G3
  WARRW/BUR WA5 ........... 119 H1
Jubilee Av DV/KA/FCH L14 ... 114 F4
  ORM L39 .................. 51 H7
  WARR WA1 ................. 122 B5
  WARRW/BUR WA5 ........... 136 A1
  WGNW/BIL/O WN5 .......... 77 M1
Jubilee Crs PS/BROM CH62 ... 128 D8
  RNFD/HAY WA11 ............ 91 H6
Jubilee Dr EHL/KEN L7 ....... 113 K3
  NTHTN L30 ................ 84 C4
  RAIN/WH L35 .............. 116 F3
  SKEL WN8 ................. 65 G5
  WKBY CH48 ................ 124 C1
Jubilee Gv LYMM WA13 ....... 139 L1
Jubilee Rd CSBY/BLUN L23 ... 82 E2
  FMBY L37 ................. 58 F4
  LITH L21 ................. 83 K6
Jubilee Wy WDN WA8 ......... 134 A2
Jubits La WDN WA8 .......... 118 C5
Juddfield St RNFD/HAY WA11.. 90 C7
Judeland CHLY/EC PR7 ....... 32 C3
Judges Dr NPK/KEN L6 ....... 113 G1
Judges Wy NPK/KEN L6 ....... 113 L1
Julian Wy WDN WA8 .......... 134 B1
Julie Gv WD/CROXPK L12 ..... 99 G8
Juliet Av BEB CH63 ......... 128 A6
July Rd NPK/KEN L6 ......... 97 M8
July St BTL L20 ............ 7 H1
Junction La BRSC L40 ....... 52 A1
  NEWLW WA12 ............... 104 D2
  STHEL WA9 ................ 103 C6
Junction Rd RNFD/HAY WA11 .. 76 A5
Junction Ter WGNS/IIMK WN3 .. 5 K5
June Av LEIGH WN7 .......... 81 L7
  PS/BROM CH62 ............. 144 A5
June Rd NPK/KEN L6 ......... 97 M8
June St BTL L20 ............ 7 H2
Juniper Cl ECCL WA10 ....... 8 A2
  GR/UP/WCH CH49 ........... 125 L3
  STBRV L28 ................ 99 K6
Juniper Dr GTS/LS CH66 ..... 163 G4
  WGNE/HIN WN2 ............. 80 A1
Juniper Gdns CSBY/BLUN L23 . 71 K7
Juniper Gv GTS/LS CH66 ..... 163 H4
Juniper La GOL/RIS/CU WA3 .. 123 J5
Juniper St BTL L20 ......... 96 E5
Jupiter Gv WGNS/IIMK WN3 ... 79 G3
Jurby Ct WARRN/WOL WA2 .... 122 A4
  WARRN/WOL WA2 ........... 122 B4
Justin Wy RAIN/WH L35 ...... 101 K3
Juvenal Pl VAUX/LVPD L3 .... 13 J2
Juvenal St VAUX/LVPD L3 .... 13 H3

**K**

Kaigh Av CSBY/BLUN L23 ..... 70 F8
Kale Cl WKBY CH48 .......... 124 D4
Kane Ct GOL/RIS/CU WA3 ..... 93 J4
Kara Cl BTL L20 ............ 7 H4
Karan Wy MGHL L31 .......... 85 J2
Karen Cl WARRW/BUR WA5 .... 104 B7
Karen Rd WGN WN1 ........... 5 K4
Karen Wy GTS/LS CH66 ....... 162 F2
Karonga Rd AIN/FAZ L10 ..... 85 G6
Karonga Wy AIN/FAZ L10 ..... 85 H6
Karslake Rd CALD/MH L18 .... 114 B8
  WAL/EG CH44 .............. 111 M3
Kay Cl WDN WA8 ............. 5 H4
Kaye Av GOL/RIS/CU WA3 ..... 107 H3
Kearsley Cl ANF/KKDL L4 .... 97 G5
Kearsley St ANF/KKDL L4 .... 97 G5
  LEIGH WN7 ................ 81 M8
Keates St STHEL WA9 ........ 103 H5
Keats Av RAIN/WH L35 ....... 117 H2
  WGNNW/ST WN6 ............. 4 B9
  WGNS/IIMK WN3 ............ 4 B9
  WGNW/BIL/O WN5 .......... 77 M4
Keats Cl CHLY/EC PR7 ....... 30 F8
  GTS/LS CH66 .............. 163 G5
  WDN WA8 .................. 116 A3
Keats Gn HUY L36 ........... 116 A3
Keats Gv WARRN/WOL WA2 .... 121 L3
Keats St BTL L20 ........... 6 E1
  LEIGH WN7 ................ 81 M6
Keats Ter STHP PR8 ......... 25 H7
Keats Wy WGNE/HIN WN2 ..... 80 D4
Keble Dr AIN/FAZ L10 ....... 84 E2
  WAL/NB CH45 .............. 94 F7
Keble Gv LEIGH WN7 ......... 81 L5
Keble Rd BTL L20 ........... 7 G8
Keble St NPK/KEN L6 ........ 113 J2
  WDN WA8 .................. 16 E5
  WGNE/HIN WN2 ............. 80 C4
Keckwick La RUNC WA7 ....... 151 H1
  WARRS WA4 ................ 151 K3
Kedleston St TOX L8 ........ 129 J1
Keegan Dr WAL/EG CH44 ...... 112 A3
Keele Cl CL/PREN CH43 ...... 110 E4
Keenan Dr BTL L20 .......... 84 A8
Keepers La BEB CH63 ........ 127 K8
Keighley Av WAL/EG CH44 .... 95 G8
Keightley St BIRK CH41 ..... 11 C4
Keir Hardie Av BTL L20 ..... 7 M1
Keith Av ANF/KKDL L4 ....... 97 H4
  WARRW/BUR WA5 ........... 120 A7
Keith Dr BEB CH63 .......... 143 L8
Kelbrook Cl STHEL WA9 ...... 102 F7
Kelburn Ct GOL/RIS/CU WA3 .. 107 H7

Kelday Cl NWD/KWIPK L33 .... 86 A3
Kelkbeck Cl MGHL L31 ....... 73 H5
Kellaton Cl WGNS/IIMK WN3 .. 5 J7
Kellbank Rd WGNS/IIMK WN3 .. 79 G2
Kellet Cl WGNW/BIL/O WN5 ... 67 M4
Kellett Cl MOR/LEA CH46 .... 110 D2
Kellett St CHLY/EC PR7 ..... 32 E5
Kellitt Rd WAV L15 ......... 114 A6
Kelly Dr BTL L20 ........... 7 L2
Kelly St PR/KW L34 ......... 101 G7
Kelmscott Cl GTS/LS CH66 ... 162 F3
Kelmscott Dr WAL/EG CH44 .. 111 L1
Kelsall Av PS/BROM CH62 .... 155 G2
  STHEL WA9 ................ 118 D1
Kelsall Cl CL/PREN CH43 .... 127 J2
  GOL/RIS/CU WA3 ........... 122 E2
  PS/BROM CH62 ............. 155 G2
  WDN WA8 .................. 133 M3
Kelsey Cl ECCL WA10 ........ 8 A3
Kelso Cl NWD/KWIPK L33 ..... 73 M7
Kelso Rd NPK/KEN L6 ........ 113 L2
Kelton Gv AIG/SPK L17 ...... 130 A3
Kelvin Cl AIMK WN4 ......... 90 F1
  GOL/RIS/CU WA3 ........... 106 F7
Kelvin Gv TOX L8 ........... 113 J7
Kelvin Rd BIRK CH41 ........ 111 M1
  WAL/EG CH44 .............. 112 A4
Kelvinside CSBY/BLUN L23 ... 83 H3
  WAL/EG CH44 .............. 111 M4
Kelvin St GOL/RIS/CU WA3 ... 107 G7
Kelway Ter WGN WN1 ........ 5 H1
Kemberton Dr WDN WA8 ...... 118 C3
Kemble St EHL/KEN L7 ....... 113 K3
  PR/KW L34 ................ 101 G7
Kemlyn Rd ANF/KKDL L4 ..... 97 J7
Kemmel Av WARRS WA4 ....... 137 L3
Kempsell Wy HLWD L26 ...... 132 C6
Kempsey Gv STHEL WA9 ...... 102 A6
Kempson St RNFD/HAY WA11 .. 143 H1
Kempston St VAUX/LVPD L3 .. 13 K5
Kempton Cl HUY L36 ........ 115 M4
  NEWLW WA12 ............... 91 M8
Kempton Park Fold STHP PR8.. 36 B2
Kempton Park Rd
  AIN/FAZ L10 .............. 85 G3
Kempton Rd PS/BROM CH62 .. 128 D5
  WAV L15 .................. 113 M5
Kemsley Rd DV/KA/FCH L14 .. 115 H2
Kenbury Cl NWD/KWIPK L33 .. 86 C1
Kenbury Rd NWD/KWIPK L33 .. 86 C1
Kendal Av WARRN/WOL WA2 .. 121 L3
Kendal Cl BEB CH63 ......... 128 B7
  GTS/LS CH66 .............. 162 F3
  RNFD/HAY WA11 ............ 76 B3
Kendal Dr GTS/LS CH66 ...... 162 F3
  MGHL L31 ................. 72 F3
  RAIN/WH L35 .............. 117 J2
  RNFD/HAY WA11 ............ 76 B4
  RNFD/HAY WA11 ............ 89 L5
Kendal Gv AIMK WN4 ........ 91 K1
  LEIGH WN7 ................ 81 M8
Kendal Pk WD/CROXPK L12 ... 98 F7
Kendal Rd CHLDW L16 ........ 115 G6
  WAL/EG CH44 .............. 111 J3
  WDN WA8 .................. 133 L4
  WGNE/HIN WN2 ............. 69 J3
Kendal Ri RUNC WA7 ......... 149 M8
Kendal St BIRK CH41 ........ 11 L8
  WGNNW/ST WN6 ............. 4 C2
Kendal Wy STHP PR8 ......... 47 K2
Kendricks Fold RAIN/WH L35 . 117 K2
Kendrick St WARR WA1 ....... 14 C5
Kenford Dr WGNS/IIMK WN3 .. 79 G3
Kenilworth Av RUNC WA7 ..... 19 H8
Kenilworth Cl WLTN L25 ..... 131 G2
Kenilworth Ct EP CH65 ...... 164 A3
Kenilworth Dr PEN/TH CH61 .. 126 A8
  WARR WA1 ................. 122 B5
  WARR WA1 ................. 81 H1
Kenilworth Gdns
  GR/UP/WCH CH49 ........... 110 A7
  NEWLW WA12 ............... 104 C3
Kenilworth Rd CHLDW L16 .... 114 F6
  CSBY/BLUN L23 ............ 82 E2
  GOL/RIS/CU WA3 ........... 93 G6
  NSTN CH64 ................ 153 G7
  STHP PR8 ................. 47 L1
  WAL/EG CH44 .............. 111 M2
Kenilworth St BTL L20 ...... 6 F4
Kenilworth Wy WLTN L25 ..... 131 G2
Kenley Av WDN WA8 .......... 117 M8
Kenley Cl NPK/KEN L6 ....... 113 L1
Kenmare Rd WAV L15 ......... 114 A7
Kenmay Av AIMK WN4 ........ 90 F1
Kenmore Gv AIMK WN4 ........ 90 F1
Kenmore Rd CL/PREN CH43 ... 127 G4
Kennelwood Av
  NWD/KWIPK L33 ........... 86 A3
Kennessee Cl MGHL L31 ..... 73 G5
Kenneth Av LEIGH WN7 ...... 81 M7
Kenneth Cl NTHTN L30 ...... 84 A2
Kenneth Gv LEIGH WN7 ...... 81 M7
Kenneth Rd WDN WA8 ........ 133 L5
Kennet Rd BEB CH63 ........ 127 M8
  RNFD/HAY WA11 ........... 90 E7
Kennford Rd NG/CROX L11 ... 85 L8
Kensington EHL/KEN L7 ...... 113 K3
Kensington Av STHEL WA9 .... 102 E6
  WARRS WA4 ............... 138 E3
Kensington Gdns
  MOR/LEA CH46 ............ 110 A5
Kensington Rd CHLY/EC PR7 .. 32 D6
  CHTN/BK PR9 ............. 3 K4
  EP CH65 ................. 156 C8
  FMBY L37 ................ 59 C4
  WGNE/HIN WN2 ............ 80 C3
Kensington St EHL/KEN L7 ... 113 J3
Kent Av FMBY L37 .......... 59 J4
  LITH L21 ................ 83 L5
  WGNE/HIN WN2 ............ 80 C2
Kent Cl BEB CH63 .......... 143 K5
Kent Gv RUNC WA7 .......... 19 K5
Kentmere Av RNFD/HAY WA11 .. 76 B4
Kentmere Dr PEN/TH CH61 ... 141 H2
Kentmere Pl
  WARRN/WOL WA2 ........... 121 J2
Kenton Cl FMBY L37 ........ 47 H7

Kenton Rd *HLWD* L26 .......... 132 B6
Kentridge Dr *GTS/LS* CH66 ... 162 F2 🔢
Kent Rd *FMBY* L37 .......... 59 J4
  *STHEL* WA9 .......... 102 E5
  *STHP* PR8 .......... 2 F9
  *WAL/EG* CH44 .......... 111 J2
  *WARRW/BUR* WA5 .......... 136 E1
Kents Bank *WD/CROXPK* L12 ... 98 E4
Kent St *CL/PREN* CH43 .......... 10 B9
  *CLVPS* L1 .......... 112 F5
  *WARRS* WA4 .......... 15 G8
  *WDN* WA8 .......... 16 E2
  *WGN* WN1 .......... 5 H5
Kenview CI *WDN* WA8 .......... 148 C1
Kenway *RNFD/HAY* WA11 .......... 76 C7
Kenwick CI *GTS/LS* CH66 .......... 162 E2
Kenwright Crs *STHEL* WA9 .......... 102 E5
Kenwyn Rd *WAL/NB* CH45 .......... 95 K8
Kenyon Av *WARRW/BUR* WA5 ... 120 A8
Kenyon CI *NWD/KWIPK* L33 ... 74 B7 🔢
Kenyon La *GOL/RIS/CU* WA3 .......... 93 H7
  *GOL/RIS/CU* WA3 .......... 106 D2
Kenyon Rd *WAV* L15 .......... 114 C3 🔢
  *WGNNW/ST* WN6 .......... 55 M3
Kenyon's La *FMBY* L37 .......... 59 J2
  *MGHL* L31 .......... 72 F1
Kenyons La North
  *RNFD/HAY* WA11 .......... 91 H5
Kenyon's La South
  *RNFD/HAY* WA11 .......... 91 H5
Kenyon St *LEIGH* WN7 .......... 81 M5
Kepler St *LITH* L21 .......... 83 J7
Keppel St *BTL* L20 .......... 6 E2
Kerfoot's La *SKEL* WN8 .......... 64 E5
Kerfoot St *WARRN/WOL* WA2 ... 14 D1
Kerr Gv *STHEL* WA9 .......... 103 G2
Kerris CI *AIG/SPK* L17 .......... 129 L3
Kerry Cft *GTS/LS* CH66 .......... 163 G4
Kerrysdale CI *STHEL* WA9 ... 102 F6 🔢
Kersey Rd *KKBY* L32 .......... 86 B5
Kershaw Av *CSBY/BLUN* L23.... 83 H2
Kershaw St *CHLYE* PR6 .......... 33 G5
  *WDN* WA8 .......... 133 M4
  *WGNW/BIL/O* WN5 .......... 67 K7
Kershaw Wy *NEWLW* WA12 .......... 91 L8
Kerslake Wy *HTWN* L38 .......... 70 B1
Kerswell CI *STHEL* WA9 .......... 102 F7 🔢
Kestral Gv *HLWD* L26 .......... 131 M4
Kestral Pk *SKEL* WN8 .......... 65 L1
Kestrel Av
  *GR/UP/WCH* CH49 .......... 109 M7 🔢
Kestrel CI *CHLYE* PR6 .......... 33 J2 🔢
  *GR/UP/WCH* CH49 .......... 109M7
  *RNFD/HAY* WA11 .......... 89 K7 🔢
Kestrel Dr *AIMK* WN4 .......... 79 L7
Kestrel La *GOL/RIS/CU* WA3 ... 123 G1 🔢
Kestrel Ms *SKEL* WN8 .......... 65 L1
Kestrel Rd *HES* CH60 .......... 141 L6
  *MOR/LEA* CH46 .......... 109 L3
Kestrels Wy *RUNC* WA7 .......... 150 B7
Keswick Av *BEB* CH63 .......... 143 L8
  *WARRN/WOL* WA2 .......... 121 L3
Keswick CI *MGHL* L31 .......... 73 G3
  *STHP* PR8 .......... 47 L2
  *WDN* WA8 .......... 133 L4
Keswick Crs
  *WARRN/WOL* WA2 .......... 121 L3 🔢
Keswick Dr *FROD/HEL* WA6 ... 160 F5
  *LITH* L21 .......... 84 A5
Keswick PI *CL/PREN* CH43 .......... 110 F4
  *WGNE/HIN* WN2 .......... 69 J6
Keswick Rd *CALD/MH* L18 .......... 130 E3
  *ECCL* WA10 .......... 8 D2
  *WAL/NB* CH45 .......... 95 G6
Keswick Wy *CHLDW* L16 .......... 115 J1
  *RNFD/HAY* WA11 .......... 76 B3 🔢
Kettering Rd *STHP* PR8 .......... 44 A6
Kevelioc CI *BEB* CH63 .......... 143 H2 🔢
Kew Rd *FMBY* L37 .......... 58 F4
  *STHP* PR8 .......... 35 K2
Keybank Rd *WD/CROXPK* L12 ... 98 C5
Keyes CI *GOL/RIS/CU* WA3 .......... 123 H1
Keyes Gdns *GOL/RIS/CU* WA3 ... 123 H1 🔢
Kiddman St *WLT/FAZ* L9 .......... 97 H2 🔢
Kidstone CI *STHEL* WA9 .......... 102 F6 🔢
Kilbuck La *RNFD/HAY* WA11 .......... 91 J5
Kilburn Av *AIMK* WN4 .......... 91 M1
  *PS/BROM* CH62 .......... 144 A7
Kilburn Clqse *LEIGH* WN7 ... 81 M4 🔢
Kilburn Dr *WGNNW/ST* WN6 ... 55 J6
Kilburn Gv *STHEL* WA9 .......... 102 A6
  *WGNS/IIMK* WN3 .......... 78 F2
Kilburn Rd *SKEL* WN8 .......... 66 E8
Kilburn St *LITH* L21 .......... 83 K7
Kildale CI *MGHL* L31 .......... 72 E5
Kildare CI *SPK/HALE* L24 .......... 147 M3
Kildare St *WGNE/HIN* WN2 .......... 69 L8
  *WGNW/BIL/O* WN5 .......... 68 B7
Kildonan Rd *AIG/SPK* L17 .......... 129M3
  *WARRS* WA4 .......... 138 C3
Kilford CI *WARRW/BUR* WA5 ... 121 G6
Kilgraston Gdns *AIG/SPK* L17 ... 130 B4
Kilkerran CI *STHEL* WA9 .......... 32 F5
Killarney Gv *WAL/EG* CH44 ... 111 J2 🔢
Killarney Rd *CLB/OSW/ST* L13 ... 114 C2
Killester Rd *WLTN* L25 .......... 131 K1
Killingbeck CI *BRSC* L40 .......... 51 M1 🔢
Killington Wy *ANF/KKDL* L4 .......... G5
Killingworth La
  *GOL/RIS/CU* WA3 .......... 107 K8
Kilmalcolm CI *CL/PREN* CH43 ... 127 H1 🔢
Kilmore CI *WLT/FAZ* L9 .......... 84 E5
Kilmory Av *WLTN* L25 .......... 131 J3
Kilncroft *RUNC* WA7 .......... 150 D8 🔢
Kiln Hey *WD/CROXPK* L12 .......... 98 E8
Kiln La *ECCL* WA10 .......... 88 E8
  *SKEL* WN8 .......... 65 G3
Kiln Rd *GR/UP/WCH* CH49 .......... 126 C2
Kilnyard Rd *CSBY/BLUN* L23 ... 81 G6
Kilrea CI *NG/CROX* L11 .......... 98 B5
Kilrea Rd *NG/CROX* L11 .......... 98 B5
Kilsail Rd *KKBY* L32 .......... 86 C6
Kilsby Dr *WDN* WA8 .......... 135 G3
Kilshaw Rd *WARRW/BUR* WA5 ... 104 B7
Kilshaw St *NPK/KEN* L6 .......... 113 J1
  *WGNW/BIL/O* WN5 .......... 67 L8
Kilsyth CI *WARRN/WOL* WA2 .......... 122 B1

Kimberley Av *CSBY/BLUN* L23 ... 82 F2 🔢
Kimberley CI *TOX* L8 .......... 113 J6
Kimberley Dr *CSBY/BLUN* L23 ... 82 F2
  *WARRS* WA4 .......... 137 L4
Kimberley PI *AIMK* WN4 .......... 91 L2 🔢
Kimberley Rd *WAL/NB* CH45 .......... 95 K7
  *CHLY/EC* PR7 .......... 43 G4
  *WARRW/BUR* WA5 .......... 121 G8
Kimberly St *BIRK* CH41 .......... 111 H5 🔢
Kimberly St *WGNNW/ST* WN6 ... 4 A1
Kindale Rd *CL/PREN* CH43 .......... 127 G4
Kinder Gv *AIMK* WN4 .......... 79 H7
Kinder St *NPK/KEN* L6 .......... 13 M4
King Av *BTL* L20 .......... 84 A7
King Edward Rd *ECCL* WA10.... 88 F7
King Edward St *BIRK* CH41 .......... 117 K1
King Edward's Dr
  *PS/BROM* CH62 .......... 128 D7
King Edward St *VAUX/LVPD* L3... 12 D5
  *WARR* WA1 .......... 15 M2
Kingfield Rd *WLT/FAZ* L9 .......... 84 B8
Kingfisher CI *GOL/RIS/CU* WA3... 123 H1
  *NTHLY* L27 .......... 116 B8 🔢
  *NWD/KWIPK* L33 .......... 74 A7
  *RUNC* WA7 .......... 150 B8 🔢
Kingfisher Ct *AIMK* WN4 .......... 79 K7
  *CHTN/BK* PR9 .......... 3 M2
Kingfisher Dr *RNFD/HAY* WA11 ... 89 K7
Kingfisher Gv *WD/CROXPK* L12 ... 99 K4
Kingfisher Pk *SKEL* WN8 .......... 65 L1 🔢
Kingfisher Wy
  *GR/UP/WCH* CH49 .......... 109M7
King George CI *AIMK* WN4 .......... 91 K2 🔢
King George Crs *WARR* WA1 .......... 15 L2
King George Dr *WAL/NB* CH45 ... 95 L8
King George Rd
  *RNFD/HAY* WA11 .......... 91 J6
King George's Dr
  *PS/BROM* CH62 .......... 128 D7
Kingham CI *WLTN* L25 .......... 131 L3 🔢
King James Ct *RUNC* WA7 .......... 150 A7
Kinglake Rd *WAL/EG* CH44 .......... 111 M1
Kinglake St *EHL/KEN* L7 .......... 113 K4
Kinglass Rd *PS/BROM* CH62 .......... 143 K2
King's Av *GOL/RIS/CU* WA3 .......... 93 H6
  *HOY* CH47 .......... 108 F5
Kingsbrook Wy *BEB* CH63 .......... 127M5
King's Brow *BEB* CH63 .......... 127 M7 🔢
Kingsbury *WKBY* CH48 .......... 124 F2
Kingsbury CI *STHP* PR8 .......... 47 J1
Kingsbury St *SKEL* WN8 .......... 65 L1
Kings CI *AIG/SPK* L17 .......... 129 L3
  *BEB* CH63 .......... 127M6
  *FMBY* L37 .......... 59 G3
Kings Ct *HOY* CH47 .......... 108 C6 🔢
  *LITH* L21 .......... 83 H6 🔢
Kingscourt Rd *WD/CROXPK* L12... 98 E3
Kingscroft Ct *WGN* WN1 .......... 5 H5
Kingsdale Av *RAIN/WH* L35 .......... 117 M2 🔢
  *RF/TRAN* CH42 .......... 127 M3 🔢
Kingsdale Rd *CALD/MH* L18 .......... 114 C8
  *WARRW/BUR* WA5 .......... 120 B6
Kings Dock St *CLVPS* L1 .......... 112 F6
Kingsdown Crs *WGN* WN1 .......... 68 E1
  *WGNE/HIN* WN2 .......... 80 D6
Kingsdown Rd *NG/CROX* L11 ... 98 B7
Kingsdown St *BIRK* CH41 .......... 11 J9
Kingsferry CI *WARRW/WOL* WA2... 122 B1 🔢
Kings Gap *HOY* CH47 .......... 108 C6 🔢
Kingshead CI *RUNC* WA7 .......... 150 E5 🔢
Kingsheath Av *DV/KA/FCH* L14 ... 99 H8
Kings Hey Dr *CHTN/BK* PR9 .......... 25 H4
Kingshill CI *WGNNW/ST* WN6 ... 56 B6
Kingsland Crs *NG/CROX* L11 ... 98 A2
Kingsland Rd *NG/CROX* L11 .......... 97M2
  *RF/TRAN* CH42 .......... 127 L1 🔢
King's La *BEB* CH63 .......... 128 A6
Kingslea *CHLY/EC* PR7 .......... 44 B5
Kingsley Av *PS/BROM* CH62 ... 155 G2
  *WGNS/IIMK* WN3 .......... 79 H2
Kingsley Crs *RUNC* WA7 .......... 19 H6
Kingsley Dr *CHLY/EC* PR7 .......... 32 C8
  *WARRS* WA4 .......... 137 L6
Kingsley Rd *ECCL* WA10 .......... 88 F7
  *EP* CH65 .......... 20 D4
  *FROD/HEL* WA6 .......... 160 F7
  *RUNC* WA7 .......... 19 H6
  *TOX* L8 .......... 113 K6 🔢
  *WAL/EG* CH44 .......... 111 K2
Kingsley St *BIRK* CH41 .......... 10 A2
  *LEIGH* WN7 .......... 81 L6
Kingsmead *CHLY/EC* PR7 .......... 32 E8
Kingsmead Ct
  *GOL/RIS/CU* WA3 .......... 106 C5 🔢
Kingsmead Dr *WLTN* L25 .......... 131 K6
Kingsmead Gv
  *CL/PREN* CH43 .......... 111 H8 🔢
Kings Meadow *RUNC* WA7 ... 150 E5 🔢
  *STHP* PR8 .......... 47M2
Kingsmead Rd
  *CL/PREN* CH43 .......... 111 H8 🔢
  *MOR/LEA* CH46 .......... 110 B3
Kingsmead Rd North
  *CL/PREN* CH43 .......... 111 H8
Kingsmead Rd South
  *CL/PREN* CH43 .......... 111 H8
Kingsmede *WGN* WN1 .......... 68 F2
King's Moss La *RNFD/HAY* WA11 ... 77 G6
Kings Mt *CL/PREN* CH43 .......... 10 E9
Kingsnorth *RAIN/WH* L35 .......... 117 H3
Kingsoak CI *WGN* WN1 .......... 5 G3
King's Pde *WAL/NB* CH45 .......... 94 F5
Kings Pk *AIMK* WN4 .......... 79 J8 🔢
  *BEB* CH63 .......... 127M6
  *BTL* L20 .......... 7 G8
King's Rd *CSBY/BLUN* L23 .......... 82 F1
  *ECCL* WA10 .......... 101 J3
  *FMBY* L37 .......... 59 G4
  *GOL/RIS/CU* WA3 .......... 92 C6
  *GTS/LS* CH66 .......... 155 L6

  *WARRN/WOL* WA2 .......... 122 C3
Kingsthorne Pk *SPK/HALE* L24 ... 131 L7
Kingsthorne Rd *WLTN* L25 .......... 131 L7
Kingston Av
  *WARRW/BUR* WA5 .......... 120 A7 🔢
Kingston CI *MOR/LEA* CH46 .......... 110 A5
  *RUNC* WA7 .......... 150 A3 🔢
  *WD/CROXPK* L12 .......... 99 G8
  *WGNS/IIMK* WN3 .......... 79 K2
Kingston Crs *CHTN/BK* PR9.... 22 E8
King St *ALL/GAR* L19 .......... 145 L1
  *CHLY/EC* PR7 .......... 32 F7
  *CSBY/WL* L22 .......... 82 F4
  *ECCL* WA10 .......... 8 F5
  *EP* CH65 .......... 20 D2
  *NEWLW* WA12 .......... 104 D2
  *RF/TRAN* CH42 .......... 128 C4
  *RUNC* WA7 .......... 19 H2
  *STHP* PR8 .......... 2 F5
  *WAL/EG* CH44 .......... 95M8
  *WGN* WN1 .......... 4 F5
  *WGNE/HIN* WN2 .......... 69 M7 🔢
King St West *WGN* WN1 .......... 4 E4
Kingsville Rd *BEB* CH63 .......... 128 A8
Kingswalk *WKBY* CH48 .......... 124 C3
Kingsway *CHLY/EC* PR7 .......... 32 A3
  *CSBY/WL* L22 .......... 83 G3
  *FROD/HEL* WA6 .......... 160 D6
  *HES* CH60 .......... 141 L7
  *HUY* L36 .......... 115 M1
  *NEWLW* WA12 .......... 104 E3
  *RAIN/WH* L35 .......... 100 F8
  *RNFD/HAY* WA11 .......... 89 J5
  *STHP* PR8 .......... 2 E4
  *WAL/NB* CH45 .......... 95 J7
  *WDN* WA8 .......... 16 D3
  *WGN* WN1 .......... 68 F3
  *WGNE/HIN* WN2 .......... 81 L7
Kingsway North *WARR* WA1 .......... 15 M3
Kingsway South *WARR* WA4 .......... 138 B1
Kingsway (Tunnel)
  *WAL/EG* CH44 .......... 111 L3
Kingswell CI *EHL/KEN* L7 .......... 113 K5 🔢
Kings Whf *WAL/EG* CH44 .......... 112 A4
Kingswood Av *CSBY/WL* L22 .......... 83 H4
  *WLT/FAZ* L9 .......... 84 D6
Kingswood Bvd *BEB* CH63 .......... 128 A5
Kingswood Ct
  *NWD/KWIPK* L33 .......... 86 B1 🔢
Kingswood Dr *CSBY/BLUN* L23 ... 82 F2 🔢
Kingswood Rd *WAL/EG* CH44 ... 95 L8 🔢
  *WARRW/BUR* WA5 .......... 120 C3
Kington Rd *WKBY* CH48 .......... 124 C2 🔢
Kingwood Crs
  *WGNW/BIL/O* WN5 .......... 67M7
Kinlet Rd *WGNS/IIMK* WN3 .......... 78 E1
Kinley Gdns *BTL* L20 .......... 84 A8 🔢
Kinloch CI *HLWD* L26 .......... 132 C6
Kinloch Wy *ORM* L39 .......... 50 F8
Kinloss Rd *GR/UP/WCH* CH49 ... 125 L2 🔢
Kinmel CI *ANF/KKDL* L4 .......... 97 M5
  *BIRK* CH41 .......... 11 H4
Kinmel St *STHEL* WA9 .......... 102 E5
  *TOX* L8 .......... 113 J8
Kinnaird Rd *WAL/NB* CH45 .......... 95 J7
Kinnaird St *TOX* L8 .......... 129 J2
Kinnerley Rd *EP* CH65 .......... 163 J2
Kinnerton Rd *MOR/LEA* CH46 ... 109 K5
Kinnington Wy *GTS/LS* CH66 ... 163 H6 🔢
Kinniside Rd *WGNS/IIMK* WN3 ... 79 J3
Kinnock Pk *WARRW/BUR* WA5 ... 104 A7
Kinross Av *GOL/RIS/CU* WA3 ... 92 E1
Kinross CI *WARRN/WOL* WA2 .......... 122 B1
Kinross Rd *AIN/FAZ* L10 .......... 85 G6
  *CSBY/WL* L22 .......... 83 G5
  *WAL/NB* CH45 .......... 94 F7
Kinsale Dr *GOL/RIS/CU* WA3 ... 122 E1
Kinsey Rd *EP* CH65 .......... 164 A4
Kinsey's La *EP* CH65 .......... 158 B7
Kintbury St *WGNE/HIN* WN2 .......... 80 B6
Kintore CI *BEB* CH63 .......... 154 E1
Kintore Dr
  *WARRW/BUR* WA5 .......... 119 M7 🔢
Kintore Rd *ALL/GAR* L19 .......... 130 D6
Kipling Av *HUY* L36 .......... 116 C4
  *RF/TRAN* CH42 .......... 128 B4 🔢
  *WARRN/WOL* WA2 .......... 121 J4 🔢
  *WGNS/IIMK* WN3 .......... 79 J1
Kipling Crs *WDN* WA8 .......... 16 B3
Kipling Gv *LEIGH* WN7 .......... 81 M6
  *STHEL* WA9 .......... 118 C2
Kipling St *BTL* L20 .......... 83 J8
Kirby CI *WKBY* CH48 .......... 124 D4
Kirby Mt *WKBY* CH48 .......... 124 E5
Kirby Pk *WKBY* CH48 .......... 124 E5
Kirby Rd *BTL* L20 .......... 83M7
Kirkacre Av *NEWLW* WA12 .......... 104 E5
Kirkbride CI *NTHLY* L27 .......... 132 C1 🔢
Kirkburn CI *TOX* L8 .......... 129 J2
Kirkby Bank Rd *NWD/KWIPK* L33... 86 D3
Kirkby Rd *GOL/RIS/CU* WA3 .......... 107 H2
Kirkby Rw *KKBY* L32 .......... 85 L2
Kirkcaldy Av *WARRW/BUR* WA5... 119M7
Kirkdale Gdns *SKEL* WN8 .......... 66 B6 🔢
Kirkdale Rd *EV* L5 .......... 96 F7
Kirkdale V *ANF/KKDL* L4 .......... 97 G6
Kirket CI *BEB* CH63 .......... 143 J1 🔢
Kirket La *BEB* CH63 .......... 143 H1
Kirkfield Gv *RF/TRAN* CH42 ... 128 C4 🔢
Kirkham Av *GOL/RIS/CU* WA3 ... 93 H5
Kirkham Rd *CHTN/BK* PR9 .......... 23 G1
  *LEIGH* WN7 .......... 93M3
  *WDN* WA8 .......... 134 E3
Kirkham St *WGNE/HIN* WN2 .......... 80 D5 🔢
Kirkland Av *RF/TRAN* CH42 .......... 127M3
Kirkland Rd *WAL/NB* CH45 .......... 95 L5
The Kirklands *ECCL* WA10 .......... 8 E4
Kirklees St *ECCL* WA10 .......... 89 H4
Kirklees St *WGN* WN1 .......... 5 K4
Kirkless St *WGNE/HIN* WN2 .......... 69 H5
Kirkmaiden Rd *ALL/GAR* L19 ... 130 D5
Kirkman Fold *RAIN/WH* L35 .......... 117 K2

Kirkmore Rd *CALD/MH* L18 .......... 130 C3
Kirkmount *GR/UP/WCH* CH49 ... 110 C8
Kirkpatrick St *WGNE/HIN* WN2... 81 K2
Kirk Rd *BTL* L20 .......... 83 L7
Kirkside CI *WD/CROXPK* L12 .......... 98 F2 🔢
Kirkstall CI *CHLY/EC* PR7 .......... 32 E7
Kirkstall Dr *CHLY/EC* PR7 .......... 32 E7
  *FMBY* L37 .......... 59 J3 🔢
Kirkstall Rd *CHLY/EC* PR7 .......... 32 E7
  *STHP* PR8 .......... 35 H3
Kirkstone Av *RNFD/HAY* WA11 ... 89 L5
  *WARRN/WOL* WA2 .......... 121 L2
Kirkstone Crs *RUNC* WA7 .......... 161 J1
Kirkstone Rd North *LITH* L21 .......... 83 L4
Kirkstone Rd South *LITH* L21 .......... 83 K3
Kirk St *EV* L5 .......... 97 G7
Kirkwall Dr *WARRW/BUR* WA5 ... 136 C2
Kirkway *BEB* CH63 .......... 127M6
  *GR/UP/WCH* CH49 .......... 110 B8 🔢
  *WAL/NB* CH45 .......... 95 K6
Kitchener Dr *WLT/FAZ* L9 .......... 84 E7 🔢
Kitchener Av *ECCL* WA10 .......... 8 C4
Kitchen St *CLVPS* L1 .......... 112 F6
Kitling CI *PR/KW* L34 .......... 86 E8
Kitling Rd *PR/KW* L34 .......... 86 E8
Kitt Green Rd
  *WGNW/BIL/O* WN5 .......... 67 K5 🔢
Kittiwake Rd *CHLYE* PR6 .......... 33 J1
Kiverley CI *WLTN* L25 .......... 131 G2 🔢
Kiveton Dr *AIMK* WN4 .......... 91 L3
The Knap *HES* CH60 .......... 141 J7
Knaresborough Rd
  *WAL/EG* CH44 .......... 111 H1
  *WGNE/HIN* WN2 .......... 81 C7 🔢
Knighton Rd *ANF/KKDL* L4 .......... 97M4
Knight Rd *WARRW/BUR* WA5 .......... 104 B7
Knightsbridge Av *WARRS* WA4 ... 138 E2
Knightscliffe Crs
  *WGNNW/ST* WN6 .......... 68 B4
Knightshill Crs *WGNNW/ST* WN6 ... 68 B4
Knight St *CLVPS* L1 .......... 113 G5 🔢🔢
Knightsway *CSBY/WL* L22 .......... 83 H3
Knob Hall Gdns *CHTN/BK* PR9 ... 25 H2
Knob Hall La *CHTN/BK* PR9 .......... 25 H2
Knoclaid Rd *CLB/OSW/ST* L13 ... 98 A6
The Knoll *CL/PREN* CH43 .......... 127 J2
Knottingley Dr *GTS/LS* CH66 ... 155 L8
Knotty Ms *WLTN* L25 .......... 131 L2 🔢
The Knowe *NSTN* CH64 .......... 154 C5
Knowle Av *STHP* PR8 .......... 47 L8
Knowle CI *GTS/LS* CH66 .......... 163 G2
  *NG/CROX* L11 .......... 98 E3
Knowles Av *WGNS/IIMK* WN3 ... 79 H1
Knowles House Av *ECCL* WA10... 101 H2
Knowles St *BIRK* CH41 .......... 10 F4
  *CHLY/EC* PR7 .......... 32 E7 🔢
  *WDN* WA8 .......... 134 E3
  *WGNS/IIMK* WN3 .......... 5 H8
Knowsley Brow *CHLYE* PR6 .......... 33 G3
Knowsley Av *GOL/RIS/CU* WA3... 93M3
Knowsley CI *RF/TRAN* CH42 ... 128 C4 🔢
Knowsley Dr *LEIGH* WN7 .......... 93M3
  *WDN* WA8 .......... 133 G5
Knowsley Expy *RAIN/WH* L35 ... 116 F7
Knowsley La *CHLYE* PR6 .......... 44 F1
  *PR/KW* L34 .......... 86 E8
Knowsley Park La *PR/KW* L34 ... 100 E6
Knowsley Rd *ALL/GAR* L19 .......... 130 C7
  *BTL* L20 .......... 83 K8
  *CHTN/BK* PR9 .......... 24 D4
  *ORM* L39 .......... 63 H1
  *RAIN/WH* L35 .......... 117M3
  *RF/TRAN* CH42 .......... 128 C4
  *WAL/NB* CH45 .......... 95 J7
  *WCNNW/ST* WN6 .......... 56 B6
Knowsley St *ANF/KKDL* L4 .......... 97 H3 🔢
  *LEIGH* WN7 .......... 81 M8 🔢🔢
Knowsley Vw *RNFD/HAY* WA11 ... 76 A5
Knox CI *EP* CH65 .......... 96 F7 🔢
Knox St *BIRK* CH41 .......... 11 L6
Knutsford CI *ECCL* WA10 .......... 101 K3 🔢
Knutsford Gn *MOR/LEA* CH46 ... 110 A4
Knutsford Old Rd *WARRS* WA4 ... 138 C3
Knutsford Rd *MOR/LEA* CH46 ... 110 A4
  *WARRS* WA4 .......... 14 F8
Knutsford Wk *MGHL* L31 .......... 72 F1
Kremlin Dr *CLB/OSW/ST* L13 ... 98 B8
  *WD/CROXPK* L12 .......... 98 C8
Kronsbec Av *GTS/LS* CH66 .......... 155M7
Kylemore Av *CALD/MH* L18 .......... 130 B2
Kylemore CI *PEN/TH* CH61 .......... 141 G2
Kylemore Dr *PEN/TH* CH61 .......... 141 G2
Kylemore Rd *CL/PREN* CH43 .......... 127 J1
Kylemore Wy *HLWD* L26 .......... 131M6
  *PEN/TH* CH61 .......... 141 G2 🔢
Kynance Rd *NG/CROX* L11 .......... 85M8

# L

Laburnum Av *HUY* L36 .......... 116 A5
  *RNFD/HAY* WA11 .......... 89 M6
  *WARR* WA1 .......... 122 E6
  *WGNS/IIMK* WN3 .......... 5 L7
Laburnum Crs *KKBY* L32 .......... 85M2
Laburnum Dr *SKEL* WN8 .......... 64 F4
  *WCNNW/ST* WN6 .......... 68 C1
Laburnum Farm CI
  *NSTN* CH64 .......... 153 J8 🔢
Laburnum Gv *BRSC* L40 .......... 39 G7 🔢
  *GTS/LS* CH66 .......... 163 J3
  *MGHL* L31 .......... 73 H4 🔢
  *PEN/TH* CH61 .......... 125 M7
  *RUNC* WA7 .......... 19 K8
  *STHP* PR8 .......... 25 H6
Laburnum La
  *WARRW/BUR* WA5 .......... 119 J2
Laburnum PI *BTL* L20 .......... 7 J4
Laburnum Rd *CHLYE* PR6 .......... 33 K6
  *EHL/KEN* L7 .......... 113 M2 🔢
  *GOL/RIS/CU* WA3 .......... 93 H5
  *WAL/NB* CH45 .......... 95 K6
Laburnum St *AIMK* WN4 .......... 91 K3 🔢

Lace St *VAUX/LVPD* L3 .......... 13 G5
Lacey Ct *WDN* WA8 .......... 16 E6
Lacey Rd *PR/KW* L34 .......... 101 G8
Lacey St *ECCL* WA10 .......... 101 M5
  *WDN* WA8 .......... 16 D6
Ladies La *WGNE/HIN* WN2 .......... 69M7
Ladies Wk *NSTN* CH64 .......... 153 C5
Lad La *VAUX/LVPD* L3 .......... 12 D5 🔢
Lady Alice's Dr *BRSC* L40 .......... 52 A5
Ladybarn Av *GOL/RIS/CU* WA3 ... 92 B6 🔢
Ladybower CI *EHL/KEN* L7 .......... 113 K5
Ladycroft CI *WARR* WA1 .......... 123 G6 🔢
Ladywood Rd *WAL/EG* CH44 .......... 111 L2
Ladyfield *CL/PREN* CH43 .......... 110 E6
Ladyfields *WD/CROXPK* L12 .......... 98 D8
Lady Green La *HTWN* L38 .......... 71 G2 🔢
Lady Green La *HTWN* L38 .......... 70 F1
Lady La *GOL/RIS/CU* WA3 .......... 106 E4
  *WGNS/IIMK* WN3 .......... 79 G1
Ladypool *SPK/HALE* L24 .......... 147 L4
Ladysmith Av *GOL/RIS/CU* WA3 ... 91 L2
Ladysmith Rd *AIN/FAZ* L10 .......... 85 H6
Lady's Wk *BRSC* L40 .......... 51 L7
Ladywood Rd
  *WARRW/BUR* WA5 .......... 120 C4
Laffak Rd *RNFD/HAY* WA11 .......... 89M5
Lafford La *SKEL* WN8 .......... 51 G5
Laggan St *EHL/KEN* L7 .......... 113 K3 🔢
Laira St *WARRN/WOL* WA2 .......... 15 G2
Laird CI *CL/PREN* CH43 .......... 111 H5 🔢
Lairds PI *VAUX/LVPD* L3 .......... 13 G2
Laird St *BIRK* CH41 .......... 10 A2
  *CL/PREN* CH43 .......... 111 H5
Laithwaite CI *STHEL* WA9 .......... 118 D2 🔢
Laithwaite Rd
  *WGNW/BIL/O* WN5 .......... 67M6
Lakeland Av *AIMK* WN4 .......... 91 L3 🔢
Lakeland CI *CLVPS* L1 .......... 13 G9
Lakeland Gdns *CHLY/EC* PR7 .......... 32 C5
Lakemoor CI *STHEL* WA9 .......... 102 F6 🔢
Lakenheath Rd *HLWD* L26 .......... 132 A7
Lake PI *HOY* CH47 .......... 108 D6
Lake Rd *HOY* CH47 .......... 108 D6
  *WAV* L15 .......... 114 C6
Lakes Dr *WGNW/BIL/O* WN5 ... 67 G7
Lake Side *LEIGH* WN7 .......... 81 M7
Lakeside Av *WGNW/BIL/O* WN5 ... 74 F2
Lakeside CI *WDN* WA8 .......... 133 J6
Lakeside Ct *RNFD/HAY* WA11 ... 76 C7
  *WAL/NB* CH45 .......... 95 L5
Lakeside Dr *WARR* WA1 .......... 138 C3
Lakeside Gdns *RNFD/HAY* WA11... 76 C7
Lakeside Rd *LYMM* WA13 .......... 139M4
Lake St *ANF/KKDL* L4 .......... 97 J6
Lake Vw *RAIN/WH* L35 .......... 117 G4
Laleston CI *WDN* WA8 .......... 134 A5
Lamberhead Rd
  *WGNW/BIL/O* WN5 .......... 67 K7
Lambert St *VAUX/LVPD* L3 .......... 13 K5 🔢
Lambert Wy *VAUX/LVPD* L3 .......... 13 K5 🔢
Lambeth Rd *EV* L5 .......... 96 F6
Lambeth Wk *ANF/KKDL* L4 .......... 96 F6
Lambley CI *LEIGH* WN7 .......... 81 M5
Lambourn Av *WDN* WA8 .......... 117 L8
Lambourne *SKEL* WN8 .......... 65 K1
Lambourne CI *GTS/LS* CH66 ... 163 H5 🔢
Lambourne Gv *STHEL* WA9 .......... 103 J1 🔢
Lambourne Rd *ANF/KKDL* L4 .......... 97M4
Lambshear La *MGHL* L31 .......... 72 C1
Lambsickle CI *RUNC* WA7 .......... 149 H7 🔢
Lambsickle La *RUNC* WA7 .......... 149 H7
Lambs La *WARR* WA1 .......... 122 C5
Lamb St *WGN* WN1 .......... 5 J1
Lambton Rd *AIG/SPK* L17 .......... 129 K2
Lambton St *WGNW/BIL/O* WN5 ... 67 K8
Lamerton CI
  *WARRW/BUR* WA5 .......... 135 M1 🔢
Lammermoor Rd
  *CALD/MH* L18 .......... 130 C3 🔢
Lampeter CI
  *WARRW/BUR* WA5 .......... 121 G3 🔢
Lampeter Rd *NPK/KEN* L6.... 97 L7
Lamport CI *WDN* WA8 .......... 135 G2 🔢
Lamport St *TOX* L8 .......... 113 G7
Lanark CI *ECCL* WA10 .......... 8 E7
Lancaster Av *AIG/SPK* L17 .......... 113M8
  *CSBY/BLUN* L23 .......... 82 F2
  *GOL/RIS/CU* WA3 .......... 92 E5
  *RAIN/WH* L35 .......... 116 F2
  *RAIN/WH* L35 .......... 133 J3
  *RUNC* WA7 .......... 18 D8
  *WAL/NB* CH45 .......... 95 K8
Lancaster CI *CHLYE* PR6 .......... 44 D5 🔢
  *EV* L5 .......... 96 F7 🔢
  *MGHL* L31 .......... 73 H4 🔢
  *NEWLW* WA12 .......... 91 H8
  *PS/BROM* CH62 .......... 128 D7 🔢
  *STHP* PR8 .......... 25 H6 🔢
  *WARRN/WOL* WA2 .......... 122 B3 🔢
Lancaster Crs *SKEL* WN8 .......... 65 G4
Lancaster Dr *CHTN/BK* PR9 .......... 23 G8
Lancaster Ga *CHTN/BK* PR9 .......... 23 H8
Lancaster La *SKEL* WN8 .......... 53 L2
Lancaster PI *CHLYE* PR6 .......... 44 C5 🔢
Lancaster Rd *FMBY* L37 .......... 59 G4
  *HUY* L36 .......... 116 C1
  *STHP* PR8 .......... 35 G1
  *WDN* WA8 .......... 134 C2
Lancaster St *CHLY/EC* PR7 .......... 43 H4
  *EV* L5 .......... 96 F7
  *WARRW/BUR* WA5 .......... 121 G8 🔢
  *WGNS/IIMK* WN3 .......... 5 J7
  *WLT/FAZ* L9 .......... 97 H2
Lance Gv *WAV* L15 .......... 114 C6
Lance La *WAV* L15 .......... 114 C6
Lancelyn Ter *BEB* CH63 .......... 143 H1 🔢
Lancer Ct *RUNC* WA7 .......... 150 A2
Lancers Cft *GTS/LS* CH66 .......... 163 G4
Lance Wood PI
  *WGNW/BIL/O* WN5 .......... 67M7
Lancing Av *WARRN/WOL* WA2 ... 121 J1
Lancing CI *WLTN* L25 .......... 131M4
Lancing Dr *AIN/FAZ* L10 .......... 84 F3
Lancing Rd *EP* CH65 .......... 20 E6
  *WLTN* L25 .......... 131 M4
Lancing Wy *WLTN* L25 .......... 131M4
Lancots La *STHEL* WA9 .......... 102 F5

Land Cut La *GOL/RIS/CU* WA3 .. 122 F2
Land End *MGHL* L31 .......... 73 L4
Lander Cl *WARRW/BUR* WA5 .. 120 F6
Lander Rd *LITH* L21 .......... 83 K7
Landford Av *WLT/FAZ* L9 .... 98 A1
Landford Pl *WLT/FAZ* L9 ...... 98 A1
Land Gate La *AIMK* WN4 ...... 79 J6
Landican La *BEB* CH63 ........ 127 J7
  *GR/UP/WCH* CH49 .......... 126 E4
Landican Rd *GR/UP/WCH* CH49 .. 126 D4
Land La *CHTN/BK* PR9 ........ 25 L1
Landor Cl *GOL/RIS/CU* WA3 .. 93 G5
Landscape Dene
  *FROD/HEL* WA6 ............ 166 F1
Landseer Av *NSTN* CH64 ...... 153 H6
  *WARRS* WA4 .............. 137 K4
Landseer Rd *EV* L5 .......... 97 H8
Lane Head Av *GOL/RIS/CU* WA3 .. 93 G5
Lanfranc Cl *CHLDW* L16 ...... 115 G5
Lanfranc Wy *CHLDW* L16 ...... 115 G5
Langbar *RAIN/WH* L35 ........ 117 G3
Langcliffe Cl
  *GOL/RIS/CU* WA3 .......... 107 G2
Langdale Av *FMBY* L37 ........ 58 F2
  *GOL/RIS/CU* WA3 .......... 92 E4
  *LEY/BBR* PR5 .............. 29 K2
  *PEN/TH* CH61 ............ 141 H1
  *WGN* WN1 ................ 68 D2
  *WGNE/HIN* WN2 ............ 69 K5
Langdale Cl *FMBY* L37 ........ 58 F3
  *KKBY* L32 ................ 86 B4
  *WARRN/WOL* WA2 .......... 122 A2
  *WDN* WA8 ................ 133 L5
Langdale Crs *WGNE/HIN* WN2 .. 80 D5
  *WGNW/BIL/O* WN5 .......... 67 K5
Langdale Dr *BRSC* L40 ........ 52 A1
  *MGHL* L31 ................ 73 G3
Langdale Gdns *STHP* PR8 ...... 35 H4
Langdale Gv *RNFD/HAY* WA11 .. 89 K2
  *WGNE/HIN* WN2 ............ 80 D2
Langdale Rd *BEB* CH63 ...... 143 G1
  *RUNC* WA7 ................ 19 J5
  *WAL/NB* CH45 .............. 95 J6
  *WAV* L15 ................ 114 A7
  *WGNW/BIL/O* WN5 .......... 67 K6
Langdale St *BTL* L20 .......... 7 J5
Langdale Wy *FROD/HEL* WA6 .. 160 E4
Langfield *GOL/RIS/CU* WA3 .... 93 G6
Langford *SPK/HALE* L24 ...... 147 L4
Langford Gv *PS/BROM* CH62 .. 143 M8
Langford Rd *ALL/GAR* L19 .. 130 B5
Langham Av *AIG/SPK* L17 .... 129 L2
Langham Rd
  *WGNNW/ST* WN6 .......... 55 M4
Langham St *ANF/KKDL* L4 .... 97 H5
Langholm La *WGNS/IIMK* WN3 .. 78 F3
Langholm Rd *AIMK* WN4 ...... 90 E1
Langland Cl *ANF/KKDL* L4 .... 97 M5
  *WARRW/BUR* WA5 .......... 121 G3
Lang La *WKBY* CH48 .......... 124 D2
Lang La South *WKBY* CH48 .. 124 E2
Langley Cl *BEB* CH63 ........ 143 H4
  *GOL/RIS/CU* WA3 .......... 92 E4
  *HTWN* L38 ................ 70 B3
  *WD/CROXPK* L12 .......... 99 H2
  *WGNNW/ST* WN6 .......... 56 A3
Langley Pl *BRSC* L40 .......... 51 K1
Langley Rd *BEB* CH63 ...... 143 H4
  *BRSC* L40 ................ 51 K1
Langley St *TOX* L8 .......... 113 G7
  *WGNW/BIL/O* WN5 .......... 67 M7
Langrove St *EV* L5 .......... 97 G8
Langsdale St *VAUX/LVPD* L3 .. 13 L4
Langset Av *WGNE/HIN* WN2 .. 69 M7
Langstone Av
  *GR/UP/WCH* CH49 .......... 125 K3
Langton Av *WGNNW/ST* WN6 .. 56 A4
Langton Brow *CHLY/EC* PR7 .. 30 F8
Langton Cl *CHLY/EC* PR7 ...... 30 F8
  *NEWLW* WA12 .............. 104 C1
  *WDN* WA8 ................ 133 K2
Langton Gn *WARR* WA1 ...... 122 F6
Langton Rd *NWD/KWIPK* L33 .. 74 B3
  *WAV* L15 ................ 113 M6
Langtree *SKEL* WN8 .......... 65 K2
Langtree La *WGNNW/ST* WN6 .. 55 M2
Langtree St *STHEL* WA9 ...... 9 L5
Langtry Cl *ANF/KKDL* L4 ...... 96 F5
Langtry Rd *ANF/KKDL* L4 .... 96 F5
Langwell Cl *GOL/RIS/CU* WA3 .. 107 J8
Langwood La *RNFD/HAY* WA11 .. 76 E4
Lansbury Av *STHEL* WA9 ...... 103 G3
Lansbury Rd *HUY* L36 ........ 116 C3
Lansbury St *WGNW/BIL/O* WN5 .. 67 J7
Lansdown *WD/CROXPK* L12 .... 98 C7
Lansdowne *FROD/HEL* WA6 .. 160 F7
  *GOL/RIS/CU* WA3 .......... 107 G3
Lansdowne Cl *BIRK* CH41 .... 10 A1
Lansdowne Pl
  *CL/PREN* CH43 ............ 111 H5
  *EV* L5 .................... 97 H7
Lansdowne Rd *CL/PREN* CH43 .. 111 H5
  *STHP* PR8 ................ 25 G7
  *WAL/NB* CH45 .............. 95 H5
Lanville Rd *ALL/GAR* L19 .... 130 D4
Lanyork Rd *VAUX/LVPD* L3 .... 12 D4
Lapford Crs *NWD/KWIPK* L33 .. 86 C1
Lapwing Cl *GOL/RIS/CU* WA3 .. 92 F5
  *WD/CROXPK* L12 .......... 99 G4
Lapwing Ct *HLWD* L26 ...... 132 M4
Lapwing Gv *RUNC* WA7 ...... 150 F2
Lapwing La *WARRS* WA4 ...... 144 A3
Lapworth St *MOR/LEA* CH46 .. 109 K5
Lapworth St *EV* L5 .......... 96 F7
Larch Av *CHLYE* PR6 ........ 33 G3
  *NEWLW* WA12 .............. 104 C3
  *WARRW/BUR* WA5 .......... 120 A8
  *WDN* WA8 ................ 134 D3
  *WGNW/BIL/O* WN5 .......... 67 M7
Larch Cl *ALL/GAR* L19 ...... 130 B6
  *GOL/RIS/CU* WA3 .......... 93 H7
  *RUNC* WA7 ................ 19 M9
  *SKEL* WN8 ................ 65 G4
  *WGNW/BIL/O* WN5 .......... 77 M8
Larchdale Cl *GTS/LS* CH66 .. 163 H5
Larchdale Gv *WLT/FAZ* L9 .... 97 K3
Larchfield Rd *CSBY/BLUN* L23 .. 71 J8

Larch Gv *CL/PREN* CH43 ...... 111 G5
Larch Lea *NPK/KEN* L6 ...... 97 K8
Larch Rd *HUY* L36 .......... 115 L3
  *RF/TRAN* CH42 ............ 10 F8
  *RNFD/HAY* WA11 .......... 91 G6
  *RUNC* WA7 ................ 149 L6
Larch St *STHP* PR8 .......... 25 G8
Larch Wy *FMBY* L37 .......... 58 F1
Larchways *WARRS* WA4 ...... 137 M8
Larchwood Av *MGHL* L31 .... 72 E6
Larchwood Cl *PEN/TH* CH61 .. 141 H2
  *WLTN* L25 ................ 115 K8
Larchwood Dr *BEB* CH63 .... 128 B6
  *WGN* WN1 ................ 68 D1
Larcombe Av
  *GR/UP/WCH* CH49 .......... 110 B8
Larkfield *CHLY/EC* PR7 ...... 30 D7
Larkfield Av *WARR* WA1 ...... 122 B6
  *WGN* WN1 ................ 68 D1
Larkfield Cl *AIG/SPK* L17 .... 129 L3
Larkfield Gv *AIG/SPK* L17 .... 129 L3
Larkfield La *CHTN/BK* PR9 .... 25 J2
Larkfield Rd *AIG/SPK* L17 .... 129 L3
Larkfield Vw *WAV* L15 ...... 114 A5
Larkhill *SKEL* WN8 .......... 65 K1
Larkhill Av *GR/UP/WCH* CH49 .. 110 C7
  *WGNNW/ST* WN6 .......... 56 B5
Larkhill Cl *CLB/OSW/ST* L13 .. 98 A6
Larkhill Gv *HTWN* L38 ...... 70 B2
Larkhill La *CLB/OSW/ST* L13 .. 98 A6
  *FMBY* L37 ................ 58 E1
Larkhill Pl *CLB/OSW/ST* L13.. 98 A6
Larkhill Vw *CLB/OSW/ST* L13 .. 98 B6
Larkhill Wy *GR/UP/WCH* CH49 .. 110 C6
Larkspur Cl *RUNC* WA7 ...... 161 H1
  *STHP* PR8 ................ 3 L6
Larkstoke Cl *WARRS* WA4 .... 138 A7
Larksway *HES* CH60 ........ 141 K5
Lark Wy *AIG/SPK* L17 ...... 129 K2
Larton Rd *WKBY* CH48 ...... 124 F2
Lascelles Rd *AIG/GAR* L19 .. 130 F6
Lascelles St *STHEL* WA9 ...... 9 M5
Laskey La *WARRS* WA4 ...... 139 H1
Latchford Cl *HES* CH60 ...... 141 K7
Latchford St *WARRS* WA4 .. 138 C2
Late Moffatt Rd West
  *WLT/FAZ* L9 .............. 84 D6
Latham Av *FROD/HEL* WA6 .. 166 D4
  *NEWLW* WA12 ............ 104 E1
  *ORM* L39 ................ 51 J8
  *RUNC* WA7 ................ 19 L5
Latham La *WGNW/BIL/O* WN5 .. 67 F5
Latham Rd *HOR/BR* BL6 ...... 57 L2
Latham St *EV* L5 .......... 96 F7
Latham Wy *BEB* CH63 ...... 143 K3
Lathbury La *AIG/SPK* L17 .... 114 A8
Lathom Av *LITH* L21 ........ 83 H7
  *SKEL* WN8 ................ 53 K2
  *WAL/EG* CH44 ............ 111 K1
  *WARRN/WOL* WA2 .......... 121 K5
Lathom Cl *BRSC* L40 ........ 52 A1
Lathom Dr *MGHL* L31 ........ 73 G2
  *RNFD/HAY* WA11 .......... 76 B6
Lathom La *BRSC* L40 ........ 51 L2
Lathom Rd *BTL* L20 .......... 83 L8
  *CHTN/BK* PR9 ............ 24 E4
  *HUY* L36 ................ 116 A2
  *ORM* L39 ................ 64 B6
Lathum Cl *RAIN/WH* L35 .... 101 G8
Latimer Cl *WGNW/BIL/O* WN5 .. 67 H6
Latimer St *EV* L5 .......... 96 F8
Latrigg Rd *AIG/SPK* L17 ...... 130 A3
Lauder Cl *NWD/KWIPK* L33 .. 73 M7
Launceston Cl *RUNC* WA7 .. 150 E7
Launceston Dr
  *WARRW/BUR* WA5 .......... 136 A2
Launceston Rd *WGNE/HIN* WN2 .. 81 L2
The Laund *WAL/NB* CH45 .... 95 H8
Laurel Av *BEB* CH63 ........ 143 G1
  *BRSC* L40 ................ 39 G7
  *CHLY/EC* PR7 ............ 31 K2
  *HES* CH60 ................ 141 H4
  *NEWLW* WA12 ............ 104 F3
  *WARR* WA1 ................ 122 F6
Laurel Bank *WARRS* WA4 .... 138 E4
  *WDN* WA8 ................ 134 C2
Laurelbanks *HES* CH60 ...... 141 G4
Laurel Crs *WGNE/HIN* WN2 .. 81 J2
Laurel Dr *ECCL* WA10 ...... 101 H1
  *EP* CH65 ................ 163 K3
  *NSTN* CH64 .............. 154 D4
  *SKEL* WN8 ................ 65 G3
Laurel Gv *AIMK* WN4 ........ 91 K1
  *CHTN/BK* PR9 ............ 25 G6
  *CSBY/WL* L22 ............ 82 F3
  *GOL/RIS/CU* WA3 .......... 92 F5
  *HUY* L36 ................ 116 A5
Laurelhurst Av *PEN/TH* CH61 .. 141 J1
Laurel Rd *ECCL* WA10 ...... 8 A7
  *EHL/KEN* L7 ............ 113 M3
  *PR/KW* L34 .............. 101 G7
  *RF/TRAN* CH42 ............ 11 G9
  *RNFD/HAY* WA11 .......... 90 B8
Laurels Farm Ct *CHNE* CH2 .. 165 K2
The Laurels *CHLY/EC* PR7 .... 43 H2
Laurelwood Dr *GTS/LS* CH66 .. 163 G5
Lauriston Rd *ANF/KKDL* L4 .. 97 L4
Laurus Cl *NTHLY* L27 ...... 116 B8
Lavan Cl *NPK/KEN* L6 ...... 113 J2
Lavan St *EP* CH65 .......... 20 F7
Lavender Cl *ANF/KKDL* L4 .. 19 M6
Lavender Crs *PR/KW* L34 .... 101 G7
Lavender Gv *CHLY/EC* PR7 .... 32 E8
Lavender Rd *WGNNW/ST* WN6 .. 68 B2
Lavender Wy *RNFD/HAY* WA11 .. 89 K2
Lavrock Bank *TOX* L8 ...... 129 G3
Lawler St *HES* CH60 ........ 141 L5
  *SKEL* WN8 ................ 53 L5
Lawler St *LITH* L21 .......... 83 K7
Lawn Av *WARR* WA1 ........ 122 B5
Lawns Av *BEB* CH63 ........ 143 K7
  *SKEL* WN8 ................ 66 E8
Lawnside Cl *RF/TRAN* CH42 .. 128 D4
The Lawns *CHTN/BK* PR9 .... 25 H3
  *CL/PREN* CH43 ............ 110 F6

Lawnswood Gv *CHNE* CH2 .. 165 K2
Lawnwood Av *CHLY/EC* PR7 .. 32 C8
Lawrence Cl *ALL/GAR* L19 .. 130 C6
Lawrence Ct *WGNE/HIN* WN2 .. 80 D5
Lawrence Gv *WAV* L15 ...... 114 A6
Lawrence La *CHLY/EC* PR7 .... 30 E6
Lawrence Rd *CHLY/EC* PR7 .. 32 D6
  *ECCL* WA10 .............. 88 E7
  *WAV* L15 ................ 113 M6
Lawrence St *NEWLW* WA12 .. 104 C2
Lawson Cl *WARR* WA1 ...... 123 G6
  *CHTN/BK* PR9 ............ 25 J6
Lawson Av *BTL* L20 .......... 84 F2
Lawton Cl *WD/CROXPK* L12 .. 98 A8
Lawton Rd *CSBY/WL* L22 .... 82 F3
  *HUY* L36 ................ 115 L3
  *RAIN/WH* L35 ............ 117 M3
Lawton St *CLVPS* L1 ........ 13 J8
Laxey Av *WARR* WA1 ........ 122 F7
Laxey Crs *LEIGH* WN7 ...... 81 L6
Laxey St *TOX* L8 .......... 113 G7
Laxton Cl *GTS/LS* CH66 .... 163 H5
Laxton Rd *WLTN* L25 ...... 131 L7
Layford Cl *HUY* L36 ........ 99 M7
Layford Rd *HUY* L36 ...... 99 M8
Layland Av *GOL/RIS/CU* WA3 .. 107 G1
Layton Av *CL/PREN* CH43 .. 127 H3
Layton Cl *GOL/RIS/CU* WA3 .. 123 G2
  *WGNW/BIL/O* WN5 .......... 67 M8
  *WLTN* L25 ................ 131 L3
Layton Rd *WLTN* L25 ...... 131 L3
Lazenby Crs *AIMK* WN4 .... 91 H2
Leach Cft *STBRV* L28 ........ 99 J6
Leach La *STHEL* WA9 ........ 102 F8
  *ECCL* WA10 .............. 8 F3
Leach Wy *PEN/TH* CH61 .... 125 L7
Lea Cl *CL/PREN* CH43 ...... 127 G1
Lea Crs *ORM* L39 .......... 51 G6
Leacroft *GOL/RIS/CU* WA3.. 107 J7
Lea Cross Gv *WDN* WA8 .... 133 L2
Leadale Cl *WGNNW/ST* WN6 .. 55 M4
Leadenhall Cl *EV* L5 ........ 97 H7
Leader St *WGN* WN1 ........ 5 K4
  *WGNW/BIL/O* WN5 .......... 67 L7
Leafield Cl *PEN/TH* CH61 .. 126 B7
Leafield Rd *WLTN* L25 ...... 131 K7
Leagate *AIN/FAZ* L10 ...... 85 H5
Lea Gate Cl *WGNS/IIMK* WN3 .. 79 G2
Lea Green Rd *STHEL* WA9 .. 102 C8
Leal Holme Av *WGNE/HIN* WN2 .. 69 J3
Leamington Av
  *NEWLW* WA12 ............ 104 E4
Leamington Cl *NSTN* CH64 .. 153 G7
  *WARRW/BUR* WA5 .......... 120 C5
Leamington Rd *NG/CROX* L11 .. 97 M3
  *STHP* PR8 ................ 34 E8
Leander Rd *WAL/NB* CH45 .. 95 J8
Lea Rd *WAL/EG* CH44 ...... 95 L8
Leas Cl *GTS/LS* CH66 ...... 155 L8
Leaside *RUNC* WA7 ........ 149 M4
Leasowe Av *WAL/NB* CH45 .. 95 G7
Leasowe Gdns *MOR/LEA* CH46 .. 110 A2
Leasowe Rd *MOR/LEA* CH46 .. 110 C1
  *WLT/FAZ* L9 .............. 84 D6
Leasoweside *MOR/LEA* CH46 .. 110 C1
The Leas *PEN/TH* CH61 ...... 126 D7
  *WAL/NB* CH45 ............ 95 G6
Lea St *WGNS/IIMK* WN3 .... 4 B5
Leatham Cl *GOL/RIS/CU* WA3 .. 123 G2
Leatherbarrows La *MGHL* L31 .. 73 J6
Leather's La *HLWD* L26 .... 132 B6
Leathwood *MGHL* L31 ...... 73 G4
Lea Vw *WGN* WN1 .......... 5 L2
Leaway *GR/UP/WCH* CH49 .. 125 M1
  *WGNE/HIN* WN2 ............ 80 B6
Leawood Gv *MOR/LEA* CH46 .. 110 B5
Leckwith Rd *NTHTN* L30 .... 84 D2
Ledburn *SKEL* WN8 ........ 65 G3
Ledbury Cl *CL/PREN* CH43 .. 127 G3
  *ECCL* WA10 .............. 101 K2
  *WD/CROXPK* L12 .......... 99 H1
Ledger Rd *RNFD/HAY* WA11 .. 90 C8
Ledmore Gv *AIMK* WN4 .... 90 F2
Ledsham Cl *CL/PREN* CH43 .. 127 G1
  *GOL/RIS/CU* WA3 .......... 122 G2
Ledsham La *GTS/LS* CH66 .. 162 B2
Ledsham Park Dr
  *GTS/LS* CH66 ............ 155 J7
Ledsham Rd *GTS/LS* CH66 .. 155 J8
  *KKBY* L32 ................ 85 L3
Ledson Gv *ORM* L39 ........ 62 E6
Ledston Cl *RUNC* WA7 ...... 150 F4
Ledyard Cl *WARRW/BUR* WA5.. 120 F6
Leece St *CLVPS* L1 .......... 13 J9
Lee Cl *RAIN/WH* L35 ...... 118 F8
Leecourt Cl *WD/CROXPK* L12 .. 98 F8
Leeds St *VAUX/LVPD* L3 .... 12 E4
Lee Hall Rd *WLTN* L25 ...... 115 L8
Lee La *BRSC* L40 .......... 40 E6
  *WGNE/HIN* WN2 ............ 80 D5
Leeming Cl *ALL/GAR* L19 .. 130 E8
Lee Park Av *WLTN* L25 .... 115 L8
Lee Rd *HOY* CH47 .......... 108 E6
  *WARRW/BUR* WA5 .......... 120 D7
Lees Av *RF/TRAN* CH42 .... 128 B3
Leeside Av *KKBY* L32 ...... 86 B5
Leeside Cl *KKBY* L32 ...... 86 B4
Lees La *EP* CH65 .......... 20 F7
  *NSTN* CH64 .............. 153 K5
  *SKEL* WN8 ................ 53 L5
  *SKEL* WN8 ................ 54 C6
  *WD/CROXPK* L12 .......... 98 F6
Leeson Av *CHLY/EC* PR7 .... 42 F1
Lees Rd *CHLYE* PR6 ........ 44 D5
  *NWD/KWIPK* L33 .......... 86 D3
Lee St *STHEL* WA9 .......... 103 G5
Leeswood *SKEL* WN8 ...... 65 K2
Leeswood Rd
  *GR/UP/WCH* CH49 .......... 126 C2
Lee Vale Rd *WLTN* L25 .... 131 L1
Legh Av *KIRK/FR/WA* PR4 .. 27 J1
Legh Rd *PS/BROM* CH62 .. 128 D6

  *RNFD/HAY* WA11 .......... 90 C7
Legh St *AIMK* WN4 .......... 91 K3
  *GOL/RIS/CU* WA3 .......... 92 C5
  *NEWLW* WA12 ............ 104 C2
  *WARR* WA1 ................ 14 D5
Legion La *PS/BROM* CH62 .. 146 D1
Legion Rd *ECCL* WA10 ...... 101 M5
Leicester Av *CSBY/WL* L22.. 82 F3
Leicester Rd *BTL* L20 ...... 7 K2
Leicester St *CHTN/BK* PR9 .. 3 H1
  *STHEL* WA9 .............. 101 M3
  *WARRW/BUR* WA5 .......... 121 G8
Leigh Av *WDN* WA8 ........ 16 C2
Leigh Rd *WGNE/HIN* WN2 .. 81 K4
  *WKBY* CH48 .............. 124 D2
Leighs Hey Crs *KKBY* L32 .. 86 B3
Leigh St *LEIGH* WN7 ........ 81 L8
  *WGN* WN1 ................ 5 H5
  *WGNE/HIN* WN2 ............ 81 K4
Leighton Av *HOY* CH47 .... 109 G5
  *MGHL* L31 ................ 72 F3
Leighton Cha *NSTN* CH64 .. 152 F4
Leighton Ct *NSTN* CH64 .... 152 F5
Leighton Dr *LEIGH* WN7 .... 93 K4
Leighton Pk *NSTN* CH64 .... 152 F5
Leighton Rd *BIRK* CH41 .... 128 A1
  *NSTN* CH64 .............. 152 E2
The Leightons *NSTN* CH64 .. 152 F5
Leighton St *ANF/KKDL* L4 .. 7 L9
Leinster Rd *CLB/OSW/ST* L13 .. 114 D2
Leinster St *WGN* WN1 ...... 18 E2
Leison St *ANF/KKDL* L4 .... 96 F6
Leiston Cl *PEN/TH* CH61 .. 126 A6
Lemon Gv *TOX* L8 .......... 113 L4
Lemon St *EV* L5 ............ 96 F7
Lemon Tree Wk *ECCL* WA10 .. 101 M4
Lendel Cl *FMBY* L37 ........ 59 G2
Lenfield Dr *RNFD/HAY* WA11.. 90 B7
Lenham Wy *SPK/HALE* L24 .. 146 D1
Lennon St *CHLY/EC* PR7 .... 32 E6
Lennox Av *WAL/NB* CH45 .. 95 K6
Lennox La *CL/PREN* CH43 .. 110 E4
Lenthall St *ANF/KKDL* L4 .. 97 H3
Lenton Av *FMBY* L37 ........ 58 F1
Lenton Rd *WLTN* L25 ...... 115 L8
Leo Cl *DV/KA/FCH* L14 .... 115 H1
Leominster Rd *WAL/EG* CH44 .. 111 K1
Leonard Cheshire Dr *NTHTN* L30.. 84 B2
Leonard St *RUNC* WA7 .... 148 F6
  *STHEL* WA9 .............. 103 H6
  *WARRN/WOL* WA2 .......... 15 G2
  *WARRS* WA4 .............. 137 L4
Leon Cl *WARRW/BUR* WA5 .. 119 M6
Leonora St *TOX* L8 ........ 129 J1
Leopold Gv *STHEL* WA9 .... 102 E8
Leopold Rd *CSBY/WL* L22 .. 82 E3
  *EHL/KEN* L7 ............ 113 K3
Leopold St *WAL/EG* CH44 .. 112 A2
  *WGNW/BIL/O* WN5 .......... 67 K8
Lesley Rd *STHP* PR8 ........ 25 G6
Leslie Av *GR/UP/WCH* CH49 .. 125 M2
Leslie Rd *ECCL* WA10 ...... 101 L5
Lesseps Rd *TOX* L8 ........ 113 L6
Lessingham Av *WGN* WN1 .. 68 D2
Lessingham Rd *WDN* WA8 .. 134 B2
Lester Cl *ANF/KKDL* L4 .... 97 G6
Lester Dr *ECCL* WA10 ...... 88 C8
  *PEN/TH* CH61 ............ 125 K8
Lester Gv *HUY* L36 ........ 116 B1
Lestock St *TOX* L8 .......... 113 G6
Leta St *ANF/KKDL* L4 ...... 97 H4
Letchworth Dr *CHLY/EC* PR7 .. 32 D7
Letchworth St *NPK/KEN* L6 .. 97 L8
Letchworth Wks
  *CHLY/EC* PR7 ............ 32 D7
Lethbridge Cl *EV* L5 ........ 96 F7
Lethbridge Rd *STHP* PR8.... 3 M7
Letitia St *TOX* L8 .......... 113 H8
Levens Hey *WD/CROXPK* L12 .. 98 F7
  *WGNW/BIL/O* WN5 .......... 69 J5
Levens Pl *WGNE/HIN* WN2 .. 69 J5
Leven Cl *ANF/KKDL* L4 .... 97 G5
Leven Wk *EP* CH65 ........ 156 C5
Lever Av *WAL/EG* CH44 .... 112 A3
Lever Cswy *BEB* CH63 ...... 127 K6
Leveret Rd *SPK/HALE* L24 .. 147 J2
Lever Park Av *HOR/BR* BL6 .. 45 J8
Lever St *STHEL* WA9 ........ 118 F1
Leveson Rd *CLB/OSW/ST* L13.. 114 D4
Levisham Gdns
  *WARRW/BUR* WA5 .......... 121 G6
Lewis Av *WARRW/BUR* WA5 .. 121 H3
Lewis Cl *CHLY/EC* PR7 ...... 44 A7
  *WGNS/IIMK* WN3 .......... 4 A9
Lewis Crs *WDN* WA8 ...... 16 C5
Lewis Gv *WDN* WA8 ........ 133 M4
Lewisham Rd *NG/CROX* L11 .. 98 C4
  *PS/BROM* CH62 ............ 128 C7
Lewis St *ECCL* WA10 ........ 8 D1
Lexden St *WARRW/BUR* WA5 .. 121 G7
Lexham Rd *DV/KA/FCH* L14 .. 114 C2
Lexton Dr *CHTN/BK* PR9 .... 25 K2
Leybourne Av *STHP* PR8 .... 35 H6
Leybourne Cl *WLTN* L25 .... 115 J7
Leybourne Gn *WLTN* L25 .. 115 J7
Leybourne Gv *WLTN* L25 .. 115 J7
Leyburn Cl *KKBY* L32 ...... 86 A3
  *WGN* WN1 ................ 5 L2
Leyburn Rd *WAL/NB* CH45 .. 95 H6
Ley Cl *STHEL* WA9 .......... 118 F1
Leyfield Cl *WD/CROXPK* L12 .. 98 F7
Leyfield Rd *WD/CROXPK* L12 .. 98 F7
Leyland Av *WGNE/HIN* WN2 .. 80 F2
Leyland Gn Rd *AIMK* WN4 .. 78 E6
Leyland Gv *RNFD/HAY* WA11.. 90 B7
Leyland La *LEY/BBR* PR5 .... 30 C2
Leyland Mill La *WGN* WN1 .. 68 C2
Leyland Rd *CHTN/BK* PR9 .... 3 L1
  *RNFD/HAY* WA11 .......... 76 B7
  *STHP* PR8 ................ 24 E4
Leyland St *PR/KW* L34 ...... 100 F7
  *WGNE/HIN* WN2 ............ 80 D4
Leyland Wy *ORM* L39 ...... 51 H8
Leyton Cl *RUNC* WA7 ...... 149 K7

Liberty St *WAV* L15 ........ 114 A6
Libra Cl *DV/KA/FCH* L14 .... 99 J8
Library St *CHLY/EC* PR7 .... 32 E6
  *WGN* WN1 ................ 4 F4
Libson Cl *WARRN/WOL* WA2 .. 122 C3
Lichen Cl *CHLY/EC* PR7 .... 42 F1
Lichfield Av *CSBY/WL* L22.. 82 F2
  *GOL/RIS/CU* WA3 .......... 92 F5
Lichfield Cl *NTHTN* L30 .... 84 C4
Lichfield Dr *GTS/LS* CH66 .. 163 G5
Lichfield Gv *AIMK* WN4 .... 91 L3
Lichfield Rd *CHLY/EC* PR7 .. 32 D7
  *HLWD* L26 ................ 132 A7
  *WAV* L15 ................ 114 C7
Lichfield St *WAL/NB* CH45 .. 95 L6
  *WGNW/BIL/O* WN5 .......... 67 L8
Lickers La *RAIN/WH* L35 .... 117 G3
Liddell Av *MGHL* L31 ...... 85 J1
Liddell Rd *WD/CROXPK* L12 .. 98 B6
Lidderdale Rd *WAV* L15 .... 114 A7
Lidgate Cl *NWD/KWIPK* L33 .. 74 A8
Liebig St *WGN* WN1 ........ 16 E4
Lifeboat Rd *FMBY* L37 ...... 58 C4
Liffey St *TOX* L8 .......... 113 K6
Lifton Rd *NWD/KWIPK* L33 .. 86 B3
Lightbody St *EV* L5 ........ 96 D8
Lightburn St *RUNC* WA7 .... 18 F6
Lightfoot Cl *HES* CH60 .... 141 K6
Lightfoot La *HES* CH60 .... 141 K6
Lighthorne Dr *STHP* PR8 .... 47 J1
Lighthouse Rd *HOY* CH47 .. 108 C7
  *SPK/HALE* L24 ............ 148 A6
Lighthurst Av *CHLY/EC* PR7 .. 32 E7
Lighthurst La *CHLY/EC* PR7 .. 32 E8
Lightshaw La *GOL/RIS/CU* WA3 .. 92 D1
Lightwood Dr *EHL/KEN* L7 .. 113 L5
Lightwood St *EHL/KEN* L7 .. 113 L5
Lilac Av *AIMK* WN4 ........ 78 E6
  *STHP* PR8 ................ 47 M3
  *WARRW/BUR* WA5 .......... 120 A8
  *WDN* WA8 ................ 134 D3
  *WGNNW/ST* WN6 .......... 68 C2
Lilac Crs *RUNC* WA7 ........ 19 L7
Lilac Gdns *WGNE/HIN* WN2 .. 80 B1
Lilac Gv *GTS/LS* CH66 ...... 163 J5
  *HUY* L36 ................ 115 M5
  *RNFD/HAY* WA11 .......... 90 B8
  *SKEL* WN8 ................ 65 G4
  *WARRS* WA4 .............. 138 A4
  *WGNS/IIMK* WN3 .......... 89 H1
Lilac Rd *GOL/RIS/CU* WA3 .. 92 C4
Lilford Av *WARRW/BUR* WA5 .. 121 H8
  *WLT/FAZ* L9 .............. 84 B7
Lilford Dr *WARRW/BUR* WA5 .. 120 B7
Lilford St *WARRW/BUR* WA5 .. 14 B2
Lilian Dr *WGNNW/ST* WN6 .. 68 C2
Lilley Rd *EHL/KEN* L7 ...... 113 M2
Lillian Rd *ANF/KKDL* L4 .... 97 K7
Lillie Cl *CL/PREN* CH43 .... 110 E5
Lillyfield *HES* CH60 ........ 141 H7
Lilly Gv *ANF/KKDL* L4 ...... 97 K4
Lilly V *EHL/KEN* L7 ........ 113 M2
Lily Av *NEWLW* WA12 ...... 104 E3
Lily Pl *AIMK* WN4 .......... 91 L3
Lily Rd *LITH* L21 .......... 83 K7
Lily St *AIMK* WN4 .......... 91 L3
Limbrick Rd *CHLYE* PR6 .... 33 G3
Lime Av *BEB* CH63 ........ 142 F1
  *FROD/HEL* WA6 ............ 160 E5
  *WDN* WA8 ................ 134 D3
Lime Cl *CLB/OSW/ST* L13 .. 114 C1
  *WGNE/HIN* WN2 ............ 80 D6
Limedale Rd *CALD/MH* L18 .. 114 C8
Lime Gv *CHLY/EC* PR7 ...... 32 E8
  *CHNE* CH2 ................ 165 J2
  *GOL/RIS/CU* WA3 .......... 92 F7
  *LITH* L21 ................ 83 J7
  *RNFD/HAY* WA11 .......... 76 B7
  *RUNC* WA7 ................ 19 L7
  *SKEL* WN8 ................ 65 G4
  *TOX* L8 .................. 113 L7
  *WGNE/HIN* WN2 ............ 81 H2
Limehurst Gv *PS/BROM* CH62 .. 143 M7
Limekiln La *EV* L5 .......... 96 F8
  *VAUX/LVPD* L3 ............ 13 G3
  *WAL/EG* CH44 ............ 111 J3
  *WARRW/BUR* WA5 .......... 120 A2
Limes Av *CHLY/EC* PR7 .... 31 L1
  *WGNE/HIN* WN2 ............ 56 D7
The Limes *GOL/RIS/CU* WA3 .. 106 C1
  *GR/UP/WCH* CH49 .......... 110 B8
  *WGNNW/ST* WN6 .......... 56 C7
Lime St *CLVPS* L1 .......... 13 H6
  *EP* CH65 ................ 20 C1
  *STHP* PR8 ................ 25 G7
  *VAUX/LVPD* L3 ............ 13 J7
  *WGN* WN1 ................ 5 G3
Limetree Av *WARR* WA1 .... 122 B5
  *WARRS* WA4 .............. 138 A4
Lime Tree Cl *GTS/LS* CH66 .. 163 J5
  *WLT/FAZ* L9 .............. 97 K2
Lime Tree Gv *HES* CH60 .... 141 L5
Lime Tree Wy *FMBY* L37 .... 58 F3
Lime V *WGNE/HIN* WN2 .... 80 B1
Lime Vale Rd *RNFD/HAY* WA11 .. 89 G2
Limeways *WARRS* WA4 .... 138 A8
Limont Rd *STHP* PR8 ........ 34 F8
Linacre La *BTL* L20 ........ 83 L8
  *HTWN* L38 ................ 60 F3
Linacre Rd *LITH* L21 ...... 83 K7
Linaker Dr *ORM* L39 ........ 49 K5
Linaker St *STHP* PR8 ...... 3 H7
Linbeck Gv *GOL/RIS/CU* WA3 .. 93 G4
Linbridge Rd *DV/KA/FCH* L14 .. 99 H1
Lincoln Av *GOL/RIS/CU* WA3 .. 93 L3
  *HUY* L36 ................ 116 C2
  *NPK/KEN* L6 .............. 113 K1
  *RUNC* WA7 ................ 149 L7
  *WARR* WA1 ................ 123 G7
Lincoln Crs *RNFD/HAY* WA11.. 89 K7
Lincoln Dr *AIMK* WN4 ...... 91 L3
  *AIN/FAZ* L10 ............ 84 F2
  *WAL/NB* CH45 ............ 95 L7
  *WGNE/HIN* WN2 ............ 57 M8

Lincoln Gn *MGHL* L31 ...... 72 D5
Lincoln Pl *WGNW/BIL/O* WN5 ..... 67 L5
Lincoln Rd *ECCL* WA10 ...... 8 A3
  *GTS/LS* CH66 ...... 162 F2
  *STHP* PR8 ...... 35 J4
Lincoln Sq *WDN* WA8 ...... 134 D3
Lincoln St *ALL/GAR* L19 ...... 145 L1
  *BIRK* CH41 ...... 10 A1
Lincoln Wy *RAIN/WH* L35 ...... 117 M4
Lincombe Rd *HUY* L36 ...... 115 K1
Lincroft Rd *WGNE/HIN* WN2 ...... 81 J2
Lindale Dr *STHEL* WA9 ...... 118 E1
Lindale Rd *EHL/KEN* L7 ...... 114 A2
Lindby Cl *KKBY* L32 ...... 86 C5
Lindby Rd *KKBY* L32 ...... 86 C5
Linden Av *AIMK* WN4 ...... 79 H8
  *CSBY/BLUN* L23 ...... 82 E1
  *NTHTN* L30 ...... 84 B3
  *WGNW/BIL/O* WN5 ...... 67 G7
Linden Cl *GTS/LS* CH66 ...... 163 H5
  *WARR* WA1 ...... 122 F6
Linden Ct *WDN* WA8 ...... 134 B1
Linden Dr *CL/PREN* CH43 ...... 127 G4
  *FROD/HEL* WA6 ...... 166 D4
  *HUY* L36 ...... 116 A3
Linden Gv *CHLYE* PR6 ...... 32 F2
  *RNFD/HAY* WA11 ...... 89 L2
  *WAL/NB* CH45 ...... 95 K6
  *WGNW/BIL/O* WN5 ...... 67 G7
Linden Rd *NTHLY* L27 ...... 116 A8
Lindens *SKEL* WN8 ...... 65 K1
The Lindens *MGHL* L31 ...... 72 E6
Linden Wy *WGNW/ST* WN6 ...... 67 L8
  *ECCL* WA10 ...... 101 K1
  *WDN* WA8 ...... 134 B1
Lindenwood L32 ...... 86 B5
Lindeth Av *WAL/EG* CH44 ...... 111 K3
Lindfield Cl *WARRS* WA4 ...... 136 D8
Lindholme *SKEL* WN8 ...... 65 L2
Lindi Av *WARRS* WA4 ...... 138 D4
Lindisfarne Av *EP* CH65 ...... 163 L4
  *GOL/RIS/CU* WA3 ...... 93 L5
Lindisfarne Dr *WD/CROXPK* L12 ...... 99 J2
Lindley Av *WARRS* WA4 ...... 138 B1
  *WGNW/BIL/O* WN5 ...... 66 E8
Lindley Cl *EHL/KEN* L7 ...... 113 L5
Lindley Dr *SKEL* WN8 ...... 53 L2
Lindley St *EHL/KEN* L7 ...... 113 L5
Lindow St *LEIGH* WN7 ...... 81 M7
Lindrick Cl *RAIN/WH* L35 ...... 117 J1
Lindsay Dr *CHLYE* PR7 ...... 32 C6
Lindsay St *STHEL* WA9 ...... 119 G2
Lindsay Ter *WGNE/HIN* WN2 ...... 57 K8
Lind St *ANF/KKDL* L4 ...... 97 H4
Lindsworth Cl
  *WARRW/BUR* WA5 ...... 120 E7
Lindwall Cl *RAIN/WH* L35 ...... 110 E4
Linear Pk *MOR/LEA* CH46 ...... 109 L4
Linear Vw *NEWLW* WA12 ...... 104 C5
Lineside Cl *WLTN* L25 ...... 115 K8
Linford Gv *RNFD/HAY* WA11 ...... 9 M1
Lingdale Av *CL/PREN* CH43 ...... 111 H7
Lingdale Rd *CL/PREN* CH43 ...... 111 H6
  *WKBY* CH48 ...... 124 C2
Lingdales *FMBY* L37 ...... 57 K8
Lingfield Cl *HUY* L36 ...... 115 L4
Lingfield Crs *WGNNW/ST* WN6 ...... 68 A2
Lingfield Gv *DV/KA/FCH* L14 ...... 114 F3
Lingfield Rd *DV/KA/FCH* L14 ...... 114 F3
  *RUNC* WA7 ...... 18 D7
Lingford Cl *NTHLY* L27 ...... 132 B1
Lingham Cl *MOR/LEA* CH46 ...... 109 M3
Lingham La *MOR/LEA* CH46 ...... 109 L3
Lingholme Rd *ECCL* WA10 ...... 8 D3
Lingley Green Av
  *WARRW/BUR* WA5 ...... 119 L7
Lingley Rd *WARRW/BUR* WA5 ...... 119 M7
Lingmell Av *RNFD/HAY* WA11 ...... 89 K4
Lingmell Rd *WD/CROXPK* L12 ...... 98 D5
Lingmoor Cl *WGNS/IIMK* WN3 ...... 79 J4
Ling St *EHL/KEN* L7 ...... 113 K3
Lingtree Rd *KKBY* L32 ...... 86 C3
Lingwell Av *WDN* WA8 ...... 133 M3
Lingwood Rd
  *WARRW/BUR* WA5 ...... 120 A7
Linhope Wy *AIG/SPK* L17 ...... 129 L2
Link Av *CSBY/BLUN* L23 ...... 71 J8
  *RNFD/HAY* WA11 ...... 90 A8
Link Rd *HUY* L36 ...... 116 D4
Links Av *CHTN/BK* PR9 ...... 25 C3
  *GTS/LS* CH66 ...... 155 L6
Links Cl *BEB* CH63 ...... 143 K7
  *WAL/NB* CH45 ...... 95 H5
Links Hey Rd *WKBY* CH48 ...... 125 G7
Linkside *BEB* CH63 ...... 127 M6
Linkside Av *WARRN/WOL* WA2 ...... 105 K3
Linkside Wy *GTS/LS* CH66 ...... 163 H5
Links Cl *KKBY* L32 ...... 86 C4
Linkstor Rd *WLTN* L25 ...... 131 H3
Links Vw *CL/PREN* CH43 ...... 111 G8
  *WAL/NB* CH45 ...... 95 H5
Links View Cl *WLTN* L25 ...... 131 H2
Linkway *WAL/NB* CH45 ...... 95 H6
Linkway *ECCL* WA10 ...... 88 D7
  *RUNC* WA7 ...... 19 L8
Linkway Av *AIMK* WN4 ...... 80 A8
Linkway East *STHEL* WA9 ...... 9 J7
Linkway West *ECCL* WA10 ...... 8 F6
Linley Cl *WGNNW/ST* WN6 ...... 67 L1
Linley Rd *WGNW/BIL/O* WN5 ...... 67 M8
Linner Rd *SPK/HALE* L24 ...... 146 F2
Linnet Cl *NEWLW* WA12 ...... 104 E2
  *WARRN/WOL* WA2 ...... 121 M2
Linnet Gv *GOL/RIS/CU* WA3 ...... 123 G2
Linnet La *AIG/SPK* L17 ...... 113 K8
Linnets Wy *HES* CH60 ...... 141 L5
Linnet Wy *NWD/KWIPK* L33 ...... 74 A6
Linosa Cl *NPK/KEN* L6 ...... 113 L1
Linslade Cl *NWD/KWIPK* L33 ...... 86 B1
Linslade Crs *NWD/KWIPK* L33 ...... 86 B1
Linton Av *GOL/RIS/CU* WA3 ...... 92 B3
Linton St *ANF/KKDL* L4 ...... 97 H4
Linville Av *CSBY/BLUN* L23 ...... 82 D1
Linwood Cl *RUNC* WA7 ...... 150 E8
  *WGNE/HIN* WN2 ...... 80 D1
Linwood Gv *RAIN/WH* L35 ...... 117 G3
Linwood Rd *RF/TRAN* CH42 ...... 128 A2

Lionel St *STHEL* WA9 ...... 103 H6
Lion La *HOR/BR* BL6 ...... 57 L3
Lipton Cl *BTL* L20 ...... 6 F7
Liptrot St *WGNW/BIL/O* WN5 ...... 68 B6
Liptrott Rd *CHLY/EC* PR7 ...... 32 C8
Lisburn Cl *ALL/GAR* L19 ...... 145 L1
Lisburn La *AIG/SPK* L17 ...... 130 K3
Liscard Gv *WAL/EG* CH44 ...... 111 J1
Liscard Rd *WAL/EG* CH44 ...... 111 M2
  *WAV* L15 ...... 113 M6
Liscard Village *WAL/EG* CH44 ...... 95 K8
Liscard Wy *WAL/EG* CH44 ...... 111 K1
Liskeard Cl *RUNC* WA7 ...... 150 D7
Lisleholme Crs *WD/CROXPK* L12 ...... 98 E7
Lisleholme Rd *WD/CROXPK* L12 ...... 98 E7
Lismore Rd *CALD/MH* L18 ...... 130 C4
Lister Crs *EHL/KEN* L7 ...... 113 L3
Lister Dr *CLB/OSW/ST* L13 ...... 114 A1
Lister Rd *EHL/KEN* L7 ...... 113 L3
  *RUNC* WA7 ...... 19 L2
Liston St *ANF/KKDL* L4 ...... 97 H3
Litcham Cl *GR/UP/WCH* CH49 ...... 110 C6
Litchborough Gv *RAIN/WH* L35 ...... 101 J7
Litherland Av
  *MOR/LEA* CH46 ...... 109 M5
Litherland Crs *RNFD/HAY* WA11 ...... 89 L6
Litherland Pk *LITH* L21 ...... 83 K5
Litherland Rd *BTL* L20 ...... 83 L7
Lithou Cl *EV* L5 ...... 96 F8
Little Acre *MGHL* L31 ...... 73 C5
Little Barn Hey *NTHTN* L30 ...... 83 M1
Little Brook La *KKBY* L32 ...... 85 M5
Little Canning St *TOX* L8 ...... 113 H6
Little Carr La *CHLY/EC* PR7 ...... 32 F8
Little Catharine St *TOX* L8 ...... 113 H6
Littlecote Cl *STHEL* WA9 ...... 118 E1
Littlecourt *VAUX/LVPD* L3 ...... 12 E1
Little Crosby Rd *CSBY/BLUN* L23 ...... 71 C6
Littledale Rd *DV/KA/FCH* L14 ...... 114 F2
  *WAL/EG* CH44 ...... 111 M2
  *WARRW/BUR* WA5 ...... 120 B6
Little Delph *RNFD/HAY* WA11 ...... 90 F6
Littlegate *RUNC* WA7 ...... 150 A5
Little Gn *GTS/LS* CH66 ...... 162 F2
Little Hardman St *CLVPS* L1 ...... 13 K9
Little Heath Rd *SPK/HALE* L24 ...... 147 G3
Little Heyes St *EV* L5 ...... 97 J7
Little Hey La *FMBY* L37 ...... 59 K1
Little Howard St *VAUX/LVPD* L3 ...... 12 D2
Little Huskisson St *TOX* L8 ...... 113 H6
Little La *CL/PREN* CH43 ...... 127 G1
  *WARRW/BUR* WA5 ...... 136 F1
Little London *WGN* WN1 ...... 4 F2
Little Meadow La *BRSC* L40 ...... 39 M1
Littlemore
  *GR/UP/WCH* CH49 ...... 109 M8
Little Moss Hey *STBRV* L28 ...... 99 K6
Little Parkfield Rd *AIG/SPK* L17 ...... 129 K1
Little Pasture *LEIGH* WN7 ...... 81 M6
Littler Rd *RNFD/HAY* WA11 ...... 90 C8
Little St Bride St *TOX* L8 ...... 113 H5
Little Scotland *HOR/BR* BL6 ...... 57 K3
Little Stanney La *CHNE* CH2 ...... 164 A5
Littlestone Cl *WDN* WA8 ...... 134 C1
Little Storeton La *BEB* CH63 ...... 127 J7
Little St *STHEL* WA9 ...... 103 G4
Littleton Cl *CL/PREN* CH43 ...... 127 G1
  *WARRW/BUR* WA5 ...... 136 F1
Little Woolton St *EHL/KEN* L7 ...... 113 J4
Little Wissage *GTS/LS* CH66 ...... 163 H3
Littondale Av *RAIN/WH* L35 ...... 117 M3
Liverpool Av *STHP* PR8 ...... 47 M1
Liverpool Loop Line *WLTN* L25 ...... 115 H6
Liverpool Old Rd
  *KIRK/FR/WA* PR4 ...... 28 C3
  *STHP* PR8 ...... 47 L4
Liverpool Rd *AIMK* WN4 ...... 91 H2
  *BRSC* L40 ...... 28 D7
  *CH/BCN* CH1 ...... 163 H6
  *CSBY/BLUN* L23 ...... 83 G1
  *FMBY* L37 ...... 59 J3
  *HUY* L36 ...... 99 L8
  *KIRK/FR/WA* PR4 ...... 28 C1
  *MGHL* L31 ...... 72 F1
  *NSTN* CH64 ...... 153 H3
  *ORM* L39 ...... 62 D3
  *PR/KW* L34 ...... 100 D7
  *RNFD/HAY* WA11 ...... 90 E4
  *SKEL* WN8 ...... 64 F5
  *STHP* PR8 ...... 34 F8
  *WARRW/BUR* WA5 ...... 14 B6
  *WDN* WA8 ...... 16 A2
  *WGNE/HIN* WN2 ...... 69 J8
Liverpool Rd North *BRSC* L40 ...... 52 A1
  *MGHL* L31 ...... 72 E3
Liverpool Rd South *BRSC* L40 ...... 51 M2
  *MGHL* L31 ...... 72 F3
Liverpool Rw *NEWLW* WA12 ...... 104 F5
Liverpool St *ECCL* WA10 ...... 8 F6
Liversidge Rd *RF/TRAN* CH42 ...... 127 M1
Liver St *CLVPS* L1 ...... 112 C5
Livesley's La *FMBY* L37 ...... 60 B3
Livingston Dr *AIG/SPK* L17 ...... 129 L1
Livingston Dr North
  *AIG/SPK* L17 ...... 129 L2
Livingston Dr South
  *AIG/SPK* L17 ...... 129 L2
Livingston Cl
  *WARRW/BUR* WA5 ...... 120 F6
Livingstone Rd *EP* CH65 ...... 20 C1
  *MOR/LEA* CH46 ...... 110 C1
  *RF/TRAN* CH42 ...... 128 B2
Livingstone St *BIRK* CH41 ...... 10 F3
Llandaff Cl *GTS/LS* CH66 ...... 163 G4
Llanrwst Cl *TOX* L8 ...... 113 G8
Lloyd Av *BIRK* CH41 ...... 10 D3
Lloyd Cl *NPK/KEN* L6 ...... 13 M1
Lloyd Crs *NEWLW* WA12 ...... 104 B2
Lloyd Dr *EP* CH65 ...... 163 M4
  *GR/UP/WCH* CH49 ...... 125 M2
Lloyd Rd *PR/KW* L34 ...... 101 G6
Lobelia Av *WLT/FAZ* L9 ...... 90 B7
Lobelia Gv *RUNC* WA7 ...... 161 H1
Local Board St *WGNE/HIN* WN2 ...... 5 M6

Lochinvar Av *GTS/LS* CH66 ...... 155 H7
Lochinvar St *WLT/FAZ* L9 ...... 97 H2
Lochmore Rd *CALD/MH* L18 ...... 130 C4
Lochryan Rd *ALL/GAR* L19 ...... 130 D5
Loch St *RUNC* WA7 ...... 19 G2
  *WGNW/BIL/O* WN5 ...... 67 K7
Locker Av *WARRN/WOL* WA2 ...... 121 K3
Lockerbie Av *WARRN/WOL* WA2 ...... 122 A1
Lockerbie Pl *WGNS/IIMK* WN3 ...... 79 G3
Lockerby Rd *EHL/KEN* L7 ...... 113 M2
Locker La *AIMK* WN4 ...... 92 B1
Locker Pk *GR/UP/WCH* CH49 ...... 125 L1
Locke St *ALL/GAR* L19 ...... 145 L1
  *WDN* WA8 ...... 134 C3
Lockett Rd *AIMK* WN4 ...... 79 L8
Lockett St *WARRS* WA4 ...... 138 B2
Lockgate East *RUNC* WA7 ...... 150 E3
Lockgate West *RUNC* WA7 ...... 150 E3
Locking Stumps La
  *WARRN/WOL* WA2 ...... 122 D2
Lockington Cl *TOX* L8 ...... 129 J1
Lock La *KIRK/FR/WA* PR4 ...... 28 D3
Lock Rd *PS/BROM* CH62 ...... 144 D6
  *WARR* WA1 ...... 122 B6
Lock St *STHEL* WA9 ...... 9 L2
Locks Vw *WGN* WN1 ...... 5 M4
Lockton La *WARRW/BUR* WA5 ...... 121 G6
Loddon Cl *GR/UP/WCH* CH49 ...... 110 D6
Lodge Dr *GOL/RIS/CU* WA3 ...... 107 H2
Lodge Hollow *FROD/HEL* WA6 ...... 166 D1
Lodge La *NEWLW* WA12 ...... 91 K4
  *PS/BROM* CH62 ...... 128 D7
  *RNFD/HAY* WA11 ...... 75 J4
  *RUNC* WA7 ...... 150 A5
  *TOX* L8 ...... 113 K6
  *WARRW/BUR* WA5 ...... 121 G6
  *WDN* WA8 ...... 133 K1
Lodge Rd *WGNW/BIL/O* WN5 ...... 78 A1
Lodwick St *BTL* L20 ...... 6 F9
Loeminster Pl *WGNE/HIN* WN2 ...... 5 L6
Lofthouse Ga *WDN* WA8 ...... 134 B2
Logan Rd *BIRK* CH41 ...... 111 K4
Lognor Rd *KKBY* L32 ...... 85 L3
Logwood Av *WGNW/BIL/O* WN5 ...... 67 M6
Logwood Pl *WGNW/BIL/O* WN5 ...... 68 A5
Logwood Rd *HUY* L36 ...... 116 C5
Loire Dr *WGNW/BIL/O* WN5 ...... 68 B5
Lomax St *WGNE/HIN* WN2 ...... 80 C3
Lombard Rd *MOR/LEA* CH46 ...... 110 B3
Lombardy Av
  *GR/UP/WCH* CH49 ...... 125 K3
Lomond Gv *EP* CH65 ...... 163 H2
  *MOR/LEA* CH46 ...... 110 B5
Lomond Rd *EHL/KEN* L7 ...... 114 A3
London Cl *WGNW/BIL/O* WN5 ...... 68 A5
Londonderry Rd
  *CLB/OSW/ST* L13 ...... 97 M6
London Flds *WGNW/BIL/O* WN5 ...... 78 A4
London Rd *FROD/HEL* WA6 ...... 160 D5
  *VAUX/LVPD* L3 ...... 13 L6
  *WARRS* WA4 ...... 137 M5
London Rw *NEWLW* WA12 ...... 104 F5
London Sq *STHP* PR8 ...... 3 G3
London St *CHTN/BK* PR9 ...... 3 H3
Longacre *CHTN/BK* PR9 ...... 25 H2
Longacre Cl *WAL/NB* CH45 ...... 94 F8
Long Acres Rd *NSTN* CH64 ...... 153 G3
Longbarn Bvd
  *WARRN/WOL* WA2 ...... 122 E3
Long Barn La *WARR* WA1 ...... 122 F5
Longborough Rd *PR/KW* L34 ...... 99 L2
Longbrook *WGNNW/ST* WN6 ...... 55 K7
Longcliffe Dr *STHP* PR8 ...... 47 K1
Long Copse *CHLY/EC* PR7 ...... 32 B4
Longcroft Av *ALL/GAR* L19 ...... 130 F6
Long Croft Meadow
  *CHLY/EC* PR7 ...... 32 D3
Longcroft Sq *ALL/GAR* L19 ...... 130 F6
Longdale La *SFTN* L29 ...... 71 M6
Longdin St *WARRS* WA4 ...... 15 M9
Longdown Rd *NG/CROX* L11 ...... 85 K7
Longendale Rd *WGNNW/ST* WN6 ...... 55 M5
Longfellow Cl
  *WGNS/IIMK* WN3 ...... 68 C8
Longfellow Dr *RF/TRAN* CH42 ...... 128 C8
Longfellow St *BTL* L20 ...... 6 D1
  *TOX* L8 ...... 113 L6
Longfield *FMBY* L37 ...... 47 K8
Longfield Av *CHLY/EC* PR7 ...... 43 C3
  *CSBY/BLUN* L23 ...... 71 G7
Longfield Cl
  *GR/UP/WCH* CH49 ...... 125 M1
Longfield Mnr *CHLY/EC* PR7 ...... 32 C8
Longfield Rd *LITH* L21 ...... 83 K7
  *WARRN/WOL* WA2 ...... 121 L4
Longfold *MGHL* L31 ...... 73 G4
Longford Rd *STHP* PR8 ...... 35 J3
Longford St *TOX* L8 ...... 129 J2
  *WARR* WA1 ...... 14 E1
Long Hey *RAIN/WH* L35 ...... 116 F3
Long Hey Rd *WKBY* CH48 ...... 125 G6
Long Heys La *SKEL* WN8 ...... 54 B8
Long Heys or Back La *SKEL* WN8 ...... 54 C8
Longhurst Rd *WGNE/HIN* WN2 ...... 81 H1
Longland Rd *WAL/NB* CH45 ...... 95 K7
Long La *ALL/GAR* L19 ...... 130 E6
  *CHLYE* PR6 ...... 44 C1
  *CHTN/BK* PR9 ...... 23 K7
  *ORM* L39 ...... 62 E2
  *SFTN* L29 ...... 71 J5
  *SKEL* WN8 ...... 77 G2
  *WARRN/WOL* WA2 ...... 121 L4
  *WAV* L15 ...... 114 B5
  *WGNE/HIN* WN2 ...... 81 J1
  *WLT/FAZ* L9 ...... 84 E8
Longlooms Rd *EP* CH65 ...... 163 M4
Long Meadow *AIMK* WN4 ...... 91 L1
Long Meanygate *CHTN/BK* PR9 ...... 26 B5
Long Meadow *CHLY/EC* PR7 ...... 32 D3
  *ECCL* WA10 ...... 101 K1
  *HES* CH60 ...... 141 H5
Longmeadow Rd *PR/KW* L34 ...... 99 M1
Long Moss *AIN/FAZ* L10 ...... 85 G6
Longmoor Gv *WLT/FAZ* L9 ...... 84 D7

Longmoor La *AIN/FAZ* L10 ...... 85 J6
  *WLT/FAZ* L9 ...... 84 D7
Longreach Rd *DV/KA/FCH* L14 ...... 115 H2
Longridge Av
  *GR/UP/WCH* CH49 ...... 110 A7
  *RNFD/HAY* WA11 ...... 89 M8
  *WGNNW/ST* WN6 ...... 56 B5
Longridge Wk *ANF/KKDL* L4 ...... 97 G5
Longshaw Av *WGNW/BIL/O* WN5 ...... 78 A4
Longshaw Cl
  *WGNW/BIL/O* WN5 ...... 78 A4
Longshaw Common
  *WGNW/BIL/O* WN5 ...... 78 A5
Longshaw Old Rd
  *WGNW/BIL/O* WN5 ...... 78 A4
Longshaw St
  *WARRW/BUR* WA5 ...... 121 H5
Long Spinney *RUNC* WA7 ...... 150 E5
Longster Trail *FROD/HEL* WA6 ...... 166 E2
Longstone Wk *EHL/KEN* L7 ...... 113 K5
Longton Av *GOL/RIS/CU* WA3 ...... 92 C5
Longton Dr *FMBY* L37 ...... 47 J3
Longton La *RAIN/WH* L35 ...... 101 K8
Longton Rd *CHLYE* PR6 ...... 33 C5
  *WGNE/HIN* WN2 ...... 80 E1
Longview Av *RAIN/WH* L35 ...... 117 J1
  *WAL/NB* CH45 ...... 95 J8
Longview Crs *HUY* L36 ...... 116 B2
Longview Dr *HUY* L36 ...... 116 C2
Longview La *HUY* L36 ...... 100 B8
Longview Rd *HUY* L36 ...... 116 B1
  *RAIN/WH* L35 ...... 117 J1
Longville St *TOX* L8 ...... 113 G8
Longwood Cl *RNFD/HAY* WA11 ...... 88 D4
Longwood Rd *WARRS* WA4 ...... 138 A8
Longworth Av *CHLY/EC* PR7 ...... 43 H3
  *HOR/BR* BL6 ...... 57 J7
Longworth St *CHLY/EC* PR7 ...... 32 D7
Longworth Wy *WLTN* L25 ...... 131 J2
Lonie Gv *ECCL* WA10 ...... 101 L5
Lonsboro Rd *WAL/EG* CH44 ...... 111 L2
Lonsdale Av *ECCL* WA10 ...... 101 K6
  *LEIGH* WN7 ...... 93 H3
  *ORM* L39 ...... 51 H6
  *WAL/NB* CH45 ...... 95 J7
Lonsdale Cl *LITH* L21 ...... 83 K3
  *WDN* WA8 ...... 133 L5
Lonsdale Dr *LEY/BBR* PR5 ...... 29 K2
Lonsdale Ms *LITH* L21 ...... 83 K3
Lonsdale Rd *FMBY* L37 ...... 59 G2
  *HLWD* L26 ...... 132 A7
  *LITH* L21 ...... 83 K3
  *STHP* PR8 ...... 3 L9
Looe Cl *WDN* WA8 ...... 134 A3
Looe Rd *NG/CROX* L11 ...... 85 M8
The Looms *NSTN* CH64 ...... 152 D5
Loomsway *PEN/TH* CH61 ...... 125 L7
Loraine St *EV* L5 ...... 97 H8
Lordens Cl *DV/KA/FCH* L14 ...... 99 J8
Lordens Rd *DV/KA/FCH* L14 ...... 99 K7
Lord Nelson St *CLVPS* L1 ...... 13 G6
  *WARR* WA1 ...... 15 G6
Lords Av *CL/PREN* CH43 ...... 110 E5
Lord Sefton Wy *FMBY* L37 ...... 59 M3
Lordsgate Dr *BRSC* L40 ...... 52 A2
Lordsgate La *BRSC* L40 ...... 51 K3
Lordship La *FROD/HEL* WA6 ...... 159 H7
Lords La *GOL/RIS/CU* WA3 ...... 92 D4
Lord St *AIMK* WN4 ...... 91 M1
  *ALL/GAR* L19 ...... 130 E8
  *BIRK* CH41 ...... 11 K4
  *BRSC* L40 ...... 39 G8
  *CHLY/EC* PR7 ...... 30 E8
  *CHLYE* PR6 ...... 32 F6
  *CHTN/BK* PR9 ...... 3 H2
  *CLVP* L2 ...... 12 F7
  *CLVPS* L1 ...... 12 F7
  *ECCL* WA10 ...... 9 G2
  *GOL/RIS/CU* WA3 ...... 106 C5
  *NEWLW* WA12 ...... 104 C2
  *RUNC* WA7 ...... 18 F2
  *STHP* PR8 ...... 2 E5
  *WARRS* WA4 ...... 14 F8
  *WGN* WN1 ...... 4 F1
  *WGNE/HIN* WN2 ...... 69 M8
Lord Street Boulevards
  *STHP* PR8 ...... 2 E5
Lord St West *STHP* PR8 ...... 2 E6
Lordy Cl *WGNNW/ST* WN6 ...... 56 D6
Loreburn Rd *WAV* L15 ...... 114 C7
Lorenzo Dr *NG/CROX* L11 ...... 98 B4
Loretto Dr *GR/UP/WCH* CH49 ...... 110 C7
Loretto Rd *WAL/EG* CH44 ...... 111 H1
Lorne Rd *CL/PREN* CH43 ...... 10 B9
  *CSBY/WL* L22 ...... 82 F4
Lorne St *CHLY/EC* PR7 ...... 30 E8
  *EHL/KEN* L7 ...... 114 A2
  *WGN* WN1 ...... 5 J4
Lorn St *BIRK* CH41 ...... 11 K5
Lorton Av *RNFD/HAY* WA11 ...... 89 J5
Lostock Av
  *WARRW/BUR* WA5 ...... 121 H5
Lostock Cl *WGNW/BIL/O* WN5 ...... 78 A8
Lostock Rd *LEY/BBR* PR5 ...... 29 L2
Lothair Rd *ANF/KKDL* L4 ...... 97 J6
Lothian St *TOX* L8 ...... 113 J7
Loudon Gv *TOX* L8 ...... 113 J7
Lough Gn *BEB* CH63 ...... 143 J3
Loughlin Dr *NWD/KWIPK* L33 ...... 74 B8
Loughrigg Av *RNFD/HAY* WA11 ...... 89 K4
Louis Braille Cl *NTHTN* L30 ...... 84 B1
Louis Pasteur Av *NTHTN* L30 ...... 84 B1
Loushers La *WARRS* WA4 ...... 138 B1
Lovage Cl *WARRN/WOL* WA2 ...... 122 E4
Lovelace Rd *ALL/GAR* L19 ...... 130 D6
Love La *VAUX/LVPD* L3 ...... 12 E2
  *WAL/EG* CH44 ...... 111 K2
Lovel Rd *SPK/HALE* L24 ...... 146 F3
Lovel Ter *WDN* WA8 ...... 133 K8
Lovel Wy *SPK/HALE* L24 ...... 146 F2
Lovely La *WARRW/BUR* WA5 ...... 121 G7
Lovett Dr *RAIN/WH* L35 ...... 101 G8
Low Bank Rd *AIMK* WN4 ...... 91 G1
Lowcroft *SKEL* WN8 ...... 65 L2
Lowden Av *LITH* L21 ...... 83 K3
Lowe Av *WARRS* WA4 ...... 138 D1
Lowell St *ANF/KKDL* L4 ...... 97 H4

Lower Alt Rd *HTWN* L38 ...... 70 B1
Lower Appleton Rd *WDN* WA8 ...... 16 F1
Lower Bank Vw *BTL* L20 ...... 6 E9
Lower Breck Rd *NPK/KEN* L6 ...... 97 L7
Lower Burgh Wy *CHLY/EC* PR7 ...... 43 J1
Lower Carr La *HTWN* L38 ...... 60 D6
Lower Castle St *CLVP* L2 ...... 12 E7
Lower Church St *WDN* WA8 ...... 16 C9
Lower Farm Rd *WLTN* L25 ...... 115 H6
Lower Flaybrick Rd
  *CL/PREN* CH43 ...... 111 C5
Lower Gn *GR/UP/WCH* CH49 ...... 126 C2
Lower Hey *CSBY/BLUN* L23 ...... 71 K8
Lower Hill Dr *CHLYE* PR6 ...... 44 C4
Lower House La *NG/CROX* L11 ...... 98 C2
  *WDN* WA8 ...... 16 B5
Lower La *WLT/FAZ* L9 ...... 85 G6
Lower Longshoot *WGN* WN1 ...... 5 H3
Lower Lyndon Av
  *WGNNW/ST* WN6 ...... 55 J7
Lower Mersey St *EP* CH65 ...... 156 F6
Lower Mill St *WGNE/HIN* WN2 ...... 6 F9
Lower Milk St *VAUX/LVPD* L3 ...... 12 F5
Lower Prom *STHP* PR8 ...... 2 E3
Lower Rake La *FROD/HEL* WA6 ...... 166 D1
Lower Rd *HLWD* L26 ...... 132 D5
  *PS/BROM* CH62 ...... 128 D7
Lower Robin Hood La
  *FROD/HEL* WA6 ...... 166 D2
Lower St Stephen St
  *WGNW/BIL/O* WN5 ...... 4 B3
Lowerson Crs *NG/CROX* L11 ...... 98 A5
Lowerson Rd *NG/CROX* L11 ...... 98 A5
Lower Thingwall La
  *PEN/TH* CH61 ...... 126 E7
Lower Wash La *WARRS* WA4 ...... 15 M9
Lowes Gn *FMBY* L37 ...... 59 K2
Lowe's La *SKEL* WN8 ...... 53 L5
Lowe St *ECCL* WA10 ...... 8 F4
  *GOL/RIS/CU* WA3 ...... 92 C5
Lowe St South *ECCL* WA10 ...... 8 F5
Loweswater Cl
  *WARRN/WOL* WA2 ...... 121 K2
Loweswater Crs
  *RNFD/HAY* WA11 ...... 90 C7
Loweswater Wy
  *NWD/KWIPK* L33 ...... 73 M8
  *NWD/KWIPK* L33 ...... 85 H1
Lowfield La *STHEL* WA9 ...... 102 B8
Lowfield Rd *DV/KA/FCH* L14 ...... 114 E2
Lowfields Av *PS/BROM* CH62 ...... 154 F2
Lowfields Cl *PS/BROM* CH62 ...... 155 G2
Low Hl *FROD/HEL* WA6 ...... 165 M8
Lowlands Rd *RUNC* WA7 ...... 18 F3
Lowndes Rd *NPK/KEN* L6 ...... 97 M7
Lowood St *LEIGH* WN7 ...... 81 M8
Lowry Bank *WAL/EG* CH44 ...... 112 A2
Lowry Cl *WARRW/BUR* WA5 ...... 120 F7
Lowry Hill La *BRSC* L40 ...... 52 D3
Lowther Av *AIN/FAZ* L10 ...... 84 F3
  *GOL/RIS/CU* WA3 ...... 107 H1
  *MGHL* L31 ...... 73 G3
Lowther Crs *ECCL* WA10 ...... 101 K5
Lowther Dr *RAIN/WH* L35 ...... 117 K2
Lowther St *TOX* L8 ...... 13 J6
Lowton Gdns *GOL/RIS/CU* WA3 ...... 92 D8
Lowton Rd *GOL/RIS/CU* WA3 ...... 92 D4
Lowwood Gv *BIRK* CH41 ...... 11 H7
Low Wood Gv *PEN/TH* CH61 ...... 141 L1
Lowwood Rd *BIRK* CH41 ...... 11 H7
Loxdale Cl *TOX* L8 ...... 129 J1
Loxdale Dr *EP* CH65 ...... 163 H1
Loxley Cl *WARRW/BUR* WA5 ...... 120 C5
Loxley Rd *STHP* PR8 ...... 3 M9
Loxton Crs *WGNS/IIMK* WN3 ...... 79 K2
Loyola Hey *RAIN/WH* L35 ...... 118 A5
Lucania St *ALL/GAR* L19 ...... 145 L1
Lucan Rd *AIG/SPK* L17 ...... 130 A3
Lucas Av *CHLY/EC* PR7 ...... 31 M5
Lucerne Rd *WAL/EG* CH44 ...... 111 M3
Lucerne St *AIG/SPK* L17 ...... 129 L2
Lucius Cl *WLT/FAZ* L9 ...... 84 B6
Lucknow St *AIG/SPK* L17 ...... 129 L1
Ludlow *SKEL* WN8 ...... 65 L1
Ludlow Av *WGNE/HIN* WN2 ...... 81 J1
Ludlow Crs *RUNC* WA7 ...... 19 J8
Ludlow Dr *EP* CH65 ...... 21 G8
  *ORM* L39 ...... 50 F6
  *WKBY* CH48 ...... 124 D4
Ludlow Gv *PS/BROM* CH62 ...... 143 M4
Ludlow St *ANF/KKDL* L4 ...... 97 H4
  *WGNNW/ST* WN6 ...... 55 L2
Ludovic Ter *WGN* WN1 ...... 68 L1
Ludwig Rd *ANF/KKDL* L4 ...... 97 K8
Lugard Rd *AIG/SPK* L17 ...... 130 A3
Lugsdale Rd *WDN* WA8 ...... 16 D5
Lugsmore La *ECCL* WA10 ...... 101 L4
Luke St *AIMK* WN4 ...... 79 M8
  *TOX* L8 ...... 113 H7
  *WAL/EG* CH44 ...... 112 A3
Lulworth *SKEL* WN8 ...... 65 L1
Lulworth Av *CSBY/WL* L22 ...... 82 E4
Lulworth Dr *WGNE/HIN* WN2 ...... 81 J1
Lulworth Rd *STHP* PR8 ...... 2 C8
  *WLTN* L25 ...... 115 L8
Lumb Brook Rd *WARRS* WA4 ...... 138 C7
Lumber La *WARRW/BUR* WA5 ...... 104 A5
Lumby Av *HUY* L36 ...... 116 A2
Lumley Rd *WAL/EG* CH44 ...... 111 M2
Lumley St *ALL/GAR* L19 ...... 130 D7
Lunar Dr *NTHTN* L30 ...... 72 B8
Lunar Rd *WLT/FAZ* L9 ...... 84 D7
Lundy Dr *EP* CH65 ...... 163 L5
Lune Av *MGHL* L31 ...... 73 G3
Lune Gv *LEIGH* WN7 ...... 81 L3
Lunehurst *GOL/RIS/CU* WA3 ...... 93 G5
Lunesdale Av *WLT/FAZ* L9 ...... 84 D6
Lune St *CSBY/BLUN* L23 ...... 83 G1
Lunsford Rd *DV/KA/FCH* L14 ...... 115 H1
Lunt Av *NTHTN* L30 ...... 84 C3
  *RAIN/WH* L35 ...... 117 G2
Lunt Rd *BTL* L20 ...... 83 L8
  *SFTN* L29 ...... 72 A6
Lunt's Heath Rd *WDN* WA8 ...... 118 C8
Lupin Dr *RNFD/HAY* WA11 ...... 91 H7
Lupton Dr *CSBY/BLUN* L23 ...... 83 J1

Lupton St CHLY/EC PR7 ........ 32 E7 5
Lupus Wy GTS/LS CH66 ........ 163 H2
Lurdin La WGN WN1 ........ 56 D6
Luscombe Cl HLWD L26 ........ 132 C5 2
Lusitania Rd ANF/KKDL L4 ........ 97 J3
Luther Gv STHEL WA9 ........ 103 K3
Luton Gv ANF/KKDL L4 ........ 97 H5
Luton Rd EP CH65 ........ 156 C8
Luton St EV L5 ........ 96 E7
WDN WA8 ........ 16 D6 2
Lutyens Cl ANF/KKDL L4 ........ 97 H6
Luxmore Rd ANF/KKDL L4 ........ 97 J4 3
Lycett Rd ANF/KKDL L4 ........ 97 L6
WAL/EG CH44 ........ 95 G8
Lychgate WARRS WA4 ........ 137 H6 1
WGNW/BIL/O WN5 ........ 68 A8 3
Lycroft Cl RUNC WA7 ........ 149 K7
Lydbrook Cl RF/TRAN CH42 ........ 128 B2 3
Lydbury Cl WARRW/BUR WA5 ........ 120 F3
Lydbury Crs KKBY L32 ........ 86 B5
Lydd Cl SPK/HALE L24 ........ 146 D1
Lydden Rd EP CH65 ........ 20 B1
Lydd Gv CHLY/EC PR7 ........ 32 C6
Lydford Gn WGNNW/ST WN6 ........ 56 B5
Lydford Rd WD/CROXPK L12 ........ 98 D5
Lydgate CHLY/EC PR7 ........ 32 C8
Lydia Ann St CLVPS L1 ........ 13 H9
Lydiate La CHLY/EC PR7 ........ 30 D4
CSBY/BLUN L23 ........ 71 K7
NSTN CH64 ........ 154 A5
RUNC WA7 ........ 149 G6
WLTN L25 ........ 131 M3
Lydiate Pk CSBY/BLUN L23 ........ 71 K7
Lydiate Rd BTL L20 ........ 83 L8
Lydiate Station Rd MGHL L31 ........ 61 G8
The Lydiate HES CH60 ........ 141 H6
Lydieth Lea NTHLY L27 ........ 116 A7
Lydney Rd HUY L36 ........ 115 K1
Lydstep Ct
WARRW/BUR WA5 ........ 121 G3 5
Lyefield Av WGN WN1 ........ 5 L2
Lyelake Cl KKBY L32 ........ 86 B4
Lyelake La BRSC L40 ........ 64 B4
Lyelake Rd KKBY L32 ........ 86 B4
Lyle St EV L5 ........ 96 F8
Lymbridge Dr HOR/BR BL6 ........ 57 M3
Lyme Cl HUY L36 ........ 100 C7
Lyme Cross Rd HUY L36 ........ 100 B7
Lyme Gv HUY L36 ........ 100 B8
LYMM WA13 ........ 139 L3
Lyme St NEWLW WA12 ........ 104 A1
RNFD/HAY WA11 ........ 91 G7
Lymington Gv NTHTN L30 ........ 84 B2 3
Lymmington Av LYMM WA13 ........ 139 L2
Lymm Rd CL/PREN CH43 ........ 110 E6 5
WARRS WA4 ........ 139 H2
Lymn St WGNE/HIN WN2 ........ 80 D2 5
Lynas Gdns ALL/GAR L19 ........ 130 D5
Lynas St BIRK CH41 ........ 11 G2
Lyncot Rd WLT/FAZ L9 ........ 84 D5 3
Lyncroft Rd WAL/EG CH44 ........ 111 L3
Lyndale SKEL WN8 ........ 65 K1 1
Lyndale Av PS/BROM CH62 ........ 155 G1
WARRN/WOL WA2 ........ 121 M5
Lyndene Rd WLTN L25 ........ 115 J7
Lyndhurst SKEL WN8 ........ 65 K1
Lyndhurst Av CALD/MH L18 ........ 130 B2
PEN/TH CH61 ........ 141 J2
Lyndhurst Cl PEN/TH CH61 ........ 126 C8 5
Lyndhurst Rd CALD/MH L18 ........ 130 B1
CSBY/BLUN L23 ........ 83 J1
HOY CH47 ........ 109 G4
PEN/TH CH61 ........ 125 L8
STHP PR8 ........ 35 J3
WAL/NB CH45 ........ 95 H7
Lyndhurst Wy HUY L36 ........ 116 A3 4
Lyndon Av WGNNW/ST WN6 ........ 55 K6
Lyndon Dr CALD/MH L18 ........ 130 D1
Lyndon Gv RUNC WA7 ........ 19 J7
Lyndor Cl WLTN L25 ........ 131 K4
Lyndor Rd WLTN L25 ........ 131 K4
Lyneal Av GTS/LS CH66 ........ 162 E3
Lyneham RAIN/WH L35 ........ 117 H3
Lynham Av
WARRW/BUR WA5 ........ 120 D8 4
Lynholme Rd ANF/KKDL L4 ........ 97 K6
Lynmouth Cl WGNNW/ST WN6 .. 68 C3 2
Lynmouth Rd AIG/SPK L17 ........ 130 A5
Lynnbank CL/PREN CH43 ........ 10 D9
Lynnbank Rd CALD/MH L18 ........ 114 F8
Lynn Cl ECCL WA10 ........ 101 L1
RUNC WA7 ........ 149 L6
Lynndene GTS/LS CH66 ........ 155 M6
Lynscott Pl CHLDW L16 ........ 114 F5
Lynsted Rd DV/KA/FCH L14 ........ 115 H2
Lynton Av WGNNW/ST WN6 ........ 68 C2
Lynton Cl ALL/GAR L19 ........ 130 D5
HES CH60 ........ 141 K7
WARRW/BUR WA5 ........ 136 A1
Lynton Crs WDN WA8 ........ 134 A3
Lynton Dr BEB CH63 ........ 143 J2
STHP PR8 ........ 35 G4
Lynton Gn WLTN L25 ........ 131 H1
Lynton Gv STHEL WA9 ........ 102 E8
Lynton Rd HUY L36 ........ 116 D2
STHP PR8 ........ 35 G5
WAL/NB CH45 ........ 95 G7
Lynton St LEIGH WN7 ........ 81 M8
Lynton Wy ECCL WA10 ........ 88 D7
Lynwood Av GOL/RIS/CU WA3 ........ 93 G7
ORM L39 ........ 62 E2
WAL/EG CH44 ........ 111 J2 2
WARRS WA4 ........ 137 L6
Lynwood Dr PEN/TH CH61 ........ 126 A7
Lynwood End ORM L39 ........ 62 E2 2
Lynwood Gdns WLT/FAZ L9 ........ 84 B8
Lynwood Rd WLT/FAZ L9 ........ 84 B8
The Lynxway WD/CROXPK L12 ........ 98 F8
Lyon Cl ECCL WA10 ........ 8 E5
Lyon Rd ANF/KKDL L4 ........ 97 K7 1
Lyons Cl MOR/LEA CH46 ........ 110 A4 2
Lyons La CHLY/EC PR7 ........ 32 F6
CHLYE PR6 ........ 32 F6
WARRS WA4 ........ 137 M7
Lyons Rd MOR/LEA CH46 ........ 110 A4
STHP PR8 ........ 2 F8
WARRW/BUR WA5 ........ 136 B1
Lyon St AIMK WN4 ........ 79 H6
ALL/GAR L19 ........ 145 L1
ECCL WA10 ........ 8 D5
WARRS WA4 ........ 138 B2
WGNS/IIMK WN3 ........ 4 D5
Lyra Rd CSBY/WL L22 ........ 82 F4
Lyster Cl GOL/RIS/CU WA3 ........ 123 H2
Lyster Rd BTL L20 ........ 6 D4
Lytham Cl WLT/FAZ L9 ........ 85 H4
Lytham Ct KKBY L32 ........ 85 L1 1
Lytham Rd AIMK WN4 ........ 79 H8
CHTN/BK PR9 ........ 25 J1
WDN WA8 ........ 134 D3
Lytham St CHLYE PR6 ........ 33 G6
Lytham Wy WD/CROXPK L12 ........ 99 H7 2
Lythgoes La WARRN/WOL WA2 ........ 14 F3
Lytles Cl FMBY L37 ........ 59 J3
Lyttelton Rd AIG/SPK L17 ........ 130 A3
Lytton Av RF/TRAN CH42 ........ 128 B4 3
Lytton Gv LITH L21 ........ 83 J7 5
Lytton St NPK/KEN L6 ........ 13 M3


# M


Mabel St WGNW/BIL/O WN5 ........ 68 A7
Maberry Cl WGNNW/ST WN6 ........ 54 F6
Mab La WD/CROXPK L12 ........ 99 H5
Macalpine Cl
GR/UP/WCH CH49 ........ 110 C7 1
Macarthur Rd
WARRW/BUR WA5 ........ 120 D7 4
Macauley Pl WGNS/IIMK WN3 ........ 79 H1
Macbeth St BTL L20 ........ 7 H9
Macclesfield Cl
WGNE/HIN WN2 ........ 69 L8 1
Macdermott Rd WDN WA8 ........ 16 A9
Macdona Dr WKBY CH48 ........ 124 D5
Macdonald Av
RNFD/HAY WA11 ........ 90 A8 1
WGNS/IIMK WN3 ........ 79 J2 1
Macdonald Dr
GR/UP/WCH CH49 ........ 125 M2 1
Macdonald Rd MOR/LEA CH46 ........ 109 L5
Macdonald St WAV L15 ........ 114 A5
WGNW/BIL/O WN5 ........ 67 K7
Mace Rd NG/CROX L11 ........ 98 E2
Macfarren St
CLB/OSW/ST L13 ........ 114 C2 2
Mackay Cft CHLYE PR6 ........ 32 F5 7
Mackenzie Av WGNS/IIMK WN3 ........ 79 J2
Mackenzie Rd MOR/LEA CH46 ........ 110 D2
Mackenzie St NPK/KEN L6 ........ 97 J8 5
Mackenzie Cl CHLYE PR6 ........ 32 F5 8
Mackets Cl WLTN L25 ........ 131 L4
Macket's La WLTN L25 ........ 131 L4
Mack Gv NTHTN L30 ........ 83 M3
Macqueen St CLB/OSW/ST L13 ........ 114 C3
Maddock Rd WAL/EG CH44 ........ 95 M8
Maddocks St CLB/OSW/ST L13 ........ 114 C3
Maddock St BIRK CH41 ........ 10 F2
Maddrell St VAUX/LVPD L3 ........ 12 D1
Madelaine St TOX L8 ........ 113 J7
Madeley Cl WGNS/IIMK WN3 ........ 79 G2 3
WKBY CH48 ........ 124 D4 1
Madeley Dr WKBY CH48 ........ 124 D4
Madeley St NPK/KEN L6 ........ 113 L2 2
Madeline Mckenna Ct
WDN WA8 ........ 133 L2 3
Madiera Dr WLTN L25 ........ 115 K7
Madryn Av NWD/KWIPK L33 ........ 86 C3
Madryn St TOX L8 ........ 113 J8
Maelor Cl BEB CH63 ........ 143 K7
Maesbrook Cl CHTN/BK PR9 ........ 23 K8 1
Mafeking Cl WAV L15 ........ 114 B5 2
Mafeking Pl AIMK WN4 ........ 91 L2 5
Magazine Av WAL/NB CH45 ........ 95 K6 2
Magazine Brow WAL/NB CH45 ........ 95 L6
Magazine La PS/BROM CH62 ........ 144 A2
WAL/NB CH45 ........ 95 L6
Magazine Rd PS/BROM CH62 ........ 143 M2
Magazines Prom WAL/NB CH45 ........ 95 L6
Magdala St TOX L8 ........ 113 L6
Magdalen Dr AIMK WN4 ........ 91 H1
Magdalene Sq NTHTN L30 ........ 84 B1 4
Maggots Nook Rd
RNFD/HAY WA11 ........ 76 C4
Maghull La MGHL L31 ........ 73 K4
Maghull St CLVPS L1 ........ 112 E5 5
Magnolia Cl GTS/LS CH66 ........ 163 H4
HLWD L26 ........ 131 M3 5
RNFD/HAY WA11 ........ 90 B8 5
WARR WA1 ........ 123 G6 4
Magnolia Dr RUNC WA7 ........ 161 H1 5
Magnolia Wk
GR/UP/WCH CH49 ........ 125 L3
Magnum St EV L5 ........ 97 G8
Maguire Av BTL L20 ........ 7 M3
Mahon Av BTL L20 ........ 83 M7
Maiden La CLB/OSW/ST L13 ........ 97 M6
Maidford Rd DV/KA/FCH L14 ........ 99 H8
Maidstone Cl WGNE/HIN WN2 ........ 81 L3
Main Av ECCL WA10 ........ 101 L5
Main Cl RNFD/HAY WA11 ........ 90 C7
Main Dr RAIN/WH L35 ........ 117 G4
Main Front RAIN/WH L35 ........ 117 G4
Main La GOL/RIS/CU WA3 ........ 106 A2
Main Rd PS/BROM CH62 ........ 143 K1
Mains Av WGNE/HIN WN2 ........ 80 B6
Mainside Rd KKBY L32 ........ 86 B4
Mains La BRSC L40 ........ 40 B7
Main St FROD/HEL WA6 ........ 160 C5
RUNC WA7 ........ 150 B5
WGNW/BIL/O WN5 ........ 78 A8
Maintree Crs SPK/HALE L24 ........ 147 J1
Mainwaring Rd PS/BROM CH62 ........ 143 M5
WAL/EG CH44 ........ 111 M2
Mairesfield Av WARRS WA4 ........ 138 D3
Mairscough La ORM L39 ........ 61 J5
Maitland Cl TOX L8 ........ 113 K6
Maitland Rd WAL/NB CH45 ........ 95 L5 1
Maitland St TOX L8 ........ 113 K6 3
Major Cross St WDN WA8 ........ 16 D5 1
Major St EV L5 ........ 96 F7 8
WGNW/BIL/O WN5 ........ 67 L7
Makerfield Dr NEWLW WA12 ........ 91 J8
Makerfield Wy WGNE/HIN WN2 ........ 69 K6
Makinson Av WGNE/HIN WN2 ........ 69 M6
Makin St ANF/KKDL L4 ........ 97 H3
Malcolm Av WARRN/WOL WA2 ........ 121 M4
Malcolm Crs BEB CH63 ........ 143 L7
Malcolm Gv BTL L20 ........ 7 J8
Malcolm Pl WAV L15 ........ 114 B4 1
Malcolm St RUNC WA7 ........ 19 K4
Malden Rd NPK/KEN L6 ........ 113 L2
Maldon Cl HLWD L26 ........ 132 B7
WGNE/HIN WN2 ........ 69 H3
Maldon Rd WGNNW/ST WN6 ........ 56 B5
Maldwyn Rd WAL/EG CH44 ........ 95 K8
Maley Cl TOX L8 ........ 129 J1
Malham Av WGNS/IIMK WN3 ........ 79 J3
Malham Cl LEIGH WN7 ........ 81 L8
STHP PR8 ........ 36 A2
Malhamdale Av RAIN/WH L35 ........ 117 M3
Malin Cl SPK/HALE L24 ........ 147 M3
Maliston Rd WARRW/BUR WA5 ........ 120 D8
Mallaby St BIRK CH41 ........ 10 B2
Mallard Cl HLWD L26 ........ 132 A4
ORM L39 ........ 62 E3 1
RUNC WA7 ........ 150 B8 4
WARRN/WOL WA2 ........ 121 M2
WD/CROXPK L12 ........ 99 H2 2
Mallard Gdns STHEL WA9 ........ 102 A7
Mallard La GOL/RIS/CU WA3 ........ 123 H2
Mallard Wy MOR/LEA CH46 ........ 109 L4
RNFD/HAY WA11 ........ 89 K7
Mallee Av CHTN/BK PR9 ........ 25 J2
Mallee Crs CHTN/BK PR9 ........ 25 J2
Malleson Rd CLB/OSW/ST L13 ........ 98 A6
Mallins Cl TOX L8 ........ 129 J1 13
Mallom Av CHLY/EC PR7 ........ 32 A4
Mallory Av MGHL L31 ........ 72 D1
Mallory Gv RNFD/HAY WA11 ........ 89 M7
Mallory Rd EP CH65 ........ 163 J1
RF/TRAN CH42 ........ 127 M3
Mallowdale Cl PS/BROM CH62 ........ 144 A8
Mallow Rd NPK/KEN L6 ........ 113 L2
Mallow Wy HUY L36 ........ 116 B5
Malmesbury Cl
GR/UP/WCH CH49 ........ 125 L1 4
Malmesbury Pk RUNC WA7 ........ 150 F2
Malmesbury Rd NG/CROX L11 ........ 98 A3
Malpas Av CL/PREN CH43 ........ 127 J3 2
WGN WN1 ........ 5 H1
Malpas Dr BEB CH63 ........ 128 A6
WARRW/BUR WA5 ........ 136 E1
Malpas Gv WAL/NB CH45 ........ 95 J7
Malpas Rd EP CH65 ........ 163 H1
NG/CROX L11 ........ 85 M8
RUNC WA7 ........ 149 K6
WAL/NB CH45 ........ 95 H7
Malpas Wy
WARRW/BUR WA5 ........ 136 E1 2
Malta Cl HUY L36 ........ 115 M2
Malta St TOX L8 ........ 113 H8
Maltkiln La BRSC L40 ........ 40 D5
ORM L39 ........ 63 G5
Maltmans Rd LYMM WA13 ........ 139 M2
Malton Av GOL/RIS/CU WA3 ........ 93 G6
Malton Cl LEIGH WN7 ........ 81 L7
WDN WA8 ........ 117 L8
Malton Rd WLTN L25 ........ 131 L4
Malt St TOX L8 ........ 113 K5
Malvern Av DV/KA/FCH L14 ........ 115 H3
EP CH65 ........ 20 D8
WGNE/HIN WN2 ........ 81 J1
Malvern Cl AIMK WN4 ........ 91 K1
HOR/BR BL6 ........ 45 L8
KKBY L32 ........ 85 L1
WARRW/BUR WA5 ........ 120 C5
WGNS/IIMK WN3 ........ 78 E2
Malvern Crs DV/KA/FCH L14 ........ 115 H3 1
WGNE/HIN WN2 ........ 80 B1
Malvern Gv RF/TRAN CH42 ........ 127 M3
WLT/FAZ L9 ........ 84 E3
Malvern Rd BTL L20 ........ 83 L6
NPK/KEN L6 ........ 113 L2
STHEL WA9 ........ 103 H2
WAL/NB CH45 ........ 94 F8
Malvern St WGNNW/ST WN6 ........ 55 L2
Malwood St TOX L8 ........ 129 H1 10
Manchester Rd CHTN/BK PR9 ........ 3 J2
GOL/RIS/CU WA3 ........ 123 K6
HOR/BR BL6 ........ 57 M4
PR/KW L34 ........ 100 F8
WARR WA1 ........ 15 J4
WARR WA1 ........ 123 J6 1
WGN WN1 ........ 5 L4
WGNE/HIN WN2 ........ 69 J6
Manchester Rw
NEWLW WA12 ........ 104 F5 1
Manchester St (Queensway)
CLVPS L1 ........ 13 G6
Mancroft Cl WARR WA1 ........ 123 G6 5
Manderville Cl
WGNS/IIMK WN3 ........ 78 F3 2
Mandeville Rd STHP PR8 ........ 34 D8
Mandeville St ANF/KKDL L4 ........ 97 H3
Manesty's La CLVPS L1 ........ 13 G8
Manfield SKEL WN8 ........ 65 J2
Manica Crs AIN/FAZ L10 ........ 85 H7
Manion Av MGHL L31 ........ 61 K8
Manion Cl MGHL L31 ........ 61 K8
Manley Av GOL/RIS/CU WA3 ........ 92 B3
Manley Cl CL/PREN CH43 ........ 127 H2
LEIGH WN7 ........ 81 M5
Manley Gdns WARRW/BUR WA5 ........ 14 A4
Manley La FROD/HEL WA6 ........ 166 A8
Manley Pl STHEL WA9 ........ 102 A6 3
Manley Rd CSBY/WL L22 ........ 82 E3
FROD/HEL WA6 ........ 166 F5
HUY L36 ........ 116 C5
Manley St WGNS/IIMK WN3 ........ 5 J8
Manley Vw CHNE CH2 ........ 165 L2
Manna Dr CHNE CH2 ........ 165 L2 3
Mannering Rd AIG/SPK L17 ........ 129 K1
Manners La HES CH60 ........ 141 G7
Manning Av WGNNW/ST WN6 ........ 68 C3
Manningham Rd NPK/KEN L6 ........ 97 K7
Manning Rd STHP PR8 ........ 25 G7
Manning St ECCL WA10 ........ 8 E6
Mannington Cl HOY CH47 ........ 109 G5 3
Mann Island VAUX/LVPD L3 ........ 12 D8
Mann St TOX L8 ........ 113 G7
Manor Av BRSC L40 ........ 51 M3
CSBY/BLUN L23 ........ 70 F8
GOL/RIS/CU WA3 ........ 92 E5
NEWLW WA12 ........ 104 B1
RAIN/WH L35 ........ 117 L3
Manorbier Crs WLT/FAZ L9 ........ 97 J2
Manor Cl AIMK WN4 ........ 90 E2
BTL L20 ........ 7 M6
NSTN CH64 ........ 152 E6
WARR WA1 ........ 122 F6
WD/CROXPK L12 ........ 98 F2
Manor Ct GOL/RIS/CU WA3 ........ 92 E5
Manor Crs BRSC L40 ........ 51 M3
WLTN L25 ........ 131 K4
Manor Dr BRSC L40 ........ 51 M3
CSBY/BLUN L23 ........ 70 F8
GR/UP/WCH CH49 ........ 110 B6
NTHTN L30 ........ 84 D2
Manor Farm Crs CH/BCN CH1 ........ 162 D5
Manor Farm Rd HUY L36 ........ 116 B4
RUNC WA7 ........ 150 F1
Manor Fell RUNC WA7 ........ 150 D6
Manorfield Cl CH/BCN CH1 ........ 162 C5
Manor Gdns BRSC L40 ........ 51 M3
Manor Gv KKBY L32 ........ 85 K3
SKEL WN8 ........ 65 H4
WGNE/HIN WN2 ........ 57 K8
WGNW/BIL/O WN5 ........ 67 K5
Manor Hl CL/PREN CH43 ........ 10 A6
Manor House Cl MGHL L31 ........ 72 E4
RNFD/HAY WA11 ........ 89 J3
Manor House Dr SKEL WN8 ........ 77 G2
Manorial Rd NSTN CH64 ........ 152 E5
Manorial Rd South NSTN CH64 ........ 152 E5
Manor La GTS/LS CH66 ........ 162 F2
RF/TRAN CH42 ........ 128 C3
WAL/NB CH45 ........ 95 L8
Manor Ldg FMBY L37 ........ 59 G1
Manor Park Av RUNC WA7 ........ 150 E1
Manor Park Dr GTS/LS CH66 ........ 162 F3
Manor Pl PS/BROM CH62 ........ 128 F8
WGNS/IIMK WN3 ........ 5 L8
Manor Rd BEB CH63 ........ 142 B4
BRSC L40 ........ 51 M3
CHTN/BK PR9 ........ 25 J3
CSBY/BLUN L23 ........ 70 E7
FROD/HEL WA6 ........ 160 E4
HOY CH47 ........ 108 E5
PEN/TH CH61 ........ 125 M7
PS/BROM CH62 ........ 144 A7
RNFD/HAY WA11 ........ 91 J6
RUNC WA7 ........ 149 M3
WAL/EG CH44 ........ 95 K8
WDN WA8 ........ 133 K4
WGNNW/ST WN6 ........ 55 H7
WLTN L25 ........ 131 K4
Manorside Cl
GR/UP/WCH CH49 ........ 110 B7 3
Manor St GOL/RIS/CU WA3 ........ 92 D4 2
STHEL WA9 ........ 9 L8
WGN WN1 ........ 4 D4
WGNW/BIL/O WN5 ........ 68 B7
Manor Vw WD/CROXPK L12 ........ 99 H4
Manor Wy WLTN L25 ........ 131 K4
Manorwood Dr RAIN/WH L35 ........ 117 G3
Manse Av WGNNW/ST WN6 ........ 42 B7
Manse Gdns NEWLW WA12 ........ 104 F1
Mansell Cl WDN WA8 ........ 118 E8 1
Mansell Dr HLWD L26 ........ 132 A7
Mansell Rd NPK/KEN L6 ........ 113 L2
Mansfield Cl GOL/RIS/CU WA3 ........ 123 J1
Mansfield Rd EP CH65 ........ 163 J3
Mansfield St GOL/RIS/CU WA3 ........ 92 A4
VAUX/LVPD L3 ........ 13 J4
Manston Gv CHLY/EC PR7 ........ 33 C8
Manston Rd WARRW/BUR WA5 ........ 136 B2
Manton Rd NPK/KEN L6 ........ 113 L2
Manuel Perez Rd
WARRW/BUR WA5 ........ 120 D7 5
Manvers Rd CHLDW L16 ........ 115 G4
Manville Rd WAL/NB CH45 ........ 95 K6
Manville St STHEL WA9 ........ 102 E4
Manx Jane's La CHTN/BK PR9 ........ 25 J1
Manx Rd WARRS WA4 ........ 137 K2
Maori Dr FROD/HEL WA6 ........ 160 C5
Maple Av BRSC L40 ........ 52 A1 3
GOL/RIS/CU WA3 ........ 93 H6
GTS/LS CH66 ........ 155 L7
NEWLW WA12 ........ 104 F3
RNFD/HAY WA11 ........ 90 D6
RUNC WA7 ........ 19 M7
WDN WA8 ........ 16 F1 2
WGNE/HIN WN2 ........ 5 M7
Maple Cl FMBY L37 ........ 58 E4
LITH L21 ........ 83 J7
RAIN/WH L35 ........ 117 G2
WD/CROXPK L12 ........ 98 F2 4
WGNW/BIL/O WN5 ........ 77 M8
Maple Crs HUY L36 ........ 115 M3
WARRW/BUR WA5 ........ 136 B1
Mapledale Rd CALD/MH L18 ........ 114 C8
Maple Dr WGNE/HIN WN2 ........ 80 D6
Maple Gv CHLYE PR6 ........ 32 F2
ECCL WA10 ........ 101 L2
GTS/LS CH66 ........ 163 J4
PS/BROM CH62 ........ 143 L5
RAIN/WH L35 ........ 101 G8
TOX L8 ........ 113 L7
WARRS WA4 ........ 137 M2
WGNNW/ST WN6 ........ 68 C2
Maple Rd WARR WA1 ........ 123 G6
WARRN/WOL WA2 ........ 105 K7
Maple St AIMK WN4 ........ 79 J7
BIRK CH41 ........ 11 G8
STHP PR8 ........ 3 M6
Mapleton Cl CL/PREN CH43 ........ 127 G4
Mapleton Dr RUNC WA7 ........ 161 H2
Maple Tree Gv HES CH60 ........ 141 L4 1
Maplewood KKBY L32 ........ 86 B5 4
SKEL WN8 ........ 65 J1
Maplewood Cl NTHLY L27 ........ 116 A8 3
Maplewood Gv CL/PREN CH43 ........ 111 G5
Mapplewell Crs
WARRW/BUR WA5 ........ 120 C7
Marathon Cl NPK/KEN L6 ........ 13 M2
Marble Cl BTL L20 ........ 83 M6
Marbury Gdns EP CH65 ........ 156 B7
Marbury Gv WGNNW/ST WN6 ........ 56 A5
Marbury Rd KKBY L32 ........ 85 L3
Marbury St WARRS WA4 ........ 15 G8
Marc Av MGHL L31 ........ 85 K1
Marcham Wy NG/CROX L11 ........ 98 D4
Marchant Cl NTHTN L30 ........ 84 C5
Marchbank WGNE/HIN WN2 ........ 69 J3 4
Marchbank Rd SKEL WN8 ........ 64 F4
Marchfield Rd WLT/FAZ L9 ........ 84 B8
March Rd NPK/KEN L6 ........ 97 M8
Marchwiel Rd EP CH65 ........ 20 F6
Marchwood Wy WLTN L25 ........ 115 J6 1
Marcien Wy WDN WA8 ........ 134 B2
Marcot Rd NPK/KEN L6 ........ 113 M1
Marcross Cl WARRW/BUR WA5 ........ 121 G4
Marcus St BIRK CH41 ........ 11 J3
Mardale Av RNFD/HAY WA11 ........ 89 K5
WARRN/WOL WA2 ........ 121 L2
Mardale Cl NTHLY L27 ........ 132 C2 1
STHP PR8 ........ 47 K1
Mardale Rd HUY L36 ........ 99 L8
NTHLY L27 ........ 132 C2
Mareth Cl CALD/MH L18 ........ 130 C3
Marewood CHLY/EC PR7 ........ 32 D3
Marford Rd WD/CROXPK L12 ........ 98 D6
Marfords Av BEB CH63 ........ 143 L6
Margaret Av BTL L20 ........ 83 L6
STHEL WA9 ........ 102 E5 4
WARR WA1 ........ 122 D6
WGNNW/ST WN6 ........ 67 L1
Margaret Ct WDN WA8 ........ 16 E6 2
Margaret Rd ANF/KKDL L4 ........ 7 M7
CSBY/BLUN L23 ........ 70 C8
Margaret's La GTS/LS CH66 ........ 155 J6
Margaret St NPK/KEN L6 ........ 113 J1
STHEL WA9 ........ 119 G2 3
WGNE/HIN WN2 ........ 69 M7
WGNNW/ST WN6 ........ 4 B2
Margery Rd ECCL WA10 ........ 101 L4 1
Marian Av NEWLW WA12 ........ 104 A2
Marian Cl RAIN/WH L35 ........ 117 L3
The Marian Cl NTHTN L30 ........ 84 A1 3
Marian Dr MOR/LEA CH46 ........ 110 A5
RAIN/WH L35 ........ 117 K3
Marian Rd RNFD/HAY WA11 ........ 91 G6
Marians Dr ORM L39 ........ 51 G5
The Marian Sq NTHTN L30 ........ 84 A2 1
The Marian Wy NTHTN L30 ........ 84 A2
Maria Rd WLT/FAZ L9 ........ 97 H2
Marie Curie Av NTHTN L30 ........ 84 B1 5
NTHTN L30 ........ 84 B2 3
Marie Dr WARRS WA4 ........ 138 F3
Marigold St WGNW/BIL/O WN5 ........ 67 M6
Marina Av LITH L21 ........ 83 K5
STHEL WA9 ........ 102 E6
WARRW/BUR WA5 ........ 136 D1
Marina Crs HUY L36 ........ 115 M4
NTHTN L30 ........ 84 C4
Marina Dr EP CH65 ........ 20 C5 1
WARRN/WOL WA2 ........ 121 L4
WGNW/BIL/O WN5 ........ 67 M8
Marina Gv RUNC WA7 ........ 19 K4
Marina La RUNC WA7 ........ 151 G6
Marina Rd FMBY L37 ........ 59 H4
Marina Village RUNC WA7 ........ 151 G6 1
Marine Crs CSBY/WL L22 ........ 82 F4
Marine Dr CHTN/BK PR9 ........ 22 A8
HES CH60 ........ 140 F6
STHP PR8 ........ 2 C2
Marine Pde STHP PR8 ........ 2 E1
Marine Pk WKBY CH48 ........ 124 D1
Marine Prom WAL/NB CH45 ........ 95 K4
Mariner Cl RUNC WA7 ........ 150 F7
Marine Rd HOY CH47 ........ 108 C6
Mariners Rd CSBY/BLUN L23 ........ 82 D3
WAL/NB CH45 ........ 95 L6 7
Mariners Whf VAUX/LVPD L3 ........ 112 E7
Marine Ter CSBY/WL L22 ........ 82 F5
Marion Dr RUNC WA7 ........ 149 H7
Marion Gv CALD/MH L18 ........ 130 E3
Marion Pl WGNE/HIN WN2 ........ 80 B5
Marion Rd BTL L20 ........ 83 M7
Marion St BIRK CH41 ........ 11 K5
Maritime Cl NEWLW WA12 ........ 91 L8 1
Maritime Ct NTHTN L30 ........ 72 B8
Maritime Pk BIRK CH41 ........ 10 F7 2
Maritime Pl VAUX/LVPD L3 ........ 13 K4 1
Maritime Vw RF/TRAN CH42 ........ 127 M2 3
Maritime Wy CLVPS L1 ........ 13 G9
Mariton Cl CALD/MH L18 ........ 130 F3
Marius Cl ANF/KKDL L4 ........ 97 H5 5
Mark Av GTS/LS CH66 ........ 162 E1
Market Pl BIRK CH41 ........ 11 K6
CHLY/EC PR7 ........ 44 C6
PR/KW L34 ........ 100 F7
WGN WN1 ........ 4 E4
WGNNW/ST WN6 ........ 56 A4 5
Market St BIRK CH41 ........ 11 L5
CHLY/EC PR7 ........ 32 E5
CHLY/EC PR7 ........ 44 C7
EP CH65 ........ 20 B6
HOY CH47 ........ 108 D6
NEWLW WA12 ........ 104 C1
STHP PR8 ........ 2 F4
WDN WA8 ........ 16 D5
WGN WN1 ........ 4 E3
WGNE/HIN WN2 ........ 69 M8
WGNNW/ST WN6 ........ 56 A4
Markfield Crs RNFD/HAY WA11 ........ 9 M1
WLTN L25 ........ 131 M4
Markfield Rd BTL L20 ........ 83 K8
Markham Dr STHP PR8 ........ 36 A3
Marklands Rd HOR/BR BL6 ........ 45 M8
Markland St WGN WN1 ........ 5 K5
Mark Rake PS/BROM CH62 ........ 143 M4
Mark Rd HTWN L38 ........ 70 B1
Mark St EV L5 ........ 97 G7
Marksway PEN/TH CH61 ........ 141 J1
Marlborough SKEL WN8 ........ 65 J1 2
Marlborough Av MGHL L31 ........ 72 F2 2
NTHTN L30 ........ 84 C3
WGNE/HIN WN2 ........ 80 B1
Marlborough Crs WARRS WA4 ........ 138 B3
WDN WA8 ........ 118 C8 3
Marlborough Dr
FROD/HEL WA6 ........ 166 D3 2
Marlborough Gv CL/PREN CH43 ........ 10 E9
Marlborough Pl
VAUX/LVPD L3 ........ 12 F4 2
Marlborough Rd CHTN/BK PR9 ........ 3 K3
CLB/OSW/ST L13 ........ 97 M7

CSBY/BLUN L23 .......... 82 F2
CSBY/WL L22 .......... 83 C5
EP CH65 .......... 20 E9
PR/KW L34 .......... 101 G6
WAL/NB CH45 .......... 95 L6 ②
Marlborough St CHLYE PR6 .......... 33 G4
VAUX/LVPD L3 .......... 12 F4
Marlbrook Rd WLTN L25 .......... 115 K7 ②
Maridon Av CSBY/BLUN L23 .......... 83 C3
Maridon Rd WD/CROXPK L12 .......... 98 D5
Marled Hey STBRV L28 .......... 99 J5
Marley Cl RAIN/WH L35 .......... 118 A4 ②
Marlfield La PEN/TH CH61 .......... 141 J1
Marlfield Rd WARRS WA4 .......... 138 C3
WD/CROXPK L12 .......... 98 D7
Marl Gv WGNW/BIL/O WN5 .......... 77 M1
Marline Av BEB CH63 .......... 143 L7
Marling Cl FROD/HEL WA6 .......... 160 F7
Marling Pk WDN WA8 .......... 133 K4
Marlow Cl GOL/RIS/CU WA3 .......... 106 E8 ②
Marlowe Cl ALL/GAR L19 .......... 130 E8 ②
WDN WA8 .......... 16 A2
WGNS/IIMK WN3 .......... 68 C8 ②
Marlowe Dr WD/CROXPK L12 .......... 98 C7
Marlowe Rd NSTN CH64 .......... 153 C5 ②
WAL/EG CH44 .......... 111 J1
Marl Rd NTHTN L30 .......... 84 D2
NWD/KWIPK L33 .......... 86 E2
Marlsford St NPK/KEN L6 .......... 113 L2 ②
Marlston Av PEN/TH CH61 .......... 126 B7
Marlston Pl RUNC WA7 .......... 149 K7
Marlwood Av WAL/EG CH44 .......... 95 G8
Marmaduke St EHL/KEN L7 .......... 113 K4
Marmion Av BTL L20 .......... 84 A6
Marmion Cl GOL/RIS/CU WA3 .......... 93 C4
Marmion Rd AIG/SPK L17 .......... 129 K1
HOY CH47 .......... 108 D6
Marmonde St ANF/KKDL L4 .......... 97 C5 ②
Marnwood Rd KKBY L32 .......... 85 M4
Marple Cl CL/PREN CH43 .......... 127 G2
WGNW/ST WN6 .......... 55 J3
Marquis St BIRK CH41 .......... 11 J9
PS/BROM CH62 .......... 128 D6
VAUX/LVPD L3 .......... 13 K6
Marram Cl MOR/LEA CH46 .......... 110 C4
Marrick Cl WGNS/IIMK WN3 .......... 79 J3
Marron Av WARRN/WOL WA2 .......... 121 K3
Marsden Av WARR WA4 .......... 8 A3
WARRS WA4 .......... 121 H3
Marsden Cl CHLY/EC PR7 .......... 30 D6 ②
WAL/EG CH44 .......... 95 M8 ②
Marsden Rd CHTN/BK PR9 .......... 25 G6
HLWD L26 .......... 132 B7
Marsden St NPK/KEN L6 .......... 113 L2
WGN WN1 .......... 4 E3
WGNE/HIN WN2 .......... 80 B1 ②
WGNW/BIL/O WN5 .......... 68 B6
Marsden Wy NPK/KEN L6 .......... 113 J2 ①
Marshall Av STHEL WA9 .......... 102 E5 ②
WARRW/BUR WA5 .......... 121 H3
Marshall Pl VAUX/LVPD L3 .......... 12 F2 ②
Marshall Rd WARR WA1 .......... 122 F6
Marshallsay FMBY L37 .......... 59 J3 ②
Marshall's Cl FMBY L37 .......... 72 E1
Marshalls Cross Rd STHEL WA9 .......... 102 E5
Marshall St BIRK CH41 .......... 10 F2
Marsham Cl
GR/UP/WCH CH49 .......... 110 C6 ②
Marsham Rd WLTN L25 .......... 115 L8
Marsh Av BTL L20 .......... 84 A7
Marsh Brows FMBY L37 .......... 59 G3
The Marshes La
KIRK/FR/WA PR4 .......... 27 J3
Marshfield Cl WGN WN1 .......... 116 B2 ②
Marshfield Ct MOR/LEA CH46 .......... 110 A2
Marshfield Rd NG/CROX L11 .......... 98 D4
Marshgate WDN WA8 .......... 133 K7
Marshgate Rd NG/CROX L11 .......... 98 D3
Marsh Gn WGNW/BIL/O WN5 .......... 67 M4
Marsh Hall Rd WDN WA8 .......... 134 D1
Marsh House La
WARRN/WOL WA2 .......... 15 H2
Marshlands Rd NSTN CH64 .......... 153 G8
WAL/NB CH45 .......... 95 G7
Marsh La BEB CH63 .......... 127 L6
BTL L20 .......... 6 E2
CHNE CH2 .......... 158 C7
CHNE CH2 .......... 165 K2
FROD/HEL WA6 .......... 160 C5
HTWN L38 .......... 70 F1
RUNC WA7 .......... 150 B2 ②
WARRW/BUR WA5 .......... 135 L3
WGN WN1 .......... 4 F5
Marsh Moss La BRSC L40 .......... 38 E6
Marsh Rd CHTN/BK PR9 .......... 23 L4
Marsh Rw WGNE/HIN WN2 .......... 81 J1
Marshside Cl TOX L8 .......... 113 H8 ②
Marshside Rd CHTN/BK PR9 .......... 22 A8
Marsh St BTL L20 .......... 7 J9
STHEL WA9 .......... 9 M5
WARR WA1 .......... 15 K2
WDN WA8 .......... 16 C8
Marsland Gv STHEL WA9 .......... 103 G5
Marson St WARRN/WOL WA2 .......... 14 D4
Marston Cl CL/PREN CH43 .......... 127 H3
PS/BROM CH62 .......... 155 G2
Marston Crs HTWN L38 .......... 70 C3
Marten Av BEB CH63 .......... 143 L6
Martensen St EHL/KEN L7 .......... 113 K4
Martham Cl WARRS WA4 .......... 138 C2
Martin Av ECCL WA10 .......... 89 H7
NEWLW WA12 .......... 91 K8
WARRN/WOL WA2 .......... 121 M4
Martin Cl CALD/MH L18 .......... 130 C4
PEN/TH CH61 .......... 125 L7
RAIN/WH L35 .......... 117 J1
RUNC WA7 .......... 150 C1
Martindale Crs
WGNW/BIL/O WN5 .......... 68 A7
Martindale Gv RUNC WA7 .......... 149 M8
Martindale Rd CALD/MH L18 .......... 114 F8
PS/BROM CH62 .......... 144 A4
RNFD/HAY WA11 .......... 89 K3
WGNW/BIL/O WN5 .......... 89 M1
Martine Cl MGHL L31 .......... 85 L1 ②
Martin Gv RAIN/WH L35 .......... 101 C8
Martinhall Rd WLT/FAZ L9 .......... 98 B1 ②

Martin La BRSC L40 .......... 38 A5
Martin Rd CALD/MH L18 .......... 130 C4
FROD/HEL WA6 .......... 160 D5
Martins Av CHLY/EC PR7 .......... 44 A3
Martins La SKEL WN8 .......... 65 M6
WAL/EG CH44 .......... 111 L1
Martland Av AIN/FAZ L10 .......... 85 G2
GOL/RIS/CU WA3 .......... 92 F6
WGNNW/ST WN6 .......... 55 H8
Martland Gv WGNNW/ST WN6 .......... 68 A2
Martland Mill La
WGNW/BIL/O WN5 .......... 67 M3
Martland Rd WLTN L25 .......... 131 L1
Mart La BRSC L40 .......... 39 G8
Martlesham Crs
GR/UP/WCH CH49 .......... 125 K2
Martlett Rd WD/CROXPK L12 .......... 98 F8
Martock RAIN/WH L35 .......... 117 H3
Marton Cl GOL/RIS/CU WA3 .......... 107 G1 ②
SPK/HALE L24 .......... 146 F3 ②
Marton Gn SPK/HALE L24 .......... 146 F3 ②
Marton Rd HUY L36 .......... 100 A7
Marton St WGN WN1 .......... 4 E2
Marus Av WGNS/IIMK WN3 .......... 79 H2
Marvin St NPK/KEN L6 .......... 113 J2 ②
Marwick Cl WGNNW/ST WN6 .......... 55 M3
Mary Av STHP PR8 .......... 35 G7
Marybone VAUX/LVPD L3 .......... 12 F5
Maryfield Cl GOL/RIS/CU WA3 .......... 92 C6 ②
Maryhill Rd RUNC WA7 .......... 19 G8
Maryland La MOR/LEA CH46 .......... 109 M4
Maryland St CLVPS L1 .......... 13 K9 ②
Marylebone Av STHEL WA9 .......... 102 B7
Marylebone Pl WGN WN1 .......... 68 F2
Mary Rd BTL L20 .......... 83 M7
Mary St STHEL WA9 .......... 119 G2 ②
WDN WA8 .......... 17 K5
Maryton Gra CALD/MH L18 .......... 130 F3 ②
Maryville Rd PR/KW L34 .......... 101 C7
Marywell Cl STHEL WA9 .......... 102 F6 ②
Masefield Av LEIGH WN7 .......... 81 M6
WDN WA8 .......... 16 B4
WGNW/BIL/O WN5 .......... 67 J7
Masefield Crs NTHTN L30 .......... 83 M5
Masefield Dr WGNS/IIMK WN3 .......... 79 H1
Masefield Gv CHLDW L16 .......... 115 H5
ECCL WA10 .......... 8 A1
Masefield Pl NTHTN L30 .......... 84 A5
Masefield Rd CSBY/BLUN L23 .......... 71 L7
Maskell Rd CLB/OSW/ST L13 .......... 114 B2
Mason Av WARR WA1 .......... 122 A5
WDN WA8 .......... 134 C1
Mason Cl AIMK WN4 .......... 91 M1 ②
GTS/LS CH66 .......... 162 F3
Mason St CHLY PR6 .......... 33 G3
CSBY/WL L22 .......... 82 F4
EHL/KEN L7 .......... 113 J4
RUNC WA7 .......... 19 L2
WAL/NB CH45 .......... 95 K5 ②
WARR WA1 .......... 15 H6
WGNE/HIN WN2 .......... 80 D5 ②
WGNS/IIMK WN3 .......... 4 C5
WLTN L25 .......... 131 J3
Massam's La FMBY L37 .......... 47 G7
Massey Av LYMM WA13 .......... 139 J3
WARRW/BUR WA5 .......... 121 H3
Massey Brook La LYMM WA13 .......... 139 K3
Masseyfield Rd RUNC WA7 .......... 150 C8
Massey Pk WAL/NB CH45 .......... 95 J8
Massey St BIRK CH41 .......... 11 G2
STHEL WA9 .......... 102 E5
Mather Av ALL/GAR L19 .......... 130 F6
CALD/MH L18 .......... 130 D1
GOL/RIS/CU WA3 .......... 93 G7
RUNC WA7 .......... 18 B9
STHEL WA9 .......... 103 G2 ②
Mathers Cl WARRN/WOL WA2 .......... 122 C1 ②
Matheson Dr WGNW/BIL/O WN5 .......... 67 M5
Mather St CLVP L2 .......... 12 F7
Mathieson Rd WDN WA8 .......... 134 A8
Matlock Av WLT/FAZ L9 .......... 84 C7 ②
Matlock Cl WARRW/BUR WA5 .......... 120 C4 ②
Matterdale Cl FROD/HEL WA6 .......... 160 F6
Matthew Cl WAL/EG CH44 .......... 112 A3 ②
Matthews St WARR WA1 .......... 15 J2
Matthew St WAL/EG CH44 .......... 112 A3
Matty's La FROD/HEL WA6 .......... 160 D5
Maud St CHLY/EC PR7 .......... 32 D7
TOX L8 .......... 113 J7
Maunders Ct CSBY/BLUN L23 .......... 71 H8
Mauretania Rd ANF/KKDL L4 .......... 97 J3
Mavis Dr CHLY/EC PR7 .......... 43 C4
GR/UP/WCH CH49 .......... 126 C2
Mawdsley Av WARR WA1 .......... 123 C6
Mawdsley Rd FMBY L37 .......... 59 K2 ②
Mawdsley Ter ORM L39 .......... 51 H5
Mawson Cl WARRW/BUR WA5 .......... 120 F5
Max Rd DV/KA/FCH L14 .......... 99 H8
Maxton Rd NPK/KEN L6 .......... 113 L2
Maxwell Cl EP CH65 .......... 163 J3
GR/UP/WCH CH49 .......... 110 C7 ②
Maxwell Pl CLB/OSW/ST L13 .......... 98 B7
Maxwell Rd CLB/OSW/ST L13 .......... 98 B7
Maxwell St ECCL WA10 .......... 8 D6
GOL/RIS/CU WA3 .......... 107 G7
May Av LEIGH WN7 .......... 81 M7
WAL/EG CH44 .......... 111 M3
WGNE/HIN WN2 .......... 80 E6
Maybank Cl CHTN/BK PR9 .......... 25 J4
Maybank Rd RF/TRAN CH42 .......... 127 M1
Mayberry Gv WARRS WA4 .......... 122 C4
Maybury Wy AIG/SPK L17 .......... 129 L3 ②
Mayew Rd PEN/TH CH61 .......... 126 B7
Mayfair Av WARRS WA4 .......... 137 M8
Mayfair Cl CSBY/BLUN L23 .......... 71 K8
DV/KA/FCH L14 .......... 115 H3
Mayfair Cl HTWN L38 .......... 70 B3
NPK/KEN L6 .......... 113 K1 ②
Mayfair Dr WGNE/HIN WN2 .......... 69 M3 ②
WGNS/IIMK WN3 .......... 79 H3
Mayfayre Av MGHL L31 .......... 61 K8 ②
Mayfield Av CHLYE PR6 .......... 44 C6
FMBY L37 .......... 58 E4

STHEL WA9 .......... 102 A5
WDN WA8 .......... 133 K4
Mayfield Cl WD/CROXPK L12 .......... 98 E7 ②
Mayfield Cl FMBY L37 .......... 47 G8
Mayfield Dr GOL/RIS/CU WA3 .......... 93 L5
LEIGH WN7 .......... 93 L5
PS/BROM CH62 .......... 144 D7
Mayfield Gdns ALL/GAR L19 .......... 130 B6
BEB CH63 .......... 143 J2
CHLYE PR6 .......... 32 F4
SKEL WN8 .......... 66 D6
WAL/NB CH45 .......... 95 G8
WGNW/BIL/O WN5 .......... 67 K5
Mayfields North
PS/BROM CH62 .......... 128 D6
Mayfields South
PS/BROM CH62 .......... 128 D6 ②
Mayfield St AIMK WN4 .......... 91 J2 ②
Mayflower Av SPK/HALE L24 .......... 131 J7
Maynard St TOX L8 .......... 113 K6 ②
May Pl VAUX/LVPD L3 .......... 13 K8
May Rd HES CH60 .......... 141 J5
Maypole Ct NTHTN L30 .......... 71 M8 ②
May St BTL L20 .......... 7 H2
GOL/RIS/CU WA3 .......... 92 D3
LEIGH WN7 .......... 81 L8
VAUX/LVPD L3 .......... 13 K8
Maythorn Av GOL/RIS/CU WA3 .......... 106 C6
Maytree Cl HLY L27 .......... 115 L7 ②
May Tree Dr WGN WN1 .......... 68 D2
Maytree Wk SKEL WN8 .......... 65 K1
Mayville Rd CALD/MH L18 .......... 114 D8
Mazzini Cl EV L5 .......... 97 C8
Mcbride St ALL/GAR L19 .......... 130 E7
Mc Carthy Cl GOL/RIS/CU WA3 .......... 123 J2
Mc Clellan Pl WDN WA8 .......... 16 E2
Mccormack Av STHEL WA9 .......... 103 G1
Mccormack Dr WGN WN1 .......... 5 H4
Mcculloch St STHEL WA9 .......... 9 K5
Mcfarlane Av ECCL WA10 .......... 101 L1
Mcgarva Wy EP CH65 .......... 20 C7
Mcgough Cl STHEL WA9 .......... 118 C2 ②
Mcgregor St EV L5 .......... 97 G8 ②
Mckee Av WARRN/WOL WA2 .......... 121 K3
Mckeown Cl EV L5 .......... 96 F8 ②
Mcminnis Av STHEL WA9 .......... 103 J3
Mcvinnie Rd RAIN/WH L35 .......... 101 H7
Mead Av LITH L21 .......... 83 L5
Meade Cl RAIN/WH L35 .......... 118 A7
Meade Rd CLB/OSW/ST L13 .......... 98 A7
Meadfoot Rd MOR/LEA CH46 .......... 109 M4
Meadow Av STHEL WA9 .......... 118 F2 ②
STHP PR8 .......... 35 L1
WARRS WA4 .......... 137 J3
Meadow Bank MGHL L31 .......... 72 D3 ②
ORM L39 .......... 51 H8 ②
Meadowbank Cl
WD/CROXPK L12 .......... 99 G8
Meadowbridge Cl BRSC L40 .......... 64 A1 ②
Meadowbrook BRSC L40 .......... 51 M3
Meadow Brook Cl AIN/FAZ L10 .......... 85 K6
Meadowbrook Rd
MOR/LEA CH46 .......... 109 M6
Meadow Brow CHTN/BK PR9 .......... 22 F8
Meadow Cl BRSC L40 .......... 64 A1
FROD/HEL WA6 .......... 166 D2 ②
NSTN CH64 .......... 153 G7
NSTN CH64 .......... 154 B5 ②
SKEL WN8 .......... 65 M6
WDN WA8 .......... 133 M2
Meadow Clough SKEL WN8 .......... 65 K1 ②
Meadow Crs GR/UP/WCH CH49 .......... 126 D3
Meadow Cft NSTN CH64 .......... 154 A5
Meadowcroft AIMK WN4 .......... 79 H7
CHLY/EC PR7 .......... 31 K2
FMBY L37 .......... 59 H3 ②
HES CH60 .......... 141 L4
SKEL WN8 .......... 65 K1 ②
STHEL WA9 .......... 102 E7
Meadowcroft Pk
WD/CROXPK L12 .......... 114 F1
Meadowcroft Rd HOY CH47 .......... 109 G4 ②
Meadow Dr HUY L36 .......... 116 B5
ORM L39 .......... 62 E3
Meadowfield Cl
RF/TRAN CH42 .......... 128 B3 ②
Meadow Hey BTL L20 .......... 83 J8
Meadow Hey Cl WLTN L25 .......... 131 K2 ②
Meadowlands CHLY/EC PR7 .......... 42 F1
Meadow La BRSC L40 .......... 39 L5
BRSC L40 .......... 52 E2
EP CH65 .......... 20 E3
LEY/BBR PR5 .......... 28 F4
MGHL L31 .......... 73 G4
NSTN CH64 .......... 154 A4
RF/TRAN CH42 .......... 128 B3
STHEL WA9 .......... 103 H4
STHP PR8 .......... 47 L2
WARRN/WOL WA2 .......... 122 C3
WD/CROXPK L12 .......... 98 D6
Meadow Oak Dr WLTN L25 .......... 131 J1
Meadow Pk RF/TRAN CH42 .......... 128 B3 ②
Meadow Pit La WGNE/HIN WN2 .......... 57 K5
Meadow Rd WKBY CH48 .......... 125 H2
Meadows Cl
WGNE/HIN WN2 .......... 69 M8 ②
Meadows Gn GOL/RIS/CU WA3 .......... 93 G8
Meadowside LEY/BBR PR5 .......... 29 J3
MOR/LEA CH46 .......... 110 D1
Meadowside Av AIMK WN4 .......... 79 J5 ②
Meadowside Dr
NWD/KWIPK L33 .......... 74 B7
Meadowside Rd
PS/BROM CH62 .......... 143 M6
WGNE/HIN WN2 .......... 81 J3 ②
Meadow St CHLYE PR6 .......... 44 C7
WAL/NB CH45 .......... 95 J5
The Meadow
GR/UP/WCH CH49 .......... 126 D3
Meadowvale Dr
WGNW/BIL/O WN5 .......... 67 L7 ②
Meadow Vw CHNE CH2 .......... 165 J2

LITH L21 .......... 83 K2
STHP PR8 .......... 35 M1 ②
Meadow View Dr
FROD/HEL WA6 .......... 160 C6 ②
Meadow Wk PEN/TH CH61 .......... 141 G2
Meadow Wy CHLY/EC PR7 .......... 42 F5
NG/CROX L11 .......... 98 D4
Mead Rd HES CH60 .......... 141 C7
Meadway GOL/RIS/CU WA3 .......... 92 F5
GR/UP/WCH CH49 .......... 110 D7
GTS/LS CH66 .......... 155 K6
HES CH60 .......... 141 H7
MGHL L31 .......... 72 D6
NTHTN L30 .......... 84 B3
PS/BROM CH62 .......... 143 L3
RAIN/WH L35 .......... 117 H1
RUNC WA7 .......... 149 M4
WAL/NB CH45 .......... 95 J8 ②
WAV L15 .......... 114 E5
WDN WA8 .......... 133 J4
WGNE/HIN WN2 .......... 81 J1 ②
Mealhouse La CHLY/EC PR7 .......... 32 E5 ②
The Meander RF/TRAN CH42 .......... 99 C4
Measham Cl RNFD/HAY WA11 .......... 9 L1
Measham Wy WD/CROXPK L12 .......... 99 G2
Medbourne Crs KKBY L32 .......... 86 B5
Medea St EV L5 .......... 97 G7
Medlar Wy AIMK WN4 .......... 79 H8
Medlock St ANF/KKDL L4 .......... 97 C5
Medlock Wy WGNE/HIN WN2 .......... 80 C3 ②
Medway Cl AIMK WN4 .......... 79 H7 ②
LEIGH WN7 .......... 93 L5
WARRN/WOL WA2 .......... 122 A3 ②
Medway Pl WGNW/BIL/O WN5 .......... 67 M6
Medway Rd GOL/RIS/CU WA3 .......... 107 J3
RF/TRAN CH42 .......... 128 C3 ②
Meeting La WARRW/BUR WA5 .......... 119 M8
Melbreck SKEL WN8 .......... 65 J1
Melbreck Rd CALD/MH L18 .......... 130 D4
Melbury Ct GOL/RIS/CU WA3 .......... 107 H7
Melbury Rd DV/KA/FCH L14 .......... 99 K7
Melda Cl NPK/KEN L6 .......... 6 13 M4
Meldon Cl NG/CROX L11 .......... 98 E3
Meldreth Cl FMBY L37 .......... 58 E4
Meldrum Rd WAV L15 .......... 114 D7
Melford Cl CHLYE PR6 .......... 33 G2
CL/PREN CH43 .......... 127 G4
RUNC WA7 .......... 19 L6
WGNW/BIL/O WN5 .......... 77 M2
Melford Gv NPK/KEN L6 .......... 97 M7
Meliden Gdns STHEL WA9 .......... 103 H6 ②
Meliden Gv CHLY/EC PR7 .......... 30 D5 ②
Melksham Dr PEN/TH CH61 .......... 125 M6 ②
Melling Av WLT/FAZ L9 .......... 84 D6
Melling Dr KKBY L32 .......... 86 A2
Melling La MGHL L31 .......... 73 G6
Melling Rd BTL L20 .......... 7 H1
CHTN/BK PR9 .......... 25 C5
WAL/NB CH45 .......... 95 J6
WLT/FAZ L9 .......... 84 D5
Mellings Av
WGNW/BIL/O WN5 .......... 78 A4 ②
Melling St WGNW/BIL/O WN5 .......... 68 A8
Melling Wy KKBY L32 .......... 86 A2
WGNS/IIMK WN3 .......... 78 F4
Mellock Cl NSTN CH64 .......... 153 H7
Mellock La NSTN CH64 .......... 153 H6
Melloncroft Dr WKBY CH48 .......... 124 D5
Melloncroft Dr West
WKBY CH48 .......... 124 E6
Mellor Brook Dr
WGNE/HIN WN2 .......... 80 C3 ②
Mellor Cl RAIN/WH L35 .......... 116 C6
RUNC WA7 .......... 150 F5 ②
WGNNW/ST WN6 .......... 56 A3 ②
Mellor Rd RF/TRAN CH42 .......... 127 L3
Melly Rd AIG/SPK L17 .......... 129 K2
Melmerby Cl AIMK WN4 .......... 91 H2 ②
Melrose Av CHTN/BK PR9 .......... 22 D8
CSBY/BLUN L23 .......... 83 G2
ECCL WA10 .......... 88 D8
HOY CH47 .......... 108 D6 ②
LEIGH WN7 .......... 81 M4
WARRS WA4 .......... 137 M5 ②
WARRW/BUR WA5 .......... 104 B6
Melrose Crs AIMK WN4 .......... 90 E2 ②
Melrose Dr GTS/LS CH66 .......... 163 H5 ②
WGNS/IIMK WN3 .......... 78 F2
Melrose Gdns LEY/BBR PR5 .......... 29 L3
Melrose Rd ANF/KKDL L4 .......... 96 F5
CSBY/WL L22 .......... 83 G5
NWD/KWIPK L33 .......... 73 M7
Melrose Wy CHLY/EC PR7 .......... 32 F7
Melton Av WARRS WA4 .......... 137 K5
Melton Cl GR/UP/WCH CH49 .......... 110 A8 ②
Melton Rd RUNC WA7 .......... 149 K7
Melverley Rd KKBY L32 .......... 85 K3
Melverley St WGNS/IIMK WN3 .......... 4 B6
Melville Av RF/TRAN CH42 .......... 128 C4
Melville Cl WARRN/WOL WA2 .......... 14 C2
Melville Pl EHL/KEN L7 .......... 113 J5
Melville Rd BEB CH63 .......... 128 A8
BTL L20 .......... 83 L6
Melville St TOX L8 .......... 113 H8
Melwood Dr WD/CROXPK L12 .......... 98 E6
Menai Rd BTL L20 .......... 83 M7
Menai St BIRK CH41 .......... 10 F6
Mendell Cl PS/BROM CH62 .......... 144 A5
Mendip Av WARRN/WOL WA2 .......... 121 K2
WGNS/IIMK WN3 .......... 78 E2
Mendip Cl GTS/LS CH66 .......... 163 G2 ②
HLWD L26 .......... 132 A6 ②
HOR/BR BL6 .......... 45 L8
RF/TRAN CH42 .......... 127 L4
Mendip Gv STHEL WA9 .......... 103 H4
Mendip Rd RF/TRAN CH42 .......... 127 L4
WAV L15 .......... 114 C7
Menin Av WARRS WA4 .......... 137 L2
Menivale Cl CHTN/BK PR9 .......... 22 C7
Menlo Av NSTN CH64 .......... 126 D7
Menlo Cl CL/PREN CH43 .......... 127 C1
Menlove Av CALD/MH L18 .......... 130 E1
Menlove Gdns North
CALD/MH L18 .......... 114 D8
Menlove Gdns South
CALD/MH L18 .......... 114 D8

Menlove Gdns West
CALD/MH L18 .......... 114 D8
Menlove Man CALD/MH L18 .......... 114 E7 ①
Menlow Cl WARRS WA4 .......... 138 E4
Menstone Rd
CLB/OSW/ST L13 .......... 114 B1 ②
Mentmore Crs NG/CROX L11 .......... 98 D4
Mentmore Gdns WARRS WA4 .......... 138 B8
Mentmore Rd CALD/MH L18 .......... 130 D4
Menzies St TOX L8 .......... 129 J1 ② ⑥
Meols Cl FMBY L37 .......... 59 G3
GTS/LS CH66 .......... 163 G1 ②
Meols Cop Rd STHP PR8 .......... 25 H8
Meols Dr HOY CH47 .......... 124 C1
Meols Pde HOY CH47 .......... 108 D5
Mercer Av KKBY L32 .......... 85 L4
Mercer Ct CHLY/EC PR7 .......... 44 B4
WD/CROXPK L12 .......... 99 G8 ②
Mercer Rd CL/PREN CH43 .......... 111 G5
RNFD/HAY WA11 .......... 90 F7
Mercer's La ORM L39 .......... 74 D1
Mercer St ALL/GAR L19 .......... 130 E8 ②
NEWLW WA12 .......... 104 F1
WARRW/BUR WA5 .......... 104 C5
Merchants Crs GOL/RIS/CU WA3 .......... 93 G4
Mere Av BEB CH63 .......... 143 K7
BRSC L40 .......... 39 G7
LEIGH WN7 .......... 81 M8 ②
Merebank CL/PREN CH43 .......... 127 G1 ②
Merebrook Gv
NWD/KWIPK L33 .......... 74 B8 ②
Mere Brow La KIRK/FR/WA PR4 .......... 27 J3
Mere Cl GTS/LS CH66 .......... 162 F3
SKEL WN8 .......... 65 H3
Merecroft Av WAL/EG CH44 .......... 111 L3
Meredale Rd CALD/MH L18 .......... 130 C1
Meredith Av WARRS WA4 .......... 138 C3
Meredith St ALL/GAR L19 .......... 131 G8 ②
Mere Farm Gv
CL/PREN CH43 .......... 127 H1 ②
Mere Farm Rd CL/PREN CH43 .......... 127 G1
Merefield CHLY/EC PR7 .......... 32 C4
Mere Fold CHLY/EC PR7 .......... 42 F2
Mere Gn ANF/KKDL L4 .......... 97 J4
Mere Gv RNFD/HAY WA11 .......... 89 K4
Mereheath MOR/LEA CH46 .......... 110 A2
Mere Hey ECCL WA10 .......... 101 J2
Mereland Cv
WGNW/BIL/O WN5 .......... 67 G7 ②
Mere La BRSC L40 .......... 38 F2
CHTN/BK PR9 .......... 26 C2
EV L5 .......... 97 H8
HES CH60 .......... 141 C3
KIRK/FR/WA PR4 .......... 27 J6
WAL/NB CH45 .......... 95 G6
Merepark Dr CHTN/BK PR9 .......... 25 K1
Mere Park Rd
GR/UP/WCH CH49 .......... 125 L2
Mere Rd AIMK WN4 .......... 91 L1 ②
FMBY L37 .......... 58 F3
NEWLW WA12 .......... 105 H1
WARRN/WOL WA2 .......... 122 C3
Mere St LEIGH WN7 .......... 81 M8
WGNW/BIL/O WN5 .......... 68 B7 ②
Merevale Cl RUNC WA7 .......... 150 A7
Mereview Crs WD/CROXPK L12 .......... 98 F2
Merewood KKBY L32 .......... 86 B5 ②
SKEL WN8 .......... 65 J1
Merewood Cl
WARRN/WOL WA2 .......... 121 M2
Mereworth WKBY CH48 .......... 124 F7
Meribel Cl CSBY/BLUN L23 .......... 71 J8
Meriden Av BEB CH63 .......... 143 J4 ②
Meriden Cl RNFD/HAY WA11 .......... 89 M7
STHP PR8 .......... 34 D8
Meriden St WLTN L25 .......... 115 K7 ②
Merland Wy STHEL WA9 .......... 103 H3
Merlewood Av CHTN/BK PR9 .......... 25 K2
Merlin Av GR/UP/WCH CH49 .......... 109 M7
Merlin Cl CHLYE PR6 .......... 33 J2
GR/UP/WCH CH49 .......... 109 L7
RNFD/HAY WA11 .......... 89 K7 ②
RUNC WA7 .......... 150 C5
Merlin Ct HLWD L26 .......... 131 M4
Merlin St TOX L8 .......... 113 H7
Merrick Cl WARRN/WOL WA2 .......... 122 A3
Merrills La GR/UP/WCH CH49 .......... 110 C8
Merrilocks Rd CSBY/BLUN L23 .......... 82 E1
Merrion Cl WLTN L25 .......... 131 H2
Merritt Av BIRK CH41 .......... 10 C1
Merrivale Rd WLTN L25 .......... 131 L3
Merscar La BRSC L40 .......... 37 M7
Mersey Av ALL/GAR L19 .......... 130 B5
FMBY L37 .......... 47 G7
MGHL L31 .......... 73 H3
Merseybank Rd
PS/BROM CH62 .......... 128 D5
Mersey Cl WGNE/HIN WN2 .......... 81 L2
Mersey La South
RF/TRAN CH42 .......... 128 C3
Mersey Mt RF/TRAN CH42 .......... 128 A2
Mersey Rd AIG/SPK L17 .......... 130 A5
CSBY/BLUN L23 .......... 82 E2
RF/TRAN CH42 .......... 128 C3
RUNC WA7 .......... 19 G2
WDN WA8 .......... 149 J1
WGNE/HIN WN2 .......... 80 B3
WGNW/BIL/O WN5 .......... 67 H6
Mersey St LEIGH WN7 .......... 81 L8
RUNC WA7 .......... 19 H2
STHEL WA9 .......... 103 J2
WAL/EG CH44 .......... 112 A3
WARR WA1 .......... 14 F7
Merseyton Rd EP CH65 .......... 156 C9
Mersey Vw ALL/GAR L19 .......... 130 E7 ②
CSBY/WL L22 .......... 82 E3
Mersey View Rd WDN WA8 .......... 148 D1
Mersey View South Rd
RF/TRAN CH42 .......... 18 A9
Mersey Wk WARRS WA4 .......... 122 B8
Mersey Wy SPK/HALE L24 .......... 145 M3
WARRW/BUR WA5 .......... 136 E1
Mersham Ct WDN WA8 .......... 134 B1 ②
Merstone Cl HLWD L26 .......... 132 C6 ②
Merthyr Gv CHLDW L16 .......... 115 G4
Merton Bank Rd STHEL WA9 .......... 9 M1

Merton Cl NSTN CH64 153 G8
Merton Crs HUY L36 115 K3
Merton Dr GR/UP/WCH CH49 126 C2
HUY L36 115 J3
Merton Gv BTL L20 7 G5
CHLYE PR6 33 G2
CSBY/BLUN L23 82 E2
Merton Pl CL/PREN CH43 10 E6
Merton Rd BTL L20 6 F5
GTS/LS CH66 163 G2
PS/BROM CH62 155 K2
WAL/NB CH45 95 J8
WGNS/IIMK WN3 78 E1 1
Merton St STHEL WA9 9 L2
Mertoun Rd WARRS WA4 137 K4 2
Mervyn Pl WGNS/IIMK WN3 79 J1
Mesham Cl GR/UP/WCH CH49 110 A8 7
Mesnes Av WGNS/IIMK WN3 4 A9
Mesnes Park Ter WGN WN1 4 E2
Mesnes Rd WGN WN1 4 E2
Mesnes Ter WGN WN1 4 E3
Meteor Crs WARRN/WOL WA2 121 M3
Methuen St BIRK CH41 10 A2
WAV L15 114 A6
Mevagissey Rd RUNC WA7 150 E8
The Mews AIG/SPK L17 130 B4
STBRV L28 99 L6
WGNE/HIN WN2 69 M8 18
Meyrick Rd NG/CROX L11 98 A3
Meyrick St WGNW/BIL/O WN5 68 B7
Micawber Cl TOX L8 113 H8 6
Michaels Cl FMBY L37 59 G2
Michael's La ORM L39 48 E2
Mickering La ORM L39 62 E7
Micklefield Rd WAV L15 114 B7 6
Micklegate RUNC WA7 150 F6 6
Mickleton Dr STHP PR8 34 C8 1
Middlefield Rd CALD/MH L18 131 G2
Middleham Cl KKBY L32 85 L4 2
Middlehey Rd PR/KW L34 99 M1
Middlehurst Av ECCL WA10 8 F3 2
Middlehurst Cl PR/KW L34 101 J6 1
Middlehurst Rd WARRS WA4 138 C3
Middle La FROD/HEL WA6 167 M3
Middlemass Hey NTHLY L27 116 A8
Middle Moss La FMBY L37 60 B2
Middle Rd SPK/HALE L24 132 B8
Middlesex Rd BTL L20 7 K2
Middleton Rd CSBY/WL L22 83 H3
EHL/KEN L7 114 A3
Middle Wk FROD/HEL WA6 160 D6
Middle Wy NG/CROX L11 85 M8
Middle Withins La HTWN L38 60 B6
Middlewood GOL/RIS/CU WA3 93 H5 6
KKBY L32 86 B5
SKEL WN8 65 J1
Middlewood Cl CHLY/EC PR7 30 E7
ORM L39 62 E6 2
Middlewood Dr ORM L39 62 E6
Middlewood Rd ORM L39 62 E6
Midge Hall La CHTN/BK PR9 37 L3
Midghall St VAUX/LVPD L3 12 F4
Midhurst Dr STHP PR8 47 K1
Midhurst Rd WD/CROXPK L12 99 H2 3
Midland Cl LEIGH WN7 81 L7
Midland St BIRK CH41 10 F7 3
WDN WA8 16 F2
Midland Ter CSBY/WL L22 82 F4 6
Midland Wy WARR WA1 14 C4
Midlothian Dr CSBY/BLUN L23 82 E2 2
Midway Rd HUY L36 116 A1
Midwood St WDN WA8 16 E4 2
Milbrook Crs KKBY L32 85 M2
Milbrook Dr KKBY L32 86 A2
Mildenhall Rd WLTN L25 115 J7
Mildmay Rd BTL L20 83 K8
NG/CROX L11 98 A3 2
Mile End EV L5 13 G1
Miles Cl GOL/RIS/CU WA3 123 H2
GR/UP/WCH CH49 125 L3
Miles La GR/UP/WCH CH49 125 L3
WGNNW/ST WN6 55 G6
Miles St TOX L8 129 J1
Milestone Hey STBRV L28 99 K5
Mile Stone Meadow
CHLYE PR6 31 M1 1
Milford Cl FMBY L37 58 E4
Milford Dr WD/CROXPK L12 99 G2
Milford Rd WGNE/HIN WN2 69 H3
Milford St EV L5 96 D7
WGNS/IIMK WN3 5 J7
Milk St ECCL WA10 9 G5
WGNS/IIMK WN3 4 E5
Milland Cl NG/CROX L11 98 E2
Millar Crs WDN WA8 16 C5
Millar's Pace CHTN/BK PR9 22 D8
Mill Av WARRW/BUR WA5 120 A6
Mill Bank CLB/OSW/ST L13 98 B7
NSTN CH64 153 J8
WGNNW/ST WN6 54 F6
Millbank Brow BRSC L40 52 B2 4
Millbank La MGHL L31 73 H2
Millbank Rd WAL/EG CH44 111 J2 10
Millbeck Farm
WGNW/BIL/O WN5 67 M8
Millbeck Gv RNFD/HAY WA11 89 K4
Millbrook Cl SKEL WN8 65 G3
Millbrook La ECCL WA10 101 K1
Millbrook Rd BIRK CH41 111 K3
Mill Brow BEB CH63 127 M7
ECCL WA10 101 K1
STHEL WA9 102 F8
WDN WA8 17 H1
Mill Brow Cl STHEL WA9 102 F8
Millbutt Cl BEB CH63 127 M7
Mill Cl CSBY/BLUN L23 71 G7 1
EP CH65 163 L4
WARRN/WOL WA2 122 A1 2
Mill Ct NTHTN L30 71 M8
Millcroft CSBY/BLUN L23 71 J8
Millcroft Av WGNW/BIL/O WN5 66 F8
Millcroft Pk
GR/UP/WCH CH49 125 K2 1
Millcroft Rd WLTN L25 131 L4
Milldale Rd LEIGH WN7 93 K4
Mill Dam Cl BRSC L40 51 L3
Mill Dam La BRSC L40 51 M3 1
Miller Av CSBY/BLUN L23 70 F8
Miller Cl TOX L8 129 J1 17
Miller's Br BTL L20 6 E7
Millers Cl MOR/LEA CH46 109 K6 4
Millers Ct ORM L39 51 H8 2
Millerscroft KKBY L32 85 L2 2
Millersdale STHEL WA9 118 E1 13
Millersdale Av WLT/FAZ L9 84 D6 11
Millersdale Cl PS/BROM CH62 144 B8
Millersdale Gv RUNC WA7 149 M8
Millersdale Rd CALD/MH L18 130 C1
Millers Fold ECCL WA10 101 K1
Miller's La WGNE/HIN WN2 80 C3
Miller St WARRS WA4 15 H8
Millers Wy MOR/LEA CH46 109 L5 2
Mill Farm Cl WARRN/WOL WA2 122 A2
Mill Fld SKEL WN8 53 L4
Millfield Cl CLB/OSW/ST L13 98 C7
Millfield La RNFD/HAY WA11 91 H5
Millfield Rd CHLY/EC PR7 32 D4
WDN WA8 134 E3
Millfields ECCL WA10 101 J2
Millgate WGN WN1 4 F4
Mill Gn NSTN CH64 154 B5
Millgreen Cl WD/CROXPK L12 99 G2 8
Mill Green La WDN WA8 118 F8
Mill Hey RAIN/WH L35 118 A4
Mill Hey La BRSC L40 39 L2
Mill Hey Rd WKBY CH48 124 F7
Mill Hl CL/PREN CH43 127 J2
Mill Hill Rd PEN/TH CH61 125 L6
Millhouse Av WARRS WA4 137 M4
Millhouse Cl HOY CH47 109 K4
Millhouse La GOL/RIS/CU WA3 106 C7
HOY CH47 109 K4
MOR/LEA CH46 109 K5
Mill House Vw SKEL WN8 66 E6
Millingford Av GOL/RIS/CU WA3 92 B3
Millingford Gv AIMK WN4 91 K2 7
Millington Cl CL/PREN CH43 127 G4 1
RUNC WA7 161 H1 9
WDN WA8 16 A3
Mill La BRSC L40 39 G8
BTL L20 7 J4
CHLY/EC PR7 31 J4
CHLY/EC PR7 42 C3
CHLY/EC PR7 43 G3
CHTN/BK PR9 25 J4
CLB/OSW/ST L13 114 C3
FROD/HEL WA6 161 G3
GR/UP/WCH CH49 125 L4
GTS/LS CH66 162 F1
HES CH60 141 K5
KKBY L32 85 L1
NEWLW WA12 105 G2
NSTN CH64 153 L8
NSTN CH64 154 A4
NSTN CH64 154 C5
ORM L39 62 B4
PR/KW L34 86 F8
RAIN/WH L35 117 L4
RNFD/HAY WA11 88 D2
SKEL WN8 53 L4
SKEL WN8 65 H3
SKEL WN8 66 C5
STHEL WA9 102 E8
VAUX/LVPD L3 13 J5 2
WAL/EG CH44 111 J2
WARRN/WOL WA2 105 G8
WARRS WA4 137 G6
WAV L15 114 C5
WD/CROXPK L12 98 C7
WDN WA8 117 M8
WDN WA8 118 F8 1
WDN WA8 134 E1
WGNNW/ST WN6 54 E6
Mill Leat Cl SKEL WN8 53 L3 2
Mill Meadow NEWLW WA12 105 G2 2
WGN WN1 5 G5
Millom Av RAIN/WH L35 117 K1
Millom Gv ECCL WA10 101 L5
WD/CROXPK L12 98 E4 3
Mill Park Dr PS/BROM CH62 155 G2
Mill Rd BEB CH63 127 M6
NPK/KEN L6 13 M2
PEN/TH CH61 126 C7
PS/BROM CH62 143 M2
STHP PR8 34 F8
WGNW/BIL/O WN5 66 F8
Mill Sq AIN/FAZ L10 85 G3 3
Millstead Rd WAV L15 114 C5
Mill St AIMK WN4 91 L3
CHLY/EC PR7 43 G4
CHLYE PR6 44 C5
ECCL WA10 8 F3
GOL/RIS/CU WA3 92 C5
NSTN CH64 153 G5
ORM L39 63 H1
PR/KW L34 100 F7 11
RF/TRAN CH42 11 H9
STHP PR8 3 K5
TOX L8 113 G8
WGNE/HIN WN2 69 M8 19
WGNS/IIMK WN3 4 D5
WLTN L25 131 J3
Millthwaite Rd WAL/EG CH44 111 H1 6
Millvale St NPK/KEN L6 113 L1
Mill View Ct ORM L39 64 A7 1
Mill View Dr BEB CH63 127 L7
Millway Rd SPK/HALE L24 147 J1 2
Millwood BEB CH63 127 M7 2
Mill Wood Av ECCL WA10 101 H2
Millwood Cl AIMK WN4 79 J8 3
Millwood Gdns RAIN/WH L35 117 H3 6
Millwood Gld CHLY/EC PR7 32 D4
Millwood Rd SPK/HALE L24 147 G2
Milman Cl GR/UP/WCH CH49 126 B1 6
ORM L39 62 F2
Milman Rd ANF/KKDL L4 97 H4
Milner Cop HES CH60 141 J5
Milne Rd CLB/OSW/ST L13 98 A5 1
Milner Rd AIG/SPK L17 130 A4
HES CH60 141 J5
Milner St BIRK CH41 10 A1
WARRW/BUR WA5 14 B6
Milnthorpe Cl ANF/KKDL L4 97 G5 9
Milnthorpe Rd
WARRW/BUR WA5 104 A7
Milnthorpe St ALL/GAR L19 130 E7 5
Milroy St EHL/KEN L7 113 K4
Milton Av DV/KA/FCH L14 115 H3
NEWLW WA12 104 D2
RAIN/WH L35 117 G2
WDN WA8 16 A4
Milton Cl RAIN/WH L35 117 G2
Milton Crs HES CH60 141 J4
Milton Dr ORM L39 63 J1
Milton Gn PEN/TH CH61 126 D7
Milton Gv FROD/HEL WA6 166 C4
WARRS WA4 137 M2
WGN WN1 68 E2
WGNW/BIL/O WN5 67 J7
WGNW/BIL/O WN5 77 M4
Milton Rd ANF/KKDL L4 7 M6
CHLY/EC PR7 43 G5
CSBY/WL L22 83 G3
EHL/KEN L7 114 A3
EP CH65 20 F7
GOL/RIS/CU WA3 92 F6
RF/TRAN CH42 10 F9
WAL/EG CH44 111 M3
WDN WA8 16 C4
WKBY CH48 124 C2
Milton Rd East RF/TRAN CH42 11 G9
Milton St BTL L20 6 E2
CHTN/BK PR9 25 J6
STHEL WA9 118 C3
WDN WA8 16 C9
Milton Ter CHLYE PR6 32 F3 6
Milton Wy MGHL L31 72 D4
Milvain Dr WARRN/WOL WA2 121 L4
Milverton St NPK/KEN L6 113 L1 2
Mimosa Cl CHLY/EC PR7 32 C2
Mimosa Rd WAV L15 114 D6
Minehead Av LEIGH WN7 81 M3
Minehead Gv STHEL WA9 102 F8 2
Minehead Rd AIG/SPK L17 130 A4
Miners Wy SPK/HALE L24 147 J2
WDN WA8 16 D6
Minerva Cl WARRS WA4 137 M3
Mines Av AIG/SPK L17 130 B6
PR/KW L34 101 G7
Mine Wy RNFD/HAY WA11 91 H6 5
Minshull St EHL/KEN L7 113 J4
Minstead Av NWD/KWIPK L33 86 C3
Minstrel Cl WGNE/HIN WN2 80 D6 1
Minto Cl EHL/KEN L7 113 L3
Minton Cl WD/CROXPK L12 99 H2
Minton Wy WDN WA8 118 D8
Mintor Rd NWD/KWIPK L33 86 C3
Minto St EHL/KEN L7 113 K3 5
Minver Rd WD/CROXPK L12 98 F6
Miranda Rd BTL L20 7 J7
Mirfield Cl GOL/RIS/CU WA3 92 F6
HLWD L26 132 B7
Mirfield St NPK/KEN L6 113 K2
Miriam Rd ANF/KKDL L4 97 J7
Miry La SKEL WN8 53 M3
WGNNW/ST WN6 4 A3
Miskelly St BTL L20 96 E5
Mission Wk NPK/KEN L6 113 K2 8
Missouri Rd CLB/OSW/ST L13 97 M6
Mistlethrush Wy
WD/CROXPK L12 99 H2 4
Misty Cl WDN WA8 133 L3
Mitchell Av WARRW/BUR WA5 104 A8
Mitchell Crs LITH L21 83 K5 2
Mitchell Rd ECCL WA10 101 L4
PR/KW L34 100 E7
WGNW/BIL/O WN5 78 A8
Mitchell St AIMK WN4 91 L3
GOL/RIS/CU WA3 92 C6
LEIGH WN7 81 K8
WARRS WA4 137 L5
WGNE/HIN WN2 69 J6
WGNW/BIL/O WN5 68 A7
Mithril Cl WDN WA8 135 G2
Mitre Cl RAIN/WH L35 116 F4
Mitylene St EV L5 97 G7 7
Moat House St WGNE/HIN WN2 69 J6
Mobberley Cl WARRS WA4 138 F2
Mobberley Wy BEB CH63 143 J2
Mockbeggar Dr WAL/NB CH45 94 F6
Mockbeggar Whf
WAL/NB CH45 95 G6 1
Modred St TOX L8 113 H8
Moel Famau Vw AIG/SPK L17 129 K3
Moffatdale Rd ANF/KKDL L4 97 L5
Moffat Rd WLT/FAZ L9 84 E6 1
Molesworth Gv CHLDW L16 115 H4 1
Molineux Av DV/KA/FCH L14 114 F4
Molland Cl WD/CROXPK L12 98 F5 1
Mollington Av NG/CROX L11 98 B3
Mollington Rd KKBY L32 85 L3
WAL/EG CH44 111 L2 5
Mollington St BIRK CH41 11 J7
Molly Pitcher Wy
WARRW/BUR WA5 120 D8
Molly's La NWD/KWIPK L33 86 F6
Molton Rd CHLDW L16 114 E5
Molyneux Av WARRW/BUR WA5 121 H5
Molyneux Cl
GR/UP/WCH CH49 110 B8 3
HUY L36 116 B3
RAIN/WH L35 116 F1 1
Molyneux Dr RAIN/WH L35 116 F1
WAL/NB CH45 95 K5
Molyneux Rd CALD/MH L18 130 B1
CSBY/WL L22 83 G3
MGHL L31 73 H6
NPK/KEN L6 113 K2
ORM L39 62 E6
Molyneux St WGN WN1 5 H3
Molyneux Wy AIN/FAZ L10 84 E2
Monaghan Cl WLT/FAZ L9 84 C6
Monash Rd NG/CROX L11 98 B5
Monastery La STHEL WA9 102 F6
Monastery Rd NPK/KEN L6 97 L7 2
STHEL WA9 103 G6
Mona St BIRK CH41 111 H6
BTL L20 83 M7
ECCL WA10 8 A6
WGN WN1 4 D3
Mond Rd AIN/FAZ L10 85 H6
WDN WA8 16 C4
Monfa Rd BTL L20 83 L7
Monica Dr WDN WA8 118 C8
Monica Rd WLTN L25 131 K4
Monica Ter AIMK WN4 91 K3 4
Monkfield Wy ALL/GAR L19 145 M1
Monk Rd WAL/EG CH44 111 K1
Monks Carr La HTWN L38 60 C7
Monks Cl FMBY L37 59 J4
Monksdown Rd NG/CROX L11 98 C4
Monks Dr FMBY L37 59 J4
Monks Ferry BIRK CH41 11 M6
Monksferry Wk ALL/GAR L19 130 B6
Monks Gv EP CH65 20 B3 1
Monks St WARRW/BUR WA5 121 G7 3
Monk St EV L5 97 H7 4
Monks Wy BEB CH63 143 H1
WKBY CH48 124 D3
WLTN L25 131 K3
Monkswell Dr WAV L15 114 C5
Monkswell St TOX L8 129 J2 5
Monkswood Cl
WARRW/BUR WA5 121 G3 6
Monmouth Cl WARR WA1 123 G6
Monmouth Crs AIMK WN4 91 L3
Monmouth Dr AIN/FAZ L10 85 H4
Monmouth Gv STHEL WA9 102 F3 1
Monro Cl TOX L8 129 H1 11
Monroe Cl WARR WA1 122 D6
WGNS/IIMK WN3 79 J2 2
Monro St TOX L8 129 H1
Montague Rd CLB/OSW/ST L13 114 C3
Montagu Rd FMBY L37 47 G8
Montclair Dr CALD/MH L18 114 D8
Montclare Crs WARRS WA4 138 A4
Montcliffe Cl GOL/RIS/CU WA3 106 E8
Montcliffe Rd CHLYE PR6 33 G4
Monterey Rd CLB/OSW/ST L13 114 D3
Montford Ri WGNE/HIN WN2 69 J3
Montfort Dr ALL/GAR L19 130 C6
Montgomery Av CHTN/BK PR9 25 J7
Montgomery Cl
RAIN/WH L35 116 F3 4
Montgomery Hl WKBY CH48 125 J5
Montgomery Rd HUY L36 115 M1
WDN WA8 133 M5
WLT/FAZ L9 84 C7
Montgomery Wy
NPK/KEN L6 113 K1 5
Montpelier Av RUNC WA7 149 H7
Montpellier Crs WAL/NB CH45 95 J5
Montrey Crs AIMK WN4 90 E2 2
Montrose Av WAL/EG CH44 112 A4
WGNW/BIL/O WN5 67 L6
WGNW/BIL/O WN5 68 A5
Montrose Cl CHLYE PR6 33 G7 2
WARRN/WOL WA2 122 B1
Montrose Dr CHTN/BK PR9 25 H4
Montrose Rd CLB/OSW/ST L13 98 A7
Montrose Wy CLB/OSW/ST L13 114 B3
Montrovia Crs AIN/FAZ L10 85 H6
Monument Rd WGN WN1 68 F3
Monville Rd WLT/FAZ L9 84 E6
Monyash Vw WGNE/HIN WN2 81 H2
Moody La BRSC L40 41 G4
Moody St WGNNW/ST WN6 56 A4 5
Moor Av WGNNW/ST WN6 55 G5
Moorbridge Cl NTHTN L30 84 C1
Moor Cl CSBY/BLUN L23 71 H8
STHP PR8 47 M3
Moor Coppice CSBY/BLUN L23 71 H8
Moorcroft Rd CALD/MH L18 130 E4
HUY L36 100 A8
WAL/NB CH45 94 F8
Moorditch La FROD/HEL WA6 159 K4
Moor Dr CSBY/BLUN L23 71 G8
SKEL WN8 65 M6
Moore Av RF/TRAN CH42 128 A3
STHEL WA9 103 J2
WARRS WA4 138 F2
Moore Cl WDN WA8 134 F3 3
Moore Dr RNFD/HAY WA11 91 H7
Moore La WARRS WA4 136 D6
Moores La WGNNW/ST WN6 55 M3
Moore St BTL L20 6 E1
WGN WN1 68 F3
Moore St East WGN WN1 5 J1
Mooreway RAIN/WH L35 118 A4
Moorfield NWD/KWIPK L33 74 B8
Moorfield Crs GOL/RIS/CU WA3 93 J6
Moorfield Dr NSTN CH64 152 E3
Moorfield La BRSC L40 50 D2
Moorfield Rd CSBY/BLUN L23 71 J8
ECCL WA10 88 E8
WDN WA8 134 F3
Moorfields CHLYE PR6 33 G4
CLVP L2 12 F6
Moorfields Av CL/PREN CH43 126 F1
Moorfield St WGNE/HIN WN2 80 D2 6
Moorfoot Rd STHEL WA9 103 H2
Moorfoot Wy NWD/KWIPK L33 73 M7
Moorgate ORM L39 63 G1
Moorgate Av CSBY/BLUN L23 83 G2
Moorgate Rd NWD/KWIPK L33 86 B7
Moorgate St EHL/KEN L7 113 K4 7
Moorhey Rd MGHL L31 72 F6 2
Moorhouses HTWN L38 70 B2
Mooring Cl RUNC WA7 150 F7
Moorings Cl NSTN CH64 152 D4
WGN WN1 5 L4
The Moorings CHLYE PR6 33 G5 8
HES CH60 140 E5
MGHL L31 72 D1
Moorland Av CSBY/BLUN L23 71 G8
Moorland Cl HES CH60 141 J6 1
Moorland Dr RUNC WA7 151 G6
Moorland Ga CHLYE PR6 33 H7
Moorland Pk HES CH60 141 J6
Moorland Rd AIMK WN4 80 A8
GTS/LS CH66 156 A5
MGHL L31 72 E7
RF/TRAN CH42 128 A2
WGNE/HIN WN2 69 L8
Moorlands Rd CSBY/BLUN L23 71 K7
Moor La AIN/FAZ L10 85 K5
ANF/KKDL L4 97 J2
CSBY/BLUN L23 71 G8
FROD/HEL WA6 160 D5
FROD/HEL WA6 166 A4
HES CH60 141 H5
HTWN L38 70 F2
SFTN L29 71 M4
STHP PR8 47 L3
WDN WA8 16 B6
Moor La South WDN WA8 16 B6
Moor Pl VAUX/LVPD L3 13 K6
Moor Rd CHLY/EC PR7 32 C8 6
LEY/BBR PR5 29 L2
WGNW/BIL/O WN5 67 G7
Moorside Av NSTN CH64 152 E5
Moorside Cl CSBY/BLUN L23 83 H1
Moorside Ct WDN WA8 16 B5
Moorside La NSTN CH64 152 E6
Moorside Rd CSBY/BLUN L23 83 H1
Moor St CLVP L2 12 E8
ORM L39 51 H8
Moorway HES CH60 141 K5
Moorwood Crs STHEL WA9 118 E1
Moray Cl ECCL WA10 8 D1
Morcott La SPK/HALE L24 147 M3
Morden Av AIMK WN4 91 K2
Morden St NPK/KEN L6 113 L1
Morecambe St NPK/KEN L6 97 L8 4
Morecroft Rd RF/TRAN CH42 128 C3
Morella Rd ANF/KKDL L4 97 L5
Morello Dr BEB CH63 143 K3
Moresby Cl LEIGH WN7 81 M8 12
RUNC WA7 151 G6 2
Moret Cl CSBY/BLUN L23 71 J8
Moreton Av STHEL WA9 118 E1 14
Moreton Cl GOL/RIS/CU WA3 92 B4
Moreton Gv WAL/NB CH45 95 G7 7
Moreton Rd GR/UP/WCH CH49 110 B7
Morgan Av WARRN/WOL WA2 121 L3
Morgan Ms NTHTN L30 83 M2 1
Morgan St STHEL WA9 102 F3
Morland Av NSTN CH64 153 H6
PS/BROM CH62 143 M6
Morley Av BIRK CH41 10 C3
Morley Rd CHTN/BK PR9 25 G5
RUNC WA7 19 G6
WAL/EG CH44 111 J2
WARRS WA4 137 J4
Morley St ANF/KKDL L4 97 G6 12
ECCL WA10 8 F3 3
WARR WA1 15 H4
Morningside CSBY/BLUN L23 83 H2
Morningside Pl NG/CROX L11 98 B4
Morningside Rd NG/CROX L11 98 B5
Morningside Wy
NG/CROX L11 98 B5 1
Mornington Av CSBY/BLUN L23 83 G3
EP CH65 20 D5
Mornington Rd CHLYE PR6 44 D5
CHTN/BK PR9 3 J3
WAL/NB CH45 95 K7 3
Mornington St TOX L8 113 G8 5
Morpeth Cl MOR/LEA CH46 109 K5 8
Morpeth Rd HOY CH47 108 C8 1
Morpeth St TOX L8 113 H6 10
Morpeth Whf BIRK CH41 11 K2
Morris Av WARRS WA4 138 B1
Morris Cl RNFD/HAY WA11 90 C8
Morris Hey ORM L39 49 M2
Morris La ORM L39 49 M2
Morrison Cl
WARRW/BUR WA5 120 C8 1
Morrison St CHLYE PR6 32 F3 7
Morris Rd CHLYE PR6 33 G4 2
SKEL WN8 66 C6
Morrissey Cl ECCL WA10 8 A3
Morris St STHEL WA9 103 G4
WGN WN1 5 G3
WGNE/HIN WN2 69 M8 20
WGNS/IIMK WN3 80 A1
Morston Av KKBY L32 86 A5
Morston Crs KKBY L32 86 A5
Mort Av WARRS WA4 138 C1
Mortimer Av WARRN/WOL WA2 121 K5
Mortimer St BIRK CH41 11 L5 4
Mortlake Cl WDN WA8 133 L2
Morton Av FROD/HEL WA6 166 D4 1
WGNS/IIMK WN3 4 C9
Morton Cl WARRW/BUR WA5 120 E5
WGNS/IIMK WN3 78 E3 3
Morton Rd RUNC WA7 150 F5
Morton St TOX L8 113 H8 7
Mort St WGNNW/ST WN6 4 A1
Morvah Cl NG/CROX L11 98 E3 3
Morval Crs ANF/KKDL L4 7 M6
RUNC WA7 19 M6
Morven Cl WARRN/WOL WA2 122 A2 5
Morven Gv STHP PR8 25 G6
Morville Dr WGNS/IIMK WN3 79 K1
Moscow Dr CLB/OSW/ST L13 98 B8
Mosedale Av RNFD/HAY WA11 89 K4
Mosedale Gv RUNC WA7 150 A8 3
Mosedale Rd PS/BROM CH62 144 A3
WLT/FAZ L9 84 C8
Moseley Av WAL/NB CH45 111 J1
WARRS WA4 138 C1
Moseley Rd BEB CH63 143 J4
Moses St TOX L8 129 H1
Mosley St STHP PR8 3 G9
Moss Av WGNW/BIL/O WN5 77 M2
Moss Bank CHLY/EC PR7 43 G4 5
ORM L39 62 F3
Moss Bank Pk LITH L21 83 J5
Moss Bank Rd RNFD/HAY WA11 89 J4
WDN WA8 17 J5
Mossborough Hall La
RNFD/HAY WA11 87 L2
Mossborough Rd
RNFD/HAY WA11 76 B8
Moss Bridge La BRSC L40 52 E3
Moss Brow RNFD/HAY WA11 76 A6
Mossbrow Rd HUY L36 116 A1
Moss Cl CHLYE PR6 33 G5
NSTN CH64 154 C5
WARRS WA4 138 A3
Mosscroft Cl HUY L36 116 C1
Mossdale Cl WARRW/BUR WA5 120 C6
Mossdale Dr RAIN/WH L35 117 M2
Mossdale Rd AIMK WN4 79 J5
NWD/KWIPK L33 74 B8 4
Moss Delph La ORM L39 62 D3
Mossdene Rd WAL/EG CH44 111 H1
Moss End Wy NWD/KWIPK L33 86 F2
Mossfield Rd CHLYE PR6 33 G5

WLT/FAZ L9 84 B7
Moss Ga GOL/RIS/CU WA3 107 J8
Moss Gate Gv DV/KA/FCH L14 115 J2
Moss Gate Rd DV/KA/FCH L14 115 J2
Mossgiel Av STHP PR8 47 K1
Moss Green Wy STHEL WA9 103 J4
Moss Gv RF/TRAN CH42 127 K3
TOX L8 113 L7
WGNNW/ST WN6 56 A5
Moss Hey Hey KIRK/FR/WA PR4 27 J2
Mosslands ECCL WA10 101 J1
Mosslands Cl GTS/LS CH66 163 G3
Mosslands Dr WAL/EG CH44 111 G1
Moss La BRSC L40 39 J6
BTL L20 84 A7
CHLY/EC PR7 43 G4
CHTN/BK PR9 23 L7
CHTN/BK PR9 25 K5
FMBY L37 59 L1
GOL/RIS/CU WA3 92 D8
HTWN L38 59 K8
HTWN L38 70 E3
LEY/BBR PR5 29 J5
LITH L21 83 M4
MGHL L31 61 M8
NWD/KWIPK L33 74 B5
NWD/KWIPK L33 86 D2
ORM L39 75 H3
RF/TRAN CH42 127 J3
RNFD/HAY WA11 77 G8
RNFD/HAY WA11 88 B5
SKEL WN8 65 H7
STHEL WA9 103 J4
WARRS WA4 136 C7
WGNE/HIN WN2 80 C2
WGNNW/ST WN6 54 E1
WLT/FAZ L9 84 B7
Moss Lane Vw SKEL WN8 65 H7
Mosslawn Rd KKBY L32 86 C4
Mosslea Pk CALD/MH L18 130 B1
Mossley Av CALD/MH L18 114 B8
PS/BROM CH62 143 M5
Mossley Hill Dr AIG/SPK L17 113 M8
Mossley Hill Rd CALD/MH L18 130 B3
Mossley Rd RF/TRAN CH42 128 A2
Moss Nook BRSC L40 39 G7
ORM L39 62 E3 2
Moss Nook La MGHL L31 73 K5
RNFD/HAY WA11 76 A7
Moss Pits Cl AIN/FAZ L10 85 H6 4
Moss Pits La AIN/FAZ L10 85 G6
WAV L15 114 D7
Moss Rd STHP PR8 35 L3
WARRS WA4 138 C2
WGNW/BIL/O WN5 77 M2
Moss Side DV/KA/FCH L14 115 J2
FMBY L37 59 K1
Moss Side La KIRK/FR/WA PR4 27 H2
WARRS WA4 136 A6
Moss St ALL/GAR L19 130 E7
NPK/KEN L6 13 M5
PR/KW L34 100 F6
WDN WA8 17 K5
WGNE/HIN WN2 80 B2
WGNNW/ST WN6 4 A1
WGNW/BIL/O WN5 67 K8 2
Moss Ter WGNW/BIL/O WN5 67 K8 3
Mossvale GTS/LS CH66 155 M5
Moss Vw LITH L21 83 L5
MGHL L31 73 H4
STHP PR8 35 G8
Mossville Cl CALD/MH L18 130 C3
Mossville Rd CALD/MH L18 130 D3
Moss Wy NG/CROX L11 98 E1
Mossy Bank Rd
WAL/EG CH44 111 M1 11
Mossy Lea Fold
WGNNW/ST WN6 55 H2
Mossy Lea Rd WGNNW/ST WN6 42 A7
Moston Gv LYMM WA13 139 M2
Moston Wy GTS/LS CH66 163 H2 1
Mostyn Av AIN/FAZ L10 84 E3
ALL/GAR L19 130 F5
HES CH60 140 E5
WKBY CH48 124 D4
Mostyn Cl ANF/KKDL L4 97 G6 13
Mostyn St WAL/EG CH44 111 K2
Motherwell Crs STHP PR8 36 B2
Mottershead Rd WDN WA8 16 C4
Mottram Cl NWD/KWIPK L33 86 B3 4
WARRS WA4 138 D2
Mottram Dr WGNS/IIMK WN3 68 D8
Moughland La RUNC WA7 19 G7
Moulders La WARR WA1 14 F7
Mould St EV L5 96 F8 4
Moulton Cl RUNC WA7 161 H1
Mounsey Rd RF/TRAN CH42 11 G8
Mountain Rd CHLY/EC PR7 43 G5
Mountain Vw FROD/HEL WA6 166 D2
Mount Av BEB CH63 127 M6
BTL L20 83 M7
HES CH60 141 H5 1
Mountbatten Rd CHLY/EC PR7 32 C7
Mount Cl KKBY L32 85 L1
Mount Crs KKBY L32 85 L1
WGNW/BIL/O WN5 67 H7
Mount Dr BEB CH63 127 L6
Mount Farm Wy GTS/LS CH66 162 E3
Mount Gilmour CL/PREN CH43 10 D9
Mount Gv BIRK CH41 10 F8
Mount Haven Cl
GR/UP/WCH CH49 110 C8
Mount House Cl FMBY L37 47 K8
Mount House Rd FMBY L37 47 K8
Mount Olive CL/PREN CH43 127 J2
Mount Pk BEB CH63 127 M6
WLTN L25 131 J2
Mount Park Ct WLTN L25 131 J2
Mount Pleasant CHLYE PR6 44 C5
CHNE CH2 165 J1
CL/PREN CH43 127 K2
CSBY/WL L22 82 F4
VAUX/LVPD L3 13 K8
WDN WA8 134 D3 4
Mount Pleasant Av STHEL WA9 103 J2
Mount Pleasant Rd
WAL/NB CH45 95 J6
Mount Rd BEB CH63 127 L7
GR/UP/WCH CH49 110 C8
KKBY L32 85 K2
RF/TRAN CH42 127 L4
RUNC WA7 150 B5
WAL/NB CH45 95 J5
WKBY CH48 124 E4
Mount St CHTN/BK PR9 3 L3
CLVPS L1 113 G5
CSBY/WL L22 82 F4
LEIGH WN7 93 L1 2
WLTN L25 131 J3
The Mount HES CH60 141 H5
SKEL WN8 65 K5 1
WAL/EG CH44 111 L1
Mount Vernon EHL/KEN L7 113 J3
Mount Vernon St
EHL/KEN L7 113 J3 6
Mount Vernon Vw
EHL/KEN L7 113 J3 7
Mount Vw WGNS/IIMK WN3 5 H9
Mountview Cl TOX L8 113 J8 3
Mountway BEB CH63 127 M6 2
Mountwood SKEL WN8 65 J1
Mount Wood Rd
RF/TRAN CH42 127 L5
Mourne Cl GTS/LS CH66 155 J7 3
Mowbray Av RNFD/HAY WA11 9 M1
Mowbray Gv CLB/OSW/ST L13 114 C4
Mowcroft La WARRW/BUR WA5 135 K2
Moxon Av WARRS WA4 122 B8 1
Moxon St ECCL WA10 101 L3
Moxon Wy AIMK WN4 91 M1
Moyles Cl WDN WA8 133 M3 3
Mozart Cl TOX L8 113 K7 3
Muirfield Cl
WARRN/WOL WA2 122 C2 3
WD/CROXPK L12 99 G7 1
Muirfield Dr STHP PR8 47 L1
Muirfield Rd HUY L36 115 L4
Muirhead Av CLB/OSW/ST L13 98 B5
Muirhead Av East
WD/CROXPK L12 98 C5
Mulberry Av ECCL WA10 101 L2
GOL/RIS/CU WA3 93 H6
Mulberry Cl CHNE CH2 165 L2
NWD/KWIPK L33 74 B7 6
WARR WA1 123 G7 2
WGNW/BIL/O WN5 67 M7
Mulberry Gv WAL/EG CH44 111 M2 10
Mulberry Pl EHL/KEN L7 13 M9 1
Mulberry Rd RF/TRAN CH42 128 B3
Mulberry St EHL/KEN L7 13 M9
Mulcrow Cl STHEL WA9 102 F1
Mulgrave St TOX L8 113 J6
Mullberry St EHL/KEN L7 13 M8
Mullein Cl GOL/RIS/CU WA3 92 F5
Mulliner St EHL/KEN L7 113 L6
Mullins Av NEWLW WA12 91 L8 2
Mullion Cl CHTN/BK PR9 22 D8 3
HLWD L26 132 A5
RUNC WA7 150 D7 3
Mullion Gv WARRN/WOL WA2 122 C4 3
Mullion Rd NG/CROX L11 98 F1
Mullion Wk NG/CROX L11 85 L8 1
Mulveton Rd BEB CH63 143 H2 3
Mumfords La HOY CH47 109 G4 2
Muncaster Cl
PS/BROM CH62 143 M4 2
Muncaster Dr RNFD/HAY WA11 76 C6
Munro Av WGNW/BIL/O WN5 67 G7
Munster Rd CLB/OSW/ST L13 114 D2
Murat Gv CSBY/WL L22 82 E4
Murat St CSBY/WL L22 82 E4
Murcote Rd DV/KA/FCH L14 99 H8
Murdishaw Av RUNC WA7 150 E8
Muriel Cl WARRW/BUR WA5 119 M7
Muriel St ANF/KKDL L4 97 J5 1
Murphy Cl WGNS/IIMK WN3 4 A9
Murphy Gv STHEL WA9 103 G1
Murrayfield Dr MOR/LEA CH46 110 B1
Murrayfield Rd WLTN L25 115 J7
Murray Gv WKBY CH48 124 C2 4
Museum St WARR WA1 14 C7
Musker Dr NTHTN L30 83 L2
Musker St CSBY/BLUN L23 83 H2
Muspratt Rd LITH L21 83 J8
Mustard La GOL/RIS/CU WA3 106 D5
Myddleton La
WARRN/WOL WA2 105 K7
Myers Av RAIN/WH L35 101 J8
Myerscough Av BTL L20 7 M1 1
Myers Rd East CSBY/BLUN L23 83 G2
Myers Rd West CSBY/BLUN L23 82 F2
Mynsule Rd BEB CH63 143 H2
Myrtle Av AIMK WN4 79 H7 3
NEWLW WA12 104 E3
RNFD/HAY WA11 90 D6
Myrtle Gv CHTN/BK PR9 3 M5
CSBY/WL L22 82 F4
STHP PR8 25 G7
WAL/EG CH44 112 A2 3
WARRS WA4 15 K9
WGNW/BIL/O WN5 89 M1 3
Myrtle Pde TOX L8 113 H5 18
Myrtle St EHL/KEN L7 13 J9
EP CH65 156 E6
WGN WN1 4 D3


## N


Nab Rd CHLYE PR6 33 G4
Nairn Av SKEL WN8 53 K8
Nairn Cl BEB CH63 154 F1
WARRN/WOL WA2 122 C2
WGNNW/ST WN6 55 M4 4
Nangreaves St LEIGH WN7 81 L8
Nansen Cl WARRW/BUR WA5 120 F6
Nansen Gv ANF/KKDL L4 97 J4
Nant Park Ct WAL/NB CH45 95 L5 2
Nantwich Cl GR/UP/WCH CH49 126 C3
Nantwich Rd GTS/LS CH66 163 H2
Napier Cl ECCL WA10 8 D5
Napier Dr MOR/LEA CH46 110 B5
Napier Rd PS/BROM CH62 128 D5
Napier St BTL L20 6 E8
ECCL WA10 8 D5
WARR WA1 15 G6
Napier Ter STHP PR8 2 F8
Naples Rd WAL/EG CH44 111 M2
Napps Cl WLTN L25 115 H6 3
Napps Wy PEN/TH CH61 141 J3
WLTN L25 115 H5
Narborough Cl
WGNE/HIN WN2 81 G1 3
Nares Cl WARRW/BUR WA5 120 E4
Narrow Croft Rd ORM L39 62 D4
Narrow La ORM L39 62 D4
Narrow La (Clieves Hills)
ORM L39 49 M6
Narrow Moss La BRSC L40 50 F3
Naseby Cl CL/PREN CH43 126 E1 1
Naseby St ANF/KKDL L4 97 H3
Natal Rd WLT/FAZ L9 84 D7 3
Nathan Dr RNFD/HAY WA11 91 G7
Nathan Gv NWD/KWIPK L33 86 B1 5
Naunton Av LEIGH WN7 81 L8
Navenby Rd WGNS/IIMK WN3 79 J3
Navigation Cl NTHTN L30 84 C1
RUNC WA7 150 F7 2
Navigation St WARR WA1 15 J6
Navigation Whf VAUX/LVPD L3 112 F7
Naylor Av GOL/RIS/CU WA3 92 D5
Naylorfarm Av WGNNW/ST WN6 55 H8
Naylor Rd CL/PREN CH43 111 G5
WDN WA8 17 J2
Naylorsfield Dr NTHLY L27 115 L7
Naylor's Rd NTHLY L27 115 M6
WLTN L25 115 M8 1
Naylor St VAUX/LVPD L3 12 F4
WARR WA1 14 F5
Nazeby Av CSBY/BLUN L23 83 H2
Neale Dr GR/UP/WCH CH49 126 A2
Neales Fold CHTN/BK PR9 22 F8 2
Neargates CHLY/EC PR7 42 F2
Neasham Cl HLWD L26 132 B5 4
Nedens Gv MGHL L31 72 E2
Nedens La MGHL L31 72 E2
Needham Cl RUNC WA7 149 M3 2
Needham Rd EHL/KEN L7 113 L3
Needham Wy SKEL WN8 53 K8
Needwood Dr BEB CH63 143 H2
Neills Rd STHEL WA9 103 K7
Neilson Rd AIG/SPK L17 129 K2 3
Neil St WDN WA8 134 D3
Nell's La ORM L39 62 B8
Nel Pan La LEIGH WN7 81 L5
Nelson Av RAIN/WH L35 117 G3
Nelson Dr PEN/TH CH61 141 G2
WGNE/HIN WN2 69 J5
Nelson Pl RAIN/WH L35 117 G3 6
Nelson Rd CHLY/EC PR7 32 E6 10
EHL/KEN L7 113 K4
EP CH65 20 C1
GOL/RIS/CU WA3 122 F1
LITH L21 83 K6 3
RF/TRAN CH42 128 C4
Nelson's Cft BEB CH63 143 J2
Nelson St BTL L20 6 E7
CLVPS L1 13 G7
NEWLW WA12 104 C2
RUNC WA7 19 H3
STHP PR8 2 F5
WAL/NB CH45 95 J6
WAV L15 114 A6
WDN WA8 16 C8
WGNE/HIN WN2 69 M7 2
Nelville Rd WLT/FAZ L9 84 E6
Nemos Cl FROD/HEL WA6 166 E3 1
Neptune Cl RUNC WA7 150 F6 2
Neptune St BIRK CH41 11 H3
Ness Gv KKBY L32 85 L3
Neston Av STHEL WA9 118 D1 2
Neston Gn GTS/LS CH66 162 F1
Neston Rd BEB CH63 142 B8
NSTN CH64 153 H8
Neston St ANF/KKDL L4 97 H4
Netherby Rd WGNNW/ST WN6 68 C2
Netherby St TOX L8 129 H1 12
Netherfield WDN WA8 133 M5
Netherfield Cl CL/PREN CH43 126 E1 1
Netherfield Rd North EV L5 97 G6
Netherfield Rd South EV L5 13 K1
Netherfields LEIGH WN7 81 M6 3
Netherley Rd CHLY/EC PR7 43 G5
RAIN/WH L35 116 D8
Netherpool Rd GTS/LS CH66 156 B5
Netherton Dr
FROD/HEL WA6 160 C6 2
Netherton Gra NTHTN L30 84 D2
Netherton Gn NTHTN L30 72 B8
Netherton La NTHTN L30 72 A8
Netherton Park Rd LITH L21 83 M5
Netherton Rd BTL L20 83 M7
CALD/MH L18 130 C4
MOR/LEA CH46 110 A5 3
Netherton Wy NTHTN L30 84 A5
Netherwood Rd NG/CROX L11 98 A3
Netley St ANF/KKDL L4 97 G5 10
Nettlestead Rd NG/CROX L11 98 C5
Neva Av MOR/LEA CH46 109 M5
Nevada Cl WARRW/BUR WA5 120 D5
Neverstitch Cl SKEL WN8 65 H3 2
Neverstitch Rd SKEL WN8 64 F3
Neville Av STHEL WA9 103 K3
WARRN/WOL WA2 121 M4
Neville Cl CL/PREN CH43 126 E1
Neville Crs WARRW/BUR WA5 136 C2
Neville Rd CSBY/WL L22 83 G4 4
PS/BROM CH62 144 A6
WAL/EG CH44 111 J1
Neville St NEWLW WA12 104 C1 3
WGNE/HIN WN2 80 C2
Nevill St STHP PR8 3 G2
Nevin St NPK/KEN L6 113 J2 13
Nevison St EHL/KEN L7 113 K4 8
Nevitte Cl STBRV L28 99 J5
New Acres SKEL WN8 53 H4
New Acres Cl CL/PREN CH43 110 E5 6
Newark Cl CL/PREN CH43 126 E1 3
HUY L36 99 M7
Newark Rd WGNE/HIN WN2 80 E1
Newark St ANF/KKDL L4 7 M9
WGNNW/ST WN6 68 B4
New Bank Rd WDN WA8 133 K4
New Barn Av AIMK WN4 91 L2 6
New Barnet WDN WA8 134 B1 3
New Bird St CLVPS L1 112 F6
Newbold Crs WKBY CH48 125 G2
Newbold Gv WD/CROXPK L12 99 H3
Newborough Av
CALD/MH L18 114 B8 10
CSBY/BLUN L23 83 J1
Newborough Cl
WARRW/BUR WA5 120 F3
Newbridge Cl AIMK WN4 90 F2 2
GR/UP/WCH CH49 126 D1
RUNC WA7 150 E7 3
WARRW/BUR WA5 120 E3
New Bridge Rd EP CH65 21 J7
Newbridge Rd EP CH65 21 J9
Newburgh Cl RUNC WA7 150 F4
Newburn Cl SKEL WN8 53 K8
WGNS/IIMK WN3 79 G1 1
Newburns La CL/PREN CH43 127 K2
Newburn St ANF/KKDL L4 97 H4
Newbury Cl HUY L36 115 M4
WDN WA8 134 B2
Newbury Dr SKEL WN8 53 K8 2
Newbury Rd SKEL WN8 53 K8
Newbury Wy WD/CROXPK L12 99 G8
Newby Av RAIN/WH L35 117 J1 4
Newby Cl STHP PR8 47 K2
Newby Dr HUY L36 115 L2
Newby Gv WD/CROXPK L12 98 E3
Newby Sq WGNW/BIL/O WN5 67 K8 4
Newby St ANF/KKDL L4 97 H5
Newcastle Rd WAV L15 114 C7 6
New Cswy HTWN L38 59 K5
New Chester Rd BIRK CH41 128 B1
PS/BROM CH62 128 E8
RF/TRAN CH42 128 C4
Newchurch La
GOL/RIS/CU WA3 107 H3
Newcombe Av
WARRN/WOL WA2 122 A5 2
Newcombe St NPK/KEN L6 97 K8
New Court Wy ORM L39 51 H8
Newcroft Rd WLTN L25 131 H1 2
New Cross St ECCL WA10 8 F4 2
ECCL WA10 8 F5 1
PR/KW L34 100 F6 1
New Cut La NWD/KWIPK L33 87 J5
STHP PR8 35 J5
WARR WA1 122 D7
Newdales Cl CL/PREN CH43 110 E6
Newdown Rd NG/CROX L11 85 M8
Newell Rd WAL/EG CH44 111 K1
Newenden Rd WGN WN1 68 D1
Newenham Crs DV/KA/FCH L14 115 G2
New Ferry By-Pass
PS/BROM CH62 128 D6
New Ferry Rd PS/BROM CH62 128 D6
Newfield Cl CSBY/BLUN L23 71 L7
Newfield Rd LYMM WA13 139 M2
Newfield Ter FROD/HEL WA6 166 D3 3
New Fold WGNW/BIL/O WN5 77 L1
New Fort Wy BTL L20 83 J7
New Foul La STHP PR8 36 B1
Newgate Av WGNNW/ST WN6 55 G5
Newgate Rd SKEL WN8 66 B6
New Glade Hl RNFD/HAY WA11 89 M7
New Grosvenor Rd EP CH65 20 B1
New Hall Dr STHP PR8 36 E4
New Hall La GOL/RIS/CU WA3 107 J3
Newhall La HOY CH47 108 D7
New Hall La NG/CROX L11 98 A5
Newhall St CLVPS L1 113 G6 5
Newhaven Rd WAL/NB CH45 95 L6 9
WARRN/WOL WA2 121 K1
New Hedley Gv EV L5 96 E8
New Henderson St TOX L8 113 G7
New Hey WD/CROXPK L12 98 C8
New Hey La NSTN CH64 154 C6
New Hey Rd GR/UP/WCH CH49 126 D1
Newholme Cl
WD/CROXPK L12 99 G2 9
Newhope Rd BIRK CH41 10 E3
Newhouse Rd WAV L15 113 M6 4
New Hutte La HLWD L26 132 B7
Newick Rd KKBY L32 85 L4
Newington CLVPS L1 13 J8
New Islington VAUX/LVPD L3 13 K5
Newland Av WGNW/BIL/O WN5 67 M8
Newland Cl WDN WA8 133 L2 3
Newland Ct AIG/SPK L17 129 L2 3
Newland Dr WAL/EG CH44 111 J1
Newlands CHLY/EC PR7 30 E7
Newlands Av BRSC L40 52 B1 2
Newlands Cl FROD/HEL WA6 160 E7
Newlands Dr GOL/RIS/CU WA3 92 E5
Newlands Rd BEB CH63 143 K1 1
RNFD/HAY WA11 89 L6
WARRS WA4 138 B3
New La BRSC L40 38 D7
CHLY/EC PR7 30 C3
CHTN/BK PR9 25 M1
GOL/RIS/CU WA3 106 C6
ORM L39 61 G2
ORM L39 63 G3
WARRS WA4 138 D8
New Lane Pace CHTN/BK PR9 23 K5
Newling St BIRK CH41 10 E4
New Ldg WGN WN1 68 E3
Newlyn Av LITH L21 83 J4
MGHL L31 73 G4
Newlyn Cl HOY CH47 109 G3
RUNC WA7 150 D7
Newlyn Dr AIMK WN4 91 K3
SKEL WN8 65 M6 1
Newlyn Gdns
WARRW/BUR WA5 135 M2
Newlyn Gv RNFD/HAY WA11 89 M6
Newlyn Rd HOY CH47 109 G4
NG/CROX L11 85 M8
Newlyn Wk NG/CROX L11 85 M8 3
Newman Av WGNNW/ST WN6 68 C3
New Manchester Rd
WARR WA1 122 C6
Newman Cl WGNE/HIN WN2 69 L7
New Manor Rd WARRS WA4 151 K7
Newman St ANF/KKDL L4 96 F5
WARRS WA4 138 B2
WGN WN1 69 G3 1
New Market St CHLY/EC PR7 32 E5
WGN WN1 4 E3
New Meadow La FMBY L37 60 A5
New Miles La WGNNW/ST WN6 55 H7
New Mill Stile WLTN L25 131 J2
New Mill St CHLY/EC PR7 30 E7
Newmoore La RUNC WA7 151 H1
Newmorn Ct AIG/SPK L17 129 L3 7
Newnham Dr EP CH65 20 D7
New Pale Rd FROD/HEL WA6 167 K5
Newport Av WAL/NB CH45 94 F6 2
Newport Cl CL/PREN CH43 126 E1 4
Newport Ct EV L5 96 E8 1
New Quay VAUX/LVPD L3 12 D6
Newquay Cl RUNC WA7 150 D7
New Rd BRSC L40 39 K1
CHLY/EC PR7 43 H2
CHLYE PR6 44 F5
CLB/OSW/ST L13 98 A8
FMBY L37 47 J8
GTS/LS CH66 155 J5
LEY/BBR PR5 29 K6
PR/KW L34 101 G6
WARRS WA4 14 F8
WGNE/HIN WN2 57 J7
New School La GTS/LS CH66 155 K5
Newsham Cl WDN WA8 133 K1 2
Newsham Dr NPK/KEN L6 97 L8
Newsham Rd HUY L36 116 C5
Newsham St EV L5 96 F8 5
Newsholme Cl
GOL/RIS/CU WA3 107 H2 2
News La RNFD/HAY WA11 76 B3
Newstead Av CSBY/BLUN L23 82 D2
Newstead Rd TOX L8 113 L6 4
WGNS/IIMK WN3 79 G2
Newstet Rd NWD/KWIPK L33 86 D3
New St BRSC L40 40 E3
CHLY/EC PR7 30 E7
HOR/BR BL6 57 M3
NSTN CH64 153 G8
ORM L39 49 K4
RUNC WA7 19 G4
STHEL WA9 102 E7
WAL/EG CH44 112 A3
WGNE/HIN WN2 80 C4
WGNW/BIL/O WN5 67 K8
Newton Av GOL/RIS/CU WA3 107 G8 1
Newton Cl WD/CROXPK L12 98 D5 3
WGN WN1 68 F3
Newton Ct CLB/OSW/ST L13 114 A4
Newton Cross La WKBY CH48 125 G3
Newton Dr WKBY CH48 125 G3
Newton Gv
WARRN/WOL WA2 122 B2 2
Newton Hollow
FROD/HEL WA6 167 K5
Newton La NEWLW WA12 92 A7
WARRS WA4 151 L5
Newton Park Dr NEWLW WA12 105 H3
Newton Park Rd WKBY CH48 125 G3
Newton Rd CLB/OSW/ST L13 114 A1
EP CH65 20 D4
GOL/RIS/CU WA3 93 G7
HOY CH47 108 E6
STHEL WA9 103 J2
WAL/EG CH44 111 J1
WARRN/WOL WA2 105 H5
WARRN/WOL WA2 121 J2
WGNW/BIL/O WN5 78 B7
Newton St BIRK CH41 10 F4
CHTN/BK PR9 25 J6
Newton Wy
GR/UP/WCH CH49 110 B8 4
VAUX/LVPD L3 13 L7
New Tower Ct WAL/NB CH45 95 L5
Newtown NSTN CH64 153 H7
New Wy ORM L39 74 D3
Nicander Rd CALD/MH L18 114 B8
Nicholas Rd CSBY/BLUN L23 82 D1
WDN WA8 133 L5
Nicholas St VAUX/LVPD L3 13 G3 1
Nicholl Rd ECCL WA10 88 C7
Nicholls Dr PEN/TH CH61 141 H1
Nicholls St WARRS WA4 138 D3
Nicholson St STHEL WA9 103 G1 2
WARR WA1 14 B5
Nichol St CHLY/EC PR7 32 E4 5
Nick Hilton's La CHLYE PR6 44 F2
Nickleby Cl TOX L8 113 H8 3
Nickleton Brow CHLYE PR6 44 E3
Nicol Av GOL/RIS/CU WA3 123 H4
Nicol Mere Dr AIMK WN4 79 K8 2
Nicol Rd AIMK WN4 79 J8
Nidderdale Av RAIN/WH L35 117 M2 3
Nigel Rd HES CH60 141 L5
Nightingale Cl
GOL/RIS/CU WA3 123 H1 3
KKBY L32 85 K2 2
NTHLY L27 116 B8 2
RUNC WA7 150 A8
Nightingale Rd HOR/BR BL6 57 L2
WD/CROXPK L12 99 H2
Nightingale St CHLYE PR6 44 C5 6
Nimrod St ANF/KKDL L4 97 H4
Nipe La SKEL WN8 65 K8
Nithsdale Rd WAV L15 114 A7 1
Nixons La SKEL WN8 65 M6
STHP PR8 35 G6
Nixon St ANF/KKDL L4 97 H3
Noble Cl GOL/RIS/CU WA3 123 G2
Noctorum Av
GR/UP/WCH CH49 110 E8
Noctorum Dell CL/PREN CH43 126 F1
Noctorum La CL/PREN CH43 111 G7
Noctorum Rd CL/PREN CH43 110 F8
Noctorum Wy CL/PREN CH43 126 F1
Noel Ga ORM L39 62 D4
Noel St TOX L8 113 K6
Nolan St STHP PR8 3 K8
Nook La BRSC L40 30 A8
GOL/RIS/CU WA3 92 D5
STHEL WA9 103 H4
WARRN/WOL WA2 122 D3
WARRS WA4 138 C2
Nook Ri WAV L15 114 D5
The Nook CL/PREN CH43 10 D7

ECCL WA10 .............................. 88 D7
WGNNW/ST WN6 ........................ 55 G6
WKBY CH48 ............................ 125 K3
WLTN L25 .............................. 131 K2
Nora St WARR WA1 ...................... 15 H6
Norbreck Av DV/KA/FCH L14 ............ 115 C5
Norbreck Cl WARRW/BUR WA5 ........... 136 C1
Norbreck Crs
    WARRW/BUR WA5 ..................... 136 C1
    WGNNW/ST WN6 ...................... 68 C3
Norburn Crs FMBY L37 ................. 59 H3
Norbury Av BEB CH63 ................. 128 A8
    CALD/MH L18 ....................... 114 B8
    WARRN/WOL WA2 .................... 121 M5
    WCNW/BIL/O WN5 .................... 77 M7
Norbury Cl BEB CH63 ................. 128 B8
    CHTN/BK PR9 ........................ 22 E8
Norbury Fold RAIN/WH L35 ........... 118 A4
Norbury Gv KKBY L32 ................. 85 M3
Norbury St LEIGH WN7 ................ 81 M8
Norcliffe Rd RAIN/WH L35 ........... 117 K1
Norcott Av WARRS WA4 ............... 137 M3
Norcott Dr
    WARRW/BUR WA5 .................... 104 B7
Norden Cl GOL/RIS/CU WA3 ........... 106 E8
Norfolk Cl CL/PREN CH43 ............ 110 E8
Norfolk Dr WARRW/BUR WA5 .......... 120 A7
    WKBY CH48 ......................... 124 E4
Norfolk Gv STHP PR8 ................. 35 H4
    WDN WA8 ........................... 133 L5
Norfolk Pl LITH L21 .................. 83 J6
    WDN WA8 ........................... 133 L5
Norfolk Rd ECCL WA10 ................. 8 A9
    EP CH65 ............................ 20 C5
    MGHL L31 ........................... 72 E6
    STHP PR8 ........................... 35 H4
    WCNW/BIL/O WN5 .................... 78 A4
Norfolk St CLVPS L1 ................. 112 F6
    RUNC WA7 ........................... 19 K2
    WGNNW/ST WN6 ...................... 68 C3
    WCNW/BIL/O WN5 .................... 68 B7
Norgate St ANF/KKDL L4 .............. 97 H6
Norgrove Cl RAIN/WH L35 ............ 150 F5
Norland's La RAIN/WH L35 ........... 118 A4
    WDN WA8 ........................... 118 A6
Norland St WDN WA8 .................. 17 J1
Norleane Crs RUNC WA7 ............... 19 J8
Norley Av EP CH65 ................... 156 B7
    PS/BROM CH62 ...................... 155 C2
Norley Dr ECCL WA10 ................ 101 J2
Norley Hall Av
    WCNW/BIL/O WN5 ..................... 67 L7
Norley Pl HLWD L26 ................. 132 A7
Norley Rd LEIGH WN7 ................. 93 K1
    WCNW/BIL/O WN5 ..................... 67 K6
Norman Av NEWLW WA12 ............... 105 C2
    RNFD/HAY WA11 ...................... 91 J6
Normanby Cl
    WARRW/BUR WA5 .................... 121 C6
Normanby St WGNW/BIL/O WN5 ......... 67 K7
Norman Cl GTS/LS CH66 .............. 163 H5
Normandale Rd ANF/KKDL L4 .......... 97 K4
Normanhurst RUNC WA7 ............... 19 C6
Normandy Rd HUY L36 ................ 115M2
Normanhurst LEIGH WN7 ............... 63 J1
Norman Rd BTL L20 ................... 83 L6
    CSBY/BLUN L23 ...................... 82 F2
    RUNC WA7 ........................... 19 C6
    WAL/EG CH44 ....................... 112 A3
Normans Rd STHEL WA9 ............... 103 H6
Normanston Rd
    CL/PREN CH43 ..................... 127 K1
Norman St BIRK CH41 ................ 111 H5
    VAUX/LVPD L3 ....................... 13 L6
    WARRN/WOL WA2 ...................... 14 F3
Normanton Cl AIG/SPK L17 .......... 129 L2
Normanton Cl
    WGNNW/ST WN6 ...................... 68 A1
Norma Rd CSBY/WL L22 ............... 83 C4
Norreys Av WARRW/BUR WA5 .......... 121 K5
Norris Cl CL/PREN CH43 ............ 110 E8
Norris Green Crs NC/CROX L11 ...... 98 C4
Norris Green Rd
    WD/CROXPK L12 ...................... 98 D7
Norris Green Wy NC/CROX L11 ....... 98 C4
Norris House Dr ORM L39 ............ 62 E5
Norris Rd PR/KW L34 ............... 100 E7
Norris St CHLY/EC PR7 ............... 32 E7
    WARRN/WOL WA2 .................... 121 L5
Norris Wy FMBY L37 .................. 59 K2
Norseman Cl WD/CROXPK L12 ......... 98 B8
Northam Cl CHTN/BK PR9 ............. 22 C8
North Av AIN/FAZ L10 ............... 85 C3
    SPK/HALE L24 ...................... 131 J7
    WARRN/WOL WA2 .................... 121 K5
North Barcombe Rd
    CHLDW L16 ......................... 114 F6
Northbrook Cl TOX L8 ............... 113 J6
Northbrook Rd WAL/EG CH44 ......... 111M2
Northbrook St TOX L8 ............... 113 J6
Northbury Rd GTS/LS CH66 .......... 163 G4
North Cantril Av
    WD/CROXPK L12 ...................... 99 C5
North Cl PS/BROM CH62 ............. 143 L1
Northcote Cl EV L5 ................... 13 M1
Northcote Rd WAL/NB CH45 ........... 94 F7
    WLT/FAZ L9 ......................... 97 H2
Northcroft WGN WN1 ................... 5 M2
Northdale Rd WARR WA1 ............. 122 C5
    WAV L15 ........................... 114 B5
Northdene SKEL WN8 .................. 53 K3
North Dingle ANF/KKDL L4 ........... 96 F5
North Dr HES CH60 ................. 141 J6
    WAV L15 ........................... 114 B5
    WD/CROXPK L12 ...................... 98 D8
Northdunes HTWN L38 ................. 70 B1
Northenden Rd CHLY/EC PR7 ......... 43 C4
North End La HLWD L26 ............. 132 A2
    HTWN L38 ............................ 59 J8
Northern La RAIN/WH L35 ........... 133 J2
Northern Perimeter Rd
    NTHTN L30 .......................... 72 A8
Northern Ri GTS/LS CH66 ........... 163 G1
Northern Rd SPK/HALE L24 ......... 147 L2
The Northern Rd
    CSBY/BLUN L23 ...................... 83 G1
Northfield SKEL WN8 ................. 65 K1
Northfield Cl NWD/KWIPK L33 ........ 86 C3
    STHEL WA9 ......................... 118 F2
Northfield Rd BTL L20 ............... 84 A7

North Florida Rd
    RNFD/HAY WA11 ...................... 90 F5
North Front RAIN/WH L35 ........... 117 C4
Northgate Dr CHLYE PR6 ............. 33 C3
Northgate Rd CL/OSW/ST L13 ......... 98 B8
North Gv CALD/MH L18 .............. 130 E4
North Hill St TOX L8 ............... 113 J7
North John St CLVP L2 .............. 12 F7
North Leach Dr STHP PR8 ........... 34 C8
North Linkside Rd WLTN L25 ........ 131 L4
North Manor Wy WLTN L25 .......... 131 L4
North Meade MGHL L31 .............. 72 D3
Northmead Rd ALL/GAR L19 ......... 131 C6
North Moor La ORM L39 ............. 50 B5
North Moss La FMBY L37 ............. 47M6
North Mossley Hill Rd
    CALD/MH L18 ...................... 130 B1
North Mount Rd KKBY L32 ............ 85 K1
Northolt Ct
    WARRN/WOL WA2 .................... 122 A4
North Pde HOY CH47 ................ 108 C6
    KKBY L32 ............................ 86 A3
    NSTN CH64 ......................... 152 C3
    SPK/HALE L24 ...................... 147 G2
North Park Brook Rd
    WARRW/BUR WA5 .................... 121 C4
North Park Rd KKBY L32 ............. 85 L1
North Perimeter Rd
    NWD/KWIPK L33 ...................... 86 F1
Northridge Rd PEN/TH CH61 ......... 126 D7
North Rd ALL/GAR L19 .............. 130 B7
    CHTN/BK PR9 ........................ 25 K1
    DV/KA/FCH L14 ..................... 114 E3
    ECCL WA10 ........................... 8 A7
    EP CH65 ........................... 156 A2
    RF/TRAN CH42 ...................... 127 L2
    SPK/HALE L24 ...................... 132 C8
    WKBY CH48 ......................... 124 C3
Northside CHLY/EC PR7 .............. 31 L2
North St AIMK WN4 .................. 79 M8
    CHLYE PR6 .......................... 32 E3
    CHTN/BK PR9 ......................... 3 J1
    NEWLW WA12 ....................... 104 B1
    RNFD/HAY WA11 ...................... 91 G7
    VAUX/LVPD L3 ....................... 13 C5
North Sudley Rd AIG/SPK L17 ....... 130 A3
Northumberland Av HUY TOX L8 ..... 112 F8
Northumberland St
    CHLY/EC PR7 ........................ 32 F6
    TOX L8 ............................ 113 C8
    WGN WN1 ............................. 5 J3
Northumberland Ter EV L5 .......... 97 C7
Northumberland Wy NTHTN L30 ....... 83 L2
North V CHLYE PR6 .................. 44 B4
North Vw EHL/KEN L7 ............... 113 J4
    HUY L36 ........................... 116 C3
    WARRW/BUR WA5 .................... 120 A6
Northway HES CH60 ................. 141 M4
    LYMM WA13 ......................... 139 M1
    MGHL L31 ............................ 72 F3
    RUNC WA7 .......................... 150 B5
    SKEL WN8 ............................ 65 K4
    WARRN/WOL WA2 .................... 121 K3
    WAV L15 ........................... 114 D5
    WDN WA8 ........................... 133M4
    WGN WN1 ............................. 5 J3
Northways PS/BROM CH62 ............ 143 M2
    WGNNW/ST WN6 ...................... 55 M3
Northwich Cl CSBY/BLUN L23 ........ 71 K7
Northwich Rd RUNC WA7 ............. 150 E8
North William St
    WAL/EG CH44 ....................... 112 A3
Northwold Cl WGNS/IIMK WN3 ........ 78 E2
Northwood Av
    NEWLW WA12 ....................... 105 H2
Northwood Rd CL/PREN CH43 ........ 127 H3
    HUY L36 ........................... 116 B1
    RUNC WA7 .......................... 150 A3
Norton Av WARRW/BUR WA5 .......... 120 A8
Norton Dr PEN/TH CH61 ............. 125 L6
Norton Ga RUNC WA7 ................ 150 E5
Norton Gv MGHL L31 ................. 72 F7
    RAIN/WH L35 ...................... 101 M6
Norton Hl RUNC WA7 ................ 150 E5
Norton La RUNC WA7 ................ 150 E5
Norton Rd WKBY CH48 .............. 124 C2
Norton Station Rd RUNC WA7 ....... 150 F5
Norton St BTL L20 ................... 6 L1
    VAUX/LVPD L3 ....................... 13 J5
Norton Vw RUNC WA7 ............... 150 E5
Norton Village RUNC WA7 ........... 150 F5
Nortonwood La RUNC WA7 .......... 150 E4
Norville GTS/LS CH66 .............. 155 M6
Norville Rd DV/KA/FCH L14 ......... 114 E3
Norwich Av WAV L15 ................ 114 C7
Norwich Dr GR/UP/WCH CH49 ........ 110 C6
    GTS/LS CH66 ....................... 163 C5
Norwich Rd WAV L15 ................ 114 C7
Norwich Wy KKBY L32 ............... 86 A3
Norwood Av AIMK WN4 ................ 79 H7
    CHTN/BK PR9 ........................ 25 C5
    GOL/RIS/CU WA3 ..................... 93 C6
    LITH L21 ........................... 83 K4
    WGNNW/ST WN6 ...................... 68 C2
Norwood Cl CHLYE PR6 .............. 44 C5
    NPK/KEN L6 ........................ 113 K1
Norwood Ct
    GR/UP/WCH CH49 ................... 125 M2
Norwood Crs CHTN/BK PR9 ........... 25 C5
Norwood Gv NPK/KEN L6 ............ 113 K1
    RNFD/HAY WA11 ...................... 76 C7
Norwood Rd GR/UP/WCH CH49 ....... 125 M1
    STHP PR8 ........................... 25 H6
    WAL/EG CH44 ....................... 111 K3
Norwyn Rd NC/CROX L11 ............. 98 B8
Nostell Rd AIMK WN4 ................ 79 J8
Nottingham Cl RAIN/WH L35 ........ 101 L8
    WARR WA1 .......................... 122 F7
Nottingham Pl WGN WN1 .............. 5 K1
Nottingham Rd HUY L36 ............ 115 L4
Nuffield Cl GR/UP/WCH CH49 ....... 126 B1
Nun Cl CL/PREN CH43 ............... 127 K1
Nunn St STHEL WA9 ................ 102 F2
Nunsford Cl LITH L21 ............... 83 M3
Nunthorpe Rd PR/KW L34 ............ 86 D8

The Nurseries FMBY L37 ............. 59 J3
Nurse Rd PEN/TH CH61 .............. 126 D7
Nursery Av ORM L39 ................. 51 J7
Nursery Cl CHLY/EC PR7 ............. 42 F1
    CL/PREN CH43 ..................... 127 K2
    WDN WA8 ........................... 134 F2
    WLTN L25 .......................... 131 L5
Nursery Dr RAIN/WH L35 ........... 101 M6
Nursery La ALL/GAR L19 ........... 130 E6
Nursery Rd MGHL L31 ................ 72 E1
    RAIN/WH L35 ...................... 101 M6
Nutgrove Av RAIN/WH L35 ........... 101 M6
Nutgrove Hall Dr RAIN/WH L35 .... 101 M6
Nutgrove Rd RAIN/WH L35 .......... 101 L7
Nuthall Rd STHP PR8 ................ 36 A2
Nut St WGN WN1 .................... 5 J4
Nuttall Ct GOL/RIS/CU WA3 ........ 122 E1
Nuttall La SKEL WN8 ............... 65 M2
Nuttall St EHL/KEN L7 ............. 113 L4
Nutt St WGN WN1 .................... 5 J4
Nyland Rd HUY L36 ................. 99 M8

O

Oak Av CHLY/EC PR7 ................. 31 M2
    GOL/RIS/CU WA3 ..................... 92 D5
    GR/UP/WCH CH49 ................... 109 M7
    NEWLW WA12 ....................... 104 C2
    ORM L39 ............................ 62 F1
    RNFD/HAY WA11 ...................... 91 G6
    WGNE/HIN WN2 ...................... 80 E6
    WGNE/HIN WN2 ...................... 81 J2
    WGNNW/ST WN6 ...................... 56 B5
    WLT/FAZ L9 ......................... 84 D7
Oak Bank BIRK CH41 ................. 10 F8
Oakbank Rd AIG/SPK L17 ........... 114 A8
Oakbank St WAL/EG CH44 ........... 111 L2
Oakbourne Cl AIG/SPK L17 ......... 129 L3
Oak Cl MOR/LEA CH46 .............. 109 M6
    RAIN/WH L35 ...................... 117 C2
    WD/CROXPK L12 ...................... 99 H4
Oak Crs SKEL WN8 ................... 64 F4
Oakdale Av FROD/HEL WA6 .......... 160 F1
    WAL/EG CH44 ...................... 111 M3
    WARRS WA4 ......................... 137 M4
Oakdale Dr GR/UP/WCH CH49 ......... 125 L3
Oakdale Rd CALD/MH L18 ........... 114 C8
    CSBY/WL L22 ........................ 82 F3
    WAL/EG CH44 ...................... 111 M4
Oakdene Av GTS/LS CH66 ........... 155 L8
    WARR WA1 .......................... 122 E6
Oakdene Cl PS/BROM CH62 .......... 143 M8
Oakdene Rd ANF/KKDL L4 ............ 97 K6
    RF/TRAN CH42 ...................... 127 L2
Oak Dr CHLYE PR6 ................... 32 E2
    RUNC WA7 ........................... 19 M9
Oakenden Cl AIMK WN4 ............... 79 J7
Oakengates WGNNW/ST WN6 .......... 56 B4
Oakenholt Rd
    MOR/LEA CH46 ...................... 110 A4
Oakes St VAUX/LVPD L3 .............. 13 L6
Oakfield ANF/KKDL L4 ............... 97 K7
Oakfield Av GOL/RIS/CU WA3 ....... 92 B4
    WLTN L25 .......................... 131 J1
Oakfield Cl RAIN/WH L35 .......... 101 M6
Oakfield Crs WGNE/HIN WN2 ........ 57 L8
Oakfield Dr FMBY L37 ................ 58 F7
    HUY L36 ........................... 116 B5
    WDN WA8 ........................... 133 L3
Oakfield Gv ANF/KKDL L4 ........... 97 J7
    GTS/LS CH66 ....................... 155 C5
    HTWN L38 ............................ 70 B3
    PS/BROM CH62 ...................... 143 L5
Oakford Cl CHTN/BK PR9 ............. 23 K8
Oak Gn ORM L39 .................... 51 H8
Oak Gv EP CH65 ................... 163 J2
Oakham Dr AIN/FAZ L10 ............. 85 H4
    MOR/LEA CH46 ...................... 109 K4
Oakham St TOX L8 ................. 112 F7
Oakhill Cl MGHL L31 ................. 72 F1
Oakhill Dr MGHL L31 ................ 72 E1
Oakhill Pk CLB/OSW/ST L13 ........ 114 D3
Oakhill Rd CLB/OSW/ST L13 ........ 114 D3
    MGHL L31 ........................... 72 F3
Oakhurst Cl WLTN L25 ............. 131 K1
Oakland Cl LITH L21 ................ 83 L7
Oakland Dr GR/UP/WCH CH49 ....... 110 C7
Oakland Rd ALL/GAR L19 .......... 130 B5
Oaklands AIMK WN4 ................ 115 L2
Oaklands Av CSBY/BLUN L23 ........ 71 G8
Oaklands Ct STHEL WA9 ............ 118 E1
Oaklands Dr BEB CH63 ............. 128 C7
    HES CH60 .......................... 141 J4
    LYMM WA13 ......................... 139M3
Oaklands Rd GOL/RIS/CU WA3 ....... 93 H6
Oaklands Ter PEN/TH CH61 ......... 141 J3
Oakland St WARR WA1 .............. 15 M1
    WDN WA8 ........................... 149 J1
Oak La WD/CROXPK L12 .............. 98 E3
Oak La North WD/CROXPK L12 ....... 98 E3
Oaklea WGNNW/ST WN6 .............. 55 J3
Oakleaf Ms CL/PREN CH43 ......... 110 F8
Oaklea Rd PEN/TH CH61 ............ 126 B7
Oaklee Gv NWD/KWIPK L33 ......... 86 C1
Oak Leigh CLB/OSW/ST L13 ......... 98 A8
Oakleigh SKEL WN8 .................. 76 F3
Oakleigh Gv BEB CH63 ............. 128 B7
Oakley Av WGNW/BIL/O WN5 ........ 77 M7
Oakley Cl WD/CROXPK L12 .......... 98 E3
The Oaklings WGNE/HIN WN2 ....... 81 J2
Oakmere Cl RAIN/WH L35 ........... 118 A4
Oakmere Dr GR/UP/WCH CH49 ....... 125 L1
    CTS/LS CH66 ....................... 163 H5
    WARRW/BUR WA5 .................... 136 B2
Oakmere St RUNC WA7 ............... 19 G4
Oakridge Cl PS/BROM CH62 ......... 143 L3
Oakridge Rd PS/BROM CH62 ......... 143 L3
Oak Rd BEB CH63 ................... 128 B6
    GTS/LS CH66 ...................... 155 C4
    HUY L36 ........................... 115M5
    LYMM WA13 ......................... 139 L2
    RAIN/WH L35 ...................... 117 C2

WARRW/BUR WA5 .................... 136 B2
Oaks Cl STHEL WA9 ................. 118 F2
Oaks La PEN/TH CH61 .............. 141 J1
Oaksmeade Cl WD/CROXPK L12 ...... 99 H2
Oaks Pl WDN WA8 ................... 16 C5
The Oaks CHLY/EC PR7 .............. 43 K1
    WD/CROXPK L12 ...................... 99 H4
Oaks PS/BROM CH62 ................. 143 L5
    WDN WA8 ........................... 134 F2
    WLTN L25 .......................... 131 L5
Oakston Av RAIN/WH L35 ........... 117 M3
Oak St BTL L20 ...................... 7 H2
    EP CH65 ........................... 156 E6
    GOL/RIS/CU WA3 ................... 106 C6
    STHEL WA9 ......................... 103 C5
    STHP PR8 ........................... 25 C7
    WGN WN1 ............................. 5 J4
Oaksway HES CH60 ................. 141 K7
Oakthorn Gv RNFD/HAY WA11 ....... 90 E7
Oak Tree Cl SKEL WN8 .............. 65 M2
Oaktree Pl RF/TRAN CH42 ......... 128 B2
Oaktree Rd ECCL WA10 ............. 88 C8
Oak V CLB/OSW/ST L13 ............. 114 D3
Oak Vw SPK/HALE L24 .............. 147 J2
Oakways WARRS WA4 ............... 137 M8
Oakwood SKEL WN8 .................. 65 M2
Oakwood Av AIMK WN4 ............... 91 J3
    STHEL WA9 .......................... 34 F7
    WARR WA1 ........................... 15 K2
    WGNNW/ST WN6 ...................... 55 H8
Oakwood Cl WLTN L25 .............. 115 K8
Oakwood Dr CL/PREN CH43 ......... 111 C5
    HUY L36 ........................... 116 B4
    STHP PR8 ........................... 35 C8
Oakwood Ga GOL/RIS/CU WA3 ...... 122 F1
Oakwood Rd CHLY/EC PR7 ........... 32 D7
    CHLY/EC PR7 ........................ 43 H3
    HLWD L26 .......................... 132 A6
Oakwood Vw CHLY/EC PR7 .......... 43 K1
Oakworth Dr HUY L36 .............. 116 C6
Oarside Dr WAL/NB CH45 ............ 95 J7
Oasis Cl BRSC L40 .................. 39 K2
Oatfield La LITH L21 ................ 83 L6
Oatlands Rd KKBY L32 .............. 85 L3
The Oatlands WKBY CH48 .......... 124 E4
Oban Dr AIMK WN4 .................. 90 E1
    HES CH60 .......................... 141 J5
Oban Gv WARRN/WOL WA2 .......... 122 C2
Oban Rd ANF/KKDL L4 ............... 97 K7
Oban Wy WGNE/HIN WN2 ............ 57 M8
Oberon St BTL L20 ................... 7 H9
O'brien Gv STHEL WA9 .............. 103 G1
Observatory Rd CL/PREN CH43 ..... 110 F5
Oceanic Rd CLB/OSW/ST L13 ....... 114 B2
Ocean Rd LITH L21 ................. 83 K6
O'connell Cl RNFD/HAY WA11 ...... 90 E7
O'connell Rd VAUX/LVPD L3 ........ 13 C2
Octavia Hill Rd LITH L21 ......... 83 L4
Odsey St EHL/KEN L7 .............. 113 L3
Off Botanic Rd CHTN/BK PR9 ...... 25 J4
Ogle La RAIN/WH L35 ............. 101 C8
Oglet La SPK/HALE L24 ............ 146 E3
Oil Sites Rd EP CH65 ............... 20 E2
Oil St VAUX/LVPD L3 ............... 12 C2
O'keeffe Rd STHEL WA9 .............. 9 M4
Okehampton Rd CHLDW L16 ......... 114 F5
Okell Dr HLWD L26 ................ 132 A3
Okell St RUNC WA7 ................. 19 G4
Okell Gv WLTN L25 ................. 81 M7
Okell St RUNC WA7 ................. 19 G4
Old Acre HTWN L38 ................. 70 B2
Old Barn Rd ANF/KKDL L4 .......... 97 K7
    WAL/EG CH44 ...................... 111 J2
Old Bidston Rd BIRK CH41 .......... 10 D2
Old Boston RNFD/HAY WA11 ........ 91 J6
Old Boundary Wy ORM L39 ......... 51 H7
Oldbridge Dr WGNW/BIL/O WN2 ..... 69 M7
Old Chester Rd BEB CH63 ......... 128 B6
    FROD/HEL WA6 ...................... 166 D2
    GTS/LS CH66 ...................... 155 M8
    RF/TRAN CH42 ...................... 128 B3
    WARRS WA4 ......................... 137 H6
Old Church Cl EP CH65 ............. 20 D1
Old Church Yd CLVP L2 ............. 12 E7
Old Colliery Rd RAIN/WH L35 ..... 116 F2
Old Colliery Yd AIMK WN4 .......... 90 E2
Old Dawber's La CHLY/EC PR7 ..... 31 K4
Old Distillery Rd SPK/HALE L24 ... 131 K8
Old Dover Rd HUY L36 ............. 115 L5
Old Eccleston La ECCL WA10 ...... 101 L2
Old Engine La SKEL WN8 ............ 64 E3
Old Farm Cl NSTN CH64 ........... 154 C5
Old Farm Rd CSBY/BLUN L23 ....... 83 H1
    KKBY L32 ........................... 86 B7
Oldfield Cl HES CH60 ............. 141 C3
Oldfield Dr HES CH60 ............. 140 E4
Oldfield Gdns HES CH60 ........... 140 E4
Oldfield La WKBY CH48 ............ 109 J8
Oldfield Rd ALL/GAR L19 .......... 130 C4
    EP CH65 ............................ 20 B5
    HES CH60 .......................... 140 F3
    LYMM WA13 ......................... 139 K1
Oldfield St ECCL WA10 .............. 8 F1
Old Fold HES CH60 ................ 140 F3
Old Fold Rd WGNW/BIL/O WN5 ...... 67 K7
Old Fold Rd WGNE/HIN WN2 ........ 57 M8
Oldgate WDN WA8 .................. 133 L7
Old Gorsey La WAL/EG CH44 ....... 111 K3
Old Hall RAIN/WH L35 ............ 117 C3
Old Hall Cl MGHL L31 .............. 72 F6
    WARRS WA4 ......................... 137 J5
Old Hall Dr AIMK WN4 ............. 91 J3
    EP CH65 ............................ 20 B7
Old Hall Gdns RNFD/HAY WA11 ..... 76 C7
Old Hall La CHLY/EC PR7 ........... 31 K7
    CHNE CH2 .......................... 165 K2
    KKBY L32 ........................... 85 M3
Old Hall Rd MGHL L31 ............. 72 F6
    PS/BROM CH62 ..................... 144 A4
    WARRW/BUR WA5 ................... 120 C5
    WGNS/IIMK WN3 ...................... 5 L5
Oldham Pl CLVPS L1 ................. 13 J8
Oldham St CLVPS L1 ................. 13 J7
    WARRS WA4 ......................... 15 H9
Old Haymarket CLVPS L1 ........... 13 H6

Old Higher Rd WDN WA8 ............ 132 F8
Old Hutte La SPK/HALE L24 ........ 132 C8
Old Kennel Cl STBRV L28 ........... 99 H5
Old Lea BRSC L40 .................. 40 F5
    FMBY L37 ............................ 47 H7
    MGHL L31 ........................... 73 G1
    ORM L39 ............................ 61 G2
    PR/KW L34 ......................... 101 H7
    RAIN/WH L35 ...................... 117 K3
    RNFD/HAY WA11 ...................... 76 B6
    WGNNW/ST WN6 ...................... 55 K7
Old Leeds St VAUX/LVPD L3 ......... 12 C5
Old Links Cl CHTN/BK PR9 .......... 25 K5
Old Liverpool Rd
    WARRW/BUR WA5 ...................... 14 A7
Old Lord's Crs HOR/BR BL6 ......... 45 K8
Old Maryland La
    MOR/LEA CH46 ...................... 110 A4
Old Meadow PR/KW L34 ............. 86 F8
Old Meadow Rd
    PEN/TH CH61 ...................... 141 H1
Old Mill Av STHEL WA9 ............ 102 F8
Old Mill Cl HES CH60 ............. 141 K6
Old Mill Hl ORM L39 ............... 62 F2
Old Mill La FMBY L37 ............... 59 H1
    PR/KW L34 ......................... 100 A1
    WAV L15 ........................... 114 C5
Old Moss La ORM L39 ............... 48 E8
Old Nook La RNFD/HAY WA11 ....... 90 A7
Old Orch RAIN/WH L35 ............ 117 C4
Old Park La CHTN/BK PR9 .......... 25 J6
Old Pepper La WGNNW/ST WN6 ...... 55 K3
Old Post Office Pl CLVPS L1 ....... 13 C8
Old Prescot Cl MGHL L31 ........... 73 L3
Old Pump La
    GR/UP/WCH CH49 ................... 125 L2
The Old Quarry WLTN L25 ......... 131 J3
Old Quay Cl NSTN CH64 ........... 152 E6
Old Quay La NSTN CH64 ........... 152 F6
Old Quay St RUNC WA7 ............ 19 G4
Old Racecourse Rd MGHL L31 ...... 72 D5
Old Rake HOR/BR BL6 .............. 45 M8
Old Rectory Gn ORM L39 ........... 62 C6
    SFTN L29 ............................ 72 A6
Old Riding DV/KA/FCH L14 ......... 99 H8
Old Rd AIMK WN4 .................... 91 G8
    WARRS WA4 ......................... 14 F8
Old Ropery CLVP L2 ................. 12 E7
Old Rough La NWD/KWIPK L33 ...... 86 A5
Old School Cl NSTN CH64 ......... 153 H8
Old School House La
    WARRN/WOL WA2 .................... 105 J6
Old School La CHLY/EC PR7 ........ 31 M2
    CHLY/EC PR7 ........................ 31 M2
    CHLY/EC PR7 ........................ 44 A8
Old School Pl AIMK WN4 ............ 91 J2
Old School Wy
    CL/PREN CH43 ..................... 111 C6
Old Smithy La LYMM WA13 ......... 139 L3
Old Thomas La DV/KA/FCH L14 ..... 114 F4
Old Town La FMBY L37 .............. 59 C1
Old Upton La WDN WA8 ............ 134 A1
Old Vicarage Rd NSTN CH64 ....... 154 C5
Old Wargrave Rd NEWLW WA12 ..... 104 D2
Old Whint Rd RNFD/HAY WA11 ..... 90 C7
Old Will's La HOR/BR BL6 ......... 45 K7
Old Wood Rd PEN/TH CH61 ......... 141 H1
Oleander Dr ECCL WA10 ........... 101 L1
O'leary St WARRN/WOL WA2 ........ 15 H1
Olga Rd STHEL WA9 ................ 102 E6
Olinda St PS/BROM CH62 .......... 128 D6
Olive Cl MGHL L31 ................. 85 J3
Olive Crs BIRK CH41 ............... 11 K9
Olivedale Rd CALD/MH L18 ......... 130 B1
Olive Dr NSTN CH64 ............... 153 C5
Olive Gv HUY L36 ................. 115M3
    NTHTN L30 .......................... 84 C4
    SKEL WN8 ........................... 65 C4
    STHP PR8 ........................... 25 C6
    WAV L15 ........................... 114 C4
    WGNNW/ST WN6 ...................... 68 B2
Olive La WAV L15 ................. 114 C5
Olive Mt BIRK CH41 ................ 11 K9
Olive Mount Rd WAV L15 .......... 114 C5
Olive Mt BIRK CH41 ................ 11 J6
    GTS/LS CH66 ...................... 162 F1
Oliver Lyme Rd PR/KW L34 ......... 101 C7
Oliver Rd ECCL WA10 .............. 101 L4
Oliver St BIRK CH41 ............... 11 J6
    WARRN/WOL WA2 ...................... 14 E3
Oliver St East BIRK CH41 .......... 11 J6
Olivetree Rd WAV L15 ............. 114 D5
Olive V WAV L15 .................. 114 B5
Olivia Cl CL/PREN CH43 ........... 126 E1
Olivia St BTL L20 ................... 7 J8
Ollerton Cl CL/PREN CH43 ......... 126 E1
    WARRS WA4 ......................... 138 D2
    WCNE/HIN WN2 ...................... 69 J3
Ollerton St CHLYE PR6 ............. 44 C5
Ollery Gn NTHTN L30 .............. 84 D1
Olney St ANF/KKDL L4 ............. 97 H3
Olton St WAV L15 ................. 114 B5
Olympia St NPK/KEN L6 ........... 113 J2
Olympic Wy WLT/FAZ L9 ............ 84 C5
O'neill St BTL L20 ................. 6 E2
Onslow Crs STHP PR8 .............. 35 J3
Onslow Rd NPK/KEN L6 ............ 113 L2
    PS/BROM CH62 ..................... 128 D5
    WAL/NB CH45 ....................... 95 K5
Opal Cl LITH L21 ................... 83 L5
Openfields Cl HLWD L26 .......... 132 A3
Oppenheim Av ECCL WA10 .......... 101 L5
Orange Gv TOX L8 ................. 113 L2
    WARRN/WOL WA2 .................... 122 A3
Orange Tree Cl STBRV L28 ......... 99 K5
Oran Wy HUY L36 ................. 115M2
Orb Cl NC/CROX L11 ............... 98 E2
Orchard Av CHLDW L16 ............ 114 F4
Orchard Cl CHLY/EC PR7 ........... 31 M1
    FROD/HEL WA6 ...................... 160 F4
    GTS/LS CH66 ...................... 163 H4
    PR/KW L34 .......................... 101 H3
    RAIN/WH L35 ...................... 117 C4
    RNFD/HAY WA11 ...................... 89M3
    WGNNW/ST WN6 ...................... 55 M3
Orchard Ct BIRK CH41 ............. 128 B2

Orchard Dl CSBY/BLUN L23 83 H1
Orchard Dr NSTN CH64 153 G8
Orchard Gra MOR/LEA CH46 109 L6
Orchard Hvn GTS/LS CH66 163 G4
Orchard Hey ECCL WA10 101 J2
MGHL L31 73 G5
NTHTN L30 84 D2
Orchard La GTS/LS CH66 155 J5
STHP PR8 47 M1
Orchard Park La CHNE CH2 165 K1
Orchard Pl FROD/HEL WA6 166 E1 4
Orchard Rd EP CH65 163 J3
MOR/LEA CH46 110 A4
Orchard St AIMK WN4 91 L2
WARR WA1 15 G5
WARRN/WOL WA2 122 C3
WARRS WA4 137 L5
WGN WN1 5 G3
The Orchard AIG/SPK L17 130 B4 2
FROD/HEL WA6 166 C3
HUY L36 116 A4
LEY/BBR PR5 29 L2
ORM L39 50 F8
WAL/NB CH45 95 J6
Orchard Vw ORM L39 62 F4
Orchard Wy BEB CH63 127 M7
WDN WA8 133 J2 1
Orchid Gv AIG/SPK L17 129 H2 2
Orchil Cl GTS/LS CH66 155 J7
Ordnance Av GOL/RIS/CU WA3 123 H1
O'reilly Ct VAUX/LVPD L3 12 E1
Orford Av WARRN/WOL WA2 15 G1
Orford Gn WARRN/WOL WA2 121 M4
Orford La WARRN/WOL WA2 14 F2
Orford Rd WARRN/WOL WA2 121 M5
Orford St WARR WA1 14 F5
WAV L15 114 B5
Organ St WGNE/HIN WN2 81 K2
Oriel Cl AIN/FAZ L10 84 F2
Oriel Crs BTL L20 7 H9
Oriel Dr AIN/FAZ L10 84 F2
Oriel Rd AIMK WN4 91 H1
BTL L20 6 F6
RF/TRAN CH42 128 A2
Oriel St VAUX/LVPD L3 12 F3
Orient Dr WLTN L25 131 K2
Origen Rd CHLDW L16 114 F4
Oriole Cl ECCL WA10 101 K6
Orith Av ECCL WA10 101 H2
Orkney Cl EP CH65 163 L4 4
RNFD/HAY WA11 89 M6
WDN WA8 135 G2
Orlando Cl CL/PREN CH43 126 E1 6
Orlando St BTL L20 7 H9
Orleans Rd CLB/OSW/ST L13 114 C2
Ormande St STHEL WA9 102 D4
Ormesby Gv BEB CH63 143 J7
Ormiston Rd WAL/NB CH45 95 K6
Ormond Av BRSC L40 63 M1
Ormonde Av MGHL L31 72 E6
Ormonde Crs NWD/KWIPK L33 86 C3
Ormonde Dr MGHL L31 72 E5
Ormond St VAUX/LVPD L3 12 E6
WAL/NB CH45 95 K8 6
Ormond Wy CL/PREN CH43 126 E1
Ormsby Cl WGNNW/ST WN6 56 A4
Ormsby St WAV L15 114 A6 3
Ormside Cl WGNE/HIN WN2 81 K2
Ormside Gv STHEL WA9 102 F6
Ormskirk Old Rd ORM L39 64 B6
Ormskirk Rd ORM L39 63 L4
PR/KW L34 86 F8
RNFD/HAY WA11 75 M4
SKEL WN8 64 E4 1
SKEL WN8 66 C6
WGNW/BIL/O WN5 67 L7
WLT/FAZ L9 84 D3
Ormskirk St ECCL WA10 8 F4
Ormston Av HOR/BR BL6 45 K8
Orms Wy FMBY L37 59 G2
Orphan Dr NPK/KEN L6 97 M8
Orphan St EHL/KEN L7 113 J5
Orpington St
WGNW/BIL/O WN5 67 L7 4
Orrell Cl WARRW/BUR WA5 120 C7 2
Orrell Gdns WGNW/BIL/O WN5 67 H7
Orrell Hall Cl WGNW/BIL/O WN5 67 K6
Orrell Hey BTL L20 83 M6
Orrell Hill La HTWN L38 70 E1
Orrell La BRSC L40 38 F8
BTL L20 84 B6
WLT/FAZ L9 84 C7
Orrell Mt BTL L20 83 L6
Orrell Rd BTL L20 83 L6
WAL/NB CH45 95 L6
WGNW/BIL/O WN5 67 G6
Orrell St STHEL WA9 9 M5
WGN WN1 5 G6
Orret's Meadow Rd
GR/UP/WCH CH49 126 D2
Orrysdale Rd WKBY CH48 124 C2
Orry St EV L5 96 F8
Orsett Rd KKBY L32 86 B5
Orston Crs BEB CH63 143 J3
Ortega Cl PS/BROM CH62 128 E6 1
Orthes St VAUX/LVPD L3 13 L8 1
Orton Rd CHLDW L16 114 E5
Orton Wy AIMK WN4 91 H2
Orville St STHEL WA9 103 H6 2
Orwell Cl FMBY L37 58 E4
STHEL WA9 118 C2
Orwell Rd ANF/KKDL L4 96 F5
Osbert Rd CSBY/BLUN L23 82 D1
Osborne Av WAL/NB CH45 95 K6
WARRN/WOL WA2 121 M4 2
Osborne Gv WAL/NB CH45 95 K7
Osborne Rd AIMK WN4 91 J1
CL/PREN CH43 10 D7
CLB/OSW/ST L13 98 A7
ECCL WA10 88 C8
FMBY L37 59 G4
GOL/RIS/CU WA3 93 G6
LITH L21 83 L4
STHP PR8 34 D7
WAL/NB CH45 95 L6 10
WARRS WA4 137 K4
Osborne Wd AIG/SPK L17 129 M4
Osbourne Cl PS/BROM CH62 144 A6 1
Osier Cl CHNE CH2 165 L2
Osmaston Rd RF/TRAN CH42 127 J3
Osprey Cl CHLYE PR6 33 J2
NTHLY L27 116 B8 3
RUNC WA7 150 B8
WARRN/WOL WA2 122 A2
The Ospreys WGNS/IIMK WN3 78 E1 2
Ossett Cl CL/PREN CH43 126 E1 7
RUNC WA7 150 F5 4
Osterley Gdns WLT/FAZ L9 84 B7
O'sullivan Crs RNFD/HAY WA11 90 A8
Oteley Av PS/BROM CH62 143 M5
Othello Cl BTL L20 7 H9
Otterburn Cl MOR/LEA CH46 109 K5
Otterspool Dr AIG/SPK L17 129 M5
Otterspool Rd AIG/SPK L17 129 M4
Otterton Rd NG/CROX L11 85 L8 2
Otterwood Sq
WGNW/BIL/O WN5 67 L3
Ottery Cl CHTN/BK PR9 22 C8
Ottley St NPK/KEN L6 113 L2
Otway St ALL/GAR L19 145 L1
Oueenswood Av BEB CH63 128 A5
Oulton Cl CL/PREN CH43 127 G2
MGHL L31 72 D1 2
Oulton La HUY L36 115 L5
Oulton Rd CHLDW L16 114 F7
Oulton Wy CL/PREN CH43 127 G2 2
Oundle Dr AIN/FAZ L10 84 E2 2
Oundle Pl WLTN L25 131 K6
Oundle Rd MOR/LEA CH46 110 A4
Outer Central Rd SPK/HALE L24 132 A8
Outer Forum NG/CROX L11 98 A3
Out La LEY/BBR PR5 29 K3
WLTN L25 131 K3
Outlet La MGHL L31 74 A4
Outterside St CHLY/EC PR7 44 C7
The Oval EP CH65 20 D8
WAL/NB CH45 95 H7
WGNNW/ST WN6 55 H8
Overbeck Cl WGNNW/ST WN6 68 C1
Overbrook La PR/KW L34 86 E8
Overbury St EHL/KEN L7 113 K4
Overchurch Rd
GR/UP/WCH CH49 110 A7
Overdale Av PEN/TH CH61 126 F8
Overdale Rd NSTN CH64 154 C4
Overdene Wk KKBY L32 86 B4
Overgreen Gv
MOR/LEA CH46 109 M4 2
Overhill Wy WGNS/IIMK WN3 78 F2
Overpool Gdns GTS/LS CH66 163 H2 2
Overpool Rd EP CH65 156 B8
GTS/LS CH66 156 A7
Overton Av LITH L21 83 K4
Overton Cl CL/PREN CH43 127 H2
KKBY L32 85 M4
Overton Dr FROD/HEL WA6 160 E7
Overton Rd WAL/EG CH44 111 K1 5
Overton St EHL/KEN L7 113 K4
Overton Wy CL/PREN CH43 127 H2
Ovington Cl RUNC WA7 161 H1 10
Ovington Dr STHP PR8 36 A2
Ovolo Rd CLB/OSW/ST L13 114 C1
Owen Av ORM L39 51 H7 5
Owen Cl ECCL WA10 101 L4
Owen Dr SPK/HALE L24 146 D3
Owen Rd ANF/KKDL L4 96 F5
NWD/KWIPK L33 86 E6
RAIN/WH L35 117 L3
Owen's La ORM L39 61 G3
Owens St CHLYE PR6 33 G6 6
Owen St ECCL WA10 101 L4
LEIGH WN7 81 M8 13
WARRN/WOL WA2 14 D2
Oxborough Cl WDN WA8 134 B1 4
Oxbow Rd WD/CROXPK L12 99 G5
Oxburgh Rd WGNE/HIN WN2 80 B1
Oxendale Cl TOX L8 113 K6 7
Oxenham Rd WARRN/WOL WA2 121 J2
Oxenholme Crs NG/CROX L11 98 C3 1
Oxford Av BTL L20 7 L5
LITH L21 83 K5
Oxford Cl AIG/SPK L17 129 L3 3
GTS/LS CH66 163 G5
Oxford Ct STHP PR8 35 H1
WGN WN1 5 G4
Oxford Dr BEB CH63 142 B7
CSBY/WL L22 82 E4
HLWD L26 132 B5
Oxford Gdns STHP PR8 2 B9
Oxford Rd BTL L20 7 K5
CSBY/WL L22 82 E3
HUY L36 116 C1
RUNC WA7 19 G6
SKEL WN8 65 G4
STHP PR8 2 A8
WAL/EG CH44 111 L1 5
WGNW/BIL/O WN5 67 H6
WLT/FAZ L9 84 D5
Oxford St CHLY/EC PR7 32 E6 11
CHLY/EC PR7 44 B7
ECCL WA10 8 E3
EHL/KEN L7 13 L8
NEWLW WA12 104 D2 11
WARRS WA4 15 H8
WDN WA8 16 E5
Oxheys RUNC WA7 150 E5
Oxhouse Rd WGNW/BIL/O WN5 77 L1
Ox La RAIN/WH L35 116 E7
Oxley Av MOR/LEA CH46 110 D2
Oxley St STHEL WA9 102 F6 5
Oxmead Cl WARRN/WOL WA2 122 D4
Oxmoor Cl RUNC WA7 150 C8 2
Oxton Cl AIG/SPK L17 129 L3
KKBY L32 85 K5
WDN WA8 133 L1
Oxton Gn GTS/LS CH66 162 F1 4
Oxton Rd BIRK CH41 10 F8
WAL/EG CH44 111 K2
Oxton St ANF/KKDL L4 97 H5


# P


Pacific Rd BIRK CH41 11 M3
BTL L20 6 E3
Packenham Rd
CLB/OSW/ST L13 98 B7 1
Paddington EHL/KEN L7 113 J4 4
Paddington Bank WARR WA1 122 B7
Paddock Cl CSBY/BLUN L23 70 D7
Paddock Dr NSTN CH64 152 F3
Paddock Gv STHEL WA9 118 F2
Paddock Hey NTHLY L27 115 M7
Paddock Ri RUNC WA7 161 G1
WGNNW/ST WN6 68 A2
Paddock Rd SKEL WN8 65 L8
The Paddock AIMK WN4 79 H7
BRSC L40 39 L1
CHNE CH2 165 J2
FMBY L37 47 J8
FROD/HEL WA6 166 E3
GR/UP/WCH CH49 110 D8
GTS/LS CH66 162 F2
HES CH60 141 L5
KKBY L32 85 M6 1
MOR/LEA CH46 109 L6
ORM L39 62 E2
PR/KW L34 101 H6
STHP PR8 47 K1
WLTN L25 131 K1
Padeswood Cl STHEL WA9 102 F7 5
Padgate La WARR WA1 15 L2
WARR WA1 122 A5
Padstow Cl CHTN/BK PR9 22 C8
HLWD L26 132 A4
WARRW/BUR WA5 136 A2
Padstow Dr ECCL WA10 88 D7
Padstow Rd CHLDW L16 114 F5
GR/UP/WCH CH49 125 L3
Pagebank Rd DV/KA/FCH L14 115 J2
Page Ct FMBY L37 59 H2
Pagefield Cl WGNNW/ST WN6 4 B1
Pagefield Rd WAV L15 114 C7 2
Pagefield St WGNNW/ST WN6 4 B1
Page La WDN WA8 17 H2
Page Moss Av HUY L36 115 K1
Page Moss La PR/KW L34 115 J2
Page Wk VAUX/LVPD L3 13 K4
Pagewood Cl CL/PREN CH43 126 F1 5
Paignton Cl HUY L36 116 D2 2
WARRW/BUR WA5 136 A1
WGNW/BIL/O WN5 78 A5
Paignton Rd CHLDW L16 114 F5
WAL/NB CH45 95 G7
Painswick Rd GTS/LS CH66 163 G3
Paisley Av PS/BROM CH62 155 G1
RNFD/HAY WA11 89 M6
Paisley St VAUX/LVPD L3 12 C4
Palace Ar AIMK WN4 91 K2
Palace Fields Av RUNC WA7 150 C6
Palace Hey NSTN CH64 153 J8
Palace Rd STHP PR8 2 A8
WLT/FAZ L9 84 C7
Palatine Cl WGNS/IIMK WN3 79 G1
Palatine Rd PS/BROM CH62 143 L4
STHP PR8 2 C7
WAL/EG CH44 111 M3
Palatine Sq LEIGH WN7 81 M8
Palermo Cl WAL/EG CH44 111 M3
Palewood Cl WGN WN1 5 H1
Paley Cl ANF/KKDL L4 97 H6
Palin Dr WARRW/BUR WA5 120 B7 4
Palin St WGNE/HIN WN2 81 K2 5
Palladio Rd CLB/OSW/ST L13 114 D1
Palliser Cl GOL/RIS/CU WA3 123 J2
Pall Ml CHLY/EC PR7 32 E7
VAUX/LVPD L3 12 E3
Palm Av AIMK WN4 78 F8
Palm Cl WLT/FAZ L9 97 L2
Palm Ct SKEL WN8 65 G3
Palmer Cl ECCL WA10 8 E4
Palmer Crs WARRW/BUR WA5 120 F5
Palmerston Av LITH L21 83 J7 6
Palmerston Cl CALD/MH L18 130 B2
Palmerston Dr LITH L21 83 K7
Palmerston Rd ALL/GAR L19 130 E7
CALD/MH L18 130 B2
CHTN/BK PR9 25 H7
WAL/EG CH44 111 H1
Palmerston St
RF/TRAN CH42 128 B3 10
Palm Gv CHTN/BK PR9 3 M5
CL/PREN CH43 10 C7
GTS/LS CH66 163 J4
STHP PR8 25 G7 1
WGNW/BIL/O WN5 67 M7
WLTN L25 131 K4
Palm Hl CL/PREN CH43 10 C9
Palmwood Av RAIN/WH L35 117 M3
Palmwood Cl CL/PREN CH43 127 G4
Palmyra Sq North WARR WA1 14 D6
Palmyra Sq South WARR WA1 14 D7
Paltridge Wy PEN/TH CH61 141 H1 2
Pamela Cl AIN/FAZ L10 85 K6
Pampas Gv WLT/FAZ L9 97 K1 3
Pangbourne Cl WARRS WA4 138 A7
Pankhurst Rd LITH L21 83 L3
Pansy St EV L5 96 F6
Parade Crs SPK/HALE L24 147 G3
Parade St ECCL WA10 9 H4
The Parade NSTN CH64 152 D4
Paradise La FMBY L37 47 G4
RAIN/WH L35 116 F3
Paradise St CHLYE PR6 33 H2
CLVPS L1 13 G7 1
Paragon Cl WDN WA8 118 D8 2
Parbold Av RNFD/HAY WA11 89 M8
Parbold Cl BRSC L40 52 A2 2
Parbold Hl SKEL WN8 53 M3
Parbrook Cl HUY L36 99 M7
Parbrook La WGNNW/ST WN6 55 K6
Parbrook Rd HUY L36 99 M8
The Parchments NEWLW WA12 104 F1
Paris Av WGNS/IIMK WN3 78 E2
Park Av CALD/MH L18 130 A2
CHLY/EC PR7 31 M3
CHTN/BK PR9 25 G4
CSBY/BLUN L23 71 G8
FMBY L37 59 H4
GOL/RIS/CU WA3 92 B3
MGHL L31 72 F2
ORM L39 51 G8
PR/KW L34 101 H6
RAIN/WH L35 117 L1
RNFD/HAY WA11 90 C7
WAL/EG CH44 111 M2 11
WARRS WA4 137 M2
WDN WA8 16 E1
WGNNW/ST WN6 55 K6
WGNW/BIL/O WN5 78 A4
WLT/FAZ L9 84 F6
Park Av North NEWLW WA12 104 E3
Park Av South NEWLW WA12 104 E3
Park Bvd WARR WA1 14 E8
Parkbourn MGHL L31 73 J3
Parkbourn Dr MGHL L31 73 J3
Parkbourn North MGHL L31 73 J3
Parkbourn Sq MGHL L31 73 J3 1
Parkbridge Rd
RF/TRAN CH42 127 L2 4
Park Brow Dr KKBY L32 86 B5
Park Cl BIRK CH41 10 F5
FMBY L37 59 G5
KKBY L32 85 K2
SKEL WN8 53 L2
Park Ct CSBY/WL L22 83 G4
RUNC WA7 19 G8
Park Crs CHTN/BK PR9 24 F4
ORM L39 61 H1
WARRS WA4 137 M7
WGN WN1 4 C2
Park Crs West WGN WN1 4 C2
Parkdale Av WLT/FAZ L9 84 C6
Parkdale Rd WARR WA1 122 C6
Park Dr BIRK CH41 10 A3
CL/PREN CH43 10 A4
CSBY/BLUN L23 71 J6
CSBY/BLUN L23 82 C1
EP CH65 20 A8
Parkend Dr LEIGH WN7 93 M3
Parkend Rd RF/TRAN CH42 127 L2
Parker Av LITH L21 83 H6
Parker Cl NTHTN L30 84 D4
Parker Crs ORM L39 51 H6
Parkers Ct RUNC WA7 150 A7
Parker St CHLY/EC PR7 32 E4
CLVPS L1 13 H8
RUNC WA7 19 J2
WARR WA1 14 C7
Parkfield WGNNW/ST WN6 55 K6
Parkfield Av BIRK CH41 11 H5
NTHTN L30 84 C4
WARRS WA4 138 C1
Parkfield Cl BIRK CH41 10 F3
ORM L39 62 E2
Parkfield Dr EP CH65 163 J3
FROD/HEL WA6 166 D2
WAL/EG CH44 111 K1
Parkfield Gv MGHL L31 72 E4
Parkfield Pl BIRK CH41 11 G5
Parkfield Rd AIG/SPK L17 129 K1
BEB CH63 143 J2
CSBY/WL L22 83 G3
Parkfields WGNE/HIN WN2 80 D6
Parkfields La WARRN/WOL WA2 122 B3
Parkgate La NSTN CH64 142 A8
Parkgate Rd CH/BCN CH1 162 B7
NSTN CH64 152 E5
WARRS WA4 137 M4
Parkgate Wy RUNC WA7 150 E6
Park Gv BIRK CH41 11 G8
Park Hall Rd CHLY/EC PR7 42 B2
Park Hey Dr WGNNW/ST WN6 55 G6
Parkhill Rd RF/TRAN CH42 127 L2
Park Hill Rd TOX L8 129 H1
Parkhurst Rd NG/CROX L11 98 B4
RF/TRAN CH42 127 L3 2
Parkinson Rd WLT/FAZ L9 97 J1
Parkland Ct CL/PREN CH43 110 E5
Parkland Dr CHNE CH2 165 K2
Parklands CHTN/BK PR9 25 G5
GTS/LS CH66 155 M8
PR/KW L34 99 M2
RNFD/HAY WA11 76 B6
SKEL WN8 65 M2 5
WDN WA8 133 L2
Parklands Dr HES CH60 141 K7
WGNE/HIN WN2 57 L7
Parklands Gdns GTS/LS CH66 155 M7
Parklands Vw GTS/LS CH66 155 M7
Parklands Wy CSBY/WL L22 83 H4
Park La BTL L20 84 A6
CLVPS L1 13 G9
CLVPS L1 112 F5
FROD/HEL WA6 160 D5
HOY CH47 109 J3
KIRK/FR/WA PR4 27 K3
MGHL L31 73 G2
NTHTN L30 84 B3
WARRS WA4 137 H8
WGNE/HIN WN2 80 D6
WGNE/HIN WN2 81 G7
Park Lane Dr MGHL L31 73 K3 1
Park La West NTHTN L30 84 B2
Parklea GTS/LS CH66 155 M7
Park Link ORM L39 62 D4
Park Pl BTL L20 7 H5
TOX L8 113 H7
Park Rd CHLY/EC PR7 32 E4
CHLY/EC PR7 43 G4
CHLY/EC PR7 44 A7
CHNE CH2 165 G4
CSBY/WL L22 83 G4
EP CH65 20 C7
FMBY L37 59 G4
HES CH60 141 K4
HOY CH47 109 G4
KKBY L32 85 L1 2
NEWLW WA12 92 B6
NSTN CH64 154 D5
ORM L39 51 G8
PR/KW L34 100 E6
PS/BROM CH62 128 D8
PS/BROM CH62 144 B7
RF/TRAN CH42 128 A2
RUNC WA7 18 F8
STHEL WA9 9 M4
TOX L8 113 H8
TOX L8 129 J1 18
WAL/EG CH44 111 L2
WARRN/WOL WA2 121 M4
WARRW/BUR WA5 119 L6
WDN WA8 16 F1
WGNE/HIN WN2 81 G2
WGNNW/ST WN6 4 B1
WGNW/BIL/O WN5 67 J7
WGNW/BIL/O WN5 78 A4
WKBY CH48 124 C3
Park Rd East BIRK CH41 10 F6
Park Rd North BIRK CH41 10 A3
NEWLW WA12 105 G2
Park Rd South NEWLW WA12 104 F3
Park Rd West CHTN/BK PR9 24 E4
CL/PREN CH43 10 A4
Parkside WAL/EG CH44 111 L2
Parkside Av AIMK WN4 79 H5
CHLY/EC PR7 32 E5
STHEL WA9 118 D2
Parkside Cl BEB CH63 128 C7
NTHLY L27 132 A1 2
Parkside Crs WGNW/BIL/O WN5 67 H7
Parkside Dr WD/CROXPK L12 98 C5
Parkside Rd BEB CH63 128 C7
NEWLW WA12 105 K4
RF/TRAN CH42 128 A2
Parkside St NPK/KEN L6 13 M3
The Parks RNFD/HAY WA11 91 K4
Parkstile La NG/CROX L11 98 E1
Parkstone Rd RF/TRAN CH42 127 L2
Park St BIRK CH41 11 H5
BIRK CH41 11 H4
BTL L20 7 H5
CHLY/EC PR7 30 E7 1
CHLY/EC PR7 32 E5
NSTN CH64 153 G5
RNFD/HAY WA11 90 B7
STHEL WA9 9 M4
TOX L8 113 G8
WAL/EG CH44 111 L1
WGNS/IIMK WN3 4 D7
Parksway WARR WA1 122 F6
Park Ter CSBY/WL L22 83 G5
The Park HUY L36 116 A4
WARRW/BUR WA5 135 M2
Parkvale Av CL/PREN CH43 127 G5
Park Vale Rd WLT/FAZ L9 84 C7
Park Vw AIMK WN4 91 K3
CSBY/WL L22 82 F3
HUY L36 115 L1
NPK/KEN L6 97 M8
PS/BROM CH62 143 L5
WGNE/HIN WN2 80 D4
Parkview Dr NTHLY L27 132 A1
Parkview Rd NG/CROX L11 98 F1
Park Wall Rd HTWN L38 71 H2
SFTN L29 71 J4
Park Wy FMBY L37 59 H4
HOY CH47 109 G5
HUY L36 99 M6 1
TOX L8 113 H6 11
Parkway CSBY/BLUN L23 83 H3
NTHTN L30 72 A8
WAL/NB CH45 95 G6
WGNNW/ST WN6 55 J3
Parkway Cl
GR/UP/WCH CH49 126 B6 1
Park Wy West KKBY L32 85 K2 3
Park West HES CH60 140 F6
Parkwood Cl LYMM WA13 139 M3
PS/BROM CH62 144 A5 2
WGNS/IIMK WN3 5 K8
Parkwood Rd RAIN/WH L35 117 G3
WLTN L25 131 J1 1
Parlane St STHEL WA9 9 L3
Parliament Pl TOX L8 113 H6 12
Parliament St RAIN/WH L35 101 M6
SKEL WN8 66 E5
TOX L8 112 F6
WGNS/IIMK WN3 5 H7
Parliament Wy GTS/LS CH66 163 H5
Parlington Cl WDN WA8 133 L6
Parlow Rd NG/CROX L11 98 A5
Parnell Rd BEB CH63 143 J3
Parr Cottage Cl CHLY/EC PR7 30 E6 3
Parren Av RAIN/WH L35 116 E4
Parr Gv GR/UP/WCH CH49 125 L1
RNFD/HAY WA11 90 C7 5
Parr La CHLY/EC PR7 30 D6
Parr Mount St STHEL WA9 9 M5
Parr's La ORM L39 62 F5
Parrs Rd CL/PREN CH43 127 K2
Parr St CLVPS L1 13 H9
LITH L21 83 K4
STHEL WA9 9 J6
WARR WA1 14 F7
WDN WA8 17 G1 1
Parrs Wood View WARRS WA4 138 C4
Parry Dr WARRS WA4 139 G2
Parry St WAL/EG CH44 111 M3 2
Parsonage Brow SKEL WN8 66 B5
Parsonage Cl SKEL WN8 66 C6
Parsonage Rd SKEL WN8 66 C6
WDN WA8 149 J1 5
Parsonage Wy
WARRW/BUR WA5 120 C8 2
Parson's Brow CHLY/EC PR7 32 E6 12
RNFD/HAY WA11 76 A7
Parson's Wk WGN WN1 4 D2
Parthenon Dr NG/CROX L11 97 M2
Partington Av BTL L20 7 L2
Partington St
WGNW/BIL/O WN5 68 A5 2
Parton St NPK/KEN L6 113 L2
Partridge Cl GOL/RIS/CU WA3 123 G1
WD/CROXPK L12 99 H5
Partridge Rd CSBY/BLUN L23 82 D1 3
KKBY L32 85 K2
Part St STHP PR8 2 F7
Pasture Av MOR/LEA CH46 110 A3
Pasture Cl AIMK WN4 79 G7
STHEL WA9 118 E1
WLTN L25 131 K4
Pasture Crs MOR/LEA CH46 110 A4
Pasture Dr GOL/RIS/CU WA3 106 C6
Pasture La RNFD/HAY WA11 88 C1
WARRN/WOL WA2 122 D4
Pasture Rd MOR/LEA CH46 109 M2
The Pastures CHTN/BK PR9 22 F8 3
WKBY CH48 125 H3 1

Pateley Cl KKBY L32 ..... 85 L4
Paterson St BIRK CH41 ..... 10 F6
Patmos Ct EV L5 ..... 97 G7
Paton Cl WKBY L48 ..... 124 E2
Patricia Av BIRK CH41 ..... 111 G4
Patricia Gv BTL L20 ..... 83 M7
Patrick Av BTL L20 ..... 83 M6
Patricroft Rd WGNE/HIN WN2 ..... 5 L6
Patten La WARR WA1 ..... 14 E6
Patten's Cl NTHTN L30 ..... 83 M1
Patten St BIRK CH41 ..... 10 C2
Patten's Wk PR/KW L34 ..... 87 G8
Patterdale Av WARRN/WOL WA2 ..... 121 L3
Patterdale Cl STHP PR8 ..... 47 K2
Patterdale Crs MGHL L31 ..... 73 G3
Patterdale Dr ECCL WA10 ..... 101 K5
Patterdale Pl WGNE/HIN WN2 ..... 69 J6
Patterdale Rd AIMK WN4 ..... 79 J5
   BEB CH63 ..... 143 H2
   WAV L15 ..... 114 B7
Patterson Cl GOL/RIS/CU WA3 ..... 123 G2
Patterson St NEWLW WA12 ..... 104 D1
Paul Cl WARRW/BUR WA5 ..... 119 M7
Pauline St WGNE/HIN WN2 ..... 81 K4
Paul MacCartney Wy NPK/KEN L6 ..... 113 K2
Paul Orr Ct VAUX/LVPD L3 ..... 12 E2
Paulsfield Dr MOR/LEA CH46 ..... 110 A6
Paul's La CHTN/BK PR9 ..... 25 K7
Paul St VAUX/LVPD L3 ..... 12 F3
   WARRN/WOL WA2 ..... 14 C4
Paulton Cl TOX L8 ..... 129 H1
Paveley Bank NTHLY L27 ..... 115 M8
Pavilion Cl TOX L8 ..... 113 K6
Pavilion Vw LEY/BBR PR5 ..... 29 K3
Paxton Cl SKEL WN8 ..... 76 E1
Paxton Rd HUY L36 ..... 116 A1
Payne Cl WARRW/BUR WA5 ..... 120 F7
Paythorne Cl GOL/RIS/CU WA3 ..... 107 H2
Peacehaven Cl CHLDW L16 ..... 115 H5
Peach Gv MGHL L31 ..... 85 K1
   RNFD/HAY WA11 ..... 91 G6
Peacock Av WARR WA1 ..... 15 M3
Peacock Fold LEIGH WN7 ..... 81 M7
Pearce Cl WLTN L25 ..... 115 H7
Pear Gv NPK/KEN L6 ..... 113 K2
Pearl St WGNW/ST WN6 ..... 68 D2
Pearson Av WARRS WA4 ..... 137 M3
Pearson Dr BTL L20 ..... 84 A6
Pearson Rd BIRK CH41 ..... 11 J8
Pearson St WAV L15 ..... 114 B6
Pear Tree Av CHLY/EC PR7 ..... 7 J8
   RUNC WA7 ..... 19 M9
Peartree Av WD/CROXPK L12 ..... 99 H4
Peartree Cl FROD/HEL WA6 ..... 160 F4
Pear Tree La CHLY/EC PR7 ..... 32 A2
Peartree Pl WARRS WA4 ..... 15 G8
Pear Tree Rd HUY L36 ..... 116 A5
Peartree Rd LEY/BBR PR5 ..... 29 K2
Pear Tree Wy GTS/LS CH66 ..... 163 G4
Peasefield Rd DV/KA/FCH L14 ..... 115 J1
Peasley Cl WARRN/WOL WA2 ..... 122 D4
Peasley Cross La STHEL WA9 ..... 9 L8
Peatwood Av KKBY L32 ..... 86 B6
Peckers Hill Rd STHEL WA9 ..... 103 G6
Peckfield Cl RUNC WA7 ..... 150 C8
Peckforton Cl CLB/OSW/ST L13 ..... 98 A7
Peckforton Dr GTS/LS CH66 ..... 163 G2
   RUNC WA7 ..... 161 H1
Peckmill Gn NTHLY L27 ..... 132 B1
Peck Mill La FROD/HEL WA6 ..... 166 C6
Peebles Av RNFD/HAY WA11 ..... 89 M7
Peebles Cl AIMK WN4 ..... 90 E1
   GTS/LS CH66 ..... 155 H7
   NWD/KWIPK L33 ..... 73 M7
Peech St EHL/KEN L7 ..... 13 M8
Peel Av BIRK CH41 ..... 128 B2
Peel Cl RAIN/WH L35 ..... 117 G2
   WARR WA1 ..... 122 F7
Peel House La WDN WA8 ..... 134 D2
Peel Pl TOX L8 ..... 113 H6
Peel Rd BTL L20 ..... 6 C1
   SKEL WN8 ..... 66 A8
Peel St CHLY/EC PR7 ..... 32 E6
   CHLYE PR6 ..... 44 D5
   NEWLW WA12 ..... 104 C2
   RUNC WA7 ..... 18 F2
   STHP PR8 ..... 25 H7
   TOX L8 ..... 129 J1
   WGNE/HIN WN2 ..... 80 C3
Peerswood Ct NSTN CH64 ..... 153 G8
Peet Av ECCL WA10 ..... 101 L1
   ORM L39 ..... 62 F1
Peet's La CHTN/BK PR9 ..... 25 J4
Peet St EHL/KEN L7 ..... 113 K4
Pelham Gv AIG/SPK L17 ..... 129 L1
Pelham Rd WAL/EG CH44 ..... 111 J2
   WARRS WA4 ..... 138 E2
Pemberlei Rd WGNE/HIN WN2 ..... 69 M3
Pemberton Cl NSTN CH64 ..... 154 C5
Pemberton Rd CLB/OSW/ST L13 ..... 114 C2
   GR/UP/WCH CH49 ..... 126 D2
   WGNS/IIMK WN3 ..... 78 D4
Pembertons Ct PR/KW L34 ..... 101 G7
Pemberton St ECCL WA10 ..... 8 D6
Pembrey Wy WLTN L25 ..... 131 M5
Pembroke Ct MOR/LEA CH46 ..... 110 A6
Pembroke Dr EP CH65 ..... 163 J2
Pembroke Gdns VAUX/LVPD L3 ..... 13 L6
Pembroke Pl CHLY/EC PR7 ..... 32 D7
   VAUX/LVPD L3 ..... 13 L6
Pembroke Rd BTL L20 ..... 7 G5
   VAUX/LVPD L3 ..... 13 L6
   WGNE/HIN WN2 ..... 81 L2
   WGNW/BIL/O WN5 ..... 67 M4
Pembroke St VAUX/LVPD L3 ..... 13 L6
Pembury Cl WD/CROXPK L12 ..... 99 G2
Penare Gorran Hvn RUNC WA7 ..... 150 E7
Penarth Cl EHL/KEN L7 ..... 113 K5
Penbury Rd WGN WN1 ..... 56 D8

Pencombe Rd HUY L36 ..... 115 K1
Pendennis Crs WGNE/HIN WN2 ..... 81 J2
Pendennis Rd WAL/EG CH44 ..... 111 K2
Pendine Cl NPK/KEN L6 ..... 113 L1
   WARRW/BUR WA5 ..... 120 E3
Pendle Av RNFD/HAY WA11 ..... 89 M8
Pendlebury La WGN WN1 ..... 56 E7
Pendlebury St STHEL WA9 ..... 118 E1
   WARRS WA4 ..... 138 B2
Pendle Cl GR/UP/WCH CH49 ..... 110 A7
   WGNW/BIL/O WN5 ..... 67 M8
Pendle Dr HOR/BR BL6 ..... 45 L8
   LITH L21 ..... 83 L1
   ORM L39 ..... 51 J7
Pendle Gdns GOL/RIS/CU WA3 ..... 107 G2
Pendle Hill Cl GOL/RIS/CU WA3 ..... 92 E4
Pendle Rd GOL/RIS/CU WA3 ..... 92 E4
Pendleton Gn HLWD L26 ..... 132 A6
Pendleton Rd ANF/KKDL L4 ..... 97 J3
Penfold Cl CALD/MH L18 ..... 114 F8
   CH/BCN CH1 ..... 162 D5
Penfolds RUNC WA7 ..... 149 M4
Pengallo Hey NTHLY L27 ..... 116 B8
Pengwern Gv WAV L15 ..... 113 M5
Pengwern St TOX L8 ..... 113 J8
Penhale Cl AIG/SPK L17 ..... 129 K3
Peninsula Cl WAL/NB CH45 ..... 95 G5
Penistone Dr GTS/LS CH66 ..... 155 K8
Penketh Av WARRW/BUR WA5 ..... 121 H5
Penketh Gn SPK/HALE L24 ..... 147 G1
Penketh Pl SKEL WN8 ..... 65 L8
Penketh Rd WARRW/BUR WA5 ..... 136 C1
Penketh's La RUNC WA7 ..... 19 G2
Penketh St WGNNW/ST WN6 ..... 68 D3
Penkett Gv WAL/NB CH45 ..... 95 L7
Penkett Rd WAL/NB CH45 ..... 95 L7
Penkford La WARRW/BUR WA5 ..... 103 M4
Penkmans La STHEL WA9 ..... 103 G6
Penley Crs KKBY L32 ..... 85 K3
Penmann Cl HLWD L26 ..... 132 B6
Penmann Crs HLWD L26 ..... 132 B6
Penmark Cl WARRW/BUR WA5 ..... 120 E3
Penmon Dr PEN/TH CH61 ..... 141 H2
Pennant Cl GOL/RIS/CU WA3 ..... 123 J2
Pennard Av HUY L36 ..... 99 M8
Pennell Dr WGNS/IIMK WN3 ..... 68 B8
Pennine Av CHLY/EC PR7 ..... 31 M4
   WGNS/IIMK WN3 ..... 78 E2
Pennine Dr STHEL WA9 ..... 103 H2
Pennine Gv LEIGH WN7 ..... 81 L5
Pennine La GOL/RIS/CU WA3 ..... 92 E4
Pennine Pl SKEL WN8 ..... 65 K7
Pennine Rd CHLYE PR6 ..... 33 G4
   HOR/BR BL6 ..... 45 L8
   RF/TRAN CH42 ..... 127 L4
   WAL/EG CH44 ..... 111 H1
   WARRN/WOL WA2 ..... 122 A3
Pennine Wy KKBY L32 ..... 85 L1
Pennington Av BTL L20 ..... 83 M8
   ORM L39 ..... 51 G7
Pennington Gn GTS/LS CH66 ..... 162 E2
Pennington Green La WGNE/HIN WN2 ..... 69 M3
Pennington La WARRW/BUR WA5 ..... 103 L2
   WGNE/HIN WN2 ..... 57 G5
   WGNE/HIN WN2 ..... 69 J5
Pennington Rd LITH L21 ..... 83 L7
Pennington St ANF/KKDL L4 ..... 97 H3
   ORM L39 ..... 69 M7
Penn La RUNC WA7 ..... 18 E5
Pennsylvania Rd CLB/OSW/ST L13 ..... 97 M6
Pennygate Cl WGNE/HIN WN2 ..... 69 M7
Pennyhurst St WGNS/IIMK WN3 ..... 4 B5
Penny La CALD/MH L18 ..... 114 C3
   RAIN/WH L35 ..... 117 J6
   RNFD/HAY WA11 ..... 91 J6
   WARRW/BUR WA5 ..... 103 M5
Pennystone Cl WGNE/HIN WN2 ..... 69 K6
Penrhos Rd HOY CH47 ..... 108 B7
Penrhyd Rd PEN/TH CH61 ..... 125 M8
Penrhyn Av LITH L21 ..... 83 K6
   PEN/TH CH61 ..... 126 C7
Penrhyn Crs RUNC WA7 ..... 19 J9
Penrhyn Rd PR/KW L34 ..... 86 E7
Penrhyn St EV L5 ..... 96 F8
Penrith Av STHP PR8 ..... 47 K2
   WARRN/WOL WA2 ..... 121 L3
Penrith Cl FROD/HEL WA6 ..... 160 F5
Penrith Crs AIMK WN4 ..... 91 K1
   MGHL L31 ..... 72 F1
Penrith Rd ECCL WA10 ..... 101 K5
Penrith St BIRK CH41 ..... 10 F8
Penrose Av East DV/KA/FCH L14 ..... 115 G3
Penrose Av West DV/KA/FCH L14 ..... 115 G3
Penrose Gdns WARRW/BUR WA5 ..... 135 M2
Penrose Pl SKEL WN8 ..... 77 G1
Penrose St EV L5 ..... 97 H7
Penryn Av RNFD/HAY WA11 ..... 89 M6
Penryn Cl WARRW/BUR WA5 ..... 136 A1
Pensall Dr PEN/TH CH61 ..... 141 H3
Pensarn Gdns WARRW/BUR WA5 ..... 120 F3
Pensarn Rd CLB/OSW/ST L13 ..... 114 B3
Pensby Cl PEN/TH CH61 ..... 126 C3
Pensby Dr GTS/LS CH66 ..... 162 F1
Pensby Hall La PEN/TH CH61 ..... 141 H3
Pensby Rd HES CH60 ..... 141 M5
   PEN/TH CH61 ..... 126 C7
Penshaw Av WGNS/IIMK WN3 ..... 79 K2
Penshaw Ct RUNC WA7 ..... 150 A6
Penson St BIRK CH41 ..... 11 J2
Pentire Av ECCL WA10 ..... 88 D7
Pentire Cl NG/CROX L11 ..... 98 D5
Pentland Av ANF/KKDL L4 ..... 97 J4
   STHEL WA9 ..... 103 H2
   WARRN/WOL WA2 ..... 121 K2

Pentland Pl WARRN/WOL WA2 ..... 121 K2
Pentland Rd NWD/KWIPK L33 ..... 86 C1
Penuel Rd ANF/KKDL L4 ..... 97 H3
Peover St VAUX/LVPD L3 ..... 13 H5
Peploe Rd ANF/KKDL L4 ..... 97 M3
Peplow Rd KKBY L32 ..... 85 K3
Pepper La WGNNW/ST WN6 ..... 55 K2
Pepper Mill La WGN WN1 ..... 5 G6
Pepper St SPK/HALE L24 ..... 147 M4
Pepys Pl WGNW/BIL/O WN5 ..... 67 M8
Pera Cl NPK/KEN L6 ..... 113 J2
Perch Pool La CHTN/BK PR9 ..... 26 B8
Percival La RUNC WA7 ..... 18 D3
Percival St WARR WA1 ..... 15 G6
Percival Wy ECCL WA10 ..... 88 E8
Percy Rd WAL/EG CH44 ..... 112 A3
Percy St BTL L20 ..... 6 E1
   CHLY/EC PR7 ..... 32 F6
   STHEL WA9 ..... 103 H6
   TOX L8 ..... 113 H6
   WARRW/BUR WA5 ..... 121 G8
Perimeter Rd CHNE CH2 ..... 158 E8
   NWD/KWIPK L33 ..... 86 F5
Perrey St WAV L15 ..... 19 K3
Perriam Rd ALL/GAR L19 ..... 130 F5
Perrin Av RUNC WA7 ..... 18 D8
Perrins Rd WARRW/BUR WA5 ..... 104 B7
Perrygate Cl EHL/KEN L7 ..... 113 K5
Perryn Pl WGNNW/ST WN6 ..... 56 B4
Perry St TOX L8 ..... 112 F7
Pershore Gv STHP PR8 ..... 47 J1
Pershore Rd KKBY L32 ..... 86 A5
Perth Av STHEL WA9 ..... 102 A6
   WGNE/HIN WN2 ..... 69 J5
Perth Cl NWD/KWIPK L33 ..... 73 M7
   WARRN/WOL WA2 ..... 122 B1
Perth St NPK/KEN L6 ..... 113 J2
Peterborough Cl GTS/LS CH66 ..... 163 H6
Peterborough Dr NTHTN L30 ..... 84 A1
Peterborough Rd WAV L15 ..... 114 C7
Peterlee Cl STHEL WA9 ..... 102 B6
Peter Mahon Wy BTL L20 ..... 6 E3
Peter Price's La BEB CH63 ..... 143 G1
Peter Rd ANF/KKDL L4 ..... 7 M8
Peter Salem Dr WARRW/BUR WA5 ..... 104 B6
Peters Av BRSC L40 ..... 52 A1
Petersfield Cl NTHTN L30 ..... 84 B4
Petersfield Gdns GOL/RIS/CU WA3 ..... 107 G1
Petersgate RUNC WA7 ..... 150 F6
Petersham Dr WARRS WA4 ..... 138 A8
Peter's La CLVPS L1 ..... 13 G8
Peterstone Cl WARRW/BUR WA5 ..... 120 F3
Peter St AIMK WN4 ..... 91 L2
   CHLY/EC PR7 ..... 32 E5
   CLVPS L1 ..... 13 G6
   ECCL WA10 ..... 8 E2
   GOL/RIS/CU WA3 ..... 92 C5
   WAL/EG CH44 ..... 112 A3
   WGNE/HIN WN2 ..... 69 M8
   WGNW/BIL/O WN5 ..... 67 K7
Peterwood RF/TRAN CH42 ..... 128 C4
Petherick Rd NG/CROX L11 ..... 98 E1
Petticoat La WGNE/HIN WN2 ..... 69 K6
Petunia Cl DV/KA/FCH L14 ..... 115 J1
Petworth Av WARRN/WOL WA2 ..... 121 K2
Petworth Cl SPK/HALE L24 ..... 146 D1
Petworth Rd STHP PR8 ..... 34 D7
Peveril Cl WARRS WA4 ..... 137 M5
Peveril St WLT/FAZ L9 ..... 97 H2
Pheasant Cl GOL/RIS/CU WA3 ..... 123 H1
Pheasant Fld SPK/HALE L24 ..... 147 L3
Pheasant Gv HLWD L26 ..... 132 A4
Philbeach Rd ANF/KKDL L4 ..... 97 M3
Philip Cl WGNW/BIL/O WN5 ..... 67 M8
Philip Dr STHP PR8 ..... 35 G7
Philip Gv STHEL WA9 ..... 102 E6
Philip Rd WDN WA8 ..... 133 K5
Philips Dr WARRW/BUR WA5 ..... 120 A7
Philips St GTS/LS CH66 ..... 162 E1
Phillimore Rd NPK/KEN L6 ..... 113 L2
Phillip Gv WD/CROXPK L12 ..... 99 H8
Phillips Cl CSBY/BLUN L23 ..... 71 K7
   FMBY L37 ..... 59 H3
Phillip's La FMBY L37 ..... 59 H3
Phillips St VAUX/LVPD L3 ..... 12 F4
Phillips Wy HES CH60 ..... 141 G5
Phipps' La WARRW/BUR WA5 ..... 104 A6
Phoenix Av WARRW/BUR WA5 ..... 121 H3
Physics Rd SPK/HALE L24 ..... 131 L8
Phythian Cl NPK/KEN L6 ..... 113 K2
Phythian Crs WARRW/BUR WA5 ..... 136 B1
Phythian St NPK/KEN L6 ..... 113 L1
   RNFD/HAY WA11 ..... 90 B7
Picadilly WGNW/BIL/O WN5 ..... 78 A8
Pichael Nook WARRS WA4 ..... 138 C1
Pickerill Rd GR/UP/WCH CH49 ..... 125 M2
Pickering Crs WARRS WA4 ..... 138 F2
Pickering Rd WAL/NB CH45 ..... 95 K5
   WDN WA8 ..... 133 K8
Pickerings Cl RUNC WA7 ..... 149 L7
Pickering St NPK/KEN L6 ..... 97 J8
Pickles Dr BRSC L40 ..... 51 M1
Pickmere Dr PS/BROM CH62 ..... 155 H2
   RUNC WA7 ..... 150 B4
Pickmere St WARRW/BUR WA5 ..... 120 C1
Pickop St VAUX/LVPD L3 ..... 12 F5
Pickthorn Cl WGNE/HIN WN2 ..... 80 D2
Pickup St WGNE/HIN WN2 ..... 5 M6
Pickwick St TOX L8 ..... 113 H7
Picow Farm Rd RUNC WA7 ..... 18 B7
Picow St RUNC WA7 ..... 18 D5
Picton Av EP CH65 ..... 20 D5
Picton Cl CL/PREN CH43 ..... 127 H1
   GOL/RIS/CU WA3 ..... 122 C1
   PS/BROM CH62 ..... 154 F2
Picton Crs WAV L15 ..... 114 A3
Picton Gv WAV L15 ..... 113 M5

Picton La CHNE CH2 ..... 164 C6
Picton Rd CSBY/WL L22 ..... 82 F4
   WAV L15 ..... 114 A5
Piele Rd RNFD/HAY WA11 ..... 91 G6
Piercefield Rd STHEL WA9 ..... 59 H1
Pierpoint St NEWLW WA12 ..... 92 C6
Pighue La CLB/OSW/ST L13 ..... 114 A4
Pigot Pl WARRS WA4 ..... 122 B8
Pigot St ECCL WA10 ..... 8 D5
   WGNW/BIL/O WN5 ..... 67 K7
Pike House Rd ECCL WA10 ..... 88 D8
Pikelaw Pl SKEL WN8 ..... 65 L8
Pike Pl ECCL WA10 ..... 101 K1
Pikes Bridge Fold ECCL WA10 ..... 101 J1
Pikes Hey Rd WKBY CH48 ..... 125 H6
Pike St WARRS WA4 ..... 137 L4
Pilchbank Rd DV/KA/FCH L14 ..... 115 G1
Pilch La DV/KA/FCH L14 ..... 115 G3
Pilch La East HUY L36 ..... 115 H3
Pilgrim Cl WARRN/WOL WA2 ..... 105 J7
Pilgrim St BIRK CH41 ..... 113 G5
   CLVPS L1 ..... 113 G5
Pilgrims Wy WGNNW/ST WN6 ..... 56 C6
Pilkington Rd STHP PR8 ..... 3 M7
Pilkington St RNFD/HAY WA11 ..... 76 B7
   WGNE/HIN WN2 ..... 69 M7
Pilling Cl CHLY/EC PR7 ..... 32 F7
   CHTN/BK PR9 ..... 22 B8
Pilling La CHLY/EC PR7 ..... 32 E8
   MGHL L31 ..... 61 J8
Pilling Pl SKEL WN8 ..... 65 L8
Pilling St LEIGH WN7 ..... 81 K8
Pilot Gv WAV L15 ..... 113 M5
Pilsley Cl WGNW/BIL/O WN5 ..... 67 J4
Pimblett Rd RNFD/HAY WA11 ..... 91 G6
Pimblett St GOL/RIS/CU WA3 ..... 92 C6
Pimbley Gv East MGHL L31 ..... 72 E7
Pimbley Gv West MGHL L31 ..... 72 E7
Pimbo La SKEL WN8 ..... 77 H2
Pimbo Rd RNFD/HAY WA11 ..... 77 G5
   SKEL WN8 ..... 65 M8
Pimhill Cl TOX L8 ..... 113 J7
Pimlico Rd RUNC WA7 ..... 18 D5
Pincock Brow CHLY/EC PR7 ..... 31 L5
Pincock St CHLY/EC PR7 ..... 31 L5
Pine Av BEB CH63 ..... 143 H2
   ECCL WA10 ..... 89 H7
   NEWLW WA12 ..... 104 E3
   ORM L39 ..... 61 J6
   WDN WA8 ..... 134 D3
Pine Cl HUY L36 ..... 115 M1
   KKBY L32 ..... 85 L2
   RAIN/WH L35 ..... 117 G2
   RNFD/HAY WA11 ..... 90 E7
   SKEL WN8 ..... 65 L8
Pine Crest ORM L39 ..... 62 D3
Pine Dl RNFD/HAY WA11 ..... 76 A4
Pinedale Cl CL/PREN CH43 ..... 126 F1
   GTS/LS CH66 ..... 163 H5
Pine Dr ORM L39 ..... 51 H7
Pine Gv BTL L20 ..... 7 J3
   CHTN/BK PR9 ..... 3 M5
   CSBY/WL L22 ..... 82 F3
   GOL/RIS/CU WA3 ..... 92 E5
   GTS/LS CH66 ..... 163 J4
   ORM L39 ..... 51 J6
   WARR WA1 ..... 122 C6
Pinehey NSTN CH64 ..... 152 F4
Pinehurst Av ANF/KKDL L4 ..... 97 K6
Pinehurst Rd ANF/KKDL L4 ..... 97 K6
Pinellas RUNC WA7 ..... 19 J8
Pine Ms CLVPS L1 ..... 113 G6
Pinemore Rd CALD/MH L18 ..... 130 C3
Pineridge Cl PS/BROM CH62 ..... 143 L2
Pine Rd HES CH60 ..... 141 L4
   RUNC WA7 ..... 19 M9
   WGNW/BIL/O WN5 ..... 68 A7
The Pines BEB CH63 ..... 143 K2
   WD/CROXPK L12 ..... 99 H1
Pine Tree Av CL/PREN CH43 ..... 126 E1
Pine Tree Cl MOR/LEA CH46 ..... 110 B5
Pinetree Cl NTHTN L30 ..... 84 B2
Pinetree Dr WKBY CH48 ..... 124 F4
Pine Tree Gv MOR/LEA CH46 ..... 110 B5
Pine Tree Rd HUY L36 ..... 115 M5
Pinevale WGNNW/ST WN6 ..... 56 C6
Pine View Dr PEN/TH CH61 ..... 141 H4
Pine Wks RF/TRAN CH42 ..... 127 K4
Pine Wy HES CH60 ..... 141 G3
Pineways WARRS WA4 ..... 137 M8
Pinewood AIMK WN4 ..... 91 J3
   SKEL WN8 ..... 65 M2
Pinewood Av FMBY L37 ..... 58 F4
   WARR WA1 ..... 15 L1
   WD/CROXPK L12 ..... 98 F2
Pinewood Cl CHNE CH2 ..... 165 L2
   FMBY L37 ..... 58 F3
   NTHLY L27 ..... 116 A7
   STHP PR8 ..... 36 E4
   WGNE/HIN WN2 ..... 80 D6
Pinewood Crs WGNW/BIL/O WN5 ..... 2 L7
   WGNW/BIL/O WN5 ..... 67 L7
Pinewood Gdns NWD/KWIPK L33 ..... 74 A8
Pinewood Rd WARRW/BUR WA5 ..... 104 B6
Pinfold Cl NTHTN L30 ..... 71 M8
Pinfold Crs KKBY L32 ..... 86 C5
Pinfold Dr ECCL WA10 ..... 101 J3
Pinfold La BRSC L40 ..... 50 B2
   PR/KW L34 ..... 99 K2
   STHP PR8 ..... 47 J2
   WKBY CH48 ..... 125 G6
Pinfold Pl SKEL WN8 ..... 76 F1
Pinfold Rd WLTN L25 ..... 131 L6
Pinfold Rd WGNE/HIN WN2 ..... 69 J6
Pingot Rd WGNW/BIL/O WN5 ..... 78 A8
The Pingot LEIGH WN7 ..... 81 M8
Pingwood La NWD/KWIPK L33 ..... 74 C7
Pinmill Brow FROD/HEL WA6 ..... 160 D6
Pinmill Cl FROD/HEL WA6 ..... 160 D6

Pinners Brow WARRN/WOL WA2 ..... 14 E3
Pinners Fold RUNC WA7 ..... 150 D4
Pinnington Fld HUY L36 ..... 116 A3
Pinnington Rd RAIN/WH L35 ..... 117 G2
Pintail Cl RNFD/HAY WA11 ..... 89 K7
Pipe La WARR WA1 ..... 122 D4
Piper's End HES CH60 ..... 140 F5
Piper's La HES CH60 ..... 140 E3
The Pipers GOL/RIS/CU WA3 ..... 93 H5
Pipit Av NEWLW WA12 ..... 104 E2
Pipit Cl HLWD L26 ..... 132 A3
Pipit La GOL/RIS/CU WA3 ..... 123 G2
Pippin St BRSC L40 ..... 51 J3
Pippits Rw RUNC WA7 ..... 161 G5
Pirrie Rd WLT/FAZ L9 ..... 97 M2
Pitch Cl GR/UP/WCH CH49 ..... 125 M1
Pit Hey Pl SKEL WN8 ..... 65 L8
Pit La WDN WA8 ..... 134 C1
Pit Pl WLTN L25 ..... 131 J3
Pitsmead Rd KKBY L32 ..... 86 A4
Pitts Heath La RUNC WA7 ..... 150 F5
Pitts House La CHTN/BK PR9 ..... 25 K5
Pitt St CHTN/BK PR9 ..... 25 H7
   CLVPS L1 ..... 112 F5
   STHEL WA9 ..... 9 L4
   WARRN/WOL WA2 ..... 14 B3
   WDN WA8 ..... 16 C9
   WGNS/IIMK WN3 ..... 4 D5
Pitville Av CALD/MH L18 ..... 130 C2
Pitville Cl CALD/MH L18 ..... 130 C3
Pitville Gv CALD/MH L18 ..... 130 C2
Pitville Rd CALD/MH L18 ..... 130 C2
Pitville Ter WDN WA8 ..... 16 A9
Plaistow Ct RUNC WA7 ..... 150 A6
Plane Av WGNW/BIL/O WN5 ..... 68 A8
Plane Cl WLT/FAZ L9 ..... 97 L2
Plane Tree Gv RNFD/HAY WA11 ..... 91 J6
Plane Tree Rd BEB CH63 ..... 143 G1
Planetree Rd WD/CROXPK L12 ..... 99 H6
Plank La LEIGH WN7 ..... 93 J1
Plantation Cl RUNC WA7 ..... 150 C4
Plantation Dr GTS/LS CH66 ..... 156 A6
Plantation Gates WGN WN1 ..... 69 G3
Plantation Rd BRSC L40 ..... 51 K1
   PS/BROM CH62 ..... 144 B4
The Planters GR/UP/WCH CH49 ..... 125 L1
   NTHTN L30 ..... 84 D1
Platt Gv RF/TRAN CH42 ..... 127 L5
Platt La WGN WN1 ..... 5 J3
   WGNE/HIN WN2 ..... 69 M8
Platts La BRSC L40 ..... 51 M3
Platts St RNFD/HAY WA11 ..... 90 C7
Platt St WGNE/HIN WN2 ..... 80 C3
Plattsville Rd CALD/MH L18 ..... 114 C8
Playfield Rd WD/CROXPK L12 ..... 99 H6
Pleasance Wy NEWLW WA12 ..... 104 F1
Pleasant Hill St TOX L8 ..... 112 F7
Pleasant St BTL L20 ..... 7 G8
   VAUX/LVPD L3 ..... 13 K8
   WAL/NB CH45 ..... 95 K6
Pleasant Vw BTL L20 ..... 6 E6
   CHLY/EC PR7 ..... 43 H3
Pleasington Cl CL/PREN CH43 ..... 127 G1
Pleasington Dr CL/PREN CH43 ..... 127 G1
Pleck Rd EP CH65 ..... 163 J3
Plemont Rd CLB/OSW/ST L13 ..... 98 A1
Plex La ORM L39 ..... 49 K7
Plex Moss La ORM L39 ..... 48 C5
   STHP PR8 ..... 47 M4
Plimsoll St EHL/KEN L7 ..... 113 K4
Plinston Av WARRS WA4 ..... 138 B1
Plough La BRSC L40 ..... 64 C2
Ploughmans Wy GTS/LS CH66 ..... 163 G4
Plover Cl NEWLW WA12 ..... 104 E2
Plover Dr RUNC WA7 ..... 150 F5
Plovers La FROD/HEL WA6 ..... 159 L8
Plover Wy GOL/RIS/CU WA3 ..... 93 G5
Pluckington Rd HUY L36 ..... 116 D3
Plumbers Wy HUY L36 ..... 116 B3
Plumer St BIRK CH41 ..... 10 B2
   WAV L15 ..... 114 A6
Plumley Gdns RAIN/WH L35 ..... 133 J4
Plumpstons La FROD/HEL WA6 ..... 160 D4
Plumpton La ORM L39 ..... 49 G3
Plumpton St NPK/KEN L6 ..... 13 M2
Plumtre Av WARRW/BUR WA5 ..... 121 H5
Plum Tree Cl RAIN/WH L35 ..... 101 H7
   STBRV L28 ..... 99 K5
Plymouth Cl RUNC WA7 ..... 151 G7
Plymouth Gv CHLYE PR6 ..... 33 G5
   WGNNW/ST WN6 ..... 56 C6
Plymyard Av PS/BROM CH62 ..... 143 M7
Plymyard Cl PS/BROM CH62 ..... 143 L7
Poachers' La WARRS WA4 ..... 138 B2
Pochard Ri RUNC WA7 ..... 150 F5
Pocket Nook La GOL/RIS/CU WA3 ..... 93 K3
Pocket Nook St STHEL WA9 ..... 9 K4
Pocklington Ct WARRN/WOL WA2 ..... 122 B4
Podium St CLB/OSW/ST L13 ..... 114 C1
Poets Cnr PS/BROM CH62 ..... 128 D8
Poke St WGNW/BIL/O WN5 ..... 67 K7
Poleacre Dr WDN WA8 ..... 133 M3
Polegate Dr WGNE/HIN WN2 ..... 81 L3
Pole St WGNNW/ST WN6 ..... 56 A4
Pollard Rd WAV L15 ..... 114 C4
Poll Hill Rd HES CH60 ..... 141 H4
Pollitt Crs STHEL WA9 ..... 118 E2
Pollitt Sq PS/BROM CH62 ..... 128 E5
Polperro Cl WARRW/BUR WA5 ..... 136 A2
Pomfret St TOX L8 ..... 113 H7
Pomona St TOX L8 ..... 13 K8
Pond Green Wy STHEL WA9 ..... 103 H4
Pond View Cl HES CH60 ..... 141 L5
Pond Wk STHEL WA9 ..... 103 H4
Ponsonby Rd WAL/EG CH44 ..... 95 G8
Ponsonby St TOX L8 ..... 113 J7
Pool Bank PS/BROM CH62 ..... 128 D6
Poolbank Rd PS/BROM CH62 ..... 128 D6
Poole Av WARRN/WOL WA2 ..... 121 K3

Poole Crs *WARRN/WOL* WA2 .... **121** K3 🔲
Poole Hall La *GTS/LS* CH66 .... **156** A5
Poole Hall Rd *EP* CH65 .... **156** B5
Poole La *CHNE* CH2 .... **165** C3
Pool End *STHEL* WA9 .... **103** H3
Pool Hey *STBRV* WA8 .... **99** K5
Pool Hey *STHP* PR8 .... **36** D2
Pool La *CHNE* CH2 .... **158** B8
  *GR/UP/WCH* CH49 .... **126** C3
  *LYMM* WA13 .... **139** L1
  *PS/BROM* CH62 .... **143** L1
  *RUNC* WA7 .... **19** J2
  *WARRS* WA4 .... **137** J4
Poolside Rd *RUNC* WA7 .... **19** J5
Poolside Wk *CHTN/BK* PR9 .... **25** K1
Poolstock *WGNS/IIMK* WN3 .... **4** D8
Poolstock La *WGNS/IIMK* WN3 .... **79** J1
Pool St *BIRK* CH41 .... **11** H3
  *CHTN/BK* PR9 .... **25** L1
  *WDN* WA8 .... **16** F5
  *WGNE/HIN* WN2 .... **80** F1
  *WGNS/IIMK* WN3 .... **4** D8
Pooltown Rd *EP* CH65 .... **156** B7
Poolwood Rd
  *GR/UP/WCH* CH49 .... **126** D1
Pope St *BTL* L20 .... **83** K8
Poplar Av *AIMK* WN4 .... **78** F8
  *CHLY/EC* PR7 .... **31** L1
  *CSBY/BLUN* L23 .... **71** H8
  *ECCL* WA10 .... **101** J1
  *GOL/RIS/CU* WA3 .... **107** H2
  *GR/UP/WCH* CH49 .... **110** B8 🔲
  *NEWLW* WA12 .... **104** F2
  *RUNC* WA7 .... **19** M9
  *WARRW/BUR* WA5 .... **136** A1
  *WGNW/BIL/O* WN5 .... **67** M7
Poplar Bank *HUY* L36 .... **116** A3
Poplar Cl *EP* CH65 .... **20** A7
  *RUNC* WA7 .... **149** L6
Poplar Dr *BEB* CH63 .... **143** J1
  *EV* L5 .... **97** J8
  *KKBY* L32 .... **85** M2
  *SKEL* WN8 .... **65** H4
Poplar Farm Cl
  *MOR/LEA* CH46 .... **109** L7 🔲
Poplar Gv *CHNE* CH2 .... **165** J2
  *ECCL* WA10 .... **101** L2
  *LITH* L21 .... **83** H7
  *RAIN/WH* L35 .... **101** G8
  *RNFD/HAY* WA11 .... **90** E7 🔲
  *WGNE/HIN* WN2 .... **81** K3
Poplar Rd *CL/PREN* CH43 .... **127** K1
  *RNFD/HAY* WA11 .... **90** E7
  *WLTN* L25 .... **131** H2
Poplars Av *WARRN/WOL* WA2 .... **121** J1
The Poplars *CHLY/EC* PR7 .... **44** B7
  *LEIGH* WN7 .... **93** L5
  *LYMM* WA13 .... **139** M1 🔲
Poplar St *CHLY/EC* PR7 .... **32** F7
  *GOL/RIS/CU* WA3 .... **92** D4 🔲
  *STHP* PR8 .... **25** G7
Poplar Wy *PR/KW* L34 .... **96** F5 🔲
Poppleford Cl *WLTN* L25 .... **131** L1 🔲
Poppy Av *CHLYE* PR6 .... **32** F3
Poppy La *ORM* L39 .... **63** K4
Porchester Rd *NG/CROX* L11 .... **98** B4
Porlock Av *CHLDW* L16 .... **115** G8
  *STHEL* WA9 .... **102** E8
Porlock Cl *HES* CH60 .... **141** K7
  *WARRW/BUR* WA5 .... **136** A1
  *WGNE/HIN* WN2 .... **80** C4
Portal Ms *PEN/TH* CH61 .... **141** H2
Portal Rd *PEN/TH* CH61 .... **141** H2
Port Cswy *PS/BROM* CH62 .... **143** M1
Portelet Rd *CLB/OSW/ST* L13 .... **114** B1
Porter Av *NEWLW* WA12 .... **91** L8
Porter Cl *RAIN/WH* L35 .... **117** M4
Porter St *RUNC* WA7 .... **19** M3
  *VAUX/LVPD* L3 .... **12** C2
Porters Wood Cl
  *WGNW/BIL/O* WN5 .... **67** K6 🔲
Portgate Cl *NG/CROX* L11 .... **98** E4 🔲
Porthcawl Cl *WDN* WA8 .... **133** L2
Porthleven Rd *RUNC* WA7 .... **150** D8
Portia Av *BEB* CH63 .... **128** A6
Portia St *BTL* L20 .... **96** E5
Portico Av *RAIN/WH* L35 .... **101** J7
Portico La *RAIN/WH* L35 .... **101** J7
Portland Av *CSBY/WL* L22 .... **82** E3 🔲
Portland Cl *WGNE/HIN* WN2 .... **80** C4
Portland Pl *EV* L5 .... **13** J1
  *FROD/HEL* WA6 .... **166** E1 🔲
Portland St *BIRK* CH41 .... **10** A2
  *CHLY/EC* PR7 .... **32** F5 🔲
  *EV* L5 .... **12** F1 🔲
  *NEWLW* WA12 .... **104** B1 🔲
  *RUNC* WA7 .... **18** E2
  *STHP* PR8 .... **2** F5
  *WAL/NB* CH45 .... **95** J4
  *WGNW/BIL/O* WN5 .... **68** A7 🔲
Portland Wy *STHEL* WA9 .... **103** H4
Portlemouth Rd *NG/CROX* L11.. **85** L8
Portloe Av *HLWD* L26 .... **132** B4
Portman Rd *WAV* L15 .... **113** M6
Portola Cl *WARRS* WA4 .... **138** E3
Porton Rd *KKBY* L32 .... **85** L4
Portreath Wy *ECCL* WA10 .... **88** D7
Portree Av *BEB* CH63 .... **143** M8 🔲
Portree Cl *CLB/OSW/ST* L13 .... **98** A7
Portrush St *CLB/OSW/ST* L13 .... **98** A7
Portsmouth Dr *CHLYE* PR6 .... **33** G5
Portsmouth Pl *RUNC* WA7 .... **151** C7 🔲
Portwood Cl *TOX* L8 .... **113** K5 🔲
Post Office Av *CHTN/BK* PR9 .... **3** H3
Post Office La *RUNC* WA7 .... **18** A9
Potter Pl *SKEL* WN8 .... **65** M8
Potters La *WDN* WA8 .... **148** B1
Pottery Flds *PR/KW* L34 .... **100** F7 🔲
Pottery La *RAIN/WH* L35 .... **116** E2
Pottery Rd *WGNS/IIMK* WN3 .... **4** B6
Pottery Ter *WGNS/IIMK* WN3 .... **4** C6
Poulsom Dr *NTHTN* L30 .... **83** L3
Poulter Rd *WLT/FAZ* L9 .... **84** D6 🔲
Poulton Cl *HLWD* L26 .... **131** M7
Poulton Crs *WARR* WA1 .... **122** F5
Poulton Dr *AIMK* WN4 .... **91** H1 🔲

*WDN* WA8 .... **133** M5 🔲
Poulton Green Cl *BEB* CH63 .... **143** H4
Poulton Hall Rd *BEB* CH63 .... **143** J3
  *WAL/EC* CH44 .... **111** J2 🔲🔲
Poulton Rd *BEB* CH63 .... **143** J3
  *CHTN/BK* PR9 .... **25** H6
  *WAL/EC* CH44 .... **111** J2
Poulton Royd Dr *BEB* CH63 .... **143** H3
Pound Rd *GTS/LS* CH66 .... **155** L6
Poverty La *MGHL* L31 .... **73** H5
Povey Rd *WARRS* WA4 .... **121** M4 🔲
Powderworks La *MGHL* L31 .... **73** L2
Powell Av *GOL/RIS/CU* WA3 .... **123** G1
Powell Dr *WGNW/BIL/O* WN5 .... **89** M2
Powell St *BIRK* CH41 .... **111** H5
  *STHEL* WA9 .... **103** G6
  *WARRS* WA4 .... **138** B2
  *WGN* WN1 .... **4** F2
  *WGNE/HIN* WN2 .... **80** D4
Power Rd *PS/BROM* CH62 .... **144** B4
  *RF/TRAN* CH42 .... **128** C5
Powey La *CH/BCN* CH1 .... **162** D8
Powis St *TOX* L8 .... **113** J8
Pownall St *CLVPS* L1 .... **12** F9
  *CLVPS* L1 .... **112** F5 🔲🔲
Powys St *WARRW/BUR* WA5 .... **14** A6
Poynter St *STHEL* WA9 .... **102** A7
Poynton St *WARRS* WA4 .... **138** C2
Pratt Rd *PR/KW* L34 .... **100** E7
Preece Cl *WDN* WA8 .... **133** M2
Preesall Cl *CHTN/BK* PR9 .... **22** B8
Preesall Wy *NG/CROX* L11 .... **85** L8 🔲
Prefect Pl *WGNW/BIL/O* WN5 .... **67** L5
Premier St *EV* L5 .... **97** H8
Prentice Rd *RF/TRAN* CH42 .... **128** A4
Prenton Av *STHEL* WA9 .... **103** K5
Prenton Dell Av *CL/PREN* CH43.. **127** J5
Prenton Dell Rd *CL/PREN* CH43.. **127** G4
Prenton Farm Rd
  *CL/PREN* CH43 .... **127** J6
Prenton Gn *SPK/HALE* L24 .... **147** G2 🔲
Prenton Hall Rd *CL/PREN* CH43.. **127** H4
Prenton La *RF/TRAN* CH42 .... **127** K4
Prentonpark Rd *RF/TRAN* CH42 .. **127** L3
Prenton Rd East
  *RF/TRAN* CH42 .... **127** M3
Prenton Rd West
  *RF/TRAN* CH42 .... **127** L3
Prenton Village Rd
  *CL/PREN* CH43 .... **127** H4
Prenton Wy *CL/PREN* CH43 .... **126** F4
Presbyterian Fold
  *WGNE/HIN* WN2 .... **69** M7 🔲🔲
Prescot Dr *NPK/KEN* L6 .... **113** M2
Prescot Gn *ORM* L39 .... **62** F2 🔲
Prescot Rd *CLB/OSW/ST* L13 .... **114** A2
  *ECCL* WA10 .... **101** K5
  *MGHL* L31 .... **73** L7
  *ORM* L39 .... **73** M1
  *WDN* WA8 .... **117** H8
Prescot St *EHL/KEN* L7 .... **13** M5
  *WAL/NB* CH45 .... **95** J5
Prescott Av *BRSC* L40 .... **39** J2
  *GOL/RIS/CU* WA3 .... **92** B3 🔲
Prescott Br *BRSC* L40 .... **39** L5
Prescott La *WGNW/BIL/O* WN5 .... **67** K5
Prescott Rd *SKEL* WN8 .... **66** A8
Prescott St *GOL/RIS/CU* WA3 .... **92** C4 🔲
  *WARRS* WA4 .... **138** A2
  *WGNE/HIN* WN2 .... **69** M8 🔲🔲
  *WGNNW/ST* WN6 .... **4** B4
Preseland Rd *CSBY/BLUN* L23 .... **83** G2
Prestbury Av *CL/PREN* CH43 .... **127** G3
  *STHP* PR8 .... **34** D8
  *WGNS/IIMK* WN3 .... **79** G6
Prestbury Cl *CL/PREN* CH43 .... **127** G3 🔲
Prestbury Dr *ECCL* WA10 .... **101** K3
  *WARRS* WA4 .... **138** F2
Prestbury Rd *NG/CROX* L11 .... **98** B1
Preston Av *PR/KW* L34 .... **100** E8
Preston Gv *NPK/KEN* L6 .... **97** L8 🔲
Preston New Rd *CHTN/BK* PR9 .. **25** J2
Preston Nook *CHLY/EC* PR7 .... **30** E8 🔲
Preston on the Hl *WARRS* WA4 .. **151** H7 🔲
Preston Rd *CHLY/EC* PR7 .... **32** E3
  *CHLYE* PR6 .... **32** F1
  *CHTN/BK* PR9 .... **25** G5
Preston St *CLVPS* L1 .... **13** G6
  *STHEL* WA9 .... **118** C3 🔲
Preston Wy *CSBY/BLUN* L23 .... **83** J1
Prestt Gv *WGNS/IIMK* WN3 .... **4** A8
Prestwich Av *WGNS/IIMK* WN3 .. **4** A8
Prestwich Dr *WARRW/BUR* WA5 .. **107** G2
Prestwick Dr *CSBY/BLUN* L23 .... **70** E7
Prestwood Rd *DV/KA/FCH* L14 .. **115** H1
Pretoria Rd *AIMK* WN4 .... **91** J1
  *WLT/FAZ* L9 .... **84** D7
Price Gv *STHEL* WA9 .... **103** J3
Price's La *CL/PREN* CH43 .... **127** K1 🔲
Price St *BIRK* CH41 .... **10** C1
  *CLVPS* L1 .... **13** G9 🔲
Priestfield Rd *EP* CH65 .... **20** B4
Priesthouse Cl *FMBY* L37 .... **59** J2
Priesthouse La *FMBY* L37 .... **59** J2
Primrose Cl *CHTN/BK* PR9 .... **22** E8 🔲
  *FMBY* L37 .... **47** K8
  *RUNC* WA7 .... **150** C5
  *WARRN/WOL* WA2 .... **121** L4
  *WDN* WA8 .... **134** A4
Primrose Dr *HUY* L36 .... **100** A8
Primrose Gv *RNFD/HAY* WA11 .... **91** G6
  *WAL/EG* CH44 .... **112** A3 🔲🔲
  *WGNW/BIL/O* WN5 .... **68** A6 🔲
Primrose Hl *PS/BROM* CH62 .... **128** D7
  *VAUX/LVPD* L3 .... **13** G5
Primrose Hill Rd *CHLY/EC* PR7 .. **31** K1
Primrose La *FROD/HEL* WA6 .... **166** C4
  *WGNNW/ST* WN6 .... **55** M3
Primrose Rd *BIRK* CH41 .... **111** H6
  *CALD/MH* L18 .... **114** E8
Primrose St *ANF/KKDL* L4 .... **96** F6
  *CHLYE* PR6 .... **32** F5
  *LEIGH* WN7 .... **81** M8 🔲🔲
Primrose Vw *AIMK* WN4 .... **91** K3 🔲
Primula Cl *RNFD/HAY* WA11 .... **97** K1
Prince Albert Ms *CLVPS* L1 .... **113** G6 🔲
Prince Alfred Rd *WAV* L15 .... **114** C6
Prince Andrew's Gv *ECCL* WA10.. **88** E7

Prince Charles Gdns *STHP* PR8 .... **2** D8
Prince Edward St *BIRK* CH41 .... **10** F4
Prince Edwin St *EV* L5 .... **13** J2
Princes Av *CSBY/BLUN* L23 .... **82** F1
  *PS/BROM* CH62 .... **144** A7
  *TOX* L8 .... **113** H6
  *WKBY* CH48 .... **124** D3
Princes Bvd *BEB* CH63 .... **127** M5
Princes Gdns *VAUX/LVPD* L3 .... **12** E5
Princes Ga West *TOX* L8 .... **113** K7 🔲
Prince's Pk *WGNNW/ST* WN6 .... **67** H1
Princes Rd *ECCL* WA10 .... **101** L4 🔲
  *EP* CH65 .... **156** B7
  *TOX* L8 .... **113** H6
Princess Av *AIMK* WN4 .... **91** L2
  *ECCL* WA10 .... **89** G7
  *RNFD/HAY* WA11 .... **91** J6
  *WARR* WA1 .... **122** B7
  *WARRW/BUR* WA5 .... **120** A7
Princess Crs *WARR* WA1 .... **122** B7 🔲
Princess Dr *DV/KA/FCH* L14 .... **99** M7
  *WD/CROXPK* L12 .... **99** G6
Princess Rd *AIMK* WN4 .... **91** K2
  *CHLYE* PR6 .... **44** D5
  *LYMM* WA13 .... **139** L2
  *WAL/NB* CH45 .... **95** K6
  *WGNNW/ST* WN6 .... **67** L1
Princes St *CHLY/EC* PR7 .... **32** F7
  *CLVP* L2 .... **12** F7
  *RUNC* WA7 .... **19** G2
  *WARRW/BUR* WA5 .... **136** F1 🔲
  *WGNE/HIN* WN2 .... **69** L8 🔲
  *WGNS/IIMK* WN3 .... **4** E6
Princess Wy *CHLY/EC* PR7 .... **31** M3 🔲
  *LITH* L21 .... **83** J6
Prince St *CLVPS* L1 .... **12** F9
  *CSBY/WL* L22 .... **82** E5
Princes Wy *RNFD/HAY* WA11 .... **89** J5 🔲
Princesway *WAL/NB* CH45 .... **95** J7
Princeway *FROD/HEL* WA6 .... **160** D5
Prince William St *TOX* L8 .... **113** G7
Prior Farm Cl *ALL/GAR* L19 .... **130** C6 🔲
Priors Cl *WLTN* L25 .... **131** K3
Priorsfield *MOR/LEA* CH46 .... **110** A5 🔲
Priorsfield Rd *WLTN* L25 .... **131** K3
Prior St *BTL* L20 .... **83** J7
Priorswood Pl *SKEL* WN8 .... **77** H1
Priory Cl *AIG/SPK* L17 .... **129** K3
  *BEB* CH63 .... **143** J2
  *BRSC* L40 .... **38** F8
  *FMBY* L37 .... **59** K3
  *RAIN/WH* L35 .... **116** E4
  *RUNC* WA7 .... **150** C4
  *WGNW/BIL/O* WN5 .... **67** K8 🔲
Priory Gdns *ECCL* WA10 .... **89** H6
Priory Gra *STHP* PR8 .... **2** E9
Priory Gv *ORM* L39 .... **62** F1 🔲
Priory Ms *STHP* PR8 .... **2** D5
Priory Nook *SKEL* WN8 .... **66** E6
Priory Rd *AIMK* WN4 .... **79** H8
  *ANF/KKDL* L4 .... **97** J5
  *SKEL* WN8 .... **66** E6
  *WAL/EC* CH44 .... **112** A2
  *WKBY* CH48 .... **124** D3
Priory St *ALL/GAR* L19 .... **145** M1
  *BIRK* CH41 .... **11** M6
  *WARRS* WA4 .... **14** F9
The Priory *NSTN* CH64 .... **152** F4
  *WARRN/WOL* WA2 .... **105** J6
Priory Wy *WLTN* L25 .... **131** K3
Priory Whf *BIRK* CH41 .... **11** M5
Pritchard Av *LITH* L21 .... **83** H6
Pritt St *VAUX/LVPD* L3 .... **13** J3
Private Dr *PEN/TH* CH61 .... **126** F8
Prizett Rd *ALL/GAR* L19 .... **130** D6 🔲
Probyn Rd *WAL/NB* CH45 .... **95** G8
Proctor Cl *WGNW/BIL/O* WN5 .... **68** A4
Proctor Rd *FMBY* L37 .... **58** E1
  *HOY* CH47 .... **108** E7
Proctors Cl *WDN* WA8 .... **134** E3
Prodesse Ct *WGNE/HIN* WN2 .... **69** M7
Proe's Ct *WGN* WN1 .... **4** D3
Proffits La *FROD/HEL* WA6 .... **167** G1
Progress St *CHLYE* PR6 .... **33** G5
  *WGNE/HIN* WN2 .... **69** M8 🔲🔲
Promenade *STHP* PR8 .... **2** B3
Promenade Gdns *AIG/SPK* L17 .. **129** H3
Prophet Wk *TOX* L8 .... **113** G8
Prospect La *GOL/RIS/CU* WA3 .... **123** L2
Prospect Pl *SKEL* WN8 .... **66** B8
Prospect Rd *RF/TRAN* CH42 .... **127** K4
  *STHEL* WA9 .... **102** F1 🔲
  *WGNNW/ST* WN6 .... **56** A6
Prospect St *EHL/KEN* L7 .... **9** M8
Prospect V *NPK/KEN* L6 .... **113** M1
  *WAL/NB* CH45 .... **95** H8
Prospect Wy *NTHTN* L30 .... **84** D2 🔲
Providence Crs *TOX* L8 .... **113** G7 🔲
Provident Cl *STHEL* WA9 .... **103** J2
Province Rd *BTL* L20 .... **83** M7
Prussia St *VAUX/LVPD* L3 .... **12** E5 🔲
Pryce Av *WGNE/HIN* WN2 .... **5** L5
Public Hall St *RUNC* WA7 .... **19** H2
Pudsey St *CLVPS* L1 .... **13** J6
Pugin St *ANF/KKDL* L4 .... **97** G6
Pulford Av *CL/PREN* CH43 .... **127** J3
Pulford Cl *RUNC* WA7 .... **149** M7
Pulford Rd *BEB* CH63 .... **128** B8
  *EP* CH65 .... **163** H1
Pulford St *ANF/KKDL* L4 .... **97** H6
Pullman Cl *HES* CH60 .... **141** M5
Pump La *RUNC* WA7 .... **150** B5
  *WGNE/HIN* WN2 .... **69** M8
Pump Rd *BIRK* CH41 .... **11** K1
Pump St *WGNE/HIN* WN2 .... **69** M8 🔲🔲
Punnell's La *MGHL* L31 .... **61** H8
Purbeck Dr *PEN/TH* CH61 .... **125** M6
Purdy Cl *WARRW/BUR* WA5 .... **120** F4

Purley Gv *CALD/MH* L18 .... **130** C3
Purley Rd *CSBY/WL* L22 .... **82** E3 🔲
Purser Gv *WAV* L15 .... **113** M5 🔲
Putney Ct *RUNC* WA7 .... **150** A6 🔲
Pye Cl *RNFD/HAY* WA11 .... **91** K5
Pyecroft Cl *WARRW/BUR* WA5 .. **119** M7
Pyecroft Rd *WARRW/BUR* WA5 .. **119** M7
Pye Rd *HES* CH60 .... **141** J5
Pyes Gdns *RNFD/HAY* WA11 .... **89** K6 🔲
Pyes La *STBRV* L28 .... **99** L6
Pye St *WAV* L15 .... **114** C6
Pygon's Hill La *MGHL* L31 .... **61** M6
Pyke St *WGN* WN1 .... **5** H1
Pym St *ANF/KKDL* L4 .... **97** H3
Pyrus Gv *FROD/HEL* WA6 .... **166** E3 🔲

## Q

The Quadrangle
  *CALD/MH* L18 .... **130** D1 🔲
Quadrant Cl *RUNC* WA7 .... **150** F7 🔲
Quail Cl *WARRN/WOL* WA2 .... **121** M2
Quaker La *HES* CH60 .... **141** G4
Quakers Meadow *PR/KW* L34 .... **99** M1
Quakers' Pl *WGNNW/ST* WN6 .... **56** A4 🔲
Quantock Cl *GTS/LS* CH66 .... **155** J7 🔲
  *WGNS/IIMK* WN3 .... **78** E3
Quarry Av *BEB* CH63 .... **143** H1
Quarry Bank *BIRK* CH41 .... **11** C7
Quarrybank St *BIRK* CH41 .... **10** F7
Quarry Cl *CLB/OSW/ST* L13 .... **98** B8
  *HES* CH60 .... **141** H5
  *NWD/KWIPK* L33 .... **86** B2
  *RUNC* WA7 .... **149** M4
Quarry Dl *NWD/KWIPK* L33 .... **86** B2 🔲
Quarry Dr *ORM* L39 .... **62** E4
Quarry Gn *NWD/KWIPK* L33 .... **86** B2
Quarry Hey *NWD/KWIPK* L33 .... **86** B2
Quarry La *NSTN* CH64 .... **153** K4
  *PEN/TH* CH61 .... **126** C7
  *WARRS* WA4 .... **137** M7
Quarry Mt *ORM* L39 .... **51** J7 🔲
Quarry Rd *BTL* L20 .... **7** K6
  *CHLYE* PR6 .... **33** G7
  *CLB/OSW/ST* L13 .... **98** C8
  *CSBY/BLUN* L23 .... **71** J7
  *NSTN* CH64 .... **153** L4
Quarry Rd East *BEB* CH63 .... **143** J1
  *HES* CH60 .... **141** G4
Quarry Rd West *HES* CH60 .... **141** G4
Quarryside Dr *NWD/KWIPK* L33 .. **86** C3
Quarry St *WLTN* L25 .... **131** H2
Quarry St South *WLTN* L25 .... **131** J3
Quartz Wy *LITH* L21 .... **83** L5
Quay Fold *WARRS* WA4 .... **137** G1
Quayle Cl *RNFD/HAY* WA11 .... **90** D7
Quay Pl *RUNC* WA7 .... **151** G6
Quay Side *FROD/HEL* WA6 .... **160** F3
Quayside *NSTN* CH64 .... **152** F8
The Quay *FROD/HEL* WA6 .... **160** F3
Queen Anne St *STHP* PR8 .... **3** G4
  *VAUX/LVPD* L3 .... **13** J4
Queen Mary's Dr
  *PS/BROM* CH62 .... **128** D7
Queen's Av *AIMK* WN4 .... **91** K1
  *EP* CH65 .... **163** J2
  *FMBY* L37 .... **47** G8
  *HOY* CH47 .... **108** F5
  *WARR* WA1 .... **15** M1
  *WDN* WA8 .... **133** K5
Queensberry St *TOX* L8 .... **113** H8 🔲
Queensbury *WKBY* CH48 .... **124** F2
Queensbury Av *PS/BROM* CH62.. **144** A4
Queensbury Wy *WDN* WA8 .... **133** M2
Queen's Cl *RUNC* WA7 .... **18** F6
Queens Ct *NPK/KEN* L6 .... **97** J8
Queenscourt Rd
  *WD/CROXPK* L12 .... **98** E8
Queens Crs *WARR* WA1 .... **122** C5 🔲
Queens Cft *FMBY* L37 .... **58** F3
Queensdale Rd *CALD/MH* L18 .... **114** C8
Queens Dr *CL/PREN* CH43 .... **127** J4
  *ECCL* WA10 .... **88** E7
  *FROD/HEL* WA6 .... **166** D2
  *GOL/RIS/CU* WA3 .... **92** E5
  *HES* CH60 .... **141** G5
  *NEWLW* WA12 .... **91** L8
  *WARRS* WA4 .... **138** B3
Queens Dr Mossley Hl
  *CALD/MH* L18 .... **130** B1
Queens Dr Stoneycroft
  *CLB/OSW/ST* L13 .... **114** D1
Queens Dr Walton *ANF/KKDL* L4 .. **97** J3
Queens Dr Wavertree
  *DV/KA/FCH* L14 .... **114** E4
Queens Dr West Derby
  *CLB/OSW/ST* L13 .... **98** A5
Queens Gdns *EP* CH65 .... **20** A4
Queensgate *CHLY/EC* PR7 .... **32** D6 🔲
Queens Gn *ORM* L39 .... **49** H8
Queen's Gv *RF/TRAN* CH42 .... **32** E5
Queensland Av *STHEL* WA9 .... **102** A6
Queensland St *EHL/KEN* L7 .... **113** K4
Queens Ms *NPK/KEN* L6 .... **97** J8 🔲
Queen's Rd *AIMK* WN4 .... **91** K1 🔲
  *BTL* L20 .... **7** G7
  *CHLY/EC* PR7 .... **32** D5
  *CHTN/BK* PR9 .... **3** K2
  *CSBY/BLUN* L23 .... **83** G1
  *ECCL* WA10 .... **101** L4
  *FMBY* L37 .... **58** F3
  *GTS/LS* CH66 .... **155** L6
  *HOY* CH47 .... **108** C6
  *NPK/KEN* L6 .... **113** M1
  *PR/KW* L34 .... **101** G7 🔲
  *RF/TRAN* CH42 .... **128** C4
  *RNFD/HAY* WA11 .... **91** J6
  *WAL/EG* CH44 .... **112** A2
  *WGNW/BIL/O* WN5 .... **68** C3
Queen St *ALL/GAR* L19 .... **130** E8
  *BIRK* CH41 .... **11** K9
  *CSBY/WL* L22 .... **82** E5
  *ECCL* WA10 .... **8** F2
  *EP* CH65 .... **20** D1

*GOL/RIS/CU* WA3 .... **92** D5 🔲
  *NEWLW* WA12 .... **104** D2
  *ORM* L39 .... **63** G1 🔲
  *RUNC* WA7 .... **19** G2
  *WAL/NB* CH45 .... **95** K8
  *WGNE/HIN* WN2 .... **69** M7 🔲🔲
  *WGNE/HIN* WN2 .... **80** C3
  *WGNS/IIMK* WN3 .... **4** E5
  *WGNW/BIL/O* WN5 .... **67** M8
Queen St East *CHLY/EC* PR7 .... **32** F7
Queensway *CHLY/EC* PR7 .... **32** A3
  *CSBY/WL* L22 .... **83** H3
  *FROD/HEL* WA6 .... **160** D6
  *HES* CH60 .... **141** L7
  *RNFD/HAY* WA11 .... **76** C8 🔲
  *RNFD/HAY* WA11 .... **89** J5
  *RUNC* WA7 .... **18** F2
  *WAL/NB* CH45 .... **95** J7
  *WDN* WA8 .... **134** A6
  *WGN* WN1 .... **68** D3
  *WGNE/HIN* WN2 .... **69** J5 🔲
  *WGNNW/ST* WN6 .... **67** H1
Queensway Entrance (Mersey Tunnel)
  *CLVPS* L1 .... **13** G6 🔲
Queensway (Mersey Tunnel)
  *BIRK* CH41 .... **11** J3
  *VAUX/LVPD* L3 .... **12** D6
Queens Whf *VAUX/LVPD* L3 .... **112** E6
Quernmore Rd *NWD/KWIPK* L33 .. **86** C2
Quernmore Wk
  *NWD/KWIPK* L33 .... **86** C2 🔲
Quickswood Cl *WLTN* L25 .... **115** H8
Quickswood Dr *WLTN* L25 .... **115** H8
Quickswood Gn *WLTN* L25 .... **115** H8 🔲
Quickthorn Crs *STBRV* L28 .... **99** K6 🔲
Quigley Av *NTHTN* L30 .... **84** C4
Quigley St *BIRK* CH41 .... **128** A1
The Quillet *NSTN* CH64 .... **153** H6
Quinesway
  *GR/UP/WCH* CH49 .... **110** C8 🔲
Quinn St *WDN* WA8 .... **16** E5
Quintbridge Cl *HLWD* L26 .... **132** A6
Quinton Cl *STHP* PR8 .... **47** J1
Quorn St *EHL/KEN* L7 .... **113** K3

## R

Rabbit La *BRSC* L40 .... **51** H1
Raby Av *BEB* CH63 .... **143** K7
Raby Cl *BEB* CH63 .... **143** J6
  *HES* CH60 .... **141** H6
  *WDN* WA8 .... **134** F3
Raby Dr *BEB* CH63 .... **143** J6
  *MOR/LEA* CH46 .... **109** M6
Raby Gdns *NSTN* CH64 .... **153** G5
Raby Gv *RF/TRAN* CH42 .... **127** M5
Raby Hall Rd *BEB* CH63 .... **143** G8
Raby Mere Rd *BEB* CH63 .... **142** E8
Raby Park Cl *NSTN* CH64 .... **153** G5
Raby Park Rd *NSTN* CH64 .... **153** G5
Raby Rd *BEB* CH63 .... **142** D7
  *NSTN* CH64 .... **153** G5
Rachel St *EV* L5 .... **13** H1
Radburn Cl *CSBY/BLUN* L23 .... **71** G3
Radcliffe Av *GOL/RIS/CU* WA3 .... **107** G2
Radford Av *BEB* CH63 .... **143** K3
Radford Cl *WDN* WA8 .... **133** L6
Radlett Cl *WARRW/BUR* WA5 .... **136** A2
Radley Dr *AIN/FAZ* L10 .... **84** E2
  *BEB* CH63 .... **142** B7
Radley La *WARRN/WOL* WA2 .... **121** M2
Radley Rd *WAL/EG* CH44 .... **95** H8
Radley St *STHEL* WA9 .... **102** A6
Radmore Rd *DV/KA/FCH* L14 .... **114** F2
Radnor Av *HES* CH60 .... **141** H4
Radnor Cl *HLWD* L26 .... **131** M7
  *WGNE/HIN* WN2 .... **81** J2
Radnor Dr *BTL* L20 .... **7** H1 🔲
  *CHTN/BK* PR9 .... **25** H2 🔲
  *LEIGH* WN7 .... **81** L8
  *WAL/NB* CH45 .... **95** L7
  *WDN* WA8 .... **133** M3
Radnor Pl *CL/PREN* CH43 .... **10** E6
  *NPK/KEN* L6 .... **97** M8
Radnor St *WARRW/BUR* WA5 .... **121** G7
Radstock Gv *STHEL* WA9 .... **102** F8
Radstock Rd *NPK/KEN* L6 .... **113** L2
  *WAL/EG* CH44 .... **95** G8
Radway Gn *GTS/LS* CH66 .... **156** A8
Radway Rd *HUY* L36 .... **100** B7
Raeburn Av *NSTN* CH64 .... **153** H6
  *PS/BROM* CH62 .... **143** M7
  *WKBY* CH48 .... **124** E2
Raffles Rd *RF/TRAN* CH42 .... **10** F8
Raffles St *CLVPS* L1 .... **113** G6
Rafter Av *BTL* L20 .... **83** A6 🔲
Raglan Ct *GOL/RIS/CU* WA3.. **107** H7
Rail Cl *RNFD/HAY* WA11 .... **76** B3
Railside Ct *EV* L5 .... **96** E3 🔲
Railton Av *RAIN/WH* L35 .... **117** M3
Railton Cl *RAIN/WH* L35 .... **117** M4 🔲
Railton Rd *NG/CROX* L11 .... **98** A3
Railway Ap *ORM* L39 .... **51** H8
Railway Pth *ORM* L39 .... **63** G1
Railway Rd *CHLYE* PR6 .... **32** F4
  *CHLYE* PR6 .... **44** C6
  *GOL/RIS/CU* WA3 .... **92** D4
  *RF/TRAN* CH42 .... **128** B3
  *SKEL* WN8 .... **64** F5
Railway St *ALL/GAR* L19 .... **130** E8
  *CHLY/EC* PR7 .... **32** F6
  *NEWLW* WA12 .... **104** D2
  *STHEL* WA9 .... **9** J3
  *STHP* PR8 .... **3** G7
  *WGNNW/ST* WN6 .... **4** A2
Railway Ter *STHP* PR8 .... **2** F7
Rainbow Cl *WDN* WA8 .... **133** L2
Rainbow Dr *HLWD* L26 .... **132** A5
  *MGHL* L31 .... **85** K1
Raines Cl *GR/UP/WCH* CH49 .... **126** A1
Rainford Av *BTL* L20 .... **84** A8
Rainford By-pass
  *RNFD/HAY* WA11 .... **75** M6
Rainford Rd *ECCL* WA10 .... **88** E7
  *ORM* L39 .... **64** C7
  *RNFD/HAY* WA11 .... **75** M4

WGNW/BIL/O WN5 77 M8
Rainham Cl ALL/GAR L19 130 E5
Rainhill Rd RAIN/WH L35 101 L8
Raithby Dr WGNS/IIMK WN3 79 J3 2
Rake Hey MOR/LEA CH46 109 K5
Rake Hey Cl MOR/LEA CH46 109 L5
Rake La CHNE CH2 163 M8
FROD/HEL WA6 159 J7
FROD/HEL WA6 165 M6
GR/UP/WCH CH49 126 C1
WAL/NB CH45 95 K7
Rakersfield Ct WAL/NB CH45 95 L5 3
Rakersfield Rd WAL/NB CH45 95 L5
The Rake PS/BROM CH62 143 L5
Raleigh Av RAIN/WH L35 116 F3
Raleigh Cl WARRW/BUR WA5 120 F4
Raleigh Rd MOR/LEA CH46 110 D1
NSTN CH64 153 G4
Raleigh St BTL L20 6 E9
Ralph's Wife's La CHTN/BK PR9 23 H7
Rame Cl NG/CROX L11 85 K7 3
Ramford St STHEL WA9 102 F3
Ramilies Rd CALD/MH L18 114 B8
Ramleh Cl CSBY/BLUN L23 82 C2
Rampit Cl RNFD/HAY WA11 91 H6 3
Ramsay Cl GOL/RIS/CU WA3 123 G2 3
Ramsbrook Cl SPK/HALE L24 146 E1 1
Ramsbrook La SPK/HALE L24 147 L2
Ramsbrook Rd SPK/HALE L24 146 E1
Ramsden Cl WGNS/IIMK WN3 4 A9
Ramsey Cl AIMK WN4 91 K3 3
ALL/GAR L19 130 F5
RAIN/WH L35 117 G2 2
WDN WA8 135 G2
Ramsey Ct WKBY CH48 124 D4
Ramsey Rd ALL/GAR L19 130 F5
EP CH65 163 L4
Ramsfield Rd SPK/HALE L24 147 J1
Ramsons Cl HLWD L26 132 A4 7
Randall Av WGNNW/ST WN6 55 J8
Randall Dr NTHTN L30 83 L3
Randle Av RNFD/HAY WA11 76 A5
Randle Brook Ct
RNFD/HAY WA11 76 A5
Randle Cl BEB CH63 143 J3 3
Randle Meadow GTS/LS CH66 163 H3
Randles Rd PR/KW L34 86 C8
Randolph St ANF/KKDL L4 97 H6 10
Randon Gv ECCL WA10 8 E4
Ranelagh Av LITH L21 83 J5
Ranelagh Dr STHP PR8 35 H6
Ranelagh Dr North
ALL/GAR L19 130 C5
Ranelagh Dr South
ALL/GAR L19 130 C6
Ranelagh St CLVPS L1 13 H8
Ranfurly Rd ALL/GAR L19 130 D6
Rangemoor Cl
GOL/RIS/CU WA3 107 J7 4
Rangemore Rd CALD/MH L18 130 C4
Rangletts Av CHLY/EC PR7 32 E7
Ranicar Steet WGNE/HIN WN2 81 L2 1
Rankin St WAL/EG CH44 111 J3
Ranleigh Dr SKEL WN8 53 J4 5
Ranmore Av AIMK WN4 90 F1 4
Rannoch Cl GTS/LS CH66 163 H2
Ranulph Ct FROD/HEL WA6 160 E6
Ranworth Cl NG/CROX L11 98 A2 2
Ranworth Dr GOL/RIS/CU WA3 93 G6
Ranworth Pl NG/CROX L11 98 B2 1
Ranworth Rd
WARRW/BUR WA5 120 A7 4
Ranworth Sq NG/CROX L11 98 B2 2
Ranworth Wy NG/CROX L11 98 B2 3
Rappart Rd WAL/EG CH44 111 M2
Rassey Cl WGNNW/ST WN6 56 C6
Ratcliffe Rd WGNE/HIN WN2 57 L7
Ratcliffe St WGNNW/ST WN6 4 A2
Ratcliff Pl RAIN/WH L35 117 K1
Rathbone Rd HTWN L38 70 B1 1
WAV L15 114 B5
Rathen Av WGNE/HIN WN2 69 J4
Rathlin Cl WDN WA8 135 G2
Rathmell Cl GOL/RIS/CU WA3 107 G2 2
Rathmore Av CALD/MH L18 130 C2
Rathmore Cl CL/PREN CH43 127 J2
Rathmore Crs CHTN/BK PR9 25 K2
Rathmore Dr CL/PREN CH43 127 J1
Rathmore Rd CL/PREN CH43 127 J1
Raven Cl NPK/KEN L6 113 J2 16
Ravendale Cl CL/PREN CH43 126 F1 7
Ravenfield Cl HLWD L26 132 A5 3
Ravenfield Dr WDN WA8 133 L2
Ravenglass Av MGHL L31 72 F3
Ravenhead Av KKBY L32 86 A6
Ravenhead Dr SKEL WN8 66 C6
Ravenhead Rd ECCL WA10 8 D9
Ravenhead Wy SKEL WN8 66 B7
Ravenhill Crs MOR/LEA CH46 110 B2
Ravenhill Dr CHLY/EC PR7 32 E4
Ravenhurst Ct
GOL/RIS/CU WA3 107 H8
Ravenhurst Wy RAIN/WH L35 116 E4
Raven Meols La FMBY L37 59 G3
Ravenna Rd ALL/GAR L19 130 F5
Ravenscroft FMBY L37 59 H3
Ravenscroft Av ORM L39 63 G1
Ravenscroft Rd CL/PREN CH43 10 E7
Ravensdale Cl
WARRN/WOL WA2 121 M2 2
The Ravens FMBY L37 59 H3
Ravensthorpe Gn NG/CROX L11 98 B2
Ravenstone Dr STHEL WA9 102 F6
Ravenstone Rd ALL/GAR L19 130 D5
Ravenswood Av RF/TRAN CH42 128 B5
WGNS/IIMK WN3 78 F2
Ravenswood Rd
CLB/OSW/ST L13 114 C2
PEN/TH CH61 141 J3
Rawcliffe Cl WDN WA8 134 B1 5
Rawcliffe Rd CHLY/EC PR7 32 E6 13
RF/TRAN CH42 11 G8
WLT/FAZ L9 97 H1
Rawdon Cl RUNC WA7 150 C6
Rawlings Cl GOL/RIS/CU WA3 123 H2
Rawlinson Crs HLWD L26 132 D5 1
Rawlinson Gv CHTN/BK PR9 25 G4 1
Rawlinson La CHLY/EC PR7 44 A4
Rawlinson Rd CHTN/BK PR9 25 G4
CLB/OSW/ST L13 114 C2 3
Rawlins St EHL/KEN L7 113 M2
Rawson Cl LITH L21 83 H6
Rawson Rd LITH L21 83 H7
Rawthey Pl WGNE/HIN WN2 80 B3 2
Raydale Cl GOL/RIS/CU WA3 93 G4 3
WLT/FAZ L9 97 J2
Raymond Av NTHTN L30 84 C4
WARRS WA4 137 M3
Raymond Pl EV L5 13 G1
Raymond Rd WAL/EG CH44 111 J2
Raymond Wy NSTN CH64 153 J6
Rayner Av WGNE/HIN WN2 80 F3
Raynham Rd
CLB/OSW/ST L13 114 B3 1
Reade Cl BEB CH63 143 J4
Reading St EV L5 96 F6
Reads Ct WLT/FAZ L9 84 B7
Reaper Cl WARRW/BUR WA5 120 F7
Reapers Wy NTHTN L30 84 C1
Reay St WDN WA8 134 E3
Rebecca Gdns STHEL WA9 102 E6
Recreation Av AIMK WN4 91 M1
Recreation Dr
WGNW/BIL/O WN5 78 A8 2
Rector Rd NPK/KEN L6 97 L6
Rectory Av GOL/RIS/CU WA3 92 E5
Rectory Cl CHLY/EC PR7 32 E4
HES CH60 141 H6
LEY/BBR PR5 29 L3 1
RF/TRAN CH42 11 H9 1
WARRN/WOL WA2 105 J7
Rectory Dr HLWD L26 132 B4
Rectory La CH/BCN CH1 162 B4
HES CH60 141 G6
WARRN/WOL WA2 105 J7
WGNNW/ST WN6 56 B4
Rectory Rd AIMK WN4 78 F8
CHTN/BK PR9 25 H4
WKBY CH48 124 D4
Red Bank Av NEWLW WA12 105 H4
Red Banks WKBY CH48 124 F7
Red Barnes FMBY L37 47 H7
Red Barn Rd WGNW/BIL/O WN5 77 K7
Redbourne Av HLWD L26 132 B7
Redbourne Dr WDN WA8 133 K1
Redbourn St NPK/KEN L6 97 L7
Red Br BRSC L40 28 E3
Redbrook Cl PS/BROM CH62 143 M7 1
Redbrook Rd WGNS/IIMK WN3 5 J7
Redbrook St NPK/KEN L6 97 L7
Red Brow La WARRS WA4 151 H5
Redbrow Wy NWD/KWIPK L33 86 A1
Redburn Cl TOX L8 129 J1 19
WGNS/IIMK WN3 4 D8
Redcap Cl WAL/NB CH45 95 G5 3
Redcar Cl STHP PR8 36 B2
Redcar Dr PS/BROM CH62 143 M8
Redcar Rd WAL/NB CH45 94 F7
Redcar St NPK/KEN L6 97 L7
Red Cat La BRSC L40 39 G5
Redcliffe Gdns ORM L39 63 G2
Red Cross St CLVPS L1 12 E8
Red Cut La NWD/KWIPK L33 87 H5
Red Delph La RNFD/HAY WA11 75 M4
Redditch Cl
GR/UP/WCH CH49 125 L1 5
Redesdale Cl
WARRN/WOL WA2 122 A3 4
Redfern St BTL L20 96 E5
Redfield Cl WAL/EG CH44 111 M1 2
Red Fold ORM L39 62 E3
Redford Cl GR/UP/WCH CH49 125 L1 6
Redford St NPK/KEN L6 97 L8
Redgate FMBY L37 59 J3
ORM L39 62 F1
Redgate Av CSBY/BLUN L23 83 J1
Redgate Dr FMBY L37 59 K3
STHEL WA9 102 F2
Redgate Rd AIMK WN4 79 K7
Redgrave Ri WGNS/IIMK WN3 78 F2
Redgrave St EHL/KEN L7 113 L3 8
Redhill Av KKBY L32 86 B5
Redhill Gv CHLYE PR6 33 G2
Red Hill Rd BEB CH63 127 K8
Redhills Dr STHP PR8 36 B2 1
Redhills Ms EP CH65 20 B2
Red Hill Wy WGNE/HIN WN2 69 M7 12
Redhouse Bank WKBY CH48 124 C2 6
Red House La CHLY/EC PR7 30 D7
Redhouse La WKBY CH48 124 C2
Redington Rd ALL/GAR L19 130 F5
Redland Ct WGNE/HIN WN2 80 A6
Redland Rd WLT/FAZ L9 84 D5
Red La CHLY/EC PR7 31 G7
FROD/HEL WA6 160 E5
WARRS WA4 137 L6
Red Lion Cl MGHL L31 72 E4
Red Lion La GTS/LS CH66 155 L6
Red Lomes NTHTN L30 71 M8
Redmain Gv GOL/RIS/CU WA3 93 G5
Redmain Wy WD/CROXPK L12 99 H3 1
Redmayne Cl NEWLW WA12 104 D1 3
Redmere Dr HES CH60 141 L5
Redmires Cl EHL/KEN L7 113 K5 7
Redmond St BIRK CH41 11 J9 2
Redmoor Crs NWD/KWIPK L33 86 A1
Red Pike GTS/LS CH66 155 M6
Redpoll Gv HLWD L26 132 A3
Redpoll La GOL/RIS/CU WA3 123 G1 4
Red Rock Cl NPK/KEN L6 113 K1
Red Rock La WGNE/HIN WN2 56 F5
Red Rock St NPK/KEN L6 113 K1
Red Rum Cl WLT/FAZ L9 84 F5
Redruth Av RNFD/HAY WA11 89 M6
Redruth Cl RUNC WA7 150 E7
Redruth Rd NG/CROX L11 85 M8
Red Sands ORM L39 62 F2
Redshank Cl NEWLW WA12 104 E1 5
Redshank La GOL/RIS/CU WA3 123 H1
Redstart Cl GOL/RIS/CU WA3 93 G5 7
Redstone Cl HOY CH47 108 F5 2
Redstone Dr HES CH60 140 E4
Red Stone Hl FROD/HEL WA6 166 D1
Redstone Ri CL/PREN CH43 110 F7
Redvales Ct GOL/RIS/CU WA3 122 E1 4
Redvers Av GTS/LS CH66 155 J3
Redvers Dr WLT/FAZ L9 84 B7
Redwing La WLTN L25 131 J1
Redwing Wy HLWD L26 131 M3
Redwood WGNNW/ST WN6 55 K7
Redwood Av MGHL L31 72 E2 2
WGNNW/ST WN6 68 A2
WGNW/BIL/O WN5 67 J7
Redwood Cl CL/PREN CH43 127 H3 3
WARR WA1 123 G7
Redwood Dr CHNE CH2 165 L1
GTS/LS CH66 163 H4
ORM L39 62 F1
RNFD/HAY WA11 90 B8
Redwood Gv BTL L20 7 H3 1
Redwood Rd WLTN L25 115 K8
Redwood Wy NWD/KWIPK L33 74 A7
Reedale Cl CALD/MH L18 130 C1
Reedale Rd CALD/MH L18 130 C1
Reed Crs WGNS/IIMK WN3 79 J1
Reeds Av East MOR/LEA CH46 110 B2
Reeds Av West MOR/LEA CH46 110 B2
Reeds Brow RNFD/HAY WA11 76 D5
Reeds La MOR/LEA CH46 110 B2
RNFD/HAY WA11 88 B2
Reedsmere Cl WARRS WA4 138 A3 1
WGNW/BIL/O WN5 68 B7 10
Reeds Rd HUY L36 116 A1
The Reeds ORM L39 50 F7
Reedville Gv MOR/LEA CH46 110 B3
Reedville Rd BEB CH63 128 B8
Reepham Cl WGNS/IIMK WN3 78 F2
Rees Pk BRSC L40 52 B2
Reeves Av BTL L20 7 L1
Reeves St STHEL WA9 103 G2 2
Reeve St GOL/RIS/CU WA3 93 K5
Reeveswood CHLY/EC PR7 30 D7
Regal Cl GTS/LS CH66 163 G2
Regal Dr ECCL WA10 88 E8
Regal Rd NG/CROX L11 98 E2
Regency Gdns STHP PR8 35 G1
Regent Av AIMK WN4 79 H8
DV/KA/FCH L14 115 G3
NTHTN L30 84 B2
RNFD/HAY WA11 90 D6
WARR WA1 122 C5
Regent Cl STHP PR8 35 H1
Regent Rd BTL L20 6 B2
CHLY/EC PR7 32 D6
CSBY/BLUN L23 82 F1
EV L5 96 D7
STHP PR8 35 G1
WAL/NB CH45 94 F7
WDN WA8 16 E1
WGNE/HIN WN2 80 C2
Regents Cl PEN/TH CH61 126 D7
Regents Rd ECCL WA10 101 L4
Regent St CHLY/EC PR7 43 G4
EP CH65 156 C8
NEWLW WA12 104 C2
RUNC WA7 19 G2
VAUX/LVPD L3 12 C2
WARR WA1 14 D6
WGNE/HIN WN2 69 M8 26
Regents Wy BEB CH63 127 M6
CHLY/EC PR7 31 M3
Regina Av CSBY/WL L22 82 E3
Reginald Rd STHEL WA9 103 G7
Regina Rd WLT/FAZ L9 84 C7
Reid Av WARRW/BUR WA5 121 H5 2
Reid Ct GTS/LS CH66 155 L6
Reigate CHLYE PR6 33 H2
Reigate Cl WLTN L25 131 L3
Renacres La ORM L39 36 A8
Rendal Cl EV L5 97 J8 7
Rendcombe Gn NG/CROX L11 98 B2
Rendel Cl NEWLW WA12 104 F3
Rendelsham Cl
GR/UP/WCH CH49 110 A8 3
Rendel St BIRK CH41 11 H3
Rendlesham Cl
GOL/RIS/CU WA3 107 K7
Renfrew Av PS/BROM CH62 144 A8
RNFD/HAY WA11 90 A6
Renfrew Cl WGNS/IIMK WN3 79 J2
Renfrew Rd WGNE/HIN WN2 57 M8
Renfrew St EHL/KEN L7 113 J3
Renfrey Cl ORM L39 51 G5
Rennell Rd DV/KA/FCH L14 114 E2
Rennie Av ECCL WA10 101 L1 1
Renown Cl GOL/RIS/CU WA3 122 F1 5
Renown Wy SPK/HALE L24 131 J7
Renshaw St CLVPS L1 13 J8
Renton Av RUNC WA7 149 M3
Renville Rd DV/KA/FCH L14 114 E4
Renwick Av RAIN/WH L35 117 J1
Renwick Sq AIMK WN4 91 H2 2
Repton Av WGNE/HIN WN2 80 B1
Repton Gv WLT/FAZ L9 84 E3
Repton Rd CHLDW L16 114 F5
EP CH65 20 F7
Reservoir Rd RF/TRAN CH42 127 K4
WLTN L25 131 H2
Reservoir Rd North
RF/TRAN CH42 127 K3
Reservoir St NPK/KEN L6 113 J1 6
RAIN/WH L35 101 L6
WGNE/HIN WN2 69 J5 9
Rest Hill Rd BEB CH63 127 K8
Restormel Av WGNE/HIN WN2 57 M8
Retford Rd NWD/KWIPK L33 86 B3 5
Reva Rd DV/KA/FCH L14 115 H3
Revesby Cl WDN WA8 133 M3 4
Rexmore Rd CALD/MH L18 130 C3
Rexmore Wy WAV L15 114 A6 10
Reynolds Av GOL/RIS/CU WA3 107 G8
STHEL WA9 103 K3
Reynolds Cl NPK/KEN L6 113 J1
Reynolds St WARRS WA4 138 B2
Reynolds Wy WLTN L25 131 J3
Rhiwlas St TOX L8 113 J8
Rhodesia Rd WLT/FAZ L9 84 D7
Rhodes St WARRN/WOL WA2 15 G1
Rhodesway HES CH60 141 K6
Rhona Cl BEB CH63 154 E1
Rhona Dr WARRW/BUR WA5 120 A7 5
Rhosesmor Cl KKBY L32 86 B7 1
Rhosesmor Rd KKBY L32 86 B7
Rhuddlan Ct EP CH65 163 M3
Rhum Cl EP CH65 163 L4
Rhyl St TOX L8 113 H8 10
WDN WA8 16 B6 1
Ribbesford Rd WGNS/IIMK WN3 78 E1
Ribble Av CHTN/BK PR9 25 L1
MGHL L31 73 G3
RAIN/WH L35 117 L2
Ribble Cl GOL/RIS/CU WA3 107 H3
WDN WA8 135 H2
Ribble Crs WGNW/BIL/O WN5 89 L2
Ribbledale Rd CALD/MH L18 130 C1
Ribble Dr WGNW/BIL/O WN5 67 L6
Ribble Gv LEIGH WN7 81 L8
Ribble Rd WGNE/HIN WN2 80 C3
WGNNW/ST WN6 55 K3
WLTN L25 131 L2
Ribbler's La KKBY L32 85 M6
PR/KW L34 86 B7
Ribblesdale EP CH65 20 A9
Ribblesdale Av WLT/FAZ L9 84 D6 13
Ribblesdale Cl
PS/BROM CH62 144 B8 1
Ribblesdale Pl CHLY/EC PR7 32 D5 2
Ribble St BIRK CH41 111 H4
Ribchester Gdns
GOL/RIS/CU WA3 107 J2
Ribchester Wy RAIN/WH L35 116 C6
Rice Hey Rd WAL/EG CH44 95 L8
Rice La WLT/FAZ L9 97 J1
Rice St CLVPS L1 113 G5 16
Richard Gv WD/CROXPK L12 99 G8 3
Richard Hesketh Dr KKBY L32 85 L3
Richard Kelly Cl ANF/KKDL L4 97 M5 2
Richard Kelly Dr ANF/KKDL L4 97 M3
Richard Kelly Pl ANF/KKDL L4 97 M5 3
Richard Martin Rd LITH L21 83 L4 2
Richard Rd CSBY/BLUN L23 70 C7
Richards Gv STHEL WA9 103 G1
Richardson Rd RF/TRAN CH42 128 A4
Richardson St EHL/KEN L7 113 L6 5
WARRN/WOL WA2 121 L5 1
Richards Rd WGNNW/ST WN6 55 K2 1
Richard St WGNS/IIMK WN3 5 G7
Richland Rd CLB/OSW/ST L13 98 B8
Richmond Av BRSC L40 52 A2
LITH L21 83 J5
RNFD/HAY WA11 90 D6
RUNC WA7 150 A3
WARRS WA4 138 B1
WARRS WA4 138 E2
Richmond Cl BEB CH63 128 B7
ECCL WA10 101 H1
GOL/RIS/CU WA3 106 F1
HTWN L38 70 B3
WGN WN1 56 D6
Richmond Ct CHLY/EC PR7 32 E7 8
LITH L21 83 K6 5
Richmond Cresent NTHTN L30 84 B2
Richmond Gdns
NEWLW WA12 104 E3 3
Richmond Gv MGHL L31 73 G2 3
Richmond Hl WGNW/BIL/O WN5 67 L7
Richmond Ms BRSC L40 52 B2 5
Richmond Pk NPK/KEN L6 97 K7
Richmond Rd AIMK WN4 79 H8
BEB CH63 128 B7 1
CHLY/EC PR7 30 E6
CHLYE PR6 33 G7
CSBY/BLUN L23 71 G8
STHP PR8 35 H3
WGNE/HIN WN2 81 J2
Richmond Rw VAUX/LVPD L3 13 J3
Richmond St WAL/NB CH45 95 K4 4
WARRS WA4 138 C2
WDN WA8 17 G1 2
WGN WN1 4 D3
WGNS/IIMK WN3 68 C8
Richmond Ter NPK/KEN L6 97 J8
Richmond Wy HUY L36 116 C6
PEN/TH CH61 126 C7 4
PEN/TH CH61 141 H3
Rickaby Cl BEB CH63 143 L5
Rickman St ANF/KKDL L4 96 F5
Rickman Wy HUY L36 116 B5
Ridding La RUNC WA7 150 D8
Riddock Rd LITH L21 83 K8
Ridge Av WGN WN1 56 D6
Ridgeborne Cl
WARRW/BUR WA5 120 F3
Ridge Cl CHTN/BK PR9 22 E8 6
Ridgefield Rd PEN/TH CH61 126 B8
Ridgemere Rd PEN/TH CH61 126 B8
Ridge Rd CHLYE PR6 33 G6
The Ridge HES CH60 140 F3
Ridgetor Rd WLTN L25 131 J2
Ridgeview Rd CL/PREN CH43 110 F8
Ridgeway GOL/RIS/CU WA3 93 G6
Ridgeway Cl GTS/LS CH66 162 E3
Ridgeway Dr MGHL L31 72 F2
Ridgeway Gdns LYMM WA13 139 M2
The Ridgeway BEB CH63 127 M5 1
FROD/HEL WA6 167 J3
HES CH60 141 K6
HOY CH47 109 G6
RUNC WA7 150 F7
WDN WA8 117 L7
WLTN L25 131 J2
Ridgewell Av
GOL/RIS/CU WA3 92 F5 4
Ridgewood Dr PEN/TH CH61 141 H1
STHEL WA9 102 F7
Ridgewood Wy WLT/FAZ L9 84 C6
Ridgmont Av NG/CROX L11 98 B3
Ridgway HOR/BR BL6 57 L3
Ridgway St WARRN/WOL WA2 15 J1
Riding Cl STHEL WA9 118 E1 16
Riding Fold HLWD L26 131 M3 6
Riding Hill Rd PR/KW L34 99 M3
Riding La AIMK WN4 80 A8
ORM L39 61 G1
Ridings Hey CL/PREN CH43 126 F1 8
The Ridings CHTN/BK PR9 25 J2
CL/PREN CH43 110 F8 5
Riding St STHP PR8 3 G6
VAUX/LVPD L3 13 L6
Ridley Dr WARRW/BUR WA5 136 E1
Ridley Gv WKBY CH48 124 C2 7
Ridley La BRSC L40 41 H3
LEY/BBR PR5 29 M2
MGHL L31 72 F4
Ridley Rd NPK/KEN L6 113 L2
Ridley St CL/PREN CH43 10 E7
Ridyard St WGNE/HIN WN2 80 D2
WGNW/BIL/O WN5 68 A6
Riesling Dr NWD/KWIPK L33 73 M8
Rigby Av HOR/BR BL6 57 L3 2
Rigby Dr GR/UP/WCH CH49 125 M3
Rigby Rd MGHL L31 72 D2
Rigbys La AIMK WN4 91 M2
Rigby St AIMK WN4 91 J2
ECCL WA10 8 F4 3
GOL/RIS/CU WA3 92 C5 4
VAUX/LVPD L3 12 D5
Riley Av BTL L20 7 K1
Riley Dr RUNC WA7 19 H7
Riley La WGNE/HIN WN2 57 K6
Riley Sq WGN WN1 5 H3
Rilston Av GOL/RIS/CU WA3 106 F2
Rimington Av
GOL/RIS/CU WA3 92 E4 6
Rimington Cl
GOL/RIS/CU WA3 107 G2 5
Rimmer Av CHLDW L16 115 J4
Rimmer Cl LITH L21 83 K6
Rimmer Gn STHP PR8 36 F4
Rimmer Gv STHEL WA9 103 G2
Rimmer's Av FMBY L37 47 G7
STHP PR8 3 G6
Rimmers Ct BIRK CH41 111 H6 4
Rimmer St VAUX/LVPD L3 13 K5
Rimmington Rd AIG/SPK L17 130 A3 3
Rimrose Rd BTL L20 6 D4
Rimrose Valley Rd
CSBY/BLUN L23 83 J2
Ringcroft Rd CLB/OSW/ST L13 114 D2
Ringley Av GOL/RIS/CU WA3 92 B4
Ring O'bells La BRSC L40 52 D3
Ringo Starr Dr NPK/KEN L6 113 K2 11
Ringsfield Rd SPK/HALE L24 147 J2 2
Ringtail Ct BRSC L40 51 K1
Ringtail Pl BRSC L40 51 K2
Ringtail Rd BRSC L40 51 K1
Ringway CHLY/EC PR7 32 C6
GTS/LS CH66 163 G1
NSTN CH64 153 H3
Ringway Rd RUNC WA7 149 M3
WLTN L25 115 L8 3
Ringways PS/BROM CH62 143 M2
Ringwood CL/PREN CH43 127 J2
Ringwood Av DV/KA/FCH L14 115 H3
Ringwood Cl GOL/RIS/CU WA3 107 K8
Ripley Av LITH L21 83 K4
Ripley Cl MGHL L31 73 G4
Ripley Dr WGNS/IIMK WN3 78 E1
Ripley St WARRW/BUR WA5 121 G6
Ripon Av GOL/RIS/CU WA3 92 F5
Ripon Cl HUY L36 116 C2
NEWLW WA12 91 L8 3
NTHTN L30 84 B4 1
STHP PR8 36 B2
Ripon Dr AIMK WN4 91 M3
Ripon Rd WAL/NB CH45 95 G7
Ripon St ANF/KKDL L4 97 H4
BIRK CH41 11 J9
Rippon Av GTS/LS CH66 155 L8
Risbury Cl NG/CROX L11 98 B3
The Rise WGNNW/ST WN6 67 L2
Rishton Cl EV L5 97 J8
Risley Rd GOL/RIS/CU WA3 107 H7
Ritchie Av WLT/FAZ L9 84 E6
Ritherup La RAIN/WH L35 117 L1
Ritson St TOX L8 113 K7
Rivacre Brow GTS/LS CH66 156 A6
Rivacre Rd EP CH65 155 L3
GTS/LS CH66 156 A6
PS/BROM CH62 155 J1
River Avon St TOX L8 113 L6 6
Riverbank Cl HES CH60 141 H7
Riverbank Rd ALL/GAR L19 130 C6
HES CH60 141 G7
River Cl FMBY L37 59 K4
Riverdale Cl WGNNW/ST WN6 67 M2
River Gv PS/BROM CH62 128 D5
Rivermeade STHP PR8 35 M1
River Rd WARRS WA4 14 F9
Riversdale FROD/HEL WA6 160 E4
WARR WA1 123 H6
Riversdale Ct AIG/SPK L17 130 B5
Riversdale Ms ALL/GAR L19 130 B5 3
Riversdale Rd ALL/GAR L19 130 B6
LITH L21 83 H6 3
RUNC WA7 150 A4
WAL/EG CH44 111 M1
WKBY CH48 124 C3
Riverside HTWN L38 70 B1
PS/BROM CH62 128 D8
WD/CROXPK L12 99 G4
WKBY CH48 124 D5
Riverside Av WGN WN1 5 H1
Riverside Cl BTL L20 83 J8
WARR WA1 15 H7
Riverside Crs LEY/BBR PR5 29 J3
Riverside Dr AIG/SPK L17 129 J3
VAUX/LVPD L3 129 H2
Riverside Gv STHEL WA9 102 F6 10
Riverside Wk NSTN CH64 152 F8
Riverslea Rd CSBY/WL L22 82 D3
Rivers St WGNW/BIL/O WN5 67 G7
River St BIRK CH41 11 G6
River Vw CSBY/WL L22 82 D3
Riverview Rd NSTN CH64 153 H8
WAL/EG CH44 112 A2
River Wy WGN WN1 4 F5
Riverwood Rd PS/BROM CH62 144 B4
Riviera Dr RF/TRAN CH42 127 M4
Rivington Av CHLYE PR6 44 C6
CL/PREN CH43 127 G1
ECCL WA10 89 G7
GOL/RIS/CU WA3 92 E4
WGN WN1 68 D3
WGNE/HIN WN2 80 D2
Rivington Cl STHP PR8 35 J2
Rivington Dr BRSC L40 52 A2 3
SKEL WN8 66 E6
WGNE/HIN WN2 81 H4

Rivington La CHLYE PR6 ... 44 F6
HOR/BR BL6 ... 45 H4
Rivington Pl CHLY/EC PR7 ... 42 F7
Rivington Rd CHLYE PR6 ... 33 G4
ECCL WA10 ... 8 B4
EP CH65 ... 20 B5
WAL/EG CH44 ... 111 M2
Rivington St ECCL WA10 ... 8 A7
HOR/BR BL6 ... 57 M3 5
Rivington Wy WGNNW/ST WN6 ... 56 B5
Rixton Av WARRW/BUR WA5 ... 121 H5
Roach Gn WGN WN1 ... 5 K1
Roadside Ct GOL/RIS/CU WA3 ... 92 E5
Roadwater Cl WLTN L25 ... 115 K6
Robarts Rd ANF/KKDL L4 ... 97 J7
Robeck Rd CLB/OSW/ST L13 ... 114 D4 2
Robert Dr GR/UP/WCH CH49 ... 126 A2
Robert Gv WD/CROXPK L12 ... 99 G8
Roberts Av RNFD/HAY WA11 ... 90 C8
Roberts Ct RUNC WA7 ... 150 A7
Roberts Dr BTL L20 ... 84 A7
Robertson St TOX L8 ... 113 G8
Roberts St CHLY/EC PR7 ... 32 E6 14
VAUX/LVPD L3 ... 12 C4
Robert St BIRK CH41 ... 11 H4
RUNC WA7 ... 19 L3
WARRW/BUR WA5 ... 14 A4
WDN WA8 ... 16 F2
WGNE/HIN WN2 ... 80 C2 1
Robina Rd STHEL WA9 ... 102 F5
Robin Cl CHLY/EC PR7 ... 42 F2 1
RUNC WA7 ... 150 F6
Robin Hill Dr WGNNW/ST WN6 ... 55 K3
Robin Hill La WGNNW/ST WN6 ... 55 L2
Robin Hood La FROD/HEL WA6 ... 166 D3
WGNNW/ST WN6 ... 54 D2
Robin La SKEL WN8 ... 40 E8
Robin Park Rd WGNW/BIL/O WN5 ... 4 A6
Robins Cft GTS/LS CH66 ... 163 H3
Robins La GOL/RIS/CU WA3 ... 106 F3
RNFD/HAY WA11 ... 77 H5
STHEL WA9 ... 102 E5
Robinson Rd LITH L21 ... 83 L4
Robin Wy GR/UP/WCH CH49 ... 126 D3
Rob La NEWLW WA12 ... 105 G1
Robsart St EV L5 ... 97 G8
Robson St CLB/OSW/ST L13 ... 114 B4
EV L5 ... 97 H7
WARR WA1 ... 15 J3
Roby Cl RAIN/WH L35 ... 117 L1
Roby Gv WARRW/BUR WA5 ... 120 C7 3
Roby Ml SKEL WN8 ... 66 D2
Roby Mount Av HUY L36 ... 115 M3
Roby Rd HUY L36 ... 115 J3
Roby St BTL L20 ... 7 H2
ECCL WA10 ... 8 A9
WAV L15 ... 114 A6
Roby Well Wy
WGNW/BIL/O WN5 ... 77 M8
Rocastle Cl NPK/KEN L6 ... 113 J2
Rochester Av NTHTN L30 ... 84 B4
Rochester Cl GOL/RIS/CU WA3 ... 92 C5 5
WARRW/BUR WA5 ... 120 E8 5
Rochester Dr EP CH65 ... 20 F9
Rochester Gdns ECCL WA10 ... 8 A9
Rochester Rd RF/TRAN CH42 ... 128 C3
Roch Pl WGNE/HIN WN2 ... 80 B3 3
Rock Av HES CH60 ... 141 H4 2
Rockbank Rd CLB/OSW/ST L13 ... 98 B8
Rockbourne Av WLTN L25 ... 115 H8
Rockbourne Cl WGNE/HIN WN2 ... 80 E1
Rockbourne Gn WLTN L25 ... 115 H8
Rockbourne Wy WLTN L25 ... 115 H8 2
Rock Cl RF/TRAN CH42 ... 128 B3 11
Rock Ct CLB/OSW/ST L13 ... 114 C2
Rock Dr FROD/HEL WA6 ... 160 E4
Rock Farm Cl NSTN CH64 ... 153 J7
Rock Farm Dr NSTN CH64 ... 153 J7
Rock Farm Gv NSTN CH64 ... 153 J7 1
Rock Ferry By-pass
RF/TRAN CH42 ... 128 C3
Rockfield Cl WDN WA8 ... 133 M3
Rockfield Dr FROD/HEL WA6 ... 166 E3
Rockfield Rd ANF/KKDL L4 ... 97 H6
Rockford Av KKBY L32 ... 86 A6
Rockford Cl KKBY L32 ... 86 A6 2
Rockford Wk KKBY L32 ... 86 A6 3
Rock Gv CLB/OSW/ST L13 ... 114 C2
Rockhill Rd WLTN L25 ... 131 K4
Rockhouse St NPK/KEN L6 ... 97 L8
Rockingham Cl
GOL/RIS/CU WA3 ... 107 K7
Rockingham Ct
NWD/KWIPK L33 ... 86 B1 6
Rockland Rd CSBY/WL L22 ... 82 F3
Rocklands Av RF/TRAN CH42 ... 128 C6 5
Rocklands La BEB CH63 ... 142 E6
Rock La MGHL L31 ... 73 H8
WDN WA8 ... 134 A2
Rock La East RF/TRAN CH42 ... 128 C4
Rock La West RF/TRAN CH42 ... 128 B4
Rocklee Gdns NSTN CH64 ... 153 J7
Rockley St ANF/KKDL L4 ... 97 G5 11
ANF/KKDL L4 ... 97 G5 11
Rock Mount Cl WLTN L25 ... 131 H2
Rockmount Rd AIG/SPK L17 ... 130 B4 3
Rock Park Rd RF/TRAN CH42 ... 128 D4
Rockpoint Av WAL/NB CH45 ... 95 L6 11
Rocksavage Expy RUNC WA7 ... 149 L8
Rockside Rd CALD/MH L18 ... 130 C3
Rock St CLB/OSW/ST L13 ... 114 B2
GOL/RIS/CU WA3 ... 92 C3
STHEL WA9 ... 101 L5 3
The Rock FROD/HEL WA6 ... 166 D3
Rock Vw MGHL L31 ... 85 J2
Rockville Rd DV/KA/FCH L14 ... 114 E4
Rockville St RF/TRAN CH42 ... 128 B3
Rockwell Rd WD/CROXPK L12 ... 98 F5
Rockybank Rd RF/TRAN CH42 ... 127 M2
Rocky La CHLDW L16 ... 114 E5
HES CH60 ... 141 H5
NPK/KEN L6 ... 97 L8
Rocky La South HES CH60 ... 141 J5
Roderick Rd ANF/KKDL L4 ... 97 J3
Roderick St VAUX/LVPD L3 ... 13 K4 2
Rodgers Cl FROD/HEL WA6 ... 160 D4
Rodick St WLTN L25 ... 131 H3
Rodmell Rd WLT/FAZ L9 ... 84 D7
Rodney St BIRK CH41 ... 11 H8
CLVPS L1 ... 13 K9
ECCL WA10 ... 8 C5
WARRN/WOL WA2 ... 14 E3
WGN WN1 ... 4 F5
Roe Aly CLVPS L1 ... 13 H8
Roebuck St WGNE/HIN WN2 ... 81 L2 2
Roeburn Wy WARRW/BUR WA5 ... 135 M2
Roecliffe Cl WGNS/IIMK WN3 ... 4 C8
Roedean Cl MGHL L31 ... 72 F3
WLTN L25 ... 131 K5 2
Roehampton Dr CSBY/BLUN L23 ... 70 E7
RUNC WA7 ... 150 A6
Roe Hey Dr CHLY/EC PR7 ... 43 H3
Roe La CHTN/BK PR9 ... 25 G5
Roemarsh Ct RUNC WA7 ... 150 A7
Roe St CLVPS L1 ... 13 H6
Rogers Av BTL L20 ... 7 M1
Rogerson's Gn HLWD L26 ... 132 A3 5
Rokeby Av GOL/RIS/CU WA3 ... 92 F4
Rokeby Cl VAUX/LVPD L3 ... 13 K3
Rokeby Ct RUNC WA7 ... 135 M8
Rokeby St VAUX/LVPD L3 ... 13 K3
Rokeden NEWLW WA12 ... 104 F1 3
Roker Av WAL/EG CH44 ... 111 J2 12
Rokesmith Av EHL/KEN L7 ... 113 L5
Roland Av BEB CH63 ... 127 M7
RNFD/HAY WA11 ... 89 L6
RUNC WA7 ... 18 E5
Roleton Cl NTHTN L30 ... 84 D1
Rolleston Dr BEB CH63 ... 143 J1 4
WAL/NB CH45 ... 95 H6
Rolleston St WARRN/WOL WA2 ... 14 C4
Rolling Mill La STHEL WA9 ... 103 H5
Rollo St ANF/KKDL L4 ... 96 F6
Roman Cl NEWLW WA12 ... 104 E3
RUNC WA7 ... 150 E4
Roman Ct NSTN CH64 ... 153 H6
Roman Rd AIMK WN4 ... 79 J8 10
BEB CH63 ... 127 J7
CL/PREN CH43 ... 127 J5
HOY CH47 ... 108 F5 3
WARRS WA4 ... 137 L4 3
Rome Cl HUY L36 ... 115 M2
Romer Rd NPK/KEN L6 ... 113 L2
Romford Wy HLWD L26 ... 132 B7 3
Romiley Dr SKEL WN8 ... 65 H3
Romiley Rd GTS/LS CH66 ... 156 A7
Romiley Sq WGNNW/ST WN6 ... 56 A5 2
Romilly St NPK/KEN L6 ... 113 J2
Romley St ANF/KKDL L4 ... 97 H4
Romney Cl WDN WA8 ... 134 F3
Romney Wy NSTN CH64 ... 153 H6
WGN WN1 ... 68 D2
Romsey Av FMBY L37 ... 59 K3
Romsey Gv WGNS/IIMK WN3 ... 78 F3
Romulus St EHL/KEN L7 ... 113 M3 4
Ronald Cl CSBY/WL L22 ... 83 H4
Ronald Dr WARRN/WOL WA2 ... 122 D3
Ronald Rd CSBY/WL L22 ... 83 H4
Ronald Ross Av NTHTN L30 ... 84 B2
Ronaldshay WDN WA8 ... 135 G3 2
Ronald St CLB/OSW/ST L13 ... 114 B2
Ronaldsway AIN/FAZ L10 ... 85 J6
CSBY/BLUN L23 ... 71 J7
GR/UP/WCH CH49 ... 110 B7
HES CH60 ... 141 H7
HLWD L26 ... 132 C5
Ronan Cl BTL L20 ... 6 D2
Ronan Rd WDN WA8 ... 134 A8
Rone Cl MOR/LEA CH46 ... 109 M5
Roocroft Sq HOR/BR BL6 ... 57 L3 3
Rookery Av AIMK WN4 ... 91 K3
WGNNW/ST WN6 ... 55 G5
Rookery Cl CHLY/EC PR7 ... 32 C7
Rookery Dr RNFD/HAY WA11 ... 76 C8
Rookery La RNFD/HAY WA11 ... 76 C8
Rookery Rd CHTN/BK PR9 ... 25 G4
The Rookery NEWLW WA12 ... 104 F1 4
Rook Rd WARRS WA4 ... 15 M8
Rooks Wy HES CH60 ... 141 G5
Rookwood CHLY/EC PR7 ... 30 D7
Rookwood Av CHLY/EC PR7 ... 32 E3
The Rooley HUY L36 ... 115 M4
Roome St WARRN/WOL WA2 ... 15 G1
Roosevelt Dr WLT/FAZ L9 ... 84 D5
Ropers Bridge Cl RAIN/WH L35 ... 116 F3
Roper St STHEL WA9 ... 9 M3
TOX L8 ... 113 H8 11
The Ropewalk NSTN CH64 ... 152 E5 1
Rosalind Av BEB CH63 ... 128 A6
Rosalind Wy BTL L20 ... 7 K8
Rosam Ct RUNC WA7 ... 150 A7
Rosclare Dr WAL/NB CH45 ... 95 H7
Roscoe Av NEWLW WA12 ... 105 G2 3
WARRN/WOL WA2 ... 121 M5
Roscoe Cl RAIN/WH L35 ... 116 C6 1
Roscoe Crs RUNC WA7 ... 18 C9
Roscoe La CLVPS L1 ... 13 J9
Roscoe Lowe Brow CHLYE PR6 ... 44 F6
Roscoe Pl CLVPS L1 ... 13 J9
Roscoe St ECCL WA10 ... 8 B6
WGN WN1 ... 5 J5
Roscommon St EV L5 ... 13 J1
Roscote Cl HES CH60 ... 141 H6 2
The Roscote HES CH60 ... 141 H6 1
Roseacre WKBY CH48 ... 124 C2 3
Rose Av BTL L20 ... 83 L6
RNFD/HAY WA11 ... 91 G7
STHEL WA9 ... 102 E6
WGNE/HIN WN2 ... 80 D6
WGNNW/ST WN6 ... 68 B2
Rose Bank Cl WGN WN1 ... 68 D1
Rose Bank Rd CHLDW L16 ... 114 F6
Rosebank Rd HUY L36 ... 99 L7
Rosebank Wy HUY L36 ... 99 L8
Rosebay Cl FMBY L37 ... 59 J2 2
Roseberry Rd AIMK WN4 ... 79 J8 11
Rosebery Av CSBY/WL L22 ... 82 E3
WAL/EG CH44 ... 111 L1
Rosebery Gv RF/TRAN CH42 ... 127 K3 1
Rosebery Rd ECCL WA10 ... 88 F7
Rosebery St CHTN/BK PR9 ... 25 J7
TOX L8 ... 113 J6
Rosebourne Cl AIG/SPK L17 ... 129 L3 10
Rose Brae CALD/MH L18 ... 130 D1
Rosebridge Wy WGN WN1 ... 5 L5
Rose Brow WLTN L25 ... 131 J1
Rose Cl RUNC WA7 ... 150 F8
WAV L15 ... 114 A6
Rose Crs SKEL WN8 ... 65 G4
STHP PR8 ... 47 L3
WDN WA8 ... 16 B5
Rosecroft PS/BROM CH62 ... 143 L7 2
Rosecroft Cl ORM L39 ... 51 G7
Rosedale Av CSBY/BLUN L23 ... 83 G1
GOL/RIS/CU WA3 ... 92 E6
WARR WA1 ... 122 E6
Rosedale Cl WLT/FAZ L9 ... 97 K1
Rosedale Rd CALD/MH L18 ... 130 C1
RF/TRAN CH42 ... 128 A2
Rose Dr RNFD/HAY WA11 ... 76 C8
Rosefield Av BEB CH63 ... 128 A6
Rosefield Rd WLTN L25 ... 131 L4
Roseheath Dr HLWD L26 ... 132 B7
Rose Hl STHP PR8 ... 3 L6
VAUX/LVPD L3 ... 13 H3
Rosehill Av STHEL WA9 ... 103 K8
Rose Hill Av WGNW/BIL/O WN5 ... 67 L7
Rosehill Ct WLTN L25 ... 131 J1
Rosehill Dr ORM L39 ... 62 E3
Rose Hill Vw AIMK WN4 ... 79 H6
Roseland Cl MGHL L31 ... 72 D1
Roselands Ct RF/TRAN CH42 ... 128 A4
Rose La CALD/MH L18 ... 130 B2
Rose Lea Cl WDN WA8 ... 134 C1 2
Roselea Dr CHTN/BK PR9 ... 25 L1
Rosemary Av RUNC WA7 ... 150 B8 5
WARRS WA4 ... 138 A3
Rosemary Cl CL/PREN CH43 ... 111 G5 4
EHL/KEN L7 ... 113 J5 6
WARRW/BUR WA5 ... 120 E7 2
Rosemary Crs WGN WN1 ... 68 F3
Rosemary Dr NEWLW WA12 ... 105 H2
Rosemary La FMBY L37 ... 59 G2
ORM L39 ... 49 J8
Rosemead Av PEN/TH CH61 ... 141 H1
Rosemere Dr GTS/LS CH66 ... 163 H6
Rosemont Rd AIG/SPK L17 ... 130 B3
Rosemoor Dr CSBY/BLUN L23 ... 71 J8
Rosemoor Gdns WARRS WA4 ... 138 B8
Rose Mt CL/PREN CH43 ... 127 K2
Rose Mount Cl CL/PREN CH43 ... 127 J2
Rose Mount Dr WAL/NB CH45 ... 95 J7
Rose Pl BIRK CH41 ... 128 B2 11
ORM L39 ... 62 F3
RF/TRAN CH42 ... 11 H9
RNFD/HAY WA11 ... 76 C8
VAUX/LVPD L3 ... 13 J3
Rose St CLVPS L1 ... 13 H6 1
WDN WA8 ... 16 B5
WGN WN1 ... 5 L5
WGNE/HIN WN2 ... 69 M8 27
WLTN L25 ... 131 H3
Rose V EV L5 ... 97 G8
Rose View Av WDN WA8 ... 134 C3
Rose Vls WAV L15 ... 114 B6
Rosewarne Cl AIG/SPK L17 ... 129 K3 1
Rosewell Ct STBRV L28 ... 99 K7 1
Rosewood Av
FROD/HEL WA6 ... 160 F6 1
WARR WA1 ... 15 L1
Rosewood Cl NTHLY L27 ... 116 A8 4
STBRV L28 ... 99 K6 4
WGNE/HIN WN2 ... 80 D6 2
Rosewood Dr MOR/LEA CH46 ... 109 K5
Rosewood Gdns
NG/CROX L11 ... 98 D4 1
Roseworth Av WLT/FAZ L9 ... 84 C6
Rosina Cl AIMK WN4 ... 79 H7
Roskell Rd WLTN L25 ... 131 L6
Rosklyn Rd CHLYE PR6 ... 33 G6
Rosley Rd WGNS/IIMK WN3 ... 79 K2
Roslin Rd CL/PREN CH43 ... 127 K1
PEN/TH CH61 ... 125 M7
Roslyn St BIRK CH41 ... 128 B2
Rossall Av AIN/FAZ L10 ... 84 F2
Rossall Gv GTS/LS CH66 ... 155 M7
Rossall Rd CHLYE PR6 ... 33 G4 4
CLB/OSW/ST L13 ... 114 D3
MOR/LEA CH46 ... 110 A6
WARRW/BUR WA5 ... 136 D1
WDN WA8 ... 134 F3
Ross Av MOR/LEA CH46 ... 110 E1
Rossbank Rd EP CH65 ... 156 C6
Rosscliffe Rd EP CH65 ... 156 C6
Ross Cl PR/KW L34 ... 99 M2
WARRW/BUR WA5 ... 120 F5
WGNE/HIN WN2 ... 69 H3
WGNW/BIL/O WN5 ... 78 A8
Rossdale Gv WGNNW/ST WN6 ... 56 C6
Ross Dr GTS/LS CH66 ... 155 L8
Rossendale Cl CL/PREN CH43 ... 126 F1
Rossendale Dr
GOL/RIS/CU WA3 ... 107 J8 2
Rossett Av AIG/SPK L17 ... 113 M7
Rossett Cl WARRW/BUR WA5 ... 121 G3 2
WGNS/IIMK WN3 ... 78 F3 3
Rossett Rd CSBY/BLUN L23 ... 82 E2
Rossett St NPK/KEN L6 ... 97 L8
Rossfield Rd EP CH65 ... 156 C7
Rossini St LITH L21 ... 83 J7
Rosslyn Av MGHL L31 ... 72 D5
Rosslyn Crs MOR/LEA CH46 ... 110 A5 7
Rosslyn Dr MOR/LEA CH46 ... 110 A5
Rosslyn Pk MOR/LEA CH46 ... 110 A6
Rosslyn St AIG/SPK L17 ... 129 K2
Rossmore Gdns ANF/KKDL L4 ... 97 K6
GTS/LS CH66 ... 155 M7
Rossmore Rd East EP CH65 ... 156 B6
Rossmore Rd West
GTS/LS CH66 ... 155 M6
Rossmount Rd EP CH65 ... 156 C7
Ross Rd EP CH65 ... 156 C7
Ross St STHEL WA9 ... 9 M4
WDN WA8 ... 16 F2
Ross Tower Ct WAL/NB CH45 ... 95 L5
Rosswood Rd EP CH65 ... 156 C7
Rostherne Av GOL/RIS/CU WA3 ... 92 F5
GTS/LS CH66 ... 163 G1
WAL/EG CH44 ... 111 J2
Rostherne Cl WARRW/BUR WA5 ... 136 F1
Rostherne Crs WDN WA8 ... 133 M3
Rosthwaite Cl
WGNS/IIMK WN3 ... 79 J3 3
Rosthwaite Gv RNFD/HAY WA11 ... 89 K4
Rosthwaite Rd WD/CROXPK L12 ... 98 E7
Rostron Crs FMBY L37 ... 59 G4
Rothay Dr WARRW/BUR WA5 ... 135 M2
Rothbury Cl MOR/LEA CH46 ... 109 L5
RUNC WA7 ... 150 A7 3
Rothbury Ct STHEL WA9 ... 118 D3 2
Rothbury Rd DV/KA/FCH L14 ... 99 H7
Rother Dr EP CH65 ... 156 C6
Rotherham Cl HUY L36 ... 116 A1
Rotherwick Av CHLY/EC PR7 ... 32 D6
Rotherwood Cl BEB CH63 ... 127 M7 3
Rothesay Dr CSBY/BLUN L23 ... 83 G2
PS/BROM CH62 ... 154 F1
Rothley Av STHP PR8 ... 47 J1
Rothsay Cl RNFD/HAY WA11 ... 90 A6
Rothwell Cl ORM L39 ... 50 F8
Rothwell Dr ORM L39 ... 62 D3
STHP PR8 ... 34 C8
Rothwell Rd CHLYE PR6 ... 44 D6
GOL/RIS/CU WA3 ... 92 E4
Rothwells La CSBY/BLUN L23 ... 71 K7
Rothwell St NPK/KEN L6 ... 113 J1 7
Rotten Rw STHP PR8 ... 2 B7
Rotunda St EV L5 ... 96 F8 6
Roughdale Av KKBY L32 ... 86 B6
STHEL WA9 ... 118 D1 3
Roughdale Cl KKBY L32 ... 86 B6 3
Roughlea Av GOL/RIS/CU WA3 ... 106 F1
Roughley Av
WARRW/BUR WA5 ... 136 F1 9
Roughwood Dr NWD/KWIPK L33 ... 86 B2
The Roundabout WDN WA8 ... 117 M7
Round Hey STBRV L28 ... 99 J5
Round House Av WGN WN1 ... 5 K1
The Round Meade MGHL L31 ... 72 D3
Roundmoor Rd
WGNNW/ST WN6 ... 56 C6 1
Round Thorn GOL/RIS/CU WA3 ... 106 C6
The Roundway HTWN L38 ... 70 B2
Roundwood Dr STHEL WA9 ... 9 K9
Routledge St WDN WA8 ... 16 F1 3
Rowan Av GOL/RIS/CU WA3 ... 93 H6
WD/CROXPK L12 ... 99 H4
WGNNW/ST WN6 ... 68 B2
Rowan Cl RNFD/HAY WA11 ... 89 M6 1
RUNC WA7 ... 19 L9
WARRW/BUR WA5 ... 120 B7
Rowan Ct AIG/SPK L17 ... 130 A3 4
GR/UP/WCH CH49 ... 125 K3
Rowan Dr KKBY L32 ... 85 M2
Rowan Gv BEB CH63 ... 143 G1
CHLYE PR6 ... 32 E2
HUY L36 ... 115 M5
Rowanhill WGN WN1 ... 5 H1
Rowan La SKEL WN8 ... 65 K1
The Rowans ORM L39 ... 62 C6
Rowan Tree Cl
GR/UP/WCH CH49 ... 125 K2 2
Rowbottom Sq WGN WN1 ... 4 E4
Rowena Cl CSBY/BLUN L23 ... 83 H1 2
Rowland Cl WARRN/WOL WA2 ... 122 C2
Rowsley Gv WLT/FAZ L9 ... 84 D6 14
Rowson St PR/KW L34 ... 100 F6
WAL/NB CH45 ... 95 K5
Rowthorn Cl WDN WA8 ... 134 A5 1
Rowton Cl CL/PREN CH43 ... 127 H2
Rowton Ri WGN WN1 ... 56 D5
Roxborough Cl
WARRW/BUR WA5 ... 104 C7 1
Roxborough Wk WLTN L25 ... 131 L2
Roxburgh Av AIG/SPK L17 ... 129 L2
RF/TRAN CH42 ... 127 M3
Roxburgh Rd GTS/LS CH66 ... 155 H7
Roxburgh St ANF/KKDL L4 ... 7 L7
Royal Av WDN WA8 ... 133 K5
Royal Cl FMBY L37 ... 59 J4
Royal Crs FMBY L37 ... 59 J4
Royal Cft WD/CROXPK L12 ... 114 D1
Royal Gv ECCL WA10 ... 101 M4
Royal Mail St VAUX/LVPD L3 ... 13 J7
Royal St ANF/KKDL L4 ... 97 G6
Royal Ter STHP PR8 ... 2 F4
The Royal HOY CH47 ... 108 B7
Royden Av RUNC WA7 ... 18 F7
WAL/EG CH44 ... 95 M8
WGNS/IIMK WN3 ... 79 H3
Royden Crs WGNW/BIL/O WN5 ... 78 A8
Royden Rd
GR/UP/WCH CH49 ... 110 A7 5
WGNW/BIL/O WN5 ... 78 A8
Royden St TOX L8 ... 129 H1 13
Royden Wy VAUX/LVPD L3 ... 129 G2
Royhsay Cl EV L5 ... 13 K1
Royleen Dr FROD/HEL WA6 ... 160 F7
Royle Rd CHLY/EC PR7 ... 32 D5 3
Roynton Rd HOR/BR BL6 ... 45 K7
Roysten Gdns STHEL WA9 ... 102 F3
Royston Av WAL/EG CH44 ... 111 M1 13
WARR WA1 ... 122 B6
Royston Cl GOL/RIS/CU WA3 ... 93 G5 3
GTS/LS CH66 ... 163 H3
Royston St EHL/KEN L7 ... 113 K4
Royton Rd CSBY/WL L22 ... 83 H3
Rozel Crs WARRW/BUR WA5 ... 136 D1
Ruabon Crs WGNE/HIN WN2 ... 81 H1
Rubbing Stone WKBY CH48 ... 124 F7 3
Ruby St TOX L8 ... 129 H2
Rudd Av STHEL WA9 ... 103 J3
Ruddington Rd STHP PR8 ... 36 A3
Rudd St HOY CH47 ... 108 D6
Rudgate RAIN/WH L35 ... 117 G3
Rudgrave Ms WAL/EG CH44 ... 95 M8 2
Rudgrave Pl WAL/EG CH44 ... 95 M8 3
Rudgrave Sq WAL/EG CH44 ... 95 M8
Rudloe Ct WARRN/WOL WA2 ... 122 B4
Rudstone Cl GTS/LS CH66 ... 155 K8
Rudston Rd CHLDW L16 ... 114 F6
Rudyard Av WGNNW/ST WN6 ... 56 A3
Rudyard Cl DV/KA/FCH L14 ... 114 E2 1
Rudyard Rd DV/KA/FCH L14 ... 114 E2
Ruff La ORM L39 ... 63 J1
Rufford Av MGHL L31 ... 73 G2 4
Rufford Cl AIN/FAZ L10 ... 85 H4
RAIN/WH L35 ... 101 H8
WDN WA8 ... 133 L3 1
Rufford Dr CHTN/BK PR9 ... 23 H8
Rufford Rd BRSC L40 ... 40 B4
BTL L20 ... 83 L8
CHTN/BK PR9 ... 25 L2
NPK/KEN L6 ... 113 L2
RNFD/HAY WA11 ... 76 B5
WAL/EG CH44 ... 111 L2 7
Rugby Dr AIN/FAZ L10 ... 85 G4
WGNW/BIL/O WN5 ... 67 H5
Rugby Rd EP CH65 ... 20 D9
WAL/EG CH44 ... 95 H8
WLT/FAZ L9 ... 84 D5
Ruislip Cl WLTN L25 ... 131 L3
Ruislip Ct WARRN/WOL WA2 ... 122 B4
Rullerton Rd WAL/EG CH44 ... 111 J1
Rumford Pl VAUX/LVPD L3 ... 12 D6
Rumford St CLVP L2 ... 12 E6
Rumney Rd ANF/KKDL L4 ... 97 G5
Rumney Rd West ANF/KKDL L4 ... 96 F5
Runcorn Docks Rd RUNC WA7 ... 18 D4
Runcorn Rd WARRS WA4 ... 136 E8
Runcorn Spur Rd RUNC WA7 ... 19 K5
Runcorn-Widnes Br RUNC WA7 ... 149 J1
Rundle Rd AIG/SPK L17 ... 130 A3
Rundle St BIRK CH41 ... 10 A1
Runic St CLB/OSW/ST L13 ... 114 B3
Runnell's La CSBY/BLUN L23 ... 71 K8
The Runnell NSTN CH64 ... 152 F1
The Runnel ORM L39 ... 49 K3
Runnymede WARR WA1 ... 122 E6
Runnymede Cl WLTN L25 ... 131 J1
Runnymede Dr
RNFD/HAY WA11 ... 90 C7 7
Runshaw Av WGNNW/ST WN6 ... 55 G5
Runshaw La CHLY/EC PR7 ... 30 F3
Runton Rd WLTN L25 ... 115 L8
Rupert Dr NPK/KEN L6 ... 113 J2
Rupert Rd HUY L36 ... 115 L2
Rupert St WGN WN1 ... 5 H4
Ruscar Cl HLWD L26 ... 132 A3 6
Ruscolm Cl
WARRW/BUR WA5 ... 119 M6 3
Ruscombe Rd DV/KA/FCH L14 ... 99 H7
Rushdene WGNS/IIMK WN3 ... 79 J1
Rushden Rd KKBY L32 ... 86 C4
Rushey Hey Rd KKBY L32 ... 86 A4
Rushfield Crs RUNC WA7 ... 150 D8
Rushgreen Cl CL/PREN CH43 ... 110 E6 7
Rushlake Dr NTHLY L27 ... 115 M8
Rushmere Rd NG/CROX L11 ... 98 B3
Rushmoor Av AIMK WN4 ... 92 A1
Rushmore Gv WARR WA1 ... 122 C6
Rusholme Cl HLWD L26 ... 132 C7 2
Rushton Av LEIGH WN7 ... 81 M5
NEWLW WA12 ... 104 D1
Rushton Cl WDN WA8 ... 134 B2
Rushton Pl WLTN L25 ... 131 J3
Rushy Vw NEWLW WA12 ... 104 C1
Ruskin Av NEWLW WA12 ... 104 E1
RF/TRAN CH42 ... 128 B4 5
WAL/EG CH44 ... 111 J2
WARRN/WOL WA2 ... 121 L3 5
WGNS/IIMK WN3 ... 79 H2
Ruskin Cl BTL L20 ... 7 G5
Ruskin Crs WGNE/HIN WN2 ... 80 D4
Ruskin Dr ECCL WA10 ... 8 B3
EP CH65 ... 20 F8
Ruskin St ANF/KKDL L4 ... 7 L9
Ruskin Wy HUY L36 ... 115 M4
Rusland Av PEN/TH CH61 ... 141 H1
Rusland Rd KKBY L32 ... 86 B5
Russeldene Rd WGNS/IIMK WN3 ... 79 G2
Russell Av CHTN/BK PR9 ... 25 J6
Russell Rd ALL/GAR L19 ... 130 E7
CALD/MH L18 ... 114 B8
CHTN/BK PR9 ... 25 J6
HUY L36 ... 116 D3
RF/TRAN CH42 ... 128 B2
RUNC WA7 ... 18 C6
WAL/EG CH44 ... 95 G8
Russell Sq CHLYE PR6 ... 32 F4
Russell Sq West CHLYE PR6 ... 32 F4
Russell St BIRK CH41 ... 11 J4
VAUX/LVPD L3 ... 13 K6
WGNE/HIN WN2 ... 69 J5 10
WGNE/HIN WN2 ... 81 L3
Russet Cl ECCL WA10 ... 8 F2
NTHLY L27 ... 116 A8
Russian Dr CLB/OSW/ST L13 ... 98 B8
Rutherford Cl CLB/OSW/ST L13 ... 114 A4
Rutherford Rd CALD/MH L18 ... 114 D7
ECCL WA10 ... 88 E7
MGHL L31 ... 73 G6
Rutherglen Av CSBY/BLUN L23 ... 83 H3
Ruth Evans Ct RAIN/WH L35 ... 117 J1
Ruthin Cl WARRW/BUR WA5 ... 121 G2 2
Ruthven Rd
CLB/OSW/ST L13 ... 114 D4 3
LITH L21 ... 83 J6
Rutland Av AIG/SPK L17 ... 113 M7
GOL/RIS/CU WA3 ... 92 F6
HLWD L26 ... 132 B5
WARRS WA4 ... 137 K5
Rutland Cl EV L5 ... 97 J8 8
Rutland Crs ORM L39 ... 50 F6
Rutland Dr AIMK WN4 ... 91 L1
Rutland Rd STHP PR8 ... 3 L8
Rutland St BTL L20 ... 7 J2
ECCL WA10 ... 8 E2
RUNC WA7 ... 18 F3
Rutter Av WARRW/BUR WA5 ... 121 H3
Rutter St TOX L8 ... 113 G8 6
Ryburn Rd ORM L39 ... 62 F1
Rycot Rd SPK/HALE L24 ... 146 E1
Rycroft Rd AIN/FAZ L10 ... 85 G5
HOY CH47 ... 109 G5
WAL/EG CH44 ... 111 L3
Rydal Av CL/PREN CH43 ... 110 E8
CSBY/BLUN L23 ... 83 H3
FMBY L37 ... 58 F3
PR/KW L34 ... 101 H7
WARRS WA4 ... 137 J3
WGNW/BIL/O WN5 ... 67 H6
Rydal Bank BEB CH63 ... 128 C6
WAL/EG CH44 ... 111 L1
Rydal Cl AIMK WN4 ... 91 L1
AIN/FAZ L10 ... 85 H3
EP CH65 ... 163 L3
HOR/BR BL6 ... 57 L2 5
NSTN CH64 ... 153 H7
NWD/KWIPK L33 ... 85 M1

PEN/TH CH61 ................ 141 H1
Rydal Gv FROD/HEL WA6 .. 166 D4
RNFD/HAY WA11 ......... 89 J6
RUNC WA7 ............... 19 K8
Rydal Pl CHLY/EC PR7 ..... 32 E7
WGNE/HIN WN2 ......... 69 K5
WGNE/HIN WN2 ......... 80 D5
Rydal Rd HUY L36 ........ 116 A4
Rydal St EV L5 ........... 97 J7
NEWLW WA12 ........... 104 E2
Rydal Wy WDN WA8 ...... 133 L5
Ryder Cl ORM L39 ........ 62 E3
RAIN/WH L35 ........... 117 J1
Ryder Crs ORM L39 ....... 62 E4
STHP PR8 ............... 35 C5
Ryder Rd WARR WA1 ..... 122 E5
WDN WA8 ............... 134 D1
Ryde St WGNW/BIL/O WN5 . 68 A7
The Rydinge FMBY L37 .... 47 J7
Ryding's La CHTN/BK PR9 .. 23 M4
Rye Cl STHEL WA9 ........ 118 E1
Ryecote KKBY L32 ........ 86 A6
Ryecroft CHNE CH2 ....... 165 K2
Rye Cft LITH L21 ......... 83 K2
Ryecroft Av GOL/RIS/CU WA3 . 93 G4
Ryecroft HES CH60 ....... 141 L6
Ryedale Cl TOX L8 ....... 113 K6
Ryefield La LITH L21 ...... 83 K2
Ryeford Cl WGNS/IIMK WN3 .. 5 L8
Ryegate Rd ALL/GAR L19 ... 130 D6
Rye Gv WD/CROXPK L12 ... 99 G7
Rye Hey Rd KKBY L32 ..... 86 A3
Rye Moss La FMBY L37 .... 60 C5
Ryland Pk PEN/TH CH61 ... 126 C8
Rylands Av WGNNW/ST WN6 . 68 C3
Rylands Hey GR/UP/WCH CH49 . 125 M1
Rylands Rd CHLY/EC PR7 ... 32 E6
Rylands St WARR WA1 ..... 14 E6
WDN WA8 ............... 16 E3
Ryleys Gdns CLVP L2 ...... 12 F6
Rymer Gv ANF/KKDL L4 .... 97 J4
Rymers Gn FMBY L37 ...... 59 G1
Ryton Cl WGNS/IIMK WN3 ... 4 C8

## S

Sabden Brook Dr
    WGNE/HIN WN2 ......... 80 B3
Sabre Cl RUNC WA7 ....... 150 F6
Sackville Rd ECCL WA10 .... 88 E7
Sackville St CHLYE PR6 .... 33 G6
Saddleback Crs
    WGNW/BIL/O WN5 ...... 67 K6
Saddleback Rd
    WGNW/BIL/O WN5 ...... 67 K6
Saddle Cl WLT/FAZ L9 ..... 84 F5
Saddlers Ri RUNC WA7 ..... 150 E5
Sadler's La RNFD/HAY WA11 .. 88 A6
Sadler St WDN WA8 ....... 17 G1
Saffron Cl GOL/RIS/CU WA3 .. 93 G5
    WARRN/WOL WA2 ....... 122 D4
Saffron Gdns STHEL WA9 ... 102 F3
Sagar Fold ORM L39 ...... 62 F5
Sagar St CHLY/EC PR7 ..... 30 E7
Sage Cl WARRN/WOL WA2 .. 122 E3
St Agnes Rd ANF/KKDL L4 .. 96 F5
    HUY L36 ............... 116 B3
St Aidan's Cl WGNW/BIL/O WN5... 78 A7
St Aidan's Ter CL/PREN CH43 .. 111 H7
St Aidan's Wy NTHTN L30 ... 83 M2
St Aiden's Gv HUY L36 ..... 99 L6
St Alban Rd WARRW/BUR WA5 .. 120 A8
St Albans NPK/KEN L6 ...... 97 M8
St Albans Ct RNFD/HAY WA11 . 91 H6
St Albans Ct EV L5 ....... 96 E8
St Alban's Pl CHLY/EC PR7 ... 32 F8
St Alban's Rd BTL L20 ..... 7 H5
    CL/PREN CH43 .......... 10 C4
    WAL/EG CH44 .......... 111 K1
St Alban's Sq BTL L20 ..... 7 H6
St Ambrose Cft NTHTN L30 .. 84 A1
St Ambrose Gv ANF/KKDL L4 . 97 K7
St Ambrose Rd WDN WA8 ... 17 H1
St Andrew Rd ANF/KKDL L4 . 97 K7
St Andrews Av WD/CROXPK L12 .. 99 C7
St Andrews Cl
    WARRN/WOL WA2 ....... 122 C1
St Andrew's Crs WGNE/HIN WN2... 69 M8
St Andrew's Dr CSBY/BLUN L23 .. 70 D7
    PR/KW L34 ............ 99 L6
    WGNNW/ST WN6 ........ 68 B3
St Andrew's Pl STHP PR8 ... 3 G5
St Andrews Rd BEB CH63 ... 143 J2
    BTL L20 ............... 83 L8
    CSBY/BLUN L23 ........ 70 D6
    EP CH65 .............. 20 F8
St Andrew St VAUX/LVPD L3 .. 13 K7
St Andrew's Vw
    NWD/KWIPK L33 ........ 74 A8
St Annes Av WARRS WA4 ... 138 D3
St Annes Av East WARRS WA4 .. 138 D3
St Anne's Cl BIRK CH41 .... 11 H4
    FMBY L37 ............. 47 H7
St Anne's Ct EV L5 ........ 55 H8
St Anne's Dr WGNNW/ST WN6 .. 55 J8
St Annes Gdns AIG/SPK L17 .. 130 A4
St Annes Gv AIG/SPK L17 ... 130 A4
St Anne's Pth FMBY L37 .... 47 H7
St Anne's Pl BIRK CH41 .... 10 E2
St Anne's Rd AIG/SPK L17 ... 130 A4
    CHLYE PR6 ............ 33 G6
    CHTN/BK PR9 .......... 25 H1
    FMBY L37 ............. 47 H7
    HUY L36 .............. 116 A4
    ORM L39 .............. 62 F1
    WDN WA8 ............. 134 D3
St Anne St BIRK CH41 ..... 10 E2
    BIRK CH41 ............ 11 G2
    VAUX/LVPD L3 ......... 13 J3
St Ann Pl RAIN/WH L35 .... 117 L1
St Ann Rd ECCL WA10 ..... 101 L2
St Anthony's Cl PR/KW L34 .. 99 L6
St Anthony's Gv NTHTN L30 .. 83 M2

St Anthony's Rd CSBY/BLUN L23 .. 82 D1
St Asaph Dr WARRW/BUR WA5... 120 F3
St Asaph Gv NTHTN L30 ..... 84 B4
St Asaph Rd GTS/LS CH66 ... 163 G5
St Aubyn's Rd WGN WN1 .... 68 E1
St Augustine's Av
    WARRS WA4 ........... 138 B1
St Augustine St EV L5 ..... 96 F8
St Augustine's Wy NTHTN L30 .. 83 M1
St Austell Cl WARRW/BUR WA5 .. 136 A2
St Austell Cl MOR/LEA CH46 .. 109 K4
    RUNC WA7 ............. 150 D7
St Austells Rd ANF/KKDL L4 .. 7 M7
St Austins La WARR WA1 .... 14 D7
St Barnabas Pl
    WARRW/BUR WA5 ....... 121 G7
St Bedes Cl ORM L39 ...... 62 F2
St Benedicts Cl
    WARRN/WOL WA2 ....... 14 F2
St Benedict's Gv PR/KW L34 .. 99 L6
St Benet's Wy NTHTN L30 ... 84 A2
St Bernard's Cl NTHTN L30 .. 83 M2
St Bernard's Dr NTHTN L30 .. 83 M2
St Brendan's Cl HUY L36 ... 99 L6
St Brides Cl WARRW/BUR WA5 .. 136 A2
St Bride's Rd WAL/EG CH44 .. 95 M8
St Bride St TOX L8 ........ 113 H5
St Bridget's Cl
    WARRN/WOL WA2 ....... 122 B2
St Bridget's Gv NTHTN L30 .. 83 M2
St Bridget's La WKBY CH48 .. 124 D2
St Catherine's
    RF/TRAN CH42 ......... 127 M1
St Catherines Cl HUY L36 ... 116 A4
St Catherines Gdns
    RF/TRAN CH42 ......... 127 M1
St Catherine's Rd BTL L20 .. 7 G5
St Chad's Dr KKBY L32 ..... 86 A3
St Christopher Ct
    WGNNW/ST WN6 ....... 67 L1
St Christopher's Av NTHTN L30 .. 83 M1
St Christopher's Dr PR/KW L34 .. 99 L6
St Clair Dr CHTN/BK PR9 ... 25 J4
St Clement's Rd WGN WN1 .. 68 E2
St Clement's St
    WGNE/HIN WN2 ........ 80 B1
St Columba's Cl
    WAL/EG CH44 .......... 95 M8
St Cuthbert's Cl
    WD/CROXPK L12 ........ 99 G2
St Cuthbert's Rd CHTN/BK PR9 .. 25 K3
St Cyrils Cl NTHLY L27 ..... 115 L6
St Damian's Cft NTHTN L30 .. 84 A2
St David Rd PS/BROM CH62 .. 144 C7
St Davids Cl RAIN/WH L35 .. 117 L1
St David's Crs WGNE/HIN WN2 .. 57 K8
St Davids Dr GTS/LS CH66 .. 163 H5
    WARRW/BUR WA5 ....... 121 G3
St Davids Gv NTHTN L30 ... 83 M3
St Davids La CL/PREN CH43 .. 110 F8
St David's Rd ANF/KKDL L4 .. 97 K7
    DV/KA/FCH L14 ........ 99 K8
St Domingo Gv EV L5 ...... 97 J7
St Domingo Rd EV L5 ...... 97 G7
St Domingo V EV L5 ....... 97 J7
St Dunstan's Gv NTHTN L30 .. 83 M2
St Edmond's Rd BTL L20 ... 7 G6
St Edmunds Rd BEB CH63 ... 128 B8
St Edwards Cl BIRK CH41 ... 10 D2
St Elizabeth's Rd
    WGNE/HIN WN2 ........ 57 K8
St Elmo Rd WAL/EG CH44 ... 95 M8
St Elphins Cl WARR WA1 .... 15 H5
St Gabriel's Av WARR WA1 .. 15 J5
St George's Av ECCL WA10 .. 88 E8
    GTS/LS CH66 .......... 163 H5
    RF/TRAN CH42 ......... 127 M3
St Georges Gv NTHTN L30 .. 83 M3
St George's Hl EV L5 ...... 97 H8
St George's Mt WAL/NB CH45 .. 95 K5
St George's Pk WAL/NB CH45 .. 95 K5
St George's Pl CHTN/BK PR9 .. 3 G3
    CLVPS L1 ............. 13 H6
St Georges Rd ECCL WA10 .. 8 A7
    FMBY L37 ............. 59 G1
    HTWN L38 ............. 59 H8
    HUY L36 .............. 100 A8
    WAL/NB CH45 .......... 95 G7
St George's St CHLY/EC PR7 .. 32 E6
St George's Wy BEB CH63 .. 142 C6
St Gregory's Cft NTHTN L30 .. 84 A1
St Gregory's Pl CHLY/EC PR7 .. 32 E8
St Helen's Cl BIRK CH41 .... 10 D6
St Helens Linkway
    RAIN/WH L35 .......... 118 B4
    STHEL WA9 ............ 9 H8
St Helens Rd LEIGH WN7 .... 93 L4
    ORM L39 .............. 62 B6
    PR/KW L34 ............ 100 F7
    PR/KW L34 ............ 101 G6
    PR/KW L34 ............ 101 H6
    RNFD/HAY WA11 ....... 89 L5
St Hilary Brow WAL/EG CH44 .. 111 H1
St Hilary Dr WAL/EG CH44 .. 95 H8
St Hilda's Cl CHLY/EC PR7 .. 43 L1
St Hilda's Dr FROD/HEL WA6 .. 160 E4
St Hilda St ANF/KKDL L4 .. 97 G5
St Hugh's Cl CL/PREN CH43 .. 10 D6
St Ives Cl CLB/OSW/ST L13 .. 114 B2
St Ives Rd CL/PREN CH43 ... 10 A5
St Ives Wy HLWD L26 ...... 132 B5
St James Cl BRSC L40 ..... 63 L2
    GR/UP/WCH CH49 ...... 125 M1
    WD/CROXPK L12 ........ 98 C7
St James Crs WGNE/HIN WN2 .. 81 H5
St James Dr BTL L20 ...... 6 F3
St James Gv WGNS/IIMK WN3 .. 4 D8
St James Mt RAIN/WH L35 .. 117 L3
St James Pl TOX L8 ....... 113 G6
St James Rd CLVPS L1 ..... 113 G6
    HUY L36 .............. 116 A4
    PR/KW L34 ............ 101 G7
    RAIN/WH L35 .......... 117 L3
    WAL/NB CH45 .......... 95 K5
    WGNW/BIL/O WN5 ...... 66 E8
St James's Pl CHLYE PR6 ... 33 G6
St James St CLVPS L1 ..... 112 F6
    STHP PR8 ............. 3 H7

St Jerome's Wy NTHTN L30 .. 84 A1
St John Av WARRS WA4 .... 137 K3
St John's Av WLT/FAZ L9 ... 84 C8
St John's Brow RUNC WA7 .. 19 J2
St John's Cl HOY CH47 ..... 108 F5
St Jude's La CLVPS L1 ..... 13 H6
St John's Pl CSBY/WL L22 .. 82 F4
St John's Rd BTL L20 ...... 6 F8
    CSBY/WL L22 .......... 82 F4
    HUY L36 .............. 116 B4
    PS/BROM CH62 ......... 144 C8
    STHP PR8 ............. 35 H4
    WAL/NB CH45 .......... 95 G8
    WGNE/HIN WN2 ........ 57 K8
St John's St RUNC WA7 .... 19 J2
    WGNE/HIN WN2 ........ 80 D5
St John's Ter BTL L20 ..... 6 F8
St John St BIRK CH41 ..... 11 H6
    ECCL WA10 ............ 101 M5
    NEWLW WA12 .......... 104 C2
    WGNW/BIL/O WN5 ...... 67 K7
St Joseph's Cl
    WARRW/BUR WA5 ....... 120 A8
St Josephs Crs VAUX/LVPD L3 .. 13 J4
St Jude's Cl HUY L36 ...... 99 L6
St Katherines Dr HOR/BR BL6 .. 57 L2
St Katherines Wy WARR WA1 .. 15 J5
St Kilda Cl EP CH65 ....... 163 L4
St Kilda's Rd MOR/LEA CH46 .. 109 M6
St Laurence Cl BIRK CH41 .. 11 H4
St Laurence Dr BIRK CH41 .. 11 H5
St Laurence Gv KKBY L32 .. 86 B5
St Lawrence Cl TOX L8 .... 129 J1
St Lawrence Rd
    FROD/HEL WA6 ........ 160 D6
St Leonard's Cl NTHTN L30 .. 83 M1
St Lucia Rd WAL/EG CH44 .. 95 M8
St Luke's Av GOL/RIS/CU WA3 .. 92 F5
St Luke's Church Rd FMBY L37 .. 58 E3
St Lukes Cl DV/KA/FCH L14 .. 99 H7
St Luke's Crs WDN WA8 ... 134 D1
St Luke's Dr FMBY L37 .... 58 E3
    WGNW/BIL/O WN5 ...... 77 M1
St Luke's Gv CHTN/BK PR9 .. 3 M4
    NTHTN L30 ............ 83 M1
St Luke's Rd CHTN/BK PR9 .. 3 M4
    CSBY/BLUN L23 ........ 82 F1
    ECCL WA10 ............ 8 A5
St Luke's Wy FROD/HEL WA6 .. 160 D4
    HUY L36 .............. 99 L6
St Malo Rd WGN WN1 ..... 68 E2
St Margaret's Av
    WARRN/WOL WA2 ....... 121 M4
St Margaret's Gv NTHTN L30 .. 83 L2
St Margaret's Rd HOY CH47 .. 108 C6
St Mark's Av WGNW/BIL/O WN5 .. 68 B6
St Marks Crs GTS/LS CH66 .. 163 H6
St Mark's Gv NTHTN L30 ... 83 L1
St Mark's Rd HUY L36 ..... 116 B4
St Mark's Wy RNFD/HAY WA11 .. 90 C7
St Martins Dr GTS/LS CH66 .. 162 F3
St Martins Gv KKBY L32 ... 86 B6
St Martins La RUNC WA7 ... 150 F6
St Martin's Ms EV L5 ...... 13 J1
St Mary's Av ANF/KKDL L4 .. 97 J3
    WGNW/BIL/O WN5 ...... 89 L1
St Mary's Cl WARRS WA4 .. 137 L7
    WGNE/HIN WN2 ........ 57 K8
St Marys Ct WLTN L25 .... 131 J3
St Mary's Dr NTHTN L30 ... 83 L3
St Mary's Ga BIRK CH41 ... 11 G6
    CHLY/EC PR7 .......... 31 L2
St Mary's Gv ANF/KKDL L4 .. 97 J3
St Mary's La ANF/KKDL L4 .. 97 J3
St Mary's Pl ANF/KKDL L4 .. 97 J3
    WLTN L25 ............. 131 J3
St Mary's Rd ALL/GAR L19 .. 130 D7
    CSBY/WL L22 .......... 83 H5
    HUY L36 .............. 116 A3
    RUNC WA7 ............. 150 B4
    WARRW/BUR WA5 ....... 120 B8
    WDN WA8 ............. 149 J1
    WGNE/HIN WN2 ........ 57 K7
St Mary's St WAL/EG CH44 .. 111 K1
    WARRS WA4 ........... 15 H9
St Matthews Cl ANF/KKDL L4 .. 97 M3
St Matthews Av LITH L21 ... 83 M8
St Matthew's Cl HUY L36 .. 116 B2
    WARRS WA4 ........... 137 M6
    WGNS/IIMK WN3 ....... 78 E3
St Matthews Gv ECCL WA10 .. 101 L5
St Mawes Cl WDN WA8 .... 134 A3
St Mawes Wy ECCL WA10 .. 88 D7
St Mawgan Ct
    WARRN/WOL WA2 ....... 122 B3
St Michael Rd ORM L39 ... 62 B6
St Michael's Church Rd
    AIG/SPK L17 .......... 129 K3
St Michael's Cl AIG/SPK L17 .. 129 L3
    CHLY/EC PR7 .......... 32 D4
    CHTN/BK PR9 .......... 25 H2
    WDN WA8 ............. 133 L6
St Michaels Ct HUY L36 ... 116 A2
    WGN WN1 ............. 68 E3
St Michael's Gv NPK/KEN L6 .. 113 K1
    NTHTN L30 ............ 83 L2
St Michaels Pk ORM L39 ... 62 C6
St Michael's Rd AIG/SPK L17 .. 129 K2
    CSBY/BLUN L23 ........ 70 D8
    STHEL WA9 ............ 118 C2
    WDN WA8 ............. 133 L6
St Monicas Cl WARRS WA4 .. 137 M6
St Monica's Dr NTHTN L30 .. 83 M1
St Nicholas Dr NTHTN L30 .. 83 M2
St Nicholas Pl VAUX/LVPD L3 .. 12 D7
St Nicholas Rd GOL/RIS/CU WA3 .. 93 M7
    RAIN/WH L35 .......... 116 E4
    WAL/NB CH45 .......... 94 F8
St Oswald's Av CL/PREN CH43 .. 110 C5
St Oswalds Cl
    WARRN/WOL WA2 ....... 105 K7
St Oswald's La NTHTN L30 .. 84 B2
St Oswalds Ms CL/PREN CH43 .. 110 E4
St Oswalds Rd AIMK WN4 .. 91 J3
St Oswald's St CLB/OSW/ST L13 .. 114 C3

St Paschal Baylon Bvd
    CHLDW L16 ........... 115 H5
St Patrick's Cl
    NWD/KWIPK L33 ....... 74 A8
St Patrick's Dr NTHTN L30 .. 83 M1
St Patrick Wy WGN WN1 ... 5 H4
St Patricks Wy WGN WN1 .. 5 H4
St Paul's Cl CHLYE PR6 .... 44 C5
    NWD/KWIPK L33 ....... 73 M8
    RF/TRAN CH42 ......... 128 A3
St Pauls Gdns GTS/LS CH66 .. 155 K6
St Paul's Pas STHP PR8 .... 2 F6
St Paul's Rd RF/TRAN CH42 .. 128 B3
    WAL/EG CH44 ......... 111 M3
    WDN WA8 ............. 16 D5
St Paul's Sq STHP PR8 .... 2 E6
    VAUX/LVPD L3 ......... 12 E5
St Paul St ECCL WA10 ..... 8 D5
St Paul's Vls RF/TRAN CH42 .. 128 A3
St Peter's Av FMBY L37 .... 58 F1
St Peter's Cl FMBY L37 .... 58 F1
    HES CH60 ............. 141 H6
    NWD/KWIPK L33 ....... 73 M8
St Peter's Ms RF/TRAN CH42 .. 128 C4
St Peter's Rd RF/TRAN CH42 .. 128 C4
    STHP PR8 ............. 35 J2
    WLT/FAZ L9 ........... 84 E7
St Peter's St CHLYE PR6 ... 33 C4
St Peter's Wy CL/PREN CH43 .. 126 E1
    WARRN/WOL WA2 ....... 14 F3
St Philip's Av LITH L21 .... 83 L5
St Seiriol Gv CL/PREN CH43 .. 10 A6
St Stephen Rd
    WARRW/BUR WA5 ....... 120 B8
St Stephen's Av
    WARRN/WOL WA2 ....... 121 K2
    WGN WN1 ............. 69 G3
St Stephens Cl HES CH60 .. 141 L7
    WLTN L25 ............. 115 L8
St Stephen's Gv NTHTN L30 .. 83 M2
St Stephen's Rd HTWN L38 .. 70 B1
    RF/TRAN CH42 ......... 127 K3
    WGNNW/ST WN6 ....... 55 L4
St Teresa's Rd ECCL WA10 .. 8 A4
St Thomas Cl WDN WA8 ... 134 A4
St Thomas's Dr NTHTN L30 .. 83 M2
St Thomas's Rd CHLY/EC PR7 .. 32 D5
St Thomas St WGNS/IIMK WN3 .. 4 A6
St Thomas Vw EP CH65 .... 20 A7
St Vincent Rd CL/PREN CH43 .. 10 A6
    WAL/EG CH44 ......... 95 M8
    WARRW/BUR WA5 ....... 120 B8
St Vincent's Cl
    WD/CROXPK L12 ........ 99 G7
St Vincent St VAUX/LVPD L3 .. 13 K6
St Vincent Wy STHP PR8 .. 2 D9
St Vincent Wy VAUX/LVPD L3 .. 13 K6
St Werburgh's Sq BIRK CH41 .. 11 J6
St Wilfrid's Dr WARRS WA4 .. 148 C8
St Wilfrid's Rd WGNNW/ST WN6 .. 56 B5
St William Rd CSBY/BLUN L23 .. 71 K8
St Winifred Rd RAIN/WH L35 .. 101 K8
    WAL/NB CH45 .......... 95 K6
Saker St ANF/KKDL L4 .... 97 H6
Salacre Cl GR/UP/WCH CH49 .. 126 D1
Salacre Crs GR/UP/WCH CH49 .. 126 C1
Salacre La GR/UP/WCH CH49 .. 110 C8
Salcombe Cl WGN WN1 ... 69 G3
Salcombe Dr CHTN/BK PR9 .. 22 C8
    WLTN L25 ............. 131 K6
Salem Vw CL/PREN CH43 .. 127 K2
Salerno Dr HUY L36 ...... 115 M2
Salesbury Wy WGNS/IIMK WN3 .. 79 J2
Saleswood Av ECCL WA10 .. 101 J2
Salford Rd STHP PR8 ..... 34 C4
Salisbury Av NTHTN L30 ... 84 C4
    WKBY CH48 ........... 124 C3
Salisbury Dr PS/BROM CH62 .. 128 C6
Salisbury Pk CHLDW L16 .. 115 C8
Salisbury Rd AIMK WN4 ... 79 J8
    ALL/GAR L19 .......... 130 C7
    BTL L20 .............. 6 E2
    EV L5 ................ 97 J7
    RNFD/HAY WA11 ....... 91 C4
    WAL/NB CH45 .......... 95 J5
    WAV L15 ............. 113 M6
Salisbury St BIRK CH41 ... 11 G7
    CHLY/EC PR7 .......... 32 F6
    CHTN/BK PR9 .......... 25 J7
    GOL/RIS/CU WA3 ....... 92 C5
    PR/KW L34 ............ 100 F7
    RUNC WA7 ............ 19 G5
    VAUX/LVPD L3 ......... 13 L3
    WARR WA1 ............ 15 J4
    WDN WA8 ............. 16 E3
Salisbury Ter WAV L15 .... 114 B5
Salkeld Av AIMK WN4 ..... 91 H2
Sallowfields
    WGNW/BIL/O WN5 ...... 66 F8
Sally's La CHTN/BK PR9 ... 25 J3
Salop St ANF/KKDL L4 .... 96 F6
Saltash Cl HLWD L26 ..... 132 A5
Saltburn Rd WAL/NB CH45 .. 94 F8
Saltersgate GTS/LS CH66 .. 163 H3
Salthouse Quay VAUX/LVPD L3 .. 12 E9
Saltney St VAUX/LVPD L3 .. 12 C1
Salton Gdns WARRW/BUR WA5 .. 121 G6
Salt Pit La CHLY/EC PR7 ... 41 H1
Saltpit La MGHL L31 ...... 73 C4
Saltram Rd WGNS/IIMK WN3 .. 78 E1
Saltwood Dr RUNC WA7 ... 150 E8
Saltworks Cl FROD/HEL WA6 .. 160 F3
Salvin Cl AIMK WN4 ...... 91 M2
Salvia Wy NWD/KWIPK L33 .. 73 M8
Samaria Av PS/BROM CH62 .. 128 E6
Sambourn Fold STHP PR8 .. 34 C8
Samuel St RAIN/WH L35 ... 101 M6
    WARRW/BUR WA5 ....... 137 G1
Sanbec Gdns WDN WA8 ... 117 M8
Sandalwood RUNC WA7 ... 150 E4
Sandalwood Cl
    WARRN/WOL WA2 ....... 121 M3
Sandalwood Dr CL/PREN CH43 .. 126 F1

WGNNW/ST WN6 ........ 68 B2
Sandalwood Gdns
    STHEL WA9 ............ 102 E6
Sandbeck St TOX L8 ...... 129 H2
Sandbrook Gdns
    WGNW/BIL/O WN5 ...... 66 F8
Sandbrook La MOR/LEA CH46 .. 110 A5
Sandbrook Rd STHP PR8 .. 66 E8
    WGNW/BIL/O WN5 ...... 66 E8
    WLTN L25 ............. 115 J5
Sandcliffe Rd WAL/NB CH45 .. 95 G5
Sandelwood Cl NPK/KEN L6 .. 97 K4
Sandeman Rd ANF/KKDL L4 .. 97 M4
Sanderling Rd NWD/KWIPK L33 .. 86 C2
Sanders Hey Cl RUNC WA7 .. 150 C8
Sanderson Cl
    WARRW/BUR WA5 ....... 119 M7
Sanderson La CHLY/EC PR7 .. 41 J5
Sanderson St LEIGH WN7 ... 81 M8
Sandfield HUY L36 ....... 115 M3
Sandfield Av HOY CH47 ... 108 F4
Sandfield Cl BEB CH63 .... 127 M7
    GOL/RIS/CU WA3 ....... 93 H5
    WD/CROXPK L12 ........ 98 E8
Sandfield Crs ECCL WA10 .. 8 E6
Sandfield Pk HES CH60 .... 140 F5
Sandfield Pk East
    WD/CROXPK L12 ........ 98 E7
Sandfield Pl BTL L20 ..... 6 E2
Sandfield Rd BEB CH63 ... 127 M7
    BTL L20 .............. 7 K6
    ECCL WA10 ............ 88 C8
    GR/UP/WCH CH49 ...... 126 D4
    WAL/NB CH45 .......... 95 K6
    WLTN L25 ............. 131 K1
Sandfields FROD/HEL WA6 .. 160 D5
Sandfield Wk CLB/OSW/ST L13 .. 114 D1
Sandford Dr MGHL L31 .... 72 F3
Sandforth Cl WD/CROXPK L12 .. 98 E8
Sandforth Rd WD/CROXPK L12 .. 98 D8
Sandgate CHLY/EC PR7 ... 32 F8
Sandgate Cl SPK/HALE L24 .. 146 D1
Sandham Gv HES CH60 ... 141 L6
Sandham Rd SPK/HALE L24 .. 147 J2
Sandhey Rd CHLYE PR6 ... 32 F5
Sandhead St EHL/KEN L7 .. 113 M5
Sandheys Av CSBY/WL L22 .. 82 E4
Sandheys Cl ANF/KKDL L4 .. 97 G6
Sandheys Dr CHTN/BK PR9 .. 25 H4
Sandheys Gv CSBY/WL L22 .. 82 E3
Sandheys Rd WAL/NB CH45 .. 95 K6
Sandheys Ter CSBY/WL L22 .. 82 E4
Sandhills HTWN L38 ...... 70 B2
Sandhills La EV L5 ....... 96 E6
The Sandhills MOR/LEA CH46 .. 110 A2
Sandhills Vw WAL/NB CH45 .. 94 F8
Sandhurst Cl FMBY L37 ... 58 E4
    LITH L21 ............. 83 H6
Sandhurst Dr AIN/FAZ L10 .. 85 G3
Sandhurst Rd HLWD L26 .. 132 C7
    RAIN/WH L35 .......... 101 J8
Sandhurst St AIG/SPK L17 .. 129 K2
    WARRS WA4 ........... 138 B2
Sandhurst Wy MGHL L31 .. 61 K8
Sandiacre WGNNW/ST WN6 .. 56 A5
Sandicroft Rd WD/CROXPK L12 .. 98 E8
Sandilands Gv HTWN L38 .. 70 B2
Sandino St TOX L8 ....... 113 G7
Sandirngham Dr AIG/SPK L17 .. 129 K1
Sandiway BEB CH63 ...... 143 L7
    HOY CH47 ............ 108 F5
    HUY L36 .............. 116 B4
    RAIN/WH L35 .......... 116 F3
Sandiway Av WDN WA8 ... 133 J4
Sandiways NTHTN L30 .... 84 B3
Sandiways Rd WAL/NB CH45 .. 95 G4
Sandlea Pk WKBY CH48 ... 124 C3
Sandlewood Gv
    NWD/KWIPK L33 ....... 86 E1
Sandon Cl RAIN/WH L35 ... 117 K1
Sandon Crs NSTN CH64 ... 153 G8
Sandon Gv RNFD/HAY WA11 .. 76 C7
Sandon Pl WDN WA8 ..... 17 K1
Sandon Rd STHP PR8 ..... 35 H4
    WAL/EG CH44 ......... 111 M1
Sandon St CSBY/WL L22 .. 82 F4
    TOX L8 ............... 113 H5
Sandown Cl
    GOL/RIS/CU WA3 ....... 107 H1
    RUNC WA7 ............ 149 L7
Sandown La WAV L15 ..... 114 B5
Sandown Park Rd AIN/FAZ L10 .. 85 G2
Sandown Rd WAV L15 .... 114 B5
    WGNNW/ST WN6 ....... 68 A2
Sandpiper Cl GR/UP/WCH CH49 .. 109 M7
    NEWLW WA12 .......... 104 E1
Sandpiper Gv HLWD L26 .. 132 A4
Sandpiper Rd WGNS/IIMK WN3 .. 78 D1
Sandra Dr NEWLW WA12 .. 104 F2
Sandridge Av CHLY/EC PR7 .. 33 J2
Sandridge Rd PEN/TH CH61 .. 126 B8
    WAL/NB CH45 .......... 95 K6
Sandringham Av
    CSBY/WL L22 .......... 83 G3
    FROD/HEL WA6 ........ 166 D2
    HOY CH47 ............ 108 F5
Sandringham Cl CHLY/EC PR7 .. 44 A7
    HOY CH47 ............ 108 E6
    NWD/KWIPK L33 ....... 74 A8
    PS/BROM CH62 ......... 128 C6
    WGNW/BIL/O WN5 ...... 68 A8
Sandringham Dr STHEL WA9 .. 102 F2
    WAL/NB CH45 .......... 95 J5
    WARRW/BUR WA5 ....... 136 E1
Sandringham Gdns EP CH65 .. 163 H3
    CHLY/EC PR7 .......... 30 E5
    CLB/OSW/ST L13 ....... 98 A7
    CSBY/WL L22 .......... 83 G5
    FMBY L37 ............. 59 G4
    MGHL L31 ............. 72 E5
    STHP PR8 ............. 34 E8
    WDN WA8 ............. 16 B4

WGNE/HIN WN2 ............ 81 G1
Sandrock Rd WAL/NB CH45 ... 95 K6
Sands CI RAIN/WH WA6....... 130 B1
Sandstone Dr RAIN/WH L35 ... 117 L4
Sandstone CI RAIN/WH L35 ... 101 H8
WKBY CH48................. 125 C3
Sandstone Rd East
 CLB/OSW/ST L13 ........... 114 C1
Sandstone Rd West
 CLB/OSW/ST L13 .......... 114 B1
Sandstone Trail FROD/HEL WA6.. 167 H3
Sandstone Wk HES CH60....... 141 J6
Sandwash CI RNFD/HAY WA11... 88 D1
Sandway WGNNW/ST WN6 ...... 68 B3
Sandway Crs NG/CROX L11..... 98 C3
Sandwith CI RAIN/WH L35 ..... 79 K3
Sandy Brow La
 GOL/RIS/CU WA3 ......... 106 A3
 NWD/KWIPK L33........... 87 G6
Sandycroft Av WCN WN1....... 4 F1
Sandy Gn WLT/FAZ L9 ......... 84 E7
Sandy Gv CLB/OSW/ST L13 .... 98 B7
Sandy La BRSC L40 .......... 28 C6
 BRSC L40.................. 51 M6
 CHLY/EC PR7 .............. 44 A6
 CLB/OSW/ST L13 .......... 98 B7
 FROD/HEL WA6 ........... 166 D3
 GOL/RIS/CU WA3 .......... 93 J3
 GOL/RIS/CU WA3 ......... 106 C4
 HES CH60 ................ 141 J4
 HTWN L38 ................ 70 C2
 KIRK/FR/WA PR4 .......... 27 L7
 LITH L21................. 83 H6
 MGHL L31 ................ 61 L8
 MGHL L31 ................ 73 L8
 NEWLW WA12............... 92 B5
 NSTN CH64 .............. 153 J7
 ORM L39 ................. 62 D7
 PEN/TH CH61............. 125 L6
 RNFD/HAY WA11............ 88 F5
 RUNC WA7 ................ 18 B9
 SKEL WN8................. 53 H4
 SKEL WN8................. 64 F4
 WAL/NB CH45 ............. 95 C7
 WARRN/WOL WA2 .......... 121 K2
 WARRS WA4 .............. 137 M5
 WARRW/BUR WA5 ......... 136 C1
 WDN WA8 ................ 119 K7
 WGNE/HIN WN2 ........... 77 M1
 WKBY CH48............... 124 D5
 WLT/FAZ L9 .............. 84 D7
Sandy La North PEN/TH CH61.. 125 L5
Sandy La West
 WARRN/WOL WA2 ......... 121 J3
Sandy Moor La RUNC WA7 .... 150 F2
Sandymoor La RUNC WA7 .... 150 F2
 WAL/NB CH45 ............. 95 J6
Sandymount Dr BEB CH63 ... 143 H1
Sandy Rd LITH L21........... 83 J6
Sandyville Gv ANF/KKDL L4 ... 98 A5
Sandyville Rd ANF/KKDL L4 ... 97 M5
Sandy Wy SKEL WN8........... 38 F1
 CL/PREN CH43.............. 10 A7
Sanfield CI ORM L39 ......... 51 C7
Sangness Dr STHP PR8........ 36 A2
Sankey Rd MGHL L31 ........ 72 F6
 RNFD/HAY WA11............ 90 B8
Sankey St CLVPS L1 ........ 113 G5
 GOL/RIS/CU WA3 .......... 92 C5
 NEWLW WA12............... 104 C2
 STHEL WA9 ............... 102 F3
 WARR WA1 ................ 14 C6
 WDN WA8 ................. 16 E8
Sankey Wy WARRW/BUR WA5 .. 120 C8
Santon Av CLB/OSW/ST L13 ... 98 A3
Santon Dr GOL/RIS/CU WA3 .. 93 C5
Sanvino Av STHP PR8......... 34 F8
Sapphire Dr NWD/KWIPK L33 .. 74 A8
Sapphire St CLB/OSW/ST L13 . 114 B4
Sarah's Cft NTHTN L30........ 84 A2
Sarah St WGNE/HIN WN2 .... 81 K3
Sarscow La LEY/BBR PR5 .... 30 A4
Sarsfield Av GOL/RIS/CU WA3 . 92 F5
Sartfield CI CHLDW L16 ...... 115 C5
Sarum Rd WLTN L25 ........ 115 J6
Satinwood CI AIMK WN4 .... 91 H2
Satinwood Crs MGHL L31 ... 85 J2
Saughall Massie La
 GR/UP/WCH CH49 ........ 110 A8
Saughall Massie Rd
 GR/UP/WCH CH49 ........ 109 L7
 WKBY CH48............... 125 J1
Saughall Rd MOR/LEA CH46 .. 109 L6
Saunby St ALL/GAR L19 ..... 145 L1
Saunders Av RAIN/WH L35 .. 116 F1
Saundersfoot CI
 WARRW/BUR WA5 ......... 121 C3
Saunders Ms CHLY/EC PR7 ... 43 L2
Saunders St CHTN/BK PR9 ... 24 D4
Saunderton CI
 RNFD/HAY WA11........... 90 E6
Saville Av WARRW/BUR WA5... 14 B1
Saville Rd CLB/OSW/ST L13 .. 114 D3
 MGHL L31 ................ 72 E2
Saville St CHLY/EC PR7 ...... 32 E8
Savon Hook FMBY L37 ....... 59 K4
Savoylands CI AIG/SPK L17 .. 129 L3
Sawdon Av STHP PR8......... 36 A1
Sawley Av GOL/RIS/CU WA3 .. 92 F4
 WGNNW/ST WN6 ........... 68 B2
Sawley CI GOL/RIS/CU WA3 .. 107 J3
 RUNC WA7 ............... 151 C6
Sawpit La HUY L36 .......... 116 B3
Saxby Rd DV/KA/FCH L14 .... 99 J7
Saxon CI NPK/KEN L6 ....... 97 K8
Saxonia Rd ANF/KKDL L4...... 97 K3
Saxon Rd CSBY/BLUN L23 .... 82 F2
 HOY CH47................. 108 C5
 MOR/LEA CH46 ........... 110 B4
 RUNC WA7 ................ 19 L4
 STHP PR8................. 2 D8
Saxon Ter WDN WA8.......... 16 F2
Saxon Wy GTS/LS CH66 ..... 163 H5
 NWD/KWIPK L33........... 74 A7
Saxony Rd EHL/KEN L7 ...... 113 J3
Saxthorpe CI WGNS/IIMK WN3.. 78 F2

Sayce St WDN WA8.......... 16 E2
Scafell Av WARRN/WOL WA2 . 121 L1
Scafell CI BEB CH63......... 154 F2
 NTHLY L27............... 132 C2
Scafell Gv WGNE/HIN WN2 ... 80 D3
Scafell Rd ECCL WA10....... 89 J6
Scaffold La HTWN L38 ........ 59 L8
Scape La CSBY/BLUN L23 .... 71 C8
Scargreen Av NG/CROX L11 .. 98 B2
Scarisbrick Av LITH L21...... 83 K6
 SKEL WN8................. 53 L3
Scarisbrick CI MGHL L31 ..... 73 C2
Scarisbrick Crs NG/CROX L11 . 97 M2
Scarisbrick Dr NG/CROX L11 .. 97 M2
Scarisbrick New Rd STHP PR8 .. 3 J7
Scarisbrick PI NG/CROX L11 .. 97 M3
 RNFD/HAY WA11........... 76 B6
Scarisbrick St CHTN/BK PR9 ... 3 H4
 ORM L39 ................. 51 C7
 WCN WN1 ................ 4 F1
Scarlet St CHLYE PR6 ....... 33 C6
Scarsdale Rd NG/CROX L11 .. 98 B4
Scarth Hill La BRSC L40 ..... 63 K3
 ORM L39 ................. 63 G3
Scarth Pk SKEL WN8......... 65 L6
Scawfell Rd CHLY/EC PR7 ... 32 D8
Sceptre CI NEWLW WA12 .... 104 C2
Sceptre Rd NG/CROX L11 ... 98 E2
Sceptre Wk NG/CROX L11 ... 98 E2
Scholar St EHL/KEN L7 ..... 113 L6
Scholefield La WGN WN1 ..... 5 H3
Scholes WGN WN1 .......... 5 H3
Scholes Bank HOR/BR BL6 ... 45 J8
Scholes La ECCL WA10...... 101 K6
 RAIN/WH L35............. 101 L6
Scholes Pk ECCL WA10...... 101 K6
Schomberg St NPK/KEN L6... 113 J2
School Av FMBY L37 ........ 59 H2
 NSTN CH64 .............. 153 H7
 WGN WN1 ................ 5 J1
School Brow WARR WA1 .... 15 C5
 WGNW/BIL/O WN5 ........ 78 A8
School CI MOR/LEA CH46 ... 110 B4
 NTHLY L27............... 115 L6
 ORM L39 ................. 62 E4
 STHP PR8................. 35 K3
School Dr WGNW/BIL/O WN5 .. 78 A8
Schoolfield CI
 GR/UP/WCH CH49 ........ 126 D3
Schoolfield Rd
 GR/UP/WCH CH49 ........ 126 D3
School HI HES CH60......... 141 H6
School House Gn ORM L39 .. 51 H8
School House Gv BRSC L40 .. 38 F8
School La AIMK WN4 ........ 90 E2
 AIN/FAZ L10 .............. 84 F4
 BEB CH63 ............... 127 M8
 BRSC L40................. 39 H8
 BRSC L40................. 40 D4
 BRSC L40................. 64 A2
 CHLY/EC PR7 .............. 31 M2
 CHNE CH2 ............... 165 J2
 CL/PREN CH43............ 110 E4
 CLVPS L1 ................. 13 C8
 FMBY L37 ................ 59 H2
 FROD/HEL WA6........... 160 E6
 FROD/HEL WA6........... 167 J8
 GOL/RIS/CU WA3 ........ 107 L8
 GTS/LS CH66............. 155 C5
 HOY CH47................ 108 D6
 HOY CH47................ 108 F4
 HUY L36 ................. 116 C3
 LITH L21................. 83 K5
 MGHL L31 ............... 73 J4
 MGHL L31 ............... 73 J8
 NSTN CH64 ............. 152 D4
 NSTN CH64 ............. 153 H7
 NSTN CH64 ............. 153 K3
 ORM L39 ................ 61 H2
 PEN/TH CH61............ 125 K7
 PR/KW L34 .............. 86 C7
 PS/BROM CH62 .......... 128 D6
 RAIN/WH L35............ 118 B4
 RUNC WA7 .............. 150 B5
 WGNNW/ST WN6 ......... 68 C3
 WLT/FAZ L9 ............. 84 E6
Schooner CI RUNC WA7 ... 150 F7
Schwartzman Dr CHTN/BK PR9... 23 J7
Science Rd SPK/HALE L24 .. 146 E1
Scilly CI EP CH65 .......... 163 L4
Scone CI NG/CROX L11 ..... 98 E2
Scorecross STHEL WA9 ..... 102 D5
Score La CHLDW L16 ....... 114 F5
The Score STHEL WA9 ..... 102 C7
Scorton St NPK/KEN L6 ..... 97 L8
Scotchbarn La PR/KW L34 .. 101 G7
Scoter Rd NWD/KWIPK L33 .. 86 B3
Scotia Av PS/BROM CH62 ... 128 L6
Scotia Rd CLB/OSW/ST L13 . 114 C1
Scotland PI VAUX/LVPD L3 .. 13 H4
Scotland Rd EV L5 .......... 96 F5
 VAUX/LVPD L3 ........... 13 H3
 WARR WA1 ............... 14 E5

Scot La WGNE/HIN WN2 ..... 57 M7
 WGNW/BIL/O WN5 ........ 68 A3
Scott Av HUY L36 ......... 116 C5
 RAIN/WH L35 ........... 117 H2
 WDN WA8 ................ 16 A3
Scott CI ANF/KKDL L4 ...... 97 H6
 WARR WA1 ............... 72 F4
Scott Dr ORM L39 ......... 51 H6
Scotton Av GTS/LS CH66 ... 155 K8
Scott Rd GOL/RIS/CU WA3... 92 F4
Scotts Av STHEL WA9 ..... 118 C2
Scotts Quays WAL/EG CH44 .. 112 A4
Scott St BTL L20 ........... 6 E1
 CHTN/BK PR9 ............ 25 J6
 LEIGH WN7 .............. 81 M8
 WAL/NB CH45............ 95 K6
 WARRN/WOL WA2 ........ 14 F3
 WGNS/IIMK WN3 ......... 79 H1
Scow Croft La CHLYE PR6 ... 33 L1
The Scythes GR/UP/WCH CH49 .. 125 L1
 NTHTN L30............... 84 D1
Scythia CI PS/BROM CH62.. 128 E5
Seabank Av WAL/EG CH44 .. 95 L8
Seabank Rd CHTN/BK PR9 ... 3 H1
 HES CH60 ............... 141 C7
 WAL/NB CH45............ 95 L6
Seabury St WARRS WA4 ... 138 C2
Seacombe Dr GTS/LS CH66 . 163 C2
Seacombe Prom WAL/EG CH44 .. 112 A2
Seacombe Vw WAL/EG CH44 .. 112 A3
Seacroft CI DV/KA/FCH L14 . 99 J7
Seacroft Crs CHTN/BK PR9 .. 22 D8
Seacroft Rd DV/KA/FCH L14 . 99 J7
Seafield FMBY L37 ......... 59 J3
Seafield Av CSBY/BLUN L23 . 83 H1
 HES CH60 ............... 141 C7
Seafield Rd BTL L20 ........ 6 E2
 PS/BROM CH62 .......... 128 D5
 STHP PR8................ 34 E7
Seaford CI RUNC WA7 ..... 150 F4
Seaford PI WARRN/WOL WA2 . 121 J1
Seaford Rd MGHL L31 ..... 72 D1
Seaforth Dr MOR/LEA CH46 . 110 A6
Seaforth Rd LITH L21 ...... 83 J7
Seaforth V North LITH L21 .. 83 J6
Seaforth V West LITH L21 ... 83 J7
Seagram CI WLT/FAZ L9 .... 84 E5
Sealand Av FMBY L37 ...... 58 F3
Sealand CI FMBY L37 ...... 58 F3
 WARRN/WOL WA2 ........ 122 A4
Sea La RUNC WA7 ......... 149 M3
Sealy CI BEB CH63 ........ 143 J4
Seaman Rd WAV L15 ....... 114 A6
Seaman Wy WGNE/HIN WN2.. 69 J7
Sea Rd WAL/NB CH45....... 95 H5
Seascale Av ECCL WA10.... 101 K5
Seascale Crs WGN WN1 .... 68 E2
Seath Av STHEL WA9 ...... 103 C1
Seathwaite CI CSBY/BLUN L23 . 82 D1
Seathwaite Crs NWD/KWIPK L33.. 85 M1
Seathwaite Grove CI
 RUNC WA7 .............. 150 A8
Seatoller PI WGNW/BIL/O WN5 .. 67 K6
Seaton CI WD/CROXPK L12 .. 99 J3
Seaton Gv RAIN/WH L35 ... 101 M7
Seaton Pk RUNC WA7 ..... 151 C2
Seaton PI SKEL WN8........ 65 C2
Seaton Rd RF/TRAN CH42 ... 10 F9
 WAL/NB CH45............ 95 J7
Seaton Wy CHTN/BK PR9 ... 22 C8
Sea Vw HOY CH47.......... 108 D6
Seaview Av PEN/TH CH61... 125 M7
 PS/BROM CH62 .......... 144 D7
 WAL/NB CH45............ 95 J8
Sea View La PEN/TH CH61.. 125 M7
Sea View Rd BTL L20 ...... 6 D3
Seaview Rd WAL/NB CH45 .. 95 J7
Seawood Gv MOR/LEA CH46 .. 109 M6
Secker Av WARRS WA4 .... 137 M3
Secker CI WARRS WA4 .... 137 M3
Second Av CL/PREN CH43 .. 110 D7
 CSBY/BLUN L23 .......... 82 F1
 RAIN/WH L35............ 117 K1
 RUNC WA7 .............. 150 B5
 WGNNW/ST WN6 ........ 68 C3
 WLT/FAZ L9 ............. 84 E6
Sedbergh Av AIN/FAZ L10 .. 84 E2
Sedbergh Gv RUNC WA7 ... 150 A8
Sedburgh Rd WAL/EG CH44 . 95 H8
Sedburgh Gv HUY L36 .... 115 L2
Sedburn Rd KKBY L32 ..... 86 C6
Seddon CI ECCL WA10..... 101 H2
Seddon House Dr
 WGNNW/ST WN6 ........ 68 A2
Seddon PI SKEL WN8....... 65 C2
Seddon Rd ALL/GAR L19 .. 130 E7
 WGNW/BIL/O WN5 ...... 67 L7
Seddon St CLVPS L1 ....... 13 C9
 ECCL WA10............... 89 H6
Sedgefield Dr WGNNW/ST WN6.. 68 A2
Sedgefield Rd MOR/LEA CH46 . 110 C5
Sedgely WGNNW/ST WN6 ... 56 C6
Sedgemoor Rd NG/CROX L11 . 98 A2
Sedgewick Crs
 WARRW/BUR WA5 ....... 104 A7
Sedley St NPK/KEN L6 ..... 97 K7
Sedum Gv NWD/KWIPK L33 . 73 M8
Sedwyn St WGN WN1 ...... 5 J1
Seeds La WLT/FAZ L9 ..... 84 E6
Seeley Av BIRK CH41 ...... 10 A3
Seel Rd HUY L36 .......... 116 B3
Seel St CLVPS L1 .......... 13 H9
Sefton Av LITH L21 ........ 83 K6
 WDN WA8 ............... 134 C2
 WGNW/BIL/O WN5 ...... 66 F8
Sefton CI KKBY L32......... 86 C6
 WGNW/BIL/O WN5 ...... 66 F8
Sefton Coastal Footpath
 CSBY/WL L22 ............ 82 D3
 HTWN L38 ............... 70 B7
Sefton Dr AIN/FAZ L10 .... 85 C3
 CSBY/BLUN L23 .......... 71 J6
 KKBY L32................ 85 L2
 MGHL L31 ............... 72 C5
 TOX L8.................. 113 L8
Sefton Fold Dr
 WGNW/BIL/O WN5 ....... 77 M8

Sefton Fold Gdns
 WGNW/BIL/O WN5 ...... 77 M8
Sefton Gdns ORM L39 ..... 62 F6
Sefton Gv AIG/SPK L17 .... 129 L1
Sefton La MGHL L31 ...... 72 D5
Sefton Mill La SFTN L29.... 72 B6
Sefton Moss La NTHTN L30.. 83 M2
Sefton Moss Vls LITH L21 .. 83 K5
Sefton Park Rd TOX L8 .... 113 K7
Sefton Rd AIMK WN4 ...... 79 H7
 BTL L20................. 83 M8
 FMBY L37 ............... 59 C3
 LITH L21................ 83 K5
 RF/TRAN CH42 .......... 128 C4
 WAL/NB CH45............ 95 K6
 WGNS/IIMK WN3 ........ 79 H1
 WGNW/BIL/O WN5 ....... 66 F8
 WLT/FAZ L9 ............. 97 J1
Sefton St LITH L21 ........ 83 K6
 NEWLW WA12............ 104 B2
 STHP PR8................ 3 J6
 VAUX/LVPD L3 .......... 112 F8
Sefton Vw CSBY/BLUN L23 . 83 H1
 WGNW/BIL/O WN5 ...... 66 F8
Segar's La STHP PR8 ...... 34 F8
Selborne RAIN/WH L35 .... 117 H3
Selborne CI TOX L8........ 113 J8
Selborne St TOX L8........ 113 J8
Selbourne CI GR/UP/WCH CH49.. 126 D2
Selby CI ECCL WA10....... 8 B7
 RUNC WA7 .............. 151 G1
Selby Dr WARRS WA4 ..... 59 K3
 WGNS/IIMK WN3 ........ 78 E1
Selby Gn GTS/LS CH66 .... 155 K8
Selby Gv HUY L36 ........ 116 D1
Selby PI SKEL WN8......... 64 F2
Selby Rd WLT/FAZ L9 ...... 84 C7
Selby St WAL/NB CH45 .... 95 K8
 WARRW/BUR WA5 ....... 121 C8
Seldon CI ANF/KKDL L4 .... 97 L6
Seldon Rd CSBY/WL L22 ... 82 E3
Selsey CI BEB CH63 ....... 143 J3
Selside WGNS/IIMK WN3 ... 79 K3
Selside Rd NTHLY L27...... 132 C2
Selston CI BEB CH63....... 143 J3
Selwood CI GTS/LS CH66 .. 155 H8
Selworthy Dr WARRS WA4 .. 138 F2
Selworthy Gn CHLDW L16 .. 115 G7
Selworthy Rd STHP PR8 ... 34 F2
Selwyn CI WDN WA8 ...... 134 F2
Selwyn St ANF/KKDL L4 ... 7 L8
Selworthy Rd WARRS WA4 .. 69 K3
Seneschal Ct RUNC WA7 .. 150 A7
Sennen CI RUNC WA7 ..... 150 D8
Sennen Rd KKBY L32 ..... 86 B5
Sennicar La WGN WN1 ... 56 E8
Sentinel Wy NTHTN L30.... 84 D5
Sephton Av GOL/RIS/CU WA3 .. 107 C2
Sephton Dr ORM L39 ..... 51 H6
Sephton St WGNS/IIMK WN3.. 5 L7
September Rd NPK/KEN L6 . 97 L8
Serenade Rd NWD/KWIPK L33.. 74 B7
Sergeant York Loop
 WARRW/BUR WA5 ....... 120 D8
Sergrim Rd HUY L36 ...... 115 M2
Serin CI NEWLW WA12 .... 104 E2
Serpentine Rd WAL/EG CH44 . 95 L8
The Serpentine South
 CSBY/BLUN L23 .......... 82 C1
The Serpentine ALL/GAR L19 . 130 C5
 CSBY/BLUN L23 .......... 82 C1
 ORM L39 ................ 62 F5
Servia Rd LITH L21 ........ 83 K6
Servite CI CSBY/WL L22 ... 82 E3
 EP CH65 ................ 156 B7
Sessions Rd ANF/KKDL L4 .. 97 G5
Seth Powell Wy HUY L36 .. 99 L7
Settrington Rd NG/CROX L11 . 98 A3
Seven Acre Rd CSBY/BLUN L23 . 71 K8
Seven Acres La PEN/TH CH61.. 126 C7
Sevenoaks CHLY/EC PR7 ... 43 L1
Sevenoaks Av STHP PR8 ... 34 D8
Sevenoaks CI EV L5 ....... 97 G8
Seven Stars Rd WGNS/IIMK WN3... 4 B5
Seventh Av WLT/FAZ L9 ... 84 F6
Severn CI STHEL WA9 ..... 102 E8
 WARRN/WOL WA2 ....... 122 A3
 WDN WA8 ............... 135 H2
 WGNW/BIL/O WN5 ...... 89 M1
Severn Dr WGNE/HIN WN2 . 81 L2
 WGNW/BIL/O WN5 ...... 67 L7
Severn Rd AIMK WN4 ..... 80 A8
 GOL/RIS/CU WA3 ........ 107 H3
 NWD/KWIPK L33......... 74 B7
 RAIN/WH L35............ 117 K2
Severn St BIRK CH41 ..... 111 J4
 EV L5................... 96 F5
Severnvale EP CH65........ 20 A8
Severs St NPK/KEN L6 .... 113 J1
Sewell St PR/KW L34 ..... 100 F7
 RUNC WA7 ............... 19 K4
Sextant CI RUNC WA7 .... 150 F7
Sexton Av STHEL WA9 .... 103 K3
Sexton Wy DV/KA/FCH L14 . 115 H3
Seymour Dr GTS/LS CH66 .. 156 A7
 MGHL L31 ............... 73 C2
 WARR WA1 .............. 122 C6
Seymour PI West
 WAL/NB CH45............ 95 K5
Seymour Rd DV/KA/FCH L14 . 114 F4
 LITH L21................ 83 K6
Seymour St BTL L20 ....... 6 E7
 CHLYE PR6 .............. 32 F6
 RF/TRAN CH42 .......... 127 M1
 VAUX/LVPD L3 .......... 13 K6
Sgt York Loop
 WARRW/BUR WA5 ....... 120 D7
Shacklady Rd NWD/KWIPK L33.. 86 C1

Shackleton CI
 WARRW/BUR WA5 ....... 120 F5
Shackleton Rd MOR/LEA CH46.. 110 D1
Shadewood Crs WARRS WA4.. 138 D3
Shadwell CI EV L5 ........ 96 E8
Shadwell Gv LEIGH WN7 ... 81 L5
Shadwell St EV L5......... 96 D8
Shaftesbury PI STHP PR8... 35 J5
 WARRW/BUR WA5 ....... 136 A3
Shaftesbury Gv STHP PR8 .. 35 J4
Shaftesbury PI CHLY/EC PR7 . 32 D5
Shaftesbury Rd
 CSBY/BLUN L23 .......... 82 F1
 STHP PR8................ 35 J5
Shaftesbury St TOX L8 .... 113 G7
Shaftesbury Ter
 CLB/OSW/ST L13 ........ 114 C2
Shaftesbury Wy
 WARRW/BUR WA5 ....... 104 B6
Shaftsbury Av NWD/KWIPK L33.. 73 M8
Shaftsbury Rd
 WGNW/BIL/O WN5 ...... 67 J5
Shaftsbury St WGNNW/ST WN6.. 68 B2
Shaftway CI RNFD/HAY WA11.. 91 H6
Shakespeare Av RF/TRAN CH42.. 128 B4
Shakespeare Gv
 WARRN/WOL WA2 ....... 121 K3
 WGNS/IIMK WN3 ........ 79 J1
Shakespeare Rd NPK/KEN L6 . 113 J1
 NSTN CH64 ............. 153 G4
 STHEL WA9 ............. 118 C3
 WAL/EG CH44 .......... 111 M3
 WDN WA8 ............... 16 C2
Shakespeare St ALL/GAR L19 . 130 E8
 BTL L20................. 6 D1
 STHP PR8................ 3 G8
Shakespeare Ter CHLYE PR6.. 32 F3
Shakspeare CI NPK/KEN L6.. 113 J1
Shalcombe CI HLWD L26 .. 132 C6
Shaldon CI KKBY L32 ..... 86 C5
Shaldon Gv KKBY L32 .... 86 C5
Shaldon Rd KKBY L32..... 86 C6
Shalford Gv WKBY CH48 .. 124 F5
Shallacres EP CH65 ...... 156 B6
Shallcross PI NPK/KEN L6 .. 113 J1
Shallmarsh CI BEB CH63 .. 127 M8
Shallmarsh Rd BEB CH63 .. 127 M8
Shalom CI AIG/SPK L17 ... 114 A8
Shamrock Rd BIRK CH41 .. 111 H6
Shanklin CI WARRW/BUR WA5 . 119 L1
Shanklin Rd WAV L15 ..... 114 B4
Shannon St BIRK CH41 .... 111 H4
Shap Ga WGNW/BIL/O WN5 .. 67 K6
Shard CI NG/CROX L11 .... 85 K8
Shard St STHEL WA9 ..... 103 C6
Shared St WCN WN1 ..... 5 H5
Sharon Park CI WARRS WA4 . 138 E4
Sharon Sq WGNE/HIN WN2 . 80 B5
Sharpeville CI ANF/KKDL L4 . 96 F6
Sharples Crs CSBY/BLUN L23 . 83 H2
Sharp St WARRN/WOL WA2 . 14 F2
 WDN WA8 ............... 16 D3
 WGNS/IIMK WN3 ........ 5 J8
Sharrats Pth CHLY/EC PR7 . 43 H1
Sharwood Rd NTHLY L27... 132 B1
Shavington Av CL/PREN CH43.. 127 H2
Shawbury Av BEB CH63 ... 127 M6
Shawbury CI HOR/BR BL6 .. 57 M4
Shaw CI GTS/LS CH66 .... 163 C1
 ORM L39 ................ 36 B7
Shaw Crs FMBY L37 ...... 59 K1
Shawell Ct WDN WA8 ..... 135 C3
Shaw Entry WDN WA8..... 117 J6
Shawes Dr CHLYE PR6 .... 44 E6
Shaw Hill St CHLY/EC PR7 . 32 E6
 CLVPS L1 ................ 13 C6
Shaw La GR/UP/WCH CH49.. 125 L3
 ORM L39 ................ 48 F7
 RAIN/WH L35............ 117 G1
Shaw Rd HOR/BR BL6 .... 45 K8
 SPK/HALE L24............ 131 M8
Shaws Aly CLVPS L1 ...... 112 E5
Shaw's Av STHP PR8 ..... 35 J4
 WARRN/WOL WA2 ....... 121 K5
Shaws Dr HOY CH47....... 108 F5
Shaws Garth ORM L39..... 36 B7
Shaw's Rd STHP PR8 ..... 35 J4
Shaw St AIMK WN4........ 79 K8
 BIRK CH41 .............. 11 C8
 ECCL WA10.............. 9 J4
 GOL/RIS/CU WA3 ........ 107 J2
 HOY CH47............... 108 D6
 NPK/KEN L6 ............. 13 L3
 RNFD/HAY WA11......... 91 C7
 RUNC WA7 .............. 18 F4
 STHEL WA9 ............. 9 J6
 WARRN/WOL WA2 ....... 14 D2
 WGN WN1 ............... 4 F1
Shawton Rd CHLDW L16 .. 114 F5
Shearman CI PEN/TH CH61.. 141 H1
Shearman Rd PEN/TH CH61 . 141 H1
Sheen Rd WAL/NB CH45 ... 95 L6
Sheepfield CI GTS/LS CH66 . 155 L6
Sheep House La HOR/BR BL6.. 45 H3
Sheerwater CI WARR WA1 .. 122 B6
Sheffield CI
 WARRW/BUR WA5 ....... 120 E8
Shefford Crs WGNS/IIMK WN3.. 78 E3
The Sheilings
 GOL/RIS/CU WA3 ........ 93 H5
Sheil Rd NPK/KEN L6 ..... 113 L2
Shelagh Av WDN WA8 .... 16 D2
Sheldon CI BEB CH63 .... 143 J3
Sheldon Rd WD/CROXPK L12 . 98 F5
Sheldrake Gv NSTN CH64 . 153 G4
Shelley CI CHLY/EC PR7 ... 43 H5
 HUY L36 ................ 116 B4
Shelley Dr CHLY/EC PR7 .. 30 F8
 ORM L39 ................ 50 F7
 WGNE/HIN WN2 ......... 80 D4
 WGNW/BIL/O WN5 ...... 67 J7
Shelley Gv ALL/GAR L19 .. 130 E8
 STHP PR8................ 25 H6
 WARRS WA4 ............ 138 E3
Shelley PI RAIN/WH L35 ... 117 H2
Shelley Rd WDN WA8 ..... 16 C1
Shelley St BTL L20 ....... 6 E2

LEIGH WN7 .......... 81 L6
STHEL WA9 .......... 118 D3
Shelley Wy WKBY CH48 .......... 124 D5
Shellfield Rd CHTN/BK PR9 .......... 25 J2
Shellingford CI WGNNW/ST WN6 .. 54 F6
**Shellingford Rd**
  DV/KA/FCH L14 .......... 115 J1
Shellway Rd EP CH65 .......... 21 L8
Shelmore Dr TOX L8 .......... 129 H1
Shelton CI CLB/OSW/ST L13 .. 114 C3
  WDN WA8 .......... 135 K1
Shelton Dr STHP PR8 .......... 47 J1
Shelton Rd WAL/NB CH45 .......... 95 J7
Shenley CI BEB CH63 .......... 128 B7
Shenley Rd WAV L15 .......... 114 E5
Shenley Wy CHTN/BK PR9 .......... 22 F8
Shenstone St EHL/KEN L7 .......... 113 K4
Shenton Av RNFD/HAY WA11 .......... 89 M7
**Shepherd CI**
  GR/UP/WCH CH49 .......... 125 L1
Shepherds CI HOR/BR BL6 .......... 57 L2
Shepherd's La ORM L39 .......... 49 M8
Shepherd St NPK/KEN L6 .......... 13 M5
Shepherds Wy CHLY/EC PR7 .......... 32 F5
Sheppard Av CHLDW L16 .......... 115 J5
Shepperton CI WARRS WA4 .......... 137 M7
Shepsides CI GTS/LS CH66 .......... 162 E2
Shepston Av ANF/KKDL L4 .......... 97 J4
Shepton Av WGNE/HIN WN2 .......... 80 C4
Shepton Rd GTS/LS CH66 .......... 163 C3
  HUY L36 .......... 99 M7
Sheraton CI WGNW/BIL/O WN5 .. 67 K4
Sherborne CI RUNC WA7 .......... 151 H2
**Sherborne Rd**
  WGNW/BIL/O WN5 .......... 67 J5
Sherbourne Rd EP CH65 .......... 20 F8
Sherbourne St CHLYE PR6 .......... 32 F6
**Sherbourne Wy**
  WARRW/BUR WA5 .......... 104 B7
Sherbrooke CI WLT/FAZ L9 .. 99 C8
Sherburn CI WLT/FAZ L9 .......... 84 F5
Sherdley Park Dr STHEL WA9 .. 102 D7
Sherdley Rd STHEL WA9 .......... 102 D7
Sheridan Av GOL/RIS/CU WA3 .. 92 F6
Sheri Dr NEWLW WA12 .......... 104 F3
**Sheringham CI**
  GR/UP/WCH CH49 .......... 110 C6
  STHEL WA9 .......... 102 F2
**Sheringham Rd**
  WARRW/BUR WA5 .......... 120 A7
Sherlock Av RNFD/HAY WA11 .......... 91 C6
Sherlock La WAL/EG CH44 .......... 111 K2
Sherman Dr RAIN/WH L35 .......... 117 M4
Sherrat St SKEL WN8 .......... 64 F4
Sherringham Rd STHP PR8 .......... 35 C3
Sherry La GR/UP/WCH CH49 .. 126 C3
Sherwell CI WAV L15 .......... 114 C4
Sherwood Av AIMK WN4 .......... 91 L1
  CSBY/BLUN L23 .......... 70 F8
  ORM L39 .......... 62 E3
  PEN/TH CH61 .......... 125 L6
  WDN WA8 .......... 133 L4
Sherwood Ct HUY L36 .......... 116 B3
  WD/CROXPK L12 .......... 99 H2
**Sherwood Crs**
  WARRW/BUR WA5 .......... 104 A7
  WGNE/HIN WN2 .......... 80 C3
  WGNW/BIL/O WN5 .......... 67 M6
Sherwood Dr BEB CH63 .......... 128 A6
  SKEL WN8 .......... 65 M2
  WGNW/BIL/O WN5 .......... 67 M7
Sherwood Gv FROD/HEL WA6 .. 166 C2
  HOY CH47 .......... 109 H6
  WGNW/BIL/O WN5 .......... 67 M6
Sherwood PI CHLYE PR6 .......... 32 F5
Sherwood Rd CSBY/BLUN L23 .. 70 E8
  HOY CH47 .......... 109 H5
  WAL/EG CH44 .......... 111 L2
Sherwood's La AIN/FAZ L10 .. 85 H5
Sherwood St VAUX/LVPD L3 .. 12 D1
Sherwyn Rd ANF/KKDL L4 .......... 97 L6
**Shetland CI**
  WARRN/WOL WA2 .......... 122 A1
  WDN WA8 .......... 135 G2
Shetland Dr EP CH65 .......... 163 L4
  PS/BROM CH62 .......... 144 A5
**Shevington Cswy**
  LEY/BBR PR5 .......... 29 K3
Shevington CI STHEL WA9 .. 102 E6
  WDN WA8 .......... 135 G2
Shevington La WGNNW/ST WN6 .. 55 K6
**Shevington Moor**
  WGNNW/ST WN6 .......... 55 J3
Shevington's La NWD/KWIPK L33 .. 74 D3
Shewell CI RF/TRAN CH42 .. 11 H9
Shiel Rd WAL/NB CH45 .......... 95 J6
Shiggins CI WARRW/BUR WA5 .. 120 F7
Shildon CI WGNE/HIN WN2 .. 69 H3
Shillingford CI WARRS WA4 .. 138 A8
Shimmin St EHL/KEN L7 .......... 113 J4
Shipham CI LEIGH WN7 .......... 81 M5
Ship St FROD/HEL WA6 .......... 160 E3
Shipton CI ALL/GAR L19 .......... 130 D5
  CL/PREN CH43 .......... 127 G4
  WARRW/BUR WA5 .......... 120 D5
  WDN WA8 .......... 133 M2
Ship Yd WGN WN1 .......... 4 F4
Shirdley Av KKBY L32 .......... 86 B6
Shirdley Crs STHP PR8 .......... 47 L2
Shirdley Wk KKBY L32 .......... 86 B6
**Shirebourne Av**
  RNFD/HAY WA11 .......... 89 K6
Shireburn Rd FMBY L37 .......... 46 F3
Shire Gn STHEL WA9 .......... 102 E7
The Shires ECCL WA10 .......... 8 D7
Shirley Dr WARRS WA4 .......... 138 C3
Shirley Rd ALL/GAR L19 .......... 130 E5
Shirley St WAL/EG CH44 .......... 112 A2
Shirwell Ct STHEL WA9 .......... 118 E1
Shobdon CI WD/CROXPK L12 .. 99 H1
Shones Ct NSTN CH64 .......... 153 J8
Shop La MGHL L31 .......... 72 E4
Shop Rd BK PR9 .......... 99 L1
Shore Bank PS/BROM CH62 .. 128 E5
Shore Dr PS/BROM CH62 .......... 128 E7

Shorefields PS/BROM CH62 .. 128 D5
Shorefields Village TOX L8 .. 129 H2
**Shoreham Dr**
  WARRW/BUR WA5 .......... 136 C2
Shore Rd BIRK CH41 .......... 11 L3
  BTL L20 .......... 6 B1
  LITH L21 .......... 6 B1
  STHP PR8 .......... 34 C7
  WKBY CH48 .......... 124 E6
Short CI NEWLW WA12 .......... 104 A2
Short Croft La FMBY L37 .......... 59 M4
**Shortfield Rd**
  GR/UP/WCH CH49 .......... 126 C1
**Shortfield Wy**
  GR/UP/WCH CH49 .......... 126 C1
Shortland PI WGNE/HIN WN2 .. 81 J5
Short St GOL/RIS/CU WA3 .. 92 D4
  NEWLW WA12 .......... 104 A2
  RNFD/HAY WA11 .......... 91 C7
  WDN WA8 .......... 134 C8
  WGNW/BIL/O WN5 .......... 67 K7
Shortwood Rd DV/KA/FCH L14 .. 115 H2
Shorwell CI WARRW/BUR WA5 .. 119 L6
Shotwick La CH/BCN CH1 .. 162 A7
Shrewsbury Av AIN/FAZ L10 .. 84 E2
  CSBY/WL L22 .......... 82 F2
**Shrewsbury CI**
  CL/PREN CH43 .......... 111 H7
**Shrewsbury Dr**
  GR/UP/WCH CH49 .......... 110 C7
Shrewsbury Rd ALL/GAR L19 .. 130 E7
  CL/PREN CH43 .......... 10 B9
  HES CH60 .......... 141 J4
  WAL/NB CH45 .......... 95 H8
  WKBY CH48 .......... 124 C4
Shrewsbury St WARRS WA4 .. 15 J9
Shrewton Rd WLTN L25 .......... 115 J6
Shropshire CI NTHTN L30 .. 84 C1
  WARR WA1 .......... 123 C7
Shropshire Rd EP CH65 .......... 21 J9
**Shuttle Hillock Rd**
  WGNE/HIN WN2 .......... 81 H6
**Sibbering Brow Preston Rd**
  CHLY/EC PR7 .......... 31 L6
Sibford Rd WD/CROXPK L12 .. 98 F8
Sibley Av AIMK WN4 .......... 91 M1
Sidbrook St WGNE/HIN WN2 .. 69 L8
Siddall St ECCL WA10 .......... 89 H6
Siddeley Dr NEWLW WA12 .. 104 B2
Siddeley St AIG/SPK L17 .......... 129 L2
  LEIGH WN7 .......... 81 M8
Sidgreave St ECCL WA10 .......... 8 D6
Siding La RNFD/HAY WA11 .. 75 M4
The Sidings RF/TRAN CH42 .. 128 B3
Sidlaw Av STHEL WA9 .......... 103 H2
Sidlaw CI GTS/LS CH66 .......... 155 J7
Sidmouth CI WARRW/BUR WA5 .. 136 A1
Sidmouth Gv WGNS/IIMK WN3 .. 79 C2
Sidney Av WAL/NB CH45 .......... 95 J5
Sidney PI EHL/KEN L7 .......... 113 J4
Sidney Powell Av KKBY L32 .. 85 L3
Sidney Rd BIRK CH41 .......... 128 A1
  BTL L20 .......... 7 K6
  CHTN/BK PR9 .......... 25 H5
  NSTN CH64 .......... 153 H4
Sidney St BIRK CH41 .......... 11 K4
  ECCL WA10 .......... 8 B4
Sidwell St ALL/GAR L19 .......... 130 E8
Signal Works Rd WLT/FAZ L9 .. 85 C5
Silcock St GOL/RIS/CU WA3 .. 92 C5
Silcroft Rd KKBY L32 .......... 86 A5
Silkstone CI ECCL WA10 .......... 8 C6
  EHL/KEN L7 .......... 113 K5
Silkstone Crs RUNC WA7 .. 150 D6
Silkstone St ECCL WA10 .......... 8 C6
Sillitoe Dr WGNNW/ST WN6 .. 4 B2
Silsbury Gv WGNE/HIN WN2 .. 56 C5
Silsden Av GOL/RIS/CU WA3 .. 93 K5
Silver Av RNFD/HAY WA11 .. 90 C8
Silverbeech Av CALD/MH L18 .. 130 D1
Silverbeech Rd WAL/EG CH44 .. 111 J2
Silver Birch Gv AIMK WN4 .. 79 J8
Silverbirch Wy GTS/LS CH66 .. 163 H5
Silver Birch Wy MGHL L31 .. 61 K8
**Silverburn Av**
  MOR/LEA CH46 .......... 110 A4
Silverdale WGN WN1 .......... 68 E3
Silverdale Av CLB/OSW/ST L13 .. 98 A8
  WGNE/HIN WN2 .......... 69 J5
Silverdale CI FROD/HEL WA6 .. 166 A5
  HUY L36 .......... 116 A5
Silverdale Dr LITH L21 .......... 83 M5
Silverdale Gv RNFD/HAY WA11 .. 89 J5
Silverdale Rd BEB CH63 .......... 128 B6
  CHLYE PR6 .......... 33 C6
  CL/PREN CH43 .......... 10 A9
  NEWLW WA12 .......... 104 D1
  WARRS WA4 .......... 137 K3
  WGNW/BIL/O WN5 .......... 67 K5
Silverlea Av WAL/NB CH45 .. 111 J1
Silver Leigh AIG/SPK L17 .. 129 M4
Silverlime Gdns RAIN/WH L35 .. 101 L6
Silverne Dr EP CH65 .......... 163 J3
Silverstone Dr HUY L36 .......... 115 M5
Silverstone Gv MGHL L31 .. 61 K8
Silver St WARRN/WOL WA2 .. 16 E3
  WGNE/HIN WN2 .......... 80 D3
Silverthorne Dr CHTN/BK PR9 .. 25 H4
Silverton Rd AIG/SPK L17 .. 130 A5
Silverwell Rd WG/CROX L11 .. 85 M8
Silvester CI CHLY/EC PR7 .. 32 E7
Silvester St L5 .......... 96 F8
  HOR/BR BL6 .......... 57 M3
Simfield CI WGNNW/ST WN6 .. 55 M4
Simkin Av WARRS WA4 .......... 138 B1
Simms Av STHEL WA9 .......... 103 C2
Simm's Rd NPK/KEN L6 .......... 97 M7
Simnel CI WLTN L25 .......... 115 K7
Simonsbridge WKBY CH48 .. 124 F7
Simons CI RAIN/WH L35 .......... 116 E5
Simon's Cft NTHTN L30 .......... 83 L2
Simonside WDN WA8 .......... 133 L3
Simons La FROD/HEL WA6 .. 160 D7
Simonstone Gv STHEL WA9 .. 102 F6
**Simonswood La**
  NWD/KWIPK L33 .......... 86 C3
  ORM L39 .......... 74 B2

Simpkin St WGNE/HIN WN2 .. 80 D4
Simpson St BIRK CH41 .......... 111 H5
  CLVPS L1 .......... 112 F6
Sim St VAUX/LVPD L3 .......... 13 K4
Sinclair Av RAIN/WH L35 .......... 101 H8
  WARRN/WOL WA2 .......... 121 K3
  WDN WA8 .......... 16 B3
Sinclair CI RAIN/WH L35 .......... 101 H7
Sinclair Dr CALD/MH L18 .. 114 D7
Sinclair PI WGNW/BIL/O WN5 .. 68 A5
Sinclair St ALL/GAR L19 .......... 130 E8
Sineacre La ORM L39 .......... 75 G4
Singleton Av HOR/BR BL6 .. 45 L8
  RF/TRAN CH42 .......... 127 L2
  RNFD/HAY WA11 .......... 89 M8
Singleton Dr PR/KW L34 .......... 99 M2
Singleton Rd EP CH65 .......... 163 H1
Sirdar CI EHL/KEN L7 .......... 113 K5
Sir Thomas St CLVPS L1 .. 12 F4
  CLVPS L1 .......... 13 G6
Siskin CI NEWLW WA12 .......... 104 E2
Siskin Gn WLTN L25 .......... 131 H1
Sisters Wy BIRK CH41 .......... 11 G5
Sittingbourne Rd WGN WN1 .. 68 C1
Six Acre Gdns WARRS WA4 .. 136 C8
Six Acre La RUNC WA7 .......... 136 C6
Sixth Av WLT/FAZ L9 .......... 84 F6
  WLT/FAZ L9 .......... 85 G6
Skeffington RAIN/WH L35 .. 117 C3
Skelhorne St VAUX/LVPD L3 .. 13 J7
Skellington Fold NTHLY L27 .. 116 A8
Skelmersdale Rd ORM L39 .. 64 C6
Skelton CI RNFD/HAY WA11 .. 89 J6
Skelton St AIMK WN4 .......... 79 H7
Skerries Rd ANF/KKDL L4 .. 97 J7
Skiddaw CI RUNC WA7 .......... 161 J1
Skiddaw PI WGNW/BIL/O WN5 .. 67 L7
Skiddaw Rd PS/BROM CH62 .. 144 A3
Skipton Av CHTN/BK PR9 .. 22 E7
  WGNE/HIN WN2 .......... 81 J1
Skipton Dr GTS/LS CH66 .. 162 E1
Skipton Rd ANF/KKDL L4 .. 97 K2
  HUY L36 .......... 116 D2
Skirving PI EV L5 .......... 96 F7
Skirving St EV L5 .......... 96 F7
Skull House La WGNNW/ST WN6 .. 54 F5
Skye CI EP CH65 .......... 163 L4
  WDN WA8 .......... 135 G2
Slackey Fold WGNE/HIN WN2 .. 81 K4
Slack's La CHLYE PR6 .......... 44 D3
Slag La GOL/RIS/CU WA3 .. 93 H3
  RNFD/HAY WA11 .......... 90 D6
Slaidburn CI WGNS/IIMK WN3 .. 79 J2
Slaidburn Crs CHTN/BK PR9 .. 22 E8
  GOL/RIS/CU WA3 .......... 92 B3
Slate La SKEL WN8 .......... 64 E2
Slater PI CLVPS L1 .......... 13 H9
Slater St CLVPS L1 .......... 13 H9
  WARRS WA4 .......... 15 H8
Slater St North LEIGH WN7 .. 81 M7
Slatey Rd CL/PREN CH43 .. 10 C6
Sleaford Rd DV/KA/FCH L14 .. 99 K8
**Sledbrook St**
  WGNW/BIL/O WN5 .......... 67 L8
Sleepers HI ANF/KKDL L4 .. 97 H6
Slienna CI NTHLY L27 .......... 115 L7
Slessor Av WKBY CH48 .......... 124 F2
Slim Rd HUY L36 .......... 116 A1
Slingsby Dr GR/UP/WCH CH49 .. 126 C1
Sluice La BRSC L40 .......... 39 K2
Slutchers La WARR WA1 .......... 14 D8
Small Av WARRN/WOL WA2 .. 121 L3
Small Crs WARRN/WOL WA2 .. 121 L3
Smalley St WGNNW/ST WN6 .. 56 A4
Small La BRSC L40 .......... 38 A5
  ORM L39 .......... 62 B2
  ORM L39 .......... 63 H1
Small La North ORM L39 .. 49 M3
Small La South ORM L39 .. 49 L8
Smallridge CI PEN/TH CH61 .. 141 G1
Smallshaw CI AIMK WN4 .. 79 H7
Smallwoods Ms HES CH60 .. 141 G4
Smeaton St ANF/KKDL L4 .. 7 L9
**Smethurst La**
  WGNW/BIL/O WN5 .......... 67 L8
**Smethurst Park Hall**
  WGNW/BIL/O WN5 .......... 77 L3
**Smethurst Rd**
  WGNW/BIL/O WN5 .......... 77 L3
**Smethurst St**
  WGNW/BIL/O WN5 .......... 67 L8
Smilie Av MOR/LEA CH46 .. 109 L4
Smith Av BIRK CH41 .......... 10 C1
  WGNW/BIL/O WN5 .......... 67 K5
Smith Brow HOR/BR BL6 .. 57 L2
Smith Crs WARRN/WOL WA2 .. 121 M5
Smithdown La EHL/KEN L7 .. 113 J5
  TOX L8 .......... 113 J7
**Smithdown PI**
  CALD/MH L18 .......... 114 C8
Smithdown Rd AIG/SPK L17 .. 114 A7
  EHL/KEN L7 .......... 113 L6
  WAV L15 .......... 114 B7
Smith Dr BTL L20 .......... 84 A8
  WARRN/WOL WA2 .......... 121 M5
Smithfield St CLVP L2 .......... 12 F5
Smithills CI CHLYE PR6 .......... 33 G4
  GOL/RIS/CU WA3 .......... 106 F8
Smith Rd WDN WA8 .......... 16 B5
Smith's La KIRK/FR/WA PR4 .. 28 C4
  WGNE/HIN WN2 .......... 81 J5
Smith St CHLY/EC PR7 .......... 32 F7
  CHLY/EC PR7 .......... 44 B7
  EV L5 .......... 97 G6
  PR/KW L34 .......... 101 G7
  SKEL WN8 .......... 64 F4
  STHEL WA9 .......... 103 C6
  WARR WA1 .......... 14 F6
  WGNE/HIN WN2 .......... 81 H6
Smithy Brow GOL/RIS/CU WA3 .. 106 B6
  SKEL WN8 .......... 53 J4
  WGNNW/ST WN6 .......... 41 L5
Smithy CI FMBY L37 .......... 59 K1
  WDN WA8 .......... 133 L3
Smithy Gn FMBY L37 .......... 59 K1
Smithy Hey WKBY CH48 .. 124 E3
Smithy HI BEB CH63 .......... 142 C7
Smithy La BRSC L40 .......... 40 D3

BRSC L40 .......... 50 E1
FROD/HEL WA6 .......... 159 L8
GOL/RIS/CU WA3 .......... 106 C6
GTS/LS CH66 .......... 155 L7
KIRK/FR/WA PR4 .......... 27 L7
NSTN CH64 .......... 154 C5
ORM L39 .......... 49 J7
ORM L39 .......... 62 B7
WDN WA8 .......... 117 L8
Smithy Wk BRSC L40 .......... 39 C8
Smock La AIMK WN4 .......... 90 E1
Smollett St BTL L20 .......... 97 G7
  EHL/KEN L7 .......... 113 K3
Smugglers Wy WAL/NB CH45 .. 95 C5
Smyth Rd WDN WA8 .......... 134 F3
Snabwood CI NSTN CH64 .. 153 G8
Snaefell Av CLB/OSW/ST L13 .. 98 A8
Snaefell Gv CLB/OSW/ST L13 .. 98 A8
Snaefell Ri WARRS WA4 .......... 137 L6
Snape Gn STHP PR8 .......... 36 F5
Snave CI LITH L21 .......... 83 K8
Snipewood CHLY/EC PR7 .. 30 D7
Snottesbrook La NG/CROX L11 .. 98 B2
Snowberry CI WDN WA8 .......... 135 C1
Snowberry Rd NG/CROX L11 .. 98 B2
Snowden Av WGNS/IIMK WN3 .. 79 J1
Snowden Rd MOR/LEA CH46 .. 109 L5
Snowdon CI GTS/LS CH66 .. 155 J7
  WARRW/BUR WA5 .......... 120 A7
Snowdon Dr HOR/BR BL6 .. 45 L8
Snowdon Gv STHEL WA9 .. 102 E6
Snowdon La EV L5 .......... 96 E8
Snowdon Rd RF/TRAN CH42 .. 127 M3
Snowdrop Av BIRK CH41 .. 111 H6
Snowdrop CI RUNC WA7 .. 161 H1
Snowdrop St EV L5 .......... 96 F6
Snowshill Dr WGNS/IIMK WN3 .. 78 E1
Soane CI AIMK WN4 .......... 91 M2
Soham CI WGNE/HIN WN2 .. 81 C1
Soho PI VAUX/LVPD L3 .......... 13 K3
Soho St VAUX/LVPD L3 .......... 13 K3
  VAUX/LVPD L3 .......... 68 B6
Solar Rd WLT/FAZ L9 .......... 84 D7
Sole St WGN WN1 .......... 5 K1
Sollom La BRSC L40 .......... 28 D3
Solly Av RF/TRAN CH42 .......... 128 A3
Solomon St EHL/KEN L7 .. 113 K3
Solway CI AIMK WN4 .......... 91 J1
  WARRN/WOL WA2 .......... 122 B1
Solway Gv RUNC WA7 .......... 149 M8
Solway St TOX L8 .......... 113 K6
  WARRS WA4 .......... 15 L8
Soma Av LITH L21 .......... 83 L5
Somerford Rd DV/KA/FCH L14 .. 115 J1
Somerset Av CHLY/EC PR7 .. 32 E4
  STHP PR8 .......... 47 L3
Somerset PI NPK/KEN L6 .. 97 M8
Somerset Rd BTL L20 .......... 7 K2
  CSBY/WL L22 .......... 82 E3
  PEN/TH CH61 .......... 141 G1
  WAL/NB CH45 .......... 95 C8
  WGNW/BIL/O WN5 .......... 67 L7
  WKBY CH48 .......... 124 E2
Somerset St STHEL WA9 .. 102 F3
Somerset Wy WARR WA1 .. 122 D8
Somerton St WAV L15 .......... 114 A5
Somerville CI BEB CH63 .......... 143 K7
  NSTN CH64 .......... 153 C8
Somerville Crs EP CH65 .......... 20 D7
Somerville Gv CSBY/WL L22 .. 82 F3
Somerville Rd CSBY/WL L22 .. 82 F3
  WDN WA8 .......... 133 M5
  WGN WN1 .......... 68 E1
Sommer Av WD/CROXPK L12 .. 98 C6
Sonning Av LITH L21 .......... 83 K4
Sonning Rd ANF/KKDL L4 .. 97 M3
Sorany CI CSBY/BLUN L23 .. 71 K7
Sorbus CI CHNE CH2 .......... 165 L2
Sorogold St STHEL WA9 .......... 9 L6
Sorrel CI CL/PREN CH43 .......... 110 F8
  WARRN/WOL WA2 .......... 122 E3
Sougher's La AIMK WN4 .......... 79 H7
South Albert Rd AIG/SPK L17 .. 129 K1
**Southampton Wy**
  RUNC WA7 .......... 151 G7
South Av CHLY/EC PR7 .......... 32 F7
  PR/KW L34 .......... 100 E8
  WARRN/WOL WA2 .......... 14 F1
  WARRS WA4 .......... 137 L4
South Bank CL/PREN CH43 .. 127 K2
South Bank Rd ALL/GAR L19 .. 130 D6
  EHL/KEN L7 .......... 113 M3
Southbank Rd STHP PR8 .......... 3 H7
South Bank Ter RUNC WA7 .. 18 F1
**South Barcombe Rd**
  CHLDW L16 .......... 115 C6
**South Boundary Rd**
  NWD/KWIPK L33 .......... 86 D5
Southbourne Rd WAL/NB CH45 .. 94 E8
Southbrook Rd NTHLY L27 .. 115 L7
**South Cantril Av**
  WD/CROXPK L12 .......... 99 H6
South Chester St TOX L8 .. 113 J4
South Cloughton Rd BIRK CH41 .. 10 F6
Southcroft NWD/KWIPK L33 .. 86 A1
Southcroft Rd WAL/NB CH45 .. 94 F8
Southdale Rd RF/TRAN CH42 .. 127 L2
  WARRW/BUR WA5 .......... 120 B8
South DI WARRW/BUR WA5 .. 120 B8
Southdean Rd DV/KA/FCH L14 .. 99 K7
Southdene SKEL WN8 .......... 53 K3
Southdowns Rd CHLY/EC PR7 .. 32 F8
South Dr GR/UP/WCH CH49 .. 110 C8
  HES CH60 .......... 141 J6
  PEN/TH CH61 .......... 125 L8
  WAV L15 .......... 114 B5
  WD/CROXPK L12 .......... 98 D8
South Av WARRS WA4 .......... 137 M6
Southend Rd SPK/HALE L24 .. 147 C3
Southern Rd SPK/HALE L24 .. 147 C3
  STHP PR8 .......... 36 C3
Southern's Fold WGNE/HIN WN2 .. 69 J2
Southern's La RNFD/HAY WA11 .. 76 C7
Southern St WARRS WA4 .. 137 L4
  WGNW/BIL/O WN5 .......... 67 M8
Southey Av WGNS/IIMK WN3 .. 78 F2
Southey CI WDN WA8 .......... 16 A3
Southey Gv MGHL L31 .......... 72 F7

Southey Rd ECCL WA10 .. 101 L5
  STHEL WA9 .......... 6 E2
  WAV L15 .......... 114 A6
**South Ferry Quay**
  VAUX/LVPD L3 .......... 112 F7
Southfield WGNE/HIN WN2 .. 80 D3
Southfield Gv GTS/LS CH66 .. 155 L7
  WLT/FAZ L9 .......... 84 B7
**Southfields Av**
  WARRW/BUR WA5 .......... 120 B7
South Front RAIN/WH L35 .. 117 C5
**Southgate CI**
  WD/CROXPK L12 .......... 99 C2
Southgate Rd CLB/OSW/ST L13 .. 114 D2
Southgates CHLY/EC PR7 .. 42 F2
South Gv CALD/MH L18 .......... 130 E4
  TOX L8 .......... 129 J1
South Hey LEIGH WN7 .......... 81 L8
South Hey Rd PEN/TH CH61 .. 140 F1
South Highville Rd CHLDW L16 .. 114 F7
South Hill Rd CL/PREN CH43 .. 10 E9
  FROD/HEL WA6 .......... 166 F2
  TOX L8 .......... 129 H2
South Hunter St CLVPS L1 .. 13 L9
South John St CLVPS L1 .......... 12 F7
  L9 .......... 9 L5
**Southlands Av**
  WARRW/BUR WA5 .......... 136 B2
  WGNNW/ST WN6 .......... 56 A5
Southlands Ms RUNC WA7 .. 18 F7
South La WDN WA8 .......... 119 C8
South Manor Wy WLTN L25 .. 131 L4
South Meade MGHL L31 .......... 72 D4
Southmead Gdns ALL/GAR L19 .. 131 C6
Southmead Rd ALL/GAR L19 .. 131 C6
**South Mossley Hill Rd**
  ALL/GAR L19 .......... 130 C4
Southney CI KKBY L32 .......... 85 K3
South Pde KKBY L32 .......... 86 A3
  RUNC WA7 .......... 18 A9
  WKBY CH48 .......... 147 C3
South Park Rd KKBY L32 .. 85 L2
**South Parkside Dr**
  WD/CROXPK L12 .......... 98 E6
South Park Wy BTL L20 .......... 7 J6
South Pier Rd EP CH65 .......... 20 F6
**Southport New Rd**
  CHTN/BK PR9 .......... 26 D1
  KIRK/FR/WA PR4 .......... 28 A1
Southport Old Rd FMBY L37 .. 47 K6
Southport Rd BTL L20 .......... 7 M1
  CHLY/EC PR7 .......... 32 C5
  CSBY/BLUN L23 .......... 71 J6
  FMBY L37 .......... 82 B1
  LEY/BBR PR5 .......... 30 C3
  MGHL L31 .......... 61 J6
  MGHL L31 .......... 72 D1
  ORM L39 .......... 49 J7
  STHP PR8 .......... 36 C3
Southport St STHEL WA9 .. 103 J2
Southport Ter CHLYE PR6 .. 33 C6
Southridge Rd PEN/TH CH61 .. 126 C8
South Rd ALL/GAR L19 .......... 130 B7
  CHLY/EC PR7 .......... 43 C4
  CSBY/WL L22 .......... 82 F5
  DV/KA/FCH L14 .......... 114 F2
  EP CH65 .......... 20 D8
  RF/TRAN CH42 .......... 127 L3
  SPK/HALE L24 .......... 147 J1
  WKBY CH48 .......... 124 C4
Southside CHLY/EC PR7 .......... 31 L2
South Station Rd WLTN L25 .. 115 K8
South St RAIN/WH L35 .......... 101 M6
  TOX L8 .......... 113 J8
  WDN WA8 .......... 16 E3
South Sudley Rd ALL/GAR L19 .. 130 B4
South Ter CHLYE PR6 .......... 31 M1
  HUY L36 .......... 63 C1
South Vw CSBY/WL L22 .......... 83 C5
  HUY L36 .......... 116 D3
  PS/BROM CH62 .......... 128 F8
South Vis WAL/NB CH45 .......... 95 K6
Southward Rd RNFD/HAY WA11 .. 91 J6
Southway WAV L15 .......... 114 D5
Southway RUNC WA7 .......... 150 A6
  SKEL WN8 .......... 65 L4
  WDN WA8 .......... 133 M5
Southway Av WARRS WA4 .. 137 M6
Southwell CI GOL/RIS/CU WA3 .. 92 E5
**Southwick Rd**
  RF/TRAN CH42 .......... 128 A2
Southwood Av RUNC WA7 .. 150 E3
Southwood CI KKBY L32 .......... 86 C5
Southwood Rd AIG/SPK L17 .. 129 K2
**Southworth Av**
  WARRW/BUR WA5 .......... 121 H5
**Southworth La**
  WARRN/WOL WA2 .......... 105 M6
Southworth Rd NEWLW WA12 .. 105 H1
Sovereign CI GOL/RIS/CU WA3 .. 93 C6
  RUNC WA7 .......... 150 F6
**Sovereign Ct**
  GOL/RIS/CU WA3 .......... 122 E1
Sovereign Rd NG/CROX L11 .. 98 E2
  WGN WN1 .......... 5 C5
Sovereign Wy NG/CROX L11 .. 98 E2
Spa La BRSC L40 .......... 64 D1
Spark La BRSC L40 .......... 28 D7
  RUNC WA7 .......... 150 B4
Sparks La PEN/TH CH61 .. 126 D7
Sparrow Hall CI WLT/FAZ L9 .. 98 B1
Sparrow Hall Rd WLT/FAZ L9 .. 98 B1
Sparrowhawk CI HLWD L26 .. 132 A4
Sparrow HI SKEL WN8 .......... 54 C3
Spawell CI GOL/RIS/CU WA3 .. 93 C6
Speakman Dr WGNNW/ST WN6 .. 54 E7
Speakman Rd NEWLW WA12 .. 91 K8
Speakman Rd ECCL WA10 .. 88 C7
Speakman St RUNC WA7 .. 18 F2
**Speedwell CI**
  GOL/RIS/CU WA3 .......... 93 C5
  HES CH60 .......... 141 L5
Speedwell Dr HES CH60 .. 141 L5
Speedwell Rd BIRK CH41 .. 111 H6
Speke Bvd SPK/HALE L24 .. 131 K8

Speke Church Rd
 SPK/HALE L24 ............ 146 D2
Speke Hall Av SPK/HALE L24 ... 146 D1
Speke Hall Rd SPK/HALE L24 ... 131 K8
 WLTN L25 ............ 131 K7
Spekeland Rd EHL/KEN L7 ..... 113 L5
Speke Rd ALL/GAR L19 ......... 130 F8
 HLWD L26 ............ 132 D7
 SPK/HALE L24 ............ 131 K8
 WDN WA8 ............ 133 K7
 WLTN L25 ............ 131 K4
Speke Town La SPK/HALE L24 ... 146 D1
Spelding Dr WGNNW/ST WN6 ... 67 M2
Spellow La ANF/KKDL L4 ....... 97 H5
Spence Av BTL L20 ............ 83 M8
Spencer Av MOR/LEA CH46 ...... 110 C4
Spencer Cl HUY L36 ............ 116 B5
 WDN WA8 ............ 16 A2
Spencer Gdns STHEL WA9 ..... 102 F5
Spencer Pl BTL L20 ............ 83 M6
Spencer Rd WGN WN1 ........... 68 D2
Spencer Rd West
 WGNNW/ST WN6 ........... 68 C2
Spencer's La MGHL L31 ........ 85 H2
 ORM L39 ............ 48 D2
 SKEL WN8 ............ 65 K5
 WGNW/BIL/O WN5 ........... 66 F6
Spencer St BTL L20 ............ 6 E2
 NPK/KEN L6 ............ 13 M2
Spendmore La CHLY/EC PR7 .... 42 F5
Spennymoor Ct RUNC WA7 ... 150 A6
Spenser Av RF/TRAN CH42 ..... 128 B4
Spenser Rd NSTN CH64 ........ 155 G4
Spey Cl WLT/FAZ WN6 ......... 55 M4
Spicer Gv KKBY L32 ........... 86 A3
Spice St WLT/FAZ ............ 84 D8
Spilsby Sq WGNS/IIMK WN3 .... 79 J3
Spindle Cl NPK/KEN L6 ........ 13 M1
Spindle Hillock AIMK WN4 ..... 90 F1
Spindlewood Rd
 WGNS/IIMK WN3 ........... 5 K8
Spindus Rd SPK/HALE L24 ..... 146 C2
Spinnaker Cl RUNC WA7 ...... 150 F7
Spinney Av WDN WA8 ......... 133 J4
Spinney Cl NWD/KWIPK L33 ... 86 E5
 ORM L39 ............ 62 F2
 STHEL WA9 ............ 118 E1
Spinney Crs CSBY/BLUN L23 ... 70 D2
Spinney Dr GTS/LS CH66 ...... 162 F3
Spinney Gn ECCL WA10 ....... 101 J3
Spinney Rd NWD/KWIPK L33 ... 86 E5
The Spinney BEB CH63 ........ 143 K2
 CHLYE PR6 ............ 32 E2
 FMBY L37 ............ 47 J8
 HES CH60 ............ 141 L8
 NSTN CH64 ............ 152 F5
 PR/KW L34 ............ 100 E6
 RNFD/HAY WA11 ........... 76 B6
 STBRV L28 ............ 99 J6
 WGNW/BIL/O WN5 ........... 68 A4
 WKBY CH48 ............ 124 F3
Spinney Vw NWD/KWIPK L33 ... 86 F5
Spion Kop AIMK WN4 ......... 91 J2
Spiredale Brow
 WGNNW/ST WN6 ........... 56 B3
Spital Heyes BEB CH63 ....... 143 K2
Spital Rd BEB CH63 .......... 143 K2
 PS/BROM CH62 ........... 143 M3
Spitfire Rd ALL/GAR L19 ...... 131 K8
Spofforth Rd WAV L15 ........ 113 M5
Spooner Av LITH L21 ......... 83 L6
Sportsman St LEIGH WN7 ..... 81 M8
Sprainger St VAUX/LVPD L3 ... 12 D2
Sprakeling Pl BTL L20 ........ 84 A6
Spray St ECCL WA10 ......... 8 D3
Spreyton Cl NG/CROX L11 ..... 98 E3
Sprig Cl WLT/FAZ L9 ......... 84 F5
Spring Av GTS/LS CH66 ....... 155 L7
Springbank Cl RUNC WA7 ..... 97 K8
Spring Bank Rd ANF/KKDL L4 ... 97 K8
Springbourne FROD/HEL WA6 ... 166 D2
 WGNNW/ST WN6 ........... 68 B3
Springbrook Rd
 AIG/SPK L17 ............ 129 K3
Spring Cl NWD/KWIPK L33 .... 74 C8
 STHP PR8 ............ 2 E8
Springcroft NSTN CH64 ....... 152 F4
Springdale Cl
 WD/CROXPK L12 ........... 98 E6
Spring Fld RNFD/HAY WA11 .... 76 A3
Springfield VAUX/LVPD L3 .... 13 J4
Springfield Av FROD/HEL WA6 ... 166 D2
 GOL/RIS/CU WA3 ........... 92 B5
 LITH L21 ............ 83 L5
 WARR WA1 ............ 122 B5
 WARRS WA4 ............ 138 C2
 WKBY CH48 ............ 125 G2
Springfield Cl BRSC L40 ...... 51 M3
 FMBY L37 ............ 47 J8
 GR/UP/WCH CH49 ........... 126 E3
Springfield La ECCL WA10 .... 88 C3
Springfield Pk
 RNFD/HAY WA11 ........... 90 E6
Springfield Rd CHLY/EC PR7 ... 32 E5
 CHLY/EC PR7 ............ 43 G5
 CHLYE PR6 ............ 44 C5
 ECCL WA10 ............ 101 L5
 ORM L39 ............ 62 B8
 WDN WA8 ............ 133 J6
 WGNE/HIN WN2 ........... 69 K7
 WGNNW/ST WN6 ........... 68 B3
Springfield Rd North
 CHLY/EC PR7 ............ 43 G5
Springfield Sq WARR WA1 ..... 14 C5
 WGN WN1 ............ 5 G4
Springfield Wy WD/CROXPK L12 ... 99 G5
Spring Gdns GTS/LS CH66 ..... 155 L7
 MGHL L31 ............ 73 G5
 WGN WN1 ............ 4 D4
Spring Gv WD/CROXPK L12 .... 98 E7
 WGN WN1 ............ 5 H5
Springhill Av PS/BROM CH62 ... 143 M7
Spring La GOL/RIS/CU WA3 .... 106 D7
Springmeadow Rd WLTN L25 ... 115 J8
Springmount
 GOL/RIS/CU WA3 ........... 93 G6

Springmount Dr SKEL WN8 .... 40 E8
Springpool STHEL WA9 ....... 102 F6
 WGNS/IIMK WN3 ........... 78 D3
Springs Cl BTL L20 .......... 7 J3
Springs Rd WGNW/BIL/O WN5 ... 67 H5
Spring St RF/TRAN CH42 ...... 128 B2
 WDN WA8 ............ 16 D7
 WGN WN1 ............ 5 H5
 WGNE/HIN WN2 ........... 80 A1
Springville Rd WLT/FAZ L9 ... 84 E6
Springwell Rd BTL L20 ....... 83 M7
Springwood Av ALL/GAR L19 ... 130 F5
 WLTN L25 ............ 131 H6
Springwood Dr BRSC L40 ..... 28 C8
 CHLYE PR6 ............ 33 G8
Springwood Gv KKBY L32 .... 86 B6
Springwood Wy RF/TRAN CH42 ... 128 C5
Sprodley Dr WGNNW/ST WN6 ... 54 D3
Spruce Cl GOL/RIS/CU WA3 .... 93 H6
 RF/TRAN CH42 ........... 11 G9
Spruce Gv STBRV L28 ......... 99 K6
Spruce Rd WGNNW/ST WN6 .... 68 A2
Spruce Wy FMBY L37 ......... 58 E2
Sprucewood Cl NPK/KEN L6 .... 97 K8
Spun Cl NG/CROX L11 ........ 98 E2
Spurgeon Cl EV L5 .......... 97 H8
Spurling Rd WARRW/BUR WA5 ... 104 B7
Spurrier's La MGHL L31 ...... 73 M5
Spurstow Cl CL/PREN CH43 ... 127 H2
The Spur CSBY/BLUN L23 ..... 82 F2
Spymers Cft FMBY L37 ....... 47 J7
Square House La CHTN/BK PR9 ... 23 K6
The Square NSTN CH64 ....... 152 D4
Squares La BRSC L40 ........ 52 A2
The Square NSTN CH64 ...... 152 D4
Squires Cl WDN WA8 ......... 16 C3
Squires Cl RNFD/HAY WA11 .... 90 D7
Squire St EHL/KEN L7 ........ 113 J4
Squirrel Gn FMBY L37 ....... 46 E8
Stable Cl GR/UP/WCH CH49 ... 125 L1
The Stackfield WKBY CH48 .... 125 G2
Stadium Cl PS/BROM CH62 ... 144 B4
Stadium Wy WGNW/BIL/O WN5 ... 68 A4
Stafford Cl HUY L36 ......... 116 C1
Stafford Moreton Wy
 MGHL L31 ............ 72 E4
 MGHL L31 ............ 72 F4
Stafford Rd ECCL WA10 ...... 8 A9
 STHP PR8 ............ 35 J4
 WARRS WA4 ............ 137 L3
Stafford St SKEL WN8 ....... 64 F4
 VAUX/LVPD L3 ........... 13 K5
 WGNE/HIN WN2 ........... 69 L8
Stainburn Av NG/CROX L11 .... 98 B2
Stainburn Cl WGNNW/ST WN6 ... 54 F7
Stainer Cl DV/KA/FCH L14 ... 99 H8
Staines Cl WARRS WA4 ....... 138 A3
Stainmore Cl GOL/RIS/CU WA3 ... 107 K7
 RNFD/HAY WA11 ........... 89 K5
Stairgate WDN WA8 .......... 4 F4
Stairhaven Rd ALL/GAR L19 ... 130 D4
The Stakes MOR/LEA CH46 .... 110 A2
Stalbridge Av CALD/MH L18 ... 114 D8
Staley Av CSBY/BLUN L23 ..... 83 H2
Staley St BTL L20 ........... 83 L7
Stalisfield Av NG/CROX L11 ... 98 C3
Stalisfield Gv NG/CROX L11 ... 98 C3
Stalisfield Pl NG/CROX L11 ... 98 C3
Stalmine Rd WLT/FAZ L9 ..... 97 J1
Stamfordham Dr ALL/GAR L19 ... 130 F6
Stamfordham Gv ALL/GAR L19 ... 130 F6
Stamfordham Pl
 ALL/GAR L19 ............ 130 F6
Stamford Rd STHP PR8 ....... 35 J5
Stamford St EHL/KEN L7 ...... 113 L3
 EP CH65 ............ 156 C8
Stanbury Av BEB CH63 ....... 128 C7
Stancliffe Gv WGNE/HIN WN2 ... 57 L7
Standale Rd WAV L15 ........ 114 B5
Standard Pl RF/TRAN CH42 ... 128 B2
Standard Rd NG/CROX L11 ... 98 E1
Standen Cl ECCL WA10 ....... 8 D4
Stand Farm Rd
 WD/CROXPK L12 ........... 99 H2
Standhouse La ORM L39 ...... 62 D3
Standish Av WGNW/BIL/O WN5 ... 78 A3
Standish Dr RNFD/HAY WA11 ... 76 C6
Standishgate WGN WN1 ...... 4 F3
Standish St CHLY/EC PR7 .... 32 E6
 ECCL WA10 ............ 9 J3
 VAUX/LVPD L3 ........... 13 G5
Standish Wood La
 WGNNW/ST WN6 ........... 56 A6
Stand Park Av NTHTN L30 .... 84 B3
Stand Park Cl NTHTN L30 .... 84 B3
Stand Park Rd CHLDW L16 ... 114 F7
Stand Pkwy NTHTN L30 ...... 84 A3
Standring Gdn ECCL WA10 ... 101 K5
Stanedge Gv WGNS/IIMK WN3 ... 79 K3
Stanfield Av EV L5 .......... 97 H8
Stanfield Dr BEB CH63 ...... 143 H2
Stanford Av WAL/NB CH45 .... 95 K6
Stanford Crs WLTN L25 ...... 131 M5
Stangate MGHL L31 ......... 72 D3
Stanhope Dr HUY L36 ....... 115 L2
 PS/BROM CH62 ........... 143 M4
Stanhope St ECCL WA10 ..... 8 F1
 LEIGH WN7 ............ 81 M7
 TOX L8 ............ 112 F7
Stanley Bank Rd
 RNFD/HAY WA11 ........... 90 C6
Stanley Cl ANF/KKDL L4 ..... 96 F6
 WAL/EG CH44 ........... 112 A3
 WDN WA8 ............ 134 E3

Stanley Ct BRSC L40 ........ 39 G8
 RF/TRAN CH42 ........... 128 B2
Stanley Crs PR/KW L34 ...... 100 E7
Stanley Dr LEIGH WN7 ....... 81 M5
Stanley Gdns WLT/FAZ ...... 84 B8
Stanley La PS/BROM CH62 .... 144 B8
 WGNE/HIN WN2 ........... 57 L6
Stanley Pk LITH L21 ......... 83 K4
Stanley Park Av North
 ANF/KKDL L4 ............ 97 K4
Stanley Park Av South
 ANF/KKDL L4 ............ 97 K5
Stanley Pl CHLY/EC PR7 ..... 32 E5
 WARRS WA4 ............ 138 B3
Stanley Rd BIRK CH41 ....... 111 H4
 BTL L20 ............ 7 G1
 CSBY/WL L22 ............ 83 G5
 EP CH65 ............ 156 D6
 FMBY L37 ............ 47 G7
 HOY CH47 ............ 108 C7
 HUY L36 ............ 116 A3
 LITH L21 ............ 83 K7
 MGHL L31 ............ 72 E7
 RF/TRAN CH42 ........... 128 C5
 SKEL WN8 ............ 66 C6
 WGNE/HIN WN2 ........... 57 L7
 WGNW/BIL/O WN5 ........... 80 C2
Stanley St ALL/GAR L19 ..... 145 L1
 CHTN/BK PR9 ............ 3 G3
 CLVP L2 ............ 12 F7
 CLVPS L1 ............ 12 F6
 EHL/KEN L7 ............ 114 A2
 NEWLW WA12 ............ 104 C2
 RUNC WA7 ............ 19 J2
 WAL/EG CH44 ........... 112 A3
 WARR WA1 ............ 16 A1
 WGNW/BIL/O WN5 ........... 68 B7
Stanley Wy SKEL WN8 ....... 65 G2
Stanlowe Vw ALL/GAR L19 ... 130 B7
Stanmoor Dr WGNE/HIN WN2 ... 57 L8
Stanmore Pk
 GR/UP/WCH CH49 ........... 125 K2
Stanmore Rd WAV L15 ....... 114 D7
Stannanought Rd SKEL WN8 ... 65 M2
Stanner Cl WARRW/BUR WA5 ... 120 F3
Stanney Cl PS/BROM CH62 ... 155 G2
Stanney La EP CH65 ......... 155 H3
 EP CH65 ............ 20 D9
Stanney Mill La CHNE CH2 ... 164 B4
Stanney Mill Rd EP CH65 .... 164 B3
Stanney Woods Av EP CH65 ... 155 H2
Stannyfield Cl CSBY/BLUN L23 ... 71 K7
Stanny Field Dr CSBY/BLUN L23 ... 71 K7
Stansfield Av MGHL L31 ..... 73 H4
 WARR WA1 ............ 122 B7
Stanstead Av
 WARRW/BUR WA5 ........... 136 B2
Stanstead Rd WGNE/HIN WN2 ... 69 H3
Stansted Rd CHLY/EC PR7 .... 32 C6
Stanton Av LITH L21 ........ 83 J4
Stanton Cl NTHTN L30 ...... 71 M8
 RNFD/HAY WA11 ........... 90 E7
 WGNS/IIMK WN3 ........... 79 K2
Stanton Crs KKBY L32 ....... 85 L3
Stanton Ct NSTN CH64 ...... 153 H5
Stanton Rd BEB CH63 ....... 143 G2
 CALD/MH L18 ............ 114 D8
 WARRS WA4 ............ 138 F2
Stanwood Cl ECCL WA10 ..... 101 H2
Stanwood Gdns RAIN/WH L35 ... 118 D3
Stapehill Cl CLB/OSW/ST L13 ... 114 D3
Stapeley Gdns HLWD L26 .... 132 C7
Stapehill Rd DV/KA/FCH L14 ... 114 F3
Staplands Rd DV/KA/FCH L14 ... 114 F3
Stapleford Rd WLTN L25 ..... 115 L7
Staplehurst Cl
 WD/CROXPK L12 ........... 99 G2
 WGNE/HIN WN2 ........... 81 L3
Stapleton Av
 GR/UP/WCH CH49 ........... 125 M1
 RAIN/WH L35 ............ 117 L1
 SPK/HALE L24 ............ 146 F2
 WARRN/WOL WA2 ........... 121 M5
Stapleton Cl RAIN/WH L35 ... 101 L8
 WLTN L25 ............ 115 K6
Stapleton Rd FMBY L37 ..... 58 F5
 RAIN/WH L35 ............ 101 K8
Stapleton St WGNE/HIN WN2 ... 80 A2
Stapley Rd RUNC WA7 ....... 18 E5
Starbeck Dr GTS/LS CH66 .... 155 K7
Starkey Gv WARRS WA4 ...... 138 B1
Star La LYMM WA13 ......... 139 L1
Starling Cl RUNC WA7 ....... 150 F6
Starling Gv WD/CROXPK L12 ... 99 H4
Star St TOX L8 ............ 132 D1
Startham Av WGNW/BIL/O WN5 ... 89 M2
Starworth Dr PS/BROM CH62 ... 128 E6
Statham Av LYMM WA13 ..... 139 L2
 WARRN/WOL WA2 ........... 121 L3
Statham Cl LYMM WA13 ..... 139 M2
Statham La LYMM WA13 ..... 123 K8
Statham Rd CL/PREN CH43 ... 110 E5
 SKEL WN8 ............ 64 F2
Station Ap BRSC L40 ........ 39 G8
 HOY CH47 ............ 109 G5
 MOR/LEA CH46 ........... 110 A3
 ORM L39 ............ 51 H8
Station Br FROD/HEL WA6 .... 166 D7
 GTS/LS CH66 ............ 155 L6
 WGNE/HIN WN2 ........... 80 F4
 WGNW/BIL/O WN5 ........... 66 F4
Station Cl NSTN CH64 ....... 153 H6
Station Gn GTS/LS CH66 ..... 155 L7
Station Ms AIMK WN4 ....... 90 F2
Station Rd AIMK WN4 ....... 90 E2
 BEB CH63 ............ 127 J8
 BIRK CH41 ............ 111 H4
 BRSC L40 ............ 39 M1
 CHLY/EC PR7 ............ 43 H1
 CHLY/EC PR7 ............ 44 B7
 CHNE CH2 ............ 158 C8
 CHTN/BK PR9 ............ 23 H8
 EP CH65 ............ 20 D3
 GTS/LS CH66 ............ 155 L7
 HES CH60 ............ 141 H7
 HOY CH47 ............ 108 D7
 HUY L36 ............ 115 L3

 LEY/BBR PR5 ............ 29 K2
 MGHL L31 ............ 61 J7
 MGHL L31 ............ 73 G5
 MGHL L31 ............ 85 G8
 NSTN CH64 ............ 152 E5
 NSTN CH64 ............ 153 G6
 ORM L39 ............ 49 H7
 ORM L39 ............ 51 H7
 PEN/TH CH61 ............ 127 G8
 PR/KW L34 ............ 100 F7
 RAIN/WH L35 ............ 117 L2
 RNFD/HAY WA11 ........... 90 E7
 RUNC WA7 ............ 18 F3
 SKEL WN8 ............ 53 L3
 STHEL WA9 ............ 103 G6
 STHP PR8 ............ 34 E8
 WAL/EG CH44 ........... 111 J1
 WARRS WA4 ............ 138 A3
 WARRW/BUR WA5 ........... 120 B8
 WARRW/BUR WA5 ........... 135 M2
 WLTN L25 ............ 115 K8
Station Rd North
 WARRN/WOL WA2 ........... 122 C3
Station Rd South
 WARRN/WOL WA2 ........... 122 C4
Station St RAIN/WH L35 ..... 117 L2
Statton Rd CLB/OSW/ST L13 ... 114 D4
Staveley Av BRSC L40 ....... 52 A1
Staveley Rd ALL/GAR L19 .... 130 D5
 SKEL WN8 ............ 65 G2
 STHP PR8 ............ 47 M1
Stavert Cl NG/CROX L11 ..... 98 D2
Staverton Rd KKBY L32 ..... 85 L4
Stavordale Rd MOR/LEA CH46 ... 110 C5
Steble St TOX L8 ........... 113 H8
Steel Av WAL/NB CH45 ....... 95 L7
Steel Ct EV L5 ............ 96 E8
Steeley La CHLYE PR6 ....... 32 F6
Steel St WARR WA1 ......... 15 K1
Steeplechase Cl WLT/FAZ L9 ... 84 E5
Steeple Cl NSTN CH64 ...... 153 G6
The Steeple WKBY CH48 ..... 124 F7
Steeple Vw NWD/KWIPK L33 ... 74 B8
Steers Cft STBRV L28 ....... 99 H5
Stein Av GOL/RIS/CU WA3 .... 93 G5
Steinberg Ct VAUX/LVPD L3 ... 12 E1
Stenhills Crs RUNC WA7 ..... 19 K4
Stephens La CLVP L2 ........ 12 F6
Stephenson Rd
 CLB/OSW/ST L13 ........... 114 C3
 NEWLW WA12 ............ 104 E3
Stephenson St CHLYE PR6 .... 33 G6
 WGNE/HIN WN2 ........... 80 D5
Stephenson Wy FMBY L37 .... 59 L2
 WAV L15 ............ 114 A4
Stephens Ter GTS/LS CH66 .... 155 K7
Stephen St WARR WA1 ...... 15 K3
 WGNE/HIN WN2 ........... 80 D7
Stephen Wy RAIN/WH L35 .... 101 K8
Stepney Gv ANF/KKDL L4 .... 97 J4
Sterling Wy EV L5 .......... 96 F7
Sterndale Av WGNNW/ST WN6 ... 56 A3
Sterrix Av LITH L21 ........ 83 L3
Sterrix Gn LITH L21 ........ 83 L3
Sterrix La LITH L21 ........ 83 L3
Stetchworth Rd WARRS WA4 ... 137 K4
Stevenage Cl STHEL WA9 ..... 102 B6
Stevenson Cl WGNS/IIMK WN3 ... 68 C3
Stevenson Dr BEB CH63 ..... 143 H2
Stevenson St WAV L15 ...... 114 B5
Stevens Rd HES CH60 ....... 141 L6
Stevens St STHEL WA9 ...... 101 M5
Steventon RUNC WA7 ....... 151 G1
Steward Ct RAIN/WH L35 .... 101 H8
Steward's Av WDN WA8 ...... 16 A3
Stewart Av BTL L20 ......... 7 L3
Stewart Cl PEN/TH CH61 .... 141 H2
Stewart St WGNS/IIMK WN3 ... 79 J2
Stewerton Cl
 GOL/RIS/CU WA3 ........... 92 B3
Stile Hey CSBY/BLUN L23 .... 71 K8
Stiles Rd NWD/KWIPK L33 ... 74 B7
The Stiles ORM L39 ......... 51 G8
Stillington Rd TOX L8 ...... 132 D1
Stirling Av CSBY/BLUN L23 ... 83 G2
 WGNE/HIN WN2 ........... 69 J5
Stirling Cl CHLYE PR6 ...... 33 G6
 WARR WA1 ............ 123 G6
Stirling Crs STHEL WA9 ..... 102 D7
Stirling Dr AIMK WN4 ...... 90 F1
Stirling Rd SPK/HALE L24 ... 146 D2
 WGNE/HIN WN2 ........... 81 H1
Stirling St WAL/EG CH44 .... 111 K3
 WGN WN1 ............ 68 D3
Stirrup Cl WARRN/WOL WA2 ... 122 C2
Stockbridge La HUY L36 ..... 99 L7
Stockbridge Pl EV L5 ....... 97 J8
Stockbridge St EV L5 ....... 97 J8
Stockdale Cl VAUX/LVPD L3 ... 12 F4
Stockham Cl RUNC WA7 ..... 150 D5
Stockham La RUNC WA7 ..... 150 E8
Stockley Crs ORM L39 ...... 64 A7
Stockmoor Rd NG/CROX L11 ... 98 B2
Stockpit Rd NWD/KWIPK L33 ... 86 F3
Stockport Rd WARRS WA4 ... 138 F2
Stocks Av STHEL WA9 ....... 103 G2
Stocks La CHLY/EC PR7 ..... 42 A2
 WARRW/BUR WA5 ........... 119 M8
Stockswell Rd RAIN/WH L35 ... 133 H1
Stockton Gv RAIN/WH L35 ... 101 M7
Stockton La WARRS WA4 .... 138 A4
Stockton Wood Rd
 SPK/HALE L24 ............ 146 E2
Stockville Rd CALD/MH L18 ... 131 G1
Stockwell St WGNS/IIMK WN3 ... 78 E7
Stoddart Rd ANF/KKDL L4 ... 97 J3
Stoke Cl PS/BROM CH62 ..... 155 G2
Stoke Gdns EP CH65 ........ 20 D7
Stokesay CL/PREN CH43 ..... 110 F7
Stokesley Av KKBY L32 ..... 85 L3
Stokes St GOL/RIS/CU WA3 ... 107 K3
Stoke St BIRK CH41 ........ 10 E2
Stonebank Dr NSTN CH64 ... 153 J7
Stonebarn Dr MGHL L31 .... 72 E2
Stone Barn La RUNC WA7 .... 150 B7
Stonebridge La AIN/FAZ L10 ... 85 J7
 NG/CROX L11 ............ 85 K8

Stoneby Dr WAL/NB CH45 .... 95 J6
Stonechat Cl
 GOL/RIS/CU WA3 ........... 93 G5
 NTHLY L27 ............ 132 L1
 RUNC WA7 ............ 150 A8
Stonecroop CALD/MH L18 .... 115 G8
Stonecrop GOL/RIS/CU WA3 ... 122 E1
 RUNC WA7 ............ 161 H1
Stonecross Dr RAIN/WH L35 ... 117 M4
Stone Cross La North
 GOL/RIS/CU WA3 ........... 92 E6
Stone Cross La South
 GOL/RIS/CU WA3 ........... 92 E7
Stonedale Crs NG/CROX L11 ... 98 D1
Stonefield Rd DV/KA/FCH L14 ... 115 H1
Stonegate Dr TOX L8 ........ 129 H1
Stonegate Fold CHLYE PR6 ... 44 D4
Stone Hall La SKEL WN8 ..... 66 B1
Stone Hvn WGNS/IIMK WN3 ... 78 F3
Stonehaven Cl CHLDW L16 ... 115 H5
Stonehaven Dr
 WARRN/WOL WA2 ........... 122 C2
Stone Hay RAIN/WH L35 .... 116 F4
Stonehey Dr WKBY CH48 .... 124 E4
Stonehey Rd KKBY L32 ...... 86 A5
Stonehill Av ANF/KKDL L4 ... 97 K7
 BEB CH63 ............ 128 C7
Stonehills La RUNC WA7 .... 19 M4
Stonehill St ANF/KKDL L4 ... 97 K7
Stonehouse Ms CALD/MH L18 ... 130 F2
Stonehouse Rd WAL/EG CH44 ... 95 G8
Stonelea RUNC WA7 ........ 150 D3
Stoneleigh Cl STHP PR8 .... 47 L1
Stoneleigh Gdns WARRS WA4 ... 138 F4
Stoneleigh Gv
 RF/TRAN CH42 ........... 128 B5
Stone Pit Cl GOL/RIS/CU WA3 ... 93 G4
Stone Pit La GOL/RIS/CU WA3 ... 106 B3
Stoneridge Ct CL/PREN CH43 ... 110 E5
Stone Sq BTL L20 .......... 84 A8
Stone St VAUX/LVPD L3 ..... 12 D1
Stoneville Rd CLB/OSW/ST L13 ... 114 C1
Stoney Brow SKEL WN8 ..... 66 D3
Stoneycroft WD/CROXPK L12 ... 114 D1
Stoneycroft Cl CLB/OSW/ST L13 ... 98 B8
 HOR/BR BL6 ............ 45 M8
Stoneycroft Crs
 CLB/OSW/ST L13 ........... 98 C8
Stoneygate La WGNNW/ST WN6 ... 54 D3
Stoney Hey Rd WAL/NB CH45 ... 95 J6
Stoney Holt RUNC WA7 ..... 150 E5
Stoneyhurst Av AIN/FAZ L10 ... 84 E2
Stoney La CHLY/EC PR7 ..... 57 G1
 RAIN/WH L35 ............ 117 H1
Stonham Cl
 GR/UP/WCH CH49 ........... 110 A8
Stonor Rd CHLY/EC PR7 ..... 44 B6
Stonyfield NTHTN L30 ...... 72 A8
Stonyhurst CHLY/EC PR7 .... 43 L1
Stonyhurst Av WGNS/IIMK WN3 ... 5 H8
Stonyhurst Cl
 RNFD/HAY WA11 ........... 89 K6
Stony La BIRK CH41 ........ 54 A1
Stopford St TOX L8 ........ 129 H1
 WGNE/HIN WN2 ........... 5 M5
Stopgate La NWD/KWIPK L33 ... 74 C7
 WLT/FAZ L9 ............ 97 M1
Store St BTL L20 .......... 7 K8
Storeton Cl CL/PREN CH43 ... 127 J2
Storeton La PEN/TH CH61 ... 141 L1
Storeton Rd RF/TRAN CH42 ... 127 L4
Stormont Rd ALL/GAR L19 ... 130 D6
Storrington Av NG/CROX L11 ... 98 D2
Storrington Heys NG/CROX L11 ... 98 D2
Storrsdale Rd CALD/MH L18 ... 130 D3
Stour Av RAIN/WH L35 ..... 117 L2
Stourcliffe Rd WAL/EG CH44 ... 111 J2
Stour Ct EP CH65 .......... 20 B1
Stourport Cl
 GR/UP/WCH CH49 ........... 125 L1
Stourton Rd KKBY L32 ...... 86 A5
 STHP PR8 ............ 47 L1
Stourton St WAL/EG CH44 ... 111 K3
Stourvale Rd HLWD L26 ..... 132 B6
Stout St LEIGH WN7 ........ 81 L8
Stowe Av AIN/FAZ L10 ...... 85 G3
Stowe Cl WLTN L25 ......... 131 K6
Stowell St EHL/KEN L7 ...... 13 L9
Stowford Cl NG/CROX L11 ... 98 E3
Strada Wy VAUX/LVPD L3 ... 13 L4
Stradbroke Rd GOL/RIS/CU WA3 ... 93 J6
Strafford Dr BTL L20 ...... 7 L3
Straight Length
 FROD/HEL WA6 ........... 160 A6
Straight Up La CHTN/BK PR9 ... 25 L5
Straker Av EP CH65 ........ 156 B7
Strand Av AIMK WN4 ....... 91 K1
Strand Rd BTL L20 ......... 7 H3
 HOY CH47 ............ 108 D6
Strand St CLVPS L1 ........ 12 E8
The Strand AIMK WN4 ...... 91 K1
 VAUX/LVPD L3 ........... 12 D7
Strange Rd AIMK WN4 ...... 90 F2
Strange St LEIGH WN7 ...... 93 K1
Stranraer Rd WGNW/BIL/O WN5 ... 67 L4
Stratford Cl STHP PR8 ..... 34 C7
Stratford Rd ALL/GAR L19 ... 130 B5
 CHLYE PR6 ............ 32 F5
 NSTN CH64 ............ 152 F7
Stratford St WGNNW/ST WN6 ... 4 A1
Strathallan Cl HES CH60 ... 141 G3
Strathcona Rd WAL/NB CH45 ... 95 K7
 WAV L15 ............ 114 A6
Strathearn Rd HES CH60 ... 141 H7
Strathlorne Cl
 RF/TRAN CH42 ........... 128 B2
Strathmore Av AIMK WN4 ... 79 J8
Strathmore Dr CSBY/BLUN L23 ... 83 G2
Strathmore Gv CHLY/EC PR7 ... 32 D6
 STHEL WA9 ............ 102 F2
Strathmore Rd NPK/KEN L6 ... 113 L1
Stratton Cl RUNC WA7 ..... 150 D7
 WLTN L25 ............ 131 G3
Stratton Dr WGNE/HIN WN2 ... 80 B4
Stratton Pk WDN WA8 ...... 118 B8
Stratton Rd KKBY L32 ...... 85 L4

WARRW/BUR WA5 ..... 120 D8
Strauss Cl *TOX* L8 ..... 113 K7
Strawberry Cl *GOL/RIS/CU* WA3.. 122 E1
Strawberry Dr *EP* CH65 ..... 163 J5
Strawberry La *CH/BCN* CH1 ..... 162 E8
Strawberry Rd *NG/CROX* L11 ..... 98 A3
Streatham Av *CALD/MH* L18 ..... 114 B8
Street Hey La *NSTN* CH64 ..... 154 D3
Stretford Cl *NWD/KWIPK* L33 ..... 74 A8
Stretton Av *GOL/RIS/CU* WA3 ..... 93 G6
  *STHEL* WA9 ..... 103 H2
  *WAL/EG* CH44 ..... 111 J1
  *WGNW/BIL/O* WN5 ..... 78 A8
Stretton Cl *CL/PREN* CH43 ..... 127 G2
  *PS/BROM* CH62 ..... 155 G2
  *WD/CROXPK* L12 ..... 99 J2
  *WGNNW/ST* WN6 ..... 56 A5
Stretton Dr *CHTN/BK* PR9 ..... 25 H5
Stretton Wy *WGNE/HIN* WN2 ..... 116 D5
Strickland St *ECCL* WA10 ..... 9 J2
Strines Cl *WGNE/HIN* WN2 ..... 69 M7
The Strine *BRSC* L40 ..... 28 C4
Stringer Crs *WARRS* WA4 ..... 15 M7
Stringhey Rd *WAL/EG* CH44 ..... 95 L8
Stroma Rd *CALD/MH* L18 ..... 130 D4
Stromness Cl
  *WARRN/WOL* WA2 ..... 122 D2
Stroud Cl *GR/UP/WCH* CH49 ..... 125 L2
  *WGNE/HIN* WN2 ..... 69 H3
Stuart Av *MOR/LEA* CH46 ..... 110 B4
  *WGNE/HIN* WN2 ..... 81 K2
  *WLTN* L25 ..... 131 L6
Stuart Cl *MOR/LEA* CH46 ..... 110 C5
Stuart Crs *WGNW/BIL/O* WN5 ..... 77 M8
  *WARRS* WA4 ..... 138 B3
Stuart Dr *DV/KA/FCH* L14 ..... 115 G2
Stuart Gv *BTL* L20 ..... 7 K8
Stuart Rd *ANF/KKDL* L4 ..... 7 M6
  *BTL* L20 ..... 7 M5
  *CSBY/WL* L22 ..... 83 C3
  *ECCL* WA10 ..... 88 E7
  *MGHL* L31 ..... 85 K2
  *RF/TRAN* CH42 ..... 127 M2
  *RUNC* WA7 ..... 150 D1
Stuart Rd North *BTL* L20 ..... 7 M4
Stub La *BRSC* L40 ..... 51 J3
Studfold *CHLY/EC* PR7 ..... 32 D3
Studholme St *BTL* L20 ..... 96 E6
Studland St *WAL/NB* CH45 ..... 98 A1
Studley Rd *WAL/NB* CH45 ..... 95 G7
Stump La *CHLYE* PR6 ..... 32 F5
Sturdee Rd *CLB/OSW/ST* L13 ..... 114 D4
Sturgess Cl *ORM* L39 ..... 51 H6
Sturgess St *NEWLW* WA12 ..... 104 B2
Sturton Av *WGNS/IIMK* WN3 ..... 79 G2
Suburban Rd *NPK/KEN* L6 ..... 97 L7
Sudbrook Cl
  *GOL/RIS/CU* WA3 ..... 93 G5
Sudbury Cl *WGNS/IIMK* WN3 ..... 79 K3
  *WLTN* L25 ..... 131 M3
Sudbury Rd *CSBY/WL* L22 ..... 82 D3
Sudbury Wy *SPK/HALE* L24 ..... 146 D1
Sudell Av *MGHL* L31 ..... 73 H3
Sudell La *MGHL* L31 ..... 61 M7
Sudley Gra *AIG/SPK* L17 ..... 130 A4
Sudworth Rd *WAL/NB* CH45 ..... 95 J6
Suez St *NEWLW* WA12 ..... 104 C2
  *WARR* WA1 ..... 14 D6
Suffield Rd *ANF/KKDL* L4 ..... 96 F5
Suffolk Av *EP* CH65 ..... 156 B8
Suffolk Cl *WARR* WA1 ..... 122 F7
  *WGN* WN1 ..... 56 D5
Suffolk Gv *LEIGH* WN7 ..... 81 L8
Suffolk Pl *WDN* WA8 ..... 133 L6
Suffolk Rd *STHP* PR8 ..... 35 J5
Suffolk St *BTL* L20 ..... 7 J2
  *CLVPS* L1 ..... 13 H9
  *CLVPS* L1 ..... 112 F5
  *RUNC* WA7 ..... 18 E2
Suffton Pk *KKBY* L32 ..... 85 L4
Sugar La *CHTN/BK* PR9 ..... 26 E1
  *PR/KW* L34 ..... 99 M2
Sugar Stubbs La *CHTN/BK* PR9 ..... 26 E1
Sugnall St *EHL/KEN* L7 ..... 13 L9
Sulby Av *CLB/OSW/ST* L13 ..... 98 A8
  *WARRS* WA4 ..... 137 K2
Sulby Cl *STHP* PR8 ..... 35 H2
Sulgrave Cl *CHLDW* L16 ..... 114 E4
Sullington Dr *NTHLY* L27 ..... 116 A7
Sullivan Av *GR/UP/WCH* CH49 ..... 126 B1
Sullivan Wy *WGN* WN1 ..... 5 H2
Sumley Cl *RNFD/HAY* WA11 ..... 9 M1
  *RNFD/HAY* WA11 ..... 89 M8
Summerfield
  *PS/BROM* CH62 ..... 143 M3
  *WARRW/BUR* WA5 ..... 121 H3
Summerfield Av *ECCL* WA10 ..... 101 H2
  *WARRW/BUR* WA5 ..... 121 H3
Summerfields *CHLY/EC* PR7 ..... 43 H6
Summerhill Dr *MGHL* L31 ..... 73 H6
Summer La *RUNC* WA7 ..... 150 B4
  *WARRS* WA4 ..... 151 K7
Summers Av *BTL* L20 ..... 7 L2
  *VAUX/LVPD* L3 ..... 12 F2
Summer Seat *BTL* L20 ..... 6 D5
  *VAUX/LVPD* L3 ..... 12 F2
Summers Rd *VAUX/LVPD* L3 ..... 112 F8
Summer St *SKEL* WN8 ..... 65 H1
Summertrees Av
  *GR/UP/WCH* CH49 ..... 125 M1
Summertrees Cl
  *GR/UP/WCH* CH49 ..... 125 M1
Summerville Gdns *WARRS* WA4 ..... 138 B4
Summerwood *PEN/TH* CH61 ..... 125 M6
Summerwood La *ORM* L39 ..... 49 L4
The Summit *WAL/EG* CH44 ..... 95 L8
Summit Wy *WLTN* L25 ..... 131 H2
Sumner Av *ORM* L39 ..... 61 H1
Sumner Cl *EV* L5 ..... 96 E8
  *RAIN/WH* L35 ..... 117 M4
Sumner Gv *NWD/KWIPK* L33 ..... 74 B8
Sumner Rd *CL/PREN* CH43 ..... 111 H5
  *FMBY* L37 ..... 59 H2
Sumner's La *BRSC* L40 ..... 29 J6
Sumner Rd *RNFD/HAY* WA11 ..... 90 C7
  *WGNE/HIN* WN2 ..... 57 M8
Sunbeam Cl *CLB/OSW/ST* L13 ..... 114 C2
Sunbeam St *NEWLW* WA12 ..... 104 E2
Sunbourne Rd *AIG/SPK* L17 ..... 129 K3

Sunbury Dr *STHP* PR8 ..... 47 K1
Sunbury Gdns *WARRS* WA4 ..... 138 A6
Sunbury Rd *ANF/KKDL* L4 ..... 97 K6
  *WAL/EG* CH44 ..... 111 L2
Sunbury St *ECCL* WA10 ..... 101 L5
Suncroft Cl *WARR* WA1 ..... 123 G6
Suncroft Rd *HES* CH60 ..... 141 M6
Sundale Av *RAIN/WH* L35 ..... 101 H8
Sunderland Pl
  *WGNW/BIL/O* WN5 ..... 67 M4
Sundew Cl *BTL* L20 ..... 84 B6
Sundridge St *TOX* L8 ..... 129 J1
Sunfield Cl *GTS/LS* CH66 ..... 162 F2
Sunfield Rd *MOR/LEA* CH46 ..... 110 B3
Sunlight St *NPK/KEN* L6 ..... 97 L8
Sunloch Cl *WLT/FAZ* L9 ..... 84 F5
Sunningdale Av *WDN* WA8 ..... 133 K4
  *WARRW/BUR* WA5 ..... 104 B7
Sunningdale Cl *HUY* L36 ..... 115 L4
  *WARRW/BUR* WA5 ..... 104 B7
Sunningdale Dr *BEB* CH63 ..... 143 K7
  *CSBY/BLUN* L23 ..... 70 E7
  *PEN/TH* CH61 ..... 126 C8
Sunningdale Gdns *FMBY* L37 ..... 59 G2
Sunningdale Rd *WAL/NB* CH45 ..... 95 H5
  *WAV* L15 ..... 114 B5
Sunny Bank *BEB* CH63 ..... 127 M7
  *GR/UP/WCH* CH49 ..... 110 B7
Sunnybank Av
  *CL/PREN* CH43 ..... 126 F1
Sunnybank Cl *NEWLW* WA12 ..... 104 E1
Sunny Bank Rd *CHLDW* L16 ..... 114 F6
Sunny Brow *CHLY/EC* PR7 ..... 43 J3
Sunnydale *RAIN/WH* L35 ..... 117 M2
Sunnyfields *ORM* L39 ..... 51 J8
  *WGNS/IIMK* WN3 ..... 78 E3
Sunnygate Rd *ALL/GAR* L19 ..... 130 D5
Sunnymede Dr *MGHL* L31 ..... 72 F2
Sunny Rd *CHTN/BK* PR9 ..... 25 J3
Sunnyside *ORM* L39 ..... 62 E6
  *GR/UP/WCH* CH49 ..... 110 B7
Sunnyside La *RUNC* WA7 ..... 151 G1
Sunnyside Rd *AIMK* WN4 ..... 79 H7
  *CSBY/WL* L22 ..... 82 E2
Sunsdale Rd *CALD/MH* L18 ..... 114 C8
Surby Cl *CHLDW* L16 ..... 115 G5
Surrey Av *GR/UP/WCH* CH49 ..... 110 A8
Surrey Dr *WKBY* CH48 ..... 124 E5
Surrey St *BTL* L20 ..... 7 J3
  *CLVPS* L1 ..... 112 F5
  *RUNC* WA7 ..... 19 G4
  *WAL/EG* CH44 ..... 111 J2
  *WARRS* WA4 ..... 138 B3
Susan Dr *WARRW/BUR* WA5 ..... 119 M8
Susan Gv *MOR/LEA* CH46 ..... 109 M5
Susan St *WDN* WA8 ..... 134 E3
Sussex Cl *BTL* L20 ..... 7 J2
  *PEN/TH* CH61 ..... 141 G1
  *WGN* WN1 ..... 56 D4
Sussex Gv *STHEL* WA9 ..... 9 M7
Sussex Rd *CHTN/BK* PR9 ..... 3 K4
  *MGHL* L31 ..... 72 F6
  *STHP* PR8 ..... 25 G7
  *WKBY* CH48 ..... 124 E2
Sussex St *BTL* L20 ..... 7 K3
  *CSBY/WL* L22 ..... 82 E3
  *WDN* WA8 ..... 17 J1
Sutch La *BRSC* L40 ..... 52 D1
Sutcliffe St *CHLY/EC* PR7 ..... 32 F6
  *NPK/KEN* L6 ..... 113 K2
Sutherland Dr *PS/BROM* CH62 ..... 154 F1
Sutherland Rd *PR/KW* L34 ..... 101 G7
  *WGNS/IIMK* WN3 ..... 79 J2
Sutherland St *WGNE/HIN* WN2 ..... 69 L8
  *WGNW/BIL/O* WN5 ..... 68 B7
Sutton Av *GOL/RIS/CU* WA3 ..... 107 G1
  *NSTN* CH64 ..... 153 G7
Sutton Cswy *FROD/HEL* WA6 ..... 161 G3
Sutton Cl *PS/BROM* CH62 ..... 155 G2
Sutton Gv *CHLYE* PR6 ..... 33 H1
Sutton Hall Dr *GTS/LS* CH66 ..... 155 J7
Sutton Hall Gdns *GTS/LS* CH66 ..... 155 J7
Sutton Heath Rd *STHEL* WA9 ..... 102 F2
Sutton La *CHLYE* PR6 ..... 44 D5
Sutton Moss Rd *STHEL* WA9 ..... 103 H5
Sutton Oak Dr *STHEL* WA9 ..... 102 F3
Sutton Park Dr *STHEL* WA9 ..... 102 E6
Sutton Rd *FMBY* L37 ..... 59 G4
  *STHEL* WA9 ..... 9 L3
  *WAL/NB* CH45 ..... 95 K6
Sutton's La *FMBY* L37 ..... 60 A2
  *WDN* WA8 ..... 16 E6
Sutton St *CLB/OSW/ST* L13 ..... 98 A8
  *RUNC* WA7 ..... 19 K4
  *WARR* WA1 ..... 15 G7
Sutton Wy *EP* CH65 ..... 156 C8
  *GTS/LS* CH66 ..... 163 G1
Sutton Wood Rd *SPK/HALE* L24 ..... 146 E2
Swainson Rd *AIN/FAZ* L10 ..... 85 G6
Swale Av *RAIN/WH* L35 ..... 117 L2
Swaledale Av *RAIN/WH* L35 ..... 117 M2
Swaledale Cl *PS/BROM* CH62 ..... 144 A8
  *WARRW/BUR* WA5 ..... 120 B6
Swalegate *MGHL* L31 ..... 72 E3
Swale Rd *EP* CH65 ..... 156 C6
Swallow Cl *GOL/RIS/CU* WA3 ..... 123 H1
  *NTHLY* L27 ..... 116 B8
  *NWD/KWIPK* L33 ..... 74 A6
  *WD/CROXPK* L12 ..... 99 H2
Swallow Flds *WLT/FAZ* L9 ..... 98 B1
Swallowhurst Crs *NG/CROX* L11 ..... 98 C3
Swanage Ct *WARRS* WA4 ..... 138 A3
Swan Av *STHEL* WA9 ..... 103 J3
Swan Cl *GTS/LS* CH66 ..... 162 E5
Swan Crs *WAV* L15 ..... 114 D5
Swan Delph *ORM* L39 ..... 62 E3
Swan Gdns *STHEL* WA9 ..... 102 A7
Swan Hey *MGHL* L31 ..... 73 G6
Swan La *ORM* L39 ..... 62 A7
  *WGNE/HIN* WN2 ..... 81 K1
Swan Meadow Rd
  *WGNS/IIMK* WN3 ..... 4 C6
Swann St *WGNS/IIMK* WN3 ..... 4 C5
Swanpool La *ORM* L39 ..... 62 B3
Swan Rd *NEWLW* WA12 ..... 104 A1
Swanside Av *DV/KA/FCH* L14 ..... 115 G2

Swanside Rd *DV/KA/FCH* L14 ..... 115 G2
Swanston Av *ANF/KKDL* L4 ..... 97 J4
Swan St *CLB/OSW/ST* L13 ..... 114 B2
Swan Wk *MGHL* L31 ..... 73 G6
Sweden Gv *CSBY/WL* L22 ..... 82 F4
Sweetfield Gdns *GTS/LS* CH66 ..... 155 M6
Sweetfield Rd *GTS/LS* CH66 ..... 155 M6
Sweeting St *CLVP* L2 ..... 12 F7
Swift Cl *WARRN/WOL* WA2 ..... 122 A2
Swift Gv *WD/CROXPK* L12 ..... 99 H1
Swift's Cl *NTHTN* L30 ..... 83 M1
Swift's La *NTHTN* L30 ..... 83 M1
  *NTHTN* L30 ..... 84 A2
Swift St *ECCL* WA10 ..... 9 H2
  *TOX* L8 ..... 113 G8
Swinbrook Gn *NG/CROX* L11 ..... 98 B3
Swinburne Cl *CHLDW* L16 ..... 115 H5
Swinburne Rd *ECCL* WA10 ..... 101 L1
Swinburn Gv
  *WGNW/BIL/O* WN5 ..... 77 M4
Swindale Av
  *WARRN/WOL* WA2 ..... 121 K2
Swindale Cl *TOX* L8 ..... 113 K6
Swinden Cl *RUNC* WA7 ..... 150 F3
Swinderby Dr *KKBY* L32 ..... 85 K2
Swindon Cl *EV* L5 ..... 96 F6
  *GR/UP/WCH* CH49 ..... 125 L1
Swindon St *EV* L5 ..... 96 F6
Swinford Av *WDN* WA8 ..... 135 G3
Swinley La *WGN* WN1 ..... 68 E3
Swinley St *WGN* WN1 ..... 68 E3
Swinside *WGN* WN1 ..... 5 M2
Swireford Rd *FROD/HEL* WA6 ..... 166 D3
Swisspine Gdns *RAIN/WH* L35 ..... 101 L6
Swiss Rd *NPK/KEN* L6 ..... 113 L2
Swords Cross Cl *CHLY/EC* PR7 ..... 32 C8
Sword Wk *NG/CROX* L11 ..... 98 E2
Swynnerton Wy *WDN* WA8 ..... 118 D3
Sybil Rd *ANF/KKDL* L4 ..... 97 J6
Sycamore Av *CHLY/EC* PR7 ..... 31 M2
  *CSBY/BLUN* L23 ..... 71 H7
  *GOL/RIS/CU* WA3 ..... 92 C4
  *GR/UP/WCH* CH49 ..... 109 M7
  *HLWD* L26 ..... 132 A7
  *NEWLW* WA12 ..... 104 E2
  *RNFD/HAY* WA11 ..... 90 C8
  *WDN* WA8 ..... 134 D3
  *WGNE/HIN* WN2 ..... 81 H2
  *WGNNW/ST* WN6 ..... 68 B1
Sycamore Cl *BRSC* L40 ..... 40 E3
  *ECCL* WA10 ..... 101 K1
  *GR/UP/WCH* CH49 ..... 109 M6
  *WLT/FAZ* L9 ..... 97 L2
Sycamore Ct *CHLY/EC* PR7 ..... 32 D8
Sycamore Dr *GTS/LS* CH66 ..... 163 H4
  *LYMM* WA13 ..... 139 M1
  *RUNC* WA7 ..... 161 J1
  *SKEL* WN8 ..... 65 G3
  *WGNS/IIMK* WN3 ..... 78 D3
Sycamore Gdns *ECCL* WA10 ..... 89 G7
Sycamore Gv *FMBY* L37 ..... 58 E4
Sycamore La
  *WARRW/BUR* WA5 ..... 120 D7
Sycamore Pk *CALD/MH* L18 ..... 130 F3
Sycamore Ri *GR/UP/WCH* CH49 ..... 125 L3
Sycamore Rd *CHLYE* PR6 ..... 32 F3
  *CSBY/WL* L22 ..... 83 G3
  *HUY* L36 ..... 116 A5
  *RF/TRAN* CH42 ..... 11 G9
  *RUNC* WA7 ..... 19 M7
Syd Brook La *BRSC* L40 ..... 30 A7
Sydenham Av *AIG/SPK* L17 ..... 113 L8
Syderstone Cl *WGNE/HIN* WN2 ..... 81 G1
Sydney Av *RUNC* WA7 ..... 148 F6
Sydney St *RUNC* WA7 ..... 148 F6
  *WGNE/HIN* WN2 ..... 80 C2
  *WLT/FAZ* L9 ..... 84 C7
Syers Ct *WARR* WA1 ..... 15 L1
Sykes Crs *WGNS/IIMK* WN3 ..... 78 E4
Sylvan Ct *WLTN* L25 ..... 131 J4
Sylvandale Gv
  *PS/BROM* CH62 ..... 143 M3
Sylvania Rd *ANF/KKDL* L4 ..... 97 J5
Sylvia Cl *NG/CROX* L11 ..... 98 C3
Sylvia Crs *WARRN/WOL* WA2 ..... 121 M4
Synge St *WARRN/WOL* WA2 ..... 15 G1
Syren St *BTL* L20 ..... 96 E5
Syresham St *WGNE/HIN* WN2 ..... 80 D3
Syston Av *RNFD/HAY* WA11 ..... 89 L7
Sytch Cft *NSTN* CH64 ..... 153 G5

## T

Tabby Nook *KIRK/FR/WA* PR4 ..... 27 H4
Tabby's Nook *SKEL* WN8 ..... 53 J4
Taberner St *WGNNW/ST* WN6 ..... 56 B4
Taberner St *WGNE/HIN* WN2 ..... 80 D3
Tabley Av *WDN* WA8 ..... 133 M9
Tabley Cl *CL/PREN* CH43 ..... 127 H2
Tabley Rd *WAV* L15 ..... 113 M6
Tadgers La *FROD/HEL* WA6 ..... 159 M4
Tadlow Cl *FMBY* L37 ..... 58 E4
Taggart Av *CHLDW* L16 ..... 114 F7
Tagus Cl *TOX* L8 ..... 113 K7
Tagus St *TOX* L8 ..... 113 K7
Tailor's La *MGHL* L31 ..... 73 G5
Talaton Cl *CHTN/BK* PR9 ..... 22 C8
Talbot Av *BEB* CH63 ..... 142 C4
  *NSTN* CH64 ..... 153 H7
Talbot Cl *ECCL* WA10 ..... 8 E4
  *GOL/RIS/CU* WA3 ..... 123 G2
  *NSTN* CH64 ..... 153 H7
Talbot Ct *HUY* L36 ..... 115 M4
Talbot Dr *CHLY/EC* PR7 ..... 31 M3
  *STHP* PR8 ..... 3 G5
Talbot Gdns *NSTN* CH64 ..... 153 H7
Talbot Rd *CL/PREN* CH43 ..... 127 J1
  *FROD/HEL* WA6 ..... 166 A6
  *GTS/LS* CH66 ..... 163 H7
Talbot St *AIMK* WN4 ..... 91 M1
  *CHLYE* PR6 ..... 33 G4
  *GOL/RIS/CU* WA3 ..... 92 C5
  *STHP* PR8 ..... 2 F6
Talbotville Rd *CLB/OSW/ST* L13 ..... 114 C4
Talgarth Wy *WLTN* L25 ..... 115 J6
Taliesin St *EV* L5 ..... 96 F3
Talisman Cl *RUNC* WA7 ..... 151 G6

Talisman Wy *BTL* L20 ..... 6 D2
Talland Cl *HLWD* L26 ..... 132 A4
Tallarn Rd *KKBY* L32 ..... 85 K3
Talman Gv *AIMK* WN4 ..... 91 M2
Talton Rd *WAV* L15 ..... 113 M6
Tamar Cl *NPK/KEN* L6 ..... 113 K2
Tamar Rd *RNFD/HAY* WA11 ..... 90 E7
Tamer Gv *LEIGH* WN7 ..... 81 L5
Tamerton Cl *WLTN* L25 ..... 131 G3
Tamneys The *SKEL* WN8 ..... 65 H4
Tamworth Dr *WGNE/HIN* WN2 ..... 69 H3
Tamworth St *ECCL* WA10 ..... 8 C4
  *TOX* L8 ..... 113 G8
Tanar Cl *PS/BROM* CH62 ..... 143 K2
Tanat Dr *CALD/MH* L18 ..... 130 D1
Tancred Rd *ANF/KKDL* L4 ..... 97 J6
  *WAL/NB* CH45 ..... 95 J8
Tanfield Nook *SKEL* WN8 ..... 53 L3
Tanfields *SKEL* WN8 ..... 65 H4
Tan House Cl *SKEL* WN8 ..... 53 L2
Tan House Dr *WGNS/IIMK* WN3 ..... 78 E4
Tan House La *SKEL* WN8 ..... 53 L3
  *WARRW/BUR* WA5 ..... 120 C1
  *WDN* WA8 ..... 17 H5
  *WGNS/IIMK* WN3 ..... 78 E3
Tanhouse Rd *CSBY/BLUN* L23 ..... 71 K8
  *SKEL* WN8 ..... 65 M4
Tankersley Gv
  *WARRW/BUR* WA5 ..... 120 C8
Tanner's La *GOL/RIS/CU* WA3 ..... 92 D5
  *WARRN/WOL* WA2 ..... 14 D4
Tannersmith La *CHLY/EC* PR7 ..... 30 B8
Tannery La *NSTN* CH64 ..... 153 G5
  *WARRW/BUR* WA5 ..... 135 L2
Tansley Av *CHLY/EC* PR7 ..... 42 F4
Tansley Cl *WKBY* CH48 ..... 125 G3
Tansley Sq *WGNW/BIL/O* WN5 ..... 67 M8
Tanworth Gv *HOY* CH47 ..... 109 K4
  *MOR/LEA* CH46 ..... 109 K5
Tanyard Cl *CHLY/EC* PR7 ..... 42 F4
Taplow Pl *CLB/OSW/ST* L13 ..... 114 B3
Taplow St *NPK/KEN* L6 ..... 97 M7
Tarbock Rd *HUY* L36 ..... 115 M4
  *SPK/HALE* L24 ..... 146 F1
Tarbot Hey *MOR/LEA* CH46 ..... 109 L5
Target Rd *HES* CH60 ..... 140 D5
Tariff St *EV* L5 ..... 96 F8
Tarleswood *SKEL* WN8 ..... 65 H4
Tarleton Cl *HLWD* L26 ..... 132 A5
Tarleton St *CLVPS* L1 ..... 13 G7
Tarleton Rd *CHTN/BK* PR9 ..... 25 J5
Tarlscough La *BRSC* L40 ..... 38 E4
Tarlton Cl *RAIN/WH* L35 ..... 101 J8
Tarnbeck Dr *BRSC* L40 ..... 40 E2
Tarn Brow *ORM* L39 ..... 62 E2
Tarn Cl *AIMK* WN4 ..... 79 K8
Tarn Ct *WARR* WA1 ..... 123 H6
Tarn Gv *RNFD/HAY* WA11 ..... 89 K5
Tarn Hows Cl *CHLY/EC* PR7 ..... 32 D8
Tarnrigg Cl *WGNS/IIMK* WN3 ..... 79 G2
Tarn Rd *FMBY* L37 ..... 58 F2
Tarnside Rd *WGNW/BIL/O* WN5 ..... 67 G7
Tarnway *WAL/NB* CH45 ..... 93 H6
Tarporley Cl *CL/PREN* CH43 ..... 127 H2
Tarporley Rd *GTS/LS* CH66 ..... 163 G1
Tarran Dr *MOR/LEA* CH46 ..... 109 M3
Tarran Rd *MOR/LEA* CH46 ..... 109 M3
Tarrant Cl *WGNS/IIMK* WN3 ..... 78 F3
Tarran Wy East
  *MOR/LEA* CH46 ..... 109 M3
Tarran Wy North
  *MOR/LEA* CH46 ..... 109 M3
Tarran Wy South
  *MOR/LEA* CH46 ..... 109 M3
Tarran Wy West
  *MOR/LEA* CH46 ..... 109 M3
Tarvin Cl *CHTN/BK* PR9 ..... 22 F8
  *EP* CH65 ..... 20 D7
  *GOL/RIS/CU* WA3 ..... 93 G6
  *RUNC* WA7 ..... 149 L7
  *STHEL* WA9 ..... 118 D1
Tarvin Rd *FROD/HEL* WA6 ..... 166 F3
  *PS/BROM* CH62 ..... 155 H1
Tasker Ter *RAIN/WH* L35 ..... 117 L1
Tasman Cl *WARRW/BUR* WA5 ..... 120 E5
Tasman Gv *STHEL* WA9 ..... 102 A6
Tate Cl *WDN* WA8 ..... 133 M3
Tate St *ANF/KKDL* L4 ..... 97 H5
Tatham Gv *WGNS/IIMK* WN3 ..... 78 F4
Tatlock Cl *WGNE/HIN* WN2 ..... 78 A8
Tatlock St *EV* L5 ..... 12 F1
Tattersall Rd *LITH* L21 ..... 83 J6
Tatton Dr *AIMK* WN4 ..... 91 H1
Tatton Rd *RF/TRAN* CH42 ..... 11 G8
  *WLT/FAZ* L9 ..... 84 C7
Taunton Av *LEIGH* WN7 ..... 81 M3
  *STHEL* WA9 ..... 102 F8
Taunton Dr *AIN/FAZ* L10 ..... 85 G3
Taunton Rd *HUY* L36 ..... 116 D3
  *WAL/NB* CH45 ..... 95 G7
Taunton St *WAV* L15 ..... 114 A5
Taurus Rd *DV/KA/FCH* L14 ..... 115 J1
Tavener Cl *BEB* CH63 ..... 143 L8
Tavistock Dr *STHP* PR8 ..... 34 D7
Tavistock Rd *WAL/NB* CH45 ..... 95 G7
  *WARRW/BUR* WA5 ..... 136 A1
  *WGNE/HIN* WN2 ..... 81 J1
Tavlin Av *WARRW/BUR* WA5 ..... 121 H4
Tavy Rd *NPK/KEN* L6 ..... 113 J1
Taylors Rw *RUNC* WA7 ..... 19 M4
Taylor St *BIRK* CH41 ..... 11 K3
  *CHLY/EC* PR7 ..... 32 D8
  *EV* L5 ..... 96 F1

  *LEIGH* WN7 ..... 81 M5
  *SKEL* WN8 ..... 64 E4
  *STHEL* WA9 ..... 103 G5
  *WARRS* WA4 ..... 137 J4
  *WDN* WA8 ..... 17 G1
  *WGNS/IIMK* WN3 ..... 4 C4
Teakwood Cl *NPK/KEN* L6 ..... 97 K8
Teal Cl *ORM* L39 ..... 62 E3
  *RNFD/HAY* WA11 ..... 89 K7
  *WARRN/WOL* WA2 ..... 122 A2
  *WGNS/IIMK* WN3 ..... 78 D1
Teal Gv *GOL/RIS/CU* WA3 ..... 123 H2
  *HLWD* L26 ..... 132 A4
Teals Wy *HES* CH60 ..... 140 F5
Tears La *SKEL* WN8 ..... 53 H5
Teasville Rd *CALD/MH* L18 ..... 131 G1
Tebay Cl *MGHL* L31 ..... 73 H3
Tebay Rd *PS/BROM* CH62 ..... 144 A5
Tedburn Cl *WLTN* L25 ..... 131 L1
Tedbury Cl *KKBY* L32 ..... 86 A6
Tedbury Wk *KKBY* L32 ..... 86 A5
Tedder Av *CHTN/BK* PR9 ..... 25 J6
Tedder Sq *WDN* WA8 ..... 133 M5
Teddington Cl *WARRS* WA4 ..... 138 A3
Teehey Cl *BEB* CH63 ..... 127 M7
Teehey Gdns *BEB* CH63 ..... 127 M7
Teehey La *BEB* CH63 ..... 127 M7
Tees Cl *ANF/KKDL* L4 ..... 7 K9
Teesdale Rd *BEB* CH63 ..... 143 G1
  *RNFD/HAY* WA11 ..... 90 E6
Tees St *ANF/KKDL* L4 ..... 7 K9
  *BIRK* CH41 ..... 111 H4
Teilo St *TOX* L8 ..... 113 J8
Telary Cl *EV* L5 ..... 96 E8
Telegraph Rd *WKBY* CH48 ..... 125 J7
Telford Cl *CL/PREN* CH43 ..... 10 C9
  *WDN* WA8 ..... 133 M1
Telford Crs *WGNE/HIN* WN2 ..... 81 M5
Telford Rd *EP* CH65 ..... 21 G7
Temperance St *CHLYE* PR6 ..... 33 G5
Tempest Hey *CLVP* L2 ..... 12 E6
Temple Ct *CLVP* L2 ..... 12 F7
  *GOL/RIS/CU* WA3 ..... 107 G7
Templegate Cl
  *WGNNW/ST* WN6 ..... 56 B5
Temple La *CLVP* L2 ..... 12 F6
Templemore Av *CALD/MH* L18 ..... 130 C2
Templemore Rd *CL/PREN* CH43 ..... 127 J1
Temple Rd *RF/TRAN* CH42 ..... 127 L3
Temple St *CLVP* L2 ..... 12 F6
Templeton Crs *WD/CROXPK* L12 ..... 98 D4
Templeton Rd *WGNE/HIN* WN2 ..... 80 C4
Temple Wy *CHLYE* PR6 ..... 32 F2
Tenbury Dr *AIMK* WN4 ..... 91 H1
Tenby Av *LITH* L21 ..... 83 J4
Tenby Dr *WARRW/BUR* WA5 ..... 121 H3
Tenby Dr *MOR/LEA* CH46 ..... 110 B6
  *RUNC* WA7 ..... 149 M3
Tenby St *EV* L5 ..... 97 J7
Tenement St *WGNE/HIN* WN2 ..... 80 D4
Tennis St *ECCL* WA10 ..... 8 B2
Tennis St North *ECCL* WA10 ..... 8 C1
Tennyson Av *CHLY/EC* PR7 ..... 32 E7
  *LEIGH* WN7 ..... 81 L5
  *RF/TRAN* CH42 ..... 128 B4
Tennyson Dr *ORM* L39 ..... 50 F7
  *WARRN/WOL* WA2 ..... 121 L3
  *WGN* WN1 ..... 68 E2
  *WGNW/BIL/O* WN5 ..... 77 M4
Tennyson Rd *EP* CH65 ..... 163 J1
  *HUY* L36 ..... 116 C5
  *WDN* WA8 ..... 139 G8
Tennyson St *BTL* L20 ..... 6 E1
  *STHEL* WA9 ..... 118 C3
Tensing Cl *WARRW/BUR* WA5 ..... 120 D5
Tensing Rd *MGHL* L31 ..... 72 F4
Tenterden St *EV* L5 ..... 13 G1
Tenter Dr *WGNNW/ST* WN6 ..... 56 D6
Terence Av *WARR* WA1 ..... 122 B6
Terence Rd *CHLDW* L16 ..... 114 F7
Terminus Rd *HUY* L36 ..... 99 K8
  *PS/BROM* CH62 ..... 143 M2
Tern Cl *NWD/KWIPK* L33 ..... 74 A6
  *WDN* WA8 ..... 134 D1
Ternhall Rd *WLT/FAZ* L9 ..... 98 B1
Ternhall Wy *WLT/FAZ* L9 ..... 98 B1
Tern Wy *MOR/LEA* CH46 ..... 109 K4
  *PR/KW* L34 ..... 101 J6
Terrace Rd *WDN* WA8 ..... 134 C8
Terret Cft *STBRV* L28 ..... 99 K6
Tetbury Cl *WGNW/BIL/O* WN5 ..... 67 M4
Tetbury St *BIRK* CH41 ..... 10 F7
Tetchill Cl *GTS/LS* CH66 ..... 162 F3
  *RUNC* WA7 ..... 150 F5
Tetlow St *ANF/KKDL* L4 ..... 97 H5
Tetlow Wy *ANF/KKDL* L4 ..... 97 H5
Teversham *SKEL* WN8 ..... 65 H3
Tewit Hall Cl *SPK/HALE* L24 ..... 146 E2
Tewit Hall Rd *SPK/HALE* L24 ..... 146 E2
Tewkesbury *SKEL* WN8 ..... 65 G3
Tewkesbury Cl *GTS/LS* CH66 ..... 163 G6
  *WD/CROXPK* L12 ..... 99 H1
  *WLTN* L25 ..... 131 L3
Tewkesbury Rd
  *GOL/RIS/CU* WA3 ..... 92 D5
Teynham Av *PR/KW* L34 ..... 99 M1
Teynham Crs *NG/CROX* L11 ..... 98 B3
Thackeray Gdns *NTHTN* L30 ..... 83 M5
Thackeray Pl
  *WGNS/IIMK* WN3 ..... 68 C8
Thackeray Sq *TOX* L8 ..... 113 H7
Thackeray St *TOX* L8 ..... 113 H7
Thackray Rd *ECCL* WA10 ..... 101 L5
Thamesdale *EP* CH65 ..... 20 A7
Thames Dr *STHEL* WA9 ..... 102 E7
Thames Gdns *EP* CH65 ..... 163 J2
Thames Rd *GOL/RIS/CU* WA3 ..... 107 H3
  *STHEL* WA9 ..... 102 E7
Thames Side *EP* CH65 ..... 20 A8
Thames St *TOX* L8 ..... 113 K7
Thanet *SKEL* WN8 ..... 65 G3
Thatto Heath Rd *ECCL* WA10 ..... 101 M5
Thealby Cl *SKEL* WN8 ..... 65 G3
Thelwall Cl *LEIGH* WN7 ..... 93 K1
Thelwall La *WARRS* WA4 ..... 138 C2
Thelwall New Rd *WARRS* WA4 ..... 138 D2

Thelwall Rd GTS/LS CH66 163 G1
Thermal Rd PS/BROM CH62 143 M1
Thetford Cl WGNE/HIN WN2 81 G1
Thetford Rd WGNW/BIL/O WA5 120 A7
Thewlis St WARRW/BUR WA5 121 G8
Thickness St WGNNW/ST WN6 68 B2
Thickwood Moss La
  RNFD/HAY WA11 76 B8
Thingwall Av DV/KA/FCH L14 114 C4
Thingwall Dr PEN/TH CH61 126 C7
Thingwall Hall Dr
  DV/KA/FCH L14 114 F3
Thingwall La DV/KA/FCH L14 114 F2
Thingwall Rd PEN/TH CH61 125 M8
  WAV L15 114 D5
Thingwall Rd East
  PEN/TH CH61 126 C7
Third Av CL/PREN CH43 110 E7
  CSBY/BLUN L23 82 F1 3
  RUNC WA7 150 B6
  WGNNW/ST WN6 68 C3
  WLT/FAZ L9 85 G6 1
Thirlmere Av AIMK WN4 91 L1 3
  CL/PREN CH43 110 E7
  FMBY L37 59 J3
  LITH L21 83 M5 2
  RNFD/HAY WA11 89 K5
  SKEL WN8 66 D6 1
  WARRN/WOL WA2 121 L2 3
  WGNE/HIN WN2 69 K6
  WGNE/HIN WN2 80 D5 7
  WGNNW/ST WN6 68 C3
  WGNW/BIL/O WN5 67 H6 2
Thirlmere Cl CHLYE PR6 44 D5
  FROD/HEL WA6 160 F5
  MGHL L31 73 G3
Thirlmere Dr LITH L21 83 M5
  STHP PR8 47 K2
  WAL/NB CH45 95 K8
Thirlmere Gn EV L5 97 J8 10
Thirlmere Rd CHLY/EC PR7 32 C7
  EP CH65 163 L3
  EV L5 97 J8
  GOL/RIS/CU WA3 92 E4 7
  HOR/BR BL6 57 L2
  HTWN L38 70 C1
  NSTN CH64 153 G7
  WGNW/BIL/O WN5 67 K6
Thirlmere Wk
  NWD/KWIPK L33 85 M1 4
Thirlstane St AIG/SPK L17 129 J2
Thirsk SKEL WN8 65 G3 4
Thirsk Rd RUNC WA7 149 L7 2
Thistle Cl CHLYE PR6 33 G5
Thistledown Cl AIG/SPK L17 129 J2 6
  WGNNW/ST WN6 68 C3
Thistleton Av RAIN/WH L35 111 H5
Thistleton Ms CHTN/BK PR9 3 K7
Thistlewood Rd EHL/KEN L7 114 A3
Thistley Hey Rd KKBY L32 86 B5
Thomas Cl ALL/GAR L19 130 E3
  EP CH65 163 K3 3
Thomas Ct RUNC WA7 150 B6 1
Thomas Dr DV/KA/FCH L14 114 E3
  RAIN/WH L35 116 E1
Thomas La DV/KA/FCH L14 114 F2
Thomasons Bridge La
  WARRS WA4 137 G7
Thomas St BIRK CH41 11 K7
  GOL/RIS/CU WA3 92 C5 7
  RUNC WA7 19 J2
  WDN WA8 16 C6
  WGNE/HIN WN2 81 K2
Thomaston St EV L5 97 G7 3
Thompson Av GOL/RIS/CU WA3 107 G2
  ORM L39 51 J8
Thompson St AIMK WN4 91 M1
  BIRK CH41 11 J9
  ECCL WA10 101 M4 2
  GOL/RIS/CU WA3 107 G8
  LEIGH WN7 81 K8
  WGN WN1 5 J1
Thomson Rd LITH L21 83 J6 3
Thomson St NPK/KEN L6 113 K1
Thorburn Cl RF/TRAN CH42 128 D5 5
Thorburn Crs
  PS/BROM CH62 128 D5 3
Thorburn Rd PS/BROM CH62 128 D5
  WGNW/BIL/O WN5 67 L7
Thorburn St EHL/KEN L7 113 K4
Thoresby Cl WGNS/IIMK WN3 79 G2
Thoriby Rd GOL/RIS/CU WA3 107 H2
Thorley Cl WAV L15 114 C4 1
Thornaby Gv RAIN/WH L35 117 M5
Thornbeck Av HTWN L38 70 B2 6
Thornbeck Ct
  WD/CROXPK L12 99 H2 4
Thornbridge Av BRSC L40 52 A2 3
  LITH L21 83 M5
Thornbury SKEL WN8 65 H3
Thornbury Av
  GOL/RIS/CU WA3 93 G5 3
Thornbury Rd ANF/KKDL L4 97 L6
Thornbush Cl GOL/RIS/CU WA3 93 G4
Thorncliffe Rd WAL/EG CH44 111 J2
Thorn Cl WARRW/BUR WA5 136 B2
Thorncroft Dr PEN/TH CH61 141 K1
Thorndale Rd CSBY/WL L22 82 F3
Thorndyke Cl RAIN/WH L35 118 A4
Thorne Dr GTS/LS CH66 162 D1
Thornes Rd NPK/KEN L6 113 K2 1
Thorness Cl
  GR/UP/WCH CH49 125 L3 1
Thorneycroft St BIRK CH41 10 A2
Thornfield Cl GOL/RIS/CU WA3 92 E5 3
Thornfield Hey BEB CH63 143 J3
Thornfield Rd CSBY/BLUN L23 71 J7
  WLT/FAZ L9 84 B8 3
Thornham Av STHEL WA9 102 E5
Thornham Cl
  GR/UP/WCH CH49 110 C6
Thornhead La WD/CROXPK L12 98 F7
Thornhill ORM L39 62 D5 3
Thornhill Rd AIMK WN4 90 E1
  CHLYE PR6 32 F3
  WAV L15 114 C6 2
Thornholme Crs NG/CROX L11 98 C4
Thornhurst KKBY L32 86 A6 3

Thornleigh Av PS/BROM CH62 155 H2
Thornleigh Dr GTS/LS CH66 156 A7
Thornley Rd LYMM WA13 139 L2
  MOR/LEA CH46 109 K6
Thorn Rd ECCL WA10 101 L2
  RUNC WA7 19 M9
  WARR WA1 122 C5
Thorns Dr GR/UP/WCH CH49 125 L3 5
The Thorns MGHL L31 72 D3 3
Thorn St WGNE/HIN WN2 80 F1 2
Thornton WDN WA8 134 A5 3
Thornton Av BEB CH63 127 M5
  BTL L20 83 M7
Thornton Cl AIMK WN4 91 H1
  BRSC L40 39 L1 1
Thornton Common Rd
  BEB CH63 142 D6
Thornton Crs HES CH60 141 K7
Thorntondale Dr
  WARRW/BUR WA5 120 B6
Thornton Green La CHNE CH2 165 G4
Thornton Gv BEB CH63 127 L5
Thornton Rd BEB CH63 127 M5
  BTL L20 83 L8 2
  CHLDW L16 115 G4
  CHTN/BK PR9 25 H6
  EP CH65 21 G7
  WAL/NB CH45 95 J7 3
  WARRN/WOL WA2 136 D1
  SKEL WN8 66 D6 2
Thornton St BIRK CH41 10 A2
  LITH L21 83 K7
Thorntree Cl AIG/SPK L17 129 J2 7
Thorntree Gn WARRS WA4 138 D8
Thorntree Vale WGNE/HIN WN2 80 E6
Thornwood Cl NPK/KEN L6 97 K8 10
Thornwythe Gv GTS/LS CH66 163 G1
Thornycroft Rd WAV L15 113 M7
Thoroughgood Cl BRSC L40 51 M3 2
Thorpe SKEL WN8 65 H3
Thorpe Bank RF/TRAN CH42 128 B5
Thorstone Dr PEN/TH CH61 125 L6
Thorsway RF/TRAN CH42 128 B3
  WKBY CH48 124 F5
Three Butt La WD/CROXPK L12 98 B7
Three Oaks Cl BRSC L40 52 D3
Three Pools CHTN/BK PR9 25 L2
Three Sisters Rd AIMK WN4 79 K7
Three Tuns La FMBY L37 59 H2
Threlfall CHLY/EC PR7 32 B3
Threlfalls La CHTN/BK PR9 25 H3
Threlfall St TOX L8 129 J1
Thresher Av
  GR/UP/WCH CH49 125 L1 6
The Threshers NTHTN L30 84 D1 3
Throne Rd NG/CROX L11 98 E2
Throstle Nest Av
  WGNNW/ST WN6 4 A1
Thurcroft Dr SKEL WN8 66 C1 5
Thurlby Cl AIMK WN4 91 M1 3
Thurlow GOL/RIS/CU WA3 93 G6 3
Thurne Wy WLTN L25 115 J7
Thurnham St NPK/KEN L6 97 L8
Thursby Cl KKBY L32 86 B5 7
  STHP PR8 47 K2 2
Thursby Crs KKBY L32 86 B5
Thursby Rd PS/BROM CH62 144 A3
Thursford Gv HOR/BR BL6 57 M4
Thurstaston Rd HES CH60 141 G4
  PEN/TH CH61 125 K7
Thurston SKEL WN8 65 G3
Thurston Av WGNS/IIMK WN3 46 C1
Thurston Cl WARRW/BUR WA5 120 F7
Thurston Rd ANF/KKDL L4 97 K7
Thynne St WARR WA1 14 C7
Tibbs Cross La WDN WA8 118 F4
Tichbourne Wy NPK/KEN L6 13 M4
Tickle Av STHEL WA9 102 F2
Tidal La WARRN/WOL WA2 122 F1
Tideswell Av WGNW/BIL/O WN5 67 J4
Tide Wy WAL/NB CH45 95 G5
Tilbrook Dr STHEL WA9 102 F7
Tilbury Gv WGNNW/ST WN6 54 F6
Tilbury Pl RUNC WA7 151 G7
Tilcroft SKEL WN8 65 G3
Tildsley Crs RUNC WA7 149 H7
Tilley St WARR WA1 15 G4
Tillotson Cl TOX L8 113 G8
Tilman Cl WARRW/BUR WA5 120 D5 3
Tilstock Av PS/BROM CH62 128 D5
Tilstock Crs CL/PREN CH43 127 H4
Tilston Av WARRS WA4 138 C1
Tilston Cl WLT/FAZ L9 97 M2
Tilston Rd KKBY L32 85 L3
  WAL/NB CH45 95 J7 3
  WLT/FAZ L9 97 M1
Timbercombe Gdns
  WARR WA1 123 G7
Time Pk RAIN/WH L35 101 H8
Timmis Cl WDN WA8 16 C2
Timmis Crs WDN WA8 16 C2
Timms Cl FMBY L37 47 H8
Timms La FMBY L37 47 H8
Timon Av BTL L20 7 L2
Timor Av STHEL WA9 102 A5 3
Timperley Av WARRS WA4 138 C1
Timperley St EHL/KEN L7 113 L5
Timway Dr WD/CROXPK L12 99 G5
Tinas Wy GR/UP/WCH CH49 110 C8 3
Tincklers La BRSC L40 30 B7
Tinkersfield LEIGH WN7 81 M6
Tinsley Av STHP PR8 36 A2
Tinsley's La ANF/KKDL L4 36 B4
Tinsley St ANF/KKDL L4 97 K1 1
Tintagel SKEL WN8 64 F3 3
Tintagel Cl RUNC WA7 150 E7 2
Tintagel Rd NG/CROX L11 85 M8
Tintern Av AIMK WN4 91 M2
Tintern Cl WARRW/BUR WA5 121 G3 3
Tintern Dr FMBY L37 59 K3 4
Tinwald Pl WGN WN1 5 L2
Tipping St WGNS/IIMK WN3 4 C8

Tiptree Cl WD/CROXPK L12 99 H1
Titchfield St EV L5 12 F1
Tithebarn Cl HES CH60 141 H6 8
Tithebarn Dr NSTN CH64 152 D3
The Barn La CHLYE PR6 33 J1
  KKBY L32 85 M4
Tithebarn Gv WAV L15 114 C6
Tithebarn La AIMK WN4 90 E3
  CSBY/BLUN L23 71 H8
  PR/KW L34 99 M1
  STHP PR8 3 M5
  SKEL WN8 66 D6 2
Tithebarn St CLVP L2 12 E6
  WGNE/HIN WN2 5 K6
Tiverton Av LEIGH WN7 81 M3
  SKEL WN8 65 G3
  WAL/EG CH44 111 K1 6
Tiverton Cl HUY L36 116 D3 9
  WDN WA8 133 L2
Tiverton Rd HLWD L26 132 A7 2
Tiverton Sq
  WARRW/BUR WA5 136 A1 3
Tiverton St WAV L15 114 A5
Tobermory Cl RNFD/HAY WA11 90 C8
Tobin Av EV L5 12 F1
Tobin St WAL/EG CH44 111 M1
Tobruk Rd HUY L36 115 M1
Toddington La WGNE/HIN WN2 57 K5
Todd Rd STHEL WA9 9 J6
Todd's La CHTN/BK PR9 23 J7
Toft Cl WDN WA8 16 A2
Toft St EHL/KEN L7 113 L3
Toftwood Av RAIN/WH L35 118 A4 3
Toll Bar Rd WARRN/WOL WA2 121 J2
Tollemache Rd BIRK CH41 111 G5
  CL/PREN CH43 111 H6
Tollemache St WAL/NB CH45 95 G4
Tollerton Rd WD/CROXPK L12 98 B7
Tollgate Rd BRSC L40 51 K2
Tollgreen Cl WGNE/HIN WN2 69 M6
Toll St WGNE/HIN WN2 80 C4
Tolpuddle Rd WLTN L25 131 H2
Tolpuddle Wy ANF/KKDL L4 96 F5 3
Tolver St ECCL WA10 9 H4
Tomlinson Av
  WARRN/WOL WA2 121 M5
Tom Mann Cl VAUX/LVPD L3 13 H5
Tonbridge Cl SPK/HALE L24 146 D1
Tonbridge Dr AIN/FAZ L10 84 F2
Tongbarn SKEL WN8 65 G3
Tontine Rd SKEL WN8 66 E7
Toogood La WGNNW/ST WN6 41 M6
Tootell St CHLY/EC PR7 32 D7
Toothill Cl AIMK WN4 79 K8
Tootle La BRSC L40 39 H7
Top Acre Rd SKEL WN8 65 L6
Topaz Cl ANF/KKDL L4 7 M6
Topcliffe Gv WD/CROXPK L12 99 G2
Topgate Cl HES CH60 141 K5
Topping Ct GOL/RIS/CU WA3 122 D1
Top Rd FROD/HEL WA6 160 F8
Topsham Cl WLTN L25 131 L1 8
Torcross Cl CHTN/BK PR9 22 C8
Torcross Wy HLWD L26 132 A5
  WLTN L25 131 L1 8
Tordelow Cl NPK/KEN L6 113 J1
Tormore Cl CHLYE PR6 33 J3
Toronto Cl HUY L36 99 M7 2
Toronto St WAL/EG CH44 112 A2 7
Torquay Dr
  WGNW/BIL/O WN5 78 A5 3
Torridon Cl WGNNW/ST WN6 56 D6 1
Torridon Gv GTS/LS CH66 163 H2 6
Torrington Dr HLWD L26 132 A7
  PEN/TH CH61 126 D7
Torrington Gdns
  PEN/TH CH61 126 D6 1
Torrington Rd ALL/GAR L19 130 D6
  WAL/EG CH44 111 J1
Torrisholme Rd WLT/FAZ L9 97 M2
Torr St EV L5 97 G7
Torside Cl WGNE/HIN WN2 69 M7
Torus Rd CLB/OSW/ST L13 114 C1
Torver Cl WGNS/IIMK WN3 79 J3
Tor View Rd WAV L15 114 C7
Torwood CL/PREN CH43 110 F6
Tothale Turn NTHLY L27 132 B1
Totland Cl WARRW/BUR WA5 119 L6
Totnes Av HLWD L26 132 B4
Totnes Dr CHTN/BK PR9 22 C8
Totnes Rd NG/CROX L11 85 L8
Tourney Gn WARRW/BUR WA5 120 C3
Towcester St LITH L21 83 K7
Tower End FMBY L37 46 E8
Tower Gdns VAUX/LVPD L3 12 D7
Tower Hill ORM L39 51 J8
Tower Hill Rd SKEL WN8 66 C8
Tower La RUNC WA7 150 E6
Tower Nook SKEL WN8 66 C8
Tower Prom WAL/NB CH45 95 L4
Tower Rd BIRK CH41 11 J2
  RF/TRAN CH42 127 M2 8
Tower Rd North HES CH60 141 G3
Tower Rd South HES CH60 141 H4
Towers Av MGHL L31 72 E3
Towers La FROD/HEL WA6 166 D6
Towers Rd CHLDW L16 114 E7
Tower St VAUX/LVPD L3 112 F8
Tower Wy WLTN L25 131 J2
Tower Whf BIRK CH41 11 J2
Towneley Ct WDN WA8 16 C2
Towneley Av AIMK WN4 91 K3
Townfield CL/PREN CH43 127 G2 8
Townfield Gdns BEB CH63 128 B6 3
Townfield La BEB CH63 128 B6
  CL/PREN CH43 127 H2
  FROD/HEL WA6 160 E6
Townfield Rd RUNC WA7 150 D3 8
  WKBY CH48 124 D3
Townfields AIMK WN4 91 J2
Townfield Vw CHLY/EC PR7 30 D5
Towngate CHLY/EC PR7 30 D5
Town Green La ORM L39 62 E5
Town Hl WARR WA1 14 E5
Town La BEB CH63 128 C4

  CHLY/EC PR7 41 L4
  NSTN CH64 153 H7
  SPK/HALE L24 147 K6
  STHP PR8 35 M1
Town La (Kew) STHP PR8 36 A2
Townley St CHLYE PR6 32 F6
Town Meadow La
  MOR/LEA CH46 109 K5 10
Town Rd LEY/BBR PR5 29 K3
  RF/TRAN CH42 127 M2
Town Rw WD/CROXPK L12 98 D6
Townsend Av NG/CROX L11 98 A3
Townsend La CLB/OSW/ST L13 97 M6
  NPK/KEN L6 97 L6
Townsend St BIRK CH41 111 G4
  EV L5 96 D7
Townsend Vw LITH L21 83 K3 3
  NG/CROX L11 98 A2
Townshend Av PEN/TH CH61 125 M8
Town Vw CL/PREN CH43 10 E7
Towson St EV L5 97 H7
Toxteth Gv TOX L8 129 J1
Toxteth St TOX L8 113 H8
Tracks La WGNW/BIL/O WN5 77 M2
Tracy Dr NEWLW WA12 105 G2
Trafalgar Av WAL/EG CH44 95 M8
Trafalgar Dr BEB CH63 143 J1
Trafalgar Rd STHP PR8 35 G2
  WAL/EG CH44 95 L8
  WGN WN1 4 E1
  WGNE/HIN WN2 69 M8 21
Trafalgar St CHLY/EC PR7 32 E4 8
  ECCL WA10 8 C3
Trafalgar Wy NPK/KEN L6 13 M4
Trafford Av WARRW/BUR WA5 121 G5
Trafford Crs RUNC WA7 149 L7
Trafford Rd WGNE/HIN WN2 69 L8
Tragan Dr WARRW/BUR WA5 135 M2
Tram St WGNE/HIN WN2 80 C4
Tramway Rd AIG/SPK L17 129 L2
Trans Pennine Trail CHLDW L16 115 H6
  CLVPS L1 12 F8
  NTHTN L30 72 D7
  NTHTN L30 84 D2
  TOX L8 113 K8
  WARRW/BUR WA5 135 M4
  WD/CROXPK L12 114 E1
  WDN WA8 84 D8
Trap Hl FMBY L37 58 E4
Trapwood Cl ECCL WA10 101 K2
Travandon Cl NG/CROX L11 85 K7 2
Travers' Entry STHEL WA9 103 J7
Traverse St STHEL WA9 9 L5
Travis St WDN WA8 18 D5
Treborth St TOX L8 113 J8 8
Trecastell Cl WGN WN1 5 L2
Trecastle Rd NWD/KWIPK L33 86 C1
Tree Bank Cl RUNC WA7 19 G7
Treen Cl CHTN/BK PR9 22 D7
Treesdale Cl STHP PR8 35 H1
Tree Tops NSTN CH64 153 G8
Treetops Dr BIRK CH41 110 F4
Trefoil Cl WD/CROXPK L12 98 C7
Treforris Rd WAL/NB CH45 95 H6 1
Trefula Pk WD/CROXPK L12 98 C7
Tregaron Gv WGNE/HIN WN2 81 J2 3
Trelawney Cl WLTN L25 115 K7 3
Tremore Cl NG/CROX L11 98 E4 3
Trenance Cl RUNC WA7 150 D8
Trendeal Rd NG/CROX L11 85 M8 3
Trent Av DV/KA/FCH L14 115 H2
  MGHL L31 73 H3
Trent Cl BRSC L40 39 H8
  RAIN/WH L35 117 K2
  STHEL WA9 102 E8
  WD/CROXPK L12 98 F2
  WDN WA8 134 D1
Trent St EV L5 96 E7 2
Trent Wy HES CH60 141 K7
Trescott Ms WGNNW/ST WN6 56 A5
Tressel Dr STHEL WA9 118 C2
Tressell St WLT/FAZ L9 97 H2 3
Trevelyan Dr WGNW/BIL/O WN5 74 M4
Trevelyan St WLT/FAZ L9 97 H2 8
Treviot Cl NWD/KWIPK L33 73 M7
Trevor Dr CSBY/BLUN L23 83 H2
Trevor Rd BRSC L40 51 M1 1
  BRSC L40 52 A1 3
  STHP PR8 47 L1
  WLT/FAZ L9 84 C7
Trimley Cl
  GR/UP/WCH CH49 110 A8 11
Tring Cl GR/UP/WCH CH49 110 C6
Trinity Ct GOL/RIS/CU WA3 107 H8
Trinity Gdns AIMK WN4 91 H1 3
  STHP PR8 2 F6
Trinity Gv CSBY/BLUN L23 82 D3 3
Trinity La BIRK CH41 11 J4
Trinity Ms CHTN/BK PR9 3 K3
Trinity Pl BTL L20 7 J5
  WDN WA8 16 E5
Trinity Rd BTL L20 7 G6
  CHLY/EC PR7 32 D6 3
  HOY CH47 108 D6
  WAL/EG CH44 95 M8
Trinity St BIRK CH41 10 F4
  STHEL WA9 9 L5
Trispen Cl HLWD L26 132 A5
Trispen Rd NG/CROX L11 98 F1
Triumph Wy SPK/HALE L24 131 H7
Trlam Rd BTL L20 6 E3
Troon Cl BEB CH63 143 L8
  RNFD/HAY WA11 90 C8
  WD/CROXPK L12 99 G7

Trossach Cl WARRN/WOL WA2 122 A3
Trotwood Cl WLT/FAZ L9 84 F5 3
Troutbeck Av MGHL L31 73 G3
  NEWLW WA12 104 A1
  WARRW/BUR WA5 14 A1
Troutbeck Cl GR/UP/WCH CH49 126 C3
  RUNC WA7 150 C8
Troutbeck Ri
  WGNW/BIL/O WN5 67 K7 3
Troutbeck Rd AIMK WN4 79 L8 11
  CALD/MH L18 114 F8
  CHLY/EC PR7 32 D8
Trouville Rd ANF/KKDL L4 97 L6
Trowbridge St VAUX/LVPD L3 13 K7
Trueman Cl CL/PREN CH43 110 E5
Trueman St VAUX/LVPD L3 13 G5
Trumans La GTS/LS CH66 155 L6
Truro Av CHTN/BK PR9 22 D8
  NTHTN L30 84 B1
Truro Cl GTS/LS CH66 163 H5 11
  RNFD/HAY WA11 89 M6
  RUNC WA7 150 E7 3
  WARR WA1 122 D5
Truro Rd WAV L15 114 C7
Truscott Rd BRSC L40 51 M1
Tucker's Hill Brow
  WGNE/HIN WN2 57 K4
Tudor Av BEB CH63 143 J2
  WAL/EG CH44 112 A3 10
Tudor Cl GTS/LS CH66 163 H5
  RNFD/HAY WA11 76 A5
  WARRS WA4 138 C3
Tudor Gra GR/UP/WCH CH49 125 M2 3
Tudor Gv WGNS/IIMK WN3 79 G3
Tudor Rd CSBY/BLUN L23 82 F2
  RF/TRAN CH42 128 A2
  RUNC WA7 150 D2
  STHP PR8 34 D7
  WLTN L25 131 L6
Tudor St NPK/KEN L6 113 K2
Tudor Vw WD/KWIPK L33 74 A8
Tudorville Rd BEB CH63 128 B8
Tudorway HES CH60 141 K5
Tue La WDN WA8 117 K7
Tuffins Cnr NTHLY L27 115 M8
Tulip Av BIRK CH41 111 H5
Tulip Dr WGNNW/ST WN6 68 B2
Tulip Rd RNFD/HAY WA11 91 H7
  WAV L15 114 C6
Tulketh St STHP PR8 3 H4
Tullimore Rd CALD/MH L18 130 C4
Tullis St ECCL WA10 8 D7
Tulloch St NPK/KEN L6 113 K2
Tully Av NEWLW WA12 104 A2
Tumilty Av BTL L20 7 L2
Tunbridge Cl WARRW/BUR WA5 120 C5
Tunley La WGNNW/ST WN6 42 A8
Tunley Moss WGNNW/ST WN6 55 G1
Tunnel Rd BIRK CH41 11 L6
  EHL/KEN L7 113 K5
Tunstall
  GR/UP/WCH CH49 110 A8 11
Tunstall La WGNW/BIL/O WN5 67 M8
Tunstall St EHL/KEN L7 113 L6
Tunstall's Wy STHEL WA9 118 F1 1
Tupelo Cl WD/CROXPK L12 99 H1
Tupman St TOX L8 113 H8 12
Turflands LEY/BBR PR5 29 K4
Turmar Av PEN/TH CH61 126 D7
Turnacre DV/KA/FCH L14 115 G2
  FMBY L37 47 K7
Turnall Rd WDN WA8 133 K6
Turnberry SKEL WN8 64 F3
Turnberry Cl HUY L36 115 L4 7
  LYMM WA13 139 L1
  MOR/LEA CH46 108 F8
  WD/CROXPK L12 99 H7 3
Turnberry Wy CHTN/BK PR9 22 F8
Turnbridge Rd MGHL L31 72 E2
Turnbury Cl CHLYE PR6 31 M1
Turnditch Cl WGNNW/ST WN6 68 C1
Turner Av BTL L20 84 A7
  WGNE/HIN WN2 81 G4
Turner Cl WDN WA8 133 M2 3
  WGN WN1 5 G3
  WGNE/HIN WN2 69 M7 13
Turner St BIRK CH41 10 F8 3
  WGN WN1 5 G3
  WGNE/HIN WN2 69 M7 13
Turney Rd WAL/EG CH44 111 J1
Turnill Dr AIMK WN4 91 K3
Turning La STHP PR8 36 C5
Turnpike Rd ORM L39 62 C4
Turnstone Av NEWLW WA12 104 E1
Turnstone Cl WD/CROXPK L12 99 G2
Turnstone Dr HLWD L26 132 A4
Turret Hall Dr
  GOL/RIS/CU WA3 93 G5 13
Turret Rd WAL/NB CH45 95 J7
Turriff Dr BEB CH63 154 E1
Turriff Gv WGNE/HIN WN2 69 J4
Turriff Rd DV/KA/FCH L14 115 J1
Turrocks Cl NSTN CH64 153 G8 3
Turrocks Cft NSTN CH64 153 G8
Turton Cl GOL/RIS/CU WA3 106 E8
  WDN WA8 118 C2
Turton Dr CHLYE PR6 33 G4 3
Turton St EV L5 96 F7 3
  GOL/RIS/CU WA3 92 C5
Tuscan Cl WDN WA8 118 D8
Tuson Dr WDN WA8 134 B1
Tutor Bank NEWLW WA12 104 F2
Tweed Cl NPK/KEN L6 113 L1 3
Tweedsmuir Cl
  WARRN/WOL WA2 122 C1 3
Tweed St BIRK CH41 111 J4
Twenty Acre Rd
  WARRW/BUR WA5 120 E5
Twickenham Dr HUY L36 115 L4
  MOR/LEA CH46 110 C2
Twigden Cl AIN/FAZ L10 85 H5
Twig La HUY L36 115 L3
  MGHL L31 72 E4
Twiss Green Dr
  GOL/RIS/CU WA3 107 G1
Twiss Green La
  GOL/RIS/CU WA3 106 F1
Twist Av GOL/RIS/CU WA3 92 E5
Twistfield Cl STHP PR8 2 D7
Twist La LEIGH WN7 81 M8

Two Acre Gv GTS/LS CH66...... 163 H4
Two Butt La RAIN/WH L35........ 101 J8
Twomey Cl EV L5................ 12 F1
Twyford Av LITH L21............ 83 K4
Twyford Cl MGHL L31............ 73 G4
  WDN WA8...................... 134 D1
Twyford La WDN WA8............ 118 F7
Twyford St NPK/KEN L6.......... 97 K7
Tyberton Pl SPK/HALE L24....... 131 L7
Tyburn Cl BEB CH63............. 143 H3
Tyburn Rd BEB CH63............. 143 H3
Tyndall Av CSBY/WL L22......... 83 H5
Tyne Cl ANF/KKDL L4............ 97 C3
  RAIN/WH L35.................. 101 M7
  WARRN/WOL WA2............... 122 A3
Tynemouth Cl EV L5............. 97 J8
Tynemouth Rd RUNC WA7........ 150 E7
Tynesdale EP CH65.............. 20 A9
Tyne St BIRK CH41.............. 111 H4
Tynron Gv CL/PREN CH43........ 126 F1
Tynville Rd WLT/FAZ L9......... 84 E6
Tynwald Cl CLB/OSW/ST L13..... 114 B1
Tynwald Crs WDN WA8........... 118 B8
Tynwald Dr WARRS WA4.......... 137 L6
Tynwald Hl CLB/OSW/ST L13..... 114 B1
Tynwald Pl CLB/OSW/ST L13..... 114 B1
Tynwald Rd WKBY CH48.......... 124 C3
Tyrer Av WGNS/IIMK WN3........ 68 B3
Tyrer Rd NEWLW WA12.......... 104 E4
  ORM L39...................... 51 H6
Tyrer's Av MGHL L31............ 61 L8
Tyrers Cl FMBY L37............. 59 H5
Tyrer St BIRK CH41............. 111 H4

**U**

Uldale Cl NG/CROX L11.......... 98 C3
  STHP PR8..................... 47 K2
Uldale Wy NG/CROX L11......... 98 C3
Ullapool Cl GTS/LS CH66........ 155 H7
Ullet Rd AIG/SPK L17........... 113 M8
Ullswater Av CL/PREN CH43..... 110 E7
  RNFD/HAY WA11............... 89 J5
  WARRN/WOL WA2.............. 121 L2
  WGNW/BIL/O WN5............. 67 H6
Ullswater Cl NWD/KWIPK L33.... 85 M1
Ullswater Gv RUNC WA7......... 149 M8
Ullswater Rd CHLY/EC PR7...... 32 D7
  GOL/RIS/CU WA3.............. 92 E4
Ullswater St EV L5............. 97 J7
Ulnes Walton La LEY/BBR PR5... 30 B1
Ulster Rd CLB/OSW/ST L13...... 114 D2
Ultonia St ALL/GAR L19......... 145 L1
Ulverston Av WARRN/WOL WA2.. 121 K2
Ulverston Cl MGHL L31.......... 73 G3
  RNFD/HAY WA11............... 90 C7
Ulverston Lawn NTHLY L27...... 132 B1
Ulverston Rd
  WGNS/IIMK WN3.............. 79 H2
Umbria St ALL/GAR L19......... 145 L1
Underbridge La WARRS WA4..... 137 L2
Undercliffe Rd
  CLB/OSW/ST L13.............. 114 C1
Underhill Rd ECCL WA10......... 8 B7
Underley St EHL/KEN L7......... 113 L6
The Underway RUNC WA7........ 150 B5
Underwood Dr EP CH65.......... 163 K6
Unicorn Rd NG/CROX L11........ 98 C1
Unicorn Wy BIRK CH41.......... 11 L8
Union Bank La WDN WA8........ 118 D4
Union Cl CLVP L2............... 12 F7
Union St BIRK CH41............. 128 B2
  CHLY/EC PR7.................. 32 E5
  CHTN/BK PR9.................. 3 H2
  ECCL WA10.................... 9 C2
  RUNC WA7.................... 19 K4
  VAUX/LVPD L3................ 12 D6
  WAL/EG CH44................. 111 M1
  WARR WA1.................... 14 E6
  WGNE/HIN WN2................ 69 J5
Unit Rd STHP PR8.............. 34 F8
Unity Gv PR/KW L34............ 86 C9
University Rd BTL L20.......... 7 J5
Unsworth Av GOL/RIS/CU WA3... 92 F4
Unsworth Ct
  WARRN/WOL WA2............. 122 B4
Upavon Av
  GR/UP/WCH CH49............. 125 K2
Upholland Rd
  WGNW/BIL/O WN5............. 77 M1
Upland Dr AIMK WN4............ 91 M1
Upland Rd ECCL WA10........... 101 K5
  GR/UP/WCH CH49............. 110 B7
Uplands Cl BRSC L40........... 101 K5
Uplands Rd PS/BROM CH62...... 143 L4
Upper Aughton Rd STHP PR8.... 2 F8
Upper Baker St NPK/KEN L6..... 113 J2
Upper Beau St VAUX/LVPD L3... 13 J2
Upper Beckwith St BIRK CH41... 10 C2
Upper Bute St EV L5........... 13 K2
Upper Dicconson St WGN WN1... 4 F2
Upper Duke St CLVPS L1........ 113 G5
Upper Essex St TOX L8......... 113 H8
Upper Flaybrick Rd
  CL/PREN CH43................ 111 C6
Upper Frederick St CLVPS L1... 112 F5
Upper Hampton St TOX L8...... 113 H7
Upper Harrington St TOX L8.... 113 C7
Upper Hill St TOX L8........... 113 H7
  TOX L8....................... 113 H7
Upper Hope Pl TOX L8.......... 13 L9
  TOX L8....................... 113 H5
Upper Huskisson St TOX L8..... 113 J6
Upper Mann St TOX L8......... 113 G8
Upper Mersey Rd WDN WA8..... 16 C9
Upper Mersey St EP CH65...... 20 D1
  EP CH65...................... 20 D1
Upper Newington CLVPS L1..... 13 J8
Upper Park St TOX L8.......... 113 H8
Upper Parliament St TOX L8 .. 113 L9
Upper Pitt St CLVPS L1........ 112 F5
Upper Pownall St CLVPS L1.... 112 F5
Upper Raby Rd NSTN CH64..... 153 J3
Upper Rice La WAL/EG CH44... 95 L8

Upper St Stephen St
  WGNNW/ST WN6............... 4 C3
Upper Stanhope St TOX L8...... 113 G6
Upper Warwick St TOX L8....... 113 H7
Upper William St VAUX/LVPD L3. 12 D1
Uppingham SKEL WN8........... 64 F8
Uppingham Av AIN/FAZ L10..... 85 G3
Uppingham Rd CLB/OSW/ST L13.. 98 B8
  WAL/EG CH44................. 95 H8
Upton Av CLB/OSW/ST L13...... 34 D7
Upton Barn MGHL L31.......... 72 E3
Upton Bridle Pth WDN WA8 .. 134 B1
Upton By-Pass
  GR/UP/WCH CH49............. 110 A8
Upton Cl GOL/RIS/CU WA3...... 92 F5
  GR/UP/WCH CH49............. 110 B8
  SPK/HALE L24................. 147 G2
Upton Dr WARRW/BUR WA5...... 120 B8
Upton Gra WDN WA8........... 133 M1
Upton Gn SPK/HALE L24........ 147 G2
Upton La WDN WA8............ 134 B1
Upton Park Dr
  GR/UP/WCH CH49............. 110 C7
Upton Rd CL/PREN CH43........ 110 C7
  GTS/LS CH66.................. 162 F1
Upwood Rd GOL/RIS/CU WA3.... 92 F6
Ure Ct EP CH65................ 156 C6
Urmson Rd WAL/NB CH45....... 95 K8
Urmston Av NEWLW WA12....... 91 K8
Urmston St LEIGH WN7......... 81 M8
Ursula St BTL L20.............. 7 K8
Utkinton Cl CL/PREN CH43..... 127 H2
Utting Av ANF/KKDL L4......... 97 K5
Utting Av East NG/CROX L11 .. 98 A4
Uxbridge St EHL/KEN L7........ 113 K4

**V**

Vahler Ter RUNC WA7........... 19 L3
Vale Av WARRN/WOL WA2...... 121 K5
Vale Cl WGNNW/ST WN6....... 55 G5
  WLTN L25.................... 131 H3
Vale Crs STHP PR8............. 47 L3
Vale Dr WAL/NB CH45.......... 95 L6
Vale Gdns EP CH65............ 20 A7
  FROD/HEL WA6............... 166 D1
Vale Gv KKBY L32.............. 86 C4
Vale La BRSC L40.............. 53 G8
Valencia Gv PR/KW L34........ 101 J6
Valencia Rd WAV L15.......... 114 C5
Valentia Rd HOY CH47......... 108 C7
Valentine Gv AIN/FAZ L10...... 85 G4
Valentine Rd NEWLW WA12.... 104 B2
Vale Owen Rd
  WARRN/WOL WA2............. 121 M4
Valerian Rd BIRK CH41......... 111 H6
Vale Rd AIN/FAZ L10........... 85 K7
Vale Rd CSBY/BLUN L23........ 82 F1
  EP CH65...................... 20 A7
  WLTN L25.................... 131 H3
Valescourt Rd WD/CROXPK L12. 98 E8
The Vale WGNNW/ST WN6...... 54 F5
Valiant Cl WARRN/WOL WA2... 122 B3
  WD/CROXPK L12.............. 99 J3
Valiant Rd WGNW/BIL/O WN5.. 67 M5
Valiant Wy BIRK CH41.......... 11 L9
Valkyrie Rd WAL/NB CH45...... 95 J8
Vallance Rd ANF/KKDL L4...... 97 L6
Valleybrook Gv BEB CH63...... 143 K3
Valley Cl AIN/FAZ L10......... 85 H4
  CSBY/BLUN L23............... 83 K1
Valley Ct WARRN/WOL WA2.... 122 B4
Valley Dr GTS/LS CH66......... 155 M8
Valley Rd AIN/FAZ L10......... 85 K6
  ANF/KKDL L4................. 97 J7
  BIRK CH41.................... 110 F3
  KKBY L32.................... 85 M4
  PS/BROM CH62............... 143 M5
  WGNW/BIL/O WN5............ 67 M8
Valley Vw CHLYE PR6........... 33 G6
  GTS/LS CH66................. 155 M8
  NEWLW WA12................. 104 D4
Vanbrugh Crs ANF/KKDL L4.... 97 L6
Vanbrugh Rd WGNW/BIL/O WN5. 67 K4
Vandries St VAUX/LVPD L3..... 12 C2
Vandyke St TOX L8............ 113 L6
Vanguard Ct
  GOL/RIS/CU WA3............. 122 F1
Vanguard St EV L5............ 97 H7
Vardon Cl BIRK CH41........... 11 G2
Varley Rd ALL/GAR L19......... 130 C4
  STHEL WA9................... 9 L4
Varlian Cl BRSC L40........... 63 L2
Varthen St EV L5.............. 97 J6
Vaudrey Dr WARR WA1......... 122 F6
Vaughan Cl FMBY L37.......... 58 F1
Vaughan Rd STHP PR8.......... 35 J1
  WAL/NB CH45................. 95 L5
Vaughan St BIRK CH41......... 111 H5
Vaux Crs BTL L20.............. 83 M8
Vauxhall Cl WARRW/BUR WA5.. 136 B1
Vauxhall Rd EV L5............. 96 E8
  VAUX/LVPD L3................ 12 F4
Vaux Pl BTL L20............... 7 K1
Vauze Av HOR/BR BL6......... 57 M4
Vauze House Cl HOR/BR BL6... 57 M3
Venables Cl BRSC L40......... 143 K4
Venables Dr BEB CH63......... 143 J3
Venice St EV L5............... 97 H7
Venmore St WARRN/WOL WA2.. 15 J1
Ventnor Cl
  WARRW/BUR WA5............. 119 M6
Ventnor Rd CHLY/EC PR7...... 32 D7
  WAV L15...................... 114 C5
Verbena Cl RUNC WA7......... 161 H1
Verda St WGNE/HIN WN2...... 80 C5
Verdi Av LITH L21............. 83 J7
Verdi St LITH L21............. 83 H8
Vere St TOX L8................ 113 G8
Vermont Av CSBY/BLUN L23.... 82 F1
Vermont Cl WARRW/BUR WA5.. 120 E6

Vermont Rd CSBY/BLUN L23.... 82 F1
Vermont Wy BTL L20........... 7 G3
Verney Crs ALL/GAR L19....... 130 E5
Verney Crs South ALL/GAR L19. 130 E5
Vernon Av GTS/LS CH66........ 155 J3
  WAL/EG CH44................. 111 M3
Vernon Rd CHTN/BK PR9....... 25 J5
Vernon St CLVP L2............. 12 F5
  STHEL WA9................... 9 L4
  WARR WA1.................... 14 F7
Verona St EV L5............... 97 H7
Veronica Av GTS/LS CH66...... 155 M6
Verulam Cl TOX L8............. 113 J6
Verulam Rd CHTN/BK PR9...... 25 K2
Verwood Cl PEN/TH CH61...... 125 M6
Verwood Dr WD/CROXPK L12... 99 J2
Veryan Cl HLWD L26........... 132 B4
Vetch Hey NTHLY L27.......... 116 A8
Viaduct St NEWLW WA12....... 104 C2
Vicarage Cl CALD/MH L18...... 130 D3
  CHLY/EC PR7................. 31 M2
  CHLYE PR6................... 44 C5
  FMBY L37.................... 59 G1
  ORM L39..................... 63 K2
  RF/TRAN CH42................ 127 K4
  SPK/HALE L24................ 148 A4
  WGNE/HIN WN2............... 80 C3
Vicarage Dr RNFD/HAY WA11... 90 C6
Vicarage Gdns BRSC L40....... 51 M1
Vicarage Gv WAL/EG CH44..... 95 L8
Vicarage Hl FROD/HEL WA6.... 166 E1
Vicarage La BRSC L40......... 63 M2
  CHTN/BK PR9................. 23 H6
  FROD/HEL WA6............... 160 E6
  FROD/HEL WA6............... 166 E1
  WGNNW/ST WN6............... 5 J1
Vicarage Lawn WLTN L25...... 115 L8
Vicarage Rd AIMK WN4......... 91 K3
  FMBY L37.................... 58 F1
  HOR/BR BL6.................. 57 M3
  RNFD/HAY WA11.............. 90 D6
  WDN WA8.................... 16 D5
  WGNE/HIN WN2............... 80 D4
  WGNW/BIL/O WN5............. 77 M1
Vicarage Rd West HOR/BR BL6.. 57 L3
Vicarage St CHLYE PR6........ 32 F4
Vicarage Wk ORM L39.......... 51 G8
Vicar Rd NPK/KEN L6.......... 97 H2
Viceroy St EV L5.............. 97 H7
Vickers Rd WDN WA8.......... 149 G1
Victor Cl WGNW/BIL/O WN5.... 67 M5
Victoria Av CSBY/BLUN L23.... 82 E1
  DV/KA/FCH L14............... 114 F3
  HES CH60.................... 141 H7
  RNFD/HAY WA11.............. 89 J5
  WARRS WA4................... 138 C3
  WARRW/BUR WA5.............. 119 M7
  WAV L15..................... 114 B5
  WDN WA8.................... 134 C3
  WGNE/HIN WN2............... 81 G4
  WGNNW/ST WN6............... 4 B1
Victoria Bridge Rd STHP PR8... 3 J5
Victoria Cl AIG/SPK L17....... 130 A2
  WGNE/HIN WN2............... 57 K7
Victoria Crs WAV L15......... 114 C5
  WGNNW/ST WN6............... 56 A5
Victoria Dr RF/TRAN CH42..... 128 C4
  WKBY CH48................... 124 C3
  WLT/FAZ L9.................. 84 B7
Victoria Flds RF/TRAN CH42... 127 L1
Victoria Gv WDN WA8.......... 134 C2
Victoria La CL/PREN CH43..... 127 K1
Victoria Mt CL/PREN CH43..... 127 K1
Victoria Pde WAL/NB CH45.... 95 L4
Victoria Pk SKEL WN8......... 64 E4
Victoria Park Rd
  RF/TRAN CH42................ 127 M3
Victoria Pl CLB/OSW/ST L13... 114 C2
  RAIN/WH L35................. 117 L2
  WARRS WA4................... 137 L4
Victoria Rd AIG/SPK L17....... 130 A3
  AIMK WN4.................... 90 F2
  BEB CH63.................... 127 M7
  CLB/OSW/ST L13.............. 98 A7
  CSBY/BLUN L23............... 82 F1
  CSBY/WL L22................. 83 G5
  EP CH65..................... 20 B4
  FMBY L37.................... 46 D8
  HTWN L38.................... 71 G2
  HUY L36..................... 116 B3
  NEWLW WA12................. 104 E1
  NSTN CH64................... 153 J7
  ORM L39..................... 62 E2
  RF/TRAN CH42................ 11 C9
  RUNC WA7.................... 19 H4
  WAL/NB CH45................. 95 J5
  WARRS WA4................... 137 M4
  WARRW/BUR WA5.............. 136 A1
  WDN WA8.................... 16 D5
  WGNE/HIN WN2............... 80 C4
  WKBY CH48................... 124 C4
Victoria St BRSC L40.......... 39 G8
  CHLY/EC PR7................. 32 F6
  CLVP L2..................... 12 F7
  ECCL WA10................... 9 G2
  HOR/BR BL6.................. 57 M3
  PS/BROM CH62................ 128 D8
  RAIN/WH L35................. 117 L2
  RNFD/HAY WA11.............. 76 B6
  STHP PR8.................... 3 G2
  WARR WA1.................... 15 L1
  WDN WA8.................... 16 E5
  WGNE/HIN WN2............... 80 C3
  WGNW/BIL/O WN5............. 68 A7
Victoria Ter CHLYE PR6....... 32 F4
  RAIN/WH L35................. 117 L2
  WGNE/HIN WN2............... 81 H5
Victoria Wy FMBY L37......... 46 F8
  STHP PR8.................... 2 D4
Victor St EV L5............... 113 M5
Victory Av CHTN/BK PR9....... 25 J6
Victory Cl NTHTN L30......... 84 A5
Vienna St EV L5............... 97 H7
Viennese Rd WLTN L25........ 115 K6
Viewpark Cl CHLDW L16....... 115 H6
View Rd RAIN/WH L35.......... 117 L3
Vigo St WGNE/HIN WN2........ 69 H3

Viking Cl LITH L21............. 83 J6
Villa Av WGNW/BIL/O WN6...... 68 B3
Village Cl RUNC WA7........... 150 C5
  WAL/NB CH45................. 95 G7
  WARRS WA4................... 139 G1
Village Cft CHLY/EC PR7....... 31 L2
Village Green Ct
  CL/PREN CH43................ 110 E5
Village Rd BEB CH63........... 127 M7
  CL/PREN CH43................ 127 J1
  HES CH60.................... 141 H6
  WKBY CH48................... 124 E4
Village St NPK/KEN L6......... 13 L2
  RUNC WA7.................... 151 G3
Village Wy HTWN L38.......... 70 B1
  WAL/NB CH45................. 95 G8
Villa Gloria Cl ALL/GAR L19... 130 C5
Villars St WA1 WA1........... 15 H6
Villas Rd MGHL L31............ 73 K3
Villiers Crs ECCL WA10........ 88 B8
Villiers Rd PR/KW L34......... 86 D7
Vincent Cl WARRW/BUR WA5... 120 D5
  RAIN/WH L35................. 117 K1
Vincent Ct CLVPS L1........... 112 F5
Vincent Rd LITH L21........... 83 L4
  RAIN/WH L35................. 117 K1
Vincent St CLB/OSW/ST L13.... 114 B4
  ECCL WA10................... 9 H4
Vincent Wy WCNW/BIL/O WN5.. 67 M5
Vine Gv WGNS/IIMK WN3....... 4 E5
The Vineries WLTN L25........ 131 G2
Vine Gv GTS/LS CH66.......... 163 H5
Vineside Rd WD/CROXPK L12... 98 F8
Vine St CHLY/EC PR7.......... 32 E4
  EHL/KEN L7.................. 113 J5
  RUNC WA7.................... 19 G4
  WDN WA8.................... 16 D5
  WGN WN1.................... 5 H1
Vineyard St ALL/GAR L19...... 131 G4
Vining Rd RAIN/WH L35........ 107 M1
Vining St TOX L8.............. 113 H7
Viola Cl WGNNW/ST WN6....... 55 M3
Viola St BTL L20.............. 7 H8
Viola Wy WGNNW/ST WN6...... 55 M3
Violet Cl GOL/RIS/CU WA3..... 122 E1
Violet Rd BIRK CH41........... 111 H6
  LITH L21.................... 83 K7
Violet St AIMK WN4........... 91 K3
  WDN WA8.................... 16 D6
  WGNS/IIMK WN3.............. 5 K8
Virgil St ECCL WA10........... 8 C4
  EV L5....................... 13 H1
Virginia Av MGHL L31.......... 72 E2
Virginia Gv MGHL L31.......... 72 F2
Virginia Rd WAL/NB CH45...... 95 K4
Virginia St STHP PR8.......... 2 J5
  VAUX/LVPD L3................ 12 D5
Virginia Wy WGNW/BIL/O WN5.. 67 L5
Virgin's La CSBY/BLUN L23..... 71 H6
Viscount Rd WGNW/BIL/O WN5.. 67 M5
Vista Av NEWLW WA12......... 104 C1
Vista Rd NEWLW WA12......... 104 C1
  RUNC WA7.................... 19 H7
Vista Wy NEWLW WA12......... 104 C1
Vitesse Rd ALL/GAR L19....... 131 H7
Vittoria Cl BIRK CH41......... 11 G4
Vittoria St BIRK CH41......... 10 F4
Vivian Av WAL/EG CH44........ 112 A3
Vivian Dr STHP PR8........... 35 J3
Voelas St TOX L8.............. 113 J8
Vogan Av CSBY/BLUN L23...... 83 J2
Volunteer St ECCL WA10....... 8 F3
  FROD/HEL WA6............... 160 E4
Vose Cl WARRW/BUR WA5...... 120 F7
Vronhill Cl TOX L8............ 113 J7
Vulcan Cl CL/PREN CH43....... 111 H5
  NEWLW WA12................. 104 E4
  WARRN/WOL WA2............. 122 B3
Vulcan Dr WGN WN1........... 5 H5
Vulcan Rd WGNW/BIL/O WN5... 67 M5
Vulcan St ALL/GAR L19........ 145 L1
  BTL L20..................... 6 D3
  CHTN/BK PR9................. 3 J4
  CL/PREN CH43................ 111 H5
  VAUX/LVPD L3................ 12 C2
Vyner Cl CL/PREN CH43........ 111 G7
Vyner Rd WAL/NB CH45........ 95 H8
Vyner Rd North CL/PREN CH43. 110 F6
  WLTN L25.................... 115 J8
Vyner Rd South CL/PREN CH43. 110 F7
  WLTN L25.................... 115 J8
Vyrnwy St EV L5............... 97 J7

**W**

Waddicar La MGHL L31......... 73 K8
Waddington Cl
  GOL/RIS/CU WA3............. 93 H5
  WARRN/WOL WA2............. 122 B4
Wadebridge Rd NG/CROX L11... 85 J7
Wadeson Rd ANF/KKDL L4...... 97 M3
Wadeson Wy GOL/RIS/CU WA3.. 106 D6
Wadham Rd BTL L20........... 7 G8
Wagon La RNFD/HAY WA11...... 90 D7
Waine Gv RAIN/WH L35........ 101 J3
Waine St RNFD/HAY WA11...... 90 B7
  STHEL WA9................... 102 F1
Wainfleet Cl WGNS/IIMK WN3.. 79 G2
Wainwright Cl EHL/KEN L7..... 113 L5
Wainwright Gv ALL/GAR L19... 130 D7
Wakefield Crs WGNNW/ST WN6. 56 C6
Wakefield Rd GTS/LS CH66.... 163 G4
  NTHTN L30................... 84 D2
Wakefield St GOL/RIS/CU WA3. 92 C6
  VAUX/LVPD L3................ 13 J4
Walby Cl GR/UP/WCH CH49..... 126 E3
Walcot Pl WGNS/IIMK WN3..... 79 J3
Walden Cl WARRS WA4......... 138 F2
Walden Rd DV/KA/FCH L14..... 114 E2
Waldgrave Rd WAV L15........ 114 D4
Waldgrave Rd WAV L15........ 114 C4
Waldorf St WGNS/IIMK WN3.... 78 F3

Walford Cl BEB CH63.......... 143 H3
Walford Rd AIMK WN4......... 91 L2
Walgarth Dr CHLY/EC PR7..... 32 C6
Walkden Av WGN WN1.......... 68 D3
Walkden Av East WGN WN1.... 68 E3
Walker Av STHEL WA9.......... 118 D2
Walker Cl FMBY L37........... 59 H3
Walker Dr BTL L20............ 83 J6
Walker Pl RF/TRAN CH42....... 127 M2
Walker St BIRK CH41.......... 83 J6
  CHTN/BK PR9................. 113 J2
  HES CH60.................... 141 H6
  NPK/KEN L6.................. 113 J2
  PS/BROM CH62................ 128 D7
  RF/TRAN CH42................ 127 M2
  WARRN/WOL WA2.............. 14 C7
Walker Wy WLT/FAZ L9........ 84 B7
The Walk SPK/HALE L24....... 146 C3
Wallace Av HUY L36........... 116 B1
Wallace Dr HUY L36........... 116 B1
Wallace La WGN WN1.......... 5 J1
Wallace St WDN WA8.......... 16 D3
  WLT/FAZ L9.................. 84 C7
Wallacre Rd WAL/EG CH44..... 111 G1
Wallasey Bridge Rd BIRK CH41. 111 H4
Wallasey Rd WAL/EG CH44.... 111 H1
Wallasey Village WAL/EG CH44. 95 G8
  WAL/NB CH45................. 95 G7
Wallbrook Av WGNW/BIL/O WN5. 77 M4
Wallcroft NSTN CH64.......... 154 C6
Wallcroft St SKEL WN8......... 62 B8
Waller Cl ANF/KKDL L4........ 97 G6
Waller St BTL L20............. 83 J7
Walletts Cl CHLY/EC PR7...... 32 D7
Wallgarth Cl WCNS/IIMK WN3.. 79 G3
Wallgate WGNS/IIMK WN3...... 4 D5
  WGNW/BIL/O WN5............. 4 D5
Wallgate Rd WLTN L25......... 115 H7
Wallgate Wy WLTN L25........ 115 H7
Wallingford Rd
  GR/UP/WCH CH49............. 110 B8
Wallis St WARRS WA4......... 137 K2
Wallrake HES CH60............ 141 H6
Wallsend Ct WDN WA8......... 134 B2
Walls St WGNE/HIN WN2....... 81 L3
Walmer Ct STHP PR8.......... 35 H2
Walmer Rd CSBY/WL L22....... 83 C5
  STHP PR8.................... 35 J2
Walmesley Dr RNFD/HAY WA11. 76 C3
  WGNE/HIN WN2............... 69 K6
Walmesley Rd ECCL WA10...... 88 C3
  WGNW/BIL/O WN1............. 5 G5
Walmsley St EV L5............ 96 E8
  NEWLW WA12................. 104 F1
  WAL/EG CH44................. 95 L8
  WDN WA8.................... 17 H3
Walney Rd WD/CROXPK L12.... 98 F3
  WGNS/IIMK WN3.............. 78 F3
Walnut Av WGN WN1........... 68 F3
  WLT/FAZ L9.................. 97 L2
Walnut Cl WARR WA1.......... 123 C6
Walnut Gv GTS/LS CH66....... 163 H4
  MGHL L31.................... 85 J2
Walnut St STHP PR8........... 3 K9
Walpole Av RAIN/WH L35....... 117 H2
  WGNS/IIMK WN3.............. 79 H2
Walpole Gv WARRN/WOL WA2.. 121 L4
Walpole Rd RUNC WA7......... 149 K7
Walsh Cl EV L5............... 12 F1
  NEWLW WA12................. 91 L8
Walsh Rd DV/KA/FCH L14...... 114 E3
Walsingham Dr RUNC WA7..... 150 F3
Walsingham Rd CHLDW L16.... 115 G5
  WARRW/BUR WA5.............. 111 M2
  WARRW/BUR WA5.............. 120 B8
Walter Gv STHEL WA9.......... 103 H6
Walter Scott Av WGN WN1..... 68 D1
Walters Green Crs
  GOL/RIS/CU WA3............. 92 C3
Walter St AIMK WN4........... 91 M1
  LEIGH WN7...................
  VAUX/LVPD L3................ 96 D8
  WARR WA1.................... 15 L1
  WDN WA8.................... 17 J1
Waltham Av WGNNW/ST WN6... 68 B2
Waltham Ct RUNC WA7......... 151 G1
Waltham Rd NPK/KEN L6....... 97 L2
Walthew House La
  WGNW/BIL/O WN5............. 67 K4
Walthew La WGNE/HIN WN2.... 80 C3
  WGNW/BIL/O WN5............. 67 M3
Waltho Av MGHL L31........... 73 G4
Walton Av WARRW/BUR WA5.... 120 A8
Walton Breck Rd ANF/KKDL L4. 97 J7
Walton Hall Av ANF/KKDL L4... 97 K3
  NG/CROX L11................. 97 M2
Walton Heath Rd WARRS WA4.. 137 K4
Walton La ANF/KKDL L4........ 97 H6
Walton Lea Rd WARRS WA4.... 137 K5
Walton New Rd WARRS WA4.... 137 K5
Walton Pk WLT/FAZ L9......... 97 J1
Walton Rd ANF/KKDL L4........ 97 G5
  ECCL WA10................... 88 F7
  GOL/RIS/CU WA3.............. 107 H2
  WARRS WA4................... 137 L5
Walton St BIRK CH41.......... 11 J6
  CHLY/EC PR7................. 44 C7
  CHTN/BK PR9................. 3 J2
  RUNC WA7.................... 19 H4
Walton V WLT/FAZ L9......... 97 J1
Walton Village ANF/KKDL L4... 97 H3
Wambo La WLTN L25........... 131 H4
Wandsworth Rd NG/CROX L11.. 98 B4
Wandsworth Wy WDN WA8..... 16 D8
Wanes Blades Rd BRSC L40.... 53 G1
Wango La AIN/FAZ L10......... 85 G4
Wanishar La LEIGH WN7....... 49 J8
Wansfell Pl
  WARRN/WOL WA2............. 121 J2
Wantage Vw HUY L36.......... 115 L5
Wapping VAUX/LVPD L3........ 112 E5

Wapshare Rd NG/CROX L11 ........ 98 A4
Warbeck Cl WGNE/HIN WN2 ..... 81 G2
Warbler Cl HLWD L26 ............ 131 H5
Warbreck Moor WLT/FAZ L9 ...... 84 C7
Warbreck Moor WLT/FAZ L9 ...... 84 D6
Warbreck Rd WLT/FAZ L9 ......... 84 C7
Warburton Hey RAIN/WH L35 ..... 117 K1
Warburton St WARRS WA4 ........ 137 M4
Ward Av FMBY L37 ................ 58 F3
Ward Cl WARRW/BUR WA5 ....... 120 D4
Warden St ANF/KKDL L4 .......... 97 G5 13
Wardgate Av
   WD/CROXPK L12 .............. 99 G2 14
Ward Gv RF/TRAN CH42 .......... 128 B4 7
Wardley St WGNW/BIL/O WN5 .... 67 K8
Wardlow Av WGNW/BIL/O WN5.... 67 J5
Wardour St WARRW/BUR WA5 .... 121 G7
Ward Rd CSBY/BLUN L23 .......... 70 C7
Ward St CHLYE PR6 ................ 33 G6
   ECCL WA10 ...................... 9 G3
   PR/KW L34 ...................... 100 F6
   VAUX/LVPD L3 ................... 13 J6
   WGNE/HIN WN2 ................. 69 M6
Wareham Cl WARR WA1 .......... 122 E5
Wareing Rd WLT/FAZ L9 .......... 84 E7
Waresley Crs WLT/FAZ L9 ......... 98 A1
Wargrave Ms NEWLW WA12 ..... 104 E4
Wargrave Rd NEWLW WA12 ...... 104 E4
Warham Rd ANF/KKDL L4 ......... 97 L6
Waring Av RF/TRAN CH42 ........ 127 M3
   STHEL WA9 ..................... 103 K3
   WARRS WA4 ................... 122 B8
The Warings CHLY/EC PR7 ....... 41 M1
Warkworth Cl WDN WA8 ......... 133 L2 10
Warlow Dr LEIGH WN7 ............ 81 M4
Warmington Rd
   DV/KA/FCH L14 ............... 114 E2
Warminster Gv WGNS/IIMK WN3 .. 78 F3
Warncliffe St
   WGNW/BIL/O WN5 ............. 67 M8
Warner Dr ANF/KKDL L4 .......... 97 L5
Warnerville Rd CLB/OSW/ST L13 .114 D4
Warnford St WGN WN1 ............ 68 E3
Warnley Cl WDN WA8 ............ 133 M2 11
Warpers Moss Cl BRSC L40 ........ 39 H8
Warper's Moss La BRSC L40 ....... 39 J8
Warren Cl FROD/HEL WA6 ........ 160 F7
   GTS/LS CH66 .................. 162 F2
   STHP PR8 ........................ 2 B7
Warren Cft RUNC WA7 ........... 150 E4
Warren Dr CL/PREN CH43 ........ 110 E7
   GTS/LS CH66 .................. 156 A6
   NEWLW WA12 ................. 105 H1
   WAL/NB CH45 ................... 95 H5
   WARRS WA4 .................... 137 L5
Warren Gn FMBY L37 .............. 58 F1
Warren Hey BEB CH63 ............ 143 J4
Warren House Rd CSBY/WL L22 .. 82 D3
Warrenhouse Rd
   NWD/KWIPK L33 ............... 86 C1
Warren La WARR WA1 ............ 122 F5
Warren La CHTN/BK PR9 .......... 25 J5
   CSBY/BLUN L23 ................. 70 C8
   HOY CH47 ...................... 108 C6
   WARRN/WOL WA2 ............. 121 M4
   WARRS WA4 .................... 137 L6
The Warren GR/UP/WCH CH49 .. 110 D8
Warren Wy HES CH60 ............. 140 F4
Warrington Av EP CH65 .......... 163 K3
Warrington La WGN WN1 .......... 5 L4
Warrington New Rd STHEL WA9 .. 9 K6
Warrington Old Rd STHEL WA9 ... 9 J7
Warrington Rd AIMK WN4 ....... 91 K3
   GOL/RIS/CU WA3 .............. 105 K2
   GOL/RIS/CU WA3 .............. 107 H2 4
   LYMM WA13 ................... 139 K1
   NEWLW WA12 ................... 92 C7
   RAIN/WH L35 .................. 101 G8
   RUNC WA7 ..................... 150 A3 9
   WARRS WA4 .................... 137 H1
   WARRW/BUR WA5 ............. 135 M1
   WDN WA8 ...................... 17 G4
   WGNE/HIN WN2 ................. 80 C3
   WGNS/IIMK WN3 ................. 5 H1
Warrington St BIRK CH41 ........ 11 J9
Warton Cl WARRW/BUR WA5 .. 136 C2 1
   WLTN L25 ..................... 131 L3
Warton Pl CHLY/EC PR7 .......... 32 C5
Warton St BTL L20 ................. 83 J7
Warwick Av AIMK WN4 ......... 91 M3 2
   CSBY/BLUN L23 ................. 82 F2
   NEWLW WA12 ................. 104 F3
   WARRW/BUR WA5 ............... 14 A1
Warwick Cl CL/PREN CH43 ....... 10 F7
   HUY L36 ....................... 116 C2
   NSTN CH64 .................... 153 G8
   STHP PR8 ........................ 35 K2
Warwick Dr WAL/NB CH45 ........ 95 L7
   WKBY CH48 ................... 124 E5
Warwick Rd BTL L20 ............... 7 K3
   CHLY/EC PR7 ................... 30 E6
   GR/UP/WCH CH49 ............ 110 B7
   HUY L36 ....................... 116 C2
   WGNE/HIN WN2 ................ 57 L8 1
Warwick St CHLY/EC PR7 ......... 44 B7
   ECCL WA10 ...................... 8 A6
   STHP PR8 ........................ 35 K1
   TOX L8 ......................... 113 G8
Wasdale Av MGHL L31 ............ 73 H3
   RNFD/HAY WA11 ............... 89 K5
Wasdale Rd AIMK WN4 .......... 79 J5
   WLT/FAZ L9 ..................... 84 C8
Washbrook Av
   CL/PREN CH43 ................ 110 E5 9
Washbrook Cl ECCL WA10 ....... 101 K1
Washbrook Wy ORM L39 .......... 63 G1
Washington Dr
   WARRW/BUR WA5 ............. 120 D7
Washington La CHLY/EC PR7 ..... 32 A7
Washington Pde BTL L20 ........... 7 G3
Wash La WARRS WA4 ............ 138 A3
Washway La ECCL WA10 .......... 89 J6
Wasley Cl WARRN/WOL WA2 .... 122 B2
Wastdale Ct MOR/LEA CH46 .... 109 L4 8
Wastdale Dr MOR/LEA CH46 .... 109 L4
Wastdale Ms MOR/LEA CH46 .... 109 L4 2
Wastle Bridge Rd HUY L36 ...... 100 A8
Watchyard La FMBY L37 .......... 59 J2

Waterbeck Cl WGN WN1 ........... 5 L2
Waterbridge Ct WARRS WA4 .... 137 M5
Waterdale Crs STHEL WA9 ....... 102 F6
Waterhouse St EV L5 ............. 13 L1
Waterfield Pl STHEL WA9 ....... 102 F6 16
Water Dr WGNNW/ST WN6 ...... 56 D6
Waterfield Cl BEB CH63 .......... 127 M8
Waterfoot Av STHP PR8 .......... 47 K2 3
Waterford Dr NSTN CH64 ........ 153 J6
Waterford Rd CL/PREN CH43 ... 111 G8
Waterford Wy RUNC WA7 ....... 150 E7
Watergate La WLTN L25 ......... 131 K3
Watergate Wy WLTN L25 ........ 131 K5
Waterhouse Cl NPK/KEN L6 ..... 97 K7 2
Waterhouse St EV L5 ............. 13 L1
Waterland La STHEL WA9 ....... 103 H3
Water La CHTN/BK PR9 ........... 22 F8
   RAIN/WH L35 .................. 132 F1
Waterloo Cl CSBY/WL L22 ........ 83 G5 5
Waterloo La FROD/HEL WA6 .... 167 L4
Waterloo Pl BIRK CH41 .......... 11 K7
Waterloo Rd CSBY/WL L22 ....... 83 G5
   RUNC WA7 ...................... 18 F3 1
   STHP PR8 ........................ 35 G4 1
   VAUX/LVPD L3 ................... 12 C2
   WAL/NB CH45 ................... 95 K4
   WDN WA8 ........................ 16 C9
Waterloo St CHLY/EC PR7 ....... 32 E4 7
   CHLY/EC PR7 ................... 32 F4 3
   ECCL WA10 ...................... 8 F5
   WAV L15 ....................... 114 C6
   WGNNW/ST WN6 ................. 4 A1
Watermede
   WGNW/BIL/O WN5 ............. 78 A2 1
Waterpark Cl CL/PREN CH43 ... 127 H4 6
Waterpark Dr STBRV L28 ......... 99 H5
Waterpark Rd CL/PREN CH43 ... 127 J4
Watersedge FROD/HEL WA6 .... 160 F3
Waterside NTHTN L30 ............ 72 A8
   STHEL WA9 ....................... 9 K3
   WARRS WA4 .................... 137 M5
Waterside Av RUNC WA7 ....... 150 E7
Waterside Pk HUY L36 .......... 115 M4
Waters Reach WGN WN1 .......... 5 L4
Water St BIRK CH41 .............. 11 L5
   CHLY/EC PR7 ................... 32 E5
   CHLY/EC PR7 ................... 44 C7
   CLVP L2 ......................... 12 E7
   CSBY/BLUN L23 ................. 71 K7
   CSBY/WL L22 ................... 83 G5 3
   ECCL WA10 ...................... 8 F5
   NEWLW WA12 ................. 104 E1 3
   PS/BROM CH62 ................ 128 D7
   RUNC WA7 ....................... 19 H2
   VAUX/LVPD L3 ................... 12 D7
   WAL/EG CH44 ................. 111 M4
   WDN WA8 ........................ 16 C8
   WGN WN1 ......................... 4 F3
Water Tower Rd NSTN CH64 .... 153 G3
Waterway Av NTHTN L30 ......... 84 D2
Waterways WARRW/BUR WA5 .. 120 F7
Waterworks Dr
   NEWLW WA12 ................. 105 H1 1
Waterworks La GTS/LS CH66 .. 155 C4
Waterworks Rd ORM L39 ......... 51 J7
Waterworks St BTL L20 ............ 7 J4
Watery La FROD/HEL WA6 ...... 161 G8
   STHEL WA9 ..................... 103 G5
   WARRS WA4 ................... 105 G7
Watford Rd ANF/KKDL L4 ........ 97 K6
Watkin Cl NTHTN L30 ............ 84 D4
Watkins Av NEWLW WA12 ..... 104 B3
Watkinson St CLVPS L1 ......... 112 F6
Watkinson Wy WDN WA8 ........ 17 G3
Watkin St WARRN/WOL WA2 ... 14 E1
   WGN WN1 ......................... 4 F3
Watling Av LITH L21 .............. 83 J4
Watling Wy RAIN/WH L35 ...... 101 J8
Watmough St EV L5 ............... 13 K2
Watson Av AIMK WN4 .......... 91 L2 7
   GOL/RIS/CU WA3 .............. 92 B4
Watson St BIRK CH41 ............. 11 H3
Watton Beck Cl MGHL L31 ...... 73 H3
Watton Cl WARRS WA4 ......... 138 E2
   WD/CROXPK L12 ................ 99 J3 3
Watts Cl NWD/KWIPK L33 ....... 86 C1
Watts La BTL L20 ................. 84 A7
Wauchope St WAV L15 ......... 114 A5
   WDN WA8 ...................... 133 L5
Wavell Av CHTN/BK PR9 ......... 25 K6
   WDN WA8 ...................... 133 L5
Wavell Rd HUY L36 .............. 116 A1 2
Waverley SKEL WN8 .............. 64 F4
Waverley Av WARRS WA4 ..... 137 M5
Waverley Ct WGNS/IIMK WN3 .. 78 F2 3
Waverley Gv RF/TRAN CH42 ... 127 L3 3
Waverley Rd AIG/SPK L17 ....... 129 L1
   CSBY/BLUN L23 ................. 82 E2
   GOL/RIS/CU WA3 .............. 92 F4
   HOY CH47 ...................... 108 E6
   WGNE/HIN WN2 ................ 69 L8 3
Waverley St BTL L20 .............. 6 F4
   STHP PR8 ........................ 2 F3
Waverton Av CL/PREN CH43 ... 127 C3
Waverton Rd GTS/LS CH66 .... 156 A8
Wavertree Av CLB/OSW/ST L13 . 114 C4
   WDN WA8 ........................ 16 C3
Wavertree Bvd EHL/KEN L7 ... 113 M4
Wavertree Bvd South
   EHL/KEN L7 ................... 114 A4
Wavertree Gn WAV L15 ......... 114 C6
Wavertree Nook Rd WAV L15 ... 114 E5
Wavertree Rd EHL/KEN L7 ..... 113 K4
   WAV L15 ....................... 113 M5 5
Wayfarers Dr NEWLW WA12 ... 105 J3
Waylands Dr WLTN L25 ......... 131 K6
Wayte Cl LYMM WA13 ......... 139 M3
Wayville Cl CALD/MH L18 ...... 130 D3
Waywell Cl WARRN/WOL WA2 .. 122 B2
Weardale Rd WAV L15 ......... 114 A7 7
Wearhead Cl GOL/RIS/CU WA3 .. 92 C6 3
Weasdale Cl STHEL WA9 ....... 102 F6 3
Weaste La WARRS WA4 ......... 138 F3
Weates Cl WDN WA8 ........... 135 G2
Weaver Av BRSC L40 ............. 39 H8

   NWD/KWIPK L33 ............... 74 B7
   WARRS WA4 .................... 137 K2
Weaver Crs FROD/HEL WA6 .... 160 F4
Weaver Gv LEIGH WN7 ......... 93 L1 3
   STHEL WA9 ..................... 103 J2
Weaver La FROD/HEL WA6 .... 160 D3
   WARRS WA4 .................... 136 A2
Weaver Rd EP CH65 .............. 20 D9
   FROD/HEL WA6 ................ 160 F4
   GOL/RIS/CU WA3 .............. 107 J3 2
   WARRS WA4 .................... 149 J7
Weaver's Brow CHLYE PR6 ...... 33 H7
Weaverside Av RUNC WA7 ... 161 H1 14
Weavers La MGHL L31 ............ 73 H7
Weaver St WLT/FAZ L9 ......... 97 H2 7
Webb Cl EHL/KEN L7 .......... 113 L4 10
Webb Dr WARRW/BUR WA5 ... 104 B7
Webber Rd NWD/KWIPK L33 ... 86 D4
Webb St EHL/KEN L7 ........... 113 L6
   STHEL WA9 ..................... 102 F4
Webster Av BTL L20 ............... 7 L2
   WAL/EG CH44 .................. 95 M8
Webster Dr KKBY L32 ............. 86 A3
Webster Rd WAV L15 .......... 113 M6
Websters La GTS/LS CH66 ..... 163 H3
Webster's St LITH L21 ........... 83 K7
   VAUX/LVPD L3 .................. 13 G5 3
Weddell Cl WARRW/BUR WA5 . 120 F6
Wedge Av RNFD/HAY WA11 ..... 90 C8
Wedgewood Dr
   WGNNW/ST WN6 ............. 67 M2 3
Wedgewood Dr WDN WA8 .... 134 D1
Wednesbury Dr
   WARRW/BUR WA5 ............. 120 B7
Weedon Av WARRW/BUR WA5 . 120 B7
Weightman Gv WLT/FAZ L9 .... 84 C7 7
Weir La WARR WA1 .............. 123 G7
Weir St WARRS WA4 ............ 137 J4 2
Welbeck Av CALD/MH L18 .... 114 B8 13
   NEWLW WA12 ................. 104 F3
Welbeck Rd AIMK WN4 .......... 79 K8
   STHP PR8 ........................ 35 H1
   WGNS/IIMK WN3 ................. 79 G2
Welbeck Ter STHP PR8 ........... 35 H1
Welbourne Rd CHLDW L16 ..... 114 E4
Weld Av CHLY/EC PR7 ........... 32 E8
Weldbank La CHLY/EC PR7 ..... 32 E8
Weldbank St CHLY/EC PR7 .... 32 E8 3
Weld Blundell Av MGHL L31 .... 72 D1
Weld Dr FMBY L37 ............... 58 F1
Weldon Dr ORM L39 ............. 63 H1
Weldon Gv WGN WN1 ........... 69 G3
Weldon St ANF/KKDL L4 ........ 97 H3
Weld Pde STHP PR8 ............... 2 D9
Weld Rd CSBY/BLUN L23 ........ 82 E2
   STHP PR8 ........................ 2 B7
Welfield Pl TOX L8 .............. 129 J1
Welford Av CL/PREN CH43 .... 127 H3
   GOL/RIS/CU WA3 .............. 92 C6
Welland Cl HLWD L26 .......... 132 A8
Welland Rd AIMK WN4 .......... 80 A8
   BEB CH63 ..................... 127 M8 8
Wellbank Dr HLWD L26 ....... 132 C4 8
Wellbrae Cl
   GR/UP/WCH CH49 ............ 109 M8 3
Wellbrook Cl RUNC WA7 ....... 150 E8 8
   SPK/HALE L24 ................. 146 F1 8
Wellbrooke Cl AIMK WN4 ...... 91 L2 3
Wellbrook Gn SPK/HALE L24 .. 146 F1 8
Well Brow Rd ANF/KKDL L4 .... 97 K3
Wellcroft Rd HUY L36 .......... 116 A1
Wellcross Rd SKEL WN8 ......... 66 D7
Weller St TOX L8 ................. 113 H8
Weller Wy TOX L8 ............... 129 J1
Wellesbourne Pl
   NG/CROX L11 ................... 98 C3 3
Wellesbourne Rd NG/CROX L11 . 98 C2
Wellesley Av EP CH65 ............ 20 D5
Wellesley Cl NEWLW WA12 .... 91 K8 1
   WGNW/BIL/O WN5 ............. 68 A5
Wellesley Rd TOX L8 ........... 129 J1 22
   WAL/EG CH44 ................. 111 K1
Wellfield RNFD/HAY WA11 ..... 88 C1
   RUNC WA7 ..................... 151 G8
   WDN WA8 ...................... 134 C1
Wellfield Av KKBY L32 .......... 86 A4
Wellfield La BRSC L40 ............ 63 L3
Wellfield Rd GOL/RIS/CU WA3 .. 107 G1
   WGNE/HIN WN2 ................ 81 J1 8
   WGNNW/ST WN6 ................ 68 B1
   WLT/FAZ L9 ..................... 97 J1
Wellfield St WARRW/BUR WA5 . 121 G8
Wellgreen Rd WLTN L25 ....... 115 H6
Wellham Rd WGNS/IIMK WN3 .. 79 K2
Wellington Av WAV L15 ....... 113 M6
Wellington Cl AIN/FAZ L10 .... 84 E2 1
   EP CH65 ........................ 20 D4
   WARRN/WOL WA2 ........... 122 D3 8
Wellington Flds WAV L15 ..... 113 M7 8
Wellington Ga SPK/HALE L24 .. 148 A3 8
   WGNS/IIMK WN3 ................. 5 H9
Wellington Rd BEB CH63 ...... 128 C7
   CL/PREN CH43 .................. 10 A8
   EP CH65 ........................ 20 B6
   LITH L21 ......................... 83 J6 3
   TOX L8 ......................... 129 H1
   WAL/NB CH45 ................... 95 K4
   WAV L15 ....................... 113 M6
Wellington Rd North EP CH65 .. 20 D5
Wellington St ALL/GAR L19 .... 130 E8
   CHLY/EC PR7 ................... 32 E4 3
   CSBY/WL L22 ................... 82 F4
   NEWLW WA12 ................. 104 C2
   RUNC WA7 ....................... 2 E5
   STHP PR8 ........................ 2 E5
   VAUX/LVPD L3 ................... 13 G3
   WARR WA1 ..................... 15 G6
   WDN WA8 ........................ 16 C8
   WGNS/IIMK WN3 ................. 5 H4
Wellington Ter BIRK CH41 ...... 11 H8
   ECCL WA10 ...................... 9 H9
   RF/TRAN CH42 ................ 11 H9
   TOX L8 ......................... 113 J8 2
Well La BEB CH63 ............... 127 M7
   BTL L20 ........................... 7 J4

   GR/UP/WCH CH49 ............. 125 L1
   HES CH60 ...................... 141 J7
   NSTN CH64 .................... 153 H8
   ORM L39 ........................ 49 G7
   RF/TRAN CH42 ............... 128 A3
   WARRW/BUR WA5 ............ 136 A2
   WLTN L25 ..................... 115 H6
Wells Av WGNW/BIL/O WN5 .... 77 M8
Wells Cl GTS/LS CH66 .......... 163 G5 3
   WARR WA1 ..................... 122 D5
Wells Dr WGNE/HIN WN2 ....... 69 H3
Wells St WAV L15 .............. 114 B6 8
Wellstead Cl WAV L15 .......... 114 C5
Wellstead Rd WAV L15 ......... 114 C5
Well St WGN WN1 .................. 5 K3
Wellwood Rd GTS/LS CH66 ... 156 A6
Welsby Cl WARRN/WOL WA2 .. 122 B2
Welshampton Cl GTS/LS CH66 . 162 F3
Welshpool Cl
   WARRW/BUR WA5 ............. 120 F2
Welsh Rd GTS/LS CH66 ......... 155 J4
Welton Av GR/UP/WCH CH49 . 110 B8
Welton Cl SPK/HALE L24 ...... 146 F2 2
Welton Gn SPK/HALE L24 ..... 146 F2 1
Welton Rd PS/BROM CH62 .... 143 M3
Welwyn Av STHP PR8 ............ 34 F7
Welwyn Cl STHEL WA9 ......... 102 A7
   WARRS WA4 .................... 138 E2
Wembley Gdns WLT/FAZ L9 .... 84 B7
Wembley Rd CALD/MH L18 ... 114 D8 8
   CSBY/BLUN L23 ................ 83 H2 1
Wendell St TOX L8 .............. 113 L6
Wendover Av AIG/SPK L17 .... 129 L2
Wendover Cl CL/PREN CH43 .. 126 F1
Wendron Rd NG/CROX L11 ..... 85 M8 3
Wenger Rd WDN WA8 .......... 118 D8
Wenlock Cl HOR/BR BL6 ........ 45 L7
   WARR WA1 ..................... 122 C5
Wenlock Dr HLWD L26 ......... 132 A6
Wenlock Gdns GTS/LS CH66 .. 163 H3
Wenlock Rd WGNE/HIN WN2 .. 80 F1
Wenlock La ANF/KKDL L4 ....... 97 K6
   RUNC WA7 ..................... 161 J1
   WGNE/HIN WN2 ................ 69 M8
Wenlock St WGNE/HIN WN2 .. 80 F1 3
Wenning Av MGHL L31 .......... 73 G3
Wennington Rd CHTN/BK PR9 . 25 H5
Wensley Av HLWD L26 ........ 132 A6
Wensleydale WLT/FAZ L9 ...... 84 C6 3
Wensleydale Av
   PS/BROM CH62 ................ 144 A8
   RAIN/WH L35 ................. 117 M2
Wensleydale Cl MGHL L31 ..... 72 D3 3
   WARRW/BUR WA5 ............. 120 B5
Wensley Rd GOL/RIS/CU WA3 .. 93 G6
   WLT/FAZ L9 ..................... 84 C6
Wentworth Av WAL/NB CH45 .. 95 K6
   WARR WA1 ..................... 122 D6
Wentworth Cl CL/PREN CH43 . 126 F1
   STHP PR8 ........................ 47 L1
   WDN WA8 ...................... 118 C3 2
Wentworth Dr BEB CH63 ..... 143 K8
   EV L5 .......................... 13 M1
Wentworth Gv HUY L36 ...... 115 K3 1
Wentworth Rd AIMK WN4 ..... 79 H8
Wernbrook Cl CL/PREN CH43 . 126 F1
Wernbrook Rd ANF/KKDL L4 .. 97 L6
Wervin Cl CL/PREN CH43 ..... 127 C3
Wervin Rd CL/PREN CH43 .... 127 G3
   KKBY L32 ....................... 85 M4
Wescoe Cl WGNW/BIL/O WN5 . 67 G8 3
Wesley Av RNFD/HAY WA11 ... 91 G6 3
   WAL/EG CH44 ................... 95 L8
Wesley Cl NSTN CH64 .......... 152 F6
Wesley Gv WAL/EG CH44 ..... 112 A2 3
Wesley St CSBY/WL L22 ......... 82 F5
   STHP PR8 ......................... 3 C5
   WGNW/BIL/O WN5 ............. 78 F1
Wessex Cl WARR WA1 ......... 123 C6 7
   WGN WN1 ........................ 56 D4 3
Wessex Rd WGNW/BIL/O WN5 . 67 M4
West Albert Rd AIG/SPK L17 .. 129 K1
West Av GOL/RIS/CU WA3 ...... 92 D4
   WARRN/WOL WA2 ............ 121 K5
   WARRS WA4 .................... 137 L4
West Bank CHLY/EC PR7 ........ 32 E5 13
Westbank Av WAL/NB CH45 ... 95 L6 3
West Bank Rd EHL/KEN L7 ... 114 A3
Westbank Rd RF/TRAN CH42 .. 127 L2
West Bank St WDN WA8 ........ 16 C9
Westbourne Av CSBY/BLUN L23 . 71 K7
Westbourne Gdns STHP PR8 ..... 2 A9
Westbourne Gv WKBY CH48 .. 143 J8
Westbourne Rd CHLY/EC PR7 . 32 D7 3
   CL/PREN CH43 .................. 10 E7
   STHP PR8 ........................ 34 F1
   WAL/EG CH44 ................. 111 H1
   WARRS WA4 .................... 137 K6
   WKBY CH48 ................... 124 C3
Westbridge Ms WGN WN1 ........ 4 F5
Westbrook Av PR/KW L34 ..... 100 D7
   WARRS WA4 ................... 137 M3
Westbrook Centre
   WARRW/BUR WA5 ............. 120 E4
Westbrook Crs
   WARRW/BUR WA5 ............. 120 D4
Westbrook Rd MOR/LEA CH46 . 109 L4
   WLTN L25 ..................... 115 L8
Westbrook Wy
   WARRW/BUR WA5 ............. 120 C4
Westbury Av WGNS/IIMK WN3 .. 78 F3
Westbury Cl AIG/SPK L17 ...... 129 L4
   WARR WA1 ..................... 122 C5
Westbury St BIRK CH41 ......... 11 J9 3
Westcliffe Rd STHP PR8 ........... 2 B3
   WD/CROXPK L12 ................ 98 C6
West Cl CL/PREN CH43 ......... 110 F8
   PR/KW L34 .................... 101 J6
Westcombe Rd ANF/KKDL L4 .. 97 L6 3
   NPK/KEN L6 .................... 97 L6
Westcott Dr WGNS/IIMK WN3 .. 78 E1
Westcott Rd ANF/KKDL L4 ..... 97 K7
Westcott Wy
   CL/PREN CH43 ................ 126 F1 11
Westdale Rd RF/TRAN CH42 .. 128 A3
   WARR WA1 ..................... 122 C6
   WAV L15 ....................... 114 B5

Westdale Vw WAV L15 ......... 114 B5 5
West Dene SKEL WN8 ............ 53 K3 2
West Derby Rd CLB/OSW/ST L13 .98 A7
   NPK/KEN L6 .................... 113 K1
West Derby St VAUX/LVPD L3 .. 13 M6
West Derby Village
   WD/CROXPK L12 ............... 98 D6
West Dr GR/UP/WCH CH49 ... 110 C8
   HES CH60 ...................... 141 J6
   NSTN CH64 .................... 152 F7
   WARRW/BUR WA5 ............ 136 D1
Westend CHLY/EC PR7 ........... 42 F4
West End Gv RNFD/HAY WA11 . 90 B7
West End Rd RNFD/HAY WA11 . 90 B7
Westenra Av EP CH65 .......... 156 B7
Westerdale Dr CHTN/BK PR9 .. 23 K8
Western Av HUY L36 ............ 115 K2
   PS/BROM CH62 ................ 143 M1
   SPK/HALE L24 ................. 146 E2
Western Dr ALL/GAR L19 ...... 130 C6
Westerton Rd WD/CROXPK L12 . 99 G7
Westfield Av AIMK WN4 .......... 91 J1
   DV/KA/FCH L14 ............... 115 G3
Westfield Crs RUNC WA7 ....... 18 E6
Westfield Dr WD/CROXPK L12 . 99 G2
Westfield Gv WGN WN1 ......... 68 D2
Westfield Ms RUNC WA7 ........ 18 E5
Westfield Rd WARRS WA4 ....... 18 D6
   WAL/EG CH44 ................. 111 M4
   WLT/FAZ L9 ..................... 84 A7
Westfields LEY/BBR PR5 ......... 29 J3
Westfield St ECCL WA10 .......... 8 B3
Westfield Wk KKBY L32 ........ 85 K4 2
Westford Rd WARRS WA4 ..... 137 J4 3
Westgate SKEL WN8 .............. 64 F4 3
Westgate Dr
   WGNW/BIL/O WN5 ............. 66 F8 3
Westgate Rd PS/BROM CH62 .. 143 K1
   WAV L15 ....................... 114 C8 12
West Gv HES CH60 .............. 141 H5
Westhaven Crs ORM L39 ......... 62 E5
Westhay Crs
   GOL/RIS/CU WA3 .............. 107 J8 3
Westhead Av GOL/RIS/CU WA3 . 93 G5
Westhead Cl NWD/KWIPK L33 . 86 C4 3
Westhead Rd LEY/BBR PR5 ..... 29 K3
Westhead Wk NWD/KWIPK L33 . 86 B3
West Heath Gv LYMM WA13 ... 139 L1
Westhoughton Rd CHLY/EC PR7 . 44 B4
Westhouse Cl BEB CH63 ...... 143 L8 3
West Hyde LYMM WA13 ....... 139 L2
Westinghouse Cl
   WGNNW/ST WN6 ................. 4 B4
West Kirby Rd RF/TRAN CH42 . 109 L8
Westlake Gv WGNE/HIN WN2 .. 81 K1
Westlands Cl NSTN CH64 ...... 153 H4
West La FMBY L37 ............... 47 H7
   RUNC WA7 ..................... 150 A6
Westleigh La LEIGH WN7 ....... 81 M3
Westleigh Pl STHEL WA9 ...... 102 E8 3
Westlock Methodist
   WGNNW/ST WN6 ................. 4 D8
West Mains SPK/HALE L24 .... 147 J2
Westmead WGNNW/ST WN6 ... 56 A5
West Meade MGHL L31 .......... 72 D3
Westminster Av NTHTN L30 .... 84 A1
Westminster Cl WARRS WA4 .. 138 E3
   WDN WA8 ...................... 133 K5 1
Westminster Dr
   PS/BROM CH62 ................ 143 M7
   RNFD/HAY WA11 ................ 91 H7
   STHP PR8 ........................ 34 C8
Westminster Gv EP CH65 ........ 20 C3
   PR/KW L34 .................... 100 C8 3
Westminster Pl CHLY/EC PR7 .. 30 C5
   WARR WA1 ...................... 14 E5
Westminster Rd ANF/KKDL L4 .. 97 K8
   BTL L20 ......................... 7 K8
   CHLY/EC PR7 ................... 32 E6 13
   EP CH65 ........................ 20 C2
   WAL/EG CH44 ................. 111 K1 2
Westminster St
   WGNW/BIL/O WN5 ............. 68 B7 13
Westmoorland St WGN WN1 ..... 5 J2
Westmoreland Pl EV L5 .......... 96 F8 3
Westmoreland Rd STHP PR8 ..... 3 K8
   WAL/NB CH45 ................... 95 L6 13
Westmorland Av NTHTN L30 .. 83 L2 3
   WDN WA8 ........................ 16 E1
Westmorland Rd HUY L36 .... 116 A3
West Mt WGN WN1 ............... 68 F3
   WGNW/BIL/O WN5 ............. 67 H7
West Oakhill Pk
   CLB/OSW/ST L13 ............. 114 C3
Weston Crs RUNC WA7 ........ 149 H7
Weston Gv MGHL L31 ............ 72 F7
Weston Pk WGNNW/ST WN6 .. 67 M2 3
Weston Point Expy RUNC WA7 . 18 C5
West Orchard La WLT/FAZ L9 .. 84 F5
Westover Rd MGHL L31 .......... 72 E4
   WARR WA1 ..................... 122 B6
West Park Dr GTS/LS CH66 ... 163 H5 12
West Park Rd ECCL WA10 ........ 8 B7
West Quay Rd
   WARRN/WOL WA2 ............ 121 H2
West Rd CL/PREN CH43 ....... 110 F8
   DV/KA/FCH L14 ............... 114 E3
   EP CH65 ........................ 20 D8
   RUNC WA7 ...................... 18 A9
   SPK/HALE L24 ................. 131 M8
Westry Cl MOR/LEA CH46 .... 109 K5
West Side STHEL WA9 ............. 9 L7
West Side Av RNFD/HAY WA11 . 90 C7
West St CHLY/EC PR7 ........... 32 E6
   ECCL WA10 .................... 101 M4
   PR/KW L34 .................... 100 E7
   STHP PR8 ......................... 3 K8
   WAL/NB CH45 ................... 95 K8 3
   WARRN/WOL WA2 ............. 69 J5
   WGNE/HIN WN2 ................ 69 J5
   WGNE/HIN WN2 ................ 81 K2
West Ter CHLYE PR6 ............. 31 M1
West Vw NSTN CH64 ........... 153 G7
West Vw HUY L36 .............. 116 D3
   SKEL WN8 ....................... 53 K3
   WARRN/WOL WA2 ........... 122 L4 3
West View Av HUY L36 ........ 116 D3

Westview Cl CL/PREN CH43 .. 126 F1 12
Westward Ho WKBY CH48 124 F7
Westward Vw AIG/SPK L17 129 J2
CSBY/WL L22 82 D3 4
West Wy CHLY/EC PR7 32 C3
MOR/LEA CH46 110 A4
Westway CL/PREN CH43 126 F1
GR/UP/WCH CH49 125 M1
HES CH60 141 H7
HTWN L38 70 B1
MGHL L31 72 E3
WAV L15 114 D5
Westwell Rd CHLYE PR6 32 F4 4
Westwick Pl HUY L36 115 K2 2
Westwood RUNC WA7 150 E4
Westwood Cl STHP PR8 36 A2
Westwood Ct NSTN CH64 153 G3
Westwood Gv WAL/EG CH44 111 J1 3
Westwood La WGNS/IIMK WN3 5 G9
Westwood Rd CALD/MH L18 130 E5
CL/PREN CH43 110 E7
WGNS/IIMK WN3 4 E7
Westy La WARRS WA4 15 M8
Wetheral Cl WGNE/HIN WN2 81 L2
Wetherby Av WAL/EG CH44 95 G8 5
Wetherby Cl NEWLW WA12 91 L8 4
Wetherby Ct HUY L36 99 L8 3
Wetherby Wy GTS/LS CH66 155 K8
Wethersfield Rd CL/PREN CH43 .. 127 G1
Wetstone La WKBY CH48 124 E4
Wexford Av SPK/HALE L24 147 M3
Wexford Cl CL/PREN CH43 127 G1
Wexford Rd CL/PREN CH43 127 H1
Wexham Gdns WGNE/HIN WN2 80 C2
Wexwood Gv RAIN/WH L35 117 H3 7
Weybourne Cl
GR/UP/WCH CH49 110 C6
Weybourne Dr WGNS/IIMK WN3 .. 79 G2
Weybridge Cl WARRS WA4 138 A6
Weyman Av RAIN/WH L35 117 G2
Weymoor Cl BEB CH63 143 H3 6
Weymouth Av STHEL WA9 103 H4
Weymouth Cl CHLDW L16 115 H5 5
RUNC WA7 151 G7 4
Weymouth Dr WGNE/HIN WN2 81 J1
Weymouth Rd
WARRW/BUR WA5 104 B7
Whaley La PEN/TH CH61 126 B7
Whalley Av ECCL WA10 89 G6
RNFD/HAY WA11 76 B7 2
Whalley Cl WGNS/IIMK WN3 79 J2
Whalley Ct NTHTN L30 83 M1
Whalley Dr FMBY L37 59 J3
ORM L39 62 E5
Whalley Gv LEIGH WN7 81 M4
WDN WA8 134 F2
Whalley Rd CHLY/EC PR7 42 A1
RF/TRAN CH42 11 G8
Whalleys Rd SKEL WN8 53 J8
Whalley St CHLY/EC PR7 32 E6 16
TOX L8 129 H1 15
WARR WA1 15 H4
Wharf BRSC L40 50 B1
Wharfdale Cl
WARRW/BUR WA5 120 C6 1
Wharfedale RUNC WA7 150 D7 4
Wharfedale Av RF/TRAN CH42 127 K3
Wharfedale Dr PS/BROM CH62 .. 144 B8
RAIN/WH L35 117 M2
Wharfedale Rd WAL/NB CH45 .. 95 H7 1
Wharfe La EP CH65 156 C6
Wharford La RUNC WA7 151 G2
Wharf Rd NEWLW WA12 104 A3
Wharf St PS/BROM CH62 128 D8
WARR WA1 15 H7
Wharmby Rd RNFD/HAY WA11 91 G7
Wharncliffe Rd
CLB/OSW/ST L13 114 C2
Wharncliffe St
WGNE/HIN WN2 69 M8 29
Wharton Cl GR/UP/WCH CH49 109 M7
Whatcroft Cl RUNC WA7 149 M7
Wheatacre SKEL WN8 65 G5
Wheat Cft WARRW/BUR WA5 .. 120 E7 3
Wheatcroft Rd CALD/MH L18 130 E3
Wheatear Cl NTHLY L27 132 A1
Wheatfield Cl GTS/LS CH66 162 E2
MOR/LEA CH46 110 B6 2
NTHTN L30 84 D2 2
Wheatfield Rd WDN WA8 117 L8
Wheatfield Vw LITH L21 83 K3 4
Wheat Hill Rd NTHLY L27 116 A6
Wheatland Cl STHEL WA9 118 E1 19
Wheatland Rd HES CH60 141 L6
Wheatlands RUNC WA7 150 A4
Wheatlands Cl NTHLY L27 115 M7
Wheat La BRSC L40 52 C2
Wheatlea Rd WGNS/IIMK WN3 79 H4
Wheatley Av BTL L20 84 A8
NEWLW WA12 91 L8
Wheatsheaf Av STHEL WA9 102 F7
Wheatsheaf Wk
WGNNW/ST WN6 55 M4
Wheeler Dr MGHL L31 85 K2
Wheldrake Cl GTS/LS CH66 155 K8
Whelley WGN WN1 69 G3
WGNE/HIN WN2 69 H3
Whernside WDN WA8 133 L3
Whetstone Hey GTS/LS CH66 155 M8
Whetstone La BIRK CH41 11 H8
RF/TRAN CH42 127 M3
Whickham Cl WDN WA8 134 B2 5
Whimberry Cl CHLYE PR6 33 G5 11
Whimbrel Av NEWLW WA12 104 E2
Whimbrel Cl RUNC WA7 150 B8
Whimbrel Pk HLWD L26 132 A4
Whinbury Ct STHEL WA9 118 E1 20
Whinchat Av NEWLW WA12 104 E1
Whinchat Dr GOL/RIS/CU WA3 123 H2
Whinfell Gv RUNC WA7 150 A8 5
Whinfell Rd WD/CROXPK L12 98 E8
Whinfield Av CHLYE PR6 32 F4 5
Whinfield Rd CSBY/BLUN L23 71 J7
WLT/FAZ L9 84 B7
Whinhowe Rd NG/CROX L11 98 D3
Whinmoor Cl CL/PREN CH43 110 F7 2
Whinmoor Rd AIN/FAZ L10 85 J6
WD/CROXPK L12 98 E8
Whinney Gv East MGHL L31 72 E7 3
Whinney Gv West MGHL L31 72 E7 4
Whinny La CHLY/EC PR7 32 A2
Whistlecroft Ct WGNS/IIMK WN3 5 L8
Whistley St WGNE/HIN WN2 80 D2 7
Whiston La HUY L36 116 C1
Whitbarrow Rd LYMM WA13 139 L1
Whitbeam Gv WGNE/HIN WN2 81 G3
Whitburn Cl AIMK WN4 90 F1 5
Whitburn Rd NWD/KWIPK L33 .. 86 C1 7
Whitby Av CHTN/BK PR9 22 E7
WAL/NB CH45 95 G8
WARRN/WOL WA2 121 M3
Whitby La CH/BCN CH1 163 J6
Whitby Rd EP CH65 20 D4
RUNC WA7 19 H6
Whitby St NPK/KEN L6 97 M7 3
Whitchurch Cl WARR WA1 122 C5
Whitchurch Wy RUNC WA7 149 M7 5
Whitcroft Rd NPK/KEN L6 113 M2
Whiteacre WGNNW/ST WN6 55 J3
Whitebeam GTS/LS CH66 163 H4
Whitebeam Cl NWD/KWIPK L33 74 B7
RUNC WA7 150 E4
Whitebeam Dr
WD/CROXPK L12 98 F2 6
Whitebeam Gdns RAIN/WH L35 .. 101 L7
Whitebeam Wk
GR/UP/WCH CH49 125 K3
White Br BRSC L40 39 M1
Whitechapel CLVPS L1 13 G7
Whitecroft Av
GOL/RIS/CU WA3 93 G4 7
Whitecroft Rd GTS/LS CH66 163 G3
WGNS/IIMK WN3 79 J3
Whitecross Rd
WARRW/BUR WA5 121 G8
Whiteeside Cl
GR/UP/WCH CH49 126 C1 2
Whitefield Av ANF/KKDL L4 97 G5
Whitefield Cl
GR/UP/WCH CH49 126 D2
HTWN L38 70 B3 1
Whitefield Dr KKBY L32 85 K3
Whitefield La BRSC L40 39 L2
RAIN/WH L35 116 C7
Whitefield Rd ECCL WA10 8 A1
NPK/KEN L6 113 K1
WARRS WA4 137 K5
WLT/FAZ L9 84 C8
Whitefields CHNE CH2 165 K2
Whitefield Wy NPK/KEN L6 113 J1 9
Whitegate Av GOL/RIS/CU WA3 .. 107 H3
Whitegate Cl PR/KW L34 99 M1
White Gate Fold CHLY/EC PR7 43 G2
Whitegates Cl NSTN CH64 154 A4
Whitegates Crs NSTN CH64 154 A5
Whitehall Av WGNNW/ST WN6 55 G5
Whitehall La HOR/BR BL6 57 M2
Whitehall Pl FROD/HEL WA6 ... 160 D5 3
FROD/HEL WA6 160 E5 1
Whitehall St WGNS/IIMK WN3 5 J7
Whitehart Cl ANF/KKDL L4 97 K4
Whitehaven Cl STHP PR8 47 K2 4
Whitehedge Rd ALL/GAR L19 130 D6
Whitehey Rd SKEL WN8 65 G5
Whitehorn Dr STBRV L28 99 K6
White Horse Cl HOR/BR BL6 45 L8 3
Whitehouse Av FMBY L37 59 J2 3
White House Cl RNFD/HAY WA11 .. 90 D7
White House Dr WARR WA1 123 G6 8
Whitehouse Expy RUNC WA7 150 B8
White House La BRSC L40 37 L4
Whitehouse La FMBY L37 59 J2
HES CH60 141 M4
Whitehouse Rd
CLB/OSW/ST L13 114 D3 3
Whitelands Meadow
GR/UP/WCH CH49 110 A8
Whiteledge Rd SKEL WN8 65 K5
Whiteley's La BRSC L40 63 L3
White Lodge Av HUY L36 115 M2
White Lodge Cl PS/BROM CH62 .. 144 A8
White Lodge Dr AIMK WN4 91 M1
Whitely Gv NWD/KWIPK L33 74 C7 4
White Meadow Dr
CSBY/BLUN L23 71 J7
Whitemere Ct EP CH65 20 C1 3
White Moss Rd SKEL WN8 64 E6
White Moss Rd South SKEL WN8 .. 65 G6
Whiterails Dr ORM L39 50 F7
White Rock St NPK/KEN L6 113 K1 8
Whitesands Rd LYMM WA13 139 L1
Whiteside Av RNFD/HAY WA11 90 A8
WGNE/HIN WN2 69 M6
WGNNW/ST WN6 4 A1
Whiteside Cl EV L5 96 F8 10
Whiteside Rd RNFD/HAY WA11 90 D7
Whitestock SKEL WN8 65 G5
Whitestone Cl PR/KW L34 99 L3 1
White St CLVPS L1 112 F5
WARR WA1 14 C6
WARRS WA4 137 L4
WDN WA8 134 C8 6
WGNW/BIL/O WN5 67 K7 9
Whitethorn Av
WARRW/BUR WA5 120 B8
Whitewell Dr
GR/UP/WCH CH49 110 B7
Whitewood Cl AIMK WN4 79 J7 2
Whitewood Pk WLT/FAZ L9 84 F7
Whitfield Av WARR WA1 122 B6
Whitfield Gv
RNFD/HAY WA11 90 C7 10
Whitfield La HES CH60 141 J4
Whitfield St RF/TRAN CH42 .. 127 M1 11
Whitford Rd RF/TRAN CH42 127 L1
Whitham Av CSBY/BLUN L23 83 H3
Whithorn St EHL/KEN L7 113 M5 10
Whitland Rd NPK/KEN L6 113 M2
Whitledge Gn AIMK WN4 79 J8
Whitledge Rd AIMK WN4 79 J8
Whitley Av WARRS WA4 138 C1
Whitley Cl RUNC WA7 18 F7
Whitley Crs WGN WN1 68 D1
WGNE/HIN WN2 80 D6
Whitley Rd SKEL WN8 66 F4
Whitley St VAUX/LVPD L3 12 D2
Whitlow Av GOL/RIS/CU WA3 92 B4
Whitman St WAV L15 114 A6
Whitmoor Cl RAIN/WH L35 118 A4 4
Whitney Pl WLTN L25 131 L3 6
Whitney Rd WLTN L25 131 L2
Whitsbury Av WGNE/HIN WN2 80 F1
Whitstable Pk WDN WA8 134 A1
Whitstone Cl WLTN L25 131 G3
Whitstone Dr SKEL WN8 65 M6
Whittaker Av
WARRN/WOL WA2 121 M3 9
Whittaker Cl
CLB/OSW/ST L13 114 B4 2
Whittam Rd CHLY/EC PR7 32 D8
Whittier St TOX L8 113 L6
Whittle Av RNFD/HAY WA11 90 C8
WARRW/BUR WA5 120 C6
Whittle Cl EV L5 97 G7 9
Whittle Dr ORM L39 51 G6
Whittle Hall La
WARRW/BUR WA5 120 B7
Whittle La WGNNW/ST WN6 41 G8
Whittle St ECCL WA10 101 M4
EV L5 97 G7
Whittlewood Cl
GOL/RIS/CU WA3 107 J8 4
Whittlewood Ct
NWD/KWIPK L33 86 B1
Whitwell Cl WARRW/BUR WA5 119 M6
WGNNW/ST WN6 55 M3 3
Whitworth Cl GOL/RIS/CU WA3 .. 123 G2
Whitworth Dr CHLY/EC PR7 32 C7
Wholesome La CHTN/BK PR9 37 L3
Wicket Cl NG/CROX L11 85 M8 7
Wickham Cl WAL/EG CH44 111 M3
Wicklow Cl GTS/LS CH66 155 J7
Wicks Crs FMBY L37 58 E1
Wicks Gdns FMBY L37 59 G2
Wicks Gn FMBY L37 58 E2
Wicks Green Cl FMBY L37 58 E1
Wicks La FMBY L37 58 E2
Wicksten Dr RUNC WA7 19 L4
Widdale Av RAIN/WH L35 117 M2 4
Widdale Cl WARRW/BUR WA5 120 B6
Widdrington Rd WGN WN1 68 F3
Widgeons Covert BEB CH63 142 B8
Widmore Rd WLTN L25 131 L1
Widnes Rd WARRW/BUR WA5 135 J3
WDN WA8 16 E4
Wiend WGN WN1 4 F4
The Wiend BEB CH63 128 C8
RF/TRAN CH42 127 M4
Wigan La CHLY/EC PR7 43 M6
WGN WN1 4 F1
Wigan Lower Rd
WGNNW/ST WN6 67 L1
Wigan Rd AIMK WN4 91 K1
CHLY/EC PR7 31 L1
GOL/RIS/CU WA3 92 D2
LEIGH WN7 81 L6
ORM L39 51 H8
SKEL WN8 65 H5
WGNE/HIN WN2 69 J2
WGNNW/ST WN6 55 K8
WGNW/BIL/O WN5 78 B6
Wigan St WGNE/HIN WN2 80 C3
Wiggins La BRSC L40 27 J8
Wight Cl EP CH65 163 L4
Wightman Av NEWLW WA12 91 L8 5
Wightman St NPK/KEN L6 113 K2 14
Wight Moss Wy STHP PR8 35 M2
Wigmore Cl GOL/RIS/CU WA3 .. 107 J8 5
Wignall Cl KKBY L32 86 A6 5
Wignalls Meadow HTWN L38 70 B2 3
Wigshaw La GOL/RIS/CU WA3 106 F3
Wigston Cl STHP PR8 47 K1
Wilberforce Rd ANF/KKDL L4 97 K4
Wilbraham Pl EV L5 96 F8 11
Wilbraham St EV L5 96 F8
LEIGH WN7 81 L8 5
STHEL WA9 119 G2
Wilburn St ANF/KKDL L4 97 H4
Wilbur St STHEL WA9 103 G6 3
Wilcock Cl EV L5 96 F8
Wilcock Rd RNFD/HAY WA11 91 J5
Wilcock St WGNS/IIMK WN3 4 B5
Wilcote Cl WDN WA8 134 E1
Wilcove SKEL WN8 65 H4
Wild Arum Cl
GOL/RIS/CU WA3 93 G5 14
Wildbrook Dr BIRK CH41 110 F3
Wildcherry Gdns RAIN/WH L35 .. 101 K6
Wilderspool Cswy WARRS WA4 14 E8
Wilderspool Crs WARRS WA4 137 K4
Wilde St VAUX/LVPD L3 13 J6 1
Wilding Av RUNC WA7 19 K3
Wildings Old La
GOL/RIS/CU WA3 106 C5
Wilding St WGNS/IIMK WN3 5 J8
Wild Pl BTL L20 84 A6
Wildwood Gv WARR WA1 122 D6
Wilfer Cl EHL/KEN L7 113 L5 11
Wilfred Owen Dr
CL/PREN CH43 111 G6
Wilfred St WGNW/BIL/O WN5 68 B6
Wilfrid's Pl WGNNW/ST WN6 56 A4
Wilkes Av MOR/LEA CH46 110 D2
Wilkesley Av WGNNW/ST WN6 55 M5
Wilkie St WAV L15 114 A6 13
Wilkinson Av WARR WA1 122 B7
Wilkinson Cl WDN WA8 134 C8 7
Wilkinson St BIRK CH41 10 F7
WARRN/WOL WA2 15 H1
Wilkinson St North EP CH65 20 C2
Wilkin St ANF/KKDL L4 97 G6 17
Willan St CL/PREN CH43 127 K1
Willard Av WGNW/BIL/O WN5 77 M2
Willard St BTL L20 83 M7
Willaston Dr HLWD L26 132 C7
Willaston Rd ANF/KKDL L4 97 K4
BEB CH63 142 F7
MOR/LEA CH46 109 M4 3
NSTN CH64 153 M3
Willedstan Av CSBY/BLUN L23 83 G2
William Brown St CLVPS L1 13 H6
William Harvey Cl NTHTN L30 84 B2
William Henry St BTL L20 6 F7
VAUX/LVPD L3 13 K3
William Morris Av BTL L20 84 A8
William Moult St EV L5 96 F8
William Penn Cl
WARRW/BUR WA5 136 A1 5
William Rd RNFD/HAY WA11 90 B8
William Roberts Av KKBY L32 85 L3
Williams Av BTL L20 7 M1
NEWLW WA12 91 L8
Williamson St STHEL WA9 9 M4
Williams St PR/KW L34 100 F7
William St BIRK CH41 11 K5
ECCL WA10 9 G4 2
WAL/EG CH44 112 A3 21
WDN WA8 134 E3
WGNS/IIMK WN3 5 H8
William Wall Rd LITH L21 83 K3
Willingdon Rd CHLDW L16 115 G4
Willington Av PS/BROM CH62 155 G2
Willink Rd RNFD/HAY WA11 89 L6 1
Willis Cl RAIN/WH L35 116 F3
Willis La RAIN/WH L35 116 F3
Willis St WARR WA1 15 J3
Williton Rd CHLDW L16 115 G8
Willmer Rd ANF/KKDL L4 97 K6
RF/TRAN CH42 10 F8
Willoughby Cl
WARRW/BUR WA5 120 E4
Willoughby Dr ECCL WA10 101 K5
Willoughby Rd CSBY/WL L22 83 G4
DV/KA/FCH L14 115 G3
Willow Av HUY L36 116 A5
KKBY L32 85 L2
NEWLW WA12 104 F1
RAIN/WH L35 116 F2
WDN WA8 134 D3
Willow Bank FROD/HEL WA6 167 G3
Willowbank Cl HUY L36 99 L8 4
Willow Bank Est NEWLW WA12 .. 105 H2
Willowbank Rd
PS/BROM CH62 128 D7 6
RF/TRAN CH42 127 M2
Willow Brook ORM L39 36 C7
Willowbrook Dr
WGNNW/ST WN6 55 K6
Willowbrow Rd BEB CH63 153 M2
Willow Cl CHLYE PR6 44 D5
RUNC WA7 19 K9
Willow Crs BRSC L40 39 H7 1
WARR WA1 122 D5
Willowcroft Rd WAL/EG CH44 . 111 L2 9
Willowdale NEWLW WA12 105 G2
Willowdale Rd
CALD/MH L18 114 B8 14
WLT/FAZ L9 97 J1
Willowdale Wy GTS/LS CH66 163 H5
Willow Dr CHLY/EC PR7 42 F1 2
SKEL WN8 65 G4
WARRS WA4 137 M4 4
WGNE/HIN WN2 81 H2
Willow End BRSC L40 52 B1
Willowfield Gv AIMK WN4 91 J3
Willow Gn BRSC L40 39 J2
ORM L39 51 H8 5
WLTN L25 131 H1
Willow Gv AIMK WN4 80 A8 3
CHNE CH2 165 J3
CHTN/BK PR9 25 G6
FMBY L37 59 H1
GOL/RIS/CU WA3 92 C4
GTS/LS CH66 163 J4
MOR/LEA CH46 109 M6
RAIN/WH L35 101 G8
WAV L15 114 C5
Willowhey CHTN/BK PR9 25 H2
Willow Hey MGHL L31 73 G6
SKEL WN8 65 H4
Willow La BEB CH63 153 M2
Willow Lea CL/PREN CH43 127 H1
Willow Ldg WGNE/HIN WN2 80 D4 8
Willow Pk GR/UP/WCH CH49 125 L1
Willow Rd CHLYE PR6 33 G3
ECCL WA10 101 L2
NEWLW WA12 105 G1
RNFD/HAY WA11 91 G6
WAV L15 114 A5 8
WGNNW/ST WN6 68 B1
The Willows BRSC L40 40 E3
FROD/HEL WA6 160 E5
STHEL WA9 118 E1 21
WAL/NB CH45 95 G6
Willow Tree Av STHEL WA9 118 F1
Willow Tree Cl WGN WN1 68 D1
Willow Wk SKEL WN8 65 K1 4
Willow Wy CSBY/BLUN L23 71 G8
NG/CROX L11 85 M7
Wills Av MGHL L31 72 E3
Willsford Av KKBY L32 85 K2
Wilmcote Gv STHP PR8 47 K1
Wilmere La WDN WA8 118 C7
Wilmot Av WARRW/BUR WA5 120 B7
Wilmot Dr GOL/RIS/CU WA3 92 B6
Wilmslow Av GTS/LS CH66 156 A8 3
Wilmslow Crs WARRS WA4 138 F1
Wilmslow Dr GTS/LS CH66 156 A8
Wilne Rd WAL/NB CH45 95 J7 7
Wilsden Rd WDN WA8 133 K4 3
Wilsford Cl GOL/RIS/CU WA3 92 D4 6
Wilson Av WAL/EG CH44 112 A1 1
WGNNW/ST WN6 68 D3
Wilson Cl ECCL WA10 8 D5
WARRS WA4 138 F2
Wilson Gv ALL/GAR L19 130 E7 6
Wilson La GOL/RIS/CU WA3 107 G8
Wilson Patten St WARR WA1 14 C7
Wilson Rd HUY L36 116 D5
RAIN/WH L35 116 F2
WAL/EG CH44 112 A1 2
Wilsons La LITH L21 83 K5
Wilson St TOX L8 129 J1 23
WARRW/BUR WA5 14 C1
Wilstan Av BEB CH63 127 M8 5
Wilton Av WGNE/HIN WN2 69 H3
Wilton Gv CLB/OSW/ST L13 114 C3 4
Wilton La GOL/RIS/CU WA3 93 J8
Wilton Rd HUY L36 115 M3
RF/TRAN CH42 128 C4
WGNNW/ST WN6 55 J6
Wiltons Dr PR/KW L34 99 L2
Wilton St AIMK WN4 79 H7 5
WAL/EG CH44 111 K1
WGN WN1 5 G6
Wiltshire Cl WARR WA1 122 F7
Wiltshire Pl WGNW/BIL/O WN5 67 L7
Wimbledon St WAL/NB CH45 95 K8
WAV L15 114 A6 14
Wimborne Cl DV/KA/FCH L14 99 K7
Wimborne Pl DV/KA/FCH L14 99 K8
Wimborne Rd DV/KA/FCH L14 99 K8
WGNW/BIL/O WN5 67 J5
Wimborne Wy PEN/TH CH61 125 M6
Wimbourne Av PEN/TH CH61 126 C8
Wimbrick Cl MOR/LEA CH46 110 B5 3
Wimbrick Crs ORM L39 62 F2
Wimbrick Hey MOR/LEA CH46 110 B5
Wimpole St EHL/KEN L7 113 K3
Winchester Av AIMK WN4 91 J2
AIN/FAZ L10 84 F2
CHLY/EC PR7 44 A2
CSBY/WL L22 82 E3
EP CH65 20 F7
WARRW/BUR WA5 120 E8
Winchester Cl
WGNW/BIL/O WN5 67 H6
WLTN L25 131 K6
Winchester Gv WGNS/IIMK WN3 5 H8
Winchester Pl WDN WA8 133 L5 2
Winchester Rd NPK/KEN L6 97 L7
RNFD/HAY WA11 91 G4
WGNW/BIL/O WN5 77 M4
Winchfield Rd WAV L15 114 B7 8
Windbourne Rd AIG/SPK L17 .. 129 K3 4
Windermere Av
RNFD/HAY WA11 89 J5
WARRN/WOL WA2 121 L2
WDN WA8 134 D1 10
Windermere Cl NSTN CH64 153 H6 2
Windermere Crs STHP PR8 47 L2
Windermere Dr CHLYE PR6 44 D4
MGHL L31 73 G3
NWD/KWIPK L33 85 M1
RNFD/HAY WA11 76 B3
WD/CROXPK L12 98 E4
Windermere Rd CHLYE PR6 33 G6 14
CL/PREN CH43 110 E7
EP CH65 163 L3
HTWN L38 70 C1
RNFD/HAY WA11 90 D7
WGNE/HIN WN2 69 J6
WGNE/HIN WN2 80 D5
WGNW/BIL/O WN5 67 H5
Windermere St EV L5 97 J7
WDN WA8 134 D1
WGN WN1 5 J2
Windermere Ter TOX L8 113 K8 2
Windfield Cl NWD/KWIPK L33 74 C7 5
Windfield Gdns GTS/LS CH66 155 M6
Windfield Gn ALL/GAR L19 145 M2
Windfield Rd ALL/GAR L19 145 M1
Windgate SKEL WN8 65 H4
Windle Ash MGHL L31 72 E3
Windle Av CSBY/BLUN L23 83 J1
Windlebrook Crs ECCL WA10 88 D7
Windle City ECCL WA10 89 H7
Windle Ct GOL/RIS/CU WA3 122 E1 6
NSTN CH64 153 G3
Windle Gv ECCL WA10 88 E7
Windle Hall Dr ECCL WA10 89 G6
Windlehurst Av ECCL WA10 89 G7
Windleshaw Rd ECCL WA10 8 B1
Windleshaw St WGNS/IIMK WN3 5 J8
Windle St ECCL WA10 8 E2
Windle V ECCL WA10 8 C2
Windmill Av CSBY/BLUN L23 71 H8
ORM L39 51 H8
Windmill Cl NWD/KWIPK L33 ... 74 A8 12
WARRS WA4 137 L7
WGN WN1 5 H3
Windmill Gdns STHEL WA9 102 F1 3
Windmill Hts SKEL WN8 66 C5
Windmill Hill Av RUNC WA7 150 F3
Windmill Hill Av East
RUNC WA7 150 F5
Windmill Hill Av North
RUNC WA7 150 E2
Windmill Hill Av South
RUNC WA7 150 F4
Windmill Hill Av West
RUNC WA7 150 E3
Windmill La WARRS WA4 137 L7
WARRS WA4 151 J6
WARRW/BUR WA5 120 A8
Windmill Rd SKEL WN8 66 B6
Windmill St RUNC WA7 19 K3
Window La ALL/GAR L19 145 L1
Windrows SKEL WN8 65 H4
Windscale Rd
WARRN/WOL WA2 122 C3
Windsor Av CHLY/EC PR7 44 A7
LITH L21 83 J5
NEWLW WA12 104 F3
Windsor Cl BRSC L40 52 A2
CHLY/EC PR7 32 D6 6
GR/UP/WCH CH49 125 M2 4
NTHTN L30 72 B8 1
PS/BROM CH62 128 C6
Windsor Ct STHP PR8 2 B9
Windsor Crs WGNE/HIN WN2 57 M8
Windsor Dr EP CH65 163 J2
RNFD/HAY WA11 91 J6
WARRS WA4 138 D2
Windsor Gv RUNC WA7 19 K7
WGNE/HIN WN2 81 K2 6
Windsor Park Rd AIN/FAZ L10 85 G2
Windsor Rd AIMK WN4 91 K3
BTL L20 84 A8 4
CHLY/EC PR7 30 E6
CHLY/EC PR7 32 D6
CHTN/BK PR9 3 L4
CLB/OSW/ST L13 97 M7
ECCL WA10 8 A5
FMBY L37 59 G4
GOL/RIS/CU WA3 92 E5
HUY L36 115 K2 3
MGHL L31 72 E5
RAIN/WH L35 117 G1
SKEL WN8 66 C5

WDN WA8 .... 134 C1
WGNW/BIL/O WN5 .... 78 B8
WLT/FAZ L9 .... 84 C7 [7]
**Windsor St** BIRK CH41 .... 10 F7 [7]
TOX L8 .... 113 H6
WAL/NB WA45 .... 95 K4
WARRW/BUR WA5 .... 121 G7
WGN WN1 .... 5 H2
**Windsor Vw** TOX L8 .... 113 K6
**Windus St** ECCL WA10 .... 8 D5
**Windways** GTS/LS CH66 .... 155 M6
**Windy Arbor Cl** RAIN/WH L35 .... 116 F4
**Windy Arbor Rd** RAIN/WH L35 .... 116 K5
**Windy Bank** PS/BROM CH62 .... 128 C7 [3]
**Windy Bank Av**
  GOL/RIS/CU WA3 .... 93 G5 [13]
**Windy Harbour La** STHP PR8 .... 35 G6
**Wineva Gdns** CSBY/BLUN L23 .... 83 H2
**Win Field Cl** WGNNW/ST WN6 .... 4 B4
**Winfield Wy** WDN WA8 .... 16 F3
**Winford St** WAL/EG CH44 .... 111 M2 [12]
**Winfrith Cl** BEB CH63 .... 143 H3 [7]
**Winfrith Dr** BEB CH63 .... 143 H3
**Winfrith Rd** WARRN/WOL WA2 .... 122 C4
  WLTN L25 .... 131 L1
**Wingate Av** RAIN/WH L35 .... 101 M7
**Wingate Cl** CL/PREN CH43 .... 127 G1 [3]
**Wingate Rd** AIG/SPK L17 .... 130 A3
  NWD/KWIPK L33 .... 86 B1
  PS/BROM CH62 .... 144 A8
**Wingates Rd** WGN WN1 .... 56 E8
**Wingfield Cl** SFTN L29 .... 71 M5
  WGNNW/ST WN6 .... 68 C1
**Wingrave Wy** NG/CROX L11 .... 98 D4
**Winhill** WLTN L25 .... 131 J1
**Winifred La** ORM L39 .... 62 D4
**Winifred Rd** AIN/FAZ L10 .... 85 K6 [3]
**Winifred St** EHL/KEN L7 .... 113 K4
  WARRN/WOL WA2 .... 15 G2
  WGNS/IIMK WN3 .... 5 J7
**Winkle St** TOX L8 .... 113 H8 [7]
**Winmarleigh St** WARR WA1 .... 14 C6
**Winmoss Dr** NWD/KWIPK L33 .... 74 B8
**Winnington Rd** HOY CH47 .... 124 C1 [3]
**The Winnows** RUNC WA7 .... 149 M4 [3]
**Winscar Rd** WGNE/HIN WN2 .... 69 M7
**Winsford Dr** RNFD/HAY WA11 .... 91 H6 [7]
**Winsford Dr** WARRW/BUR WA5 .... 104 A6
**Winsford Gv** GTS/LS CH66 .... 162 E2
**Winsford Rd** CLB/OSW/ST L13 .... 98 B7 [3]
**Winsham Cl** KKBY L32 .... 86 B5 [3]
**Winsham Rd** KKBY L32 .... 86 A5
**Winskill Rd** NG/CROX L11 .... 98 C4
**Winslade Rd** ANF/KKDL L4 .... 97 K4
**Winslow Cl** RUNC WA7 .... 150 F5
**Winslow St** ANF/KKDL L4 .... 97 H5
**Winsmoor Dr** WGNE/HIN WN2 .... 81 G1
**Winstanley Cl**
  WARRW/BUR WA5 .... 120 E8 [7]
**Winstanley Pl** WGNS/IIMK WN3 .... 5 J8
**Winstanley Rd** AIMK WN4 .... 78 D6
  CSBY/WL L22 .... 83 G3
  NSTN CH64 .... 153 G8
  PS/BROM CH62 .... 128 D6
  SKEL WN8 .... 65 H5
  WGNE/HIN WN2 .... 80 B5
  WGNW/BIL/O WN5 .... 78 B2
**Winstanley St**
  WGNW/BIL/O WN5 .... 68 B7 [14]
**Winster Dr** NTHLY L27 .... 132 C2
  WGNE/HIN WN2 .... 80 B3 [3]
**The Winsters** SKEL WN8 .... 65 H4 [3]
**Winston Av** NEWLW WA12 .... 104 D2
  STHEL WA9 .... 103 K3
**Winston Crs** STHP PR8 .... 36 A3
**Winston Dr** CL/PREN CH43 .... 110 E8 [3]
**Winstone Rd** DV/KA/FCH L14 .... 115 J1
**Winston Gv** MOR/LEA CH46 .... 110 A5
**Winterburn Crs** WD/CROXPK L12 .. 98 F6
**Winter Gv** STHEL WA9 .... 103 K2
**Winterhey Av** WAL/EG CH44 .... 111 K3
**Winter St** NPK/KEN L6 .... 113 J2
**Winthrop Pk** CL/PREN CH43 .... 111 G8
**Winton Av** WGNW/BIL/O WN5 .... 67 M8
**Winton Cl** WAL/NB CH45 .... 95 J1
**Winton Gv** RUNC WA7 .... 150 F4 [3]
**Winton Rd** GOL/RIS/CU WA3 .... 93 G8
**Winward St** LEIGH WN7 .... 81 K8
**Winwick La** GOL/RIS/CU WA3 .... 105 M3
**Winwick Link Rd**
  WARRN/WOL WA2 .... 105 K7
**Winwick Rd** NEWLW WA12 .... 105 G3
  WARRN/WOL WA2 .... 14 E3
**Winwick St** WARRN/WOL WA2 .... 14 E4
**Winwick Vw** WARRW/BUR WA5 .... 103 M4
**Wirral Cl** BEB CH63 .... 143 H2
  GOL/RIS/CU WA3 .... 107 G2
**Wirral Crs** NSTN CH64 .... 153 H8
**Wirral Dr** WGNS/IIMK WN3 .... 78 E3
**Wirral Gdns** BEB CH63 .... 143 H2
**Wirral Mt** WAL/NB CH45 .... 95 H8
  WKBY CH48 .... 124 F3
**Wirral Vw** ALL/GAR L19 .... 130 B7
**Wirral Vis** WAL/NB CH45 .... 95 G7 [3]
**Wirral Wy** CL/PREN CH43 .... 110 E8
  NSTN CH64 .... 152 C2
  WKBY CH48 .... 124 D3
**Wisenholme Cl** RUNC WA7 .... 161 G1
**Witham Cl** NTHTN L30 .... 84 C1
  WGNNW/ST WN6 .... 55 M4
**Witham Rd** SKEL WN8 .... 64 F4
**Withburn Cl**
  GR/UP/WCH CH49 .... 110 A8 [3]
**Withensfield** WAL/NB CH45 .... 95 K7
**Withen's La** WAL/NB CH45 .... 95 K8
**Withens Rd** MGHL L31 .... 72 F2
**The Withens** STBRV L28 .... 99 K6
**Withers Av** WARRN/WOL WA2 .... 121 M5
**Wither's La** KNUT WA16 .... 139 L8
**Withert Av** BEB CH63 .... 143 M5 [3]
**Withington Av**
  GOL/RIS/CU WA3 .... 107 J1
**Withington La** CHLY/EC PR7 .... 42 A3
  WGNE/HIN WN2 .... 69 K3
**Withington Rd** SPK/HALE L24 .... 147 H2
  WAL/EG CH44 .... 111 L2
**Withins Fld** HTWN L38 .... 70 B2

**Withins La** HTWN L38 .... 60 B6
**Withins Rd** GOL/RIS/CU WA3 .... 107 H2
  RNFD/HAY WA11 .... 91 G5
**Within Wy** SPK/HALE L24 .... 148 A4
**Withnell Cl** CLB/OSW/ST L13 .... 114 D3
**Withnell Gv** CHLYE PR6 .... 33 G4
**Withnell Rd** CLB/OSW/ST L13 .... 114 D3
**Withy Cl** FROD/HEL WA6 .... 160 E5 [3]
**Withycombe Rd**
  WARRW/BUR WA5 .... 136 A1 [3]
**Witley Av** MOR/LEA CH46 .... 110 A4
**Witley Cl** MOR/LEA CH46 .... 110 A4
**Witney Cl** GR/UP/WCH CH49 .... 125 L2 [3]
**Witney Gdns** WARRS WA4 .... 138 B7
**Wittenham Cl**
  GR/UP/WCH CH49 .... 126 B1 [7]
**Wittering La** HES CH60 .... 140 F6
**Wittom Rd** CLB/OSW/ST L13 .... 97 M7
**Witton Wy** RNFD/HAY WA11 .... 76 C6
**Witt Rd** WDN WA8 .... 16 C6
**Wivern Pl** RUNC WA7 .... 19 K2
**Woburn Cl** LEIGH WN7 .... 81 M4
  NEWLW WA12 .... 104 F3
**Woburn Cl** CLB/OSW/ST L13 .... 114 B1 [7]
  RNFD/HAY WA11 .... 91 H6 [3]
**Woburn Dr** WDN WA8 .... 117 M8
**Woburn Hl** CLB/OSW/ST L13 .... 114 B1 [3]
**Woburn Pl** RF/TRAN CH42 .... 128 B3 [13]
**Woburn Rd** WAL/NB CH45 .... 95 K7
  WARRN/WOL WA2 .... 121 J1
**Wokefield Wy** ECCL WA10 .... 101 K1
**Wokingham Gv** HUY L36 .... 116 A5
**The Wold** CHLYE PR6 .... 33 J2
**Wolfenden Av** BTL L20 .... 84 A8
**Wolferton Cl**
  GR/UP/WCH CH49 .... 110 D6 [3]
**Wolfe St** TOX L8 .... 113 C8 [10]
**Wolfrick Dr** BEB CH63 .... 143 K4
**Wolfson Sq** AIMK WN4 .... 91 H1
**Wollaton Dr** STHP PR8 .... 36 B2
**Wolmer St** AIMK WN4 .... 91 J1
**Wolseley Rd** ECCL WA10 .... 8 E2
**Wolsey Cl** AIMK WN4 .... 79 J8
**Wolsey St** BTL L20 .... 7 H9
**Wolstenholme Sq** CLVPS L1 .... 13 H9
**Wolverham Rd** EP CH65 .... 20 D8
**Wolverton St** NPK/KEN L6 .... 97 L7
**Woodacre Rd** GTS/LS CH66 .... 156 B5
**Woodale Cl** WARRW/BUR WA5 .... 120 A6
**Woodall Dr** RUNC WA7 .... 19 J6
**Wood Av** BTL L20 .... 7 M1
**Woodbank Cl** CHLDW L16 .... 115 H5
**Woodbank Pk** CL/PREN CH43 .... 127 G1
**Woodbank Rd** EP CH65 .... 163 K3
  WARRW/BUR WA5 .... 136 C1
**Woodberry Cl**
  CL/PREN CH43 .... 126 F1 [13]
  NWD/KWIPK L33 .... 74 B7 [7]
**Woodbine St** EV L5 .... 96 F6
**Woodbourne Rd**
  DV/KA/FCH L14 .... 114 F1 [3]
**Woodbridge Av** HLWD L26 .... 131 M3
**Woodbrook Av** WLT/FAZ L9 .... 84 B7
**Woodbrook Dr** WGNS/IIMK WN3 .... 78 F1 [7]
**Woodburn Bvd** BEB CH63 .... 128 A5
**Woodburn Dr** HES CH60 .... 141 H7 [7]
**Woodchurch** WGN WN1 .... 5 L1
**Woodchurch La** GTS/LS CH66 .... 156 A8 [3]
  RF/TRAN CH42 .... 127 K3
**Woodchurch Rd** CL/PREN CH43.. 127 G4
  CLB/OSW/ST L13 .... 114 C1
  GR/UP/WCH CH49 .... 126 D4
  RF/TRAN CH42 .... 127 L2
**Woodcock Dr**
  WGNE/HIN WN2 .... 80 D3 [3]
**Woodcock Fold** CHLY/EC PR7 .... 30 E6
**Woodcote Av** EP CH65 .... 163 K3
**Woodcote Bank** RF/TRAN CH42.. 128 B6
**Woodcote Cl** NWD/KWIPK L33 .. 86 C1 [3]
  WARRN/WOL WA2 .... 121 M4 [7]
**The Woodcotes**
  PS/BROM CH62 .... 143 M7
**Woodcot La** HES CH60 .... 141 G4
**Woodcourt** WGNS/IIMK WN3 .... 4 D8
**Woodcroft** SKEL WN8 .... 65 H5 [3]
  WGNNW/ST WN6 .... 55 C7 [7]
**Woodcroft Dr** PEN/TH CH61 .... 141 H3
**Woodcroft La** BEB CH63 .... 128 B5 [3]
**Woodcroft Wy** WAV L15 .... 113 M6
**Woodedge** WARRN/WOL WN4 .... 91 J2
**Woodend** PEN/TH CH61 .... 141 H1
**Woodend Av** CSBY/BLUN L23 .... 71 G2
  MGHL L31 .... 72 E6
  SPK/HALE L24 .... 131 L8
**Woodend La** GOL/RIS/CU WA3 .... 123 M3
  SPK/HALE L24 .... 146 E1
**Woodend Rd** EP CH65 .... 156 B7
**Woodene Cl** KKBY L32 .... 86 C6 [3]
**Woodfall** CHLY/EC PR7 .... 32 D3
**Woodfall Cl** NSTN CH64 .... 153 J7
**Woodfall Gv** NSTN CH64 .... 153 J7
**Woodfall La** NSTN CH64 .... 153 H7
**Woodfarm Hey** STBRV L28 .... 99 J5
**Woodfield Av** BEB CH63 .... 128 A5 [3]
**Woodfield Crs** AIMK WN4 .... 91 J3 [3]
**Woodfield Rd** BEB CH63 .... 143 J2
  CHLY/EC PR7 .... 32 E4 [3]
  ORM L39 .... 62 E2
  PEN/TH CH61 .... 141 G1
  WLT/FAZ L9 .... 84 B8 [3]
**Woodfield Rd North** EP CH65 .... 20 C4
**Woodfield Rd South** WGNE/HIN WN2 .... 69 J3 [7]
**Woodford Cl** FROD/HEL WA6 .. 166 D3 [3]
  RUNC WA7 .... 149 K7 [7]
  WARRS WA4 .... 138 C2
**Woodford Copse** CHLY/EC PR7 .... 32 D6
**Woodford Rd** DV/KA/FCH L14 .... 115 G1
  ECCL WA10 .... 88 E7 [7]
  PS/BROM CH62 .... 128 D5
**Woodford St** WGNW/BIL/O WN5 .. 67 K7
**Woodgarth** LEIGH WN7 .... 81 L8 [3]

**Woodgate** NTHLY L27 .... 115 L7
**Woodger St** ALL/GAR L19 .... 130 E8 [7]
**Wood Gn** CL/PREN CH43 .... 110 E5 [10]
**Woodgreen Cl**
  WGNE/HIN WN2 .... 80 F1 [14]
**Woodgreen Rd**
  CLB/OSW/ST L13 .... 114 C1
**Wood Gv** CLB/OSW/ST L13 .... 114 B3
**Woodhall Av** WAL/EG CH44 .... 111 M1 [13]
**Woodhall Rd** WARRW/BUR WA5 .. 120 C5
**Woodham Gv** NSTN CH64 .... 153 H8 [3]
**Woodhart La** CHLY/EC PR7 .... 30 E8
**Woodhatch Rd** RUNC WA7 .... 150 C8
**Woodhead Gv**
  WGNS/IIMK WN3 .... 79 K3 [3]
**Woodhead Rd** PS/BROM CH62 .. 128 E7
**Woodhead St**
  PS/BROM CH62 .... 128 D6 [3]
**Woodhey Gv** BEB CH63 .... 128 B6 [7]
**Woodhey Rd** ALL/GAR L19 .... 130 C6 [7]
  BEB CH63 .... 128 B6
**Woodhouse Cl** ANF/KKDL L4 .. 97 C6 [13]
  GOL/RIS/CU WA3 .... 93 C5 [3]
**Woodhouse Dr** WGNNW/ST WN6.. 68 A2
**Woodhouse La** WGNNW/ST WN6 .. 4 A1
**Woodhurst Dr** WGNNW/ST WN6 .. 55 M4
**Woodin Rd** RF/TRAN CH42 .... 128 C5
**Woodkind Hey** BEB CH63 .... 143 J3
**Woodland Av** BRSC L40 .... 37 H6
  HOY CH47 .... 108 F4
  NEWLW WA12 .... 105 H2 [3]
  WDN WA8 .... 16 B1
  WGNE/HIN WN2 .... 81 J2
**Woodland Gv** RF/TRAN CH42 .... 128 B5
  WGN WN1 .... 68 F3
**Woodland Rd** ANF/KKDL L4 .... 97 M5
  EP CH65 .... 163 K3
  GR/UP/WCH CH49 .... 126 C2 [3]
  HLWD L26 .... 132 A6
  LITH L21 .... 85 J1
  MGHL L31 .... 85 J1
  RF/TRAN CH42 .... 128 B5
  WKBY CH48 .... 125 G3
**Woodlands Av** WGNS/IIMK WN3 .. 5 L8
**Woodlands Cl** CHTN/BK PR9 .... 3 M1
  FMBY L37 .... 58 F3 [7]
  NSTN CH64 .... 152 F5
  ORM L39 .... 63 J1
**Woodlands Dr** PEN/TH CH61 .... 141 L1
  WARRS WA4 .... 138 F2
  WGN WN1 .... 67 H1
**Woodlands Meadow**
  CHLY/EC PR7 .... 43 L2
**Woodlands Pk** WD/CROXPK L12 .. 98 C3
**Woodlands Rd** AIG/SPK L17 .... 130 A3
  FMBY L37 .... 58 F3
  HUY L36 .... 115 L2 [3]
  NSTN CH64 .... 152 F5
  PEN/TH CH61 .... 125 M8
  RNFD/HAY WA11 .... 89 L6
**Woodlands St** ECCL WA10 .... 9 J4
**Woodlands Ter** NPK/KEN L6 .... 97 K8
**Woodland Vw** NWD/KWIPK L33 .. 86 L1
  RF/TRAN CH42 .... 128 C5
**Woodway** GR/UP/WCH CH49 .... 125 M1
**Woodyates St**
  WGNW/BIL/O WN5 .... 68 B7 [13]
**Woodyear Rd** PS/BROM CH62 .. 144 A6
**Woolacombe Av** STHEL WA9 .... 102 E8
**Woolacombe Cl** WARRS WA4 .... 137 M2
**Woolacombe Rd** CHLDW L16 .... 115 C5
**Woolden St**
  WGNW/BIL/O WN5 .... 68 B7 [13]
**Wooler Cl** MOR/LEA CH46 .... 109 L5
**Woolfall Cl** HUY L36 .... 115 K1
**Woolfall Crs** HUY L36 .... 115 K1
**Woolfall Heath Av** NEWLW WA12.. 99 K8
**Woolfall Ter** LITH L21 .... 83 J7 [3]
**Woolhope Rd** WLT/FAZ L9 .... 97 K3
**Woolley Cl** FROD/HEL WA6 .... 160 F5 [3]
**Woolmer Cl** GOL/RIS/CU WA3 .... 107 K7
**Woolston Grange Av**
  WARR WA1 .... 123 G5
  WARRN/WOL WA2 .... 122 E3
**Woolston Rd** RNFD/HAY WA11 .... 90 E6
**Woolton Cl** AIMK WN4 .... 79 H8
**Woolton Hill Rd** WLTN L25 .... 131 G1
**Woolton Mt** WLTN L25 .... 131 J2
**Woolton Pk** WLTN L25 .... 131 J2
**Woolton Park Cl** WLTN L25 .... 131 J2 [3]
**Woolton Rd** ALL/GAR L19 .... 130 E7
  CHLDW L16 .... 114 F8
  WAV L15 .... 114 C6
  WLTN L25 .... 115 H8
**Woolton St** WLTN L25 .... 131 K3
**Worcester Av**
  CLB/OSW/ST L13 .... 97 M6 [3]
  CSBY/WL L22 .... 82 E3
  GOL/RIS/CU WA3 .... 92 D5 [3]
**Worcester Cl** WARRW/BUR WA5.. 120 D8
**Worcester Dr** CLB/OSW/ST L13 .... 97 M6
**Worcester Dr North**
  CLB/OSW/ST L13 .... 97 M6
**Worcester Pl** CHLY/EC PR7 .... 44 A2
**Worcester Rd** BTL L20 .... 7 K2
  CL/PREN CH43 .... 110 F5
**Worcester St** EP CH65 .... 20 D2 [3]
**Worcester Wk** EP CH65 .... 20 D2 [3]
**Wordsworth Av** LEIGH WN7 .... 81 M6
  RF/TRAN CH42 .... 128 B4 [3]
  STHEL WA9 .... 118 C2 [3]
  WARRS WA4 .... 137 K2
  WDN WA8 .... 16 A3
  WGN WN1 .... 68 E2
  WGNW/BIL/O WN5 .... 67 H7
  WGNW/BIL/O WN5 .... 67 H7
**Wordsworth Cl** ORM L39 .... 50 F7 [3]
**Wordsworth St** BTL L20 .... 6 D1
  TOX L8 .... 113 L6
**Wordsworth Ter** CHLYE PR6 .... 32 F5 [3]
**Wordsworth Wk** WKBY CH48 .. 124 F7 [3]
**Wordsworth Wy**
  GTS/LS CH66 .... 163 G4 [3]
  HUY L36 .... 116 B4
**Worrow Cl** NG/CROX L11 .... 98 D2
**Worrow Rd** NG/CROX L11 .... 98 D2
**Worsborough Av**
  WARRW/BUR WA5 .... 120 D8
**Worsley Av** MGHL L31 .... 72 F2
**Worsley Brow** STHEL WA9 .... 103 G3
**Worsley Cl** WGNW/BIL/O WN5 .. 67 L8 [3]
**Worsley Gn** WGNW/BIL/O WN5 .. 67 K8
**Worsley Mesnes Dr**
  WGNS/IIMK WN3 .... 68 C8 [3]
**Worsley Rd** WARRS WA4 .... 137 K4
**Worsley St** GOL/RIS/CU WA3.... 92 C5

RNFD/HAY WA11 .... 90 B7 [3]
  WARRW/BUR WA5 .... 14 B1
  WGNW/BIL/O WN5 .... 67 K8
**Worsley Ter** WGN WN1 .... 4 F2
**Worthing Cl** STHP PR8 .... 35 H2
**Worthing St** CSBY/WL L22 .... 82 E3 [3]
**Worthington Cl** RUNC WA7 .... 150 C6
**Worthington St** TOX L8 .... 112 F7 [3]
  WGNE/HIN WN2 .... 69 M7 [13]
**Worthington Wy**
  WGNS/IIMK WN3 .... 79 G3
**Worthy St** CHLYE PR6 .... 33 G6
**Wortley Rd** AIN/FAZ L10 .... 85 G5
**Wotton Dr** AIMK WN4 .... 91 M2
**Wraxhall Crs** LEIGH WN7 .... 81 M6
**Wray Av** STHEL WA9 .... 118 F1
**Wrayburn Cl** EHL/KEN L7 .... 113 L5 [12]
**Wray St** WGN WN1 .... 5 K4
**Wrekin Cl** WLTN L25 .... 131 K5
**Wrekin Dr** AIN/FAZ L10 .... 85 G3
**Wrenbury Cl** CL/PREN CH43 .. 127 H3 [3]
  WGNW/BIL/O WN5 .... 67 K8 [3]
**Wrenbury St** EHL/KEN L7 .... 113 L3
**Wren Gv** GOL/RIS/CU WA3 .... 123 H1 [3]
  RUNC WA7 .... 150 C7
  WGNW/BIL/O WN5 .... 67 K4
**Wrenfield Gv** AIG/SPK L17 .. 129 G2 [3]
**Wren Gv** HLWD L26 .... 132 A4 [10]
**Wrennalls La** CHLY/EC PR7 .... 30 D8
**Wrexham Cl**
  WARRW/BUR WA5 .... 121 G3 [3]
**Wright Crs** WDN WA8 .... 149 J1
**Wrightington St** WGN WN1 .... 4 E1
**Wright's La** WARRW/BUR WA5 .. 120 A2 [3]
  WDN WA8 .... 135 H3
**Wrights Ter** STHP PR8 .... 35 H2 [3]
  WAV L15 .... 114 C6 [3]
**Wright St** AIMK WN4 .... 79 J7 [3]
  CHLYE PR6 .... 33 G5
  CHTN/BK PR9 .... 3 H3
  EV L5 .... 96 F3
  WAL/EG CH44 .... 111 M1
  WGN WN1 .... 5 J2
  WGNE/HIN WN2 .... 80 C2
  WGNE/HIN WN2 .... 80 D6
**Wrigley Rd** RNFD/HAY WA11 .... 91 G7
**Wrigleys Cl** FMBY L37 .... 47 H8
**Wrigleys La** FMBY L37 .... 47 H8
**Wrington Cl** LEIGH WN7 .... 81 M5 [3]
**Wroxham Cl** FROD/HEL WA6 .. 166 D1 [3]
  GR/UP/WCH CH49 .... 126 C1
**Wroxham Dr** GR/UP/WCH CH49.. 126 C1
**Wroxham Rd**
  WARRW/BUR WA5 .... 120 A7
**Wroxham Wy**
  GR/UP/WCH CH49 .... 110 C8 [4]
**Wryneck Cl** ECCL WA10 .... 101 K6 [3]
**Wrynose Rd** PS/BROM CH62 .. 144 A5
**Wulstan St** ANF/KKDL L4 .... 96 F6 [3]
**Wyatt Gv** AIMK WN4 .... 91 M2
**Wycherley Rd** RF/TRAN CH42 .. 127 M2
**Wycherley St** PR/KW L34 .... 100 F7 [16]
**Wychwood Av** LYMM WA13 .... 139 L2
**Wycliffe Rd** ANF/KKDL L4 .... 97 L2
  GTS/LS CH66 .... 163 H2
  RNFD/HAY WA11 .... 91 H4
**Wycliffe St** RF/TRAN CH42 .... 128 B3 [14]
**Wye Cl** RF/TRAN CH42 .... 128 B3 [15]
**Wyedale** EP CH65 .... 20 A9
**Wyedale Rd** RNFD/HAY WA11 .... 90 E7
**Wye St** EV L5 .... 97 H7
**Wyke Cop Rd** STHP PR8 .... 36 F2
**Wykeham St** WGNS/IIMK WN3 .... 5 L8
**Wykeham St** ANF/KKDL L4 .... 96 F6
**Wyke La** CHTN/BK PR9 .... 25 L6
**Wyken Gv** RNFD/HAY WA11 .... 9 M1
**Wyke Rd** RAIN/WH L35 .... 101 L3
**Wyke Wood La** CHTN/BK PR9 .. 26 B5
**Wyllin Rd** NWD/KWIPK L33 .... 86 C3
**Wylva Av** CSBY/BLUN L23 .... 83 J2
**Wylva Rd** ANF/KKDL L4 .... 97 J7
**Wymundsley** CHLY/EC PR7 .... 32 B4
**Wynard Av** WGN WN1 .... 5 H2
**Wyncroft Cl** EP CH65 .... 163 J2
  WDN WA8 .... 133 L6
**Wyncroft Rd** WDN WA8 .... 133 L6
**Wyncroft St** TOX L8 .... 129 J1 [3]
**Wyndale Cl** CALD/MH L18 .... 130 D2
**Wyndcote Rd** CALD/MH L18 .... 130 D2
**Wyndham Av** DV/KA/FCH L14 .... 115 J3
**Wyndham Crs** GTS/LS CH66 .... 163 J2
**Wyndham Rd** WAL/NB CH45 .... 94 F8 [3]
**Wyndham St** ANF/KKDL L4 .... 97 H1 [3]
**Wynne Rd** ECCL WA10 .... 8 D2
**Wynnstay Av** MGHL L31 .... 72 F2
**Wynnstay Cl** TOX L8 .... 113 J7
**Wynstay Rd** HOY CH47 .... 108 E5
**Wynwood Pk** HUY L36 .... 115 L4
**Wyre Av** WGNE/HIN WN2 .... 80 C3
**Wyre Rd** EV L5 .... 96 F1 [3]
**Wyrescourt Rd** WD/CROXPK L12 .. 98 F3
**Wyresdale Av** ECCL WA10 .... 89 G6
  STHP PR8 .... 3 M9
**Wyresdale Rd** WLT/FAZ L9 .... 84 D6
**Wyrevale Gv** AIMK WN4 .... 91 L2 [3]
**Wysall Cl** RNFD/HAY WA11 .... 89 M8 [3]
**Wyswall Cl** HLWD L26 .... 132 A4
**Wythburn Crs** RNFD/HAY WA11.. 89 K5
**Wythburn Gv** RUNC WA7 .... 150 M8 [3]
**Wyvern Rd** MOR/LEA CH46 .... 110 A5

# Y

**Yanwath St** TOX L8 .... 113 K6 [3]
**Yarcombe Cl** HLWD L26 .... 132 B4 [3]
**Yardley Av** WARRW/BUR WA5 .. 121 H5
**Yardley Dr** BEB CH63 .... 143 J4
**Yardley Rd** NWD/KWIPK L33 .... 86 E4
**Yarmouth Rd**
  WARRW/BUR WA5 .... 120 A7
**Yarrow Av** MGHL L31 .... 73 H3
**Yarrow Cl** LEY/BBR PR5.... 29 K3
**Yarrow Ga** CHLY/EC PR7 .... 33 G7
**Yarrow Gv** CHLYE PR6 .... 33 G7
**Yarrow St** WGNE/HIN WN2 .... 80 L1 [3]
**Yates Cl** WARRW/BUR WA5 .... 120 E8 [3]

Yates' Ct PR/KW L34 .......... 100 F8 ◻
Yates Gv WGNNW/ST WN6 .......... 68 B1
Yates Rd CHLY/EC PR7 .......... 32 D8
  CHNE CH2 .......... 165 G4
Yates St TOX L8 .......... 113 G8
  WGNS/IIMK WN3 .......... 4 B5
Yeadon SKEL WN8 .......... 65 K4
Yeadon Gv CHLY/EC PR7 .......... 32 C6
Yeald Brow LYMM WA13 .......... 139 K2
Yellow Brook Cl
  WGNE/HIN WN2 .......... 57 L7 ◻
Yellow House La STHP PR8 .......... 3 G6
Yelverton Cl HLWD L26 .......... 132 B4
Yelverton Rd ANF/KKDL L4 .......... 97 L6
  RF/TRAN CH42 .......... 127 M2
Yeoman Cottages HOY CH47 .......... 108 E7
Yeoman Wy GTS/LS CH66 .......... 163 G4
Yeovil Cl WARR WA1 .......... 122 E5
Yew Bank Rd CHLDW L16 .......... 114 F6
Yewdale SKEL WN8 .......... 65 J4
  WGNNW/ST WN6 .......... 55 K7

Yewdale Av RNFD/HAY WA11 .......... 89 K4
Yewdale Crs WGN WN1 .......... 68 D2 ◻
Yewdale Dr GTS/LS CH66 .......... 163 H4
Yewdale Pk CL/PREN CH43 .......... 127 K2
Yewdale Rd AIMK WN4 .......... 79 J6
  WLT/FAZ L9 .......... 97 K1
Yewlands Av CHLY/EC PR7 .......... 42 B2 ◻
Yew Tree Av CHLY/EC PR7 .......... 31 L1
  NEWLW WA12 .......... 104 C1
  STHEL WA9 .......... 102 E7
Yew Tree Cl CHNE CH2 .......... 165 G4
  WD/CROXPK L12 .......... 99 G7
Yewtree Cl CHLY/EC PR7 .......... 43 K2 ◻
  GR/UP/WCH CH49 .......... 126 C3
  NSTN CH64 .......... 153 H6
Yew Tree Gn MGHL L31 .......... 85 K1 ◻
Yew Tree La WARRS WA4 .......... 138 E3
  WD/CROXPK L12 .......... 99 G8
Yewtree La WKBY CH48 .......... 124 D5 ◻
York Cl ECCL WA10 .......... 8 E3
  FMBY L37 .......... 47 H7
  NTHTN L30 .......... 72 B8
York Dr WARRS WA4 .......... 138 C3
York Gdns STHP PR8 .......... 2 E8
York Pl CHLYE PR6 .......... 44 C5

  HUY L36 .......... 115 M5
  MOR/LEA CH46 .......... 110 B3
  ORM L39 .......... 51 H7
  WLT/FAZ L9 .......... 97 H1
  WLTN L25 .......... 131 L5
York Rd AIMK WN4 .......... 91 L3
  CSBY/BLUN L23 .......... 83 G1
  EP CH65 .......... 20 C5
  FMBY L37 .......... 59 H2
  HUY L36 .......... 116 C2
  MGHL L31 .......... 72 F7
  STHP PR8 .......... 2 D9
  WAL/EG CH44 .......... 111 M3
  WARRS WA4 .......... 138 C3
  WDN WA8 .......... 133 L5
York Rd South AIMK WN4 .......... 91 L3
Yorkshire Gdns ECCL WA10 .......... 8 E8
York St ALL/GAR L19 .......... 145 L1
  CHLY/EC PR7 .......... 32 F6 ◻
  CLVPS L1 .......... 13 G9
  CSBY/WL L22 .......... 82 F5
  GOL/RIS/CU WA3 .......... 92 C4
  PS/BROM CH62 .......... 128 F8
  RUNC WA7 .......... 19 G4
  WARRS WA4 .......... 15 G8

  RUNC WA7 .......... 19 H4

  WGNS/IIMK WN3 .......... 4 C5
  WLT/FAZ L5 .......... 97 H2
York Ter EV L5 .......... 97 G7
York Wy ALL/GAR L19 .......... 145 M1
Youatt Av RAIN/WH L35 .......... 117 G1
Youens Dr DV/KA/FCH L14 .......... 115 G1
Yvonne Cl AIMK WN4 .......... 79 M8

## Z

Zander Gv WD/CROXPK L12 .......... 99 J2
Zetland Rd CALD/MH L18 .......... 114 B8 ◻
  WAL/NB CH45 .......... 95 H6
Zetland St CHTN/BK PR9 .......... 3 L4
Zig Zag Rd WAL/NB CH45 .......... 95 K7
  WD/CROXPK L12 .......... 98 F8

## Index - featured places

Abbey Lakes Sports Centre
  WGNW/BIL/O WN5 .......... 66 F6
Abbey Lane Industrial Estate
  BRSC L40 .......... 51 L4
Abbey Sefton Hospitals
  CSBY/WL L22 .......... 83 G6
Abbeystead Medical Centre
  WAV L15 .......... 114 D6
Abbots Lea Special School
  WLTN L25 .......... 131 G1
A B C Cinema
  CALD/MH L18 .......... 130 D1
A B C Cinema
  STHP PR8 .......... 3 G4
Abercromby Health Centre
  TOX L8 .......... 113 J5
Abingdon Medical Centre
  ANF/KKDL L4 .......... 97 L4
Abraham Guest High School
  WGNW/BIL/O WN5 .......... 67 J7
Abram C of E Primary School
  WGNE/HIN WN2 .......... 80 D4
The Academy
  Liverpool Football Club
  NWD/KWIPK L33 .......... 86 C4
Ackhurst Business Park
  CHLY/EC PR7 .......... 32 B4
Ackhurst Park
  Industrial Estate
  CHLY/EC PR7 .......... 32 A5
Acorn Business Centre
  NWD/KWIPK L33 .......... 86 D4
Acorn Surgery
  STHEL WA9 .......... 103 G6
Adlington CP School
  CHLY/EC PR7 .......... 44 B6
Adlington Cricket Club
  CHLY/EC PR7 .......... 44 C7
Adlington Medical Centre
  CHLYE PR6 .......... 44 D5
Ainsdale CE Primary School
  STHP PR8 .......... 47 M1
Ainsdale Clinic
  STHP PR8 .......... 47 M2
Ainsdale High School
  STHP PR8 .......... 34 E7
Aintree Hospitals NHS Trust
  WLT/FAZ L9 .......... 84 F6
Aintree Hospitals NHS Trust
  WLT/FAZ L9 .......... 85 G6
Aintree Osteopathic Clinic
  WLT/FAZ L9 .......... 84 E6
Aintree Park Group Practice
  WLT/FAZ L9 .......... 84 B7
A K Business Park
  CHTN/BK PR9 .......... 25 J7
Alban Retail Park
  WARRN/WOL WA2 .......... 121 J3
Albany High School
  CHLYE PR6 .......... 33 G8
Albert Road Medical Centre
  WDN WA8 .......... 16 F1
Albion Street Doctors Surgery
  EV L5 .......... 97 G7
Alder Hey Hospital Trust
  CALD/MH L18 .......... 130 C2
Alderwood CP School
  SPK/HALE L24 .......... 147 G2
Alexander House Health Centre
  WGNE/HIN WN2 .......... 80 C2
Alexandra Industrial Estate
  WDN WA8 .......... 16 F3
Allanson Street Primary School
  STHEL WA9 .......... 102 F3
Allerton Health Centre
  WAV L15 .......... 114 C8
Allerton Remedial Clinic
  AIG/SPK L17 .......... 114 A8
Allerton Surgery
  CALD/MH L18 .......... 114 D8
Allport Doctors Surgery
  PS/BROM CH62 .......... 143 M5
All Saints C of E Junior School
  WDN WA8 .......... 133 K2
All Saints C of E Primary School
  CHLY/EC PR7 .......... 32 D8
All Saints C of E Primary School
  WGNNW/ST WN6 .......... 54 E4
All Saints RC High School
  KKBY L32 .......... 86 A4
All Saints RC Infant School
  ANF/KKDL L4 .......... 97 K7
All Saints RC Junior
  Mixed School
  NPK/KEN L6 .......... 97 L7
Alsop High Community
  Comprehensive School
  ANF/KKDL L4 .......... 97 J3
Alternative Medical Centre
  ECCL WA10 .......... 8 F4

Alvanley Primary School
  FROD/HEL WA6 .......... 166 F4
Anfield Community
  Comprehensive School
  ANF/KKDL L4 .......... 97 K6
Anfield CP School
  ANF/KKDL L4 .......... 97 K7
Anfield Medical Centre
  ANF/KKDL L4 .......... 97 K6
Archbishop Beck RC
  High School
  WLT/FAZ L9 .......... 84 D7
Archbishop Blanch School
  EHL/KEN L7 .......... 113 J4
Argyle Health Centre
  BIRK CH41 .......... 11 K6
Argyle Lawn Tennis Club
  CHTN/BK PR9 .......... 25 G3
Arrowe Hall Residential School
  GR/UP/WCH CH49 .......... 126 C5
Arrowe Hill Primary School
  GR/UP/WCH CH49 .......... 126 C2
Arrowe Park Hospital Annexe
  GR/UP/WCH CH49 .......... 126 C4
Art Gallery
  NSTN CH64 .......... 153 H3
Ashfield Special School
  CHLDW L16 .......... 115 G7
Ashley Business Centre
  PR/KW L34 .......... 100 F7
Ashley Retail Park
  WDN WA8 .......... 16 F5
Ashley School
  WDN WA8 .......... 133 M4
Ash Surgery
  AIG/SPK L17 .......... 129 M3
Ashton Grange
  Industrial Estate
  AIMK WN4 .......... 79 K7
Ashton Medical Centre
  AIMK WN4 .......... 79 J8
Ashton Town Associated
  Football Club
  AIMK WN4 .......... 91 M1
Ashurst C P School
  RNFD/HAY WA11 .......... 89 M7
Ashurst Health Centre
  SKEL WN8 .......... 65 K1
Ashville Football Club
  WAL/NB CH45 .......... 110 F1
Ashworth Hospital
  MGHL L31 .......... 73 J3
Asmall CP School
  ORM L39 .......... 50 F7
Aspull Clinic
  WGNE/HIN WN2 .......... 57 L8
Aspull New Springs
  County Infant School
  WGNE/HIN WN2 .......... 69 J2
Aspull St John C of E
  Junior School
  WGNE/HIN WN2 .......... 69 J2
Astley Park School
  CHLY/EC PR7 .......... 32 D5
Astmoor County
  Primary School
  RUNC WA7 .......... 150 B3
Aston CP School
  RUNC WA7 .......... 161 L4
Atherton County
  Infant School
  EP CH65 .......... 156 B8
Atherton House School
  CSBY/BLUN L23 .......... 82 F1
Atkinson Art Gallery
  STHP PR8 .......... 3 G4
Aughton Christ Church
  C of E Primary School
  ORM L39 .......... 62 C2
Aughton St Michaels
  C of E School
  ORM L39 .......... 62 D4
Aughton Surgery
  ORM L39 .......... 62 E5
Austin Rawlinson
  Sports Centre
  SPK/HALE L24 .......... 147 G2
Avalon Preparatory School
  WKBY CH48 .......... 124 D5
Bankfield High School
  WDN WA8 .......... 133 L4
Bank Quay Trading Estate
  WARRW/BUR WA5 .......... 14 B3
Banks Health Centre
  CHTN/BK PR9 .......... 23 H7
Banks Methodist
  Primary School
  CHTN/BK PR9 .......... 23 K7
Banks Road CP School
  ALL/GAR L19 .......... 145 M1

Barlows CP School
  WLT/FAZ L9 .......... 84 F6
Barnston Primary School
  HES CH60 .......... 141 L6
Barrow Hall
  Community Primary School
  WARRW/BUR WA5 .......... 119 M6
Baycliff Road Health Centre
  WD/CROXPK L12 .......... 99 H6
Bbc Radio Merseyside
  CLVPS L1 .......... 12 F8
Beamont Community
  Junior School
  WARRN/WOL WA2 .......... 15 H1
Beauford Park School
  TOX L8 .......... 113 H8
Beauford Park School
  TOX L8 .......... 129 H1
Bebington High School
  BEB CH63 .......... 128 B8
Bedford Drive Primary School
  RF/TRAN CH42 .......... 127 M4
Bedford Primary School
  BTL L20 .......... 7 K6
Beechenhurst School
  CALD/MH L18 .......... 130 E1
Beech Hill Medical Practice
  WGNNW/ST WN6 .......... 68 C3
Beech Hill Primary &
  Infant School
  WGNNW/ST WN6 .......... 68 C2
Beechwood County
  Primary School
  RUNC WA7 .......... 149 M8
Belle Green Industrial Estate
  WGNE/HIN WN2 .......... 69 J5
Belle Vale Health Centre
  WLTN L25 .......... 115 K7
Belle Vale Primary School
  WLTN L25 .......... 115 L8
Belle Vale Swimming Pool
  WLTN L25 .......... 115 L7
The Belvidere School
  TOX L8 .......... 113 J8
Bennett & Batty Art Gallery
  CALD/MH L18 .......... 114 D8
Bewley Drive Doctors Surgery
  KKBY L32 .......... 86 A5
Bewsey Lodge
  Community Primary School
  WARRW/BUR WA5 .......... 14 A2
Bewsey Old School
  WARRW/BUR WA5 .......... 121 G6
B I C C Athletic Club
  RAIN/WH L35 .......... 101 H8
Bickershaw C of E School
  WGNE/HIN WN2 .......... 81 J5
Bickerstaffe C of E
  Junior School
  ORM L39 .......... 64 A8
Bidston Avenue Junior & Infant
  School
  CL/PREN CH43 .......... 111 G6
Bidston Village C of E
  Primary School
  CL/PREN CH43 .......... 110 E4
Bigdale Medical Centre
  NWD/KWIPK L33 .......... 86 C2
Bigham Road Medical Centre
  NPK/KEN L6 .......... 113 J2
Billinge Chapel End
  Parish Council
  WGNW/BIL/O WN5 .......... 78 A8
Billinge Clinic
  WGNW/BIL/O WN5 .......... 89 M1
Billinge Hospital
  WGNW/BIL/O WN5 .......... 77 M3
Birchfield CP School
  EHL/KEN L7 .......... 114 A3
Birch Green CP School
  SKEL WN8 .......... 65 K2
Birchwood C of E
  Primary School
  GOL/RIS/CU WA3 .......... 123 H2
Birchwood Community
  High School
  GOL/RIS/CU WA3 .......... 122 F2
Birchwood Medical Centre
  GOL/RIS/CU WA3 .......... 123 G2
Birkdale High School
  STHP PR8 .......... 35 G6
Birkdale Primary School
  STHP PR8 .......... 35 K2
Birkdale School for
  Hearing Impaired Children
  STHP PR8 .......... 35 G2
Birkdale Trading Estate
  STHP PR8 .......... 35 H3
Birkenhead Boys School
  CL/PREN CH43 .......... 111 H8

Birkenhead County Court
  BIRK CH41 .......... 11 L6
Birkenhead High
  School for Girls
  CL/PREN CH43 .......... 10 B7
Birkenhead Park Cricket Club
  BIRK CH41 .......... 10 C5
Birkenhead Park Rugby Union
  Football Club
  BIRK CH41 .......... 10 B3
Birkenhead Preparatory School
  CL/PREN CH43 .......... 10 A8
Birkenhead Priory and Museum
  BIRK CH41 .......... 11 M6
Birkenhead Sixth Form College
  CL/PREN CH43 .......... 111 H6
Birleywood Health Centre
  SKEL WN8 .......... 65 M7
Bishop David Sheppard C of E
  School
  CHTN/BK PR9 .......... 25 K6
Bishop Martin C of E
  Primary School
  WLTN L25 .......... 131 J3
Bishop Martins Junior &
  Infant School
  SKEL WN8 .......... 65 M7
Bishop Rawstone School
  LEY/BBR PR5 .......... 29 L3
Bispham Hall Business Park
  WGNW/BIL/O WN5 .......... 77 L3
Blackbrook RC Junior &
  Infant School
  RNFD/HAY WA11 .......... 90 A7
Black Cat Industrial Estate
  WDN WA8 .......... 16 C3
Blackheath Medical Practice
  MOR/LEA CH46 .......... 110 B2
Black Horse Hill Infant School
  WKBY CH48 .......... 124 F2
Black Horse Hill Junior School
  WKBY CH48 .......... 124 F2
Blacklow Brow Primary School
  HUY L36 .......... 115 M4
Blackmoor Park Infant School
  WD/CROXPK L12 .......... 98 F7
Blackmoor Park Junior School
  WD/CROXPK L12 .......... 98 F8
Black Moss Special School
  SKEL WN8 .......... 64 F3
Blackrod Church School
  HOR/BR BL6 .......... 57 L3
Blackrod Galleries
  HOR/BR BL6 .......... 57 M3
Blackthorn Galleries
  BIRK CH41 .......... 11 K4
Bleak Hill Primary School
  ECCL WA10 .......... 88 D8
Blessed Sacrament
  Infant School
  WLT/FAZ L9 .......... 84 F6
Blessed Sacrament RC
  Primary School
  WLT/FAZ L9 .......... 84 D7
Blowick Business Centre
  CHTN/BK PR9 .......... 25 J7
Bluecoat Gallery
  CLVPS L1 .......... 13 G8
The Blue Coat School
  WAV L15 .......... 114 C7
Blue Planet Aquarium
  EP CH65 .......... 163 M4
Boaler Street Industrial Estate
  NPK/KEN L6 .......... 113 J2
Boat Museum
  EP CH65 .......... 20 E1
Bold Industrial Estate
  WDN WA8 .......... 118 E8
Bold Street Medical Centre
  WARR WA1 .......... 14 D7
Bolton County Junior &
  Infant School
  WARRS WA4 .......... 15 M9
Bolton County Junior &
  Infant School
  WARRS WA4 .......... 138 B2
Bolton Metropolitan
  Borough Council
  HOR/BR BL6 .......... 57 L3
Booker Avenue Infant &
  Junior School
  CALD/MH L18 .......... 130 D3
Bootle Cricket Club
  BTL L20 .......... 7 J7
Bootle High School
  NTHTN L30 .......... 84 C1
Bootle Stadium Sports Centre
  BTL L20 .......... 7 M3
Borron Road Industrial Estate
  NEWLW WA12 .......... 104 E1

Borsdane Brook Special School
  WGNE/HIN WN2 .......... 80 E1
Botanic Estate
  EHL/KEN L7 .......... 113 M4
Botanic Gardens Museum
  CHTN/BK PR9 .......... 25 K3
Bousfield Health Centre
  ANF/KKDL L4 .......... 97 G6
Bowers Business Park
  WDN WA8 .......... 16 F5
Bowers Business Park
  WDN WA8 .......... 17 G4
Bowring Comprehensive School
  HUY L36 .......... 115 K2
The Bowry Health Centre
  STHEL WA9 .......... 101 M5
The Boydell Galleries
  CSBY/BLUN L23 .......... 70 D8
Brackenbield Infant School
  BEB CH63 .......... 128 B8
Brackenwood Junior School
  BEB CH63 .......... 128 A8
Bradley Hall Trading Estate
  WGNNW/ST WN6 .......... 56 C3
Bradshaw Community
  Primary School
  WARRS WA4 .......... 138 D3
Breckfield Community
  Comprehensive School
  EV L5 .......... 97 H8
Breckfield & North
  Everton Council
  EV L5 .......... 97 H7
Breckfield Primary School
  EV L5 .......... 97 H7
Breckfield Road North Doctors
  Surgery
  EV L5 .......... 97 H7
Brentwood Gallery &
  Framing Centre
  WARRS WA4 .......... 137 L4
Brewery
  TOX L8 .......... 113 G7
Briars Hey School
  RAIN/WH L35 .......... 117 M4
Bridgehouse Clinic
  BEB CH63 .......... 127 M7
Bridge Industrial Estate
  SPK/HALE L24 .......... 131 K8
Bridgewater Community
  High School (Lower)
  WARRS WA4 .......... 137 M7
Bridgewater Community
  High School (Upper)
  WARRS WA4 .......... 137 M6
Britannia Bridge
  Primary School
  WGNS/IIMK WN3 .......... 5 J7
Britonwood Trading Estate
  NWD/KWIPK L33 .......... 86 D6
Broadgreen Community
  Comprehensive School
  CLB/OSW/ST L13 .......... 114 D3
Broadgreen Hospital NHS Trust
  DV/KA/FCH L14 .......... 114 E3
Broad Green Junior &
  Infant School
  CLB/OSW/ST L13 .......... 114 C3
Broad Oak Community Primary
  School
  STHEL WA9 .......... 103 J2
Broad Square CP School
  NG/CROX L11 .......... 98 B5
Broadway Community
  High School
  ECCL WA10 .......... 101 L5
Bromborough Pool
  Primary School
  PS/BROM CH62 .......... 128 F8
Brook Acre Community Primary
  School
  WARRN/WOL WA2 .......... 122 A4
Brookdale Primary School
  GR/UP/WCH CH49 .......... 126 A2
Brookfield CP School
  SKEL WN8 .......... 64 F3
Brookfield High School
  KKBY L32 .......... 85 M5
The Brookfield School
  WDN WA8 .......... 134 F3
Brook House Business Centre
  WKBY CH48 .......... 124 C3
Brookhurst Primary School
  BEB CH63 .......... 143 L7
Brook Lodge Primary School
  RNFD/HAY WA11 .......... 76 B5
Brookside Infant School
  GTS/LS CH66 .......... 162 F1
Brookside Primary School
  STBRV L28 .......... 99 K6

Brookvale County Comprehensive School *RUNC* WA7 ... 150 E8
Brookvale County Junior School *RUNC* WA7 ... 150 D8
Brookvale Recreation Centre *RUNC* WA7 ... 150 E7
Broomfields Community Junior School *WARRS* WA4 ... 138 A4
Broughton Hall High School *WD/CROXPK* L12 ... 99 G8
Brow CP School *RUNC* WA7 ... 150 B4
Bruche Community Junior & Infant School *WARR* WA1 ... 122 C6
Bryn Cross Surgery *AIMK* WN4 ... 79 J1
Bryn Gates CP School *WGNE/HIN* WN2 ... 80 B7
Buckshaw CP School *CHLY/EC* PR7 ... 32 C3
Burscough Bridge Methodist School *BRSC* L40 ... 38 F8
Burscough County Primary School *BRSC* L40 ... 39 H8
Burscough Cricket Club *BRSC* L40 ... 52 B1
Burscough Health Centre *BRSC* L40 ... 39 G8
Burscough Priory High School *BRSC* L40 ... 38 F8
Burscough RC Primary School *BRSC* L40 ... 52 A3
Burscough Sports Centre *BRSC* L40 ... 39 G8
Burtonwood Community Primary School *WARRW/BUR* WA5 ... 104 A6
Burtonwood Industrial Centre *WARRW/BUR* WA5 ... 104 A6
Business Centre *WARR* WA1 ... 14 E5
Business Centre *WARRW/BUR* WA5 ... 14 B3
Byrchall High School *AIMK* WN4 ... 91 K4
Byrne Avenue Recreation Centre *RF/TRAN* CH42 ... 128 B4
Cabinet War Rooms *CLVP* L2 ... 12 E6
Cafe & Cricket Club *CHLDW* L16 ... 115 H4
Calday Grange Grammar School *WKBY* CH48 ... 124 F4
Calderstones Community Comprehensive School *CALD/MH* L18 ... 130 E1
Callands Community Primary School *WARRW/BUR* WA5 ... 121 G6
Camberley Medical Centre *WLTN* L25 ... 131 L5
Cambridge Road CP School *EP* CH65 ... 20 D5
Cammell Laird's Sports Club *RF/TRAN* CH42 ... 128 C4
Campion RC High School *EV* L5 ... 13 K1
Canalside Industrial Estate *EP* CH65 ... 20 F1
Canning Road Industrial Estate *CHTN/BK* PR9 ... 25 J7
Cansfield High School *AIMK* WN4 ... 91 J1
Capenhurst Grange School *GTS/LS* CH66 ... 163 G3
Capenhurst Primary School *CH/BCN* CH1 ... 162 D5
Cardinal Heenan RC High School *WD/CROXPK* L12 ... 98 F8
Carleton House Preparatory School *CALD/MH* L18 ... 130 B2
Cariton Lawn Tennis Club *STHP* PR8 ... 35 H3
Carmel RC 6th Form College *ECCL* WA10 ... 101 K4
Carr Lane Industrial Estate *HOY* CH47 ... 108 C6
Carr Mill Infant School *RNFD/HAY* WA11 ... 89 K5
Castlefields Health Centre *RUNC* WA7 ... 150 A8
Castle View CP School *RUNC* WA7 ... 149 M5
Castleway Primary School *MOR/LEA* CH46 ... 110 C1
Catalyst Museum *WDN* WA8 ... 134 C8
Causeway Medical Centre *WARRS* WA4 ... 137 K2
Cavendish Medical Centre *BIRK* CH41 ... 10 C2
Cavendish School *RUNC* WA7 ... 149 K8
Cavern Mecca *CLVP* L2 ... 12 F7
Cedar Cross Medical Centre *RAIN/WH* L35 ... 116 F2
Cedar Farm Gallery *BRSC* L40 ... 40 E5
Centec Business Centre *NG/CROX* L11 ... 85 K8
Central Shopping Centre *CLVPS* L1 ... 13 J8
Central Surgery *ECCL* WA10 ... 8 E3
Chaigley School *WARRS* WA4 ... 139 G1
Chalon Way Industrial Estate *STHEL* WA9 ... 9 H7

Chapel End CP School *WGNW/BIL/O* WN5 ... 90 A1
Chapelfield Clinic *WDN* WA8 ... 133 K4
Chapel Lane Business Park *CHLY/EC* PR7 ... 43 H5
Chapel Street Clinic *WDN* WA8 ... 16 D6
Charnock Richard C of E Primary School *CHLY/EC* PR7 ... 42 F1
Chatfield Community Primary School *GOL/RIS/CU* WA3 ... 123 G2
Cherryfield Primary School *KKBY* L32 ... 86 B6
Cherry Tree Community Primary School *LYMM* WA13 ... 139 L3
Cheshire County Council *GTS/LS* CH66 ... 163 H3
Cheshire County Council *RUNC* WA7 ... 151 M3
Chesire County Council *WDN* WA8 ... 16 E4
Chesnut Lodge Special School *WDN* WA8 ... 134 A4
Chesterfield High School *CSBY/BLUN* L23 ... 83 J1
Childcare Practice *SKEL* WN8 ... 65 M7
Childer Thornton CP School *GTS/LS* CH66 ... 155 K5
Childrens Centre Nhs Trust *CHTN/BK* PR9 ... 3 J2
Childwall Chiropodist Surgery *CHLDW* L16 ... 114 F6
Childwall C of E Primary School *CHLDW* L16 ... 114 F8
Childwall Community Comprehensive School *WAV* L15 ... 114 E6
Childwall Community Comprehensive School *WAV* L15 ... 114 C6
Childwall Park Avenue Doctors Surgery *CHLDW* L16 ... 114 F7
Chorley Associated Football Club *CHLY/EC* PR7 ... 32 E7
Chorley Cricket Club *CHLY/EC* PR7 ... 32 D5
Chorley & District Hospital *CHLY/EC* PR7 ... 32 E3
Chorley Golf Club *CHLYE* PR6 ... 44 C2
Chorley Mayfield School *CHLY/EC* PR7 ... 32 E8
Chorley North Business Park *CHLYE* PR6 ... 32 F2
Chorley & South Ribble Health Authority *CHLY/EC* PR7 ... 42 F4
Chorley Sports Centre *CHLY/EC* PR7 ... 32 F4
Chorley West Business Park *CHLY/EC* PR7 ... 32 B5
Christchurch C of E Primary School *BIRK* CH41 ... 10 F9
Christ Church C of E Primary School *BTL* L20 ... 7 J3
Christ Church C of E Primary School *MOR/LEA* CH46 ... 110 A5
Christian Fellowship School *EHL/KEN* L7 ... 113 K5
Christ the King Primary School *WAV* L15 ... 114 E5
Christ the King RC Primary School *PS/BROM* CH62 ... 144 A6
Christ the King School *STHP* PR8 ... 35 K3
Chromolyte Industrial Estate *STHP* PR8 ... 3 G7
Church Drive Primary School *PS/BROM* CH62 ... 128 D7
Churchill Industrial Estate *WLT/FAZ* L9 ... 84 E5
Church Road Medical Centre *BEB* CH63 ... 143 J1
Church Street Industrial Estate *WARR* WA1 ... 15 G6
Churchtown County Junior & Infant School *CHTN/BK* PR9 ... 25 K3
Churchtown Medical Centre *CHTN/BK* PR9 ... 25 J3
Cinnamon Brow C of E Primary School *WARRN/WOL* WA2 ... 122 B2
Civic Buildings *WGN* WN1 ... 4 E2
Claremont Medical Centre *MGHL* L31 ... 72 D5
Claremont Special School *WAL/NB* CH45 ... 95 H7
Clare Mount School *MOR/LEA* CH46 ... 110 B4
Clarence House School *FMBY* L37 ... 47 G7
Claughton Medical Centre *BIRK* CH41 ... 10 A3
Clayton Square Shopping Centre *CLVPS* L1 ... 13 H7
Cleveland Business Park *BIRK* CH41 ... 10 F2
Clifford Holroyde Special School *DV/KA/FCH* L14 ... 114 F2
Clinic for the Handicapped *WARRN/WOL* WA2 ... 14 D4
Clinic & Welfare Centre *WARR* WA1 ... 122 D6

Clough Fold Primary School *SKEL* WN8 ... 65 L3
Cobbs Brow CP School *SKEL* WN8 ... 65 J2
The Cobbs Community Infant School *WARRS* WA4 ... 138 A5
Cole Street Primary School *BIRK* CH41 ... 10 E6
Collins Industrial Estate *STHEL* WA9 ... 9 M1
Colwell CP School *DV/KA/FCH* L14 ... 99 J7
Commercial Business Centre *RAIN/WH* L35 ... 117 L2
Common Bank Employment Area *CHLY/EC* PR7 ... 32 A6
Common Bank Industrial Estate *CHLY/EC* PR7 ... 32 B6
Commonfield Road Surgery *GR/UP/WCH* CH49 ... 126 D4
Common Ground Sign Dance Theatre *CLVPS* L1 ... 13 G8
Community Care for Health *WDN* WA8 ... 16 D5
Community Centre *TOX* L8 ... 113 H5
Constance Industrial Estate *WDN* WA8 ... 16 D8
Coops Business Centre *WGN* WN1 ... 4 D4
Copplehouse Medical Centre *AIN/FAZ* L10 ... 85 J6
Coppull CP School *CHLY/EC* PR7 ... 43 G4
Coppull Medical Practice *CHLY/EC* PR7 ... 43 G5
Coppull Parish Church School *CHLY/EC* PR7 ... 43 H4
Corinthian CP School *CLB/OSW/ST* L13 ... 114 C1
Corner House Clinic *WKBY* CH48 ... 124 D3
Cornerways Medical Centre *HUY* L36 ... 99 L8
Corpus Christi RC Primary School *RNFD/HAY* WA11 ... 76 B6
Cottage Crafts & Gallery *GOL/RIS/CU* WA3 ... 106 C5
Council Offices *RNFD/HAY* WA11 ... 76 B7
County Fire HQ *CLVP* L2 ... 12 F5
The County Gallery *ANF/KKDL* L4 ... 97 H3
County Police Hq *CLVPS* L1 ... 12 F9
County Sessions House *VAUX/LVPD* L3 ... 13 J5
Court Hey Drive Doctors Surgery *CHLDW* L16 ... 115 H4
Court Hey Road Doctors Surgery *CHLDW* L16 ... 115 H4
Cowley High School *ECCL* WA10 ... 89 G7
Cowling Brow Industrial Estate *CHLYE* PR6 ... 33 G7
Craighurst CP School *WLTN* L25 ... 115 J6
Crawford County School *SKEL* WN8 ... 77 G2
The Cricketer Sports Club *WGNS/IIMK* WN3 ... 4 C9
Cricket Street Business Centre *WCNNW/ST* WN6 ... 4 B3
Croft Community Primary School *GOL/RIS/CU* WA3 ... 106 D5
Cromdale Way Community Hall & Health Centre *WARRW/BUR* WA5 ... 120 A7
Cronton C of E School *WDN* WA8 ... 117 L7
Crosby Baths *CSBY/BLUN* L23 ... 82 D3
Crosby Road North Primary School *CSBY/WL* L22 ... 83 G4
The Crosby Surgery *CSBY/BLUN* L23 ... 83 G2
Crossens C of E Primary School *CHTN/BK* PR9 ... 22 E8
Crossens Cricket Club *CHTN/BK* PR9 ... 25 M1
Cross Farm CP School *NTHLY* L27 ... 132 B1
Cross Hall High School *BRSC* L40 ... 51 K8
Cross Lane Surgery *RAIN/WH* L35 ... 116 F1
Croston Medical Centre *LEY/BBR* PR5 ... 29 L2
Croston Sports Club *LEY/BBR* PR5 ... 29 K5
Croston Village Surgery *LEY/BBR* PR5 ... 29 K3
Crowland Street Industrial Estate *CHTN/BK* PR9 ... 25 H7
Croxteth Community Comprehensive School *NG/CROX* L11 ... 85 L8
Croxteth CP School *NG/CROX* L11 ... 98 F1
Croxteth Family Health Centre *NG/CROX* L11 ... 98 E1
Croxteth Sports Centre *NG/CROX* L11 ... 98 E1
Culcheth Clinic *GOL/RIS/CU* WA3 ... 107 G2
Culcheth Community Primary School *GOL/RIS/CU* WA3 ... 107 J1

Culcheth High School *GOL/RIS/CU* WA3 ... 107 J2
Culcheth Sports Club *GOL/RIS/CU* WA3 ... 107 H2
Cunard Building *VAUX/LVPD* L3 ... 12 D7
The Curtain Gallery *PR/KW* L34 ... 100 E7
The Cutting Gallery *FMBY* L37 ... 59 H2
Daleacre Primary School *NTHTN* L30 ... 83 L2
Dallam Community Primary School *WARRW/BUR* WA5 ... 121 H4
Dalweb Trading Estate *CHTN/BK* PR9 ... 26 E2
Daresbury CP School *WARRS* WA4 ... 151 K3
Davenhill CP School *AIN/FAZ* L10 ... 84 F3
Dawpool C of E Primary School *PEN/TH* CH61 ... 125 K7
Deacon Trading Estate *NEWLW* WA12 ... 104 C3
Deanery C of E High School *WGN* WN1 ... 4 C2
De La Salle RC High School *NG/CROX* L11 ... 98 D3
De La Salle School *ECCL* WA10 ... 101 L1
The Dell Primary School *RF/TRAN* CH42 ... 128 D4
Delphside Primary School *SKEL* WN8 ... 65 K5
Derby Lane Medical Centre *CLB/OSW/ST* L13 ... 114 C2
Devaney Medical Centre *CL/PREN* CH43 ... 10 D8
Devonshire Park Primary School *RF/TRAN* CH42 ... 127 L3
Deyes High School *MGHL* L31 ... 72 F4
Deysbrook Medical Centre *WD/CROXPK* L12 ... 98 F6
Diamond Business Park *RNFD/HAY* WA11 ... 88 D1
Dinas Lane Medical Centre *HUY* L36 ... 115 L1
District C E Primary School *NEWLW* WA12 ... 104 C1
Ditton C of E Primary School *WDN* WA8 ... 133 J4
Ditton CP School *WDN* WA8 ... 133 M4
Ditton Hall St Michaels RC Primary School *WDN* WA8 ... 133 L6
Ditton Medical Centre *WDN* WA8 ... 133 L4
Dobson Park Industrial Estate *WGNE/HIN* WN2 ... 69 J7
Dock Board Offices *VAUX/LVPD* L3 ... 12 D8
Douglas Farm Riding School *SKEL* WN8 ... 53 L4
Douglas Valley Business Park *WGN* WN1 ... 56 E8
Dovecot CP School *DV/KA/FCH* L14 ... 115 J2
Dovecot Health Clinic *DV/KA/FCH* L14 ... 115 H1
Dovedale CP School *CALD/MH* L18 ... 114 C8
Downall Green RC Primary School *AIMK* WN4 ... 79 G7
Drug Dependency Clinic *CLVPS* L1 ... 13 K8
Drug Dependency Clinic *WDN* WA8 ... 16 D6
Drugs Clinic *CSBY/WL* L22 ... 83 G5
Duke Street County Infant School *CHLY/EC* PR7 ... 32 E7
Duke Street Doctors Surgery *FMBY* L37 ... 59 H3
Dunham on Hill CP School *FROD/HEL* WA6 ... 166 A7
Dunkirk Trading Estate *CH/BCN* CH1 ... 162 F7
Dunnys Sports Club *WLT/FAZ* L9 ... 97 J1
Duxbury Park Golf Club *CHLY/EC* PR7 ... 43 M1
Dyson Hall Special School *WLT/FAZ* L9 ... 84 F8
Eagle Sports Club *WARRW/BUR* WA5 ... 136 D1
Earle Primary School *EHL/KEN* L7 ... 113 L5
Earle Road Medical Centre *EHL/KEN* L7 ... 113 L5
East Chorley Business Centre *CHLYE* PR6 ... 32 F5
Eastcroft Park Primary School *NWD/KWIPK* L33 ... 74 B8
Eastside Industrial Estate *STHEL* WA9 ... 9 M7
EastView Surgery *CSBY/BLUN* L23 ... 83 G3
Eastway Primary School *MOR/LEA* CH46 ... 110 B4
Eaton Road Medical Centre *WD/CROXPK* L12 ... 98 E8
Eaves CP School *STHEL* WA9 ... 102 E7
Eccleston CP School *CHLY/EC* PR7 ... 30 D7
Eccleston Health Centre *CHLY/EC* PR7 ... 30 D6
Eccleston Lane Ends Primary School *PR/KW* L34 ... 101 G6

Eccleston Medical Centre *ECCL* WA10 ... 88 D8
The Edgebright Clinic *CLVPS* L1 ... 13 K9
Edge Hill Enterprise Training Centre *WLT/FAZ* L9 ... 85 G7
Edge Hill Health Centre *EHL/KEN* L7 ... 113 L4
Edge Hill University College *ORM* L39 ... 63 J2
Edge Lane Medical Centre *EHL/KEN* L7 ... 113 K4
Egremont Medical Centre *WAL/EG* CH44 ... 111 M1
Egremont Primary School *WAL/EG* CH44 ... 111 M1
Elaine Norris Sports Centre *VAUX/LVPD* L3 ... 12 F1
Elimu Study School *TOX* L8 ... 113 K6
Elleray Park School *WAL/NB* CH45 ... 95 J6
Ellesmere Port Business Centre *EP* CH65 ... 20 B5
Ellesmere Port Catholic High School *EP* CH65 ... 163 J2
Ellesmere Port Clinic *EP* CH65 ... 20 B7
Ellesmere Port Hospital *EP* CH65 ... 163 J3
Ellesmere Port Stadium *EP* CH65 ... 21 H8
Elliott Clarke School *CLVPS* L1 ... 113 G5
Elmers Green CP School *SKEL* WN8 ... 65 M4
Elms School *STBRV* L28 ... 99 K5
Elsie Smith College of Theatre Arts *EV* L5 ... 97 J8
Eltham Green Clinic *GR/UP/WCH* CH49 ... 126 D3
Elton County Primary School *CHNE* CH2 ... 165 J1
Emmaus School *WD/CROXPK* L12 ... 99 H2
Empress Industrial Estate *WGNE/HIN* WN2 ... 5 L5
Endowed Primary School *BRSC* L40 ... 40 F7
English Martyrs RC Primary School *LITH* L21 ... 83 K5
English Martyrs RC Primary School *RNFD/HAY* WA11 ... 91 G6
Epic Leisure Centre *EP* CH65 ... 20 C7
Eric Moore Health Centre *WARRN/WOL* WA2 ... 14 D4
Ernest Cookson Special School *WD/CROXPK* L12 ... 98 D7
Euxton C of E Primary School *CHLY/EC* PR7 ... 31 L2
Euxton CP School *CHLY/EC* PR7 ... 31 K1
Euxton Hall Hospital *CHLY/EC* PR7 ... 31 L4
Evelyn Primary School *PR/KW* L34 ... 101 G6
Evelyn Street Community Primary School *WARRW/BUR* WA5 ... 137 G1
Everite Road Industrial Estate *WDN* WA8 ... 133 K6
Everton Football Club Co *ANF/KKDL* L4 ... 97 H5
Everton Park Sports Centre *EV* L5 ... 97 G8
Everton Road Health Clinic *NPK/KEN* L6 ... 13 M2
Everyman Theatre *VAUX/LVPD* L3 ... 13 L8
Express Industrial Estate *WDN* WA8 ... 133 J6
Fairfield C of E School *WARR* WA1 ... 15 H3
Fairfield County High School *WDN* WA8 ... 134 E2
Fairfield County Junior & Infant School *WDN* WA8 ... 134 D3
Fairfield Hospital *RNFD/HAY* WA11 ... 89 G3
Fairfield Medical Centre *NPK/KEN* L6 ... 113 L2
Fairfield R F Football Club *RF/TRAN* CH42 ... 128 B3
Fairway Trading Estate *WDN* WA8 ... 134 A6
Faith House Yoga & Natural Health Centre *WAL/NB* CH45 ... 95 J7
Falcongate Industrial Estate *BIRK* CH41 ... 111 K4
Family Health Centre *KKBY* L32 ... 85 L3
Family Surgery *STHP* PR8 ... 35 J2
Farnborough Road Junior School *STHP* PR8 ... 35 J5
Farnworth C of E Junior & Infant School *WDN* WA8 ... 134 C1
Fazakerley CP School *AIN/FAZ* L10 ... 85 H6
Fazakerley High School *AIN/FAZ* L10 ... 85 H6
Fazakerley Sports Centre *AIN/FAZ* L10 ... 85 H5
Fearnhead Cross Medical Centre *WARRN/WOL* WA2 ... 122 B3

Fender Primary School
GR/UP/WCH CH49 ............... 126 E2
Fernhill Sports Centre
BTL L20 ............... 83 M7
Ferries Industrial Estate
RF/TRAN CH42 ............... 128 B2
Fingerpost Surgery
STHEL WA9 ............... 9 L4
Fire Station
CLVPS L1 ............... 12 F9
Firsdale Industrial Estate
LEIGH WN7 ............... 81 H2
Fir Tree Drive South Medical Centre
WD/CROXPK L12 ............... 99 H2
Fishwicks Industrial Estate
RNFD/HAY WA11 ............... 91 H5
Fishwicks Industrial Estate
STHEL WA9 ............... 102 F5
Fleet Lane Industrial Estate
STHEL WA9 ............... 103 G3
Fleming Industrial Estate
WARR WA1 ............... 15 G5
Floral Pavilion Theatre
WAL/NB CH45 ............... 95 L4
Florence Melly Junior School
ANF/KKDL L4 ............... 97 L4
Flower Gallery
WARRS WA4 ............... 138 F2
Ford Medical Practice
LITH L21 ............... 83 K3
Fordton Leisure Centre
WARRN/WOL WA2 ............... 121 J2
Forefield Infant School
CSBY/BLUN L23 ............... 83 J1
Forefield Junior School
CSBY/BLUN L23 ............... 83 H1
The Forge Shopping Centre
WARRS WA4 ............... 137 L4
Formby Associated
Football Club
FMBY L37 ............... 59 H2
Formby Cricket Club
FMBY L37 ............... 47 H8
Formby Golf Club
FMBY L37 ............... 46 F8
Formby Hall Golf Club
FMBY L37 ............... 47 L5
Formby High Lower School
FMBY L37 ............... 59 H1
Formby High School
FMBY L37 ............... 59 G1
Formby Junior Sports Club
FMBY L37 ............... 47 J8
Formby Ladies Golf Club
FMBY L37 ............... 46 F8
Formby Lawn Tennis Club
FMBY L37 ............... 47 H8
The Fountains Abbey
ANF/KKDL L4 ............... 97 G6
Four Acre Health Centre
STHEL WA9 ............... 118 D1
Foxfield School
MOR/LEA CH46 ............... 109 M5
Freshfield Primary School
FMBY L37 ............... 59 J1
Freshfield Surgery
FMBY L37 ............... 59 H1
Freshlea Private Clinic
FMBY L37 ............... 58 F4
Friary Primary School
EV L5 ............... 13 K2
Friends of St Helens College
ECCL WA10 ............... 8 F5
Frodsham C of E
Primary School
FROD/HEL WA6 ............... 160 E6
Frodsham County High School
FROD/HEL WA6 ............... 160 D5
Frodsham Golf Club
FROD/HEL WA6 ............... 160 D8
Frodsham Town Council
FROD/HEL WA6 ............... 160 C5
Frodsham Weaver Vale CP
School
FROD/HEL WA6 ............... 160 E3
Fylde Road Industrial Estate
CHTN/BK PR9 ............... 25 K1
The Gallery
AIG/SPK L17 ............... 129 K1
The Gallery
CLVPS L1 ............... 13 H8
The Gallery
ECCL WA10 ............... 8 F4
The Gallery
WKBY CH48 ............... 124 C3
Garston Industrial Estate
ALL/GAR L19 ............... 145 L1
Garston Leisure Centre
ALL/GAR L19 ............... 130 E7
Garston RC Primary School
ALL/GAR L19 ............... 130 E7
Garston Sports Centre
ALL/GAR L19 ............... 130 E6
Garswood CP School
AIMK WN4 ............... 90 L1
Garswood Football Club
AIMK WN4 ............... 78 D8
Garven Place Clinic
WARR WA1 ............... 14 C6
Gateacre Community
Comprehensive School
WLTN L25 ............... 115 J8
Gateworth Industrial Estate
WARRW/BUR WA5 ............... 136 F2
Gayton Primary School
HES CH60 ............... 141 J9
Gemini Business Park
WARRW/BUR WA5 ............... 121 H2
General Medical Practice
HUY L36 ............... 116 A1
George's Dock
VAUX/LVPD L3 ............... 12 C7
Gilbrook School
BIRK CH41 ............... 11 M5
Gilded Hollins School
LEIGH WN7 ............... 93 L4
Gillibrand Primary School
CHLY/EC PR7 ............... 32 D7

Gillmoss Medical Centre
NG/CROX L11 ............... 85 L8
Gilmour Infant School
ALL/GAR L19 ............... 130 D6
Gilmour Junior School
ALL/GAR L19 ............... 130 D6
Gladstone Theatre
PS/BROM CH62 ............... 143 K1
Glenburn High School
SKEL WN8 ............... 65 J4
Glenda Jackson Theatre
RF/TRAN CH42 ............... 127 L2
Glovers Lane Practice
NTHTN L30 ............... 84 B2
The Glucksman Practice
WGN WN1 ............... 4 E4
Golborne All Saints RC School
GOL/RIS/CU WA3 ............... 92 D5
Golborne Clinic
GOL/RIS/CU WA3 ............... 92 D4
Golborne CP School
GOL/RIS/CU WA3 ............... 92 C5
Golborne High School
GOL/RIS/CU WA3 ............... 92 E4
Golden Triangle I
ndustrial Estate
WDN WA8 ............... 133 L7
Golf Club Bungalow
WGNW/BIL/O WN5 ............... 66 F6
The Golf Gallery
WGN WN1 ............... 4 E3
Gorse Covert Primary School
WARRW/BUR WA5 ............... 107 K7
Gorsewood CP School
RUNC WA7 ............... 151 G6
Gorsthills CP School
GTS/LS CH66 ............... 162 E2
Grain Industrial Estate
TOX L8 ............... 129 G1
Granada TV
VAUX/LVPD L3 ............... 12 E9
The Grange Country Club
NSTN CH64 ............... 153 H1
Grange Primary School
NTHTN L30 ............... 72 A8
Grange Surgery
STHP PR8 ............... 2 E9
Grange Valley Primary School
RNFD/HAY WA11 ............... 90 F8
Grantside Special School
NPK/KEN L6 ............... 113 J1
Grappenhall Clinic
WARRS WA4 ............... 138 D3
Grappenhall Cricket Club
WARRS WA4 ............... 138 C4
Grappenhall Hall School
WARRS WA4 ............... 138 D4
Grappenhall Sports Club
WARRS WA4 ............... 138 B4
Grassendale Medical Practice
ALL/GAR L19 ............... 130 C5
Greasby Health Centre
GR/UP/WCH CH49 ............... 125 M2
Greasby Infant School
GR/UP/WCH CH49 ............... 125 L3
Greasby Junior School
GR/UP/WCH CH49 ............... 125 L4
Great Crosby RC Primary School
CSBY/BLUN L23 ............... 83 G1
Great Homer Street
Medical Centre
EV L5 ............... 97 G8
Great Meols Primary School
HOY CH47 ............... 109 G4
Great Sankey Community
High School
WARRW/BUR WA5 ............... 119 M5
Great Sankey Community
Primary School
WARRW/BUR WA5 ............... 120 C8
Great Sutton Health Centre
GTS/LS CH66 ............... 162 F1
Greenbank Galleries
WAV L15 ............... 114 A7
Greenbank High School
STHP PR8 ............... 35 G4
Greenbank Surgery
NSTN CH64 ............... 154 B5
Green Lane Medical Centre
CLB/OSW/ST L13 ............... 98 A8
Green Lane School
WARR WA1 ............... 122 D5
Greenleas Primary School
WAL/NB CH45 ............... 94 E7
Greenoaks Farm Industrial
Estate
WDN WA8 ............... 17 H3
Green Park Primary School
MGHL L31 ............... 72 D3
Greenways Special School
ALL/GAR L19 ............... 130 B6
Greetby Hill C of E Junior
School
ORM L39 ............... 51 H4
Gresford Medical Centre
DV/KA/FCH L14 ............... 115 H2
Grimefold Industrial Estate
CHLYE PR6 ............... 44 F7
Group Practice
WAL/NB CH45 ............... 95 G4
Grove House Practice
RUNC WA7 ............... 19 H3
Grove Park Industrial Estate
CHLY/EC PR7 ............... 30 E8
Grove Street
Community Primary School
PS/BROM CH62 ............... 128 C6
Guardian Medical Centre
WARRW/BUR WA5 ............... 14 A4
Guardian Street
Industrial Estate
WARRW/BUR WA5 ............... 14 B4
Guinea Gap Baths &
Recreation Centre
WAL/EG CH44 ............... 112 A2
Gwladys Street CP School
ANF/KKDL L4 ............... 97 J4

Gwydrin Road Doctors Surgery
CALD/MH L18 ............... 114 E8
Halebank C of E
Controlled Primary School
WDN WA8 ............... 148 C1
Hale C of E School
SPK/HALE L24 ............... 148 A4
The Halefield Family
Medical Centre
ECCL WA10 ............... 8 F3
Hale Primary School
SPK/HALE L24 ............... 147 M4
Halewood C of E Primary School
HLWD L26 ............... 132 C4
Halewood Community
Comprehensive School
WLTN L25 ............... 131 M6
Halewood Health Centre
HLWD L26 ............... 132 B6
Halewood Sports Centre
HLWD L26 ............... 132 C6
Hall Green Clinic
SKEL WN8 ............... 66 D6
Hall Green Surgery
SKEL WN8 ............... 66 C6
Hall Street Medical Centre
ECCL WA10 ............... 9 H5
Hallwood Health Centre
RUNC WA7 ............... 150 B6
Hallwood Park CP School
RUNC WA7 ............... 150 A7
Halton Borough Council
RUNC WA7 ............... 150 B5
Halton Borough Council
WDN WA8 ............... 16 E4
Halton Borough Council
WDN WA8 ............... 16 C5
Halton Borough Council
WDN WA8 ............... 16 F3
Halton Borough Council
WDN WA8 ............... 16 A6
Halton Borough Council
WDN WA8 ............... 133 K5
Halton College
WDN WA8 ............... 16 D5
Halton College of
Further Education
WDN WA8 ............... 16 C4
Halton General Hospital
NHS Trust
RUNC WA7 ............... 150 B7
Halton Health Authority
WDN WA8 ............... 134 F3
Halton Lodge County
Junior & Infant School
RUNC WA7 ............... 19 M8
Halton Magistrates Court
RUNC WA7 ............... 150 B5
Halton St Marys C of E
Primary School
RUNC WA7 ............... 150 C5
Hamblett School
ECCL WA10 ............... 88 F7
Hanover Galleries
CLVPS L1 ............... 13 G9
Hanson Road Business Park
WLT/FAZ L9 ............... 84 E8
Harold Magnay Special School
WLTN L25 ............... 131 H1
Hartley Trading Estate
WLT/FAZ L9 ............... 84 D8
Haskayne C of E School
ORM L39 ............... 61 G2
Haslemere Industrial Estate
AIMK WN4 ............... 79 J5
Hatton Garden Industrial Estate
CLVP L2 ............... 12 F5
Hatton Hill Primary School
LITH L21 ............... 83 K3
Hawkley Brook Surgery
WGNS/IIMK WN3 ............... 79 H2
Hawkley Brook Trading Estate
WGNS/IIMK WN3 ............... 79 G3
Hawkley Hall High School
WGNS/IIMK WN3 ............... 79 L2
Hawthorne Business Park
WARRW/BUR WA5 ............... 121 J5
Haydock Cricket Club
RNFD/HAY WA11 ............... 90 F6
Haydock Cricket Club
RNFD/HAY WA11 ............... 90 E7
Haydock High School
RNFD/HAY WA11 ............... 90 D7
Haydock Medical Centre
RNFD/HAY WA11 ............... 90 F7
Hayfield School
GR/UP/WCH CH49 ............... 110 C7
Hazel Business Park
RNFD/HAY WA11 ............... 88 E1
Health Authority
SPK/HALE L24 ............... 147 G2
The Health Centre Surgery
HLWD L26 ............... 132 B6
Heath Road Medical Centre
RUNC WA7 ............... 19 J7
Helsby County High School
FROD/HEL WA6 ............... 160 A8
Helsby Health Centre
FROD/HEL WA6 ............... 166 D2
Her Majesty's Prison
WLT/FAZ L9 ............... 84 B8
Hermes Galleries
WAL/EG CH44 ............... 111 J1
Hesketh Golf Club
CHTN/BK PR9 ............... 25 G3
Heskin Football Club
CHLY/EC PR7 ............... 41 M2
Heskin Pembertons
Primary School
CHLY/EC PR7 ............... 42 B3
Heswall County Primary School
PEN/TH CH61 ............... 141 J4
Heswall Football Club
HES CH60 ............... 141 L6
Heswall Health Centre
HES CH60 ............... 141 H4
Heswall Preparatory School
HES CH60 ............... 141 G3

Hey Comprehensive School
HUY L36 ............... 116 B3
Heygarth Junior School
PS/BROM CH62 ............... 144 A8
Hey Green Jmi School
WAV L15 ............... 114 A5
Higher Bebington
Junior School
BEB CH63 ............... 127 L7
Higher Primary School
BEB CH63 ............... ... 
Higher Side Community
Comprehensive School
RAIN/WH L35 ............... 117 J2
Highfield C of E School
WGNS/IIMK WN3 ............... 78 A3
Highfield CP School
CHLYE PR6 ............... 32 F5
Highfield Cricket Club
WGNS/IIMK WN3 ............... 78 E1
Highfield Industrial Estate
CHLYE PR6 ............... 32 E3
Highfield School
HLWD L26 ............... 132 C6
High Pastures Surgery
MGHL L31 ............... 72 E3
Hightown Village Surgery
HTWN L38 ............... 70 C1
Hilbre High School
WKBY CH48 ............... 124 F2
Hillside CP School
FROD/HEL WA6 ............... 166 F1
Hillside CP School
SKEL WN8 ............... 65 M5
Hillside Golf Club
STHP PR8 ............... 35 G4
Hillside Health Centre
SKEL WN8 ............... 65 L4
Hillside High School
BTL L20 ............... 7 M5
Hillside House Surgery
HUY L36 ............... 100 B8
Hillside Infant School
CL/PREN CH43 ............... 110 E8
Hillside Junior School
CL/PREN CH43 ............... 110 F8
Hillside Road Doctors Surgery
HUY L36 ............... 100 A8
Hill Street Business Centre
VAUX/LVPD L3 ............... 112 F7
Hill View CP School
RUNC WA7 ............... 161 G1
Hinderton School
EP CH65 ............... 163 J2
Hindley Business Centre
WGNE/HIN WN2 ............... 69 M8
Hindley CP School
WGNE/HIN WN2 ............... 69 M8
Hindley Green C of E School
WGNE/HIN WN2 ............... 81 K2
HM Coroners Court
CLVP L2 ............... 12 F7
HM Remand Centre
GOL/RIS/CU WA3 ............... 107 G5
Holcroft Clinic
GOL/RIS/CU WA3 ............... 107 G2
Holgate CP School
WGNW/BIL/O WN5 ............... 67 G8
Holland Moor CP School
SKEL WN8 ............... 66 A6
Hollies Surgery
FMBY L37 ............... 59 H2
Holly Lodge Comprehensive
School
WD/CROXPK L12 ............... 98 C7
Hollywood Superbowl
CLB/OSW/ST L13 ............... 114 B4
Holmbrook School
WLTN L25 ............... 131 G2
Holmeswood Methodist School
KIRK/FR/WA PR4 ............... 27 K7
Holy Angels Infant School
KKBY L32 ............... 85 L3
Holy Angels Primary School
KKBY L32 ............... 85 M2
Holy Cross RC High School
CHLY/EC PR7 ............... 43 L1
Holy Cross RC Primary School
BIRK CH41 ............... 111 G4
Holy Cross RC Primary School
ECCL WA10 ............... 9 J4
Holy Cross & St Marys
Primary School
VAUX/LVPD L3 ............... 13 G4
Holy Family High School
CSBY/BLUN L23 ............... 71 J7
Holy Family Primary School
WLTN L25 ............... 131 M4
Holy Family RC Primary School
CHTN/BK PR9 ............... 25 G6
Holy Family RC Primary School
WDN WA8 ............... 117 M7
Holy Family RC Primary School
WGNE/HIN WN2 ............... 69 J3
Holy Family RC Primary School
WGNE/HIN WN2 ............... 80 C4
Holy Name RC Primary School
WLT/FAZ L9 ............... 85 G6
Holy Rosary RC Primary School
AIN/FAZ L10 ............... 84 E2
Holy Spirit RC Primary School
NTHTN L30 ............... 83 M2
Holy Spirit School
RUNC WA7 ............... 149 M5
Holy Trinity C of E Primary
School
CHTN/BK PR9 ............... 3 J3
Holy Trinity C of E Primary
School
FMBY L37 ............... 59 H2
Holy Trinity C of E Primary
School
HOY CH47 ............... 108 E6
Holy Trinity Primary School
ALL/GAR L19 ............... 130 F8
Homoeopathic Medical Centre
CLB/OSW/ST L13 ............... 114 C2
Hood Manor Community
Primary School
WARRW/BUR WA5 ............... 120 E7

Hood Manor Medical Centre
WARRW/BUR WA5 ............... 120 E8
Hope Special School
WGNS/IIMK WN3 ............... 79 G3
Hope Street Natural
Health Centre
CLVPS L1 ............... 113 G5
Hope Valley CP School
EV L5 ............... 97 H6
Horns Mill CP School
FROD/HEL WA6 ............... 166 C4
Hornspit Medical Centre
NG/CROX L11 ............... 98 C5
Howley Quay Industrial Estate
WARR WA1 ............... 15 J5
Hoylake Business Centre
HOY CH47 ............... 108 E5
Hoylake Cottage Hospital
HOY CH47 ............... 108 E5
Hoylake Cottage Hospital Trust
HOY CH47 ............... 108 E5
Hoylake Road Surgery
MOR/LEA CH46 ............... 109 M5
Hoylake Rugby Football Club
HOY CH47 ............... 108 D6
Hudson Primary School
MGHL L31 ............... 72 F6
Hugh Baird College
BTL L20 ............... 7 H7
Hulmes Bridge Business Centre
ORM L39 ............... 49 M3
Hunts Cross CP School
WLTN L25 ............... 131 L7
Hunts Cross Group Practice
WLTN L25 ............... 131 K6
Hurlston Hall Golf Club
BRSC L40 ............... 50 E3
Hurst Special School
ECCL WA10 ............... 89 G7
Huyton St Michaels
Primary School
HUY L36 ............... 115 M2
Ince Clinic & Community Centre
WGNE/HIN WN2 ............... 69 J6
Ince C of E Primary School
WGNE/HIN WN2 ............... 5 M6
Ince In Makerfield C of E Junior
& Infant School
WGNE/HIN WN2 ............... 69 J6
Ince Spring View Cs School
WGNE/HIN WN2 ............... 80 B1
Interchange Motorway
Industrial Estate
HUY L36 ............... 116 C2
Irby Cricket Club
PEN/TH CH61 ............... 125 M5
Irby Primary School
PEN/TH CH61 ............... 126 A6
Irwin Road Health Centre
STHEL WA9 ............... 102 F6
Isle of Man Ferry Terminal
VAUX/LVPD L3 ............... 12 C6
Islington House Medical Centre
NPK/KEN L6 ............... 13 M4
Ivy Farm Court Doctors Surgery
SPK/HALE L24 ............... 147 M4
John Moores University
CLVPS L1 ............... 113 G5
John Street CP School
EP CH65 ............... 20 C2
John Street Medical Centre
GOL/RIS/CU WA3 ............... 92 C4
Jubilee Medical Centre
NG/CROX L11 ............... 98 E2
The Kenneth Macrae
Medical Centre
RNFD/HAY WA11 ............... 76 B7
Kensington CP Junior &
Infant School
EHL/KEN L7 ............... 113 K3
Kensington Medical Centre
NPK/KEN L6 ............... 113 J2
Kerfoot Business Park
WARRN/WOL WA2 ............... 121 J5
Kew Medical Centre
STHP PR8 ............... 36 A2
Kew Woods CP School
STHP PR8 ............... 36 A2
King David High School
WAV L15 ............... 114 E6
King David Primary School
WAV L15 ............... 114 E6
King Edward Industrial Estate
VAUX/LVPD L3 ............... 12 C5
Kingfisher Business Park
BTL L20 ............... 83 L6
King George Vi Sixth Form
College
STHP PR8 ............... 25 G8
Kingsbury School
ORM L39 ............... 51 G8
Kings Business Park
PR/KW L34 ............... 100 C8
Kingsdown High School
WGNW/BIL/O WN5 ............... 67 L6
Kingsley Community School
TOX L8 ............... 113 J6
Kingsmead School
HOY CH47 ............... 108 E5
Kingsway Christian School
WGN WN1 ............... 4 F2
Kingsway Primary School
WAL/EG CH44 ............... 111 L3
Kingsway Surgery
CSBY/WL L22 ............... 83 G3
Kinsbury Estate
SKEL WN8 ............... 64 D3
Kirkby Industrial Estate
Post Office
NWD/KWIPK L33 ............... 86 D5
Kirkby Sports Centre
KKBY L32 ............... 85 L5
Kirkdale CP School
ANF/KKDL L4 ............... 96 F5
Kirkless Industrial Estate
WGNE/HIN WN2 ............... 69 K4
The Knoll Surgery Partnership
FROD/HEL WA6 ............... 160 D4

Knotty Ash CP School
 *DV/KA/FCH* L14 .................. **114** F1
Knowsley Borough Council
 *HUY* L36 .......................... **116** A3
Knowsley Community College
 *KKBY* L32 ......................... **85** M3
Knowsley Community College
 *PR/KW* L34 ....................... **100** A2
Knowsley Industrial Park
 *NWD/KWIPK* L33 ................. **86** E3
Knowsley Magistrates Court
 *HUY* L36 .......................... **116** A3
Knowsley Medical Centre
 *PR/KW* L34 ....................... **99** M2
Knowsley Metropolitan
 Borough Council
 *DV/KA/FCH* L14 .................. **99** K8
Knowsley Metropolitan
 Borough Council
 *HLWD* L26 ........................ **132** B6
Knowsley Metropolitan
 Borough Council
 *HUY* L36 .......................... **115** M3
Knowsley Metropolitan
 Borough Council
 *HUY* L36 .......................... **116** A3
Knowsley Metropolitan
 Borough Council
 *KKBY* L32 ......................... **85** M3
Knowsley Metropolitan
 Borough Council
 *KKBY* L32 ......................... **86** B4
Knowsley Metropolitan
 Borough Council
 *PR/KW* L34 ....................... **100** E7
Knowsley Parish Council
 *PR/KW* L34 ....................... **99** L1
Knowsley Village
 Primary School
 *PR/KW* L34 ....................... **99** L3
Ktis Art Gallery
 *CALD/MH* L18 ..................... **114** C8
Lady Lever Art Gallery
 *PS/BROM* CH62 ................... **128** D7
Ladymount RC Primary School
 *PEN/TH* CH61 ..................... **141** H2
Lakeside Surgery
 *LYMM* WA13 ...................... **139** M3
Lamberhead Green
 County Infants School
 *WGNW/BIL/O* WN5 ............... **67** J6
Lamberhead Green CP School
 *WGNW/BIL/O* WN5 ............... **67** K6
Lamberhead Industrial Estate
 *WGNW/BIL/O* WN5 ............... **67** K8
The Lamplighters Gallery
 *STHP* PR8 ......................... **34** F8
Lancashire College for Adult
 Education
 *CHLY/EC* PR7 ..................... **32** B5
Lancashire County Council
 *BRSC* L40 ......................... **52** A2
Lancashire County Council
 *CHLYE* PR6 ........................ **44** C6
Lancashire Schools I C T Centre
 *CHLY/EC* PR7 ..................... **32** C5
Lancaster House
 Medical Centre
 *ECCL* WA10 ....................... **9** G3
Lance Lane Medical Centre
 *WAV* L15 .......................... **114** C6
Lander Road Primary School
 *LITH* L21 .......................... **83** L7
Landgate Industrial Estate
 *AIMK* WN4 ......................... **79** J5
Langbank Medical Centre
 *NG/CROX* L11 ..................... **98** B4
Langham Street
 Industrial Estate
 *ANF/KKDL* L4 ..................... **97** H5
Larkfield CP School
 *CHTN/BK* PR9 ..................... **25** J2
Latchford Medical Centre
 *WARRS* WA4 ...................... **138** A2
Lathom High School
 *SKEL* WN8 ......................... **65** H1
Lathom House Surgery
 *BRSC* L40 ......................... **39** H8
Lathom Park C of E
 Primary School
 *BRSC* L40 ......................... **52** C5
Lathom Road Health Centre
 *HUY* L36 .......................... **116** A4
Laurel Business Centre
 *EHL/KEN* L7 ....................... **113** M3
Lawrence CP School
 *WAV* L15 .......................... **113** M6
Lea Green Business Park
 *STHEL* WA9 ....................... **118** B1
Leamington CP School
 *NG/CROX* L11 ..................... **97** M3
Leasowe Primary School
 *MOR/LEA* CH46 ................... **110** D1
Leasowe Recreation Centre
 *MOR/LEA* CH46 ................... **110** C2
Lee Manor High School
 *NTHLY* L27 ........................ **115** M8
Legh Vale CP School
 *RNFD/HAY* WA11 ................. **90** D7
Lewisham Medical Centre
 *ANF/KKDL* L4 ..................... **97** L5
Leyland House Surgery
 *ORM* L39 .......................... **51** H8
Lidderdale CP School
 *WAV* L15 .......................... **114** A1
Linacre Primary School
 *BTL* L20 ........................... **83** L8
Linaker County Primary School
 *STHP* PR8 ......................... **3** G8
Lincoln Road Health Centre
 *STHP* PR8 ......................... **35** J4
Lingham CP School
 *MOR/LEA* CH46 ................... **109** M4
Lingholme Health Centre
 *ECCL* WA10 ....................... **8** F4
Liscard Primary School
 *WAL/NB* CH45 ..................... **95** L8

Lister Drive CP School
 *CLB/OSW/ST* L13 ................. **114** A1
Litherland High School
 *LITH* L21 .......................... **83** M3
Litherland Moss Primary School
 *LITH* L21 .......................... **83** M4
Little Crosby Road
 Doctors Surgery
 *CSBY/BLUN* L23 ................... **70** F8
Little Digmoor CP School
 *SKEL* WN8 ......................... **65** K7
Little Theatre
 *CHLY/EC* PR7 ..................... **32** E5
Little Theatre
 *CHTN/BK* PR9 ..................... **3** H3
Liver Industrial Estate
 *WLT/FAZ* L9 ...................... **97** L1
Liverpool Airport
 *SPK/HALE* L24 .................... **146** E3
Liverpool Anglican Cathedral
 *CLVPS* L1 ......................... **113** G6
Liverpool Art School
 *EHL/KEN* L7 ....................... **13** L9
Liverpool Art School
 *TOX* L8 ............................ **113** H5
Liverpool Chinese
 Medical Centre
 *CLVPS* L1 ......................... **13** G7
Liverpool City Council
 *AIG/SPK* L17 ...................... **129** M3
Liverpool City Council
 *ANF/KKDL* L4 ..................... **97** G6
Liverpool City Council
 *CALD/MH* L18 ..................... **130** F1
Liverpool City Council
 *CLB/OSW/ST* L13 ................. **114** A3
Liverpool City Council
 *CLVP* L2 .......................... **12** E6
Liverpool City Council
 *CLVPS* L1 ......................... **12** F6
Liverpool City Council
 *CLVPS* L1 ......................... **13** G6
Liverpool City Council
 *NPK/KEN* L6 ...................... **113** L1
Liverpool City Council
 *NPK/KEN* L6 ...................... **114** A2
Liverpool City Council
 *TOX* L8 ............................ **113** G7
Liverpool City Council
 *VAUX/LVPD* L3 .................... **12** C3
Liverpool City Council
 *VAUX/LVPD* L3 .................... **12** E6
Liverpool City Council
 *VAUX/LVPD* L3 .................... **13** L5
Liverpool City Council
 *WLT/FAZ* L9 ...................... **84** E7
Liverpool Community College
 *AIG/SPK* L17 ...................... **130** A4
Liverpool Community College
 *CLB/OSW/ST* L13 ................. **98** B7
Liverpool Community College
 *CLVPS* L1 ......................... **13** J9
Liverpool Community College
 *EHL/KEN* L7 ....................... **13** L9
Liverpool Community College
 *EHL/KEN* L7 ....................... **113** J5
Liverpool Community College
 *EV* L5 ............................. **96** F7
Liverpool Community College
 *VAUX/LVPD* L3 .................... **112** F6
Liverpool Cricket Club
 *ALL/GAR* L19 ..................... **130** D5
Liverpool Crown & High Court
 *CLVPS* L1 ......................... **12** F8
Liverpool Empire Theatre
 *CLVPS* L1 ......................... **13** H6
Liverpool Football Club
 *BTL* L20 ........................... **6** E2
Liverpool Football Club
 *WD/CROXPK* L12 ................. **98** E6
Liverpool Football Club
 *ANF/KKDL* L4 ..................... **97** J6
Liverpool Health Authority
 *VAUX/LVPD* L3 .................... **12** E5
Liverpool Hope University
 *CLVPS* L1 ......................... **13** L9
Liverpool Hope
 University College
 *CHLDW* L16 ....................... **114** F7
Liverpool Hope
 University College
 *VAUX/LVPD* L3 .................... **13** L4
Liverpool John
 Moores University
 *AIG/SPK* L17 ...................... **130** B4
Liverpool John
 Moores University
 *BIRK* CH41 ........................ **11** K2
Liverpool John
 Moores University
 *CALD/MH* L18 ..................... **130** A2
Liverpool John
 Moores University
 *CLVPS* L1 ......................... **13** K8
Liverpool John
 Moores University
 *VAUX/LVPD* L3 .................... **12** F5
Liverpool John
 Moores University
 *VAUX/LVPD* L3 .................... **13** H4
Liverpool John
 Moores University
 *VAUX/LVPD* L3 .................... **13** G5
Liverpool Magistrates Court
 *CLVP* L2 .......................... **13** G6
Liverpool Museum
 *VAUX/LVPD* L3 .................... **13** H5
Liverpool Playhouse Theatre
 *CLVPS* L1 ......................... **13** H7
Liverpool St Helens Rugby Union
 Football Club
 *RNFD/HAY* WA11 ................. **88** C6
Liverpool Theatre School
 *AIG/SPK* L17 ...................... **129** M1
Liverpool Theatre School
 *AIG/SPK* L17 ...................... **130** B4
Liverpool University
 *NSTN* CH64 ....................... **153** M6

Liverpool Womens
 Hospital Trust
 *TOX* L8 ............................ **113** J6
Locking Stumps
 Community Primary School
 *GOL/RIS/CU* WA3 ................. **106** E8
Longbarn Community
 Primary School
 *WARRN/WOL* WA2 ............... **122** D4
Longford Street Surgery
 *WARRN/WOL* WA2 ............... **14** E1
Long Lane Community
 Primary School
 *WARRN/WOL* WA2 ............... **121** K4
Long Lane Doctors Surgery
 *ALL/GAR* L19 ..................... **130** F6
Long Lane Medical Centre
 *WLT/FAZ* L9 ...................... **98** B1
Longshoot Health Centre
 *WGN* WN1 ........................ **5** J2
Longton Lane CP School
 *RAIN/WH* L35 ..................... **101** K8
Longton Medical Centre
 *RAIN/WH* L35 ..................... **117** K2
Longview Primary School
 *HUY* L36 .......................... **100** A7
Lordsgate Township C of E
 Primary School
 *BRSC* L40 ......................... **52** A2
Lourdes Hospital
 *CALD/MH* L18 ..................... **130** B1
Loushers Lane Special School
 *WARRS* WA4 ...................... **137** M3
Lower Lee Special School
 *WLTN* L25 ......................... **131** G1
Low Hall County Primary School
 *WGNE/HIN* WN2 ................. **80** C2
Lowton High School
 *GOL/RIS/CU* WA3 ................. **93** K5
Lowton Junior & Infant School
 *GOL/RIS/CU* WA3 ................. **93** J6
Lowton St Marys C of E School
 *GOL/RIS/CU* WA3 ................. **93** K5
Lowton West Primary School
 *GOL/RIS/CU* WA3 ................. **92** E5
Lunts Heath CP School
 *WDN* WA8 ........................ **118** D8
Lydiate Primary School
 *MGHL* L31 ........................ **72** E1
Lyme County Infant School
 *NEWLW* WA12 .................... **104** B1
Lyndale School
 *PS/BROM* CH62 ................... **144** B8
Mab Lane Junior & Infant School
 *STBRV* L28 ........................ **99** H6
Mabs Cross Primary School
 *WGN* WN1 ........................ **5** G1
Mackets Primary School
 *WLTN* L25 ......................... **131** L4
Macmillan Surgery
 *KKBY* L32 ......................... **86** C4
Maghull Health Centre
 *MGHL* L31 ........................ **72** F4
Maghull High School
 *MGHL* L31 ........................ **72** D6
Maghull Primary School
 *MGHL* L31 ........................ **72** D6
Maidford CP School
 *DV/KA/FCH* L14 .................. **99** H8
Malvern Primary School
 *DV/KA/FCH* L14 .................. **115** H3
Manchester Port Health
 Authority
 *RUNC* WA7 ........................ **19** G2
Manley Village School
 *FROD/HEL* WA6 ................... **167** J7
The Manor C of E Junior School
 *NEWLW* WA12 .................... **104** B1
Manor Farm Medical Centre
 *HUY* L36 .......................... **116** B4
Manor High School
 *CSBY/BLUN* L23 ................... **70** E7
Manor House CP School
 *FROD/HEL* WA6 ................... **160** E4
Manor Industrial Estate
 *WARRS* WA4 ...................... **15** M8
Manor Primary School
 *CL/PREN* CH43 .................... **110** E7
Mansfield CP School
 *EP* CH65 .......................... **163** H2
Marble Place Shopping Centre
 *STHP* PR8 ......................... **3** G4
Margaret Beavan Special School
 *WD/CROXPK* L12 ................. **98** C6
The Margaret Thompson
 Medical Centre
 *SPK/HALE* L24 .................... **147** J1
Maricourt High School
 *MGHL* L31 ........................ **73** G5
Marine Football Club
 *CSBY/BLUN* L23 ................... **82** F2
Market Hall
 *EP* CH65 .......................... **20** C6
Market Hall
 *SKEL* WN8 ......................... **65** K4
Market Street Medical Centre
 *WGNE/HIN* WN2 ................. **69** M7
Marsh Green Health Centre
 *WGNW/BIL/O* WN5 ............... **67** M4
Marsh Green Primary School
 *WGNW/BIL/O* WN5 ............... **67** M5
Marsh Green Surgery
 *WGNW/BIL/O* WN5 ............... **67** M4
Martlew Day Hospital
 *RAIN/WH* L35 ..................... **101** L8
Marus Bridge Health Centre
 *WCNS/IIMK* WN3 ................. **79** H3
Maryland Health Centre
 *CLVPS* L1 ......................... **13** L9
Marymount Convent School
 *WAL/EG* CH44 .................... **111** K2
Massey Hall Special School
 *WARRS* WA4 ...................... **139** H3
Maternity & Child
 Welfare Clinic
 *STHEL* WA9 ....................... **103** H2

Maternity & Child
 Welfare Clinic
 *WGNE/HIN* WN2 ................. **69** L8
Mather Avenue
 Doctors Surgery
 *CALD/MH* L18 ..................... **130** E4
Matthew Arnold School
 *TOX* L8 ............................ **129** J2
Mawdesley C of E School
 *BRSC* L40 ......................... **40** E2
Max Road Surgery
 *DV/KA/FCH* L14 .................. **99** H7
Maypole Industrial Estate
 *WGNE/HIN* WN2 ................. **80** E6
Meadow Bank Special School
 *AIN/FAZ* L10 ...................... **85** H5
Meadow County Junior School
 *CTS/LS* CH66 ..................... **163** G3
Meadowside
 *GR/UP/WCH* CH49 ............... **126** C3
Megabowl
 *NTHTN* L30 ....................... **84** C2
Melling CP School
 *MGHL* L31 ........................ **85** K1
Melrose Abbey
 *ANF/KKDL* L4 ..................... **7** K9
Mendell Primary School
 *PS/BROM* CH62 ................... **144** A5
Meols Cop High School
 *STHP* PR8 ......................... **25** H8
Merchant Taylors School
 *CSBY/BLUN* L23 ................... **83** G1
Merchant Taylors
 School for Girls
 *CSBY/BLUN* L23 ................... **83** G2
Mere Brow C of E School
 *KIRK/FR/WA* PR4 ................. **27** H3
Merefield School
 *STHP* PR8 ......................... **47** K1
Mere Oaks School
 *WGN* WN1 ........................ **56** D8
Merkmal Gallery
 *TOX* L8 ............................ **113** H5
Mersey Ferries
 *VAUX/LVPD* L3 .................... **12** D8
Mersey Park Primary School
 *RF/TRAN* CH42 ................... **127** M2
Mersey Regional Health
 Authority
 *RUNC* WA7 ........................ **19** M2
Merseyside Car Hospital
 *BIRK* CH41 ........................ **11** J4
Merseyside Maritime Museum
 *VAUX/LVPD* L3 .................... **12** E9
Mersey View School
 *AIG/SPK* L17 ...................... **130** A4
Merton Bank Junior &
 Infant School
 *STHEL* WA9 ....................... **9** M3
Metropolitan Borough Council
 *ECCL* WA10 ....................... **9** G4
Metropolitan Cathedral Rc
 *VAUX/LVPD* L3 .................... **13** L8
Millbrook CP School
 *WGNNW/ST* WN6 ................. **55** K7
Millbrook Primary School
 *KKBY* L32 ......................... **85** M2
Millfields Primary School
 *PS/BROM* CH62 ................... **155** G1
Mill Green Special School
 *NEWLW* WA12 .................... **105** G2
Millhouse Gallery
 *WGN* WN1 ........................ **53** L4
Millingford Industrial Estate
 *GOL/RIS/CU* WA3 ................. **92** D5
Mill Lane Industrial Estate
 *EP* CH65 .......................... **21** J9
Millstead Special Schools
 *WAV* L15 .......................... **114** D5
Mill Street Medical Centre
 *ECCL* WA10 ....................... **8** F4
Millwood CP School
 *SPK/HALE* L24 .................... **147** H3
Millwood Road
 Doctors Surgery
 *SPK/HALE* L24 .................... **147** H1
Miriam Health Centre
 *BIRK* CH41 ........................ **111** H5
Monksdown CP School
 *NG/CROX* L11 ..................... **98** C4
Montrose Special School
 *WGNW/BIL/O* WN5 ............... **67** M6
Moore CP School
 *WARRS* WA4 ...................... **136** C8
Moore Rugby Union
 Football Club
 *WARRS* WA4 ...................... **136** D7
Moorfield CP School
 *WDN* WA8 ........................ **134** F2
Moor Lane Business Centre
 *WDN* WA8 ........................ **16** C6
Moorside CP School
 *SKEL* WN8 ......................... **66** A6
Moreton Medical Centre
 *MOR/LEA* CH46 ................... **110** A5
Mosscroft Primary School
 *HUY* L36 .......................... **116** C2
Moss Industrial Estate
 *LEIGH* WN7 ....................... **93** K4
Mosslands School
 *WAL/EG* CH44 .................... **111** G1
Moss Lane Sports Centre
 *LITH* L21 .......................... **83** M4
Mossock Hall Golf Club
 *ORM* L39 .......................... **74** A1
Moss Pits CP School
 *WAV* L15 .......................... **114** D7
Mossy Lea CP School
 *WGNNW/ST* WN6 ................. **42** A7
Mostyn House School
 *NSTN* CH64 ....................... **152** E5
Mother Teresa RC
 Primary School
 *EV* L5 ............................. **13** G1
Mount Carmel School
 *ORM* L39 .......................... **62** F3
Mount Primary School
 *WAL/NB* CH45 ..................... **95** J5

Multibowl
 *PS/BROM* CH62 ................... **143** M3
Murdishaw Health Centre
 *RUNC* WA7 ........................ **150** F6
Murdishaw West CP School
 *RUNC* WA7 ........................ **150** F7
Murrayfield Hospital
 *PEN/TH* CH61 ..................... **126** F8
Museum & Art Gallery
 *WARR* WA1 ....................... **14** D7
Museum of Liverpool Life
 *VAUX/LVPD* L3 .................... **12** D9
National Discovery Park
 *CLVPS* L1 ......................... **12** F8
National Museums & Galleries
 Merseyside
 *CLVPS* L1 ......................... **12** F6
National Museums &
 Galleries on Merseyside
 *BTL* L20 ........................... **6** D4
Natural History Clinic
 *PR/KW* L34 ....................... **100** F7
Neptune Theatre
 *CLVPS* L1 ......................... **13** H8
Neston County High School
 *NSTN* CH64 ....................... **153** H4
Neston CP School
 *NSTN* CH64 ....................... **153** G6
Neston Cricket Club
 *NSTN* CH64 ....................... **152** E5
Neston Medical Centre
 *NSTN* CH64 ....................... **153** G5
Neston Recreation Centre
 *NSTN* CH64 ....................... **153** H4
Neston St Marys C of E Primary
 School
 *NSTN* CH64 ....................... **153** H4
Neston Surgery
 *NSTN* CH64 ....................... **153** H6
Netherfield Family Health Clinic
 *EV* L5 ............................. **97** G8
Netherley Health Centre
 *NTHLY* L27 ........................ **116** A8
Netherley Sports Centre
 *NTHLY* L27 ........................ **115** M8
Netherpool County
 Infant School
 *CTS/LS* CH66 ..................... **156** A6
Netherton Moss Primary School
 *NTHTN* L30 ....................... **84** A2
Netherton Park Primary School
 *NTHTN* L30 ....................... **84** B4
Newborough School
 *WLTN* L25 ......................... **131** H2
New Brighton Primary School
 *WAL/NB* CH45 ..................... **95** L5
New Brighton Rugby
 Union Football Club
 *MOR/LEA* CH46 ................... **110** B1
Newburgh C of E School
 *SKEL* WN8 ......................... **53** J4
Newburgh Cricket Club
 *SKEL* WN8 ......................... **53** J4
Newchurch Community Primary
 School
 *GOL/RIS/CU* WA3 ................. **107** G3
Newfield School
 *CSBY/BLUN* L23 ................... **71** K8
New Heys Community
 Comprehensive School
 *CALD/MH* L18 ..................... **130** F4
New Hutte Junior School
 *HLWD* L26 ........................ **132** A7
New Lodge Industrial Estate
 *NWD/KWIPK* L33 ................. **86** D5
Newman RC High School
 *WARRS* WA4 ...................... **122** B8
New Mersey Retail Park
 *SPK/HALE* L24 .................... **131** H8
New Park School Butler Wing
 *NPK/KEN* L6 ...................... **113** K2
New Park School Newsham
 Wing
 *NPK/KEN* L6 ...................... **113** L1
News Gallery
 *NSTN* CH64 ....................... **153** G6
Newspaper Office
 *VAUX/LVPD* L3 .................... **12** D6
Newstead Abbey
 *TOX* L8 ............................ **113** L6
Newton Bank Preparatory
 School
 *NEWLW* WA12 .................... **105** G1
Newton Community Hospital
 *NEWLW* WA12 .................... **104** D4
Newton Health Clinic
 *NEWLW* WA12 .................... **104** D1
Newton Le Willows CP School
 *NEWLW* WA12 .................... **104** E2
Newton-le-willows
 Sports Club
 *NEWLW* WA12 .................... **104** E1
Newton West Park CP School
 *LEIGH* WN7 ....................... **81** L5
New Way Business Centre
 *WAL/EG* CH44 .................... **111** M3
Nicol Mere Primary School
 *AIMK* WN4 ......................... **79** J8
Nine Tree Primary School
 *STBRV* L28 ........................ **99** J4
Norley Hall Cricket Club
 *WGNW/BIL/O* WN5 ............... **67** K6
Norman Pannell CP School
 *NTHLY* L27 ........................ **115** M8
Norris Green Family
 Health Clinic
 *NG/CROX* L11 ..................... **98** A4
North Cheshire Health Authority
 *RUNC* WA7 ........................ **19** L2
Northcote CP School
 *WLT/FAZ* L9 ...................... **97** J2
Northern Cricket Club
 *CSBY/BLUN* L23 ................... **71** H7
North Meols Lawn Tennis Club
 *CHTN/BK* PR9 ..................... **25** J4
North Mersey Business Centre
 *NWD/KWIPK* L33 ................. **86** E1

North Mersey Community
NHS Trust
*BTL* L20 .................... **7** J4
North Mersey Community
NHS Trust
*CALD/MH* L18 .................... **130** A1
North Mersey Community
NHS Trust
*CLB/OSW/ST* L13 .................... **114** C3
North Mersey Community
NHS Trust
*NTHTN* L30 .................... **84** A1
North Mersey Community
NHS Trust
*TOX* L8 .................... **113** M7
North Mersey Community
NHS Trust
*WLT/FAZ* L9 .................... **84** F7
North Park Health Centre
*BTL* L20 .................... **6** F1
North Quarry Business Park
*WGNNW/ST* WN6 .................... **54** F4
North Road Doctors Surgery
*ECCL* WA10 .................... **9** G3
North Road Surgery
*ECCL* WA10 .................... **8** F3
Northway CP School
*WAV* L15 .................... **114** D4
Northway Primary School
*MGHL* L31 .................... **72** F2
Norton Priory County
High School
*RUNC* WA7 .................... **150** D4
Norton Priory
Recreation Centre
*RUNC* WA7 .................... **150** D3
Norwood CP School
*CHTN/BK* PR9 .................... **25** G6
Notre Dame High School
*EV* L5 .................... **97** H6
Nugent House School
*WGNW/BIL/O* WN5 .................... **89** M1
Nutgrove Methodist
Primary School
*RAIN/WH* L35 .................... **101** M6
Nye Bevan Swimming Pool
*SKEL* WN8 .................... **65** K4
Oak Cottage Medical Centre
*HUY* L36 .................... **116** A4
Oakdene Primary School
*RAIN/WH* L35 .................... **117** L3
Oakfield County
Junior & Infant School
*WDN* WA8 .................... **133** J5
Oakhouse Surgery
*STHEL* WA9 .................... **103** G6
Oak Remedial Clinic
*WD/CROXPK* L12 .................... **99** G1
Oak Vale Medical Practice
*CLB/OSW/ST* L13 .................... **114** E3
Oakwood Avenue Community
Primary & Infant School
*WARR* WA1 .................... **15** K1
Odeon Cinema
*CLVPS* L1 .................... **13** H6
Odeon Cinema
*NTHTN* L30 .................... **84** C2
Odeon Multiscreen Cinema
*PS/BROM* CH62 .................... **143** M2
The Oldershaw Lower School
*WAL/NB* CH45 .................... **95** K8
The Oldershaw School
*WAL/NB* CH45 .................... **95** J8
Old Foundry Estate
*WDN* WA8 .................... **16** F6
Old Hall Community
Primary School
*WARRW/BUR* WA5 .................... **120** B5
Old Hall Farm Business Park
*CHTN/BK* PR9 .................... **25** H8
Old Hall Farm Business Park
*CHTN/BK* PR9 .................... **25** K7
Old Hall Surgery
*EP* CH65 .................... **20** B6
Old Parkonians Rugby Club
*CL/PREN* CH43 .................... **127** H2
Old Rockerrians Rugby Club
*CL/PREN* CH43 .................... **127** H5
Old Swan Health Centre
*CLB/OSW/ST* L13 .................... **114** C3
Ophthalmic Surgery
*CLVPS* L1 .................... **13** K9
Ormskirk College
*ORM* L39 .................... **51** G7
Ormskirk Cricket Club
*ORM* L39 .................... **63** H1
Ormskirk & District
General Hospital
*ORM* L39 .................... **51** J8
Ormskirk Golf Club
*BRSC* L40 .................... **52** A6
Ormskirk Grammar School
*ORM* L39 .................... **63** H1
Ormskirk Rugby Union
Football Club
*ORM* L39 .................... **51** G7
Ormskirk Swimming Pool
*ORM* L39 .................... **51** G8
Orrell Clinic
*WGNW/BIL/O* WN5 .................... **67** G6
Orrell County Primary School
*BTL* L20 .................... **83** L8
Orrell Holgate Primary School
*WGNW/BIL/O* WN5 .................... **67** G8
Orrell Lane Doctors Surgery
*WLT/FAZ* L9 .................... **84** C7
Orrell Newfold CP School
*WGNW/BIL/O* WN5 .................... **77** M1
Orrell Rugby Union
Football Club
*WGNW/BIL/O* WN5 .................... **67** G8
Orrets Meadow School
*MOR/LEA* CH46 .................... **110** A4
Our Lady & All Saints RC School
*SKEL* WN8 .................... **53** L3
Our Lady Immaculate
Primary School
*EV* L5 .................... **97** G7

Our Lady of Compassion
RC Primary School
*FMBY* L37 .................... **59** J2
Our Lady of Fatima High School
*NPK/KEN* L6 .................... **113** J1
Our Lady of Good Help Primary
School
*WAV* L15 .................... **114** C5
Our Lady of Mount
Carmel Primary School
*TOX* L8 .................... **113** H8
Our Lady of Perpetual
Succour Junior School
*WDN* WA8 .................... **133** H5
Our Lady of Perpetual
Succour RC Infant School
*WDN* WA8 .................... **133** K4
Our Lady of Pity RC Prim
School
*GR/UP/WCH* CH49 .................... **125** M3
Our Lady of Reconciliation
Primary School
*VAUX/LVPD* L3 .................... **12** F2
Our Lady of the Assumption
Infant School
*WLTN* L25 .................... **115** K7
Our Lady of the Assumption
Primary School
*WLTN* L25 .................... **115** K7
Our Lady of the Rosary RC
School
*LEIGH* WN7 .................... **81** K8
Our Lady of Walsingham RC
Infant School
*NTHTN* L30 .................... **84** B3
Our Lady of Walsingham RC
Primary School
*NTHTN* L30 .................... **84** A3
Our Lady Queen of Peace RC
High School
*SKEL* WN8 .................... **65** H1
Our Lady Queen of Peace RC
Primary School
*LITH* L21 .................... **83** K3
Our Lady & St Edwards RC
Primary School
*BIRK* CH41 .................... **10** D1
Our Lady & St Philomenas R C
Primary School
*WLT/FAZ* L9 .................... **98** B1
Our Lady & St Swithens Primary
School
*NG/CROX* L11 .................... **85** L8
Our Ladys Bishop Eton School
*CALD/MH* L18 .................... **114** E8
Our Ladys Catholic
Primary School
*WARRS* WA4 .................... **138** A2
Our Ladys Primary School
*PR/KW* L34 .................... **100** F6
Our Ladys RC Infant School
*EP* CH65 .................... **163** J2
Our Ladys RC Junior School
*EP* CH65 .................... **163** J2
Our Ladys RC Primary School
*RUNC* WA7 .................... **150** C7
Our Ladys RC Primary School
*STHEL* WA9 .................... **103** G2
Our Ladys RC Primary School
*WGNE/HIN* WN2 .................... **57** K8
Our Lady Star of the Sea RC
Primary School
*LITH* L21 .................... **83** J7
Outlet Village
*EP* CH65 .................... **164** A3
The Oval Sports Centre
*BEB* CH63 .................... **128** C6
Overchurch Junior & Infant
School
*GR/UP/WCH* CH49 .................... **110** B7
Overdale Primary School
*NWD/KWIPK* L33 .................... **86** B1
Oxton Cricket Club
*CL/PREN* CH43 .................... **127** H1
Oxton St Saviours C of E
Primary School
*CL/PREN* CH43 .................... **127** J2
Padgate Business Centre
*WARR* WA1 .................... **122** D5
Padgate Business Centre
*WARR* WA1 .................... **122** C5
Padgate C of E Primary School
*WARRN/WOL* WA2 .................... **122** C4
Padgate Community
High School
*WARRN/WOL* WA2 .................... **122** B3
Padgate Medical Centre
*WARRN/WOL* WA2 .................... **122** C4
Pagefield Industrial Estate
*WGNNW/ST* WN6 .................... **68** B4
Palacefields County
Infant School
*RUNC* WA7 .................... **150** C7
Palace Theatre
*WARR* WA1 .................... **14** E6
Palatine Industrial Estate
*WARRS* WA4 .................... **15** G9
Parbold Douglas C of E Primary
School
*SKEL* WN8 .................... **53** M2
Parish C of E Primary School
*ECCL* WA10 .................... **9** H3
Park Brow CP School
*KKBY* L32 .................... **86** C5
Park Business Centre
*WGNE/HIN* WN2 .................... **80** F2
The Park CP School
*RUNC* WA7 .................... **150** C4
Parkdale Industrial Estate
*WARR* WA1 .................... **15** H7
Parkfield Medical Centre
*PS/BROM* CH62 .................... **128** D5
Parkfield School
*KKBY* L32 .................... **86** A5
Parkgate CP School
*NSTN* CH64 .................... **152** E4
Park Golf Club
*CHTN/BK* PR9 .................... **24** E4

Park Hall Leisure Centre
*CHLY/EC* PR7 .................... **42** C1
Park High Lower School
*BIRK* CH41 .................... **10** A3
Park High School
*BIRK* CH41 .................... **10** D6
Park House Medical Centre
*PR/KW* L34 .................... **100** F7
Park House Surgery
*STHEL* WA9 .................... **9** L5
Park Industrial Estate
*AIMK* WN4 .................... **91** G2
Parklands CP Infant School
*GTS/LS* CH66 .................... **155** L1
Park Medical Centre
*WKBY* CH48 .................... **124** D3
Park Primary School
*WAL/EG* CH44 .................... **111** G2
Park Road Community Primary
School
*WARRW/BUR* WA5 .................... **120** A7
Park Road Group Practice
*TOX* L8 .................... **129** J1
Park Road Sports Centre
*TOX* L8 .................... **113** H8
Park View Primary School
*HUY* L36 .................... **115** L1
Parr Community High School
*STHEL* WA9 .................... **103** G3
Parr Flat Community
Infant School
*STHEL* WA9 .................... **103** J2
Parrs Corner Trading Estate
*BTL* L20 .................... **7** H2
Parr Swimming Baths
*STHEL* WA9 .................... **9** M5
Pasture Road Health Centre
*MOR/LEA* CH46 .................... **110** A4
Patterdale Lodge Group
Practice
*NEWLW* WA12 .................... **104** F1
Patterdale Lodge
Medical Centre
*NEWLW* WA12 .................... **104** C2
Peatwood Medical Centre
*KKBY* L32 .................... **86** B6
Peelhouse Lane Surgery
*WDN* WA8 .................... **17** C1
Pemberton Business Centre
*WGNW/BIL/O* WN5 .................... **67** L7
Pemberton Clinic
*WGNW/BIL/O* WN5 .................... **67** M7
Pemberton CP School
*WGNW/BIL/O* WN5 .................... **67** L7
Penketh Business Park
*WARRW/BUR* WA5 .................... **136** D1
Penketh Community
High School
*WARRW/BUR* WA5 .................... **120** C8
Penketh Community
Primary School
*WARRW/BUR* WA5 .................... **135** M1
Penketh Health Clinic
*WARRW/BUR* WA5 .................... **136** A1
Penketh South
Community Primary School
*WARRW/BUR* WA5 .................... **136** B2
Penketh Swimming Baths
*WARRW/BUR* WA5 .................... **120** A8
Penkford Technology School
*NEWLW* WA12 .................... **104** A3
Penlake Industrial Estate
*STHEL* WA9 .................... **103** G7
Penny Lane Surgery
*WAV* L15 .................... **114** C7
Pensby Clinic
*PEN/TH* CH61 .................... **141** J2
Pensby High School
*PEN/TH* CH61 .................... **140** F1
Pensby Infant School
*PEN/TH* CH61 .................... **141** H2
Pensby Junior School
*PEN/TH* CH61 .................... **141** H2
Pensby Park Primary School
*PEN/TH* CH61 .................... **140** F2
Pensby Recreation Centre
*PEN/TH* CH61 .................... **126** C8
Pepper Mill Business Centre
*WGN* WN1 .................... **5** G5
Perry Brook Community Primary
School
*AIMK* WN4 .................... **79** J6
Pershore House School
*RF/TRAN* CH42 .................... **127** K4
Peterhouse School
*CHTN/BK* PR9 .................... **25** K2
Peterhouse School
*STHP* PR8 .................... **3** L7
Peter Lloyd Leisure Centre
*CLB/OSW/ST* L13 .................... **98** B8
Pewithall CP School
*RUNC* WA7 .................... **19** J9
Philharmonic Hall
*CLVPS* L1 .................... **13** L9
Phoenix Medical Centre
*ECCL* WA10 .................... **8** F4
Picton Road Surgery
*WAV* L15 .................... **114** A5
Pilch Lane Surgery
*DV/KA/FCH* L14 .................... **115** J2
Pinehurst Junior School
*ANF/KKDL* L4 .................... **97** L6
Pinehurst Road County
Infant School
*ANF/KKDL* L4 .................... **97** L6
Pink Museum
*AIG/SPK* L17 .................... **129** L1
Pioneer Industrial Estate
*WGNW/BIL/O* WN5 .................... **68** A7
Pius XII RC School
*GTS/LS* CH66 .................... **155** M7
Plantation Business Park
*PS/BROM* CH62 .................... **144** B3
Plantation Primary School
*HLWD* L26 .................... **132** B5
Platt Bridge Clinic
*WGNE/HIN* WN2 .................... **80** C3

Pleasant Street CP School
*VAUX/LVPD* L3 .................... **13** K8
Plessington RC High School
*BEB* CH63 .................... **128** C6
Pontville School
*ORM* L39 .................... **62** F2
Pooltown CP School
*EP* CH65 .................... **156** B8
Portland Primary School
*BIRK* CH41 .................... **10** A2
Portrait Gallery
*WDN* WA8 .................... **134** C3
Poulter Road Medical Centre
*WLT/FAZ* L9 .................... **84** D6
Poulton Lancelyn
Primary School
*BEB* CH63 .................... **143** J3
Poulton Primary School
*WAL/EG* CH44 .................... **111** J2
Prenton High School for Girls
*RF/TRAN* CH42 .................... **127** M4
Prenton Infant & Junior School
*CL/PREN* CH43 .................... **127** J4
Prenton Preparatory School
*CL/PREN* CH43 .................... **127** K2
Prescot Associated
Football Club
*PR/KW* L34 .................... **100** E6
Prescot CP School
*PR/KW* L34 .................... **101** G7
Prescot Leisure Centre
*RAIN/WH* L35 .................... **101** G8
Prescot Medical Centre
*PR/KW* L34 .................... **100** F7
Prescot Museum
*PR/KW* L34 .................... **100** E7
Prescot Primary School
*RAIN/WH* L35 .................... **116** F1
Prescot School
*PR/KW* L34 .................... **100** E6
Prestfield School
*CHTN/BK* PR9 .................... **25** J2
Price Street Business Centre
*BIRK* CH41 .................... **10** E2
Priestley Business Centre
*WARRW/BUR* WA5 .................... **14** A5
Priestley College
*WARRS* WA4 .................... **137** L2
Princes Park Health Centre
*TOX* L8 .................... **113** K7
Princess Drive Medical Centre
*DV/KA/FCH* L14 .................... **99** J7
Princes Special School
*TOX* L8 .................... **113** J6
The Priory Medical Centre
*NPK/KEN* L6 .................... **97** L8
Priory Parish C of E
Primary School
*BIRK* CH41 .................... **10** F4
Prospect House
Medical Centre
*WGNW/BIL/O* WN5 .................... **67** J7
Prospect Industrial Estate
*WGNE/HIN* WN2 .................... **69** M8
Pump House Museum
*BIRK* CH41 .................... **11** L4
The Quadrangle Business
Centre
*WGNE/HIN* WN2 .................... **81** K1
Quay Business Centre
*WARRN/WOL* WA2 .................... **121** J2
Queen Mary Community
Comprehensive School
*WLT/FAZ* L9 .................... **97** M1
Queens Drive Family
Health Clinic
*WLT/FAZ* L9 .................... **97** J2
Queens Drive Recreation
Centre
*ANF/KKDL* L4 .................... **97** H3
Queens Park C of E U RC
Primary School
*ECCL* WA10 .................... **8** B3
Queensway Business Centre
*WDN* WA8 .................... **16** C9
Racecourse Retail Park
*WLT/FAZ* L9 .................... **84** D3
Radio City
*CLVP* L2 .................... **12** F6
Radnor Medical Centre
*NPK/KEN* L6 .................... **97** M8
Raeburn Primary School
*PS/BROM* CH62 .................... **143** M7
Rainbow Medical Centre
*STHEL* WA9 .................... **103** G6
Rainford C of E Primary School
*RNFD/HAY* WA11 .................... **76** B7
Rainford Health Centre
*RNFD/HAY* WA11 .................... **76** C7
Rainford High School
*RNFD/HAY* WA11 .................... **76** C5
Rainhill Clinic
*RAIN/WH* L35 .................... **117** L2
Rainhill High School
*RAIN/WH* L35 .................... **117** M3
Rainhill Parish Council
*NTHTN* L30 .................... **84** C4
Rainhill Village Surgery
*RAIN/WH* L35 .................... **117** L2
Range High School
*FMBY* L37 .................... **58** E5
Ranworth Square Jmi School
*NG/CROX* L11 .................... **98** B2
Ravenscroft Primary School
*NWD/KWIPK* L33 .................... **74** A8
Rawson Road Primary School
*LITH* L21 .................... **83** H7
Record Business Park
*WARRN/WOL* WA2 .................... **121** J5
Rectory C of E Primary School
*AIMK* WN4 .................... **78** F8
Red Bank School
*NEWLW* WA12 .................... **105** G4
Redbridge High School
*AIN/FAZ* L10 .................... **85** H5
Redgate Primary School
*FMBY* L37 .................... **59** J3

Regent House Surgery
*CHLY/EC* PR7 .................... **32** D6
Regional College of Art
*WAV* L15 .................... **114** B5
Renacres Hall Hospital
*ORM* L39 .................... **36** D8
Retail Park
*VAUX/LVPD* L3 .................... **12** D3
Rice Lane County Junior School
*WLT/FAZ* L9 .................... **84** C8
Richard Evans County
Infant School
*RNFD/HAY* WA11 .................... **90** C7
Richard Evans Primary School
*RNFD/HAY* WA11 .................... **90** B7
Ridgeway High School
*CL/PREN* CH43 .................... **126** F1
Rimrose Business Park
*BTL* L20 .................... **6** D3
Rivacre Valley CP School
*GTS/LS* CH66 .................... **156** A6
Riverside Bowl
*WAL/NB* CH45 .................... **95** K4
Riverside Primary School
*WAL/EG* CH44 .................... **112** A2
Riverside Surgery
*RF/TRAN* CH42 .................... **128** C3
Rivington & Blackrod
High School
*HOR/BR* BL6 .................... **45** K7
Rivington CP School
*ECCL* WA10 .................... **8** C1
Rivington Primary School
*HOR/BR* BL6 .................... **45** H4
R L Hughes County
Junior & Infant School
*AIMK* WN4 .................... **91** J2
R N I B Sunshine House School
*STHP* PR8 .................... **2** A8
Roberts Primary School
*BTL* L20 .................... **84** A6
Robins Lane
Community Primary School
*STHEL* WA9 .................... **102** E5
Robson Street Clinic
*WARR* WA1 .................... **15** J4
Roby Medical Centre
*HUY* L36 .................... **115** J3
Roby Mill C of E School
*SKEL* WN8 .................... **66** D2
Roby Park Primary School
*HUY* L36 .................... **115** J2
Rock Court Surgery
*CLB/OSW/ST* L13 .................... **114** C2
Rocket Trading Centre
*DV/KA/FCH* L14 .................... **114** E4
Rock Ferry High School
*RF/TRAN* CH42 .................... **128** B5
Rock Ferry Medical Centre
*RF/TRAN* CH42 .................... **128** B2
Rock Ferry Primary School
*RF/TRAN* CH42 .................... **128** B3
Rock Surgery
*FROD/HEL* WA6 .................... **160** D4
Rodney Fertility Clinic
*CLVPS* L1 .................... **13** K9
Roma Galleries
*CL/PREN* CH43 .................... **10** E8
Ronald House School
*CSBY/BLUN* L23 .................... **71** G7
Roscoe CP School
*CLB/OSW/ST* L13 .................... **98** A6
Rose Bridge High School
*WGN* WN1 .................... **5** L3
Rose Cottage Surgery
*WARRW/BUR* WA5 .................... **136** A1
Roseheath Primary School
*HLWD* L26 .................... **132** B6
Rosehill Business Park
*CHTN/BK* PR9 .................... **3** M5
Rose Hill School
*AIMK* WN4 .................... **80** A8
Ross Business Centre
*WGNW/BIL/O* WN5 .................... **67** M8
Rossmore CP School
*GTS/LS* CH66 .................... **155** L6
Rother Drive Business Park
*EP* CH65 .................... **156** C5
Royal Albert Edward Infirmary
*WGN* WN1 .................... **68** E3
The Royal Birkdale Golf Club
*STHP* PR8 .................... **34** E5
Royal College of Nursing
*CLVP* L2 .................... **12** E7
Royal College of Nursing
*MGHL* L31 .................... **73** K3
Royal Court Theatre
*CLVPS* L1 .................... **13** H6
Royal Liver Building
*VAUX/LVPD* L3 .................... **12** D7
Royal Liverpool Childrens
NHS Trust
*WD/CROXPK* L12 .................... **114** E1
Royal Liverpool University
Hospital
*EHL/KEN* L7 .................... **113** J3
Royal Mail Sorting Office
*VAUX/LVPD* L3 .................... **13** K7
Roy Castle International
Centre for Lung Cancer
*EHL/KEN* L7 .................... **13** M5
Rudston CP School
*CHLDW* L16 .................... **114** F5
Rufford C of E School
*BRSC* L40 .................... **39** K1
Ruffwood Community
Comprehensive School
*NWD/KWIPK* L33 .................... **86** B2
Runcorn All Saints C of E
Primary School
*RUNC* WA7 .................... **19** G2
Runcorn County Court
*RUNC* WA7 .................... **150** B5
Runcorn Football Club
*RUNC* WA7 .................... **19** K2
Runcorn Rowing Club
*RUNC* WA7 .................... **160** F1

Runshaw College
*CHLY/EC* PR7 .................... **32** E6
Rutherford Medical Centre
*CALD/MH* L18 .................... **114** D7
Sacred Heart High School
*CSBY/BLUN* L23 .................... **83** G2
Sacred Heart RC High School
*CSBY/BLUN* L23 .................... **83** G1
Sacred Heart RC
Primary School
*CHLYE* PR6 .................... **33** G6
Sacred Heart RC
Primary School
*MOR/LEA* CH46 .................... **110** B4
Sacred Heart RC
Primary School
*NWD/KWIPK* L33 .................... **86** B3
Sacred Heart RC
Primary School
*WARRW/BUR* WA5 .................... **121** G8
Sacred Heart RC School
*WGNE/HIN* WN2 .................... **81** K2
Sacred Heart RC School
*WGNNW/ST* WN6 .................... **68** B3
St Aelreds RC High School
*NEWLW* WA12 .................... **104** F1
St Agnes Primary School
*HUY* L36 .................... **116** B4
St Aidans C of E
Community Primary School
*STHEL* WA9 .................... **119** G2
St Aidans C of E Primary School
*WGNW/BIL/O* WN5 .................... **78** A8
St Aidans Primary School
*HUY* L36 .................... **116** B1
St Aidans RC Primary School
*WGNS/IIMK* WN3 .................... **78** F3
St Albans Catholic
Primary School
*WARRW/BUR* WA5 .................... **14** B3
St Albans RC Primary School
*WAL/EG* CH44 .................... **111** J1
St Alberts Primary School
*STBRV* L28 .................... **99** J4
St Aloysius RC Junior &
Infant School
*HUY* L36 .................... **115** L1
St Ambrose Barlow RC
High School
*NTHTN* L30 .................... **72** C8
St Ambrose Primary School
*SPK/HALE* L24 .................... **147** J2
St Andrews Ce Primary School
*WARRN/WOL* WA2 .................... **121** L2
St Andrews C of E Junior &
Infant School
*WGNNW/ST* WN6 .................... **68** B3
St Andrews C of E
Primary School
*BEB* CH63 .................... **128** B7
St Andrews Maghull C of E
Primary School
*MGHL* L31 .................... **72** F4
St Annes C of E Primary School
*CLB/OSW/ST* L13 .................... **114** B2
St Annes RC Junior School
*RF/TRAN* CH42 .................... **128** B5
St Annes RC Primary School
*EHL/KEN* L7 .................... **113** K5
St Annes RC Primary School
*HUY* L36 .................... **115** M4
St Annes RC Primary School
*ORM* L39 .................... **62** F1
St Annes RC Primary School
*STHEL* WA9 .................... **102** F6
St Anns C of E Primary School
*RAIN/WH* L35 .................... **117** L2
St Anns C of E Primary School
*WARRN/WOL* WA2 .................... **121** L5
St Anselms College
*CL/PREN* CH43 .................... **10** B7
St Anthony of Padua
Primary School
*CALD/MH* L18 .................... **130** B1
St Augustine of Canterbury
RC High School
*RNFD/HAY* WA11 .................... **90** A8
St Augustines RC
Primary School
*RUNC* WA7 .................... **150** C3
St Austins Primary School
*ALL/GAR* L19 .................... **130** D6
St Barnabas C E Aided
Primary School
*WARRW/BUR* WA5 .................... **14** A5
St Bartholomews RC
Primary School
*RAIN/WH* L35 .................... **118** A4
St Basils RC Primary School
*RAIN/WH* L35 .................... **133** J3
St Bedes RC Junior &
Infant School
*WDN* WA8 .................... **16** D1
St Bedes RC School
*ORM* L39 .................... **62** F1
St Benedicts Catholic
Primary School
*WARRN/WOL* WA2 .................... **15** J1
St Benedicts RC High School
*GR/UP/WCH* CH49 .................... **126** D1
St Benedicts RC Primary School
*WGNE/HIN* WN2 .................... **69** L7
St Bernadettes RC
Primary School
*WGNNW/ST* WN6 .................... **55** J7
St Bertelines Primary School
*RUNC* WA7 .................... **150** E5
St Bridgets Catholic
Primary School
*WARRN/WOL* WA2 .................... **122** B2
St Bridgets C of E
Primary School
*WKBY* CH48 .................... **124** D4
St Brigids Primary School
*STBRV* L28 .................... **99** J6
St Catherines C of E
Primary School
*WGN* WN1 .................... **5** J4

St Catherines RC Primary School
*GOL/RIS/CU* WA3 .................... **93** G6
St Cecilias Primary School
*CLB/OSW/ST* L13 .................... **98** A8
St Chads RC School
*RUNC* WA7 .................... **149** M6
St Charles Primary School
*AIG/SPK* L17 .................... **129** L3
St Christophers Infant School
*SPK/HALE* L24 .................... **146** F1
St Christophers Junior School
*SPK/HALE* L24 .................... **146** F1
St Clares Primary School
*WAV* L15 .................... **114** A4
St Clements RC Primary School
*RUNC* WA7 .................... **19** G7
St Cleopas C of E Primary School
*TOX* L8 .................... **129** H1
St Columbas Primary School
*HUY* L36 .................... **100** A8
St Cuthbert RC Junior Mixed School
*WGNW/BIL/O* WN5 .................... **67** M7
St Cuthberts C of E
Primary School
*ORM* L39 .................... **49** K4
St Cuthberts Primary School
*CLB/OSW/ST* L13 .................... **114** B2
St Davids C of E Primary School
*WGNE/HIN* WN2 .................... **57** J6
St Dominics Junior &
Infant School
*DV/KA/FCH* L14 .................... **99** K7
St Edmund Arrowsmith
Comprehensive School
*RAIN/WH* L35 .................... **101** H8
St Edmund Arrowsmith RC
High School
*AIMK* WN4 .................... **91** K3
St Edmund of Canterbury
Comprehensive School
*DV/KA/FCH* L14 .................... **99** K7
St Edmunds RC Primary School
*CSBY/WL* L22 .................... **82** F4
St Edmunds RC Primary School
*SKEL* WN8 .................... **65** H4
St Edwards College
*WD/CROXPK* L12 .................... **98** D8
St Edwards RC Junior &
Infant School
*WGNW/BIL/O* WN5 .................... **68** B6
St Edwards RC Primary School
*RUNC* WA7 .................... **19** K2
St Francis de Sales Infant School
*ANF/KKDL* L4 .................... **7** M7
St Francis de Sales Junior
Boys School
*ANF/KKDL* L4 .................... **7** M9
St Francis de Sales Junior
Girls School
*ANF/KKDL* L4 .................... **7** M9
St Francis Xavier Lower School
*WAV* L15 .................... **114** E5
St Francis Xaviers College
*WLTN* L25 .................... **131** G1
St Gabriels C of E
Primary School
*HUY* L36 .................... **116** C3
St George of England
High School
*BTL* L20 .................... **83** M7
St George's Hall
*CLVPS* L1 .................... **13** H6
St Georges Medical Centre
*WAL/NB* CH45 .................... **95** K4
St Georges Primary School
*CHLY/EC* PR7 .................... **33** G8
St Georges Primary School
*WAL/NB* CH45 .................... **95** H8
St Georges RC Primary School
*MGHL* L31 .................... **72** F6
St Gerards RC School
*EV* L5 .................... **96** F7
St Gregorys Catholic
High School
*WARRW/BUR* WA5 .................... **120** F8
St Gregorys RC Jmi School
*NTHLY* L27 .................... **116** A8
St Gregorys RC Junior School
*MGHL* L31 .................... **72** E1
St Helens Associated
Football Club
*STHEL* WA9 .................... **103** H6
St Helens Borough Council
*ECCL* WA10 .................... **9** G5
St Helens Borough Council
*ECCL* WA10 .................... **101** J2
St Helens College
*ECCL* WA10 .................... **8** F5
St Helens College
*NEWLW* WA12 .................... **104** D1
St Helens College
*STHEL* WA9 .................... **9** K3
St Helens County Court
*ECCL* WA10 .................... **9** G5
St Helens Cricket Club
*ECCL* WA10 .................... **8** C2
St Helens Hospital
*STHEL* WA9 .................... **102** E4
St Helens & Knowsley
Hospitals Trust
*RAIN/WH* L35 .................... **117** H1
St Helens Metropolitan Borough
Council
*ECCL* WA10 .................... **8** D6
St Helens Metropolitan Borough
Council
*ECCL* WA10 .................... **101** M5
St Helens Metropolitan Borough
Council
*NEWLW* WA12 .................... **104** D2
St Helens Metropolitan Borough
Council
*RNFD/HAY* WA11 .................... **89** L5
St Helens Metropolitan Borough
Council
*RNFD/HAY* WA11 .................... **90** A8
St Helens Metropolitan Borough
Council
*STHEL* WA9 .................... **9** K3

St Helens Metropolitan Borough
Council
*STHEL* WA9 .................... **9** M4
St Helens Museum & Art Gallery
*ECCL* WA10 .................... **9** G4
St Helens Retail Park
*STHEL* WA9 .................... **9** K6
St Helens Rugby League
Football Club
*ECCL* WA10 .................... **101** L2
St Helens Theatre Royal
*ECCL* WA10 .................... **9** H5
St Hilary Brow Group Practice
*WAL/EG* CH44 .................... **111** H1
St Hildas C of E High School
*AIG/SPK* L17 .................... **113** L8
St James C of E Infant School
*RNFD/HAY* WA11 .................... **91** G7
St James C of E Junior School
*RNFD/HAY* WA11 .................... **91** G7
St James C of E Primary School
*WARRS* WA4 .................... **14** F8
St James C of E School
*BRSC* L40 .................... **64** A1
St James C of E School
*CHLYE* PR6 .................... **33** G6
St James C of E School
*WGNS/IIMK* WN3 .................... **68** B8
St James RC Primary School
*BTL* L20 .................... **6** F2
St James RC Primary School
*SKEL* WN8 .................... **65** K1
St James RC Primary School
*WGNW/BIL/O* WN5 .................... **77** M1
St Jeromes RC Primary School
*FMBY* L37 .................... **58** E2
St Joan of Arc RC Primary School
*BTL* L20 .................... **6** C1
St John Almond High School
*ALL/GAR* L19 .................... **130** F7
St John Bosco High School
*NG/CROX* L11 .................... **98** D2
St John Bosco RC
Primary School
*MGHL* L31 .................... **72** D3
St John Fisher Junior &
Infant School
*WDN* WA8 .................... **17** K1
St John Fisher Primary School
*PR/KW* L34 .................... **99** L1
St John Fisher RC High School
*WGNNW/ST* WN6 .................... **68** B2
St John Rigby College
*WGNW/BIL/O* WN5 .................... **67** H3
St Johns Catholic Infant School
*BEB* CH63 .................... **128** B6
St Johns C of E County
Primary School
*BRSC* L40 .................... **39** H8
St Johns C of E Primary School
*CSBY/WL* L22 .................... **82** F3
St Johns C of E Primary School
*WGNE/HIN* WN2 .................... **81** K2
St Johns C of E School
*WGNW/BIL/O* WN5 .................... **67** K7
St Johns Junior School
*ANF/KKDL* L4 .................... **97** G5
St John Southworth RC Primary
School
*AIMK* WN4 .................... **91** M1
St Johns RC Primary School
*SKEL* WN8 .................... **65** L4
St Johns School
*CHLY/EC* PR7 .................... **42** F7
St Johns Shopping
Precinct & Market
*CLVPS* L1 .................... **13** H7
St Johns Surgery
*HUY* L36 .................... **116** B4
St John Stone RC
Primary School
*STHP* PR8 .................... **47** M3
St John Vianney RC
Primary School
*STHEL* WA9 .................... **102** A7
St Josephs Catholic
Primary School
*WARRW/BUR* WA5 .................... **120** A8
St Josephs Junior &
Infant School
*KKBY* L32 .................... **86** A4
St Josephs Primary School
*HUY* L36 .................... **116** B2
St Josephs RC College
*SKEL* WN8 .................... **66** D3
St Josephs RC Primary School
*CHLYE* PR6 .................... **44** D6
St Josephs RC Primary School
*CL/PREN* CH43 .................... **127** K3
St Josephs RC Primary School
*GR/UP/WCH* CH49 .................... **110** C8
St Josephs RC Primary School
*WAL/EG* CH44 .................... **111** M3
St Josephs RC School
*CHLYE* PR6 .................... **32** F3
St Josephs RC School
*WGNNW/ST* WN6 .................... **55** J2
St Judes RC Junior &
Infant School
*WGNS/IIMK* WN3 .................... **68** B8
St Julie RC Primary School
*ECCL* WA10 .................... **101** J1
St Julies High School
*WLTN* L25 .................... **131** K4
St Laurence Medical Centre
*KKBY* L32 .................... **86** B4
St Laurences Primary School
*BIRK* CH41 .................... **11** G4
St Laurences Primary School
*KKBY* L32 .................... **86** B4
St Lawrence C of E
Primary School
*ANF/KKDL* L4 .................... **7** L9
St Leos Primary School
*RAIN/WH* L35 .................... **117** G3
St Lewis's Catholic
Primary School
*GOL/RIS/CU* WA3 .................... **106** D4

St Lukes C E Primary School
*FMBY* L37 .................... **58** F4
St Lukes C of E School
*GOL/RIS/CU* WA3 .................... **93** G6
St Lukes Halsall C of E
Primary School
*CSBY/BLUN* L23 .................... **70** F8
St Lukes Primary School
*RAIN/WH* L35 .................... **117** H1
St Lukes RC Primary School
*FROD/HEL* WA6 .................... **160** E5
St Lukes RC Primary School
*SKEL* WN8 .................... **66** A7
St Malachys RC Primary School
*TOX* L8 .................... **113** G8
St Margaret Marys Junior &
Infant School
*DV/KA/FCH* L14 .................... **115** H2
St Margarets Ce Junior School
*WARRN/WOL* WA2 .................... **121** L4
St Margarets C of E
Controlled Infant School
*WARRN/WOL* WA2 .................... **121** L3
St Margarets C of E High School
*AIG/SPK* L17 .................... **130** A4
St Margarets C of E Jmi School
*TOX* L8 .................... **113** H6
St Margarets C of E
Primary School
*NPK/KEN* L6 .................... **97** L8
St Maries RC Primary School
*WGNNW/ST* WN6 .................... **56** A3
St Maries RC School
*NWD/KWIPK* L33 .................... **86** C2
St Marks C of E Junior School
*WGNW/BIL/O* WN5 .................... **68** B6
St Marks R C Primary School
*HLWD* L26 .................... **132** C5
St Marks RC Primary School
*SKEL* WN8 .................... **66** A5
St Marks School
*BRSC* L40 .................... **36** F5
St Martins RC Primary School
*RUNC* WA7 .................... **151** G6
St Mary & St. John RC
Primary School
*WGN* WN1 .................... **5** G2
St Marys C of E Primary School
*CHLY/EC* PR7 .................... **30** E7
St Marys C of E Primary School
*PS/BROM* CH62 .................... **144** C8
St Marys C of E School
*BTL* L20 .................... **6** F5
St Marys College
*CSBY/BLUN* L23 .................... **83** G1
St Marys College
*WAL/NB* CH45 .................... **95** G7
St Marys Primary School
*CSBY/BLUN* L23 .................... **71** G5
St Marys RC High School
*AIG/SPK* L17 .................... **113** M8
St Marys RC High School
Bellerive
*TOX* L8 .................... **113** K8
St Marys RC Infant School
*NEWLW* WA12 .................... **104** D1
St Marys RC Junior School
*NEWLW* WA12 .................... **104** D2
St Marys RC Primary School
*CHLY/EC* PR7 .................... **32** C6
St Marys RC Primary School
*WGNW/BIL/O* WN5 .................... **89** M1
St Marys & St. Thomas C of E
Primary School
*ECCL* WA10 .................... **8** E4
St Marys School
*CHLY/EC* PR7 .................... **31** L2
St Marys West Derby C of E
Primary School
*WD/CROXPK* L12 .................... **98** D6
St Matthews C of E
Primary School
*RAIN/WH* L35 .................... **101** L6
St Matthews Primary School
*ANF/KKDL* L4 .................... **98** A5
St Matthews RC Primary School
*SKEL* WN8 .................... **65** M6
St Michael In the
Hamlet Infant School
*AIG/SPK* L17 .................... **129** K2
St Michaels & All Angels
RC Infant School
*GR/UP/WCH* CH49 .................... **126** E3
St Michaels C of E High School
*CHLY/EC* PR7 .................... **32** E3
St Michaels C of E
Primary School
*SKEL* WN8 .................... **53** M8
St Michaels Primary School
*NPK/KEN* L6 .................... **113** K1
St Monicas Catholic
Primary School
*WARRS* WA4 .................... **137** M6
St Monicas RC Primary School
*BTL* L20 .................... **7** L2
St Nathaniels Primary &
Infant School
*WGNE/HIN* WN2 .................... **80** D2
St Nicholas C of E
Primary School
*CSBY/BLUN* L23 .................... **82** D2
St Nicholas RC Primary School
*VAUX/LVPD* L3 .................... **13** L8
St Oswalds Catholic
Primary School
*WARR* WA1 .................... **122** B5
St Oswalds C of E
Primary School
*NTHTN* L30 .................... **84** B2
St Oswalds Junior School
*CLB/OSW/ST* L13 .................... **114** C3
St Oswalds Primary School
*AIMK* WN4 .................... **91** K4
St Oswalds RC Primary School
*CHLY/EC* PR7 .................... **42** E5
St Paschal Baylon
Primary School
*CHLDW* L16 .................... **115** H5

St Patricks Junior School
*WGN* WN1 .................... **5** H4
St Patricks Primary School
*CHTN/BK* PR9 .................... **25** J3
St Patricks Primary School
*TOX* L8 .................... **113** H7
St Patricks Primary School
*WGN* WN1 .................... **5** H5
St Paul of the Cross Catholic
Primary School
*WARRW/BUR* WA5 .................... **104** A7
St Pauls C of E Junior &
Infant School
*WGNS/IIMK* WN3 .................... **79** H2
St Pauls C of E School
*CHLYE* PR6 .................... **44** C5
St Pauls Junior School
*WD/CROXPK* L12 .................... **98** E7
St Paul's RC Primary School
*CL/PREN* CH43 .................... **110** D6
St Pauls & St. Timothys
Infant School
*WD/CROXPK* L12 .................... **98** E6
St Peter & St. Paul High School
*WDN* WA8 .................... **134** B3
St Peter & St. Paul RC
Primary School
*RNFD/HAY* WA11 .................... **89** K6
St Peter & St. Paul RC School
*WAL/NB* CH45 .................... **95** K5
St Peter & St. Pauls
Primary School
*NWD/KWIPK* L33 .................... **74** B8
St Peters Catholic
Primary School
*WARR* WA1 .................... **122** E6
St Peters C of E Junior School
*CHLYE* PR6 .................... **33** G3
St Peters C of E Junior School
*LEIGH* WN7 .................... **81** K8
St Peters C of E Primary School
*FMBY* L37 .................... **47** J8
St Peters C of E Primary School
*HES* CH60 .................... **141** H6
St Peters C of E Primary School
*NEWLW* WA12 .................... **104** F1
St Peters C of E School
*WGNE/HIN* WN2 .................... **69** L8
St Peters Infants Mixed School
*LEIGH* WN7 .................... **81** L8
St Peters Primary School
*AIMK* WN4 .................... **79** H7
St Peters RC High School
*WGNW/BIL/O* WN5 .................... **67** H6
St Peters RC Primary School
*CL/PREN* CH43 .................... **126** E1
St Philips Church & Community
Primary School
*WARRW/BUR* WA5 .................... **120** D4
St Philips (Controlled) C of E
Primary School
*LITH* L21 .................... **83** L5
St Phillips C of E Primary School
*STHP* PR8 .................... **3** K6
St Raymonds RC Primary School
*NTHTN* L30 .................... **83** M1
St Richards RC Primary School
*SKEL* WN8 .................... **64** F4
St Robert Bellarmine RC Primary
School
*BTL* L20 .................... **83** M6
St Saviours RC Aided School
*GTS/LS* CH66 .................... **163** G2
St Sebastians JMI School
*EHL/KEN* L7 .................... **113** M3
St Stephen's Primary School
*WARRN/WOL* WA2 .................... **121** L4
St Stephens Primary School
*WGN* WN1 .................... **69** G3
St Stephens School
*CHTN/BK* PR9 .................... **23** H7
St Teresa RC Primary School
*ECCL* WA10 .................... **8** B4
St Teresas Infant School
*NG/CROX* L11 .................... **98** B3
St Teresas Junior School
*NG/CROX* L11 .................... **98** B3
St Theresas RC Primary School
*STHEL* WA9 .................... **118** E2
St Theresa's School
*SKEL* WN8 .................... **66** D4
St Thomas Becket RC
High School
*HUY* L36 .................... **116** C2
St Thomas Ce Primary School
*WARRS* WA4 .................... **137** M4
St Thomas C of E
Junior & Infant School
*GOL/RIS/CU* WA3 .................... **92** C4
St Thomas C of E
Primary School
*MGHL* L31 .................... **72** F1
St Thomas C of E School
*AIMK* WN4 .................... **91** L2
St Thomas More RC High School
*WGNW/BIL/O* WN5 .................... **68** B6
St Thomas of Canterbury
RC School
*CSBY/WL* L22 .................... **83** G5
St Thomas the Martyr C of E
Primary School
*SKEL* WN8 .................... **66** D6
St Vincents Catholic
Primary School
*WARRW/BUR* WA5 .................... **136** A2
St Vincents Primary School
*CLVPS* L1 .................... **112** F5
St Weburgh C of E
Primary School
*WARRS* WA4 .................... **137** K3
St Werburghs RC
Primary School
*BIRK* CH41 .................... **11** G8
St Wilfrieds C of E
Primary School
*WARRS* WA4 .................... **138** D4

St Wilfrids C of E
Primary School
WGNNW/ST WN6 ...... 56 B4
St Wilfrids High School
LITH L21 ...... 83 L6
St William of York RC
Primary School
CSBY/BLUN L23 ...... 71 K8
St Williams RC School
WGNE/HIN WN2 ...... 5 M6
St Winefrides R C Aided Primary
School
NSTN CH64 ...... 153 H6
St Winefrides RC Infant School
BTL L20 ...... 7 G6
St Winefrides RC Junior School
BTL L20 ...... 6 F5
Salisbury Road Doctors Surgery
ALL/GAR L19 ...... 130 C7
Sandbrook Primary School
MOR/LEA CH46 ...... 110 B3
Sandfield Medical Centre
ECCL WA10 ...... 8 E6
Sandfield Park School
WD/CROXPK L12 ...... 98 D8
Sandhills Business Park
EV L5 ...... 96 E7
Sandon Industrial Estate
VAUX/LVPD L3 ...... 96 D7
Sandringham Medical Centre
TOX L8 ...... 129 K1
Sandy Lane Health Centre
SKEL WN8 ...... 64 F4
Sankey Bridge Industrial Estate
WARRW/BUR WA5 ...... 136 E1
Sankey Medical Centre
WARRW/BUR WA5 ...... 120 A6
Sankey Valley Industrial Estate
NEWLW WA12 ...... 104 D3
Savio RC High School
NTHTN L30 ...... 84 A4
Scarisbrick CP School
BRSC L40 ...... 50 B2
School Clinic
SKEL WN8 ...... 65 M7
School of Good Shepherd
ANF/KKDL L4 ...... 97 H4
Scot Lane Junior &
Infant School
WGNW/BIL/O WN5 ...... 68 B6
Seabank Medical Centre
WAL/NB CH45 ...... 95 K6
Seaforth Health Clinic
LITH L21 ...... 83 J6
Sefton Cricket Club
AIG/SPK L17 ...... 129 M1
Sefton Metropolitan
Borough Council
BTL L20 ...... 7 H5
Sefton Metropolitan
Borough Council
BTL L20 ...... 7 H3
Sefton Metropolitan
Borough Council
BTL L20 ...... 7 J3
Sefton Metropolitan
Borough Council
CSBY/WL L22 ...... 83 G5
Sefton Metropolitan
Borough Council
MGHL L31 ...... 72 E4
Sefton Metropolitan
Borough Council
NTHTN L30 ...... 83 L2
Sefton Metropolitan
Borough Council
NTHTN L30 ...... 84 B1
Sefton Park Medical Centre
WAV L15 ...... 113 M7
Sefton Road Health Clinic
LITH L21 ...... 83 K5
Sewage Works
HTWN L38 ...... 60 F5
Sherdley CP School
STHEL WA9 ...... 102 E7
Shevington County High School
WGNNW/ST WN6 ...... 55 K6
Shevington CP School
WGNNW/ST WN6 ...... 55 H7
Shevington Vale CP School
WGNNW/ST WN6 ...... 55 C5
Shizhen Chinese Medical Centre
WAL/EG CH44 ...... 111 K2
The Shopping Centre
STHEL WA9 ...... 118 D1
Shorefields Community
Comprehensive School
AIG/SPK L17 ...... 129 K1
Shorefiels Comm Comp School
TOX L8 ...... 129 J2
Shoreshird School
STHP PR8 ...... 47 K1
Shorrocks Hill Country Club
FMBY L37 ...... 58 D4
Showcase Cinemas
NG/CROX L11 ...... 98 C1
Silverdale Medical Centre
HES CH60 ...... 141 H5
Simms Cross County
Primary School
WDN WA8 ...... 16 C4
Simonswood County
Primary School
NWD/KWIPK L33 ...... 86 C3
Sir Alfred Jones
Memorial Hospital
ALL/GAR L19 ...... 130 E7
Sir Thomas Boteler
High School
WARRS WA4 ...... 138 A2
Skelmersdale College
SKEL WN8 ...... 65 J4
Skelmersdale Crow
Orchard County
Primary School
SKEL WN8 ...... 65 H3
Skelmersdale Park CP School
SKEL WN8 ...... 65 G4

Skelmersdale Sports Centre
SKEL WN8 ...... 65 L6
Skelmersdale United
Football Club
SKEL WN8 ...... 64 F5
Slaidburn Industrial Estate
CHTN/BK PR9 ...... 25 J1
Small Business Centre
VAUX/LVPD L3 ...... 112 F8
Smm Business Park
WAL/EG CH44 ...... 111 L4
Snaefell Avenue
Doctors Surgery
CLB/OSW/ST L13 ...... 98 A8
Somerville Medical Practice
WAL/EG CH44 ...... 111 L2
Somerville Primary School
WAL/EG CH44 ...... 111 L2
Southbank Tennis Club
STHP PR8 ...... 36 A1
Southdene Medical Centre
KKBY L32 ...... 86 C5
Southlands High School
CHLY/EC PR7 ...... 32 C8
Southmead Junior &
Infant School
RAIN/WH L35 ...... 117 G3
Southport & Ainsdale Golf Club
STHP PR8 ...... 34 F7
Southport & Birkdale
Cricket Club
STHP PR8 ...... 35 G2
Southport Business Centre
CHTN/BK PR9 ...... 3 H3
Southport Business Park
STHP PR8 ...... 35 J2
Southport College
CHTN/BK PR9 ...... 3 J3
Southport Football Club
STHP PR8 ...... 25 G8
Southport & Formby
District General Hospital
STHP PR8 ...... 3 M8
Southport & Formby Hospital
CHTN/BK PR9 ...... 3 H3
Southport General Infirmary
STHP PR8 ...... 3 M7
Southport Girls Football Club
STHP PR8 ...... 25 H7
Southport New Synagogue
STHP PR8 ...... 3 G5
Southport Pier
STHP PR8 ...... 24 B4
Southport Rugby Club
STHP PR8 ...... 35 G4
Southport Sailing Club
STHP PR8 ...... 24 C4
Southport Swimming Baths
STHP PR8 ...... 2 D4
Southport Zoo &
Conservation Trust
STHP PR8 ...... 2 D3
South Sefton Business Centre
BTL L20 ...... 6 F6
South Wirral High School
PS/BROM CH62 ...... 154 F1
Sovereign Business Park
WGN WN1 ...... 5 G5
Speke Community
Comprehensive School
SPK/HALE L24 ...... 146 F3
Speke Comprehensive School
SPK/HALE L24 ...... 146 F2
Speke Family Health Clinic
SPK/HALE L24 ...... 147 G2
Sphynx Tennis Club
STHP PR8 ...... 36 A1
Springbank Industrial Estate
WGNE/HIN WN2 ...... 80 D2
Springfield School
KKBY L32 ...... 86 A5
Spring View Cricket Club
WGNE/HIN WN2 ...... 5 H6
Springwood CP School
ALL/GAR L19 ...... 131 G5
Standish Clinic
WGNNW/ST WN6 ...... 56 A4
Standish Cricket Club
WGNNW/ST WN6 ...... 56 A5
Standish High School
WGNNW/ST WN6 ...... 55 L3
Standish Lower Ground C of E
School
WGNNW/ST WN6 ...... 67 M2
Standish Medical Practice
WGNNW/ST WN6 ...... 56 A4
Stanlaw Abbey CP School
EP CH65 ...... 163 M3
Stanley High School
CHTN/BK PR9 ...... 25 H1
Stanley Medical Centre
EV L5 ...... 96 F7
Stanley School
PEN/TH CH61 ...... 126 C7
Stanney Grange CP School
EP CH65 ...... 163 L3
Stanney High School
EP CH65 ...... 163 L3
Stanney Mill Industrial Estate
CHNE CH2 ...... 164 B4
Stanney Mill Industrial Estate
EP CH65 ...... 21 K9
Stanton Road Primary School
BEB CH63 ...... 143 H2
Statham Community
Primary School
LYMM WA13 ...... 139 L1
Stockbridge Primary School
HUY L36 ...... 99 L7
Stockbridge Village
Health Centre
STBRV L28 ...... 99 J5
Stockton Heath
Community Primary School
WARRS WA4 ...... 137 L4
Stockton Heath Medical Centre
WARRS WA4 ...... 137 L4

Stockton Wood Jmi School
SPK/HALE L24 ...... 146 E2
Stopgate Medical Centre
WLT/FAZ L9 ...... 97 M2
Storrsdale Medical Centre
CALD/MH L18 ...... 130 D2
The Strand Medical Centre
BTL L20 ...... 7 G2
Streatham House School
CSBY/BLUN L23 ...... 82 F1
Studio Gallery
BEB CH63 ...... 142 C3
Stutelea Hotel & Leisure Club
CHTN/BK PR9 ...... 24 E4
Sudley Art Gallery
AIG/SPK L17 ...... 130 B3
Sudley Infant School
AIG/SPK L17 ...... 130 A3
Sudley Junior School
AIG/SPK L17 ...... 130 A4
Sullivan Way Surgery
WGN WN1 ...... 5 G2
Summerhill Primary School
MGHL L31 ...... 73 H5
Sunnymede School
STHP PR8 ...... 2 C6
Superbowl 2000 & Laserquest
WGNS/IIMK WN3 ...... 4 D5
Sutton C of E Junior & I
nfant School
STHEL WA9 ...... 103 G5
Sutton C of E Primary School
STHEL WA9 ...... 103 G5
Sutton Community
High School
STHEL WA9 ...... 102 D7
Sutton Community
High School Sports Centre
STHEL WA9 ...... 102 D7
Sutton County High School
GTS/LS CH66 ...... 156 A8
Sutton Cricket Club
STHEL WA9 ...... 102 E7
Sutton Green CP School
GTS/LS CH66 ...... 155 K8
Sutton Hall Golf Club
RUNC WA7 ...... 161 J2
Sutton Manor Community
Primary School
STHEL WA9 ...... 118 C3
Sutton Way County
Junior School
EV L5 ...... 163 G1
Swan Meadow Industrial Estate
WGNS/IIMK WN3 ...... 4 C7
Sycamore Lane Community
Primary School
WARRW/BUR WA5 ...... 120 D8
Sylvester Primary School
HUY L36 ...... 116 B4
Tarbock Road Doctors Surgery
HUY L36 ...... 116 A4
Temple of Praise
EV L5 ...... 97 J7
Thatto Heath CP School
STHEL WA9 ...... 102 A5
Theatre Building Surgery
ECCL WA10 ...... 9 H5
Thelwall Community
Infant School
WARRS WA4 ...... 138 E2
Thelwall Community
Junior School
WARRS WA4 ...... 138 F2
Thelwall New Road Surgery
WARRS WA4 ...... 138 D2
Theta Gallery
TOX L8 ...... 112 F6
Thingwall Primary School
PEN/TH CH61 ...... 126 C7
Thingwall Recreation Centre
PEN/TH CH61 ...... 126 D7
Thomas Gray Infant School
BTL L20 ...... 6 E2
Thomas Gray Junior School
BTL L20 ...... 6 F1
Thornton Hough
Primary School
BEB CH63 ...... 142 D6
Thornton Primary School
CSBY/BLUN L23 ...... 71 K7
Titanic Memorial
VAUX/LVPD L3 ...... 12 C7
Tower Dene Preparatory School
CHTN/BK PR9 ...... 25 H1
Tower Hill Health Centre
NWD/KWIPK L33 ...... 74 B8
Townfield Primary School
CL/PREN CH43 ...... 127 G2
Town Green CP School
ORM L39 ...... 62 E5
Town House Practice
WDN WA8 ...... 16 F2
Town Lane Infant School
BEB CH63 ...... 128 A7
Toxteth Sports Centre
TOX L8 ...... 113 H7
Tranmere Rovers Football Club
RF/TRAN CH42 ...... 127 L3
Transport Museum
BIRK CH41 ...... 11 L3
Trent Avenue Doctors Surgery
MGHL L31 ...... 73 J3
Trentham Road Medical Centre
KKBY L32 ...... 85 L3
Trident Industrial Estate
GOL/RIS/CU WA3 ...... 107 G7
Trinity CP School
SKEL WN8 ...... 65 G4
Twelve Apostles Mixed &
Infants School
LEIGH WN7 ...... 81 M5
Twig Lane Clinic
HUY L36 ...... 115 L1
Twin Lakes Industrial Park
LEY/BBR PR5 ...... 29 J2

Twiss Green Community Primary
School
GOL/RIS/CU WA3 ...... 107 G1
Unity Theatre
CLVPS L1 ...... 13 K9
University of Liverpool
AIG/SPK L17 ...... 130 A1
University of Liverpool
AIG/SPK L17 ...... 130 B3
University of Liverpool
EHL/KEN L7 ...... 13 M8
University of Liverpool
NSTN CH64 ...... 153 M6
University of Liverpool
VAUX/LVPD L3 ...... 13 L6
University of Liverpool
VAUX/LVPD L3 ...... 13 M6
University Propagation Centre
AIG/SPK L17 ...... 130 B2
The Unsworth Group Practice
HOR/BR BL6 ...... 57 L2
Upholland High School
WGNW/BIL/O WN5 ...... 77 L1
Upper Parliament
Medical Centre
EHL/KEN L7 ...... 113 K5
Upton County Infants School
WDN WA8 ...... 133 K2
Upton Cricket Club
GR/UP/WCH CH49 ...... 110 A8
Upton Group Practice
GR/UP/WCH CH49 ...... 110 D8
Upton Hall Convent School
GR/UP/WCH CH49 ...... 110 B8
Upton Medical Centre
WDN WA8 ...... 133 K2
Ursuline RC Primary School
CSBY/BLUN L23 ...... 82 D2
Uveco Business Centre
BIRK CH41 ...... 111 K4
Valewood Primary School
CSBY/BLUN L23 ...... 70 F8
Valley Medical Centre
ANF/KKDL L4 ...... 97 G6
Valley Medical Centre
CHLDW L16 ...... 115 G6
VAT House & HM Customs &
Excise
VAUX/LVPD L3 ...... 112 E6
Vauxhall Business Centre
VAUX/LVPD L3 ...... 12 E3
Vauxhall Health Centre
EV L5 ...... 13 C1
Vernon Sangster Sports Centre
ANF/KKDL L4 ...... 97 J6
Victoria Road CP School
RUNC WA7 ...... 19 C5
Victoria Trading Estate
RAIN/WH L35 ...... 117 L2
The Village Gallery
HES CH60 ...... 141 H6
Village Medical Centre
WLTN L25 ...... 131 J3
The Village Surgery
FMBY L37 ...... 59 G3
Villa Medical Centre
CL/PREN CH43 ...... 127 J5
Virgin Cinemas
CLB/OSW/ST L13 ...... 114 B4
Virgin Cinemas
WGNW/BIL/O WN5 ...... 68 D7
Vittoria Medical Centre
BIRK CH41 ...... 11 G3
Vyner Primary School
CL/PREN CH43 ...... 110 F4
Waddicar Lane Surgery
MGHL L31 ...... 85 J1
Wade Deacon High School
WDN WA8 ...... 134 B3
Walker Art Gallery
VAUX/LVPD L3 ...... 13 H5
Wallasey Rugby Club
WAL/NB CH45 ...... 94 F8
Wallasey School
MOR/LEA CH46 ...... 110 C2
Walray Pictures Gallery
NSTN CH64 ...... 152 E6
Walton Breck Surgery
EV L5 ...... 97 J7
Walton Hall
WARRS WA4 ...... 137 J7
Walton Hall Medical Centre
ANF/KKDL L4 ...... 97 J4
Walton Hospital
WLT/FAZ L9 ...... 97 H2
Walton Medical Centre
ANF/KKDL L4 ...... 97 H3
Walton St Mary C of E
Primary School
ANF/KKDL L4 ...... 97 H3
Walton Sports Centre
WLT/FAZ L9 ...... 97 K3
Walton Village Medical Centre
ANF/KKDL L4 ...... 97 J4
Wargrave C of E Primary School
NEWLW WA12 ...... 104 E4
Wargrave House School
NEWLW WA12 ...... 104 E4
Warren Road Doctors Surgery
CSBY/BLUN L23 ...... 82 D2
Warrington Borough Council
GOL/RIS/CU WA3 ...... 107 H2
Warrington Borough Council
WARR WA1 ...... 14 C5
Warrington Borough Council
WARR WA1 ...... 15 J4
Warrington Borough Council
WARR WA1 ...... 122 D6
Warrington Borough Council
WARR WA1 ...... 123 H6
Warrington Borough Council
WARRN/WOL WA2 ...... 121 K3
Warrington Borough Council
WARRN/WOL WA2 ...... 122 B3
Warrington Borough Council
WARRS WA4 ...... 138 A6
Warrington Borough Council
WARRS WA4 ...... 138 B1

Warrington Borough Council
WARRW/BUR WA5 ...... 121 H5
Warrington Borough Council
WARRW/BUR WA5 ...... 121 H3
Warrington Business Park
WARRN/WOL WA2 ...... 121 L1
Warrington Central
Trading Estate
WARRN/WOL WA2 ...... 14 C3
Warrington Community
Health Care NHS Trust
WARRN/WOL WA2 ...... 105 H7
Warrington New Town
Cricket Club
WARRW/BUR WA5 ...... 120 F8
Warrington Rugby
League Football Club
WARRS WA4 ...... 15 G9
Warrington Sports Club
WARRS WA4 ...... 137 J6
Warrington Town A F C
WARRS WA4 ...... 138 A3
Watergate School
WLTN L25 ...... 131 K3
Waterloo Football Club
CSBY/BLUN L23 ...... 70 D8
Wavertree Cricket Club
WAV L15 ...... 114 B5
Wavertree Health Clinic
WAV L15 ...... 114 C7
Wavertree Retail Park
EHL/KEN L7 ...... 113 L4
Wavertree Town Hall
WAV L15 ...... 114 C6
Weatherhead High School
WAL/NB CH45 ...... 95 J6
Weatherstone Business Centre
NSTN CH64 ...... 153 L5
Weaver Industrial Estate
ALL/GAR L19 ...... 145 L2
Weaver Park Industrial Estate
FROD/HEL WA6 ...... 160 F3
Wellesbourne County
Primary School
NG/CROX L11 ...... 98 B3
West Bank County
Primary School
WDN WA8 ...... 149 H1
West Bank Medical Centre
WDN WA8 ...... 16 C9
West Bank Medical Centre
WDN WA8 ...... 134 C8
Westbourne Preparatory School
WAL/NB CH45 ...... 95 L7
Westbrook Medical Centre
WARRW/BUR WA5 ...... 120 D4
West Cheshire College
EP CH65 ...... 20 A5
West Cheshire College
EP CH65 ...... 156 C8
West Derby
Comprehensive School
CLB/OSW/ST L13 ...... 98 B7
West End County Primary School
ORM L39 ...... 51 G6
West Kirby Foot Health Clinic
WKBY CH48 ...... 124 D3
West Kirby Grammar
School for Girls
WKBY CH48 ...... 124 B2
West Kirby Health Centre
WKBY CH48 ...... 124 C2
West Kirby Primary School
WKBY CH48 ...... 124 C1
West Kirby Residential School
WKBY CH48 ...... 124 C2
West Lancashire District Council
SKEL WN8 ...... 65 M5
West Lancs District Council
SKEL WN8 ...... 64 F4
West Lancs Yacht Club
STHP PR8 ...... 24 C4
Westleigh Cricket Club
LEIGH WN7 ...... 81 M8
Westleigh Methodist School
LEIGH WN7 ...... 81 M5
Westminster Industrial Park
EP CH65 ...... 156 B7
Westminster Medical Centre
ANF/KKDL L4 ...... 7 L9
Westminster Road
Swimming Pool
ANF/KKDL L4 ...... 97 G6
Westminster Surgery
EP CH65 ...... 20 C1
Weston Point County
Primary School
RUNC WA7 ...... 18 D9
Weston Primary School
RUNC WA7 ...... 149 J7
West Park Rugby Football Club
STHEL WA9 ...... 101 K4
Westside Industrial Estate
ECCL WA10 ...... 9 L8
WesTVale Health Centre
KKBY L32 ...... 85 L3
WesTVale Primary School
KKBY L32 ...... 85 K3
West Wirral Group Practice
HES CH60 ...... 141 H5
West Wirral Group Practice
PEN/TH CH61 ...... 125 M7
West Wirral Group Practice
PEN/TH CH61 ...... 126 C7
Wheathill Industrial Estate
NTHLY L27 ...... 115 M7
Wheathill Special School
HUY L36 ...... 115 M6
Wheatlea Industrial Estate
WGNS/IIMK WN3 ...... 79 H3
Whelley Hospital
WGN WN1 ...... 69 G3
Whetstone Lane Health Centre
BIRK CH41 ...... 11 G7
Whiston Health Centre
RAIN/WH L35 ...... 116 F2
Whitby County High School
GTS/LS CH66 ...... 163 J4

Whitby Heath County
Primary School
EP CH65 .................................. 20 A9
Whitechapel Gallery
CLVPS L1 ................................... 13 G7
Whitefield JMI School
NPK/KEN L6 ............................. 113 J1
Widnes Community
Midwifery & Ante Natal
WDN WA8 ............................... 134 B3
Widnes Cricket Club
WDN WA8 ............................... 134 D1
Widnes Public Baths
WDN WA8 .................................. 16 D4
Widnes Rugby Football Club
WDN WA8 .................................. 16 B4
Widnes Sixth Form College
WDN WA8 ................................ 118 A8
Wigan Area Health Authority
WGNE/HIN WN2 ........................ 69 M7
Wigan & Bolton
Health Authority
WGN WN1 .................................. 4 F3
Wigan & Leigh College
LEIGH WN7 ................................ 93 M2
Wigan & Leigh College
WGN WN1 ................................... 4 E3
Wigan & Leigh Technical College
WGN WN1 ................................... 4 D3
Wigan Little Theatre
WGN WN1 ................................... 5 G3
Wigan Magistrates Court
WGN WN1 ................................... 5 G5
Wigan Metro Borough Coun
WGN WN1 ................................... 4 F4
Wigan Metropolitan
Borough Council
GOL/RIS/CU WA3 ....................... 92 D5
Wigan Metropolitan
Borough Council
GOL/RIS/CU WA3 ....................... 93 J5
Wigan Metropolitan
Borough Council
LEIGH WN7 ................................ 81 M5

Wigan Metropolitan
Borough Council
WGN WN1 ................................... 4 E2
Wigan Metropolitan
Borough Council
WGNE/HIN WN2 ......................... 57 H8
Wigan Metropolitan
Borough Council
WGNE/HIN WN2 ......................... 57 L8
Wigan Metropolitan
Borough Council
WGNE/HIN WN2 ......................... 69 L8
Wigan Metropolitan
Borough Council
WGNE/HIN WN2 ......................... 80 C3
Wigan Metropolitan
Borough Council
WGNS/IIMK WN3 ......................... 4 D6
Wigan Metropolitan
Borough Council
WGNS/IIMK WN3 ......................... 5 G6
Wigan Metropolitan
Borough Council
WGNW/BIL/O WN5 ...................... 67 H7
Wigan Metropolitan
Borough Council
WGNW/BIL/O WN5 ...................... 68 A6
Wigan Rugby Union
Football Club
WGN WN1 ................................... 56 F8
Willaston C of E
Primary School
NSTN CH64 .............................. 154 B5
William Beaumont
Community High School
WARRN/WOL WA2 .................... 121 K4
Williamson Art Gallery &
Museum
CL/PREN CH43 ........................... 10 C8
William Stockton CP School
EP CH65 .................................. 20 A4
Willow Tree Primary School
STHEL WA9 .............................. 118 F1
Wilson Business Centre
HUY L36 .................................. 116 B4

Windmill Hill County
Primary School
RUNC WA7 ............................... 150 E3
Wingate Medical Centre
NWD/KWIPK L33 ........................ 86 C2
Winstanley College
WGNW/BIL/O WN5 ..................... 78 A2
Winstanley CP School
WCNS/IIMK WN3 ......................... 78 E3
Winstanley Industrial Estate
WARRN/WOL WA2 .................... 121 K4
Winstanley Medical Centre
WGNS/IIMK WN3 ......................... 78 F2
Winwick C of E Primary School
WARRN/WOL WA2 .................... 105 K7
Winwick Parish Leisure Centre
WARRN/WOL WA2 .................... 105 K7
Wirral Area Health Authority
WAL/EG WA4 ........................... 111 K1
Wirral Borough Council
CL/PREN CH43 ......................... 111 H5
Wirral Borough
Magistrates Court
BIRK CH41 ................................. 11 M5
Wirral Community Centre
WAL/EG WA4 ........................... 111 L4
Wirral Community
Healthcare N H S Trust
BEB CH63 ............................... 128 C8
Wirral Community
Healthcare Nhs Trust
MOR/LEA WA6 ......................... 110 C2
Wirral Community
Healthcare N H S Trust
RF/TRAN CH42 ........................ 127 M2
Wirral Community
Healthcare N H S Trust
WAL/EG WA4 ........................... 111 K2
Wirral Community
Healthcare N H S Trust
WAL/EG WA4 ........................... 111 L1
Wirral County Grammar
School for Girls
BEB CH63 ............................... 143 G1

Wirral Grammar School
for Boys
BEB CH63 ............................... 143 G1
Wirral Health Authority
BIRK CH41 ................................. 11 L3
Wirral Health Authority
RF/TRAN CH42 ........................ 128 A3
Wirral Hospital
BEB CH63 ............................... 143 G4
Wirral Hospital NHS Trust
GR/UP/WCH CH49 ................... 126 B3
Wirral Metropolitan Borough Council
BIRK CH41 ................................. 11 M4
Wirral Metropolitan Borough Council
BIRK CH41 ................................. 11 G8
Wirral Metropolitan Borough Council
WAL/EG WA4 ........................... 111 L3
Wirral Metropolitan College
BIRK CH41 ................................. 11 J5
Wirral Metropolitan College
PS/BROM CH62 ........................ 144 C7
Wirral Metropolitan College
RF/TRAN CH42 ........................ 127 L1
Wirral Museum
BIRK CH41 ................................. 11 L4
Wirral Stroke & Head Injury Clinic
CL/PREN CH43 ........................ 127 H4
Wirral Tennis & Sports Centre
BIRK CH41 ............................... 110 F3
Wirral & West Cheshire Community
NHS Trust
CL/PREN CH43 ........................... 10 B9
Woodchurch C of E Primary School
GR/UP/WCH CH49 ................... 126 C3
Woodchurch High School
GR/UP/WCH CH49 ................... 126 F2
Woodchurch Leisure Centre
GR/UP/WCH CH49 ................... 126 E2
Woodchurch Road Primary School
RF/TRAN CH42 ........................ 127 L1
Woodend Industrial Estate
SPK/HALE L24 ......................... 131 M8
Woodfall County Junior & Infant
School
NSTN CH64 .............................. 153 J7

Woodfield Primary School
WGN WN1 .................................. 68 E1
Wood Fold Primary School
WGNNW/ST WN6 ....................... 55 M5
Woodlands County Infant School
GTS/LS CH66 .......................... 163 H3
Woodlands County Junior School
GTS/LS CH66 .......................... 163 H4
Woodlands Industrial Estate
NEWLW WA12 ............................ 91 L7
Woodlands Primary School
BIRK CH41 ................................. 11 H8
Woodlands Primary School
FMBY L37 .................................. 58 F2
Woodside County Primary School
RUNC WA7 ............................... 150 A6
Woodslee Primary School
PS/BROM CH62 ........................ 143 M3
Woodvale CP School
STHP PR8 .................................. 47 M2
Woolston C of E Primary School
WARR WA1 ............................... 122 E5
Woolston Community High School
WARR WA1 ............................... 122 D5
Woolston Community Primary School
WARR WA1 ............................... 122 E6
Woolston Surgery
WARR WA1 ............................... 122 F6
Woolton County Infant School
WLTN L25 ............................... 131 K2
Woolton House Medical Centre
WLTN L25 ............................... 131 J3
Woolton Surgery
WLTN L25 ............................... 131 J3
Woolton Swimming Pool
WLTN L25 ............................... 131 J3
Worsley Mesnes County Primary
School
WGNS/IIMK WN3 ....................... 79 J1
Wrightington Hospital NHS Trust
WGNNW/ST WN6 ....................... 55 G4
YMCA
CLVPS L1 ................................... 13 K8
York Road Group Practice
EP CH65 .................................. 20 C5

## Page 100

**F7**
1. Atherton St
2. Bond St
3. Cambridge St
4. Carlton St
5. Chapel St
6. Church St
7. Duke St
8. Highfield Pl
9. Leyland St
10. Market Pl
11. Mill St
12. Pottery Flds
13. Salisbury St
14. Seddons Ct
15. Wood St
16. Wycherley St

## Page 101

**G7**
1. Cliftonville Rd
2. Derby Sq
3. East St
4. Evelyn Av
5. Kelly St
6. Kemble St
7. Lavender Crs
8. Pembertons Ct
9. Queens Rd
10. Smith St

**J7**
1. Ancholme Cl
2. Brockhall Cl
3. Farthingstone Cl
4. Georgian Cl
5. Helford Cl

**J8**
1. Ariss Gv
2. Duncote Cl
3. Waine Gv

**K1**
1. The Cloisters
2. Linden Wy

**L7**
1. Buckthorn Gdns
2. Fountain St

**M1**
1. Caraway Gv
2. Hearne Rd
3. Hopkins Cl
4. Juniper Cl
5. Kitchener St
6. Melville Cl
7. Newfields
8. St Luke's Rd
9. St Teresa's Rd

**M2**
1. Belmont St
2. Roscoe St
3. Warwick St

**M3**
1. Constance St
2. Selby St

**M4**
1. Alexandra Rd
2. Carlow St
3. Crosby Gv
4. Derringstone Cl
5. Thompson St

**M5**
1. Beech St
2. Legion Rd
3. Leicester St

**M6**
1. Blaydon Gv
2. Common St
3. Crown St
4. Fernlea Av
5. Corsefield
6. Nutgrove Av
7. Oakfield Cl
8. Samuel St

**M7**
1. Aycliffe Rd
2. Bevan Cl
3. Hexham St

## Page 102

**A1**
1. Greenall St
2. Tamworth St
3. Trafalgar St

**A2**
1. Bruce St
2. Crispin St
3. Duncan St
4. Lawrenson St
5. Maxwell St
6. Napier Cl
7. Pemberton St
8. Windus St

**A3**
1. Ayrshire Gdns
2. Boundary Rd
3. Eldon Cl
4. Tullis St

**A5**
1. Timor Av

**A6**
1. Denison Gv
2. Kempsey Gv
3. Manley Pl

**A7**
1. Basildon Cl

**B1**
1. Barton Cl
2. Burnell Cl
3. Chorley St
4. Halefield St
5. Lowe St
6. New Cross St
7. Palmer Cl
8. Randon Gv
9. Rigby St
10. Volunteer St

**B2**
1. Copperas St
2. Headley Cl
3. Lowe St South
4. Manning St
5. Rigby St

**B3**
1. Berkshire Gdns
2. Buckingham St
3. Cardigan Cl
4. Duncan Cl
5. Flintshire Gdns
6. Clamorgan Cl

**B7**
1. Cheyne Wk
2. Farringdon St

**C1**
1. Baldwin St
2. Claughton St
3. College St
4. Ditcconson St
5. John St
6. Ward St
7. William St

**D2**
1. Bickerstaffe St

**E1**
1. Bolton St
2. Earl St
3. Johnson St
4. Parlane St

**E2**
1. Ardwick St
2. Higher Parr St
3. Ivy Ct
4. Mcculloch St
5. Orrell St
6. Parr Mount St
7. South John St
8. Trinity St

**E3**
1. Clarence St
2. Hunter St

**E4**
1. Ada St
2. Cleveland St
3. Cowper St
4. Emmett St

**E5**
1. Bridle Ct
2. Dellside Gv
3. Green End La
4. Margaret Av
5. Marshall Av

**E6**
1. Eton Hall Dr
2. Sandalwood Gdns
3. Shevington Cl
4. Snowdon Gv

**E7**
1. Bracewell Cl
2. Cotterdale Cl
3. Evenwood
4. Freda Av
5. Heward Av
6. Thames Rd

**E8**
1. Westleigh Pl

**F1**
1. Blackhorse St
2. Prospect Rd
3. Windmill Gdns

**F3**
1. Monmouth Gv

**F5**
1. Crouch St
2. Spencer Gdns

**F6**
1. Ambergate Cl
2. Boscow Crs
3. Dunscroft
4. Eaglesfield Cl
5. Kerrysdale Cl
6. Kidstone Cl
7. Lakemoor Cl
8. Marywell Cl
9. Oxley St
10. Riverside Gv
11. St Nicholas Gv
12. Simonstone Gv
13. Springpool
14. Waterdale Pl
15. Weasdale Cl

**F7**
1. Clovelly Av
2. Drybeck Gv
3. Elsbeck Gv
4. Freshford
5. Holywell Cl
6. Kelbrook St
7. Kerswell Cl
8. Padeswood Cl

**F8**
1. Colyton Av
2. Minehead Cl

## Page 104

**B1**
1. Camelot Cl
2. Cherry Cl
3. North St
4. Parkland Cl

**B2**
1. Birket St
2. Farnworth Av
3. Findley Dr
4. Greenheath Wy

**B4**
1. School Cl
2. Yew Wy

**B5**
1. Grampian Av
2. Leawood Av
3. Wilmbrick Cl

**B6**
1. Blackthorn Cl
2. Wheatfield Cl

**B7**
1. Edgewood Rd
2. Hereford Av
3. Manorside Cl

**B7**
1. Arncliffe Dr
2. Colne Av
3. Dorchester Wy
4. Exmouth Wy
5. Gleave Rd
6. Norcott Dr
7. Sherbourne Wy

**C2**
1. Alpine St
2. Back Booth St
3. Back Lawrence St
4. Back Legh St
5. Booth St
6. Lord St
7. Sceptre Ct
8. Stanley St

**C2**
1. Barford Cl
2. College Cl
3. Copplice Cl
4. Corwen Cl
5. Deeside Cl
6. Delamere Cl

**C3**
1. Buttercup Cl

**C6**
1. Blakeney Cl
2. Hunstanton Cl
3. Marsham Cl
4. Sheringham Cl

**C8**
1. Garfield Ter
2. Quineeway
3. Tinas Wy
4. Wroxham Wy

**D2**
1. Alma St
2. Back Bridge St
3. Chemical St
4. Derby Cl
5. Duke St
6. Grafton St
7. Hotel St
8. Houghton St
9. Houghton St
10. Junction La
11. Oxford St
12. Princess St

**D2**
1. Kellett Cl

**D2**
1. Ford Dr

**D6**
1. Broadfield Cl
2. Deniston Cl
3. Edgemoor Cl
4. Loddon Cl
5. Wolferton Cl

**E1**
1. Dean Meadow
2. Dunlin Av
3. Greenfields Cl
4. Greenshank Cl
5. Redshank Cl
6. Sandpiper Cl
7. Sunnybank Cl
8. Water St

**E3**
1. Cedar St
2. Findlay Cl
3. Richmond Gdns

## Page 107

**G2**
1. Crofton Gdns
2. Langcliffe Cl
3. Lawton Cl
4. Rathmell Cl
5. Rimington Cl

## Page 109

**K5**
1. Barberry Cl
2. Cardus Cl
3. Earlswood Cl
4. Ebony Cl
5. Hornbeam Cl
6. Huntingdon Cl
7. Lapworth Cl
8. Morpeth Cl
9. Tanworth Gv
10. Town Meadow La

**L4**
1. Wastdale Cl
2. Wastdale Ms

**L5**
1. Belford Dr
2. Snowden Rd

**L6**
1. Amberley Cl
2. Brunsfield Cl

**M3**
1. Lingham Cl
2. Tarran Dr
3. Tarran Rd

## Page 110

**A1**
1. Castlegrange Cl

**A2**
1. Castleford Ri
2. Castleheath Cl
3. The Heathlands

**A4**
1. Garden La
2. Lyons Cl
3. Oakenholt Rd
4. Old Maryland La
5. Silverburn Av

**A5**
1. Barnston La
2. Chadwick St
3. Kensington Gdns
4. Kingston Cl
5. Netherton Rd
6. Priorsfield
7. Rosslyn Crs

**A7**
1. Bleasdale Cl
2. Broadoaks
3. Kenilworth Gdns
4. Pendle Cl
5. Royden Rd

**A8**
1. Bowscale Rd
2. Bramford Cl
3. Brookside Dr
4. Devonshire Rd
5. Dunning Cl
6. Melton Cl
7. Rendelsham Cl
8. Stonham Cl
9. Trimley Cl
10. Tunstall Cl
11. Withburn Cl

**B2**
1. Bala Gv
2. Breck Rd
3. Chester St
4. Courtney Av
5. Dundee Gv
6. Heathbank Av
7. Ingleby Rd
8. Killarney Gv
9. Lynwood Av
10. Millbank Rd
11. Poulton Hall Rd
12. Roker Av

**B7**
1. Austin St
2. Chamberlain St

**J5**
1. Colwyn St
2. Danescourt Rd
3. Dundonald St
4. Falkland St
5. Lansdowne Cl
6. Methuen St
7. Thornton St

**J6**
1. Seeley Av

**J8**
1. Beresford Cl
2. Chetwynd Rd

**K1**
1. Acland Rd
2. Ashburton Rd
3. Conway St
4. Devonshire Rd
5. Overton Rd
6. Tiverton Av
7. Westminster Rd

**K2**
1. Alderley Rd
2. Sherlock La

**K3**
1. Burnside Av

**K5**
1. Churchview Rd
2. Dawson Av
3. St Edwards Cl
4. Upper Beckwith St

**K6**
1. Asquith St
2. Curzon Av
3. Hartington Av

**K7**
1. St Helen's Cl

**K8**
1. Barnard Rd
2. Claughton Gn
3. Devonshire Cl
4. Enfield Ter
5. The Nook

**L1**
1. Belgrave Av
2. Bristol Av
3. Brompton Av
4. Bryn Bank
5. Chatsworth Av
6. Chepstow Av
7. Ferndale Av
8. The Grange
9. Oxford Rd

**L3**
1. Cranford St
2. Stourton St

**L6**
1. Stoke St

**L6**
1. Aberdeen St
2. Newhope Rd

**L8**
1. Winston Dr

**F8**
1. Compton Cl

## Page 111

**G1**
1. Kelmscott Dr

**G5**
1. Crossway
2. Elmtree Gv
3. Lower Flaybrick Rd
4. Rosemary Cl

**G8**
1. Old School Wy

**H1**
1. Bletchley Av
2. Braemore Rd
3. Brynmoss Av
4. Cromarty Rd
5. Loretto Rd
6. Millthwaite Rd
7. St Hilary Brow

**H4**
1. Brenig St
2. Shannon St

**H5**
1. Bertha St
2. Deans Wy
3. Effet St
4. Goschen St
5. Laird St
6. Lansdowne Pl
7. Vulcan Cl
8. Vulcan St

**H6**
1. Broom Hl
2. Buckingham Av
3. Foxglove Rd
4. Rimmers Ct
5. Snowdrop Av

**H7**
1. Brancote Mt
2. Hanover Cl
3. Shrewsbury Cl

**H8**
1. Kingsmead Pk
2. Kingsmead Rd

**J1**
1. Frankby Av
2. Stretton Av
3. Westwood Gv

**M6**
1. Beckwith St East
2. Brook St
3. Keightley St
4. Kimmel Cl
5. Newton St
6. Robert St
7. St Anne St
8. St Laurence Av
9. Vittoria St
10. Watson St

**M7**
1. Bentinck Cl
2. Cardigan Av
3. Catherine St
4. Corfu St
5. Coventry St
6. Exmouth Cl
7. Exmouth Gdns
8. Exmouth Wy
9. Florence St
10. Hilton Cl
11. Parkfield Av
12. St Laurence Ct
13. Simpson St

**M8**
1. Brookland Rd
2. Cedar St
3. Cook St
4. Fearnley Av
5. Hazel Rd
6. Hollybank Rd
7. Lowwood Rd
8. Maple St
9. Mounsey Rd
10. Quarry Bank
11. Rawcliffe Rd
12. Wellington Ter
13. Whalley Rd

**L8**
1. Barton St
2. Belmont
3. Carnforth St
4. Cartmel St
5. Clayton Pl
6. Clayton St
7. Henthorne St
8. Maritime Pk
9. Morant Cw
10. Oak Bank
11. Penrith St
12. Quarrybank St
13. Ravenscroft Rd
14. Town Vw
15. Town View Ms
16. Turner St
17. Warwick Ct
18. Wilkinson St
19. Windsor St

**M1**
1. Askew Cl
2. Church Gdns
3. Church La
4. Churchmeadow La
5. Clydesdale Rd
6. Comely Bank Rd
7. Dalehurst Cl
8. Darlington Cl
9. Darlington St
10. Glenalmond Rd
11. Mossy Bank Rd
12. Redfield Cl
13. Royston Av
14. Woodhall Av

**M2**
1. Addington St
2. Bulkeley Rd
3. Ethel Rd
4. Gladstone Rd
5. Glenburn Rd
6. Hood St
7. Hotfifield Rd
8. Illchester Rd
9. Mulberry Gv
10. Park Av
11. Winford St

**M3**
1. Corsedale Pk
2. Parry St

## Page 112

**A3**
1. Abbotsford Cl
2. Acacia Gv
3. The Birches
4. Borough Rd East
5. Briardale Rd
6. Church Crs
7. Delamere Gv
8. Denman Gv
9. Dickenson St
10. Duke Street La
11. Greetham St
12. Hanover St
13. Lakeland Cl
14. Powrall St
15. Price St
16. Seddon St
17. Surrey St
18. Upper Pownall St
19. Vincent Ct
20. Wolstenholme Sq

**A5**
1. Freeman St

**A7**
1. Alma St
2. Back Oliver St
3. Bank St
4. Borough Pl
5. Clifton Crs
6. Conway St
7. Grange Av
8. Oliver La
9. Walton St

**B7**
1. Albion St
2. Brandon St
3. Camperdown St
4. Cross St
5. Duncan St
6. Gertrude St
7. Hamilton St
8. Hornby St
9. Ivy St
10. Knox St
11. Market Pl
12. Market St
13. Mortimer St

**E1**
1. Archbishop Worlock Ct
2. Bishop Sheppard Ct
3. Clement Gdns
4. Fitzpatrick Ct
5. Hughes Cl
6. Jack Mcbain Ct
7. James Clarke St
8. Marshall St
9. Portland St
10. Tobin Cl
11. Twomey Cl
12. Walsh Cl

**F5**
1. Back Seel St
2. Burton Cl
3. Carpenters Rw
4. Cleveland Buildings
5. Cleveland Sq
6. Dickenson St
7. Duke Street La
8. Greetham St
9. Hanover St
10. Lakeland Cl
11. Powrall St
12. Price St
13. Seddon St
14. Surrey St
15. Upper Pownall St
16. Vincent Ct
17. Wolstenholme Sq

**F7**
1. The Anchorage
2. Dwerryhouse St
3. Cranary Wy
4. Pleasant Hill St
5. Worthington St

**F8**
1. Northumberland Gv

## Page 113

**C2**
1. Abram St
2. Back Beau St
3. Beresford St
4. Clifton Gv
5. Douro St
6. Duncan St
7. Juvenal St
8. St Martin's Ms
9. Upper Beau St
10. Watmough St

**C2**
1. Bickerstaffe St
2. Birchfield St
3. Drinkwater Gdns
4. Field St
5. Maritime Pl
6. Page Wk
7. Pritt St
8. Roderick St
9. Rokeby Cl
10. Soho Pl

**G3**
1. Back Bridport St
2. Burgess St
3. Camden St
4. Clifford St
5. Craven St
6. Fraser St
7. Hotham St
8. Kempston St
9. Lambert St
10. London Rd
11. Pudsey St
12. St Vincent St
13. St Vincent Wy
14. Ward St
15. Wilde St

**J1**
1. Aubrey Ct
2. Burnley Cl
3. Cranwell St
4. Dawber Cl
5. Harewood St
6. Reservoir St
7. Rothwell St
8. Shakespeare Rd
9. Wedgwood St

## Page 114

**J2**
1. Baker St
2. Churton St
3. Dunkeld Cl
4. Dunkeld St
5. Fitzroy Wy
6. Gloucester Pl
7. Henglers Cl
8. Hughes St
9. Lavan St
10. Marsden Wy
11. Marvin St
12. Nevin St
13. Olympia St
14. Pera Cl
15. Raven Cl

**J3**
1. Back Mount Vernon
2. Battenberg St
3. Bengal St
4. Fielding St
5. Kensington St
6. Mount Vernon Gn
7. Mount Vernon Vw

**J4**
1. Albert St
2. Brydges St
3. Heldsy St
4. Paddington
5. Shimmin St

**J5**
1. Back Falkner St South
2. Cambridge St
3. Freedom Cl
4. Pilot Gv
5. Purser Gv
6. Sandhead St
7. victor St
8. Wavertree V
9. Whithorn St

**J6**
1. Adele Thompson Dr
2. Crown St
3. Daniel Davies Dr
4. Harrowby St
5. Montgomery Wy
6. Northbrook Cl
7. Northbrook St
8. Upper Huskisson St

**J7**
1. Arnold St
2. Back Kelvin Gv
3. Celtic St
4. Eversley St
5. North Hill St
6. Pimhill Cl
7. Vronhill Cl

**J8**
1. Devonshire Rd West
2. Hawkstone St
3. Mountview Cl
4. Pengwern St
5. Treborth St
6. Voelas St
7. Willow Rd

**K1**
1. Berwick Cl
2. Every St
3. Guion St
4. Mayfair Cl
5. Montgomery Wy
6. Norwood Cl
7. Norwood Gv
8. White Rock St

**K2**
1. Alexandra Ct
2. Bourne St
3. Cottenham St
4. Denman St
5. George Harrison Cl
6. Goldsmith St
7. Owenfron St
8. Mission St
9. Paul Maccartney Wy
10. Phythian Cl
11. Ringo Starr Dr
12. Sutcliffe St
13. Thornes Rd
14. Wightman St

**H4**
1. Bedford St North
2. Great Orford St
3. Newton Wy
4. Pilgrim St

**H5**
1. Abercromby Sq
2. Arrad St
3. Back Bedford St
4. Back Canning St
5. Back Catharine St
6. Back Hope St
7. Back Mulberry St
8. Back Sir Howard St
9. Back St Bride St
10. Bedford Cl
11. Blackburne Pl
12. Caledonia St
13. Falkner St
14. Hope Wy
15. Maryland St
16. Mulberry St
17. Myrtle Pde
18. South Hunter St
19. Stowell St
20. Sugnall St
21. Upper Hope Pl

**H6**
1. Back Egerton St North
2. Back Huskisson St
3. Back Little Canning St
4. Back Sandon St
5. Birley Ct
6. Gibson St
7. Grey St
8. Little Catharine St
9. Little Huskisson St
10. Morpeth St
11. Park Wy
12. Parliament Pl
13. Peel St

**K3**
1. Adderley Pl
2. Edinburgh Rd
3. Kemble St
4. Laggan St
5. Minto St
6. Seldon St
7. Smollett St
8. Solomon St

**K4**
1. Agnes Wy
2. Back Chatham Pl
3. Back Holland Pl
4. Back Towerlands St
5. Church Mt
6. Hawthorn Gv
7. Moorgate St
8. Nevison St
9. Uxbridge St

**K5**
1. Boothwood Cl
2. Brightgate Cl
3. Dovestone Cl
4. Kingswell Cl
5. Perrygate Cl
6. Portwood Cl
7. Redmires Cl
8. Silkstone Cl
9. Upper Parliament St

**K6**
1. Askham Cl
2. Back Windsor Vw
3. Buttermere St
4. Kingsley Rd
5. Maitland St
6. Maynard St
7. Oxendale Cl
8. Swindale Cl
9. Yanwath St

**K7**
1. Bentley Rd
2. Brahms Cl
3. Mozart Cl
4. Princes Ga West
5. Strauss Cl

**K8**
1. Albert Pk
2. Windermere Ter

**L1**
1. Celt St
2. Milverton St
3. Tweed Cl

**L2**
1. Derwent Sq
2. Podium Rd

**L3**
1. Chiswell St
2. Dell St
3. Flaxman St
4. Frost St
5. Holdsworth St
6. Houlton St
7. Wilton Gv

**L4**
1. Beames Cl
2. Bremner Cl
3. Chris Ward Cl
4. Claughton Cl
5. Fowler Cl
6. Gresley Cl
7. Hughes Cl
8. Lemon Cl
9. Webb Cl

## Page 115

**G1**
1. Churchdown Gv

**G2**
1. Greystone Crs

**G7**
1. Selworthy Rd

**H2**
1. Ashfarm Ct

**H3**
1. Malvern Crs
2. Sexton Wy

**H4**
1. Molesworth St

**H5**
1. Glen Vine Cl
2. Harwich Gv
3. Peacehaven Cl
4. Swinburne Cl
5. Weymouth Cl

**H6**
1. Dronfield Wy
2. Hartsbourne Cl
3. Napps Cl

**H8**
1. Quickswood Gn
2. Rockbourne Wy

**J1**
1. Dinas La
2. Petunia Cl

**J6**
1. Marchwood Wy

**J7**
1. Cranleigh Pl
2. Hayles Cl
3. Holmleigh Rd
4. Leybourne Av

## Page 116

**A4**
1. The Brooklands
2. Evanville
3. Greenlands
4. St Catherines Cl
5. St James' Cl

**B2**
1. Bramblewood Cl
2. Bramley Cl
3. Maplewood Cl
4. Rosewood Cl

**B2**
1. Huyton La
2. Longview Crs
3. St Matthew's Cl

**B5**
1. Kingfisher Cl
2. Nightingale Cl
3. Osprey Cl
4. Swallow Cl

**D3**
1. Taunton Rd
2. Tiverton Cl

**F1**
1. Molyneux Cl

**F2**
1. Cherry Tree Cl

**F3**
1. Eglington Av
2. Fisher Pl
3. Hostock Cl
4. Montgomery Cl

## Page 117

**H2**
1. Brackenwood Gv
2. Braemar Ct
3. Gresford Cl
4. Shelley Pl

**J1**
1. Hadden Cl
2. Lindrick Cl
3. Longview Av
4. Newby Av

**K1**
1. Sandon Cl

**L2**
1. Braithwaite Cl
2. Brandreth Cl
3. Exchange Pl
4. Houghton St
5. Oaklands
6. Station St
7. Victoria St

## Page 118

**H6**
1. Acorn Cl
2. Beacon La
3. Brock Hall Cl
4. Churchfields
5. Cottage Pl
6. Falcow Cl
7. Farrier Wk
8. Harvest Wy
9. Hazelfield Ct
10. Hoylake Gv
11. Lindale Dr
12. Littlecote Cl
13. Millersdale
14. Moreton Av
15. Oaklands St
16. Ride Cl
17. Rye Cl
18. Spinney Cl
19. Wheatland Cl
20. The Willows
21. Woodcroft Wy

## Page 120

**J3**
1. Clovelly Av
2. Coogee Av
3. Greenway
4. Hall Ter

**F3**
1 Cresswell Cl
2 Gresford Cl
3 Pensarn Gdns
4 Peterstone Cl
5 Stanner Cl

**F4**
1 Drake Cl

**F5**
1 Frobisher Ct

**F6**
1 Bewsey Farm Cl

**F7**
1 Shiggins Cl

## Page 121

**G3**
1 Bala Cl
2 Cartmel Cl
3 Granston Cl
4 Lampeter Cl
5 Lydstep Ct
6 Monkswood Cl
7 Rossett Cl
8 Tintern Cl
9 Wrexham Cl

**G7**
1 Bostock Cl
2 Cartwright St
3 Monks St
4 St Barnabas Pl

**G8**
1 Baxter St
2 Green St
3 Lancaster St
4 Percy St
5 Selby St

**J2**
1 Brendon Av
2 Chiltern Av
3 Chiltern Crs
4 Crawley Av
5 Harvard Ct
6 Kentmere Pl
7 Wansfell Pl

**K3**
1 Achilles Ct
2 Armour Av
3 Brandwood Av
4 Clough Av
5 Dean Crs
6 Poole Av
7 Poole Crs

**K7**
1 Ashton St
2 Chorley St
3 Erwood St
4 Hardy St
5 Rodney St
6 St Peter's Wy
7 Silver St

**K8**
1 Bank St
2 Bennett St
3 Bewsey St
4 Blackhurst St
5 Cockhedge Wy
6 James St
7 Naylor St
8 Patten La
9 Rylands St
10 Town Hl
11 Union St
12 Westminster Pl

**L2**
1 Ambleside Crs
2 Cartmel Av
3 Scafell Av
4 Thirlmere Av

**L3**
1 Byron Ct
2 The Coppins
3 Keswick Crs
4 Penrith Av
5 Ruskin Av

**L4**
1 Cossack Av
2 Kipling Av

**L5**
1 Richardson St

**L6**
1 Adam St
2 Alamein Crs
3 Arnhem Crs
4 Garner St
5 Synge St

**L7**
1 Chester St
2 Hopwood St
3 Morley St

**L8**
1 Cockhedge La
2 Crossley St
3 Dutton St
4 High St
5 Parr St
6 Percival St

**M2**
1 Bittern Cl
2 Ravensdale Cl

**M3**
1 Caldbeck Av
2 Catterall Av
3 Cherwell Cl
4 Concorde Pl
5 Greenwood Crs
6 Halifax Cl
7 Hughes Pl
8 Sandalwood Cl
9 Whittaker Av

**M4**
1 Ferguson Dr
2 Osborne Av
3 Povey Rd
4 St Margaret's Av
5 Sylvia Crs
6 Vale Owen Rd
7 Woodcote Cl

**M5**
1 Norbury Av

**M6**
1 Matthews St

## Page 122

**A2**
1 Dovedale Cl
2 Dunnock Cl
3 Horseshoe Crs
4 Langdale Cl
5 Morven Cl
6 Swift Cl

**A4**
1 Andover Cl
2 Biggin Ct
3 Duxford St
4 Finningley Ct
5 Jurby Ct
6 Northolt Ct
7 Sealand Cl
8 Woodvale Cl

**B2**
1 Briers Cl
2 Newton Gv
3 St Bridget's Cl

**B4**
1 Jurby Ct
2 Pocklington Cl
3 Unsworth Ct

**C3**
1 Edgars Dr

**C5**
1 Queens Crs

**D2**
1 Stromness Cl

**D6**
1 Aveley Cl

**E1**
1 Aspull Cl
2 Campion Cl
3 Holmes Cl
4 Redvales Cl
5 Sovereign St
6 Windle Ct

**E3**
1 Blackburne Cl

**E4**
1 Lovage Cl

**E6**
1 Abstone Cl
2 Greenfields Cl

**F1**
1 Beeston Cl
2 Bickerton Cl
3 Carden Cl
4 Centurion Cl
5 Renown Cl
6 Vanguard Ct

**F2**
1 Land Cut La

**F6**
1 Hereford Cl
2 Laurel Av

**F7**
1 Laxey Av
2 Peel Cl

## Page 124

**C2**
1 Broughton Av
2 Hilton Gv
3 Kington Rd
4 Murray Gv
5 Norton Rd
6 Redhouse Bank
7 Ridley Gv
8 Roseacre

**D2**
1 De Grouchy St
2 Heatherdene Rd

## Page 125

**L1**
1 The Carters
2 Finchdean Cl
3 Harvester Wy
4 Malmesbury Cl
5 Redditch Cl
6 Redford Cl
7 Shepherd Cl
8 Stourport Cl
9 Swindon Cl
10 Thresher Av

**M1**
1 The Barncroft
2 Birchdale Cl
3 Dryfield Cl
4 Heygarth Dr
5 Holcombe Cl
6 Ingleton Cl
7 Longfield Cl
8 Pitch Cl
9 St James Cl

## Page 126

**B1**
1 Benson Cl
2 Brightwell Cl
3 Cholsey Cl
4 Crowmarsh Cl
5 Dorchester Cl
6 Milman Cl
7 Wittenham Cl

**C7**
1 Ambleside Cl
2 Berwyn Av
3 Heywood Cl
4 Richmond Wy

**E1**
1 Naseby Cl
2 Netherfield Cl
3 Newark Cl
4 Newport Cl
5 Ollerton Cl
6 Orlando Cl
7 Ossett Cl

**F1**
1 Dodleston Cl
2 Eastview Cl
3 Edgefield Cl
4 Fern Gv
5 Pagewood Cl
6 Pinedale Cl
7 Ravendale Cl
8 Ridings Hey
9 Sunnybank Av
10 Tynron Gv
11 Westcott Wy
12 Westview Cl
13 Woodberry Cl

## Page 127

**G2**
1 Hargrave Cl
2 Oulton Wy
3 Townfield Cl

**G4**
1 Millington Cl
2 Shipton Cl

**H1**
1 Ince Cl
2 Kilmalcolm Cl
3 Mere Farm Gv

**H2**
1 Aston Cl
2 Bollington Cl
3 Duddon Cl
4 Gawsworth Cl
5 Hatchmere Cl
6 Spurstow Cl

**H3**
1 Davenham Cl
2 Holm Cottages
3 Redwood Cl
4 Wrenbury Cl

**H4**
1 Dickens Av
2 Dickens Cl
3 Goldsmith Rd
4 Goldsmith Wy
5 Waterpark Rd

**L1**
1 Ashford Rd
2 Brimstage Rd
3 Falcon Rd
4 Halcyon Rd
5 Harrowby Rd South
6 Heathfield Rd
7 James St
8 Kingsland Rd
9 Laburnum Rd

**M1**
1 Ash Rd
2 Aspendale Rd
3 Charlecombe St
4 Dewberry Cl
5 Rectory Cl
6 St Catherine's
7 St Catherines Gdns
8 Shewell Cl
9 Spruce Cl
10 Sycamore Rd
11 Whitfield St

**M6**
1 Beckett Gv
2 Mountway

**M7**
1 King's Brow
2 Millwood
3 Rotherwood Cl
4 Sandfield Cl
5 Victoria Rd

**M8**
1 Derwent Cl
2 Glenmarsh Cl
3 Shallmarsh Cl
4 Welland Rd
5 Wilstan Av

## Page 128

**A1**
1 Acuba Gv
2 Chamberlain St
3 Hampden Gv
4 Holly Gv
5 Kingsdown St
6 Leighton Rd
7 Olive Crs
8 Redmond St
9 Ripon St
10 Westbury St

**B2**
1 Alison Av
2 Beaconsfield Cl
3 Brougham Av
4 Cobden Cl
5 Cobden Pl
6 Gladstone Rd
7 Grenville Wy
8 Livingstone Rd
9 Lydbrook Cl
10 Orchard Cl
11 Rose Rd
12 Standard Pl
13 Stanley Ct
14 Strathlorne Cl
15 Wye Cl

**B3**
1 Aldersgate
2 Ashley St
3 Birchcliffe Rd
4 Byrne Av
5 Corinthian St
6 Doric St
7 Fairhaven Cl
8 Meadowfield Cl
9 Meadow Pk
10 Palmerston St
11 Rock Cl
12 The Sidings
13 Woburn Pl
14 Wycliffe St

**C7**
1 Apsley Gv
2 Wellesley Gv
3 Windy Bank

**D5**
1 Apsley Rd
2 Esher Rd
3 Field Cl
4 Kempton Rd
5 Thorburn Cl
6 Thorburn Crs

**D6**
1 Beaconsfield Rd
2 Mayfields South
3 Poolbank Rd
4 Woodhead St

**D7**
1 Causeway Cl
2 Elmbank Rd
3 Lancaster Cl
4 Lower Rd
5 Walker St
6 Willowbank Rd

**D8**
1 Cross St
2 Gardens Rd
3 Poets Cnr
4 Victoria St

**E5**
1 Pollitt Sq

**E6**
1 Ortega Cl

**E7**
1 The Anzacs

## Page 129

**H1**
1 Anglesea Wy
2 Barclay St
3 Chatburn Wk
4 Chilhem Cl
5 Cleopas St
6 Greaves St
7 Hawkhurst Cl
8 Haylock Cl
9 Kirkburn Cl
10 Malwood St
11 Monro Cl
12 Netherby St
13 Royden St
14 Shelmore Dr
15 Whalley St
16 Woodruff St

**H2**
1 Armstrong Quay
2 Badminton St
3 Bowood St
4 The Bulrushes
5 Charlecote St
6 Herculaneum Ct
7 Orchid Gv
8 Sandbeck St

**J1**
1 Back Wellesley Rd
2 Bowring Cl
3 Bowring St
4 Bruce St
5 Dentwood St
6 Dingle Gv
7 Drysdale St
8 Drysdale Wk
9 Fair View Pl
10 Gredington St
11 Hawkstone St
12 Leonora St
13 Lockington Cl
14 Loxdale Cl
15 Mallins Cl
16 Menzies St
17 Miller Cl
18 Park Rd
19 Redburn Cl
20 St Lawrence Cl
21 Sundridge St
22 Wellesley Rd
23 Wilson St
24 Wyncroft St

**J2**
1 Dingle Brow
2 Emerald St
3 Hindlip St
4 Jasmine Ms
5 Moniswell St
6 Thistledown Cl
7 Thorntree Cl

**L3**
1 Battery Cl
2 Burgundy Cl
3 Hythedale Cl
4 Larkfield Cl
5 Larkfield Gv
6 Maybury Wy
7 Newmorn Ct
8 Oakbourne Cl
9 Oxford Cl
10 Sycamore Rd
11 St Michael's Cl
12 Wrenfield Gv

## Page 130

**A3**
1 Ashlar Gv
2 Bessbrook Rd
3 Rimmington Rd
4 Rowan Ct

**C6**
1 Beechwood Cl
2 Bennison Dr
3 Convent Cl
4 Dugdale Cl
5 Eslington St
6 Fletcher Dr
7 Lawrence Cl
8 Prior Farm Cl
9 Woodhey Rd

**E7**
1 Granville Rd
2 Island Pl
3 Jackson St
4 Mersey Vw
5 Milnthorpe St
6 Wilson Gv

**E8**
1 Leeming Cl
2 Lord St
3 Marlowe Cl
4 Mercer St
5 Shakespeare St
6 Thomas Cl
7 Woodger St

**F2**
1 Beech Ct

**F3**
1 Maryton Gra
2 Sycamore Pk

**F5**
1 Danefield Pl

**F6**
1 Stamfordham Pl

**F7**
1 Haxted Gdns

**F8**
1 Arthur St
2 Aston St

## Page 131

**J1**
1 Parkwood Rd

**J2**
1 Woolton Park Cl

**L2**
1 Davids Wk
2 Halewood Pl
3 Knotty Ms

**L3**
1 Budworth Dr
2 Felsted Av
3 Halewood Wy
4 Kingham Cl
5 Warton Cl
6 Whitney Pl

**L5**
1 Dunmow Wy

**L7**
1 Braydon Cl

**M3**
1 Blackberry Gv
2 Edenhall Dr
3 Hazelwood Gv
4 Honeysuckle Cl
5 Magnolia Cl
6 Riding Fold

**M4**
1 Lancing Rd

**M5**
1 Pembrey Wy

## Page 132

**A3**
1 Comfrey Gv
2 Okell Dr
3 Openfields Cl
4 Pipit Cl
5 Rogerson's Gn
6 Ruscar Cl

**A5**
1 Carlyon Wy
2 Cheriton Cl
3 Ravenfield Cl
4 Stainton Cl
5 Tarleton Cl

**B5**
1 Cambridge Dr
2 Catterick Cl
3 Fernwood Dr
4 Neasham Cl

**D5**
1 Rawlinson Crs

## Page 133

**L2**
1 Auburn Cl
2 Broxton Cl
3 Burnham Cl
4 Caxton Cl
5 Chatsworth Dr
6 Fenton Cl
7 Hambleton Cl
8 Madeline Mckenna Ct
9 Newland Cl
10 Warkworth Cl

**L3**
1 Rufford Cl

**L4**
1 Gaisgill Ct
2 Graham Cl
3 Kendal Rd
4 Sherwood Cl

**L5**
1 Kenneth Rd
2 Winchester Rd

## Page 134

**B2**
1 Battersea Ct
2 Burton Cl
3 Giltbrook Cl
4 Grundy Cl
5 Whickham St

**C6**
1 Alexandra Cl
2 Alforde St
3 Bold St
4 Chapel St
5 Darlington St
6 Eleanor St
7 Ellis St
8 Emily St
9 Finlan Rd
10 Guest St
11 Lewis Crs
12 Luton St
13 Major Cross St
14 Market St
15 Millar Crs
16 Miners Wy
17 St Paul's Rd
18 Thomas St
19 Vicarage Rd
20 Victoria Rd
21 Violet St
22 Witt Rd

**C8**
1 Chidlow Cl
2 Constance Wy
3 Dock Rd
4 Queensway
5 Short St
6 White St
7 Wilkinson Cl

**D2**
1 Boxgrove Cl
2 Durham Rd
3 Griffin Ms

**D3**
1 Hawthorn Av
2 Larch Av
3 Lime Av
4 Mount Pleasant
5 Pine Av

**D4**
1 Bradley Wy
2 Cross St
3 Lower Appleton Rd
4 Maple Av
5 Mount St
6 Robert St
7 Routledge St
8 Saxon Ter
9 Westmorland Av

**D5**
1 Alfred Cl
2 Elliot St
3 Gerrard St
4 Grenfell St
5 Hibbert St
6 Liebig St
7 Lugsdale Rd
8 Midwood St
9 Rylands St
10 Salisbury St
11 Timperley St
12 Travis St

**D6**
1 Batherton Cl
2 Caroline St
3 Elizabeth Ct
4 Lacey Ct
5 Margaret Ct
6 Pool St
7 Sutton's La
8 Trinity Pl

**E1**
1 Claremont Av

**E3**
1 Doward St
2 Stanley Cl
3 Susan St

**E4**
1 Bell House Rd
2 Black Denton's Pl
3 Cliffe St
4 Edwin St
5 Esther St
6 Harris St
7 Henry St
8 Parr St
9 Richmond St
10 Sadler St
11 Taylor St

**F2**
1 Crow Wood Pl
2 Selwyn Cl

**F3**
1 Barnes Cl
2 Drummond St
3 Moore Cl

**F4**
1 East St
2 Edward St
3 Hargreaves Cl
4 Norland St
5 Sussex St
6 Walter St

## Page 137

**K1**
1 Barbauld St
2 Bridge St
3 Friars Ga
4 Friars La
5 School St
6 Stanley St
7 Wilson Patten St

**K5**
1 Hill Cliffe Rd

**K6**
1 Cambridge Cl

**L2**
1 Causeway Av
2 Clelland St

**M2**
1 Beatrice St
2 Birch Gv
3 Cedar Gv
4 Florence St

## Page 141

**H2**
1 Hawthorn Dr
2 Kentmere Rd
3 Stewart Cl

**L5**
1 Brimstage Gv
2 Speedwell Cl

**M4**
1 Northway

**M5**
1 Aspen Cl
2 Brimstage Gn
3 Cottesmore Dr

**M6**
1 Dovesmead Rd

## Page 143

**H2**
1 Heath Dl
2 Kevelioc Cl
3 Mulveton Rd
4 Stanfield Dr

**J1**
1 Abbots Dr
2 Eversleigh Dr
3 Kirket Cl
4 Rolleston Dr

**J3**
1 Burdett Cl
2 Henley Cl
3 Hockenhull Cl
4 Langley Rd
5 Randle Cl
6 Sheldon Cl

## Page 149

**H2**
1 Brackley Cl
2 Clarence St
3 Edith St
4 Egerton St
5 Greek St
6 Grove St
7 Handley St
8 Lord St
9 Speakman St

**H3**
1 Cavendish St
2 Hankey St
3 High St
4 Lowlands Rd
5 Rutland St
6 Shaw St
7 Waterloo Rd

**H4**
1 Burland Cl
2 Curzon St
3 Drayton Cl
4 The Elms
5 Havergal St
6 Lightburn St
7 Queen's Cl
8 Southlands Ms
9 Stapley Cl
10 Westfield Ms

**H7**
1 Ashton Cl
2 Company's Cl
3 Cresta Dr
4 Lambsickle Cl

**J1**
1 Beamont St
2 Bridge View Cl
3 Cholmondeley St
4 Hurst St
5 Parsonage Rd

**J2**
1 Alcock St
2 Bridgewater St
3 Canon St
4 Clarence Ter
5 Cooper St
6 Egerton St
7 Granville St
8 Loch St
9 Penketh's La
10 Princess St
11 Public Hall St
12 Wellington St

**J3**
1 Albert St
2 Arthur St
3 Back High St
4 Brook St
5 Devonshire Pl
6 Eaton St
7 Greenway Rd
8 High St
9 Nelson St
10 New St
11 Oakmere St
12 Queensway
13 Surrey St
14 Vine St
15 Walton St

**L4**
1 Bickley Cl
2 Lavender Cl

**M3**
1 Henley Ct
2 Needham Cl
3 Tenby Dr

**M4**
1 The Winnows

**M5**
1 Davenport Rw

**M6**
1 Cranage Cl

**M7**
1 Cantley Cl
2 Danby Cl
3 Handforth La
4 Hyde Cl
5 Whitchurch Wy

**M8**
1 Braithwaite Cl
2 Kendal Ri

## Page 150

**A7**
1 Hobby Ct
2 Hunters Ct
3 Rothbury Cl
4 Seneschal Ct

**A8**
1 Bowland Cl
2 Brambling Cl
3 Mosedale Gv
4 Stonechat Cl
5 Whinfell Gv

**D7**
1 Allendale
2 Bodmin Cl
3 Mullion Cl
4 Wharfedale

**D8**
1 Bartlegate
2 Broome Ct
3 Clover Ct
4 Coney Gv
5 Goulders Ct
6 Kilncroft

**E3**
1 Priory Rd
2 Southwood Av
3 Townfield Rd

**E4**
1 Sandalwood

**E5**
1 Kings Meadow
2 Saddlers Ri
3 Stoney Holt

**E6**
1 Cloverfield

**E7**
1 Camborne Cl
2 Launceston Cl
3 Newbridge Cl
4 Penare Corran Hvn
5 Tintagel Cl
6 Truro Cl

**E8**
1 Backford Cl
2 Calverly Cl
3 Granby Cl
4 Halsall Cl
5 Linwood Cl
6 Wellbrook Cl

**F3**
1 Adlington Rd
2 Ashbury Cl
3 Harvard Cl
4 Haywood Crs
5 Swinden Cl

**F4**
1 Camden Ct
2 Chorlton Cl
3 Culford Cl
4 Gooseberry La
5 Winton Gv

**F5**
1 Dorrington Cl
2 Heron Cl
3 Mellor Cl
4 Ossett Cl

**F6**
1 Barton Cl
2 Aster Crs
3 Chiswick Cl
4 Hitchen's Cl
5 Humphrey's Cl
6 Micklegate
7 Neptune Cl
8 Sabre Cl
9 Sovereign Cl

**F7**
1 Bournemouth Cl
2 Navigation Cl
3 Quadrant Cl
4 Schooner Cl

## Page 161

**H1**
1 Ashbrook Av
2 Aster Cl
3 Audlem Cl
4 Azalea Gv
5 Bluebell Cl
6 Larkspur Cl
7 Lobelia Gv
8 Magnolia Dr
9 Millington Cl
10 Salisbury Cl
11 Peckforton Dr
12 Stonecrop Cl
13 Verbena Cl
14 Weaverside Av

## Page 163

**H2**
1 Moston Wy
2 Overpool Gdns
3 Torridon Gv

**H4**
1 Badgers Cl
2 Bangor Cl
3 Bramley Cl
4 Gloucester Cl
5 Green Lawns Dr
6 Lambourne Cl
7 Larchdale Cl
8 Laxton Cl
9 St Georges Av
10 Truro Cl
11 Truro Cl
12 West Park Dr

**K1**
1 Chapel Ms

**K2**
1 Coronation Rd
2 Mcgarva Wy
3 Stanlaw Rd
4 Tarvin Cl

**L5**
1 Farne Cl

**Notes**

**Notes**

**Notes**